Discover 2008
One Tank Trips

New York/New England States: CT, NY, ME, NH, RI, VT, MA

This region is where America began over 230 years ago, and the states included here are rich in the sights, sounds, and flavors of early American history. Just one look at the map will reveal a profusion of destinations that define "New England." From the relaxed atmosphere and seafood dining pleasures of its seaside summer resort towns to the bucolic splendor of its national forests; and from Revolutionary War-era historical sites to the metropolitan excitement of New York City – America's Northeast delivers the goods.

The Mid-Atlantic States: DE, MD, NJ, PA, VA, WV, DC

Bordered by Pennsylvania to the north and Virginia to the south, there's so much to see that you'll run out of energy before you run out of your tank of gas. In Washington, D.C. there's a museum, memorial, or government building for virtually anything you can think of. Pennsylvania offers attractions connected to everything from chocolate to cheese steaks, and plenty more. New Jersey's Atlantic City provides visitors with casino kicks while the Appalachian Mountains running through the midst of the Mid-Atlantic region furnish outdoor recreation enthusiasts with its biggest playground.

The South: AL, FL, GA, KY, LA, MS, NC, SC, TN

With much to delight all the senses, a trip within the states of the South amply provides all the things you'd expect. The states affected by Hurricane Katrina are recovering well and are joined by their neighboring states in welcoming you back for a visit. Most of the South is a gentler place, and not so hurried. Every visitor, from fans of the space program to anglers, golfers, horse racing and thrill ride enthusiasts will find something to cheer about in The South; it's a rich, deep showcase of America's past, present and future.

The Midwest: IL, IN, IA, MI, MN, OH, WI

The Great Lakes states that make up much of this region have some of the hardiest inhabitants, and they have to be to thrive in this winter "meat locker." For the majority of the year, however, you can experience plenty of entertainment in and around the Lakes and surrounding areas within one-tank-of-gas proximity. The Lake Michigan and Lake Superior shorelines account for a large part of the recreational offerings here. RVers can enjoy gorgeous scenery, wineries, artist colonies, gardens, breweries, and nature preserves unique to the Midwest region.

The Frontier West/Great Plains & Mountain States: AR, CO, KS, MO, MT, NE, NM, ND, OK, SD, TX, UT, WY

"Thirteen" may be your lucky number if you're looking for the number of states with the most Lewis & Clark-based adventures to offer. Part of the famous duo's transcontinental route stretches through here from Missouri to Montana, but modern-day explorers can cover ground more quickly, if they want. You'll want to spend time touring the Rocky Mountains, The Black Mountains, The Ozarks, Four Corners, Salt Lake, Yellowstone National Park. The Frontier West region spans such a variety of Arcadian landscapes that you're sure to see something unique on every trip.

The Far West: AK, AZ, CA, ID, NV, OR, WA, MX

As expansive and remote as some parts of the Far West can be, you'll still find a passel-full of pastimes within a short drive of each other. This rugged territory incorporates almost non-stop views of remarkable mountain ranges and very different climates; note the bold contrast of Washington's Olympic Mountain range with Arizona's Yuma Desert. Alaska and Mexico are also included in this group, at opposite ends of the climatic spectrum. But whether you're enticed by the "civilized" attractions of its major cities or inspired to search for rustic remnants of its storied past, The Far West is a great place to roam, pardner!

Canada: AB, BC, MB, NB, NL, NT, NS, ON, PE, QC, SK, YT, NWT

It's really a case of perception vs. reality. The common (mis) perception may be that the "Great White North" is just that, but unless you're here in the off-season, much of it is beautiful country where myriad adventures await you. Intrepid RVers are rewarded with beautiful natural vistas, flower gardens, historic districts, as well as the nation's own versions of British and French culture. Several provinces, such as Nova Scotia and Newfoundland/Labrador are almost entirely detached from the mainland but contain plenty of sights and places of their own to explore in this distinctive region.

Published by Woodall's Publications Corp.
2575 Vista Del Mar, Ventura, CA 93001
Phone: 805-667-4100 or 800-323-9076
Website: www.woodalls.com

Also Publishers of *Woodall's Tenting Directory and Woodall's Go & Rent, Rent & Go.*

Woodall's Camperways, Woodall's Southern RV, Woodall's Northeast Outdoors, Woodall's Florida RV Traveler, Woodall's Midwest RV Traveler: (800) 323-9076 ext. 356; *Woodall's Campground Management :* (219) 457-3370; *Woodall's RV Buyer's Guide:* (800) 323-9076, ext. 284.

MULTI-MEDIA DIVISION
VICE PRESIDENT Joe Daquino
Associate Publisher Ann Emerson
Executive Assistant Christina Din

Senior Director of Production and Editorial Christine Bucher
Senior Database Manager Stephen Welthe, Clarinda De La Paz
Systems and Editorial Staff Susan Shapiro

Production Manager Yvette L. Brownstone
Electronic Prepress Systems Specialist Milt Phelps
Production Staff Artists Gary Guthrie, Jessa Riley
Ad Traffic Coordinator Alyssa Halberg, Tanya Paz

Production/Editorial Assistants Corey Grant, Marcos Jimenez, Princesa Rodriguez

Cover Design Quebecor World Premedia
Feature Writers Brent Peterson, Cathy Williams
Feature Designs Jessa Riley

Electronic Media Dept. Web Specialist Jonathan Blackburn

Marketing Manager Genevieve Branco, Donna Brown
Circulation Manager Liz Shura
Marketing Fulfillment Coordinator Lance Tully
Business Manager Dawn Watanabe
Lead Account Coordinator Christine Distl
Account Coordinators Nelly Beraun, Olivia Long, Sherri Ohnemus

Marketing Consultants Jim & Sally Bryan

NATIONAL ADVERTISING
Scott Oakes - Eastern Sales
206-283-9545
1818 Westlake Ave. N., Ste. 420
Seattle, WA 98109
John Marciano - Western Sales
206-283-9545
1818 Westlake Ave. N., Ste. 420
Seattle, WA 98109

WOODALL REPRESENTATIVES

- Bill & Juanita Adkins
- Larry & Glenna Baird
- Greg & Maureen Baron
- Randy & Debbie Block
- Jeff & Lynnaine Borock
- Paul & Debra Bokei
- Dave & Jaynie Carlson
- Neal & Marion Carmickle
- Joe & Rita Comer
- Pete & Joan Dawes
- Chip & Pat Dennis
- John & Jean Everett
- Duane & Bev Finger
- Lee & Mary Franck
- A.J. & Kathleen Goodale
- Chuck & Nancy Hanson
- Don & Lovena Hickman
- Pierre Hebert & Dorys Lamothe
- Michael & Ellen McNamee
- Frank & Linda Mintken
- John & Mary Michaud
- Fred & Joanne Playle
- John & Michele Pynenburg
- Travis & Sharon Rymer
- Bob & Joann Schaefer
- John & Carla Skolburg
- Bob & Joan Stevens
- Marcia Waggoner

PRINTED IN THE U.S.A.
Book Trade Distribution by The Globe-Pequot Press
246 Goose Lane
P.O. Box 480
Guilford, CT 06437 (203) 458-4500
ISBN-10: 0-7627-4618-1
ISBN-13: 978-0-7627-4618-7

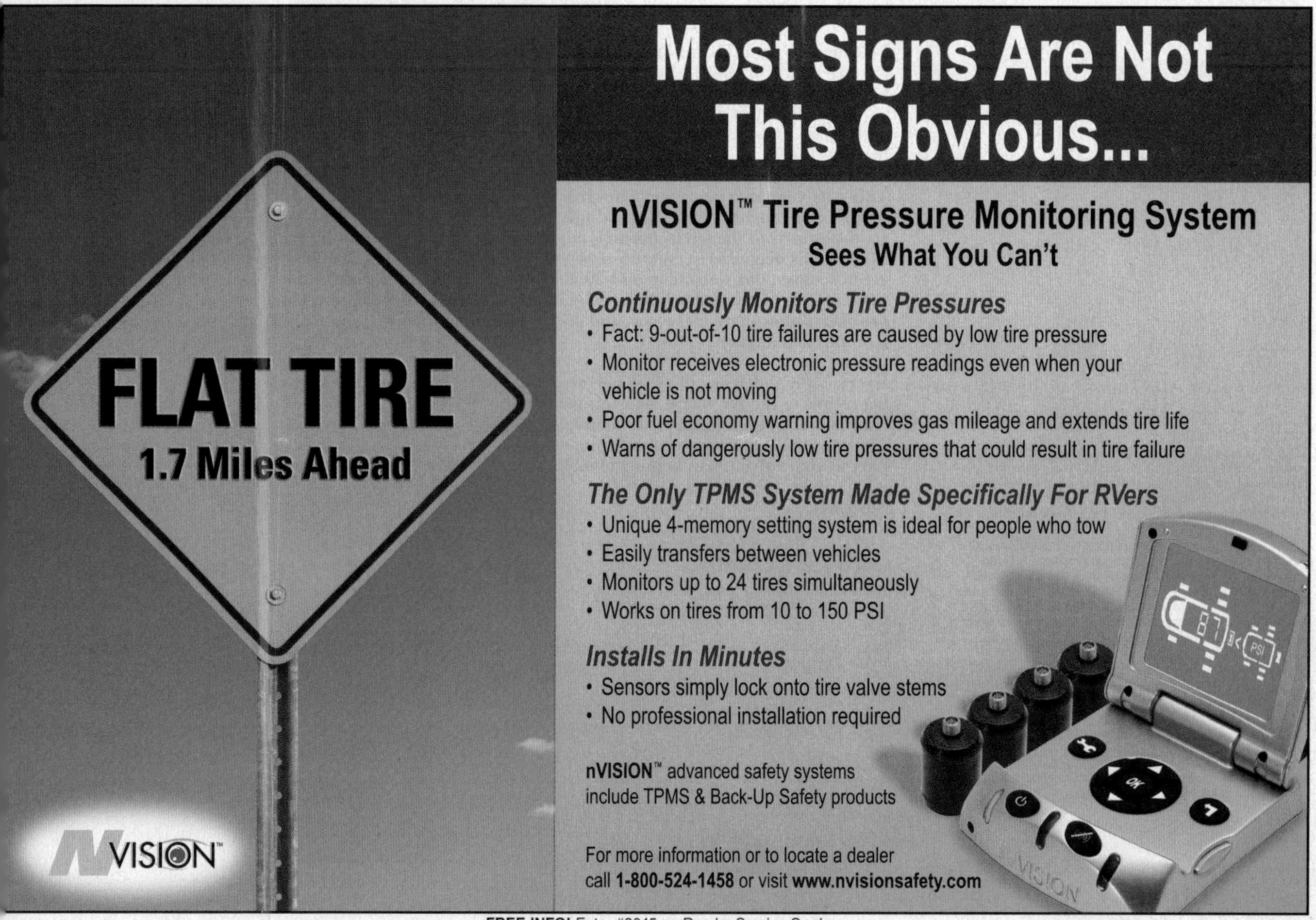

2008
The South Edition Directory Listings

Dear Readers

2007 saw a lot of changes in camping and RV travel. Whether it was a growing conscientiousness of the environment, the influx of new technology, or the rising gas prices, where we go, and how we get there, has dramatically changed.

Gone are the days where twenty bucks will get you a full tank of gas and a pack of gum. With the ever-increasing gas prices, we are spending more money at the pump than ever before. As a society, we seemed to have all "tightened our collective belts" as we try to absorb the added cost of fuel. For some of us, it means making a concerted effort at car-pooling—whether to work, the kids' practice or social events. For others, it means finding alternate forms of travel, like bikes, or buses. And for many of us, higher gas prices have caused us to spend less days, or shorten the miles, on our vacations.

But you shouldn't have to choose between spending time exploring the outdoors, or buying a tank of gas. To help you in your efforts to enjoy the freedom of RV travel (while still keeping an eye on fuel expenses) we have put together a special editorial—Discover One Tank Trips. These articles highlight some of North America's most interesting trips that you can experience on a single tank of gas. From the rugged, mountainous beauty of Alaska, to the stylish and chic cities of Atlanta and Annapolis, we will show you the best routes to take to see all that this continent has to offer. Each trip is chock full of appealing attractions and electrifying events that make North America so unique. You can visit a Cookie Cutter museum in Missouri, go bourbon tasting in Kentucky, tap your feet in jazz clubs in Alabama, participate in a kite festival in Oregon, or eat your way through the lobster festival in Maine. Tour America's "favorite drive," eat America's "favorite food," visit America's "favorite playground," and shop at America's "favorite mall." Take pictures by the world's largest road-runner, largest ball of twine, or largest sculpture made from old cars. Every route is designed to make your vacation both appealing and memorable.

You can also find this article on www.woodalls.com, along with an electronic version of our Campground Directory. Every RV Park and campground, attraction, and RV dealer offering sales and services, is found in our online Directory; just a click away. You'll also find a variety of articles about the RV lifestyle—from tips on choosing the best park to camp, to the latest offering of gadgets and gizmos. And the more you visit, the more you stay informed, as we update the website weekly with features like finding used RVs for sale or the latest RV destination hot spots.

This past year also saw a move towards greater environmental awareness—a lean towards "green"—which has brought about new products and services. As outdoor enthusiasts, we have a desire to be good stewards of the environment—ensuring that future generations have the same opportunities to explore this magnificent country as we have enjoyed. In keeping with the recent advancements in green ecology, our website in mid-2008 will be debuting a series of articles on the growing trend of Green RVing. Included will be articles on using eco-friendly camping supplies—like biodegradable products, phosphate-free soap, and green dishes—and how to use your RV to both save gas and protect the environment.

Every edition of Woodall's Campground Directory strives to inform our readers of current and exciting trends in the RV world, and this edition is no exception. The 2008 Directory continues the Woodall tradition of providing the most complete, accurate, and up-to-date information, so that our readers can have the best camping and RVing experience possible. Thank you for allowing Woodall's to play a part in your adventures helping to make them as enjoyable as they can be.

Sincerely,

Ann Emerson
Associate Publisher

Please see page two for the Table of Contents for *Discover 2008— One Tank Trips*

WOODALL'S IS THE OFFICIAL CAMPGROUND DIRECTORY RECOGNIZED by the FAMILY MOTOR COACH ASSOCIATION and FAMILY CAMPERS AND RVERS

FORD RV
commtruck.ford.com

THE BEST-SELLING RV CHASSIS OUT THERE.
NOW APPEARING IN A LIFE NEAR YOU.

Why is the Ford Super Duty® frame the RV chassis sales leader? Nothing else delivers the same Built Ford Tough peace of mind. What's more, our Class A chassis features the best-in-class power and torque of the 362-hp Triton® V10 engine. And our Class C chassis boasts best-in-class towing. No wonder they're so easy to get sold on.

FREE INFO! Enter #3438 on Reader Service Card

Sometimes life on the road can seem like a boundless puzzle as we connect the dots around our nation visiting friends and family, making it to the next festival or gathering, or finally making it to that one destination we've always promised ourselves we'd visit. With the constant rise in gas prices, it's time to change our strategy a bit. Driving for hours on the road, going from one far-flung destination to another costs a big chunk of change these days. However, these changing times play into the RV lifestyle that we came to love in the first place. Shorter road trips don't necessarily mean any less of an escape, merely a chance to stop and smell the roses closer to home. This season we offer up an assortment of shorter trips geared around one tank of gas; where you get more bang for your buck, you might say. The goal is to provide you, our dear reader, with an array of getaways all within a fuel tank's worth of travel. We're talking anywhere from 200-400 miles roundtrip, so you know. Each adventure is special in its own way as these shorter routes reveal the unturned stones and the unsung sights, all within an easy drive of one another.

During these times when we're trying to cut back on excessive driving, touring the northeastern U.S. seems made to order. Where else can you be enjoying major art museums in the heart of a sprawling metropolis, and only a half-tank of fuel later have your toes deep in the sand of an Atlantic coast beach? True, the northeast corridor isn't the boundless open road you'll find in the big sky country of the American West, but the region does hold innumerable opportunities to explore American history, quaint New England Villages, and areas that preserve our natural heritage.

MAINE

Escaping to Maine in summer can be some of the most rewarding road tripping you ever might experience. Touring "Downeast," Maine's central coast, reveals many hidden treasures in enchanting seaside towns. All along Hwy 1 from Rockland to Bar Harbor, Maine's picturesque rocky coast is your travel partner.

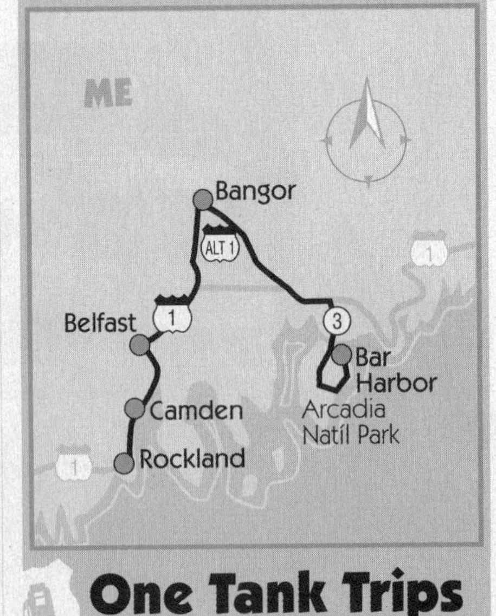

MAINE

Start your Downeast Hwy 1 tour in the town of Rockland. The first of many towns nestled along Penobscot Bay, picturesque Rockland serves as an ideal welcome mat to the area. Catch up on some local culture at the Farnsworth Art Museum and Wyeth Center, where you can learn about three generations of Maine's most beloved art family, the Wyeths. If you're lucky enough to be here during the first week of August, don't miss the Maine Lobster Festival. Sure, it seems every town in coastal Maine has a "lobster fest", but this is truly the granddaddy of 'em all and not to be missed.

Just a few miles up the road you'll find yourself in Camden, a town that promises to get you connected with the heritage of coastal Maine. One favorite activity while visiting this charming little town is to climb aboard one of several old-time schooners that offer half-day and full-day cruises around scenic Penobscot Bay. Like other small Maine towns, Camden comes alive especially during the summer months, when local artisans seem to come from all around to sell their wares. It all makes for great summer days strolling the streets of this appealing village.

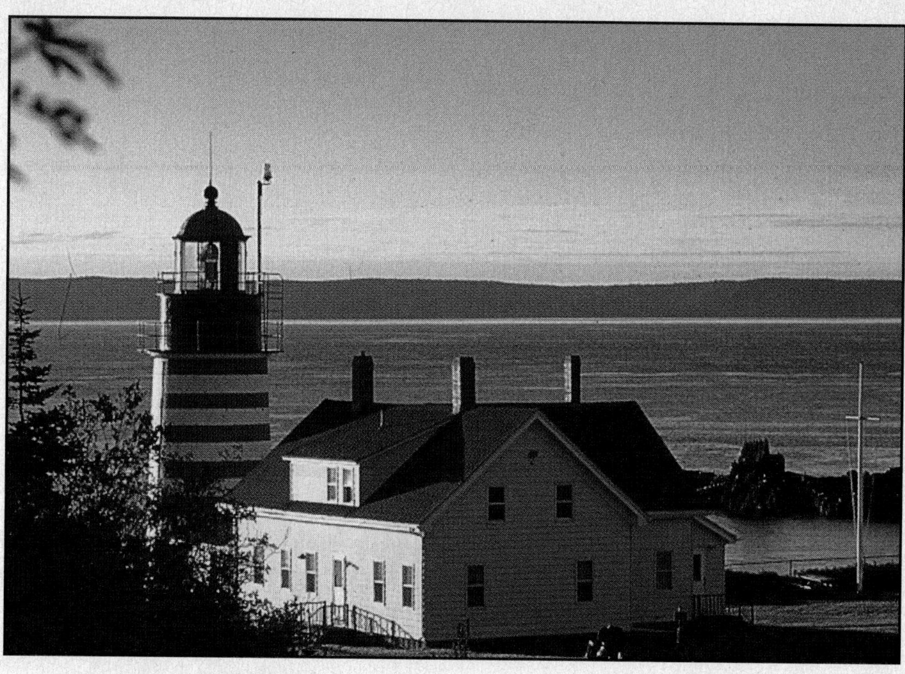
West Quoddy Head Lighthouse, Lubec. Maine Department of Tourism

If you're into this idea of exploring charming small towns in search of hidden treasures and alluring eateries, and learning what Maine is all about, head up the road along the coast to Belfast, a town with oodles of authentic Maine charm. You can also take a ride on the famous Belfast Moosehead Railroad or enjoy a relaxing seaside lunch, watching the sailboats and kayaks out on the water.

Just across the bay from Belfast lies the town of Searsport. Brush up on your maritime history with a visit to the state's oldest maritime museum, the Penobscot Marine Museum. It includes several buildings that capture 18th century life in this nautical village and presents exhibits with artifacts of Maine's heritage, including the unique Glass Plate Image Archive.

Travel the highway a spell, and soon you will reach Bangor, home to two American cultural giants. One is the famous lumberjack, Paul Bunyan, whose statue towers over tourists in Bass Park. Said to be the largest statue of Paul Bunyan in the country, the likeness is over 31 feet tall. The other giant here is the famous author Stephen King, who made his residence in Bangor for a number of years, and who includes the town in many of his novels. If you want a good scare, visit King's home, and you will find it as macabre as any place in his stories. If children are in your traveling party, be sure to head over to the Maine Discovery Museum, where exhibits on anatomy, geography, and nature both delight, and inform, kids and adults alike. And if you are lucky enough to wander into town at the right time, you will be able to experience the annual American Folk Festival, held at the Bangor waterfront. This festival draws people from all over the country to join in the celebration of Folk music, dance, and crafts. It is an event not to be missed.

Nature lover's will adore the Standwood Wildlife Sanctuary, located just a few miles due east Hwy 1 in the town of Ellsworth. This 200-acre sanctuary offers a meditative respite for strolling the miles of foot paths while becoming acquainted with Maine's natural spectacles.

Summer life in Maine reaches its extremes in the town of Bar Harbor. Normally a quiet village of 2,000 residents, ten times that many pack in for the summer months. However, it's for good reason: Bar Harbor is an enticing New England summer resort town which also provides the gateway to some of the finest natural wonders east of the Mississippi River, in Acadia National Park. The park itself encompasses more than half of the enormous Mount Desert Island as well as several smaller islands. Take time to explore the 27-mile

Other Area Locations

BANGOR
Pumpkin Patch RV Resort

ROCKPORT
Camden Hills RV Resort (Morgan RV Resorts)

Megunticook Campground By The Sea (Morgan RV Resorts)

Loop Road. Along the way you'll encounter places to fish, sea-kayak, bicycle, ride horseback, picnic, or just sit back and enjoy the views of the Atlantic seashore.
www.visitmaine.com; 888/624-6345.

CONNECTICUT

It's hard to believe that right here along Hwy 1, you're less than two hours outside of the most populated city in the United States. However, it won't take long to realize that this sojourn down Hwy 1 is a fine change of pace from the crowded city streets of New York City and will take you deep into the beauty of New England.

You can follow Hwy 1 as it skirts the north shore of Long Island Sound. Sure I-95 runs a parallel route, but

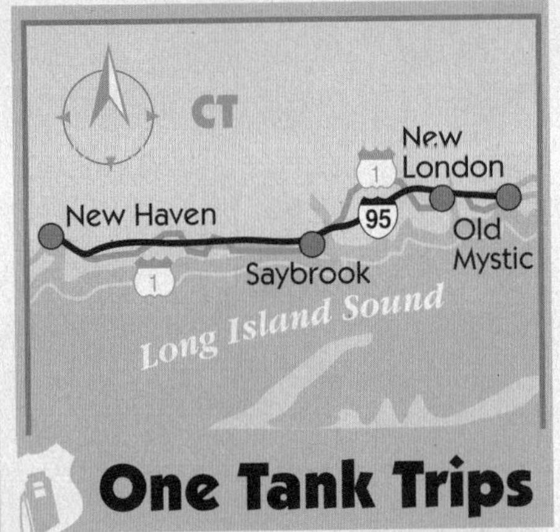

CONNECTICUT

it's a good idea to skip the super highway since it is the main (busier) route between New York City and Boston. New Haven is the perfect starting point for exploring Connecticut. Home of Yale University, New Haven has a lot going for it no matter what the time of year. Explore the New Haven Green, an historic 16-acre public park and the central square of the nine-square settlement plan of the original Puritan colonists. Spend some time milling about the 84-acre Lighthouse Point Park, the jewel of New Haven's park system, which includes a circa 1840 lighthouse as well as an authentically restored Coney Island carousel. Other highlights around town include the Connecticut Audubon Coastal Center and the Eli Whitney Museum, a tribute to New Haven's favorite son and inventor of the cotton gin.

Heading east along Hwy 1, don't miss a chance to pull over and explore the plethora of New England villages dotting the coastline. In Guilford, stop by the Henry Whitfield State Historical Museum, which features one of the oldest homes in all of New England (and there are a lot of old homes in New England). Dip your toes in the Long Island Sound at the largest beach park in the state, Hammonasett Beach State Park, found in the town of Madison. Down the road in Old Lyme lie the remnants of an old ship captains' town, which has been nicely preserved. One of the town's best attractions is the Florence Griswold Museum and its renowned collection of 18th- and 19th-century American art.

Further east on Hwy 1, as you travel to New London, you can visit the boyhood home of famed playwright Eugene O'Neill. The Eugene O'Neill Theater Center stands in his honor and hosts a variety of theater events throughout the year. O'Neill's restored boyhood home, the Monte Cristo Cottage, can also be seen.

In nearby Groton, be sure to stop by the impressive Submarine Force Museum, which features the U.S.S. Nautilus, the world's first nuclear-powered submarine.

The spirited town of Mystic is (sigh) our last stop along coastal Hwy 1. As one of the premier destinations in all of New England, the town features a period village virtually restored in its entirety, to depict its glory years as a famed 19th-century seaport. Mystic is the perfect place to explore the whaling and fishing history that made this town the jewel it is today.

www.tourism.state.ct.us
888/CT-VISIT.

NEW YORK

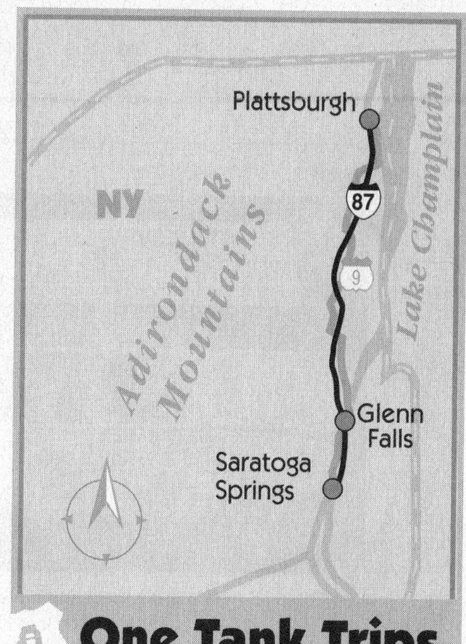

NEW YORK

THIS ROUTE BROUGHT TO YOU BY:

Lake George RV Park
www.lakegeorgervpark.com
info@lakegeorgervpark.com
(518)792-3775

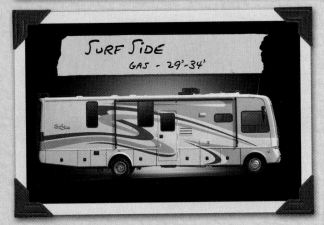

Naturally, we all know about the high-energy magnetism of New York City. However, when we think of nature, we think a tour of the state's Adirondack Park and its six million acres might be New York's most deserving attraction.

Let's start our Adirondack tour in one of New York's pleasant big towns, Saratoga Springs. Be sure to explore the city's downtown area, a large yet unassuming collection of unique shops and eateries. If you like watching the ponies race, well, this is the place for you. Spend an afternoon at the historic Saratoga Racetrack and catch up on the sport's history at the National Museum and Racing Hall of Fame. A favorite local venue for events is the Saratoga Spa State Park. Listed as a National Historic Landmark, this 2,200-acre public park offers the Saratoga Performing Arts Center, the Spa Little Theater, the National Museum of Dancc, and the Lincoln Baths. History buffs won't want to miss a chance to visit the Saratoga National Historical Park, a wonderful place to learn about the Battle of Saratoga, possibly the most important battle of the American Revolution.

After you've had your fill of Saratoga Springs, head north on US-9 to the town of Lake George. In and around its 32-mile lake are plenty of opportunities for golfing, fishing, and boating... oh, lots and lots of boating. The south side of the lake hosts the namesake village, which we consider to be a thoroughly enjoyable throwback to the heyday of 1950s East Coast resort towns. The north side of

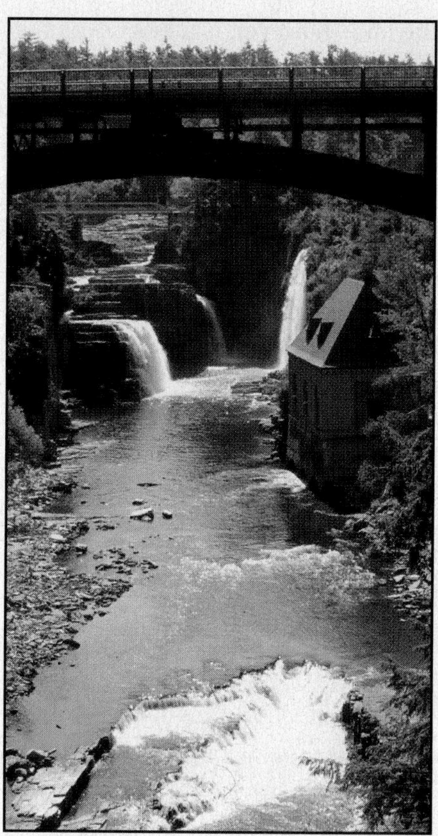

Ausable Chasm off Lake Champlain, Adirondacks.
Lake Placid/Essex County Visitors Bureau.

the lake, however, is a less developed region offering more rustic escapes and plenty of opportunities to explore the greener side of a wonderful, natural environment.

Stay on US-9 north and consider having lunch or going antiquing in the town of Warrensburg before pressing on northwards to Schroon Lake. From there, stay on Hwy 9 north to Hwy 73 north, until the town of Saranac Lake comes into view. This little town is as charming as they get in New York State. Nestled along the lake of the same name, the town is the cultural hub of the northern Adirondacks high country. These environs are noticeably different than those surrounding Lake George and Schroon Lake. Here, the terrain dazzles with thousands of green acres highlighted by towering peaks. Of course, the area's beauty was on full display during the 1980 winter Olympic Games, held in the nearby village of Lake Placid. It's hard to imagine that the world converged on this normally quiet, small town for a couple of weeks nearly 30 years ago. Despite its time on the world stage, the town retains its authentic spirit while serving as a world-class, Olympic training center and home for all sorts of competitive events.

From Lake Placid, let's cut across Hwy 86 north through the town of Jay to Keeseville, our last stop along this tour. Don't miss the impressive Ausable Chasm where, 150 feet down, you can walk along the famous Inner Sanctum trail, or ride the legendary Ausable River whitewater in a river raft. Anglers will feel right at home here since the Ausable River is world-renown for its lively trout fishing.

In Plattsburgh, New Yorkers take their history seriously. Re-enactments of the famous 1814 Battle of Plattsburgh takes place annually, and they are so realistic, you feel like you are in the thick of the war. And if you head over to the Kent-Delord House Museum, you can experience the lives of early Americans during 1812, with exhibits and artifacts showcasing this period. Hear from both "American defenders" and "British attackers" here, as they tell you first-hand the struggles they experienced. While in town, make sure to get some culture by heading over to Plattsburgh Art Museum, located on the campus of the State University of New York. This Art Museum houses the works of such masters as Cézanne, Picasso, and Peter Paul Rubens, as well as media and sculpture pieces. To finish a visit of Plattsburgh properly, take a Juniper Boat Tour around Lake Champlain, and take in the beauty of the Lake and the surrounding Adirondack Mountains.

LAKE GEORGE
Ledgeview RV Park

LAKE LUZERNE
Half Mile Ranch Camping Resort

NEWBURGH
KOA-Newburgh/New York City North

NORTH HUDSON
Yogi Bear's Jellystone Park at Paradise Pines

WARRENSBURG
Lake George/Schroon Valley Resort

www.iloveny.com
800/CALL-NYS.

NEW HAMPSHIRE

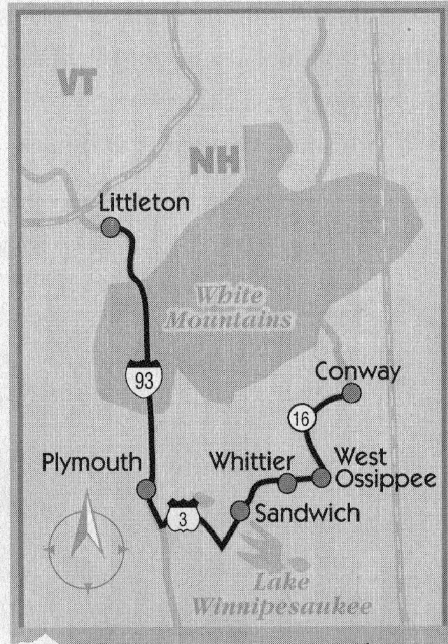

NEW HAMPSHIRE

Of all the New England states, New Hampshire seems the most intent on keeping a low profile. Let Vermont and Massachusetts attract the hordes of "Leaf Peepers" who appear each autumn. Let Rhode Island and Maine attract folks for their maritime history and picturesque coastal towns. All the better for "the Granite State", and for you, too. New Hampshire is chock-full of hidden adventures and unique treasures. You just gotta know where to look.

One way to explore New Hampshire is by touring the White Mountains, a 770,000-acre expanse that defines the northern half of the state. Let's start in the town of Littleton, a quaint little hamlet that will be your "base camp" for exploring the White Mountain National Forest, located just a few miles down the road. In nearby Bethlehem, you'll find the forest's ranger station where you can load up on all the info and ideas you need to really get the most out of exploring the forest.

From Littleton, let's head south along I-93 for just a few miles to get a taste of bucolic New Hampshire at Franconia Notch State Park. Once covered by glaciers, this spectacular setting benefits from wonderful vistas and great hiking trails left in the wake of its own personal ice age. Here, of course, lie the remains of the "Old Man of the Mountain", a rocky outcropping that, until recently, resembled the profile of a man's face. Over the years, the "Old Man" became a New Hampshire icon and it even appears on the New Hampshire issue of the U.S. quarter. Sadly, the "Old Man" finally gave in to old age and was destroyed several years ago when the rock formation collapsed from the side of the mountain.

Keep heading south along I-93 and pick up Hwy 3, a lazier, gentler way to enjoy road-tripping New Hampshire-style. By the time you hit

North Woodstock, you'll be in the heart of the White Mountain National Forest. While in town, treat yourself to a visit at Clark's Trading Post; part general store and part amusement park, reminiscent of South Dakota's famed Wall Drug.

Stay on Hwy 3 south until reaching the town of Plymouth, nestled in at the southern border of the forest. Be sure to visit the Smith Bridge, which spans the Baker River, and/or the Polar Caves Park, which showcases the work of Mother Nature from when the glaciers receded from the area some 50,000 years ago.

From Plymouth, lets head east along Hwy 113. You might try a pleasant side trip from here southward to Lake Winnipesaukee, an adventure unto itself, with nearly 300 miles of shoreline and easy New England roads to follow. Otherwise, we recommend cutting a path northeast back along Hwy 113 to the end of our White Mountain getaway in town of North Conway, a busy little New England hideaway loaded with great shopping for those fortunate enough to make it this way. One way to sit back and enjoy these environs is on the Conway Scenic Railway, an 11-mile round trip that meanders through the lush area around the national forest. You might also consider signing up with one of the many outfitters to kayak or canoe the scenic Saco River. We think you can't go wrong either way.

Heading down the road a pace, you will find the town of Sandwich, nestled between the majestic White Mountains and the sparkling lakes. Take a hike up Sandwich Mountain to soak it all in with a scenic view. Or maybe visit Squam Lakes Natural Science Center to learn about the local landscape. At the center, you can also take a moose tour, to experience the wildlife up close and personal.

Hiding away in our route is the tiny village of Whittier, named after the poet, John Greenleaf Whittier, who would frequent this spot often. Once you stop, you can see why. Whittier is a peaceful, idyllic New England town, that lends itself to quiet inspiration. It is here that you can see the historic Whittier Bridge, one of the oldest, enclosed, wood bridges in the country.

If your trip needs a little pop, head over to West Ossipee, and Mt. Madness, where there are 750 acres of open land dedicated to extreme sports. Here you can snow-broad, ride motorcycles or ATVs, play a round of paintball, and go rappelling. Bumps, bruises, and serious adrenaline rushes guaranteed. However, West Ossipee has a tamer side as well. You can learn to kayak at White Lake State Park, shop the abundance of antique stores that are around every corner, or simply take a stroll down a winding road, lined with graceful New England foliage.

Other Area Locations

LANCASTER
Roger's Campground

www.visitnh.com
800/FUN-IN-NH.

RHODE ISLAND

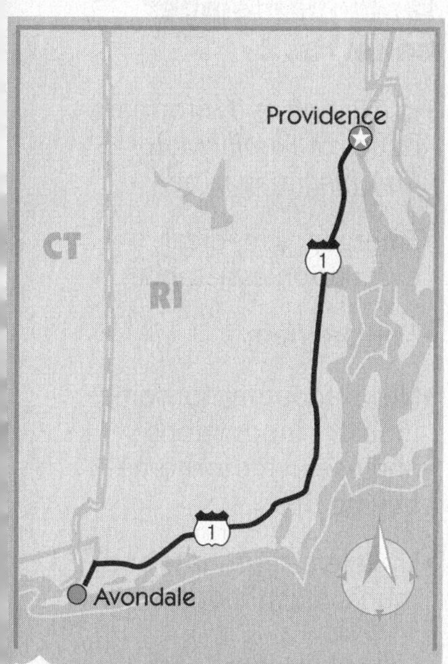

One Tank Trips

RHODE ISLAND

In most states, taking a short, one-gas-tank tour is like taking one bite of a delicious sandwich and walking away. However, Rhode Island is so small, it's perfect for one-tank road trips. Whatever the reason, you find yourself in Rhode Island, a coastal tour along Route 1 packs plenty of appeal, from Providence to Avondale, to all along the Connecticut border.

Let's start our Ocean State journey in the capital city of Providence. This city is a delightful blend of historic maritime New England as well as all the amenities of a modern city. Definitely give Benefit Street a good look, with its more than 100 historic buildings representing Colonial, Greek Revival, and Victorian architecture. Then hop on over to the Museum of Art at the world-renown Rhode Island School of Design (RISD: pronounced "Riz-Dee," by those in the know). Other city highlights include the Roger Williams Park and Zoo, taking a stroll through the Waterfront Park and Riverwalk, or spending an afternoon exploring the historic campus of Brown University.

From Providence, let's head south along Rte 1 to the town of East Greenwich. Boaters, mainly of the yachting variety, flock to the city during the summer months and its port along Greenwich Bay. Dip your toes in the water at the Goddard Memorial State Park, a 440-acre retreat complete with a popular beach, a 9-hole public golf course, hiking and biking trails, and much more.

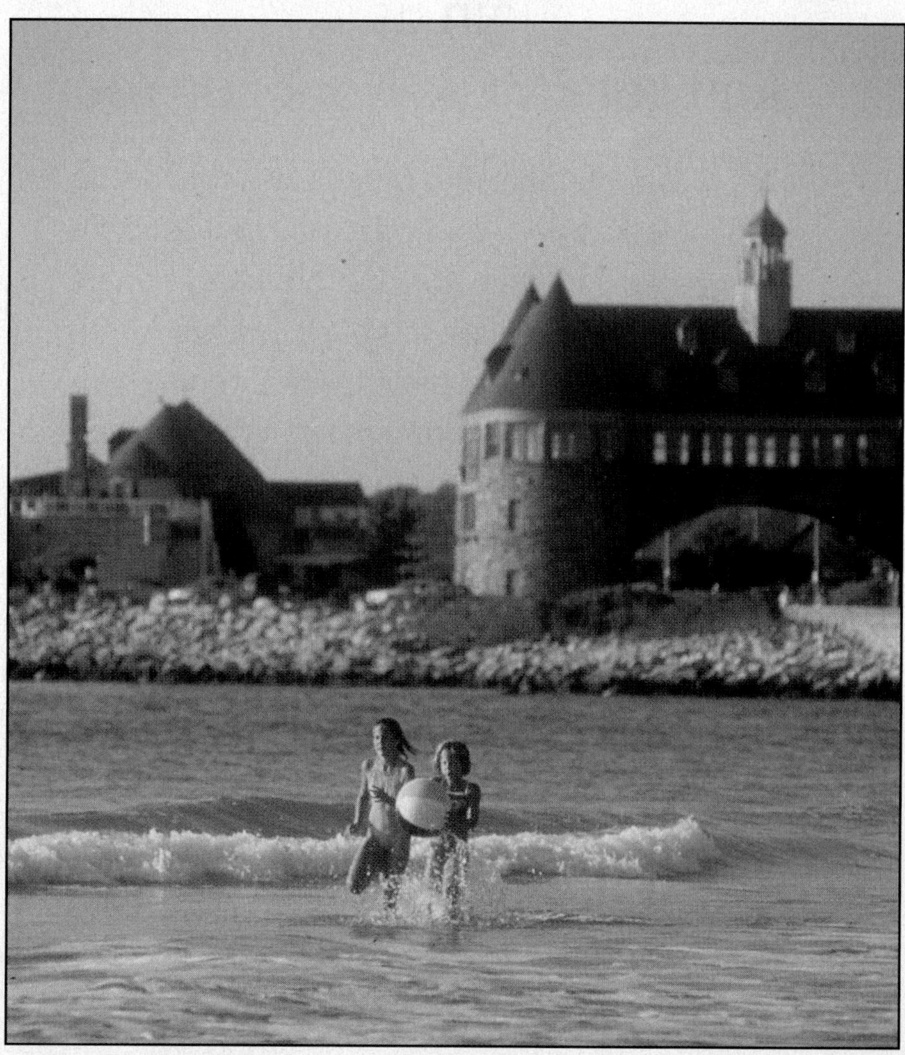

Narragansett Beach, Narragansett. Photo Credit: Rhode Island Tourism Division

The next town on our southward trek is Warwick. Best known as the childhood home of famed American contemporary novelist John Updike, the town boasts a picturesque harbor and downtown area dotted with historic homes. Further south on Hwy 1 you'd do well to stop near North Kingstown at Smith's Castle, one of the oldest plantation houses in the nation. Afterwards, enjoy a visit to the Old Narragansett Church, built in 1707.

Heading south, don't miss a stop in Narragansett, your portal to Rhode Island's South County beach country. Once a thriving casino town, today this coastal community is popular with surfers and boaters alike. Heading west along Hwy 1 you'll come across several public beaches and parks, including Roger W. Wheeler Memorial Beach and East Matunuck State Beach, ideal places to spend a quiet afternoon by the surf.

When you get to Charlestown, be sure to stop for a visit to the Kimball Wildlife Refuge run by the Rhode Island Audubon Society.

Our last stop-off in Rhode Island is near the western border, at the town of Watch Hill. This upscale resort community is full of historic homes, where everyone gets especially gussied up during the high summer season. Be sure to take a spin on the Flying Horse Carousel, an authentic 1867 carousel located right on the beach, or snap some family postcard photos at the granite Watch Hill Lighthouse, which celebrated its 200th birthday in 2007.

Step into the town of Avondale for a taste of a true rustic, New England style fishing community.

Equinox Mountain, Vermont.
Photo credit: Manchester and the Mountains Regional Chamber of Commerce.

Here in Avondale you will find the famous Watch Hill lighthouse, a pictorial piece of nautical history, which serves as both a monument, and as a symbol of Rhode Island pride. For a real scenic excursion, stop by Wilcox Park and Arboretum, which delights every sense-from lush gardens, to beautiful statues, to charming walkways, Wilcox Park is definitely worth the time. While walking the grounds, you might even stumble onto a Shakespeare performance, which takes place here often.

www.visitrhodeisland.com
401/278-9100.

VERMONT

Almost like a siren, Vermont beckons road-trippers to its many miles of lazy country roads that spin through rolling pastoral landscapes. We're thinking this sounds pretty great, too.

Vermont's capital city of Montpelier is a good place to start.

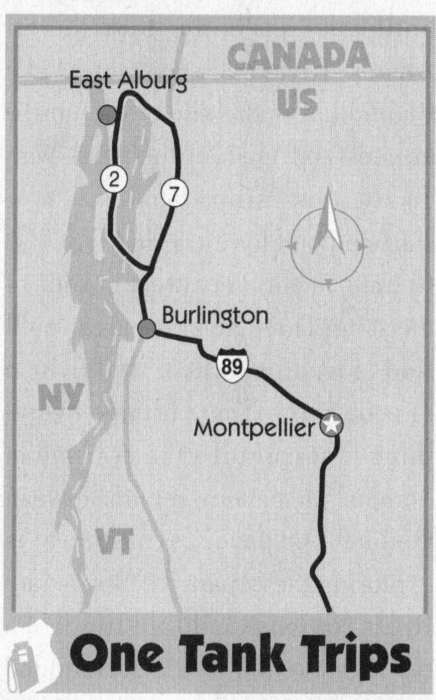

While you're in town, check out the historic State House before heading to Morse Farm, a working sugar and maple farm located just outside of town. For a unique perspective on Vermont, consider a side-trip south on US-302 to the town of Barre, where you'll find the impressive 500-foot-deep Rock of Ages Quarry; it's the world's largest granite quarry.

From Montpelier, let's head north along US-2, running parallel to I-89, to the town of Burlington. Home to the University of Vermont, Burlington is the largest city in the state, and home to nearly a third of the state's population in its greater metropolitan area. Nestled along the banks of the scenic Lake Champlain, the historic district along Church Street is excellent for spending the afternoon soaking in the local atmosphere. Just outside town, consider a visit to Shelburne Farms, an historic 1,400-acre estate-turned-city-park.

From Burlington, head north along US-7 as it parallels the eastern banks of Lake Champlain, until you reach the town of St. Albans. Trivia buffs take note: Lake Champlain is the site of the northernmost skirmish of the Civil War. Today, this railroad town is your starting point for exploring Franklin County in the northwest corner of the state. Throughout the area you'll find adventure-filled trails, lush forests, and rolling pastures-everything that captures the essence of Vermont no matter what time of year. One of our favorite pastimes is exploring the expansive Missisquoi River National Wildlife Refuge, a 6,000+-acre peninsula surrounded by the chilly waters of Lake Champlain.

Blink your eyes, and you might miss East Alburg. However, this little town offers so much that we think it is worth a stop. For nature lovers, the place to be is the Alburg Dunes, a veritable oasis near Lake Champlain, where wild deer, turkey, and a host of feathered fowl can be seen in their natural environment. If your legs need a stretch, consider taking a bike ride on many of East Alburgs short, but exciting, bike trails. And if you make it to town in August, make sure not to miss the Lake Champlain Bluegrass Festival, where some of the biggest stars in Bluegrass put on one of the best live concerts this side of the Mississippi. You will be tapping your toes the rest of the trip.

Close out your Vermont tour by taking Hwy 78 west to US-2 south. This road allows for a little island hopping thanks to a series of beautiful Lake Champlain Islands such as Isle La Motte and North Hero located on charming Grand Isle. *www.vermontvacation.com; 800/VERMONT.*

MASSACHUSETTS

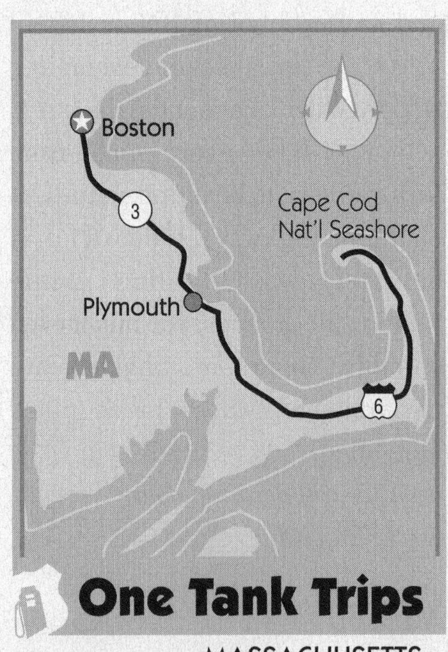

Throughout New England many worthwhile destinations are located within a tank-full of gas of one another. Massachusetts and its offerings are no different. Where else can you leave a bustling, historical metropolis and then get lost among sprawling sand beaches and endless protected green space? Well, on this trip you can, as we take you from the city environs of Boston to the rustic and inspiring peninsula of Cape Cod.

Okay, so Boston isn't the friendliest place for big rigs, but that's no reason you shouldn't try to explore New England's capital city. Maybe you'll want to park that motorhome and take a cab or carriage, or walk off the calories from the morning funnel cakes? If it's your first trip to "Beantown", be sure to get history's perspective to appreciate Boston's contribution to the formation of the United States. A great way to do that is by walking the Freedom Trail, a series of historical markers and sites tracing some of the most important events in our nation's history. Some highlight destinations in the heart of Old Boston include the Paul Revere House and the Old State House, site of the Boston Massacre. Other city highlights include the Boston Common and Public Garden, the New England Aquarium, and the John F. Kennedy Presidential Library and Museum.

We love Boston, but let's get outta town on southbound I-93 for a few minutes before jumping on US-3A south as it traces Massachusetts Bay. One of America's oldest settlements is the town of Duxbury. Founded in 1637 after some Pilgrims found Plymouth, well, a little too crowded, today, the town is popular for its stellar, nine-mile beach along the bay.

Just south of Duxbury is where this whole "America" thing got started. You have heard about Plymouth, haven't you? History buffs will no doubt enjoy a visit to the impressive Plimouth Plantation, a living-history museum that recreates the 1620-era village. Moreover, visitors can check out the Mayflower II, a replica of the 17th-century vessel that brought the Pilgrims to America, at (where else?) Plymouth Rock.

Pick up US-6A east from Plymouth towards Cape Cod and your first stop on the peninsula, at Sandwich. As the first town settled on Cape Cod, the main attraction here is a visit to the Sandwich Glass Museum, home to a truly awesome collection of more than 5,000 pieces of glassworks produced by the Sandwich Company during the 19th-century.

Skirting the northern shores of the Cape, be sure to make a stop at the Cape Cod Museum of Natural History in Brewster. While you're in the city limits, you might want to learn about firefighting history at the impressive New England Fire and History Museum, which nicely presents the equipment, and captures the history, of these brave men and women, from Revolutionary War times to modern day.

In the town of Orleans, pick up US-6 as it heads north some 30 miles to the tip of the Cape. In just a few miles there will be nothing beyond the Cape Cod National Seashore. Hey, things could be worse. Yes, you're going to need to simply put up with mile after mile of stunning flora and fauna thriving in endless acres of protected seashore, cedar swamps, and sprawling wetlands, all the way to Provincetown. We suggest a visit to the Salt Pond Visitors Center near Eastham to get caught up on what else to see and do along the seashore. However, we might also recommend visits to such standout places as the inspiring, windswept Province Lands Area, the Atlantic White Cedar Swamp Trail, and Marconi Beach near South Wellfleet.

Other Area Locations

EAST FALMOUTH
Cape Cod Campresort & Cabins
SALISBURY
Rusnik Family Campground

www.mass-vacation.com
617/973-8500.

Mid-Atlantic destinations offer exceptional variety and great fun for travelers. In New Jersey, you can go "Victorian" in Cape May or play the night away at a boardwalk casino. Pennsylvania is perfect for sampling chocolates, bologna, and fine wine. Find a seashore hideaway in Delaware or settle in for a succulent seafood feast at a Maryland restaurant. Try exploring a cave in West Virginia, an aquarium in Virginia, or the mighty Smithsonian museums in Washington, DC.

PENNSYLVANIA

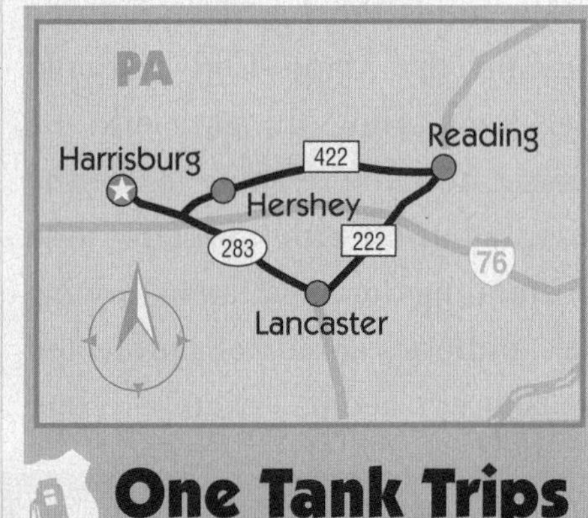

PENNSYLVANIA

Your family can't go wrong on a road tour of Pennsylvania, whether you amble through downtown Harrisburg, dip into chocolate at Hersheypark, or munch a slice of Lebanon's storied bologna. Kutztown's caves, Allentown's wineries, and the crayons and canals of Easton set the stage for a perfect Pennsylvania getaway.

We prefer to start things off in the central region around Pennsylvania's state capital of Harrisburg. Walk around the vibrant downtown district and browse through Broad Street Market among bright flowers, fresh veggies, and tempting bakery treats. See thousands of classic toys in an amazing full-scale "doll house" setting at - where else? - the Doll House Museum. The impartial National Civil War Museum, also in Harrisburg, is credited as both the largest and least subjective among Civil War centers in America.

A quick show of hands: Who's in the mood for chocolate? Yep, just like we thought. Good thing Hershey is just down the road on US-422. Stroll, ride, and smile your way around a sweet and entertaining escape at Hersheypark, Chocolate World, and bountiful Hershey Gardens. Be sure to include a visit to Hershey's big-time Antique Auto Museum, where a laudable collection of antique cars and buses steers you through 80 momentous years of transportation history.

From Hershey, pick up US-422 east to Lebanon. Hopefully, it'll be nearing lunchtime when you enter the town limits, where you'll find Weaver's Famous Lebanon Bologna store ready to fill you up on some wonderful local grub. With a full belly, continue your drive east into Reading. Just a few miles south of here, on US-422, is the town of Birdsboro and the Daniel Boone Homestead, the legendary

Pennsylvanian's 18th-century birthplace.

From Reading, follow US-222 east through Kutztown, where you can participate in an underground cave tour, go panning for gems, and check out the Rock Shop at Crystal Cave. Before you leave the area, spend a memorable hour rolling past tidy Mennonite farms on an East Penn Scenic Railroad ride.

In the town of Allentown, also on US-222, tour and taste-test at acclaimed local wineries, pedal your way through a day of scenic cycling, or learn to fly-fish on the Delaware River in Allentown. Lost River Caverns outside Bethlehem offers guided explorations of local limestone caves that contain curious stalagmite, stalactite, and flowstone formations with names such as "Crystal Chapel" and the namesake "Lost River."

From Bethlehem, follow US-22 east into Easton, where our gas-tank trip ends. First stop: the Crayola Factory, production site for the ever-popular crayons and markers. Next, take a historic cruise on a mule-drawn canal boat at the National Canal Museum. Both stops are located at Two Rivers Landing in Easton.

www.visitPA.com
800/VISIT-PA.

NEW JERSEY

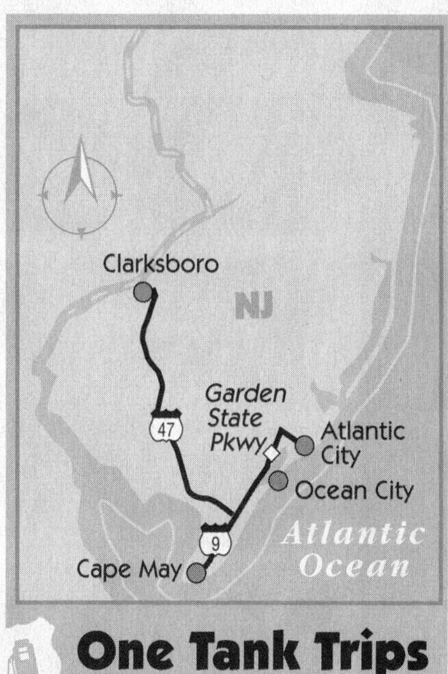

In New Jersey, the options for tourists are top-notch. You can hit the casinos or stroll the boardwalk in Atlantic City; take to the beach at Ocean City, Stone Harbor, or Wildwood; go Victorian in Cape May; or explore south-central New Jersey's glassmaking heritage in Millville and Glassboro.

Continued on page 26

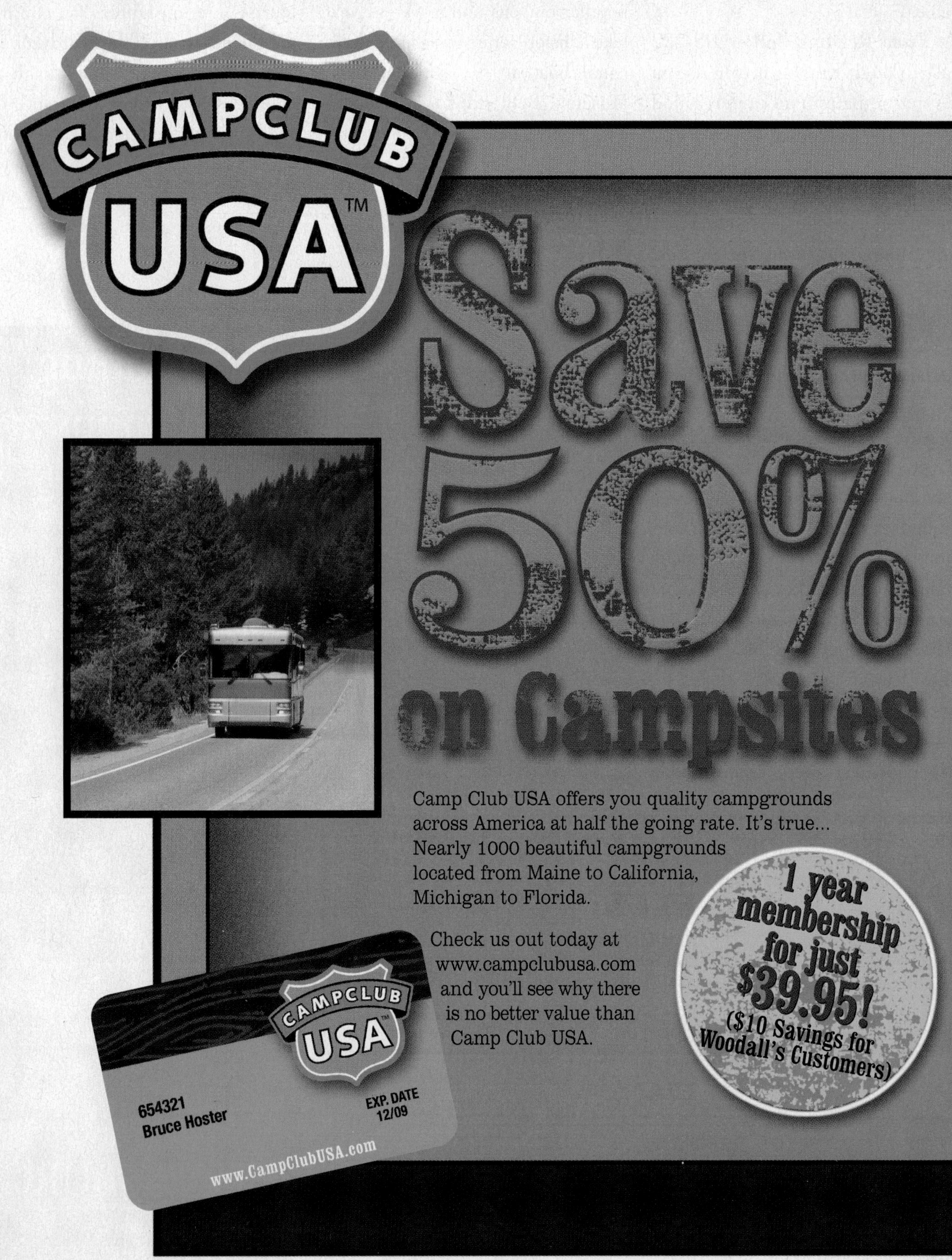

CAMPCLUB USA™
Save 50% on Campsites
Camp Club USA offers you quality campgrounds across America at half the going rate. It's true... Nearly 1000 beautiful campgrounds located from Maine to California, Michigan to Florida.
Check us out today at www.campclubusa.com and you'll see why there is no better value than Camp Club USA.
1 year membership for just $39.95! ($10 Savings for Woodall's Customers)
CAMPCLUB USA™
654321
Bruce Hoster
EXP. DATE 12/09
www.CampClubUSA.com

Prepare to be dazzled by the sights, sounds and high-rolling action in Atlantic City's numerous casino resorts. "AC" fully earns its widespread reputation as the city that's always turned on, and the constant excitement spills over into shopping venues such as Atlantic City Outlets-The Walk and Siganos Plaza, plus boardwalk-based retailers like Steel's Fudge, James Salt Water Taffy, and Boardwalk Peanut Shoppe. Atlantic City's circa 1870 boardwalk also sports arcades, a renovated 1929 concert hall, restaurants galore, and health spas. Be sure to try out the Steel Pier's abundance of games, rides, lively entertainers, and food vendors. Even though the boardwalk's hustle-bustle can be captivating, some AC visitors say the city's best attraction is under the boardwalk, lounging about on the less frenzied, sandy beaches.

From Atlantic City, take Atlantic City Expressway west to Garden State Parkway (Rte 444) south, all the way to Cape May. Whoa - what's your rush? Be sure to stop along the way at the following fun spots: In delightful Ocean City, you can take a look at thousands of shells from around the world at Ocean City's Discovery Sea Shell Museum. For family amusements and water park slides, check out Gillian's two Ocean City locations at Island and Wonderful Pier. If you're interested in eateries and shops of all varieties, walk through Downtown Ocean City. Bird watchers catch great views of shorebirds at the Stone Harbor Bird Sanctuary and Wetlands Institute and Museum. Turtle tanks, an aquarium, and salt marsh safari are but a few of the highlights.

The town of Wildwood is the home of a jammin', family-friendly boardwalk. And it's also the site of the National Marbles Hall of Fame, a collection of mementos and trophies earned by the world's top marble champions. The Hall of Fame is part of the George F. Boyer Historical Museum, a center that interprets Wildwood area history. Plan to visit Victorian Cape May's colorful Historic District via trolley or on foot. Stop to see the Victorian House Museum and restored Cape May Lighthouse, originally constructed in 1859. Hop aboard the Seashore Lines Railroad for a train ride through town

Other Area Locations

BUENA
Buena Vista Camping Resort (Morgan RV Resorts)

CAPE MAY
Lake Laurie Campground (Morgan RV Resorts)
Seashore Campsites

CLARKSBORO
Timberlane Campground

MAYS LANDING
Yogi Bear's Jellystone Park Camp Resort (Morgan RV Resorts)

OCEAN VIEW
Ocean View Resort Campground

PORT REPUBLIC
Atlantic City Blueberry Hill (Morgan RV Resorts)

WOODSTOWN
Four Seasons Campground

or sail away on a cruise to catch sightings of whales and dolphins.

From Cape May take US-9 north, then pick up NJ State Hwy 47 north to Millville, where glass production is a key factor in the past and present times of New Jersey's south-central communities. The Glasstown Arts District showcases regional artistry, including prints, pottery, and glass creations. The Riverfront Renaissance Center for the Arts contains restaurants and retail establishments as well as the work of local artists and craftspeople. Millville's cultural arts center at WheatonArts encompasses the T.J. Wheaton Glass Factory (in operation since 1888), the Museum of American Glass, and the Down Jersey Folk Life Center, where the rich creative traditions of southern New Jersey are celebrated. Another 20 miles north on Hwy 47, Glassboro's Heritage Glass Museum displays glassblowing tools, glass objects, and related keepsakes dating from as far back as the 1700s.

www.visitnj.org
800/VISIT-NJ.

DELAWARE

The state of Delaware welcomes visitors to Dover's NASCAR and harness races, Milford's hiking and boating options, and the splendid seashores of Rehoboth, Dewey, and Bethany Beaches and Fenwick Island.

The city of Dover's Air Mobility Command Museum displays a well-rounded collection of military and tanker aircraft. Cargo planes, bombers, helicopters, and fighters are all represented; there's a flight simulator that gives visitors over the age of ten a well-supervised opportunity to test their piloting skills. Accounts of several American Medal of Honor recipients' courageous

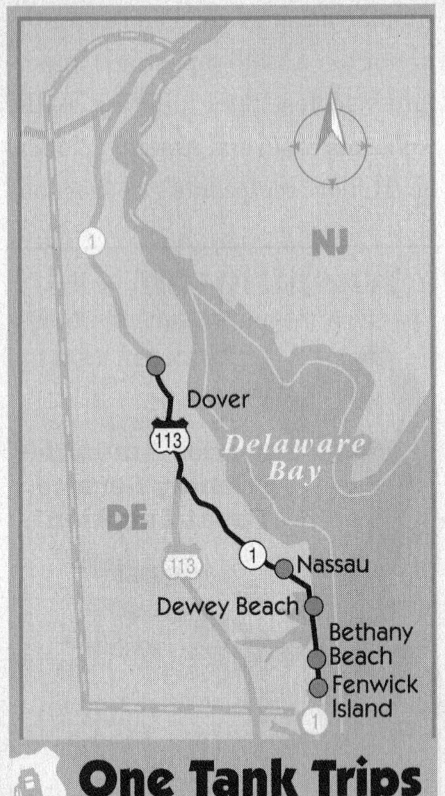

actions are told in the museum's Hall of Heroes. Dover Downs features high-energy harness racing, plenty of slot machines, live entertainment, and casino-style dining. At Dover International Speedway, join in on speedy NASCAR fun at triple-header "Monster Mile" race weekends held twice annually.

From Dover, take US-113 south to Milford. Go for an easy hike through meadows and woods at the Delaware Nature Society's Abbott's Mill Nature Center. Rent a watercraft, go for a sail, or book a seat on a charter fishing boat in Delaware Bay or the Atlantic Ocean, at Adam's Wharf and Indian River Marina.

From Milford, take Delaware Hwy 1 south all the way to Fenwick Island, stopping to see the sights at several beach communities. Start by soaking in Rehoboth Beach's quintessential resort area boardwalk. On the mile-long trek, sink your teeth into beach-style treats like fresh funnel cakes and chewy taffy. Rehoboth's Jolly Trolley can easily shuttle you to the seashore's boutiques, top-notch restaurants, and a whole host of other amusements and points of interest.

A quieter side of Delaware may be found further south at Dewey Beach, where a narrow sandbar is all that separates the Atlantic Ocean from Rehoboth Bay. Angling, boating, and a complete line-up of water sports are popular pastimes at Dewey.

Bethany Beach keeps your itinerary humming with its historic Fenwick Lighthouse, beautiful boardwalk, and challenging golf at Salt Pond Golf Club. The Made by Hand International Cooperative is a fair trade establishment that supports artisan enterprises around the world. Hand-crafted musical instruments, jewelry, apparel, and domestic wares are available for purchase inside.

At the "bottom" of the Delaware, on Hwy 1, undisturbed beaches and a relaxed pace of life grace Fenwick Island's barrier island community. See who's swimming in the fish tanks at DiscoverSea Shipwreck Museum. Look! There's silver and gold bars, coins, jewels, and pottery recovered from sunken ships by local treasure salvors. Take time to tour the museum's conservation lab and local marine history displays.

Other Area Locations

LEWES
Tall Pines
REHOBOTH BEACH
Big Oaks Family Campground

www.visitdelaware.com
866/284-7483.

WEST VIRGINIA

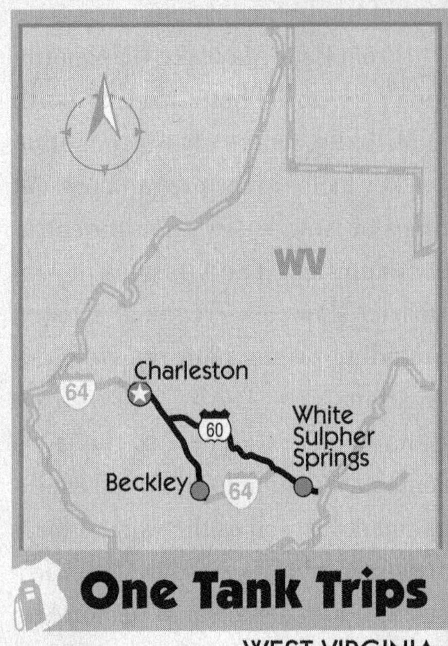

West Virginia keeps tourists engaged with its Capitol Complex in Charleston, abundant natural wonders in locales such as Ansted and White Sulphur Springs, and cultural opportunities that stretch from Charleston to Lewisburg and Beckley.

Beginning with West Virginia's State Capitol Complex in Charleston, tour the unique Capitol building with the gold-leafed dome, visit the state museum and galleries, or attend a concert at the theater in the West Virginia Cultural Center. After your Capitol tour, treat yourself to a memorable meal or shop 'til you drop in the Downtown Village District.

From Charleston, go all the way to White Sulphur Springs on US-60 east, with stops in Ansted and Lewisburg. Are you ready for some nachos? Make sure and, if so, put Ansted's Blue Smoke salsa factory on your hit-list. Through observation windows, watch the actual production of Blue Smoke's celebrated recipe and stock up on fresh-bottled salsa from the factory store. At Hawk's Nest State Park, board a fast-paced jet boat for a spin around the river or fly high above the New River Gorge Canyon on the park's aerial tramway.

Lewisburg's Carnegie Hall invites guests to browse through its art galleries or catch a live performance. At Lost World Caverns, you can go 120 feet under the surface of Greenbrier Valley for an easy, self-paced cave walk past intricate stalactite and stalagmite formations. While you're visiting Lewisburg, keep in mind that it's also a promising spot for fly-fishing. You can keep your outdoor adventure rolling with biking in Caldwell and bass fishing in White Sulphur Springs.

From White Sulphur Springs, take I-64 west to Beckley.

The town's namesake Exhibition Coal Mine operates fascinating seasonal underground tours conducted by experienced coal miners. The Youth Museum of Southern West Virginia features hands-on activities, a pioneer village complete with log cabin, and Mountain Homestead exhibit. Also in Beckley, take in a summer outdoor drama at Theatre West Virginia. At the marketplace known as Tamarack: The Best of West Virginia, allow plenty of time to savor a delicious meal then observe, and support, regional crafters while they work in their studios.

www.callwva.com
800/CALL-WVA.

MARYLAND

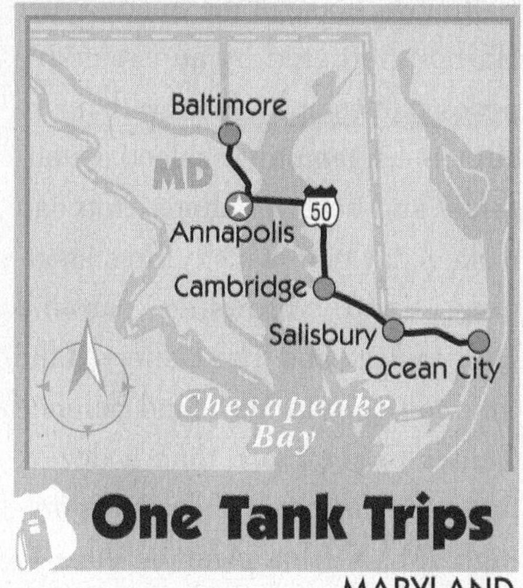

From the acclaimed National Aquarium at Baltimore's Inner Harbor and the U.S. Naval Academy in Annapolis, to Assateague Island's wild, woolly ponies and Ocean City's bustling boardwalk scene, the state of Maryland is a superb destination for RV travelers.

We like to kick things off in Baltimore, home of the trendy Inner Harbor, bordered by an expansive pedestrian complex lined with metro attractions, tempting seafood restaurants, and eclectic shops. You can make a day of it just strolling, shopping, and browsing around Harborplace and The Gallery. Take time to pop into Maryland Science Center to see more than a dozen, full-scale dinosaurs and a five-story-high IMAX film. And be sure to catch the sweeping harbor view from the Top of the World Observation Level at Baltimore's World Trade Center.

Don't depart from the Inner Harbor without visiting Maryland's premier tourist stop, the National Aquarium. Thousands of individual animals represent diverse aquatic ecosystems such as Maryland's Chesapeake Bay, the Pacific Ocean, and the otherworldly Amazon Rainforest. Sleek sharks and stingrays, performing dolphins, lively painted turtles, sizzling electric eels, and colorful coral formations are all part of the National Aquarium experience.

Just north of the I-95 junction with I-395, is the Babe Ruth Birthplace & Museum, where you'll learn about the life and times of Baltimore's larger-than-life native son, George Herman "Babe" Ruth, the renowned "Sultan of Swat." The nearby Sports Legends Museum at Camden Yards contains exhibits featuring the Orioles pro baseball team, (formerly) Baltimore Colts football team, and a selection of legendary Maryland-based sports professionals from various fields of play.

Fort McHenry National Monument & Historic Shrine is the hallowed site of a hard-fought battle against the British during the War of 1812. Based on his views of the dramatic clash at imperiled Fort McHenry, Francis Scott Key wrote the time-tested song "The Star-Spangled Banner." Go ahead, hum a few bars.

If you're a devotee of thoroughbred horse racing, Baltimore's Pimlico Race Course, official home of the Preakness, will keep you entertained with seasonal live races and year-round simulcasts.

From Baltimore, take I-695 south, then Hwy 2 south to Annapolis. The U.S. Naval Academy, the undergraduate institution of the American Navy, first opened its doors in 1845. At the Armel-Leftwich Visitor Center, you can view the film "To Lead and to Serve," and learn about past and present roles of student midshipmen. The Freedom 7 space capsule, tomb of John Paul Jones, and campus chapel are available to tour. Visit the Academy Museum to see displays of naval uniforms, weapons of war, and the circa 1951 Gallery of Ships Models Collection.

During Colonial times, the City Dock was a bustling port occupied by ship's carpenters and rowdy tavern guests. Presently preserved as a peaceful waterfront park, the location is a lovely place to relax and enjoy Annapolis' incomparable views. To gain the best perspective of the circa 1875 Thomas Point Shoal Lighthouse at the mouth of the

South River, you really ought to view it from a boat. Still operated today by the U.S. Coast Guard, the unique screwpile offshore lighthouse is a National Landmark, one of only nine such lighthouses in the entire United States that have survived to this day.

Were you aware that the Maryland State House in Annapolis served as the capitol of the United States in the late 1700s? No? Then back to 6th grade with you! It also bears the distinction of being the oldest, continuously-used state house in America, home to the Maryland General Assembly for three months each year, with offices occupied by Maryland's Governor and Lieutenant Governor.

For a breezy, invigorating close to your sweep of Annapolis' sights, take a two-hour cruise on the schooner Woodwind, a 74' sailing yacht. You can help hoist the sails as a participating crewmember or relax and rejuvenate on the sunny deck. It's your call, sailor.

From Annapolis, take US-50 east towards Ocean City, with stops in Cambridge, Salisbury, and Berlin. Harriet Tubman, famed female abolitionist and escaped slave, was instrumental in the organization of the Underground Railroad, a system of getaway routes and safe houses used by slaves seeking freedom. At the site of Cambridge's historic Bucktown Village Store, take a tour of Tubman's birthplace and learn about the freedom network's secret beginnings. As a sidelight, the store rents out bikes, kayaks, and canoes for self-paced explorations of the area's unspoiled natural surroundings. At nearby Blackwater National Wildlife Refuge, sizable flocks of swans, geese, and ducks swoop in for seasonal landings. The refuge boasts the largest nesting population of bald eagles on the eastern U.S. coast, so it's a great stopover for avid bird watchers.

Speaking of bird-lovers (and wood-carvers), the Ward Museum of Wildfowl Art in Salisbury houses the most extensive collection of contemporary and antique bird carvings found anywhere in the world. Salisbury University's affiliated museum also interprets the history of waterfowl decoy art, and everything is presented in three-dimensional splendor.

Assateague Island National Seashore and State Park, in the town of Berlin, are must-sees! These classic, undeveloped coastal retreats on a 37-mile-long island stretch from Atlantic surf and sandy shores on its eastern boundaries, to Chincoteague Bay's rippling waters on its western edge. Assateague's most famous residents are its shaggy, free-roaming ponies. View them at close range in both the national and state park sections of the island. In addition to pony watching, pleasing pastimes on

Skiing at Wisp Resort.
Photo credit: Tim Tadder.

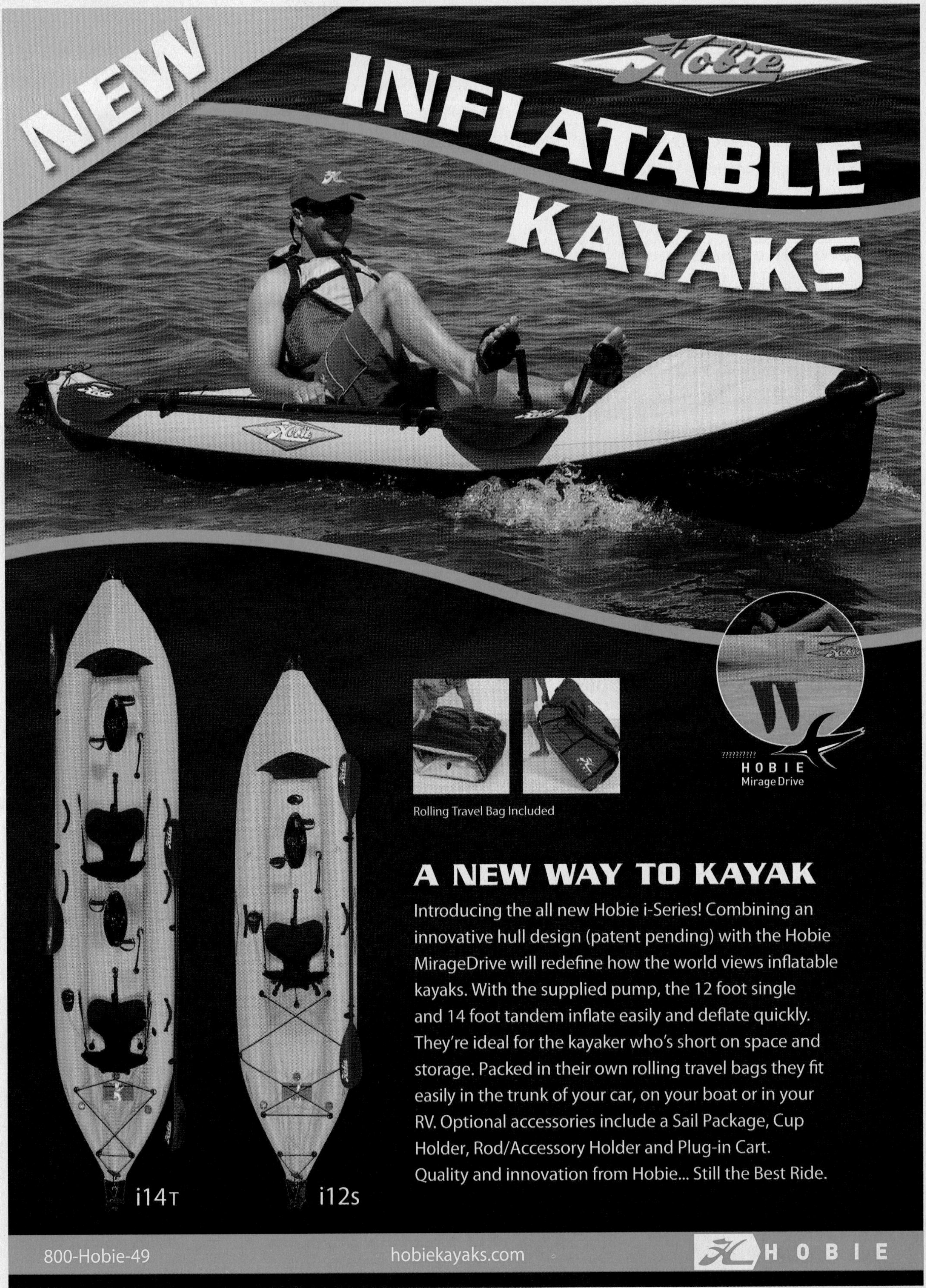

the island of Assateague include ocean swimming, surf-fishing, hiking to the lighthouse, seashell collecting, kayaking, and crabbing.

In Ocean City, Maryland, take a guided nature cruise, explore coastal bays, go for a fast ride on a giant speedboat, or book a customized fishing excursion from one of several local marinas. Play a leisurely round of golf at award-winning courses with the benefit of great ocean views, or stroll along the pier boardwalk and partake in a menagerie of rides, games, and traditional seaside amusements. Don't miss the chance to indulge in some legendary Thrasher's French Fries while you're there. And be sure to see the aquariums and local history exhibits at the circa 1891 Life-Saving Station Museum. *www.visitmaryland.org* *877/333-4455.*

WASHINGTON, DC

The National Mall in Washington, DC is within walking distance of a whole host of inspiring federal monuments, landmark buildings, and outstanding Smithsonian museums. It's the perfect place to begin your sweeping tour of America's capital city. Arlington's National Cemetery, Alexandria's mix of wildlife, arts, and inventions, and Fredericksburg's old-fashioned attractions come together nicely for an interesting DC-Virginia getaway.

Start your Capitol tour at the National Mall, a two-mile-long grassy stretch of parkland located in the heart of Washington, featuring DC's most renowned points of interest. Several major monuments and a Federal Landmark Building are located here, with the west and east ends bordered by the Lincoln Memorial and white-domed U.S. Capitol Building, respectively. The Reflecting Pool and several war memorials are situated between the Lincoln Memorial and the Washington Monument, which stands like a sentinel at the middle of the National Mall lawn. Within easy walking distance are a number of Smithsonian Institution museums, the National Gallery of Art, and U.S. Botanic Gardens, and all are well worth visiting. Other standout DC attractions include the Bureau of Engraving and Printing, where you can see U.S. paper money being produced; the Jefferson Memorial; National Zoological Park; and C&O Canal National Historic Park, where you can take a ride in a mule-drawn canal boat.

From Washington DC, take I-395 south into Arlington, Virginia. Just outside DC, Arlington National Cemetery is a hallowed burial ground for more than 285,000 honored dead, including President John Fitzgerald Kennedy, Supreme Court Justice Thurgood Marshall, and the Tomb of the Unknown Soldier.

Continue on I-395 south into Alexandria, for it's time to dig out your binoculars. Bird watching, anyone? Alexandria's Huntley Meadows Park is prime territory for observing more than 200 feathered species, as well as furry ones such as deer, fox, beaver, and otter. The park encompasses forests, wetlands, and (as its name implies) meadows. There's a boardwalk and observation tower, and a consulting naturalist is on-site to address your questions.

At the three-story Torpedo Factory Art Center in Old Town Alexandria, you can interact with working artists in 82 studios and browse through six fascinating galleries that display ceramics, photography, and mixed-media art. Find out if you have what it takes to become an inventor at Alexandria's U.S. Patent and Trademark Office Museum, where surprising facts and helpful tips about useful everyday inventions are presented. The museum's exhibits are designed to "record, share, and preserve" America's inventive spirit.

South of Alexandria, pick up I-95 south to Fredericksburg. For a handy overview of the city of Fredericksburg, then and now, consider taking a narrated trolley or carriage tour. If you'd like to step back in time at your own pace, visit George Washington's Ferry Farm, the site of Washington's childhood home.

www.washington.org; 800/422-8644.

VIRGINIA

Now let's get serious about Virginia. The charm of Colonial Williamsburg, Newport News' mariners' tales, and the Naval Air Station and aquarium in Virginia Beach add to the sense of adventure, while Suffolk's peanuts and trains, and Petersburg's museums bring your trip to an interesting conclusion.

We think the capital city of Richmond is a worthy starting point for a fabulous vacation. Tour the restored State Capitol Building designed by Thomas Jefferson. For another slice of local history, visit the Richmond National Battlefield Park Civil War Visitor Center that commemorates the Peninsular Campaign of 1862 and General Grant's 1864 Cold Harbor offensive. The center is affiliated with three other Richmond-area National Park Service sites, each memorializing a different Civil War confrontation. Be sure to make a phone appointment to tour Historic Hanover Tavern. This Richmond inn's noteworthy history includes visits by George Washington, Marquis de Lafayette, and Charles Dickens, among others.

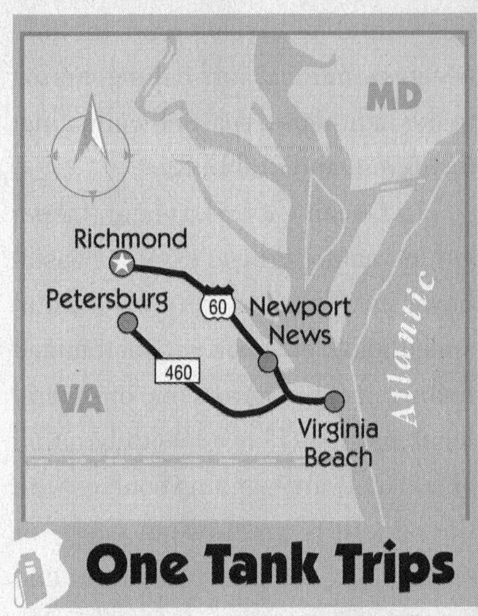

VIRGINIA

In a more contemporary setting, Paramount's Kings Dominion focuses on family-friendly entertainment. The 400-acre amusement park whitens the knuckles with a dozen meaty roller coasters, a water park that's ideal for chilling out, and the frightfully fun and interactive Scooby-Doo™ Haunted Mansion.

From Richmond, go south on US-60 all the way to Virginia Beach

American Impressionism collection.
Photo Credit: Carl Hansen, Smithsonian Institution.

with stops at Williamsburg and Newport News. Early American times are depicted in Colonial Williamsburg, the reconstructed site of Britain's most productive 18th-century New World settlement. Within Williamsburg's 'interactive museum' setting, costumed guides show-and-tell what everyday life was like for the original colony's founding families. To see statues of all U.S. chief executives since George Washington, visit Presidents Park. And to bounce back to the present, spend some time at the world-famous Busch Gardens Williamsburg, acclaimed as the world's most beautiful amusement park.

The Mariner's Museum in Newport News boasts an international collection of small watercraft, ship models, and objects recovered from the USS Monitor, America's first ironclad warship.

The Virginia Aquarium and Marine Science Center just down Hwy 60 in Virginia Beach delivers visually appealing aquariums full of fish and other sea life, plus eye-popping IMAX® theatrical presentations. Virginia Beach's Naval Air Station Oceana/Master Jet Base may be visited seasonally on the city's HRT Tours and Trolley system. Tour guests get to see more than 200 aircraft, including an F/A-18 Hornet fighter jet.

From Virginia Beach, take US-58 west to Suffolk. At Planters Peanut Center in Suffolk, stop to view (and smell) peanuts cooking in their shells in a vintage 1936 roaster. The refurbished 1885 Suffolk Seaboard Station Railroad Museum presents a genuine locomotive caboose plus exhibits of HO-scale model trains.

From Suffolk, take US-460 northwest to Petersburg, where the Army Women's Museum awaits. This is the only such center devoted to female members of the U.S. Army, from the Revolutionary War to the present. Another nice stop is Pamplin Historical Park and National Museum of the Civil War Soldier, a comprehensive, well-respected historic site and memorial to all those who fought in the Civil War.

www.virginia.org
800/VISIT-VA.

Other Area Locations

GREY'S POINT
Grey's Point Camp

The southern states of the U.S.A. have so much more to share than just hospitality, sunny days, and blue skies. Florida's sandy beaches and theme parks are just the beginning of the family fun you'll encounter in the "Sunshine State." Alabama greets guests with jazz music, fruit farms, and a landmark American battleship. Mississippi offers up camellia blossoms, quaint country stores, even an historic lighthouse. Kentucky struts its stuff in the green hills of horse country, while Tennessee serenades you with world-class country music. South Carolina boasts the sparkle of Myrtle Beach, and North Carolina's mountains are just short of heaven. Louisiana's grand cuisine delights and ignites your senses just as Georgia shines with its special balance of metropolitan chic and pastoral peace. In short, the South is a spot-on vacation destination.

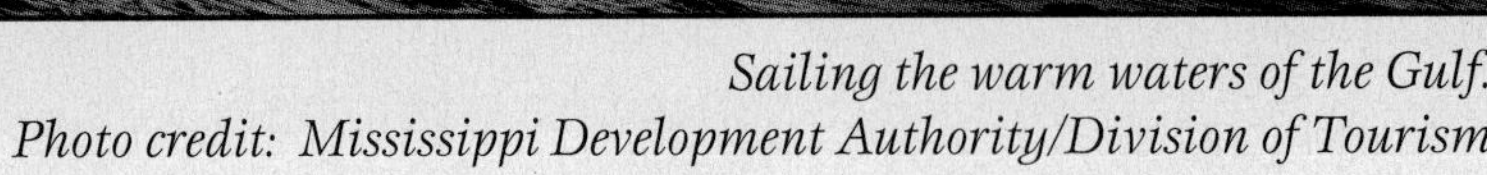

Sailing the warm waters of the Gulf.
Photo credit: Mississippi Development Authority/Division of Tourism

MISSISSIPPI

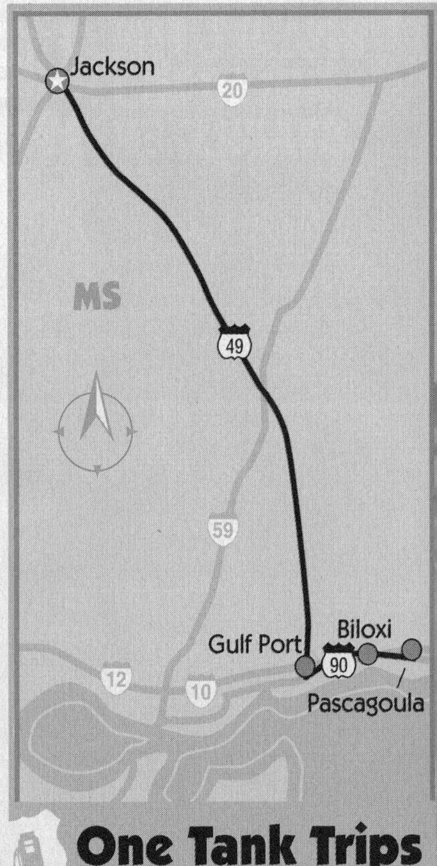

From Jackson's Governor's Mansion and the antique shops in Collins and Hattiesburg, to Biloxi's lighthouse and Pascagoula's alligators, the state of Mississippi both welcomes and entertains.

Kicking things off in the city of Jackson, our first stop is the Chimneyville Crafts Gallery, which features demonstrations, exhibits, and sales of a fabulous variety of original pieces produced by the Craftsmen's Guild of Mississippi, Inc. It's a great place to create a friendship with local artisans. Head over to the circa 1841 Mississippi Governor's Mansion, a good stop for amateur historians. The impeccable Greek Revival-style estate is a designated National Historic Landmark. For a little floral boost before departing Mississippi's state capital, walk among the camellias, azaleas, and songbirds at the city's beautiful Mynelle Gardens.

From Jackson, drive south on US-49 all the way to Gulfport. Easy on the gas pedal there, Leadfoot; there are a few nice towns we'd like you to see along the way. Start in Mendenhall and its namesake Grocery & Grain, a country store built back in 1928. All it takes is a step through its doors to transport you back in time. From whole vanilla beans and Mississippi-made foods, to handcrafted pottery and bird houses, Mendenhall's Grocery & Grain stocks up on vintage fun.

There's more old-time shopping to be found in the town of Mount Olive. You can order a custom-designed furnishing at Diehl Brothers Furniture, pick up homemade jams and a hand-stitched quilt at Martha's Kitchen, or visit Roger's Basketry for signature soaps and baskets tinted with natural nut dyes.

A great selection of time-tested wares is readily available in the antique shops of Collins. Might we also suggest loading up the rig with straight-from-the-soil goodies at Mitchell Farms, where antiques are offered alongside fruits, veggies, and fresh-harvested peanuts? Be sure to browse the shelves at Pope Company General Store, a sprawling, circa 1913 establishment that carries everything from feed n' seed to kitchen equipment and comfy shoes.

Shady Acres fruit stand yields much more than produce for the town of Seminary's lucky visitors. Make room in your basket for baked treats, rich ice cream, sweet jellies, and homespun candies. The nearby city of

Hattiesburg has several antique malls and art galleries to explore, while Gulfport is a good place to embark on a windswept offshore cruise.

From Gulfport, pick up US-90 east. Take a break in Biloxi for more appealing river cruise options. You can make reservations for sight-seeing, fishing, dinner cruises, or sunset viewing on your choice of small craft, sailing schooner, shrimp boat, or pontoon boat. From Biloxi Lighthouse, there's also a memorable adventure waiting for you aboard the street-based, open-air Biloxi Tour Train, known as the "shrimp train" by local folks, that drives through Biloxi's Historical District.

Pascagoula is the final stop on our Mississippi sojourn. On a Gulf Coast Gator Ranch visit, carve some time in the day to stroll along boardwalks that wind through alligator territory and take an airboat ride through a genuine Mississippi swamp.
www.VisitMississippi.org
866/733-6477.

Other Area Locations

BILOXI
Cajun RV Park
Lakeview RV Resort
Mazalea Travel Park
Parker's Landing RV Park
OCEAN SPRINGS
Camp Journey's End

GEORGIA

Travel through "The Peach State", and you will see why Ray Charles crooned "Georgia on my Mind." Every part of the state welcomes visitors with genuine southern hospitality. In Georgia you can find breath-taking coastal beaches, sophisticated cities, stun-

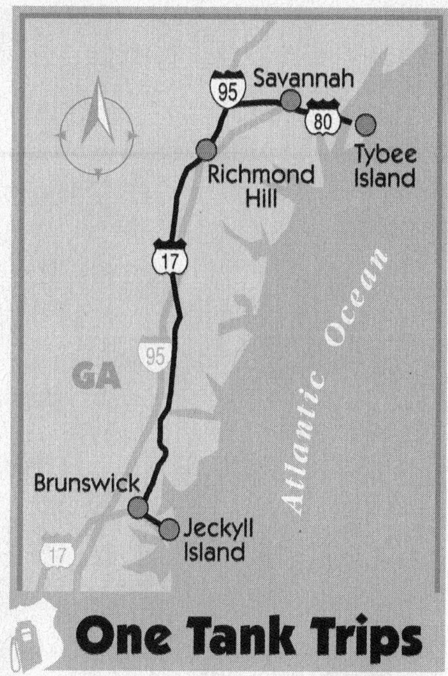

Jekyll Island Historic District. Photo credit: Georgia Department of Economic Development

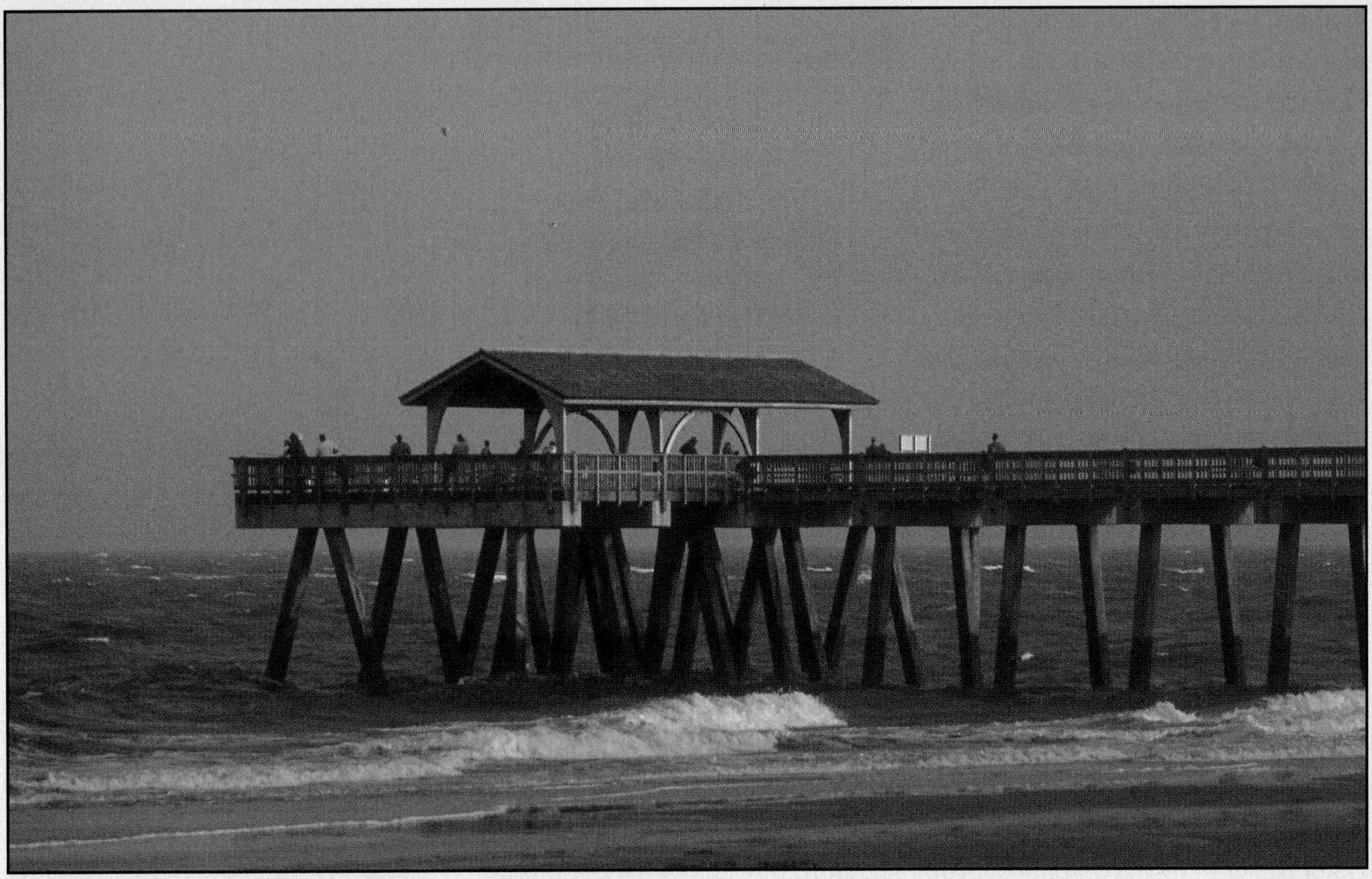

Tybee Island Beach. Photo credit: Georgia Department of Economic Development

ning southern architecture, and a rich and vibrant history that seems to pop up at every bend in the road.

Our excursion through Georgia starts in the beautiful Savannah coast. Begin in Tybee Island, a robust beach town that caters to those wishing to explore life around the southern coast. Head over to the Tybee Island Lighthouse, which has guided mariners through the Savannah River for over 200 years. If you are so inclined, climb the precisely 178 steps to the top of the lighthouse, and see the nine-foot-tall lens that still functions. Head back down and see over 100 indigenous marine animals-like alligators, polka dot batfish, and tree frogs-at the Tybee Island Marine Science Center. For a little bit of Georgia history, visit Fort Pulaski, which was designed by a young Robert E. Lee. With towering walls, a moat, artillery tunnels, and a massive drawbridge, the fort resembles a medieval castle

Hop on the US 80 east, and then get on I-95 south to continue to our next destination; Savannah. Be warned, though; according to research, Savannah is the most haunted city in the country. To experience the ghosts first-hand, take a

midnight ghost tour through the city, where guides point out the most creepy and macabre parts of Savannah. If you crave some tamer activities, head down to the Historic City Market in Savannah to visit unique art galleries, fine dining, and loads of great shopping. Or you can escape the city and go to the Savannah National Wildlife Refuge and explore 30,000 acres of freshwater marshes, tidal rivers, and bottomland forests. Whatever you do, just make sure that you finish your tour of Savannah with a carriage ride through the city at dusk to get one last look.

Off Highway 17 is Brunswick, a city drenched in American history. Tour the "Bloody Marsh" Battle Site, where in the 1700s the British repelled a Spanish attack, and thereby protected Georgia from becoming a Spanish colony. The Fort Frederica National Monument stands at the sight to honor the brave soldiers who fought there. Get knee-deep in history at the Georgia Heritage Theme Park and Animal Experience, an innovative amusement park that showcases Georgia's Victorian history with a real Main

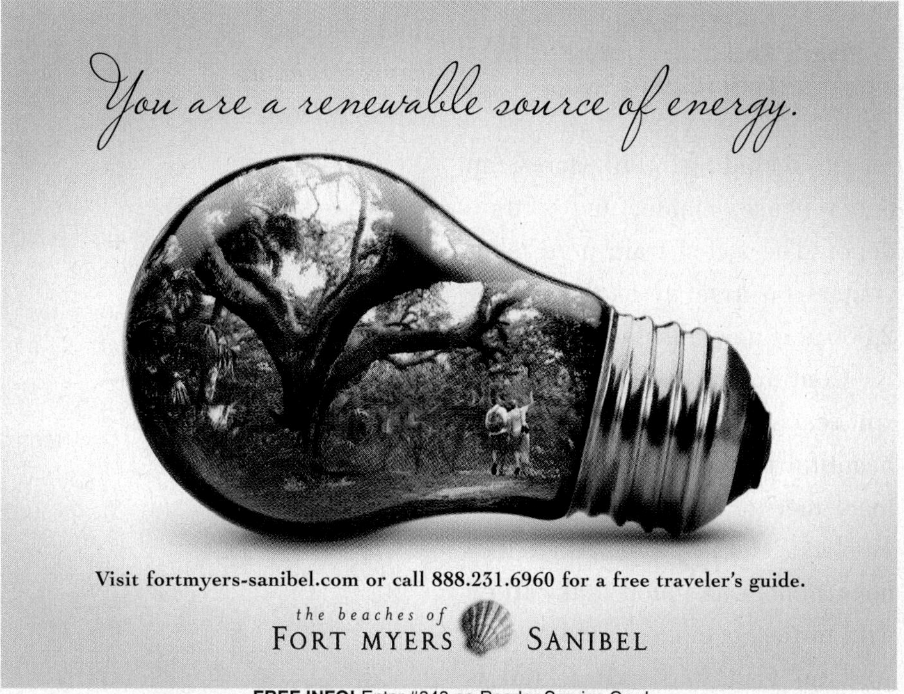

Other Area Locations

BRUNSWICK
Brunswick/Golden Isles Visitors Bureau

SAVANNAH
Savannah Oaks RV Resort

TYBEE ISLAND
River's End Campground & RV Park (City Park)

Street, including retail stores, an opera house, stable, and a train depot. The steam train here takes visitors on a safari of the nearby 2,000 acre animal habitat.

Continue on highway 17 until you reach the end of our trip, the beautiful Jekyll Island. Explore the local marine life hands-on at the Tidelands Marine Center, where they have numerous touch-tanks filled with turtles, octopuses, and sharks. And no visit to Jekyll Island is complete without touring the Historic Distinct, where you can shop at the famous open city market, eat at notable restaurants, and see the mansions built here by the likes of the Vanderbilts and the Rockefellers.

www.georgia.org
800/VISIT-GA.

KENTUCKY

Kentucky vacations cover plenty of interesting territory. There's Louisville's famed race track, Frankfort's intoxicating distillery, Lexington's horse park, and the rural railroad ride through Versailles. Historic Bardstown boasts its bourbon and Elizabethtown features cars and cola. There's something remarkable for every traveler to see in Kentucky.

Let's begin our Kentucky getaway in Louisville, the epicenter of horse racing in this country. Visit Louisville's world-famous racetrack at Churchill Downs and the Kentucky Derby Museum, where the great race is commemorated in fine detail.

Continue east on I-64 until you smell the whiskey wafting from the town of Frankfort. Thirsty? America's oldest, continuously running,

distillery, Buffalo Trace Distillery, provides a tasty factory tour. Nearby in Frankfort Cemetery, visit the final resting place of the legendary Daniel Boone, his beloved wife Rebecca, as well as 17 former Bluegrass State governors.

Assuming you can't find a mighty steed to take you there, hop back in the rig and drive east on I-64 towards Lexington, home to the Kentucky Horse Park. This unique equine attraction is where horse enthusiasts can choose their preferred entertainment from several separate options within the complex. A theme park and a working horse farm that entertains and educates guests with dozens of representative breeds. The setting also features two museums, a pair of theaters, and a full-scale show facility that hosts year-round equestrian competitions.

From Lexington, follow Martha Layne Collins Bluegrass Parkway in a southwest direction to Elizabethtown, with stops in Versailles and Bardstown. In Versailles, you can take a rambling ride through hills and farming communities on the Bluegrass Scenic Railroad. Stock up on luscious fresh fruit at Boyd Orchards and embark on a wine-tasting adventure at Castle Hill Farm Winery and Vineyard. See a vintage copper pot still in present-day operation at the refurbished Woodford Reserve distillery, and then travel back in your mind to simpler times at the Nostalgia Station Toy & Train Museum.

The "Bourbon Capital of the World" of Bardstown is home of the Heaven Hill Distilleries Bourbon Heritage Center, where the historical side of whiskey-making is highlighted. Be sure to see the "Portrait of Heaven Hill" film and attend a guided bourbon-tasting session. Before you leave the center, you can even design a personalized souvenir bourbon bottle. While in town, plan to take a carriage or trolley ride through town and a guided craft tour of area artists' studios. Students of history should see the comprehensive Civil War Museum, the Old County Jail, the specialized Women of the Civil War Museum, Oscar Getz Museum of Whiskey History, and Old Bardstown Village with its nine original log cabins. Reserve a place for a memorable, mobile meal on My Old Kentucky Dinner Train and learn about a much-celebrated American composer at the rousing outdoor theater production of "Stephen Foster - The Musical."

More regional narration may be found in Elizabethtown on the Historic Downtown Walking Tour, inside the Schmidt's Museum of Coca-Cola Memorabilia, and at the Swope's Cars of Yesteryear Museum with its approximately 50 antique cars. *www.kentuckytourism.com; 800/225-8747.*

ALABAMA

Are you ready to tour the assorted wonders of Alabama and northwest Florida? In Mobile, explore scientific marvels and the famed battleship, the U.S.S. Alabama. See colorful birds on Dauphin Island, cagey lions in Gulf Shores, and playful dolphins in Orange Beach. Pensacola, Florida is noted for its aircraft museum and Gulf Breeze for its Civil War fort.

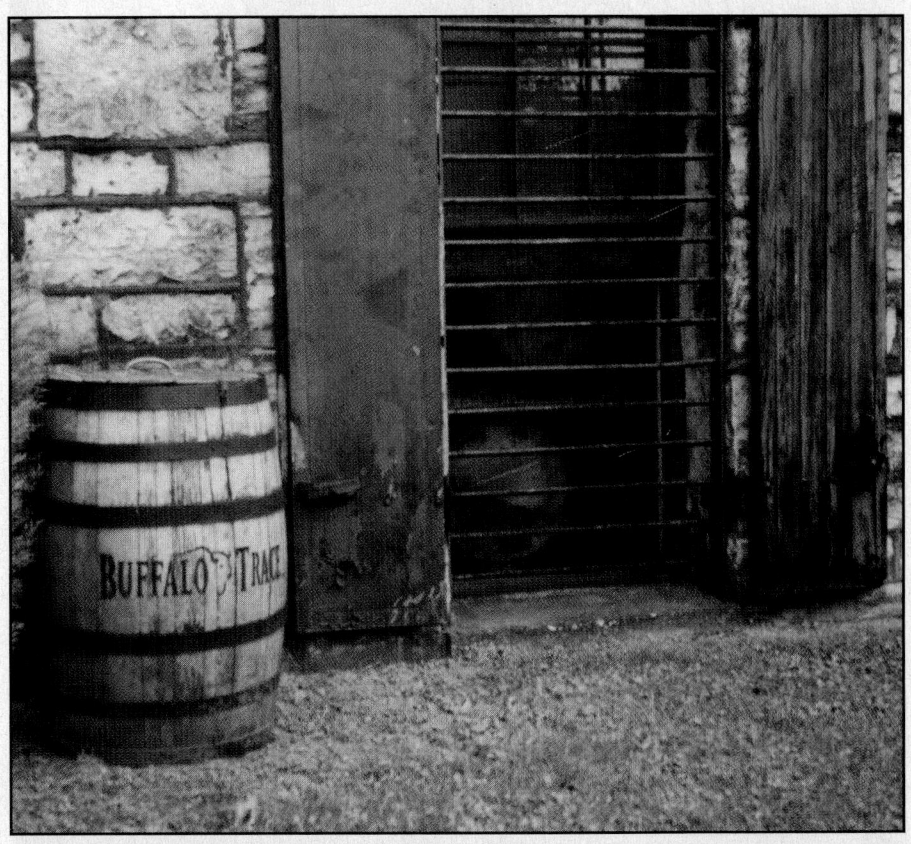

Buffalo Trace aging warehouse. Photo credit: www.kentuckytourism.com

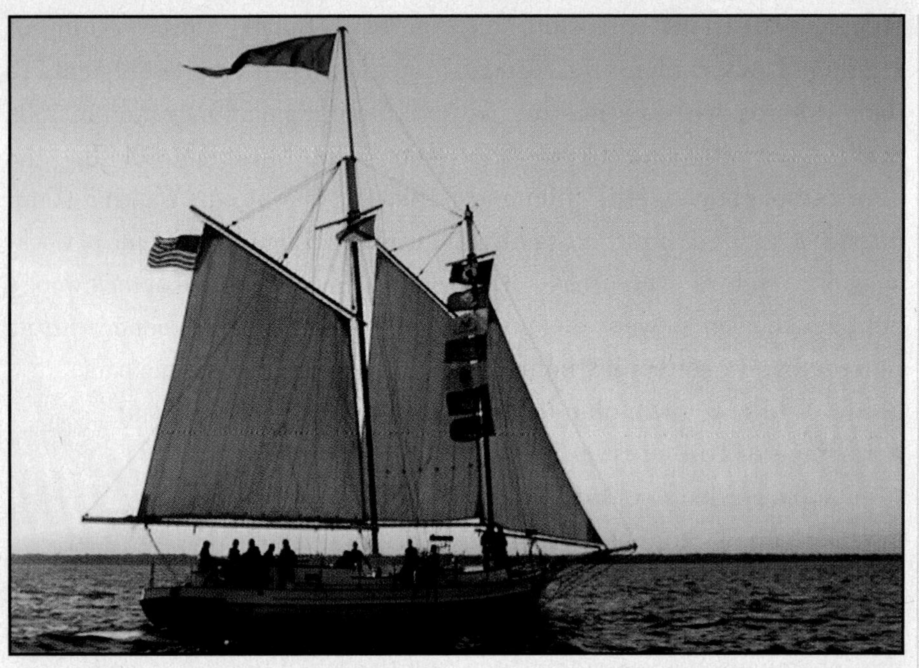

Schooner Joshua sails the Alabama Gulf Coast. Photo by Capt. Cindy Frank

Before you depart from Alabama and Florida, be sure to sail away for part of a day from the sparkling shores of Destin or Panama City Beach.

We think Mobile, Alabama, is a great place to start. While you probably wouldn't think of the region as a hotbed of naval history, the National Historic Landmark U.S.S. Alabama Battleship Memorial Park is here, with a displays of the namesake ship, as well as the U.S.S. Drum submarine, assorted military hardware, and strategic aircraft. The Gulf Coast Exploreum Science Center offers a practical introduction to the entertaining side of science. Be sure to watch a film in the center's IMAX Dome Theater. Before departing the city of Mobile, retreat to the area's fine Gulf beaches for a breezy stretch of relaxation.

From Mobile, travel east on Hwy 10 to Panama City Beach, home to mini-golf at Coconut Creek Family Fun Park, sea lions performing at Gulf World Marine Park, aquatic absurdity at Shipwreck Island Waterpark, and musical entertainment and sea views with your evening meal found onboard the Lady Anderson Dining Yacht.

From there, take Hwy 98 west to nearby Destin, board a glass-bottom boat to scope the waters for dolphin, take a charter fishing excursion, or go for a breezy ride on the historic wooden Sailing Schooner, the Daniel Webster Clements. The city provides a nice spot to shop till you drop in an open-air environment at 70 unique shops in Destin Commons. While here, be sure to visit America's biggest designer outlet center at Silver Sands Factory Stores.

Keep on Hwy 98 through Pensacola and Gulf Breeze, Florida. (See attraction information for the cities of Pensacola and Gulf Breeze in the Florida travel section under Panhandle Beaches to State Capital Run).

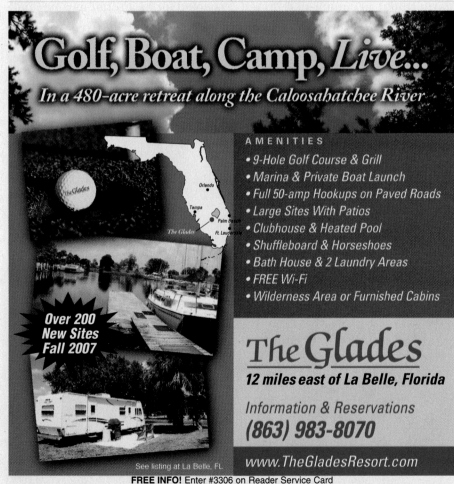

Heading west, you will soon reach Dauphin Island. Explore the trails at Dauphin Island's Audubon Bird Sanctuary, board a sightseeing cruise or deep-sea fishing boat, and go crabbing or fishing for the likes of speckled trout and flounder on the town's Fishing Pier.

Travel east via ferry from Dauphin Island across to Fort Morgan, then continue east/northeast through Gulf Shores and Orange Beach. You can see lions, tigers, and birds from the tropics at Gulf Shores' Alabama Gulf Coast Zoo, while at Bart Rockett Dinner Theater, every meal is accompanied by a variety show featuring music, magical acts, dancing, and comedy.

Orange Beach obliges water lovers with sail away opportunities as part of a dolphin watch or fishing cruise in the waters. Learn about local Native American culture at the Indian & Sea Museum. Swim with dolphins at Gulf World or cool off at the water park at Riverwalk Orange Beach.

Other Area Locations

MOBILE
I-10 Kampground
Shady Acres Campground

www.800ALABAMA.com
800/ALABAMA.

FLORIDA

Bet on Florida to deliver your vacation dreams, while taking you on adventures you never even imagined. Pensacola delights visitors with vintage airplanes and sparkling seashores. Tallahassee has an old cotton plantation and a fine Spanish mission. Orlando is tops for theme parks fans and devoted shoppers while Tampa boasts Busch Gardens, an aquarium, and a family-friendly zoo. And you can cruise off Clearwater, meet sponge divers in Tarpon Springs, and wave to swimming mermaids at Spring Hill's Weeki-Wachee. Tour art galleries, gardens, and a circus museum in Sarasota; uncover sharks' teeth in Venice and inventions in Fort Myers. And for goodness sakes, don't miss the airboat ride through the Everglades.

FLORIDA NORTH

We think Florida's panhandle is a great place to launch our adventure, so, naturally, Pensacola is where we'll start. The National Museum of Naval Aviation is one of the world's most extensive aircraft museums, with its collection of more than 150 restored planes and helicopters representing the airborne

Continued on page 54

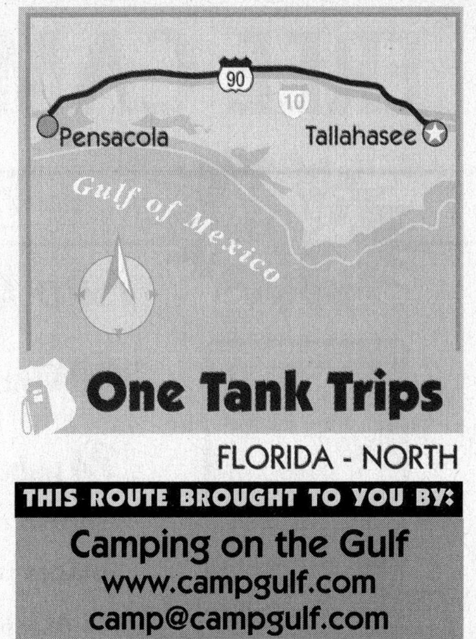

FLORIDA - NORTH

THIS ROUTE BROUGHT TO YOU BY:

Camping on the Gulf
www.campgulf.com
camp@campgulf.com
(877)226-7485

FREE CAMPING INFORMATION
by "Region"

Quick & Easy

Free Travel & Camping Information

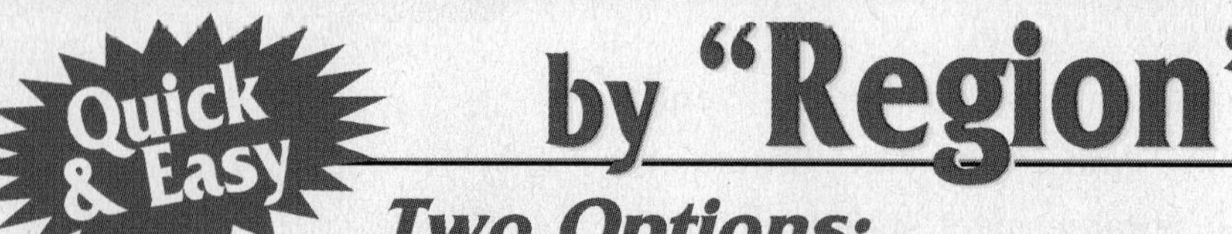

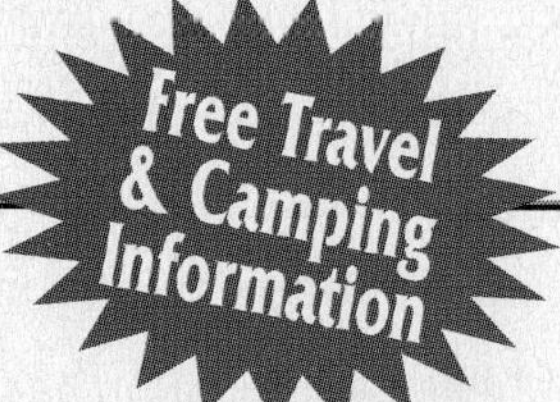

Two Options:

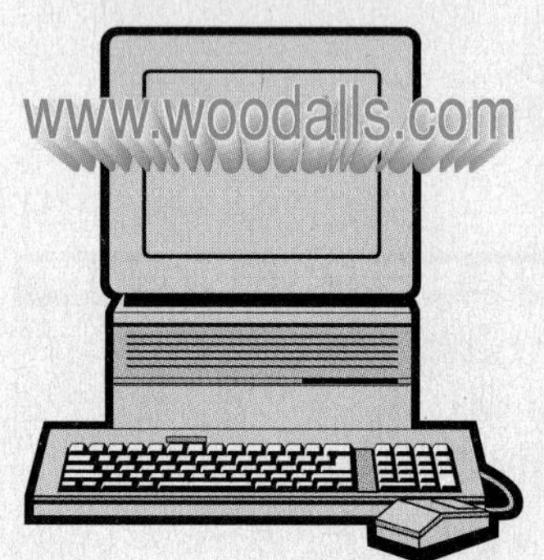

1 Visit us @ www.woodalls.com and click on "FREE CAMPING INFO"

OR

2 Indicate on one of the cards to the right the number of the "Region" shown on the map below from which you want FREE Information about places to camp and things to see & do. Your inquiry will be forwarded to ALL locations in that region who advertise in the Discover Section and/or Travel Sections.

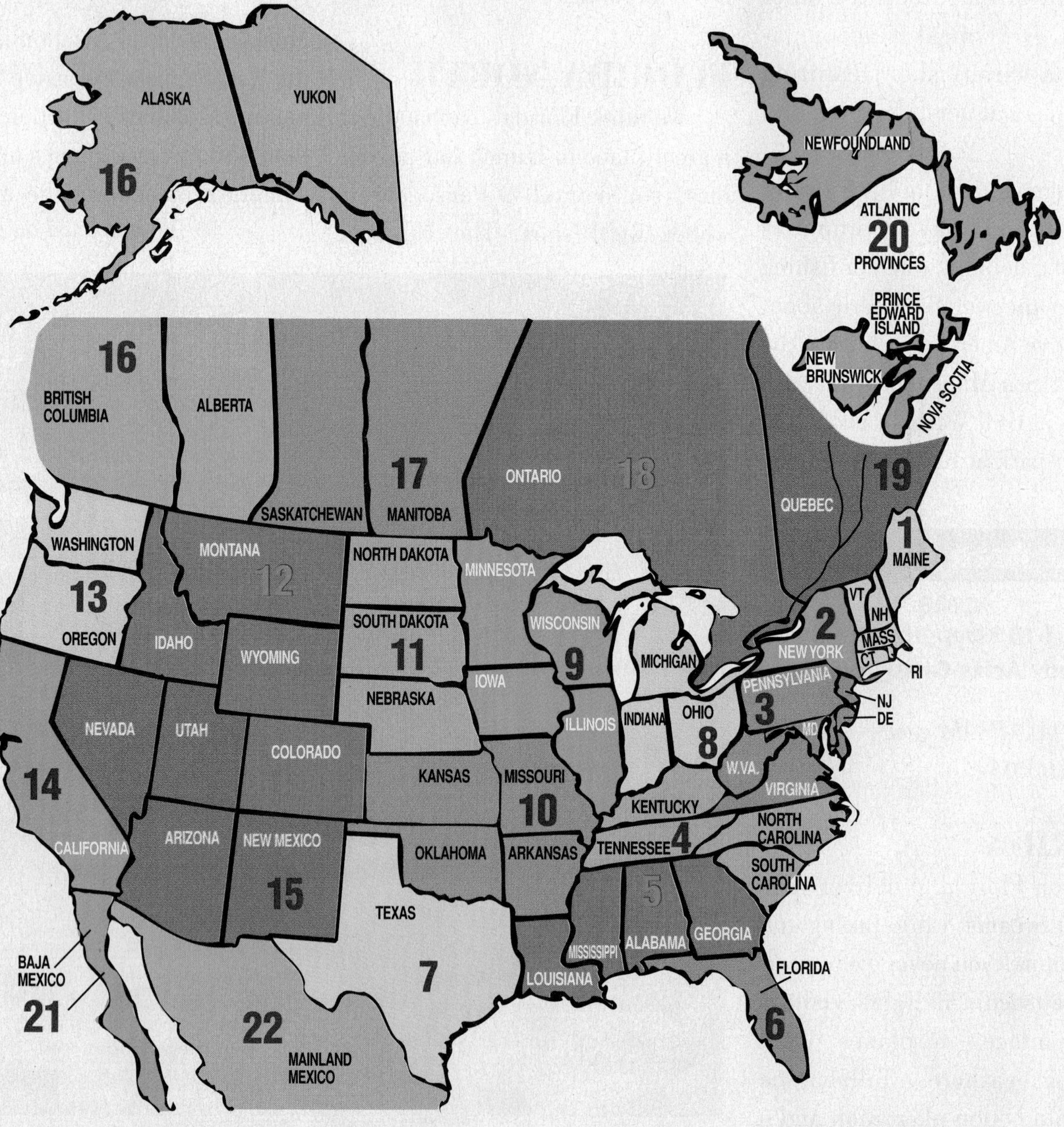

GET FREE INFORMATION ABOUT PRODUCTS & SERVICES FOUND IN THIS DIRECTORY

WOODALL'S READER QUESTIONNAIRE

lease enter your response or circle the ppropriate number on the reader ervice card indicating your answer to ur questions below. This will help us etermine how to serve you better. hank you!

. Age________

. What is your approximate annual gross family income?________

. What is your approximate family net worth?________

. Approximately how many years have you been camping / RVing? ________

. What was your camping pattern over the last 12 months? (best estimate)

a. Number of camping trips______

b. Total number of nights camped___

c. Total number of miles traveled__

d. Number of different parks at which you stayed_____

e. Number of Amusement/Tourist Attractions visited while on camping trips_____

f. Total money spent on Amusement/ Tourist Attractions_______

. How close to your home did you buy your present RV?

a. Within 50 miles b. 50 to 99 miles

c. 100 or more miles away

. Are you considering buying a new RV in the next 12 months?

a. yes b. no

. If yes, please indicate the type which interests you most: (select only one)

a. Travel Trailer

b. Park Model (Trailer)

c. Class A motor home – gas

d. Class A motor home – diesel

e. Fold-Down Trailer (Tent Trailer)

f. Truck Camper

g. Fifth Wheel

h. Class C motor home

i. Van Conversion

j. Class B motor home

l. Other-Please specify________

(continued on back)

To receive valuable information from our advertisers, simply write in the numbers on the attached card that correspond to the advertisers which interest you. Then, fill out your name and address and drop it in the mail.

Receive FREE Product Information Online at

WWW.WOODALLS.COM

The #1 Site For RVers On The Internet

(Tell all your friends to "Bookmark" this site!)

READER SERVICE
EXPIRES: DEC. 31, 2010

NAME ____________________
ADDRESS ____________________
CITY & STATE/PROV. ____________________ ZIP/P.C. ________
PHONE (____) ____________________
E-MAIL ____________________

PRINT READER SERVICE NUMBERS OF THE ADVERTISERS FROM WHOM YOU WANT MORE INFORMATION.

ENTER REGION FROM PAGE NUMBER 48 TO RECEIVE INFO. FROM ALL ADVERTISERS IN THE REGION (Max. of 8):

READER QUESTIONNAIRE: Please circle the appropriate response number for each question.

1. ________. **2.** ____________. **3.** ____________. **4.**________.
5. a_____,b_____,c________,d_____,e_____,f________. **6.** a,b,c. **7.** a,b.
8. a,b,c,d,e,f,g,h,i,j,l________. **9.** a,b,c,d. **10.** a,b,c,d,e. **11.** a,b. **12.** a,b.
13. a,b,c,d,e,f. **14.** __________ **15.** __________ **16.** a,b. **17.** a,b,c,d,e,f,g.
18. a,b. **19.** a,b. **20.** a,b.

RG-08

Use this card for additional information or fill it out for a friend.

READER SERVICE
EXPIRES: DEC. 31, 2010

NAME ____________________
ADDRESS ____________________
CITY & STATE/PROV. ____________________ ZIP/P.C. ________
PHONE (____) ____________________
E-MAIL ____________________

PRINT READER SERVICE NUMBERS OF THE ADVERTISERS FROM WHOM YOU WANT MORE INFORMATION.

ENTER REGION FROM PAGE NUMBER 48 TO RECEIVE INFO. FROM ALL ADVERTISERS IN THE REGION (Max. of 8):

READER QUESTIONNAIRE: Please circle the appropriate response number for each question.

1. ________. **2.** ____________. **3.** ____________. **4.**________.
5. a_____,b_____,c________,d_____,e_____,f________. **6.** a,b,c. **7.** a,b.
8. a,b,c,d,e,f,g,h,i,j,l________. **9.** a,b,c,d. **10.** a,b,c,d,e. **11.** a,b. **12.** a,b.
13. a,b,c,d,e,f. **14.** __________ **15.** __________ **16.** a,b. **17.** a,b,c,d,e,f,g.
18. a,b. **19.** a,b. **20.** a,b.

RG-08

Receive FREE Product Information Online at

WWW.WOODALLS.COM

The #1 Site For RVers On The Internet

(Tell all your friends to "Bookmark" this site!)

NO POSTAGE NECESSARY IF MAILED IN THE UNITED STATES

BUSINESS REPLY MAIL
FIRST-CLASS MAIL PERMIT NO. 398 NAPLES, FL

POSTAGE WILL BE PAID BY ADDRESSEE

WOODALL'S® CAMPGROUND DIRECTORY

ARGI / WOODALL'S
PO BOX 413050
NAPLES FL 34101-6804

NO POSTAGE NECESSARY IF MAILED IN THE UNITED STATES

BUSINESS REPLY MAIL
FIRST-CLASS MAIL PERMIT NO. 398 NAPLES, FL

POSTAGE WILL BE PAID BY ADDRESSEE

WOODALL'S® CAMPGROUND DIRECTORY

ARGI / WOODALL'S
PO BOX 413050
NAPLES FL 34101-6804

9. How far from your home would you consider driving in order to buy the right RV for your needs

a. Within 50 miles
b. 50 to 99 miles
c. 100 or more miles away
d. Mileage would not be a factor in locating the right RV

10. What portion of your campground stops do you pre-plan before leaving home?

a. None b. 1/4 c. 1/2
d. 3/4 e. All

11. When pre-planning your campi trips at home, do you also plan what to do and see on your trip?

a. yes b. no

12. Are you inclined to select locations that advertise their unique features over those wh don't?

a. yes b. no

13. How often do you/will you bu a new WOODALL'S Campground Directory?

a. Every year b. Every 2 years
c. Every 3 years d. Every 4 years
e. Every 5 years f. More than 5 yrs

14. How many times did you use your WOODALL'S Campground Directory in the past 12 months?_____

15. How many times have others used your WOODALL'S Campground Directory in the past 12 months? (Including ho many times you have loaned o your WOODALL'S Campground Directory)_____

16. Do you belong to any RV camping clubs?

a. yes b. no

17. If yes, please select which one (check all that apply)

a. FCRV
b. FMCA
c. Good Sam
d. KOA Value Kard
e. Camp Club USA
f. Escapees
g. Other(s)_______________

18. Do you access the internet while on RV camping trips?

a. yes b. no

19. Have you ever searched for R camping info on woodalls.com

a. yes b. no

20. Do you access websites found advertisements to learn more about that business?

a. yes b. no

USE READER SERVICE TO GET FREE INFORMATION ABOUT THE ADVERTISERS IN THIS DIRECTORY!

Here is a quick and easy way to receive free travel and camping information. Enter the Reader Service Number (listed below) on the Reader Service Card, which is located opposite page 48. Your request will be forwarded to the businesses you've indicated. You'll receive information, sent directly to your home. It's the no-hassle way to plan your next trip!

SAVE HOURS OF RESEARCH—USE READER SERVICE!

Here is a quick and easy way to receive free travel and camping information. Enter the Reader Service Number (listed below) on th Reader Service Card, which is located opposite page 48. Your request will be forwarded to the businesses you've indicated. You' receive information, sent directly to your home. It's the no-hassle way to plan your next trip!

Enter Number

ALASKA
3713 Adventure Bound Alaska
3424 Alaska Campground Owners Association
684 Alaska Marine Hwy System
3089 Alaska State Parks
3512 Alaska's Inter-Island Ferry Authority
3299 Delta Junction Chamber of Commerce
3434 Orca Enterprises
3289 Santaland RV Park
3111 Stan Stephens Glacier & Wildlife Cruises
3435 Wasilla Convention & Visitors Bureau
2690 White Pass & Yukon Route Railway

ALABAMA
678 Alabama Mountain Lakes Tourist Assoc.
3760 American Motor Coach Resorts
823 Bellingrath Gardens & Home
3310 Huntsville Convention & Visitors Bureau
3369 Little Mountain Marina Camping Resort
3651 Natchez Trace Compact
472 Noccalula Falls Park & Campground

ARKANSAS
3304 Arkansas State Parks
3464 Casino Aztar RV Park
3449 Fort Smith Visitors Center

ARIZONA
3335 Arizona State Parks
2163 Arizona Travel Parks Association
3801 El Rio RV Resort
3680 Rincon Country West RV Park
3714 Silver Sands RV Resort
3570 Sunbeam Lake RV Resort

CALIFORNIA
2837 Anaheim Harbor RV Park
3735 Blue Heron RV Park
3588 Coyote Valley Resort & RV Destination
3520 Hemet Visitor & Tourism Council
3539 Lake Shasta Caverns
3370 Riverside County Parks
3040 San Bernardino County Parks
492 San Diego County Parks
3615 Silverwood Lake
3571 Sunbeam Lake RV Resort

COLORADO
2969 Colorado Campground & Lodging Owners Assoc
3208 Colorado State Parks

CONNECTICUT
457 Connecticut Campground Owners Assoc
3712 Highland Orchards Resort Park

Enter Number

DISTRICT OF COLUMBIA
683 Aquia Pines Camp Resort
781 Bethpage Camp Resort
3323 Capitol KOA Washington DC NE
462 Cherry Hill Park
565 Fredericksburg / Washington DC KOA
562 Greenville Farm Family Campground
3687 River Riders

FLORIDA
3501 Avalon RV Resort
3401 Bay Bayou RV Resort
3477 Big Cypress RV Resort
3463 Blueberry Hill RV Resort (Morgan RV Resorts)
3784 Broward County Parks
3498 Camp Inn Resort
3657 Camp USA
3671 Como Truck & RV Sales & Service
3748 CRF Communities
3749 CRF Communities
2574 Disney's Fort Wilderness
671 Dunedin RV Resort
3775 East Lake Fish Camp
3788 Elite Resorts at Salt Springs
3583 Flagler County Chamber of Commerce
2173 Florida Association of RV Parks and Campgrounds
3658 Lake Rousseau RV & Fishing Resort
3737 Myakka RV Resort
3666 Quail Run RV Park
3684 Rob's Auto Detailing
3806 Sarasota Sunny South
3805 Siesta Bay RV Resort
3374 Sonrise Palms Christian RV Park
3555 Southern Charm RV Resort
2777 Space Coast RV Resort
3305 The Glades
3672 The Shell Factory & Nature Park
2982 Three Lakes RV Resort
3216 Travelers Rest Resort
3670 Wilderness RV Park Estates
3499 Winter Paradise Travel Resort
3752 Winterset RV Resort

GEORGIA
2424 Brunswick / Golden Isles Visitors Bureau
3696 Cedar Creek Park RV & Driving Range
3119 Country Boy's RV Park
3221 Flynn's Inn Camping Village
473 Georgia Mountain Fairgrounds Campground
465 Georgia State Parks & Historic Sites
3612 John Bleakley RV Ctr
2883 Lake Harmony RV Park & Campground
3697 Mountain Creek RV Resort
3053 Norman Campers

Enter Number

849 Old Salem Park (Georgia Power)
3734 Pine Mountain RVC
733 Stone Mountain Family Campground

IOWA
3276 Iowa Assoc of RV Park CG
3458 Truck Country

IDAHO
3633 Idaho RV Campground Association

ILLLINOIS
3522 Abel RV Center

INDIANA
3473 Amishville USA Campground
3325 Indiana Beach Camp Resort
3797 Tom Stinnett RV Freedom Center

KANSAS
3129 Boot Hill Museum
2724 Hays Convention & Visitors Bureau
458 Kansas Association RV Parks & Campgrounds
3326 Kansas RV Parks & Travel Inc
3431 Prairie Band Casino & Resort RV Park
3430 Rolling Hills Wildlife Adventure

KENTUCKY
3429 Kentucky Lake KOA @ Prizer Point
3371 Northside RV's
3388 Shepherdsville Bullitt County
3690 Wolf Creek Resort

LOUISIANA
3791 Bayou Outdoor Supercenter
2687 Cajun Coast Visitors & Convention Bureau
396 Houma Area Convention & Visitors Bureau
2843 Lafayette Convention & Visitors Commission
3255 Louisiana Campground Owners Assoc
3767 Louisiana Travel Promotion Assoc.
3303 Natalbany Creek Campground
2589 Paragon Casino
3378 Pavilion RV Park
2662 Prejean's Restaurant
3705 Randol's Restaurant & Cajun Dance Hall
837 Shreveport/Bossier Convention & Tourist Bureau
3013 Southwest Louisiana CVB
153 St Tammany Parish Tourist Convention Commission
773 Tangipahoa Parish Tourist Community

Enter Number

MASSACHUSETTS
2222 Massachusetts Association of Campground Owners

MARYLAND
461 Cherry Hill Park
3482 Yogi Bear's Jellystone Camp Resort Williamspor

MAINE
2613 Libby's Oceanside Camp
709 Maine CG Owner Assoc.
716 Point Sebago Golf & Beac RV Resort

MICHIGAN
3796 Alice Springs Campgroun
756 Bronner's Christmas Wonderland
3726 Bud's Trailer Center
3074 Crossroads Village & Huckleberry RR
3514 Dutch Village
3729 Frankenmuth Bavarian Inn
3711 Gilmore Car Museum
3804 Hidden Ridge
3777 Krenek RV Super Center
3728 Lake Huron Campground
3022 Little River Casino Resort
3702 Lloyd Bridges Traveland
3703 Monroe County KOA
3440 Oak Beach County Park
3171 Ojibwa Casino
3786 River Pines RV Park & C
3759 Sunny Brook RV Resort
3605 Thunder Bay RV & Golf Resort
3795 Vegas Kewadin Casinos
3083 Washakie Golf and RV Resort
3533 Windmill Island

MINNESOTA
3446 Dakotah Meadows RV Park & Campground
647 Lake Byllesby Campground (Dakota County Park)
3414 Lake of the Woods Area Tourism Bureau
3420 Minnesota Resort Campground Association
3560 Prairie View RV Park & CG

MISSOURI
3766 Branson Lakes Area Chamber of Commerce & CVB
3465 Casino Aztar RV Park
3525 City of Canton
3028 Division of State Parks M
3147 Missouri Association of R Parks
3338 Missouri Division of Tourism
3393 Worlds of Fun Village

MISSISSIPPI
832 Hollywood Casino RV Resort
754 Mississippi State Parks
3649 Natchez Trace Compact

Free Camping Information
Travel Sections

Enter Number	
3828	Plantation Pines RV Resort
MONTANA	
495	Campground Owners of Montana
MEXICO-MAINLAND	
3818	Sky Med
NORTH CAROLINA	
3531	Allsport RV Center
359	Camp Hatteras
3695	Cape Fear RV & Canoe Center
3386	Crisp RV Center
3527	Daly RV
3617	Franklin RV Park & CG
3721	Golden Pond Campground
3548	Happy Holiday RV Park & Campground
3548	Happy Holiday RV Park & Campground
3452	Howard RV Center
3710	Lake Norman MotorCoach Resort
3723	Mountain Camper Sales & Service
3536	Out of Doors Mart
3437	Rivers Edge Mountain RV Park
3537	The Family RV Center
3558	The Great Outdoors RV Resort
3707	The Refuge
3540	The RV Resort at Carolina Crossroads
3794	Tom Johnson Camping Ctr
3764	Valley River RV Resort
NORTH DAKOTA	
504	Medora Campground
3145	Norsk Hostfest
3144	North Dakota Lewis and Clark Interpretive Center
NEBRASKA	
999	Cabela's RV Park
NEW HAMPSHIRE	
3793	Gunstock Mountain Resort
74	Hart's Turkey Farm Restaurant
30	White Mountain Attractions Visitors Center
NEW JERSEY	
3086	Beaver Hill Campground
73	Brookville Campground
74	New Jersey Campground Assoc
58	Ocean View Resort Campground
3742	Yogi Bear's Jellystone Park Camp Resort (Morgan RV Resorts)
NEW MEXICO	
3769	Lordsburg Hildago Chamber of Commerce
NEVADA	
3761	City of West Wendover
3467	Iron Horse RV Park
3785	Lincoln County & Nevada State Parks
3662	Monaco Las Vegas Sales & Service
3566	Pioneer Territory
3566	Pioneer Territory
3665	Seibt Desert Retreat Luxury Resort
3783	Solstice Motorcoach
3629	Winnemucca Convention & Visitors Authority
NEW YORK	
3762	Camp Waubeeka Family Campground
3789	Greene County Tourism
2560	Maple Lane Campground & RV Park
665	Oswego County Dept of Promotion & Tourism
689	Sullivan County Tourism
3574	The Villages at Turning Stone RV Park
659	Yogi Bear's Jellystone Park Camp Resort at Mexico
OHIO	
2807	Cedar Point Camper Village
3725	Homestead RV Center
711	Ohio Department of Natural Resources
3790	Post's Traveland
3779	RV Wholesalers
OKLAHOMA	
3380	Bartlesville Convention & Visitors Bureau
3169	Claremore Expo Center
3454	Green Country Marketing
3521	Oak Lake Trails Naturist Park
3332	Oklahoma State Parks & Reccreation
OREGON	
3569	Albany Visitors Association
3736	Blue Heron RV Park
2917	Grants Pass Visitor & Convention Bureau
3632	Mallard Creek Golf & RV Resort
3135	Medford Visitors & Convention Bureau
3673	Outdoor Resorts Pacific Shores
3827	Schroeder Josephine & County Park
3717	Seven Feathers RV Resort
3741	The Mill Casino RV Park
PENNSYLVANIA	
3568	Bear Run Campground
3597	Bedford County Conference & Visitors Center
3708	Berks Mont Camping Center
3739	Boyer RV Center
3692	Cavalier Coach RV Inc
3743	Dale Smith's Camper Sales
3611	Endless Mountains Visitors Bureau
3768	Gettysburg Campground
3585	Greater Reading CVB
3719	Harold's RV Center
3693	Huffy's Trailer Sales
3694	Keystone RV Center
3619	Lampe Campground & Marina
3538	Lehigh Valley Convention & Visitors Bureau
3704	Mellott Brothers Trailer Sales
515	Pennsylvania Campground Owners' Association
3546	Pocono Mountain Visitors Bureau
3829	Starr's Trailer Sales
3740	Stivenson Camper Sales
3542	Susquehanna Valley Visitors Bureau
3584	The Foote Rest Campground
SOUTH CAROLINA	
3659	Broxton Bridge Plantation
3610	Cane Creek Motor Coach Resort
644	Cunningham RV Park
3545	Don Mar RV Sales
3781	Florence KOA
3660	Hardeeville RV Thomas' Parks & Sites
3667	Magnolia RV Park & Campground
3518	New Green Acres RV Park
3664	Rocks Pond Campground & Marina
522	South Carolina State Parks
3663	Tony's RV Parts & Service
SOUTH DAKOTA	
3682	Christmas Village
2805	Department of Game Fish & Parks
3709	Hart Ranch Camping Resort
2665	Lake Mitchell Campground (City Park)
2467	Rafter J Bar Ranch Camping Resort
3701	Sioux Empire Fair
2819	South Dakota Tourism
3688	The Journey Museum
2754	Wylie Park Campground
TN	
3455	Casino Aztar RV Park
3650	Natchez Trace Compact
3342	Tennessee State Parks
TEXAS	
3802	Commemorative Air Force
3614	Gulf Waters Beach Front Resort
3668	Parkview Riverside
2840	Port Aransas Chamber Of Commerce
3328	Texas Association of Campground Owners
3813	Texas State Parks
UTAH	
3631	Dinosaurland Travel Board
2685	Iron County Tourism & Convention Bureau
VIRGINIA	
3745	Aquia Pines Camp Resort
568	Bethpage Camp Resort
538	Cherrystone Family Camping Resort
3727	Chesapeake Bay Camp Resort
3601	Endless Caverns
3596	Greenway Creek RV Park
3751	New Point RV Resort (Morgan RV Resort)
3757	Virginia CG Assoc
VERMONT	
2293	Quechee Pine Valley KOA
3148	Vermont Campground Owners Assoc
WASHINGTON	
3586	Eagles Landing RV Resort Community
3620	K M Resorts of America
2533	Lake Associates Recreation Club
3689	Lakeshore RV Park & Marina
3787	Lost Lake Resort
3803	Maplewood @ Travel Inn Resort
3744	Ocean Park Area Chamber of Commerce
3606	The Cedars RV Resort
3634	Tullamoor RV & Golf Resort
3698	Two Rivers Marina, Casino & RV Resort
3720	Washington State Parks
3594	Winthrop Chamber of Commerce
3471	Yakama Nation RV Resort
WISCONSIN	
3456	Truck Country
3256	Wisconsin Association of Campgrounds
3426	Wisconsin Dells Visitor & Convention Bureau
WEST VIRGINIA	
3718	Ashland KOA West Virginia
3686	Outdoor Express RV
3716	Seneca Caverns
WYOMING	
3652	Cheyenne Area Convention & Visitors Bureau
690	Cody Country Chamber of Commerce
718	Thermopolis Hot Springs Chamber of Commerce
CANADA	
ALBERTA	
2776	Chinook County Tourist Association
3422	Historic Sites & Cultural Heritage Branch
BRITISH COLUMBIA	
3453	District of Chetwynd
MANITOBA	
741	Communications Services Manitoba
2873	Town of Morden
ONTARIO	
2720	Agawa Canyon Train Tour
3033	Glen Rouge Campground
466	Ontario Private Campground Association
2850	Toronto & Region Conservation
QUEBEC	
990	Camping Wigwam
SASKATCHEWAN	
2535	East Central SK Tourism Region
798	Saskatchewan South East Tourism
2534	Saskatchewan Southwest Tourism
2532	Saskatchewan West Central

Free Camping Information Extended Stay Guide

SAVE HOURS OF RESEARCH!

The campgrounds/RV parks, RV service centers and attractions listed below want your business! Here is a quick and easy way to receive free information about seasonal camping, fun things to do, and where to service your RV or buy a new one. Simply enter their **Reader Service Number** (listed below) on the **Reader Service Card**, which is located opposite page 48 in the front of the **Discover Section**. Your request will be forwarded to the names you've indicated. Then, you'll receive brochures and/or pricing information, sent directly to your home. It's the no-hassle way to shop for the campground, attraction or RV dealership you are interested in!

Enter Number	
ARIZONA	
3444	Towerpoint Resort
3445	Good Life RV Resort
3681	Rincon Country East RV Park
3699	Arizona Maverik RV Park
3700	Mesa Spirit RV Resort
3715	Pueblo El Mirage RV Resort
3724	Desert's Edge RV Village
CALIFORNIA	
851	Rancho Los Coches RV Park
856	TwentyNine Palms Resort
2663	Pomona Fairplex KOA
2677	La Pacifica RV Resort
2965	Bernardo Shores RV Park
3532	Morena Mobile Village Office
3534	Woods Valley Kampground
3589	San Diego RV Resort
3590	Golden Village Palms RV Resort
3675	Flag City RV Resort
CONNECTICUT	
3770	Camper's World, Inc.
DELAWARE	
3409	Leisure Point Resort
FLORIDA	
884	Club Naples RV Resort (Morgan RV Resorts)
906	Road Runner Travel Resort
919	Upriver RV Resort
3544	John Prince Memorial Park
3554	Mill Creek RV Resort
3656	The Glades
GEORGIA	
3058	River's End Campground & RV Park
MICHIGAN	
926	Creek Valley
993	Wheel Inn Campground & Whitetail Acres Archery
1076	Greenwood Acres Family Campground
2124	Clearwater Campground
3441	Lake Chemung Outdoor Resort
MISSISSIPPI	
3732	Lakeview RV Resort
3792	Indian Point RV Resort
NEW JERSEY	
3081	Pleasant Valley Family Campground
NEW YORK	
925	Cliff & Ed's Trailer Park
PENNSYLVANIA	
3765	Mountain Pines RV Resort
TEXAS	
3669	Parkview Riverside
3677	Llano Grande Lake Park
3678	Alamo Palms
3679	Victoria Palms Resort
VERMONT	
3630	Apple Island Resort
WISCONSIN	
3271	Lakeland Camping Resort
ONTARIO	
3173	Rochester Place Resort Inc
3618	Spring Lake RV Resort

Reserve Online at Woodalls.com!

It's as easy as 1-2-3...

1) Complete a search for RV Campgrounds at www.woodalls.com/rvs

2) Review our search results to determine which campground is best for you, and select Reserve Online

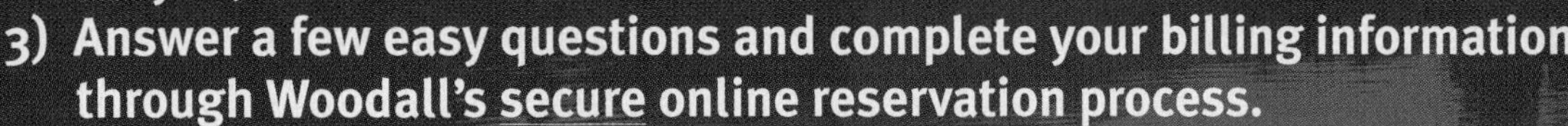
3) Answer a few easy questions and complete your billing information through Woodall's secure online reservation process.

ScanAlert™ HACKER SAFE TESTED DAILY 01-JAN

ALASKA

CANTWELL
Cantwell RV Park LLC (800)940-2210
HAINES
Oceanside RV Park (907)766-2437
TOK
Tok RV Village (907)883-5877
VALDEZ
Eagle's Rest RV Park & Cabins (800)553-7275
WASILLA
Alaskan Trails RV & Camper Park (907)376-5504

ARKANSAS

HARRISON
Parkers RV Park (870)743-CAMP

ARIZONA

BENSON
Butterfield RV Resort (800)863-8160
GILA BEND
Augie's Quail Trail RV Park (928)683-2850
MARANA
Valley of The Sun RV Mobile Home Resort (520)682-3434
MARICOPA
John Wayne RV Ranch (Formerly known as Table Top RV Ranch) (520)424-3813
PICACHO
Picacho Peak RV Resort (520)466-7841
QUARTZSITE
Desert Sunset RV Park (928)927-6443
QUARTZSITE
La Paz Valley RV Park (928) 927-6661
QUARTZSITE
Split Rail RV Park (928)927-5296
TUCSON
Rincon Country East (888)401-8989
TUCSON
Rincon Country West (800)782-7275
WILLCOX
Lifestyle RV Park (520)384-3303

CALIFORNIA

BORREGO SPRINGS
The Springs at Borrego RV Resort & Golf Course (866)330-0003
EL CAJON
Rancho Los Coches RV Park (800)630-0448
IMPERIAL BEACH
Bernardo Shores RV Park (619)429-9000
REDDING
Mountain Gate RV Park (800)404-6040
REDWAY
Dean Creek Resort (877)923-2555

FLORIDA

ARCADIA
Cross Creek Country Club & RV Resort (863)494-7300
CLERMONT
The Bee's RV Resort (352)429-2116
DAVENPORT
Themeworld RV Resort (863)424-8362
FOUNTAIN
Pine Lake RV Park (850)722-1401

IOWA

NEWTON
Rolling Acres RV Park (641)792-2428
ONAWA
On-Ur-Wa RV Park (712)423-1387

IDAHO

EDEN
Anderson Camp RV Park (888)480-9400
RIGGINS
Canyon Pines RV Resort (866)744-4006

KANSAS

TOPEKA
Capital City RV Park (785)862-5267

LOUISIANA

DUSON
Frog City RV Park (337)873-9085
NEW ORLEANS
French Quarter RV Resort (504)586-3000
ST. JOSEPH
Shiloh's Lake Bruin Resort (318)766-3334

MAINE

GEORGETOWN
Sagadahoc Bay Campground (207)371-2014

MICHIGAN

MANISTEE
Insta-Launch Campground & Marina (866)452-8642

MINNESOTA

ST. CLOUD
St. Cloud Campground & RV Park (320)251-4463

MISSOURI

POPLAR BLUFF
Bullwinkles RV Park (573)778-3535
VAN BUREN
Big Spring RV Camp (800)354-6295

MISSISSIPPI

PICAYUNE
Sun Roamers RV Resort (601)798-5818

NORTH CAROLINA

ABERDEEN
Long Leaf Pine Oasis (910)266-8372
FOREST CITY
Foothills Family Campground (828)245-4064

NEBRASKA

GREENWOOD
Pine Grove RV Park (402)944-3550

NEW HAMPSHIRE

CONWAY
Eastern Slope Camping Area (603)447-5092

OHIO

PORT CLINTON
Shade Acres Campground & Cottages (800)431-8449
SANDUSKY
Bayshore Estates Campground (800)962-3786
SANDUSKY
Camp Sandusky (800)875-1044

OREGON

BANDON
Robbin's Nest RV Park (541)347-7400
OAKLAND
Rice Hill RV Park (866)236-0121
SILVERTON
Silver Spur RV Park (503)873-2020
SUTHERLIN
Hi-Way Haven RV Park (541)459-4557

PENNSYLVANIA

COVINGTON
Tanglewood Camping (570)549-8299
KINZERS
Roamers' Retreat Campground (800)525-5605
SHEFFIELD
Whispering Winds Campground (814)968-4377

SOUTH DAKOTA

RAPID CITY
Whispering Pines Campground & Lodging (605)341-3667

TENNESSEE

GATLINBURG
Smoky Bear Campground (formerly Huc A Bee) (800)850-8372

TEXAS

COLUMBUS
Columbus KOA (979)732-9494
FORT DAVIS
RV Resort MacMillen in the Highlands (432)426-2056
GUNBARREL CITY
Lakeridge RV Park (877)451-4304
KILGORE
Shallow Creek RV Resort (903)984-4513
MANSFIELD
Texan RV Ranch (817)473-1666
MISSION
Mission Bell Tradewinds RV Resort (956)585-4833
PORT MANSFIELD
The Park @ Port Mansfield (956)746-1530
SUNSET
Sunset RV Park, Inc (940)845-2007
TYLER
Spring Creek RV Resort, Inc (903)526-1717
TYLER
Whispering Pines RV & Cabin Resort (800)559-3817
WACO
Quail Crossing RV Park (888)848-4116

VIRGINIA

LURAY
Luray RV Resort-The Country Waye (888)765-7222

WASHINGTON

BIRCH BAY
Birch Bay RV Resort (360)371-7922

WISCONSIN

BARABOO
Fox Hill RV Park (888)236-9445
WISCONSIN DELLS
Yogi Bear's Jellystone Park Camp-Resort (800)462-9644

WYOMING

RAWLINS
RV World Campground (877)328-1091

CANADA

BRITISH COLUMBIA

HOPE
Wild Rose RV Park (800)463-7999

MEXICO

MEXICO-BAJA

LORETO (B.C.S.)
Loreto Shores Villas & RV Park 011-52-613-135-1513

Shell Island. Photo credit: WWW.VISITFLORIDA.ORG

squadrons of the U.S. Navy, Marine Corps, and Coast Guard. See a rare SB2A Brewster Buccaneer from WWII, catch a thrilling Blue Angels air show, watch an IMAX film at the Memorial Theatre, or sharpen your piloting skills on the museum's flight simulator. After your aviation tour, pop over to Gulf Breeze to experience the historic and natural wonders of a Civil War-era fort, bright white sands, and blue-green salty waters at Gulf Islands National Seashore.

From Pensacola, take US-90 east to the natural delights found in the towns of Chipley and Marianna. See Florida's tallest cascade amid cool pine forests at Falling Waters State Park (Chipley). Marianna's Florida Caverns State Park offers a guided underground tour to see amazing stalagmite and stalactite configurations with descriptive names such as the "Christmas Tree" and "Wedding Cake."

In Florida's capital city of Tallahassee, visit the Challenger Learning Center to see a planetarium star show, try out your flying abilities on a Space Mission Simulator, and be dazzled by the special effects of an IMAX film. Get your feet back on the ground at Goodwood Museum & Gardens with a tour of the charming 1830s estate that was originally a working cotton and corn plantation. In today's gardens, look for botanical bonuses such as towering live oaks, heirloom roses, blooming bromeliads, and sunny yellow daffodils. At Mission San Luis, see the "Sunshine State's" only reconstructed, circa 1600s Spanish-style Apalachee Indian mission. If you're a shopping enthusiast, don't leave Tallahassee without visiting the two-story retail mall at Governor's Square.

FLORIDA CENTRAL

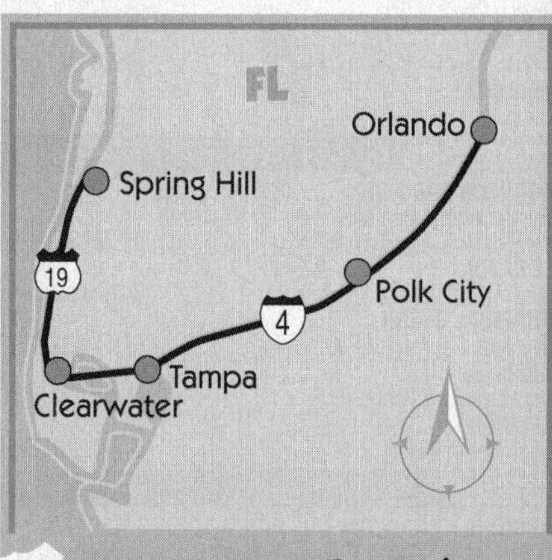

Mickey Mouse time! Florida's greater Orlando area, located mid-state, is a theme park hub extraordinaire, and all the amusement action is clustered so that you can park-hop to your heart's content. SeaWorld Adventure Park is tops for water-based entertainment, and Walt Disney World Resort seemingly has it all, from the Magic Kingdom and MGM Studio's movie madness, to Epcot's international themes and Disney's Animal Kingdom. Non-Disney standouts, Universal Studios and Islands of Adventure, offer movie-themed fun plus rides that provide thrills and chills. Shopping venues in and around town are plentiful, whether you prefer mega malls, souvenir shops, or reasonable-priced factory outlets. The local selection of dinner shows also includes a mind-boggling array of themes and backdrops, from the heart of Dixie, to stalwart medieval castles, to blustery pirate ships.

From Orlando, drive west on I-4, pausing for a breather in Polk City. Fantasy of Flight can take you up, up, up and away in a biplane or hot air balloon. Of course, you may prefer to sit in the cockpit of a static fighter jet or "soar" through the sky in a simulated hang glider. See vintage planes from both World Wars and browse through the largest private aircraft collection on earth.

Busch Gardens in Tampa Bay ranks as one of the country's great amusement parks for good reason. Big-time loops, drops, and dives on several thrilling roller coasters, safari-style rides with views of African rhinos and lanky giraffes, a number of lively shows featuring entertainers like acrobats, storytellers, and marching bands; it all combines to make up one seriously fun package of activities.

Tampa's Florida Aquarium houses thousands of captivating water-dwelling animals such as a Pacific octopus, penguins, and rare Australian sea dragons. Be sure to explore the coral reef grotto, then board a catamaran tour to set your sights on passing dolphins. To see animals of the terra firma variety you should mosey on over to the Lowry Park Zoo, with its 1,600 animals, family-friendly rides, shows, and a memorable manatee exhibit (this is Florida, after all) that gives you an insider's view of daffy sea cows. At the Museum of Science and Industry, also in Tampa, take in an eye-popping IMAX movie in the domed theater and explore exhibits about shipwrecks, pirates' treasures,

ROLLING RIDGE
RV RESORT
CLERMONT, FLORIDA

OWNERSHIP OPTIONS FROM $11,900

"REAL-ESTATE" OWNERSHIP

AT A FRACTION OF THE COST!

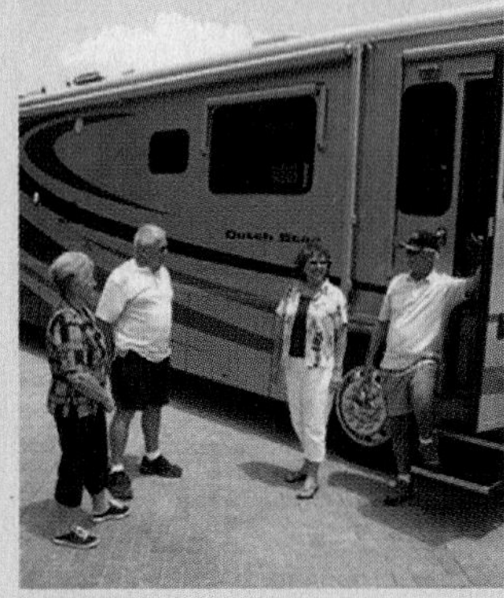

- Rolling Ridge is a unique 155-unit RV pad Community located directly off Hwy 27 in Lake County Florida. With its great location & easy access to all-major highways, Disney & other major attractions are within a 30 minute drive. Rolling Ridge is the perfect platform for full enjoyment of the RV lifestyle.

- Rolling Ridge offers multiple ownership & rental options. Whether you're a seasonal or full time resident, Rolling Ridge has the ownership option to fit your needs. Full or fractional ownership options are available.

- Each exclusive RV pad features 50 amp electrical hook-up, potable water, sewer plus beautiful brick pavers with an outdoor grill.

- From travel trailers to class "A" motor coaches, we welcome all RV's including Park Models.

- Now is the time to stop paying rent and own a place of your own…..

COMMUNITY AMENITIES INCLUDE

Tennis - Swimming Pool - Shuffleboard - Multi Use Area - Fitness Area
Event Room - Covered Veranda with Outdoor Kitchen & More...

Toll-Free: 1-877-429-3796

20285 U.S. Highway 27 North - Clermont, Florida 34715

and scientific perspectives on way-out weather patterns and natural disasters.

From Tampa Bay, travel north on US-19 to Clearwater, home of the Clearwater Marine Aquarium. Meet dolphins, sea turtles, and other such creatures rescued and rehabilitated by the center staff. Intracoastal waterway cruises are another favorite area attraction. The choice between dashing speedboats, sedate dinner cruises, and informative sightseeing tours is never easy. Better try them all.

If you choose to board a cruise in nearby Tarpon Springs, you might learn how Greek sponge divers influenced local history. Be sure to watch closely while practiced divers demonstrate their sponging skills.

Further north on US-19, Port Richey's Werner-Boyce Salt Springs State Park is noted for its unspoiled beaches and the 320' deep salt spring that gave the preserve its name. Animals such as the gray fox, gopher tortoise, and several species of songbirds and wading shorebirds may also be seen at the park.

North of Port Richey, Spring Hill is home of a whimsical, six-decade-long tradition, the Weeki Wachee Spring "City of Mermaids" daily underwater shows. Just four miles from the Gulf of Mexico, Spring Hill is awash with natural springs, streams, lakes, and rivers, and it's a notable spot for bass fishing and canoe or kayak paddling. Buccaneer Bay pleases action-oriented families with its tube rides, bumper boats, and water slides. And for quieter moments, you can stroll among the butterflies, desertscape, and herb blossoms at Spring Hill's Nature Coast Botanical Gardens.

FLORIDA-SOUTH

Take State Rte 50 east and then head south a ways on US-41, past Tampa and St. Petersburg, where we embark on the south Gulf Shore segment of the trip. Our first stop is Sarasota and the famed Ringling Estate. It includes 22 galleries of the John and Mable Ringling Museum of Art, the lavish Ca d'Zan (House of John) mansion, and Mable Ringling Rose Garden. A visit to the waterfront estate isn't complete without a leisurely tour of the Ringling Circus Museum where glitzy costumes, wagons, a miniature circus, and fascinating mementos from the historic Ringling Brothers Barnum & Bailey Circus are displayed. Mote Marine Laboratory is a research

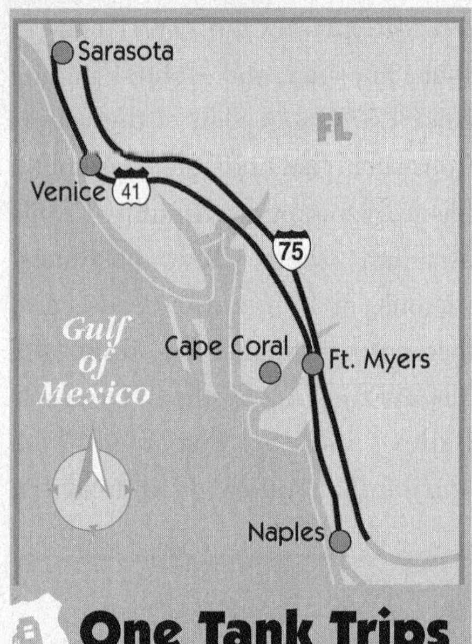

FLORIDA - SOUTH

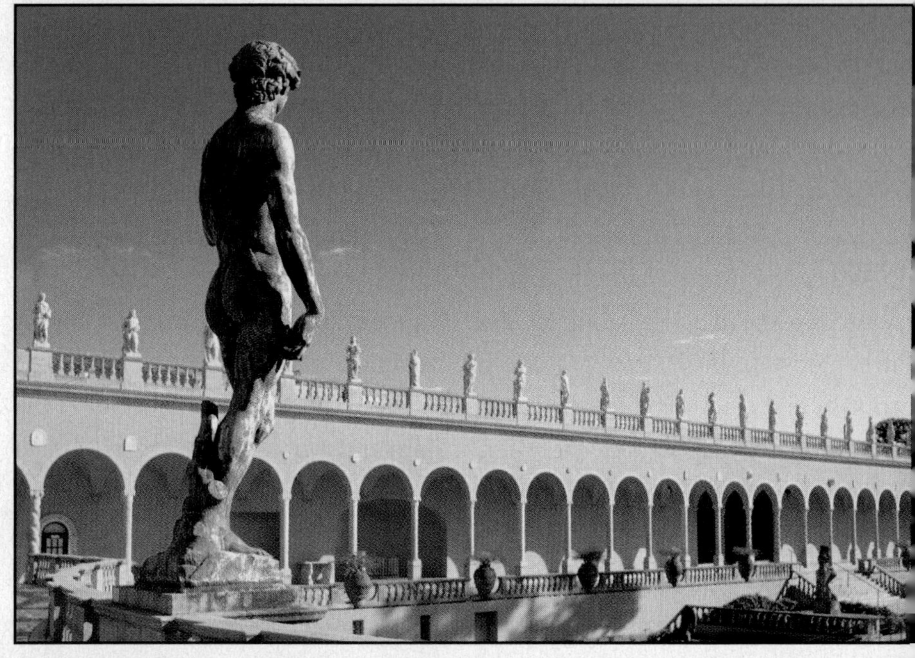

Ringling Estate and Museum. Photo credit: WWW.VISITFLORIDA.ORG

facility best known for studying dolphins and sharks. However, it's also a great place to learn about Florida's whole host of marine critters. Manatees, stingrays, horseshoe crabs, and a 27' preserved squid are all part of Mote's magic. Catch an interactive show at the aquarium's Immersion Theatre and board a pontoon boat for a narrated local cruise.

From Sarasota, we'll take US-41 south all the way to Everglades City, with sightseeing stops in Venice, Fort Myers, and Naples. A bygone sharks' burial ground just offshore makes Venice Beach a Florida hotspot for locating stray shark's teeth. Try combing the sands around Venice Pier, where numerous individual black and white teeth are routinely found.

The Edison-Ford Winter Estates in Fort Myers chronicles and celebrates the eminent careers of inventors-extraordinaire Thomas Edison and Henry Ford. While you're there take a river cruise and tour the estates' laboratory, museum full of inventions, and botanical gardens Calusa Nature Center & Planetarium may help slow your vacation pace by taking in the tranquil butterfly aviary, stargazing a the planetarium, and exploring "natural" Florida on the center's boardwalks.

Plan to hit the greens in Naples at the area's top-rated golf courses before proceeding to Everglades City an unassuming, small town that hearkens back to early-1900s Florida. As the recognized entryway to Everglades National Park and the site

of the Museum of the Everglades, it's an ideal home base for arranging guided Everglades tours via airboat, pontoon boat, jet boat, canoe, or kayak.
www.VISITFLORIDA.com

Other Area Locations

FORT MYERS
The Shell Factory & Nature Park
JACKSONVILLE
Pecan Park RV Resort
LA BELLE
The Glades RV, Golf & Marina Resort
NAPLES
Rock Creek RV Resort & Campground
PANAMA CITY BEACH
Emerald Coast RV Beach Resort
TALLAHASSEE
Tallahassee RV Park

888/735-2872 (U.S.) or 888/352-4636 (Canada).

LOUISIANA

The state of Louisiana stands ready with unique tourism opportunities. In New Orleans, there's a noteworthy aquarium and zoo to see and world-famous local cuisine to sample. Walk around a 19th century plantation in Garyville, while Baton Rouge earns its vacation accolades with an art and science center, the destroyer U.S.S. Kidd, and casino action. In Lafayette, hear colorful stories about resourceful Cajun settlers at the living history village of Vermilionville.

Naturally, we want to start things off right in "The Big Easy", New Orleans. You really can't go wrong in locating wonderful, authentic cuisine here. Eat a fresh-made praline, taste some spicy gumbo, and tap your toes to jazz music. Best of all, every dollar spent here helps rebuild one of America's most distinctive cities, severely damaged by Hurricane Katrina. We also recommend visiting the frisky otters, squishy jellyfish, and a white alligator from the bayou at Audubon Aquarium of the Americas. See more than 2,000 creatures living in realistic surroundings at Audubon Zoo. Go on a steamboat cruise and try your luck at the perpetually rocking Harrah's New Orleans Casino near the French Quarter.

Let's hit the road, taking US-61 northeast. While our ultimate destination will be Lafayette, we think a few stopovers are in order first. The restored 1850s plantation estate, schoolhouse, and slave cabin, set among 300-year-old oaks at San

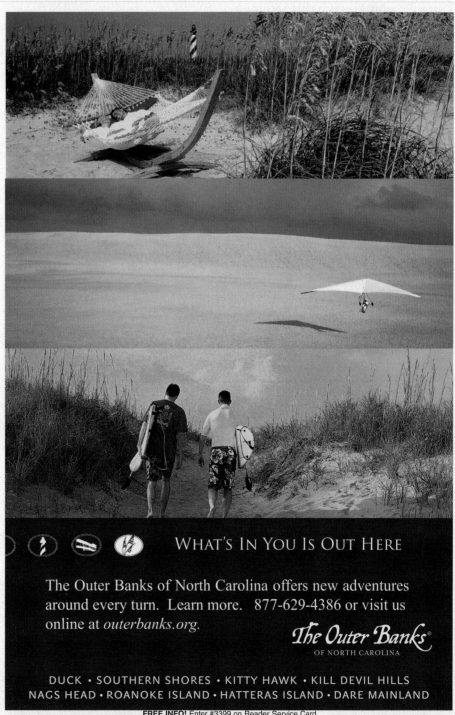

Francisco Plantation is what makes the town of Garyville a compelling respite. Meanwhile, the town of Gonzales lets you flip forward to modern times and experience the non-stop shopping options at Tanger Outlet Center.

In Baton Rouge, see a refurbished WWII destroyer at the U.S.S. Kidd & Veteran's Memorial Museum. The museum contains an aircraft exhibition, Hall of Honor, and interesting models of U.S. military ships.

You can see an Egyptian tomb, a space theater show, and fine art exhibits all in one place at the Louisiana Art & Science Museum. Feeling lucky? Of course you are, which is why a winning diversion to Argosy Casino seems like a good a bet. Take advantage of round-the-clock restaurants and upscale entertainment venues in a high-rolling casino atmosphere.

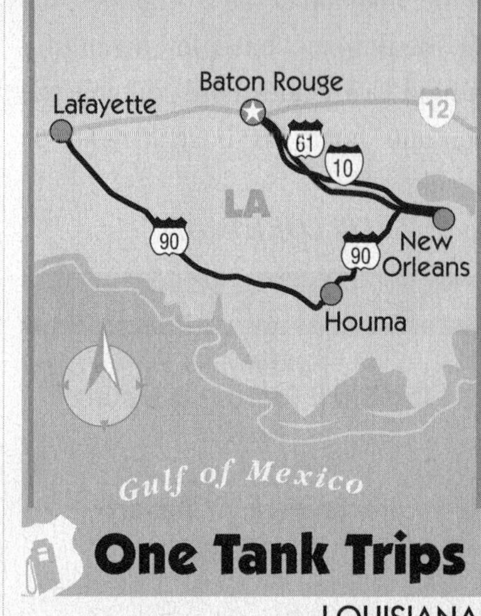

LOUISIANA

THIS ROUTE BROUGHT TO YOU BY:

Felix Poche Plantation RV Resort
www.pocheplantation.com
innkeeper@pocheplantation.com
(225)715-9510

From Baton Rouge, take I-10 south, then 90 west, to go deep into the exotic bayous of Houma. Numerous companies in the area offer swamp tours, where you have the chance to see towering cypress trees, long-legged herons, and the swamp's most famous occupant, the alligator. Any of these tours are definitely worth your time. Another worthwhile visit is the Bayou Terrebonne Waterlife Museum, and its interactive exhibits displaying the beauty, and importance, of the Louisiana waters.

Last, but not least; Lafayette. Jean Lafitte National Park Acadian Cultural Center teaches visitors about the Cajuns who migrated from Nova Scotia, Canada, to Louisiana during the mid-18th century. Nearby Vermilionville does it one better, with a restored Cajun village and living history museum located, where else, but on the bayou? In and around Lafayette, tour elegant plantation homes, dance to lilting zydeco music, and dine on succulent seafood straight from the waters of the Gulf of Mexico.

www.LouisianaTravel.com
225/342-8119

Other Area Locations

HOUMA
Houma Area Convention & Visitors Bureau
LAFAYETTE
Lafayette Convention & Visitors Commission
NEW ORLEANS
French Quarter RV Resort

NORTH CAROLINA

Travel down Blue Ridge Parkway in North Carolina and you will soon discover why it is "America's Favorite Drive." This route serves the RV traveler a heaping portion of natural beauty and enthralling attractions. From "Blowing Rock" in Boone, to Biltmore Estate in Asheville, to the mountain music of Maggie Valley, the North Carolina route may become your favorite drive as well.

Our trip begins in the town of Boone, which is notable for its most famous tourist attraction; Blowing Rock. This "rock" is an immense, 4,000 foot cliff, in which northwest winds blow through the gorge in such a way to make an upward flume, making it the only place in the world where snow falls up! But Blowing Rock isn't the only interesting attraction in Boone. Also check out "Grandfather Mountain," with its mile-high swinging bridge. Or if you prefer your feet on the ground, visit Linville Caverns, where you can explore an underground stream, a bottomless pool, and countless stalactites and stalagmites. To see how the Appalachian pioneers lived,

Continued on page 64

Cafe du Monde and lower Pontabala apartments on Decatur St. Photo credit: Louisiana Office of Tourism

Alabama
Gulf Shores/Pensacola West

Arizona
Benson
Flagstaff
Grand Canyon/Williams
Holbrook/Petrified Forest
Kingman
Seligman/Route 66
Williams/Exit 167/Circle Pines

Arkansas
Fort Smith/Alma
Little Rock North/Jct I-40
Memphis

California
Barstow/Calico
Cloverdale
Crescent City/Redwoods
Los Angeles/Pomona/Fairplex
Mt. Lassen/Shingletown
Oroville/Feather Falls Casino
San Diego Metro
San Francisco North/Petaluma
Stockton Delta
Trinity Lake
Visalia/Fresno South

Colorado
Colorado Springs
Cortez/Mesa Verde
Denver East/Strasburg
Fort Collins North/Wellington
Fort Collins/Lakeside
Fort Collins/Poudre Canyon
Grand Junction
Pueblo
Pueblo South/Colorado City

Connecticut
Mystic

Florida
Kissimmee
Milton/Gulf Pines
Orlando Southwest/Fort Summit
St Augustine Beach
Starke/Gainesville Northeast
West Palm Beach/Lion Country Safari

Georgia
Forsyth

Idaho
Mountain Home

Illinois
Lasalle/Peru
Lena
Rock Island/Quad Cities

Indiana
Elkhart Co/Middlebury Exit
Terre Haute

Iowa
Des Moines West

Kansas
Lawrence/Kansas City
Salina

Kentucky
Kentucky Lakes/Prizer Point
Louisville Metro
Louisville South
Renfro Valley

Louisiana
Baton Rouge
Lafayette
New Orleans West
Shreveport/Bossier

Maine
Bar Harbor
Saco/Old Orchard Beach

Maryland
Washington DC/Capitol

Massachusetts
Boston/Cape Cod

Michigan
Coloma/St Joseph
Covert/South Haven
Detroit/Greenfield
Gaylord
Mackinaw City/Mackinac Island
Monroe County/Toledo North
Oscoda
St Ignace/Mackinac Island
Traverse City

Minnesota
Minneapolis Northwest
Rochester/Marion

Mississippi
Meridian East/Toomsuba

Missouri
Branson
Kansas City East/Oak Grove
St. Louis Northeast/I-270/Granite City
St. Louis West/Historic Route 66

Montana
Big Timber
Dillon
Livingston/Paradise Valley
Missoula
Polson/Flathead Lake
Townsend/Canyon Ferry Lake

Nebraska
West Omaha

Nevada
Ely
Las Vegas KOA at Circus Circus
Laughlin/Avi Casino
Reno KOA at Boomtown
Wendover

New Mexico
Albuquerque Central
Carlsbad
Clayton
Grants/Cibola Sands
Las Vegas New Mexico
Santa Fe
Silver City
Tucumcari

Look for these wonderful KOA locations in Woodall's Campground Directory

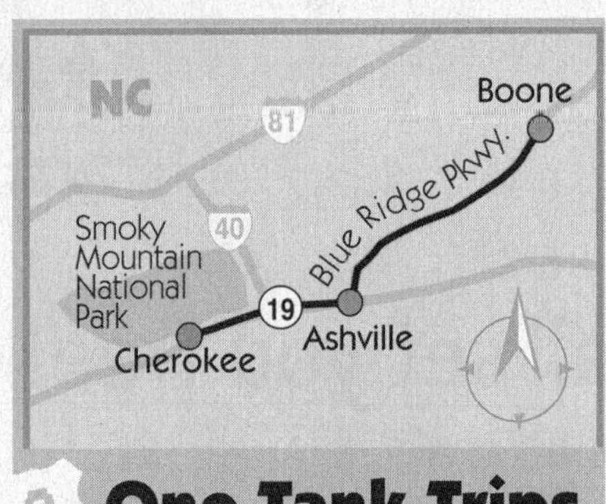

visit the Hickory Ridge Homestead & Living History Museum, where costumed actors demonstrate mountain skills-like candle-making, tin working, weaving, and fireplace baking-in a "living history" setting.

Travel down "The Blue Ridge Parkway" to get to our next destination, the town Asheville. But take your time getting there; The Blue Ridge Parkway isn't called "America's Favorite Drive" for no reason. Wildflowers dominate the road in the spring, while autumn foliage takes over in the later months, making for a truly remarkable sight.

Once you reach Asheville, be sure to visit Biltmore Estate, the famous home of the Vanderbilts. This 250-room castle houses some of the most incredible art, 16-century tapestries, and architecture that you will see anywhere in the country. Also on the grounds is a celebrated winery, with lakeside vineyards and wine-tasting tours. You can browse through a great collection of antique radios, dating from WWI to the 1960s, at Asheville's Southern Appalachian Radio Museum, or perhaps jump in a hot air balloon at one of the local touring companies in town, and go for a breath-taking scenic ride over the Blue Ridge Mountains.

Follow US Highway 19 south to Maggie Valley, where you can hear traditional Appalachian music, like bluegrass, country ballads, or country hymns, at the Valley's Opry House. Motorcycle enthusiasts shouldn't miss seeing the collection of two-wheeled wonders at the Wheels of Time Museum.

Keep on the 19 to reach the last town on our trip; Cherokee. See the story of the local tribe at the Cherokee Museum, where an interactive 3-D exhibit immerses you in their history. If you enjoy great theater, catch the production of "Unto these Hills", an outdoor drama which depicts the challenging, often heartbreaking, history of the Cherokee tribe, from the 1500s, to their relocation in Oklahoma in the 1800s. And it is Christmas all year at the nearby theme park, Santaland, where kids can meet the denizens of the North Pole in person, while riding roller coasters and eating local goodies.

www.visitnc.com
800/VISIT-NC.

Biltmore Estate, Asheville Photo credit: Asheville CVB

SOUTH CAROLINA

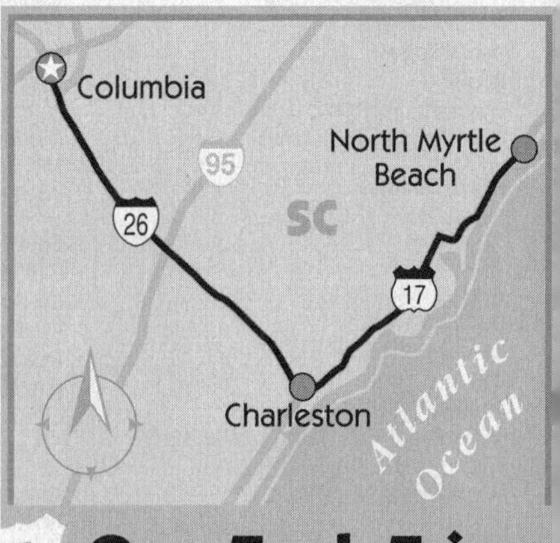

SOUTH CAROLINA

The culmination of rich colonial history, stunning architecture, and southern hospitality and charm is found in the sunny state of South Carolina. Here, you can sink your

MYRTLE BEACH – FOR YEAR-ROUND CAMPING FUN!

Lakewood Camping Resort

Toll-Free 1.877.LAKEWOOD • 843.238.5161
www.lakewoodcampground.com

Toll-Free 1.800.562.7790 • 843.448.3421
www.myrtlebeachkoa.com

Toll-Free 1.800.255.3568 • 843.449.3714
www.myrtlebeachtravelpark.com

Toll-Free 1.800.876.4306 • 843.238.5636
www.oceanlakes.com

Toll-Free 1.800.443.CAMP • 843.238.5155
www.pirateland.com

Toll-Free 1.866.207.2267 • 843.756.4334
www.willowtreervr.com

CAMPMYRTLEBEACH.COM

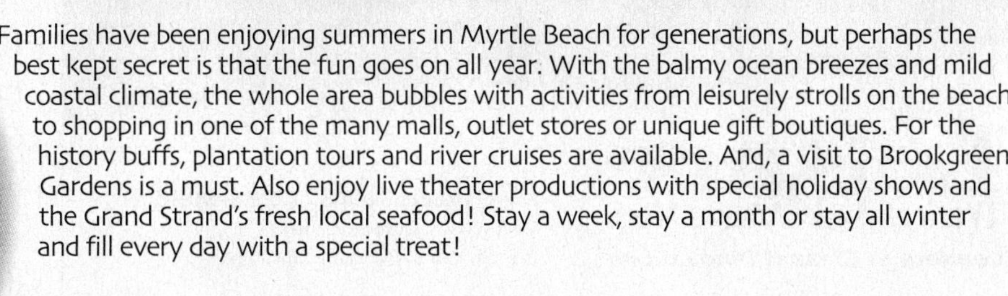

Families have been enjoying summers in Myrtle Beach for generations, but perhaps the best kept secret is that the fun goes on all year. With the balmy ocean breezes and mild coastal climate, the whole area bubbles with activities from leisurely strolls on the beach to shopping in one of the many malls, outlet stores or unique gift boutiques. For the history buffs, plantation tours and river cruises are available. And, a visit to Brookgreen Gardens is a must. Also enjoy live theater productions with special holiday shows and the Grand Strand's fresh local seafood! Stay a week, stay a month or stay all winter and fill every day with a special treat!

FREE INFO! Enter #322 on Reader Service Card

Carriage Tour, Charleston. Photo credit: Charlesotn Area CVB

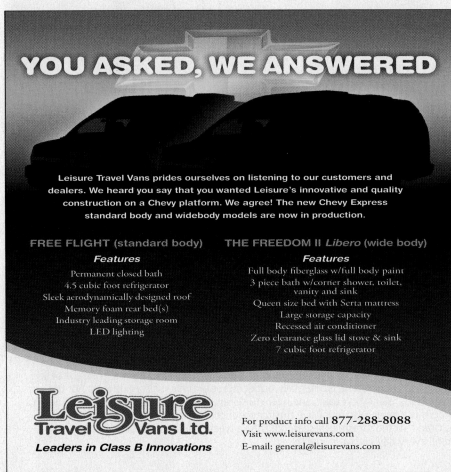

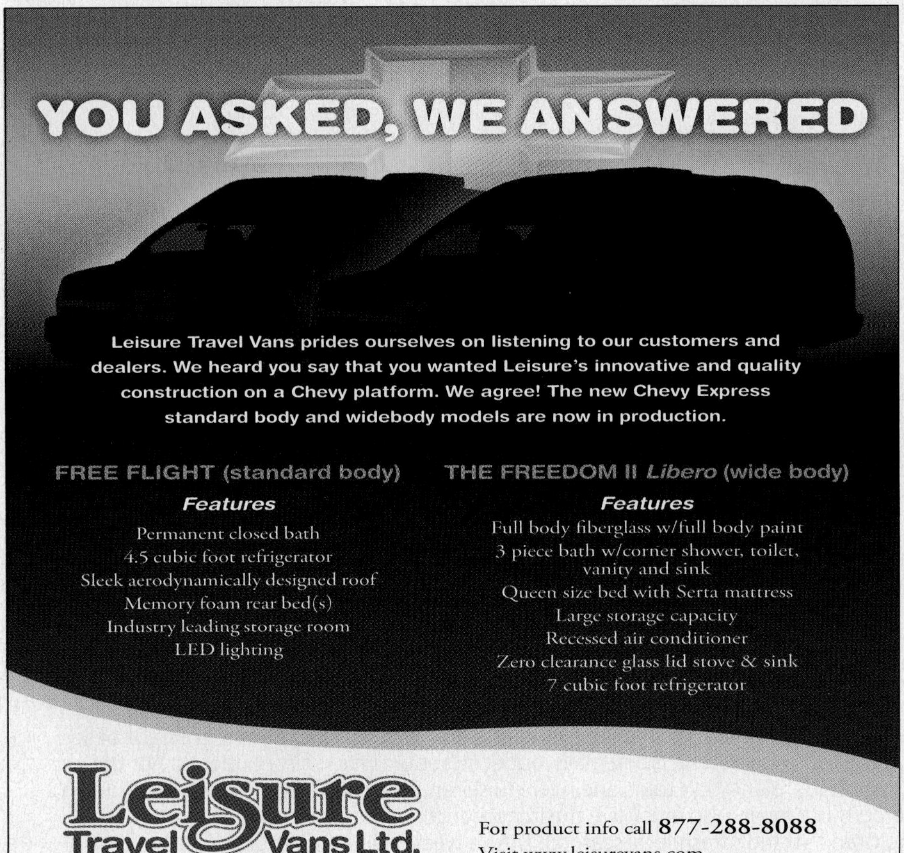

toes in beautiful beaches that rival any found on the West Coast, tour massive plantation estates and quaint 1700th century homes, unwind at the gorgeous gardens and parks, or have fun at the many zoos, museums, and concert halls scattered throughout the state. Don't let her old age fool you; South Carolina is one of the most exciting states on the East Coast.

Those who would argue that the West controls the market on beautiful beaches have never visited Myrtle Beach. Miles of white sand and crystal clear water make Myrtle Beach the perfect place to begin our tour. Along with the breath-taking coastline, the town also hosts more than 100 golf courses, malls, restaurants, boutiques, water parks, and deep-fishing venues. Some attractions that should not be missed include Dolly Parton's Dixie Stampede, where patrons can enjoy delicious southern cooking, while watching an entertaining dinner show, complete with daring horsemanship and thrilling stunts. At the Family Kingdom-South Carolina's only seaside amusement park, and one of the top ten parks in the country-you can ride over 30 hair-raising roller-coasters and munch on tasty treats.

Keep on Highway 17 to reach our next destination spot, the charming little town of Murrell's Inlet. If you are a bird enthusiast, head over to Huntington Beach State Park, where many flocks of feathered fowl gather along the banks of the freshwater lagoon, or near the salt marsh. The unique Brookegreen Gardens provides a leafy oasis of pools, flowers, and fountains, with hundreds of pieces of artistic sculpture skillfully blended into the landscape.

Farther down the 17 Highway is the historic town of Charleston. Stop in at the South Carolina Aquarium and Wharf, and you will not only get a view of amazing marine life and superb seafood, but also get a chance to see a movie at the IMAX Theater and shop at many chic boutiques. To see the historic side of the city, make a trip to Fort Sumter National Monument and see where the initial struggle between Union Soldiers and the Confederate armies began. Or hop on a carriage ride through the downtown distinct to see the wonderful 17th century homes and the Middleton Plantation.

From Charleston, travel on Interstate 26 West and 77 North to the state capital of Columbia. Your family can meander through a blooming landscape and experience close encounters with zebras, koalas,

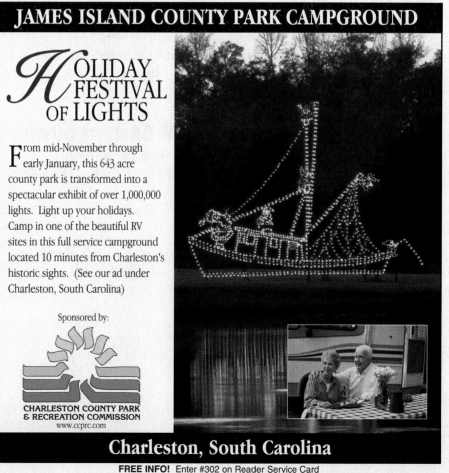

Memphis Rock and Soul Museum. Photo Courtesy Memphis Convention & Visitors Bureau

Live music at The BlueBird. Photo credit: Nashville Convention and Visitors Bureau

giraffes, and other captivating creatures at Riverbanks Zoo & Garden. Hike, or bike, your way through 120,000 acres of lakeview trails in Sumter National Forest, or get a chance to go on a space mission at the Challenger Learning Center, where high-tech simulators provide you an opportunity to boldly go into the final frontier. At the South Carolina State Museum there are four floors of exhibits on art, history, science, and technology, not to mention a 43-foot prehistoric great white shark lurking somewhere in the building. And a trip down I-26 takes you to Columbia's recently renovated Newberry Opera House, which hosts all genres of top-notch performers, from classical instrumentalists to country crooners, to dancing pop stars. South Carolina's capital is the perfect way to end the tour of this truly delightful southern state. *www.DiscoverSouthCarolina.com 866/224-9339.*

TENNESSEE

Tennessee's musical heritage is hard to beat and even harder to forget. You can visit Elvis' curious estate in Memphis and explore the vibrant history of the rock-a-billy music scene in Jackson. Our final destination on Tennessee's Music

One Tank Trips

TENNESSEE

Highway certainly earns Nashville's "Music City" moniker, thanks to the Grand Ole Opry, Country Music Hall of Fame, and renowned Ryman Auditorium.

Is there a more appropriate spot to begin our Tennessee tour than at Elvis Presley's rambling Graceland estate in Memphis? It's in the southwest corner of Tennessee. Take a self-guided audio tour of the "King's" legendary mansion and see his gold and platinum record awards in the remarkable Hall of Gold. Might we suggest picking up a fried peanut butter and banana sandwich in town beforehand to get into the mood? For Memphis magic after sundown, visit Beale Street's Historic District, which delivers three city blocks of lively nightclubs, musical venues, eateries, and shops.

From Memphis, pick up The Music Highway, I-40, east all the way to Nashville. Naturally, we've found a few gems to admire along the way. Bargains, anyone? Shop till you drop at the Factory Outlet Mall in the town of Lakeland, then push on to Jackson to do a little browsing at the Old Hickory Mall. While you're here, the Casey Jones Home & Railroad Museum honors the widely celebrated locomotive king. On another

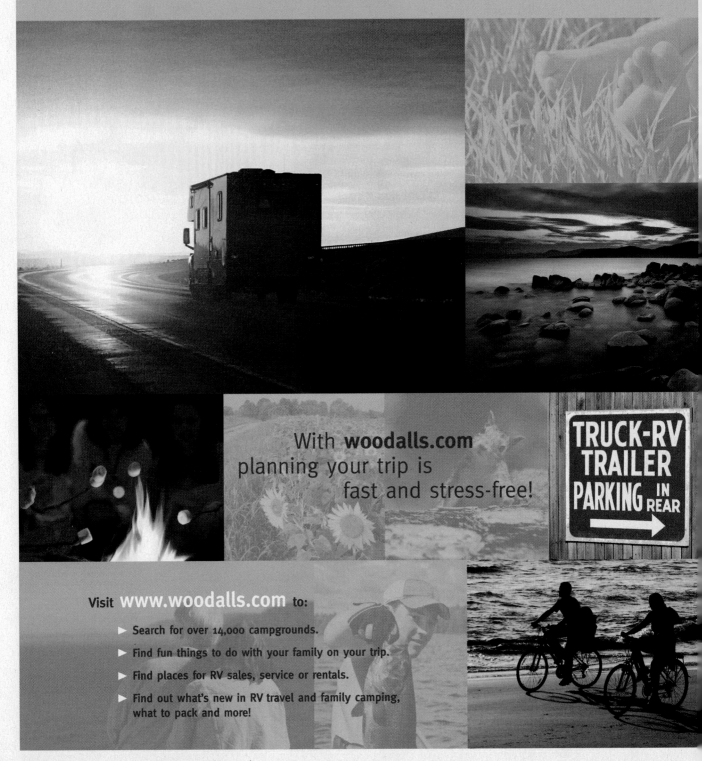

track, the International Rock-a-Billy Hall of Fame & Museum, also in Jackson, focuses its exhibits on the country/blues/rock-and-roll music style begun by legendary stars like Bill Haley and the Comets, and Carl Perkins.

In Burns, at the Old Spencer Mill, take a step back in time to a historic site where two stone grist-mills and a 20'-wide waterwheel still stand. Next, take a step forward onto the green at the 18-hole Tennessee Golf Trail at Montgomery Bell State Park Golf Course.

Those in need of an aquatic fun are in luck. The place to go for paddling a canoe and savoring the views on the picturesque Harpeth River is none other than nearby Kingston Springs.

Ah, finally, Nashville. The "Music City" rocks, rolls, and welcomes you with open arms. Begin your visit at the Grand Ole Opry, where the cream of the country music crop performs onstage. For behind-the-scenes action, a visit to the Country Music Hall of Fame and Museum is in order, to gaze upon authentic stage costumes, instruments, honest-to-goodness music videos, and interactive exhibits featuring the brightest country talents on the planet. A tour of the Ryman Auditorium is also full of pleasant surprises. You can stand on stage like one of the big stars, step backstage to the dressing rooms, and make your own one-in-a-million CD in a real Ryman recording studio. For a culinary change of pace, board Nashville's General Jackson Showboat for a lunch or dinner cruise with a musical theme. Evening cruises include memorable shows by fine entertainers. Attention, golfers! Gaylord Springs Golf Links on the Cumberland River is a Larry Nelson-designed course with 18 superb holes to impress your senses and challenge your game.

www.TNVACATION.com
800/462-8366.

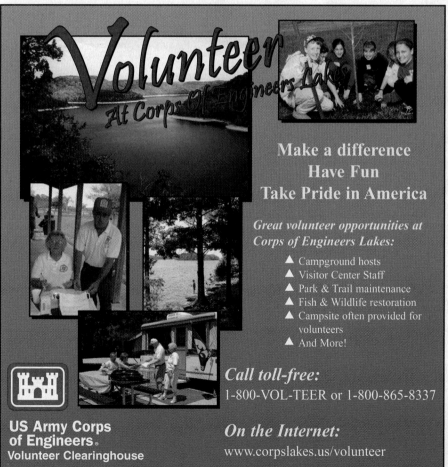

Memphis in May BBQ Championship.
Photo credit: Tennessee Department of Tourist Development

It's got the lure of the big cities (Chicago, Minneapolis-St. Paul, Milwaukee, etc.) and the kinds of rural communities that make Mayberry seem almost metropolitan. Connecting them is an assortment of highways and byways to entice any traveler to a lakeside journey, farmland field trip, or visit to a variety of can't-miss attractions, natural or man-made.

ILLINOIS

Illinois' I-55 may be a daunting, fast-paced freeway, but along the way there's plenty of places to pull off and enjoy a little slower pace. Even though I-55 replaced Route 66 as the preferred thoroughfare from Chicago to St. Louis, the remains of the famed "Mother Road" are still there, parallel to the modern interstate highway, waiting to be explored.

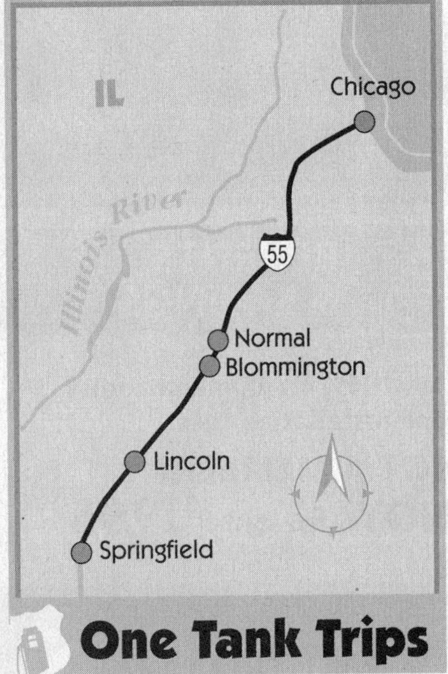

Start your I-55 trip at Springfield, Illinois, the state capital, which carries with it the hospitality and warmth of a southern city. In Springfield, of course, you'll discover the legacy of it's favorite son, Abraham Lincoln, the state's most famous resident. Today, Springfield provides a variety of terrific Lincoln-themed sights. Start off your tour at the Lincoln Home National Historic Site, where the family lived from 1844 to 1861. Other Springfield destination gems include the Lincoln Memorial Garden and Nature Center, the Old State Capital State Historic Site, and the Lincoln Tomb State Historic Site. Of course, you could just take a crash-course about the former president at the newly unveiled Abraham Lincoln Presidential Library and Museum.

While heading north, you'll soon come upon the town of Atlanta (pop 1,650). Okay, so it doesn't have many of the features of the bigger namesake city in Georgia. What Atlanta, Illinois does have is several quirky roadside attractions and fabulous stick-to-the-ribs-style eateries keeping with the tradition of fabled Route 66, including the obligatory 19-foot statue of a guy holding a hot dog! Quick, somebody get the camera! Be sure to stop by the Constitution Trail, a favorite local destination boasting miles of recreation trails winding through the most scenic areas of the city.

Pontiac is another town that provides a nice respite from the highway. And what better way to shake off those freeway blues than a visit to the Route 66 Hall of Fame and Museum, located downtown. There are even three historic swinging bridges that span the Vermillion River. And you won't just find your mother's version of "antiquing" here any more. These days, the good folks running the famous Old City Shoppes even have their own blog on the web (www.oldcityhallshoppes.blogspot.com) to bring you up to date on their antiques and collectable wares.

Soon you'll be entering the greater Chicagoland area where navigating your rig might get tricky. So ease into it with a visit to the suburbs. Naperville is one of Chicago's finest little 'burbs, about 45 minutes west of the city. With a great downtown district for shopping and eating, this fast-growing city features many of the city charms yet retains much of the warmth of its once small-town history.

Heading east, your next stop should be the historic town of Oak Park, which is a stone's throw from the Chicago city limits. The legacies of both Ernest Hemingway (born here) and Frank Lloyd Wright (lived and worked here) still loom and their historic ties to the area can be explored at the Ernest Hemingway Museum and Frank Lloyd Wright Home and Studio respectively.

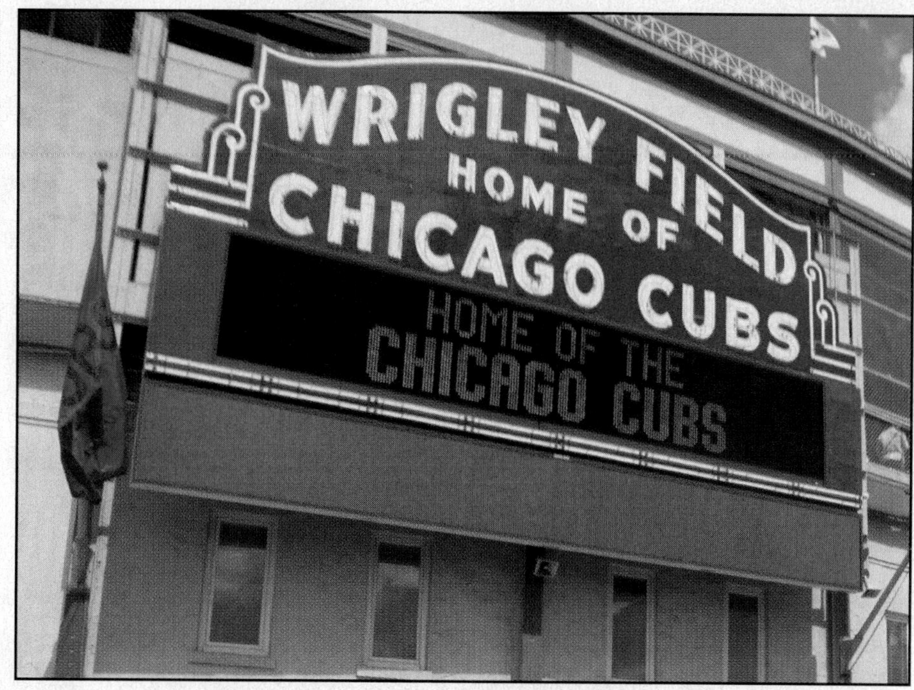

Wrigley Field. Photo courtesy of the City of Chicago/Chris McGuire

Finally, the Windy City: Chicago. You made it. So take a load off by parking your rig and taking advantage of public transportation. Trust me on this one. Besides, Chicago's train line is a destination in and of

itself. Pick up the train in the Loop (Chicago's downtown area) and enjoy the ride above the city streets as it snakes its way across town. Take it north to Wrigleyville, home of the Chicago Cubs, and a national shrine of daylight-only baseball.

INDIANA

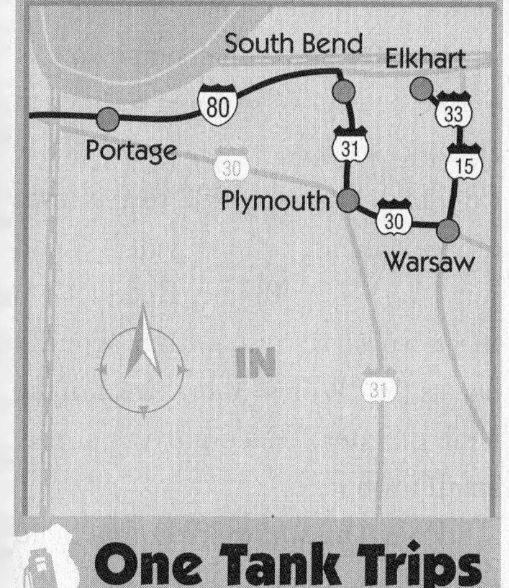

From Chicago, let's head east into the Hoosier State. Northwest Indiana presents an eclectic mix of natural beauty and good old-fashioned Midwest warmth. Best of all, this tour winds up in the RV Capital of the World!

After leaving Chicago, head south on I-90, then I-80/94 east to enter northwest Indiana. Be sure to allow some extra travel time here or pass through at an off-hour to avoid the heavy traffic. Your first stop should be the town of Portage, where you can jump head first, climb, roll down, etc. into the famed Indiana Dunes. Today, nearly 20,000 acres of Lake Michigan shoreline consists of the Indiana Dunes National Lakeshore and the adjacent Indiana Dunes State Park. Take your pick, they're equally impressive. Here, the

Sun setting over Lake View beach, Indiana Dunes National Lakeshore. Photographer Christopher Light.

sand dunes, some up to nearly 200 feet high, sprawl as far the eye can see. It is one of the Midwest's finest natural treasures, and the two parks combined offer endless opportunities for hiking, swimming, picnicking, and wildlife watching.

La Porte, Indiana, is our next stop. It's a few miles south of I-80/90 on Hwy 35, but this little town will give you a taste of northern Indiana's fascination with the automobile. Check out the popular Door Prairie Museum and explore more than 100 years of motorized toys. Keep moving east along I-80/90 until you reach the town of South Bend, the home of the Fighting Irish of Notre Dame. But don't think this college football-obsessed town is a mere one-trick pony (although the College Football Hall of Fame here is a must-see). Check out the Studebaker National Museum or the South Bend Regional Museum of Art.

From here, head south on US-31 until you reach the town of Plymouth. This historic town is a great place to spend an afternoon, especially within the town's splendid network of city parks, each with its own unique signature. If you find yourself still exploring Plymouth come sundown, head over to the Tri-Way Drive-In Theater for a double feature; it's one of only a handful of such theaters left in the state. From

Plymouth, head east along US-30 until you reach the town of Warsaw, capital of Indiana's Lake District. Here you'll discover a charming collection of lakes that serve as popular getaway destinations for regional folks.

Let's finish up our Indiana tour by heading north on State Hwy 15 to the town of Elkhart, the RV Capital of the World. Today, Elkhart is home to nearly three-dozen RV and mobile home companies, including Coachmen RV and Holiday Rambler. Without question, your first stop here has to be the RV Hall of Fame, which has recently moved into a larger facility. Another fun activity for like-minded folk is to take a tour of some of the many RV plants in and around Elkhart. Hey, maybe your rig was built here! Most tours are free.

IOWA

Americana is alive and well in the western hills of Iowa. Although "hills" and "Iowa" are not often found together in the same sentence, a meandering trip along the Loess Hill Scenic Byway might change your perception of the Hawkeye State.

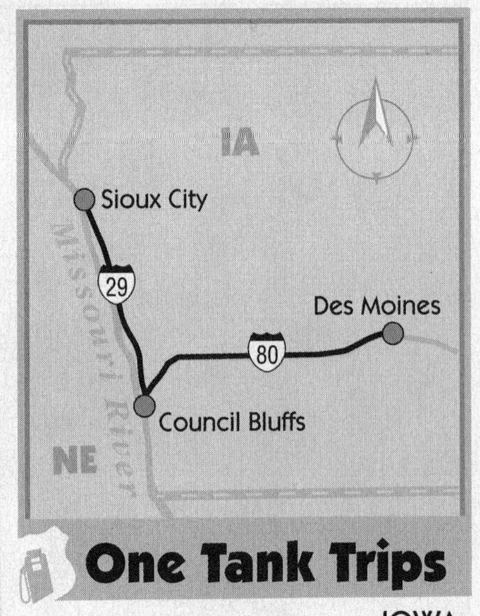

This wonderful little route begins at the thriving small/big town of Sioux City along the banks of the Missouri River. A favorite outdoor escape destination here is Stone State Park, which marks the northernmost limits of the Scenic Loess Hills. Another place to visit in town is the Sergeant Floyd Monument, an obelisk reminiscent of the Washington Memorial, and dedicated to the only man to die on the Lewis and Clark expedition. Duffers, take note. Sioux City offers up several top-notch municipal golf courses, while offering more than 1,500 acres of city parks, just perfect for picnics.

In order to stay the course on this scenic byway, we're going to have to zig-zag, so stay close. From Sioux City, take Highway 982 to the town of Smithland, where you'll head southwest along County Road L12 to the town of Onawa, which proudly boasts the "Widest Main Street in the United States." Exemplifying a true, small town feel.

From Onawa, we're gonna head east along Highway 37, past the town of Soldier, then southwest again along Hwy 183. Outside Soldier is the Loess Hills Visitors Center, a required stop for those who really want to turn over some unexplored rocks in this picturesque part of the nation. Afterwards, you'll find great picnicking opportunities at either Preparation Canyon State Park or the Loess Hills State Forest.

From there, keep riding south along Hwy 183 until you reach the town of Council Bluffs. Founded in 1804 by Lewis and Clark, this historic village is a walker's delight with a charming downtown filled with shops and restaurants.

From Council Bluffs, leave the Loess Hills behind us and head north, then eastward, along I-80. Along the way, be sure to stop in the town of Adair to experience a little of America's outlaw past. Just outside of town Jesse James and his notorious gang committed their very first robbery when they knocked off the Rock Island Railroad line on July 21, 1873.

Let's keep moving east along I-80 to our last stop, Des Moines, Iowa's capital smack dab in the middle of the state. Start exploring downtown in the city's capital district. The capitol building is nothing short of impressive and has an actual golden dome gilded with 23-karat gold tissue paper. The area also features the Principal Riverwalk, a lovely pedestrian walkway that connects all of downtown. Summer evenings find many of the locals at Gray's Lake Park, the jewel of the downtown's rejuvenation efforts, which features popular walking trails along the lakefront.

Loess Hills, Western Iowa. Photo credit: Iowa Department of Economic Development

OHIO

RVs and football go together like peanut butter and jelly. Following your favorite team, tailgating at the local game, or ensuring you're never too far away from a TV and a couch on any given Sunday in autumn is all part of the RV lifestyle. But hey, even if you don't care for the pigskin pastime, touring Northeast Ohio has plenty of thrills and chills for us all.

Let's start in Cleveland, the Buckeye State's second-largest city. Home of NBA basketball's Cavaliers and their star forward LeBron James, as well as home to the historic Cleveland Browns NFL football team. But there's more to Cleveland than football. The city boasts several waterfront parks - Euclid, Gordon, and Edgewater - that enliven the banks of Lake Erie year-round. A local favorite is Wade Park, home to the Cleveland Botanical Garden. One of the city's most famous recent additions is the Rock 'n Roll Hall of Fame, where you can catch up on the history of rock's superstars, from Elvis Presley to Bruce Springsteen.

From Cleveland, head south along I-77 until you reach Akron. Obviously, it would be almost rude to visit the "Tire Capital of the World" without touring the Goodyear World of Rubber. Don't worry, you'll definitely learn how rubber has changed the way we live. For something a bit more "green," check out the Cuyahoga Valley National Park, a 33,000-acre spread containing many historic sites and miles of trails for outdoor fun.

From Akron let's head further south on I-77 to Canton, home of the Pro Football Hall of Fame. Second only to Major League Baseball's Hall of Fame in Cooperstown, NY, no place in America houses more childhood heroes than the buildings at 2121 George Halas Drive. If you're in the neighborhood in late July or August, stick around as football greats from today and years gone by flock to Canton for the annual Hall of Fame inductions.

East of Canton, on Hwy 62, turn north on Hwy 44 until you reach I-76 East. On your way to

Youngstown, don't miss a couple of chances to get back to nature at the West Branch State Park or the Lake Milton State Park. Youngstown is our final stop in the Buckeye State, just shy of the Pennsylvania border. While there, visit the Butler Institute for American Art, the first museum dedicated solely to the works of American artists.

Other Area Locations

Canal Fulton
Clay's Park Resort

CANTON
KOA-Bear Creek Resort Ranch

DELAWARE
Cross Creek Camping Resort

LOUISVILLE
Cutty's Sunset Camping Resort

MT. EATON
Evergreen Park RV Resort

MICHIGAN

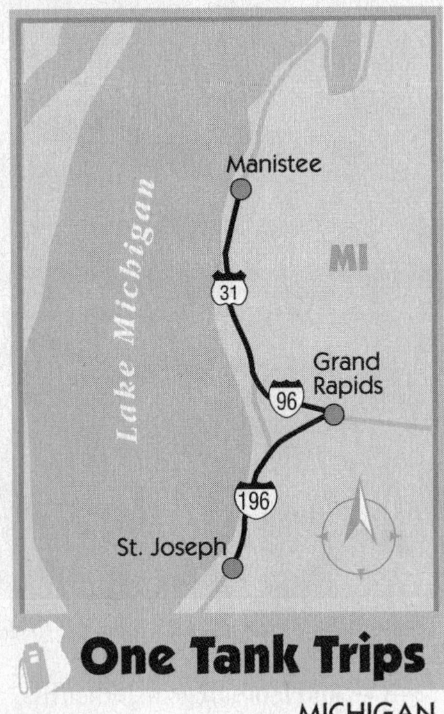

MICHIGAN

Driving the Lake Michigan shoreline ranks up there among the best of RV road trips, where winding roads connect small mid-western towns eager to please visitors year-round. As the route transitions from south to north, the scenery becomes progressively greener, evolving from small, lakeside resort towns into the great wide open spaces of northern Michigan.

Let's trace the lake's shore by starting in the town of St. Joseph, in the southwest corner of the state. "St. Joe," as the locals call it, is a small town with a big heart, complete with a charming town center chock-full of shopping and excellent bistros. South of town is the wonderful, 1,500-acre Warren Dunes State Park, which offers beaches, fine campgrounds, and plenty of hiking trails. Once you've warmed up to this neck of the woods, let's head north along scenic Hwy 63, skirting the lake's eastern shore, until you hit the town of Paw Paw Lake. This quiet little town opens its arms to summer visitors, drawing them in with its flourishing grape industry. With grapes come wines, and with wines come local vineyards. Take a tour and tasting at the several wineries in the area, or stick around in early September for the Wine and Harvest Festival.

Continuing north along the shoreline on I-196, take some time to stop at the town of South Haven, home to the impressive Lake Michigan Maritime Museum. The town is also well known for its marinas and several charters, which can take you for a spin around the lake in search of abundant (with the right bait and know-how) lake trout or Chinook salmon.

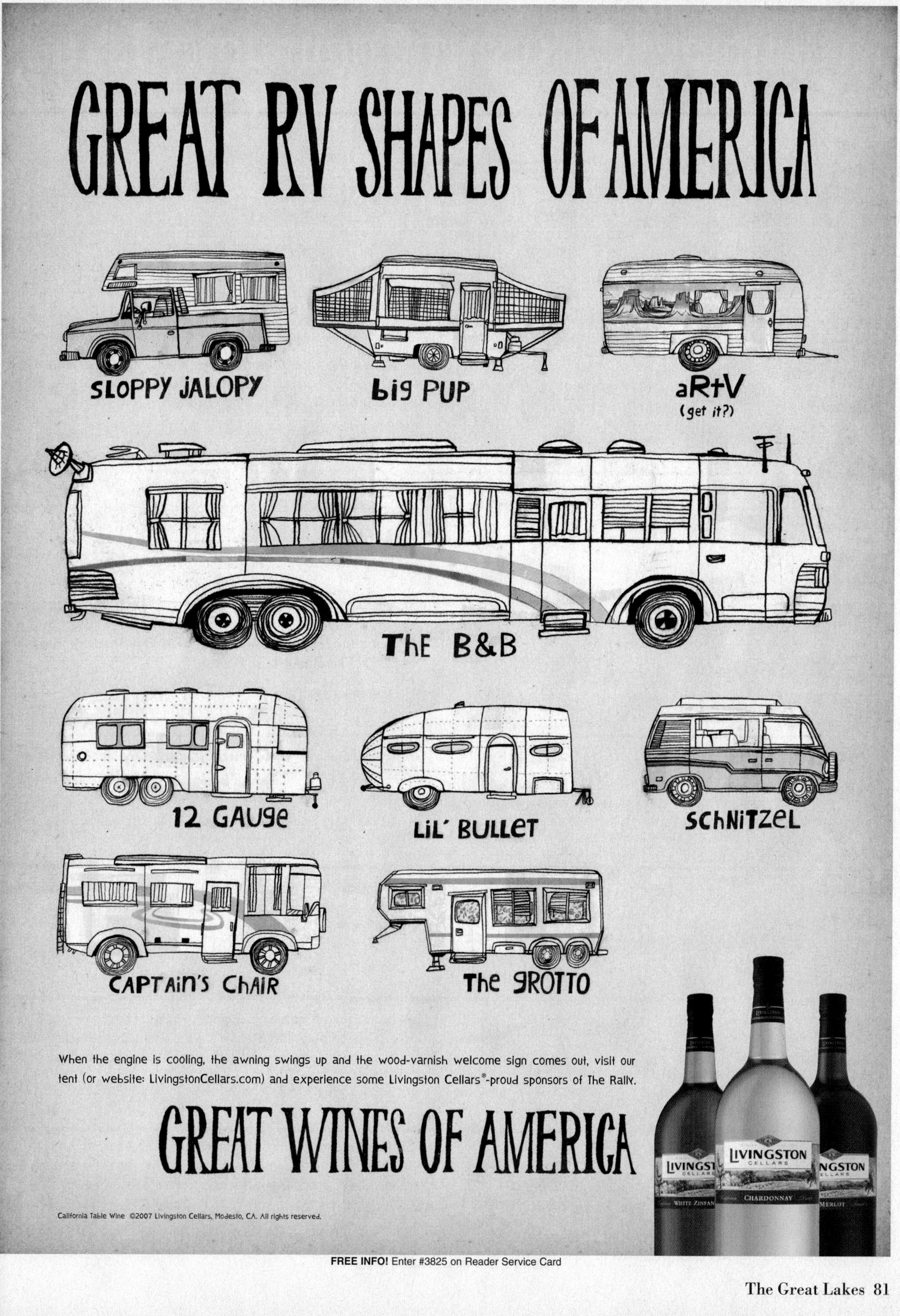

LIVINGSTON
CELLARS
CHARDONNAY
MERLOT

Redefining RV Resort Community Living

Discover the many advantages of RV Lot Ownership as well as some of the best amenities, service and activities that you'll find anywhere.

Find out more about all of LCM's great RV Resort properties at www.rvbuyalot.com Lot rentals also available.

Florence, Arizona

Set amidst the natural, undisturbed beauty of a cactus forest in the pristine Sonoran Desert, you'll find 266 of the largest, fully developed lots in warm, sunny Arizona.

9668 N. Hwy 79 Florence, AZ 85232

888-868-4888

Dickinson, Texas

Just minutes from South Houston's best attractions, this secluded, tree-lined, 42 acre property (formerly named Via Bayou) is on the edge of the bayou leading to Galveston Bay.

10000 San Leon Drive Dickinson, TX 77539

866-RVCAMP1

Lake Havasu City, Arizona

Luxurious country club living at the premier RV Resort in the Colorado River Valley. Just minutes from bustling Lake Havasu City and brilliant blue Lake Havasu.

1905 Victoria Farms Road Lake Havasu City, AZ 86404

877-407-2020

Ocala, Florida

Formerly known as Ocala Ranch, this RV resort is centrally located in *Florida's Horse Capital of the World* and an easy 1-hour drive from Orlando, the Gulf Coast, Daytona and the Atlantic Ocean.

2559 SW Hwy 484 Ocala, FL 34473

877-809-1100

Foley, Alabama

Conveniently close to the beautiful white sand beaches of Gulf Shores, a new multi-million dollar renovation brings the amenities of a premium RV Resort.

15810 Hwy 59 Foley, AL 36535

888-878-5687

Durand, Illinois

44 beautiful acres nestled in a graceful bend of the Sugar River, 1½ hours from Chicago and Milwaukee. A large heated pool, magnificent clubhouse and game room are just some of the great amenities.

9938 W. Winslow Rd Durand, IL 61024

877-517-9525

Ludington, Michigan

Situated in a natural setting and just minutes from vast Lake Michigan beaches, Vacation Station RV Resort offers 155 manicured, full hook-up sites and a private fishing pond.

4895 West US-10 Ludington, MI 49431

877-856-0390

FREE INFO! Enter #3800 on Reader Service Card

Get back on the interstate for a spell, before stopping in the wonderful artist's colony of Saugatuck and its amazing Oval Beach (rated one of the best in America by Conde Nast Traveler); it has a terrific, "artsy" downtown. This is a prime spot for a weekend getaway with some great campgrounds in the area. When you're ready, head back onto the highway to Holland, one of Michigan's most charming little towns. Settled in the mid-1800s by the Dutch (of course!), today Holland is world-famous for its tulip festival, blooming each May. For those Dutch RVers (or those willing to be Dutch for a day), check out the Dutch Village, a theme park that recreates 18th-century Holland right here in America. Take a picnic near the spinning arms of the only operating imported Dutch windmill in the U.S. at Windmill Island near downtown. Be sure to stop by the DeKlomp Wooden Shoe and Delft Factory, the only one of its kind in the entire nation and a perfect place to find a unique gift.

From Holland, let's take a side trip away from the shoreline eastward to Grand Rapids. Well-known for its city parks (there are almost 50 of them), Grand Rapids is the great place to spend an afternoon. Be sure to visit the Frederik Meijer Gardens and Sculpture Park, an enormous botanical garden complete with a 15,000-square-foot conservatory. Of course, one can't leave town without paying respects to its favorite son at the Gerald R. Ford Presidential Library and Museum, commemorating the life and work of our 38th president. If you happen to be downtown during the springtime, be sure to visit the Grand Rapids Fish Ladder, a unique device that allows spawning salmon and trout to circumvent the dam and continue their journey upstream.

From Grand Rapids, head back northwest along I-96 to the town of Muskegon. Wander some of the city's 25+ miles of Lake Michigan shoreline or enjoy a picnic in some of the city's 3,000 acres of public parks. Downtown is built on the shores of Lake Muskegon, which is popular with fishermen hoping to catch perch, walleye, pike, and other quarry. Other favorite destinations include the P.J. Hoffmaster State Park along Lake Michigan and the impressive Gillette Visitor Center, where you can learn all about dune ecology. Muskegon State Park is just north of town and offers up more than 1,000 acres of outdoor fun.

Heading north out of Muskegon you'll begin to entire another world - Michigan's North Country. You're first stop should be the Huron-Manistee National Forest. Some half-million acres large, this is your gateway to wild Michigan. In addition, along US-31 north you come across Duck Lake, Silver Lake, Hart-Montague, and Charles Mears state parks. Our last stop on this route will be the charming town of Manistee. One local hangout is the Orchard Beach State Park, a 200-acre park located on a bluff overlooking Lake Michigan, but the downtown area is still the big attraction here. Loaded with quaint shops and restaurants, the city's promenade follows the banks of the Little Manistee River as it empties into Lake Michigan.

WISCONSIN

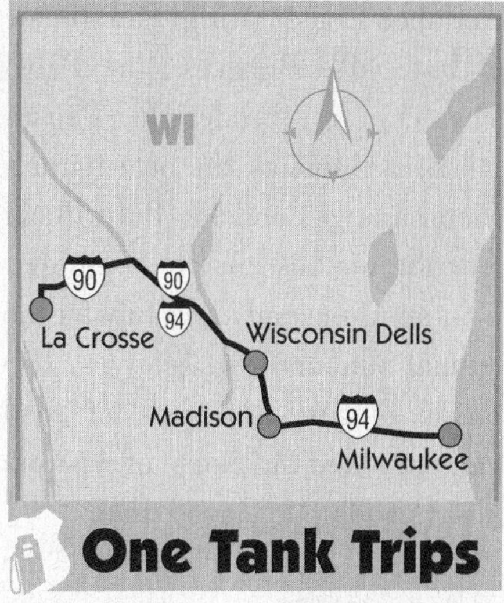

WISCONSIN

Other Area Locations

HOLLAND
Nelis' Dutch Village
Windmill Island
LUDINGTON
Poncho's Pond
ZEELAND
Dutch Treat Camping & Recreation

Let's start our central "playground" tour in Milwaukee, one of the finest, undiscovered big cities in America. One reason why Milwaukee is such a fun place to visit is because it considers itself both the beer and bowling capitals of the world. Naturally, you're going to need to tour the Miller Brewing Company, one of the largest brewing facilities in the world. We recommend you sample the wares while here. Another way to experience both the city and its suds is aboard the Brew City Queen, a pontoon boat that cruises the Milwaukee River and makes stops at some of the city's finer brew houses. There's also a bevy of other non-alcohol related sites that still come attached with a brew-related tag, such as the Schlitz Audubon Center, Miller Park (home of baseball's Brewers), the Pabst Theater, or Frederick Pabst's Historic Mansion, the beer baron's Victorian-age domicile. But without a doubt, the best time to be in town is in late June and early July for the annual SummerFest. Ten (yes, 10!) music stages, hundreds of food vendors, and millions of visitors always add up to a good time.

Let's head west along I-94 to the capital city of Madison. Home of the University of Wisconsin, the city is a thriving, progressive town. Visit the world famous Henry Vilas Park Zoo or the State Historical Museum located near the stunning state capitol building. Be sure to strap on your shoes and take a walking tour of the Madison campus on the shoreline of Lake Mendota. Some campus highlights include the Carillon Tower, the Washburn Observatory, and the Geology Museum.

From Madison, head north along I-90/94 to the town of Baraboo. The original home of the Ringling Brother's circus, its heritage is celebrated at the Circus World Museum, an enormous facility and a must-see for those in search of America's more unusual destinations. Nature lovers (and those of you who are clown-phobic) should visit the International Crane Foundation, a scientific organization and refuge dedicated to preserving the 15 species of cranes around the world.

From Baraboo, continue along the interstate until reaching the enigma that is the Wisconsin Dells. By far Wisconsin's most popular tourist destination, "the Dells" is either an essay in summertime American kitsch or a dubious portrait of the decline of American culture; you decide. Pre-packaged family fun is the "norm" here with the Tommy Bartlett Thrill Show, the Riverview Park and Waterland, or the Dell's Ducks Boat Tours. Oh, and the Dells is the unofficial water park capital of the world, with scores of mega-H20 parks to choose from.

From the Dells, head north and then west on I-90 until reaching the town of La Crosse, along the Minnesota border, on the banks of the Mississippi River. Once a trading post, today La Crosse is a thriving and warm city. Enjoy an afternoon walk along the banks of the mighty Mississippi at Riverside Park. Visit Granddad Bluffs that rise over the downtown area yielding stunning views of the legendary river. Finally, fill out your tour of central Wisconsin with a trip on the La Crosse Queen, an authentic 150-seat paddlewheel boat.

MINNESOTA

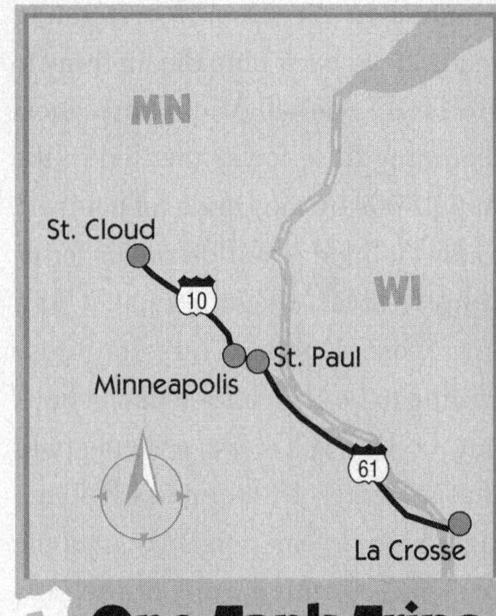

One Tank Trips

MINNESOTA

So you've just left the Badger State behind, crossed the "Old Man River" (Mississippi), and found yourself in Minnesota without a clue as to where to find fun and excitement. That's easy: Just keep the river on your right and head north along US-61. (that's the Mississippi River; pretty hard to miss) This is the highway made famous by Bob Dylan's classic album, "Highway 61 Revisited." The highway reaches from near his boyhood home in northern Minnesota, down along the Mississippi, all the way south to New Orleans.

Go north on US-61 to the town of Winona, which will welcome you to the Land of 10,000 Lakes (seriously has anyone ever really counted?) This former lumber town now hosts two colleges, St. Mary's and Winona

State, and has all the energy that goes with it. Learn all about the historic importance of steamboat culture at Wilkie Steamboat Center or explore the outdoors at the 250,000-acre Upper Mississippi River National Wildlife and Fish Refuge. Continuing north along US-61 you'll notice a pretty consistent theme, it's green everywhere. From the southern Iowa border up to the Twin Cities, nearly the entire route is surrounded by state and national parks and wildlife refuges.

If you're looking for more civilization but in a small-town sort of way, Red Wing is a worthwhile place to visit. Once an industrial center, the town embraces its history by blending in with the great outdoors. One local favorite activity is a visit to the Red Wing Pottery, opened since 1870 and one of the state's oldest businesses. Another favorite diversion is spending an afternoon or morning hiking the 20-mile Cannon Valley Trail that connects the towns of Welch, Cannon Falls, and Red Wing.

Back on US-61 you'll find yourself entering the Twin Cities region. St. Paul, the state's capital, quietly stands in the shadow of its more popular sister city, Minneapolis. A great way to introduce yourself to St. Paul can be had by exploring the historic downtown area. Here, you'll find historic Rice Park, which is surrounded by a number of fine venues including the Minnesota Museum of American Art, the St. Paul Public Library, the Ordway Music Theater, and the St. Paul Hotel. Within spittin' distance of the park lie the popular Science Museum of Minnesota, the Minnesota Capitol Building, and the Fitzgerald Theater.

Cross over the Mississippi River to reach the other half of the Twin Cities, Minneapolis, a surprisingly modern, progressive, and cosmopolitan city here in the north. The eclectic downtown area, ironically known as "Uptown," offers an array of top-notch restaurants and fancy shopping that can be enjoyed at any time of year. Minnesotans figured out that it's really cold during the winter time, so these industrious folks built an enormous network of heated walkways throughout the Uptown area, ensuring that a visit to the city is enjoyable no matter the temperature. Good thinking. A favorite walk for those enjoying the city is a stroll across Stone Arch Bridge, a Minneapolis icon that spans the Mississippi River in the city's downtown area. Other attractions include the River City Trolley with which you can explore some of the city's finest neighborhoods, or the famous Nicollet Mall, its hip commercial center.

From Minneapolis, let's take Hwy 10 northwest to a quieter region, beginning at the town of Elk River. Stretch your legs at the 30,000-acre Sherburne National Wildlife Refuge or visit the Oliver H. Kelley Farm, a state historic site and living history site that captures life in 1860's Minnesota.

From Elk River, keep heading northwest on Hwy 10 to end our Minnesota tour at St. Cloud and explore the several historic parks, including Lake George Eastman Park, Whitney Memorial Park, or Heritage Park. Finally, consider a visit to the Cathedral of St. Mary, the oldest church and largest parish in the area.

Mill City Museum, Minneapolis. Photo credit: Minnesota Historical Museum

"Go west, young man". It's been great advice for more than 150 years for both the young and the young at heart. While the West may not be as wild as it was when Horace Greeley uttered that famous advice in 1851, it remains as vast and beautiful as ever. That said, we've still carved out some nice itineraries for you, each one accomplished with a full tank of fuel and a willing spirit to roam.

OKLAHOMA

Home to America's first big oil boom, this state drips with American history. From Sooners, to ranchers and wildcat oil drillers, you'll need more than one "beautiful morning" (shameless "Oklahoma" musical reference) to take it all in.

Freedom
35
OK
16
Tulsa
35
44
40
Oklahoma City

One Tank Trips
OKLAHOMA

Start your Oklahoma adventure in Tulsa, with an old fashioned BBQ dinner and a show at Discoveryland. Named a "National Treasure" by InStyle magazine, this family destination alternates professional performances of classics "Oklahoma" and "Seven Brides for Seven Brothers" on weekend nights all summer long. You can choose to just see the show or come early for the BBQ dinner.

From there, head on down I-44 about 100 miles to Oklahoma City and soak in more of the old west at the National Cowboy and Western Heritage Museum. This must-see attraction was created to preserve and interpret the heritage of the American West, and has been doing so for more than half a century.

After taking in the history of the cowman, head north on I-35 then east on State Rte 51 to Stillwater to see how farmers plied their trade in days gone by at the Pfeiffer Farm Collection, featuring antique farm implements (call for appointment). While you're in town, grapplers among you will enjoy learning more about America's history of Greco-Roman-style wrestling at the National Wrestling Hall of Fame.

Tulsa skyline. Photo credit: Oklahoma Tourism

Got an itch to go spelunking? Then head west on I-16 to the City of Freedom, and head over to Alabaster Caverns State Park. One of the largest of its kind, the Alabaster Cavern stretches for three-quarters of a mile into the earth, which leaves plenty of space to explore. With a cave this big, it might be easy to get lost, so thankfully the park recently put in a lighting system that not only helps people find their way around, but also highlights the natural beauty of the Alabaster rock. The City of Freedom also boasts a site that help shape American archaeology; the Burnham Dig. Unearthed at this site were extremely rare fossils of extinct mammals, like wooly mammoths, and ancient tools used by men prior to the Ice Age. Most of these artifacts can be seen at the Freedom Museum, along with a large barb wire exhibit, and the most extensive collection of late 1800s house-wares and farm equipment in the country.
www.travelok.com
800/652-6552.

KANSAS

The unofficial hub of America's heartland, Kansas, delivers a surprising mix of fun and interesting diversions. For history buffs, fans of the offbeat, or just plain, old sight-seers, Kansas is the place to be.

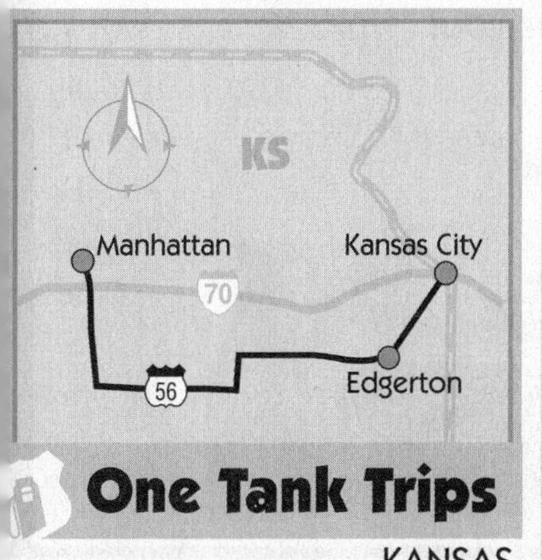

Baldknobbers Music Show, Branson. Photo Credit: Missouri Division of Tourism

The Overland Park area of Kansas City is a great place to fuel up for a short trip into the prairie. A wide variety of restaurants provide a great starting point enhanced by funky antique shops and heritage exhibits.

As soon as you are ready for more, just hop onto I-35 south towards Edgerton and bone up on the "three R's" at the Lanesfield School Historic Site. This living tribute to early American education features exhibits, re-enactors, and activities all designed to give visitors a taste of "old-time schoolin'." And once you get the living history bug, nothing can stop you from heading down the road to Wellsville for a visit to Back To Basics, everyone's favorite one-stop shop for re-enactment clothing and accessories from the 1850s to 1900.

A trip west on I-56 and north on State Rte 177 takes you to the historic and fun "Aggieville" section of downtown Manhattan, aka "The Little Apple". This town, the home of Kansas State University, features four full blocks absolutely jam-packed with more than 100 specialty shops, restaurants, and nightspots.

Finish your tour of Kansas by heading east on US-70 to state capital of Topeka. Make sure you have time to explore the six acres of history at the Ward Meade Historic Site; it's not to be missed. The botanic gardens, vintage buildings, and re-enactors bring 19th century Kansas to life.
www.travelks.com
800/2-KANSAS.

MISSOURI

The "Show Me State" aims to please with travel destinations and activities tucked away in every corner of the state. Whether you love music, history, or just a relaxing day in the country, Missouri's got you covered.

Joplin, located in the southwest corner of the state, is the perfect place to begin your adventure, and the Joplin Museum Complex in

Schifferdecker Park is the last word in all things Joplin. The complex features five different museums, with exhibits that illuminate the history of the area with an emphasis on the mining industry that gave rise to the town. Oh, and do we even need to hype the National Cookie Cutter Historical Museum?

Assuming you're not to emotionally spent from your cookie cutter excursion, jump on I-44 east and cruise into Springfield. Here you can try your hand in a Cobra flight simulator at the Air and Military Museum of the Ozarks, watch the AA-league Springfield Cardinals baseball team take on their minor league foes, or observe over 225 species of wildlife at the 92,000-square-foot Wonders of Wildlife indoor facility.

It's time to point the rig south down I-65 to one of the Midwest's true vacation meccas,. Yes, we're talking about Branson. With more than 100 shows appearing at 40 theaters, we're sure that finding a great dinner show won't be a problem. With acts ranging from Andy Williams to the Baldknobbers, it's nobody's fault but yours if you can't find something exciting to do and see in Branson.

While motoring back to Joplin, why not exit I-44 at Hwy 59 and check out the George Washington Carver National Monument? This 210-acre park is a tribute to the guy who invented peanut butter (hooray!!!) and about a zillion (okay, it was just 300) other uses for this humble legume.

www.visitmo.com
800/519-2100.

Other Area Locations

BRANSON

Acorn Acres RV Park & Campground

America's Best Campground

Branson KOA

Branson Lakes Area Chamber of Commerce & Convention & Visitors Bureau

Cooper Creek Campground

Oak Grove RV Park

CARTHAGE

Big (Red) Barn RV Park

Coachlight RV Sales

NEBRASKA

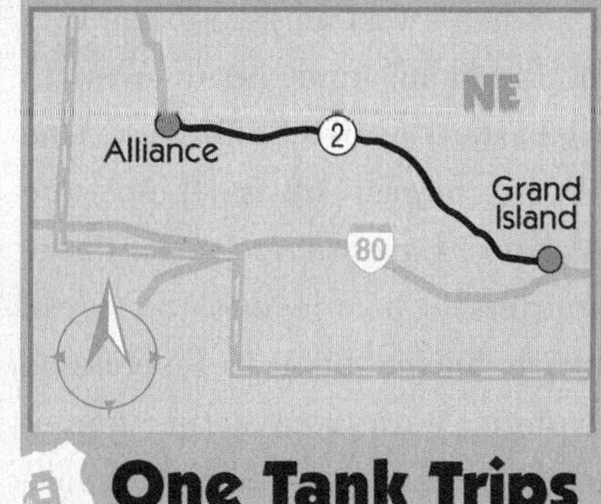

NEBRASKA

If you ever feel the need to just hit the road and let beautiful landscapes melt your cares away, then Nebraska is what you crave. This is mellow driving at its best. And you might even find a surprise or two along the way.

In America, there are a few roadside attractions that are so unusual, that they necessitate a stop. As you travel to town of Alliance, you will be able to see one of these attractions, known as "Carhenge." 38 vintage American cars, all painted grey, planted in the ground, make up Nebraska's replication of the ancient monument of Stonehenge. Though maybe not as awe-inspiring as the original, "Carhenge" does, however, portray human "engine-uity." Also in Alliance is the Knight Museum of the High Plains Heritage-a museum built to acquaint the visitor with the typical life of a Nebraskan pioneer in the early 1900s, with exhibits highlighting the farm tools and household supplies of a prairie rancher.

Our next stop is the delightfully peculiar town of Grand Island, located east on Highway 2. If you get here at the right time, you can witness the "Running of the Wieners", an annual dog race exclusively for wiener dogs. An additional prize is awarded to the best costume on the doggy contestants. For more normal races, visit Fonner Park, where live thoroughbred-racing happens year-round. If you need a respite from the prairie heat, take the kids and head down to Island Oasis Water Park, where six-story slides, wave pools, a river course, and an aquatic obstacle course, provide a refreshing diversion. Grand Island is also known for its shopping opportunities, so take some time to tour downtown, and see how many quaint, little shops you can find.

www.visitnebraska.org
877/NEBRASKA.

COLORADO

At the intersection of mountain and sky, you can cruise through some of the most beautiful landscapes America has to offer. Unsurpassed beauty is never far away in Colorado.

The San Juan Skyway, or "Road to the Sky," is the perfect antidote to another bland slog down a stretch of super-slab highway. Starting in the historic town of Durango, visitors may want to take a day in town and explore the historic downtown area which is a Nationally Registered Historic District packed

Visitors at Cliff Palace ruin at Mesa Verde National Park.
Photo credit: www.colorado.com. Photo by Tom Stillo/CTO

COLORADO

with restaurants specializing in regional fare, brewpubs, and cozy cafes. Round out the day with shopping and visiting Durango's eclectic galleries. For the history buff, Durango steams you back in time on the Durango and Silverton Narrow Gauge Railroad, which chugs along for 46 miles from Durango to the old mining town of Silverton. Your train ticket also gets you into the Railroad Museum, which explores the history of railroading through the challenging landscape of the Rocky Mountains.

Skyway travelers pick up their trail on Hwy 550, heading north, and begin the climb. The Hwy 550 leg of the skyway features three mountain passes; Coal Bank Pass (10,640'), Molas Pass (10,890'), and the Red Mountain Pass (just over 11,000'). Passing between Silverton and Ouray you will travel over the Million Dollar Highway, so named for the vast amounts of gold and silver that crossed these very same mountain passes in Colorado's mining booms. The Million Dollar Overlook along the highway is worth at least that much in stunning views.

Over the pass lies Ouray, known as the "Switzerland of America" for its alpine charm. Travelers flock to the Ouray Hot Springs and the Box Canyon Falls before continuing on the skyway along Hwy 62. On a southerly heading along the skyway, Telluride beckons as a side trip for skiers, artists, adventurers, and anyone who is thrilled at the sight of a post-card perfect town, nestled in an awe-inspiring glacial valley.

Trek north from Ouray and you will soon reach the movie town of Ridgeway, where such famous films as "How the West Was Won" and "True Grit" were shot. Many of the original props, stage fronts, and buildings from the movies can still be seen as you drive through town. Ridgeway is also famous for its three natural hot springs, where you can soak up the beautiful scenery while being pampered with massages and gourmet food. To interact with the landscape, consider visiting Ridgeway State Park, where there are sandy beaches to swim, challenging trails to hike, trout streams to fish, and meadows beckoning for an outdoor picnic.

Mountains, like the 14,246' Mt Wilson, and forest, ease you further down the skyway until reaching Cortez, the gateway to the only National Park created by humans, Mesa Verde National Park. This site preserves the 700-year history of the cliff-dwelling Anasazi people, who literally carved a home out of bare rocks hundreds of years before Columbus.

Heading back into Durango, you can reflect on passing from mountain to desert and high cliff waterfalls to ancient cliff dwellings. Not bad for a tidy little 236-mile drive.

www.colorado.com

800/COLORADO

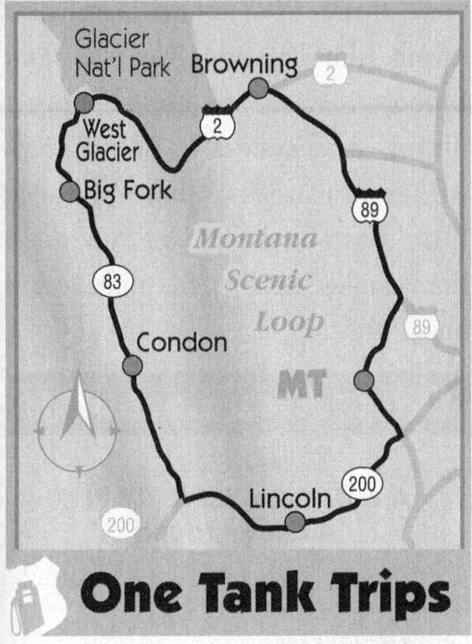

MONTANA

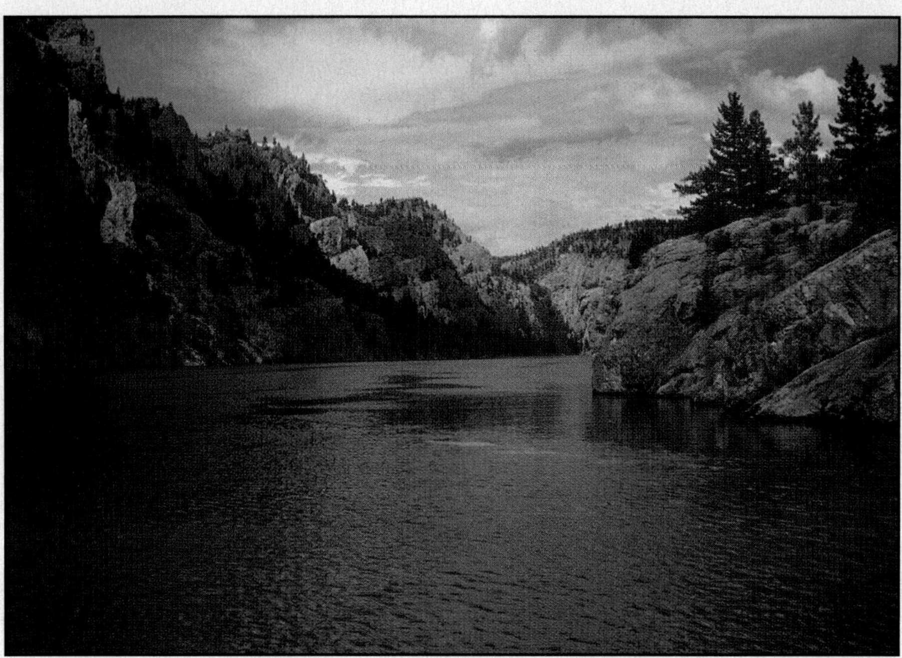

Gates of the Mountains on the Missouri River. Photo credit: Travel Montana/Donnie Sexton

The "Big Sky Country" of Montana welcomes travelers with open arms, splendid landscapes, and the mountain vistas that the Blackfeet Indians called "the backbone of the world".

The Montana Scenic Loop winds through nearly 400 miles of wilderness, rustic mountain communities, and some of America's richest national parkland. Heading just east from Missoula, not far from the border with Idaho, the Loop turns north on Hwy 83 and on to the quaint villages of Seeley Lake and Condon. As you wind northward, be sure to check out Flathead Lake, the largest freshwater lake in the West. Visitors come in droves to try out the trout fishing and ogle the magnificent stands of mature ponderosa pine trees. Wild Horse Island State Park sits in Flathead's southwestern arm and is home to bighorn sheep, bald eagles, and rarely seen wild horses.

Further north lies one of America's greatest natural treasures, Glacier National Park. With 50 glaciers, lakes, waterfalls, and meadows, this is the best places to experience one of America's most beautiful landscapes just as it's existed for thousands of years. One of the few roads in the park, Going-To-The-Sun Road, bisects the park in half and the views it affords are among the best in the world. Shutterbugs, be warned: This is a photographer's paradise.

The Blackfeet Indian Reservation lies just to the east of Glacier National Park on the Montana Scenic Loop, offering visitors a chance to explore the heritage of what once were the most dominant native people in the western plains region. Both the Museum of the Plains

Sandia tram. Photo courtesy of the New Mexico Tourism Department. Photograph by Mark Nohl

Indian, near I-89 in Browning, and the half- or full-day Blackfeet Historic Site Tours are wonderful resources in which to introduce the curious to the rich culture of the Plains Indian.

Head south on the I-89 and I-287 sections of The Loop, and then west on Hwy 200. As you do, you'll pass through small villages and towns like Bynum, Augusta, and Lincoln. Each offers shopping, dining, and access to the region's wilderness areas. Whatever these little towns lack in size, they more than make up for in charm and hospitality.

Other Area Locations

MANCOS
A & A Mesa Verde RV Park & Campground

www.visitmt.com
800/VISIT-MT.

NEW MEXICO

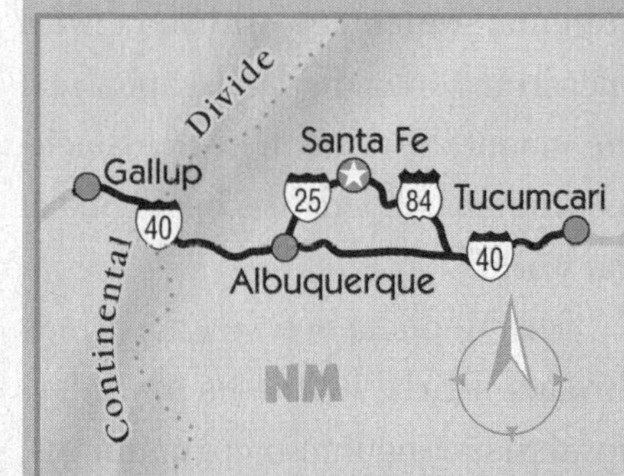

One Tank Trips

NEW MEXICO

The ancient and modern come together in New Mexico like nowhere else. New Mexico's storied past is unique, and the blending of culture and history this rich deserves to be explored.

New Mexico is well known as the "Land of Enchantment," but one of its better-known features isn't land at all, but a road. Called the "Mother Road" in Steinbeck's Grapes Of Wrath (or "Main Street USA"), Route 66 has been largely replaced by nearby interstate highways, but that hasn't diminished the romance the original name still conjures.

Between the towns of Tucumcari and Gallup you can find several stretches of the original historic route intact as well as several attractions that celebrate the famed highway. Tucumcari serves as an eastern entrance to the road and features Route 66 kitsch and fun like the famed Tee Pee Curios shop, and legendary vintage motels such as the Blue Swallow. Just down the road a bit in Santa Rosa, travelers can check out the route's namesake museum, which features "anything having to do with wheels" and has a number of restored and tricked-out cars on display.

The beautiful capital of Santa Fe is the next stop in our route. One of the oldest cities in the nation, Santa Fe is a city melded from its Native American past, its Spanish upbringing, and its recent, modern renovation. Part of what makes this city so gorgeous is the stunning architecture which can be seen in many of its structures. A good example of this is the Loretto Chapel, which displays the mysterious St. Joseph staircase. Santa Fe is also chalk full of wonderful museums, including the Museum of Fine Arts, the Palace of the Governors, and the Museum of Archaeology. To get a scenic view of the city, consider hopping on the Santa Fe Southern Railway, where you can take a take day trip through the greater Santa Fe area in the comfort of a rail-car with full amenities. Or simply walk through the capital and experience all the great shopping, exceptional restaurants, and energetic night life of the city for yourself.

Travel south on I-25 to the next stop; Albuquerque, and a visit to the National Atomic Museum. This unique museum was established in 1969 as an intriguing place to learn the story of the Atomic Age, from early weapons research and development through today's peaceful uses of nuclear technology, such as in the field of medicine. There is no better way to see this exciting city then in a Sandia Peak Tramway ride. The Tram lifts you from the Sandia foothills, 10,000 ft to the top of Sandia Peak. While you are at the top, grab lunch at one of the restaurants nearby, and enjoy a fantastic view of Albuquerque. Also, be sure to stop by the New Mexico Museum of Natural History and Science, where you can see massive dinosaurs, gaze at the stars in the

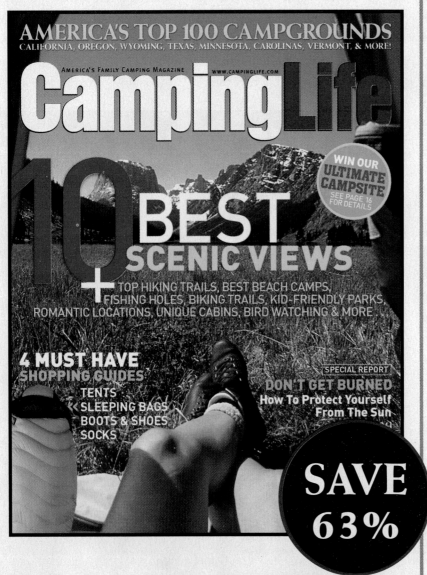

planetarium, walk through bat-filled caves, or watch a movie at the Pynamax theater.

Finish the trip in the colorful little town of Gallup. Once just a pit-stop on Route 66, Gallup is now a growing tourist town, with a jazzy downtown district full of brassy shops, throwback diners, and interesting attractions. Don't pass through without visiting the Red Rock State Park, with its beautiful desert landscape, and museum, highlighting the lives of the early Native Americans in that area.

Other Area Locations

ALBUQUERQUE
Enchanted Trails Camping Resort
GALLUP
USA RV Park
SANTA FE
Los Campos de Santa Fe RV Resort
Rancheros de Santa Fe Campground
Santa Fe KOA Campground
Santa Fe Skies RV Park
The Trailer Ranch RV Resort
SANTA ROSA
Santa Rosa Campground
TUCUMCARI
KOA of Tucumcari

www.newmexico.org
800/733-6396.

ARKANSAS

Blessed with natural features, ranging from the rugged Ozark and Ouachita Mountains to the level fields of the Mississippi River Delta region, Arkansas has beauty and nature in abundance.

Travel the beautiful Scenic 7 Byway to El Dorado. The early 20th century oil boom here financed a growth spurt that is still visible in the restored architecture of the quaint downtown area. Self-guided walking tours wind past shops and restaurants, as well as the fully restored art deco-era Rialto Theater.

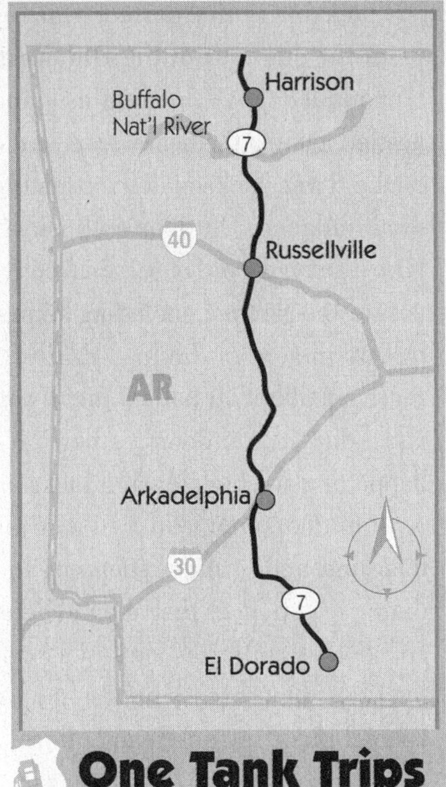

Keep on the 7 Byway, and you will soon reach Arkadelphia, a picturesque town, where the Ouachita Mountains meet the gleaming DeGray Lake. Consider staying at the DeGray Lake Resort State Park, with its 96-room lodge, 18-hole golf course, marina, and horse-back riding trails, it's the perfect place to enjoy scenic Arkansas. Venture out of the lakeside paradise to check out Reynolds Science Center Planetarium, where visitors can view the night sky using high-powered telescopes, and learn the history of space exploration.

Sooth your road-weary body in the town of Hot Springs, where you can soak away your cares in one of the famous spas of Bath House Row, or lose yourself in the simple serenity of the 210-acre Garland Woodland Gardens. It's a win-win proposition no matter which one you choose.

Our little jaunt ends near the border of Missouri, in the pleasing borough of Harrison. Pass the time fishing at the local trout farms, visiting the Boone County museum, having a picnic by the Lake, or shopping at the little boutiques downtown. However, make sure to hike over to Mystic Caverns, where you can travel into the heart of the Ozark Mountains and witness the spectacular eight-story cave dome. It is a breath-taking end to an exciting Arkansas trip. *www.arkansas.com 800/NATURAL.*

WYOMING

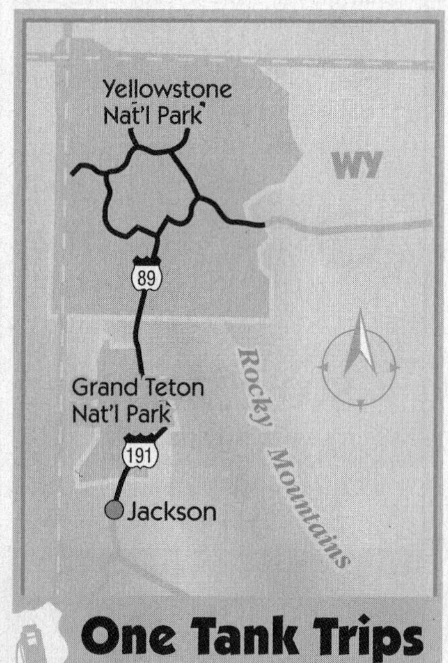

WYOMING

It's hard to imagine there being an American West without Wyoming, and vice versa. The frontier may have closed a long time ago, but Wyoming "never got the memo." This is where history actually lives.

Jackson is the perfect starting point for this tour of the Old West. Surrounded by mountains and nestled against the headwaters of the Snake River, Jackson delivers nature in abundance. Outdoor enthusiasts have a smorgasbord of seasonal activities to choose from, including hiking, mountaineering, biking, birding, rafting, and hot air ballooning. If you can do it outdoors, then it's happening at a high level in Jackson. Avid indoorsmen can while away their time at the unique shopping and dining experiences that abound here, as well as galleries and seasonal festivals that highlight the town's special place in American culture.

Heading north from Jackson, RVers can take in some of the most beautiful scenery America has to offer as Hwy 89 rolls past Jackson Lake in the Grand Teton National Park and eventually into Yellowstone Park. Obviously, you're going to spend ample time at both, right? At Yellowstone Lake, hang a right, east, onto US-14 (call ahead for seasonal road closings) and breeze into Cody. This bustling western town celebrates its namesake, Buffalo Bill, with the Buffalo Bill Historical Center and the Cody Night Rodeo, as well as pow-wows and Wild West shootouts.

South of Cody lives the other half of our western narrative. The Wind River Reservation, which begins just south of Thermopolis, is home to 4,500 Arapaho and 2,500 Shoshone Native Americans. This 2.2-million-acre expanse features historical and natural sites such as the burial place of famed Lewis and Clark guide, Sacajawea. The many original outpost buildings of Fort Washakie Historic District, along with Castle Gardens an eerie archeological formatio featuring windswept sandstone an weathered trees-are both terrific stops *www.wyomingtourism.org 800/225-5996.*

SOUTH DAKOTA

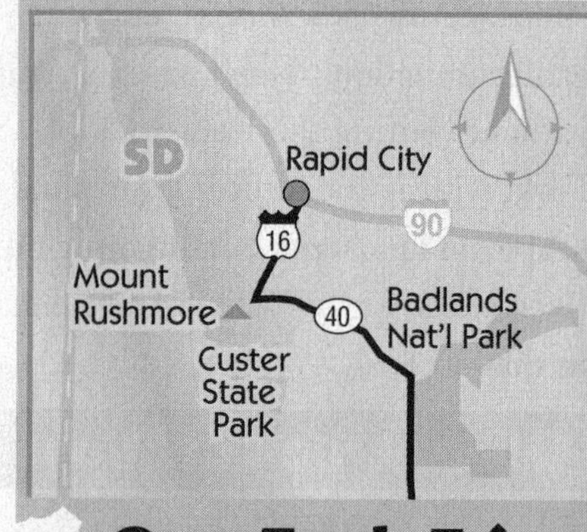

SOUTH DAKOTA

If you are looking for the plac where heroes turn into legends an legends become monuments, wher landscapes defy description an nature forges geologic wonders, the you've been looking for a place lik South Dakota all along.

Rapid City is more than just th gateway to Mt. Rushmore. No, ther are other top-notch attractions like th Journey Museum, Museum of Geolog and the Dahl Arts Center (a.k.a., "th Dahl") The town of Sturgis is just short drive up I-90, and every Augus they host the biker mega-mixer know as the Sturgis Rally. In other words this is a great place to start your Sout Dakota odyssey.

Mt. Rushmore National Monument is only 25 miles south of Rapi City, so no trip to the area would b complete without going to check ou the four presidents' faces immortalized in granite. A mere 20 miles sout

on state Hwy 244 is one of the last wild places on earth. Custer State Park's 71,000 acres has pronghorn, elk, mountain goats, and a herd of almost 2,000 bison. In September, the bison are herded by park staff and volunteers and moved to corrals. We're sure you've never seen anything like a buffalo roundup before, so be sure to catch it if you're in the area.

After you come back to the rig you should think about heading south on US-385 to Hot Springs. Soak away those wild bumps and bruises in the soothing natural spas of the Black Hills or tour the Mammoth Site Museum of South Dakota, which also just so happens to be the world's largest mammoth research facility and active dig site.

Heading further east, RVers can explore what has to be the next-to-the-last wild place on earth, in Badlands National Park. This 381-square-mile geological wonder hearkens back to another time with its slowly eroding rock formations and fossils of early mammals, such as pigs, horses, and cats. This is a sparse and challenging environment for modern creatures, but full of beauty.

Other Area Locations

HILL CITY
KOA-Mount Rushmore
Rafter J Bar Ranch Camping Resort

RAPID CITY
Happy Holiday Resort
KOA-Rapid City

SPEARFISH
Chris' Camp

www.travelsd.com
800/S-DAKOTA.

NORTH DAKOTA

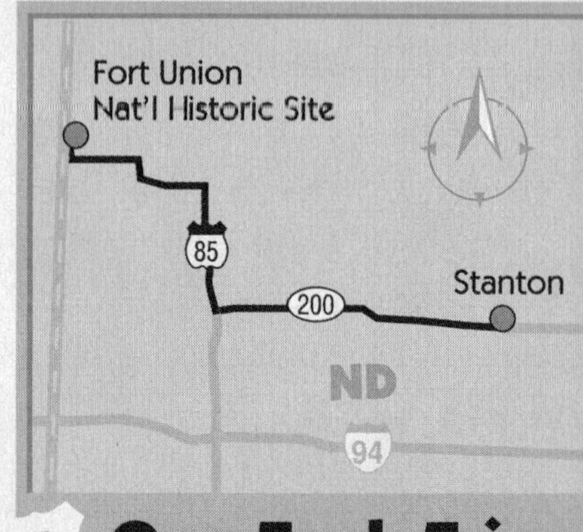

One Tank Trips

NORTH DAKOTA

Excitement and adventure have a new address. From Lewis and Clark to Native American culture North Dakota delights visitors with its western heritage and groovy lore.

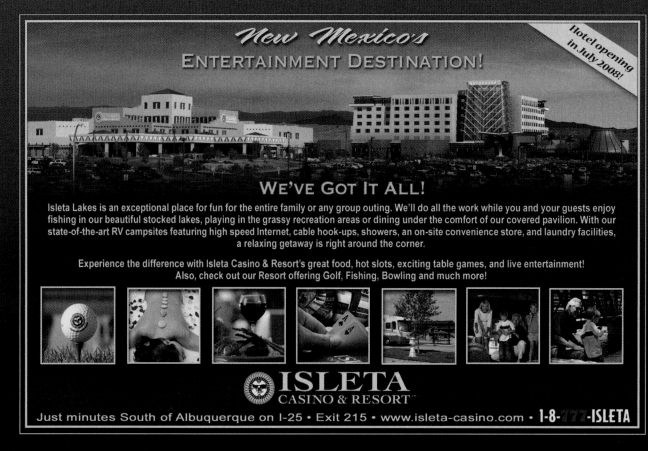

Start the trip in true pioneer fashion at the Lewis and Clark Interpretive Center in Washburn. It's complete with a replica of the expe dition's 1804-05 winter quarters as well as other displays of Native American interest, and it's a great place to pick up the old Lewis and Clark Trail as it winds its way northward.

Continue the trek west on Highway 200, to historic Stanton. Follow in the footsteps of early pioneers by learning more about the Native American tribes that inhabited North Dakota at the Knife River Indian Villages Historical Site. This site contains over 50 archaeological digs, and numerous artifacts. Discover how to interpret the artifacts at the earthlodge and visitor centre on the grounds, and learn how these early Americans lived. Then head to Lake Sakakawea State Park to enjoy a wide range of water sports, like boating, kayaking, fishing, or simply stroll around the lake and savor the untamed beauty of the area.

While in North Dakota why not head up to the Fort Union National Historic Site? Built near the junction of the Missouri and Yellowstone rivers in 1828, Fort Union was headquarters for fur trading between American pioneers and Native Americans. The longest-lasting fur trading business in the United States, Fort Union has undergone extensive reconstructions, so as to preserve its unique place in American history. Tour the Fort's huge wooden structures and snug, little nooks, to experience a place where, for a time, Frontiersmen and Native Americans peacefully conducted business.

Other Area Locations

WASHBURN
North Dakota Lewis and Clark Interpretive Center

www.ndtourism.com
800/HELLO-ND.

TEXAS

Most everyone is familiar with the old saying that "everything is bigger in Texas," right? Well, that goes for the fun and excitement a Texan vacation offers too. But since this much state won't easily fit into just one package, we've mapped out a southern and northern route. Think of it as more Texas bang for your gas buck.

TEXAS SOUTH

When people talk about "the coast" down south they don't mean New York or LA. Here, the only shoreline that matters is the beaches lapped by the warm waters and gentle breezes of the Gulf of Mexico.

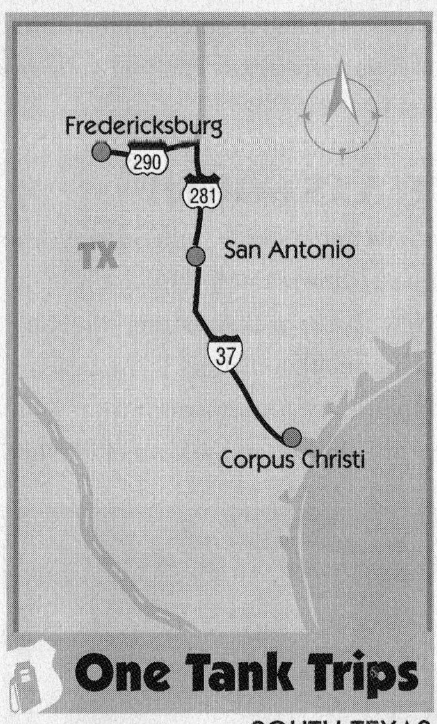

SOUTH TEXAS

Corpus Christi is the jewel of the Texas coast; where you can find a lot more to do than sit under a beach umbrella. Local attractions include the Texas State Aquarium, Corpus Christi Water Garden, and the Marina, called the "T" by locals. Sightseeing boats line the "T" as well as seaside restaurants and shrimpers selling their catch right off the boat.

Once you have soaked up all the sun, sand, and fun you can, head north up I-37 to San Antonio for a leisurely stroll down the famed River Walk, a terrific strip of tour boats, shopping, and dining al fresco along the "Paseo Del Rio". Of course, who could visit San Antonio without remembering to see the Alamo, which many consider to be the birthplace of the Republic of Texas.

Head up north just a bit and you step into a region that boasts another strong cultural heritage in New Braunfels. Settled in 1845 by German pioneers, the town still celebrates a strong sense of the old country with festivals and several restaurants featuring traditional German fare. "Tubing" down the Guadalupe River is another favorite local attraction locally as is the awesome Schlitterbahn, recently named America's number one water park by the Travel Channel.

But don't think the cultural heritage of the German pioneer in Texas is limited to New Braunfels. Heading north on Hwy 281, and then west on US 290, more of the German spirit awaits you in Fredericksburg. Established in 1846, on what at the time was Comanche territory, this charming Hill Country town still delights visitors with its closely held old world customs. Outdoor enthusiasts love Fredericksburg and the surrounding region for its abundance of plant and animal life. Just seven miles outside town, Wildseed Farms is the nation's largest wildflower farm with more than 80 acres of fields; the 3,000 sq. ft. "Butterfly Haus" and seed market features many rare varieties. And for something a little out of the ordinary, the Old Tunnel Wildlife Management Area offers the nightly spectacle of three million Mexican Bats flying from an abandoned railroad tunnel.

TEXAS NORTH

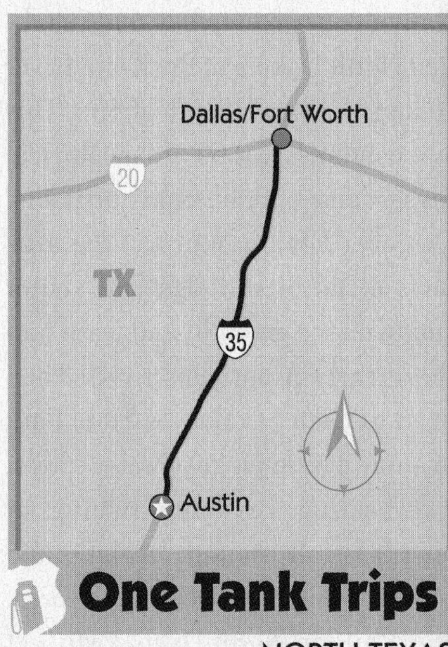

NORTH TEXAS

Let's kick our northern tour off in Austin, one of the most vibrant and energetic cities in the country, with music, water, and Hill Country all coming together in a panorama that is distinctly Texan. In addition to the many clubs and festivals that draw music-lovers, Austin is also home to PBS's longest running show, "Austin City Limits." which in many ways helped to foster the city's music boom of recent years. Free tickets to the show can be hard to come by so if you are not one of the lucky few you can tour the studios of KLRU on the UT campus. East Sixth St., also known as Old Pecan Street, is lined with several music venues that play home to well-established acts, along with up and comers. For nightlife o ı different kind, Mt. Bonnell, along)ld Bull Creek Road, offers a stunıing view of Austin's skyline. Come ust before dusk and bring your :amera.

Heading north on I-35, the once ›leepy, now suddenly bustling, town ›f Round Rock is part of the ›urgeoning I-35 corridor. Named for ı big round rock that marked a well-›orn ford in Brushy Creek for :hisholm Trail cattle drives (still ·isible wagon ruts mark the spot), this s one of the fastest growing commuıities in America. Corporate headquarters for Dell and Nolan Ryan's riple A Round Rock Express stand ›houlder to shoulder with the historic lowntown area and Old Settler's Park.

Situated along the Brazos River, Vaco is home to the Texas Sports Hall ›f Fame and the Texas Ranger Hall of 'ame and Museum, which both docuıents and definitely celebrates the xploits of those distinctly Texan ball ›layers; the Texas Rangers.

Only about an hour and a half ›orth from Waco is the shining star f Texas style, glitz, and excess:)allas. As much of an idea as a lestination, this city began with a ingle log cabin in 1841 and has rown into a major population center, omplete with sleek glass kyscrapers, fashionable neighborıoods, and nightlife galore. To say ıere is a lot to do in Dallas is like aying Texas is kind of big. Start your isit off at the Dallas Museum of Art, ›ith its world-class collection ıcluding important works from ;eorgia O'Keefe. Galleria Dallas is must see landmark for the shopaıolic in your life, while the Deep :llum District features shops, restaurants, bars, and live music all within a gentrified warehouse district. Sports more your style? Just pick your season. The Cowboys, Rangers, Stars, and Mavs fill your sports calendar with professional play. On the college level, the great Red River Rivalry, also known as the annual Texas-Oklahoma football game, is played here at the neutral site in the Cotton Bowl.

Other Area Locations

CONCAN
Parkview Riverside RV Park

800/8888-TEX
www.traveltex.com.

UTAH

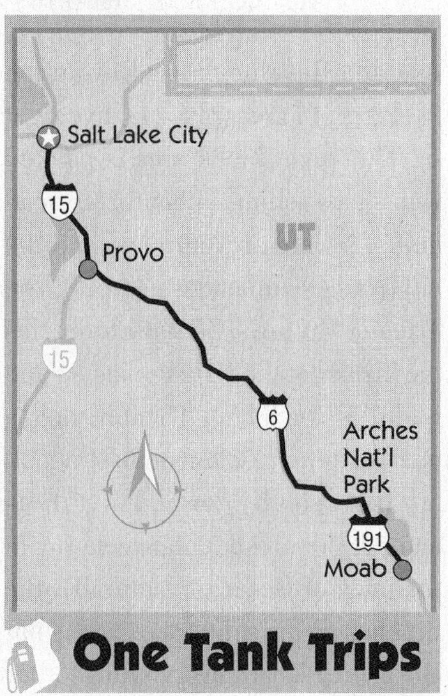

UTAH

Whether you crave outdoor adventures, landscapes, or old western flavor, you can find it in ever-surprising Utah.

Any visit to Utah should begin among the spectacular sites of Temple Square in Salt Lake City. More than 20 attractions relating to Mormon history are within easy walking distance here and the Square showcases some of the most dazzling architecture in America. The Salt Lake Temple, Salt Lake Tabernacle, and Conference Center are some of the best examples.

Just down I-15 sits Provo, with unique and relaxing spots like the Provo River and its world-class trout fishing, and the nearby Sundance Resort. Dedicated to providing a respite from the demands and stress of daily living, nearby Thanksgiving Point is a relaxing place that has so much to offer, thanks to its wonderful theme gardens, shopping, dining, golf, and the North American Museum of Ancient Life, which displays more than 50 standing dinosaurs.

Gorgeous scenery and exciting adventures await those who travel into the town of Moab. Named after the lush, green valley of the same name in the Middle East, Moab is home to many unique attractions. Start your tour with a visit to the "Hole 'N the Rock", a 5,000 sq foot home built into solid sandstone. This "house" has fourteen rooms, a bathtub, and a deep French fryer. Take lots of pictures, because most people won't believe it till they see it. After the sandstone open house, go over to Butch Cassidy's King World Waterpark, where you can indulge in watery frivolity, with 5 slides and three different pools. The waterpark is in the same canyon where Butch Cassidy and his gang housed their rustled steer and horses, as the natural springs in the area could water their stolen herds.

No visit to Utah would be complete without heading over to the Arches National Park. This park is unique to the state, and contains some of the most magnificent natural landforms in the world. Over 2,000 sandstone arches lie within this verdant valley, just waiting to be discovered by intrepid explorers. Many of the arches here are so inspiring and artistic that many early settlers have named them. Here you can see "The Organ," "The Delicate Arch," and "Dark Angel."

Those planning to return to Salt Lake City should ponder getting off the beaten path and drive US-50 west then US-6 north, to State Rte 68 along Utah Lake, for a different view of some of Utah's stunning scenery. This tour of Utah's attractions will put about another 350 miles on the odometer, but you'll be rewarded with a lot of memories for the miles.
www.utah.com
800/200-1160.

MEXICO

Bienvenidos, amigos! So exotic and yet so close, Mexico is the ultimate getaway for fun, romance, and relaxation. With so many destinations to choose from, it can be hard to decide where to begin. However, the Pacific "vibe" of Baja is a call you have to answer.

Do keep in mind before beginning your Mexican vacation that travel requirements have changed and you will need a valid U.S. passport when crossing the border. Lead times for processing passports have lengthened considerably, so give yourself plenty of time to apply if you need a new visa.

Ok, let's go. Tijuana is the beginning point for your Baja travels and

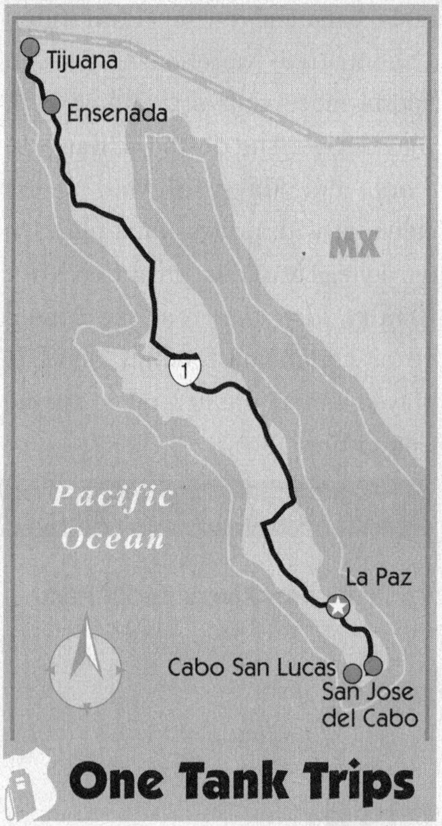

One Tank Trips

Mexico - Baja California

Avenida Revolucion, or Revolution Avenue, is a great place to dive right in. This eight block area is packed with shops selling authentic Mexican crafts, jewelry, restaurants, and the city's famous/infamous nightlife. The Tijuana Cultural Center chronicles the history of the Baja Peninsula and includes an IMAX Theater, not to mention a world-class orchestra hall.

Just south down Hwy 1 is another picturesque Baja getaway in the town of Rosarito. Naturally, the beaches are pristine and relaxing but Rosarito also offers visitors other activities including several quality golf courses to choose from. Fox Studios recently built the movie magic theme park Xploration here in conjunction with the enormous Fox Studios Baja, which, FYI, features the world's largest water tanks, used for filming Titanic, among other motion pictures.

Further down Hwy 1, Ensenada is one of the more charming and varied communities along the Baja Coast, with sea, mountains, and desert all in close proximity. Whale watchers flock to Ensenada to see gray whales in the shallower waters and other species further out. (The whale season reaches its peak in February). The temperate valleys surrounding Ensenada boast several wineries offering tours and tasting.

And no Mexico trip would be complete without a visit to one of the premier party cities; Cabo San Lucas. Within the city are a slew of nightclubs that beckon the tourist to enjoy the city's night life. One of the more famous of these clubs is "Cabo Wabo." Started by the great Sammy Hagar, "Cabo Wabo" hosts exciting bands, exotic drinks, and a party scene like no other. But Cabo San Lucas is more than just a night-life city. The city contains hundreds of pristine beaches, with glowing white sand, and crystal clear water.

The unique coastal geography of San Quintin, provides great opportunities for travelers with eco-interests. San Quintin's coastline is comprised of several, interconnected bays that provide a unique and protected habitat for sea life of all kinds. Boating and fishing are popular here and the protected bays also make for a resting area and breeding ground for flocks of migratory birds each season. Because of the protection afforded along much of the coastline, beaches here are less developed than in other areas of Baja. Fortunately, the relaxing waves and warm sands remain.
www.visitmexico.com
800/44-MEXICO.

FREE INFO! Enter #117 on Reader Service Card

The vast American West is like no other place in the world. Where else can you visit glamorous cities, explore remnants of the Wild West, tour expansive deserts, or ski on white-capped mountains all within a half-day's drive? If there's any problem, it's that, well, there's so much of it to explore. The endless adventures and long scenic highways aren't exactly conducive to these days of sky-high gas prices; at a time when we're all trying to cut back a bit. But don't fret. We've compiled a list of spectacular short road trips, each one capturing the essence of the American West, with its eclectic sights, picturesque camping opportunities, and chances to experience memorable outdoor escapes.

ALASKA

For the intrepid RVer, the ultimate frontier lies in the wilds of Alaska. Of course, just getting there is a journey unto itself. However, once there, this vast expanse is like nothing else found in the lower 48.

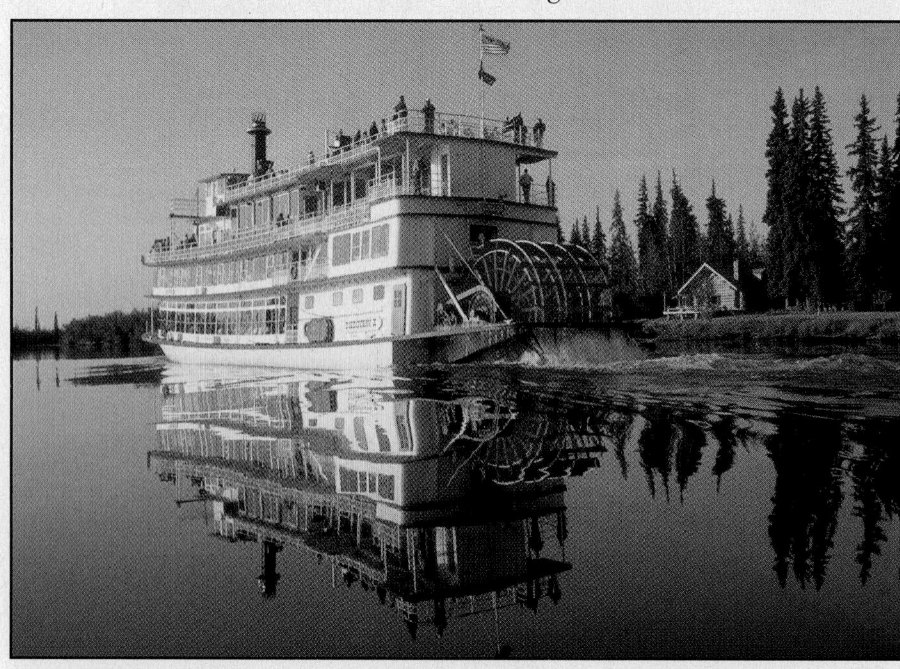

Alaska's river towns were historically served by sternwheelers like this one on the Chena River near Fairbanks. Photo Credit: Clark Mishler/ATIA

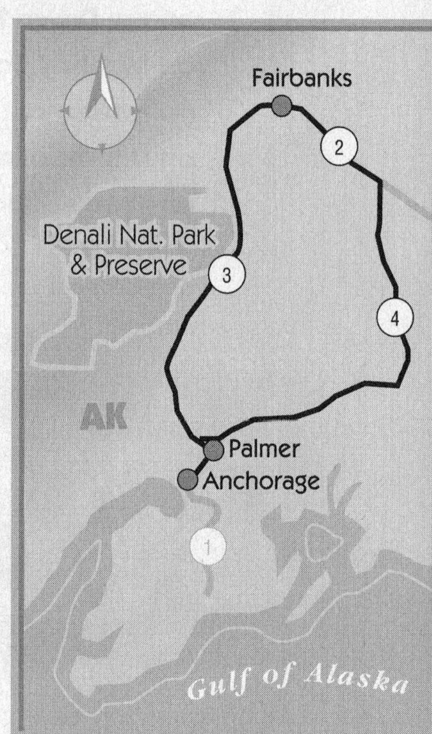

One Tank Trips

ALASKA

Let's kick things off i
Anchorage, the state's largest city with more than 250,000 residents Summertime really brings out th best in this charming city. True, th summer months are rather short (an sweet), but these folks make the bes of it. Birders always seem to enjoy visit to the Anchorage Coasta Wildlife Refuge at Potter Marsh. It more than 500 acres provides a vita habitat for its eclectic collection o

coastal birds. About 50 miles south of town lies the popular Portage Glacier, Alaska's most-visited tourist attraction. Be sure to spend time at the impressive Begich Boggs Visitor Center, which offers informative tours of the area. If you happen to be in Anchorage during the month of March, though, you can experience the granddaddy Alaskan spectacle of 'em all in the world-famous "Iditarod", a 1,100-mile dog sled race from Anchorage to Nome. Might we suggest bringing ear muffs? The Alaska Zoo, which showcases the local arctic and sub-arctic fauna that defines the region, is a great, year-round attraction.

Heading north along Hwy 3, let's get lost (not literally) in the vast expanse of Denali National Park and Preserve. At six million acres, it ranks as one of the world's largest parks and is home to more than 20 glaciers, sprawling mountain ranges, and huge herds of caribou and other stunning sub-arctic wildlife. Because Denali is known more for its pristine, undisturbed wilderness, the park offers surprisingly few trails; deep exploration of the park is limited to only the hardiest of explorers. However, one exceptional hike is the Mount Healy Overlook Trail, with dazzling vistas of the towering Alaska Range. At the park's center stands North America's tallest peak, at 20,320 feet, fabled Mt. McKinley.

From Denali, point the rig north on Hwy 3 and step on the gas. A couple of hours later you'll come into the town of Fairbanks. During the spring and fall migration, birders can't pass up a visit to Creamer's Field Migratory Waterfowl Refuge, an important respite for thousands of waterfowl venturing to and from the south. To learn the history of life in this region, stop in at the Museum of the North, located at the University of Alaska-Fairbanks. Some of their more than 1.5 million artifacts are featured in displays to narrate Alaska's natural and civilized histories.

Head south along Hwy 2, also known as the Alaska Highway. At the town of Big Delta, we'll pick up Hwy 4 and keep going further south. Use the tiny village of Gakona as a base camp for exploring the expansive Wrangell-St. Elias National Park and Preserve, which sprawls across the Alaska-Canada border.

From Gakona, let's pick up Hwy 1 west again until we reach the town of Palmer. Formerly an outpost during the late 1800s, the town was an experimental farming colony during the New Deal period of the early 1900's. Sadly, the experiment ultimately failed, but you can explore its legacy at the Colony House Museum. Another popular stop is the Musk Ox Farm, a truly unique experience. If you're lucky enough to find yourself in Palmer during September, you won't want to miss the rollicking Alaska State Fair and its 12 days of family fun.

www.travelalaska.com.

ARIZONA

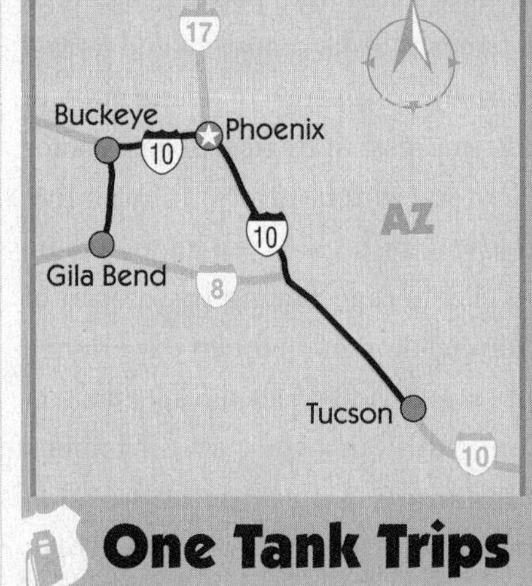

ARIZONA

Arizona provides the quintessential road trip, where sprawling desert landscapes give way to towering peaks. In between lie lively cities, hidden artist colonies, and Old West towns that provide a glimpse of bygone days. The combination of all this provides for an eclectic trip sure to provide plenty of fantastic memories. Some of the best opportunities to explore the state appear in the southern area; we can start in Tucson, explore the greater Phoenix area, and wind up in a vast desert.

Situated in the impressive and desolate landscape of the desert southwest, stands the intriguing city of Tucson. At its heart, Tucson remains a friendly resort town, bookended by the natural wonders of the Santa Catalina Mountains and the Ironwood Forest National Monument. The Tucson Museum of Art is one of the city's best attractions. A visit here only confirms the city's thriving art community. Other interesting destinations can be found at the University of Arizona, such as the Flandrau Science Center and Planetarium, and the Mineral Museum. One of the more unique and fun attractions is in the nearby town of Oracle, north of

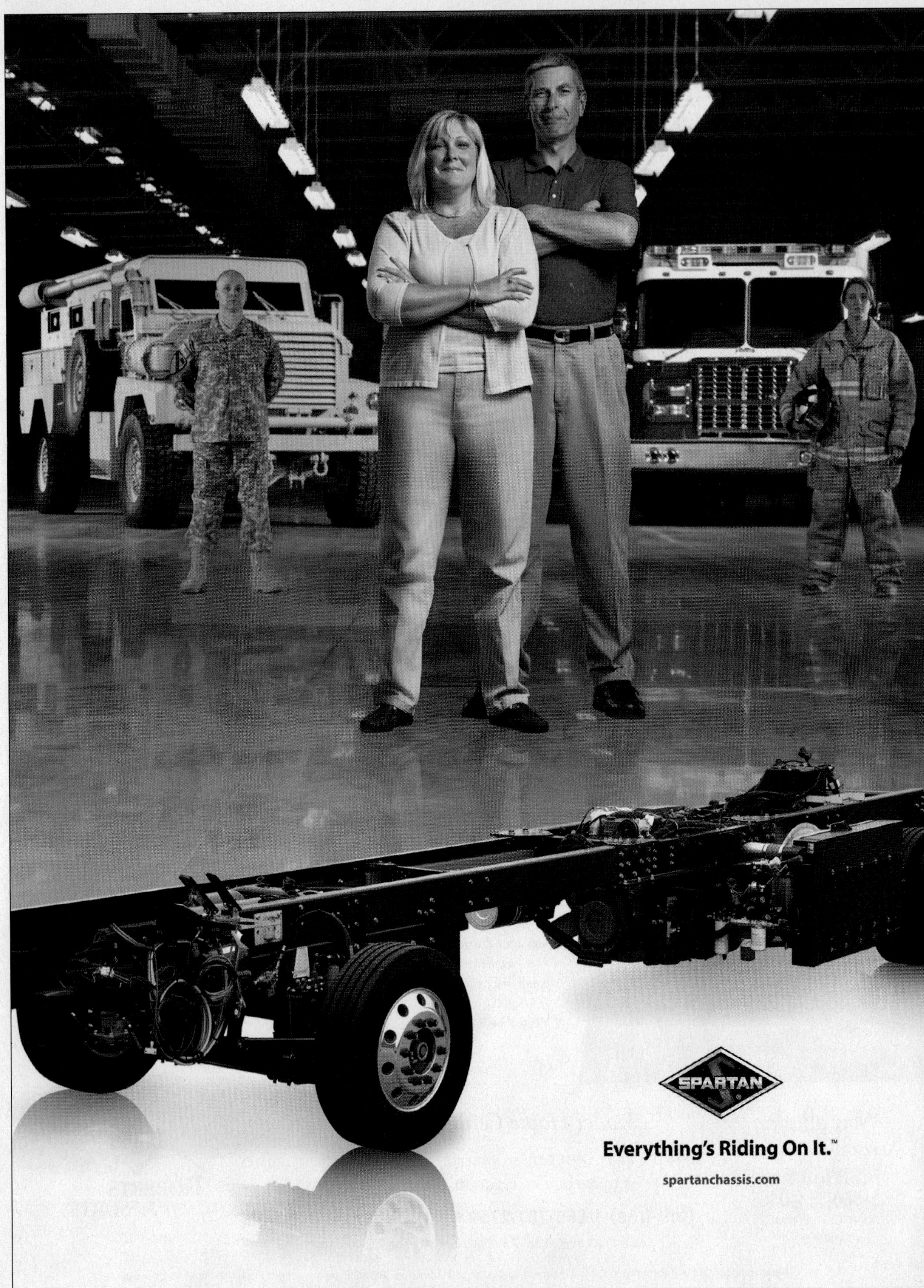

SPARTAN
Everything's Riding On It.™
spartanchassis.com

Tucson on Hwy 77. The Biosphere 2, an unusual research center founded in 1991, is an artificial closed ecological system within a 3.5-acre glass enclosure. It was recently saved from property developers, and is again open to visitors and under the temporary stewardship of the University of Arizona.

Now that you've gotten out of the city, head a few miles east to the expansive Coronado National Forest. Here you'll find nearly 2 million acres of prime forest loaded with great views and plenty of hiking and biking trails. Arguably, the best way to see it all is on horseback and plenty of outfitters are available to connect you with a friendly steed.

The ever-rising silhouette of Phoenix lies to the west. Be sure to time your visit here with care, and not just because of the seasonal high temperatures. Phoenix, with all its charms, has grown rather quickly and is beginning to earn its reputation as a sprawling metropolis. (The key word here is "sprawling."). Venturing through the city at the wrong time of day can be nightmarish, especially in a big rig. Regardless, a visit to Phoenix is worth the effort. One of the many places of interest is the famed Heard Museum, a world-class art museum that features tremendous work of southwestern artists. Other local favorite activities include a tour of the Phoenix Zoo, and spending a day exploring the Phoenix Mountain Preserve, a series of city parks built in the desert landscapes that surround the city. The vibrant sports scene, thanks much in part to transplant Jerry Colangelo, features Diamondbacks baseball, Suns basketball, and Coyotes hockey.

Later February and March mark a dazzling transition for southern Arizona. Sure, the rainbow displays of desert flowers may tell some folks that spring is on the way. However, for most, nothing demonstrates that winter's harsh grasp is melting away like baseball's spring training camps. Each year hundreds of thousands of fans come from around the country to watch their favorite team gear up for the long haul that is the Major League Baseball season. Arizona boasts 12 such teams that comprise the Cactus League for a month's worth of hardball. Smaller parks create the best chances most fans will ever have to get up close

Other Area Locations

APACHE JUNCTION
La Hacienda RV Resort
Superstition Sunrise RV Resort

CASA GRANDE
Val Vista Winter Village

EL MIRAGE
Pueblo El Mirage RV Resort & Country Club

GOODYEAR
Destiny Phoenix RV Resort

MESA
Apache Wells RV Resort
Good Life RV Resort
Mesa Convention & Visitors Bureau
Mesa Regal RV Resort
Mesa Spirit RV Resort
Orangewood Shadows RV Resort
Silveridge RV Resort
Sun Life RV Resort
Towerpoint Resort
Val Vista Village RV Resort
Valle Del Oro RV Resort

PEORIA
Pleasant Harbor RV Resort

PHOENIX
Phoenix Metro RV Park
Royal Palm

SURPRISE
Sunflower Resort

TUCSON
Mission View RV Resort
Rincon Country East
Voyager RV Resort

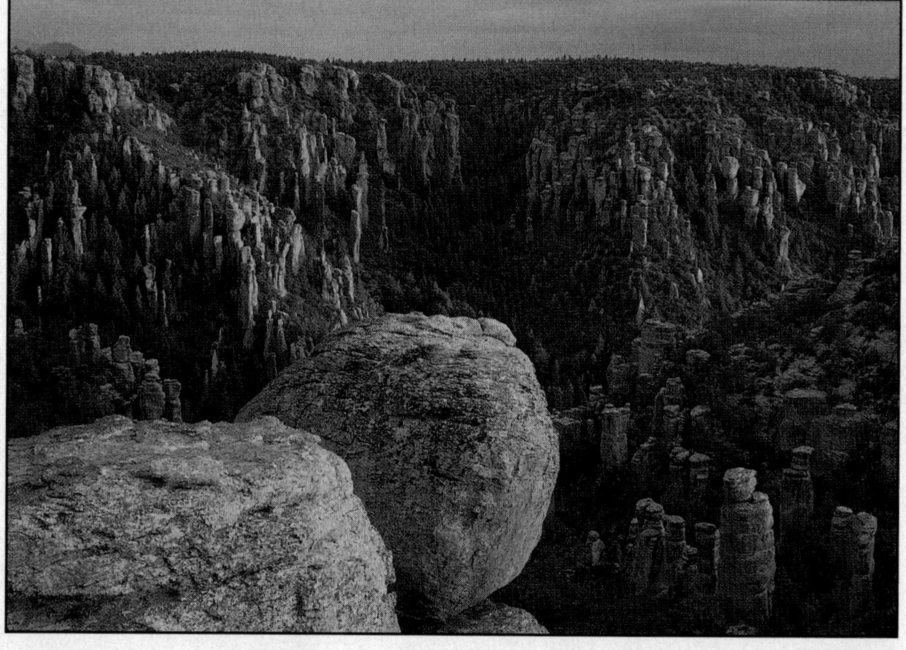

Chiricahua National Monument.
Photo by: Peter Noebels © Metropolitan Tucson Convention and Visitors Bureau.

Park Yourself in *Luxury.*

See what Luxury Living is all about

With large spaces to accommodate the finest of RV's and our most spacious home models to date, Palm Creek is all about first-class living. 18 holes of golf and every possible sport and activity under the sun, you'll never want to leave.

Reserve your space now at one of the ***Elite Rated Resorts**** in the nation.

**(based on Woodalls, Trailer Life, and Motorhome Magazine ratings)*

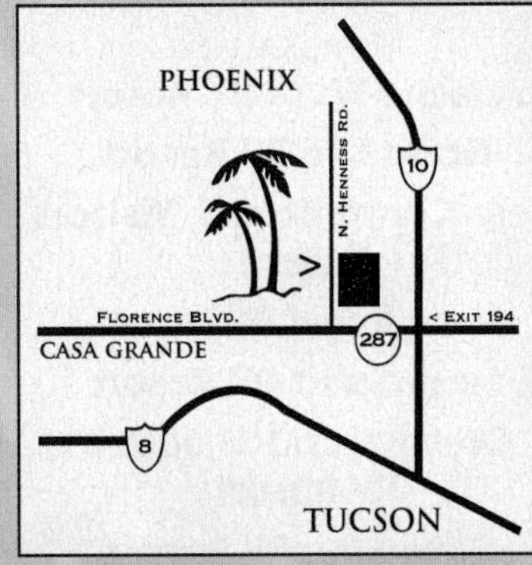

Conveniently located between Phoenix and Tucson.

Unbeatable Amenities, Unmatched Activities

- Over 100 First Class Amenities
- 6 Tennis Courts, 8 Pickleball Courts, and Fitness Facility
- Resort-Wide Highspeed Wireless Internet (WiFi)
- Presenting Over 50 Planned Entertainment Events
- Surprisingly Affordable Daily, Weekly, and Monthly Rates.

**This offer is subject to change without notice.*

*A 55 or better community.

1110 North Henness Road, Casa Grande, Arizona 85222 . 1 800 421 7004 • www.palmcreekgolf.com

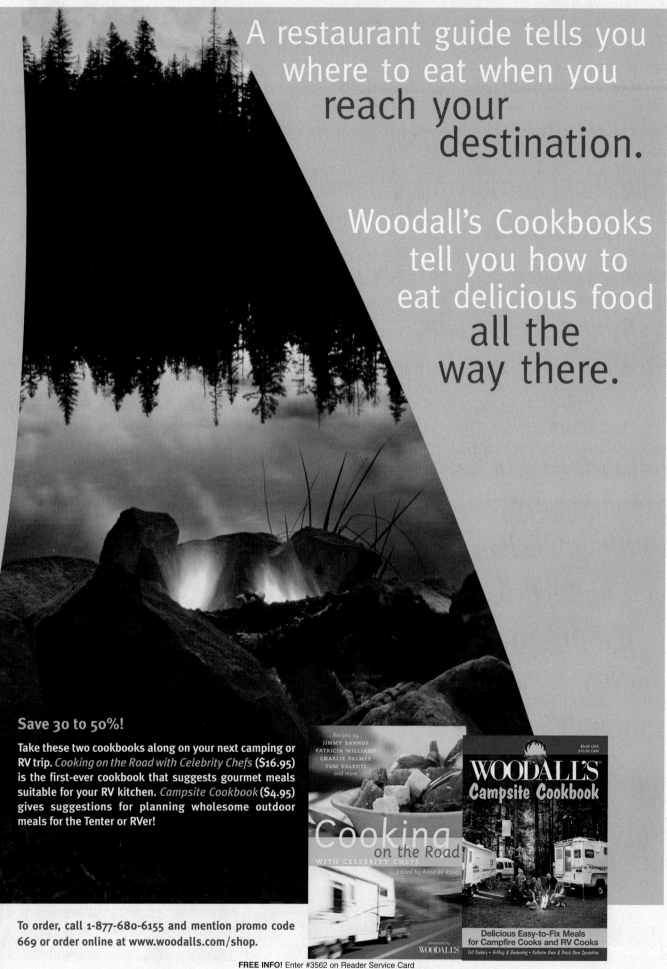

and personal with their favorite players. Cheap tickets, great seats, and plenty of sunshine make a spring training tour a truly unique event. Luckily, all of the Cactus League teams are within an hour's drive from one another. Tucson features the hometown favorite Arizona Diamondbacks, as well as the Chicago White Sox and Colorado Rockies. Phoenix hosts the Milwaukee Brewers and Oakland A's, and nearby Mesa packs in ever-loyal Chicago Cubs fans. The Los Angeles Angels of Anaheim play in Tempe, the Kansas City Royals play in Surprise, and both the San Diego Padres and Seattle Mariners stake out Peoria. And when you're in Scottsdale and hit by baseball fever, be sure to look up the San Francisco Giants and Texas Rangers. Insider's Tip: If you've never experienced a spring training game, be sure to arrive on time. During these exhibition games, most of the big-league players are replaced with minor-league prospects for the last innings of games.

Traveling through Arizona, refreshing, little oasis' seem to pop up right out of the desert. The small town of Buckeye is one such little paradise. The town is one of the prettiest, and fastest growing, suburbs in Arizona. At the White Tank Mountain Regional Park you can experience the beauty first hand, as you explore over 30,000 acres of lovely, and delicate, desert landscape. Named after the white granite exposed by river depressions, White Tank Park delivers a great hiking, or exploring, excursion. The beauty of the town can also been seen in its new Sundance Golf Course, which is nestled between the White Tank Mountains in the north, and the Estrella Mountains in the south. While in town, head over to the Buckeye Historical and Archeological Museum, to learn about the early settlers of the area-the Hohokam Indians. On display are exhibits highlighting Native American Pottery and the building of the Buckeye Canal.

For our last stop, let's take I-10 west from Buckeye, to the town of Gila Bend. From here you can explore that vast Sonoran Desert National Monument, where nearly a half-million acres of stunning desert landscape await you.
866/275-5816
www.arizonaguide.com.

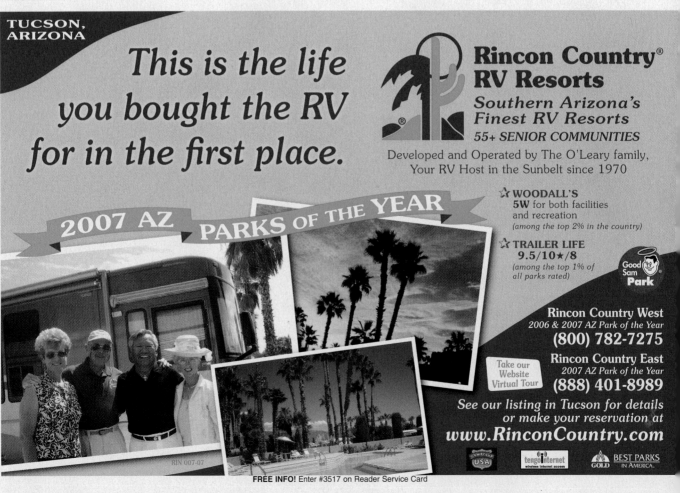

Enjoy Arizona's Finest Luxury RV Resorts

Stay with us and you'll never worry about too much idle time! Each resort has over 3 acres of recreational facilities, including heated indoor and outdoor pools and jacuzzi's, computer labs, exercise rooms, classes, parties, tennis, ball field, pickle ball, dinners and so much more!

"WHERE THE FUN NEVER SETS"

Contact us for details and reservations!

Sun Vista
RV RESORT
the Ultimate in Leisure Living

7201 E. 32nd St.
Yuma, AZ 85365

928-726-8920
1-800-423-8382

www.sunvistarvresort.com

See listing at Yuma, AZ

Superstition
Sunrise
Luxury RV Resort

702 S. Meridian Rd.
Apache Junction, AZ 85220

480-986-4524
1-800-624-7027

www.azrvresort.com

See listing at Apache Junction, AZ

Make your reservation today

FREE INFO! Enter #3385 on Reader Service Card

NORTHERN CALIFORNIA

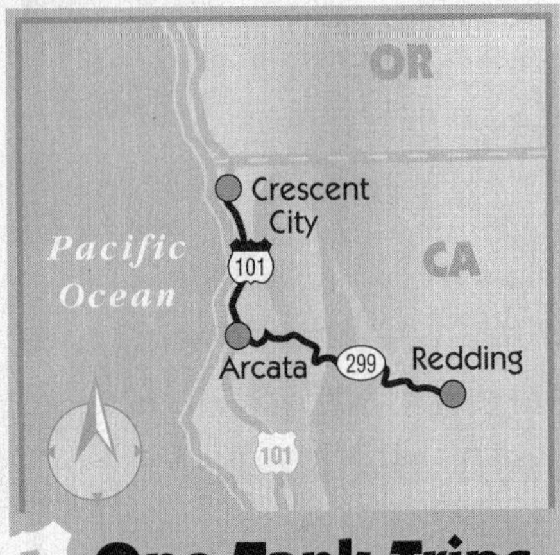

CALIFORNIA - NORTH

While the southern and central portions of the Golden State garner the most attention, California's northern region beckons us, too. It's a sometimes-overlooked beauty waiting to be discovered.

Let's tour this unsung neck of the woods by starting in the town of Redding, home to Shasta Lake, an enormous body of water with numerous opportunities for boating, fishing, and hiking. The city itself is surrounded by such mountain ranges as the Cascades, the Coast Ranges, and the Sierra Nevada, each one worthy of its own explorations for outdoor adventures. Along the shores of Lake Shasta, be sure to take time to explore the magnificent Lake Shasta Caverns. To see how northern California is balancing the delicate needs of both man and nature, check out the massive Shasta Dam and power plant then visit the Coleman National Fish Hatchery, which helps maintain the region's all-important population of salmon.

From Redding, let's head coastward along Hwy 299 a few miles and stop at Whiskeytown (yes, that's its real name). Head down along Whiskeytown Lake to enjoy the scenery before visiting its very own dam and hydroelectric power plant that helps supply the area with electricity.

Memorial Lighthouse, Trinidad. Photo Credit: Robert Holmes/California Tourism

Keep your heading westward until you find yourself entering Gold Rush country, an apt title for these parts-where cities and towns survived the boom and bust cycles with varying results. Learn about the Chinese immigrants' heritage and their major contribution to building the West at Weaverville's Joss House State Historic Park. The town's major ranger station is an ideal hub to launch your escapades into the massive Klamath National Forest.

Continuing west along Hwy 299 be sure to stop and smell the roses at the Horse Mountain Botanical Area. Okay, this is northern California, so there probably aren't many roses to stop and smell. However, with more than 1,000 acres of California's native plants within its borders, a stopover here is sure to satisfy.

Before hitting the coast, anglers won't be able to resist pulling over in this section of Six Rivers National Forest and trying their luck along the Trinity River, a particularly lively fishing area, where several pristine rivers converge to provide bounties of trout and salmon.

The coastal town of Eureka is our next stop. A town where fishing and lumber industries used to thrive, Eureka features many attributes of a frontier town. Enjoy a stroll through Old Town where some of the historic buildings, like Carson Mansion, remain from the glorious gold rush years. Other featured venues here include the Sequoia Zoo and the Humboldt Bay Maritime Museum.

Our route north along Hwy 101 takes us along the scenic coast, passing through the towns of Arcata

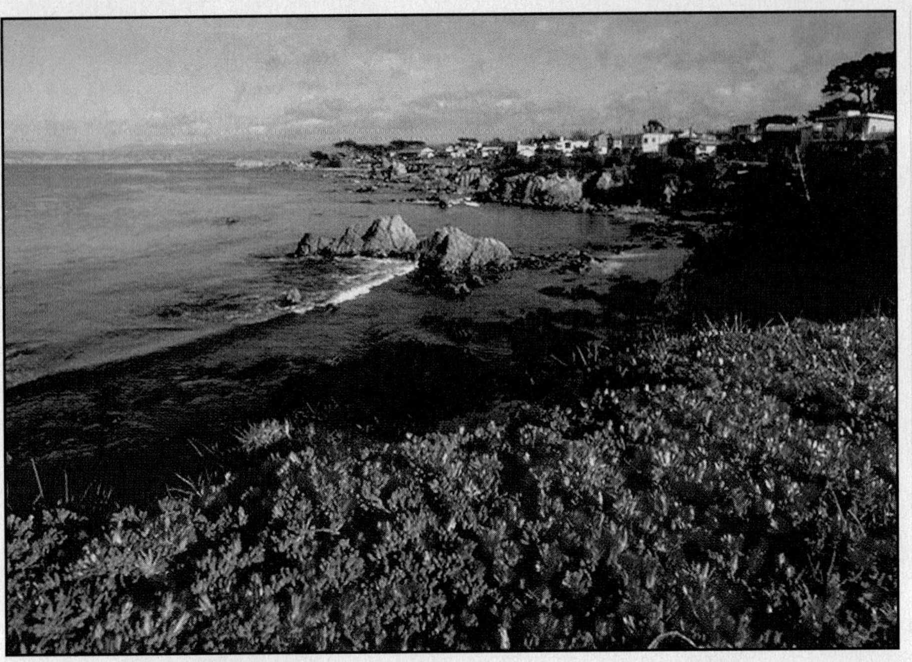

Pacific Grove at Monterey Bay Photo Credit: Robert Holmes/California Tourism

to the south and McKinleyville to the north. Be sure to enjoy Lady Bird Johnson Grove, near the town of Orick, and its 100,000-plus acres of majestic redwood forest.

Finally, let's wind up in the northernmost big town of Crescent City. Use the city as a base camp to explore the nearby Redwood National Forest. Notice the pristine Pacific Ocean backdrop to the Battery Point Lighthouse. For a unique side-trip, visit the wreckage of the S.S. Emidio, a tanker that became one of the first American casualties of World War II when it was destroyed by torpedoes from a Japanese submarine. The ship was then abandoned by survivors and drifted 85 miles north before grounding on the rocky shore off of Crescent City.

CENTRAL COASTAL CALIFORNIA

For all the great drives around North America-and there are plenty of them-few can hold up to the likes of California's majestic Hwy 1. This famous road traces the twisting western coastline of our continent, spanning from Los Angeles all the

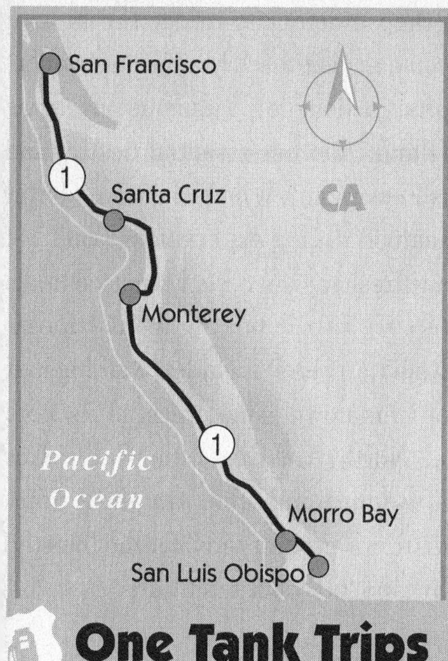

CALIFORNIA - CENTRAL

way to Eureka in the north. Of course, this epic route doesn't fit our fuel-tank criteria, but we have captured a central coast tour that's ideal for shorter getaways.

This taste of Hwy 1 begins in the town of San Luis Obispo, founded in 1772. Consider a stopover and visit the Spanish mission here, the fifth such institution in the state, as an excellent introduction to central California's missionary heritage.

Up the road apiece, past Morro Bay, is where we find the landscape beginning to change. The rolling, oak-covered hills give way to taller, greener landscapes, complete with cliffs, hills, and mountains rising straight out of the Pacific. Take some time to explore the town of Cambria, a cute-as-a-button village favored by grizzled bikers and ritzy spa-goers alike.

Roughly fifty miles north lies Los Padres National Forest, and Big Sur. More of an idea than an actual place, Big Sur still retains all the charms of its bohemian past. Be sure to visit the Henry Miller Library, a rather unique and eclectic destination along the highway, and homage to the famous author and painter.

Leaving Los Padres, Hwy 1 brings you to the Monterey Peninsula. Spend an afternoon shopping the quietly upscale downtown area of Carmel-by-the-Sea. Heading north on Hwy 1, once in the town of Monterey you must visit the famed Cannery Row, made famous by John Steinbeck's novel of the same name. Long gone are the riff-raff and bums depicted in Steinbeck's works. Today, this revitalized district is headlined by the world-class Monterey Aquarium. Take time to stroll along the city's scenic waterfront and indulge your inner clam chowder-lover at any of the several restaurants along Fisherman's Wharf.

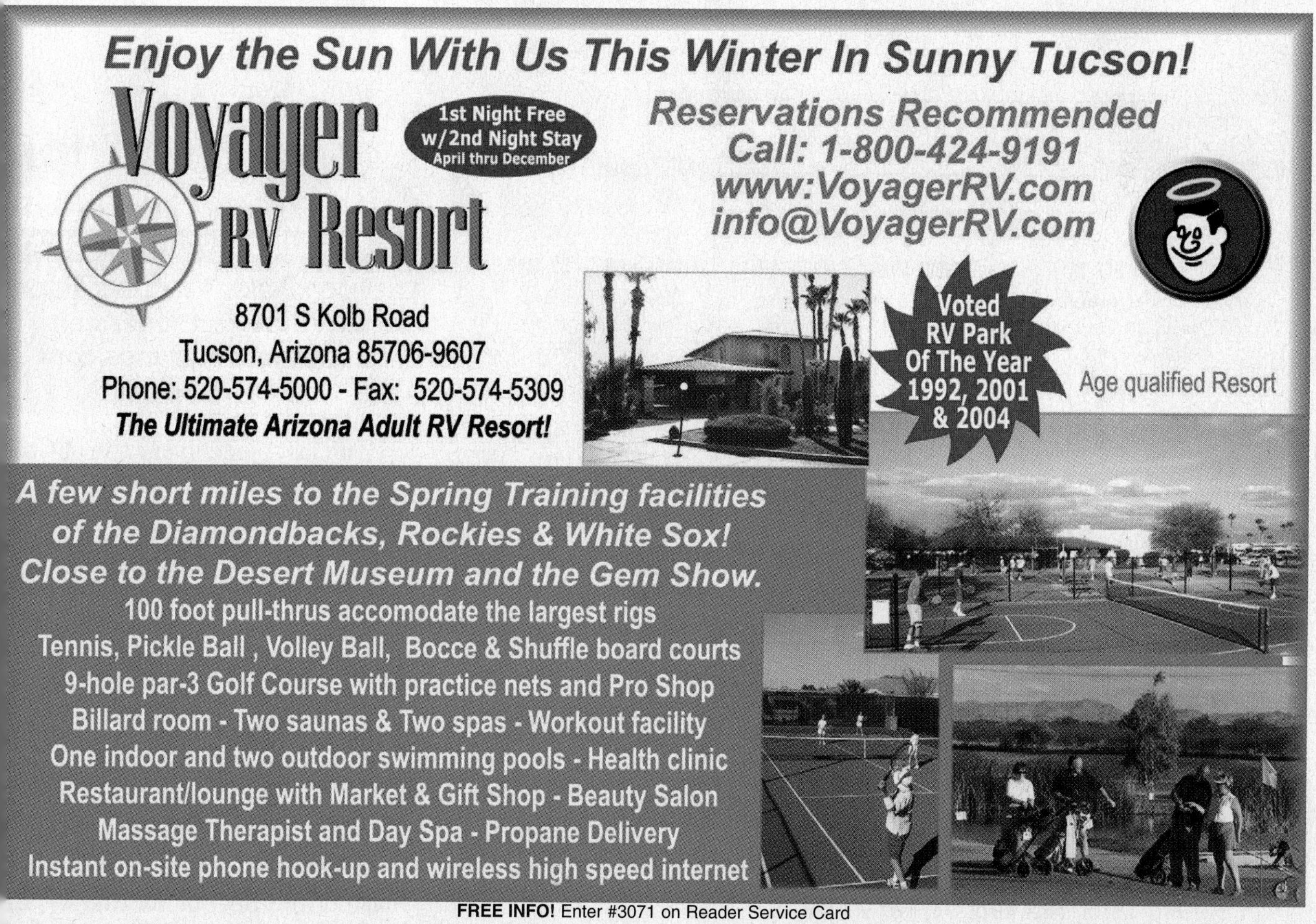

The quiet, meandering Hwy 1 morphs into a fast freeway for a spell as it carries you north around Monterey Bay to the town of Santa Cruz. With nearly 30 miles of public beach, this is a great place to be lazy. Don't miss taking a lap or two on foot along the Santa Cruz Beach Boardwalk.

Hwy 1 returns to its old leisurely self after passing through Santa Cruz, as it approaches Half Moon Bay and San Francisco. "The City by the Bay" may not offer the best topography for getting around in your rig. So drop her off and hop aboard one of the several of San Fran's famed cable cars for a fun and breathtaking tour of some of the city's most famous areas. Afterwards, consider a visit to the Golden Gate National Recreation Area, a 74,000-acre park along the bay with its magnificent centerpiece - of course - the Golden Gate Bridge. From here you can visit three beaches, as well as plan a tour of infamous Alcatraz Island. Another essential destination is Fisherman's Wharf where wonderful seafood dining experiences don't get any fresher. Other San Francisco treats (no, we're not talking 'bout Rice-a-Roni (tm) here!) include a walking tour of Chinatown (The largest of its kind in North America), the Cable Car Museum, and the Haight-Asbury district, "ground zero" for the (mostly) bygone '60s counterculture.

SOUTHERN CALIFORNIA

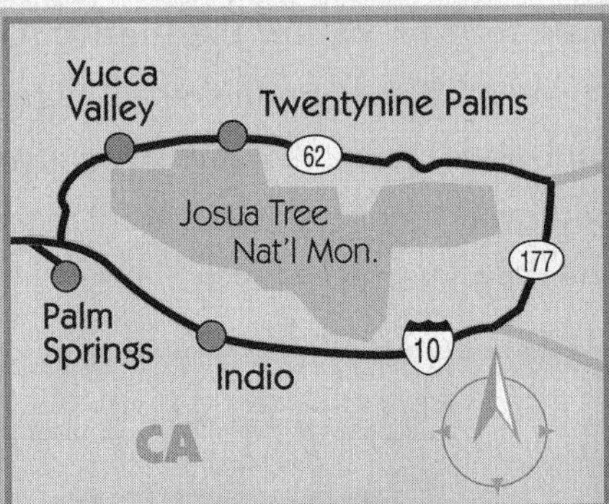

One Tank Trips

CALIFORNIA - SOUTH

THIS ROUTE BROUGHT TO YOU BY:

Newport Dunes Waterfront Resort
www.newportdunes.com
info@newportdunes.com
(800)765-7661

The last piece in our trio of Cali fornia tours takes place in storie southern California, home to ever warm climes, ubiquitous palm trees and the rich and famous. Thankfully we're skipping the latter crowd instead focusing on the interior o southern California, which invites al passersby in.

Let's start in the town of Palr Springs, a city that's sure had it share of the best of southern Cali fornia's riches during the last century. The Palm Springs Aerial Tramway remains one of the most popular attractions in all of southern California, taking visitors from the bottom of the Coachella Valley to the top of the San Jacinto Mountains.

Another worthwhile activity is spending an afternoon at the Palm Springs Desert Museum, where you can brush up on your natural history of southern California. Before leaving town, stop by the Palm Springs Air Museum featuring one of the world's largest collections of flying vintage World War II aircraft, and has an artifact collection as well as original mural art works that will impress visitors, young and old.

Down the road from Palm Springs, east on I-10, you'll pass by Indio and eventually come to the General George S. Patton Memorial Museum. Gen. Patton established the nearby U.S. Army Desert Training Center for the purpose of training fighting men and machines for action under the harsh conditions of the North African deserts. First opened in 1942, today the sites, and the museum, are major draws for military buffs. For bird watchers, The Salton Sea attracts hundreds of species of birds.

From Indio, jump on I-10 for a few minutes to exit 163. Hang a left and suddenly-gasp!-you're on another planet populated by strange aliens (just kidding). This is actually Joshua Tree National Park, one of the most unique landscapes in all of North America. More than 1,200 square miles await your exploration among forests of these unusual Joshua Trees that flourish here in the southwestern U.S.

The small city of Twentynine Palms will greet you as you exit I-10 on the park's north side, along Hwy 62. Come in mid-May and enjoy the Joshua Tree Music Festival, a three-day event held at Joshua Tree National Park. Don't miss the annual Twentynine Palms Street Fair and Car Show, the extravaganza held each year on the first weekend in June. If you make it down here in October, Pioneer Days is a multi-day celebration with over a dozen fun events and all the small-town personality you could hope for.

Driving through the Yucca Valley you might feel a bit like you are wandering around in the desert. However, you are not alone. In Desert Christ Park, biblical characters wander through the desert as well. In the park are 35 elegant, concrete statues of ancient figures-including the Hebrew prophets, the twelve apostles, the tomb of Christ, and even a replication of the Sermon on the Mount. To return to A.D., visit the Hi-Desert Nature Museum, to explore the history of the area. With exhibits on the wildlife of the desert, Native American artifacts, a fossil collection, a gem and mineral collection, and even a mini-zoo with live, desert animals, the museum is a perfect stop for the recreational naturalist.

Other Area Locations

INDIO
Outdoor Resorts Motorcoach Country Club
SAN DIEGO
Campland on the Bay

877/CALIFORNIA
www.visitcalifornia.com.

When it comes to camping, it's all about family and friends sharing memorable experiences for years to come.

Guest First™ RV Resorts is dedicated to providing its guests the finest in camping experiences by offering the Highest Level of Guest Service of any campgrounds, RV parks or camping resorts at each of our locations...

Darlings Marina
Florence, OR

Lakefront RV Sites
541-997-2841 • info@darlingsresortrv.com

Hat Creek
Old Station, CA

RV Sites, Tent Sites, Cabins & Motel
800-568-0109 • info@hatcreekresortrv.com

Yosemite Pines
Groveland, CA

RV Sites, Tent Sites, Cabins & Yurts
877-962-7690 • yosemite@yosemitepinesrv.com

High Sierra
Oakhurst, CA

Riverfront RV Sites • Tent Sites
877-314-7662 • camping@highsierrarv.com

Rancheria
Hat Creek, CA

RV Sites, Tent Sites, Cabins & Yurts
530-335-7514 • info@rancheriarv.com

The Redwoods
Crescent City, CA

RV Sites, Tent Sites & Cabins
707-487-7404 • info@redwoodsrv.com

Loon Lake Lodge
Reedsport, OR

RV Sites, Tent Sites, Motel & Cabins
866-360-3116 • loonlakerv@loonlakerv.com

El Rio Resort
Bullhead City, AZ

RV Sites, Luxury Rentals & Motel
866-357-4640 • elriorv@elriorv.com

McCloud Dance Country
McCloud, CA

RV Sites, Tent Sites & Cabins
530-964-2252 • info@mccloudrvpark.com

www.GuestFirstRVResorts.com

FREE INFO! Enter #3547 on Reader Service Card

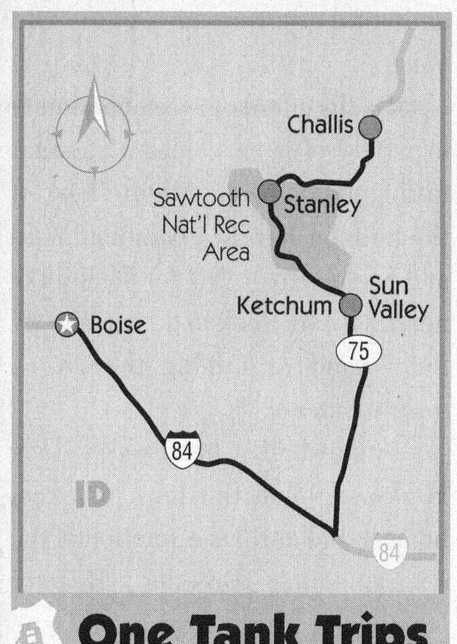

The famed Idaho spud might garner much of the state's notoriety from folks not familiar with the state's other treasures. Those bold enough to venture into the Gem State, however, are rewarded by loads of natural attractions, the best of which can be found throughout the majestic Sawtooth Range.

Let's start in the capital city of Boise, a bustling, yet charming small city in the state's southwest region. As the state's largest city with just over 100,000 residents, Boise is an original blend of the rugged Old West and the slick sophistication of the modern Northwest. Start by exploring the city's historic downtown district. Capitol Boulevard showcases the Capitol building, while Maine Street features stores and restaurants as well as historic buildings restored and preserved from the glory days of the Gold Rush. Stroll through Julia Davis Park, which skirts along the scenic Boise River, to Zoo Boise at the park's center. For something a little different, visit the Old Idaho Penitentiary, the former home to some unlucky Idaho outlaws, circa 1870. If the visit here makes you feel claustrophobic, we recommend blue skies and fresh air via drive to either the Boise National Forest to the north, or the Snake River Birds of Prey National Conservation Area, and its winged wonders, to the south.

Time to mount up from city of Boise, along I-84 south, all the way to Twin Falls. Just outside of town be sure to gander at the impressive Shoshone Falls, so called the

Boise city view from Foothills. Photographer: Tom Volk/Boise CVB

Fishing the Boise River. Photographer: Tom Volk/Boise CVB

"Niagara of the West." Another gander-worthy stop is a visit to the Perrine Bridge, towering some 1,500 feet above the roaring Snake River. Pop culture buffs might recall this as the site of the Evel Knievel's failed "Skycycle" motorcycle jump attempt over the mighty Snake River in 1974. Better luck next time, Evel.

The town of Stanley is home to the Redfish Lake Visitors Center, to help visitors get acquainted with its sprawling, green environs. Guests can also find audio tape/CD tours for the three scenic byways that converge in this area - a guided tour!

Head east along Highway 75 until the ghost towns of Bonanza and Custer come into view. Hardly tourist traps, these sites may be a little tricky to visit with a big rig, but smaller vehicles will have an easier time driving around to these sparse and authentic remnants of the Old West.

Challis affords a nice opportunity to partake of some serious whitewater rafting action at the Middle Fork of the Salmon River, a National Wild and Scenic River. Not for the faint of heart, visitors flock to this area to try their hand at taming the river's unruly waters.

From Challis, head south along Highway 93 to the town of Arco, home to the curious attraction of the Experimental Breeder Reactor Number-1. The seriously odd and enormous contraption enables the city to claim its place as "the first city in the world to be lit by atomic power." Arco also serves as a good jumping off point to explore the stunning Craters of the Moon National Monument. which features thousands of acres of ancient lava flows that left behind a scenic and unique geologic landscape.

208/334-2470
www.visitidaho.com

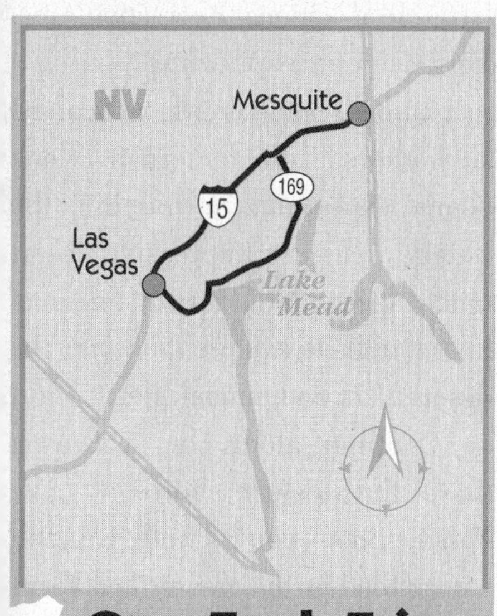
NV
Mesquite
15
169
Las Vegas
Lake Mead
One Tank Trips

NEVADA

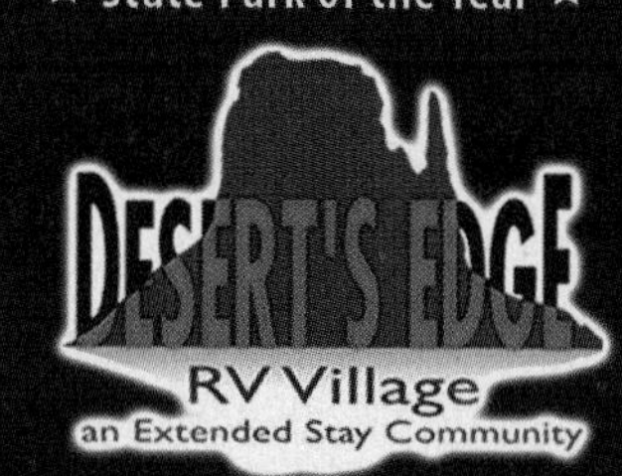
DESERT'S EDGE
RV Village
an Extended Stay Community

Photo by Ryan Photography
Visit Our Online Virtual Tour!
Reserve Today! 623-587-0940

Photo by Ryan Photography
Photo by Ryan Photography
Photo by campersview.com

VISA

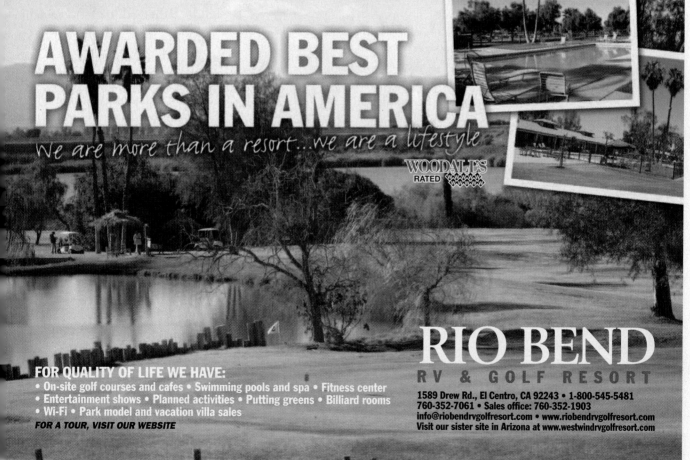

Our one-tank excursion through Nevada is going to focus on the very southeastern part of the state. A veritable playground unto itself, it won't take the odometer long to reveal we're in the man-made wonderlands of Lake Mead and Las Vegas.

Let's start by roaming the town of Mesquite, located on I-15 near the Nevada-Arizona border. Duffers won't want to miss a chance to test their skills on the many public golf courses carved into the rocky desert landscapes here. This resort town is also a prime starting point for exploring the North Rim of the Grand Canyon, located just a few miles east of town. The Valley of Fire State Park, just west of town, is another worthwhile natural wonder to check out.

Head south on Hwy 169 and consider a stop in the nearby town of Overton. The interesting Lost City Museum of Archaeology hosts an impressive collection of Native American artifacts. Overton is a convenient place to begin your exploration of Lake Mead National Recreation Area. This deep and sprawling lake is a recreational paradise where boaters, sunbathers, and fishermen flock nearly year-round. Surrounding the watery areas are impressive desert landscapes adorned with miles of hiking trails to explore the wondrous desert plant and animal life.

Continue along Hwy 169 as it skirts the western shores of Lake Mead. Soon you'll find yourself surrounded by the greater Las Vegas area. A playground like no other place on Earth, the lights and sights of Las Vegas are something to behold. Start exploring "Sin City" on the famed Vegas Strip, where casinos like the MGM Grand and the Mirage hustle to compete for your attention (and money) often with awe-inspiring results. Away from the Strip, Vegas holds other (kitschy) treasures, including the Liberace Foundation and Museum, Elvis-A-Rama Museum, and Guinness World Records Museum. Outside of town, get back to nature at the stunning Red Rock Canyon National Conservation Area, a favorite with hikers and bicyclists who enjoy the challenges of the beautiful, rocky desert terrain.

Wrap up your Nevada tour by heading south on Hwy 93/95 towards Boulder City, best known for a true engineering miracle, Hoover Dam. Take the tour to learn all about this feat of American ingenuity that transformed the southwest desert. Another massive engineering challenge is underway right now to relieve interstate traffic over Hoover Dam. Located just 1500 feet from

Hoover Dam, the new Mike O'Callaghan-Pat Tillman Memorial Bridge is due for completion in 2010. *800/NEVADA-8*

Other Area Locations

LAS VEGAS
Hitchin' Post RV Park

www.travelnevada.com.

OREGON

Talk about getting more bang for your buck. If you're looking for spectacular road trips that are easy on the mileage, look no further than a journey down Oregon's Coastal Route, US-101. Start in the most-northern town of Astoria, along the banks of the Columbia River and head south to Florence, while

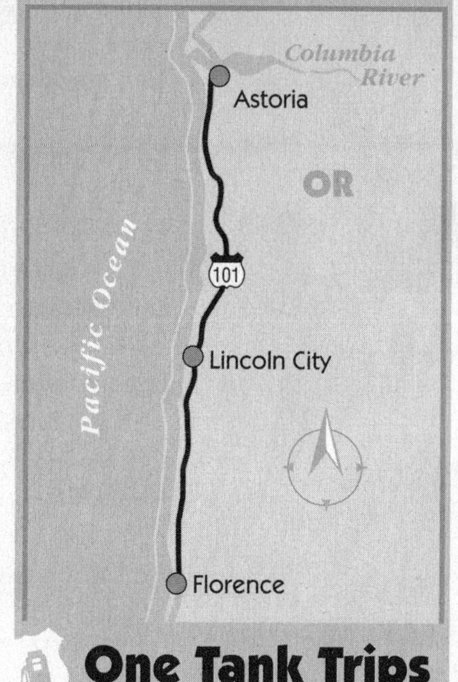

OREGON

enjoying the view of Oregon's priceless coastline.

The town of Astoria was originally established as a fur trading post-and for good reason. Strategically located along the mouth of the Columbia River and emptying into the Pacific Ocean, the site served as an important home for the fishing industry that shaped the region. Learn all about it at Columbia River Maritime Museum. Nearby is Fort Stevens State Park, while holds the distinction as the only mainland American military installation to be fired upon by foreign forces since the War of 1812. In June 1942, a Japanese submarine sent to avenge the Doolittle Raid on Tokyo approached the shore and fired seventeen rounds at the fort. None of them caused any damage, but the event did secure the fort's footnote in American history.

Head south along the 101 to the town of Seaside. The Seaside

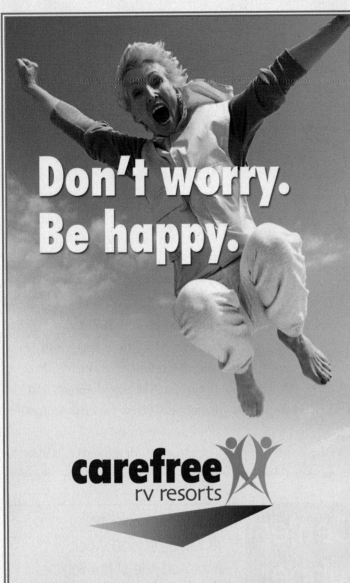

Aquarium showcases the marine environment that's so important to coastal Oregon.

Further south, round Tillamook Bay, then stop in the town of Tillamook, the county seat. A good way to explore the town and surrounding area is by a drive along the Three Capes Scenic Loop. This 38-mile circular drive starts in downtown Tillamook and ventures along the coast and into the wilderness, passing through state parks and wildlife refuges alike. Don't leave the area without touring the famous Tillamook cheese factory and also the Tillamook Air Museum, located inside a massive, historic, WWII blimp hangar.

In Lincoln City, you will find that you are never too old to fly a kite. The city boasts being the "kite capital of the world," and as you move towards D River State Recreation Site in the middle of town, you might see why. Twice a year in the park, the largest kite festival in the world is held, with some of the top "kiters" from around the world arriving to show off their amazing skills. For a more relaxing destination, check out the Connie Hansen Garden, where tidy, grass walkways meander through hundreds of flowing trees, scented flower beds, and vibrant green shrubs.

Back on US-101, let's take some time to explore the town of Newport. Situated on Yaquina Bay, this fishing village attracts visitors for its renowned crabbing, especially for the hearty Dungeness crabs. The town beckons visitors to explore the natural world that so defines the Oregon coast, and its best done at the Hatfield Maine Science Center of Oregon State University. Home to some of the world's best-known coastal ecologists, the Center offers tours of its aquarium and museum, nature trails, films, and special programs throughout the summer months. The Oregon Coast Aquarium, home to some 1,500 marine and freshwater species, is yet another way to enjoy the coastal wildlife. Otherwise, see how much of it you can find outdoors at scenic Ona Beach or the 130-acre Beverly Beach. Also nearby is the impressive Devil's Punch Bowl, an eight-acre, bowl-shaped park that fills with seawater during high tide, then reveals the wonders of tide pools during low tide.

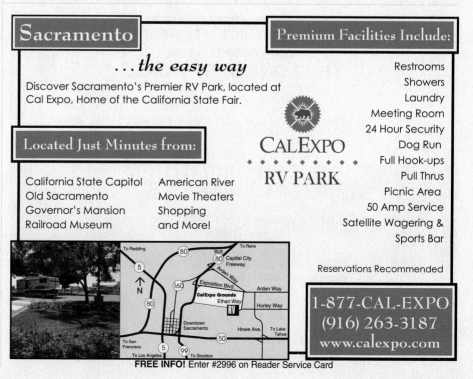

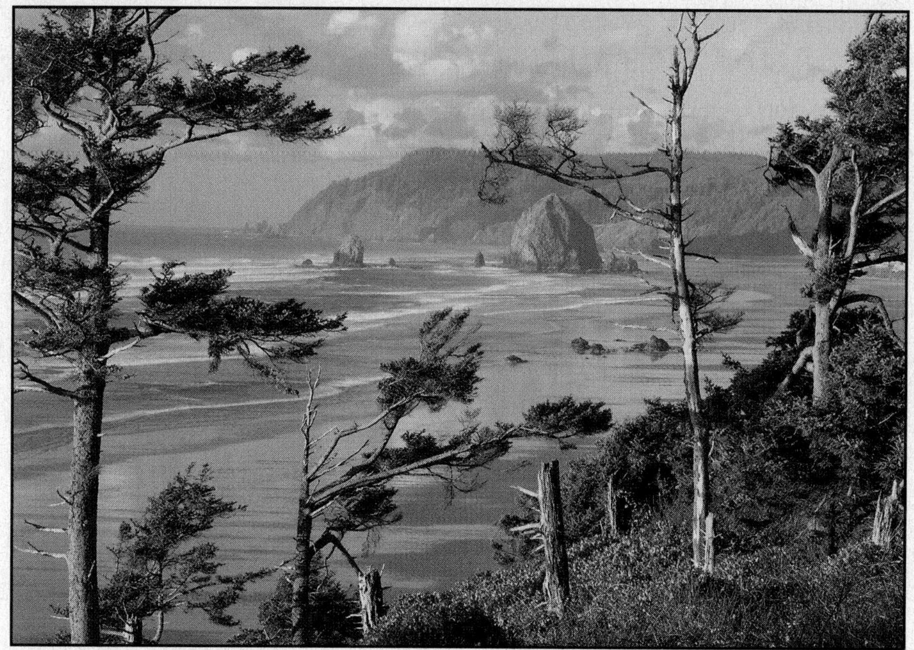

Oregon Coast. Photo by Larry Gedis

Florence is our last stop on our one-gas-tank Oregon tour. North of the town lies Sea Lion Caverns, the largest sea cave in the world. This is one impressive natural wonder, attracting hordes of sea lions for much of the year. Other favorite pastimes around town include a hike to the Heceta Head Lighthouse, located on a picturesque coastal cliff while, just south of town, the Oregon Dunes National Recreation Area boasts some of the world's largest sand dunes.
800/547-7842
www.traveloregon.com.

WASHINGTON

Northwest Washington is a gem unto itself. It's unique in that it seems to be able to comfortably blend its modern metropolitan areas within their natural surroundings. By the time we finish our tour in Puget Sound, this truth, and more, will be revealed.

Aberdeen, our starting point on the central coast, is an old harbor town nestled along scenic Grays Harbor on the Pacific Coast. Get acquainted with the city's shipping heritage at the Grays Harbor Historical Seaport. Or, for lazy summer afternoons, choose from among the city's several large city parks for a pleasant walk along the harbor's shoreline.

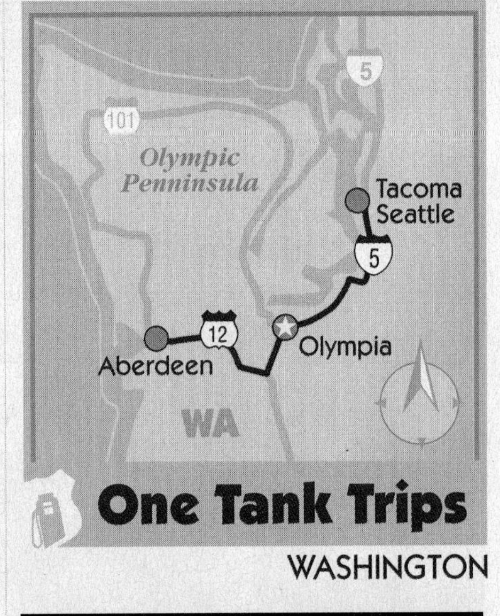

WASHINGTON

THIS ROUTE BROUGHT TO YOU BY:
Yakama Nation RV Resort
yakamanation.com
reservations@yakamanation.com
(800)874-3087

For a scenic detour, let's take Hwy 101 north, where we'll venture into the heart of the Olympic Peninsula and circle the scenic Olympic Mountains. Olympic National Park, and its nearly 1,500 square miles of protected lands, takes up the vast majority of the peninsula. Of all the unique attractions you'll find in the park, one stands out above all: since the peninsula is doused in rain and fog for much of the year, the park is home to several of the northernmost rainforests in the world, offering a truly exceptional natural wonder. Must-sees include the Queets Rain Forest, located along the park's southwest region, and the Hoh Rain Forest, in the northwest section of the park.

Hwy 101 skirts the Pacific Coast, passing though the villages of Queets and Kalaloch before headed back inland. Northwards, be sure to stop in the town of Forks, one of the largest towns in the heart of the Olympic Peninsula. Visit the Fork's Timber Museum to learn more about the industry that defined this region for nearly a century. For wild escapes, try a long hike on the scenic Rialto Beach or fishing for wild salmon along the Bogachiel River.

Next, head east along Hwy 101 until you reach the town of Port Angeles. City highlights include the Joyce General Store and a bevy of art galleries located downtown. Hop aboard the ferry that runs regularly to Victoria, British Columbia if you really want to make things interesting. The port is located just 15 miles across the Strait of Juan de Fuca.

From the scenic route, simply loop around back to the I-5. But if you prefer to plow ahead, take Highway 12, back into the interior of

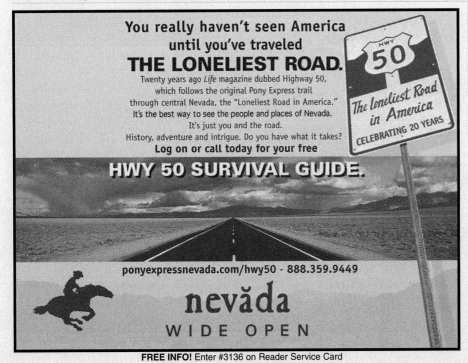

Washington, to the picturesque town of Olympia. Start your tour of Washington's capital city at, where else, but the Capitol Group, a collection of several historic buildings that house the state's government. Olympia is also an appropriate starting point to explore Olympia National Park, as well as the adjacent Olympia National Forest.

Jump on I-5 north for a few miles to the city of Tacoma. Nestled in the shadow of Seattle, Tacoma still retains much of its heritage and frontier town charms. Point Defiance Park is a 700-acre public park comprised of gardens, a zoo and aquarium, a restored fur-trading outpost, and miles of hiking and biking trails.

We can think of no better way to end our Olympic Peninsula tour than with a stop in incomparable Seattle. This hip and fashionable city offers all the big-city features you expect, accented with that unique Seattle style. Coffee may not have been invented here, but its culture sure was perfected. Maybe it was the seemingly endless rain and gloom of Seattle that spawned all those coffee shops, but it worked. Everywhere are cute and comfortable cafes, providing ample ime (and brews) to map out your itinerary. However, we suggest you nclude visits to the following attractions: The Center for Wooden Boats, a historical museum dedicated to, well, wooden boats; Discovery Park, a 500+-acre park with trails located n one of the nicest neighborhoods in he city; and a Mariner's baseball game at still-new Safeco Field.

800/544-1800
www.experiencewashington.com.

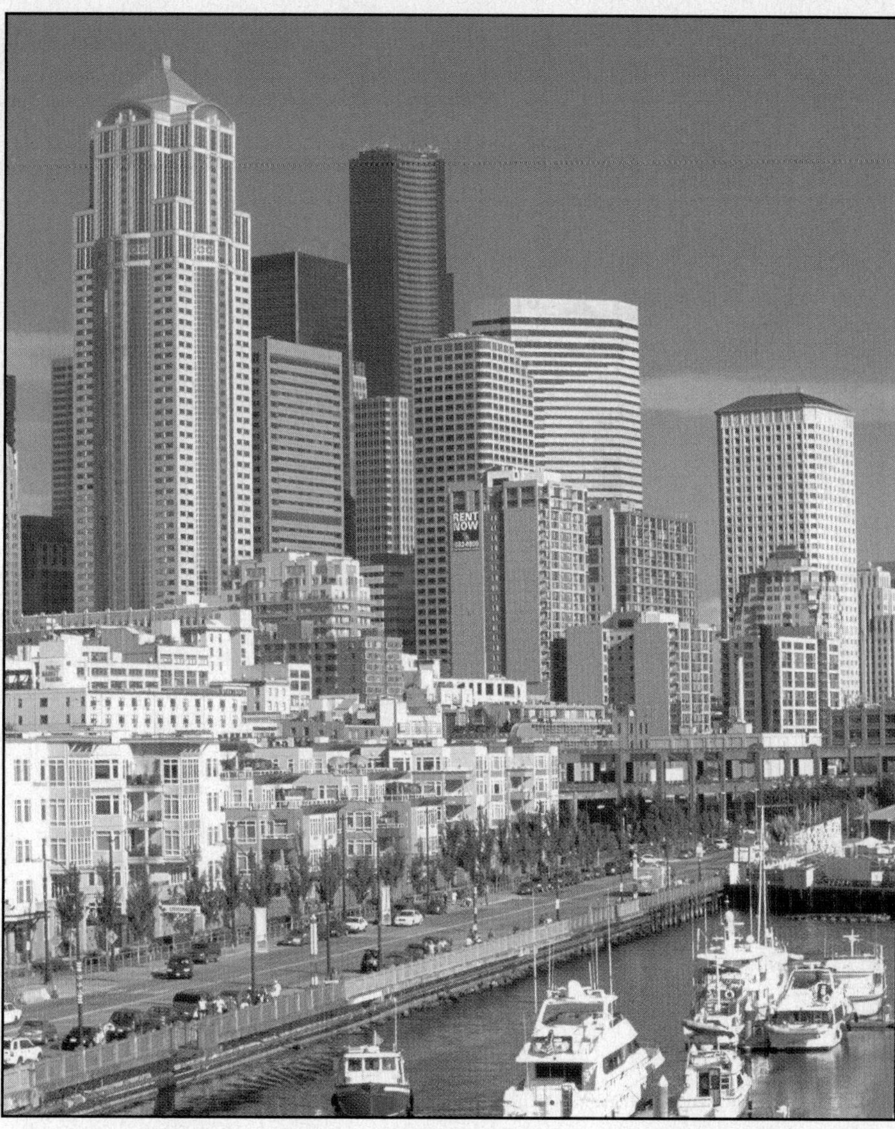

Boats move in and out of the Bell Harbor Marina, Seattle. Photo: Tim Thompson

Canada, the Western Hemisphere's largest country, offers tourists much more than its vast acreage. Northern, Western and Central wilderness areas are just the beginning of a Canadian travel adventure. Modern-day metro experiences are yours for the taking in eastward provinces such as Quebec and Ontario. And splendid seashore delights await guests who venture into Canada's southeastern coastal locales. Oh, Canada!

NEW BRUNSWICK

New Brunswick beckons travelers with flower gardens, antique autos, golf greens, and scenic waterways. Whether you want to visit historic districts, tumbling cascades, grand gorges, gardens, or the longest covered bridge on earth, the province of New Brunswick can fulfill most anyone's best vacation wishes.

We start things off at the tour in New Brunswick Botanical Garden in the town of Edmundston. Be sure nothing impedes your appreciation of the fragrances around the property.

With Edmundston now in your rearview mirror, drive on Canada Collector Hwy 144 south through Saint-Leonard and into Grand Falls/Grand Sault. It shouldn't take long before noticing how half the town of Grand Falls is surrounded by exquisite Grand Falls Gorge, a ravine carved by the cascading action of New Brunswick's biggest waterfall.From Grand Falls/Grand Sault, pick up Canada Collector Hwy 2 south and east. Cross the St. John River at a National Historic Site - Hartland Covered Bridge. The circa 1901 feat of engineering, located in Hartland, is touted as the "Longest Covered Bridge in the World."

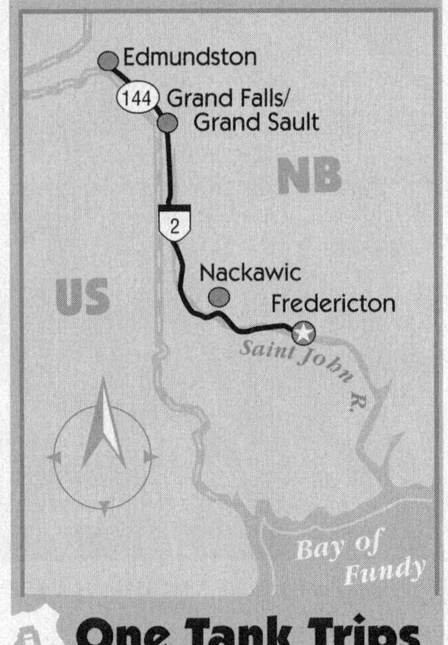

NEW BRUNSWICK

Further south on Hwy 2, the town of Nackawic has two unique attractions. First, take time to see 50+ species of trees and bushes at the town's waterfront International Garden. Next, ponder the significance of the "World's Largest Axe," a seven-ton, 66' stainless steel curiosity that stands guard nearby. *www.TourismNewBrunswick.ca 800/561-0123.*

QUEBEC

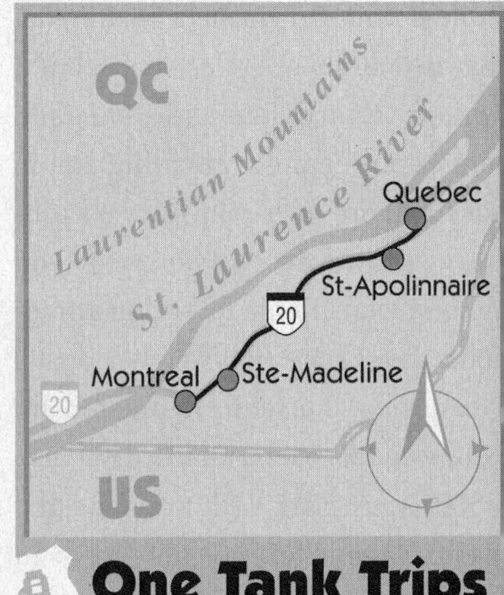

QUEBEC

From the Biodome, Casino complex, and Botanic Garden in Montreal to Quebec City's Nationa

Battlefields Park, Citadelle, and Capital Observatory, the metropolitan areas of provincial Quebec enlighten and entertain visitors.

In the second-biggest French-speaking city on earth, Montreal dazzles as a true cosmopolitan gem of the north. Be sure to visit the Montreal Biodome that now occupies the original velodrome structure built expressly for the 1976 Olympic Games. Meander through four captivating indoor ecosystems replicating a South American rainforest, North American forest, marine estuary, and polar zone. Watch carefully during your Biodome walk for animals ranging from fish to penguins that typically live in each environment. The five-story Casino de Montreal features a variety of restaurants including dinner shows, musical entertainment, thousands of slot machines, and more than 100 gaming tables. Natural offerings are best captured at Montreal's Botanic Garden, which contains more than 30 themed gardens and 10 greenhouses, representing flora from France, China, Japan, and the Sonoran Desert.

From Montreal, drive northeast on Canada Hwy 40 all the way to the province capital, Quebec City. If you're traveling Canada this year, take note that Quebec City, the birthplace of New France, celebrates its 400th anniversary, from January-October 2008 with commemorative stage performances, festivals, and unique cultural exhibits. At National Battlefields Park - The Plains of Abraham, you can view historic exhibits, go cross-country skiing, indulge in an old-timey "mystery meal," see the Martello towers, and view a multi-media show, all at one fascinating location. Be sure to tour the Official Residence of the Governor General of Canada at the Quebec City Citadelle. The elegant home has been occupied by Canada's governor generals since 1872. For the finest overviews of Quebec City and to learn about the area's colorful history, visit the 31-story Capital Observatory. Breathe deeply. Say, "Ah." Repeat.

www.bonjourquebec.com
877/BONJOUR, ext. 839.

BRITISH COLUMBIA NORTH

Whales, bears, forests, and fish provide outdoorsy amusements for travelers venturing into northern

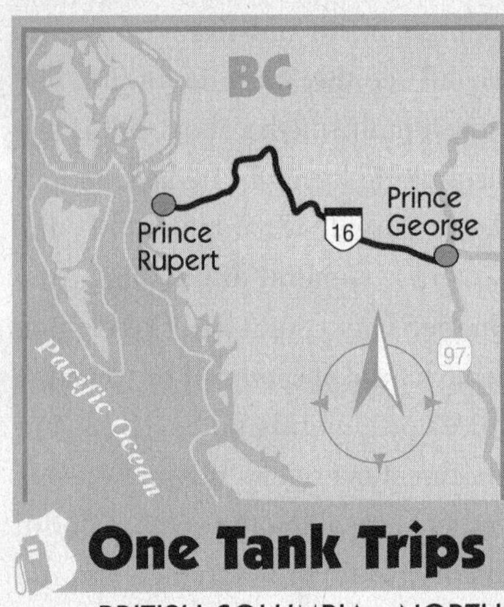

British Columbia. Meanwhile, southern BC delights visitors with abundant natural delights as well as "civilized" fun such as Kamloops' steam train excursions and the metropolitan allure of downtown Vancouver.

Starting off in the central province town of Prince George, treat yourself to the five-hour Self-Guided Cultural & Heritage Tour. A variety of galleries and unique museums are on the itinerary, including The Exploration Place and Prince George Railway & Forestry Museum.

From Prince George, drive west on Hwy 16 to Prince Rupert, through the towns of Houston, Smithers, and Terrace. Take a forestry tour or fly fish for steelhead in Houston. Smithers is a hot spot for catching salmon, as well as great views of Twin Falls and Moricetown Canyon. You can even go hiking or heli-fishing (where you're dropped from a helicopter at a secret angling spot). And while you're in the vicinity, be sure to schedule some bear watching time for black, grizzly, and rare white Kermode varieties in the wilds around Terrace.

BRITISH COLUMBIA SOUTH

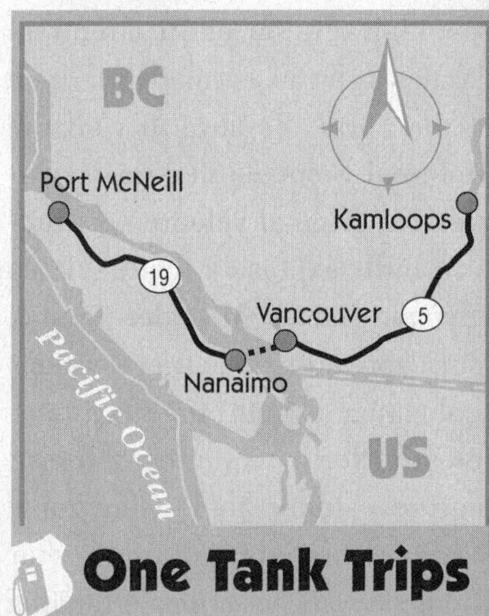

The southern portion of British Columbia ain't too shabby, either.

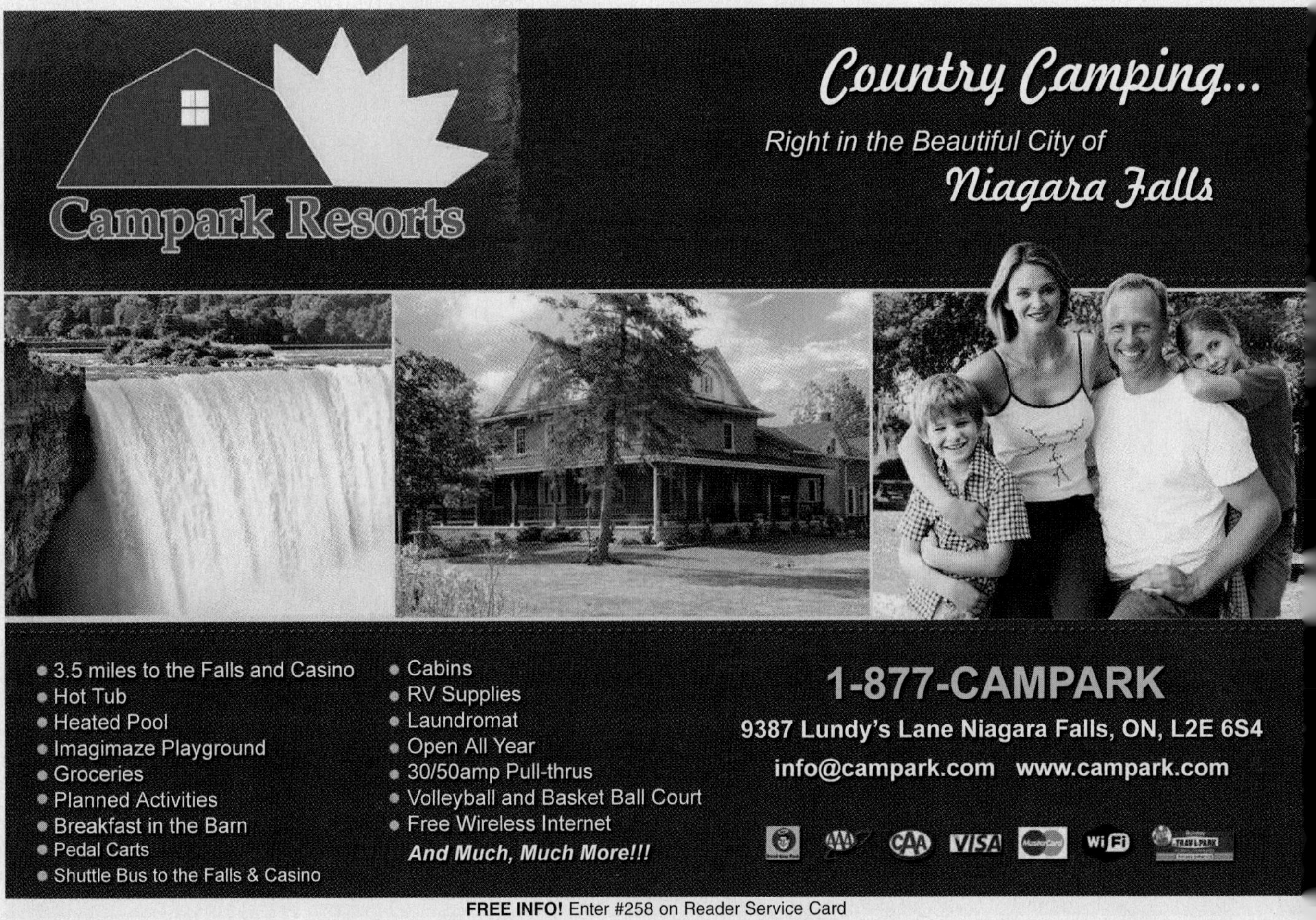

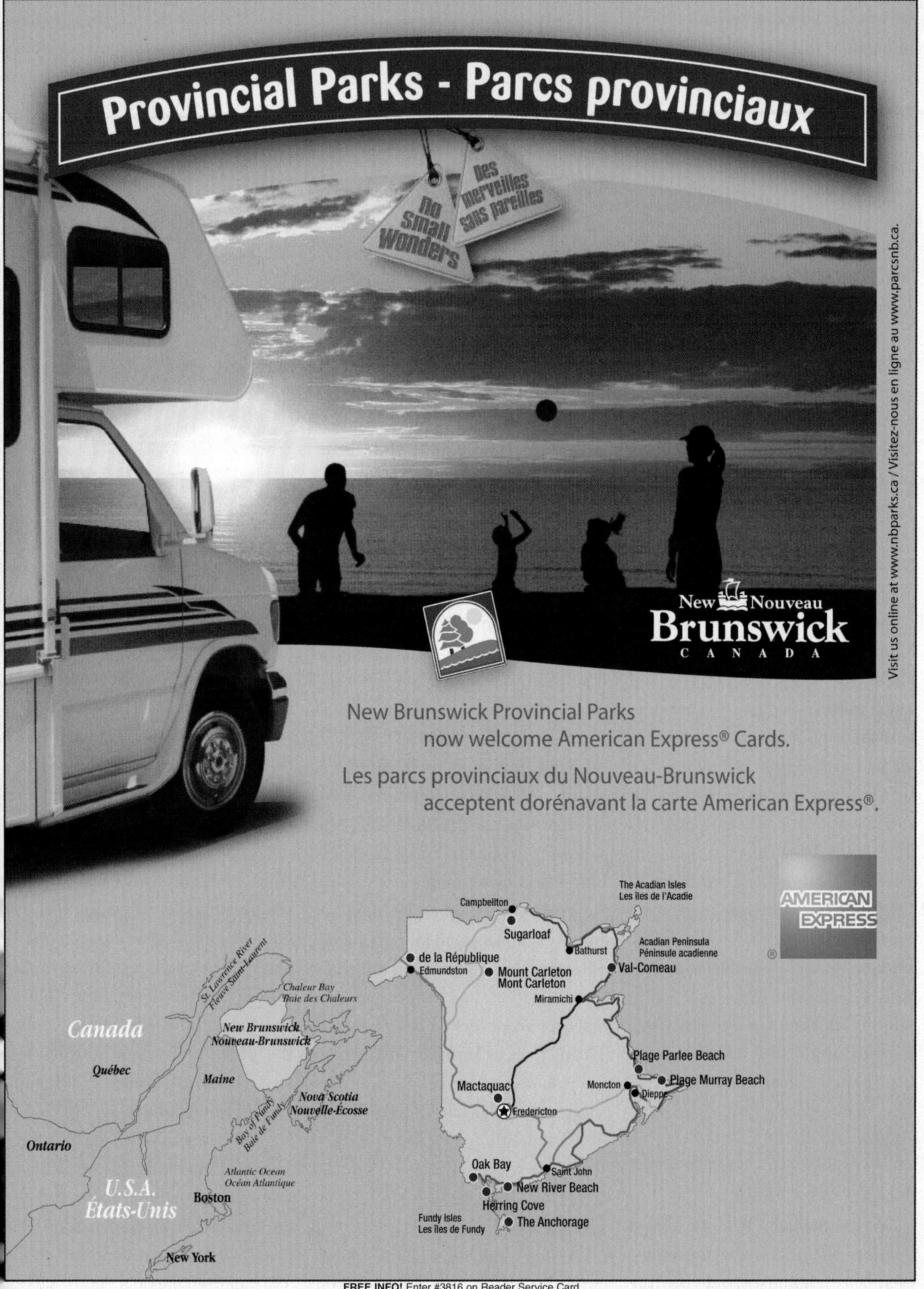

FREE INFO! Enter #3816 on Reader Service Card

Start in Kamloops, where we'll hunt for crystals, quartz, or fossils and be ready for black bear, snow geese, and heron sightings. At BC Wildlife Park, a conservation and animal rehab center, observe both local and exotic creatures at close range. And don't miss taking an authentic vintage steam train ride on the Kamloops Heritage Railway's 2141 Spirit of Kamloops or Armstrong Explorer.

From Kamloops, take Hwy 5 southwest to Vancouver. However, we'd first suggest a quick stop just east of the town of Merritt at Douglas Lake Ranch. At over 500,000 acres, it's British Columbia's largest working cattle ranch, and they offer horseback riding, fly fishing and ranch tours.

Next, take a bona fide British Columbian ferry from Vancouver to Nanaimo, on Vancouver Island, where you can park the RV and spend your day sailing, sea kayaking, scuba diving, fishing, or cruising to see harbor seals.

Once you've seen Nanaimo, pick up Hwy 19 north through Campbell River. Visit Home Lake Caves Provincial Park, fish, snorkel (yes, snorkel!) with salmon as they spawn in the river, or scuba dive Campbell River. At the northern terminus of this trip, Port McNeill, reserve your seat on a wildlife cruise to observe sea lions, dolphins, orca whales, as well as black bears roaming along the shoreline.
www.HelloBC.com
800/HELLO-BC.

NOVA SCOTIA

Nova Scotia's Atlantic coast wonders include lively museums, steadfast lighthouses, salty sailing adventures, and bountiful doses of Acadian charm.

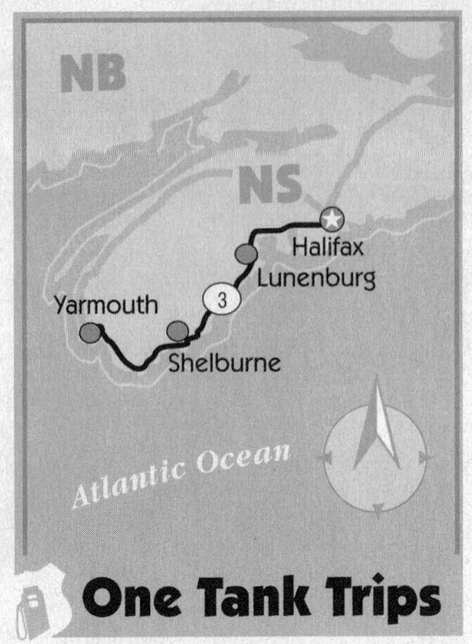

We begin our seacoast shuffle tour in the southwestern region, at the town of Yarmouth. See an old steam pump fire engine at the Firefighters' Museum of Nova Scotia and get a glimpse of the area's seafaring past at Yarmouth County Museum & Archives. Be sure to visit the Yarmouth Lighthouse on Cape Forchu Scenic Drive.

From Yarmouth, travel on Hwy 3 along Nova Scotia's southern shore, all the way to Halifax with the following stops in Pubnico, Shelburne, and Lunenburg.

Finally, we'll reach Halifax. Let singers, acrobats, and military bands entertain you at Halifax's International Tattoo, and later you can discover shipwrecked treasures and Titanic facts at Maritime Museum of the Atlantic.
www.novascotia.com
800/565-0000.

PRINCE EDWARD ISLAND

Prince Edward Island (PEI) shimmers with seaside natural beauty, historic charm, artistic opportunities, and savvy shoppers' hideaways. But that's not all! Upscale urban adventures are also available for tourists visiting the scenic capital city of Charlottetown.

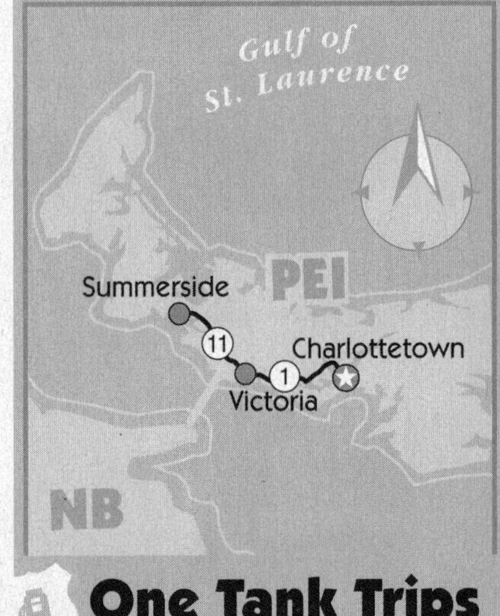

Let's kick off PEI's island holiday excursion in Summerside. From there take Hwy 11 east to nearby Reeds Corner and follow the Blue Heron Coastal Drive. Between Summerside and Victoria, browse for antiques and regional arts and crafts, stop for a bite to eat from a nice selection of local restaurants, and stroll through Gateway Village's assortment of shops. Next, take a round-trip, 20-minute drive over the famed Confederation Bridge that spans the Northumberland Strait. The sky-high view from the 200-foot-tall bridge is amazing!

Take the Trans-Canada Hwy (Hwy 1) south from the bridge, to Crapaud. The adjacent village of Victoria-by-the-Sea, with a population of 200, has charming tearooms and craft shops. You can even attend a candy-making workshop at the Island Chocolates Factory, where delicious Belgian chocolate is handmade.

A detour to Hwy 19 south along the coast takes you to Rocky Point and Port-la-Joye- Fort Amherst National Historic Site. It's a great stop for a picnic with spectacular views of Charlottetown Harbour.

www.peiplay.com
888/PEI-PLAY.

ALBERTA

The best place to start off our Alberta sojourn is in the capital city of Edmonton, always a winner in providing activities for its guests. Step back in time with costumed interpreters circa 1840s western Canada at Fort Edmonton Park. The Royal Alberta Museum and Wild Alberta Gallery showcase the histo-

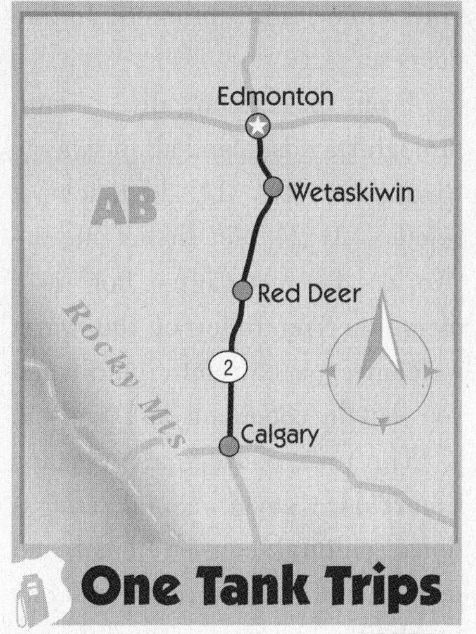

ries of Canada's people and Canadian nature, respectively.

From Edmonton, drive all the way to Calgary, south on Hwy 2. En route in Wetaskiwin and Red Deer (both off Hwy 2A) are promising locales for scenic mountain biking and out-of-the-way fishing adventures.

In Calgary, the "Heart of the New West," Calgary Tower attracts visitors with its TOPS Grill, revolving Panorama Room, and observation terrace. The Tower's cuisine alone is worth the elevator ride to the summit. Canada Olympic Park, the original site of the XV Winter Olympic Games, hosts an Olympic Hall of Fame and Museum, as well as sporting options for visitors. Are you an auto racing enthusiast? Well, then, ladies and gentlemen, start your engines! Race City Motorsport Park in Calgary sponsors seasonal car, truck, motorcycle, and drag racing contests. If you appreciate a different kind of horsepower, you can arrange your Alberta travel time accordingly, and

plan to attend the Calgary Stampede, a worldwide rodeo extraordinaire. The Stampede takes place during ten jam-packed days each summer with the chuck wagon races drawing the biggest crowds.
www.TravelAlberta.com
800/ALBERTA.

SASKATCHEWAN

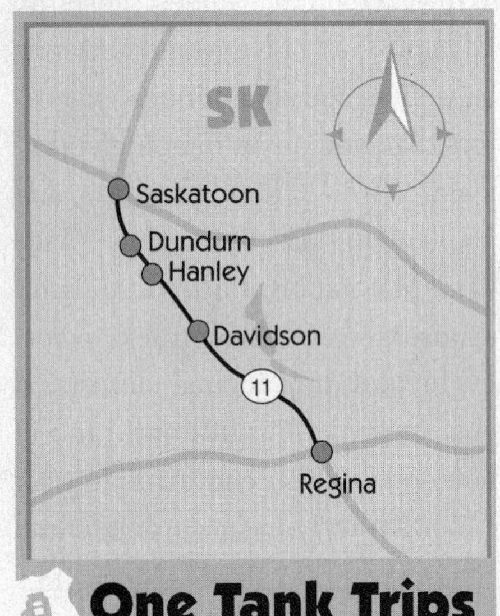

SASKATCHEWAN

From tipi rings and ceremonial dances, to fine arts, crafts, and fres picked berries, the province of Saskatchewan is a blend of the very best ingredients. Do lively casinos, an oversized coffee pot, and the Canadian Mounties sound like elements of a very special vacation? Of course, they do. Enter "Saskatchewan" on your travel itinerary.

We chose Saskatoon as our starting point and not just because of its cool name. No, it's a great place to learn about North Plains Indian history and culture at Saskatoon's Wanuskewin Heritage Park, and we're certainly always up for learning something new. Ok, we like the name, too. While in town, expect to see tipi rings, a buffalo pound, medicine wheel, and authentic Indian dances.

From Saskatoon, drive south through Davidson and all the way to Regina on Hwy 11. Java lovers, rejoice! At 24 feet in height, the 'World's Largest Coffee Pot" is a marvelous reminder of the warm welcome you can anticipate when you visit the community of Davidson.

The town of Regina's Wascana Centre is a governmental, educational, cultural, conservational, and recreational hub, all rolled into one fabulous complex. The Centre encompasses a monument, fountain, and several parks with appealing names like Goose Hill and Candy Cane.
www.sasktourism.com
877/237-2273.

MANITOBA

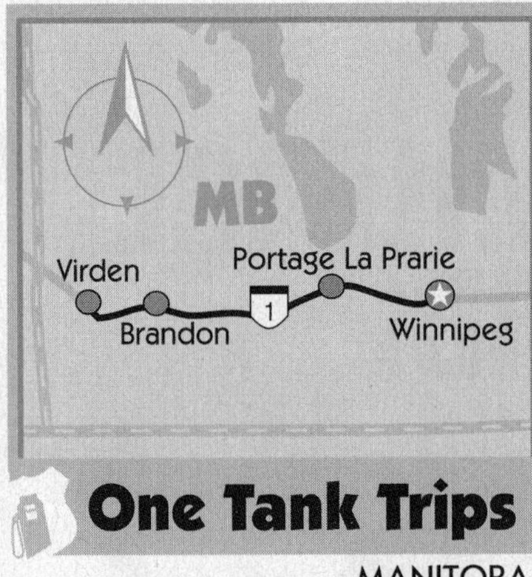

MANITOBA

Tours of Manitoba's oil fields, air museums, pioneer villages, spacious parks, government mint, and scenic waterways provide non-stop options for action-minded tourists. And there's another kind of action to be found at the province's casinos and race track.

First stop is Virden, on Trans-Canada Hwy 1. Naturally, you're going to want to take an oil field tour and step back to a Victorian lifestyle at the circa 1988 Pioneer Home Museum in town, right?

Now that we've scratched that itch, travel east on Trans-Canada Hwy 1 towards Winnipeg. However, don't "leadfoot" your way through the town of Brandon. Manitoba's "Wheat City" features the Commonwealth Air Training Plan Museum where loads of WWII-era Royal Canadian Air Force planes and memorabilia are on display.

Winnipeg time. Check out the Casinos of Winnipeg to experience zesty live entertainment, bountiful buffets, a walk-through aquarium, Millennium Express historic ride, tumbling waterfall, and first-class gaming at two locations - Club Regent and McPhillips Street Station.
www.travelmanitoba.com
800/665-0040.

NORTHWEST TERRITORIES/ NUNAVUT

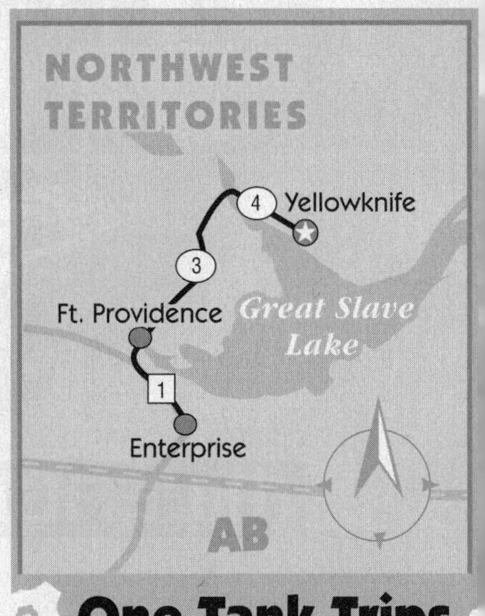

NORTHWEST TERRITORIES/NUNAVUT

Jellystone Park™ Niagara

Get A Close Up At The Falls!

TM & © Hanna-Barbera. (s08)

Fun For All Ages!

Kids Program

Falls Shuttle

Family Camping, RV/Big Rigs, Cabins & More!

Picture perfect! If it's Niagara Falls you want to see, then there's no better place than Yogi Bear's Jellystone Park™ Niagara Campground. Visit and enjoy attractions like Marineland, Casino Niagara, The Niagara Falls Casino Resort, and the roaring Falls, all just minutes away. Jellystone Park™ Niagara offers you this accessible location plus the conveniences that make camping enjoyable.

• Red Carpet RV Sites • Pull-thru sites • Sewer hookup with 30 and 50 amp service • WiFi available • Exclusive tenting • Full service Deluxe Rental Cabins and Trailers • Bare Bones Camping Cabins • Clean modern washrooms, showers and laundry facilities • Restaurant • Mini-mart • Souvenir shop

PLUS - There's an array of great on-site amenities and activities for the whole family, from our outdoor pool, games room and volleyball courts to pedal cart rentals, scheduled children's activities and so much more!

Experience the Falls from Jellystone Park™ Niagara

8676 Oakwood Dr. Niagara Falls, ON L2E 6S5 Direct Line: 905-354-1432 Fax: 905-354-2115

Reserve Online at www.jellystoneniagara.ca or call 1-800-558-2954

FREE INFO! Enter #218 on Reader Service Card

When you think about the Northwest Territories/Nunavut, do you imagine waterfalls, moose hair crafts and free-roaming bison? Well, you should, considering that's where this gas-tank friendly tour takes us. Oh, and did we mention the real Tlicho tipis, world-class fishing, sparkling diamonds, and radiant views of the Aurora Borealis?

Enterprise is the first town you come across as you enter the Northwest Territory on Hwy 1. Shop for supplies and take a short side trip to thundering Alexandra Falls in Twin Falls Gorge Territorial Park. Continue on Hwy 1 north past Kakisa and pick up Hwy 3, Yellowknife Hwy, traveling north and then east. Fort Providence is the place to buy north woods crafts designed with genuine moosehair tufting. Phew, now you can cross that off on your shopping list. Go on a sightseeing or fishing cruise on the Mackenzie River and see a 2,000-strong herd on the range at the bison sanctuary just north of town. On the shores of Great Slave Lake at Behchoko, stop for a bite to eat at the town restaurant, see traditional tipi lodges, and visit the headquarters and largest community of the new Tlicho Self Government.

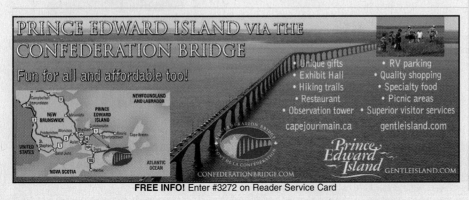

In the town of Yellowknife, a.k.a., "Diamond Capital of North America" and capital of the Northwest Territories, tour the dome-shaped legislative building. Stroll or ride a bike around Old Town, order a tasty meal at the circa 1930 log-construction Wildcat Café, and play 18 holes at Yellowknife's sandy course.

www.explorenwt.com
800/661-0788

NEWFOUNDLAND-LABRADOR

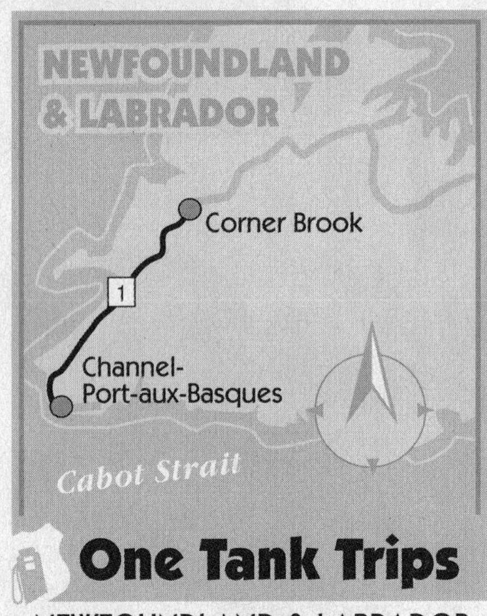

NEWFOUNDLAND & LABRADOR

Harbour boardwalks, mountaintop trails, salty Atlantic cruises, and Captain James Cook join forces to complete your Newfound-land/Labrador travel experience.

It's best to kick off our Newfoundland/Labrador adventure in Channel-Port aux Basques with a stroll and browse session through unique shops on the flag-decorated Scotts Cove Harbour Boardwalk, from Marine Atlantic to Scott's Cove Park. Burn off additional calories with a walk up the gravel Table Mountain Hiking Trail to the mountain's peak on the outskirts of town.

From Channel-Port aux Basques, drive on Trans-Canada Hwy 1 all the way to Corner Brook. On the Corner Brook Stream Trail, hike through the heart of the city, stopping to see bridges and the gorge from viewing decks equipped with seating.

www.newfoundlandandlabrador-tourism.com
800/5673-NFLD.

YUKON

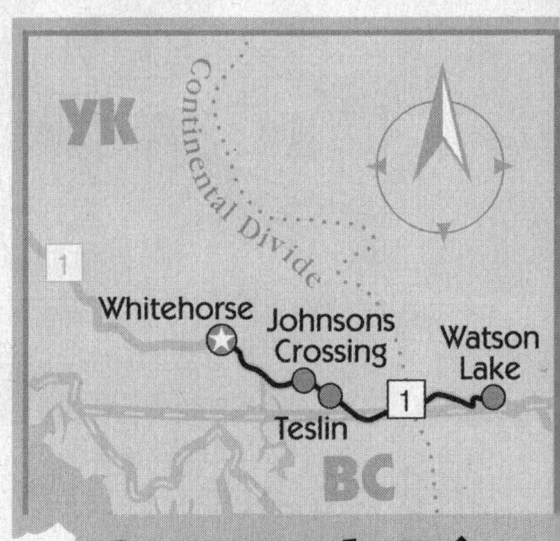

YUKON

A world apart, the Yukon gives tourists something different and a little daring. From Northern Lights ancient Tlingit tales, and woolly mammoth casts, to sternwheeler cruises, dogsled rides, and fresh brewed beer, the Yukon is a traveler's adventureland.

Where else to begin our Yukon tour in the town of Watson Lake than at Watson Lake Visitor Center? As the "Gateway to the Yukon," the center provides oodles of information about the construction of the famed Alaska Hwy and the pleasing Watson Lake Walking Tour. The Northern Lights Centre keeps visitors well-informed about the Aurora Borealis phenomenon, via several multi-media presentations. See how many signs you can read in one visit at Signpost Forest, a remarkable tourist spot that currently contains 60,000-plus individual signs, originated by homesick American soldier, Carl Lindley.

From Watson Lake, travel on Alaska Hwy 1, all the way to Teslin. At the lakeside George Johnston Museum, artifacts, exhibits and photos taken by the famous Tlingit elder and entrepreneur depict the Inland Tlingits' fascinating history. Teslin Tlingit Heritage Centre presents details about the traditional Tlingits' daily lifestyle and cultural practices.

Marsh Lake, along Alaska Hwy 1, is next. An ideal place to spend an afternoon on the beach, enjoy a tasty meal at a local café, or board a boat tour that departs from the town marina.

Tap into your adventurous side in the capital city of Whitehorse for some serious fishing, mountain biking, rafting on the wild Yukon River, or wildlife watching. Shop till you drop in the downtown district and don't be timid when sampling the selection of local restaurants.

www.touryukon.com
800/661-0494.

ONTARIO SOUTHEAST

We start this Lake Erie-friendly tour in the town Amherstburg for a tour of the Fort Malden National Historic Site on the Detroit River. The fort provides a fun glimpse into military life during the era of the War of 1812. Amherstburg's Gibson Gallery occupies a former Michigan Central Railroad Station and is well worth a visit. A variety of paintings, creative stitchery, and student art may be viewed there. Walk through a 1790s-vintage Victorian home at Park House Museum and experience tours and wine tastings at Sanson and D'Angelo Estates' Wineries before continuing on your way.

From Amherstburg, take County Road 18 east. Just before Leamington, pick up Kings Hwy 3 south-

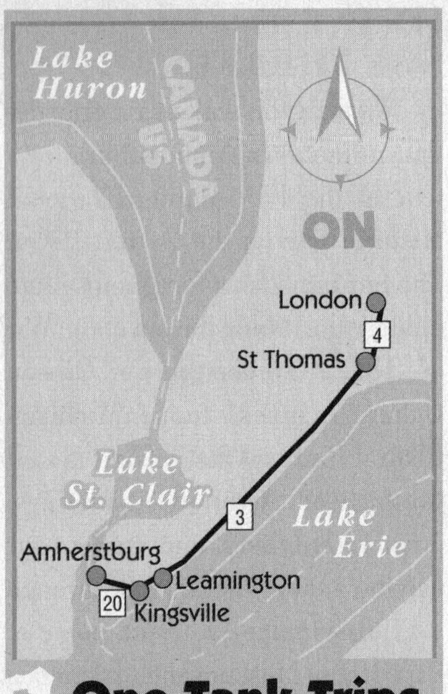

ONTARIO - SOUTHEAST

THIS ROUTE BROUGHT TO YOU BY:

Wildwood Golf & RV Resort
www.wildwoodgolfandrvresort.com
joelucier@aol.com
(866)994-9699

east into Leamington and continue onto County Road 3, heading northeast to St. Thomas. Circus history fans might recall the sad tale of Jumbo the Elephant, a famous performing pachyderm killed in a train run-over in St. Thomas, Ontario in 1885.

From St. Thomas, drive north on Kings Hwy 4 north and Kings Road 401 northeast into London. While in London, take a double-decker bus outing, shop at Covent Garden Market, and visit the town's Museum of Archaeology. Take time to tour the Bellamere Winery or stop in at the Labatt Brewery for some well-earned samples before heading over to the Fanshawe Pioneer Village where you can experience 19th century life in southern Ontario.

ONTARIO NIAGARA FALLS

ONTARIO - NIAGARA FALLS

THIS ROUTE BROUGHT TO YOU BY:

Yogi Bear's Jellystone Park Camp-Resort
www.jellystoneniagara.com
yogibear@jellystoneniagara.ca
(905)354-1432

A ways east on Kings Hwy 4, then south on Hwy 406, there's lots of fun in and around famed Niagara Falls. Naturally, you and yours are obliged to take in the falls from the observation deck of the 520-foot tall Skylon Tower, take a Maid of the Midst boat excursion, or a helicopter flight just above the waterfalls. Wave to a whale at Marineland, shop at factory outlet stores, see an IMAX film, and visit the Rossi Glass studio, where fine pieces of handmade collectible glass are produced. Visit the Niagara Parks Butterfly Conservatory, tour local wineries, take a whirlpool jet boat ride, hike the Bruce Trail or Niagara River Recreation Trail in the well-named Niagara-on-the-Lake.

When you've got your fill of water, water everywhere, head west on Hwy 420 until it connects with Queen Elizabeth Way (QEW). Continue traveling west/northwest on QEW into Hamilton, home to 60 (smaller) waterfalls in the city, as well as the African Lion Safari, just north of town. While you're there, drive through the Game Reserves, take the African Queen cruise, and go for a scenic railway ride.

Across the bay of the same name, Burlington is a great place to put those walking shoes to the test. Navigate the downtown section at Burlington's Discovery Landing, catch the lake view from the observatory, and grab a bite to eat at a waterfront restaurant.

From Burlington, head out on King's Hwy 403 northeast into Bronte and immerse yourself in the living history demonstrations at Bronte Creek Provincial Park for a quiet respite. From Bronte, travel on County Road 25 northwest until it runs into Express Toll Route 407 north. Continue on 407 until you can pick up County Road 1 north into Georgetown.

From Georgetown, backtrack south on County Road 1 and pick up Express Toll Route 407 southwest to King's Hwy 401 southwest to Morriston. Head south on King's Hwy 6, southwest on King's Hwy 3, and west on County Road 2/53 to Brantford. When you reach Brantford, it's time to work some muscles along the Grand River via canoe or kayak, or gather a basketful of fresh fruits and veggies to get your five-a-day at the Brantford Farmer's Market.

From Brantford, head west on County Road 53/King's Hwy 24, then south on King's Hwy 24. You'll take County Road 59 south to Long Point Provincial Park, on the thin strip of land jutting into Lake Erie.

For those looking to get acquainted with Ontario's superior northwest, buckle up and meet us in at Sault Ste. Marie on Lake Superior's craggy coast. First things first. Tour the Canada Bushplane Heritage Centre to learn about northern Ontario's high-flying settlers and take a one-day wilderness train ride to awesome Agawa Canyon.

ONTARIO NORTHWEST LOOP TRAIL

From North Bay's trails and South River's waterways, to Renfrew's whitewater rafting opportunities and the maple forests of Algonquin Provincial Park, northwest Ontario is a veritable outdoor playground. Tourists in the region can also sample local culture and art at Huntsville's Muskoka Heritage Place or the eclectic galleries of North Bay.

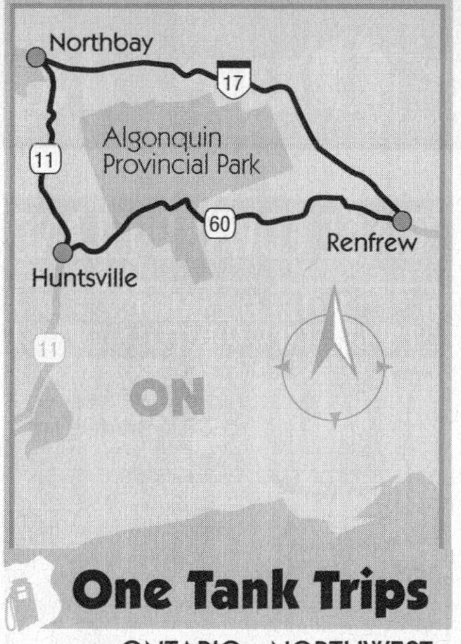

ONTARIO - NORTHWEST

Staying on the move in North Bay, is easy, considering the area's abundance of all-purpose trails. Whether you prefer walking, biking, ice-skating, or cross-country skiing, North Bay delivers a venue for your favorite mode of locomotion. The city and surrounds also accommodate the interests of snowmobilers and ATV enthusiasts; if railways are your thing, you can take a scenic train trip on the Dream Catcher Express.

From North Bay, travel south on King's Highway 11 all the way to Huntsville. The village of South River is our next stop, a popular hub for canoeists who want to paddle their way into the fabulous Algonquin Provincial Park via the water. Observant birders catch sight of species such as boreal chickadees, black-backed woodpeckers and magnolia warblers. Hikers and cyclists should plan to try out South River's Forgotten trails. Be on the look out for beavers, birds, and bunnies usually spotted from the trails.

Other Area Locations

NIAGARA FALLS
Campark Resorts
SAUBLE BEACH
Woodland Park

www.ontariotravel.net 800/ONTARIO.

Discover One Tank Trips

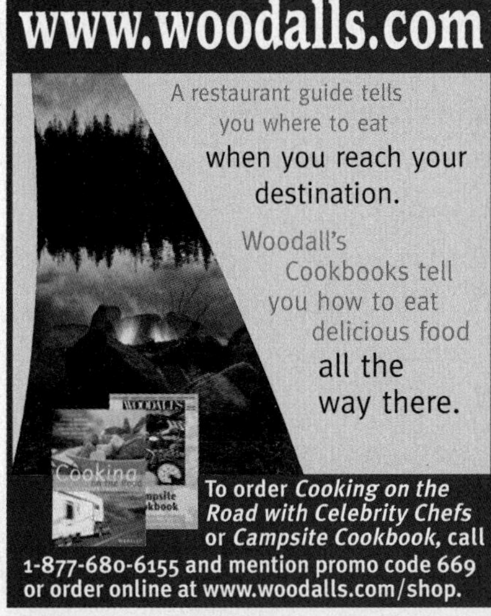

Welcome to Cal-Am Country!

If any place on earth could be described as a vacation wonderland, it's Arizona. From the breathtaking vistas of the Grand Canyon and Sedona, to the old west history of Prescott, Tombstone and Bisbee you could spend a lifetime here and never see it all. Arizona has long been a destination and haven for visitors from around the world.

Cal-Am's Arizona RV Resorts are centrally located near Phoenix in the lush Valley of the Sun allowing you to explore the local entertainment, shopping, sporting and recreational events or venture out on day trips to dozens of exciting destinations. When you stay at a Cal-Am Resort you're literally surrounded by enjoyment!

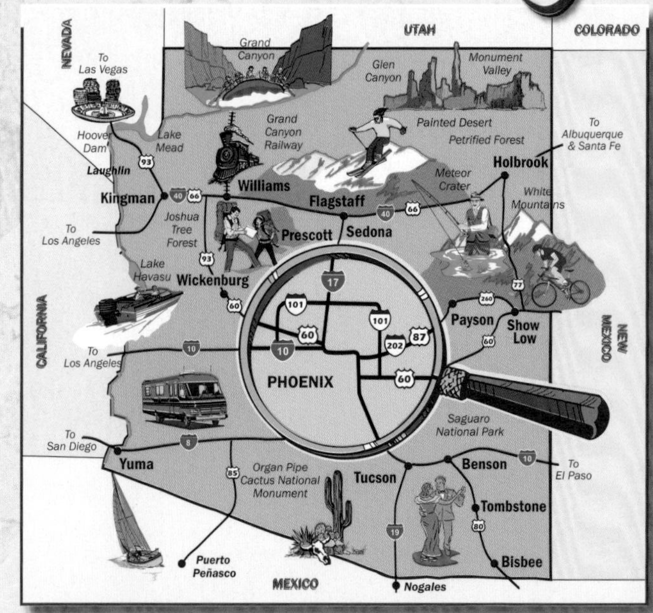

Cal-Am's Arizona RV Resorts are minutes from everything!

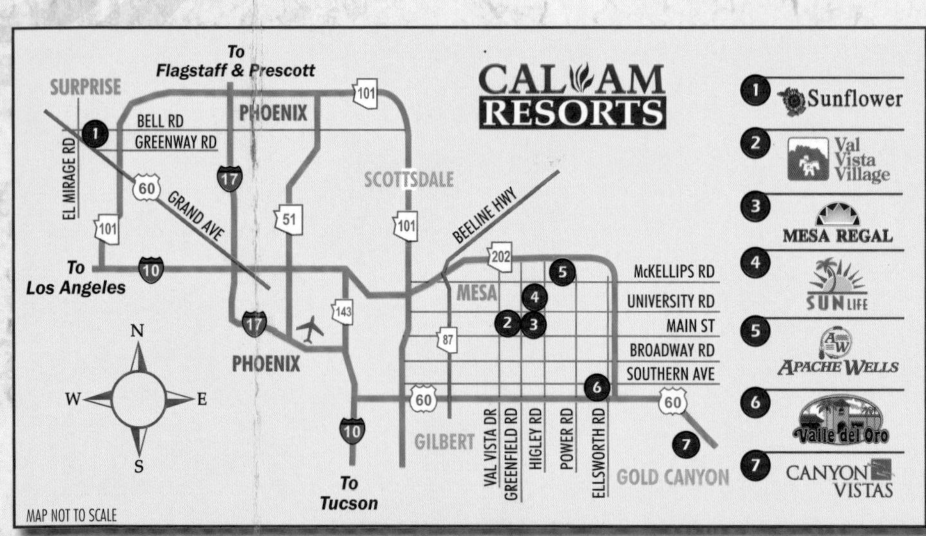

Hot Air Balloon Ride

University of Phoenix Stadium

Pink Jeep Tours, Sedona

Las Vegas, Nevada

Beautiful Golf Courses

Rodeos

FREE INFO! Enter #2584 on Reader Service Card

Call 888.940.8989 or visit www.cal-am.com

Look for Cal-Am Resort specific information in the Arizona section.

How to Use This Directory

Find it Quickly!

WOODALL'S Campground Directory

is organized alphabetically:

First by U.S. state

Then by Canadian province

Followed by Mexico.

Under these categories, the information is alphabetized by town. Each town name is followed by a letter and number (i.e., A-1) which refers to a grid coordinate on the maps found at the beginning of each state or province.

The campgrounds, RV sales/service centers and attractions/tourism locations are alphabetized under those towns.

Travel Sections are found at the beginning of each state/province

Each state/province begins with travel information and a map, both of which are updated annually. The sole purpose of the state/provincial maps is to show towns where campgrounds (indicated by diamonds ◆), attractions/tourism locations (indicated by flags ⚑), and RV sales/service centers (indicated by gears ✱) are located.

We recommend that you always travel with an official state or provincial highway map or a current road atlas. The WOODALL maps are meant to help you identify towns where parks, attractions and/or RV sales/service centers are located. Use them in conjunction with the listings to plan your travel itinerary.

The North American Split

The North American edition is split into Eastern and Western sections, each organized alphabetically starting with Alabama in the East and Alaska in the West. At the end of each section, you'll find an alphabetical index of all facilities listed in that section. The "WOODALL Alphabetical Quick Reference" provides the name of each listed campground/RV park, RV sales/service center or attraction/tourism location — in name order. It's useful when you know the name of the location you want to visit, but don't remember the town under which it's listed. Symbols in front of each name indicate the availablilty of ® RV /park trailer rentals; Δ tent rentals; □ cabin rentals; ★ RV sales/service centers; ● attractions/tourism locations. You'll also find the map coordinate after each town name for ease in using our maps. Find it quickly at the end of the Eastern and the end of the Western sections.

WOODALL Representatives make Personal Inspections

All privately-owned RV parks/campgrounds are personally inspected each year by one of our 28 Rep Teams.

Their detailed inspection reports provide the listing information and recommend the WOODALL ratings. These WOODALL Rep Teams have had years of RVing experience before joining WOODALL'S. They are professionally trained in their territory and are brought together each year for additional training. The privately-operated RV park/campground listings in this Directory are based upon Rep Teams' personal inspections made in the spring and summer of 2007. In addition to compiling information on a detailed listing form for each park, the Rep Teams also complete an evaluation form (sample shown on pages 148 and 149) to recommend the ratings.

Our Rep Teams also personally visit and gather information on RV sales/service centers and attractions/toursim locations. Those listed in this Directory are the facilities particularly interested in your business.

The listings for government campgrounds (federal, state, provincial, municipal and military) are based upon information collected from public resources.

WOODALL'S Dual Rating System

What do all those ◆s mean?

Ratings help you choose the park you are looking for.

WOODALL'S assigns two ratings to each privately-owned campground/RV park. One rating is assigned to the facilities at the park (sites, roads, service buildings, restrooms, hookups, etc.). A separate recreation rating is also assigned. Both facilities and recreation ratings range from 1◆ to 5◆. (This ◆ is WOODALL'S copyrighted rating symbol.) Keep in mind the final ratings are a composite of several different areas of interest.

The WOODALL Rating System is detailed on pages 148 and 149 with an example of how our representatives complete an evaluation form.

What do the Woodall Ratings indicate?

Ratings depend on the quality and quantity of our criteria elements. The more ◆s a park has generally reflects the presence of more development at the park, and usually more facilities. HOWEVER, THE MAINTENANCE OF THE CAMPGROUND WEIGHS HEAVILY IN ALL RATINGS ASSIGNMENTS. Cleanliness is a major factor in determining if you and your family will have an enjoyable vacation. The maintenance level at a park must meet or exceed the recommended ratings or the rating cannot be assigned at that level.

Do more ◆s mean a better park?

Emphatically, NO! The WOODALL rating system does NOT indicate good, better, best. Each RV/camping family needs to decide how much development is going to make their trip enjoyable. WOODALL lists a wide range of parks from rustic, natural settings to resort-like RV parks. Different factors may make a park attractive: convenience to the Interstate; width of sites; located near a popular attraction; a swimming pool, lake or other on-site recreation. Please take the time to understand the WOODALL Rating System and consider the ratings, along with other factors, when choosing the parks in which you want to stay. Be sure to read the listings carefully to make sure they have the facilities and amenities you want, and be sure to let the park owner know you found them in WOODALL'S.

How to Use This Directory

WOODALL'S features
8 Different Types of Listings

The top line of every listing identifies the type of listing.
Privately-owned campgrounds are rated.

(NW) RIDGEVIEW RV RESORT—(Mohave) *From jct Hwy 95 & Bullhead Pkwy (Casino Bridge) Go 1/2 mi E on Bullhead Pkwy. Enter on L.*

WELCOME

◊◊◊◊◊ FACILITIES: 302 sites, typical site width 25 ft, 302 full hkups, (30 & 50 amps), heater not allowed, cable TV, tenting, RV/park trailer rentals, RV storage, dump station, non-guest dumping ($), laundry, RV supplies, LP gas by meter, ice, patios.

◊◊◊◊◊ RECREATION: rec hall, swim pool, whirlpool, 12 bike rentals, 2 shuffleboard courts, planned activities, horseshoes, local tours.

Partial handicap access. Open all yr. Big rigs welcome. Internet friendly. Rate in 2007 $18 per vehicle. MC/VISA/DISC/AMEX. Phone: (555)392-8560.
SEE AD TRAVEL SECTION PAGE 3

✔ **ADVERTISER LISTING:**
Name is in dark, all capital letters. Shown with a Welcome diamond at the beginning of the listing.

WELCOME

Advertisers Want Your Business

The listings in this Directory are provided at no charge to the campground owner. Any campground which meets our minimum criteria requirements receives a listing. Many campground owners want to tell you more about their campground than the listing includes. These campgrounds have purchased advertising for that purpose. These ads can be a great help to you in choosing where to stay – they describe the special features and uniqueness of that campground. They can also tell you about nearby attractions, shopping and restaurants. Remember to say you "saw them in WOODALL'S."

(SW) Sunnyvale RV Resort—(Pinal) *From jct I-10 (exit 194) & Hwy 287: Go 7 mi E on Hwy 287, then 1 1/4 mi S on Eleven Mill Corner Rd, then 1/2 mi E on Sunscape Way. Enter on L.* ◊◊◊ FACILITIES: 215 sites, typical site width 28 ft, 159 full hkups, 56 E (30 & 50 amps), some extended stay sites, dump station, laundry, patios. ◊◊◊ RECREATION: rec hall, swim pool, planned activities. Partial handicap access. No tents. Open mid Sep thru early May. Big rigs welcome. Internet friendly. Rate in 2007 $20 per vehicle. Phone: (555)429-0490.

✔ **PRIVATE CAMPGROUND (NON-ADVERTISER):**
Name is in dark type, capital and lower case letters.

COPAKE FALLS AREA (Taconic SP)—*From business center: Go 13 mi NE on Hwy 22 & Hwy 344.* FACILITIES: 112 sites, 22 ft. max RV length, 112 no hkups, tenting, dump station, tables. RECREATION: river swimming, boating, canoeing, river fishing, playground, hiking trails. No pets. Open mid May thru mid Dec. Phone: (555)329-3993.

✔ **PUBLICLY-OWNED CAMPGROUND:**
Operated by a federal, state or local government agency. Name appears in light capital letters.

MILITARY PARK (Lake Martinez Recreation Area-Yuma MCAS)—*Off base. Located on Colorado River, off US 95.* FACILITIES: 20 sites, 17 W & E, 3 no hkups, tenting. RECREATION: lake swimming, boating, fishing. Open all yr. Reservations required. For Military Use Only- w/ Military ID Card. Phone: (555)341-2278.

✔ **MILITARY CAMPGROUND:**
Career-military personnel and U.S. Dept. of Defense personnel (active or retired) may camp at these parks. Proper ID is required for admittance. Call ahead to ensure eligibility. Note: use the Alphabetical Quick Reference to locate these parks — look under "M" for MILITARY PARK.

⚑ **(E) JUSTIN'S WATER WORLD**—*From jct I-10 & I-19: Go 1 1/2 mi S on I-19, then 9 mi W on Hwy 86 (Ajo Way), then 2 1/2 mi NW on San Joaquin Rd. Enter on R.* Eight swimming pools and seven giant slides in the rural Sonoran Desert. Located adjacent to Saguaro National Park. Open late May thru late Aug. Phone: (555)883-8340.
SEE AD PAGE 42

WELCOME

✔ **ATTRACTIONS AND TOURISM LOCATIONS (ADVERTISER FORMAT):**
Identified by a flag symbol. Also shown with a Welcome diamond at the beginning of the listing.

⚙ **(W) 1 STOP AUTOMOTIVE & RV REPAIR**—*From jct I-40 (exit 48) & Historic Route 66/Business I-40 (W Beale St): Go 100 feet S on Historic Route 66. Enter on L.* SERVICES: full-time mech, engine/chassis repair, RV appliance repair, body work/collision repair, LP gas by meter. Open all yr. MC/VISA/DISC/AMEX. Phone: (555)718-1400.
SEE AD THIS PAGE

WELCOME

✔ **RV SALES/SERVICE CENTER (ADVERTISER FORMAT):**
Identified by a gear symbol. Also shown with a Welcome diamond at the beginning of the listing.

⚙ **(S) Giant RV World**—*From jct I-495 (exit 6) & US-44: Go 3 mi W on US 44. Enter on R.* SALES: travel trailers, 5th wheels, van campers, motor homes, mini-motor homes, Class B motor homes, fold-down camping trailers, pre-owned unit sales. SERVICES: full-time mech, engine/chassis repair, RV appliance repair, body work/collision repair, LP gas by weight/by meter, RV storage, sells parts/accessories. Open all yr. MC/VISA/DISC/AMEX. Phone: (508)555-3338. FMCA discount.

✔ **RV SALES/SERVICE CENTER (NON-ADVERTISER FORMAT):**
Identified by a gear symbol.

⚑ **(N) The Caverns of Sonora**—*From jct US 277 & I-10: Go 8 mi W on I-10 (exit 392), then 5-1/2 mi S on RR 1989, then 1 mi E on paved road.* Over a mile of trails through caves. Gift shop, picnic grounds. Registered US Natural Landmark. Ample parking for RV's. Open all yr. Closed Xmas. MC/VISA. Phone: (325)555-3105.

✔ **ATTRACTIONS/TOURISM LOCATIONS (NON-ADVERTISER FORMAT):**
Identified by a flag symbol.

Abbreviation Key

You'll see a few selected abbreviations incorporated into some of our listings. Our editors have made every attempt to keep them simple and easy to read and understand.

mech	mechanic
emerg rd svc	emergency road service
L	left
R	right
W	water
E	electric
v-ball	volleyball
bsktball	basketball
hkups	hookups
need activ	needs activation
yr	year
wkends	weekends
Auth	Authority
BLM	Bureau of Land Management
COE	Corps of Engineers
Cons	Conservation
NF	National Forest
NP	National Park
NRA	National Recreation Area
PF	Provincial Forest
PP	Provincial Park
Reg	Regional
SF	State Forest
SNA	State Natural Area
SP	State Park
SRA	State Recreation Area

A word about camping fees...

Neither WOODALL'S nor the campground operator intends the published rate as a guaranteed rate. These rates were gathered by WOODALL Representatives during their inspections in 2007. The rates will almost always be higher by the time you get there because operators' costs have increased just like those of any other business. Rates are provided to give you a comparative overview of the camping fees within a general area. The fee will most often be shown as a range of rates for either a specific number of persons, a family (2 adults, 2 children) or per vehicle. The range represents the low to high ranges and may or may not include hookups.

How to Use This Directory

How to read the listings

PEACEFUL VALLEY – A-2

(NW) CAREFREE CAMPING RV PARK—(DuPage)
From jct I-94 (exit 24) & Hwy 120: Go 1/2 mi N on Hwy 120 (Golden Eagle Road), then 4 mi W on Hwy 80, then 1 mi N on Carefree Rd. Enter on R.

WELCOME

JUST LIKE NEW!
We've completely renovated our park for this season! Come relax in our new swimming pool or take advantage of our deluxe new bathhouses. Don't miss our annual festivities such as Christmas in July & end-of-season pig roast.

◆◆◆◆◆ FACILITIES: 320 sites, typical site width 40 ft, 175 full hkups, 100 W & E, 25 E, (20, 30 & 50 amps), 50 amps ($), 20 no hkups, some extended stay sites, 50 pull-thrus, heater not allowed, cable TV, wireless Instant Internet access at site ($), phone/cable on-site Internet access (needs activ), cable Internet access central location, tenting, RV/park trailer rentals, cabins, dump station, non-guest dumping ($), laundry, groceries, LP gas by weight/meter, LP bottle exch, ice, tables, wood.

◆◆◆◆◆ RECREATION: rec hall, equipped pavilion, coin games, 2 swim pools, wading pool, lake swimming, whirlpool, boating, 10 motorboat rentals, lake fishing, fishing supplies, mini-golf ($), 25 bike rentals, playground, planned activities, tennis, hiking trails, local tours.

Pets welcome, breed restr, size restr, quantity restr ($). Partial handicap access. Escort to site. Open all year. Big rigs welcome. Internet friendly. Clubs welcome. Rate in 2007 $18.50-23.50 per family. MC/VISA/DISC/AMEX. ATM. Member of ARVC. Phone: (999)555-6200. FCRV 10% discount. FMCA discount.
e-mail: cmpn@carefree.com
SEE AD THIS PAGE

1. WELCOME:
The Welcome symbol before a listing identifies those parks that have purchased an advertisement because they want to tell you more about their business.

2. FACILITIES:
The ratings range from 1 to 5 ◆s. All of the facilities listed are available on site.

3. PARTIAL HANDICAP ACCESS:
Indicates the park has been adapted in one or more ways to accommodate RVers/campers with disabilities. May include showers with benches and handrails, sinks and toilets that allow wheelchair access, wide doorways with no curbs or steps, wheelchair ramps, signs on buildings and/or hiking trails printed in Braille, TDD equipment, etc. If you or a family member has special needs, please call ahead to determine the type of services/facilities available.

4. TENT/RV/PARK TRAILERS/ CABIN RENTALS:
You may rent a tent, RV/park trailer or cabin at this park.

5. RECREATION:
The ratings range from 1 to 5 ◆s. All recreation listed is available right at the campground.

6. RATE INFORMATION:
Most often this will show as a range of rates from low to high which the privately-owned campground charged in 2007 (the year in which these inspections were made). THESE ARE NOT GUARANTEED RATES.

7. NATIONAL AND STATE/ PROVINCIAL CAMPGROUND AFFILIATION:
This directory identifies the campgrounds which belong to the National Association of RV Parks & Campgrounds (ARVC) and also those which are members of U.S. state or Canadian province campground associations.

8. ADVERTISER REFERENCE:
This line will refer you to the specific page for this listing's advertisement.

9. PHONE NUMBER:
Phone numbers are included for ease in calling ahead for a site.

10. DISCOUNTS:
KOA-10% Value Card Discount, CCUSA, FCRV & FMCA Discounts are shown.

11. ADDITIONAL INFO:
Information such as age restrictions, operating season and pet policy. If the listing reads "no pets" then the park has a strict policy that prevents RVers from bringing pets of any kind on the premise. If the listing reads "pets welcome" this indicates the park does accept some pets. ($) indicates charges for pets. If you are traveling with a large or unusual pet, or with several pets, we recommend you call ahead to be sure your pet is welcome. If your 6-foot iguana is your best pal, call ahead to make sure he'll be welcome.

12. BIG RIGS WELCOME:
Factors evaluated by WOODALL Requirements are: minimum 50 amps, road width, overhead access clearance, site clearance to accommodate the tallest and widest rigs built. Often, not every site at the park can accommodate a big rig, so we recommend you call ahead for availability.

13. CLUBS WELCOME:
If the park's management welcomes camping clubs, we'll indicate that in the listing.

14. TENTING:
This campground welcomes tenters. NOTE: Tenters are welcome at most campgrounds. If a campground does not have facilities for tenters, its listing will indicate "no tents" in the special info section or "accepts full hookup units only" in the facilities section.

15. DIRECTIONS/ENTRANCE:
Detailed, easy-to-read locator directions to guide you right to the park entrance. Directly following these directions, we tell you whether the park's entrance is on the left, right, or at the end of the street.

16. INTERNET FRIENDLY:
If a park offers Internet access that is active upon your arrival, or if there is wireless internet access or a central modem hookup (with a separate line, ample counter space and convenient access hours), we've designated this park as Internet Friendly.

17. MAP COORDINATES:
Matching grids on each state/provincial map help you to locate the listing town.

18. TYPICAL SITE WIDTH/ MAX RV LENGTH:
Most parks have sites of varying sizes. The listing shows the most commonly occurring site width at a park. The maximum length of RV (excluding the tow vehicle) that the campground can accommodate is shown (if under 40 ft.). Factors are turns, access and site sizes, based on the skills of an average RVer.

19. INTERNET ACCESS:
More and more RVers are staying in touch via email and utilizing the Internet. This has prompted many parks to provide Internet access at their sites and/or at a central location in the park, usually in the office or rec hall area. ($) indicates a fee may apply. Some site hookups may need activation by a service provider or the local phone/cable company before you can use them. Others noted "Instant Internet access" are immediately available.

20. COUNTY:
This appears in parentheses after the park name. May be useful when severe weather occurs as you travel, since most broadcast weather warnings are given by county.

21. CREDIT CARDS/ATMs:
MC=MasterCard;
VISA;
DISC=Discover;
DC=Diner's Club; AMEX=American Express; ATM=Automated Teller Machine; Debit=Debit Card.

22. E-MAIL ADDRESS:
When available, advertiser listings contain e-mail addresses.

23. NON-GUEST DUMPING:
If the park management allows travelers to come in off the road (non-guests) and empty their holding tanks, this is indicated in the listing. If the park charges for this service, you'll see a "$" after the phrase, i.e., non-guest dumping ($).

24. ESCORT TO SITE:
If management escorts your RV right to your site, we let you know.

25. SPECIAL INFORMATION:
Unique information provided by park owners who want you to know about special features and offers at their park. These individualized messages are highlighted in yellow and give you that little extra nugget of information not found in our standardized listing information.

26. DIRECTION LOCATOR:
The abbreviation before the facility's name indicates the direction from town. For example, "(NW)" means the facility is northwest of their listed town; "(C)" means center of town.

Special Notes

Toilets? Showers?

• Unless otherwise noted, all campgrounds have flush toilets and hot showers. If the showers in the restroom are coin operated, the listing will indicate "shower$."

Seasonal Sites?

• Many parks can accommodate seasonal or extended stay RVers. If less than 10% of a park's sites are occupied by extended stay RVers, the listing won't mention seasonals. If 10% to 49% are usually occupied by extended stay RVers, the listing will indicate "some extended stay sites." Between 50% and 74%, the listing will indicate "many extended stay sites," and between 75% to 99%, the listing will indicate "mostly extended stay sites."

Age Restrictions?

• WOODALL'S lists "Age Restrictions May Apply" based upon information believed to be correct at the time of WOODALL'S inspections. Some sunbelt area parks cater to senior adults only. Since these classifications may change because of developing legislation, we suggest that you confirm this status by telephone, if it's important to you.

CG NAME: **Forestville RV Park** TOWN: **Green Valley** STATE/PROV.: **WA**

AREAS OF INTEREST	Not Qualified	Level 1	Level 2	Level 3
ENTRANCE Includes an assessment of the following: Sign, Entrance, Access into CG, Entry Roads.	If any of these exist: No Sign, Access or Entry Roads too Dangerous or Difficult	Requires the following: **1** ___ Sign ___ Reasonable Access	Requires 2 of the following (in addition to Level 1): **2** ___ Commercial Quality Sign Lighted ___ Developed Entrance ___ Wide Easy Access ___ All Weather Entry Roads.	Requires 3 of the following: **3** ___ Commercial Quality Sign Lighted ___ Developed Entrance ___ Wide Easy Access ___ All Weather Entry Roads.
SERVICES Includes an assessment of Registration & Laundry.	If no registration system	Requires the following: **1** ___ Some system of registration (self-service accepted)	Requires: **2** ___ Part-time Management (no regular office hours)	(circled) Requires 1 of the following: **3** ✓ Management with reg. office hours ✓ Laundry (under a roof but not enclosed by walls is acceptable)
RESTROOMS AFHO/ASCO listings do not require restrooms. If restrooms are provided, numbers can be waived, but construction requirements apply for rating level suggested. If none, assign same level as hookups.	None-unless AFHO/ASCO	May be crude construction. **3** Non-flush permitted. May not have showers.	May be non-professional finish. **6** Standard flush, marine or recirculation toilets. Showers & basins required.	Over 50% professional finish. **9** Standard flush toilets, showers & basins required.
DUMP STATION If park has all Full Hookup Sites or Accepts Self-Contained units only, or if all non-full hookup sites are for *tents only,* No Requirement. If provided, assign the higher of either the dump station or hookups. If none, assign same level as Hookups.	None **0** Assign **0** point value	Some method available such as **1** ___ Sewer site, if vacant OR ___ Portable dump	Some method available on daily basis such as **2** ___ Permanent facility OR ___ Portable dump	Good quality facility with concrete pad sloped to flush inlet, closure and flushing water. Management provided pump-out service acceptable substitute. **3**
SITES Includes an assessment of Picnic Tables and/or Patios. Also Shade and/or Plantings and/or Landscaping. If sites for *tents only* exist, disregard those sites for the purpose of determining the SITES rating.	**0**	Some sites must be level & some sites must have **2** ___ picnic table (patio substitute) OR ___ shade and/or plantings and/or landscaping	**10% of the sites must:** **4** ___ be level ___ have reasonable access ___ have picnic table (patio substitute) ___ have shade and/or plantings and/or landscaping	**25% of the sites must:** **6** ___ be level ___ have good access ___ have picnic table (patio substitute) ___ have shade and/or plantings and/or landscaping
HOOKUPS If sites for *tents only* exist, disregard those sites for the purpose of determining the hookup rating.	No water available	Adequate water taps **2**	25% electric hookups plus adequate water taps. **4**	25% electric and water hookups, plus 25% electric hookups. **6**
INTERIOR ROADS An assessment of the roads within the park utilized by RVs or the towing of RVs.	**0**	Roads are not All-Weather (may be a track through grass) **1**	Some are All-Weather or paved **2**	High-use roads are All-Weather or paved **3**
GROUNDS & LIGHTING This refers to non-camping, non-recreational areas. These are the public & common areas. Include in this element an assessment of the lighting that exists overall in this campground.	No lighting	A lighted area **1**	Requires both: **2** ___ grounds development ___ lighting outside at central building	Requires All of the following: **3** ___ grounds development Lighting at: ___ registration ___ restrooms
RECREATION		1 Major recreation or 3 minors	2 Major recreations	Indoor Recreation OR Swimming TOTAL REQUIREMENT 4 Major recreations

REC HALL	(M)	MN	NC	ITC	CANOEING	M	MN	NC	ITC	PUTTING GREEN	M	MN	NC	ITC
REC ROOM/AREA	M	MN	NC	ITC	KAYAKING	M	MN	NC	ITC	PLAYGROUND	M	MN	NC	ITC
PAVILION	M	MN	NC	ITC	BOAT RENTALS	M	MN	NC	ITC	PLAY EQUIPMENT	M	MN	NC	ITC
EQUIPPED PAVILION	M	MN	NC	ITC	FLOAT TRIPS	M	MN	NC	ITC	MINI GOLF	(M)	MN	NC	ITC
SWIM	(M)	MN	NC	ITC	FISHING	(M)	MN	NC	ITC	TENNIS	M	MN	NC	ITC
WADING POOL	M	MN	NC	ITC	FISHING GUIDES	M	MN	NC	ITC	SHUFFLEBOARD CTS.	M	MN	NC	ITC
WHIRLPOOL	M	MN	NC	ITC	PLANNED GROUP ACT.	M	MN	NC	ITC	HORSESHOES	M	MN	NC	ITC
BOATING	M	MN	NC	ITC	DRIVING RANGE	M	MN	NC	ITC	BIKE RENTALS	M	MN	NC	ITC

- The circles shown above indicate the level of each AREA OF INTEREST that exists at this Campground/RV Park.
- The underlined words indicate what is lacking in each AREA OF INTEREST that does not allow it to be circled at the next level.
- Point values are given to the park based on each AREA OF INTEREST circled.
- A 4W Facility Rating would be assigned to the above park.

Remember: A park may have particular AREAS OF INTEREST that are at different levels than the rating assigned. The overall rating is a composite of all AREAS OF INTEREST.

SAMPLE EVALUATION

Level 4	Level 5	TOTAL	MAINTENANCE unacceptable	minimal	fair	good	very good	superior	2006 CD F-3-5
Requires All of the following: 4 ✓ Commercial Quality Sign Lighted ✓ Landscaped Entrance ✓ Wide Easy Access ✓ Wide All Weather Entry Roads.	Requires All of the following: 5 ✓ Superior Commercial Quality Sign Lighted ✓ Superior Landscaped Entrance ✓ Superior Paved Wide Easy Access ___ Superior Paved Wide Entry Roads	4	0	1	2	3	4	(5)	
Requires Both of the following 4 ✓ Management with Posted Daily office hrs. ___ Laundry (Enclosed)	Requires Both of the following: 5 ___ Management w/posted daily office hours and separate registration building or area ___ Superior Laundry (Commercial Quality Laundromat)	3	0	1	2	(3)	4	5	
Only a trace of non-professional finish acceptable. 12 RATIO OF 1:10 NON SEWER SITES PLUS 1:50 SEWER SITES	Full professional finish inside & out. 15 Ceramic tile floors, showers & 4 feet up the walls. Ceramic tile, Formica or Corian counters. Factory built partitions. (Certain quality equivalent materials acceptable as substitute for ceramic tile.) RATIO SAME AS LEVEL 4	12	0 (F)	2 W	4 (C)	6 (Cn)	(8) S	10 P	
			(circle Prof. Items) Indicates professional finish — F=floors; W=walls; C=ceilings; Cn=counters; S=showers; P=partitions						
4' x 6' Concrete pad sloped to flush inlet; self-closing cap, flushing water; if drinking water available, it must be at least 30' from dump. Regularly scheduled, daily, Management pump-out service acceptable substitute. 4	Same as Level 4, except must have easy access & be clearly signed. NOTE: Pump-out service is not an acceptable substitute at this level. 5	5	0	1	2	3	(4)	5	
50% of the sites must: 8 ✓ be level ✓ have easy access ✓ have picnic table (patio substitute) ✓ have shade and/or plantings and/or landscaping ✓ have surface preparation	**75% of the sites must:** 10 ✓ be level have easy access ✓ have picnic table (patio substitute) ✓ have shade and/or plantings and/or landscaping **100% of the sites must:** ✓ have surface preparation	8	0	1	2	3	4	(5)	
25% full hookups plus 25% electric & water hookups plus 25% electric plus adequate water taps. Logical hookup relationship. Will accept 2 RVs per full hookup cluster. Will accept 4 RVs per non-full hookup cluster. 8 ✓ *Minimum 20 amp* receptacles at all sites with electrical hookups.	50% *individual* full hookups plus 50% electric & water hookups with a water tap and electric stanchion for each 4 non-full hookup spaces. Logical hookup relationship. 10 ___ 30 amp receptacle at all full hookups AND ✓ 20 amp receptacle at all electrical hookups	8	0	1	2	3	(4)	5	
High-use roads are wide and All-Weather or paved. 4	All roads are wide and All-Weather or paved. 5	4	0	1	2	(3)	4	5	
Requires All of the following: 4 ___ grounds development Lighting at: ___ registration ___ restrooms ___ camping areas	Requires All of the following: 5 ✓ Extensive grounds development Lighting at: ✓ registration ✓ restrooms ✓ camping areas ✓ some activity areas	5	0	1	2	3	(4)	5	

Indoor Recreation (with 4 items) AND Swimming TOTAL REQUIREMENT 6 Major recreations					Indoor Recreation (with 6 items), Planned Group Activities AND Swimming TOTAL REQUIREMENT 10 Major recreations				
LOCAL TOURS	M	MN	NC	ITC		M	MN	NC	ITC
HIKING TRAILS	M	MN	NC	ITC		M	MN	NC	ITC
BASKETBALL	M	(MN)	NC	ITC		M	MN	NC	ITC
BADMINTON	M	(MN)	NC	ITC		M	MN	NC	ITC
VOLLEYBALL	M	(MN)	NC	ITC		M	MN	NC	ITC
SPORTS FIELD	M	MN	NC	ITC		M	MN	NC	ITC
	M	MN	NC	ITC		M	MN	NC	ITC
	M	MN	NC	ITC		M	MN	NC	ITC
	M	MN	NC	ITC		M	MN	NC	ITC
	M	MN	NC	ITC		M	MN	NC	ITC

49 FACILITIES TOTALS 36	
AREAS OF INTEREST	**MAINTENANCE**
	Delete 0-8
1W 12-21	1W 9-15
2W 22-33	2W 16-24
3W 34-45	3W 25-33
(4W 46-56)	(4W 34-42)
5W 57-60	5W 43-45
REC. LEVEL	**REC. MAINT.**
4	3

COMMENTS:

- The lower portion of the form is used to tally the recreation.
- Recreation items are assigned Major (M), Minor (MN) or No Count (NC) value based on the investment and/or quantity and/or usage of that recreation item at the park.
- The recreation items shown for the above park would result in a 3W Recreation Rating due to maintenance.
- The maintenance level at a Campground/RV Park must meet or exceed the recommended rating or the ratings cannot be assigned at that level.
- Remember: Ratings are recommended by WOODALL'S Rep Teams, and are approved (or declined) by the WOODALL Rating Committee.

Free Camping Information

✔ FREE INFORMATION

Use our Reader Service Card opposite page 48 /Discover Section as an easy way to write for FREE travel and camping information and more information about advertisers' products and services. This card also gives you the opportunity to be a part of WOODALL by sharing with us how far you travel, for how long, and in what type of unit so that we can better meet your needs.

✔ EXTENDED STAY GUIDE

When looking for a park in which to spend a month or an entire season, also refer to WOODALL'S Extended Stay Guide to RV Parks/Campgrounds (the yellow pages at the back of this directory).

Detailed listings include locator directions, facilities and recreation available on-site, and more, all verified through personal visits by WOODALL'S representatives.

Many facilities have purchased advertising in this section to tell you about its unique features, special rates, and nearby attractions. All ads are reader serviced, so you can obtain even more information, FREE!, direct from the parks.

✔ PERSONAL INSPECTIONS

And most important, WOODALL'S 28 Representative Teams spent over 5,000 days, traveling half a million miles to update our information by personal inspection. And as a result, our dependable WOODALL ratings for both facilities and recreation have been assigned to privately-operated campgrounds.

✔ TRAVEL SECTIONS

When planning your next trip be sure to refer to the travel sections located at the beginning of each state and province. You'll find helpful information on climate, topography, time zone, travel information sources, recreational information, places to see and things to do, and events.

✔ 100% MONEY BACK GUARANTEE

WOODALL has been publishing RV/camping guides, directories and magazines for over 70 years! We take pride in our efforts to provide you with the most complete, accurate and up-to-date Campground Directory available on the market. However, if for any reason you're not satisfied with this Directory, please return it to us by December 31, 2008, along with your sales receipt, and we will reimburse you for the amount you paid for the Directory. Also please share with us the reason for your dissatisfaction.

TYPES OF NON-RATED LISTINGS:

1. RV SPACES: Spaces reserved for overnight travelers as an adjunct to the main business operation. To be listed, there must be a minimum of 10 spaces for RV's; reasonable access for all units; water available; level, lighted area and evidence of maintenance.

2. TOO NEW TO RATE: These parks have been inspected by WOODALL and are fully operational, but before a rating is assigned, we want each park to have the opportunity to fully complete its development and maintenance regime.

3. UNDER CONSTRUCTION, PLANNED, REBUILDING, NOT VISITED: Please write or phone ahead when considering a stay at these parks to confirm their ability to accommodate you.

4. CAMP RESORT: Usually fewer than 10 spaces are available to non-members. Phone ahead for site availability and for more information about purchasing a site.

5. NUDIST RESORTS: WOODALL lists a few nudist and clothing-optional RV parks/campgrounds.

Do all parks qualify for a listing in WOODALL'S Campground Directory?

No, not all parks are listed. A campground must meet our standards for maintenance, access into the park, and have a minimum of 10 designated sites available for overnight camping. Parks that are deleted are re-visited after three years.

Why is a new WOODALL'S Campground Directory needed each year?

During each inspection season, our representative teams delete several hundred listings because they do not meet our minimum requirements and we think they wouldn't meet yours. Hundreds of new parks are added each year, too. And, each year over 178,000 changes are made to the listings from the previous edition involving changes in phone numbers, ratings, open and close dates, facilities and recreation available, park policy, and more—important reasons to ALWAYS use a current WOODALL'S Campground Directory.

We'd like to hear from you!

We are always glad to hear from you for any reason and we respond to all correspondence and phone calls, whether you have a suggestion, a compliment or a complaint. Your comments continue to help us improve our directory each year. There are several ways to get in touch with us, so pick the method most convenient to you:

- **Visit our Web Site at: www.woodalls.com**
- Phone us at: 877/680-6155
- Fax us at: 805/667-4468
- Write us at: WOODALL Publications Corporation
Woodall Correspondent
64 Inverness Dr. E.
Englewood, CO 80112

Every attempt is made to ensure that all phone numbers are correct. However, due to numerous changes in area codes throughout North America, your call might not go through. Please call Directory Assistance for more information.

Comment Utiliser ce Guide

L'organisation du guide WOODALL

Toutes les informations dans le **WOODALL'S CAMPGROUND DIRECTORY** sont classées par ordre alphabétique. Vous y trouverez en premier lieu les états américains, suivent les provinces canadiennes et, finalement, le Mexique. L'ordre alphabétique se maintient au niveau des états et provinces ainsi que des villes et, sous celles-ci, des inscriptions des établissements tels que terrains de camping, centres de service de véhicules récréatifs et attractions touristiques. Chaque nom de ville est suivi d'une lettre et d'un chiffre (ex: A-1) vous permettant de situer la ville que vous recherchez sur la carte géographique au début de chaque état et province.

L'édition Nord-Américaine est divisée en deux sections: Est et Ouest. Chacune de ces sections est aussi classée par ordre alphabétique en débutant par l'Alabama à l'Est et par l'Alaska à l'Ouest. L'index "WOODALL'S ALPHABETICAL QUICK REFERENCE" que vous retrouverez à la fin de chaque section fournit le nom des terrains de camping, des services et locations d'équipements ainsi que des attractions touristiques. Cet index facilite les recherches si vous connaissez le nom de l'établissement mais non la ville où il est situé. Dans cet index, le symbole ® signifie location de véhicules récréatifs; Δ location de tentes; □ location de chalets; ★ centre de services; • attractions touristiques. Vous y trouverez aussi la référence vous permettant de repérer la ville sur la carte.

Chaque état et province, ainsi que le Mexique, débute par une carte géographique et des informations pertinentes à la région. Sur la carte, les villes où sont localisés les terrains de camping sont identifiées par le losange ◈; les attractions touristiques par le drapeau ⚑ et les centres de services pour véhicules récréatifs par un ✵ . Ces cartes doivent être utilisées en complément des cartes routières officielles. Nous vous invitons à consulter les listes d'attractions touristiques et de points d'intérêt lorsque vous planifiez votre voyage.

Les représentants WOODALL effectuent des inspections annuelles

Tous les terrains de camping privés répertoriés dans ce guide sont inspectés chaque année par une équipe WOODALL.

Ces équipes comptent déjà de nombreuses années d'expérience en camping et véhicules récréatifs avant de joindre WOODALL. En plus d'être familiers avec le territoire qui leur est assigné, ils reçoivent une formation initiale intensive à laquelle vient s'ajouter une formation annuelle. Le rapport détaillé recueilli à chaque inspection complète les informations nécessaires au classement recommandé par WOODALL. Le répertoire des terrains de camping privés de ce présent guide est établi à la suite des inspections faites au printemps et à l'été 2007. En complément aux informations recueillies pour chaque terrain de camping, les représentants complètent une formule d'évaluation (exemple en pages 148 et 149) permettant d'attribuer la cote d'évaluation de WOODALL.

Les représentants WOODALL visitent aussi les centres de service de véhicules récréatifs et les attractions touristiques d'importance dont la liste s'ajoute à celle des terrains de camping.

Le répertoire des terrains de camping publics (fédéraux, provinciaux, municipaux et militaires) d'informations de public.

Le système d'évaluation jumelée de WOODALL

Les cotes d'évaluation vous aident à choisir le terrain de camping que vous recherchez.

WOODALL fixe deux cotes d'évaluation à chacue terrain de camping privé. Le système d'évaluation exclusif à WOODALL est expliqué en pages 148 et 149 à l'aide de la formule dont se servent les représentants sur le terrain. La première cote tient compte des caractéristiques de chaque terrain de camping (ex: sites, routes, toilettes, eau, égouts, électricité, etc.). La seconde cote évalue les services récréatifs. Les deux cotes vont de 1◈ à 5◈. Le ◈ est un symbole exclusif à WOODALL. La cote finale tient compte du degré d'entretien que présente le terrain de camping.

Que signifient les cotes d'évaluation WOODALL?

Les cotes dépendent non seulement des caractéristiques d'un terrain de camping donné, mais aussi du degré d'entretien qui lui est consacré. Mieux un terrain de camping est coté, non seulement plus nombreuses sont ses caractéristiques mais aussi en meilleur état d'entretien. En vue de vous assurer une satisfaction complète, à vous et à votre famille, WOODALL porte une attention particulière à la propreté et en tient compte dans sa cote d'évaluation. Le niveau d'entretien et de propreté doit être supérieur, du moins égal à la cote des caractéristiques sinon la cote générale devient celle de l'entretien.

Plusieurs ◈ indiquent-ils un meilleur terrain de camping?

Définitivement NON! Tous les terrains de camping répertoriés dans le Guide WOODALL rencontrent les normes minimales de WOODALL; cependant la cote d'évaluation ne permet pas de déterminer si un terrain de camping est bien, très bien ou excellent. Chaque campeur doit fixer son choix selon les caractéristiques énumérées dans le Guide. Plusieurs facteurs entrent alors en ligne de compte: la description des sites, la proximité d'une autoroute, d'attractions touristique, une piscine, un lac, etc. Assurez-vous de bien saisir le système de cotation exclusif à WOODALL'S; il facilitera votre choix et assurera votre satisfaction. Et ne manquez surtout pas de mentionner lors de votre inscription que vous avez fait votre choix à l'aide des informations contenues dans le Guide WOODALL.

WELCOME

Encouragez Nos Annoneurs

L'inscription dans le Guide WOODALL est offerte sans frais aux propriétaires de terrains de camping qui rencontrent les normes minimales de WOODALL. Les propriétaires qui désirent faire mieux connaître leur terrain le font à l'aide d'annonces publiées dans nos pages. Cette publicité additionnelle est destinée à vous seconder dans votre choix en mettant l'accent sur des particularités dont ils sont fiers. Si c'est le cas, n'oubliez pas d'aviser les propriétaires que vous avez fait votre choix à l'aide de leur publicité.

Comment Utiliser Ce Guide

Nous sommes à l'écoute de nos lecteurs. Basée sur les commentaires et les suggestions que vous nous avez soumis, voici une description des éléments contenus dans une inscription. Ces éléments sont ceux que vous jugez importants.

26 **PEACEFUL VALLEY – A-2** 17

(NW) CAREFREE CAMPING RV PARK—(DuPage) 20

1 WELCOME *From jct I-94 (exit 24) & Hwy 120: Go 1/2 mi N on Golden Eagle Rd, then 4 mi W on Hwy 80, then 1 mi N on Carefree Rd. Enter on R.* 15

JUST LIKE NEW!
We've completely renovated our park for this season! Come relax in our new swimming pool or take advantage of our deluxe new bathhouses. Don't miss our annual festivities such as Christmas in July & end-of-season pig roast. 25

2 ♦♦♦♦♦ FACILITIES: 320 sites, typical site width 40 ft, 175 full hkups, 100 W & E, 25 E, (20, 30 & 50 amps), 50 amps ($), 20 no hkups, some extended stay sites, 50 pull-thrus, heater not allowed, cable TV, wireless Instant Internet access at site ($), phone/cable on-site Internet access (needs activ), cable Internet access central location, tenting, RV/park trailer rentals, cabins, dump station, non-guest dumping ($), laundry, groceries, LP gas by weight/meter, LP bottle exch.,ice, tables, wood. 18 4 19 14 23

5 ♦♦♦♦♦ RECREATION: rec hall, equipped pavilion, coin games, 2 swim pools, wading pool, lake swimming, whirlpool, boating, 10 motorboat rentals, lake fishing, fishing supplies, mini-golf ($), 25 bike rentals, playground, planned activities, tennis, hiking trails, local tours. 3 24

11 Pets welcome, breed restr, size restr, quantity restr ($). 16
6 Partial handicap access. Escort to site. Open all year. 13
12 Big rigs welcome. Internet friendly. Clubs welcome.
7 Rate in 2007 $18.50-23.50 per family. 9
21 MC/VISA/DISC/AMEX. ATM. Member of ARVC. Phone: (999)555-6200. FCRV 10% discount. FMCA discount. 10
8 e-mail: cmpn@carefree.com 22
SEE AD THIS PAGE

1. LE LOSANGE WELCOME:
Le losange WELCOME devant une inscription indique que le propriétaire de ce terrain de camping dispose d'une annonce publicitaire pour vous offrir des renseignements supplémentaires à propos de son terrain.

2. CARACTÉRISTIQUES:
Évaluées et cotées de 1à 5 ♦.Toutes les caractéristiques énumérées dans l'inscription sont offertes sur ce terrain de camping.

3. ACCES PARTIEL AUX HANDICAPÉS:
Indique que le terrain présente certains éléments pouvant accommoder les personnes avec des incapacités physiques. Soit des douches avec bancs et rampes murales, des lavabos et toilettes donnant accès aux chaises roulantes, des portes admettant des chaises roulantes, des trottoirs avec rampes, signalisation en Braille. Pour en connaître davantage, informez-vous avant votre départ.

4. LOCATION DE TENTE, DE VÉHICULE RÉCRÉATIF ET DE CHALET:
Vous pouvez louer une tente, un véhicule récréatif ou un chalet à ce terrain de camping.

5. ACTIVITÉS RÉCRÉATIVES:
Évaluées et cotées de 1à 5♦,Toutes ces activités récréatives sont offertes sur ce terrain de camping.

6. CONCERNANT LES TARIFS:
Les tarifs indiquent les prix minimum et maximum au cours de la saison précédente, en vigueur lors de l'inspection par les représentants WOODALL. Ces tarifs sont sujets à changement.

7. AFFILIATIONS:
Identifie les associations que patronise ce terrain de camping.

8. PUBLICITÉ ADDITIONNELLE:
Vous réfère à la page où paraît l'annonce publicitaire.

9. NUMÉRO DE TÉLÉPHONE:
Ce numéro de téléphone vous servira à réserver votre site.

10. RABAIS:
Rabais offerts aux membres d'organismes particuliers.

11. INFORMATIONS SPÉCIFIQUES:
Restrictions telles qu'animaux interdits, motocyclistes interdits, âge minimum, dates d'ouverture, etc. Si la mention NO PETS n'apparaît pas, les animaux sont acceptés. Cependant, si vous possédez un animal domestique peu commun il vous serait préférable de vous informer au préalable.

12. GRANDS VÉHICULES ACCEPTÉS:
Si le terrain de camping est en mesure d'accueillir les grands véhicules récréatifs l'inscription l'indique. Les principaux facteurs pris en considération sont: la largeur et la longueur des sites, le dégagement vertical, l'ampérage, les routes d'accès et l'accès aux sites.

13. BIENVENUE AUX CLUBS:
Cette mention indique que le terrain accueille des clubs et des caravanes.

14. BIENVENUE AUX TENTES:
Cette mention indique que le terrain accepte les tentes. Ces campeurs sont acceptés dans la plupart des terrains, cependant si un terrain ne les accepte pas la mention NO TENTS ou ACCEPTS FULL HOOKUP UNITS ONLY paraîtra dans les informations spécifiques.

15. DIRECTIONS POUR S'Y RENDRE:
Des informations faciles et détaillées vous conduiront au terrain.

16. INTERNET FRIENDLY:
Si le Parc offre, a votre arrivee, un acces a internet sans fil ou un modem (avec ligne independante, un espace amenage et heures accessibles) nous designons ce Parc comme Internet Friendly.

17. POINT DE RÉFÉRENCE:
Vous permet de situer la ville sur la carte géographique de l'état ou de la province.

18. LONGUEUR ET LARGEUR DES SITES:
La dimension des sites varie d'un parc à l'autre. Vous trouverez ici les dimensions les plus communes de ce terrain. Si la longueur du site est inférieure à 40 pieds elle sera précisée. L'on a tenucompte de l'habileté d'un conducteur moyen.

19. L'INTERNET::
De plus en plus de VR'S veulent utiliser leur courriel ainsi que internet. Maintenant plusieurs Parcs offrent ce service directement a votre emplacement / ou a un endroit central, qui est normalement situe a l'Office ou dans la Salle Communautaire nous designons ce Parc comme "*Instant Internet access.*" Aussi un autre service, directement a votre emplacement, peut etre offert dans ce Parc mais vous devrez activer la ligne telephonique en vous abonnant au service local de la Compagnie de telephone; ceci est surtout pour ceux qui veulent y resider a long terme.

20. COMTÉS:
Le nom du comté dans lequel le parc est situé apparaît entre parenthèses. Aux États-Unis, le nom des comtés est utilisé lors d'alertes.

21. CARTES DE CRÉDIT:
MC=MasterCard;
VISA;
DISC=Discover;
DC=Diner's Club;
AMEX=American Express;
ATM=Automated Teller Machine.
Debit=Debit Card

22. COURRIER ÉLECTRONIQUE:
Si c'est le cas, l'adresse e-mail du terrain.

23. VIDANGE DES RÉSERVOIRS D'ÉGOUT:
Si le terrain accepte les voyageurs non clients ou non et s'il y a des frais ($) pour ce service

24. ESCORTER AU SITÉ:
Ceci vous indique que la Direction vous reconduit a votre emplacement designe pour votre VR.

25. L'INFORMATION SPECIALE:
Nouveau dans notre édition 2006 est l'information fournie par les propriétaires de Parc qui veulent vous informer des caractéristiques et des offres spéciales à leur Parc. Ces messages individualisés sont surlignés en 'jaune' et vous donnent des détails supplémentaires qui ne se retrouvent pas dans les informations régulières.

26. LOCALISATEUR DE LA DIRECTION:
L'abréviation avant la facilite indique la position de cette facilite versus la direction de la Ville. Par exemple, "(NW)" veut dire que cette facilite est situee au Nord-ouest de la ville ou est son inscription; "(C)" signifie le centre de la ville.

Special Notes

Toilettes? Douches?

• À moins d'indication contraire, tous les terrains de camping énumérés sont munis de toilettes à l'eau courante et de douches à l'eau chaude. Si les douches sont payantes, l'inscription "shower$" le précise.

Sites saisonniers

Plusieurs Parcs peuvent offrir des emplacements pour saisonniers ou ceux qui desirent prolonger leur sejour. Si le Parc a moins de 10% de son occupation en saisonnier cela ne sera pas mentionner dans la description de nos Guides. S'il y a entre 10% et 49% la mention se lira comme suit "some extended stay sites." S'il y a entre 50% et 74% la mention se lira comme suit "many extended stay sites." S'il y a entre 75% et 99% la mention se lira comme suit "mostly extended stay sites."

Restriction d'age

• La mention "Age Restrictions May Apply" paraîtra si le terrain en question n'offre pas des services qu'aux personnes d'un certain âge. Ces restrictions étant sujettes à certaines législations, nous vous recommandons donc de vérifier auprès des responsables.

LES CARACTÉRISTIQUES SPÉCIALES

✔ INFORMATION GRATUITE

Pour obtenir de l'information supplémentaire sur les produits et services offerts dans ce guide, il vous suffit d'utiliser notre carte "READER SERVICE CARD" de la page 48. De plus, cette carte vous offre l'opportunité de partager, avec WOODALL'S, vos informations voyage telle que la durée de votre voyage, la distance parcourue, le genre de véhicule récréatif que vous utilisez. Tous ces renseignements nous permettent de mieux répondre à vos besoins.

✔ LES SECTIONS VOYAGE

Lors de la planification de votre prochain voyage, consultez la section voyage située au début de tous les états et provinces. Vous y trouverez des informations, concernant la région que vous désirez visiter, sur le climat, la topographie, les fuseaux horaires, les bureaux d'informations touristiques, les attractions et points d'intérêt, etc.

LES RAISONS POUR LESQUELLES CERTAINS TERRAINS DE CAMPING NE SONT PAS ÉVALUÉS ET INSCRITS.

1. ESPACES POUR VÉHICULES RÉCRÉATIFS: Les terrains de camping doivent offrir un minimum de 10 sites disponibles pour les voyageurs d'un soir, tel qu'indiqué plus haut, pour être inscrits. De plus, ils doivent offrir une facilité d'accès pour tous types de véhicules récréatifs, une disponibilité d'eau, des sites bien éclairés mais surtout propres et bien entretenus.

2. SITES TROP RÉCENTS POUR ÊTRE ÉVALUÉS: Ces terrains ont été inspectés par nos représentants et sont entièrement opérationnels mais, avant de leur attribuer une cote, nous désirons leur laisser l'opportunité de compléter leur développement.

3. TERRAINS EN CONSTRUCTION, EN RÉNOVATION OU NON-VISITÉS: S'il-vous-plaît, veuillez communiquer avec ces terrain pour vous assurer qu'ils sont en mesure de vous accueillir.

4. RESORT: Habituellement, ces terrains de camping comptent moins de 10 sites disponibles pour les non-membres. Veuillez communiquer avec les responsables du terrain pour vous assurer qu'ils sont en mesure de vous accueillir.

5. PARC NATURISTE: WOODALL'S inscrit quelques-uns de ces terrains de camping dans le guide.

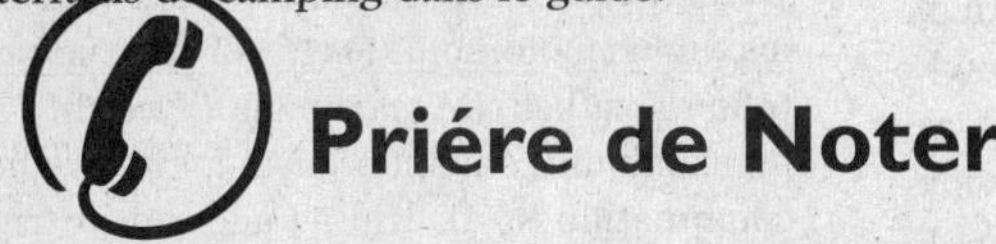

Priére de Noter

Nous tentons de nous assurer que les numéros de téléphone inscrits sont exacts. Cependant, dû aux changements de codes régionaux en Amérique du Nord, votre appel peut ne pas être acheminé. Si cela se produit, demandez l'aide des téléphonistes.

Quand vous regardez pour un Parc ou vous voudriez sejourner un mois ou une saison entiere, vous pourrez vous referer dans la section du Guide de WOODALL'S Extended Stay (les pages jaune qui se trouve a la fin de nos Guides).

Les details qui vous y retrouverez comprendront: la direction, les facilites, les recreations et un peu plus; que nos Representants auront verifies personnellement lors de leur inspection.

Certains Parcs ont voulu se demarquer en placant une publicite qui leur permet de vous donner encore plus de details comme: leur offre speciale, leur tarif, les attractions dans les environs et plus encore. Ils benificient aussi du service du "reader's service" qui vous est offert "GRATUITEMENT" en vous permettant d'obtenir plus amples informations.

✔ INSPECTIONS PERSONNALISÉES

Et, le plus important, 28 représentants dévoués de WOODALL'S parcourent plus d'un demi million de milles pendant près de 5 000 jours dans le but de mettre à jour les informations contenues dans ce guide. Suite à leurs inspections personnalisées, les cotes sont émises pour chacun des terrains de camping privés, autant pour les facilités que les activités offertes.

✔ SATISFACTION GARANTIE OU ARGENT REMIS

¡WOODALL'S publie ce guide plus de 70 ans! Nous sommes fiers de vous procurer un guide des plus complets et mis à jour annuellement. Toutefois, si, pour quelques raisons que ce soit, vous n'êtes pas satisfait de ce guide, veuillez nous le retourner avant le 31 Décembre 2007 avec votre reçu d'achat et nous vous rembourserons. Veuillez, s'il-vous-plaît, nous faire part de la raison de votre insatisfaction.

Est-ce que tous les terrains de camping sont inscrits dans le guide WOODALL'S ?

Non, ce ne sont pas tous les terrains de camping qui sont inscrits. Un terrain doit rencontrer les standards établis par WOODALL'S pour l'entretien du terrain, l'accès au terrain et aux sites et doit offrir un minimum de 10 sites disponibles pour les voyageurs d'un soir afin d'être inscrit dans le guide. Les terrains de camping non-inscrits sont revisités après 3 ans.

Pour quelles raisons WOODALL'S publie un guide à chaque années?

Lors de leur inspection annuelle, nos équipes de représentants suppriment plusieurs centaines d'inscriptions parce qu'elles ne répondent plus à nos standards minimums établis. De plus, des centaines de terrains de camping se rajoutent à chaque année. Ainsi, plus de 178,000 changements sont apportés aux inscriptions de l'édition précédente que ce soit pour les prix, les numéros de téléphone, les dates d'ouverture et de fermeture, les facilités offertes et plus encore. Voici quelques-unes des raisons d'utiliser un guide WOODALL'S actualisé.

Nous voulons connaître votre opinion!

Nous sommes toujours heureux de recevoir vos commentaires, que ce soit une plainte, un compliment ou une suggestion. Utilisez le formulaire fourni à la fin du guide pour nous faire part de vos commentaires; ils nous permettent d'améliorer le guide. Vous pouvez aussi visiter notre site internet à **www.woodalls.com**

Téléphone: (877) 680-6155 Fax: (805) 667-4468

Écrivez-nous à: WOODALL Publications Corporation
Woodall Correspondent
64 Inverness Dr. E.
Englewood, CO 80112, USA

RULES of the ROAD

The following **Rules of the Road** are compiled each year via mailings to state/provincial highway departments and/or police departments. Some changes may have been made since this data was compiled. For additional regulations not addressed in this section, we suggest that you contact the state or provincial agency listed. While every attempt has been made to check this information, the *Woodall's Campground Directory* cannot guarantee its accuracy, and assumes no responsibility for errors and omissions.

ALABAMA: Maximum RV width 102 in.; maximum motorhome length 45 ft.; maximum trailer length 40 ft.; maximum RV height 13.5 ft.; maximum combined length of two vehicles 65 ft. Triple towing is not allowed. Riding allowed in truck campers. Overnight parking in rest areas permitted where posted. **RV Safety Requirements:** At 3,000 lbs.: trailer brakes, flares and breakaway switch. **Driving Laws:** Wipers on/headlights on. Right turn on red permitted unless posted otherwise. All front-seat occupants must use seat belts; children under age 3 must be in child-restraint safety seats; ages 3-6 must wear seat belts. **More Information**: Department of Public Safety, RSA Criminal Justice Center, Bldg. C, 5th Fl., Suite C5-15, 301 S. Ripley St., Montgomery, AL 31604. Emergency number: (334) 242-4395 *HP or *47 on cellular phones.

ALASKA: Maximum RV width 102 in.; maximum motorhome length 45 ft.; maximum trailer length 40 ft.; maximum length of two-vehicle combination 75 ft. Overnight parking in rest areas allowed, unless posted. **RV Safety Requirements:** All RVs: flares or reflective signs, fire extinguisher and gas detector. Over 3,000 lbs.: trailer brakes, breakaway switch and safety chains. **Driving Laws:** Headlight use required on designated highways. Right turn on red permitted, unless posted otherwise. All passengers must wear seat belts; child-restraint safety seats are required for children up to age 4. **More Information:** Alaska State Troopers, 5700 E. Tudor, Anchorage AK 99507. Emergency number: 911, or *273 on cellular phones.

ARIZONA: Maximum RV width 102 in.(some exceptions); maximum motorhome length 45 ft.; maximum trailer length 40 ft.; maximum RV height 13.5 ft.; maximum combined length for two vehicles 65 ft. Triple-towing allowed w/fifth wheel. Riding permitted in travel trailers, fifth-wheel trailers and truck campers. Overnight parking in rest areas allowed unless posted. **RV Safety Requirements:** Over 3,000 lbs.: trailer brakes, breakaway switch and safety chains. **Driving Laws:** Right turn on red permitted, unless posted otherwise. Children under 5 years must be in child-restraint safety seats. **More Information:** Arizona Dept.of Public Safety, Box 6638, Phoenix AZ 85005; (602) 223-2000. Emergency number: 911.

ARKANSAS: Maximum RV width 102 in.; maximum motorhome length 45 ft.; maximum length for single towed trailer 43.5 ft.; maximum length for two-vehicle combination 65 ft. Overnight parking in rest areas allowed unless posted. **RV Safety Requirements:** 3,000 lbs.: trailer brakes, breakaway switches and safety chains. **Driving Laws:** Wipers on/headlights on. Right turn on red permitted unless posted otherwise. **More Information:** Arkansas State Highway and Transportation Department., P.O. Box 2261, Little Rock AR 72203. Emergency number: 911 (in some counties) or *55 on cellular phones.

CALIFORNIA: Maximum RV width 102 in.; maximum motorhome length 40 ft.(45 ft. on some highways); maximum trailer length 40 ft.; maximum RV height 14 ft.; maximum combined length for two-vehicle combination, 65 ft. Riding is allowed in truck campers if passengers are seat-belted; in fifth-wheel trailers with safety glass and an audible or visual device connected with tow vehicle, plus at least one exit must be able to be opened from both outside and inside the trailer. Vehicles towing trailers or dinghies are restricted to the right-hand lane. Overnight parking in rest areas not allowed. **RV Safety Requirements:** Over 1,500 lbs.: trailer brakes, breakaway switch and safety chains. All power-brake systems require breakaway switch. Chains may be required during winter months on mountain roads. **Driving Laws:** Right turn on red permitted, unless posted otherwise (but not on red arrow). At least two/three riders for carpool lane as posted. **More Information:** California Highway Patrol, 444 N. 3rd St., Suite 310, Sacramento CA 95814; (916) 445-1865. www.dot.ca.gov/hq/traffopr/trucks/bus-mh/bus-map.html. Emergency number: 911.

COLORADO: Maximum RV width 102 in.; maximum motor- home length 45 ft.; maxi mum trailer length not specified; maximum RV height 13 ft.; maximum length of two- or three vehicle combination 70 ft. Riding in truck campers allowed; in fifth-wheels allowed bu not recommended. Overnight parking in res areas permitted unless posted otherwise. Al towed vehicles must stop at ports of entry (only commercial vehicles are required to stop a ports of entry). **RV Safety Requirements** Chains or snow tires required when posted Trailers over 3,000 lbs. require trailer brakes and breakaway switch. **Driving Laws:** At leas two riders required for carpool lane. Firearms may be transported loaded or unloaded anywhere in a vehicle except on one's person **More Information:** Colorado State Patrol, 70 Kipling St., Suite 2000, Denver CO 80215 (303) 239-4540. Emergency number: 911 *CSP or *277 o cellular phones.

CONNECTICUT: Maximum RV width 10 in.; maximum motorhome length 45 ft.; maxi mum trailer length not specified; maximum R height 13.5 ft.; maximum combined length fo two vehicles 60 ft. RVs are not allowed in ca pool lanes. Riding allowed in truck campers Overnight parking in rest areas is permitted unless posted. **RV Safety Requirements** Over 3,000 lbs.: safety chains, breakaway switch and trailer brakes. **Driving Laws** Wipers on/headlights on. Right turn on re allowed unless posted otherwise. Front-sea passengers are required to wear seat belts **More Information:** Department. of Moto Vehicles, 60 State St., Wethersfield CT 06161 Emergency number: 911.

DELAWARE: Maximum RV width 102 in. maximum motorhome length 45 ft.; maximum trailer length 40 ft.; maximum RV height 13. ft.; maximum combined length for two-vehicle combination 65 ft. Riding allowed in truck campers. Overnight parking in rest areas allowed where posted. **RV Safety Requirements:** Over 4,000 lbs.: trailer brakes and safety chains. **Driving Laws:** Wipers on/headlights on. Right turn on red allowed unless posted otherwise. Front-seat passengers and all passengers under 16 years are required to wear seat belts. **More Information:** Delaware State Police, P.O. Box 430, Dover DE 19903; (302) 378-5230. Emergency number: 911 or *77 on cellular phones.

DISTRICT OF COLUMBIA: Maximum RV width 96 in.; maximum motorhome length 40 ft.; maximum trailer length not specified; maximum RV height 13.5 ft.; maximum length of two- or three-vehicle combination 55 ft. Riding allowed in truck campers. Overnight parking in rest areas is not allowed. **RV Safety Requirements:** Trailers over 3,000 lbs.: safety chain, breakaway switch, trailer brakes. Emergency number: (202) 727-6161

FLORIDA: Maximum RV width 102 in.; maximum motorhome length 45 ft.; maximum trailer length 40 ft.; maximum RV height 13.5 ft.; maximum combined length for two vehicles 65 ft. Triple towing is illegal. Riding allowed in truck campers. **RV Safety Requirements:** Trailers over 3,000 lbs.: trailer brakes, breakaway switch and safety chains. **Driving Laws:** Wipers on/headlights on. Right turn on red allowed unless posted otherwise. At least two riders for carpool lanes. **More Information:** Florida Highway Patrol, Office of Public Affairs, Room A425, MS44, 2900 Apalachee Pkwy., Tallahassee FL 32399-0553; (850) 617-2381. Emergency number: 911 or *FHP or *347 on cellular phones.

GEORGIA: Maximum RV width 102 in.; maximum motorhome length 45 ft.; maximum trailer length not specified; maximum RV height 13.5 ft.; maximum length for two-vehicle combination 60 ft. Riding allowed in truck campers. Overnight parking in rest areas is not allowed. **RV Safety Requirements:** One mirror required on all RVs. Over 1,500 lbs.: trailer brakes and safety chain. **More Information:** Department of Transportation, Commissioner, 2 Capitol Sq., Atlanta GA 30334. Emergency number: (404) 656-5267, or *GSP on cellular phones.

HAWAII: Maximum RV width 108 in. for both single unit motor vehicles and trailers; maximum height is 14 ft.; maximum single unit motor vehicle length is 45 ft.; maximum trailer length is 48 ft.; maximum combined length for two vehicles is 65 ft.; No triples allowed. Overnight parking in rest areas is not allowed. **RV Safety Requirements:** safety chains. Over 3,000 lbs.: trailer brakes. **Driving Laws**: Right turn on red allowed unless posted otherwise. At least two riders for carpool lanes, three riders for zipper lane. **More Information:** Public Information Office, 869 Punchbowl St., Honolulu, HI, 96813. Emergency number: 911, or *273 on cellular phones.

IDAHO: Maximum RV width 102 in.; maximum motorhome length 45 ft.; maximum trailer length 48 ft.; maximum RV height 14 ft.; maximum combined length for two- or three-vehicle combination 75 ft. Riding is allowed in truck campers. Overnight parking in rest areas is permitted where posted. **RV Safety Requirements:** Over 1,500 lbs.: trailer brakes, breakaway switch and safety chains. **Driving Laws:** Right turn on red is allowed unless posted otherwise. **More Information:** Idaho Transportation Department, P.O. Box 7129, Boise ID 82707-1129. Emergency number: *ISP or *477 on cellular phones.

ILLINOIS: Maximum RV width 102 in. (some roads 96 in.); maximum motorhome length 45 ft.; maximum trailer length 53 ft.; maximum RV height 13.5 ft.; maximum combined length of two- or three-vehicle combination (with fifth-wheel trailer only) 60 ft. Riding is allowed in truck campers. Overnight parking in rest areas only where designated. **RV Safety Requirements:** Safety chains and flares required on all trailers. Trailers over 3,000 lbs.: trailer brakes. Over 5,000 lbs.: brakes on all axles and breakaway switch. **Driving Laws:** Wipers on/headlights on. Right turn on red allowed unless posted otherwise. **More Information:** Illinois State Police Commercial Vehicle Team, 500 Iles Park, Suite 400, Springfield IL 62718; (217) 782-7820. Emergency number: 911 or (217) 786-6677; *999 on cellular phones.

INDIANA: Maximum RV width 102 in.; maximum motorhome length 45 ft.; maximum trailer length 40 ft.; maximum RV height 13.6 ft.; maximum combined length of two-vehicle combination 60 ft.; three-vehicle combination 65 ft. Riding allowed in truck campers, travel trailers and fifth-wheel trailers. Overnight parking in rest areas is not allowed. **RV Safety Requirements:** Trailers over 3,000 lbs.: trailer brakes, breakaway switch and safety chains. **Driving Laws:** Right turn on red allowed if posted. Wipers on/lights on recommended. Mobile police scanners not permitted. **More Information:** Indiana State Police, Commercial Vehicle Enforcement Div., 5252 Decatur Blvd., Suite J, Indianapolis IN 46241; (317) 615-7373 or (800) 523-2261. Emergency number: 911.

IOWA: Maximum RV width 102 in.; maximum motorhome length 45 ft.; maximum trailer length not specified; maximum RV height 13.5 ft.; maximum combined length for two-vehicle combinations 65 ft.; or three-vehicle combinations 70 ft. Riding allowed in truck campers, legal but not recommended in fifth-wheel trailers and travel trailers. Overnight parking allowed if posted. **RV Safety Requirements**: Over 3,000 lbs.: trailer brakes and safety chains. **Driving Laws:** Right turn on red allowed, unless posted otherwise. **More Information:** Iowa Department of Transportation Motor Vehicle Enforcement, P.O. Box 10473, Des Moines IA 50306-0473; (515) 237-3156. Emergency number: 911 or *55 on cellular phones.

KANSAS: Maximum RV width 108 in.; maximum motorhome length 45 ft; maximum RV height 14 ft.; maximum combined length of two- or three-vehicle combination 65 ft. Riding allowed in truck campers and trailers if 14 yrs. or older. Overnight parking in rest areas allowed in designated areas only. **RV Safety Requirements:** All trailers: safety chains. **Driving Laws:** Right turn on red is allowed, unless posted otherwise. **More Information:** Kansas Highway Patrol, 122 SW 7th, Topeka KS 66603; (785) 296-6800. Emergency number: 911, *KTA or *47 on cellular phones.

KENTUCKY: Maximum RV width is 102 in. on any public State maintained highway; maximum RV height is 13 ft 6 inches; Maximum length of two or three vehicle combinations is 65 ft. (RV, motorhome, travel trailer, camping trailer, truck camper). **RV Safety Requirements:** Trailer brakes must be sufficient to stop within legal distance of 40 ft. at 20 mph. **Driving Laws:** Wipers on/headlights on. **More Information:** Kentucky Transportation Cabinet, 200 Mero St., Division of Motor Carriers, 2nd floor, Frankfort KY 40622; (502) 564-4540. Emergency number: 911.

LOUISIANA: Maximum RV width 102 in. (on federal road systems; 96 in. elsewhere); maximum motorhome length 45 ft.; maximum trailer length 40 ft.; maximum length of two- or three-vehicle combination 70 ft. Riding allowed in truck campers. Overnight parking in rest areas is prohibited unless posted otherwise. **RV Safety Requirements:** Over 3,000 lbs.: trailer brakes, breakaway switch. **Driving Laws:** Right turn on red is allowed, unless posted otherwise. Wipers on/lights on. **More Information:** Louisiana State Police, 265 South Foster Dr., Baton Rouge LA 70806; (225) 925-4239. Emergency number: 911 (in metropolitan areas only); *ISP or *911 on cellular phones.

MAINE: Maximum RV width 102 in.; maximum motorhome length 45 ft.; maximum trailer length 48 ft.; maximum RV height 13.5 ft.; maximum combined length for two vehicles 65 ft.; triple-towing not allowed. Riding allowed in truck campers. Overnight parking in rest areas is not allowed. **RV Safety Requirements:** All trailers: 1/4-in. safety chains. Over 3,000 lbs.: brakes on all axles. **Driving Laws:** Right turn on red is allowed, unless posted otherwise. Wipers on/headlights on. **More Information:** Maine State Police, Station 20, Augusta ME 04333; (207) 624-7000. Emergency number: *77 on cellular phones.

MARYLAND: Maximum RV width 102 in.; maximum motorhome length 40 ft; maximum trailer length 40 ft.; maximum RV height 13.6 ft.; maximum combined length for two vehicles 55 ft.; triple-towing allowed unless overall length exceeds 55 feet. Riding allowed in truck campers. Overnight parking in rest areas allowed unless posted otherwise. **RV Safety Requirements:** Over 3,000 lbs.: trailer brakes, breakaway switch and safety chains required. Tunnel Regulations: Trailer hitch must be reinforced or braced to frame of towing vehicle. Safety chains must be attached to frame of towing vehicle and not to pintle hook. No propane tanks in tunnels. **Driving Laws:** Wipers on/headlights on. Right turn on red allowed, unless posted otherwise. At least two riders for carpool lane. **More Information:** State Highway Administration, Motor Carrier Division, 7491 Connelley Dr., Hanover MD 21076. Emergency number: 911; *SP or *77 on cellular phones.

MASSACHUSETTS: Maximum RV width 102 in.; maximum motorhome length 45 ft.; maximum trailer length 40 ft.; maximum RV height 13.5 ft.; maximum two-vehicle combined length 60 ft. Riding is allowed in truck campers. Overnight parking is allowed in rest areas unless posted otherwise. **RV Safety Requirements:** Trailer brakes, chains and wheel chocks. No propane allowed in tunnels (in Boston, I-90, I-93, Rt. 1A; in Newton, I-90). **Driving Laws:** Right turn on red allowed unless posted otherwise. At least two riders for carpool lane. **More Information:** Massachusetts State Police, 760 Elm St., Concord MA 01742; (978) 369-1004. Emergency number: (508) 820-2121; *SP or *77 on cellular phones.

MICHIGAN: Maximum RV width 102 in.; maximum motorhome length 45 ft.; maximum RV height 13.5 ft.; maximum combined length for two-vehicle combination 65 ft.; pickup with fifth-wheel trailer 65 ft. Riding in travel trailers, fifth-wheel trailers and truck campers allowed. Overnight parking in rest areas is not allowed. **RV Safety Requirements:** All trailers: two chains of sufficient strength are required when towing. Over 3,000 lbs.: trailer brakes. **Driving Laws:** Right turn on red allowed, unless otherwise posted. Mobile police scanners not allowed. **More Information:** Michigan State Police, Special Operations Division, Traffic Services Section, 714 Harrison Rd., East Lansing MI 48823; (517) 336-6660. Emergency number: 911.

MINNESOTA: Maximum RV width 102 in.; maximum motorhome length 45 ft; maximum trailer length 45 ft; maximum RV height 13.5 ft.; maximum lengths for two/three combination 75/70 ft. (Three-vehicle combo must be a fifth-wheel trailer, maximum length 28 ft. + watercraft, ATV, motorcycle or snowmobile). Riding allowed in travel trailers, fifth-wheel trailers and truck campers. **RV Safety Requirements:** Over 3,000 lbs.: trailer brakes, two safety chains, glass mirror and hitch to safety stands. Over 6,000 lbs.: breakaway switch also. **Driving Laws:** Headlights on during rain, sleet, snow or hail. Right turn on red is allowed, unless posted otherwise. At least two riders required for carpool lane. Mobile police scanners not allowed. **More Information:** Minnesota State Patrol, 444 Cedar St., Suite 130, St. Paul MN 55101-5130. Emergency number: 911.

MISSISSIPPI: Maximum RV width 102 in.; maximum motorhome length 45 ft; maximum trailer length 40 ft.; maximum RV height 13.5 ft. Triple-towing is allowed. Riding allowed in truck campers, fifth-wheel trailers and travel trailers. Overnight parking in rest areas is not allowed. **RV Safety Requirements:** Trailers over 2,000 lbs.: trailer brakes and safety chains. **More Information:** Mississippi Department of Public Safety, P.O. Box 958, Jackson MS 39205-0958. Emergency number: 911; *HP or *47 on cellular phones.

MISSOURI: Maximum RV width 102 in.; maximum motorhome length 45 ft.; maximum trailer length not specified; maximum RV height 14 ft. (if more than 10 miles from designated highway, width 8 ft.; height 13.5 ft.); maximum combined length for two- or three-vehicle combination 65 ft. (55 ft. if more than 10 miles from a primary or designated highway). Riding allowed in truck campers, fifth-wheel trailers and travel trailers. Overnight parking in rest areas is allowed where posted. **RV Safety Requirements:** Trailers over 3,000 lbs.: trailer brakes and breakaway switch recommended. Safety chains required for bumper hitches. **Driving Laws:** Right turn on red allowed unless posted otherwise. Wipers on/headlights on recommended. **More Information:** Missouri State Highway Patrol, Commercial Vehicle Enforcement Div., P.O. Box 568, Jefferson City MO 65102; (573) 526-6128. Road/highway information (800) 222-6400. Emergency number: 911 or *55 on cellular phones.

MONTANA: Maximum RV width 102 in.; maximum motorhome length 55 ft.; maximum trailer length not specified; maximum RV height 14 ft.; maximum combined length for three vehicles 65 ft. Towing unit must have manufacturer's rated carrying capacity in excess of 2,000 lbs. Riding allowed in truck campers and fifth-wheel trailers. Overnight parking in rest areas is allowed. **RV Safety Requirements:** All RVs should have flares or reflective signs. Trailers under 3,000 lbs.: safety chains minimum 1/4 in. in diameter. Over 3,000 lbs.: trailer brakes, breakaway switch and safety chains. **Driving Laws:** Right turn on red allowed, unless posted otherwise. **More Information:** Montana Highway Patrol, 2550 Prospect Ave., Helena MT 59620-1419. Emergency number: 911.

NEBRASKA: Maximum RV width 102 in.; maximum motorhome length 45 ft.; maximum RV height 14.5 ft.; maximum combined length for two- or three-vehicle combination 65 ft. Riding allowed in travel trailers, fifth-wheel trailers and truck campers. Overnight parking in rest areas is not allowed. **RV Safety Requirements:** All RVs are required to have flares or reflective signs. Trailers over 3,000 lbs.: trailer brakes on each wheel, breakaway switch and safety chains. **Driving Laws:** Right turn on red allowed, unless posted otherwise. **More Information:** Nebraska State Patrol, P.O. Box 94907, Lincoln NE 68509-4907; (402) 471-4545. Emergency number: (800) 525-5555 or *55 on cellular phones.

NEVADA: Maximum RV width 102 in.; maximum motorhome length 45 ft.; maximum length of trailers not specified; maximum length of two- or three-vehicle combination 70 ft. Riding is allowed in truck campers. Overnight parking in rest areas allowed in designated areas only; not to exceed 18 hours in any two-week period. **RV Safety Requirements:** All trailers over 3000 lbs.: chains and brakes on all wheels. **Driving Laws:** It is unlawful for a person to have an open container of an alcoholic beverage within the passenger area of a motor vehicle while on a highway; however, this does not apply to the living quarters of a motorhome or travel trailer. **More Information:** Planning Division Chief, Department of Transportation, 1263 S. Stewart St., Carson City NV 89712. Emergency number: 911, or dial "0" and ask for Zenith 12000 or dial *NHP on cellular phones.

NEW HAMPSHIRE: Maximum RV width 96 in.; maximum motorhome length 45 ft.; maximum trailer length 48 ft.; triple-towing is not allowed. Riding is allowed in truck campers. Overnight parking in rest areas is not allowed. **RV Safety Requirements:** Trailers over 3,000 lbs.: trailer brakes, breakaway switch, safety chains and lights. **Driving Laws:** Right turn on red allowed, unless posted otherwise. **More Information:** Director, Division of Motor Vehicles, 10 Hazen Dr., Concord NH 03305. Emergency number: 911 or *711 on cellular phones.

NEW JERSEY: Maximum RV width 96 in. (102 in. on certain federal roads); maximum motorhome length 40 ft.; maximum RV height 13.5 ft.; maximum combined length 62 ft. Riding is not allowed in truck campers or trailers. **RV Safety Requirements:** Trailers over 3,000 lbs.: trailer brakes, breakaway switch, chains and safety glass. **Driving Laws:** Wipers on/headlights on. Right turn on red is allowed, unless posted otherwise. Seat belts required. At least two riders in carpool lane. Open propane cylinders are not allowed while traveling on open highways. New Jersey Turnpike: Motorhome may tow vehicle as long as all four wheels are on the ground; no tow dollies or piggybacks. Garden State Parkway: Motorhome may tow another vehicle with tow bar, safety chains and emergency tail lights on both vehicles. **More Information:** Department of Transportation, Motor Vehicle Commission, CN-174, Trenton NJ 08666; (609) 292-6500. Emergency number: 911 or (888) SAF-ROAD; *77 on cellular phones.

NEW MEXICO: Maximum RV width 102 in.; maximum motorhome length 45 ft.; maximum trailer length 40 ft; maximum RV height 14 ft.; maximum length of two-vehicle combination 65 ft. Riding is allowed in pickup campers. Overnight parking in rest areas is allowed, but not more than 24 hours in any three-day period in the same area. **RV Safety Requirements:** Trailers over 3,000 lbs.: trailer brakes and chains. **Driving Laws:** Wipers on/headlights on. **More Information:** New Mexico Highway Department, P.O. Box 1149, Santa Fe NM 87504-1149; (505) 827-2241. Emergency number: (505) 827-9000; *911 on cellular phones.

NEW YORK: Maximum RV width 96 in. (102 in. on qualifying or access highways); maximum motorhome length 45 ft.; maximum trailer length 48 ft.; maximum RV height 13.6 ft.; maximum combined length for two-vehicle combination 65 ft. Riding is allowed in truck campers or fifth-wheel trailers. RVs are not allowed in carpool lane, unless posted. Bottled gas is prohibited in tunnels, the lower levels of the George Washington Bridge and the Verrazano-Narrows Bridge, and on I-95 through Manhattan. **RV Safety Requirements:** Trailers over 1,000 lbs. unladen and trailers having a maximum gross weight in excess of 3,000 lbs.: trailer brakes and safety chains. **Driving Laws:** Wipers on/headlights on. Right turn on red allowed, unless posted otherwise; In New York City, right turn on red is not allowed unless posted. Radar detectors and mobile police scanners are not permitted in non-commercial motor vehicles with a gvwr over 18,000 lbs. **More Information:** State of New York Department of Motor Vehicles, Empire State Plaza, Albany NY 12228; (800) CALL-DMV. Emergency number: 911 or *DWI on cellular phones.

NORTH CAROLINA: Maximum RV width 102 in.; maximum motorhome length 45 ft.; maximum trailer length 48 ft.; maximum RV height 13.5 ft.; maximum length for two-vehicle combination 60 ft. Riding allowed in truck campers. Overnight parking is permitted in some rest areas unless otherwise posted. **RV Safety Requirements:** All RVs: safety glass. Trailers over 4,000 lbs.: trailer brakes. **Driving Laws:** Wipers on/lights on. Right turn on red allowed, unless posted otherwise. **More Information**: North Carolina State Highway Patrol, 512 N. Salisbury St., Raleigh NC 27604; (919) 715-8683. Emergency number: 911 or (800) 672-4527; *HP on cellular phones.

NORTH DAKOTA: Maximum RV width 102 in.; maximum motorhome length 50 ft; maximum trailer length 53 ft.; maximum RV height 14 ft.; maximum combined length for two- or three-vehicle combination 75 ft. Riding allowed in fifth-wheel trailers but not in truck campers. Overnight parking in rest areas allowed, unless posted otherwise. **RV Safety Requirements:** All RVs: flares or reflective signs and fire extinguisher. All trailers: trailer brakes, safety chains and breakaway switch. **Driving Laws:** Right turn on red allowed, unless posted otherwise. **More Information:** North Dakota Highway Patrol, 600 E. Boulevard Ave., Bismarck ND 58505-0240. Emergency number: 911.

OHIO: Maximum RV width 102 in; maximum motorhome length 45 ft.; maximum trailer length 40 ft.; maximum length of two- or three-vehicle combination 65 ft. Riding allowed in truck campers. Overnight parking allowed in service areas, no rest areas. Trailers may be barred at any time, or tire chains required, due to hazardous road conditions. **RV Safety Requirements:** Safety chains, turn signals and brake lights. Trailers over 2,000 lbs.: trailer brakes and breakaway switch. Ohio Turnpike: Over 2,000 lbs.: trailer brakes and breakaway switch. **Driving Laws:** Rest area parking allowed for a maximum of three hours. **More Information:** Director, Department of Public Safety, 1970 W. Broad St., Columbus OH 43223. Emergency number: (800) GRAB-DUI, (888) 877-PATROL OR 911; *DUI on cellular phones.

OKLAHOMA: Maximum RV width 102 in.; maximum motorhome length 45 ft.; maximum trailer length 40 ft.; maximum RV height 13.5 ft.; maximum length of two- or three-vehicle combination 65 ft. Riding allowed in truck campers. Overnight parking in rest areas is allowed, unless posted otherwise. **RV Safety Requirements:** All trailers: coupling equipment designed to prevent swerving, trailer brakes, breakaway switch and safety chains. Rubber or fabric aprons behind rear wheels required. **Driving Laws:** Right turn on red allowed unless posted otherwise. **More Information:** Oklahoma Department of Public Safety—Size & Weight Permit Div., 3600 N. Martin Luther King Blvd., Oklahoma City OK 73136; (405) 425-2206. Emergency number: (405) 425-2385 or *55 on cell phone.

OREGON: Maximum RV width 102 in.; maximum motorhome length 45 ft.; maximum trailer length 45 ft.; maximum length of two-vehicle combination 65 ft. Riding in truck campers allowed. Passengers are allowed in fifth-wheel trailers if the trailer is equipped with the following: All windows are made of safety glazing materials; an auditory or visual signaling device that passengers can use to gain the attention of the motor-vehicle driver towing the vehicle; and at least one unobstructed exit capable of being opened from both the interior and exterior of the vehicle. **RV Safety Requirements:** All trailers must have full lighting equipment. Hitches and chains must meet SAE standards and use recommendations. Combinations of vehicles that include a motor vehicle and any other vehicle shall be equipped with a brake system on one or more of the vehicles sufficient to stop both from 20 mph without leaving a 12-foot-wide travel lane. The stopping distance must be within 25 ft. for vehicles under 8,000 GVWR, and within 35 ft. for vehicles weighing 8,000 GVWR and more. Manufacturer's requirements must be followed on towed vehicles. **Driving Laws:** Headlights must be on when limited-visibility conditions exist of 1,000 feet or less. Right turn on red after stopping is allowed unless posted otherwise. **More Information:** Oregon Department of Transportation, Transportation Safety Division, 235 Union St. NE, Salem OR 97301; 511 or (800) 977-ODOT (6368) in state; (503) 588-2941 outside of Oregon. Emergency number: 911.

PENNSYLVANIA: Maximum RV width 102 in.; maximum motorhome length 45 ft.; maximum trailer length not specified; maximum length of two-vehicle combination 60 ft. Riding allowed in fifth-wheel trailers with electronic communications. Overnight parking in rest areas is not allowed. RVs are not allowed in carpool lane. **RV Safety Requirements:** All RVs or motor vehicles towing an RV: flares or reflective signs and fire extinguisher. All trailers: brakes and breakaway system if the gross trailer weight with load exceeds 40 percent of the towing vehicle's gross weight with load; safety chains and lighting equipment (brakes, turn signals, reflectors). **Driving Laws:** Headlights must be on in inclement weather. Right turn on red allowed, unless posted otherwise. **More Information:** Pennsylvania Department of Transportation, Bureau of Highway Safety & Traffic Engineering, 55 Walnut St., Forum Pl., P.O. Box 2047, Harrisburg PA 17105-2047. Emergency number: 911.

RHODE ISLAND: Maximum RV width 102 in.; maximum motorhome length 40 ft; maximum trailer length not specified; maximum length of two-vehicle combination 60 ft. Riding allowed in truck campers. Overnight parking in rest areas allowed unless posted otherwise. **RV Safety Requirements:** Over 4,000 lbs.: trailer brakes, breakaway switch, two safety chains and flares. **Driving Laws:** All passengers must use seat belts. Children under 4 yrs. must be in child-restraint systems; children under 6 yrs. must be properly restrained in the back seat. **More Information:** Rhode Island Division of Motor Vehicles, 100 Main Street, Pawtucket, RI 02860. Emergency number: 911 or *77 on cellular phones.

SOUTH CAROLINA: Maximum RV width 102 in.; maximum motorhome length 45 ft.; maximum trailer length 48 ft.; maximum RV height 13.5 ft. Triple-towing not allowed. Riding is allowed in truck campers. Overnight parking in rest areas is not allowed. **RV Safety**

Requirements: Trailers over 10,001 lbs., other than fifth-wheel trailers: chains, cable, etc. **Driving Laws**: Wipers on/headlights on. Right turn on red (after full stop) is allowed, unless posted otherwise. Front-seat passengers must wear seat belts. Children under 4 yrs. must be in child-restraint safety seats; children 4-6 must use child-restraint safety seats or wear seat belts. **More Information:** South Carolina Department of Public Safety, State Transport Police Div., P. O. Box 1993, Blythewood SC 29016; (803) 896-5500. Emergency number: (803) 896-9621;*HP or *47 on cellular phones.

SOUTH DAKOTA: Maximum RV width 102 in.; maximum motorhome length 45 ft.; maximum trailer length 53 ft.; maximum combined length for a single motor vehicle and two trailers 75 ft. (on Needles Highway 87 in the Black Hills, maximum width 8 ft. 7 in., maximum height 10 ft. 8 in.). Riding allowed in truck campers; in fifth-wheel trailers only with two-way communication. Overnight parking in rest areas is not allowed unless posted otherwise. **RV Safety Requirements:** All RVs: flares or reflective signs. Trailers over 3,000 lbs.: breakaway switch and safety chains. **Driving Laws:** Right turn on red allowed, unless posted otherwise. Weigh-Station Requirements: All towed vehicles, motor trucks or trailers over 8,000 lbs. must stop. **More Information:** South Dakota Highway Patrol, 118 W. Capitol Ave., Pierre SD 57501-2000. (605) 773-4578 or emergency number: 911.

TENNESSEE: Maximum RV width 102 in.; maximum motorhome length 45 ft.; maximum trailer length 40 ft.; maximum RV height 13.5 ft.; maximum combined length for two- or three-vehicle combination 65 ft. Overnight parking in rest areas allowed unless posted. **RV Safety Requirements:** Trailers over 3,000 lbs.: trailer brakes, breakaway switch, safety chains (chains not required on gooseneck fifth-wheel trailers). **Driving Laws:** Wipers on/headlights on. Right turn on red allowed, unless posted otherwise. **More Information:** Tennessee Highway Patrol, 1150 Foster Ave., Nashville TN 37249-1000. Emergency number: 911, (615) 741-2069; *THP or *847 on cellular phones.

TEXAS: Maximum RV width 102 in.; maximum motorhome length 45 ft.; maximum trailer length not specified; maximum RV height 14 ft.; maximum length of two- or three-vehicle combination 65 ft. Speed limit for travel trailers: 60 during the day, 55 at night, unless otherwise posted. Overnight parking in rest areas is allowed (up to 24 hours). **RV Safety Requirements:** All trailers except fifth-wheels: safety chains. Trailers over 4,500 lbs.: trailer brakes, breakaway switch, flares and mirrors. **Driving Laws:** Headlights on 1/2 hour after sunset to 1/2 hour before sunrise. Right turn on red allowed after complete stop. **More Information:** Texas Department of Public Safety, P.O. Box 4087, Austin TX 78773; (512) 424-2000. Emergency number: 911.

UTAH: Maximum RV width 102 in.; maximum motorhome length 45 ft.; maximum trailer length 40 ft.; maximum RV height 14 ft.; maximum combined length for two- or three-vehicle combination 65 ft. or by special permit. Riding in truck campers is allowed. 12-hour maximum parking in rest areas. **RV Safety Requirements:** Trailers over 3,000 lbs.: trailer brakes, safety chains and breakaway switch. **Driving Laws:** Right turn on red is allowed, unless posted otherwise. **More Information:** Utah Department of Transportation, 4501 South 2700 West, Salt Lake City UT 84119-141265; (801) 965-4000. Emergency number: 911 or (801) 965-4219; *911 on cellular phones.

VERMONT: Maximum RV width 102 in.; maximum motorhome length 46 ft.; maximum trailer length 53 ft.; maximum combined length for two-vehicle combinaton 65 ft. Riding is allowed in truck campers. Overnight parking in rest areas is not allowed. **RV Safety Requirements:** Trailers over 3,000 lbs.: trailer brakes on one axle, breakaway switch and safety chains. Trailers over 6,000 lbs.: trailer brakes on all wheels, breakaway switch and safety chains. **Driving Laws:** Right turn on red is allowed, unless posted otherwise. Headlights on from 1/2 hour after sunset to 1/2 hour before sunrise. **More Information:** Department of Motor Vehicles, 120 State St., Montpelier VT 05603-0001; (802) 828-2000. Emergency number: 911.

VIRGINIA: Maximum RV width 102 in.; maximum motorhome length 45 ft.; maximum trailer length 45 ft.; maximum RV height 13.5 ft.; maximum combined length for two-vehicle combination 65 ft. Riding is allowed in truck campers. Overnight parking in rest areas is permitted unless posted otherwise. RVs allowed in the HOV-3 (carpool) lanes if there are three or more occupants. In the Tidewater area, RVs are allowed in the HOV-2 lanes only if there are two or more occupants and the gvw is less than 10,000 lbs. Tunnel Regulations: Maximum height 13 ft 6 in. Maximum of two approved propane gas tanks 20 lbs. each. Tanks must be turned off when going through tunnels. **RV Safety Requirements:** All trailers: safety chains. Trailers over 3,000 lbs.: trailer brakes, breakaway switch. **Driving Laws:** Right turn on red allowed, unless posted otherwise. Wipers on/lights on. Front-seat passengers are required to wear seat belts; children up to 5 yrs. must be in child-restraint safety seats. Radar detectors not permitted. **More Information:** Department of State Police, P.O. Box 27472, Richmond VA 23261-7472; (804) 674-2000. Emergency number: 911 or #77

WASHINGTON: Maximum RV width 102 in.; maximum motorhome length 46 ft.; maximum trailer length 53 ft.; maximum RV height 14 ft.; maximum combined length for two vehicles 60 ft.; triple-towing not allowed. No vehicle towing a trailer, or no vehicle or combination over 10,000 lbs. may be driven in the left-hand lane of a limited-access roadway having three or more lanes for traffic moving in one direction, except when preparing for a left turn. Riding allowed in truck campers. Minimum of two riders required in carpool lane; trailers are not allowed in carpool lanes. Overnight parking in rest areas allowed; 8-hr. maximum suggested. Mountain Pass Regulations: Tire chains are required from November 1-March 31 on RVs over 10,000 lbs. on all passes. **RV Safety Requirements:** All RVs: flares or reflective signs, fire extinguishers and safety chains. Trailers over 3,000 lbs.: trailer brakes, breakaway switch. Vehicles over 10,001 lbs. gvwr and vehicle combinatons are required to obey truck speed limits. **Driving Laws:** Right turn on red allowed, unless posted otherwise. **More Information:** Washington State Patrol, Commercial Vehicle Enforcement Section, P.O. Box 42614, Olympia WA 98504-2614; (360) 753-0350. Road and highway information number: (800) 695-ROAD. Emergency number: 911.

WEST VIRGINIA: Maximum RV width 102 in.; maximum motorhome length 45 ft; maximum trailer length 40 ft.; maximum RV height 13.5 ft.; maximum combined length for two vehicles 65 ft. (major roads)/55 ft. (other routes). Triple-towing is not allowed. Riding allowed in truck campers and fifth-wheel trailers. **RV Safety Requirements:** Safety chains required; trailers over 3,000 lbs. gvwr: trailer brakes required. **Driving Laws:** Wipers on/headlights on. Right turn on red allowed, unless posted otherwise. Overnight parking is not allowed. **More Information:** West Virginia Division of Highways, Maintenance Division, Central Permit Office, Bldg. 5, Room A-337, 1900 Kanawha Blvd. E., Charleston WV 25305-0430; (304) 558-9483. Emergency number: 911; *SP or *77 on cellular phones.

WISCONSIN: Maximum RV width 102 in.; maximum motorhome length 45 ft.; maximum trailer length 48 ft.;maximum RV height 13.5 ft.; maximum combined length for two vehicles 65 ft.; maximum combined length for three vehicles 65 ft (with permit only). Riding is allowed in truck campers. Riding is allowed in fifth-wheel trailers, but no one under age 12 unless accompanied by a person 16 or older; trailer must be equipped with a two-way voice communication between driver and occupant(s). **RV Safety Requirements:** All trailers require safety chains; trailers over 3,000 lbs. require trailer brakes. **Driving Laws:** Right turn on red is allowed, unless posted otherwise. **More Information:** Wisconsin State Patrol, 4802 Sheboygan Ave., Rm. 551, Madison WI 53707-7912; (608) 266-0264. Emergency number: 911.

WYOMING: Maximum RV width 102 in.; maximum motorhome length 60 ft.; maximum trailer length 45 ft.; maximum combined length for two or three vehicles 85 ft. Riding in truck campers is allowed. Overnight parking in rest areas is not allowed unless posted. **RV Safety Requirements:** All house trailers are required to have flares or reflective signs. All vehicles or combinations of vehicles must have sufficient brakes to stop within 40 ft. from an initial speed of 20 mph on a level, dry, smooth, hard surface. **Driving Laws:** Right turn on red is allowed, unless posted otherwise. **More Information:** Wyoming Highway Patrol, 5300 Bishop Blvd., Cheyenne WY 82003-3340; (307) 777-4306. Emergency number: (800) 442-9090 or #HELP on cellular phones.

Canada

Note: 2.6 m. = 8 1/2 ft.
12.5 m. = 41 feet; 16.15 m = 53 ft.

ALBERTA: Maximum RV height 4.0 m.; maximum RV width 2.6 m.; maximum trailer length 12.5 m.; maximum motorhome length 13 m.; combined length for two or three (w/fifth-wheel) vehicles 20 m. **RV Safety Requirements:** Trailers over 2,000 lbs. must have trailer brakes, unless the lead vehicle is twice the weight of the trailer. **Driving Laws:** Right turn on red is allowed, unless posted otherwise. Headlights on when conditions restrict visibility to 150 meters/500 ft. or less; driving with headlights on during all hours of the day is permitted. All passengers are required to wear seat belts; children up to 6 yrs./40 lbs. must be in child safety-restraint seats. **More Information:** Alberta Infrastructure and Transportation, Twin Atria Building, 4999-98 Ave., Edmonton AB T6B 2X3. Emergency number: 911.

BRITISH COLUMBIA: Maximum RV height 4.15 m.; maximum RV width 2.6 m.; maximum trailer length 12.5 m; maximum motorhome length 12.5 m.; maximum length of two-vehicle combination 20 m./65 1/2 ft.; three-vehicle combinations are prohibited. **RV Safety Requirements:** Trailers over 3,000 lbs. must have trailer brakes on all wheels, breakaway switch and safety chains (except fifth-wheel trailers). Motorhomes (only) may tow motor vehicles via a tow bar without brakes hooked up on the towed motor vehicle when the towed motor vehicle's weight is less than 4,409 lbs. and less than 40 percent of the gross vehicle weight rating (gvwr) of the motorhome towing it. **Driving Laws:** Right turn on red is allowed, unless posted otherwise. All passengers must wear seat belts; children up to 40 lbs. must be in child-restraint safety seats. **More Information:** Insurance Corporation of British Columbia, Commercial Transport and Inspection, Box 3750, Victoria BC V8W 3Y5. Emergency number: 911

MANITOBA: Maximum RV height 4.15 m.; maximum RV width 2.6 m.; maximum trailer length 12.5 m.; maximum motorhome length 12.5 m.; maximum combined length for two vehicles 21.5 m.; combined length for three vehicles (fifth-wheel combinations only) 23 m. Riding is allowed in truck campers. Open propane cylinders are not allowed while traveling on open highways. **RV Safety Requirements:** All trailers must have safety chains; trailers over 2,000 lbs. must also have trailer brakes. **Driving Laws:** Right turn on red is allowed, unless posted otherwise. All passengers are required to wear seat belts; children up to age 5 yrs./50 lbs. must be in child-restraint safety seats. Radar detectors and mobile scanners are not permitted. **More Information:** Vehicle Standards and Inspections, 1075 Portage Ave., Winnipeg MB R3G 0S1. Emergency number: (204) 983-5461.

NEW BRUNSWICK: Maximum RV height 4.15 m.; maximum RV width 2.6 m.; maximum trailer length 12.5 m.; maximum motorhome length 12.5 m.; maximum combined length for two-vehicle combination 23 m. Overnight parking is allowed if posted. **RV Safety Requirements:** All RVs are required to have flares or reflective signs and a fire extinguisher. Trailers over 3,000 lbs. must have trailer brakes, breakaway switch and safety chains. **Driving Laws:** Right turn on red is allowed, unless posted otherwise. All occupants must wear seat belts; children up to 40 lbs. (approximately 4 yrs. of age) must be in the appropriate child-restraint safety seat. Radar detectors are not allowed. **More Information:** Department of Public Safety, Licensing Registration Branch, P.O. Box 6000, Fredericton NB E3B 5H1.

NEWFOUNDLAND and LABRADOR: Maximum RV height 4.15 m.; maximum RV width 2.6 m.; maximum trailer length 12.5 m.; maximum motorhome length 12.5 m; maximum combined length for two-vehicle combination 23 m. Riding in truck campers not specified. Overnight parking is not allowed unless posted. **RV Safety Requirements:** All trailers must have safety chains. Trailers with a gvwr in excess of 1,350 kg must also have trailer brakes and breakaway switch. **Driving Laws:** Right turn on red is allowed, unless posted otherwise. All passengers are required to wear seat belts. Radar detectors and mobile police scanners are not permitted. **More Information:** Department of Government Services & Lands, Motor Registration Division, P.O. Box 8710, St. Johns NF A1B 4J5. Emergency numbers: 911 or *RCMP on cellular phones.

NORTHWEST TERRITORIES: Maximum RV height 4.2 m.; maximum RV width 3.2 m.; maximum trailer length not specified; maximum motorhome length 12.5 m.; maximum length of two-vehicle combination not specified. Overnight parking in rest areas is permitted. **RV Safety Requirements:** Brakes are required on trailers over 1,360 kg.; safety chains are required on all trailers except fifth-wheel trailers. **Driving Laws:** Headlights or daytime running lights should be on at all times. Right turn on red allowed after stop and when clear. All passengers must wear seat belts; children up to 40 lbs. must be in child-restraint safety seats. Radar-detection devices are prohibited. **More information:** Department of Transportation, Road Licensing & Safety Division, 4510 Franklin Ave., Yellowknife, NT X1A 2L9. Emergency number: (867) 669-1111.

NOVA SCOTIA: Maximum RV height 4.15 m.; maximum RV width 2.6 m.; maximum trailer length 12.5 m.; maximum motorhome length 12.5 m.; maximum combined length for two-vehicle combination 23 m. Riding in pickup camper is permitted if seats are equipped with safety belts. Open propane cylinders are not allowed while traveling on open highways. Towing mirrors must be attached to vehicle if the load or trailer obscures rear vision; however, it is illegal to drive on the highway with the extra mirrors in place without the load or trailer attached to the vehicle. **RV Safety Requirements:** All RVs are required to have flares. All trailers must have safety chains; trailers over 3,000 lbs. must also have breakaway switch; over 4,000 lbs. must also have trailer brakes. **Driving Laws:** Right turn on red is allowed, unless posted otherwise. All passengers are required to wear seat belts; children up to 40 lbs. must be in child-restraint safety seats. Radar detectors are not allowed. **More Information:** Department of Business & Consumer Services Call Center, 1505 Barrington St. N., 8th Fl., Halifax NS B3J 3E7. Emergency number: 911.

NUNAVUT: Maximum RV height 4.2 m.; maximum RV width 2.6 m.; maximum trailer length not specified; maximum motorhome length 12.0 m.; maximum length of two-vehicle combination 21.0 m. Riding is allowed in truck campers. (Note: Few roadways in Nunavut can accommodate RVs.)

ONTARIO: Maximum RV height 4.15 m.; maximum RV width 2.6 m.; maximum trailer length 12.5 m.; maximum motorhome length 12.5 m.; maximum length of two-vehicle combination 23 m. Riding in truck campers is allowed. Overnight parking is allowed in restricted areas. **RV Safety Requirements:** Over 3,000 lbs./1,360 kg. brakes are required. Safety chains are required unless the trailer is attached by a fifth-wheel attachment. **Driving Laws:** Driver and all passengers are required to wear seat belts. Children up to 9 kg./20 lbs. and under 26 in./66 cm. must be secured in a rearward-facing child-restraint system secured by the seat-belt assembly. Children between 20-40 lbs./9-18 kg. and over 26 in./66 cm. must be secured in a child-restraint system secured by the seat-belt assembly and a tether strap. Children over 40 lbs./18 kg. can use a booster seat secured by the seat-belt assembly. Radar detection and jamming devices are prohibited. **More Information:** Ministry of Transportation Information, 301 St. Paul St., St. Catharines ON L2R 7R4. Emergency number: 911.

PRINCE EDWARD ISLAND: Maximum RV height 4.15 m.; maximum RV width 2.6 m.; maximum trailer length 12.5 m; maximum motorhome length 12.5 m; maximum length for two-vehicle combination 23 m. Riding in truck campers, fifth-wheel trailers not specified. Overnight camping is allowed in rest areas unless posted otherwise. **RV Safety Requirements:** All trailers (except fifth-wheels) must have safety chains. Trailers 1,500 kgs. and over must also have trailer brakes and breakaway switch. **Driving Laws:** Right turn on red is allowed, unless posted otherwise. All passengers must wear seat belts; children up to 40 lbs. must be in child-restraint safety seats. Radar detectors are not allowed. Ferry Regulations: Propane tanks must be shut off. **More Information:** Highway Safety Operations, P.O. Box 2000, Charlottetown, PE C1A 7N8. Emergency numbers: (902) 368-5200 (during business hours); (902) 437-8534 (after hours) or 911.

QUEBEC: Maximum RV height 4.15 m.; maximum RV width 2.6 m.; maximum trailer length 12.5 m.; maximum motorhome length 12.5 m.; maximum length of two-vehicle combination 23 m. Riding is allowed in truck campers, with seat belts. Overnight parking in rest areas is not allowed. **RV Safety Requirements:** All RVs are required to have flares or reflective signs if wider than 2 m./6 1/2 ft. Trailers over 1,300 kg./2,865 lbs. or exceeding 50% of tow-vehicle weight must have trailer brakes, breakaway switch and safety chains. **Driving Laws:** Right turn on red is strictly prohibited except when allowed by an additional green arrow. All occupants are required to wear seat belts; children up to 40 lbs. must be in child-restraint safety seats; children under 8 yrs. should be secured in a booster seat. Radar detectors are not allowed, whether connected or not. **More Information:** Ministere des Transportes, Service de la normalisation technique, 700, boul. Rene Levesque, Est, Quebec PQ G1R 5H1; (418) 643-1345. Emergency number: 911.

SASKATCHEWAN: Maximum RV height 4.15m; maximum RV width 2.6 m.; maximum trailer length 12.5 m.; maximum motorhome length 12.5 m., 14 m with permit; maximum combined length for a two- or three-vehicle combination (only if fifth-wheel combination) 23 m. Triple towing is allowed only with fifth-wheel trailer. Riding is allowed but not recommended in truck campers. **RV Safety Requirements:** Trailers over 3,000 lbs. must have trailer brakes, breakaway switch and double safety chains. **Driving Laws:** Right turn on red is allowed, unless otherwise posted. All passengers are required to wear seat belts; children up to 40 lbs. must be in child-restraint safety seats. **More Information:** Saskatchewan Highways & Transportation, Trucking Policy and Programs, 8th Fl., 1855 Victoria Ave., Regina SK S4P 3T2; (306) 787-5307. Emergency number: 911.

YUKON TERRITORIES: Maximum RV height 4.9 m.; maximum RV width 2.6 m.; maximum trailer length 16.15 m.; maximum motorhome length 16.15 m.; maximum length of two-vehicle combination 25 m. Three-vehicle combinations must be fifth-wheel with one additional trailer on ball hitch connected to fifth-wheel's frame. Overnight parking is allowed unless posted. **RV Safety Requirements:** Trailers over 910 kg. must have trailer brakes and safety chains. **Driving Laws:** Headlights required at all times. Right turn on red is allowed, unless otherwise posted. All passengers are required to wear seat belts; children up to 6 yrs./44 lbs. must be in child-restraint safety seats. **More Information:** Tourism Yukon, P.O. Box 2703, Whitehorse YK Y1A 2C6; (867) 667-5315. Emergency number: 911.

Bridge, Tunnel & Ferry Regulations

RV RESTRICTIONS:

It's wise to check in advance with local authorities before traveling in the following areas, particularly if travel via ferry, bridge or tunnel is planned.

California: Pulling travel trailers may not be allowed in snow areas. Contact the California Highway Patrol before entering a snow area; chains may be required at any time. Trailers may be barred due to high winds, blowing sand, etc. RVs over 20 feet may experience difficulty in negotiating hairpin turns on State Highway 89.

Connecticut: RV size may be limited on the Connecticut River ferry between Chester and Hadlyme; also on Wilbur Cross and Merrit parkways.

Illinois: Trailers are prohibited on boulevards in and around Chicago.

Massachusetts: Trailers are prohibited on Memorial Drive in Cambridge and Storrow Drive in Boston, along the Charles River; and on many other parkways in the Boston area.

Montana: All vehicles over 21 feet long (including bumpers) and 8 feet wide (including mirrors) are not permitted through Logan Pass at the summit of Going-to-the-Sun Road in Glacier National Park. Shuttle service is available between St. Mary and West Glacier. Restriction applies from Avalanche Campground on the south side to Sun Point area on the north side.

New York: Trailers and motorhomes are not permitted on Taconic State Parkway; trailers are not permitted on most parkways.

LP-GAS PROHIBITED:

Maryland/Baltimore: Baltimore Harbor and Fort McHenry (I-95) tunnels. Alternate route for RVs with propane over the Francis Scott Key Bridge is I-695.

Massachusetts/Boston Harbor: All.

New York/East River: Between Manhattan and Brooklyn: Brooklyn Battery Tunnel. Between Manhattan and Queens: Queens Midtown Tunnel.

New York and New Jersey/Hudson River: Between Manhattan and Jersey City: Holland Tunnel. Between Manhattan and Fort Lee: Lower level George Washington Bridge (I-95 South) and George Washington Bridge Expressway. Lower level Verrazano Narrows Bridge. Between Manhattan and Weehawken: Lincoln Tunnel.

LP-GAS RESTRICTIONS:

Virginia/Chesapeake Bay Bridge/Tunnel: RVs equipped with ICC-approved compressed cooking tanks not exceeding two 45-pound capacity tanks (or two permanently mounted containers with maximum total capacity of 200 pounds) may cross the facility provided that, in the opinion of the toll collector or police sergeant after inspection, the tanks are completely shut off and securely attached.

Texas/Houston Ship Channel: Washburn Tunnel between Pasadena and Galena Park: Maximum of two 71/2-gallon containers (30 pounds gas each) or one 10-gallon container (40 pounds gas) of DOT (ICC)-approved type, with shutoff valve at discharge opening. Valve must be closed when in tunnel. LP-gas as vehicle fuel prohibited. 71/2-gallon containers (30 pounds gas each) or one 10-gallon container (40 pounds gas) of DOT (ICC)-approved type, with shutoff valve at discharge opening. Valve must be closed when in tunnel. LP-gas as vehicle fuel prohibited.

Alabama

READER SERVICE INFO

The following businesses have placed an ad in the Alabama Travel Section. To receive free information, enter their Reader Service number on the Reader Service Card opposite page 48/Discover Section in the front of this directory:

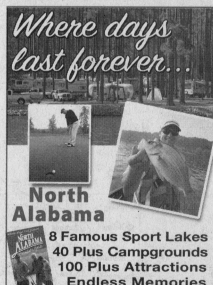

Advertiser	RS#
Alabama Mountain Lakes Tourist Assoc.	678
American Motor Coach Resorts	3760
Bellingrath Gardens & Home	823
Huntsville Convention & Visitors Bureau	3310
Little Mountain Marina Camping Resort	3369
Natchez Trace Compact	3651
Noccalula Falls Park & Campground	472

TIME ZONE

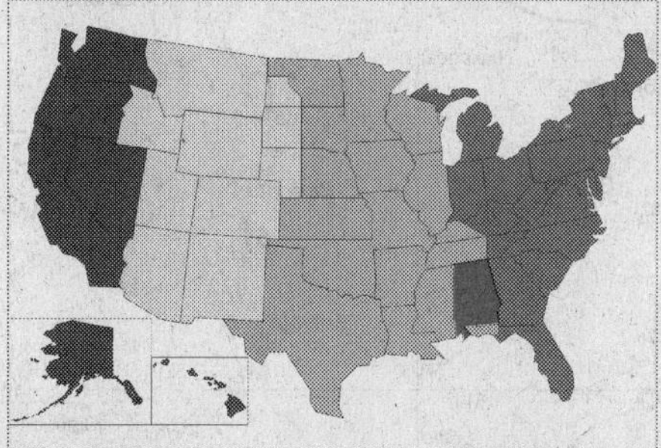

Alabama is in the Central Time Zone.

TOPOGRAPHY

The state's terrain is varied; the Appalachian Mountains enter the state from the northeast and gradually spread out into rolling hills and rich farmlands. Alabama has numerous lakes and 53 miles of gulf coastline.

TEMPERATURE

The temperature reaches 60° by March and in summer the average is in the low 80s with periods of 90° and above. Generally, November requires only a sweater or light jacket and snow is rarely found except in the high altitudes of northern Alabama. The average temperature in January is 46°.

TRAVEL & TOURISM INFO

State Agency:

Alabama Bureau of Tourism & Travel
401 Adams Ave., Suite 126,
P.O Box 4927
Montgomery, AL 36103-4927
(800/ALABAMA or 334/242-4169).
Email: info@tourism.alabama.gov
www.800alabama.com

Regional Agencies:

Tenn-Tom Tourism Association
P.O Box 671, Columbus, MS 39703
(662/328-3286) tenntom@ebicom.net;
www.tenntom.org

Alabama Mountain Lakes Tourist Association
25062 North St., P.O Box 1075
Mooresville, AL 35649
(800/648-5381)
Email:info@northalabama.org
www.northalabama.org

Alabama Sunrise Region
207 N Main Street
Tuskegee, AL 36083
pullijs@acesag.auburn.edu
www.alsunrise.com

Southeast Alabama Trails
5 County Complex
New Brockton, AL 36351
(334/894-5596)
lion265605@aol.com;
www.southeastalabamatrails.com

Local Agencies:
For local information, contact the Chamber of Commerce or Convention and Visitor's Bureau for the locality you are interested in.

RECREATIONAL INFO

Biking:
Alabama Dept. of Transportation
1409 Coliseum Blvd.
Montgomery, AL 36130
(334/242-6358).

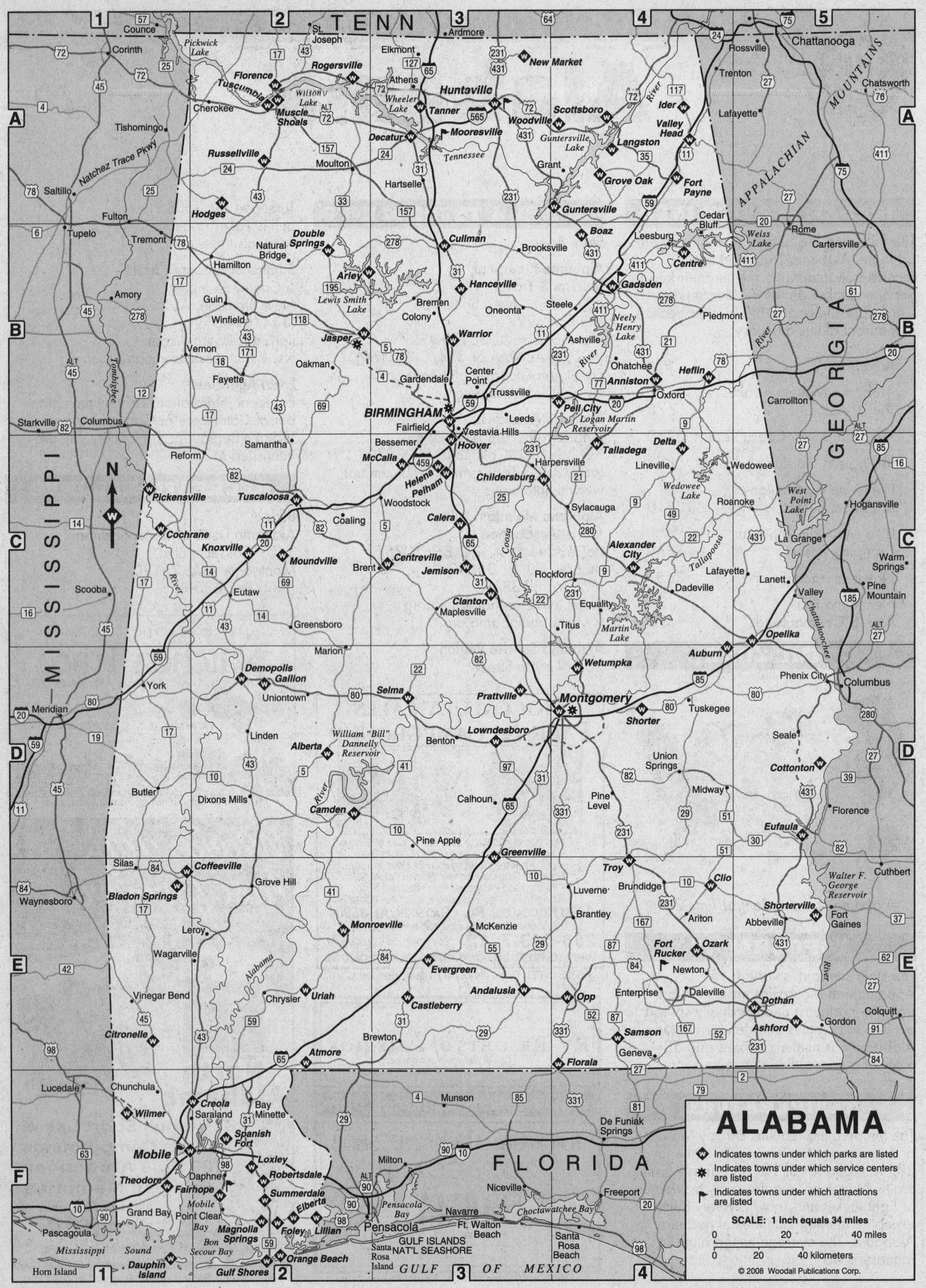
ALABAMA
Indicates towns under which parks are listed
Indicates towns under which service centers are listed
Indicates towns under which attractions are listed
SCALE: 1 inch equals 34 miles
0 20 40 miles
0 20 40 kilometers
© 2008 Woodall Publications Corp.
TENN
MISSISSIPPI
GEORGIA
FLORIDA
GULF OF MEXICO
APPALACHIAN MOUNTAINS
Natchez Trace Pkwy
GULF ISLANDS NAT'L SEASHORE
Counce
St. Joseph
Ardmore
Chattanooga
Corinth
Pickwick Lake
Rogersville
Elkmont
New Market
Rossville
Trenton
Chatsworth
Florence
Tuscumbia
Muscle Shoals
Wilson Lake
Wheeler Lake
Athens
Huntsville
Tanner
Cherokee
Scottsboro
Ider
Valley Head
Lafayette
Tishomingo
Decatur
Mooresville
Woodville
Guntersville Lake
Langston
Tennessee
Russellville
Moulton
Hartselle
Grant
Grove Oak
Fort Payne
Saltillo
Hodges
Guntersville
Fulton
Tupelo
Tremont
Double Springs
Natural Bridge
Cullman
Brooksville
Boaz
Cedar Bluff
Leesburg
Weiss Lake
Rome
Cartersville
Centre
Hamilton
Arley
Hanceville
Gadsden
Amory
Guin
Lewis Smith Lake
Bremen
Colony
Oneonta
Steele
Piedmont
Winfield
Jasper
Warrior
Neely Henry Lake
Ashville
Vernon
Oakman
Center Point
Ohatchee
Heflin
Fayette
Gardendale
Trussville
Anniston
Oxford
Carrollton
Starkville
Columbus
BIRMINGHAM
Fairfield
Vestavia Hills
Leeds
Pell City
Logan Martin Reservoir
Bessemer
Hoover
Talladega
Delta
Samantha
Reform
McCalla
Helena
Pelham
Harpersville
Lineville
Wedowee
Childersburg
Pickensville
Tuscaloosa
Woodstock
Wedowee Lake
Roanoke
West Point Lake
Hogansville
Sylacauga
Coaling
Calera
Cochrane
Coosa
Alexander City
La Grange
Knoxville
Moundville
Brent
Centreville
Jemison
Tallapoosa
Lafayette
Warm Springs
Lanett
Pine Mountain
Rockford
Scooba
Eutaw
Clanton
Dadeville
Valley
Maplesville
Equality
Chattahoochee
Greensboro
Titus
Martin Lake
Opelika
Marion
Auburn
Wetumpka
Demopolis
Gallion
Phenix City
Columbus
York
Uniontown
Selma
Prattville
Montgomery
Shorter
Tuskegee
Meridian
Linden
William "Bill" Dannelly Reservoir
Lowndesboro
Benton
Seale
Alberta
Union Springs
Cottonton
Butler
Dixons Mills
Calhoun
Pine Level
Midway
Camden
Florence
Pine Apple
Eufaula
Silas
Coffeeville
Greenville
Troy
Grove Hill
Clio
Waynesboro
Bladon Springs
Luverne
Brundidge
Walter F. George Reservoir
Cuthbert
Brantley
Ariton
Shorterville
Abbeville
Fort Gaines
Leroy
Monroeville
McKenzie
Wagarville
Evergreen
Fort Rucker
Ozark
Newton
Alabama
Andalusia
Opp
Enterprise
Daleville
Vinegar Bend
Chrysler
Uriah
Castleberry
Dothan
Ashford
Gordon
Colquitt
Citronelle
Brewton
Samson
Geneva
Atmore
Florala
Lucedale
Chunchula
Creola
Saraland
Bay Minette
Munson
Wilmer
De Funiak Springs
Spanish Fort
Mobile
Milton
Loxley
Theodore
Daphne
Robertsdale
Fairhope
Summerdale
Niceville
Freeport
Mobile Bay
Grand Bay
Point Clear
Elberta
Pensacola Bay
Navarre
Choctawhatchee Bay
Pascagoula
Magnolia Springs
Foley
Lillian
Pensacola
Ft. Walton Beach
Bon Secour Bay
Santa Rosa Beach
Mississippi Sound
Santa Rosa Island
Horn Island
Dauphin Island
Gulf Shores
Orange Beach

Fishing & Hunting:
Alabama Dept. of Conservation & Natural Resources
Game & Fish Division
64 N. Union Street
Montgomery, AL 36130
(334/242-3465)
www.dcnr.state.al.us.

Golf:
For information, call (800/ ALABAMA). For information on a complex of 23 courses and 432 holes which stretches across the state, call **Sunbelt Golf Corporation** (800/949-4444). www.rtjgolf.com

SHOPPING

Mountain Top Flea Market, Attalla, offers 2.6 miles of shopping at 1,500 vendor booths. 11301 US Hwy 278 W, Attalla, AL 35954 (800/535-2286).

Boaz Shopper's Paradise, Boaz. Shop at 140 direct factory outlets and discount retailers. Located one hour from Birmingham or Huntsville, at 306 W Mann Ave, Boaz, AL 35957 (800/SHOP-BOAZ).

Rue's Antique Mall and Deli, Brundidge. You'll find everything from antique bottles and dishes, to comic books and furniture. 123 Main St, Brundidge, AL 36010 (334/735-3125).

UNIQUE FEATURES

CIVIL RIGHTS MUSEUM TRAIL

Travel to Montgomery, Birmingham, Selma and Tuskegee and visit many of the places in Alabama that were battlegrounds from 1955 to 1965.

Montgomery: The Rosa Parks Library and Museum opened on the 45th anniversary of her arrest. Visitors to the city can now ride a replica of the 1953-era bus on which Mrs. Parks was arrested. The modest frame parsonage Dr. King and his young family called home for four years has been authentically restored and opened to the public as the **Dexter Parsonage Museum**. The Interpretive Center next door offers a short video presentation prior to tours of the parsonage. The house is furnished with period furniture, some dating from the residency of the Kings. Dr. King's church, renamed the **Dexter Avenue King Memorial Baptist Church**, is now a National Historic Landmark. A large mural depicts the struggles of the movement and landmark moments in King's life. A block behind the church is the **Civil Rights Memorial** designed by renowned sculptor Maya Lin. Other Montgomery sites include: **Holt Street Baptist Church**, the site of mass meetings leading to the bus boycott; and **The National Center for the Study of Civil Rights & African-American Culture** highlighting the involvement of the local community and Alabama State University students during the boycott and the Civil Rights Movement.

Birmingham: The **Birmingham Civil Rights Institute** is part history lesson, part audience participation and part demonstration of how the city has evolved since the 1960s. Photos, videos, audio recordings and exhibits put visitors inside the integration movement. Visitors can see "white" and "colored" drinking fountains and a 1950s lunch counter that symbolized segregation in public places. A statue of Rev. Fred Shuttlesworth honors the leader of Birmingham's 1963 demonstrations. At the **Sixteenth Street Baptist Church**, photos are on display in the basement showing the damage of a dynamite blast that ripped through the church in 1963. Walk through **Kelly Ingram Park** to see artists' images from the Civil Rights era. Alabama's largest statue of Dr. Martin Luther King Jr. faces the Sixteenth Street Church. Rent an audio wand at the **Civil Rights Institute** that guides visitors through the park.

Selma-to-Montgomery National Historic Trail: Locations along the route (primarily U.S. 80) are indicated by blue signs erected by the National Park Service. It has been designated both a National Scenic Byway and All-American Road. Some of the more prominent sites to see are: **Brown Chapel AME Church** – a bust of Dr. King is in front of the church. **The Voting Rights Trail Interpretive Center** operated by the National Park Service and the State of Alabama at the midpoint of the trail displays photographs and memorabilia from the march. It is between mile markers 105 and 106 in the rural community of White Hall in Lowndes County. Visitors can walk across the **Edmund Pettus Bridge**, one of the most recognized symbols of the Civil Rights Movement. **National Voting Rights Museum** showcases items and participants' stories related to the voting rights movement. Volunteer guides share their recollections of the struggle to gain the right to vote. **Old Depot Museum** is housed in a restored 1891 railway depot. It includes artifacts from the Civil War and voting rights eras, plus rare African-American photography of early 1900s life.

Tuskegee: The university campus offers the following highlights:

Carver Museum features National Park Service exhibits that spotlight the legacy of black scientist George Washington Carver at Tuskegee Institute. His research on peanuts, sweet potatoes and other crops revolutionized Southern agriculture.

The Oaks is the elegant 1899 home of Tuskegee Institute president Booker T. Washington, designed by black architect Robert Taylor and built by students. The National Park Service operates the house museum on the Tusk pus.

Tuskegee Airmen N The site revisits the Airmen, who help the Armed Forces set the stage for le gation. View exhi programs and en explore this prea Movement. **Motc** Tuskegee Airmen includes photos e era.

Tuskegee Huma Cultural Center ne

student involvement in the Civil Rights Movement.

HANK WILLIAMS TRAIL

The Hank Williams Trail links four museums and additional points of interest important to the life and career of country music's first superstar. Linking sites in Georgiana, Montgomery, Alexander City, Birmingham and Tuscumbia, the trail begins in the rural Mount Olive community off I-65 where young Hank sat on a stool next to the church organ his mother played in the Baptist church. The small church still has services on the second and fourth Sundays of the month and welcomes visitors. The stool is displayed along with other personal mementos nine miles away in Georgiana in the **Hank Williams Boyhood Home**. A stage behind the museum hosts the annual Hank Williams Festival the first weekend of June, reuniting fans, current country musicians and surviving members of his Drifting Cowboys band.

Sixty miles north on I-65, officially named the **Hank Williams Memorial Lost Highway**, is Montgomery, the city where the singer began his career with a live radio show while a teenager. The **Hank Williams Museum** in downtown Montgomery contains the largest collection of costumes, boots, records, photographs and documents related to the careers of Hank and Audrey Williams. The powder blue Cadillac convertible in which the singer died on Jan. 1, 1953, is on loan from his son, singer Hank Williams, Jr. The museum is two blocks from the street where Hank Sr. not only began his radio career and won his first talent contest, but it is also the street where he last performed in public four days before his death.

DESTINATIONS

MOUNTAIN REGION

Bridgeport. Preserving the record of more than 8,000 years of Native American occupation, **Russell Cave National Monument** is an archaeological cave shelter containing prehistoric artifacts in the visitor center. Living history demonstrations of weapons and tools are also available. Explore the Indian Garden and hiking trails.

Cullman is home to the amazing **Ave Maria Grotto**—over 125 miniature reproductions of famous churches, shrines and buildings from all over the world. Scenic pathways lead visitors past the Pantheon in Rome, the Hanging Garden of Babylon, Ave Maria Grotto, the city of Jerusalem and St. Peter's Basilica in Rome. The **North Alabama Museum of History and Fine Arts** is said to have one of the best collections in the world today of porcelain, antiques, bronzes, cut glass and more.

Decatur. Ducks are a big draw at this town on the Tennessee River. The 750-acre **Point Mallard Park** offers hiking and biking trails, picnic facilities, a wave pool, diving pool, duck pond, water slides, wave and kiddie pools and water bubbles. They also have the largest free 4th of July Celebration in North Alabama with family games and live entertainment. Also visit Decatur's **Historic Bank Street** and **Old Decatur and Albany Historic Districts** containing the largest concentration of Victorian homes and bungalows in Alabama. Known as the "Painted Ladies," some date back to the early 1800s. The **Civil War Walking Tour** features 11 historic markers relating events from the four day battle in 1864. **Cooks Natural Science Museum** contains over 2,000 exhibits and artifacts, science films and live and interactive exhibits. **Wheeler National Wildlife Refuge** is located 1-1/2 miles east of Decatur and is an excellent spot for observing flights of migratory waterfowl from September to May.

Double Springs. Bankhead National Forest's approximately 185,000 acres of natural beauty awaits explorers. Enjoy hiking, biking, canoeing, wildlife watching, swimming, fishing and boating. Trails lead to gorges, canyons, natural bridges, lakes and bluffs. The **Corinth Recreational Area**, part of the **William B Bankhead National Forest,** is located on the banks of beautiful 22,000 acre **Lake Lewis Smith**. Boat launches, a large beach, campgrounds and hiking trails are located in this area of diverse terrain and landscapes. Nearby are many attractions of historic, educational and geological interest.

Florence. Among the many museums to visit are **Alabama's Frank Lloyd Wright Rosenbaum House Museum**, fully restored and constructed of cypress, glass and brick; **Indian Mound & Museum**, whose temple atop the 43-ft. high mound was once a place for ceremonies honoring the sun god. An on-site museum features Native American artifacts of weaponry, culture and lifestyle dating back 10,000 years. **Pope's Tavern Museum**, a 19th century structure, was once a stagecoach stop and inn and was used as a military hospital during the Civil War. The **W.C. Handy Birthplace, Museum & Library** is composed of original hand hewn logs in the cabin. The museum contains the most complete collection in the world of personal papers and artifacts of the "Father of the Blues."

Fort Payne. Known as the "Grand Canyon of the South," **Little River Canyon** offers scenic views, rafting, rock climbing, camping and nature study. It contains the only stream in the world that has its source and runs its course entirely on the top of a mountain. Also visit the **Depot Museum**, home to a wonderful collection of relics including Native American artifacts, early 20th-century medical equipment and books, the farming tools of early settlers and military uniforms. Adorning the walls are interesting murals.

Grant. Cathedral Caverns contains wide chambers, a stalagmite "forest" and fossils estimated at 220 million years old.

Huntsville. Housed in one of America's oldest railroad structures, the **Historic Huntsville Depot** invites visitors to enjoy a sight and sound history of Huntsville, original Civil War graffiti and trolley tours of downtown Huntsville. Other attractions include:

Huntsville Museum of Art offers year-round exhibitions and educational programs.

Things to See & Do

FAIRHOPE
Wales West Train & Garden Lovers

FORT RUCKER
U.S. Army Aviation Museum

GADSDEN
Noccalula Falls

HUNTSVILLE
Alabama Constitution Village
Burritt on the Mountain
Early Works Children's Museum
Harrison Brothers Hardware
Historic Huntsville Depot
Huntsville Botanical Garden
Huntsville Convention & Visitors Bureau
Huntsville Museum of Art
Sci-Quest Hands-On Science Center
US Space & Rocket Center
Weeden House Museum

MOBILE
Bellingrath Gardens & Home

MOORESVILLE
Alabama Mountain Lakes Tourist Association

RV Sales & Service

	SALES	SERVICE
BIRMINGHAM		
Heritage Coach & RV Center		•
JASPER		
Burton's RV Service	•	•
MONTGOMERY		
Prattville Auto & RV Repair Center		•

Woodall's Quick & Easy Reference for Alabama

	BIG RIGS WELCOME	INTERNET FRIENDLY	PETS WELCOME	WEB SAVER
ANNISTON				
Country Court RV Park	▲		■	
ASHFORD				
Shallow Creek RV Park	▲		■	
AUBURN				
Leisure Time Campgrounds	▲	●	■	
BIRMINGHAM				
Heritage Coach & RV Center				$
M & J RV Park	▲		■	
CULLMAN				
Cullman Campground	▲	●	■	
DAUPHIN ISLAND				
Dauphin Island Campground (City Park)	▲	●	■	
DECATUR				
Point Mallard Campground (City Park)	▲	●	■	
ELBERTA				
Lazy Acres	▲	●	■	
FAIRHOPE				
Driftwood RV Park	▲	●	■	
Wales West Train & Garden Lovers RV Resort	▲	●	■	
FOLEY				
Anchors Aweigh RV Resort	▲	●	■	
Palm Lake Rv Park	▲	●	■	
GADSDEN				
Noccalula Falls Park & Campground (City Park)	▲	●	■	
GREENVILLE				
Sherling Lake Park & Campground (City Park)	▲		■	
GULF SHORES				
Gulf Breeze Resort	▲	●	■	
Island Retreat RV Park	▲	●	■	$
Southport Campgrounds			■	
GUNTERSVILLE				
Seibold Campground	▲		■	
HEFLIN				
Cane Creek RV Park & Campground	▲	●	■	
HUNTSVILLE				
Huntsville Convention & Visitors Bureau				$
Mountain Breeze RV Park	▲		■	
JASPER				
Sleepy Holler Campground	▲		■	
JEMISON				
Peach Queen Campground	▲	●	■	
LANGSTON				
Little Mountain Marina Camping Resort	▲	●	■	$
South Sauty Creek Resort	▲		■	
LILLIAN				
KOA-Pensacola/Perdido Bay		●	■	
MAGNOLIA SPRINGS				
Magnolia RV Park	▲	●	■	
Southwind RV Park	▲	●	■	
MCCALLA				
McCalla Campground	▲		■	
MOBILE				
Alabama Port RV Park	▲		■	
I-10 Kampground	▲		■	
Payne's RV Park	▲	●	■	
Shady Acres Campground	▲	●	■	
Shady Grove Campground	▲		■	
MONTGOMERY				
Capital City RV Park	▲	●	■	
Montgomery Campground			■	
Prattville Auto & RV Repair Center				$
The Woods RV Park and Campground	▲	●	■	
OPELIKA				
Lakeside RV Park		●	■	
OZARK				
Ozark Travel Park	▲	●	■	

▲ = Big Rigs Welcome; ● = Internet Hookups; ● = (Wi-Fi available); ■ = Pets Welcome; $ = Web Saver Coupons

Check out the "How to Use This Directory" section in the front of this book for a description of the criteria Woodall's uses in this chart.

Twickenham Historic District contains homes dating from 1814. The Weeden House Museum, built in 1819, is noted for its collection of period furnishings.

U.S. Space & Rocket Center. See the past, present and future of space exploration at this center. Take part in hands-on exhibits and demonstrations, including a Mars Mission simulator, **G Force Accelerator**, **Space Shuttle**, **Saturn V** and a bus tour that takes you through the nearby **NASA Marshall Space Flight Center**. It is also home to the **Spacedome IMAX® Theater** and the **US Space Camp**.

Killen is home to the **Pettus Museum** which brings history to life with artifacts and exhibits from every period in American history including military collectibles, postal history and the Boy Scouts of America.

Natural Bridge. The Natural Bridge of Alabama is the largest sandstone rock bridge east of the Rockies. At 60-ft. high and 148-ft. long, it spans scenic natural areas, forests and wilderness.

Valley Head. Located just off I-59 and west of the Georgia border, Valley Head's main attraction is **Sequoyah Caverns**. One of the country's most outstanding show caves, Sequoyah Caverns features fantastic formations, ancient fossils and the famous "Looking Glass Lakes."

METROPOLITAN

Alexander City. Wind Creek State Park is situated on the shores of beautiful Lake Martin and includes camping, a marina, hiking trails and 210-foot fishing pier.

Anniston. See displays of dinosaurs and fossils, a 400 species bird collection, Egyptian mummies and a replica of an Alabama cave at the **Anniston Museum of Natural History**. The **Berman Museum of World History** contains military artifacts from ancient Greece through World War II. Visit the highest point in Alabama at **Cheaha State Park**, 2,407 feet above sea level. A restaurant offers panoramic views and camping is available.

Birmingham. Not-to-be-missed attractions within Birmingham include: **Birmingham Botanical Gardens**; **McWane Center**, an exciting science museum and IMAX Theatre; **Birmingham Zoo**, with more than 700 rare and exotic animals; the **Birmingham Museum of Art**, with Asian, European and American collections; and the **Alabama Sports Hall of Fame**, honoring such greats as Joe Louis, Paul "Bear" Bryant and Jesse Owens. Ride the Rampage wooden roller coaster and other thrill rides at **Magic Adventure Theme Park** or cool off at **Splash Beach Water Park**. Take a self-guided journey through the Civil Rights Movement and human rights struggle at the **Birmingham Civil Rights Institute**. Learn about jazz greats Lionel Hampton, Sun Ra and more at the **Alabama Jazz Hall of Fame**.

In **Childersburg,** explore chambers larger than a football field at **DeSoto Caverns**. You'll travel 160 feet underground and see a laser light and sound show. You can visit a fully operational, 134-year old covered bridge at **Kymulga Grist Mill & Covered Bridge**.

Gadsden. Noccalula Falls is the famous site of the Native American legend of the princess who hurled herself from the heights into the river after her lover's death. The park features 90-foot waterfalls, a War Memorial, pioneer homestead, botanical gardens, carpet golf and hiking trails.

Talladega. Auto buffs and racing fans won't want to miss Talladega's automotive attractions. **Talladega Superspeedway** is the world's fastest speedway and the site of numerous racing events. At the **International Motorsports Hall of Fame** you can see record-breaking and special autos, ride the famous "#43" race car simulator and view memorabilia dating back to 1902.

Tuscaloosa. Wonderful old buildings within Tuscaloosa include the **Battle-Friedman House** (1835), Gorgas House (1829) and the Old Tavern Museum (1827). The **Children's Hands-on Museum of Tuscaloosa** features hands-on exhibits, in-depth programs and special events that provide a fun learning experience just for kids. Exhibits include a Choctaw Indian Village, a planetarium, a children's hospital, a bank, a TV studio, **The Wardrobe**, a print shop, a general store and Images (a color and light display). You can view 26 prehistoric platform mounds, a reconstructed

Woodall's Quick & Easy Reference for Alabama

	BIG RIGS WELCOME	INTERNET FRIENDLY	PETS WELCOME	WEB SAVER
PELHAM				
Birmingham South Campground	▲	●	■	
PELL CITY				
Lakeside Landing RV Park & Marina	▲	●	■	
Safe Harbor RV Park	▲	●	■	
PRATTVILLE				
Autauga Creek RV Campground			■	
Kountry Air RV Park	▲	●	■	
ROBERTSDALE				
Hilltop RV Park		●	■	
Styx River Resort	▲	●	■	
Wilderness RV Park	▲	●	■	
SUMMERDALE				
Royal Palm Motor Coach Villages		●		$
TALLADEGA				
Logan Landing RV Resort & Campground	▲	●	■	
Talladega Creekside Resort	▲	●	■	
THEODORE				
Azalea RV Park	▲	●	■	
TROY				
Deer Run RV Park	▲	●	■	
TUSCALOOSA				
Sunset Travel Park	▲		■	
TUSCUMBIA				
Heritage Acres RV Park	▲	●	■	

▲ = Big Rigs Welcome; ● = Internet Hookups; ● = (Wi-Fi available); ■ = Pets Welcome; $ = Web Saver Coupons

Check out the "How to Use This Directory" section in the front of this book for a description of the criteria Woodall's uses in this chart.

Native American village and a museum at **Moundville Archaeological Park**. Nature trails are also available. Public tours are available at the newly opened **Mercedes-Benz U.S. International** assembly plant with museum and gift shop.

RIVER HERITAGE REGION

Andalusia. Hiking trails at **Conecuh National Forest** lead through holly, dogwoods, longleaf pine and magnolia trees and past scenic cypress ponds and natural springs.

Enterprise. Visit the world's only monument to a pest. The **Boll Weevil Monument** was built in 1915 after the boll weevil devoured 2/3 of Coffee County's cotton crop, forcing local farmers to become more diversified.

Eufaula. Lake Eufaula, the "Bass Capital of the World," features a lodge, restaurant, camping and marina at Lakepoint Resort State Park. A fabulous historic district in the city provides a chance to visit such landmarks as Shorter Mansion and Fendall Hall.

Fort Rucker. See military airplanes, helicopters and the largest collection of archives on U.S. Army aviation at the **U.S. Army Aviation Museum.**

Montgomery. Attractions include the **Montgomery Zoo**, which features habitats from 5 continents and over 800 animals. Other attractions within Montgomery are:

Civil Rights Memorial. This tribute to the 40 Americans who died during the Civil Rights Movement from 1954 to 1968 documents the events of the Civil Rights struggle.

Dexter Parsonage Museum. Former home of Rev. Dr. Martin Luther King, Jr. family . Interpretive Center chronicles history that led to the Montgomery bus boycott and the Civil Rights Movement.

Ozark. This small Southern town almost doubles its size as visitors converge downtown the first Saturday in October. The annual **Claybank Jamboree** features arts and crafts, live music, clogging and line dancing. Anglers may want to stop by **Dale County Public Lake**—92 acres of good bass fishing!

Selma. Historic attractions abound including **Historic Water Avenue**, a 19th century restored commercial district offering scenic views, historic buildings, markers and picnicking areas. **The Old Town Historic District** is one of the largest historic districts in the state including Sturdivant Hall. There are more than 1,200 buildings dating from the 1820s. The "Windshield Tour," with brochures and tapes available from the chamber of commerce, covers 116 historic sites. Take the **Martin Luther King, Jr. Street Historic Walking Tour** and experience the history of Selma's Civil Rights movement.

Spanish Fort. See close-up views of nature's creatures at **Meaher State Park** as well as indigenous plants on two self-guided walking trails, which have boardwalks over Mobile Delta. Any angler will be lured here by a 300-ft. fishing pier. Paddleboat rentals and picnic areas are available to all. New for 2007 is the **Delta Resource Center**. Five Rivers, as the center is called, encompasses seven buildings on 81 acres at the juncture of the Mobile-Tensaw Delta and the Mobile Bay. Among the facilities are the **Shellbank Visitor Center**, **Bartram Canoe and Kayak Landing** and the **Nature Center Complex** which has three buildings.

GULF COAST REGION

Dauphin Island. Fort Gaines Historic Site was the site of a week-long naval and land battle which led to the eventual capture by Union forces. Onsite are cannons used in the Civil War battle, soldiers' quarters, tunnels and bastions.

Gulf Shores. The coastal community entices visitors with unsurpassed Gulf vistas and the following attractions:

Gulf Beaches. Enjoy 32 miles of sun and surf on miles of sugar-white sand. Among the facilities at the 6,000-acre **Gulf State Park** is the popular fishing pier, which extends 825 ft. into the Gulf.

Mobile. Your first stop in Mobile should be **Fort Conde Museum** with its partially reconstructed 1720s French fort, costumed guides and visitor information center. Also worth seeing in Mobile is the **Cathedral of the Immaculate Conception,** an 1835 Greek Revival masterpiece built on old Spanish burial grounds.

Gulf Coast Exploreum Science Center. Science is fun at this hands-on museum where visitors can ride the bicycle generator and power a television monitor. You can test the delayed shadow exhibit where shadows linger after you've gone. You can also visit the Imax Theater.

U.S.S. Alabama Battleship Memorial Park. Tour a mighty battleship, inspect aircraft and stroll through the fleet submarine, U.S.S. Drum. This 100-acre park also offers a picnic and barbeque area, a nature observatory, a model airplane flying field and a rose garden.

ANNUAL EVENTS

JANUARY

Pancake Day, Fairhope.

FEBRUARY

Mardi Gras (through March), Mobile; Heritage Arts Festival, Monroesville; Mobile Boat Show, Mobile.

MARCH

Opp Jaycees Rattlesnake Rodeo, Opp; Bridge Crossing Jubilee, Selma; Arts & Crafts Festival & Outdoor Show, Fairhope; Festival of Flowers, Mobile.

APRIL

Alabama Crawfish Festival, Faunsdale; Birmingham International Festival Salute, Birmingham; Spring Festival of Flowers.

MAY

Polk Salat Festival, Arab; Blessing of the Fleet, Bayou La Batre; Alabama Jubilee Hot-Air Balloon Classic, Decatur; Riverfest, Gadsden; Jubilee Cityfest, Montgomery; Whistlestop Festival & Rocket City Barbecue Cookoff, Huntsville; Homestead.

JUNE

The Miracle Worker Play & Helen Keller Festival (through July), Tuscumbia; Jazz Fest, Alexander City; Miss Alabama Pageant, Birmingham; Alabama Blueberry Festival.

JULY

W. C. Handy Music Festival (through August), Florence & The Shoals Area; World Championship Domino Tournament andalusia; Alabama Deep Sea Fishing Tournament, Dauphin Island; Spirit of America Festival, Decatur.

AUGUST

Black Belt Folk Roots Festival, Eutaw; World's Longest Yard Sale, Fort Payne, Gadsden, Mentone; Gulf Coast Ethnic & Heritage Jazz Festival, Mobile.

SEPTEMBER

Mullet Festival, Lillian; Jubilee Festival, Daphne; Racking Horse World Celebration, Decatur; Alabama Catfish Festival, Greensboro; Fall Festival, Theodore; Coon Dog Graveyard Labor Day Celebration; EA Sports 500 Weekend, Talladega.

OCTOBER

Harvest Festival, Boaz; Oktoberfest, Cullman; Carver Sweet Potato Festival, Tuskegee; National Shrimp Festival, Gulf Shores; Syrup Soppin' Festival, Loachapoka.

NOVEMBER

National Veterans Day Parade, Birmingham; National Peanut Festival, Dothan; Alabama Pecan Festival, Tillman's Corner; Galaxy of Lights, Huntsville; Holiday Light Festival, Montgomery; Magic Christmas in Lights, Mobile.

DECEMBER

Christmas at Arlington, Birmingham; Christmas on the River, Demopolis; Christmas in Historic Decatur, Decatur; Victorian Christmas, Dothan; Stars on the Water Boat Parade, Guntersville.

Alabama

ALBERTA—D-2

(SE) CHILATCHEE CREEK PARK (COE-Alabama River Lakes)—(Wilcox) *From jct Hwy 5 & CR 29: follow signs 9 mi on CR 29.* FACILITIES: 53 sites, 47 W&E, 6 no hkups, tenting, dump station, laundry, fire rings, grills, wood. RECREATION: pavilion, boating, ramp, dock, river fishing, playground, hiking trails. Rec open to public. Partial handicap access. Open Mar thru Nov 11. Phone: (334)573-2562.

ALEXANDER CITY—C-4

(S) WIND CREEK SP—(Tallapoosa) *From jct Hwy-63 & Hwy-128: Go 1-1/2 mi E on Hwy-128.* FACILITIES: 636 sites, 245 full hkups, 391 W&E, (30 amps), tenting, dump station, laundry, full svc store, ice, grills. RECREATION: pavilion, lake swimming, boating, ramp, dock, 8 rowboat/2 pedal boat rentals, lake fishing, playground, planned activities, hiking trails. Rec open to public. Partial handicap access. Open all yr. Phone: (256)329-0845.

ANDALUSIA—E-3

(S) CONECUH NF (Open Pond Campground)—(Covington) *From jct US-84 & US-29: Go 10 mi S on US-29, then 6 mi S on Hwy-137, then 1/2 mi E on CR-24, then 1 mi SE on FR-336.* FACILITIES: 55 sites, 32 W&E, 23 no hkups, tenting, dump station, ltd groceries, fire rings, grills. RECREATION: boating, electric motors only, canoeing, ramp, lake/pond fishing, hiking trails. Partial handicap access. Open all yr. Phone: (334)222-2555.

ANNISTON—B-4

(S) COUNTRY COURT RV PARK—(Calhoun) *E'bnd: From jct I-20 (exit 188) & Hwy 78: Go N 300 feet, then 1-1/2 mi E on Hwy 78. (Ent on L). W'bnd: From jct I-20 & Hwy 431/78 (exit 191): Go 2-3/4 mi W on Hwy 431/78 (Ent on R)*

◇◇◇FACILITIES: 45 sites, typical site width 30 ft, accepts full hkup units only, 45 full hkups, (30 & 50 amps), 19 pull-thrus, cable TV, tables, patios.

Pets welcome. No tents. Open all yr. No restrooms. Big rigs welcome. Rate in 2007 $20 per vehicle. Phone: (256)835-2045.

SEE AD THIS PAGE

ARLEY—B-2

(E) Hidden Cove Outdoor Resort—(Winston) *I-65 (Cullman exit 308) & Hwy 278: Go 16 mi W on Hwy 278 to Hwy 77: Go 9 mi S on Hwy 77 to CR 12/3919. Enter on R.* ◇◇◇◇FACILITIES: 64 sites, 60 full hkups, 4 W&E, (30 & 50 amps), 25 pull-thrus, tenting, dump station, laundry, ice, tables, fire rings, grills.

ARLEY—Continued
Hidden Cove Outdoor Resort—Continued

◇◇◇◇RECREATION: rec hall, pavilion, swim pool, boating, ramp, dock, lake fishing, mini-golf, playground, horseshoes, hiking trails, v-ball. Pets welcome. Open all yr. Rate in 2007 $31.50 per vehicle. Phone: (205)221-7042.

ASHFORD—E-5

(N) SHALLOW CREEK RV PARK—(Houston) *From jct Ross Clark Cir & Hwy 84 E: Go 7 mi E to Hwy 55, then 1-1/2 mi N on Hwy 55. Enter on R.*

◇◇◇FACILITIES: 60 sites, typical site width 30 ft, 60 full hkups, (30 & 50 amps), 10 pull-thrus, phone/cable on-site Internet access (needs activ), tenting, RV storage, laundry, tables.

◇◇RECREATION: swim pool, golf nearby, play equipment, sports field.

Pets welcome. Open all yr. Big rigs welcome. Rate in 2007 $15 for 2 persons. Phone: (877)586-4920.

SEE AD DOTHAN PAGE 12

ATMORE—E-2

CLAUDE D. KELLEY SP—(Escambia) *From jct I-65 & Hwy 21: Go 12 mi N on Hwy 21.* FACILITIES: 17 sites, 5 full hkups, 12 W&E, (30 amps), tenting, grills. RECREATION: pavilion, lake swimming, boating, canoeing, ramp, dock, 5 rowboat/canoe/4 pedal boat rentals, lake fishing, playground, hiking trails, v-ball. Open all yr. Phone: (251)862-2511.

AUBURN—D-4

(S) Bar W Campground—(Lee) *From jct I-85 (exit 51) & US 29: Go 2.2 mi S on US 29, then E 1 mi on Lee Cty Rd 20/395. Enter on L.* ◇◇FACILITIES: 31 sites, typical site width 30 ft, 25 full hkups, 6 W&E, (20, 30 & 50 amps), 10 pull-thrus, tenting. ◇◇RECREATION: pavilion, horseshoes, hiking trails. Pets welcome. Open all yr. Rate in 2007 $20-22 for 2 persons. Phone: (334) 444-0497.

(E) CHEWACLA SP—(Lee) *From jct I-85 (exit 51) & US 29: Go 1/4 mi S on US 29, then 2 mi E on Shell Toomer Pkwy.* FACILITIES: 31 sites, 16 full hkups, 15 no hkups, 9 pull-thrus,

AUBURN—Continued
CHEWACLA SP—Continued

tenting, dump station, laundry, grills. RECREATION: pavilion, lake swimming, boating, electric motors only, canoeing, 2 rowboat/13 canoe/2 pedal boat rentals, lake fishing, playground, tennis, sports field, hiking trails. Rec open to public. Partial handicap access. Open all yr. Phone: (334)887-5621.

(S) LEISURE TIME CAMPGROUNDS—(Lee) *From jct I-85 (exit 51) & US 29: Go 1/4 mi S on US 29. Enter on R.*

◇◇◇◇FACILITIES: 58 sites, typical site width 30 ft, 58 full hkups, (30 & 50 amps), 50 amps ($), some extended stay sites, 28 pull-thrus, cable TV ($), phone Internet access central location, tenting, laundry, ice, tables, grills.

RECREATION: golf nearby.

Pets welcome. Partial handicap access. Open all yr. Big rigs welcome. Internet friendly. Clubs welcome. Rate in 2007 $19-22 per family. MC/VISA/DISC/AMEX/Debit. Member ARVC, ALARVC. Phone: (334)821-2267.

SEE AD THIS PAGE

BIRMINGHAM—B-3

BIRMINGHAM SOUTH CAMPGROUND—*From jct I-459 & I-65: Go 8 mi S on I-65 (exit 242), then 3/4 mi W on Hwy 52, then 1/4 mi N on Hwy 33. Enter on R.*

SEE PRIMARY LISTING AT PELHAM AND AD NEXT PAGE

Carson Village Mobile Home Community (RV SPACES)—(Jefferson) *From jct I-65 & Walker Chapel Rd (exit 267): Go E 6.8 mi on Walker Chapel Rd/Carson Rd (Cross Red Hollow Rd.) Enter on R.* FACILITIES: 30

Carson Village Mobile Home Community—Continued on next page

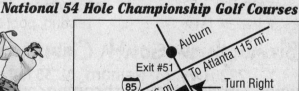

BIRMINGHAM—Continued
Carson Village Mobile Home Community—Continued

sites, typical site width 16 ft, accepts full hkup units only, 30 full hkups, (30 & 50 amps), laundry. RECREATION: rec hall. Pets welcome. No tents. Open all yr. Big rigs welcome. Rate in 2007 $20 per vehicle. Phone: (205)854-0059.

Introducing gourmet meals for your RV kitchen! Woodall's Cooking on the Road with Celebrity Chefs includes dozens of tips and sidebars that makes recipes easier to use while traveling. Go to www.woodalls.com/shop and check it out.

BIRMINGHAM—Continued

✱ **(W) HERITAGE COACH & RV CENTER**—*From jct of I-65 & I-59: Go 12 mi S on I-59 (exit 108), then 1/2 mi NW on Academy Dr, then 1/4 mi NE on Powder Plant Dr. Enter on L.* SERVICES: full-time mech, engine/chassis repair, RV appliance repair, body work/collision repair, 24-hr emerg rd svc, LP gas by weight/by meter, RV storage, sells parts/accessories, installs hitches. Open all yr. MC/VISA. Phone: (205)426-2655.

SEE AD THIS PAGE

Alabama State Rock: Marble

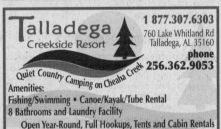

BIRMINGHAM—Continued

(S) M & J RV PARK (REBUILDING)—(Jefferson) *S'bnd: From jct I-59/I-20 (exit 118) & Valley Rd: Go 1/2 mi SW on Valley Rd, then 1-1/4 mi SE on Aaron Aronov Dr, then 1/2 mi SW on Hwy 11/State Hwy 5. Enter on L.*

FACILITIES: 72 sites, accepts full hkup units only, 72 full hkups, (15, 30 & 50 amps), 6 pull-thrus, patios.

RECREATION: golf nearby.

Pets welcome, breed restrict. No tents. Open all yr. No restrooms. Big rigs welcome. MC/VISA/DISC/AMEX/Debit. Phone: (205)788-2605. FMCA discount.

SEE AD THIS PAGE

BLADON SPRINGS—E-1

(E) BLADON SPRINGS STATE PARK—(Choctaw) *From jct US-43 & US-84: Go 25 mi on US-84 E, then turn S on CR-6 traveling approx 4 mi to park.* FACILITIES: tenting.

BOAZ—B-4

(E) Barclay RV Parking—(Marshall) *From jct US 431 & Billy Dyar Blvd: Go 3/4 mi W(under the Barclay Gold billboard.) Enter on L.* ◆◆◆FACILITIES: 22 sites,

Barclay RV Parking—Continued on next page

On December 14, 1819, Alabama became the 22nd state.

BOAZ—Continued
Barclay RV Parking—Continued

typical site width 22 ft, accepts full hkup units only, 22 full hkups, (30 & 50 amps), 50 amps ($), 6 pull-thrus, tables, grills. Pets welcome. No tents. Open all yr. No restrooms. Big rigs welcome. Rate in 2007 $12-15 per vehicle. Phone: (256)593-5913.

CALERA—C-3

(N) Rolling Hills RV Park—(Shelby) *From jct I-65 (exit 231) & US 31: Go 1 blk E to City Rd 304, then 1/2 mi S on City Rd 304. Enter on L.* ◊◊◊FACILITIES: 61 sites, typical site width 30 ft, 61 full hkups, (30 & 50 amps), some extended stay sites, 6 pull-thrus, tenting, laundry. ◊◊◊RECREATION: equipped pavilion, swim pool, boating, no motors, canoeing, canoe/pedal boat rentals, lake fishing, tennis, hiking trails, v-ball. Pets welcome. Open all yr. Rate in 2007 $22.50 per vehicle. Phone: (205)668-6893.

CAMDEN—D-2

(W) EAST BANK ACCESS AREA (COE-Alabama River Lakes)/Millers Ferry Campground—(Wilcox) *From town: Go 10 mi W on Hwy-28.* FACILITIES: 65 sites, 59 W&E, 6 no hkups, tenting, dump station, laundry, fire rings, grills, wood. RECREATION: pavilion, lake/river swimming, boating, ramp, river fishing, playground, sports field, v-ball. Rec open to public. Partial handicap access. Open all yr. Phone: (334)682-4191.

(N) ROLAND COOPER SP—(Wilcox) *From jct Hwy-10 & Hwy-41: Go 6 mi NE on Hwy-41.* FACILITIES: 60 sites, 47 full hkups, 13 no hkups, tenting, dump station, laundry, ltd groceries, grills, wood. RECREATION: pavilion, boating, ramp, lake fishing, playground, hiking trails. Rec open to public. Pets welcome. Open all yr. Phone: (334)682-4838.

CASTLEBERRY—E-3

(S) Country Sunshine RV Park—(Conecuh) *From jct I-65 (exit 83) & CR 6: Go 3-1/2 mi E on CR 6. Enter on L.* ◊◊FACILITIES: 17 sites, typical site width 20 ft, 17 full hkups, (30 & 50 amps), 50 amps ($), 11 pull-thrus, tenting, laundry, tables, grills. ◊ Pets welcome. Open all yr. Big rigs welcome. Rate in 2007 $21-23.50 for 4 persons. Phone: (251)966-5540. CCUSA discount.

CENTRE—B-4

(E) John's Campground & Grocery—(Cherokee) *In town, from jct Hwy 9 & US 411: Go 7.1 mi SE on N US 411, then 1-3/4 mi N on CR 31. Enter on R.* ◊◊FACILITIES: 58 sites, typical site width 26 ft, 26 full hkups, 32 W&E, (30 & 50 amps), some extended stay sites, tenting, dump station, portable dump, laundry, full svc store, LP gas by weight/by meter, ice, tables, patios, grills, wood. ◊◊◊RECREATION: lake swimming, boating, canoeing, ramp, dock, lake fishing, sports field. Rec open to public. Pets welcome. Partial handicap access. Open all yr. Rate in 2007 $25 per family. Phone: (256)475-3234.

At 2,405 feet Cheaha Mountain is Alabama's highest point above sea level and mean elevation is 500 feet at its lowest elevation point.

CENTREVILLE—C-3

(W) TALLADEGA NF (Payne Lake West Side)—(Hale) *From town: Go 2 mi W on US 82, then 6 mi S on Hwy 5, then 15 mi W on Hwy 25.* FACILITIES: 72 sites, 22 ft max RV length, 72 no hkups, tenting, cold showers only, dump station, grills. RECREATION: lake swimming, boating, electric motors only, canoeing, ramp, lake fishing, hiking trails. Open all yr. Phone: (205)926-9765.

CHILDERSBURG—C-3

(E) DeSoto Caverns Park Campground—(Talladega) *From jct US-280 & Hwy-76: Go 5 mi E on Hwy-76. Enter on L.* ◊◊◊◊FACILITIES: 21 sites, typical site width 30 ft, 16 full hkups, (20, 30 & 50 amps), 5 no hkups, tenting, ice, tables, grills. ◊◊RECREATION: equipped pavilion, mini-golf ($), playground, hiking trails. Pets welcome. Partial handicap access. Open all yr. Internet friendly. Rate in 2007 $25.99 for 4 persons. Phone: (800)933-2283. CCUSA discount.

CITRONELLE—E-1

(W) CITRONELLE LAKEVIEW RV PARK (City Park)—(Mobile) *From jct US 45 & Hwy 96: Go 5 mi W on Hwy 96 to Citronelle Lakeside Park entrance, then 3 mi S. Enter at end.* FACILITIES: 38 sites, 31 full hkups, 7 W&E, (30 & 50 amps), 7 pull-thrus, tenting, dump station, laundry, fire rings, grills. RECREATION: pavilion, boating, canoeing, ramp, lake fishing, sports field, hiking trails. Partial handicap access. Open all yr. Phone: (251)866-9647.

CLANTON—C-3

(E) Peach Park RV Park—(Chilton) *I-65 & Hwy 31 (exit 205): Turn E 300 yds. Enter on L.* ◊◊◊FACILITIES: 14 sites, typical site width 30 ft, accepts full hkup units only, 14 full hkups, (50 amps), tables, patios. ◊RECREATION: pavilion, playground. Pets welcome. No tents. Open all yr. No restrooms. Big rigs welcome. Rate in 2007 $17 per vehicle. Phone: (205)755-2065.

CLIO—E-4

(E) BLUE SPRINGS SP—(Barbour) *From jct Hwy-51 & Hwy-10: Go 6 mi E on Hwy-10.* FACILITIES: 50 sites, 7 full hkups, 43 W&E, (30 amps), 7 pull-thrus, tenting, dump station, grills. RECREATION: pavilion, swim pool, river fishing, playground, tennis. Rec open to public. Partial handicap access. Open all yr. Phone: (334)397-4875.

COCHRANE—C-1

(E) COCHRANE CAMPGROUND (COE-Tennessee/Tombigbee Waterway)—(Pickens) *In town, off Hwy 17, follow signs.* FACILITIES: 60 sites, 60 W&E, (30 amps), dump station, laundry, ice, patios, fire rings, grills. RECREATION: pavilion, boating, ramp, dock, lake/river fishing, playground, hiking trails, v-ball. Partial handicap access. Open Mar 1 thru Dec 31. Max stay 14 days. Phone: (205)373-8806.

COFFEEVILLE—E-1

(W) SERVICE PARK (COE-Coffeeville Lake)—(Choctaw) *From town: Go 3 mi W on US 84. Enter on R.* FACILITIES: 32 sites, 32 W&E, (50 amps), 11 pull-thrus, tenting, dump station, non-guest dumping $, laundry, fire rings, grills. RECREATION: lake swimming, boating, canoeing, ramp, lake/river fishing, playground. Rec open to public. Partial handicap access. Open all yr. Phone: (334)754-9338.

COTTONTON—D-5

(W) BLUFF CREEK PARK (COE-Walter F. George Lake)—(Russell) *From Hwy 165 in town: Go 2 mi E on park access road.* FACILITIES: 88 sites, 88 W&E, (30 amps), 6 pull-thrus, tenting, dump station, laundry, fire rings, grills, wood. RECREATION: pavilion, lake/river swimming, boating, ramp, dock, lake/river fishing. Open Feb 23 thru Oct 28. Phone: (334)855-2746.

CREOLA—F-2

(NE) DEAD LAKE MARINA & CG—(Mobile) *From I-65 (exit 22): Go 300 yards W on Sailor Rd, then 1/7-10 mi N on Creola Axis Creek Loop, then 2-1/2 mi E on Dead Lake Rd. Enter on L.* FACILITIES: 42 sites, typical site width 30 ft, 24 full hkups, 13 W&E, 5 E, (50 amps), 50 amps ($), some extended stay sites, 37

CREOLA—Continued
DEAD LAKE MARINA & CG—Continued

pull-thrus, tenting, dump station, non-guest dumping $, laundry, groceries, LP gas by meter, ice, wood. RECREATION: rec room/area, pavilion, swim pool, boating, ramp, dock, lake fishing, playground. Rec open to public. Partial handicap access. Open all yr. Phone: (251)574-2266.

CULLMAN—B-3

WELCOME

(W) CULLMAN CAMPGROUND—(Cullman) *From jct I-65 (exit 310) & Hwy 157N: Go 1-1/2 mi N on Hwy 157, then 1 mi S on paved road, following signs. Enter on L.*

◊◊◊◊FACILITIES: 75 sites, typical site width 25 ft, 75 full hkups, (20, 30 & 50 amps), 50 amps ($), some extended stay sites, 67 pull-thrus, wireless Instant Internet access at site, phone Internet access central location, tenting, RV storage, dump station, non-guest dumping $, laundry, ltd groceries, RV supplies, LP gas by weight/by meter, ice, tables, fire rings, wood.

◊◊RECREATION: pavilion, pond fishing, golf nearby, horseshoes, v-ball.

Pets welcome. Partial handicap access. Open all yr. Big rigs welcome. Internet friendly. Escort to site. Clubs welcome. Rate in 2007 $19-21 for 2 persons. MC/VISA/DISC. Phone: (256)734-5853.

e-mail: campgroundscullm@bellsouth.net

SEE AD THIS PAGE

(S) Good Hope Campground—(Cullman) *From jct I-65 & Hwy 69,(exit 304) then 1/2 mi N on Super Saver Road Enter on L.* ◊◊FACILITIES: 36 sites, typical site width 25 ft, 36 full hkups, (20 & 30 amps), 19 pull-thrus, tenting, dump station, non-guest dumping $, laundry, LP gas by weight/by meter, ice, tables, wood. ◊RECREATION: play equipment, hiking trails. Pets welcome. Partial handicap access. Open all yr. Internet friendly. Rate in 2007 $22-24 for 2 persons. Phone: (256)739-1319.

DAUPHIN ISLAND—F-1

WELCOME

(E) DAUPHIN ISLAND CAMPGROUND (City Park)—(Mobile) *At end of Hwy 193: Turn left & go 2 mi on Bienville Blvd. Enter on R.*

FACILITIES: 152 sites, typical site width 30 ft, 76 full hkups, 76 W&E, (30 & 50 amps), 8 pull-thrus, wireless Instant Internet access at site ($), tenting, dump station, laundry, groceries, RV supplies, ice, tables, controlled access gate.

RECREATION: rec hall, equipped pavilion, saltwater swimming, boating, ramp, dock, saltwater fishing, golf nearby, bsktball, playground, shuffleboard court, planned activities, horseshoes, hiking trails, v-ball.

Pets welcome. Partial handicap access. Open all yr. Big rigs welcome. Internet friendly. Clubs welcome. MC/VISA. Phone: (251)861-2742.

e-mail: dipbb@email.msn.com

SEE AD THIS PAGE

DECATUR—A-3

(W) MALLARD CREEK (TVA-Wheeler Lake)—(Lawrence) *From town: Go 11-1/2 mi W on US-72A/Hwy-20, then 3-3/4 mi N on Spring Creek Rd.* FACILITIES: 56 sites, 56 W&E, tenting, dump station, grills. RECREATION: pavilion, lake swimming, boating, ramp, lake fishing, playground. Open Mar 21 thru Nov 3. Phone: (256)386-2231.

DECATUR—Continued on next page

DECATUR—Continued

(E) POINT MALLARD CAMPGROUND (City Park)—(Morgan) *From jct I-65 (exit 340) & Alt US 72/Hwy 20: Go 3 mi W on ALT US 72/Hwy 20, then 1 mi S (across the bridge) on US 31. At the second traffic light, go 3 mi E on Church St. (Follow signs) Enter at end.*

FACILITIES: 210 sites, typical site width 25 ft, 114 full hkups, 96 W&E, (20, 30 & 50 amps), 22 pull-thrus, phone Internet access central location, tenting, dump station, laundry, ltd groceries, RV supplies, ice, tables, grills, wood.

RECREATION: rec hall, equipped pavilion, swim pool, river fishing, putting green, bsktball, playground, tennis, sports field, hiking trails, v-ball. Rec open to public.

Pets welcome. Partial handicap access. Open all yr. Big rigs welcome. Internet friendly. Clubs welcome. MC/VISA/Debit. Phone: (256)351-7772.

SEE AD THIS PAGE

DELTA—C-4

CHEAHA SP—(Cleburne) *From jct Hwy 49 & Hwy 281: Go 5 mi N on Hwy 281. Enter on L.* FACILITIES: 84 sites, 73 full hkups, 11 no hkups, 39 pull-thrus, tenting, laundry, ltd groceries, ice, grills, wood. RECREATION: pavilion, lake swimming, boating, canoeing, lake fishing, playground, hiking trails. Rec open to public. Pets welcome. Partial handicap access. Open all yr. Phone: (256)488-5111.

DEMOPOLIS—D-2

(N) FORKLAND PARK (COE-Demopolis Lake)—(Greene) *From town: Go 12 mi N on US 43, then 1 mi W on dirt road to pavement. Enter at end.* FACILITIES: 42 sites, 42 W&E, (50 amps), 13 pull-thrus, tenting, dump station, non-guest dumping $, laundry, fire rings, grills. RECREATION: equipped pavilion, lake/river swimming, boating, ramp, dock, lake fishing, playground. Rec open to public. Partial handicap access. Open all yr. Phone: (334)289-5530.

(W) FOSCUE PARK (COE-Demopolis Lake)—(Marengo) *From jct US 43/Hwy 13 & US 80/Hwy 8: Go 2 mi W on US 80/Hwy 8, then 2 mi N on Maria St. Enter on R.* FACILITIES: 54 sites, 49 full hkups, 5 W&E, (50 amps), tenting, dump station, non-guest dumping $, laundry, fire rings, grills. RECREATION: equipped pavilion, lake swimming, boating, canoeing, ramp, dock, lake fishing, playground, sports field, hiking trails, v-ball. Rec open to public. Partial handicap access. Open all yr. Phone: (334)289-5535.

DOTHAN—E-5

(S) Pecan Point RV Park—(Henry) *From S jct Ross Clark Circle & US 231 S: Go 1-1/2 mi S on US 231 S/Oates St. Enter on R.* ◆◆◆FACILITIES: 62 sites, typical site width 30 ft, accepts full hkup units only, 62 full hkups, (30 & 50 amps), many extended stay sites, 29 pull-thrus, dump station, non-guest dumping $, laundry, tables, patios. ◆RECREATION: pavilion, sports field. Pets welcome. No tents. Open all yr. Big rigs welcome. Rate in 2007 $25 for 2 persons. Member ARVC, ALARVC. Phone: (334)673-3737. CCUSA discount.

Alabama State Gem: Star Blue Quartz

DOTHAN—Continued
Pecan Point RV Park—Continued

DOUBLE SPRINGS—B-2

(W) BANKHEAD NF (Corinth Rec Area)—(Winston) *From town: Go 5-1/2 mi E on US 278, then 3-1/2 mi S on CR 57.* FACILITIES: 50 sites, 50 full hkups, 5 pull-thrus, dump station, fire rings, grills. RECREATION: pavilion, lake swimming, boating, canoeing, ramp, lake fishing. Rec open to public. Partial handicap access. Open Mar 19 thru Dec 1. No reservations. Max stay 14 days. Phone: (205)489-5111.

(E) BANKHEAD NF (Houston Rec Area)—(Winston) *From town: Go 10 mi E on US-278, then 2 mi S on CR-63, then 2 mi SW on CR-64, then 1 mi W on FR-118.* FACILITIES: 57 sites, 30 ft max RV length, 57 no hkups, 1 pull-thrus, tenting, dump station, ltd groceries, fire rings, grills. RECREATION: lake swimming, boating, canoeing, ramp, dock, lake fishing, hiking trails. Partial handicap access. Open Apr 1 thru Sep 15. No reservations. Max stay 14 days. Phone: (205)489-5111.

(W) CORINTH RECREATION AREA—(Winston) *From town: Go 5 mi E on US 278, then go 3 mi S on CR 57 (at church) to entrance. Enter at end.* FACILITIES: 58 sites, 58 full hkups, (30 & 50 amps), tenting, dump station, non-guest dumping $, fire rings, grills, wood. RECREATION: equipped pavilion, lake swimming, boating, ramp, dock, lake/3fishing. Partial handicap access. Open May 16 thru Nov 1. Phone: (205)489-3165.

ELBERTA—F-2

(E) LAZY ACRES—(Baldwin) *From jct Hwy 83 & Hwy 98: Go 9-1/2 mi E on Hwy 98.*

◆◆◆FACILITIES: 52 sites, typical site width 30 ft, 44 full hkups, 8 W&E, (20, 30 & 50 amps), some extended stay sites, 22 pull-thrus, phone Internet access central location, tenting, dump station, laundry, LP gas by weight, ice, tables, fire rings.

◆◆◆RECREATION: rec hall, swim pool, pond swimming, pond fishing, golf nearby, bsktball, playground, planned activities, horseshoes, v-ball.

Pets welcome. Partial handicap access. Open all yr. Big rigs welcome. Internet friendly. Clubs welcome. Rate in 2007 $21-30 for 2 persons. MC/VISA/DISC/AMEX. Phone: (877)986-5266.

e-mail: lazyacres@gulftel.com

SEE AD TRAVEL SECTION PAGE 4

(S) Plantation Harbor RV Resort (Wolf Bay Plantations)—(Baldwin) *From jct Hwy 98 & Hwy 59: Go 2-1/2 mi S on Hwy 59, then 5 mi E on CR 20.* ◆◆◆◆FACILITIES: 178 sites, typical site width 45 ft, 178 full hkups, (20, 30 & 50 amps), some extended stay sites, 16 pull-thrus, laundry, tables, patios. ◆◆◆◆RECREATION: rec hall, equipped pavilion, swim pool, boating, canoeing, ramp, dock, river/pond fishing, planned activities. Pets welcome, breed restrict, quantity restrict. Partial handicap access. No tents. Open all yr. Big rigs welcome. Internet friendly. Rate in 2007 $30 for 4 persons. Phone: (251)987-5131.

EUFAULA—D-5

(N) Lake Eufaula Campground—(Barbour) *From north jct US 431 & US 82: Go 1/4 mi W on Chewalla Creek Dr. (Through log yard) Enter on L.* ◆◆FACILITIES: 100 sites, typical site width 20 ft, 88 full hkups, 12 W&E, (20 & 30 amps), many extended stay sites, 49 pull-thrus, tenting, dump station, laundry, groceries, ice, tables, wood. ◆◆RECREATION: rec room/area, pavilion, swim pool, boating, ramp, dock, lake fishing. Pets welcome. Open all yr. Rate in 2007 $16-17 for 4 persons. Phone: (334)687-4425.

Alabama State Tree: Southern Pine

EUFAULA—Continued

(N) LAKEPOINT RESORT LODGE—(Barbour) *From jct US-82 & US-431: Go 7 mi N on US 431.* FACILITIES: 245 sites, 80 full hkups, 165 W&E, (30 amps), 57 pull-thrus, tenting, laundry, ltd groceries, grills. RECREATION: rec hall, pavilion, lake swimming, boating, ramp, dock, lake fishing, playground, shuffleboard court, tennis, hiking trails. Rec open to public. Open all yr. Phone: (800)544-5253.

(N) LAKEPOINT SP—(Barbour) *From jct US-82 & US-431: Go 7 mi N on US-431.* FACILITIES: 245 sites, 80 full hkups, 165 W&E, (30 amps), 57 pull-thrus, tenting, dump station, laundry, ltd groceries, grills. RECREATION: rec hall, pavilion, lake swimming, boating, ramp, dock, lake fishing, playground, shuffleboard court, tennis, hiking trails. Rec open to public. Open all yr. Phone: (334) 687-6676.

(S) WHITE OAK CREEK PARK (COE-Walter F. George Lake)—(Barbour) *From jct US-431 & Hwy-95: Go 2 mi S on Hwy-95.* FACILITIES: 130 sites, 130 W&E, tenting, dump station, laundry, fire rings, grills, wood. RECREATION: pavilion, lake/river swimming, boating, ramp, dock, lake/river fishing, playground. Open all yr. Phone: (334)687-3101.

EVERGREEN—E-3

(W) Owassa Lakeside RV—(Conecuh) *From jct I-65 (exit 101) & Hwy 29: Go 1-1/2 mi N on Hwy 29, then turn E 1/4 mi on dirt road.* ◆◆◆FACILITIES: 24 sites, typical site width 35 ft, accepts self-contained units only, 19 full hkups, 5 W&E, (20, 30 & 50 amps), 14 pull-thrus, laundry, tables. ◆◆RECREATION: rec room/area, lake fishing. Pets welcome. No tents. Open all yr. Big rigs welcome. Rate in 2007 $20 for 2 persons. Phone: (251)578-0976.

FAIRHOPE—F-2

(SE) DRIFTWOOD RV PARK—(Baldwin) *From jct I-10 (exit 35) & US 98 E: Go 18 miles on US 98 E. Enter on R.*

◆◆◆FACILITIES: 51 sites, typical site width 30 ft, 51 full hkups, (30 & 50 amps), 50 amps ($), 24 pull-thrus, cable TV, wireless Instant Internet access at site, phone Internet access central location, RV/park trailer rentals, laundry.

RECREATION: rec room/area, pavilion.

Pets welcome. No tents. Open all yr. Big rigs welcome. Internet friendly. Rate in 2007 $18-22 for 2 persons. Phone: (251)928-8233.

e-mail: driftwoodrvpark@mchsi.com

SEE AD TRAVEL SECTION PAGE 4

(E) WALES WEST TRAIN & GARDEN LOVERS—*From jct US 98 & CR 48 (near Fairhope): Go 5.6 mi E on CR 48, then 1.4 mi S on CR 9. Enter on L.* A Welsh style village with an authentic narrow gauge railway & gardens. The most westerly outpost of Welsh Victorian steam railroading in the world. Open all yr. MC/VISA. Phone: (888)569-5337.

e-mail: enquiries@waleswest.com

SEE AD THIS PAGE

FAIRHOPE—Continued on next page

FAIRHOPE—Continued

(E) WALES WEST TRAIN & GARDEN LOVERS RV RESORT—(Baldwin) *From jct US 98 & CR 48 (near Fairhope): Go 5.6 mi E on CR 48, then 1.4 mi S on CR 9.*

◊◊◊◊FACILITIES: 76 sites, typical site width 40 ft, 76 full hkups, (20, 30 & 50 amps), some extended stay sites, 37 pull-thrus, cable TV, wireless Internet access central location, RV storage, laundry, groceries, RV supplies, ice, tables.

◊◊◊◊◊RECREATION: rec hall, rec room/area, swim pool, lake swimming, whirlpool, boating, no motors, kayaking, dock, 2 pedal boat rentals, lake fishing, golf nearby, playground, planned activities, horseshoes, hiking trails.

Pets welcome. No tents. Open all yr. Behind Meadow Breeze MH Village. Big rigs welcome. Internet friendly. Clubs welcome. Rate in 2007 $35 for 2 persons. MC/VISA. Phone: (888)569-5337.

e-mail: enquiries@waleswest.com

SEE AD PAGE 12

FLORALA—E-4

(SE) FLORALA SP—(Covington) *In town off Hwy 9/US 331.* FACILITIES: 23 sites, 23 full hkups, (30 amps), tenting, dump station, laundry, grills. RECREATION: pavilion, lake swimming, boating, ramp, dock, lake fishing, playground. Rec open to public. Open all yr. Phone: (334)858-6425.

FLORENCE—A-2

(W) MC FARLAND PARK (City Park)—(Lauderdale) *From jct US 43, US 72 & Hwy 120: Go 2 blocks W on Hwy 20. (N of Tennessee River Bridge) Enter on L.* FACILITIES: 60 sites, 60 W&E, 18 pull-thrus, tenting, dump station, laundry, grills. RECREATION: pavilion, boating, ramp, river fishing, playground, hiking trails. Rec open to public. Pets welcome. Partial handicap access. Open Apr 1 thru Nov 30. Phone: (256)760-6416.

VETERANS MEMORIAL PARK (City Park)—(Lauderdale) *From jct US 43, US 72 & Hwy 133: Go 3 mi S on Hwy 133. (At the N end of Wilson Dam) Enter on L.* FACILITIES: 22 sites, 22 W&E, 10 pull-thrus, tenting, dump station, laundry, grills. RECREATION: river fishing, playground, tennis, sports field. Rec open to public. Partial handicap access. Open all yr. Phone: (256)760-6416.

FOLEY—F-2

(E) AAA RV Park—(Baldwin) *From jct Hwy 59 & Hwy 20: Go 1/2 mi E on Hwy 20, then N 1/4 mi on Juniper Street. Enter on R.* ◊◊FACILITIES: 24 sites, typical site width 40 ft, accepts full hkup units only, 24 full hkups, (20 & 30 amps), 24 pull-thrus. Pets welcome. No tents. Open all yr. Rate in 2007 $15. Phone: (251)970-1232.

(S) ANCHORS AWEIGH RV RESORT—(Baldwin) *From jct Hwy 98 & Hwy 59: Go 3 mi S on Hwy 59, then 1/4 mi W on (2nd) Hwy 20 S.*

◊◊◊◊FACILITIES: 112 sites, typical site width 30 ft, 112 full hkups, (20, 30 & 50 amps), 14 pull-thrus, cable TV, wireless/cable Instant Internet access at site, laundry, ltd groceries, ice, tables, patios.

FOLEY—Continued
ANCHORS AWEIGH RV RESORT—Continued

◊◊◊◊RECREATION: rec hall, swim pool, whirlpool, golf nearby, playground, planned activities (wkends only), horseshoes, sports field, local tours.

Pets welcome, breed restrict, quantity restrict. Partial handicap access. No tents. Open all yr. Big rigs welcome. Internet friendly. Clubs welcome. Rate in 2007 $30-36 per vehicle. MC/VISA. Member ARVC. Phone: (251)971-6644.

e-mail: aarvresort@aol.com

SEE AD THIS PAGE

(W) Magnolia Springs RV Hideaway—(Baldwin) *From jct Hwy 59 and CR 12: Go 5 mi W on CR 12, then 2 mi N on CR 49. Enter on L.* ◊◊◊FACILITIES: 62 sites, typical site width 35 ft, 62 full hkups, (30 & 50 amps), 2 pull-thrus, laundry, tables, patios. ◊◊RECREATION: rec hall. Pets welcome, quantity restrict. No tents. Open all yr. Big rigs welcome. Internet friendly. Rate in 2007 $28 per vehicle. Phone: (251)965-6777. CCUSA discount.

PALM LAKE RV PARK—(Baldwin) *From jct I-10 (exit 44) & Hwy 59: Go 14-1/2 mi S on Hwy 59. Enter on L.*

◊◊◊◊FACILITIES: 200 sites, typical site width 30 ft, 200 full hkups, (20, 30 & 50 amps), some extended stay sites, 90 pull-thrus, cable TV, wireless Instant Internet access at site, phone on-site Internet access (needs activ), phone Internet access central location, RV storage, laundry, tables.

◊◊◊◊RECREATION: rec hall, rec room/area, pavilion, 2 swim pools, pedal boat rentals, pond fishing, putting green, golf nearby, planned activities, horseshoes, hiking trails.

Pets welcome. Partial handicap access. No tents. Open all yr. Big rigs welcome. Internet friendly. Rate in 2007 $33 per family. MC/VISA/Debit. Phone: (888)878-5687.

e-mail: info@palmlake.com

SEE AD THIS PAGE AND AD DISCOVER SECTION PAGE 82

FORT PAYNE—A-4

(N) DE SOTO SP—(DeKalb) *From jct Hwy-35 & CR-89: Go 5 mi N on CR-89.* FACILITIES: 78 sites, 20 full hkups, 58 W&E, (30 & 50 amps), 10 pull-thrus, tenting, laundry, ltd groceries, ice, grills. RECREATION: swim pool, river fishing, playground, tennis, hiking trails. Rec open to public. Partial handicap access. Open all yr. Phone: (800)760-4089.

(N) DESOTO STATE PARK LODGE—(DeKalb) *From jct Hwy 35 & CR-89: Go 5 mi N on CR-89.* FACILITIES: 78 sites, 20 full hkups, 58 W&E, (30 & 50 amps), tenting, laundry, ltd groceries, ice, grills. RECREATION: swim pool, river fishing, playground, tennis, hiking trails. Rec open to public. Partial handicap access. Open all yr. Phone: (800)568-8840.

FORT RUCKER—E-4

See listings at Dothan, Ozark & Troy

Alabama State Bird: Yellowhammer

FORT RUCKER—Continued

(N) U.S. ARMY AVIATION MUSEUM—*From jct US 231 & Hwy 249: Go 9.7 mi S on Hwy 249. Enter on L.* World's largest collection of helicopters in a 87,000 sq foot facility. Many one of a kind aircraft. The aircraft displays trace the history of army aviation. Free admission. Also, gift shop. Open all yr. MC/VISA/DISC/AMEX. Phone: (888)ARMY-AVN.

e-mail: giftshopmanager@armyaunmuseum.org

SEE AD THIS PAGE

GADSDEN—B-4

NOCCALULA FALLS—*From jct US 431 & I-59: Go 5 mi N on I-59 (exit 188), then 2-1/2 mi E on Noccalula Rd. Enter on R.* City park featuring 90 foot waterfalls, pioneer village, botanical gardens, petting zoo, train rides & carpet golf. Nature trails & picnic pavilions to seat 2,000. Adjacent to Noccalula Falls Campground. Open all yr. Phone: (256)549-4663.

SEE AD NEXT PAGE AND AD TRAVEL SECTION PAGE 1

(N) NOCCALULA FALLS PARK & CAMPGROUND (City Park)—(Etowah) *From jct US 431 & I-59: Go 5 mi NE on I-59 (exit 188), then 2-1/2 mi E on Noccalula Rd. Enter on R.*

FACILITIES: 126 sites, typical site width 25 ft, 79 full hkups, 47 W&E, (30 & 50 amps), 6 pull-thrus, cable TV, cable Internet access central location, tenting, cabins, dump station, non-guest dumping $, laundry, ltd groceries, RV supplies, ice, tables, grills, wood.

RECREATION: pavilion, swim pool, mini-golf ($), playground, hiking trails.

Pets welcome. Partial handicap access. Open all yr. Big rigs welcome. Internet friendly. Clubs welcome. MC/VISA/Debit. Phone: (256)543-7412.

SEE AD NEXT PAGE AND AD TRAVEL SECTION PAGE 1

GADSDEN—Continued on next page

Whether you're dreaming about buying a new RV or are actively shopping, WOODALL'S 2008 RV Buyer's Guide is your best source. It contains all the information you need to make an intelligent buying decision. Over 450 vehicles are profiled with complete information about construction features, dimensions, popular options, and more, making comparing models easy. To order your copy go to www.woodalls.com/shop.

GADSDEN, ALABAMA

ONLY 2 MILES FROM I-59, EXIT 188

FOLLOW THE SIGNS FROM US HWYS 431 & 411

NOCCALULA FALLS

PARK & CAMPGROUND

Visit us at www.cityofgadsden.com

Known As One of The Old South's Most Beautiful Campgrounds

OPEN 365 DAYS

Discover Alabama's Noccalula Falls Park & Campground. One of Alabama's top attractions. Wake up in the morning to the sound of a rolling brook, dropping 90 feet into a natural gorge. Visit us in April and see the flowers burst into bloom.

NEW ACCOMMODATIONS

Two 2-bedroom Cabins
Enjoy all the comforts of home and the beauty of nature all in one package.

COME, RELAX AND ENJOY THE VERY FINEST IN RV RESORTS FOR A DAY OR WEEK (14 DAY LIMIT)

DELUXE RESORT FACILITIES:

- Paved Roads
- Concrete Sites
- 30 & 50 Amp Service
- Laundry
- 2 Bath Houses
- Country Store
- 24 Hour Security
- Camper Repair (Nearby)
- Restaurants Nearby
- Souvenir Shop

RECREATIONAL FACILITIES:

- Meeting Hall
- Picnic Pavilions
- Swimming Pool
- 90-Ft. Waterfall
- Petting Zoo
- Nature Trail
- Carpet Golf
- Botanical Garden
- Passenger Train
- Pioneer Village

ANNUAL EVENTS

Gadsden Street Rod Association.......June
Gadsden Antique Car Show.......July
450 Mile Outdoor Sale.......August
Ghost Town Express.......October
Kid's Hoe Down.......October
Holiday Wonderland.......December

For Reservations, Contact

1600 Noccalula Rd. • Gadsden, AL 35904
Campground Office: (256) 543-7412
Park Office: (256) 549-4663

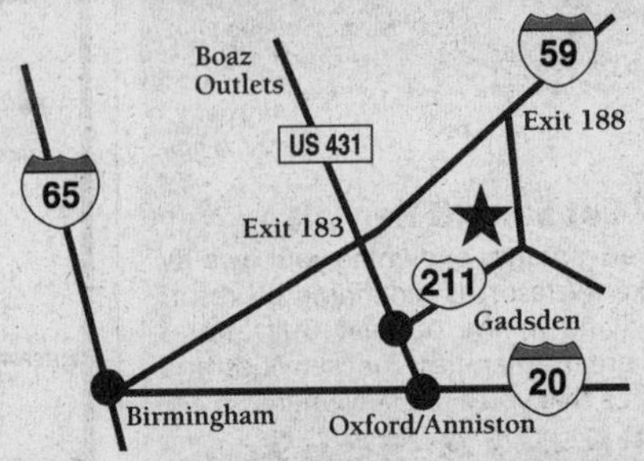

GADSDEN—Continued

(E) River Country Campground—(Etowah) *From jct I-59 (exit 182) & I-759: Go 4-1/2 mi E on I-759 to exit 4B, then 1/4 mi N on US 411, then 3/4 mi E on River Rd. Enter at end.* ◇◇◇◇FACILITIES: 235 sites, typical site width 30 ft, 185 full hkups, 50 E, (30 & 50 amps), 50 amps ($), 98 pull-thrus, portable dump, laundry, ltd groceries, LP gas by weight/hy meter, ice, tables. ◇◇◇◇RECREATION: rec hall, rec room/area, equipped pavilion, swim pool, boating, ramp, dock, river fishing. Pets welcome. Partial handicap access. No tents. Open all yr. Conference Center and computer lounge available. Big rigs welcome. Internet friendly. Rate in 2007 $26-28 for 2 persons. Phone: (256)543-7111. FMCA discount.

GALLION—D-2

(N) CHICKASAW SP—(Mobile) *From town: Go 4 mi N on US 43.* FACILITIES: 8 sites, 8 W&E, (30 amps), tenting, grills. RECREATION: pavilion, playground, hiking trails. Open all yr. No showers. Phone: (334)295-8230.

GREENVILLE—D-3

(NW) SHERLING LAKE PARK & CAMPGROUND (City Park)—(Butler) *From I-65 (exit 130) & CR 185: Go 2.5 mi NW on CR 185/CR 263, then 1 mi W on CR 263. Enter on L.*

WELCOME

FACILITIES: 41 sites, typical site width 25 ft, 30 full hkups, 11 W&E, (30 & 50 amps), some extended stay sites, 20 pull-thrus, tenting, dump station, ice, tables, patios, fire rings, grills, controlled access gate.

RECREATION: rec hall, rec room/area, pavilion, boating, electric motors only, canoeing, 4 rowboat rentals, lake fishing, golf nearby, playground, hiking trails. Rec open to public.

Pets welcome. Partial handicap access. Open all yr. Big rigs welcome. Clubs welcome. Member ARVC. Phone: (800)810-5253.

e-mail: sherlinglake@cityofgiville.com

SEE AD THIS PAGE

GROVE OAK—A-4

(N) BUCK'S POCKET SP—(Marshall) *From Hwy-227 in town follow signs N.* FACILITIES: 45 sites, 6 full hkups, 22 W&E, (30 & 50 amps), 17 no hkups, 8 pull-thrus, tenting, dump station, laundry, grills. RECREATION: pavilion, boating, ramp, river fishing, playground, hiking trails. Rec open to public. Open all yr. Phone: (256)659-2000.

GULF SHORES—F-2

See listings at Fairhope, Foley, Loxley, Orange Beach, Magnolia Springs, Robertsdale & Summerdale

Alabama State Motto: "We Dare Maintain our Rights."

Woodall's Tip #28... Woodall's ratings depend on the quality and quantity of our criteria elements. The more W's a park has generally reflects the presence of more development at the park, and usually more facilities.

Royal Palm Motor Coach Villages

Opening Spring 2008

3 Lakes • 2 pools • Shuffleboard
Steam Room • Sauna • Hot Tubs
General Store • Clubhouse
The Village Restaurant & Tiki Bar

Call us at:
251-978-1717

See listing at Summerdale, AL

SHERLING LAKE PARK & CAMPGROUND

Good Sam Park

Just Minutes to Beautiful Robert Trent Jones Golf Course!

The Most Beautiful Park in East Alabama
- Spacious Pull-thru Paved Sites
- Full Hookups • 30/50 Amps
- Clean Restrooms • Pavilions
- Fishing • Boating • New Nature Trail
- Fishing Lakes

Open Year Round

BIG RIGS WELCOME

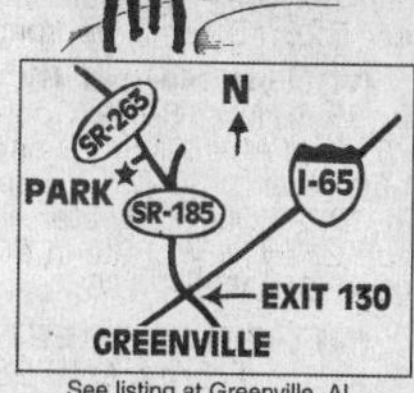

NEARBY: • Restaurants • Grocery • Laundromat
Fax: (334) 382-1948
(800) 810-5253 OR (334) 382-3638

www.sherlinglake.com
e-mail: sherlinglake@cityofgville.com

4397 Braggs Rd. - Greenville, AL 36037

SR-265 N PARK SR-185 I-65 EXIT 130 GREENVILLE

See listing at Greenville, AL

Island Retreat RV PARK

Gulf Shores' Newest & Best!

18201 Hwy 180 West • Gulf Shores, AL 36542

COME VACATION WITH US AND ENJOY OUR MANY AMENITIES:

- 173 Full Hookup Sites
- Large lots w/ Concrete Pads
- Pull Thrus Available
- Paved Roads
- 50/30 Amp Service
- Free Cable TV
- Wireless Internet
- Swimming Pool
- Bath Houses
- Laundry Facilities
- Meeting room
- RV Storage
- 5 Minutes from Beach
- Playground

NIGHTLY, WEEKLY & MONTHLY RATES

Woodalls Rated:
Fac: ◇◇◇◇
Rec: ◇◇◇

E-mail: islandretreat@gulftel.com • Web: www.islandretreatrv.com
251-967-1666 Local

Reservations: 866-974-9999 Toll Free

See listing at Gulf Shores, AL

GULF SHORES—Continued

(N) AMERICAN MOTOR COACH RESORTS (UNDER CONSTRUCTION) —(Baldwin) *From jct US 98 & Hwy 59: Go 6-1/2 mi S on Hwy 59, then 1/2 mi W on Cty Rd 6. Enter on L.*

FACILITIES: 800 sites, typical site width 45 ft, 800 full hkups, (30 & 50 amps), wireless Instant Internet access at site, tables, patios, grills, controlled access gate.

RECREATION: rec hall, swim pool, whirlpool, no motors, pond fishing, putting green, golf nearby, bsktball, playground, shuffleboard court, planned activities, tennis, horseshoes, hiking trails, v-ball.

Pets welcome, quantity restrict. Partial handicap access. No tents. Open all yr. Big rigs welcome. Clubs welcome. Phone: (251)968-7521.

SEE AD TRAVEL SECTION PAGE 1

(W) Bay Breeze RV On the Bay—(Baldwin) *From jct I-10 and Hwy 59 (Loxley Exit #44): Go 29 mi S on Hwy 59, then 6.1 mi W on Hwy 180 W (Ft Morgan Parkway). Enter on R.* ◆◆◆FACILITIES: 30 sites, typical site width 25 ft, 26 full hkups, 4 W&E, (30 & 50 amps), 50 amps ($), tenting, laundry, ice, tables. ◆◆◆RECREATION: saltwater swimming, boating, canoeing, dock, saltwater fishing. Pets welcome. Partial handicap access. Open all yr. Big rigs welcome. Internet friendly. Rate in 2007 $26-38 for 2 persons. Phone: (251)540-2362.

(W) Doc's RV Park—(Baldwin) *From jct US 98 & Hwy 59: Go 9-1/2 mi S on Hwy 59, then 2-3/10 mi W on Hwy 180. Enter on R.* ◆◆◆◆FACILITIES: 75 sites, typical site width 30 ft, 75 full hkups, (30 & 50 amps), dump station, laundry, LP gas by weight/by meter, ice, tables, grills. ◆◆◆◆RECREATION: rec room/area, pavilion, swim pool, playground, planned activities, horseshoes, v-ball. Pets welcome. Partial handicap access. No tents. Open all yr. Planned group activities winter only. Big rigs welcome. Internet friendly. Rate in 2007 $26.75 for 2 persons. Phone: (251)968-4511.

(W) Fort Morgan RV Park—(Baldwin) *From jct Hwy 59 & Hwy 180 W: Go 10 mi W on Hwy 180. Enter on R.* ◆◆FACILITIES: 20 sites, typical site width 35 ft, 20 full hkups, (30 & 50 amps), laundry, tables, patios. ◆RECREATION: saltwater fishing. Pets welcome. No tents. Open all yr. Rate in 2007 $28-34 for 2 persons. Phone: (251)540-2416.

(N) GULF BREEZE RESORT—(Baldwin) *From jct US 98 & Hwy 59: Go 6-1/2 mi S on Hwy 59, then 300 yards on CR 6. Enter on L.*

◆◆◆◆◆FACILITIES: 254 sites, typical site width 45 ft, 254 full hkups, (20, 30 & 50 amps), 50 pull-thrus, cable TV, wireless Instant Internet access at site, phone on-site Internet access (needs activ), phone Internet access central location, RV/park trailer rentals, cabins, RV storage, laundry, ice, tables, patios, grills.

◆◆◆◆◆RECREATION: rec hall, rec room/area, equipped pavilion, 2 swim pools, wading pool, whirlpool, 5 pedal boat rentals, lake fishing, mini-golf, golf nearby, bsktball, playground, 4 shuffleboard courts, planned activities, v-ball.

Pets welcome. Partial handicap access. No tents. Open all yr. Planned group activities winter only. Big rigs welcome. Internet friendly. Clubs welcome. Rate in 2007 $28 for 4 persons. MC/VISA/DISC/AMEX. Phone: (251)968-8884.

e-mail: ehodges@mindspring.com

SEE AD TRAVEL SECTION PAGE 3

Alabama State Flower: Camellia

GULF SHORES—Continued

(W) Gulf Coast RV Park (RV SPACES)—(Baldwin) *From jct Hwy 59 & CR 6: Go 3 mi W on CR 6. Enter on L.* FACILITIES: 30 sites, typical site width 35 ft, 30 full hkups, (30 & 50 amps), 3 pull-thrus, tenting, laundry, ice, tables, patios. RECREATION: rec hall, pond fishing, planned activities. Pets welcome. Rate in 2007 $20 for 4 persons. Phone: (251)968-6494.

(E) GULF SP—(Baldwin) *From jct Hwy-59 & Hwy-182: Go 3 mi E on Hwy-182. Enter on L.* FACILITIES: 260 sites, 260 full hkups, (50 amps), 40 pull-thrus, tenting, dump station, laundry, ltd groceries, ice, grills. RECREATION: pavilion, saltwater swimming, boating, ramp, dock, saltwater fishing, playground, tennis, hiking trails. Rec open to public. Open all yr. Phone: (251)948-6353.

(W) ISLAND RETREAT RV PARK—(Baldwin) *From jct I-10 and Hwy 59 (Loxley exit #44): Go 35 mi S on Hwy 59, then 1-1/2 mi W on Hwy 180 W. Enter on R.*

COME ENJOY BEAUTIFUL WHITE BEACHES!
2-1/2 miles from the beaches, close to shopping, restaurants, & golfing. Enjoy swimming pool, free wifi, full 50 amp hookups and lots of friendly people.

◆◆◆◆FACILITIES: 173 sites, typical site width 40 ft, 173 full hkups, (20, 30 & 50 amps), 16 pull-thrus, cable TV, wireless Instant Internet access at site, wireless Internet access central location, RV storage, laundry, ltd groceries, RV supplies, LP gas by meter, ice, tables, patios, fire rings.

◆◆◆RECREATION: rec hall, swim pool, golf nearby, bsktball, playground, planned activities, horseshoes, v-ball.

Pets welcome, breed restrict. Partial handicap access. No tents. Open all yr. Big rigs welcome. Internet friendly. Clubs welcome. Rate in 2007 $29.65-32.65 for 4 persons. MC/VISA/DISC/AMEX/Debit. Phone: (251)967-1666.

e-mail: islandretreat@gulftel.com

SEE AD PAGE 15

(N) Lazy Lake RV Park—(Baldwin) *From jct Hwy 59 & CR 6: Go 3/4 mi W on CR 6, then 1/4 mi S on Old Plash Island Rd. Enter on L.* ◆◆◆FACILITIES: 40 sites, typical site width 30 ft, 40 full hkups, (30 & 50 amps), laundry, tables. ◆RECREATION: boating, no motors, canoeing, lake fishing, v-ball. Pets welcome. No tents. Open all yr. Big rigs welcome. Internet friendly. Rate in 2007 $25-27 for 4 persons. Phone: (251)968-7875.

(S) Luxury RV Resort—(Baldwin) *From jct US 98 & Hwy 59: Go 9 mi S on Hwy 59. Enter on L.* ◆◆◆◆◆FACILITIES: 90 sites, typical site width 35 ft, 90 full hkups, (20, 30 & 50 amps), dump station, laundry, ltd groceries, ice, tables, patios. ◆◆◆RECREATION: rec hall, swim pool, 2 shuffleboard courts, planned activities, horseshoes, hiking trails, v-ball. Pets welcome, breed restrict. Partial handicap access. No tents. Open all yr. Big rigs welcome. Internet friendly. Phone: (800)982-3510.

(N) SOUTHPORT CAMPGROUNDS—(Baldwin) *From jct Hwy 180 & Hwy 59: Go 2 mi N on Hwy 59, then 2/10 mi W on CR 4. Enter at end.*

◆◆FACILITIES: 116 sites, typical site width 25 ft, 68 full hkups, 48 W&E, (20, 30 & 50 amps), 30 pull-thrus, cable TV, tenting, RV storage, dump station, non-guest dumping $, laundry, ice, tables.

◆◆RECREATION: rec room/area, pavilion, boating, dock, saltwater fishing, golf nearby, planned activities, horseshoes, v-ball.

GULF SHORES—Continued
SOUTHPORT CAMPGROUNDS—Continued

Pets welcome. Partial handicap access. Open all yr. Clubs welcome. Rate in 2007 $18-22 for 2 persons. Phone: (251)968-6220.

SEE AD THIS PAGE

(N) Sun-Runners RV Park—(Baldwin) *From jct US 98 & Hwy 59: Go 5-1/2 mi S on Hwy 59, then 1/2 mi W on CR 8. Enter on L.* ◆◆◆FACILITIES: 60 sites, typical site width 25 ft, 41 full hkups, 19 W&E, (20 & 30 amps), 13 pull-thrus, tenting, dump station, laundry, ice, tables. ◆◆RECREATION: rec room/area, sports field. Pets welcome, breed restrict. Partial handicap access. Open all yr. Rate in 2007 $25 for 2 persons. Phone: (251)955-5257.

GUNTERSVILLE—A-4

(N) LAKE GUNTERSVILLE STATE LODGE—(Marshall) *From jct US-431 & Hwy-227: Go 6 mi NE on Hwy-227.* FACILITIES: 321 sites, 143 full hkups, 178 W&E, (30 & 50 amps), 51 pull-thrus, tenting, laundry, ltd groceries, ice, grills. RECREATION: pavilion, lake swimming, boating, ramp, dock, rowboat/canoe rentals, lake fishing, playground, shuffleboard court, tennis, hiking trails, v-ball. Rec open to public. Open all yr. Phone: (256)571-5455.

(N) SEIBOLD CAMPGROUND—(Marshall) *From jct US 431 & Hwy 79: Go 1 mi N on Hwy 79. Enter on R.*

◆◆◆FACILITIES: 136 sites, typical site width 50 ft, 136 W&E, (20, 30 & 50 amps), many extended stay sites, tenting, dump station, portable dump, tables, grills, controlled access gate.

◆◆◆◆RECREATION: rec hall, swim pool, lake swimming, boating, canoeing, kayaking, ramp, dock, lake fishing, golf nearby, bsktball, playground.

Pets welcome. Partial handicap access. Open Mar 1 thru Oct 31. Big rigs welcome. Clubs welcome. Rate in 2007 $20-25 for 5 persons. MC/VISA/Debit. Member ARVC, ALARVC. Phone: (256)582-0040.

e-mail: seiboldcampground@charter.net

SEE AD NEXT PAGE

HANCEVILLE—B-3

(W) Country View RV Park—(Cullman) *From jct I-65 (exit 291) & Hwy 91: Go 1.5 mi N on Hwy 91 N. Enter on L.* ◆◆◆FACILITIES: 33 sites, typical site width 25 ft, 33 full hkups, (30 & 50 amps), 33 pull-thrus, tenting, laundry, ltd groceries, LP gas by weight/by meter, ice, tables. ◆◆RECREATION: rec room/area, play equipment, horseshoes. Pets welcome. Open all yr. Big rigs welcome. Rate in 2007 $26 for 2 persons. Phone: (256)352-4678.

HEFLIN—B-4

CANE CREEK RV PARK & CAMPGROUND (NOT VISITED)—(Cleburne) *From jct I-20 (exit 205) & Hwy 46: Go 1-3/4 mi N on Hwy 46. Enter on L.*

FACILITIES: 171 sites, typical site width 30 ft, 31 full hkups, 140 W&E, (20, 30 & 50 amps), 50 amps ($), some extended stay sites, wireless Instant Internet access at site, tenting, RV storage, dump station, laundry, ltd groceries, RV supplies, LP gas by weight/by meter, ice, tables, fire rings, wood.

RECREATION: rec room/area, river swimming, canoeing, stream fishing, golf nearby, play equipment, planned activities (wkends only), horseshoes, hiking trails.

Pets welcome. Partial handicap access. Open all yr. Big rigs welcome. Internet friendly. Escort to site. Clubs welcome. Rate in 2007 $17-19 for 2 persons. MC/VISA/Debit. Phone: (256)463-2602.

e-mail: canecreekrvpark@aol.com

SEE AD NEXT PAGE

(NW) TALLADEGA NF (Coleman Lake)—(Cleburne) *From town: Go 6 mi NE on US 78, then 8-1/2 mi NW on CR 61/FR 553, then 1-1/2 mi N on FR 500. Follow signs.* FACILITIES: 39 sites, 35 ft max RV length, 39 W&E, 1 pull-thrus, tenting, dump station, fire rings, grills. RECREATION: pavilion, lake swimming, boating, no motors, canoeing, ramp, hiking trails. Partial handicap access. Open Mar 15 thru Nov 27. Phone: (256)463-2272.

(N) TALLADEGA NF (Pine Glen)—(Cleburne) *From jct Hwy-46 & US-78: Go 2-1/2 mi W on US-78, then 8 mi N on FR-500.* FACILITIES: 30 sites, 22 ft max RV length, 30 no hkups, tenting, non-flush toilets only, fire rings, grills. RECREATION: hiking trails. Open all yr. No showers. Max stay 14 days. Phone: (256)463-2272.

Woodall's Tip #22... If you think Woodall's Ratings mean Good, Better, Best...think again. See the "How to Use" pages in the front of this Directory for an explanation of our Rating System.

HELENA—C-3

(S) CHEROKEE CAMPGROUND—(Shelby) *From jct I-459 (exit 6) Hwy 52: Go 4 mi SW on Hwy 52/Morgan Rd, then 3/4 mi W on Hwy 93. Enter on L.*

◊◊◊FACILITIES: 100 sites, typical site width 40 ft, 92 full hkups, 8 W&E, (30 & 50 amps), 50 amps ($), some extended stay sites, 22 pull-thrus, wireless Internet access central location, dump station, laundry, ltd groceries, LP bottle exch.

◊◊RECREATION: rec room/area, pavilion, lake fishing, golf nearby, bsktball, hiking trails.

Pets welcome. No tents. Open all yr. Big rigs welcome. Clubs welcome. Rate in 2007 $18-21 for 2 persons. Phone: (205)428-8339.

SEE AD BIRMINGHAM PAGE 10

HODGES—A-2

(E) BEAR CREEK DEV AUTH (Horseshoe Bend)—(Franklin) *From jct Hwy 24 & CR 88: Go 2 mi S on CR 88, then 5 mi E on CR 16, then 2 mi W on Horseshoe Bend Rd. Enter on R.* FACILITIES: 26 sites, typical site width 25 ft, 26 W&E, (30 amps), tenting, dump station, ltd groceries, ice, grills. RECREATION: pavilion, lake swimming, boating, ramp, dock, lake fishing. Partial handicap access. Open Apr thru Oct. Phone: (256)332-4392.

HOOVER—C-3

(S) HOOVER RV PARK—(Jefferson) *From W jct I-59 N & I-459 N: Go 10 mi NE on I-459N to exit 10, then 3/10 mi SE on Hwy 150, then 1-1/2 mi W on Stadium Trace Pkwy. Follow RV park signs. Enter on L.* FACILITIES: 144 sites, typical site width 21 ft, 144 full hkups, (20, 30 & 50 amps), 144 pull-thrus, dump station. RECREATION: Partial handicap access. No tents. Open all yr. Phone: (866)466-8378.

HUNTSVILLE—A-3

(C) ALABAMA CONSTITUTION VILLAGE *—From jct of Hwy 231 & I-565: Go 1-1/2 mi on I-565 (exit 19C) to Jefferson St, then 5 blks S to Gates Ave, then 1 blk E (Village on left). Enter on L.* Award winning reconstruction of Huntsville as it existed in 1819 when the state's first constitution was written. Open all yr. MC/VISA. Phone: (256)564-8100.

SEE AD TRAVEL SECTION PAGE 4

(E) BURRITT ON THE MOUNTAIN—*From jct I-565 & Hwy 231: Go S on US 231 to Governors Dr, then E on Governors Dr to US 431, through town & up mountain to Monte Sano Blvd, then 3/4 mi N on Sano Blvd to Burritt Dr, take sharp left turn & continue up Burritt Dr to top of mountain. Enter at end.* Burritt is a unique museum of regional history located atop Monte Sano Mountain, overlooking Huntsville. The 167 acre site contains the Burritt Mansion, a collection of 19th century historic rural structures and nature trails. Open all yr. Phone: (256)536-2882.

SEE AD TRAVEL SECTION PAGE 4

(S) DITTO LANDING MARINA CAMPGROUND (City/County Park)—(Madison) *From jct US 431 & US 231: Go 9 mi S on US 231, then 1 mi E on Hobbs Island Rd. Enter on R.*

HUNTSVILLE—Continued
DITTO LANDING MARINA CAMPGROUND (City/County Park)—Continued

FACILITIES: 26 sites, 26 W&E, tenting, dump station, laundry, ice, grills. RECREATION: pavilion, boating, canoeing, ramp, river fishing, playground, tennis, sports field, hiking trails, v-ball. Rec open to public. No pets. Partial handicap access. Open Mar thru Nov. Phone: (256)883-9420.

(C) EARLY WORKS CHILDREN'S MUSEUM—*From jct of Hwy 231 & I-565: Go 1-1/2 mi on I-565 (exit 19C) to Jefferson St, then 6 blks S. (Early Works on left). Enter on L.* The South's largest hands-on history musuem. Once inside history emerges in ways you've never seen before. Open all yr. MC/VISA. Phone: (256)564-8100.

SEE AD TRAVEL SECTION PAGE 4

(C) HARRISON BROTHERS HARDWARE *—From jct of Hwy 231 & I-565: Go 1-1/2 mi on I-565 (exit 19C) to Jefferson St, then 4 blks S past the courthouse, then E on Southside Square. (Harrison Brothers on right). Enter on R.* Alabama's oldest hardware store-virtually unchanged since its opening in 1879. Nostalgic hardware, gifts & local crafts are sold. Open all yr. Phone: (256)536-3631.

SEE AD TRAVEL SECTION PAGE 4

(C) HISTORIC HUNTSVILLE DEPOT—*From the jct of Hwy 231 & I-565: Go 1-1/2 mi on I-565 (exit 19C) to Jefferson St, go 1 blk S on Jefferson St, then W on Monroe St, then N on Church St. Enter on R.* Built in 1860, the historic Huntsville Depot brings alive the story of the Memphis & Charleston Railroad and the Depot's Civil War Connection. Open all yr. Phone: (256)564-8100.

SEE AD TRAVEL SECTION PAGE 4

(W) HUNTSVILLE BOTANICAL GARDEN *—From jct of Hwy 231 & I-565: Go W on I-565 to Bob Wallace Ave (exit 14), then go 1 mi E (follow signs). Enter on R.* Beautiful 110-acre site with stunning floral collections. Home of the nation's largest seasonal Butterfly House. Enjoy woodland paths, aquatic, perennial & annual displays ablaze with color. Open all yr. Phone: (256)830-4447.

SEE AD TRAVEL SECTION PAGE 4

HUNTSVILLE—Continued

(C) HUNTSVILLE CONVENTION & VISITORS BUREAU—*Westbound on I-565: exit 19A (Washington/Jefferson exit) go across overpass-R at light onto Monroe St, then R at light onto Church St, travel across train tracks. Eastbound use exit 19C and continue same directions. Enter on L.* Tourism & convention information office. Open all yr. Phone: (800)-SPACE-4-U.

e-mail: cwinters@huntsville.org

SEE AD TRAVEL SECTION PAGE 4

(S) HUNTSVILLE MUSEUM OF ART—*From the jct of Hwy 231 & I-565: Go 1-1/2 mi on I-565 (exit 19C) to Jefferson St, then go 1 blk S on Jefferson St, then W on Monroe St, then 3 blks S on Church St. Enter on R.* North Alabama's leading visual arts center, seven galleries filled with nationally and regionally acclaimed artists. Open all yr. Phone: (256)535-4350.

SEE AD TRAVEL SECTION PAGE 4

(E) MILITARY PARK (Redstone Arsenal Travel Camp)—(Madison) *From I-65: Take Hwy 20 (exit 340 E). On base.* FACILITIES: 23 sites, 23 W&E, tenting, dump station. RECREATION: boating. Open all yr. For Military Use Only-w/Military ID Card. Phone: (205)876-6854.

(E) MONTE SANO SP—(Madison) *From jct I-565 & Hwy 1/US 431: Go E on Hwy 1/US 431 (Governors Dr), then N on Monte Sano Blvd.* FACILITIES: 105 sites, 20 full hkups, 65 W&E, (30 & 50 amps), 20 no hkups, 4 pull-thrus, tenting, dump station, portable dump, laundry, ltd groceries, ice, fire rings, grills, wood. RECREATION: pavilion, playground, hiking trails. Rec open to public. Partial handicap access. Open all yr. Phone: (256)534-6589.

(S) MOUNTAIN BREEZE RV PARK (RV SPACES)—(Morgan) *From jct of Hwy 36 & Hwy 231: Go 4-1/2 mi S on Hwy 231 (mm 299). Enter on R.*

FACILITIES: 23 sites, typical site width 40 ft, accepts full hkup units only, 23 full hkups, (20, 30 & 50 amps), 6 pull-thrus, phone on-site Internet access (needs activ), laundry.

Pets welcome. No tents. Open all yr. No restrooms. Big rigs welcome. Rate in 2007 $20 per vehicle. Phone: (256)498-2571.

e-mail: mtbrz299@otelco.net

SEE AD THIS PAGE

HUNTSVILLE—Continued on next page

(W) SCI-QUEST HANDS-ON SCIENCE CENTER—*From jct Hwy 231 & I-565: Go 4 mi W on I-565 to Space Center Exit (exit 15), then go W on Old Madison Pike and then N on Wynn Dr at the first light. Sci Quest is located directly behind Calhoun Community College. Enter on L.* Over 120 hands-on science explorations for curious,active youngsters. 40,000 square foot facility with interactive exhibits for all ages. Open all yr. MC/VISA. Phone: (256)837-0606.

SEE AD TRAVEL SECTION PAGE 4

(W) US SPACE & ROCKET CENTER—*From jct of Hwy 231 & I-565: Go 4 mi W on I-565 to Space Center Exit (exit 15). Enter on L.* Train like an astronaut and experience simulated missions at the Earth's greatest space attraction while you learn about Huntsville's leadership in space exploration. Open all yr. MC/VISA. Phone: (256)837-3400.

SEE AD TRAVEL SECTION PAGE 4

(W) US Space & Rocket Center RV Campground—(Madison) *From jct Hwy 231 & I-565: Go 4 mi W on I-565 to Space Center exit (exit 15), then 1/4 mi S to Space Center access road, then 1/4 mi W.* ◊◊◊FACILITIES: 27 sites, typical site width 15 ft, 27 full hkups, (20 & 30 amps), 5 pull-thrus, tables. ◊ Pets welcome. No tents. Open all yr. Rate in 2007 $18-20 per vehicle. Phone: (256)830-4987.

(C) WEEDEN HOUSE MUSEUM—*From jct of Hwy 231 & I-565: Go 1-1/2 mi I-565 (exit 19C) to Jefferson St, then 1 blk S on Jefferson St to Monroe St, then 2 blks E to Greene St, then 5 blks S (Weeden House on corner). Enter on R.* The 1819 Weeden House is within the Twickenham Historic District and is only a block from Alabama Constitution Village. Open all yr. Phone: (256)536-7718.

SEE AD TRAVEL SECTION PAGE 4

IDER—A-4

(E) Thunder Canyon Campground—(Dekalb) *From jct I-59 (exit 231) & Hwy 117: Go 10 mi N on Hwy 117, then 1 mi E on CR 141 (Thunder Canyon Lane). Enter on L.* ◊◊◊FACILITIES: 30 sites, typical site width 24 ft, 18 full hkups, 7 W&E, (15, 20 & 30 amps), 5 no hkups, 20 pull-thrus, tenting, dump station, ice, tables, fire rings, wood. ◊◊RECREATION: rec hall, swim pool, pond/stream fishing, horseshoes, hiking trails, v-ball. Rec open to public. Pets welcome. Open May 1 thru Oct 31. Phone: (256)632-2103.

JASPER—B-2

BANKHEAD NF (Clear Creek Rec Area)—(Walker) *From town: Go 5 mi N on Hwy 195, then 8-1/2 mi NE on CR 27.* FACILITIES: 97 sites, 97 W&E, 10 pull-thrus, tenting, dump station, ltd groceries, patios, fire rings, grills, wood. RECREATION: pavilion, lake swimming, boating, canoeing, ramp, lake fishing, hiking trails, v-ball. Partial handicap access. Open Mar 20 thru Oct 31. Phone: (205)489-5111.

(E) BURTON'S RV SERVICE—*From jct Hwy 69 & US 78: Go 2 mi E on US 78. Enter on R.* SALES: travel trailers, pre-owned unit sales. SERVICES: full-time mech, RV appliance repair, body work/collision repair, sells parts/accessories, installs hitches. Open all yr. MC/VISA/DISC. Phone: (205)221-0826.

e-mail: burtonsrvservice@aol.com

SEE AD THIS PAGE

Official nut of Alabama: the pecan

(E) SLEEPY HOLLER CAMPGROUND—(Walker) *From jct Hwy 69 & Hwy 78: Go 3 mi E on Hwy 78, then 1 mi S on Buttermilk Rd (at caution light) Enter on L.*

◊◊◊FACILITIES: 130 sites, typical site width 25 ft, 120 full hkups, 10 W&E, (15, 30 & 50 amps), 40 pull-thrus, RV/park trailer rentals, cabins, laundry, LP gas by meter, tables.

◊◊RECREATION: pavilion, lake fishing, horseshoes, hiking trails.

Pets welcome, breed restrict. No tents. Open all yr. Big rigs welcome. Escort to site. Clubs welcome. Rate in 2007 $20-34 for 2 persons. Phone: (205)483-7947.

SEE AD THIS PAGE

JEMISON—C-3

(E) PEACH QUEEN CAMPGROUND—(Chilton) *From jct I-65 (Exit 219) & Exit Rd: Go 1/2 mi E on Exit Rd. Enter on R.*

◊◊◊FACILITIES: 54 sites, typical site width 35 ft, 54 full hkups, (20, 30 & 50 amps), 54 pull-thrus, wireless Instant Internet access at site, phone on-site Internet access (needs activ), wireless Internet access central location, tenting, laundry, ltd groceries, RV supplies, LP gas by weight/by meter, ice, tables.

◊◊◊RECREATION: rec room/area, pavilion, swim pool, boating, no motors, lake fishing, play equipment, horseshoes, sports field, v-ball.

Pets welcome. Open all yr. Big rigs welcome. Internet friendly. Clubs welcome. Rate in 2007 $24-30 for 2 persons. MC/VISA/DISC/Debit. Member ARVC, ALARVC. Phone: (205)688-2573.

e-mail: peachqueencampground@tridigital.broadband.com

SEE AD THIS PAGE

KNOXVILLE—C-2

(E) Knox Hill RV Resort—(Greene) *From jct I-20/I-59 (exit 52) & Hwy 11: Go 1/2 mi N on Hwy 11, then 500 yards E on Old Patton Rd. Enter at end.* ◊◊◊◊FACILITIES: 24 sites, typical site width 35 ft, 24 full hkups, (30 & 50 amps), 24 pull-thrus, tenting, laundry, tables, patios. ◊◊RECREATION: rec hall, equipped pavilion, swim pool, hiking trails, v-ball. Pets welcome. Open all yr. Big rigs welcome. Internet friendly. Rate in 2007 $20-28 for 4 persons. Phone: (877) 372-3911. FMCA discount.

LANGSTON—A-4

(S) LITTLE MOUNTAIN MARINA CAMPING RESORT—(Marshall) *From jct US 431 & Hwy 227: Go 12 mi S on Hwy 227 (Hwy 227 turns N), then 1/2 mi N on S Sauty Rd (Hwy 227 goes E at S Sauty Rd) to Murphy Hill Rd, then left on Murphy Hill Rd. Enter on L.*

LITTLE MOUNTAIN MARINA CAMPING RESORT

Camping in beautiful Lake Guntersville region, unspoiled natural beauty & landscape. Big rigs welcome. Large wooded & open sites. Heated pool, cozy cabins. Come and enjoy the peaceful setting in the mountains.

◊◊◊◊◊FACILITIES: 371 sites, typical site width 30 ft, 336 full hkups, 35 W&E, (20, 30 & 50 amps), some extended stay sites, 7 pull-thrus, phone Internet access central location, tenting, RV/park trailer rentals, cabins, RV storage, dump station, laundry, LP gas by weight, ice, tables, patios, grills, controlled access gate.

◊◊◊◊◊RECREATION: rec hall, rec room/area, pavilion, equipped pavilion, coin games, 2 swim pools, wading pool, lake swimming, whirlpool, boating, canoeing, ramp, dock, lake fishing, mini-golf, bsktball, playground, 3 shuffleboard courts, planned activities, tennis, sports field, v-ball.

Pets welcome. Partial handicap access. Open all yr. Big rigs welcome. Internet friendly. Clubs welcome. Rate in 2007 $28 for 4 persons. MC/VISA/DISC/AMEX. Phone: (256)582-8211. CCUSA discount.

SEE AD TRAVEL SECTION PAGE 3

(S) NORTHSHORE CAMPGROUND AT THE BIG ROCK—(Jackson) *From jct US 431 & Hwy 227: Go 12 mi S on Hwy 227 (Hwy 227 turns N) then 6 1/2 mi N on S Sauty Rd. Enter on R.*

◊◊◊FACILITIES: 51 sites, typical site width 30 ft, accepts full hkup units only, 51 full hkups, (20, 30 & 50 amps), RV storage, full svc store, RV supplies, LP bottle exch, marine gas, ice, tables, fire rings, controlled access gate.

◊◊◊RECREATION: swim pool, boating, canoeing, ramp, dock, lake fishing, fishing supplies, fishing guides, golf nearby.

Pets welcome. No tents. Open all yr. Register at South Sauty Creek Resort Store. Big rigs welcome. Rate in 2007 $25 for 5 persons. MC/VISA/DISC. Phone: (256) 582-3367.

e-mail: ssautycamp@hotmail.com

SEE AD GUNTERSVILLE PAGE 17

(S) SOUTH SAUTY CREEK RESORT—(Marshall) *From jct US 431 & Hwy 227: Go 12 mi S on Hwy 227 (Hwy 227 turns N), then 6-1/2 mi N on S Sauty Rd. Enter at end.*

◊◊◊FACILITIES: 85 sites, typical site width 30 ft, 85 W&E, (20, 30 & 50 amps), many extended stay sites, tenting, RV storage, dump station, portable dump, full svc store, RV supplies, LP gas by weight, LP bottle exch, marine gas, ice, tables, fire rings.

◊◊◊RECREATION: swim pool, lake swimming, boating, canoeing, ramp, dock, lake fishing, fishing supplies, fishing guides, golf nearby. Rec open to public.

Pets welcome. Open all yr. Big rigs welcome. Rate in 2007 $20 for 5 persons. MC/VISA/DISC. Member ALARVC. Phone: (256)582-3367.

e-mail: ssautycamp@hotmail.com

SEE AD GUNTERSVILLE PAGE 17

LILLIAN—F-2

(S) KOA-PENSACOLA/PERDIDO BAY—(Baldwin) *From jct US-98 & CR-99: Go 1-1/2 mi S on CR-99. Enter on L.*

◊◊◊FACILITIES: 112 sites, typical site width 18 ft, 103 full hkups, 9 W&E, (20, 30 & 50 amps), some extended stay sites, 80 pull-thrus, cable TV ($), wireless Instant Internet access at site, wireless Internet access central location, tenting, RV/park trailer rentals, cabins, RV storage, laundry, groceries, RV supplies, LP gas by weight/by meter, ice, tables, patios, wood.

◊◊◊RECREATION: rec hall, swim pool, saltwater swimming, whirlpool, boating, ramp, dock, saltwater/lake fishing, fishing supplies, golf nearby, bsktball, playground, planned activities (wkends only), horseshoes.

Pets welcome. Open all yr. Internet friendly. Clubs welcome. Rate in 2007 $28-35 for 2 persons. MC/VISA. Phone: (251)961-1717. KOA 10% value card discount.

e-mail: lostbayrv@hotmail.com

SEE AD TRAVEL SECTION PAGE 4 AND AD DISCOVER SECTION PAGES 62 & 63

The Monarch Butterfly is a native butterfly to Alabama.

LOWNDESBORO—D-3

(N) PRAIRIE CREEK PARK (COE-Alabama River Lakes) —(Lowndes) *From jct US 80 & CR 29: Go N on CR 29. Follow signs.* FACILITIES: 62 sites, 62 W&E, 10 pull-thrus, tenting, dump station, laundry, ice, fire rings, grills. RECREATION: pavilion, boating, canoeing, ramp, dock, river fishing, playground, hiking trails. Rec open to public. Partial handicap access. Open all yr. Phone: (334)418-4919.

LOXLEY—F-2

(S) Parkway RV Camp (RV SPACES)—(Baldwin) *From jct I-10 (exit 44) & Hwy-59: Go 2-1/2 mi S on Hwy-59. Enter on R.* FACILITIES: 26 sites, typical site width 25 ft, accepts full hkup units only, 26 full hkups, (50 amps), 50 amps ($). Pets welcome. No tents. Open all yr. No restrooms. Rate in 2007 $20 for 2 persons. Phone: (251)964-6489.

MAGNOLIA SPRINGS—F-2

(W) MAGNOLIA RV PARK—(Baldwin) *From jct Hwy 59 & Hwy 98: Go 5 mi W on Hwy 98, then 1 mi N on State Rd 49, then 1 mi W on Mannich Ln. Enter on L.*

WELCOME

◊◊◊FACILITIES: 56 sites, typical site width 28 ft, 56 full hkups, (20, 30 & 50 amps), some extended stay sites, 4 pull-thrus, wireless Instant Internet access at site, wireless Internet access central location, dump station, laundry, ltd groceries, RV supplies, ice, tables, grills.

◊◊◊RECREATION: rec hall, swim pool, golf nearby, bsktball, playground, horseshoes, sports field.

MAGNOLIA SPRINGS—Continued
MAGNOLIA RV PARK—Continued

Pets welcome. Partial handicap access. No tents. Open all yr. Big rigs welcome. Internet friendly. Clubs welcome. Rate in 2007 $20 for 2 persons. MC/VISA/DISC/AMEX. Phone: (251)965-6885.

SEE AD FOLEY PAGE 13

(W) SOUTHWIND RV PARK—(Baldwin) *From jct Hwy 59 & US 98: Go 7-1/2 mi W on US 98, then 3/10 mi N on CR 9N. Enter on L.*

WELCOME

◊◊◊FACILITIES: 120 sites, typical site width 35 ft, 120 full hkups, (20, 30 & 50 amps), some extended stay sites, 105 pull-thrus, cable TV, phone Internet access central location, cabins, RV storage, laundry, LP gas by weight/by meter, tables.

◊◊RECREATION: rec hall, rec room/area, golf nearby.

Pets welcome. Partial handicap access. No tents. Age restrictions may apply. Open all yr. Big rigs welcome. Internet friendly. Clubs welcome. Rate in 2007 $20 for 2 persons. Phone: (251)988-1216.

e-mail: swindrvpk@aol.com

SEE AD TRAVEL SECTION PAGE 4

The word Alabama means "tribal town" in the Creek Indian language.

MCCALLA—C-3

(S) MCCALLA CAMPGROUND—(Tuscaloosa) *From west jct I-459 & I-20/I-59: Go 6 mi SW on I-20/I-59 (exit 100), then 200 yards W on Hwy 216. Enter on L.*

WELCOME

◊◊◊FACILITIES: 47 sites, typical site width 30 ft, 43 full hkups, 4 W&E, (30 & 50 amps), 50 amps ($), some extended stay sites, 47 pull-thrus, cable TV, phone Internet access central location, tenting, cabins, RV storage, dump station, non-guest dumping $, laundry, groceries, RV supplies, LP gas by weight/by meter, ice, tables.

◊◊◊RECREATION: equipped pavilion, swim pool, golf nearby.

Pets welcome. Partial handicap access. Open all yr. Big rigs welcome. Clubs welcome. Rate in 2007 $25-27 for 2 persons. MC/VISA/DISC/AMEX/Debit. Phone: (877)477-4778.

SEE AD BIRMINGHAM PAGE 10

(S) TANNEHILL IRONWORKS HISTORICAL STATE PARK—(Tuscaloosa) *From I-59 (exit 100): Go 2-1/2 mi E following signs. Enter on L.* FACILITIES: 300 sites, 43 full hkups, 168 W&E, (50 amps), 89 no hkups, 60 pull-thrus, tenting, dump station, laundry, ltd groceries, LP gas by weight/by meter, ice, grills, wood. RECREATION: pavilion, stream fishing, planned activities, hiking trails. Rec open to public. Pets welcome. Partial handicap access. Open all yr. No reservations. Phone: (205)477-5711.

MOBILE—F-1

See listings at Dauphin Island, Theodore, Creola, & Wilmer

MOBILE—Continued on next page

MOBILE—Continued

(S) ALABAMA PORT RV PARK—(Mobile) *From jct SR 193 & SR 188: Go 4/10 mi N on SR 193. Enter on R.*

◆◆◆FACILITIES: 125 sites, typical site width 35 ft, 125 full hkups, (20, 30 & 50 amps), 13 pull-thrus, phone Internet access central location, tenting, laundry, tables, fire rings, controlled access gate.

◆◆RECREATION: pavilion, swim pool, saltwater fishing, golf nearby.

Pets welcome, breed restrict. Open all yr. Big rigs welcome. Clubs welcome. Rate in 2007 $20 for 4 persons. MC/VISA. Phone: (251)873-5001.

e-mail: hatanchor@aol.com

SEE AD PAGE 19

Alabama's mean elevation is 500 feet at its lowest elevation point.

(S) BELLINGRATH GARDENS & HOME—*From jct I-10 (exit 15A) & US 90: Go 2-1/2 mi SW on US 90 W, then 8 mi S on Bellingrath Rd. Enter on L.* One of the world's most beautiful gardens surrounding a 15-room home containing a magnificent collection of antiques, china, porcelain and other art objects. Cafe on property. RV day parking available. Gardens are wheel- chair accessible. Open all yr. Open 8:00 a.m. to Dusk. MC/VISA/DISC/AMEX. Phone: (251)973-2217.

SEE AD TRAVEL SECTION PAGE 4

(S) CHICKASABOGUE PARK & CG (Mobile County Pk)—(Mobile) *From I-65 (exit 13) & Hwy 158: Go 2 mi S on Hwy 213, then 3/4 mi SE on Whistler St, then 1 mi N on Aldock Rd. Enter at end.* FACILITIES: 74 sites, typical site width 25 ft, 24 full hkups, 34 W&E, (30 & 50 amps), 16 no hkups, 30 pull-thrus, tenting, dump station, non-guest dumping $, laundry, ltd groceries, ice, fire rings, grills, wood. RECREATION: equipped pavilion, river swimming, boating, canoeing, ramp, 12 canoe rentals, river fishing, playground, horseshoes, sports field, hiking trails, v-ball. Rec open to public. Partial handicap access. Open all yr. Phone: (251) 574-2267.

(W) I-10 KAMPGROUND—(Mobile) *From jct I-10 (exit 13) & Theodore Dawes Rd: Go 1/2 mi S on Theodore Dawes Rd. Enter on L.*

◆◆◆FACILITIES: 165 sites, typical site width 22 ft, 157 full hkups, 8 W&E, (30 & 50 amps), some extended stay sites, 155 pull-thrus, cable TV, phone Internet access central location, RV storage, dump station, non-guest dumping $, laundry, ltd groceries, RV supplies, LP gas by weight/by meter, ice, tables.

◆◆RECREATION: rec hall, pavilion, swim pool, golf nearby, sports field.

Pets welcome. Partial handicap access. No tents. Open all yr. Big rigs welcome. Clubs welcome. Rate in 2007 $25 for 2 persons. MC/VISA/DISC/AMEX. Phone: (800)272-1263.

e-mail: i10kamp@msn.com

SEE AD THIS PAGE

(N) I-65 RV Campground—(Mobile) *From jct I-65 (exit 19) & Hwy 43: Go 1/10 mi N on Hwy 43, then 9/10 mi W on Jackson Rd. Enter on L.* ◆◆◆FACILITIES: 90 sites, typical site width 30 ft, 76 full hkups, 10 W&E, (20, 30 & 50 amps), 50 amps ($), 4 no hkups, mostly extended stay sites, 20 pull-thrus, tenting, dump station, non-guest dumping $, laundry, ltd groceries, LP gas by weight/by meter, ice, tables. ◆◆RECREATION: rec hall, pond fishing, horseshoes. Pets welcome. Partial handicap access. Open all yr. Big rigs welcome. Rate in 2007 $27 for 2 persons. Phone: (800)287-3208. FMCA discount.

(E) MILITARY PARK (Coast Guard Rec Facility)—(Mobile) *Off base, 37 mi from ATC Mobile. Located at E end of Dauphin Island, off Hwy 193 on Agassiz St.* FACILITIES: 105 sites, 35 ft max RV length, 5 full hkups, 100 no hkups, tenting, laundry, ltd groceries, ice, grills. RECREATION: saltwater swimming, boating, motorboat rentals, saltwater fishing, playground, hiking trails, v-ball. No pets. Open all yr. For Military Use Only-w/Military ID Card. Phone: (251)861-7113.

(S) PAYNE'S RV PARK—(Mobile) *From jct I-10 & US 90 (exit 15A): Go 3 mi SW on US 90W, then 1-1/2 mi S on Bellingrath Rd/CR 59. Enter on R.*

◆◆◆◆FACILITIES: 90 sites, typical site width 35 ft, 90 full hkups, (20, 30 & 50 amps), 62 pull-thrus, wireless Instant Internet access at site, phone Internet access central location, tenting, laundry, LP gas by weight/by meter, tables, fire rings, grills.

◆◆RECREATION: rec room/area, equipped pavilion, golf nearby.

Pets welcome, breed restrict. Open all yr. Big rigs welcome. Internet friendly. Clubs welcome. Rate in 2007 $22-25 for 2 persons. MC/VISA. Phone: (251)653-1034.

e-mail: paynesrvpark@aol.com

SEE AD PAGE 19

(S) SHADY ACRES CAMPGROUND—(Mobile) *From jct I-10 and Hwy 163/Dauphin Island Parkway (exit 22B): Go 3/4 mi S on Dauphin Island Parkway, then go 1/2 mi W on Old Military Rd. Enter on R.*

◆◆◆◆FACILITIES: 92 sites, typical site width 30 ft, accepts full hkup units only, 92 full hkups, (30 & 50 amps), some extended stay sites, 10 pull-thrus, wireless Instant Internet access at site, phone Internet access central location, dump station, non-guest dumping $, laundry, LP gas by weight/by meter, tables, patios.

◆◆◆RECREATION: rec room/area, boating, canoeing, ramp, dock, river fishing, hiking trails.

Pets welcome. No tents. Open all yr. Big rigs welcome. Internet friendly. Clubs welcome. Rate in 2007 $20-36 for 2 persons. MC/VISA. Phone: (251)478-0013. CCUSA discount.

e-mail: dogriver13@aol.com

SEE AD PAGE 19

SHADY GROVE CAMPGROUND—(Mobile) *From jct I-10 (exit 15A) & US 90: Go 3-1/4 mi SW on US 90. Enter on L.*

◆◆◆FACILITIES: 93 sites, typical site width 35 ft, accepts full hkup units only, 93 full hkups, (50 amps), 50 amps ($), some extended stay sites, 20 pull-thrus, cable TV, cabins, RV storage, laundry, tables.

◆RECREATION: rec room/area.

Pets welcome. No tents. Open all yr. Big rigs welcome. Clubs welcome. Rate in 2007 $17 for 2 persons. MC/VISA/DISC/AMEX. Phone: (251)653-0835.

SEE AD TRAVEL SECTION PAGE 4

MONROEVILLE—E-2

(N) ISAAC CREEK PARK (COE - Alabama River Lakes) —(Monroe) *From town: Go 8 mi N on Hwy 41, then follow signs W on CR 17.* FACILITIES: 60 sites, 60 W&E, tenting, dump station, portable dump, laundry, ltd groceries, fire rings, grills. RECREATION: pavilion, boating, ramp, dock, lake fishing, playground, sports field, hiking trails, v-ball. Partial handicap access. Open all yr. Phone: (251)282-4254.

MONTGOMERY—D-4

(N) CAPITAL CITY RV PARK—(Pike) *From jct I-85 (exit 6) & East Blvd: Go W 4.1 mi on East Blvd to Hwy 231, then 2.6 mi N on Hwy 231 to Old Wetumpka Hwy, then 1 block E. Enter on R.*

◇◇◇◇◇FACILITIES: 80 sites, typical site width 35 ft, 80 full hkups, (20, 30 & 50 amps), some extended stay sites, 80 pull-thrus, wireless/cable Instant Internet access at site, wireless Internet access central location, dump station, non-guest dumping $, laundry, tables.

◇◇RECREATION: rec room/area, pond fishing, golf nearby, horseshoes.

Pets welcome. Partial handicap access. No tents. Open all yr. Big rigs welcome. Internet friendly. Escort to site. Clubs welcome. Rate in 2007 $25 for 4 persons. MC/VISA/Debit. Phone: (877)271-8026.

e-mail: mi@bellsouth.net

SEE AD THIS PAGE

(W) GUNTER HILL PARK (COE-Alabama River Lakes) —(Montgomery) *From jct I-65 (exit 167) & US 80W: Go 9 mi W on US 80, then 3 mi N on CR 7.* FACILITIES: 174 sites, 174 W&E, 10 pull-thrus, tenting, dump station, laundry, ltd groceries, fire rings, grills, wood. RECREATION: pavilion, boating, ramp, river fishing, playground, hiking trails. Partial handicap access. Open all yr. Phone: (334)269-1053.

(S) MONTGOMERY CAMPGROUND—(Montgomery) *From jct I-65 & US 31 (exit 164): Go 1/4 mi S on US 31. Enter on R.*

◇◇◇FACILITIES: 96 sites, typical site width 40 ft, 29 full hkups, 67 W&E, (20, 30 & 50 amps), 50 pull-thrus, phone Internet access central location, tenting, cabins, RV storage, dump station, non-guest dumping $, laundry, groceries, RV supplies, LP gas by weight/by meter, ice, tables.

◇◇RECREATION: swim pool, lake fishing, golf nearby, bsktball, playground.

Pets welcome. Partial handicap access. Open all yr. Clubs welcome. MC/VISA/Debit. Phone: (866) 308-3688.

e-mail: bcj@mindspring.com

SEE AD THIS PAGE

Helen Keller, author & educator, was from Alabama.

MONTGOMERY—Continued

(N) PRATTVILLE AUTO & RV REPAIR CENTER—*N'bnd: From jct I-65 (exit 179) & Hwy 82/W6: Go 1/2 mi W then 2 mi S & W on Hwy 82/W6, then 1 mi N on US 31. (Ent on R). S'bnd: Exit 186 & Hwy 31: Go 10 mi S on Hwy 31 (Ent on L). Enter on R.* SERVICES: full-time mech, engine/chassis repair, RV appliance repair, body work/collision repair, LP gas by weight/by meter, sells parts/accessories. Open all yr. MC/VISA/DISC/AMEX/DC/Debit. Phone: (334)365-5085. FMCA discount.

e-mail: pvillervrepair@aol.com

SEE AD THIS PAGE

(S) THE WOODS RV PARK AND CAMPGROUND—(Montgomery) *From jct I-65 S (exit 168) and South Blvd: Go 1/8 mi E to Sassafras Cir (between Arby's & BP) Enter on R.*

◇◇◇FACILITIES: 105 sites, typical site width 40 ft, 105 full hkups, (20, 30 & 50 amps), some extended stay sites, 105 pull-thrus, cable TV, wireless Instant Internet access at site, phone Internet access central location, tenting, RV storage, dump station, non-guest dumping $, laundry, RV supplies, LP gas by weight/by meter, tables, fire rings.

◇◇RECREATION: lake fishing, golf nearby, play equipment, horseshoes, v-ball.

Pets welcome. Partial handicap access. Open all yr. Big rigs welcome. Internet friendly. Escort to site. Rate in 2007 $25 per vehicle. MC/VISA/DISC/AMEX/Debit. Phone: (334)356-1887.

SEE AD THIS PAGE

MOORESVILLE—A-3

(E) ALABAMA MOUNTAIN LAKES TOURIST ASSOCIATION—*From jct I-65 & I-565: Go 2 mi E on I-565 (exit 2), then 500 feet S on Mooresville Rd to North St. Enter on R.* Northern Alabama tourist association representing camping, attractions, fishing, parks and events. Open all yr. Phone: (256)350-3500.

e-mail: info@almtlakes.org

SEE AD TRAVEL SECTION PAGE 1

MOUNDVILLE—C-2

(S) MOUNDVILLE ARCHAEOLOGICAL PARK (Univ of Alabama)—(Hale) *From I20/59 (exit 71A) go 13 miles South on Hwy 69.* FACILITIES: 36 sites, 31 W&E, (30 amps), 5 no hkups,

MOUNDVILLE—Continued
MOUNDVILLE ARCHAEOLOGICAL PARK (Univ of Alabama)—Continued

6 pull-thrus, tenting, dump station, fire rings, grills. RECREATION: lake/river/pond fishing, sports field, hiking trails. Rec open to public. No pets. Open all yr. Bathhouse is closed Dec 1 to Mar 1. Park closed Thanksgiving, Dec 24, 25, 31 & Jan 1. Phone: (205) 371 2234.

MUSCLE SHOALS—A-2

(S) WILSON DAM/ROCKPILE (TVA-Wilson Lake)—(Colbert) *From south side of Wilson Dam: Go 1/2 mi W on Hwy 133/TVA Reservation Rd, then 1/2 mi N (follow signs).* FACILITIES: 23 sites, 23 no hkups, tenting, ltd groceries, grills. RECREATION: pavilion, boating, ramp, lake/river fishing, hiking trails. Open all yr. Phone: (256)386-2560.

NEW MARKET—A-3

(N) SHARON JOHNSTON PARK—(Madison) *North on Memorial Parkway, right on Winchester, left on Coleman Rd. Enter on R.* FACILITIES: 33 sites, 33 W&E, tenting, dump station, grills. RECREATION: pavilion, swim pool, lake fishing, sports field. Pets welcome. Partial handicap access. Open all yr. Reservation necessary. Phone: (256)379-2868.

OPELIKA—C-5

(S) LAKESIDE RV PARK—(Troup) *From jct I-85 (exit 62) & US 280: Go 4-1/2 mi E on US 280. Enter on L.*

◇◇◇FACILITIES: 44 sites, typical site width 25 ft, accepts full hkup units only, 44 full hkups, (50 amps), some extended stay sites, 30 pull-thrus, cable TV, wireless Instant Internet access at site, phone on-site Internet access (needs activ), phone Internet access central location, laundry, tables.

◇RECREATION: pond fishing, golf nearby, play equipment.

Pets welcome, breed restrict. No tents. Open all yr. Internet friendly. Escort to site. Rate in 2007 $28 for 3 persons. Phone: (334)705-0701.

SEE AD AUBURN PAGE 9

OPP—E-4

(N) FRANK JACKSON SP—(Covington) *From town: Go 4 mi N on US 331.* FACILITIES: 31 sites, 26 W&E, 5 no hkups, 26 pull-thrus, tenting, laundry, fire rings, grills, wood. RECREATION: pavilion, lake swimming, boating, canoeing, ramp, dock, lake fishing, playground, hiking trails. Partial handicap access. Open all yr. Phone: (334)493-6988.

ORANGE BEACH—F-2

(E) Beech's Camping MHP—(Baldwin) *From jct Hwy 59 & Hwy 182: Go 7 mi E on Hwy 182, then 1-1/2 mi N on Hwy 161. Enter on R.* ◇◇FACILITIES: 90 sites, typical site width 30 ft, 65 full hkups, 25 W&E, (20, 30

Beech's Camping MHP—Continued on next page

ORANGE BEACH—Continued
Beech's Camping MHP—Continued

& 50 amps), some extended stay sites, 40 pull-thrus, dump station, laundry, tables, grills. ◆RECREATION: rec room/area, shuffleboard court, horseshoes. Pets welcome. No tents. Open all yr. Rate in 2007 $25 for 2 persons. Phone: (251)981-4136.

OZARK—E-4

(S) MILITARY PARK (Fort Rucker Campground)—(Dale) *From US 231 (Fort Rucker Military Res-Ozark Gate exit): Go S to Andrews Ave, then SW on Whittaker Rd, then W on Christian Rd, then N on Johnson Rd. On base. Enter at end.* FACILITIES: 18 sites, 18 W&E, 18 pull-thrus, tenting, dump station, patios, fire rings, grills. RECREATION: rec room/area, pavilion, lake swimming, boating, canoeing, dock, rowboat/canoe rentals, lake fishing, playground, tennis, sports field, hiking trails, v-ball. No pets. Open Apr thru Oct. For Military Use Only-w/Military ID Card. Phone: (334)255-4305.

(W) Mr. D's—(Coffee) *From jct US 231 & Hwy 27: Go 2 mi N on US 231 (45 mile marker). Enter on L.* ◆◆FACILITIES: 50 sites, 50 full hkups, (30 & 50 amps), 50 pull-thrus, tenting, laundry. RECREATION: hiking trails. Pets welcome. Open all yr. Big rigs welcome. Rate in 2007 $20-25 for 2 persons. Phone: (334)774-8361.

Interested in receiving special discounts on camping and RVing books, directories and maps? Looking for the latest in RV travel destination spots? Log onto www.woodalls.com and register to receive FREE information and special offerings that will make your RV travel more enjoyable.

On The Shores of Beautiful Logan Martin Lake
LAKESIDE LANDING
RV Resort & Marina
Wi-Fi
(205) 525-5701
★ RV SITES ★
• Full Hookups
• Pull-Thrus
• 30/50 AMP
• Laundry
• Meeting Room
• Modem Friendly
★ MARINA ★
• Boat Launch
• Boat Sales/Srvc.
• Fishing Piers
• Gas & Oil
• Dry Boat -RV Storage
Big Rigs Welcome
Fishing Supplies
Convenience Store
ATM Propane
Exit 158
To Birmingham
Pell City
20
231
Nearby: Talladega Speedway
Lakeside Landing
Logan Martin Lake
www.lakeloganmartin.com
See listing at Pell City, AL

OZARK—Continued

(N) OZARK TRAVEL PARK—(Dale) *From jct US 231 & Hwy 27: Go 3 mi N on US 231 (mile marker 47-east side). Enter on R.*

WELCOME

ENJOY SOUTHERN HOSPITALITY
Rest, relax and play. Serene, peaceful get-away. Play golf, visit the Army Aviation Museum. Enjoy two public fishing and recreation lakes nearby, or just sit and take in our "Boutique of a Park".

◆◆◆◆◆FACILITIES: 65 sites, typical site width 30 ft, 65 full hkups, (20, 30 & 50 amps), 47 pull-thrus, cable TV, wireless Instant Internet access at site, wireless Internet access central location, tenting, cabins, dump station, non-guest dumping $, laundry, groceries, RV supplies, LP gas by weight/by meter, ice, tables, patios, fire rings, grills, wood.

◆◆◆◆RECREATION: rec room/area, coin games, swim pool, pond fishing, fishing supplies, golf nearby, playground, horseshoes, v-ball.

Pets welcome. Open all yr. Big rigs welcome. Internet friendly. Escort to site. Clubs welcome. Rate in 2007 $27.95 for 2 persons. MC/VISA/DISC/AMEX/Debit. Member ARVC, ALARVC. Phone: (800)359-3218. FMCA discount.

e-mail: rv@charter.net

SEE AD THIS PAGE

PELHAM—C-3

(W) BIRMINGHAM SOUTH CAMPGROUND—(Shelby) *From jct I-65 (exit 242) & Hwy 52: Go 700 yards W on Hwy 52, then 300 yards N on Hwy 33. Enter on R.*

YA'LL COME - YA HEAR!
Smiling faces await you at our 5 star park in the Heart of Dixie. Located 1/2 mi from I-65, you will find fine dining, fantastic shopping, premier golf & amusement parks. Close to the bright lights of the city. We have it all.

◆◆◆◆◆FACILITIES: 108 sites, typical site width 50 ft, 102 full hkups, 6 W&E, (30 & 50 amps), 50 amps ($), many extended stay sites, 56 pull-thrus, cable TV, wireless Instant Internet access at site, phone Internet access central location, tenting, cabins, RV storage, dump station, non-guest dumping $, laundry, full svc store, RV supplies, LP gas by weight/by meter, ice, tables, patios, fire rings, grills, wood.

◆◆◆◆◆RECREATION: rec hall, rec room/area, pavilion, equipped pavilion, coin games, swim pool, whirlpool, golf nearby, bsktball, playground, planned activities, horseshoes, v-ball. Rec open to public.

Pets welcome. Partial handicap access. Open all yr. Big rigs welcome. Internet friendly. Clubs welcome. Rate in 2007 $33 for 2 persons. MC/VISA/DISC/Debit. Member ARVC, ALARVC. Phone: (205) 664-8832.

e-mail: bscampground@aol.com

SEE AD BIRMINGHAM PAGE 10

(NE) OAK MOUNTAIN SP—(Shelby) *From jct I-65 (exit 246) & Hwy 119: Follow signs.* FACILITIES: 145 sites, 85 full hkups, 60 no hkups, 24 pull-thrus, tenting, dump station, laundry,

PELHAM—Continued
OAK MOUNTAIN SP—Continued

ltd groceries, ice, grills. RECREATION: rec hall, lake swimming, boating, electric motors only, canoeing, ramp, dock, rowboat/canoe/pedal boat rentals, lake fishing, playground, tennis, hiking trails. Rec open to public. Pets welcome. Open all yr. Phone: (205)620-2527.

PELL CITY—B-4

(S) LAKESIDE LANDING RV PARK & MARINA—(St. Clair) *From jct I-20 (Eastbound exit 158, Westbound exit 158-B) & US 231: Go 6 mi S on US 231. Enter on L.*

GREAT LOCATION NEAR ALL ATTRACTIONS
On the shores of beautiful Logan Martin Lake, great fishing, wake-board competition and other great water sports. 13 miles to Tallageda Speedway. Between Birmingham and Atlanta.

◆◆◆◆FACILITIES: 193 sites, typical site width 25 ft, 193 full hkups, (15, 30 & 50 amps), some extended stay sites, 164 pull-thrus, cable TV, wireless Internet access central location, tenting, RV storage, dump station, non-guest dumping $, laundry, full svc store, RV supplies, LP gas by weight, LP bottle exch, gas, marine gas, ice, tables, patios.

◆◆◆◆RECREATION: rec hall, rec room/area, lake swimming, boating, canoeing, kayaking, ramp, dock, lake fishing, fishing supplies, golf nearby. Rec open to public.

Pets welcome. Partial handicap access. Open all yr. Big rigs welcome. Internet friendly. Clubs welcome. Rate in 2007 $20-22 for 4 persons. MC/VISA/DISC/AMEX/Debit. ATM. Phone: (205)525-5701.

e-mail: lawbse@aol.com

SEE AD THIS PAGE

(E) SAFE HARBOR RV PARK—(St. Clair) *From jct 78 & I-20 (exit 162): Go 1/2 mi E on 78. Enter on R.*

WELCOME

◆◆◆FACILITIES: 32 sites, typical site width 20 ft, accepts full hkup units only, 32 full hkups, (30 & 50 amps), 50 amps ($), 32 pull-thrus, cable TV, cable Internet access central location, RV storage, dump station, non-guest dumping $, tables.

◆◆RECREATION: lake swimming, boating, ramp, dock, lake fishing, golf nearby.

Pets welcome. No tents. Open all yr. No restrooms. Big rigs welcome. Internet friendly. Rate in 2007 $20 per vehicle. Phone: (205)338-2591.

SEE AD TRAVEL SECTION PAGE 4

PICKENSVILLE—C-1

(W) PICKENSVILLE CAMPGROUND (COE-Tennessee/Tombigbee Waterway)—(Pickens) *From town: Go 3 mi W on Hwy 86.* FACILITIES: 176 sites, 176 W&E, (30 amps), tenting, dump station, laundry, ice, patios, fire rings, grills. RECREATION: pavilion, boating, ramp, dock, lake/river/pond fishing, playground, hiking trails, v-ball. Partial handicap access. Open all yr. Facilities fully operational Jun thru Sep. Phone: (205)373-6328.

Woodall's Tip #37... 100% Money Back Guarantee... If for any reason you're not satisfied with this Directory, please return it to us by December 31, 2008 along with your sales receipt, and we'll reimburse you for the amount you paid for the Directory.

• 70-Foot, Paved Pull-Thrus
• Swimming Pool • Laundry
• 30, 50 Amp • Free Cable TV
• Golf Courses Nearby
• General Store
• Fenced Dog Run
• BIG RIGS Welcome
• Easy Propane
Good Sam Park
FREE Wi-Fi
OZARK
TRAVEL PARK
BEST PARKS IN AMERICA
Highly rated by Woodall's and Trailer Life
Visit Army Aviation Museum
HOME OF FORT RUCKER
"Award Winning Park"
EASY ON EASY OFF
MONTGOMERY (70 MILES)
TROY
MILE MARKER #47 ON US 231 N.
Ozark Trav-L-Park
FORT RUCKER 8 mi.
OZARK
DOTHAN (20 MILES)
TO PANAMA CITY
TO TALLAHASSEE
1-800-359-3218 1-334-774-3219
2414 N US 231, Ozark, AL 36360
Visit Our Web Page: http://www.ozarktravelpark.com • E-mail Us At: rv@charter.net
See listing at Ozark, AL

PRATTVILLE—D-3

(S) AUTAUGA CREEK RV CAMPGROUND —(Autauga) *From jct I-65 (exit 179) & Hwy 82/W 6: Go 1 mi W to Hwy 8 200, then 2 mi S on Hwy 82, then 1-1/2 mi S on Hwy 31, then 3 mi W on City Rd 4.*

◇◇FACILITIES: 20 sites, typical site width 35 ft, accepts full hkup units only, 20 full hkups, (20, 30 & 50 amps), fire rings, grills.

◇◇RECREATION: river swimming, canoeing, kayaking, stream fishing, golf nearby.

Pets welcome. No tents. Open all yr. No restrooms. Rate in 2007 $18 per vehicle. Phone: (334)361-3999.

e-mail: langfordllc@bellsouth.net

SEE AD THIS PAGE

(E) K & K RV Park—(Elmore) *From jct I-85 & I-65: Go 8 mi N on I-65 (exit 179), then 1/4 mi S on E Service Road. Enter at end.* ◇◇◇FACILITIES: 94 sites, typical site width 27 ft, accepts full hkup units only, 94 full hkups, (30 & 50 amps), 94 pull-thrus, laundry, groceries, LP gas by weight/by meter, ice. Pets welcome. No tents. Open all yr. No restrooms. Big rigs welcome. Internet friendly. Rate in 2007 $20.75 per family. Phone: (334)285-5251.

(W) KOUNTRY AIR RV PARK—(Autauga) *From jct I-65 (exit 179): Go 1/2 mi W on Cobbsford Rd, then 12 mi SW on Hwy 82 W (mm 131). Enter on L.*

◇◇◇FACILITIES: 30 sites, typical site width 30 ft, 30 full hkups, (20, 30 & 50 amps), some extended stay sites, 25 pull-thrus, wireless Instant Internet access at site, tenting, cabins, dump station, laundry, ltd groceries, RV supplies, LP gas by weight/by meter, ice, tables, fire rings, grills, wood.

◇◇◇RECREATION: rec room/area, swim pool, golf nearby, playground, planned activities (wkends only), horseshoes, sports field, hiking trails, v-ball.

Pets welcome. Open all yr. Big rigs welcome. Internet friendly. Rate in 2007 $20 for 4 persons. Phone: (334)365-6861.

SEE AD MONTGOMERY PAGE 21

ROBERTSDALE—F-2

(E) HILLTOP RV PARK—(Baldwin) *From jct Hwy 59 & I-10: Go 8 mi E on I-10 (exit 53), then 1/2 mi S on Hwy 64. Enter on L.*

◇◇◇FACILITIES: 81 sites, typical site width 33 ft, 81 full hkups, (30 & 50 amps), 50 amps ($), some extended stay sites, 69 pull-thrus, wireless Instant Internet access at site, phone Internet access central location, RV storage, laundry, RV supplies, LP gas by weight/by meter, tables.

◇◇RECREATION: rec hall, planned activities.

Pets welcome. No tents. Open all yr. Big rigs welcome. Internet friendly. Clubs welcome. Rate in 2007 $24-25 for 2 persons. MC/VISA. Phone: (251)960-1129. FMCA discount.

SEE AD THIS PAGE

(E) STYX RIVER RESORT (CAMP RESORT) —(Baldwin) *From I-10, take Wilson Rd (exit 53): Go N on service road. At B.P. Station, turn east 1.25 mi. on Waterworld Rd. Enter on L.*

FACILITIES: 145 sites, typical site width 25 ft, 145 full hkups, (20, 30 & 50 amps), 130 pull-thrus, wireless Internet access at site, phone Internet access central location, RV/park trailer rentals, laundry, ltd groceries, tables, controlled access gate.

RECREATION: rec hall, rec room/area, coin games, 2 swim pools, river swimming, whirlpool, boating, canoeing, kayaking, float trips, river fishing, mini-golf, putting green, bsktball, playground, shuffleboard court, planned activities, horseshoes, hiking trails, v-ball.

Pets welcome. No tents. Open all yr. Big rigs welcome. Internet friendly. MC/VISA/DISC. Phone: (251)960-1167.

e-mail: reservationsatstyx@gulftel.com

SEE AD PENSACOLA, FL PAGE 161 AND AD ATLANTA, GA PAGE 199

Find a park or campground Woodall's does not list? Tell us about it! Use Reader Comment Forms located after the Alphabetical Quick Reference pages.

ROBERTSDALE—Continued

(E) WILDERNESS RV PARK (CAMP RESORT)—(Baldwin) *From I-10 (exit 53) & CR 64: Go S 1/4 mi on CR 64, then turn left on Patterson Rd for 1.3 mi.*

FACILITIES: 74 sites, typical site width 46 ft, 74 full hkups, (20, 30 & 50 amps), 50 amps ($), some extended stay sites, 71 pull-thrus, wireless Internet access central location, dump station, laundry, LP gas by meter, tables, controlled access gate.

RECREATION: rec hall, pavilion, swim pool, whirlpool, lake/pond fishing, golf nearby, planned activities, horseshoes, sports field.

Pets welcome, quantity restrict. No tents. Open all yr. Big rigs welcome. Internet friendly. Clubs welcome. Rate in 2007 $24-28 for 4 persons. MC/VISA. Phone: (251)960-1195. CCUSA discount.

e-mail: wildernessrv@gulftel.com

SEE AD TRAVEL SECTION PAGE 4

ROGERSVILLE—A-2

(W) JOE WHEELER SP—(Lauderdale) *From town: Go 1 mi W on US-72, then 3 mi S on Park Rd.* FACILITIES: 116 sites, 110 full hkups, 6 W&E, (20 & 30 amps), 12 pull-thrus, tenting, dump station, laundry, ltd groceries, ice, grills. RECREATION: lake swimming, boating, pedal boat/motorboat rentals, lake fishing, playground, tennis, hiking trails. Rec open to public. Partial handicap access. Open all yr. Phone: (256)247-1184.

(S) JOE WHEELER STATE PARK LODGE—(Lauderdale) *From town: Go 1 mi W on US-72, then 3 mi S on Park Rd.* FACILITIES: 116 sites, 110 full hkups, 6 W&E, (20 & 30 amps), 12 pull-thrus, tenting, dump station, laundry, ltd groceries, ice, grills. RECREATION: lake swimming, boating, pedal boat/motorboat rentals, lake fishing, playground, tennis, hiking trails. Rec open to public. Partial handicap access. Open all yr. Phone: (800)544-5639.

(S) WHEELER RESERVATION CAMPGROUND—(Lauderdale) *From jct US 72 & Hwy 101: Go 3-1/2 mi S on Hwy 101 (just before crossing dam) Enter on L.* FACILITIES: 30 sites, typical site width 35 ft, 30 W&E, (20, 30 & 50 amps), 50 amps ($), tenting, dump station, grills. RECREATION: boating, dock, lake/river fishing. Partial handicap access. Open April 1 thru Oct 31. No on site management. Phone: (256)760-5878.

RUSSELLVILLE—A-2

(W) BEAR CREEK DEV AUTH (Elliott Branch)—(Franklin) *From town: Go W on Hwy 24, then 1-1/2 mi S on CR 88, then 1/4 mi E on Elliot Branch Rd. Enter at end.* FACILITIES: 30 sites, typical site width 25 ft, 30 W&E, (50 amps), some extended stay sites, tenting, dump station, ltd groceries, ice, patios, grills. RECREATION: pavilion, lake swimming, boating, ramp, dock, lake fishing. Partial handicap access. Open Mar thru Oct. Phone: (256) 332-4392.

(N) BEAR CREEK DEV AUTH (Slickrock)—(Franklin) *From town: Go 9 mi W on Hwy 24, then 6 mi N on CR 33. Enter on L.* FACILITIES: 53 sites, typical site width 25 ft, 53 W&E, (50 amps), tenting, dump station, ltd groceries, ice, patios, grills. RECREATION: pavilion, lake swimming, boating, ramp, dock, lake fishing, mini-golf. Partial handicap access. Open Mar thru Oct. Phone: (256)332-4392.

SAMSON—E-4

(W) Just Loafin' RV Park—(Geneva) *From jct 52 & Hwy 153: Go 7-1/2 mi S on Hwy 153. Enter on L.* ◇FACILITIES: 22 sites, typical site width 35 ft, 17 full hkups, 5 E, (20, 30 & 50 amps), 11 pull-thrus, tenting, laundry, tables. ◇◇RECREATION: rec room/area, pond fishing. Pets welcome. Open all yr. Rate in 2007 $26 for 2 persons. Phone: (334)898-9202.

SCOTTSBORO—A-4

(W) Crawford RV Park—*From jct 72 & Hwy 279: Go 1/2 mi E on Hwy 79. Enter on R.* ◇◇◇FACILITIES: 18 sites, typical site width 40 ft, accepts self-contained units only, 18 full hkups, (30 & 50 amps), some extended stay sites, 4 pull-thrus, tables. Pets welcome. No tents. Open all yr. No restrooms. Rate in 2007 $30-36 for 4 persons. Phone: (256)574-5366. CCUSA discount.

(W) GOOSE POND COLONY (City Park)—(Jackson) *From jct US 72 & Hwy 79: Go 3 mi S on Hwy 79. Enter on L.* FACILITIES: 117 sites, typical site width 30 ft, 37 full hkups, 80 W&E, (15, 30 & 50 amps), some extended stay sites, 1 pull-thrus, tenting, dump station, ltd groceries, ice, wood. RECREATION: rec hall, pavilion, swim pool, lake swimming, boating, canoeing, ramp, dock, lake fishing, playground, sports field, hiking trails. Rec open to public. Partial handicap access. Open all yr. Phone: (256)259-2884.

SELMA—D-3

(N) PAUL M. GRIST SP—(Dallas) *From town: Go 15 mi N on Hwy 22.* FACILITIES: 6 sites, 6 full hkups, tenting, grills. RECREATION: pavilion, lake swimming, boating, canoeing, ramp, lake fishing, playground, hiking trails. Partial handicap access. Open all yr. Phone: (334)872-5846.

(S) SIX MILE CREEK (COE-Alabama River Lakes)—(Dallas) *From the bridge in town: Go 1/2 mi E on US 80, then S on CR 77 (Kings Bend Rd).* FACILITIES: 31 sites, 31 W&E, tenting, dump station, fire rings, grills, wood. RECREATION: pavilion, boating, ramp, river fishing, v-ball. Rec open to public. Partial handicap access. Open Apr 1 thru Sept 15. Phone: (334)875-6228.

SHORTER—D-4

(N) Wind Drift Campground—(Macon) *From I-85 (exit 22, Shorter): Go 100 yards S, then turn right 500 feet. Enter on R.* ◇◇◇◇FACILITIES: 33 sites, typical site width 25 ft, 33 full hkups, (20, 30 & 50 amps), some extended stay sites, 31 pull-thrus, laundry, groceries, LP gas by weight/by meter, ice, tables, grills. ◇◇RECREATION: rec hall, lake fishing, horseshoes. Pets welcome. No tents. Open all yr. Internet friendly. Rate in 2007 $24 per family. Phone: (334)724-9428.

SHORTERVILLE—E-5

(N) HARDRIDGE CREEK PARK (COE-Walter F. George Lake)—(Henry) *From jct Hwy 10 & CR 97: Go 6 mi N on CR 97.* FACILITIES: 77 sites, 20 full hkups, 57 W&E, 19 pull-thrus, dump station, laundry, fire rings, grills. RECREATION: pavilion, lake swimming, boating, canoeing, ramp, dock, lake fishing, playground. Partial handicap access. Open Mar 2 thru Dec 3. Phone: (912)768-2516.

SPANISH FORT—F-2

(N) BLAKELEY STATE PARK—(Baldwin) *From jct I-10 & US 98: Go N 1 mi on Hwy 98 to Hwy 31, then N 4/5 mi to Hwy 225, follow signs. Enter on L.* FACILITIES: 31 sites, 31 no hkups, dump station. RECREATION: river fishing, planned activities, hiking trails. Open all yr. Phone: (251)626-0798.

MEAHER SP—FACILITIES: tenting. RECREATION: pavilion, boating, ramp, dock, saltwater/river fishing, playground, hiking trails. Open all yr.

SUMMERDALE—F-2

(W) Escapees Rainbow Plantation—(Baldwin) *From jct Hwy 59 & Cnty Rd 28: Go 5.4 mi W on Cnty Rd 28. Enter on R.* ◇◇◇FACILITIES: 98 sites, typical site width 40 ft, 98 full hkups, (30 & 50 amps), some extended stay sites, tenting, dump station, laundry. ◇◇◇RECREATION: rec hall, swim pool, shuffleboard court, planned activities, horseshoes, v-ball. Pets welcome. Partial handicap access. Open all yr. Big rigs welcome. Internet friendly. Rate in 2007 $21 for 2 persons. Phone: (251)988-8132.

(W) ROYAL PALM MOTOR COACH VILLAGES (UNDER CONSTRUCTION) —(Baldwin) *From jct I-10 (exit 42) & Hwy 59 (Gulf Shores Pkwy): Go 9-1/2 mi S on Hwy 59. Enter on R.*

FACILITIES: 159 sites, typical site width 40 ft, 159 full hkups, (30 & 50 amps), 47 pull-thrus, cable TV, wireless Instant Internet access at site, laundry, patios, controlled access gate.

RECREATION: rec hall, pavilion, swim pool, whirlpool, golf nearby, 6 shuffleboard courts, tennis, horseshoes, local tours.

Pets welcome. Partial handicap access. No tents. Open all yr. Big rigs welcome. Clubs welcome. Phone: (251)978-1717.

SEE AD GULF SHORES PAGE 15

TALLADEGA—C-4

(E) LOGAN LANDING RV RESORT & CAMPGROUND—(Talladega) *From I-20 (E'bnd exit 158, W'bnd exit 158-B): Go 3-1/2 mi S on US 231, then 5-1/2 mi E on Hwy 34 (Stemley Bridge Rd), then 6-3/4 S on CR 207, then 3/4 mi W on CR 54 (Glovers Ferry Rd), then 1 mi N on Paul Bear Bryant Rd. Enter on R.*

◇◇◇◇FACILITIES: 170 sites, typical site width 25 ft, 110 full hkups, 30 W&E, 6 E, (20, 30 & 50 amps), 24 no hkups, 20 pull-thrus, wireless Instant

LOGAN LANDING RV RESORT & CAMPGROUND—Continued on next page

TALLADEGA—Continued
LOGAN LANDING RV RESORT & CAMPGROUND—Continued

Internet access at site ($), phone Internet access central location, tenting, RV/park trailer rentals, RV storage, dump station, laundry, groceries, LP gas by weight/by meter, ice, tables, patios, fire rings, grills, wood, controlled access gate.

◇◇◇◇◇RECREATION: rec hall, swim pool, lake swimming, boating, electric motors only, canoeing, kayaking, ramp, dock, 2 rowboat/3 canoe/7 pedal boat rentals, lake/pond fishing, fishing supplies, bsktball, 12 bike rentals, playground, planned activities (wkends only), horseshoes, sports field, hiking trails, v-ball. Rec open to public.

Pets welcome. Partial handicap access. Open all yr. Big rigs welcome. Internet friendly. Escort to site. Clubs welcome. Rate in 2007 $25.50-30.50 for 4 persons. MC/VISA/Debit. Member ARVC, ALARVC. Phone: (888)564-2671. CCUSA discount. FMCA discount.

e-mail: loganlanding@hughes.net

SEE AD THIS PAGE

WELCOME **(NE) TALLADEGA CREEKSIDE RESORT** —(Talladega) *From jct I-20 & Hwy 6 (exit 173): Go S to Cty Rd 005, then 4 mi S on Cty Rd 005 to Lake Whitland Dr, then 1/4 mi E on Lake Whitland Dr. Enter on L.*

◇◇◇FACILITIES: 21 sites, typical site width 30 ft, 21 full hkups, (30 & 50 amps), some extended stay sites, 3 pull-thrus, wireless Internet access central location, tenting, cabins, laundry, ltd groceries, ice, tables, wood.

◇◇◇RECREATION: river swimming, canoeing, kayaking, dock, canoe/7 kayak rentals, float trips, river fishing, golf nearby, horseshoes.

Alabama was the 22nd state admitted to the Union.

TALLADEGA—Continued
TALLADEGA CREEKSIDE RESORT—Continued

Pets welcome, breed restrict. Open all yr. Big rigs welcome. Internet friendly. Clubs welcome. Rate in 2007 $20-30 for 4 persons. MC/VISA/Debit. Phone: (256)362-9053. CCUSA discount.

e-mail: info@talladegacreekside.com

SEE AD BIRMINGHAM PAGE 10

TALLADEGA AREA—C-4

See listings at Pell City, Anniston

TANNER—A-3

(N) Swan Creek Community (RV SPACES) —(Limestone) *From Hwy 65 & Hwy 72 (exit 351): Go 1 mi W on Hwy 72 to Hwy 31: Go 6 mi S on Hwy 31.* FACILITIES: 15 sites, typical site width 30 ft, accepts full hkup units only, 15 full hkups, (30 & 50 amps), 4 pull-thrus, laundry. RECREATION: rec hall, playground. Pets welcome. No tents. Open all yr. Rate in 2007 $20 per vehicle. Phone: (256)355-5392.

THEODORE—F-1

WELCOME **(W) AZALEA RV PARK** (UNDER CONSTRUCTION)—(Mobile) *From jct I-10 & Hwy 90 9exit 15B): Go 1/8 mi W on Tillman's corner Pkwy (first traffic light), then 1 mi W on Old Pascagoula Rd. Enter on R.*

FACILITIES: 50 sites, typical site width 35 ft, 50 full hkups, (20, 30 & 50 amps), wireless Instant Internet access at site, dump station, non-guest dumping $, ice, tables, controlled access gate.

RECREATION: pavilion, golf nearby.

Pets welcome, breed restrict, quantity restrict. Partial handicap access. No tents. Open all yr. Big rigs welcome. Internet friendly. Clubs welcome. Rate in 2007 $12.50-25 for 4 persons. MC/VISA/DISC. Phone: (251)605-0685.

e-mail: azalearv@mchsi.com

SEE AD MOBILE PAGE 19

Hank Aaron, baseball player, is from Alabama.

TROY—E-4

WELCOME **(W) DEER RUN RV PARK**—(Montgomery) *From jct US 29 & Hwy 231: Go 6-1/2 mi N on US 231 (between mile marker 83 & 84), at Cty Rd 1124. Enter on L.*

SOUTHERN HOSPITALITY AT ITS BEST!
A naturally attractive place to overnight, stay awhile or spend the winter. Enjoy our free popcorn, lemonade, coffee, Cappucino & USA Today! New Big Rig sites-50 amps, pull thrus, cable & WiFi! Close to local attractions!

◇◇◇◇◇FACILITIES: 86 sites, typical site width 35 ft, 86 full hkups, (20, 30 & 50 amps), 69 pull-thrus, cable TV, wireless Instant Internet access at site, wireless Internet access central location, laundry, RV supplies, LP gas by weight/by meter, ice, tables, fire rings.

◇◇◇◇RECREATION: rec hall, rec room/area, swim pool, whirlpool, pond fishing, golf nearby, bsktball, planned activities, horseshoes, hiking trails.

Pets welcome. Partial handicap access. No tents. Open all yr. Big rigs welcome. Internet friendly. Escort to site. Clubs welcome. Rate in 2007 $27.50 for 4 persons. MC/VISA/DISC. Phone: (800)552-3036.

e-mail: deerrun@troycable.net

SEE AD THIS PAGE

TUSCALOOSA—C-2

(NE) DEERLICK CREEK (COE-Holt Lake)—(Tuscaloosa) *From I-20/59 (exit 73): Go 4 mi W on US 82, then 3 mi N on CR 30 (Rice Mine Rd), then 3-1/2 mi E on CR 87, then 3-1/2 mi E on CR 42, then 3-3/4 mi S on CR 89.* FACILITIES: 46 sites, typical site width 15 ft, 40 W&E, (50 amps), 6 no hkups, 11 pull-thrus, tenting, dump station, laundry, ice, fire rings, grills. RECREATION: pavilion, lake swimming, boating, ramp, dock, lake fishing, playground, hiking trails. Partial handicap access. Open Mar 1 thru Nov 19. Phone: (205)759-1591.

(NW) LAKE LURLEEN SP—(Tuscaloosa) *From jct US-82 & CR-21: Go 12 mi NW on CR-21.* FACILITIES: 91 sites, 35 full hkups, 56 W&E, (30 & 50 amps), 34 pull-thrus, tenting, dump station, ltd groceries, grills. RECREATION: rec hall, pavilion, lake swimming, boating, ramp, rowboat/pedal boat rentals, lake fishing, playground, hiking trails. Rec open to public. Open all yr. Phone: (205)339-1558.

WELCOME **(E) SUNSET TRAVEL PARK**—(Tuscaloosa) *From jct I-59 (exit 76) & US 11: Go 1/10 mi N on US 11, then 500 feet E on JVC Rd. Enter on L.*

◇◇◇◇FACILITIES: 186 sites, typical site width 45 ft, accepts full hkup units only, 186 full hkups, (30 & 50 amps), some extended stay sites, 34 pull-thrus, cable TV, dump station, laundry, RV supplies, LP gas by weight/by meter, patios.

RECREATION: golf nearby.

Pets welcome. No tents. Open all yr. Big rigs welcome. Clubs welcome. Rate in 2007 $28-31 per vehicle. MC/VISA/Debit. Phone: (205)553-9233.

SEE AD THIS PAGE

TUSCUMBIA—A-2

(S) HERITAGE ACRES RV PARK—(Colbert) *From jct Hwy 43 & Hwy 72: Go 2-1/2 mi W on Hwy 72, then 1/4 mi S on Neil Morris Rd. Enter on L.*

WELCOME

◆◆◆FACILITIES: 59 sites, typical site width 30 ft, accepts full hkup units only, 59 full hkups, (20, 30 & 50 amps), some extended stay sites, 8 pull-thrus, cable TV, wireless Instant Internet access at site, phone Internet access central location, laundry, tables, fire rings.

RECREATION: golf nearby.

Pets welcome. No tents. Open all yr. No restrooms. Big rigs welcome. Internet friendly. Clubs welcome. Rate in 2007 $25 for 2 persons. MC/VISA/DISC/AMEX/Debit. Member ARVC, ALARVC. Phone: (256)383-7368.

e-mail: heritageacresrv@comcast.net

SEE AD THIS PAGE

URIAH—E-2

(S) Ponderosa RV Park—(Monroe) *From jct 65 & Hwy 21 (exit 57): Go N on Hwy 21 for 12 mi. Enter on L.* ◆◆◆FACILITIES: 16 sites, typical site width 35 ft, accepts full hkup units only, 16 full hkups, (20, 30 & 50 amps), 50 amps ($), 4 pull-thrus, laundry, tables. RECREATION: swim pool, planned activities, horseshoes. Pets welcome. No tents. Open all yr. No restrooms. Big rigs welcome. Internet friendly. Rate in 2007 $15-17.50 for 2 persons. Phone: (251)862-2670. CCUSA discount.

Alabama State Gem: Star Blue Quartz

VALLEY HEAD—A-4

(S) Sequoyah Caverns & Ellis Homestead—(DeKalb) *From jct I-59 (exit 231) & Hwy 40: Go 1 mi E on Hwy 40, then 6 mi N on US 11. Enter on L.* ◆◆◆FACILITIES: 85 sites, typical site width 20 ft, 15 full hkups, 70 W&E, (20, 30 & 50 amps), 16 pull-thrus, tenting, dump station, laundry, groceries, ice, tables, grills. ◆◆◆RECREATION: rec room/area, swim pool, pond fishing, play equipment, horseshoes, sports field, hiking trails. Rec open to public. Pets welcome. Open all yr. Big rigs welcome. Phone: (800)843-5098.

WARRIOR—B-3

(N) RICKWOOD CAVERNS SP—(Blount) *From I-65 (exit 289): Go 4 mi W.* FACILITIES: 13 sites, 13 full hkups, (30 amps), tenting, dump station. RECREATION: pavilion, swim pool, playground, hiking trails. Rec open to public. Open all yr. Phone: (205)647-9692.

WETUMPKA—D-4

(S) FORT TOULOUSE/JACKSON PARK (Ala. State Historical Commission)—(Elmore) *From US 231 (1 mi S of town): Go W on Ft Toulouse Rd.* FACILITIES: 39 sites, 39 W&E, tenting, dump station, fire rings, grills. RECREATION: pavilion, river swimming, boating, canoeing, ramp, river fishing, hiking trails. Rec open to public. Open all yr. Phone: (334)567-3002.

WILMER—F-1

(W) Escatawpa Hollow Campground—(Mobile) *Located at the Mississippi/Alabama state line on US 98 W (5 mi W of Wilmer City Limits). Enter on L.* ◆◆◆FACILITIES: 43 sites, typical site width 30 ft, 6 full hkups, 22 W&E, (20, 30 & 50 amps), 15 no hkups, some extended stay sites, 10 pull-thrus, tenting, dump

---

Alabama State Flower: Camellia

WILMER—Continued
Escatawpa Hollow Campground—Continued

station, ice, tables, fire rings, grills. ◆◆◆RECREATION: pavilion, river swimming, boating, canoeing, ramp, 56 canoe rentals, river fishing, hiking trails, v-ball. Rec open to public. Pets welcome. Open all yr. Rate in 2007 $20 per family. Phone: (251)649-4233.

WOODVILLE—A-4

(E) CATHEDRAL CAVERNS SP—(Jackson) *From Huntsville: Take Hwy 72 E to Hwy 63, then right until you see the Cathedral Caverns rock sigh. Turn left & follow signs.* FACILITIES: tenting. RECREATION: Phone: (256)728-8193.

(E) Parnell Creek Campground—(Jackson) *From jct Hwy 72 and 565 (Huntsville): Go 24 mi E on Hwy 72. From Scotsboro jct 79 and 72: Go 14 mi W on Hwy 72. Enter on R.* ◆◆◆FACILITIES: 26 sites, typical site width 20 ft, 10 full hkups, 16 W&E, (30 & 50 amps), 50 amps ($), some extended stay sites, 3 pull-thrus, tenting, dump station, portable dump, laundry, ltd groceries, ice, tables, fire rings, grills. RECREATION: rec room/area. Pets welcome. Open all yr. Internet friendly. Rate in 2007 $25 for 2 persons. Phone: (256)776-2348. CCUSA discount.

A compass tells you
east from west.
Woodall's
Campground Directories
tell you how to
make memories
in either direction.
Special pre-publication offer! Save 50% off the cover price.
Now you can get all of North America (that's all of the U.S., Mexico and Canada) in a two volume set. Just like the North American Directory, 2009 listings have been completely updated by our inspectors in the field. Find places you can park your RV for a month or for a season with the Woodall's Extended Stay Guide, which is also included. Pre-order by 11/1/08 to pay only $16.90 plus shipping and handling and receive it by the end of the year.
To pre-order, call 1-877-680-6155 and mention promo code 669 or order online at www.woodalls.com/shop.
The Complete On-the-Road Guide for Today's RV Enthusiast
WOODALL'S
EASTERN
CAMPGROUND DIRECTORY
168,000 UPDATES FOR 2009
LOADED WITH INFO!
discover one-tank t
The Complete On-the-Road Guide for Today's RV Enthusiast
WOODALL'S
WESTERN
CAMPGROUND DIRECTORY
116,000 UPDATES FOR 2009
LOADED WITH INFO!
discover one-tank trips
woodalls.com

Florida

READER SERVICE INFO

The following businesses have placed an ad in the Florida Travel Section. To receive free information, enter their Reader Service number on the Reader Service Card opposite page 48/Discover Section in the front of this directory:

Advertiser	RS#
Avalon RV Resort	3501
Bay Bayou RV Resort	3401
Big Cypress RV Resort	3477
Blueberry Hill RV Resort (Morgan RV Resorts)	3463
Broward County Parks	3784
Camp Inn Resort	3498
Camp USA	3657
Como Truck & RV Sales & Service	3671
CRF Communities	3748
CRF Communities	3749
Disney's Fort Wilderness	2574
Dunedin RV Resort	671
East Lake Fish Camp	3775
Elite Resorts at Salt Springs	3788
Flagler County Chamber of Commerce	3583
Florida Association of RV Parks and Campgrounds	2173
Lake Rousseau RV & Fishing Resort	3658
Myakka RV Resort	3737
Quail Run RV Park	3666
Rob's Auto Detailing	3684
Sarasota Sunny South	3806
Siesta Bay RV Resort	3805
Sonrise Palms	
Christian RV Park	3374
Southern Charm RV Resort	3555
Space Coast RV Resort	2777
The Glades	3305
The Shell Factory & Nature Park	3672
Three Lakes RV Resort	2982
Travelers Rest Resort	3676
Wilderness RV Park Estates	3670
Winter Paradise Travel Resort	3499

TIME ZONE

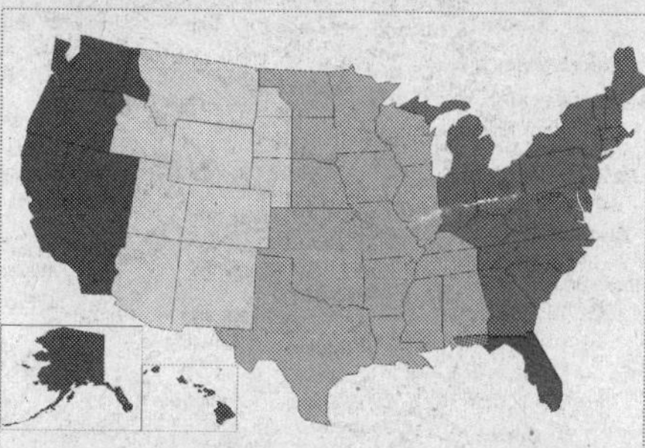

Most of Florida is in the Eastern Time Zone; the section west of the Apalachicola River is in the Central Time Zone.

TOPOGRAPHY

The terrain in Florida ranges from farm and pastureland to swampy everglades; flat cattle land to the rolling hills of orange groves. There are more than 1,800 miles of coastline.

TEMPERATURE

In the northern section, summer temperatures average 80.5° and winter temperatures average 53°. The southern areas average 82.7° in summer and 68.5° in winter. Rainfall is fairly even throughout the state and averages 53 inches per year. The heaviest rainfall occurs during June, July, August and September.

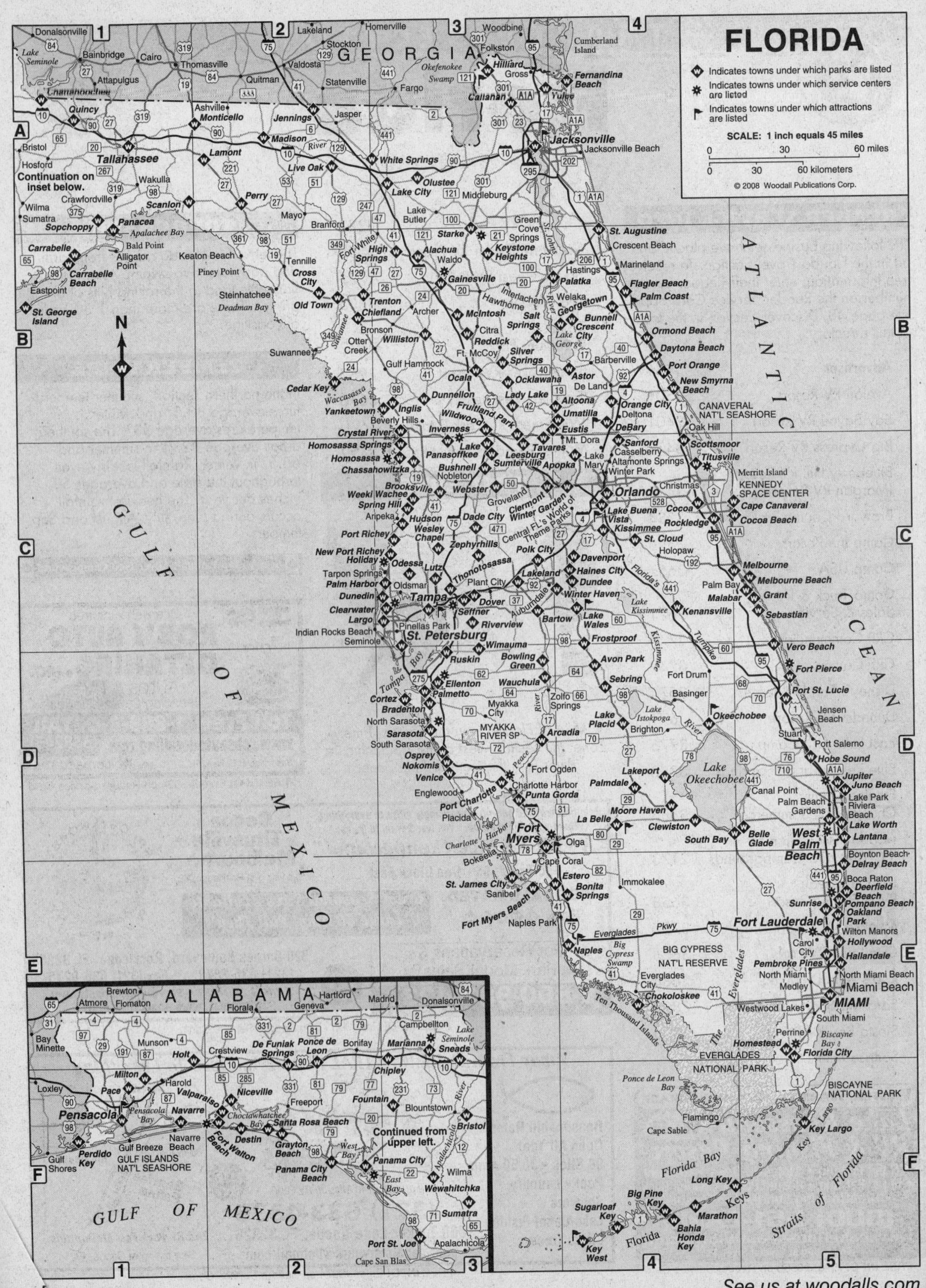

See us at woodalls.com

TRAVEL & TOURISM INFO

State Agency:

Visit Florida
661 E. Jefferson St., Ste. 300
Tallahassee, FL 32301
(888/7FLA USA)
www.visitflorida.com

Regional Agencies:

Central Florida VCB
600 N. Broadway, Suite 300
Bartow, FL 33830

Central Florida VCB (cont.)
(800/828-7655)
www.sunsational.org

Charlotte County Chamber of Commerce,
2702 Tamiami Trail
Port Charlotte, FL 33952
(941/627-2222)
www.charlottecountychamber.org

Emerald Coast CVB
1540 Miracle Strip Parkway
Fort Walton Beach, FL 32548
(800/322-3319)
www.destin-fwb.com

Florida's Freshwater Frontier
PO Box 1196
Sebring, FL
(800/620-3602)
www.floridafreshwaterfrontier.com

Florida Keys & Key West Tourist Development Council
1201 White St., Ste. 102
Key West, FL 33040
(800/352-5397)
www.fla-keys.com

Florida's Space Coast Office of Tourism
2725 Judge Fran Jamieson Way, #B-105
Viera, FL 32940
(877/57-BEACH)
www.space-coast.com

Lake County Economic Development Tourism Dept.
20763 U.S. Hwy. 27
Groveland, FL 34736
(352/429-3673 or 800/430-LAKE)
www.lakecountyfl.com

Lee County Chamber of Commerce
13601 McGregor Blvd., Ste. 16
Fort Myers, FL 33919
(239/931-0931)
www.leecountychamberofcommerce.com

Local Agencies:

Amelia Island Tourist Development
961687 Gateway Blvd., Ste. 101 G
Amelia Island, FL 32034
(800/226-3542)
www.ameliaisland.org

Cedar Key Area Chamber of Commerce
618 Second St.
Cedar Key, FL 32625
(352/543-5600)
www.cedarkey.org

Daytona Beach Area CVB
126 E. Orange Ave.
Daytona Beach, FL 32114
(800/854-1234)
www.daytonabeach.com

Greater Fort Lauderdale CVB
100 E. Broward Blvd., Ste. 200
Fort Lauderdale, FL 33316
(800/22-SUNNY)
www.sunny.org

UPGRADED FACILITIES

HAPPY CAMPERS

1,613 ACRES...315 CAMPSITES...
5 PARKS...1 GREAT TIME!

C.B. SMITH PARK
900 N. Flamingo Rd.
Pembroke Pines, FL 33028
954-437-2650
cbsmithpark@broward.org

BROWARD COUNTY FLORIDA
www.broward.org/parks

QUIET WATERS PARK
(Rent-A-Tent and Tepee camping only)
401 S. Powerline Rd.
Deerfield Beach, FL 33442
954-360-1315
quietwaterspark@broward.org

EASTERLIN PARK
1000 N.W. 38th St.
Oakland Park, FL 33309
954-938-0610
easterlinpark@broward.org

MARKHAM PARK
16001 W. State Rd. 84
Sunrise, FL 33326
954-389-2000
markhampark@broward.org

T.Y. PARK
3300 N. Park Rd.
Hollywood, FL 33021
954-985-1980
typark@broward.org

- RV sites with full hookups and tent sites
- Complete Rent-A-Tent packages with electric and water
- Two tepee sites
- Fishing, boating, biking, and hiking
- Swimming beaches, pools, and water playgrounds (open seasonally)
- Sports and water-skiing
- Nature trails and programs
- 3,000 hours sunshine annually

Reservations are recommended.
For more information,
call or e-mail the park of your choice.

Individuals with disabilities requiring accommodations in order to participate in County programs, services, and activities must contact the Special Populations Section at 954-357-8170 or TTY 954-537-2854 at least ten (10) business days prior to the scheduled meeting or event to request an accommodation.

FREE INFO! Enter #3784 on Reader Service Card

Greater Fort Myers Beach Area Chamber of Commerce
17200 San Carlos Blvd.
Fort Myers, FL 33931
(800/782-9283)
www.fmbchamber.com

Jacksonville & the Beaches CVB
550 Water St., Ste. 1000
Jacksonville, FL 32202
(800/733-2668)
www.visitjacksonville.com

Key Largo Chamber of Commerce/ Florida Keys Visitor Center
106000 Overseas Hwy.
Key Largo, FL 33037
(800/822-1088)
www.keylargochamber.org

Kissimmee CVB
1925 E. Irlo Bronson Memorial Hwy
Kissimmee, FL 34742
(800/333-KISS)
www.floridakiss.com

Melbourne/Palm Bay Area Chamber of Commerce
1005 E. Strawbridge Ave.
Melbourne, FL 32901
(800/771-9922)
www.melpb-chamber.org/

Greater Miami CVB
701 Brickell Ave., Ste. 2700
Miami, FL 33131
(888/76-MIAMI)
www.miamibeaches.com

Naples, Marco Island, Everglades CVB
3050 N. Horseshoe Dr., Ste. 218
Naples, FL 34103
(800/2-ESCAPE)
www.paradisecoast.com

Ocala-Marion County Chamber of Commerce
110 E. Silver Springs Blvd.
Ocala, FL 34470
(800/FL-OCALA)
www.ocalamarion.com

Orlando/Orange County CVB
8723 International Dr., Ste. 101
Orlando, FL 32821
(407/363-5872)
www.orlandoinfo.com

Palm Beach County CVB
1555 Palm Beach Lakes Blvd., Ste. 800
West Palm Beach, FL 33401
(800/833-5733)
www.palmbeachfl. com

Panama City Beach CVB
17001 Panama City Beach Pkwy
Panama City Beach, FL 32417
(800/553-1330)
www.thebeachloversbeach.com

Pensacola Chamber of Commerce and Visitors Information Center
735 Pensacola Beach Blvd.
Pensacola, FL 32501
(800/635-4803)
www.visitpensacolabeach.com

St. Augustine, Ponte Vedra & The Beaches Visitors and Convention Bureau
88 Riberia St., Ste. 400
St. Augustine, FL 32084
(800/653-2489)
www.getaway4florida.com

St. Petersburg/Clearwater Area CVB
13805 - 58th St. N., Ste. 2-200
Clearwater, FL 33760
(877/352-3224)
www.floridasbeach.com

Santa Rosa County Tourism Development Council
1917 Navarre School Rd.
Navarre, FL 32566
(800/480-7263)
www.beaches-rivers.com

Sarasota CVB
655 N. Tamiami Trail
Sarasota, FL 34236
(800/522-9799)
www.sarasotafl.org

Suwannee County Tourist Development Council
816 S. Ohio Ave.
Live Oak, FL 32064
(386/362-3071)
www.suwanneechamber.com

Tallahassee Area CVB/Visitor Information Center
106 E. Jefferson St.
Tallahassee, FL 32302
(800/628-2866)
www.seetallahassee.com

Tampa Bay Beaches Chamber of Commerce
6990 Gulf Blvd.
St. Pete Beach, FL
(800/944-1847)
www.tampabaybeaches.com

Zephyrhills Chamber of Commerce
38550 Fifth Ave.
Zephyrhills, FL 33542
(813/782-1913)
www.zephyrhillschamber.org

RECREATIONAL INFO

Biking: Florida Dept. of Environmental Protection, Greenways & Trails. For a free copy of a bicycle trails brochure: (888/735-2872) www.floridagreenwaysandtrails.com

Canoeing: Florida Professional Paddlesports Assn. (FPPA), PO Box 1764, Arcadia, FL 34265. www.paddleflausa.com

Fishing: Florida Fish and Wildlife Conservation Commission, Division of Freshwater Fisheries, 620 S. Meridian St., Tallahassee, FL 32399 (850/488-4676). www.floridaconservation.org

Golf: Florida Sports Foundation, 2930 Kerry Forest Parkway, Tallahassee, FL 32309 (850/488-8347). www.flasports.com

Historical Sites: Department of State, Division of Historic Resources, R.A. Gray Bldg., 500 S. Bronough St., Tallahassee, FL 32399. (850/245-6300) www.flheritage.com

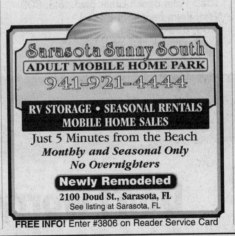

State Parks: Dept. of Environmental Protection, Div. of Rec. & Parks, MS #49, 3900 Commonwealth Blvd., Tallahassee, FL 32399-3000. (850/245-2118) www.dep.state.fl.us/mainpage

SHOPPING

Aventura Mall, 19501 Biscayne Blvd. & 196th St., Aventura. Florida's largest indoor super-regional mall with 250 stores and six department stores.

Fisherman's Village, 1200 W. Retta Esplanade, Punta Gorda. Waterfront complex featuring unique shops, restaurants, marina and museums.

Lake Buena Vista Factory Stores, 15591 Apopka Vineland Rd., Orlando. Save up to 75% on manufacturer direct merchandise. Over 400 designer and name brands.

Centro Ybor, 1600 E 8th Ave, Ste A-100, Tampa. These former brick cigar factories were converted into unique shopping, dining and entertainment attractions. Eighth Ave. & 13th St., Tampa, FL.

DESTINATIONS

NORTHWEST REGION

Apalachicola. The name means "friendly people" and the town is the site of

Apalachicola Bay, which has over 10,000 acres of oyster beds, producing 90% of Florida's oysters. This is also the home of Fort Gadsden Historic Site. Apalachicola has more antebellum sites than anywhere else in Florida. Upwards of 200 homes and commercial buildings, which hold boutiques, shops, galleries, restaurants, churches and B&Bs, are listed on the National Register of Historic Places. The circa-1912 **Dixie Theatre** hosts a summer repertory group. **John Gorrie Museum State Park** commemorates the 19th-century doctor who invented an ice-making machine, the precursor to modern air conditioning, while searching for a way to make his yellow fever victims more comfortable.

The **St. Vincent National Wildlife Refuge** is an undeveloped barrier island just offshore from the mouth of the Apalachicola River, in the Gulf of Mexico. Ten separate habitat types have been identified. The island is a haven for endangered and threatened species, including bald eagles, sea turtles, indigo snakes and gopher tortoises. Wood storks use the refuge during their migration. In addition, the refuge serves as a breeding area for endangered red wolves. Scuba divers and anglers will enjoy the **Mighty O**, the retired aircraft carrier Oriskany, that was intentionally sunk 24 miles SE of Pensacola to become the world's largest artificial reef.

Falling Waters State Recreation Area, Chipley. One of the most recognized geological features in the state is the 100-ft.-deep sinkhole.

Destin. Known for its incredible fishing, you can also sightsee in glass-bottom boats, snorkel, dive, sail, or partake of almost any water sport you can think of. At **Henderson Beach State Park** or **James W. Lee Park** you'll find amazingly soft and white sand beaches created from pulverized quartz washed, buffeted and delivered by river sweep all the way from the Appalachian Mountains. The sand's quartz origins contribute to the sparkling brightness and to the way it squeaks when you walk on it. **Big Kahuna's Water & Adventure** is a shipwreck-themed water park, with miniature golf, go-karts, food concessions and other kiddie rides.

Fort Walton Beach. The Boardwalk is an energetic center of activity with restaurants, clubs, the town's fishing pier, beach volleyball and the classic Gulfarium, home to animals such as alligators, penguins, tropical birds, otters, grey seals and fresh and saltwater fish. Featured performers are trained dolphins and sea lions. View a panorama of undersea life at the "Living Sea." The **Emerald Coast Science Center** is a hands-on haven for kids. In addition to Destin's annual fishing contests, the area hosts more than 100 festivals each year, many focused on relishing seafood. The annual Billy Bowlegs Pirate Festival celebrates Fort Walton Beach's swashbuckling past during June.

Florida Caverns State Park, Marianna. Explore calcite formations, stalactites, stalagmites and columns.

Panama City Beach offers over 27 miles of unspoiled beaches, with an average water temperature of about 72° and an average air temperature of about 78°—the climate alone is reason enough to visit again and again.

Divers won't want to miss **The Museum of Man in the Sea**, home to interesting displays of diving from the 1500's to the present.

Gulf World Marine Park features four shows, sea lions, dolphins, Penguin Island, performing parrots, underwater show and expert scuba demonstrations.

Shipwreck Island lets you slosh along water canals on inner tubes, zoom down a waterslide at 40 mph, or relax in the shade of gazebos while watching children frolic in the Tadpole Hole.

Pensacola. This thriving resort city is home to several historic districts. The Seville Historic District contains a variety of architecture dating from the 1780s to the late 1800s. North Hill Preservation District was developed between 1870 and 1930 and is on the National Register of Historic Places.

Panhandle Pioneer Settlement, Blountstown. Preserving the artifacts, history and values of the rural Florida Panhandle, the Settlement, located on 47 acres, has 16 buildings dating from 1840 to 1940. They include a general store/post office, four 19th century log homes, a church, an old jail, a country doctor's office, a 1880 two-room school, a farmstead and a dogtrot farm house. A blacksmith shop, grist mill and firehouse were built on-site.

Historic Pensacola Village. Museums span 200 years of history. Artifacts and buildings left by early pioneers tell the story of French, Spanish and English rule.

Pensacola Beach. On the western point of Santa Rosa Island, the U.S. built the mammoth Fort Pickens in 1830. Now part of a national park, its well-preserved ruins sit among the pure-white sand dunes of Gulf Islands National Seashore. At Pensacola Beach's east end, more beachscape is preserved at a long stretch known as Santa Rosa National Seashore Day Use Area. In between, the town offers seafood restaurants, beach shops, miniature golf and a couple of full-facility beach parks with watersports and fishing piers.

St. George Island. You can reach this island via a bridge from Eastpoint. Here you can enjoy the white dunes and sandy beaches of Florida's Panhandle. St. George Island State Park is a natural area of ghost crabs, salt-dwarfed pines, wild rosemary and reindeer moss. On the beach side, loggerhead and green sea turtles lumber ashore to lay eggs every summer. On the bay side, salt marshes host snakes, turtles and a variety of fish among their reeds.

Vortex Springs, Ponce de Leon. This complete underwater diving resort offers natural springs, swimming, canoeing and paddleboats.

The Zoo, Gulf Breeze. This 50-acre zoo is home to over 700 animals. Also on-site are botanical gardens and the "Safari Line" train ride, which takes passengers through almost a mile of free-roaming animals in their natural habitat.

White Springs. Home to the state's Nature & Heritage Tourism Center and to Stephen Foster Folk Culture Center State Park which maintains a museum and carillon tower that gongs out his famous compositions. Its village of old-time craftspeople stages candle making, blacksmithing and other demonstrations and every May the park hosts the Florida Folk Festival, along with 15 other annual special events.

NORTH CENTRAL REGION

If you've ever wondered where "way down upon the Suwannee River" is, you'll find it right here in North Central Florida's spring-fed oasis. Sandwiched between the Suwannee and the Santa Fe rivers, this region lays claims to more than 100 springs, pristine wilderness areas, friendly river towns, old-time festivals and intriguing historical sites.

Florida Sports Hall of Fame and Museum of Florida Sports History, Lake City. Florida sports history is preserved with memorabilia from members such as Arnold Palmer, Chris Evert, Steve Spurrier and Ted Williams.

Gainesville. Descend 232 steps into a giant sinkhole at **Devil's Millhopper State Geological Site**. The **Florida Museum of Natural History** is the largest natural history museum in the South. Visit **Paynes Prairie State Preserve** to see wild horses and a herd of bison. View natural history exhibits and archery artifacts dating back to the Stone Age at the **Fred Bear Museum**.

Ginnie Springs. High Springs features 220 acres of wilderness along the beautiful Santa Fe River. Snorkel and swim in crystal clear water, feed fish, discover artifacts, or view awesome springs such as Devil's Eye and Ear. Equipment rental, fishing, tubing, hiking, picnicking, diver training programs, nature trails and camping are also available.

Manatee Springs State Park, Chiefland, comprises over 2,000 acres surrounding a spring that puts out 49,000 gallons of water per minute. Enjoy fishing, hiking and swimming.

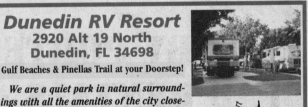

Tallahassee. You'll enjoy fragrant magnolia trees and rolling hills in and around Florida's capital city. Among the many attractions are:

The Capitol, offering a panoramic view from the 22nd-floor observatory/art gallery and a tour of the House and Senate.

Maclay State Gardens. This 250-acre display of floral beauty also features nature trails, tours and a museum. View over 200 varieties of plants.

Natural Bridge Battlefield State Historic Site is located just outside Tallahassee. This was the only Confederate capital east of the Mississippi never captured by Union forces. See the 1865 battle re-enacted in March.

Tallahassee Museum of History & Natural Science, a great place for kids, combines a natural-habitat zoo for native animals with a collection of historic structures including a 19th-century farm, one-room schoolhouse and plantation mansion. Cotton plantations dictated much of Tallahassee's history and at one, **Goodwood Museum & Gardens,** you can tour the restored buildings. Or explore Tallahassee's archaeological heritage at **Lake Jackson Mounds Archaeological State Park** and **Mission San Luis.** Its five historic "canopy roads" carry you from capital-city bustle to the tranquility of the Old South.

Nearby is St. Marks, an important harbor for Spanish conquerors and missionaries. **San Marcos de Apalache Historic State Park** preserves a fort site from the era. The lighthouse at **St. Marks National Wildlife Refuge** punctuates the port's import. Birds and butterflies – specifically monarchs during their fall migration – make the refuge a favorite with nature-lovers.

Wakulla Springs State Park. This park has one of the world's deepest freshwater springs and offers glass-bottom boat tours and ranger-led snorkeling programs.

NORTHEAST REGION

Amelia Island. Located off Florida's northeastern-most corner, Amelia Island provides a refreshing change of pace. Fernandina Beach, the island's only town, showcases more than 50 blocks of restored Victorian neighborhoods.

Flagler Beach State Recreation Area. This recreation area is noted for fishing from a long pier and a white sand beach that is sprinkled red from coquina shells. Fishing, hiking and swimming are available.

Jacksonville. A continuous stretch of beaches offers fishing from piers, swimming and a carnival-like boardwalk with concessions. The **Museum of Science & History** has a state-of-the-art planetarium and a 1,200-gallon marine aquarium. Observe the brewing and bottling process on a tour of **Anheuser-Busch Brewery.**

Jacksonville Zoological Gardens is home to over 800 birds, reptiles and mammals on 62 acres. On-site is a petting zoo, an African Veldt exhibit with an elevated walkway, a miniature train, the Okavango Trail and the Jax Landing.

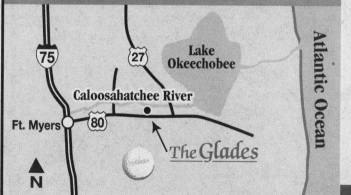

St. Augustine Area. St. Augustine, the nation's oldest city, is often called the City of the Centuries because of its antiquity. Founded in 1565, it is the oldest continuously occupied settlement of European origin in the U.S. The city was founded fifty-five years before the Pilgrims landed at Plymouth Rock and was already two centuries old at the time of the American Revolution. "Oldest" structures featuring guided tours include **The Oldest House, Oldest Store Museum** and **Oldest Wooden Schoolhouse.**

While St. Augustine is valued historically, it is also a family resort with a variety of family attractions and 50 miles of hard-packed, white sand. Attractions in the St. Augustine area include:

Ghost Tours of St. Augustine. Candlelight tours of St. Augustine's historic district with licensed professional guides in period attire await you. Meander brick-lined streets while hearing of apparitions past and present. The tour is suitable for all ages.

Marineland of Florida. Watch dolphins play and journey beneath the ocean's surface.

Ponce de Leon's Fountain of Youth. The first St. Augustine mission and colony is portrayed through exhibits, foundations and artifacts.

Scenic Cruises aboard the **Victory II** afford visitors a 1-1/4 hour scenic and historical cruise of St. Augustine waterfront and beautiful Matanzas Bay.

St. Augustine Alligator Farm. Founded in 1893, this farm boasts the "Land of crocodiles"—the world's only complete collection of all twenty-two living species. View birds, monkeys, giant tortoises and deer along an elevated nature walk. Visit the futuristic-style World Golf Village, home to the World of Golf Hall of Fame Museum. Browse the PGA Tour Golf Academy, shops and a tee off on a championship, eighteen-hole golf course.

CENTRAL EAST REGION

Daytona Beach. Renting a beach cruiser bicycle or moped is a great way to sightsee along Daytona's 23 miles of beaches. Other "toys" for rent include sailboats, jet skis and windsurfers. A boardwalk, amusements, concerts, a gondola skyride and a space needle are great additions to the beach. You won't believe the bargains you'll find at the **World's Largest Flea Market** here in Daytona. Over 1,000 vendors are under one roof and open year-round on Friday, Saturday and Sunday.

Daytona International Speedway, home of the Daytona USA World Center of Racing, offers displays and audio and visual presentations.

McKee Botanical Garden, Vero Beach. Originally established in 1932, the 18-acre garden had more than 100,000 annual visitors in its heyday. Today the garden has been restored by the Indian River Land Trust.

Merritt Island National Wildlife Refuge, Titusville. Auto routes and foot trails provide access for viewing some 25 mammals, 310 bird species and 117 varieties of fish.

Ponce de Leon Inlet Lighthouse, Ponce Inlet. Located off the Atlantic coast, this 100-year-old structure was still in use until 1970. It is now preserved as a national monument and museum.

Space Coast. Encompassing the cities of Cocoa Beach, Melbourne, Palm Bay and Titusville, the Space Coast area offers attractions such as:

Astronaut Memorial Planetarium & Observatory, Cocoa. Explore the universe through Florida's largest public telescope, planetarium programs and laser light shows.

Space Coast Science Center, Melbourne. Science exhibits allow visitors to experiment with shadows, enter a giant kaleidoscope and experience anti-gravity.

Spaceport USA (Kennedy Space Center). The International Space Station Center and the Launch Complex 39 Observation

Gantry provide a new approach to learning about the operational areas of the center. Explore the past, present and future of U.S. space programs. Motion, video and special effects create the Shuttle Launch Experience in a new exhibit at the Visitor Complex.

U.S. Astronaut Hall of Fame, Titusville. View historic artifacts, space hardware, personal mementos and rare video footage. Take a "Shuttle to Tomorrow" in the cargo bay of a full-scale space shuttle mock-up.

Sugar Mill Gardens, Port Orange. These plantation ruins of an old English sugar mill are surrounded by 12 acres of botanical gardens. Enjoy flowering trees, holly, magnolias and other blooming plants.

Turtle Watching, Loggerhead. Green and leatherback sea turtles come ashore to lay eggs in July and August at Jensen Beach, Hutchinson Island, Hobe Sound Wildlife Refuge and Blowing Rocks Preserve.

CENTRAL REGION

Central Florida Zoological Park, Sanford. Explore the world of nature and discover more than 400 animals including cheetahs, leopards, elephants, mandrills, macaws and reptiles.

Cypress Gardens Adventure Park. These lush botanical gardens also feature water ski shows, a butterfly conservatory, ice skating shows, reptile and birds of prey shows and **Nature's Way Zoo.**

Kissimmee is known as the "Gateway to the World" because millions of visitors annually pass through the Kissimmee-St. Cloud area on their way to Walt Disney World®.

A World of Orchids. Exquisite flowering orchids are displayed in a rainforest setting with exotic birds, fish, chameleons and Asian squirrels.

Old Town. This town was re-created to resemble old Florida's brick-lined streets with horse and surrey rides, floral gardens, a fountain, a gazebo and a European antique carrousel.

Wolfman Jack's Rock N' Roll Palace. Relive the fabulous '50s with dining, dancing, saddle shoes, poodle skirts and the stars of the '50s and '60s.

Lake County is aptly named for the area's 1,400 lakes. The largest of these are Lake Harris, Lake Eutis, Lake Yale, Lake Griffin and a large portion of Lake Apopka. Cast your line for shellcrackers, bluegill, speckled perch and bass.

Orlando. Attractions in and around Orlando include:

Discovery Cove. Experience once-in-a-lifetime, up-close encounters with dolphins and other exotic marine animals. Swim with dolphins, rays and thousands of tropical fish.

Gatorland is home to thousands of alligators and crocodiles. A petting zoo, a mini-water park, an eco-tour, a bird sanctuary and wildlife shows are also on-site.

Guinness World Records Experience. You'll experience first-hand what it takes to be a Guinness World Record Holder at this interactive "prototype" attraction.

Meade Botanical Gardens, Winter Park. Enjoy over 50 acres of floral paradise, rockeries, nature trails and picnic pavilions.

Orlando Science Center. Explore hundreds of interactive attractions for all ages in ten themed exhibitions. Surround yourself with images on the eight-story CineDome screen, the world's largest domed theater and planetarium.

SeaWorld Orlando. Try the water coaster and enjoy more than 200 acres of shows, attractions and exhibits.

Titanic—The Exhibition. Experience this major Titanic exhibition with authentic artifacts, historic treasures and full-scale re-creations including the Grand Staircase. Share the stories of her passengers and crew.

Universal Orlando. Set on 444 acres, this motion picture and television studio allows visitors to watch actual shootings and be a part of studio audiences. Enjoy over 40 rides, shows, movie set streets and the new Islands of Adventure.

Wet 'N Wild. This 25-acre water-theme park includes slides, chutes, flumes, floats and plunges. Ride the Bubba Tub (a three-story, triple-dip slide) in a tube big enough for the whole family.

Silver Springs. This nature theme park east of Ocala features Glass Bottom Boats and the World of Bears attraction, plus the Panther Prowl, Big Gator Lagoon, Jungle Cruise, Lost River Voyage, Jeep Safari and live animal shows.

Adjacent to Silver Springs is Wild Waters, a family water park located in a grove of oak trees featuring racing flumes, a 450,000 gallon wave pool, miniature golf, volleyball, a video arcade and a picnic area. The water park is open mid-March to September.

Walt Disney World®, Lake Buena Vista, features Magic Kingdom theme park, MGM Studio Tours, resort hotels, a campground resort and championship golf courses. Captain Jack Sparrow joins the cast of the Pirates of the Caribbean ride. Epcot Center is located on the Disney World grounds. This 260-acre entertainment showplace spotlights futuristic ideas and technologies along with the arts, culture, craftmanship, authentic foods and natural wonders of over 10 nations. Theme areas have exciting (and informative) ride-through attractions, adventure shows and visual experiences. Animal Kingdom combines thrill rides, exotic landscapes and more than a thousand wild animals to view.

CENTRAL WEST REGION

DeSoto Monument, Bradenton. A movie, a tour and nature trails pay tribute to Hernando do Soto and 600 Spaniards who first set foot in the New World.

Dinosaur World, Plant City. View more than 100 life-sized model dinosaurs, reflecting modern scientific theories, displayed in a natural landscape.

Homosassa Springs State Wildlife Park, Homosassa Springs. This display of native Florida wildlife offers unspoiled nature trails, guided boat tours, a floating observatory and fascinating nature programs.

Tampa. This city by the bay welcomes visitors with a downtown art district, state-of-the-art museums, festivals and first-class attractions, including the following:

Busch Gardens. This 300-acre African theme park presents song and dance revues, amusement rides and wild animals. A seven-acre area re-creates Egypt in the 1920s, complete with King Tut's tomb and an artifact dig for the children. The largest inverted steel roller coaster in the world, "Montu," also makes its home here. See two big babies born late 2006: a hippo and a white rhinoceros.

The Florida Aquarium. View more than 6,000 aquatic plants and animals native to Florida.

Weeki Wachee Spring, Spring Hill. At this 200-acre nature theme park, guests enjoy underwater performances, along with the Birds of Prey and Exotic Bird Show, Wilderness River Cruise and Animal Forest Petting Zoo.

SOUTHWEST REGION

Children's Science Center, Cape Coral. Children of all ages delight in optical illusions, inventions, holograms, dinosaurs, mazes, a butterfly garden, steam engines, giant bubbles and a nature trail.

Everglades Wonder Gardens, Bonita Springs. Everglades wildlife in its natural habitat includes bears, otters, wading birds, snakes, the Florida panther and the endangered saltwater crocodile. Alligator feedings and an otter show add to the experience.

Fairchild Tropical Gardens, Coral Gables. This huge 83-acre arboretum is the nation's largest subtropical botanical garden. View the rare plant house, museum, jungle flora and palm display.

Fort Myers. Hop on an old-fashioned trolley for a tour of historic Fort Myers. Visitors can catch the trolley at a variety of downtown locations. Walk the mile-long boardwalk, known as the Six-Mile Cypress Slough, through a 2,000-acre wetland ecosystem filled with subtropical ferns, wild orchids and birds such as herons, egrets, spoonbills and storks.

Calusa Nature Center & Planetarium. View over 100 animals indigenous to Florida—most have been injured and can't return to the wild.

The Shell Factory. Displayed are a huge collection of shells and the exhibit Into Africa, which features taxidermy examples of more than 100 wild animals, including a white Rhino.

J.N. "Ding" Darling National Wildlife Refuge, Sanibel Island. This 5,030-acre refuge is home to otters, raccoons, alligators, brown pelicans, roseate spoonbills and other Florida wildlife. A five-mile auto tour and guided tours led by naturalists are available.

Mote Marine Aquarium, Sarasota. 10 new exhibits, working research labs, a touch tank and interactive Sea Cinema await you. Come face-to-face with a shark or visit with resident manatees and endangered sea turtles. Eco-tours of Sarasota are available.

Pasco County. With more than 30 parks and preserves, there are numerous rivers, trails, shorelines, beaches and recreational areas to see Florida's natural coast. In **New Port Richey, Jay B. Starkey Wilderness Park** offers marked foot trails, horse trails and bicycle paths. You can also take a unique ecotour venturing through pine flatwoods, sand pine ridges and pastureland at the Anclote River Ranch. At **Sims Park**, on the Pithlachascotee River, you can stroll the riverwalk and maybe catch a glimpse of a manatee. Dade City's **Withlacoochee River Park** offers a fishing dock and canoe launch for those interested in exploring the river and its native inhabitants such as river otters, alligators and a variety of fish. **Anclote Key State Preserve** on Anclote Key has a beautiful secluded beach and a recently restored 118-year-old lighthouse. Other attractions include:

Pioneer Florida Museum & Village, which features Lacoochee School, a restored 1930's building; John Overstreet House, a two-story farmhouse built in the 1860's; The Trilby Depot, built in 1896 to haul cypress logs to a sawmill in Lacoochee; Enterprise Church, an 1878 example of rural architecture; and Jack Bromley's Shoe Repair Shop.

Ringling Museum of Art, Sarasota. This complex was willed to the state by circus king John Ringling. It includes art and circus museums, the Asolo State Theatre and the home of John and Mable Ringling.

Sarasota Jungle Gardens, Sarasota. Stroll through acres of beautiful gardens and nature trails. You'll see jungle animal exhibits, reptile encounters and bird shows.

Wooten's Everglades Airboat Tours, Naples. Tours cover the mangrove wilderness—home to 600 varieties of fish, 300 species of birds, countless mammals and 45 indigenous species of plant life found nowhere else.

SOUTHEAST & THE KEYS

St. Lucie. St. Lucie offers visitors a real Florida vacation miles away from the congested freeways and long lines found in bigger tourist destinations. Here you can bask in the golden sunshine surrounded by miles of powder white beaches and see manatees and dolphins frolicking the Indian River Lagoon.

Butterfly World, Coconut Creek. Experience a world where thousands of live exotic butterflies and hummingbirds fly around you in tropical flowering gardens.

Palm Beach County is home to museums that appeal to all ages. The International Museum of Cartoon Art in Boca Raton is the only facility of its kind, displaying masterpieces in every aspect of cartoon art. The Sports Immortals Museum showcases the largest sports memorabilia collection in the world. The Children's Science Explorium and the Children's Museum of Boca Raton at Singing Pines feature exciting and creative hands-on exhibits designed to teach children about everything from electrical fields to recycling.

Everglades National Park. Just 39 miles from Miami, the park encompasses 1.4 million acres of land and water. The visitor center offers a five-minute orientation, brochures and information. Close-up observation of wildlife is accessible through ranger-led hikes. The main entrance can be reached via U.S. Hwy. 1 at Florida City, nine miles along State Hwy. 27. Just outside the main entrance is Everglades Alligator Farm, home to more than 3,000 alligators. Guided airboat tours are available. Live alligator, snake and wildlife shows run continuously during the day. Gator Park offers narrated airboat tours of the Everglades, wildlife shows and alligator wrestling.

Fort Lauderdale is the fabled city of sun and fun. Besides miles of beaches, this city has brick pedestrian promenades lined with sidewalk cafes.

The Keys. This 126-mile string of coral islands is connected by the Overseas Highway and together these bodies of land offer a traveler much more than terrific fishing, scuba diving and Key Lime pie!

Conch Tour Train, Key West. Riding the train is the best way to get an overall view of this picturesque island and its varied attractions, which include the homes of Hemingway and Audubon, old Conch architecture and lush tropical foliage.

Dolphin Research Center, Grassy Key. Educational tours give information on these fascinating creatures. The Dolphin Encounter exhibit allows visitors to actually swim with dolphins. Reservations are required.

John Pennekamp Coral Reef State Park, Key Largo. The nation's first underwater preserve covers 75 square miles and is a refuge for dozens of living coral and almost 400 species of fish.

Key West Aquarium. Visit this home to tropical, game and exotic fish, as well as turtles, sharks and birds.

Lake Okeechobee. Excellent bass fishing is offered in the second largest freshwater lake in the continental U.S.

West Palm Beach. Lion Country Safari, America's First Cageless Zoo. A four-mile drive through the safari with over 900 animals roaming free within inches of your vehicle is a highlight on this adventure. Also included in admission is **Safari World Amusement Park** with animal encounters and demonstrations, rides, games, shopping, food and thrills. Go to www.lioncountry.com for more details.

Miami. This diverse city is home to many attractions such as:

Historical Museum of Southern Florida. Go back in time 10,000 years with hundreds of artifacts, documents and photos. Get a hands-on look at the past with

Things to See & Do

DEBARY
Swamp House Grill

FORT LAUDERDALE
Broward County Parks & Recreation Division

FORT MYERS
Lee County Visitor & Convention
The Shell Factory & Nature Park

HILLIARD
Canoe Country Outpost

HOMOSASSA SPRINGS
Homosassa Springs Wildlife State Park

JACKSONVILLE
Pecan Park Flea & Farmers Market

KEY WEST
Big Pine Key & Florida's Lower Keys

LA BELLE
The Glades Golf & Grill House
The Glades Marina

LAKE BUENA VISTA
Walt Disney World Resort

LAKE WALES
CRF Communities

MIAMI
Gator Park Airboat Tours

NAPLES
Naples Realty Services

OKEECHOBEE
Okeechobee County Tourism Development Council

PALM COAST
Flagler County Chamber of Commerce

PENSACOLA
Pensacola Convention & Visitor Information Center

TAMPA
Florida RV Trade Association (FRVTA)

RV Sales & Service

	SALES	SERVICE
CLEARWATER		
Arrow RV Sales	•	•
Harberson Swanston RV	•	•
FORT LAUDERDALE		
Dixie Trailer Supply		•
FORT MYERS		
Park Model City & RV Sales	•	•
FORT PIERCE		
Al's Motor Home & Trailer Sales	•	•
FORT WALTON BEACH		
Open Road RV Center	•	•
GAINESVILLE		
J. D. Sanders RV Center	•	•
HOLIDAY		
Harberson RV	•	•
HOMESTEAD		
K & K Trailer Supplies		•
HOMOSASSA		
Como Truck & RV Sales & Service	•	
INVERNESS		
Como Truck & RV Sales & Service	•	•
JUPITER		
Land Yachts		•
LAKELAND		
R.V. World of Lakeland	•	•
MARIANNA		
Arrowhead RV Sales	•	•
PANAMA CITY		
RV Connections	•	•
RV Connections	•	•
POMPANO BEACH		
Camp USA	•	•
PORT CHARLOTTE		
Charlotte RV Service	•	•
SARASOTA		
Campbell RV Inc	•	•
SEFFNER		
Rob's Auto Detailing Inc		•
STARKE		
Revels Nationwide RV Sales		•
TITUSVILLE		
Eagle's Pride at the Great Outdoors		•
VENICE		
RV World Inc of Nokomis	•	•
WEST PALM BEACH		
Palm Beach RV	•	•

Woodall's Quick & Easy Reference for Florida

	BIG RIGS WELCOME	INTERNET FRIENDLY	PETS WELCOME	WEB SAVER
ALACHUA				
Travelers Campground	▲	●	■	
APOPKA				
Orange Blossom RV Resort	▲	●	■	
ARCADIA				
Arcadia Peace River Campground		●	■	$
Big Tree RV Resort	▲	●	■	
Craig's RV Park		●		$
Cross Creek Country Club & RV Resort	▲	●	■	
BONITA SPRINGS				
Bonita Lake RV Resort	▲	●	■	
Imperial Bonita Estates RV Resort	▲	●	■	$
BOWLING GREEN				
Orange Blossom Adult RV Park	▲	●	■	
BRADENTON				
Arbor Terrace RV Resort	▲	●	■	
Holiday Cove RV Resort	▲	●	■	
Horseshoe Cove RV Resort	▲	●	■	
Pleasant Lake RV Resort	▲	●	■	
BUSHNELL				
Blueberry Hill RV Resort	▲	●	■	$
Red Barn Campground	▲	●	■	
The Oaks RV Resort	▲	●	■	
CALLAHAN				
Kelly's Countryside RV Park	▲	●	■	
CAPE CANAVERAL				
Carver's Cove	▲	●	■	
CEDAR KEY				
Cedar Key Sunset Isle RV Park		●	■	
CHOKOLOSKEE				
Chokoloskee Island Park & Campground		●	■	
Outdoor Resorts/Chokoloskee Island	▲	●	■	
CLEARWATER				
Avalon RV Resort	▲		■	
Clearwater Travel Resort	▲	●	■	
CLERMONT				
Elite Resorts at Citrus Valley	▲	●	■	
Rolling Ridge RV Resort	▲	●	■	
CLEWISTON				
Big Cypress RV Resort	▲	●	■	
COCOA				
Sonrise Palms Christian RV Park	▲	●	■	
CORTEZ				
Key Way RV Park			■	
CROSS CITY				
Shady Oaks RV & Mobile Home Park, Inc			■	
CRYSTAL RIVER				
Elite Resorts at Crystal River	▲	●	■	
Lake Rousseau RV & Fishing Resort	▲	●	■	
DADE CITY				
Blue Jay RV Park			■	
Citrus Hill Park & Sales	▲		■	
Grove Ridge RV Resort	▲	●	■	
Town N' Country RV Resort	▲		■	
Travelers Rest Resort	▲	●	■	
DAVENPORT				
Deer Creek Golf & RV Resort	▲		■	
Three Worlds Resort	▲	●	■	
DAYTONA BEACH				
Daytona Beach Campground	▲	●	■	$
Nova Family Campground		●	■	$
DEBARY				
Highbanks Marina & Campresort	▲		■	
DEERFIELD BEACH				
Quiet Waters Park (Broward County Park)			■	

▲ = Big Rigs Welcome; ● = Internet Hookups; ● = (Wi-Fi available); ■ = Pets Welcome; $ = Web Saver Coupons

***Check out the "How to Use This Directory" section in the front of this book for a description of the criteria Woodall's uses in this chart.**

Woodall's Quick & Easy Reference for Florida

	BIG RIGS WELCOME	INTERNET FRIENDLY	PETS WELCOME	WEB SAVER
DEFUNIAK SPRINGS				
Sunset King Lake RV Resort	▲	●	■	
DELRAY BEACH				
Del Raton RV Park		●		
DESTIN				
Camping on the Gulf	▲	●	■	$
Destin RV Beach Resort	▲	●	■	
Destin Village RV Resort	▲	●	■	
Geronimo RV Resort	▲			$
DOVER				
Tampa East RV Resort	▲	●	■	
DUNEDIN				
Dunedin RV Resort	▲	●	■	
ELLENTON				
Ellenton Gardens Travel Resort	▲	●	■	
FLAGLER BEACH				
Beverly Beach Camptown RV Resort	▲	●	■	
Bulow Plantation RV Resort		●	■	
Flagler by the Sea Campground			■	
FLORIDA CITY				
Florida City Campsite (City Park)	▲	●	■	
FORT LAUDERDALE				
Paradise Island	▲	●	■	
Yacht Haven Park & Marina	▲	●	■	
FORT MYERS				
Park Model City & RV Sales				$
Raintree RV Resort	▲	●	■	
Riverbend Motorcoach Resort	▲	●	■	
Shady Acres RV Travel Park	▲	●	■	$
Sunseeker's RV Park		●	■	
Tamiami RV Park		●	■	$
The Groves RV Resort		●	■	
The Shell Factory & Nature Park				$
Upriver RV Resort	▲	●	■	$
Woodsmoke Camping Resort	▲	●	■	$
FORT MYERS BEACH				
Indian Creek Park		●	■	
San Carlos RV Park & Islands		●	■	$
Siesta Bay RV Resort	▲	●		
FORT PIERCE				
Road Runner Travel Resort	▲	●	■	$
Treasure Coast RV Park	▲	●	■	
FORT WALTON BEACH				
Playground RV Park	▲	●	■	
FOUNTAIN				
Pine Lake RV Park	▲	●	■	
FROSTPROOF				
Camp Inn Resort	▲	●	■	
GAINESVILLE				
J. D. Sanders RV Center				$
HALLANDALE				
Holiday Park			■	
HILLIARD				
St. Mary's River Fish Camp & Campground	▲		■	
HOLLYWOOD				
Topeekeegee Yugnee (T.Y.) Park (Broward County Park)		●	■	
HOLT				
River's Edge RV Campground	▲	●	■	
HOMESTEAD				
Goldcoaster Mobile Home & RV Resort	▲	●	■	
Pine Isle Mobile Home Park	▲	●	■	
The Boardwalk	▲	●	■	
HOMOSASSA				
Nature's Resort & Marina	▲		■	
HOMOSASSA SPRINGS				
Turtle Creek Campground	▲	●	■	

▲ = Big Rigs Welcome; ● = Internet Hookups; ● = (Wi-Fi available); ■ = Pets Welcome; $ = Web Saver Coupons

*Check out the "How to Use This Directory" section in the front of this book for a description of the criteria Woodall's uses in this chart.

Woodall's Quick & Easy Reference for Florida

	BIG RIGS WELCOME	INTERNET FRIENDLY	PETS WELCOME	WEB SAVER
HUDSON				
Three Lakes RV Resort (Morgan RV Resorts)	▲	●	■	$
Winter Paradise Travel Resort			■	
INVERNESS				
Riverside Lodge	▲	●	■	$
JACKSONVILLE				
Flamingo Lake RV Resort	▲	●	■	$
Hanna Park (City Park)			■	
Pecan Park RV Resort	▲	●	■	$
JENNINGS				
Jennings Outdoor Resort Campground	▲	●	■	
JENSEN BEACH				
Nettles Island	▲		■	
JUNO BEACH				
Juno Ocean Walk RV Resort	▲	●	■	
JUPITER				
West Jupiter Camping Resort	▲	●	■	
KEY LARGO				
Kings Kamp, RV, Tent & Marina			■	
KEY WEST				
Bluewater Key RV Resort	▲	●	■	
Boyd's Key West Campground	▲	●	■	
KISSIMMEE				
East Lake Fish Camp		●	■	
KOA Orlando/Kissimmee	▲	●	■	
Orange Grove Campground	▲	●	■	
LA BELLE				
Grandma's Grove RV Park			■	
The Glades	▲	●	■	$
LAKE BUENA VISTA				
Disney's Fort Wilderness Resort & Campground	▲	●	■	
Fort Summit KOA	▲	●	■	$
LAKE CITY				
Inn & Out RV Park	▲	●	■	
Lake City Campground	▲	●	■	
LAKE PLACID				
Camp Florida Resort	▲		■	
LAKE WALES				
CRF Communities				$
LAKE WORTH				
John Prince Memorial Park (Palm Beach County Park)			■	
LAKELAND				
Lakeland RV Resort	▲	●	■	
LAKEPORT				
Aruba RV Park	▲		■	
LARGO				
Rainbow Village RV Resort	▲		■	
Yankee Traveler RV Park	▲	●	■	
LEESBURG				
Holiday Travel Resort	▲	●	■	
MALABAR				
Camelot RV Park	▲	●	■	
MARATHON				
Jolly Roger Travel Park		●	■	
MARIANNA				
Arrowhead Campsites		●	■	$
MCINTOSH				
Sportsman's Cove Resort	▲	●	■	
MIAMI				
Gator Park			■	
Gator Park Airboat Tours				$
Miami Everglades Campground	▲	●	■	

▲ = Big Rigs Welcome; ● = Internet Hookups; ● = (Wi-Fi available); ■ = Pets Welcome; $ = Web Saver Coupons

***Check out the "How to Use This Directory" section in the front of this book for a description of the criteria Woodall's uses in this chart.**

Woodall's Quick & Easy Reference for Florida

	BIG RIGS WELCOME	INTERNET FRIENDLY	PETS WELCOME	WEB SAVER
MILTON				
Gulf Pines KOA	▲	●	■	
Pelican Palms RV Park	▲	●	■	
NAPLES				
Club Naples RV Resort (Morgan RV Resorts)		●	■	$
Crystal Lake RV Resort	▲	●	■	
Kountree Kampinn RV Resort		●	■	
Lake San Marino RV Park		●	■	
Marco Naples Hitching Post Travel Resort		●	■	
Neapolitan Cove RV Resort	▲	●	■	
Pelican Lake Motorcoach Resort	▲	●	■	
Rock Creek RV Resort & Campground	▲	●	■	
Silver Lakes RV Resort and Golf Club	▲	●	■	
NAVARRE				
Emerald Beach RV Park	▲	●	■	
Navarre Beach Campground	▲	●	■	
NEW PORT RICHEY				
Seven Springs Travel Park		●		
NEW SMYRNA BEACH				
New Smyrna Beach RV Park	▲	●	■	
OAKLAND PARK				
Easterlin Park (Broward County Park)			■	
OCALA				
Holiday Trav-L-Park RV Resort	▲	●	■	
Ocala RV Camp Resort	▲	●	■	
Silver Springs Campers Garden RV Resort	▲	●	■	$
OKEECHOBEE				
Buckhead Ridge Marina Resort			■	
Silver Palms RV Village	▲	●	■	
OLD TOWN				
Old Town Campground N' Retreat		●	■	
Yellow Jacket Campground Resort		●	■	
ORANGE CITY				
Orange City RV Resort	▲	●	■	
ORMOND BEACH				
Harris Village RV Park	▲	●	■	
PALM COAST				
Flagler County Chamber of Commerce				$
PALMETTO				
Fiesta Grove RV Resort	▲	●	■	
Winterset RV Resort			■	
PANAMA CITY				
RV Connections				$
PANAMA CITY BEACH				
Camper's Inn	▲	●	■	
Emerald Coast RV Beach Resort	▲	●	■	$
Panama City Beach RV Resort	▲	●	■	
PEMBROKE PINES				
C.B. Smith Park (Broward County Park)	▲		■	
POLK CITY				
LeLynn RV Resort	▲	●	■	
POMPANO BEACH				
Camp USA				$
Highland Pines RV Resort		●	■	
PORT CHARLOTTE				
Charlotte RV Service				$
Riverside RV Resort & Campground	▲	●	■	
PORT ST. LUCIE				
Port St Lucie RV Resort	▲	●	■	
PUNTA GORDA				
Punta Gorda RV Resort		●	■	
Water's Edge RV Resort of Punta Gorda	▲	●	■	
QUINCY				
Beaver Lake Campground	▲		■	
ROCKLEDGE				
Space Coast RV Resort	▲	●	■	

▲ = Big Rigs Welcome; ● = Internet Hookups; ● = (Wi-Fi available); ■ = Pets Welcome; $ = Web Saver Coupons

**Check out the "How to Use This Directory" section in the front of this book for a description of the criteria Woodall's uses in this chart.*

Woodall's Quick & Easy Reference for Florida

	BIG RIGS WELCOME	INTERNET FRIENDLY	PETS WELCOME	WEB SAVER
RUSKIN				
Hide-A-Way RV Resort	▲	●	■	
Sun Lake RV Resort	▲		■	
Tampa South RV Resort	▲	●	■	
SALT SPRINGS				
Elite Resorts At Salt Springs	▲	●	■	$
SANFORD				
Twelve Oaks RV Resort	▲	●	■	
SARASOTA				
Sarasota Lakes Camping Resort	▲		■	
Sarasota Sunny South Adult Mobile Home Park	▲		■	
Sun-N-Fun RV Resort	▲	●	■	$
SEBASTIAN				
Pelican's Landing	▲	●	■	
SEBRING				
Buttonwood Bay	▲	●	■	
Lake Josephine RV Resort	▲	●	■	
SILVER SPRINGS				
Wilderness RV Park Estates	▲	●	■	
ST. AUGUSTINE				
North Beach Camp Resort	▲	●	■	$
St. Augustine Beach KOA Kampground Resort	▲	●	■	
Stagecoach RV Park	▲	●	■	
ST. CLOUD				
The Mark Manufactured Home Park	▲	●	■	
ST. PETERSBURG				
Robert's Mobile Home & RV Resort	▲	●	■	
STARKE				
Revels Nationwide RV Sales				$
Starke/Gainesville NE KOA	▲	●	■	
SUNRISE				
Markham Park (Broward County Park)	▲		■	
TALLAHASSEE				
Tallahassee RV Park	▲	●	■	
TAMPA				
Bay Bayou RV Resort	▲	●	■	$
Camp Nebraska	▲		■	
THONOTOSASSA				
Happy Traveler RV Park	▲	●	■	
Spanish Main RV Resort	▲	●	■	
TITUSVILLE				
The Great Outdoors RV-Nature & Golf Resort	▲	●	■	
VENICE				
Florida Pines Mobile Home Court	▲			
Myakka RV Resort	▲	●	■	$
WESLEY CHAPEL				
Quail Run RV Park	▲	●	■	
WEST PALM BEACH				
Lion Country Safari KOA		●	■	
WINTER HAVEN				
Hammondell Campground	▲	●	■	
YANKEETOWN				
Cattail Creek RV Park			■	
YULEE				
Bow & Arrow Campground	▲	●	■	
ZEPHYRHILLS				
Baker Acres RV Resort	▲	●	■	
Glen Haven RV Resort	▲	●	■	
Happy Days RV Park			■	
Hillcrest RV Resort	▲	●	■	
Leisure Days RV Resort	▲	●	■	
Majestic Oaks RV Resort	▲	●	■	
Rainbow Village RV Resort	▲	●	■	
Southern Charm RV Resort	▲	●	■	
Sweetwater RV Park	▲	●	■	
Water's Edge RV Resort	▲	●	■	

▲ = Big Rigs Welcome; ● = Internet Hookups; ● = (Wi-Fi available); ■ = Pets Welcome; $ = Web Saver Coupons

****Check out the "How to Use This Directory" section in the front of this book for a description of the criteria Woodall's uses in this chart.***

continuously changing exhibits and multimedia presentations.

ANNUAL EVENTS

JANUARY

Kumquat Festival, Dade City.

FEBRUARY

Pasco County Fair, Dade City; Race for Humanity, Dade City; Celtic Festival & Highland Games, Zephyrhills; Edison Festival of Light, Fort Myers.

MARCH

Saturday Downtown Marketplace, Tallahassee; Little Everglades Steeplechase, Dade City; Chasco Fiesta, New Port Richey; Jacksonville Flower Show, Jacksonville.

APRIL

Delray Beach Green Market in the Park, Delray Park; Annual Southern Watercolor Society Exhibit, Panama City Beach.

MAY

FreedomFest, Cape Coral; Annual Pensacola Crawfish Creole Fiesta, Pensacola; Pioneer Craft Day, Dade City; Cajun Zydeco Festival, Deerfield Beach; West Palm Beach Antique & Collectibles Show, West Palm Beach; Annual Children's Festival of the Arts, Davie; Cotee River Seafood Festival & Boat Show, New Port Richey; Florida Estate Winery's Wine Festival, Land O'Lakes.

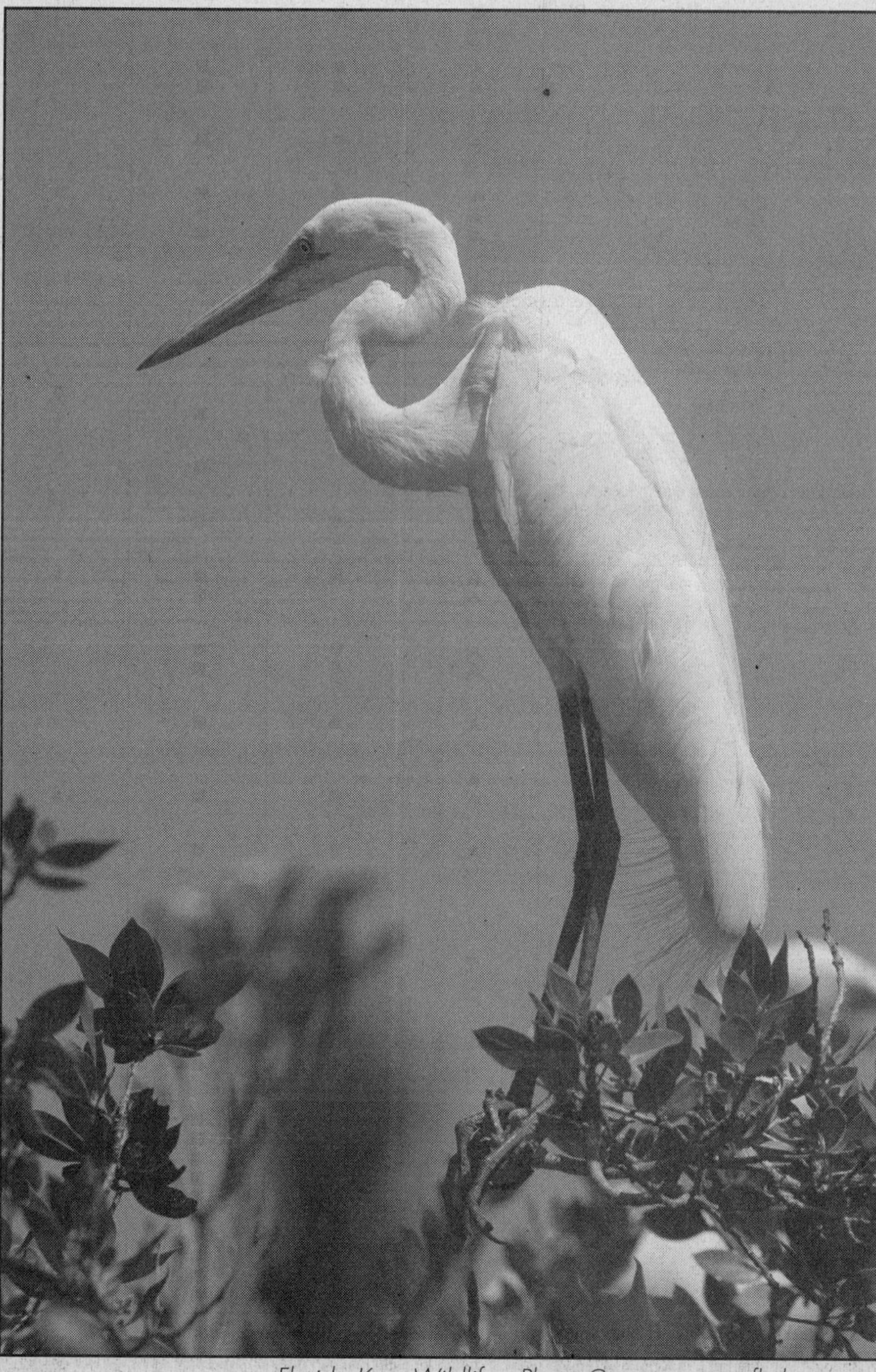

Florida Keys Wildlife. Photo Courtesy www.fla-keys.com

JUNE

San Juan Festival, Port St. Lucie; Yulee Railroad Days, North Central Florida; San Juan Festival, Port St. Lucie; Fiesta Celebration, Pensacola; Sprint Billy Bowlegs Pirate Festival & Parade, Okaloosa; John Levique Pirate Days, Madeira Beach; World Oceans Day, Fort Pierce; Jazz Jams Uptown, Altamonte Springs; Florida Gulf Coast Outdoor Festival, Bradenton Beach; Boca Grande Silver King Festival, Englewood; Main Street Blast, New Port Richey.

JULY

Bradenton Beach Fireworks Celebration, Bradenton Beach; 4th of July on Florida's Gulf Islands, Palmetto; Sertoma's 4th of July Celebration, Pensacola; Florida International Festival, Daytona Beach; Mango Mania Tropical Fruit Fair, Cape Coral; Water Lily Celebration, Vero Beach.

SEPTEMBER

Annual Las Olas Art Fair, Fort Lauderdale; Pensacola Seafood Festival, Pensacola; Delray Beach Craft Festival, Delray Beach; Art Festival, Tampa.

OCTOBER

Arts & Crafts Show, Punta Gorda; Rattlesnake Festival, San Antonio; Central Florida Peanut Festival, Williston; Amelia Book Island Festival, Amelia Island; Alligator Fest, Lake City; Pensacola Interstate Fair, Pensacola.

NOVEMBER

Annual Down Home Days, Trenton; Craft Festival, Gainesville; Flapjack Festival, Land O' Lakes; Pasco Bug Jam, Dade City; Great Gulfcoast Arts Festival, Pensacola; American Indian Arts Celebration, Clewiston; Festival of Lights, Lake City; Halifax Art Festival, Daytona Beach; Greek Festival, Pensacola; American Indian Arts Celebration, Clewiston; Daytona Turkey Run Car Show, Daytona Beach.

DECEMBER

Country Christmas Stroll, Dade City; Holiday Art & Craft Fair, Cocoa; Annual Fernandina Beach Lighted Holiday Parade, Amelia Island; Snow Days, Lake City; Skydive City Annual Christmas Boogie, Zephyrhills.

Florida

ALACHUA—B-3

(W) TRAVELERS CAMPGROUND—(Alachua) *From jct I-75 (exit 399 old 78) & US 441: Go 200 feet SE on US 441, (turn N at Waffle House), then 1 mi N on April Blvd. Enter on R.*

◆◆◆◆FACILITIES: 142 sites, typical site width 20 ft, 109 full hkups, 33 W&E, (20, 30 & 50 amps), some extended stay sites, 42 pull-thrus, cable TV, wireless Instant Internet access at site, tenting, RV storage, dump station, non-guest dumping $, laundry, ltd groceries, RV supplies, LP gas by weight/by meter, ice, tables.

◆◆RECREATION: rec room/area, swim pool, bsktball, shuffleboard court, horseshoes, v-ball. Rec open to public.

Pets welcome. Partial handicap access. Open all yr. Big rigs welcome. Internet friendly. Escort to site. Clubs welcome. Rate in 2007 $30-33 for 2 persons. Member ARVC, FLARVC. Phone: (386) 462-2505. FMCA discount.

e-mail: dreamcamper@juno.com

SEE AD GAINESVILLE PAGE 126

ALTOONA—B-4

(NE) OCALA NATIONAL FOREST (Alexander Springs Rec. Area)—(Lake) *From jct Hwy 42 & Hwy 19: Go 3.7 mi N on Hwy 19, then 5.1 mi NE on CR 445.* FACILITIES: 65 sites, typical site width 11 ft, 35 ft max RV length, 65 no hkups, tenting, dump station, ltd groceries, fire rings, grills. RECREATION: pavilion, lake swimming, boating, canoeing, 25 canoe rentals, stream fishing, hiking trails. Rec open to public. Partial handicap access. Open all yr. No reservations. 14-day limit. Phone: (352)669-3522.

Florida is larger than England & Wales combined.

ALTOONA—Continued

(W) OCALA NATIONAL FOREST (Big Bass Campground)—(Lake) *From jct Hwy 19 & Hwy 42: Go 9.6 mi W on Hwy 42, then 1/4 mi N on FR 588.* FACILITIES: 34 sites, typical site width 19 ft, 32 ft max RV length, 34 no hkups, tenting, non-flush toilets only, dump station, fire rings, grills. RECREATION: Rec open to public. Partial handicap access. Open Oct 1 thru Apr 30. No reservations. 14-day limit. Phone: (352)669-3153.

(W) OCALA NATIONAL FOREST (Big Scrub Campground)—(Lake) *From town: Go 5-1/2 mi N on Hwy 19, then 7 mi W on FR 573.* FACILITIES: 50 sites, 22 ft max RV length, 50 no hkups, tenting. RECREATION: hiking trails. Rec open to public. Open all yr. No showers. Phone: (352)699-3153.

APOPKA—C-4

(W) ORANGE BLOSSOM RV RESORT—(Orange) *From jct FL Hwy 429 (Tollway) & US 441: Go 3 mi NW on US 441. Enter on L.*

◆◆◆◆FACILITIES: 72 sites, typical site width 28 ft, 72 full hkups, (20, 30 & 50 amps), mostly extended stay sites (in winter), 12 pull-thrus, wireless Instant Internet access at site ($), phone on-site Internet access (needs activ), phone Internet access central location, tenting, dump station, non-guest dumping $, laundry, tables.

◆◆◆RECREATION: rec room/area, swim pool, golf nearby, bsktball, playground, 2 shuffleboard courts, planned activities.

Pets welcome, breed restrict, size restrict. Open all yr. Reservations recommended. Big rigs welcome. Internet friendly. Clubs welcome. Rate in 2007 $30-35 for 2 persons. MC/VISA. Member ARVC. Phone: (407)886-3260. FMCA discount.

e-mail: obrvresort@yahoo.com

SEE AD ORLANDO PAGE 150

(NE) WEKIWA SPRINGS STATE PARK—(Orange) *From jct I-4 & Hwy 436: Go 3 mi W on Hwy 436.* FACILITIES: 60 sites, 60 W&E, tenting, dump station, grills. RECREATION: pavilion, lake swimming, boating, canoeing, 60 canoe rentals, river fishing, playground, hiking trails. Pets welcome. Partial handicap access. Open all yr. Phone: (407)884-2008.

ARCADIA—D-3

(W) ARCADIA PEACE RIVER CAMPGROUND—(DeSoto) *From jct US 17 & Hwy 70: Go 2 mi W on Hwy 70. Enter on R.*

◆◆◆FACILITIES: 182 sites, typical site width 25 ft, 178 full hkups, 4 W&E, (20, 30 & 50 amps), some extended stay sites (in winter), 110 pull-thrus, wireless Internet access at site ($), wireless Internet access central location, tenting, RV storage, dump station, non-

ARCADIA—Continued
ARCADIA PEACE RIVER CAMPGROUND—Continued

guest dumping $, laundry, full svc store, RV supplies, LP gas by weight/by meter, ice, tables, patios, wood.

◆◆◆◆RECREATION: rec hall, rec room/area, pavilion, coin games, swim pool, boating, canoeing, 7 canoe rentals, river/pond fishing, fishing supplies, golf nearby, bsktball, playground, 4 shuffleboard courts, planned activities, horseshoes, hiking trails, v-ball, local tours.

Pets welcome. Partial handicap access. Open all yr. Internet friendly. Clubs welcome. Rate in 2007 $15-43 per family. MC/VISA/Debit. Member ARVC, FLARVC. Phone: (800)559-4011.

e-mail: woodalls@peacerivercampground.com

SEE AD THIS PAGE

(E) BIG TREE RV RESORT—(DeSoto) *From jct US-17 & Hwy-70: Go 2-1/2 mi E on Hwy-70. Enter on L.*

◆◆◆◆FACILITIES: 390 sites, typical site width 40 ft, 390 full hkups, (20, 30 & 50 amps), mostly extended stay sites (in winter), wireless Instant Internet access at site ($), phone Internet access central location ($), dump station, non-guest dumping $, laundry, LP gas by weight, tables, patios.

BIG TREE RV RESORT—Continued on next page

ARCADIA—Continued
BIG TREE RV RESORT—Continued

◊◊◊◊RECREATION: rec hall, rec room/area, swim pool, whirlpool, golf nearby, 6 shuffleboard courts, planned activities, horseshoes.

Pets welcome, breed restrict, size restrict, quantity restrict. Partial handicap access. No tents. Age restrictions may apply. Open all yr. Big rigs welcome. Internet friendly. Escort to site. Rate in 2007 $32-37 for 2 persons. MC/VISA. Member ARVC, FLARVC. Phone: (863)494-7247. CCUSA discount. FMCA discount.

e-mail: bigtreerv@earthlink.com

SEE AD THIS PAGE AND AD DISCOVER SECTION PAGE 128

(N) CRAIG'S RV PARK—(DeSoto) *From jct Hwy 70 & US 17 N: Go 7 mi N on US 17 N, then 200 feet SW on Cubitis Ave. Enter on L.*

WELCOME

◊◊◊◊FACILITIES: 349 sites, typical site width 35 ft, 349 full hkups, (20, 30 & 50 amps), many extended stay sites (in winter), 64 pull-thrus, wireless Instant Internet access at

ARCADIA—Continued
CRAIG'S RV PARK—Continued

site ($), phone Internet access central location ($), RV storage, dump station, non-guest dumping $, laundry, RV supplies, LP gas by weight/by meter, patios.

◊◊◊◊RECREATION: rec hall, rec room/area, pavilion, swim pool, putting green, golf nearby, bsktball, 8 shuffleboard courts, planned activities, horseshoes, hiking trails, local tours.

No pets. Partial handicap access. No tents. Open all yr. Church services & planned activities during Nov-Apr. Internet friendly. Escort to site. Clubs welcome. Rate in 2007 $30 for 2 persons. MC/VISA/DISC/Debit. Member ARVC, FLARVC. Phone: (877) 750-5129.

e-mail: craigsrv@desoto.net

SEE AD THIS PAGE

Florida misses being in the tropic zone by less than 100 miles.

ARCADIA—Continued

(N) CROSS CREEK COUNTRY CLUB & RV RESORT—(DeSoto) *From jct Hwy 70 & US 17N: Go 5 mi N on US 17, then 1/4 mi W on CR 660, then 1 mi N on Cubitis Ave (Old Hwy 17). Enter on L.*

WELCOME

◊◊◊◊◊FACILITIES: 523 sites, typical site width 40 ft, 523 full hkups, (30 & 50 amps), mostly extended stay sites (in winter), cable TV, phone/wireless Instant Internet access at site ($), RV storage, dump station, laundry, LP gas by weight/by meter, ice, tables, patios, grills, controlled access gate.

◊◊◊◊◊RECREATION: rec hall, rec room/area, pavilion, swim pool, whirlpool, pond fishing, putting green, golf nearby, bsktball, 8 shuffleboard courts, planned activities, tennis, horseshoes, v-ball.

Pets welcome, breed restrict. Partial handicap access. No tents. Open all yr. Big rigs welcome. Internet friendly. Escort to site. Clubs welcome. Rate in 2007 $40 for 2 persons. MC/VISA/DISC. Member ARVC, FLARVC. Phone: (863)494-7300. CCUSA discount.

e-mail: info@crosscreekrv.com

Reserve Online at Woodalls.com

SEE AD PAGE 93

(N) Little Willies RV Resort—(DeSoto) *From jct Hwy 70 & US 17N: Go 5 mi N on US 17, then 1/4 mi W on CR 660, then 200 feet S on Cubitus Ave. Enter on R.* ◊◊◊◊FACILITIES: 331 sites, typical site width 30 ft, 331 full hkups, (30 & 50 amps), some extended stay sites (in winter), dump station, laundry, LP gas by weight/by meter, patios. ◊◊◊◊RECREATION: rec hall, rec room/area, equipped pavilion, swim pool, 6 shuffleboard courts, planned activities, horseshoes. Pets welcome, size restrict. Partial handicap access. No tents. Age restrictions may apply. Open Sept 1 thru May 15. Big rigs welcome. Internet friendly. Rate in 2007 $37 for 2 persons. Phone: (863)494-2717. CCUSA discount.

RIVERSIDE RV RESORT & CAMPGROUND—*From Arcadia: Go 11 mi S on US 17, then 3 mi W on Hwy 761, then 1-1/2 mi S on Hwy 769. Enter on L.*

WELCOME

SEE PRIMARY LISTING AT PORT CHARLOTTE AND AD PORT CHARLOTTE PAGE 162

(E) Toby's RV Resort—(DeSoto) *From jct US 17 & Hwy 70: Go 3 mi E on Hwy 70. Enter on L.* ◊◊◊◊FACILITIES: 382 sites, typical site width 37 ft, 380 full hkups, 2 W&E, (30 & 50 amps), mostly extended stay sites (in winter), 30 pull-thrus, dump station, non-guest dumping $, laundry, LP gas by weight/by meter, tables, patios. ◊◊◊◊RECREATION: rec hall, rec room/area, pavilion, swim pool, pond fishing, 8 shuffleboard courts, planned activities, tennis, horseshoes. Pets welcome, size restrict, quantity restrict. Partial handicap access. No tents. Age restrictions may apply. Open all yr. Big rigs welcome. Internet friendly. Rate in 2007 $28-65 for 2 persons. Member ARVC, FLARVC. Phone: (800)307-0768.

ASTOR—B-4

(W) OCALA NATIONAL FOREST (Juniper Springs Rec. Area)—(Marion) *From town: Go 10 mi W on Hwy-40. Enter on R.* FACILITIES: 79 sites, typical site width 11 ft, 35 ft max RV length, 79 no hkups, 17 pull-thrus, tenting, dump station, laundry, ltd groceries, ice, fire rings, grills, wood. RECREATION: pavilion, swim pool, boating, no motors, canoeing, 25 canoe rentals, lake fishing, hiking trails. Rec open to public. Partial handicap access. Open all yr. No reservations. 14-day limit. Phone: (352)625-3147.

ASTOR—Continued on next page

ASTOR—Continued

(E) Parramore's Campground—(Volusia) *From jct St. Johns River Bridge & Hwy 40: Go 1/4 mi E on Hwy 40, then 3/4 mi N on Riley Pridgeon Rd, then 1 mi W on S Moon. Enter on L.* ◆◆◆FACILITIES: 69 sites, typical site width 30 ft, 64 full hkups, 5 W&E, (20, 30 & 50 amps), many extended stay sites, 3 pull-thrus, tenting, dump station, non-guest dumping $, laundry, ice, tables, fire rings, grills, wood. ◆◆◆◆RECREATION: rec hall, rec room/area, pavilion, swim pool, boating, canoeing, ramp, dock, river fishing, playground, planned activities, tennis, horseshoes. Rec open to public. Pets welcome, quantity restrict. Partial handicap access. Open all yr. Planned Group Activities in Winter only. Big rigs welcome. Internet friendly. Rate in 2007 $29.50-35.50 for 2 persons. Member ARVC, FLARVC. Phone: (800)516-2386. CCUSA discount. FMCA discount.

(E) St Johns River Campground—(Volusia) *From jct US 17 & SR 40: Go 6 miles W on SR 40. Enter on R.* ◆◆◆FACILITIES: 70 sites, 55 full hkups, (20, 30 & 50 amps), 15 no hkups, many extended stay sites, 4 pull-thrus, tenting, dump station, non-guest dumping $, laundry, tables, fire rings, grills. ◆RECREATION: rec hall, shuffleboard court, horseshoes. Pets welcome ($), breed restrict, size restrict. Partial handicap access. Open all yr. Rate in 2007 $20 for 2 persons. Member ARVC, FLARVC. Phone: (386)749-3995.

AVON PARK—D-4

(W) Adelaide Shores RV Resort—(Highlands) *From jct Hwy 64 & US 27: Go 4 mi N on US 27. Enter on L.* ◆◆◆◆FACILITIES: 399 sites, typical site width 40 ft, 399 full hkups, (30 & 50 amps), some extended stay sites (in winter), dump station, laundry, patios. ◆◆◆◆RECREATION: rec hall, swim pool, boating, canoeing, dock, lake fishing, 5 shuffleboard courts, planned activities, tennis, horseshoes. Pets welcome, breed restrict, size restrict, quantity restrict. No tents. Age restrictions may apply. Open all yr. Big rigs welcome. Internet friendly. Rate in 2007 $30 for 2 persons. Phone: (800)848-1924. CCUSA discount.

(SW) Lake Glenada RV Park—(Highlands) *From jct Hwy 64 & US 27: Go 2 mi S on US 27. Enter on L.* ◆◆◆◆FACILITIES: 216 sites, 216 full hkups, (30 & 50 amps), many extended stay sites (in winter), laundry, tables, patios. ◆◆◆◆RECREATION: rec hall, swim pool, boating, ramp, dock, lake fishing, 4 shuffleboard courts, planned activities, horseshoes. Pets welcome, size restrict, quantity restrict. No tents. Open all yr. Planned activities winter only. Big rigs welcome. Rate in 2007 $31-33 for 2 persons. Phone: (863)453-7007. CCUSA discount.

BAHIA HONDA KEY—F-4

(S) BAHIA HONDA STATE PARK—(Monroe) *On US 1 at milemarker 37.* FACILITIES: 80 sites, 64 W&E, 16 no hkups, tenting, dump station, ltd groceries, ice, grills. RECREATION: saltwater swimming, boating, ramp, dock, saltwater fishing, hiking trails. No pets. Open all yr. Phone: (305)872-2353.

BARTOW—C-3

(E) Good Life RV Resort—(Polk) *From jct US 98 & Hwy 60: Go 7 mi E on Hwy 60. Enter on R.* ◆◆◆FACILITIES: 397 sites, typical site width 35 ft, 397 full hkups, (30 & 50 amps), mostly extended stay sites, dump station, non-guest dumping $, laundry, patios. ◆◆◆RECREATION: rec hall, swim pool, 6 shuffleboard courts, planned activities, horseshoes. Pets welcome, breed restrict, size restrict. No tents. Age restrictions may apply. Open all yr. Planned activities & church services in winter only. Big rigs welcome. Internet friendly. Rate in 2007 $25 for 2 persons. Phone: (863)537-1971.

BELLE GLADE—D-5

(N) BELLE GLADE CAMPGROUND (City Park)—(Palm Beach) *From jct Hwy 80 & Hwy 715: Go 2-1/4 mi N on Hwy 715, then 2 mi W on Torry Rd. (Turn left immediately after crossing*

BELLE GLADE—Continued
BELLE GLADE CAMPGROUND (City Park)—Continued

bridge.) Enter at end. FACILITIES: 380 sites, 240 full hkups, 140 W&E, some extended stay sites (in winter), 20 pull-thrus, tenting, dump station, laundry, ice, patios. RECREATION: rec hall, rec room/area, boating, ramp, dock, mini-golf, 2 shuffleboard courts, planned activities, v-ball. Partial handicap access. Open all yr. Planned activities winter only. Phone: (561)996-6322.

BIG PINE KEY—F-4

(S) Breezy Pines Campground (REBUILDING) —(Monroe) *On US 1 at mile marker 29.8. Enter on R.* FACILITIES: 96 sites, typical site width 22 ft, 34 ft max RV length, 90 full hkups, 6 W&E, (20 & 30 amps), some extended stay sites (in winter), laundry, tables, patios. RECREATION: rec hall, swim pool, shuffleboard court. Pets welcome ($), size restrict. No tents. Open all yr. Planned activities winter season only. Rate in 2007 $33-48 for 2 persons. Member ARVC, FLARVC. Phone: (305)872-9041.

(SW) SUNSHINE KEY RESORT—(Monroe) *On US-1 at mile marker 39. Enter on R.*

WELCOME

◆◆◆◆FACILITIES: 400 sites, typical site width 30 ft, 385 full hkups, 15 W&E, (20, 30 & 50 amps), many extended stay sites (in winter), 340 pull-thrus, cable TV, wireless Instant Internet access at site ($), phone Internet access central location, tenting, RV/park trailer rentals, RV storage, dump station, non-guest dumping $, portable dump, laundry, full svc store, RV supplies, LP gas by weight/by meter, gas, marine gas, ice, tables, controlled access gate.

◆◆◆◆◆RECREATION: rec hall, rec room/area, coin games, swim pool, saltwater swimming, boating, canoeing, kayaking, ramp, dock, saltwater fishing, fishing supplies, golf nearby, bsktball, 2 shuffleboard courts, planned activities, tennis, horseshoes, sports field, hiking trails, v-ball.

Pets welcome. Open all yr. Planned activities in winter only. Big rigs welcome. Internet friendly. Escort to site. Clubs welcome. Rate in 2007 $63-120 for 6 persons. MC/VISA/DISC/AMEX/Debit. ATM. Member ARVC, FLARVC. Phone: (800)852-0348.

e-mail: sunshinekey@mhchomes.com

SEE AD KEY WEST PAGE 134

Titusville, known as Space City, USA, is located on the west shore of the Indian River directly across from the John F. Kennedy Space Center.

BONITA SPRINGS—E-4

(N) BONITA LAKE RV RESORT—(Lee) *From jct I-75 (exit 116) & CR 865 (Bonita Beach Rd): Go 1 mi W on Bonita Beach Rd, then 1-1/2 mi N on Old US 41. Enter on R.*

WELCOME

◆◆◆◆FACILITIES: 165 sites, typical site width 30 ft, 165 full hkups, (30 & 50 amps), some extended stay sites (in winter), wireless Instant Internet access at site, tenting, dump station, laundry, tables, patios.

◆◆◆◆RECREATION: rec hall, rec room/area, pavilion, swim pool, whirlpool, lake fishing, golf nearby, 6 shuffleboard courts, planned activities, horseshoes, local tours.

Pets welcome. Partial handicap access. Open all yr. Big rigs welcome. Internet friendly. Escort to site. Clubs welcome. Rate in 2007 $39-45 for 2 persons. MC/VISA/DISC/Debit. Member ARVC, FLARVC. Phone: (239)992-2481.

e-mail: bonitalakes@earthlink.net

SEE AD THIS PAGE

(E) IMPERIAL BONITA ESTATES RV RESORT (CAMP RESORT)—(Lee) *From jct I-75 (exit 116) & CR 865 (Bonita Beach Rd): Go 1/2 mi W on Bonita Beach Rd, then 1/4 mi N on Imperial St, then 2 blocks E on Dean St. Enter on L.*

WELCOME

A PARK FULL ON FUN!

Conveniently located between Naples & Fort Myers on the Imperial River. Beaches, golf, fishing, shopping, restaurants & beautiful sandy beaches within minutes. Calendar full of park activities. Enjoy Florida's Gulf Coast! FREE WI-FI.

FACILITIES: 312 sites, typical site width 30 ft, 312 full hkups, (30 & 50 amps), many extended stay sites (in winter), 20 pull-thrus, wireless Instant Internet access at site, RV storage, dump station, non-guest dumping $, laundry, LP gas by weight, tables, patios.

RECREATION: rec hall, rec room/area, pavilion, swim pool, boating, canoeing, kayaking, ramp, river fishing, golf nearby, 8 shuffleboard courts, planned activities, horseshoes.

Pets welcome. Partial handicap access. No tents. Age restrictions may apply. Open all yr. Group activities winter only. Big rigs welcome. Internet friendly. Escort to site. Clubs welcome. Rate in

IMPERIAL BONITA ESTATES RV RESORT—Continued on next page

BONITA SPRINGS—Continued
IMPERIAL BONITA ESTATES RV RESORT—Continued

2007 $35-50 for 2 persons. MC/VISA/DISC/ Debit. Member ARVC, FLARVC. Phone: (239)992-0511.

e-mail: ibecoop@comcast.net

SEE AD PAGE 95

BOWLING GREEN—D-3

(S) ORANGE BLOSSOM ADULT RV PARK —(Hardee) *From jct Hwy 62 & US 17: Go 1/2 mi N on US 17. Enter on L.*

WELCOME

◆◆◆FACILITIES: 170 sites, 170 full hkups, (30 & 50 amps), mostly extended stay sites (in winter), phone/cable on-site Internet access (needs activ), phone Internet access central location, RV storage, dump station, laundry, RV supplies, patios.

◆◆◆RECREATION: rec hall, rec room/area, swim pool, lake fishing, golf nearby, 6 shuffleboard courts, planned activities, horseshoes.

Pets welcome, breed restrict, size restrict. No tents. Age restrictions may apply. Open all yr. Group activities in winter only. Big rigs welcome. Internet friendly. Rate in 2007 $18 for 2 persons. Phone: (863)773-2282.

SEE AD THIS PAGE

(SW) Wagon Wheel RV Park—(Hardee) *From jct Hwy 62 & US 17: Go 1/2 mi N on US 17, then 1/2 mi W on Bostick Rd. Enter on R.* ◆◆◆◆FACILITIES: 265 sites, typical site width 25 ft, accepts full hkup units only, 265 full hkups, (30 & 50 amps), laundry, patios. ◆◆◆RECREATION: rec hall, rec room/area, 6 shuffleboard courts, planned activities, horseshoes. Pets welcome. No tents. Age restrictions may apply. Open all yr. Big rigs welcome. Phone: (863)773-3157.

BRADENTON—D-3

(S) ARBOR TERRACE RV RESORT—(Manatee) *From jct I-75 (exit 217) & Hwy 70: Go 7-1/2 mi W on Hwy 70/53rd Ave, then 1/2 mi S on US 41, then 1/2 mi E on 57 Ave W. Enter on L.*

WELCOME

◆◆◆FACILITIES: 392 sites, typical site width 20 ft, 392 full hkups, (30 & 50 amps), mostly extended stay sites (in winter), 62 pull-thrus, wireless Instant Internet access at site, phone/cable on-site Internet access (needs activ), phone Internet access central location ($), tenting, dump station, non-guest dumping $, laundry, patios.

◆◆◆◆RECREATION: rec hall, rec room/area, equipped pavilion, swim pool, golf nearby, 12 shuffleboard courts, planned activities, horseshoes.

Pets welcome, breed restrict, quantity restrict. Open all yr. Planned activities winter only. Big rigs welcome. Internet friendly. Clubs welcome. Rate in 2007 $40 for 2 persons. MC/VISA/DISC. Member ARVC, FLARVC. Phone: (941)755-6494. CCUSA discount.

e-mail: sunresv@aol.com

SEE AD TRAVEL SECTION PAGE 73

(NW) HOLIDAY COVE RV RESORT—(Manatee) *From jct I-75 (exit 217) & Hwy 70: Go 12 mi W on Hwy 70 (53rd Ave), then 4 mi W on Cortez Rd. Enter on R.*

WELCOME

BEST LITTLE PARK IN FLORIDA

3/4 mi to beautiful Gulf beaches. Heated pool, boat ramp & docks, FREE: WI-FI, cable TV, bike and canoe use. Near boat/jet ski rentals and deep sea fishing charters. It's Florida the way you always dreamed it would be.

◆◆◆◆FACILITIES: 112 sites, typical site width 20 ft, 112 full hkups, (20, 30 & 50 amps), heater not allowed, cable TV, wireless Instant Internet access at site, phone/cable on-site Internet access (needs activ), wireless Internet access central location, dump station, non-guest dumping $, laundry, RV supplies, LP gas by weight/by meter, ice, tables, patios.

◆◆◆◆RECREATION: rec hall, swim pool, boating, canoeing, ramp, dock, canoe rentals, saltwater fishing, golf nearby, 5 bike rentals, 2 shuffleboard courts, planned activities, horseshoes.

Pets welcome, quantity restrict. No tents. Open all yr. Planned activities winter only. Big rigs welcome. Internet friendly. Rate in 2007 $36-81 for 2 persons. MC/VISA/DISC. Member ARVC, FLARVC. Phone: (941)792-1111.

e-mail: holidaycoverv@aol.com

SEE AD THIS PAGE

(SE) HORSESHOE COVE RV RESORT—(Manatee) *From jct I-75 (exit 217) & Hwy 70: Go 1-1/4 mi W on Hwy 70, then 1/4 mi N on Caruso Rd. Enter on L.*

WELCOME

SARASOTA AREA'S FINEST RV RESORT!!!

Enjoy our private island - hiking - birdwatching - picknicking. Join or just enjoy our fabulous music program! Great woodworking & carving shop. Country living but within minutes to beaches, shopping, golf & attractions.

◆◆◆◆◆FACILITIES: 476 sites, typical site width 35 ft, accepts full hkup units only, 476 full hkups, (30 & 50 amps), many extended stay sites (in winter), phone/cable on-site Internet access (needs activ), wireless Internet access central location, RV/park trailer rentals, laundry, tables, patios, controlled access gate.

◆◆◆◆◆RECREATION: rec hall, rec room/area, equipped pavilion, swim pool, whirlpool, boating, dock, river fishing, golf nearby, 8 shuffleboard courts, planned activities, horseshoes, hiking trails, local tours.

Pets welcome, breed restrict, size restrict, quantity restrict. Partial handicap access. No tents. Age restrictions may apply. Open all yr. Children's visits 30 days max. Planned activities winter. Big rigs welcome. Internet friendly. Clubs welcome. Rate in 2007 $30-45 for 2 persons. MC/VISA. Phone: (800)291-3446.

e-mail: hshoecove@aol.com

SEE AD NEXT PAGE

(E) LAKE MANATEE STATE RECREATION AREA—(Manatee) *From jct I-75 (exit 42) & Hwy 64: Go 15 mi E on Hwy 64.* FACILITIES: 60 sites, 60 W&E, tenting, dump station, grills. RECREATION: pavilion, lake swimming, boating, 20 hp limit, canoeing, ramp, 2 rowboat rentals, lake fishing, hiking trails. Open all yr. Phone: (941)741-3028.

(SE) PLEASANT LAKE RV RESORT—(Manatee) *From jct I-75 (exit 217) & Hwy 70: Go 1/2 mi W on Hwy 70. Enter on R.*

WELCOME

◆◆◆◆FACILITIES: 343 sites, typical site width 40 ft, accepts full hkup units only, 343 full hkups, (30 & 50 amps), many extended stay sites (in winter), 16 pull-thrus, cable TV, wireless Instant Internet access at site, phone/cable on-site Internet access (needs activ), phone Internet access central location ($), RV storage, laundry, LP gas by weight/by meter, tables, patios, controlled access gate.

◆◆◆◆RECREATION: rec hall, swim pool, boating, electric motors only, canoeing, ramp, lake fishing, golf nearby, 10 shuffleboard courts, planned activities, horseshoes.

Pets welcome, size restrict, quantity restrict. No tents. Age restrictions may apply. Open all yr. Planned activities winter only. Big rigs welcome. Internet friendly. Clubs welcome. Rate in 2007 $25-50 for 2 persons. MC/VISA. Member ARVC, FLARVC. Phone: (941)756-5076. FCRV 10% discount. FMCA discount.

e-mail: manager@pleasantlakerv.com

SEE AD THIS PAGE

(W) Sarasota Bay RV Park—(Manatee) *From jct I-75 (exit 217) & Hwy 70: Go 12 mi W on Hwy 70/53rd Ave, then 3 mi W on Cortez Rd. Enter on L.* ◆◆◆◆FACILITIES: 240 sites, typical site width 25 ft, accepts full hkup units only, 240 full hkups, (30 & 50 amps), many extended stay sites (in winter), dump station, non-guest dumping $, laundry, patios. ◆◆◆◆RECREATION: rec hall, rec room/area, equipped pavilion, swim pool, boating, ramp, saltwater fishing, 4 shuffleboard courts, planned activities, horseshoes. Pets welcome. No tents. Age restrictions may apply. Open all yr. Planned activities winter only. Children welcome up to 2 weeks. Big rigs welcome. Internet friendly. Rate in 2007 $35-44 for 2 persons. Member ARVC, FLARVC. Phone: (941)794-1200.

(SE) Tropical Gardens RV Park—(Manatee) *From jct I-75 (exit 217) & Hwy 70: Go 6 mi W on Hwy 70 (53rd Ave). Enter on L.* ◆◆◆◆FACILITIES: 150 sites, 150 full hkups, (30 & 50 amps), many extended stay sites

Tropical Gardens RV Park—Continued on page 98

Florida's beautiful weather influences almost every part of the state's economy.

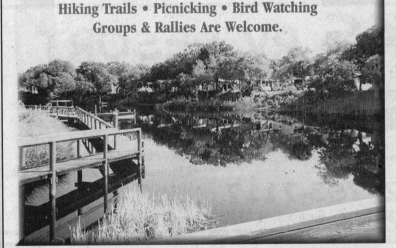

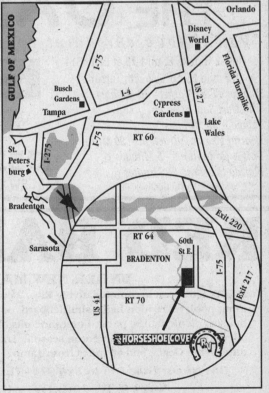

BRADENTON—Continued
Tropical Gardens RV Park—Continued

(in winter), 15 pull-thrus, dump station, non-guest dumping $, laundry, patios. ◇◇◇RECREATION: rec hall, swim pool, 2 shuffleboard courts, planned activities. Pets welcome, size restrict. No tents. Age restrictions may apply. Open all yr. Planned activities winter only. Big rigs welcome. Rate in 2007 $20-40 for 2 persons. Phone: (941)756-1135. CCUSA discount.

(NE) WINTER QUARTERS MANATEE RV RESORT—(Manatee) *From jct I-75 (exit 220) & Hwy 64: Go 3/4 mi W on Hwy 64, then 1 mi NE on 60th St Ct East. Enter on L.*

WELCOME

◇◇◇◇◇FACILITIES: 415 sites, typical site width 35 ft, 415 full hkups, (30 & 50 amps), many extended stay sites (in winter), 4 pull-thrus, wireless Instant Internet access at site, phone/cable on-site Internet access (needs activ), phone Internet access central location, tenting, RV/park trailer rentals, dump station, non-guest dumping $, laundry, LP gas by weight/by meter, tables, patios, controlled access gate.

◇◇◇◇◇RECREATION: rec hall, rec room/area, equipped pavilion, 2 swim pools, whirlpool, boating, canoeing, pedal boat rentals, lake fishing, golf nearby, 5 shuffleboard courts, planned activities, horseshoes.

Pets welcome. Partial handicap access. Open all yr. Planned activities winter only. Big rigs welcome. Internet friendly. Clubs welcome. Rate in 2007 $30-68 for 2 persons. MC/VISA/DISC/AMEX. Member ARVC, FLARVC. Phone: (800)678-2131. FCRV 10% discount, FMCA discount.

e-mail: nhcflugm@msn.com

SEE AD SARASOTA PAGE 169

BRISTOL—F-3

(N) TORREYA STATE PARK—(Liberty) *From jct Hwy 20 & Hwy 12: Go 4 mi N on Hwy 12, then 7 mi N on CR 270, then 1-1/2 mi N on CR 271.* FACILITIES: 30 sites, 30 ft max RV length, 30 W&E, tenting. RECREATION: pavilion, playground, hiking trails. No pets. Open all yr. Phone: (850)643-2674.

BROOKSVILLE—C-3

(S) Campers Holiday—*From jct US 98 & Hwy 581: Go 5-1/2 mi S on Hwy 581. Enter on L.* ◇◇◇◇FACILITIES: 60 sites, 60 full hkups, (30 & 50 amps), dump station, laundry, tables, patios.

BROOKSVILLE—Continued
Campers Holiday—Continued

◇◇◇◇RECREATION: rec hall, equipped pavilion, swim pool, playground, 6 shuffleboard courts, horseshoes. Pets welcome, breed restrict, quantity restrict. No tents. Open all yr. Big rigs welcome. Rate in 2007 $28 for 2 persons. Phone: (352)796-3707. CCUSA discount.

(N) Cloverleaf Forest RV Resort—(Hernando) *From jct I-75 (exit 301) & US 98 & Hwy 50A: Go 10 mi W on Hwy 50A, then 1 mi N on US 41. Enter on R.* ◇◇◇FACILITIES: 277 sites, 277 full hkups, (20, 30 & 50 amps), laundry, tables, patios. ◇◇◇◇RECREATION: rec hall, rec room/area, 2 swim pools, pond fishing, 6 shuffleboard courts, horseshoes. Pets welcome, quantity restrict. No tents. Age restrictions may apply. Open all yr. Planned activities winter only. Big rigs welcome. Internet friendly. Rate in 2007 $28-32 for 2 persons. Phone: (877)796-5931.

(E) Hidden Valley Campground—(Hernando) *From jct Hwy 50 & US 98: Go 1/2 mi E on US 98. Enter on L.* ◇◇◇FACILITIES: 65 sites, 65 full hkups, (30 & 50 amps), dump station, non-guest dumping $, laundry, tables, patios. ◇◇RECREATION: rec hall, horseshoes. Pets welcome, breed restrict. No tents. Open all yr. Rate in 2007 $22 for 2 persons. Member ARVC. Phone: (352)796-8710. CCUSA discount.

BUSHNELL—C-3

(W) BLUEBERRY HILL RV RESORT—(Sumter) *From jct I-75 (exit 314) & Hwy 48: Go 1 block E on Hwy 48. Enter on R.*

WELCOME

◇◇◇◇◇FACILITIES: 404 sites, typical site width 30 ft, 404 full hkups, (20, 30 & 50 amps), 96 pull-thrus, wireless Instant Internet access at site, phone on-site Internet access (needs activ), wireless Internet access central location, dump station, non-guest dumping $, laundry, RV supplies, LP gas by weight/by meter, tables.

◇◇◇◇RECREATION: rec hall, rec room/area, equipped pavilion, swim pool, golf nearby, bsktball, 6 shuffleboard courts, planned activities, horseshoes.

Pets welcome, breed restrict. Partial handicap access. No tents. Open all yr. Big rigs welcome.

BUSHNELL—Continued
BLUEBERRY HILL RV RESORT—Continued

Internet friendly. Clubs welcome. Rate in 2007 $35 for 2 persons. MC/VISA/Debit. Phone: (877) 793-4112.

SEE AD NEXT PAGE AND AND AD TRAVEL SECTION PAGE 80

(W) Breezy Oaks RV Park—(Sumter) *From jct I-75 & Hwy 673 (exit 309): Go 3/4 mi E on Hwy 673, then 1/2 mi N on Hwy 671. Enter at end.* ◇◇◇FACILITIES: 100 sites, typical site width 35 ft, 100 full hkups, (20, 30 & 50 amps), 50 pull-thrus, dump station, non-guest dumping $, laundry, ltd groceries, ice, tables, patios. ◇◇◇RECREATION: rec room/area, swim pool, boating, canoeing, 5 canoe rentals, 2 shuffleboard courts, planned activities, horseshoes. Pets welcome, breed restrict, size restrict, quantity restrict. No tents. Open all yr. Big rigs welcome. Rate in 2007 $20 for 2 persons. Member ARVC, FLARVC. Phone: (352)569-0300.

(W) RED BARN CAMPGROUND—(Sumter) *From jct I-75 (exit 314) & Hwy 48: Go 1 block E on Hwy 48. Enter on L.*

WELCOME

◇◇◇FACILITIES: 497 sites, typical site width 40 ft, 497 full hkups, (20, 30 & 50 amps), some extended stay sites (in winter), 225 pull-thrus, cable TV, wireless/cable Instant Internet access at site, phone on-site Internet access (needs activ), wireless Internet access central location, dump station, non-guest dumping $, laundry, tables, patios.

◇◇◇RECREATION: rec hall, rec room/area, swim pool, golf nearby, 11 shuffleboard courts, planned activities, horseshoes, sports field.

Pets welcome, breed restrict, size restrict, quantity restrict. No tents. Age restrictions may apply. Open all yr. Church & planned group activities winter only. Big rigs welcome. Internet friendly. Clubs welcome. Rate in 2007 $42 for 2 persons. MC/VISA/DISC/Debit. Phone: (352)793-6220.

e-mail: info@redbarn.com

SEE AD THIS PAGE

(W) Sumter Oaks RV Park—(Sumter) *From I-75 (exit 309) & Hwy 476B/673: Go 1-1/2 mi E on CR 673. Enter on L.* ◇◇◇FACILITIES: 124 sites, typical site width 35 ft, 124 full hkups, (20, 30 & 50 amps), tenting,

Sumter Oaks RV Park—Continued on page 100

BUSHNELL—Continued
Sumter Oaks RV Park—Continued

laundry, groceries, LP gas by weight/by meter, ice, patios. ◇◇◇RECREATION: rec hall, rec room/area, swim pool, 2 shuffleboard courts, planned activities, horseshoes. Pets welcome. Partial handicap access. Open all yr. Planned activities winter only. Big rigs welcome. Rate in 2007 $24 for 2 persons. Phone: (352) 793-1333.

(W) THE OAKS RV RESORT—(Sumter) *From jct I-75 (exit 314) & Hwy 48: Go 1/2 mi E on Hwy 48, then 1/2 mi N on SW 18th Terrace. Enter on R.*

◇◇◇◇FACILITIES: 515 sites, typical site width 40 ft, 515 full hkups, (30 & 50 amps), many extended stay sites (in winter), 110 pull-thrus, cable TV, wireless Instant Internet access at site, phone on-site Internet access (needs activ), phone Internet access central location, RV/park trailer rentals, dump station, non-guest dumping $, laundry, ice, tables, controlled access gate.

◇◇◇◇RECREATION: rec hall, rec room/area, equipped pavilion, swim pool, whirlpool, golf nearby, 8 shuffleboard courts, planned activities, horseshoes, local tours.

Pets welcome, breed restrict, quantity restrict. Partial handicap access. No tents. Age restrictions may apply. Open all yr. Planned activities & church services winter only. Big rigs welcome. Internet friendly. Clubs welcome. Rate in 2007 $35 for 2 persons. MC/VISA/DISC/Debit. Phone: (352)793-7117.

e-mail: info@oaksrv.com

SEE AD PAGE 98

CALLAHAN—A-3

(N) KELLY'S COUNTRYSIDE RV PARK—(Nassau) *From jct US 1 & US 301: Go 7 mi N on US 1/301. Enter on L.*

◇◇◇◇FACILITIES: 67 sites, typical site width 25 ft, 65 full hkups, 2 W&E, (30 & 50 amps), some extended stay sites, 15 pull-thrus, wireless Instant Internet access at site, tenting, RV storage, dump station, non-guest dumping $, laundry, LP bottle exch, ice, tables, patios.

◇◇RECREATION: rec hall, 2 shuffleboard courts.

Pets welcome. Partial handicap access. Open all yr. Big rigs welcome. Internet friendly. Escort to site. Clubs welcome. Rate in 2007 $25 for 2 persons. MC/VISA/DISC/AMEX/Debit. Member ARVC, FLARVC. Phone: (904)845-4252.

e-mail: pattie6830@windstream.net

SEE AD JACKSONVILLE PAGE 132

CAPE CANAVERAL—C-5

(S) CARVER'S COVE—*From jct Hwy 528 & Hwy A1A: Go 1-3/4 mi SE on Hwy A1A.*

◇◇FACILITIES: 40 sites, typical site width 44 ft, 40 full hkups, (20, 30 & 50 amps), wireless Instant Internet access at site, dump station, laundry, patios.

◇RECREATION: boating, dock, saltwater fishing.

Pets welcome, size restrict, quantity restrict. No tents. Open all yr. Big rigs welcome. Internet friendly. Rate in 2007 $35 for 2 persons. Phone: (321)799-0343.

SEE AD THIS PAGE

(NE) JETTY PARK (Canaveral Port Auth)—(Brevard) *From I95 & SR 528: Go E on 528 to Port Canaveral, then follow signs to Jetty Park.* FACILITIES: 150 sites, 35 ft max RV length, 32 full hkups, 85 W&E, 33 E, tenting, dump station, laundry, full svc store, ice, grills. RECREATION: pavilion, saltwater swimming, boating, ramp, saltwater fishing, playground, v-ball. Pets welcome. Partial handicap access. Open all yr. Phone: (321)783-7111.

CARRABELLE—B-1

(E) Ho-Hum RV Park—(Franklin) *From jct Hwy 67 & US 98/319: Go 3-1/2 mi E on US 98/319. Enter on R.* ◇◇◇◇FACILITIES: 50 sites, typical site width 30 ft,

CARRABELLE—Continued
Ho-Hum RV Park—Continued

50 full hkups, (30 & 50 amps), 50 amps ($), 20 pull-thrus, laundry, tables. ◇◇◇◇RECREATION: rec hall, saltwater swimming, boating, canoeing, saltwater fishing, planned activities, horseshoes. Pets welcome, breed restrict. Partial handicap access. No tents. Open all yr. Planned group activities in winter only. Internet friendly. Rate in 2007 $26-29 for 2 persons. Member ARVC, FLARVC. Phone: (888)884-6486. FMCA discount.

CARRABELLE BEACH—B-1

(W) Carrabelle Palms RV Park & Store—(Franklin) *From jct Hwy 67 & US 98/319: Go 2-3/4 mi W on US 98/319. Enter on R.* ◇◇◇◇FACILITIES: 82 sites, typical site width 40 ft, 82 full hkups, (30 & 50 amps), some extended stay sites, 58 pull-thrus, tenting, dump station, non-guest dumping, laundry, groceries, ice, tables. ◇◇◇RECREATION: rec hall, swim pool, playground, horseshoes. Pets welcome. Partial handicap access. Open all yr. Big rigs welcome. Internet friendly. Rate in 2007 $29.25 for 2 persons. Member ARVC, FLARVC. Phone: (850)697-2638.

CEDAR KEY—B-2

(N) CEDAR KEY SUNSET ISLE RV PARK—(Levy) *From jct US 19 and SR 24: Go 19 mi W on SR 24. Upon crossing first bridge on the island (Channel 4 Bridge) continue approximately 1 mi. Enter on R.*

◇◇◇FACILITIES: 53 sites, typical site width 30 ft, 53 full hkups, (20, 30 & 50 amps), 7 pull-thrus, cable TV, phone Internet access central location, tenting, dump station, non-guest dumping $, tables.

◇◇◇RECREATION: rec hall, canoeing, kayaking, saltwater fishing.

Pets welcome ($). Open all yr. Internet friendly. Rate in 2007 $38-42 for 2 persons. MC/VISA. Member ARVC, FLARVC. Phone: (800)810-1103. CCUSA discount.

e-mail: sunset@cedarkeyrv.com

SEE AD THIS PAGE

(NE) Rainbow Country RV Campground—(Levy) *From jct US 19/98 & Hwy 24: Go 14 mi SW on Hwy 24. Enter on R.* ◇◇◇FACILITIES: 65 sites, typical site width 25 ft, 50 full hkups, 15 W&E, (30 amps), mostly extended stay sites, 10 pull-thrus, tenting, dump station, non-guest dumping $, laundry, LP gas by weight/by meter, ice, tables, patios, fire rings, grills, wood. ◇◇RECREATION: rec hall, rec room/area, planned activities. Pets welcome. Partial handicap access. Open all yr. Rate in 2007 $19 for 2 persons. Member ARVC, FLARVC. Phone: (352)543-6268.

CENTRAL FL'S WORLD OF THEME PARKS—C-4

For facilities near Walt Disney World Vacation Kingdom, Universal Studios & Sea World see listings at Apopka, Kissimmee, Orlando, Winter Garden & Lake Buena Vista

CENTRAL FL'S WORLD OF THEME PARKS—Continued

CENTRAL FLORIDA'S WORLD OF THEME PARKS MAP

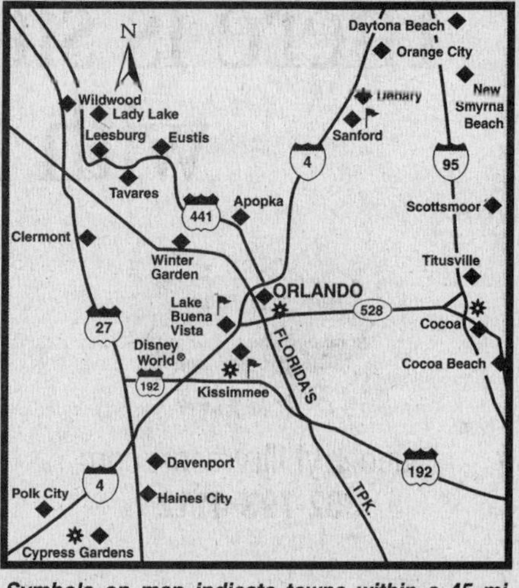

Symbols on map indicate towns within a 45 mi radius of Disney World, Universal Studios, Sea World & Cypress Gardens where campgrounds (diamonds), attractions (flags), & RV service centers & camping supply outlets (gears) are listed. Check listings for more information.
Walt Disney World Vacation Kingdom, Universal Studios, SeaWorld & Cypress Gardens are registered trademarks and/or service marks of

CAMP INN RESORT—*From jct US 192 & I-4: Go 9 mi W on I-4 to exit 23, then 33 mi S on US 27.*

SEE PRIMARY LISTING AT FROSTPROOF AND AD TRAVEL SECTION PAGE 73

ELITE RESORTS AT CITRUS VALLEY (Not Visited)—*From jct I-4 & US 192: Go 9 mi W on US 192, then 3 mi N on US 27. Enter on R.*

SEE PRIMARY LISTING AT CLERMONT AND AD TRAVEL SECTION PAGE 79

FORT SUMMIT KOA—*From jct US 192 & I-4: Go 6 mi W on I-4, then 1 block S on US 27, then 1000 feet on south frontage road.*

◇◇◇◇◇FACILITIES: 299 sites, 261 full hkups, 38 W&E, (20, 30 & 50 amps), some extended stay sites (in winter), 100 pull-thrus, cable TV, wireless Instant Internet access at site, phone on-site Internet access (needs activ), phone/wireless Internet access central location, tenting, cabins, RV storage, dump station, non-guest dumping $, laundry, full svc store, RV supplies, LP gas by weight/by meter, ice, tables, patios.

◇◇◇◇◇RECREATION: rec hall, rec room/area, coin games, swim pool, wading pool, mini-golf ($), bsktball, playground, planned activities, horseshoes, v-ball, local tours.

Pets welcome. Partial handicap access. Open all yr. Planned activities winter only. Big rigs welcome. Internet friendly. Escort to site. Clubs welcome. Rate in 2007 $39-69 for 2 persons. MC/VISA/DISC. Member ARVC, FLARVC. Phone: (800)424-1880. FCRV 10% discount. FMCA discount.

SEE PRIMARY LISTING AT LAKE BUENA VISTA AND AD ORLANDO PAGES 152-153

CHASSAHOWITZKA—C-3

(W) CHASSAHOWITZKA RIVER CAMPGROUND (City Park)—(Citrus) *From jct US-19, US-98 & CR-480: Go 1-3/4 mi W on CR-480. Enter on R.* FACILITIES: 85 sites, 35 full hkups, 17 W&E, (30 & 50 amps), 33 no hkups, 4 pull-thrus, tenting, dump station, laundry, groceries, ice, grills. RECREATION: pavilion, boating, canoeing, ramp, dock, 12 rowboat/36 canoe rentals, river fishing, shuffleboard court. Rec open to public. Partial handicap access. Open all yr. Phone: (352)382-2200.

CHATTAHOOCHEE—A-1

(S) KOA-Chattahoochee/Tallahassee West—(Gadsden) *From jct I-10 (exit 166) & Hwy 270A: Go 1 mi S on Hwy 270A. Enter on L.* ◇◇◇FACILITIES: 56 sites, typical site width 30 ft, 23 full hkups, 28 W&E, (20, 30 & 50 amps), 50 amps ($), 5 no hkups, 45 pull-thrus,

KOA-Chattahoochee/Tallahassee West—Continued on next page

CHATTAHOOCHEE—Continued
KOA-Chattahoochee/Tallahassee West—Continued

tenting, dump station, non-guest dumping $, laundry, ltd groceries, LP gas by weight/by meter, ice, tables, wood. ◆◆◆RECREATION: pavilion, equipped pavilion, swim pool, playground, horseshoes, hiking trails. Pets welcome. Partial handicap access. Open all yr. Internet friendly. Rate in 2007 $23-28.50 for 2 persons. Phone: (800)KOA-2153. KOA 10% value card discount.

CHIEFLAND—B-2

(E) Breezy Acres Campground—(Levy) *From jct US 19/98 & Alt US 27: Go 7 mi E on Alt US 27. Enter on L.* ◆◆FACILITIES: 60 sites, typical site width 30 ft, 50 full hkups, 10 W&E, (30 & 50 amps), mostly extended stay sites (in winter), 20 pull-thrus, tenting, dump station, non-guest dumping $, laundry, ice, tables. ◆◆RECREATION: rec room/area, equipped pavilion, shuffleboard court, planned activities, horseshoes, sports field. Pets welcome. Partial handicap access. Open all yr. Rate in 2007 $16 for 4 persons. Phone: (352)493-7602.

(W) MANATEE SPRINGS STATE PARK—(Levy) *From jct US 98/19 & Hwy 320: Go 7 mi W on Hwy 320.* FACILITIES: 92 sites, 92 W&E, tenting, dump station, groceries, grills. RECREATION: pavilion, lake swimming, boating, canoeing, ramp, canoe rentals, lake fishing, playground, hiking trails. Pets welcome. Open all yr. No showers. Phone: (352)493-6072.

CHIPLEY—E-3

(S) FALLING WATERS STATE PARK—(Washington) *From town: Go 3 mi S on Hwy 77A.* FACILITIES: 24 sites, 24 W&E, tenting, dump station, grills. RECREATION: lake swimming, lake fishing, playground, hiking trails. Pets welcome. Open all yr. Phone: (850)638-6130.

CHOKOLOSKEE—E-4

(W) CHOKOLOSKEE ISLAND PARK & CAMPGROUND—(Collier) *From jct US 41 & Hwy 29: Go 8 mi S on CR 29, then 1 block W on Demere Ln, then 1 block W on Hamilton Ln. Enter at end.*

WELCOME

◆◆◆FACILITIES: 54 sites, typical site width 25 ft, 27 ft max RV length, 54 full hkups, (30 amps), many extended stay sites (in winter), cable TV, wireless Instant Internet access at site ($), tenting, dump station, laundry, marine gas, ice, tables.

◆◆◆RECREATION: pavilion, boating, canoeing, kayaking, ramp, dock, saltwater/river fishing, fishing supplies, fishing guides, planned activities.

Pets welcome. Partial handicap access. Open all yr. Planned group activities winter only. Internet friendly. Clubs welcome. Rate in 2007 $38-43 for 2 persons. MC/VISA/AMEX. Member ARVC, FLARVC. Phone: (239)695-2414.

e-mail: manager@chokoloskee.com

SEE AD THIS PAGE

(N) OUTDOOR RESORTS/ CHOKOLOSKEE ISLAND—(Collier) *From jct US-41 & Hwy-29 (CR 29): Go 8 mi S on CR 29. Enter on L.*

WELCOME

◆◆◆◆◆FACILITIES: 283 sites, typical site width 35 ft, accepts full hkup units only, 283 full hkups, (20, 30 & 50 amps), some extended stay sites (in winter), cable TV, wireless Internet access central location, cabins, RV storage, laundry, groceries, RV supplies, LP gas by weight/by meter, gas, marine gas, ice, tables, patios, controlled access gate.

CHOKOLOSKEE—Continued
OUTDOOR RESORTS/ CHOKOLOSKEE ISLAND—Continued

◆◆◆◆◆RECREATION: rec hall, 3 swim pools, whirlpool, boating, canoeing, kayaking, ramp, dock, 12 canoe/4 kayak/6 motorboat rentals, saltwater fishing, fishing supplies, fishing guides, play equipment, 2 shuffleboard courts, planned activities, tennis.

Pets welcome, quantity restrict. Partial handicap access. No tents. Open all yr. Big rigs welcome. Internet friendly. Clubs welcome. Rate in 2007 $69-89 for 2 persons. MC/VISA. Phone: (239)695-3788. FMCA discount.

e-mail: orachokoloskee@aol.com

SEE AD THIS PAGE

CLEARWATER—C-3

✲ **(E) Arrow RV Sales**—*From jct US 19 & Hwy 60: Go 1/4 mi E on Hwy 60. Enter on L.* SALES: travel trailers, 5th wheels, pre-owned unit sales. SERVICES: full-time mech, RV appliance repair, sells parts/accessories, installs hitches. Open all yr. Phone: (727)796-7336.

CLEARWATER—Continued

(E) AVALON RV RESORT—(Pinellas) *From jct Hwy 60 & US 19: Go 2 mi S on US 19, then 1/4 mi S on Whitney/Frontage Rd. Enter on R.*

WELCOME

◆◆◆◆FACILITIES: 263 sites, typical site width 24 ft, accepts full hkup units only, 263 full hkups, (20, 30 & 50 amps), many extended stay sites (in winter), phone/cable on-site Internet access (needs activ), laundry, LP gas by weight/by meter, tables, patios.

◆◆◆RECREATION: rec hall, rec room/area, swim pool, golf nearby, 9 shuffleboard courts, planned activities, horseshoes.

Pets welcome, breed restrict, quantity restrict. No tents. Open all yr. Planned activities winter. Big rigs welcome. Clubs welcome. Rate in 2007 $30 for 2 persons. MC/VISA. Phone: (727)531-6124.

e-mail: avalon@newbury-management.com

SEE AD TRAVEL SECTION PAGE 75

CLEARWATER—Continued on next page

(E) CLEARWATER TRAVEL RESORT—(Pinellas) *From jct US-19 & Hwy-60: Go 1/2 mi E on Hwy-60. Enter on L.*

WELCOME

◇◇◇◇FACILITIES: 163 sites, typical site width 32 ft, 163 full hkups, (20, 30 & 50 amps), many extended stay sites (in winter), wireless Instant Internet access at site, phone on-site Internet access (needs activ), wireless Internet access central location, RV storage, dump station, non-guest dumping $, laundry, RV supplies, LP gas by weight/by meter, tables, patios.

◇◇◇RECREATION: rec hall, swim pool, golf nearby, 4 shuffleboard courts, planned activities, horseshoes.

Pets welcome, breed restrict, size restrict, quantity restrict. Partial handicap access. No tents. Age restrictions may apply. Open all yr. Planned activities winter only. Big rigs welcome. Internet friendly. Clubs welcome. Phone: (800)831-1204.

SEE AD THIS PAGE

✲ **(SE) HARBERSON SWANSTON RV**—*From jct Hwy-686 & US-19: Go 1 mi N on US-19. Enter on L.* SALES: travel trailers, 5th wheels, van campers, motor homes, mini-motor homes, micro-mini motor homes, SERVICES: full-time mech, engine/chassis repair, RV appliance repair, body work/collision repair, LP gas by weight/by meter, sells parts/accessories, installs hitches. Open all yr. Phone: (727)539-8714. FCRV 10% discount.

WELCOME

e-mail: harswan@aol.com

SEE AD PAGE 101 AND AD HOLIDAY PAGE 127

(SE) Travel World—(Pinellas) *From jct I-275 & Hwy 688: Go 4 mi W on Hwy 688, then 1/2 mi S on S'bound frontage road (parallels US 19). Enter on R.* ◇◇◇◇FACILITIES: 320 sites, typical site width 28 ft, 37 ft max RV length, accepts full hkup units only, 320 full hkups, (20, 30 & 50 amps), some extended stay sites (in winter), 6 pull-thrus, dump station, non-guest dumping $, laundry, LP gas by weight/by meter, ice, tables, patios. ◇◇◇◇RECREATION: rec hall, rec room/area, swim pool, 12 shuffleboard courts, planned activities, horseshoes. Pets welcome. Partial handicap access. No tents. Age restrictions may apply. Open all yr. Planned group activities winter only. Rate in 2007 $24 for 2 persons. Phone: (727)536-1765. FMCA discount.

WINTER PARADISE TRAVEL RESORT—*From jct Alt US 19 & US 19: Go 33 mi N on US 19. Enter on R.*

WELCOME

SEE PRIMARY LISTING AT HUDSON AND AD TRAVEL SECTION PAGE 78

CLERMONT—C-3

(NW) CLERBROOK GOLF & RV RESORT—(Lake) *From jct Hwy 50 & US 27: Go 7-1/2 mi N on US 27. Enter on L.*

WELCOME

◇◇◇◇FACILITIES: 1250 sites, 1250 full hkups, (30 & 50 amps), some extended stay sites (in winter), heater not allowed, phone/cable on-site Internet access (needs activ), tenting, RV storage, dump station, laundry, LP gas by weight/by meter, ice, tables, patios, controlled access gate.

◇◇◇◇RECREATION: rec hall, pavilion, 3 swim pools, whirlpool, pond fishing, putting green, golf nearby, bsktball, 20 shuffleboard courts, planned activities, sports field, v-ball, local tours.

Pets welcome, breed restrict, size restrict, quantity restrict. Partial handicap access. Open all yr. Tent camping summer months only. Big rigs welcome. Clubs welcome. Rate in 2007 $35 for 2 persons. MC/VISA. Member ARVC, FLARVC. Phone: (800)440-3801.

e-mail: clerbrookrv@comcast.net

SEE AD ORLANDO PAGE 154

(S) ELITE RESORTS AT CITRUS VALLEY (Not Visited)—(Lake) *From jct Hwy-50 & US-27: Go 12 mi S on US-27. Enter on L.*

WELCOME

RV RESORT NEAR ORLANDO ATTRACTIONS! Just 8 miles from Disney's gates lies Elite Resorts of Citrus Valley. 305 new full hook-up 100 amp RV sites with large pool, free WiFi and activities. Renting and selling deeded RV lots and Vacation Cottages.

◇◇◇◇FACILITIES: 305 sites, typical site width 35 ft, 305 full hkups, (30 & 50 amps), 50 amps ($), many extended stay sites (in winter), cable TV, wireless Instant Internet access at site, RV/park trailer rentals, RV storage, dump station, non-guest dumping $, laundry, groceries, RV supplies, tables, controlled access gate.

◇◇◇◇RECREATION: rec hall, rec room/area, swim pool, mini-golf, golf nearby, 4 shuffleboard courts, planned activities, horseshoes.

Pets welcome. No tents. Open all yr. Big rigs welcome. Escort to site. Clubs welcome. Rate in 2007 $24-34 for 2 persons. MC/VISA. Member FLARVC. Phone: (800)356-2460.

e-mail: info@eliteresorts.com

SEE AD TRAVEL SECTION PAGE 79

(S) LAKE MAGIC RV PARK—(Lake) *From jct US 27 & US 192: Go 1/2 mi E on US 192. Enter on R.*

WELCOME

◇◇◇◇FACILITIES: 292 sites, 292 full hkups, (30 & 50 amps), some extended stay sites (in winter), 135 pull-thrus, cable TV, wireless Instant Internet access at site, phone/cable on-site Internet access (needs activ), wireless Internet access central location, tenting, RV storage, dump station, non-guest dumping $, laundry, tables, patios.

◇◇◇◇RECREATION: rec hall, 2 swim pools, wading pool, whirlpool, golf nearby, bsktball, 10 shuffleboard courts, tennis, horseshoes, v-ball.

Pets welcome. Partial handicap access. Open all yr. Big rigs welcome. Clubs welcome. Rate in 2007 $33-56 for 2 persons. MC/VISA/DISC/AMEX. Phone: (888)558-5777.

e-mail: info@rvonthego.com

SEE AD ORLANDO PAGE 155

(W) Outdoor Resorts At Orlando—(Polk) *From jct I-4 & US-192: Go 6-1/2 mi W on US-192. Enter on L.* ◇◇◇◇◇FACILITIES: 43 sites, typical site width 35 ft, 43 full hkups, (20, 30 & 50 amps), laundry, tables, patios. ◇◇◇◇◇RECREATION: rec hall, 2 swim pools, boating, ramp, dock, lake fishing, mini-golf, playground, 6 shuffleboard courts, planned activities, tennis, horseshoes, v-ball. Pets welcome, breed restrict, size restrict, quantity restrict. Partial handicap access. No tents. Open all yr. Church & planned group activities winter only. Big rigs welcome. Rate in 2007 $36-81 per vehicle. Member ARVC. Phone: (800)531-3033.

(NW) ROLLING RIDGE RV RESORT—(Lake) *From jct Hwy 50 & US 27: Go 9 mi N on US 27. Enter on L.*

WELCOME

◇◇◇◇FACILITIES: 154 sites, typical site width 40 ft, 154 full hkups, (20, 30 & 50 amps), wireless Instant Internet access at site ($), wireless Internet access central location ($), RV storage, dump station, laundry, tables, patios.

◇◇RECREATION: bsktball, 2 shuffleboard courts, planned activities, horseshoes.

Pets welcome. No tents. Open all yr. Big rigs welcome. Internet friendly. Rate in 2007 $35 for 2 persons. VISA/DISC/AMEX/DC/Debit. Phone: (352)429-5003.

SEE AD TRAVEL SECTION PAGE 77 AND AD TRAVEL SECTION PAGE 83 AND AD DISCOVER SECTION PAGE 56

CLEWISTON—D-4

(S) BIG CYPRESS RV RESORT—(Hendry) *From west jct US 27 & Hwy 80: Go 3 mi W on Hwy 80, then 35-1/2 mi S on CR 833. Enter on L.*

WELCOME

◇◇◇◇FACILITIES: 110 sites, typical site width 40 ft, 60 full hkups, 50 W&E, (20, 30 & 50 amps), many extended stay sites (in winter), 9 pull-thrus, phone Internet access central location, tenting, cabins, RV storage, dump station, non-guest dumping $, portable dump, laundry, RV supplies, LP gas by weight/by meter, ice, tables, fire rings, grills.

◇◇◇◇RECREATION: rec hall, pavilion, swim pool, whirlpool, mini-golf, putting green, bsktball, play equipment, 2 shuffleboard courts, planned activities, horseshoes, sports field.

Pets welcome, breed restrict. Partial handicap access. Open all yr. Big rigs welcome. Internet friendly. Escort to site. Clubs welcome. Rate in 2007 $21-26 for 2 persons. MC/VISA/DISC/AMEX/DC/Debit. Member ARVC, FLARVC. Phone: (800)437-4102.

e-mail: bcrvresort@semtribe.com

SEE AD TRAVEL SECTION PAGE 80

(W) Clewiston/Lake Okeechobee KOA Campground—(Hendry) *From West jct Hwy 80 & US 27: Go 6-1/2 mi S on US 27, then 500 feet N on CR 720. Enter on R.* ◇◇◇◇FACILITIES: 124 sites, typical site width 30 ft, 118 full hkups, 6 W&E, (20, 30 & 50 amps), 50 amps ($), some extended stay sites (in winter), 90 pull-thrus, tenting, dump station, non-guest dumping $, laundry, ltd groceries, LP gas by weight/by meter, ice, tables. ◇◇◇◇RECREATION: rec hall, rec room/area, swim pool, playground, shuffleboard court, planned activities, horseshoes, v-ball. Pets welcome. Partial handicap access. Open all yr. Planned activities during season. Big rigs welcome. Internet friendly. Rate in 2007 $29-36 for 2 persons. Member ARVC, FLARVC. Phone: (863)983-7078. KOA 10% value card discount.

(SE) Crooked Hook RV Resort—(Palm Beach) *From west jct Hwy 80 & US 27: Go 12-1/2 mi S on US 27. Enter on R.* ◇◇◇◇FACILITIES: 186 sites, typical site width 30 ft, 186 full hkups, (30 & 50 amps), mostly extended stay sites (in winter), 4 pull-thrus, tenting, laundry, ice, tables, patios. ◇◇◇◇RECREATION: rec hall, rec room/area, pavilion, swim pool, playground, 3

Crooked Hook RV Resort—Continued on next page

Key West has the highest average temperature in the United States.

CLEWISTON—Continued
Crooked Hook RV Resort—Continued

shuffleboard courts, planned activities, horseshoes, sports field, hiking trails. Pets welcome, breed restrict. Partial handicap access. Open all yr. Big rigs welcome. Internet friendly. Rate in 2007 $33 for 2 persons. Member ARVC, FLARVC. Phone: (863)983-7112.

(SE) Okeechobee Landings—(Rogers) *From west jct Hwy 80 & US 27: Go 10 mi S on US 27, then 500 feet S on Holiday Isles Blvd. Enter on L.* ◊◊◊FACILITIES: 270 sites, 270 full hkups, (30 & 50 amps), some extended stay sites (in winter), heater not allowed, tenting, laundry, tables, patios. ◊◊◊RECREATION: rec hall, swim pool, lake fishing, playground, 4 shuffleboard courts, planned activities, tennis, horseshoes. Pets welcome, breed restrict, size restrict. Partial handicap access. Open all yr. Big rigs welcome. Internet friendly. Rate in 2007 $35 for 2 persons. Member ARVC, FLARVC. Phone: (863)983-4144. CCUSA discount.

COCOA—C-4

(W) Forest Village RV Resort—(Brevard) *From jct I-95 (exit 201) & Hwy 520: Go 100 yards W on Hwy 520, then 1/2 mi S on Tucker Lane. Enter on R.* ◊◊◊◊FACILITIES: 75 sites, 75 full hkups, (20, 30 & 50 amps), laundry, tables, patios. ◊◊RECREATION: rec hall, swim pool, horseshoes. Pets welcome. Partial handicap access. No tents. Open all yr. Rate in 2007 $39 for 4 persons. Phone: (321)631-0305.

(W) SONRISE PALMS CHRISTIAN RV PARK—(Brevard) *From jct I-95 (exit 201) & Hwy 520: Go 1 block W on Hwy 520, then 3/4 mi S on Tucker Ln. Enter on R.*

WELCOME

◊◊◊◊FACILITIES: 98 sites, typical site width 25 ft, 83 full hkups, 15 W&E, (15, 20, 30 & 50 amps), some extended stay sites (in winter), wireless Instant Internet access at site ($), phone on-site Internet access (needs activ), wireless Internet access central location, RV/park trailer rentals, RV storage, dump station, non-guest dumping $, laundry, tables.

◊◊RECREATION: swim pool, pond fishing, golf nearby, playground, planned activities.

Pets welcome, breed restrict, size restrict, quantity restrict. Partial handicap access. No tents. Open all yr. Planned activities winter only. Big rigs welcome. Internet friendly. Clubs welcome. Rate in 2007 $40 for 4 persons. MC/VISA. Phone: (321) 633-4335.

e-mail: sonrisepalmsrvpark@hotmail.com

SEE AD TRAVEL SECTION PAGE 71

COCOA BEACH—C-5

(E) MILITARY PARK (Manatee Cove Campground-Patrick AFB)—(Brevard) *From jct US 1 & Hwy 520: Go E on Hwy 520 to Hwy A1A, then S on Hwy A1A to main gate. On base.* FACILITIES: 80 sites, 46 full hkups, 34 W&E, 5 pull-thrus, tenting, dump station, laundry, ice, patios. RECREATION: pavilion, saltwater swimming, boating, canoeing, saltwater fishing, playground, v-ball. Partial handicap access. Open all yr. For Military Use Only-w/Military ID Card. Max stay 30 days. Phone: (407)494-4787.

Florida State Stone: Coral

CORTEZ—D-3

(E) KEY WAY RV PARK (NOT VISITED) —(Manatee) *From jct US 41 & Hwy 684 (Cortez Rd): Go 7 mi W on Hwy 684. Enter on R.*

WELCOME

FACILITIES: 47 sites, 39 ft max RV length, 47 full hkups, (30 & 50 amps), phone/cable on-site Internet access (needs activ), phone Internet access central location, RV storage, dump station, tables, patios.

RECREATION: rec hall, boating, canoeing, kayaking, ramp, dock.

Pets welcome. No tents. Open all yr. Rate in 2007 $30-45 for 2 persons. Phone: (941)798-3090.

e-mail: marty.baxter@newbymanagement.com

SEE AD BRADENTON PAGE 96

CRESCENT CITY—B-4

(N) Crescent City Campground—(Putnam) *From jct Hwy 308 & US 17: Go 1-3/4 mi N on US 17. Enter on L.* ◊◊◊FACILITIES: 92 sites, typical site width 25 ft, 82 full hkups, (20, 30 & 50 amps), 10 no hkups, many extended stay sites (in winter), 21 pull-thrus, tenting, dump station, non-guest dumping $, laundry, LP gas by weight/by meter, LP bottle exch, ice, tables, patios. ◊◊RECREATION: rec room/area, swim pool, playground, shuffleboard court, horseshoes. Rec open to public. Pets welcome. Open all yr. Big rigs welcome. Internet friendly. Rate in 2007 $27-32 for 2 persons. Member ARVC, FLARVC. Phone: (800)634-3968.

CROSS CITY—B-2

(S) SHADY OAKS RV & MOBILE HOME PARK, INC—(Dixie) *From jct US 27 Alt/US 19 and CR-349. Go 6 mi NW on US 27 - Alt/US 19, then 150 ft E on NE 300th St. Enter on L.*

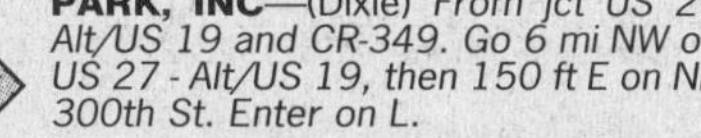

WELCOME

◊◊◊FACILITIES: 31 sites, 31 full hkups, (30 amps), some extended stay sites (in winter), 31 pull-thrus, cable TV, tenting, dump station, non-guest dumping $, laundry, ltd groceries, LP gas by weight/by meter, LP bottle exch, ice, tables.

◊◊RECREATION: rec room/area, swim pool, golf nearby, 2 shuffleboard courts, horseshoes.

Pets welcome, breed restrict. Open all yr. Rate in 2007 $17 for 2 persons. MC/VISA. Phone: (352) 498-7276.

SEE AD THIS PAGE

CRYSTAL RIVER—B-3

CRYSTAL ISLES—(Citrus) *From jct US 19 & Hwy C-44: Go 4 mi W on Hwy C-44. Enter on R.*

WELCOME

◊◊◊◊FACILITIES: 250 sites, typical site width 40 ft, 237 full hkups, 2 W&E, (30 & 50 amps), 11 no hkups, some extended stay sites (in winter), 6 pull-thrus, cable TV, wireless Instant Internet access at site ($), phone Internet access central location, tenting, cabins, dump station, non-guest dumping $, laundry, ltd groceries, RV supplies, LP gas by weight/by meter, ice, tables, patios, fire rings, wood.

◊◊◊◊◊RECREATION: rec hall, swim pool, wading pool, whirlpool, boating, kayaking, ramp, dock, 2 pontoon/3 kayak rentals, lake/river/pond fishing, golf nearby, bsktball, playground, 2 shuffleboard courts, planned activities, tennis, horseshoes, v-ball.

Pets welcome, breed restrict. Partial handicap access. Open all yr. Big rigs welcome. Internet friendly. Escort to site. Clubs welcome. Rate in 2007 $33-44 for 2 persons. MC/VISA/DISC/AMEX. Phone: (888)783-6763.

e-mail: crystal_isles@mhchomes.com

SEE AD DAYTONA BEACH PAGE 109

ELITE RESORTS AT CRYSTAL RIVER—(Citrus) *From US 19 & SR 44: Go 3.6 mi E on SR 44, then 1.2 mi S on Rock Crusher Road. Enter on L.*

WELCOME

RV RESORT ON THE GULF COAST

Nestled on 80 wooded acres, Elite Resorts at Crystal River offers for sale or rent large lots with 50 amp service, free WiFi, cable TV and full range of amenities and short distance to golf, fishing and boating on the Gulf.

◊◊◊◊◊FACILITIES: 398 sites, typical site width 30 ft, 398 full hkups, (50 amps), 4 pull-thrus, cable TV, wireless Instant Internet access at site, dump station, non-guest dumping $, laundry, RV supplies, LP gas by weight/by meter, ice, tables.

ELITE RESORTS AT CRYSTAL RIVER—Continued on next page

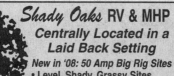

CRYSTAL RIVER—Continued
ELITE RESORTS AT CRYSTAL RIVER—Continued

◆◆◆◆◆RECREATION: rec hall, rec room/area, equipped pavilion, swim pool, whirlpool, lake fishing, golf nearby, bsktball, playground, planned activities, horseshoes, hiking trails, v-ball.

Pets welcome. Partial handicap access. No tents. Open all yr. Planned group activities from Nov - Apr. Big rigs welcome. Internet friendly. Escort to site. Clubs welcome. Rate in 2007 $23-35 for 2 persons. MC/VISA. Member ARVC, FLARVC. Phone: (800)356-2460.

e-mail: info@eliteresorts.com

SEE AD TRAVEL SECTION PAGE 79

(N) LAKE ROUSSEAU RV & FISHING RESORT—(Citrus) *From North jct Hwy 44 & US 19: Go 6 mi N on US 19, then 3.5 mi E on Hwy 488, then 1.5 mi N on Northcut Ave. Enter on R.*

WELCOME

◆◆◆FACILITIES: 125 sites, typical site width 30 ft, accepts full hkup units only, 125 full hkups, (30 & 50 amps), many extended stay sites, 2 pull-thrus, cable TV, wireless Instant Internet access at site ($), wireless Internet access central location ($), RV/park trailer rentals, RV storage, laundry, ltd groceries, RV supplies, LP gas by weight/by meter, ice, tables, wood.

◆◆◆◆RECREATION: rec room/area, swim pool, boating, canoeing, kayaking, ramp, dock, 2 canoe/pedal boat/2 motorboat rentals, lake fishing, fishing supplies, golf nearby, planned activities, horseshoes, sports field.

Pets welcome, quantity restrict. Partial handicap access. No tents. Open all yr. Big rigs welcome. Internet friendly. Clubs welcome. Rate in 2007 $29 for 4 persons. MC/VISA. Member ARVC, FLARVC. Phone: (800)561-CAMP. FMCA discount.

e-mail: info@lakerousseaurvpark.com

SEE AD TRAVEL SECTION PAGE 71

CYPRESS GARDENS—C-4

See listings at Bartow, Dundee, Haines City, Lake Wales & Winterhaven

DADE CITY—C-3

(SE) BLUE JAY RV PARK—(Pasco) *From jct Hwy 301 & US 98: Go 3/4 mi S on US 98. Enter on L.*

WELCOME

◆◆◆FACILITIES: 56 sites, 56 full hkups, (20, 30 & 50 amps), phone on-site Internet access (needs activ), RV storage, laundry.

◆◆◆RECREATION: rec hall, swim pool, golf nearby, 6 shuffleboard courts, planned activities, horseshoes.

Pets welcome, breed restrict, size restrict, quantity restrict. Partial handicap access. No tents. Age restrictions may apply. Open all yr. Rate in 2007 $28 for 2 persons. Phone: (352)567-9678.

SEE AD TAMPA PAGE 178

(SE) CITRUS HILL PARK & SALES—(Pasco) *From south jct US 301 & US 98: Go 4 mi SE on US 98. Enter on R.*

WELCOME

◆◆◆FACILITIES: 182 sites, 182 full hkups, (30 & 50 amps), phone/cable on-site Internet access (needs activ), phone Internet access central location, dump station, laundry, tables, controlled access gate.

◆◆◆RECREATION: rec hall, golf nearby, 3 shuffleboard courts, planned activities, horseshoes.

DADE CITY—Continued
CITRUS HILL PARK & SALES—Continued

Pets welcome, breed restrict, size restrict, quantity restrict. No tents. Open all yr. Big rigs welcome. Rate in 2007 $27 for 2 persons. Phone: (352)567-6045.

e-mail: bel-aire@3oaks.com

SEE AD TAMPA PAGE 179

(SE) GROVE RIDGE RV RESORT—(Pasco) *From jct Hwy 301 & US 98: Go 1 mi S on US 98. Enter on R.*

WELCOME

WELCOME TO CAREFREE RV RESORTS!
Nestled between orange groves and rolling hills, Grove Ridge offers the best scenery around. The large heated pool & Rec Hall are perfect for group get-togethers. Only 1 hour from major Florida attractions. Come join the fun!

◆◆◆◆FACILITIES: 247 sites, accepts full hkup units only, 247 full hkups, (30 & 50 amps), many extended stay sites (in winter), wireless Instant Internet access at site, phone/cable on-site Internet access (needs activ), wireless Internet access central location, RV/park trailer rentals, dump station, laundry, tables.

◆◆◆◆RECREATION: rec hall, rec room/area, swim pool, golf nearby, 12 shuffleboard courts, planned activities, horseshoes.

Pets welcome, breed restrict, size restrict. No tents. Age restrictions may apply. Open all yr. No showers. Big rigs welcome. Rate in 2007 $28 for 2 persons. Phone: (352)523-2277. CCUSA discount.

e-mail: bel-aire@3oaks.com

SEE AD TAMPA PAGE 177 AND AD TRAVEL SECTION PAGE 75 AND AD DISCOVER SECTION PAGE 128

(SE) Many Mansions RV Park—(Pasco) *From South jct US 301 & US 98: Go 3 mi SE on US 98 (Richland exit), then 1 mi S on Hwy 35A, then 1 block E on Stewart Rd. Enter on L.* ◆◆◆FACILITIES: 235 sites, typical site width 30 ft, accepts full hkup units only, 235 full hkups, (20, 30 & 50 amps), many extended stay sites (in winter), laundry, LP gas by weight/by meter. ◆◆◆RECREATION: rec hall, equipped pavilion, 4 shuffleboard courts, planned activities, horseshoes, sports field. Pets welcome. Partial handicap access. No tents. Age restrictions may apply. Open all yr. Planned activities in season. Children accepted for 2 weeks maximum. Big rigs welcome. Internet friendly. Rate in 2007 $32 for 2 persons. Phone: (800)359-0135. CCUSA discount.

(W) TOWN N' COUNTRY RV RESORT—(Pasco) *From South jct US 98 & US 301: Go 6-3/4 mi N on US 98/US 301. Enter on R.*

WELCOME

◆◆◆◆FACILITIES: 200 sites, typical site width 40 ft, 200 full hkups, (30 & 50 amps), phone on-site Internet access (needs activ), RV storage, laundry, tables, patios.

◆◆◆◆RECREATION: rec hall, swim pool, putting green, golf nearby, 4 shuffleboard courts, planned activities, horseshoes, local tours.

Pets welcome, size restrict, quantity restrict. Partial handicap access. No tents. Age restrictions may apply. Open all yr. Big rigs welcome. Rate in 2007 $28 for 2 persons. Member ARVC, FLARVC. Phone: (352)567-7707.

SEE AD THIS PAGE

(W) TRAVELERS REST RESORT—(Pasco) *From jct I-75 (exit 293) & Hwy 41: Go 1/2 mi W on Hwy 41, then 1 mi S on Hwy 577, then 1-1/2 mi W on Johnston Rd. Enter on R.*

WELCOME

◆◆◆◆FACILITIES: 557 sites, accepts full hkup units only, 557 full hkups, (30 & 50 amps), many extended stay sites, 80 pull-thrus, cable TV, wireless Instant Internet access at site, phone/cable on-site Internet access (needs activ), dump station, non-guest dumping $, laundry, LP gas by weight/by meter, patios, controlled access gate.

◆◆◆◆◆RECREATION: rec hall, rec room/area, equipped pavilion, swim pool, whirlpool, lake fishing, putting green, golf nearby, bsktball, 8 shuffleboard courts, planned activities, tennis, horseshoes, local tours.

Pets welcome, quantity restrict. Partial handicap access. No tents. Open all yr. Big rigs welcome. Internet friendly. Clubs welcome. Rate in 2007

Florida State Gem: Moonstone

DADE CITY—Continued
TRAVELERS REST RESORT—Continued

$25 for 2 persons. MC/VISA. Member ARVC, FLARVC. Phone: (800)565-8114. CCUSA discount. FMCA discount.

e-mail: reservations@travelersrestresort.com

SEE AD TAMPA PAGE 179 AND AD TRAVEL SECTION PAGE 78

DAVENPORT—C-4

(SW) 21 Palms RV Resort—(Osceola) *From jct I-4 (exit 58) & Hwy 532: Go 3 mi E on Hwy 532. Enter on L.* ◆◆◆FACILITIES: 160 sites, 160 full hkups, (30 & 50 amps), some extended stay sites (in winter), 35 pull-thrus, dump station, non-guest dumping $, laundry, tables, patios. ◆◆◆RECREATION: rec hall, swim pool, pond fishing, 2 shuffleboard courts, planned activities, horseshoes. Pets welcome. Partial handicap access. No tents. Open all yr. Big rigs welcome. Rate in 2007 $25 for 2 persons. Phone: (407)397-9110.

(NW) DEER CREEK GOLF & RV RESORT—(Polk) *From jct I-4 (exit 55) & US 27: Go 1 mi S on US 27. Enter on L.*

WELCOME

◆◆◆◆FACILITIES: 110 sites, typical site width 45 ft, 110 full hkups, (30 & 50 amps), cable TV, RV/park trailer rentals, RV storage, dump station, non-guest dumping $, laundry, RV supplies, tables, patios, controlled access gate.

◆◆◆◆RECREATION: rec hall, rec room/area, 5 swim pools, whirlpool, putting green, golf nearby, bsktball, playground, 6 shuffleboard courts, planned activities, tennis, local tours.

Pets welcome. Partial handicap access. No tents. Open all yr. Big rigs welcome. Clubs welcome. Rate in 2007 $45 for 2 persons. MC/VISA/DISC. Phone: (800)424-2931. FMCA discount.

SEE AD TRAVEL SECTION PAGE 83 AND AD TRAVEL SECTION PAGE 77 AND AD DISCOVER SECTION PAGE 56

(N) Florida Camp Inn—(Polk) *From jct I-4 (exit 55) & US 27: Go 4-1/2 mi N on US 27. Enter on L.* ◆◆◆◆FACILITIES: 471 sites, typical site width 30 ft, 447 full hkups, 24 W&E, (20, 30 & 50 amps), many extended stay sites (in winter), 30 pull-thrus, tenting, dump station, non-guest dumping $, laundry, ltd groceries, LP gas by weight/by meter, ice, tables, patios. ◆◆◆RECREATION: rec hall, swim pool, 6 shuffleboard courts, planned activities, horseshoes. Pets welcome. Partial handicap access. Open all yr. Planned activities winter only. Big rigs welcome. Internet friendly. Rate in 2007 $17 for 2 persons. Member ARVC, FLARVC. Phone: (863)424-2494.

(N) Mouse Mountain RV Camping Resort—(Polk) *From jct I-4 (exit 58) & Hwy 532: Go 1-1/2 mi E on Hwy 532. Enter on R.* ◆◆◆◆FACILITIES: 279 sites, typical site width 35 ft, 260 full hkups, (20, 30 & 50 amps), 19 no hkups, many extended stay sites (in winter), 12 pull-thrus, tenting, laundry, LP gas by weight/by meter, tables, patios. ◆◆◆◆RECREATION: rec hall, rec room/area, swim pool, playground, 3 shuffleboard courts, planned activities, horseshoes. Pets welcome, breed restrict, quantity restrict. Partial handicap access. Open all yr. Church services in winter only. Big rigs welcome. Rate in 2007 $18-30 for 2 persons. Member ARVC. Phone: (800)347-6388. CCUSA discount.

(NW) Themeworld RV Resort—(Polk) *From jct I-4 (exit 55) & US 27: Go 1 block S on US 27, then 1/2 mi W on Frontage Rd. Enter on L.* ◆◆◆◆◆FACILITIES: 272 sites, 272 full hkups, (30 & 50 amps), 150 pull-thrus, tenting, dump station, laundry, ltd groceries, LP gas by meter, ice, tables, patios, wood. ◆◆◆◆RECREATION: rec hall, rec room/area, swim pool, playground, 4 shuffleboard courts, planned activities, horseshoes, sports field. Pets welcome, breed restrict, quantity restrict. Partial handicap access. Open all yr. Big rigs welcome. Internet friendly. Rate in 2007 $34 for 2 persons. Member ARVC. Phone: (863)424-8362. CCUSA discount.

Reserve Online at Woodalls.com

(NE) THREE WORLDS RESORT—(Polk) *From jct Hwy 547 & US 17-92: Go 3 mi N on US 17-92. Enter on R.*

WELCOME

◆◆◆◆FACILITIES: 220 sites, 220 full hkups, (30 & 50 amps), 5 pull-thrus, heater not allowed, wireless Instant Internet access at site, phone/cable on-site Internet access (needs activ), wireless Internet access central location, tenting, RV/park trailer rentals, RV storage, dump station, laundry, tables, patios, controlled access gate.

◆◆◆◆RECREATION: rec hall, swim pool, pond fishing, mini-golf, golf nearby, 8 shuffleboard courts, planned activities, horseshoes, local tours.

THREE WORLDS RESORT—Continued on next page

DAVENPORT—Continued
THREE WORLDS RESORT—Continued

Pets welcome, breed restrict, quantity restrict. Partial handicap access. Age restrictions may apply. Open all yr. Big rigs welcome. Internet friendly. Escort to site. Rate in 2007 $40 for 2 persons. MC/VISA. Phone: (863)424-1286.

SEE AD ORLANDO PAGE 154

DAYTONA BEACH—B-4

See listings at Flagler Beach, New Smyrna Beach, Ormond Beach, Palm Coast & Port Orange.

WELCOME

BEVERLY BEACH CAMPTOWN RV RESORT—*From jct 1-4 & I-95: Go 23 miles N on I-95, then 3-1/4 mi E on Hwy 100, then 3 mi N on Hwy A1A. Enter on R.*

SEE PRIMARY LISTING AT FLAGLER BEACH AND AD THIS PAGE

WELCOME

(S) DAYTONA BEACH CAMPGROUND—*(Volusia) From I-95 (exit 256) & Hwy 421: Go 3/4 mi E on Hwy 421, then 1-1/4 N on Clyde Morris Blvd. Enter on R.*

LOCATION, ENVIRONMENT, AMENITIES
Close to beaches and shopping. We have it all! Located near all of the attractions in the Daytona Beach area. If you want to be where the action is, you will want to be here! Your Camping Pleasure is our business!

◆◆◆◆FACILITIES: 225 sites, typical site width 30 ft, 190 full hkups, 35 W&E, (20, 30 & 50 amps), some extended stay sites, 18 pull-thrus, cable TV, phone Internet access central location, tenting, dump station, non-guest dumping $, laundry, ltd groceries, RV supplies, LP gas by weight/by meter, ice, tables, patios.

◆◆◆◆RECREATION: rec hall, rec room/area, pavilion, swim pool, wading pool, golf nearby, play equipment, 2 shuffleboard courts, planned activities, horseshoes.

Pets welcome. Partial handicap access. Open all yr. Planned group activities winter only. Big rigs welcome. Internet friendly. Escort to site. Clubs welcome. Rate in 2007 $35-45 for 2 persons. MC/VISA. Member ARVC, FLARVC. Phone: (386) 761-2663.

e-mail: dbcampground@cfl.rr.com

SEE AD PAGE 107

(W) Daytona Speedway KOA—(Volusia) *S'bnd from I-95 (exit 261): Go 1 block W on US 92W, then 150 feet S on CR 415 (Tomoka Farms Rd). N'bnd: From I-95 (exit 87): Go 2 blocks W on US 92W, then 150 feet S on CR 415. Enter on R.* ◆◆◆◆FACILITIES: 98 sites, typical site width 20 ft, 98 full hkups, (20, 30 & 50 amps), some extended stay sites, 4 pull-thrus, dump station, non-guest dumping $, laundry, LP gas by weight/by meter, ice, tables, patios. RECREATION: rec room/area. Pets welcome, size restrict. No tents. Open all yr. Big rigs welcome. Internet friendly. Rate in 2007 $25-40 for 2 persons. Phone: (386)257-6137. KOA 10% value card discount.

WELCOME

ELITE RESORTS AT SALT SPRINGS—*From jct I-95 (exit 261) & US-92: Go 6 mi N on I-95, then 35 mi W on Hwy 40, then 16 mi N on Hwy 19. Enter on L.*

SEE PRIMARY LISTING AT SALT SPRINGS AND AD TRAVEL SECTION PAGE 79

(W) International RV Park & Campground—(Volusia) *From jct I-95 (exit 261B) & US 92: Go 1-1/3 mi W on US 92. Enter on L.* ◆◆◆◆FACILITIES: 194 sites, typical site width 35 ft, 194 full hkups, (20, 30 & 50 amps), mostly extended stay sites (in winter), 13 pull-thrus, tenting, dump station, non-guest dumping $, laun-

International RV Park & Campground—Continued on next page

DAYTONA BEACH—Continued
International RV Park & Campground—Continued

dry, ltd groceries, LP gas by weight/by meter, ice, tables, patios. ◆◆RECREATION: swim pool, pond fishing, horseshoes, sports field. Pets welcome. Partial handicap access. Open all yr. Big rigs welcome. Internet friendly. Rate in 2007 $25-30 for 2 persons. Phone: (866)261-3698. CCUSA discount. FCRV 10% discount. FMCA discount.

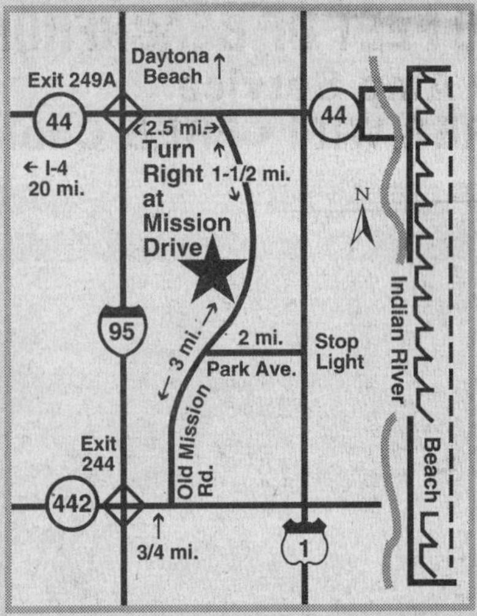

(S) NOVA FAMILY CAMPGROUND—(Volusia) *From I-95 & Hwy 421: Go 1 mi E on Hwy 421, then 1 mi N on Clyde Morris Blvd, then 3/4 mi E on Herbert St. Enter on R.*

WELCOME

◆◆◆FACILITIES: 350 sites, typical site width 30 ft, 117 full hkups, 92 W&E, (20, 30 & 50 amps), 141 no hkups, some extended stay sites (in winter), 11 pull-thrus, cable TV, cable Internet access central location ($), tenting, RV/park trailer rentals, cabins, RV storage, dump station, non-guest dumping $, portable dump, laundry, groceries, RV supplies, LP gas by weight/by meter, ice, tables, wood.

◆◆◆◆RECREATION: rec hall, rec room/area, equipped pavilion, coin games, swim pool, 2 shuffleboard courts, planned activities, horseshoes.

Pets welcome ($), breed restrict. Open all yr. RV storage Apr-Feb only. Internet friendly. Clubs welcome. Rate in 2007 $25-33.50 for 2 persons. MC/VISA/DISC/AMEX. Member ARVC, FLARVC. Phone: (386)767-0095.

e-mail: friends@novacamp.com

SEE AD NEXT PAGE

Woodall's Tip #11... Turn to the Travel Section for a list of the RV Parks & Campgrounds that are Internet Friendly.

St. Augustine is the oldest European settlement in North America.

Florida is not the southernmost state in the United States.

DEBARY—B-4

(W) HIGHBANKS MARINA & CAMPRESORT—(Volusia) *From I-4 (exit 108) (circle under cloverleaf): Go 2 mi W on Dirksen Rd, then 1 3/4 mi N on US 17/92, then 2-1/2 mi W on Highbanks Rd. Enter on R.*

◆◆◆◆◆FACILITIES: 218 sites, typical site width 32 ft, 218 full hkups, (30 & 50 amps), mostly extended stay sites, 10 pull-thrus, cable TV, cable on-site Internet access (needs activ), tenting, cabins, dump station, laundry, ltd groceries, RV supplies, LP gas by weight/by meter, gas, marine gas, ice, tables, patios.

◆◆◆◆◆RECREATION: rec hall, rec room/area, equipped pavilion, swim pool, boating, ramp, dock, 6 pontoon rentals, float trips, river/pond fishing, fishing supplies, golf nearby, playground, 2 shuffleboard courts, planned activities, horseshoes.

Pets welcome, breed restrict, size restrict, quantity restrict. Partial handicap access. Open all yr. Tenting May 1 - Sep 30. Big rigs welcome. Escort

DEBARY—Continued
HIGHBANKS MARINA & CAMPRESORT—Continued

to site. Clubs welcome. Rate in 2007 $45 for 2 persons. MC/VISA/DISC/AMEX/Debit. Member ARVC, FLARVC. Phone: (386)668-4491.

e-mail: mail@campresort.com

SEE AD NEXT PAGE

(N) LAKE MONROE PARK (Volusia County Park)—(Volusia) *From jct I-4 (exit 52) & US 17/92N: Go 1/2 mi N on US 17/92N.* FACILITIES: 44 sites, 44 W&E, tenting, dump station, ice, fire rings, grills. RECREATION: pavilion, boating, ramp, dock, river fishing, playground, hiking trails, v-ball. Rec open to public. Pets welcome. Open all yr. Phone: (386)668-3825.

(W) SWAMP HOUSE GRILL—*From I-4 (exit 108) (circle under Cloverleaf): Go 2 mi W on Dirksen Rd, then 1-3/4 mi N on US 17/92, then 2-1/2 mi W on Highbanks Rd. Enter on R.* Open air, riverfront, casual family-oriented restaurant on the beautiful St. John's River. Seafood & Steak Specialties. Open all yr. Closed on Mon, Christmas Eve, Christmas Day. MC/VISA/DISC/AMEX.

e-mail: gm@swamphousegrill.com

SEE AD NEXT PAGE

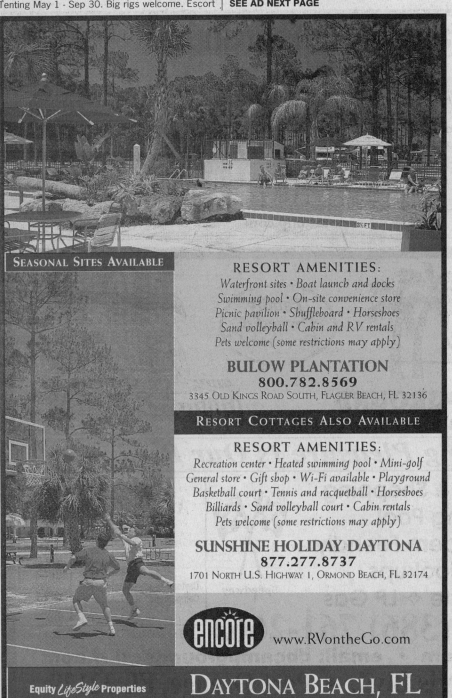

DEERFIELD BEACH—E-5

(W) QUIET WATERS PARK (Broward County Park)—(Broward) *From jct I-95 & SW 10th St: Go 2 mi W on SW 10th St, then 1/2 mi N on Powerline Rd. Enter on L.*

FACILITIES: 27 sites, 27 no hkups, tenting, tent rentals, ice, tables, fire rings, grills, wood, controlled access gate.

RECREATION: pavilion, swim pool, lake swimming, boating, electric motors only, canoeing, kayaking, 8 rowboat/16 canoe/5 kayak/15 pedal boat rentals, lake fishing, playground, horseshoes, sports field, hiking trails, v-ball. Rec open to public.

Pets welcome. Partial handicap access. Open all yr. RV sites are not available. MC/VISA/DISC. Phone: (954)360-1315.

e-mail: quietwaterspark@broward.org

SEE AD TRAVEL SECTION PAGE 74

DEFUNIAK SPRINGS—E-2

CAMPING ON THE GULF—*From I-10 (exit 85) & US 331: Go 25 mi S on US 331, then 10 mi W on US 98. Enter on L.*

SEE PRIMARY LISTING AT DESTIN, FL AND AD DISCOVER SECTION PAGE 54

(S) LongLeaf RV Park—(Walton) *From jct I-10 (exit 85) & US 331: Go 3-1/2 mi S on US 331. Enter on L.* ◆◆FACILITIES: 24 sites, typical site width 30 ft, 19 full hkups, 5 W&E, (30 & 50 amps), 50 amps ($), many extended stay sites, 15 pull-thrus, tenting, dump station, laundry, tables. RECREATION: rec room/area, horseshoes. Pets welcome. Open all yr. Big rigs welcome. Rate in 2007 $22-24 for 2 persons. Phone: (850)892-7261.

(NW) SUNSET KING LAKE RV RESORT—(Walton) *From jct I-10 (exit 85) & US 331: Go 2 mi N on US 331, then 2 mi W on US 90, then 5-1/2 mi N on US 331, then 1 mi SW on Kings Lake Rd, then 1/4 mi SE on Paradise Isl. Rd. Enter on R.*

CATCH THE DIFFERENCE AT KING LAKE!!
Home of Big Bass! Spacious Club House, Chapel, Restaurant Open Thurs - Sunday. WI-FI. 50 AMP, Long Pull Thrus, Swimming Pool, 220 Full Hookups, Rental Cabins & Boats, Family Operated. 1-800-774-5454. WWW.SUNSETKING.COM

◆◆◆◆◆FACILITIES: 230 sites, typical site width 40 ft, 220 full hkups, (20, 30 & 50 amps), 10 no hkups, some extended stay sites, 90 pull-thrus, cable TV, wireless Instant Internet access at site ($), phone Internet access central location, tenting, RV/park trailer rentals, cabins, RV storage, dump station, non-guest dumping $, laundry, groceries, RV supplies, LP gas by weight/by meter, ice, tables, patios, wood.

◆◆◆◆◆RECREATION: rec hall, rec room/area, equipped pavilion, coin games, swim pool, boating, canoeing, ramp, dock, 5 rowboat/2 canoe/6 motorboat rentals, lake fishing, fishing supplies, mini-golf, golf nearby, bsktball, playground, planned activities, horseshoes, v-ball.

Pets welcome. Partial handicap access. Open all yr. Big rigs welcome. Internet friendly. Escort to site. Clubs welcome. Rate in 2007 $27 for 4 persons. MC/VISA/DISC/Debit. Member ARVC, FLARVC. Phone: (800)774-5454. CCUSA discount.

e-mail: reservations@sunsetking.com

SEE AD DESTIN PAGE 112

DELRAY BEACH—E-5

(S) DEL RATON RV PARK—(Palm Beach) *From jct Hwy 806 & I-95: Go 1-1/2 mi S on I-95 (exit 51), then 1 mi E on Linton Blvd, then 1 mi S on US-1. Enter on R.*

◆◆◆FACILITIES: 85 sites, typical site width 30 ft, 38 ft max RV length, 60 full hkups, 25 W&E, (20, 30 & 50 amps), some extended stay sites (in winter), 25 pull-thrus, wireless Instant Internet access at site ($), shower$, dump station, non-guest dumping $, laundry, RV supplies, LP gas by weight/by meter, patios, controlled access gate.

◆◆RECREATION: rec room/area, golf nearby, planned activities.

DEL RATON RV PARK—Continued on next page

Florida was the 27th state admitted to the Union.

DELRAY BEACH—Continued
DEL RATON RV PARK—Continued

No pets. No tents. Open all yr. Planned activities during season. Internet friendly. Escort to site. Rate in 2007 $32-39 for 2 persons. Member ARVC, FLARVC. Phone: (561)278-4633.

e-mail: delraton@aol.com

SEE AD THIS PAGE

DESTIN—F-2

(E) CAMPING ON THE GULF—(Walton) *From Destin Mid Bay Bridge (293) & US 98: Go 5 mi E on US 98. Enter on R.*

WELCOME

YOU CAN'T GET ANY CLOSER THAN THIS! Beachfront camping, designer outlet shopping, gulf fishing, golfing, great seafood, heated pool, wireless Internet, deluxe luxury cabins. 22 new beautiful family-style bathrooms. 877-CAMPGUL(F) 877-226-7485 WWW.CAMPGULF.COM

◊◊◊◊◊FACILITIES: 213 sites, typical site width 30 ft, 197 full hkups, 16 W&E, (30 & 50 amps), some extended stay sites (in winter), 18 pull-thrus, cable TV, wireless Instant Internet access at site, phone on-site Internet access (needs activ), cable Internet access central location, tenting, cabins, RV storage, dump station, laundry, ltd groceries, RV supplies, LP gas by weight/by meter, ice, tables, patios, controlled access gate.

◊◊◊◊◊RECREATION: rec hall, rec room/area, equipped pavilion, 2 swim pools, saltwater swimming, whirlpool, saltwater/lake fishing, fishing supplies, putting green, golf nearby, playground, shuffleboard court, planned activities, horseshoes, v-ball.

Pets welcome. Partial handicap access. Open all yr. Big rigs welcome. Internet friendly. Escort to site. Clubs welcome. Rate in 2007 $60-109 for 5 persons. MC/VISA. Member ARVC, FLARVC. Phone: (877)226-7485.

e-mail: camp@campgulf.com

SEE AD PAGES 110-111 AND AD DISCOVER SECTION PAGE 54

Florida's beautiful weather influences almost every part of the state's economy.

DESTIN—Continued

(N) DESTIN RECREATION AREA—(Walton) *From jct US 98 & Benning Dr.: Go N on Benning Dr. to the USAIC Reac. Area* FACILITIES: 46 sites, 46 full hkups, (50 amps), dump station, laundry, ice, grills. RECREATION: rec hall, swim pool, saltwater fishing, play equipment. No tents. Open all yr. Phone: (800)642-0466.

DESTIN—Continued on next page

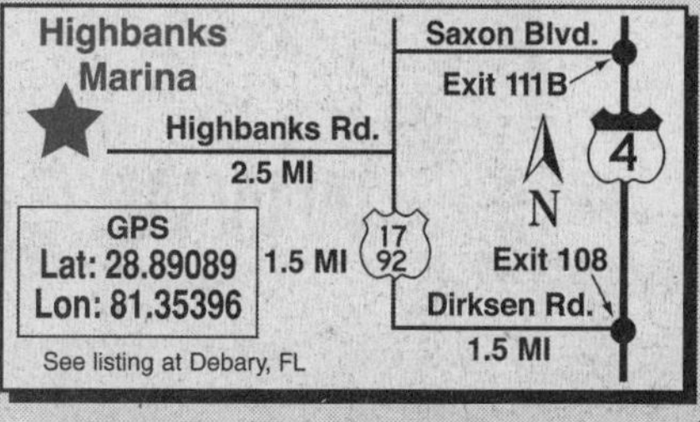

Destin,

CAMPING on

You Can't Get Any

Sandcastle Cabins, Clean Family Style Bathrooms,
Free Wifi and phone hookups at site, Near Seafood, Golfing, Fishing,
Near largest Designer Outlet in the U.S., Heated Pool, Activities,
Big Rigs Welcome, Beachfront sites, Beach sites, Grassy/Shade sites
Business Center

DESTIN—Continued

(E) DESTIN RV BEACH RESORT—(Walton) *From jct SR 293 & US 98: Go 4 mi E on US 98, then 1/4 mi S on Miramar Beach Drive. Enter on R.*

WELCOME

◆◆◆◆◆FACILITIES: 36 sites, typical site width 30 ft, 36 full hkups, (30 & 50 amps), many extended stay sites (in winter), cable TV, wireless Instant Internet access at site, laundry, tables, patios.

◆RECREATION: swim pool, saltwater swimming. Pets welcome, quantity restrict. Partial handicap access. No tents. Open all yr. Big rigs welcome. Internet friendly. Rate in 2007 $60-79 for 2 persons. MC/VISA. Member ARVC, FLARVC. Phone: (877)737-3529.

e-mail: info@destinrvresort.com

SEE AD NEXT PAGE AND AD PANAMA CITY BEACH PAGE 160

(E) DESTIN VILLAGE RV RESORT (RV SPACES)—*From jct Hwy 293 (Mid Bay Bridge) and Hwy 98: Go 2-3/10 mi E on Hwy 98 to Driftwood Rd, then 3/10 mi S to Payne St. Enter on R.*

WELCOME

FACILITIES: 27 sites, typical site width 30 ft, accepts full hkup units only, 27 full hkups, (20, 30 & 50 amps), cable TV, wireless Instant Internet access at site, laundry, tables, patios.

DESTIN VILLAGE RV RESORT—Continued on next page

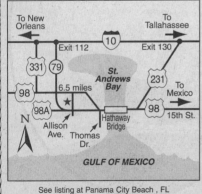

DESTIN—Continued
DESTIN VILLAGE RV RESORT—Continued

RECREATION: rec hall, swim pool, golf nearby.

Pets welcome. No tents. Open all yr. Big rigs welcome. Internet friendly. Rate in 2007 $55-60 for 4 persons. Phone: (850)496-6520.

e-mail: destinrvresort@aol.com

SEE AD PAGE 112

GERONIMO RV RESORT—(Walton) *From jct US 98 & Hwy 293 (Mid Bay Bridge): Go 4-1/4 mi E on US 98, then 1/2 mi S on South Geronimo St, then W on Arnett Ln.*

FACILITIES: 29 sites, 29 full hkups, (30 & 50 amps).

Open all yr. Rate in 2007 $35-70 per vehicle. Phone: (850)424-6801.

e-mail: info@geronimorvresort.com

SEE AD PAGE 109

(N) MILITARY PARK (Destin Recreation Area-Fort Benning GA)—(Okaloosa) *Off base. From jct US 98 & Benning Dr in town: Go N on Benning Dr to the USAIC Rec Area.* FACILITIES: 46 sites, 46 full hkups, tenting, dump station, laundry, ice, grills. RECREATION: rec room/area, swim pool, saltwater swimming, ramp, dock, 2 pedal boat/3 motorboat rentals, saltwater fishing, play equipment, v-ball. No pets. Open all yr. For Military Use Only-w/Military ID Card. Phone: (706)545-5600.

SUNSET KING LAKE RV RESORT—*From jct US 98 & CR 293: Go 6-1/2 mi N on CR 293, then 5-1/2 mi W on CR 20, then 23 mi N on CR 285, then 8-1/2 mi E on US 90, then 3-1/2 mi N on Kings Lake Rd, then 1/4 mi E on Paradise Island Rd. Enter on R.*

SEE PRIMARY LISTING AT DEFUNIAK SPRINGS AND AD PAGE 112

DOVER—C-3

(SE) **Citrus Hills RV Park**—(Hillsborough) *From jct I-75 & Hwy 60: Go 8 mi E on Hwy 60. Enter on R.* ◆◆◆FACILITIES: 228 sites, typical site width 37 ft, 228 full hkups, (30 & 50 amps), some extended stay sites (in winter), tenting, dump station, laundry, patios. ◆◆RECREATION: rec hall, planned activities. Pets welcome, breed restrict. Open all yr. Big rigs welcome. Rate in 2007 $25 for 2 persons. Member ARVC, FLARVC. Phone: (813)737-4770. CCUSA discount.

(N) TAMPA EAST RV RESORT—(Hillsborough) *From jct I-4 (exit 14) & McIntosh Rd: Go 1 block S on McIntosh Rd. Enter on R.*

◆◆◆◆FACILITIES: 694 sites, typical site width 40 ft, 659 full hkups, 35 W&E, (30 & 50 amps), some extended stay sites (in winter), wireless Instant Internet access at site, phone on-site Internet access (needs activ), wireless Internet access central location, cabins, RV storage, dump station, non-guest dumping $, laundry, ltd groceries, RV supplies, LP gas by weight/by meter, ice, tables, patios.

◆◆◆◆RECREATION: rec hall, rec room/area, 3 swim pools, whirlpool, pond fishing, golf nearby, bsktball, playground, 8 shuffleboard courts, planned activities, horseshoes, v-ball.

Pets welcome, breed restrict, size restrict. Partial handicap access. No tents. Open all yr. Planned activities winter only. Big rigs welcome. Internet friendly. Clubs welcome. Rate in 2007 $26-50 for 2 persons. MC/VISA/DISC. Member ARVC, FLARVC. Phone: (800)454-7336. CCUSA discount.

e-mail: info@rvonthego.com

SEE AD TRAVEL SECTION PAGE 73

DUNDEE—C-4

(W) **Greenfield Village**—(Polk) *From jct US 27 & Hwy 542: Go 1 block W on Hwy 542. Enter on L.* ◆◆◆◆FACILITIES: 104 sites, typical site width 30 ft, 104 full hkups, (20, 30 & 50 amps), mostly extended stay sites (in winter), laundry, tables, patios. ◆◆◆RECREATION: rec hall, swim pool, 4 shuffleboard courts, planned activities, horseshoes. Pets welcome, breed restrict, quantity restrict. Partial handicap access. No tents. Age restrictions may apply. Open all yr. Planned group activities, winter only. Big rigs welcome. Rate in 2007 $45 for 2 persons. Phone: (863)439-7409.

Safety Harbor is the home of the historic Espiritu Santo Springs, given in 1539 by the Spanish explorer Hernando de Soto, who was searching for the legendary Fountain of Youth. Known for their curative powers, the natural springs have attracted worldwide attention.

DUNEDIN—C-3

(N) DUNEDIN RV RESORT—(Pinellas) *From jct Hwy-586 & Alt US-19 N: Go 3/4 mi N on Alt US-19. Enter on R.*

WE'RE COUNTRY QUIET & CITY CLOSE
A full amenity park with lots of planned group activities. Close to all Tampa Bay area attractions, including Busch Gardens, beaches, golfing, shopping, museums and restaurants. Free wireless Internet at every site.

◆◆◆◆◆FACILITIES: 233 sites, typical site width 30 ft, 233 full hkups, (20, 30 & 50 amps), 18 pull-thrus, wireless Instant Internet access at site, phone/cable on-site Internet access (needs activ), wireless Internet access central location, tenting, RV storage, dump station, non-guest dumping $, laundry, ltd groceries, RV supplies, LP gas by weight/by meter, ice, tables, patios.

Florida's State Nickname: The Sunshine State

◆◆◆◆RECREATION: rec hall, swim pool, golf nearby, bsktball, 7 bike rentals, playground, 6 shuffleboard courts, planned activities, horseshoes, v-ball.

Pets welcome, breed restrict, quantity restrict. Partial handicap access. Open all yr. Planned group activities winter only. Big rigs welcome. Internet friendly. Clubs welcome. Rate in 2007 $30-50 for 2 persons. MC/VISA/DISC/AMEX. Member ARVC, FLARVC. Phone: (800)345-7504. FMCA discount.

e-mail: campdbc@aol.com

SEE AD TRAVEL SECTION PAGE 78

DUNNELLON—B-3

(E) RAINBOW SPRINGS STATE PARK—(Marion) *From jct I-75 (exit 341) and Hwy 484: Go 19 mi W on Hwy 484, then 2-1/4 mi N on SW 180th Ave Rd. Enter on L.* FACILITIES: 93 sites, 93 W&E, (20 & 30 amps), tenting, dump station. RECREATION: 6 canoe rentals, hiking trails. Open all yr. Phone: (352)465-8550.

DUNNELLON—Continued on next page

DUNNELLON—Continued

(W) Withlacoochee Backwaters RV Park—(Levy) *From jct US 41 & CR 40: Go 6 mi W on CR 40. Enter on L.* ◊◊◊FACILITIES: 21 sites, typical site width 30 ft, 21 full hkups, (30 amps), many extended stay sites (in winter), 3 pull-thrus, tables. ◊◊◊RECREATION: rec hall, boating, ramp, dock, lake fishing, planned activities, horseshoes. Pets welcome. Partial handicap access. No tents. Age restrictions may apply. Open all yr. Rate in 2007 $25 for 2 persons. Phone: (352)489-6691.

ELLENTON—D-3

(NE) ELLENTON GARDENS TRAVEL RESORT—(Manatee) *From jct I-75 (exit 224) & US-301: Go 1-1/4 mi NE on US-301. Enter on L.*

WELCOME

◊◊◊FACILITIES: 196 sites, typical site width 20 ft, 196 full hkups, (20, 30 & 50 amps), mostly extended stay sites (in winter), wireless Instant Internet access at site, phone/cable on-site Internet access (needs activ), phone Internet access central location, dump station, non-guest dumping $, laundry, patios.

◊◊◊RECREATION: rec hall, swim pool, pond fishing, golf nearby, 6 shuffleboard courts, planned activities, horseshoes.

Pets welcome, breed restrict, size restrict, quantity restrict. Partial handicap access. No tents. Open all yr. Planned activities winter only. Big rigs welcome. Internet friendly. Clubs welcome. Rate in 2007 $38 for 2 persons. Phone: (941)722-0341.

SEE AD SARASOTA PAGE 169

ESTERO—E-3

(W) KORESHAN STATE PARK—(Lee) *From jct I-75 (exit 19) & Corkscrew Rd: Go 2 mi W on Corkscrew Rd to US 41.* FACILITIES: 60 sites, 60 W&E, tenting, dump station, laundry, grills. RECREATION: boating, canoeing, ramp, 10 canoe rentals, saltwater fishing, playground, hiking trails, v-ball. Open all yr. Phone: (941)992-0311.

EUSTIS—B-4

(N) SOUTHERN PALMS RV RESORT—(Lake) *From jct US 441 & Hwy 19: Go 3-1/2 mi N on Hwy 19, then 1/2 mi W on CR 44 (not SR 44). Enter on R.*

WELCOME

◊◊◊◊FACILITIES: 953 sites, typical site width 28 ft, 953 full hkups, (30 & 50 amps), many extended stay sites, cable TV, wireless Instant Internet access at site ($), RV/park trailer rentals, RV storage, dump station, non-guest dumping $, laundry.

◊◊◊◊◊RECREATION: rec hall, rec room/area, 2 swim pools, whirlpool, golf nearby, 18 shuffleboard courts, planned activities, horseshoes, local tours.

Pets welcome, quantity restrict. Partial handicap access. No tents. Open all yr. Big rigs welcome.

EUSTIS—Continued
SOUTHERN PALMS RV RESORT—Continued

Internet friendly. Escort to site. Clubs welcome. Rate in 2007 $35-41 for 2 persons. MC/VISA/DISC/AMEX. Member ARVC, FLARVC. Phone: (866)778 8253.

SEE AD THIS PAGE

EVERGLADES CITY—E-4

CHOKOLOSKEE ISLAND PARK & CAMPGROUND—*From Everglades City: Go 3 mi S on CR 29, then 1 block W on Demere Ln, then 1 block W on Hamilton Ln. Enter at end.*

WELCOME

SEE PRIMARY LISTING AT CHOKOLOSKEE AND AD CHOKOLOSKEE PAGE 101

OUTDOOR RESORTS/CHOKOLOSKEE ISLAND—*From Everglades City: Go 3 mi S on CR 29. Enter on L.*

WELCOME

SEE PRIMARY LISTING AT CHOKOLOSKEE AND AD CHOKOLOSKEE PAGE 101

EVERGLADES NATIONAL PARK—F-4

See listings at Chokoloskee, Everglades City, Florida City & Homestead.

FERNANDINA BEACH—A-4

(E) FORT CLINCH STATE PARK—(Nassau) *From jct Hwy-A1A & Hwy-105: Go 3 mi NE on Hwy-A1A.* FACILITIES: 62 sites, 62 W&E, (20 & 30 amps), tenting, dump station, laundry. RECREATION: saltwater swimming, boating, canoeing, saltwater fishing, playground, hiking trails. Partial handicap access. Open all yr. Phone: (904)277-7274.

FLAGLER BEACH—B-4

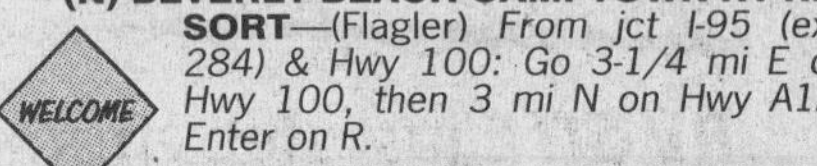

(N) BEVERLY BEACH CAMPTOWN RV RESORT—(Flagler) *From jct I-95 (exit 284) & Hwy 100: Go 3-1/4 mi E on Hwy 100, then 3 mi N on Hwy A1A. Enter on R.*

◊◊◊◊FACILITIES: 285 sites, typical site width 25 ft, 285 full hkups, (30 & 50 amps), some extended stay sites (in winter), cable TV, wireless Instant Internet access at site, tenting, dump station, non-guest dumping $, laundry, groceries, RV supplies, ice, tables.

◊◊RECREATION: saltwater swimming, saltwater fishing, fishing supplies.

Pets welcome. Partial handicap access. Open all yr. Big rigs welcome. Internet friendly. Clubs welcome. Rate in 2007 $50-85 for 2 persons. MC/VISA/DISC. Phone: (800)255-2706.

SEE AD DAYTONA BEACH PAGE 105 AND AD TRAVEL SECTION PAGE 84

Charles and John Ringling, circus entrepreneurs, were from Florida.

FLAGLER BEACH—Continued

(W) BULOW PLANTATION RV RESORT—(Flagler) *From I-95 (exit 284/Old 91) & Hwy 100: Go 1/4 mi E on Hwy 100, then 3 mi S on Old Kings Rd. Enter on L.*

WELCOME

◊◊◊FACILITIES: 385 sites, typical site width 39 ft, 250 full hkups, (30 & 50 amps), 135 no hkups, some extended stay sites, 100 pull-thrus, cable TV, wireless Internet access central location, tenting, cabins, dump station, non-guest dumping $, laundry, ltd groceries, RV supplies, LP gas by weight/by meter, ice, tables, patios, fire rings, wood.

◊◊◊RECREATION: rec hall, rec room/area, pavilion, coin games, swim pool, boating, dock, lake fishing, fishing supplies, golf nearby, 2 shuffleboard courts, planned activities, horseshoes, hiking trails, local tours.

Pets welcome. Partial handicap access. Open all yr. Rates higher during special events. Internet friendly. Escort to site. Clubs welcome. Rate in 2007 $35-45 for 2 persons. MC/VISA/DISC/AMEX. Member ARVC, FLARVC. Phone: (386)439-9200.

e-mail: rvinfo@mhchomes.com

SEE AD DAYTONA BEACH PAGE 108 AND AD TRAVEL SECTION PAGE 84

FLAGLER BY THE SEA CAMPGROUND—*From jct I-95 (exit 284) & Hwy 100: Go 3-1/4 mi E on Hwy 100, then 3-1/2 mi N on Hwy A1A. Enter on R.*

WELCOME

◊◊FACILITIES: 31 sites, 31 full hkups, (50 amps), some extended stay sites (in winter), 13 pull-thrus, cable TV, laundry, RV supplies, ice, tables.

◊◊RECREATION: saltwater swimming, saltwater fishing, golf nearby.

Pets welcome. No tents. Open all yr. Rate in 2007 $40-55 for 2 persons. MC/VISA. Member ARVC, FLARVC. Phone: (800)434-2124.

SEE AD TRAVEL SECTION PAGE 84

(S) GAMBLE ROGERS MEMORIAL STATE PARK AT FLAGLER BEACH—(Flagler) *From jct Hwy-100 & Hwy-A1A: Go 2 mi S on Hwy-A1A.*

WELCOME

FACILITIES: 34 sites, 30 ft max RV length, 34 W&E, tenting, dump station, tables, grills.

RECREATION: saltwater swimming, boating, canoeing, ramp, saltwater fishing, hiking trails.

Pets welcome ($). Open all yr. MC/VISA. Phone: (386)517-2086.

e-mail: gambler@pfl.net

SEE AD TRAVEL SECTION PAGE 84

FLORIDA CITY—E-5

(E) FLORIDA CITY CAMPSITE (City Park)—(Dade) *From jct Hwy 27, US 1 & Southern Terminus of Florida Tpk: Go 1 block W on Hwy 9336 (Palm Dr), then 1/2 mi N on Hwy 997, then 500 feet W on 336th St, then 500 feet N on 2nd Ave. Enter on R.*

WELCOME

FACILITIES: 310 sites, typical site width 20 ft, 253 full hkups, 27 W&E, (20, 30 & 50 amps), 30 no hkups, heater not allowed, phone Internet access central location, tenting, dump station, non-guest dumping $, laundry, LP gas by weight/by meter.

RECREATION: playground.

Pets welcome. Partial handicap access. Open all yr. Big rigs welcome. Internet friendly. Clubs welcome. MC/VISA. Phone: (305)248-7889.

SEE AD HOMESTEAD PAGE 127

FORT LAUDERDALE—E-5

BROWARD COUNTY PARKS & RECREATION DIVISION—5 County parks: Topeekeegee Yugnee, Easterlin, Markham, C.B. Smith & Quiet Waters. Full hookups to rustic tent camping. Recreation includes water playgrounds, Disc Golf Course, Target Gun Range, Model Airplane field, Raquetball, & a dog park. Open all yr. Phone: (954)357-8117.

WELCOME

e-mail: cybaker@broward.org

SEE AD TRAVEL SECTION PAGE 74

FORT LAUDERDALE—Continued on next page

Dwight Gooden, baseball player, is from Florida.

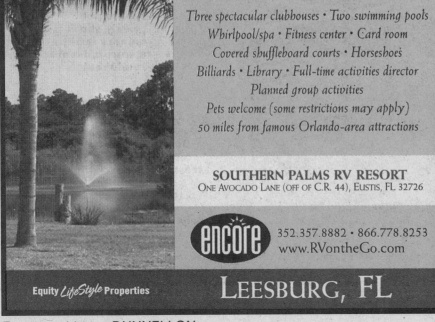

FORT LAUDERDALE—Continued

✽ **DIXIE TRAILER SUPPLY**—*From jct I-95 (exit 31) & Hwy 816 (Oakland Blvd): Go 1-3/4 mi E on Hwy 816 (Oakland Blvd), then 3/4 mi N on Hwy 811 (Dixie Hwy). Enter on L.* SERVICES: full-time mech, RV appliance repair, mobile RV svc, sells parts/accessories, installs hitches. Open all yr. MC/VISA/Debit. Phone: (954)565-9210.

SEE AD THIS PAGE

(NW) Kozy Kampers RV Park—(Broward) *From jct Hwy 816 (Oakland Park Blvd) & I-95: Go 2 mi N on I-95 (exit 32), then 2-1/2 mi W on Commercial Blvd. Enter on R.* ◊◊◊FACILITIES: 104 sites, typical site width 22 ft, 104 full hkups, (30 & 50 amps), mostly extended stay sites (in winter), 13 pull-thrus, heater not allowed, dump station, laundry, tables, patios. ◊RECREATION: rec room/area, shuffleboard court, planned activities. Pets welcome, breed restrict, quantity restrict. No tents. Open all yr. Planned group activites winter only. Big rigs welcome. Internet friendly. Rate in 2007 $35-45 for 2 persons. Member ARVC, FLARVC. Phone: (954)731-8570.

(S) North Coast RV Park & Marina—(Broward) *From Jct Hwy 816 (Oakland Park Blvd) & I-95: Go 7-3/4 mi S on I-95 (exit 23), then 1/4 mi W on Hwy 818 (Griffin Rd), then 1/4 mi N on Anglers Ave. Enter on R.* ◊◊◊◊FACILITIES: 35 sites, typical site width 35 ft, accepts full hkup units only, 35 full hkups, (20, 30 & 50 amps), many extended stay sites (in winter), heater not allowed, dump station, patios. ◊◊RECREATION: pavilion, boating, canoeing, dock, saltwater fishing. Pets welcome, size restrict. No tents. Age restrictions may apply. Open all yr. No restrooms. Big rigs welcome. Phone: (954)983-2083.

Florida has belonged to five different nations: Spain, England, France, the Confederacy and the U.S.A.

FORT LAUDERDALE—Continued

(NW) PARADISE ISLAND—(Broward) *From jct I-95 (exit 31) & Hwy 816 (Oakland Park Blvd): Go 1/2 mi W on Oakland Park Blvd, then 1 block S on NW 21st Ave. Enter on R.*

◊◊◊◊FACILITIES: 232 sites, typical site width 25 ft, 232 full hkups, (20, 30 & 50 amps), some extended stay sites (in winter), 25 pull-thrus, wireless Instant Internet access at site ($), dump station, non-guest dumping $, laundry, RV supplies, ice, tables, patios.

◊◊◊◊RECREATION: rec hall, rec room/area, equipped pavilion, swim pool, golf nearby, 2 shuffleboard courts, planned activities.

Pets welcome, breed restrict, size restrict. Partial handicap access. No tents. Open all yr. Group activities winter only. Big rigs welcome. Internet friendly. Escort to site. Clubs welcome. Rate in 2007 $33-40 for 2 persons. MC/VISA/DISC/AMEX/Debit. Member ARVC, FLARVC. Phone: (800)487-7395. CCUSA discount. FMCA discount.

e-mail: info@paradiserv.com

SEE AD THIS PAGE

(S) YACHT HAVEN PARK & MARINA—(Broward) *From jct Hwy 816 (Oakland Park Blvd) & I-95: Go 5-1/2 mi S on I-95 (exit 25), then 500 feet W on Hwy 84. Enter on R.*

◊◊◊◊FACILITIES: 250 sites, typical site width 35 ft, 250 full hkups, (20, 30 & 50 amps), many extended stay sites (in winter), phone Internet access central location, dump station, non-guest dumping $, laundry, ice, patios, controlled access gate.

◊◊◊◊RECREATION: rec hall, swim pool, whirlpool, boating, dock, saltwater/river fishing, golf nearby, 2 shuffleboard courts, planned activities.

FORT LAUDERDALE—Continued
YACHT HAVEN PARK & MARINA—Continued

Pets welcome, breed restrict, size restrict, quantity restrict. Partial handicap access. No tents. Open all yr. Planned group activities winter only. Big rigs welcome. Internet friendly. Clubs welcome. Rate in 2007 $34-65 for 2 persons. MC/VISA/Debit. Member ARVC, FLARVC. Phone: (954) 583-2322.

e-mail: yhpm@bellsouth.net

SEE AD THIS PAGE

FORT MYERS—D-3

(E) Cypress Woods RV Resort—(Lee) *From jct Hwy 82 & I-75: Go 1-1/2 mi N on I-75 (exit 139), then 1/2 mi E on Luckett Rd. Enter on L.* ◊◊◊◊◊FACILITIES: 423 sites, typical site width 46 ft, accepts full hkup units only, 423 full hkups, (20, 30 & 50 amps), laundry, patios. ◊◊◊◊◊RECREATION: rec hall, rec room/area, pavilion, 2 swim pools, boating, no motors, canoeing, lake fishing, 8 shuffleboard courts, planned

Cypress Woods RV Resort—Continued on next page

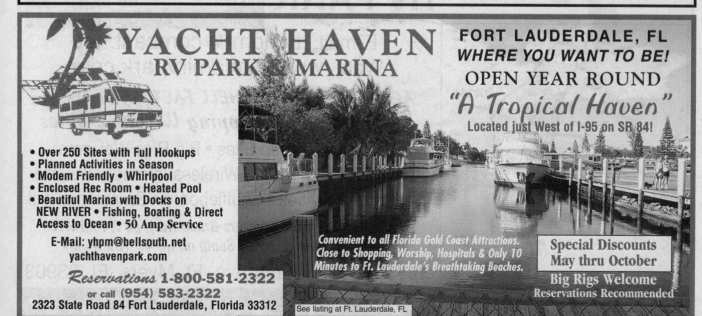

FORT MYERS—Continued
Cypress Woods RV Resort—Continued

activities, tennis, horseshoes. Pets welcome. Partial handicap access. No tents. Open all yr. Big rigs welcome. Rate in 2007 $60-75 for 2 persons. Member ARVC, FLARVC. Phone: (888)CW WOODS. FMCA discount.

IMPERIAL BONITA ESTATES RV RESORT —*From Fort Myers: Go 22 mi S on I-75 (exit 116), then 1/2 mi W on Bonita Beach Rd, then 1/4 mi N on Imperial St, then 2 blocks E on Dean St. Enter on L.*

WELCOME

SEE PRIMARY LISTING AT BONITA SPRINGS, FL AND AD BONITA SPRINGS PAGE 95

(N) Labonte's Garden RV Park (RV SPACES) —(Lee) *From jct Hwy 82 & I-75: Go 6 mi N on I-75 (exit 143), then 5-1/4 mi W on Hwy 78 (Ashore Rd), then 1-1/2 mi N on Business 41, then 1/2 mi E on Laurel Dr, then 200 yards N on Garden St. Enter on R.* FACILITIES: 31 sites, typical site width 20 ft, 31 full hkups, (20, 30 & 50 amps), mostly extended stay sites (in winter), laundry, tables, patios. RECREATION: rec hall, shuffleboard court, planned activities, horseshoes. Pets welcome, size restrict. No tents. Open all yr. Rate in 2007 $25-35 for 2 persons. Phone: (239)989-3072.

LEE COUNTY VISITOR & CONVENTION —Open all yr. Phone: (239)338-3500.

WELCOME

SEE AD DISCOVER SECTION PAGE 41

(NE) Orange Grove Mobile Home & RV Park (RV SPACES)—(Lee) *From jct Hwy 82 & I-75: Go 1-3/4 mi N on I-75 (exit 139), then 1 mi W on Luckett Rd, then 1 mi N on Nuna Ave. Enter on R.* FACILITIES: 72 sites, typical site width 30 ft, accepts full hkup units only, 72 full hkups, (30 & 50 amps), mostly extended stay sites (in winter), laundry, tables, patios. RECREATION: rec hall, swim pool, 2 shuffleboard courts, planned activities, horseshoes. Pets welcome, breed restrict. Partial handicap access. No tents. Open all yr. Planned activities during winter only. Big rigs welcome. Internet friendly. Rate in 2007 $45 for 2 persons. Phone: (239) 694-5534.

Florida State Flower: Orange Blossom

FORT MYERS—Continued

(NE) PARK MODEL CITY & RV SALES— *From jct Hwy 82 & I-75: Go 5-1/2 mi N on I-75 (exit 143), then 1-3/4 mi E on Hwy 78 (Bayshore Rd). Enter on R.* SALES: travel trailers, park trailers, pre-owned unit sales. SERVICES: LP gas by weight/by meter, RV storage. Open all yr. Phone: (800)848-1652.

WELCOME

e-mail: camping@upriver.com

SEE AD PAGE 118

Florida is the only state that has 2 rivers both with the same name. There is a Withlacoochee in north central Florida (Madison County) and a Withlacoochee in central Florida (Polk County).

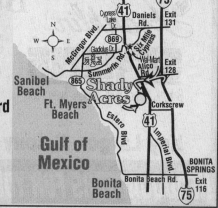

UPRIVER RV RESORT

An Adult Community

• Day - Week - Month - Season •

On the Caloosahatchee River

BOAT RAMP & DOCK

Super Rally Facilities

17021 Upriver Dr.
No. Fort Myers, FL 33917

- Heated Pool • Tennis • Shuffleboard • Planned Activities • Wi-Fi Available
- Horseshoes • Park Residents Non-Regulation Golf • Boat Ramp
- Boat Storage • Waterfront Sites Available with Docks
- Modem Friendly • All Full Hookups • 30/50 amps • FREE Cable TV
- Clean Grassy Sites with Cement Pads • Paved Roads
- EZ on EZ off I-75 Exit #143 (Hwy 78 East 1-3/4 Mi.)

100' LONG PAVED CONCRETE/PATIOS SUPER SITES

7000 Sq. Ft. Rec Hall & Recreational Complex

10 min. to Shopping -

Convenient to SW Florida Attractions & Florida's Beaches

Email address: **camping@upriver.com**

Visit Our WebSite: **www.upriver.com**

See listing at Fort Myers, FL

• Family Reunions • Week-end Getaway • New Spa

FOR GOOD FISHING & BOATING

Canal Water Lots Now Available *"While They Last"*

Come see our beautiful park on the Caloosahatchee River

We Deliver Anywhere

For Your Best Deals Around

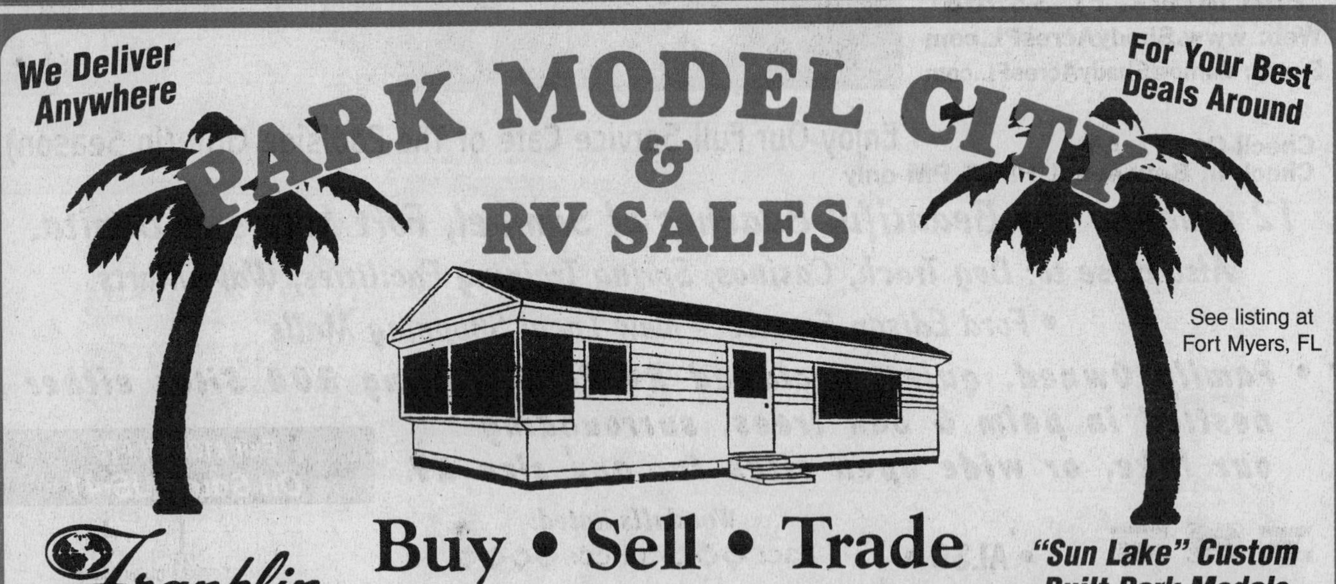

See listing at Fort Myers, FL

SKYLINE

BRINGING AMERICA HOME, BRINGING AMERICA FUN

Buy • Sell • Trade

North Fort Meyers, FL 33917

239-731-2818

or 239-994-0181

"Sun Lake" Custom Built Park Models

Chariot EAGLE

Key Largo - Colony Double Wides • Nomad Trailer • Park Trailer

HEADQUARTERS FOR YOUR BEST DEAL ON SINGLE/DOUBLEWIDE PARK UNITS

WOODSMOKE CAMPING RESORT

Fort Myers Naples

YES! Everyone from 8 to 80 comes to WOODSMOKE, near Fort Myers in Southwest Florida, because we offer the most beautiful campsites...AND, the friendliest people. In the center of the great gulf beaches, fishing, golf, Sanibel Island, Professional Ice Hockey, Outlet Malls, Edison Home and many other area attractions. Great Restaurants Nearby! Only 4 mi from I-75 (Exit 123).

WHITE SANDY BEACHES NEARBY

• 300 Wooded Campsites with Full Hookups • 75' Paved Pull-Thrus • Paved Roads • 4 Clean Bathhouses • Large A/C Rec Hall • Fishing Lake • Giant Heated Pool • Whirlpool • Nature Trail Boardwalk • Very Easy In & Out • GREAT ACTIVITIES

New Large Paved Concrete Pull-Thru Sites 50 Amp
BIG RIGS WELCOME!

BEAUTIFUL WOODED SEASONAL SITES AVAILABLE
Write or Call For Special Seasonal Rates!

We Love Seniors!

AAA

Outside 239 Area

Call 1-800-231-5053
or Local (239) 267-3456

WebSite: woodsmokecampingresort.com
E-Mail Address: woodsmok@aol.com

WOODSMOKE CAMPING RESORT 19551 US Highway 41 S., Ft. Myers, FL 33908

On US 41 South

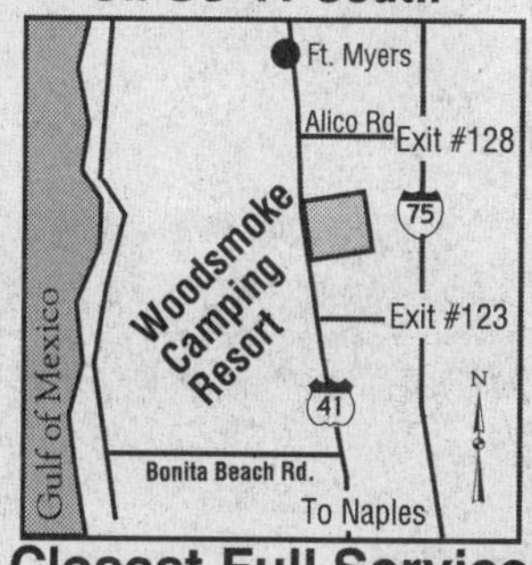

Closest Full Service RV Resort to I-75 (exit 123)

See listing at Fort Myers, FL

Florida State Bird: Mockingbird

Florida is also knows as the Peninsula State

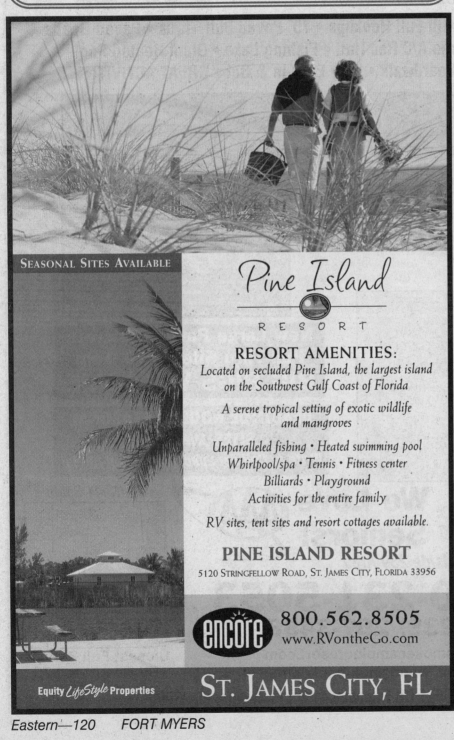

FORT MYERS—Continued

(S) PIONEER VILLAGE RV RESORT (Encore)—(Lee) *From jct Hwy 82 & I-75: Go 6 mi N on I-75 (exit 143), then 1 mi W on Hwy 78 (Bayshore Rd), then 500 feet S on Samville Rd. Enter on L.*

◊◊◊◊FACILITIES: 500 sites, 500 full hkups, (30 & 50 amps), mostly extended stay sites (in winter), wireless Instant Internet access at site ($), tenting, RV/park trailer rentals, RV storage, dump station, laundry, tables, patios.

◊◊◊◊RECREATION: rec hall, pavilion, swim pool, whirlpool, golf nearby, bsktball, 12 shuffleboard courts, planned activities, tennis, horseshoes, v-ball.

Pets welcome, breed restrict. Partial handicap access. Open all yr. Internet friendly. Escort to site. Clubs welcome. Rate in 2007 $35-40 for 2 persons. MC/VISA/DISC/AMEX. Member ARVC, FLARVC. Phone: (877)897-2757.

e-mail: info@rvonthego.com

SEE AD FORT MYERS BEACH PAGE 123

WELCOME

(NW) RAINTREE RV RESORT—(Lee) *From jct Hwy 82 & I-75: Go 6 mi N on I-75 (exit 143), then 6-1/4 mi W on Hwy 78 (Bayshore Rd), then 4-1/2 mi N on US 41. Enter on R.*

◊◊◊◊◊FACILITIES: 340 sites, typical site width 34 ft, 326 full hkups, 14 W&E, (20, 30 & 50 amps), many extended stay sites (in winter), 22 pull-thrus, heater not allowed, cable TV, wireless Instant Internet access at site, dump station, non-guest dumping $, laundry, ice, tables, patios, controlled access gate.

◊◊◊◊◊RECREATION: rec hall, rec room/area, swim pool, whirlpool, pond fishing, putting green, golf nearby, 8 shuffleboard courts, planned activities, horseshoes, local tours.

Pets welcome, breed restrict, size restrict, quantity restrict. Partial handicap access. No tents. Age restrictions may apply. Open all yr. Planned activities during winter only. Big rigs welcome. Internet friendly. Escort to site. MC/VISA. Member ARVC, FLARVC. Phone: (800)628-6095.

e-mail: jacquesc500@hotmail.com

SEE AD NEXT PAGE

WELCOME

(NE) RIVERBEND MOTORCOACH RESORT (CAMP RESORT)—(Hendry) *From jct Hwy 82 & I-75: Go 3 mi N on I-75 (exit 141), then 17 mi E on Hwy 80. Enter on L.*

FACILITIES: 315 sites, typical site width 50 ft, accepts full hkup units only, 315 full hkups, (30 & 50 amps), cable TV, wireless Instant Internet access at site, dump station, laundry, RV supplies, ice, patios, controlled access gate.

RECREATION: rec hall, rec room/area, equipped pavilion, swim pool, river/pond swimming, whirlpool, boating, canoeing, kayaking, ramp, dock, 2 pontoon rentals, river/pond fishing, golf nearby, bsktball, 4 shuffleboard courts, planned activities, tennis, horseshoes, hiking trails, v-ball, local tours.

Pets welcome, quantity restrict. Partial handicap access. No tents. Open all yr. Planned group. Big rigs welcome. Internet friendly. Escort to site. Clubs welcome. Rate in 2007 $32-85 for 2 persons. MC/VISA/Debit. Member ARVC, FLARVC. Phone: (863)674-0085.

e-mail: info@riverbendflorida.com

SEE AD PAGE 116

WELCOME

RIVERSIDE RV RESORT & CAMPGROUND—*From Fort Myers: Go 31 mi N on I-75 (exit 170), then 4-1/2 mi NE on Hwy 769. Enter on R.*

SEE PRIMARY LISTING AT PORT CHARLOTTE AND AD PORT CHARLOTTE PAGE 162

WELCOME

(S) SHADY ACRES RV TRAVEL PARK—(Lee) *From jct Hwy 82 & I-75: Go 10 mi S on I-75 (exit 128), then 1 mi W on Alico Rd, then 2-1/4 mi S on US 41 (Tamiami Trail), then 1/2 mi W on Santa Maria Dr. Enter on L.*

A VERY ACTIVE FAMILY OWNED PARK
Relax by the heated pool, enjoy a burger, hot dog, a Philly or more at the Tiki Hut or eat breakfast & dinner in our cafe. Quiet sites either nestled in Palm & Oak Trees, around the lake or large open spaces for any size RV.

◊◊◊◊FACILITIES: 307 sites, typical site width 33 ft, 299 full hkups, 8 W&E, (20, 30 & 50 amps), many extended stay sites (in winter), 2 pull-thrus,

SHADY ACRES RV TRAVEL PARK—Continued on next page

FORT MYERS—Continued
SHADY ACRES RV TRAVEL PARK—Continued

heater not allowed, wireless Internet access central location, RV/park trailer rentals, RV storage, dump station, non-guest dumping $, laundry, ltd groceries, RV supplies, LP gas by weight/by meter, ice, tables, patios.

◊◊◊◊RECREATION: rec hall, rec room/area, pavilion, swim pool, golf nearby, playground, 2 shuffleboard courts, planned activities, horseshoes.

Pets welcome, breed restrict, size restrict, quantity restrict. Partial handicap access. Open all yr. Group activities winter only. Big rigs welcome. Internet friendly. Escort to site. Clubs welcome. Rate in 2007 $30-36 for 2 persons. MC/VISA/DISC/AMEX/Debit. Member ARVC, FLARVC. Phone: (888)634-4080. CCUSA discount.

e-mail: camp@shadyacresfl.com

SEE AD PAGE 117

(NW) SUNSEEKER'S RV PARK—(Lee) *From jct Hwy 82 & I-75: Go 6 mi N on I-75 (exit 143), the 6-1/4 mi W on Hwy 78 (Bayshore Rd), then 5 mi N on US 41. Enter on L.*

◊◊◊FACILITIES: 239 sites, 35 ft max RV length, 224 full hkups, 15 W&E, (20 & 30 amps), mostly extended stay sites (in winter), 8 pull-thrus, phone Internet access central location, tenting, RV/park trailer rentals, dump station, laundry, patios, controlled access gate.

◊◊◊RECREATION: rec hall, rec room/area, swim pool, whirlpool, golf nearby, 5 shuffleboard courts, planned activities.

Pets welcome, breed restrict. Age restrictions may apply. Open all yr. Group activities in winter only. Internet friendly. Escort to site. Rate in 2007 $20-30 for 2 persons. Member ARVC, FLARVC. Phone: (239)731-1303.

e-mail: sunseekrs@aol.com

SEE AD PAGE 120

(N) Swan Lake Village Manufactured Homes & RV Resort—(Lee) *From jct Hwy 82 & I-75: Go 6 mi N on I-75 (exit 143), then 5-1/2 mi W on Hwy 78 (Bayshore Rd), then 3/4 mi N on Business 41/Hwy 739. Enter on R.* ◊◊◊FACILITIES: 104 sites, typical site width 22 ft, 104 full hkups, (30 amps), some extended stay sites (in winter), heater not allowed, laundry, tables, patios. ◊◊◊RECREATION: rec hall, rec room/area, pavilion, swim pool, lake fishing, 8 shuffleboard courts, planned activities, horseshoes. Pets welcome. Partial handicap access. No tents. Age restrictions may apply. Open all yr. Internet friendly. Rate in 2007 $18-28 for 2 persons. Member ARVC, FLARVC. Phone: (239)995-3397.

(NW) TAMIAMI RV PARK—(Lee) *From jct Hwy 82 & I-75: Go 6 mi N on I-75 (exit 143), then 6-1/4 mi W on Hwy 78 (Bayshore Rd), then 2 mi N on US 41. Enter on L.*

TAMIAMI RV PK-HOME AWAY FROM HOME

The longer you stay the less you pay! WiFi is available as well as many fun activities all season long! Meet great people and make lasting friendships. Full hookups 30-50 amp. Close to shopping and restaurants!

◊◊◊◊FACILITIES: 245 sites, typical site width 27 ft, 245 full hkups, (30 & 50 amps), some extended stay sites (in winter), wireless Instant Internet access at site ($), RV storage, dump station, non-guest dumping $, laundry, ice, tables, patios.

◊◊◊RECREATION: rec hall, rec room/area, swim pool, golf nearby, 4 shuffleboard courts, planned activities, horseshoes.

Pets welcome, breed restrict, quantity restrict. Partial handicap access. No tents. Open all yr. Planned group activities in winter only. Internet friendly. Escort to site. Clubs welcome. Rate in 2007 $20-30 for 2 persons. MC/VISA/DISC/Debit. Member ARVC, FLARVC. Phone: (239)995-7747.

e-mail: tvmgmt@comcast.net

SEE AD PAGE 116

(E) THE GLADES RV, GOLF & MARINA RESORT—(Hendry) *From Fort Myers: Go 38 mi E on Hwy 80. Enter on L.*

◊◊◊◊FACILITIES: 109 sites, typical site width 35 ft, 109 full hkups, (30 & 50 amps), many extended stay sites (in winter), 4 pull-thrus, wireless Instant Internet access at site, tenting, cabins, RV storage, dump station, non-guest dumping $, laundry, tables, patios.

◊◊◊◊RECREATION: rec hall, rec room/area, swim pool, boating, canoeing, kayaking, ramp,

FORT MYERS—Continued
THE GLADES RV, GOLF & MARINA RESORT—Continued

dock, river/pond fishing, golf nearby, 4 shuffleboard courts, planned activities, horseshoes, sports field, hiking trails.

Pets welcome, breed restrict. Partial handicap access. Open all yr. Big rigs welcome. Internet friendly. Escort to site. Clubs welcome. Rate in 2007 $30 for 2 persons. MC/VISA/DISC/AMEX/Debit. Member ARVC, FLARVC. Phone: (863)902-7034.

e-mail: info@thegladesresort.com

SEE PRIMARY LISTING AT LA BELLE AND AD TRAVEL SECTION PAGE 81

(S) THE GROVES RV RESORT—(Lee) *From jct Hwy 82 & I-75: Go 7 mi S on I-75 (exit 131), then 2-1/2 mi W on Daniels Rd, then 8-1/4 mi W on Hwy 865 (Gladiolus Dr), then 2 mi W on Hwy 867 (McGregor Blvd), then 1/2 mi N on John Morris Rd. Enter on R.*

◊◊◊◊FACILITIES: 287 sites, typical site width 32 ft, 287 full hkups, (30 & 50 amps), many extended stay sites (in winter), 35 pull-thrus, cable TV ($), wireless Instant Internet access at site ($), tenting, dump station, non-guest dumping $, laundry, tables, patios.

◊◊◊◊RECREATION: rec hall, rec room/area, swim pool, golf nearby, 4 shuffleboard courts, planned activities, horseshoes.

Pets welcome, breed restrict. Partial handicap access. Open all yr. Church services & group activities winter only. Internet friendly. Escort to site. Clubs welcome. MC/VISA/DISC/Debit. Member ARVC, FLARVC. Phone: (239)466-4300. CCUSA discount.

e-mail: sunresv@aol.com

SEE AD TRAVEL SECTION PAGE 73

(NW) THE SHELL FACTORY & NATURE PARK—*From jct Hwy 82 & I-75: Go 6 mi N on I-75 (exit 143), then 6-1/4 mi W on Hwy 78 (Bayshore Rd), then 2 mi N on US 41. Enter on R.* The Shell Factory has a collection of common & rare seashells, sponges, coral, fossils & sea life specimens with 18 acres of shopping displays dining & entertainment. The Nature Park features a petting farm & the Day of the Dinosaur Park & much more. Open all yr. MC/VISA/DISC/AMEX. Phone: (800) 282-5805.

e-mail: questions@shellfactory.com

SEE AD TRAVEL SECTION PAGE 76

(NE) UPRIVER RV RESORT—(Lee) *From jct Hwy 82 & I-75: Go 5-1/2 mi N on I-75 (exit 143), then 1-3/4 mi E on Hwy 78 (Bayshore Rd). Enter on R.*

◊◊◊◊FACILITIES: 350 sites, typical site width 35 ft, 350 full hkups, (20, 30 & 50 amps), some extended stay sites (in winter), 60 pull-thrus, cable TV, wireless Instant Internet access at site ($), phone Internet access central location, laundry, RV supplies, LP gas by weight/by meter, tables, patios.

◊◊◊◊◊RECREATION: rec hall, rec room/area, pavilion, swim pool, boating, canoeing, kayaking, ramp, dock, saltwater/river fishing, putting green, golf nearby, bsktball, 6 shuffleboard courts, planned activities, tennis, horseshoes, local tours.

Pets welcome, breed restrict, size restrict, quantity restrict. Partial handicap access. No tents. Age restrictions may apply. Open all yr. Group activities during winter season only. Big rigs welcome. Internet friendly. Escort to site. Clubs welcome. MC/

Florida became a state on March 3, 1845.

FORT MYERS—Continued
UPRIVER RV RESORT—Continued

VISA/DISC/Debit. Member ARVC, FLARVC. Phone: (800)848-1652. CCUSA discount. FCRV 10% discount. FMCA discount.

e-mail: camping@upriver.com

SEE AD PAGE 118

(S) WOODSMOKE CAMPING RESORT—(Lee) *From jct Hwy 82 & I-75: Go 14 mi S on I-75 (exit 123), then 2 mi W on Corkscrew Rd, then 2 mi N on US 41. Enter on R.*

◊◊◊◊FACILITIES: 300 sites, typical site width 35 ft, 300 full hkups, (20, 30 & 50 amps), many extended stay sites (in winter), 16 pull-thrus, heater not allowed, wireless Instant Internet access at site, wireless Internet access central location, RV/park trailer rentals, RV storage, dump station, non-guest dumping $, laundry, RV supplies, tables, patios.

◊◊◊◊◊RECREATION: rec hall, rec room/area, equipped pavilion, swim pool, whirlpool, boating, no motors, canoeing, kayaking, lake fishing, golf nearby, bsktball, playground, 5 shuffleboard courts, planned activities, horseshoes, hiking trails.

Pets welcome, breed restrict, size restrict, quantity restrict. Partial handicap access. No tents. Open all yr. Planned group activities winter only. Big rigs welcome. Internet friendly. Clubs welcome. MC/VISA/DISC/Debit. Member ARVC, FLARVC. Phone: (800)231-5053. FCRV 10% discount. FMCA discount.

e-mail: woodsmok@aol.com

SEE AD PAGE 119

FORT MYERS BEACH—E-3

(N) FORT MYERS BEACH RV RESORT—(Lee) *From jct Hwy 82 & I-75: Go 6 mi S on I-75 (exit 131), then 5-3/4 mi W on Daniels Rd, then 5-3/4 mi SW on Summerlin Rd, then 3/4 mi N on San Carlos. Enter on R.*

◊◊◊FACILITIES: 306 sites, typical site width 27 ft, 306 full hkups, (30 & 50 amps), some extended stay sites (in winter), 216 pull-thrus, cable TV, wireless Instant Internet access at site ($), tenting, RV/park trailer rentals, laundry, RV supplies, LP gas by weight/by meter, ice, tables, patios.

◊◊◊◊RECREATION: rec hall, rec room/area, swim pool, whirlpool, golf nearby, 6 shuffleboard courts, planned activities.

Pets welcome. Partial handicap access. Open all yr. Group activities winter only. Internet friendly. Escort to site. Clubs welcome. Rate in 2007 $50 for 2 persons. MC/VISA/DISC/AMEX/Debit. Member ARVC, FLARVC. Phone: (800)553-7484.

SEE AD PAGE 123

(N) GULF AIR TRAVEL RESORT—(Lee) *From Hwy 82 & I-75: Go 6 mi S on I-75 (exit 131), then 5-3/4 mi W on Daniels Rd, then 5-3/4 mi S on Summerlin Rd, then 1/4 mi S on San Carlos Blvd. Enter on L.*

◊◊◊FACILITIES: 246 sites, typical site width 30 ft, 38 ft max RV length, 246 full hkups, (30 & 50 amps), many extended stay sites (in winter), cable TV, wireless Instant Internet access at site ($), phone Internet access central location, RV/park trailer rentals, dump station, non-guest dumping $, laundry, LP gas by weight/by meter, tables, patios.

◊◊◊RECREATION: rec hall, swim pool, golf nearby, 2 shuffleboard courts, planned activities, horseshoes.

GULF AIR TRAVEL RESORT—Continued on next page

Pets welcome. No tents. Open all yr. Internet friendly. Escort to site. Clubs welcome. MC/VISA/DISC/AMEX/Debit. Member ARVC, FLARVC. Phone: (877)937-2757.

e-mail: info@RVontheGo.com

SEE AD NEXT PAGE

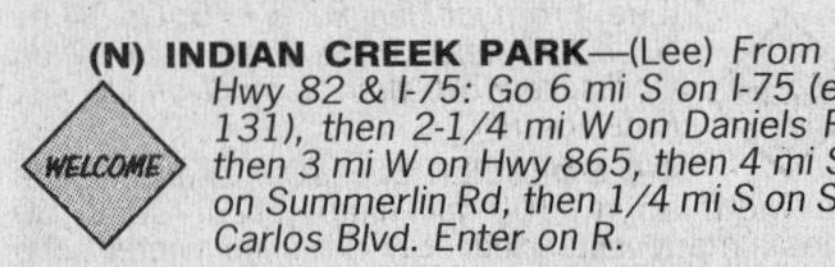

(N) INDIAN CREEK PARK—(Lee) *From jct Hwy 82 & I-75: Go 6 mi S on I-75 (exit 131), then 2-1/4 mi W on Daniels Rd, then 3 mi W on Hwy 865, then 4 mi SW on Summerlin Rd, then 1/4 mi S on San Carlos Blvd. Enter on R.*

◊◊◊◊◊FACILITIES: 1148 sites, typical site width 30 ft, accepts full hkup units only, 1148 full hkups, (30 & 50 amps), mostly extended stay sites (in winter), 159 pull-thrus, cable TV, wireless Instant Internet access at site ($), cable Internet access central location, RV storage, laundry, ice, tables, patios.

◊◊◊◊◊RECREATION: rec hall, rec room/area, 3 swim pools, whirlpool, lake fishing, golf nearby, 16 shuffleboard courts, planned activities, tennis, horseshoes, v-ball, local tours.

Pets welcome, breed restrict, quantity restrict. Partial handicap access. No tents. Age restrictions may apply. Open all yr. Church services winter only. Internet friendly. Escort to site. Clubs welcome. MC/VISA/DISC/Debit. Member ARVC, FLARVC. Phone: (239)466-6060. CCUSA discount.

e-mail: sunresv@aol.com

SEE AD TRAVEL SECTION PAGE 73

(E) Red Coconut RV Resort on the Beach—(Lee) *From jct Hwy 82 & I-75: Go 6 mi S on I-75 (exit 131), then 5-1/2 mi W on Daniels Rd/Cypress Lake Dr (Hwy 869), then 5-3/4 mi SW on Summerlin Rd/Hwy 869, then 4 mi S on San Carlos Blvd, then 1 mi SE on Estero Blvd. Enter on L.* ◊◊◊FACILITIES: 250 sites, typical site width 28 ft, 250 full hkups, (20, 30 & 50 amps), many extended stay sites (in winter), 13 pull-thrus, tenting, dump station, non-guest dumping $, laundry, LP gas by weight/by meter, ice, tables, patios. ◊◊◊RECREATION: rec hall, saltwater swimming, boating, canoeing, saltwater fishing, 5 shuffleboard courts, planned activities, v-ball. Pets welcome, breed restrict, quantity restrict. Partial handicap access. Open all yr. Group activities winter only. Internet friendly. Rate in 2007 $35-75 for 2 persons. Member ARVC, FLARVC. Phone: (239)463-7200.

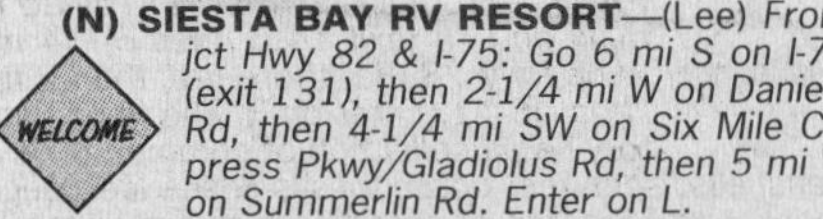

(N) SAN CARLOS RV PARK & ISLANDS—(Lee) *From jct Hwy 82 & I-75: Go 6 mi S on I-75 (exit 131), then 2-1/2 mi W on Daniels Rd, then 4-1/4 mi SW on Six Mile Cypress Pkwy/Gladiolus Rd, then 4 mi SW on Summerlin Rd, then 2 mi S on San Carlos Blvd. Enter on L.*

WATERFRONT HIGH SPEED WIRELESS
Waterfront camping. Great wildlife. Planned activities in winter season. Extremely friendly. Family owned & operated. Loyal staff. Customer satisfaction is our main goal! Wireless high speed Internet throughout park.

◊◊◊◊FACILITIES: 131 sites, typical site width 25 ft, 122 full hkups, 9 W&E, (20, 30 & 50 amps), some extended stay sites (in winter), heater not allowed, wireless Instant Internet access at site, tenting, dump station, laundry, RV supplies, ice, tables, patios.

◊◊◊◊RECREATION: rec hall, swim pool, whirlpool, boating, canoeing, kayaking, ramp, dock, 3 kayak rentals, saltwater fishing, fishing supplies, golf nearby, 2 shuffleboard courts, planned activities, horseshoes.

Pets welcome, breed restrict, quantity restrict. Partial handicap access. Open all yr. Internet friendly. Escort to site. Clubs welcome. Rate in 2007 $35-58 for 2 persons. MC/VISA/DISC/Debit. Member ARVC, FLARVC. Phone: (800)525-7275.

e-mail: mail@sancarlosrv.com

SEE AD THIS PAGE

(N) SIESTA BAY RV RESORT—(Lee) *From jct Hwy 82 & I-75: Go 6 mi S on I-75 (exit 131), then 2-1/4 mi W on Daniels Rd, then 4-1/4 mi SW on Six Mile Cypress Pkwy/Gladiolus Rd, then 5 mi W on Summerlin Rd. Enter on L.*

◊◊◊◊◊FACILITIES: 846 sites, typical site width 37 ft, accepts full hkup units only, 846 full hkups, (30 & 50 amps), mostly extended stay sites (in winter), wireless Instant Internet access at site ($), RV storage, laundry, ice, patios.

◊◊◊◊◊RECREATION: rec hall, rec room/area, pavilion, 2 swim pools, whirlpool, lake fishing, golf nearby, bsktball, 12 shuffleboard courts, planned activities, tennis, horseshoes, v-ball, local tours.

No pets. Partial handicap access. No tents. Age restrictions may apply. Open all yr. Big rigs welcome. Internet friendly. Escort to site. Clubs welcome. Rate in 2007 $21-48 for 2 persons. MC/VISA/DISC/Debit. Member ARVC, FLARVC. Phone: (239)466-8988. CCUSA discount.

e-mail: sunresv@aol.com

SEE AD TRAVEL SECTION PAGE 73

FORT PIERCE—D-5

✲ **(N) AL'S MOTOR HOME & TRAILER SALES**—*From jct Hwy 70 & I-95 (exit 129): Go 8-1/2 mi N on I-95 (exit 138), then 6 mi E on Indrio Rd, then 500 feet S on US 1. Enter on R.*

AL'S MOTORS AT ALSMOTORHOMES.COM
Motorhomes to pop-ups - all at big savings. New and used RVs. Thousands of parts & accessories. Smart RV shoppers start here. See how fun driving an RV can be. SALES - SERVICE - PARTS.

SALES: travel trailers, 5th wheels, motor homes, mini-motor homes, micro-mini motor homes, pre-owned unit sales. SERVICES: full-time mech, engine/chassis repair, RV appliance repair, body work/collision repair, bus. hrs emerg rd svc, mobile RV svc, sells parts/accessories, installs hitches. Open all yr. MC/VISA/DISC/AMEX/Debit. Phone: (888)399-9970. FMCA discount.

e-mail: sales@alsmotorhomes.fdn.com

SEE AD PAGE 124

(S) Easy Livin' RV Park (RV SPACES)—(St. Lucie) *From jct I-95 (exit 129) & Hwy 70: Go 4 mi E on Hwy 70, then 2-1/2 mi S on US 1. Enter on R. FACILITIES:*

Easy Livin' RV Park—Continued on next page

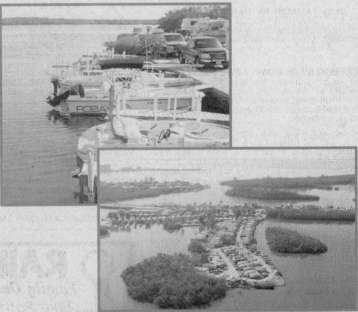

FORT PIERCE—Continued
Easy Livin' RV Park—Continued

50 sites, typical site width 30 ft, 50 full hkups, (30 & 50 amps), mostly extended stay sites (in winter), laundry, patios. Pets welcome. Partial handicap access. No tents. Open all yr. Big rigs welcome. Phone: (772)461-0800.

(NW) ROAD RUNNER TRAVEL RESORT —(St. Lucie) *From jct I-95 (exit 129) & Hwy 70: Go 3/4 mi W on Hwy 70, then 5 mi N on Hwy 713, then 1-1/4 mi E on CR 608. Enter on L.*

NESTLED IN A BEAUTIFUL FL HAMMOCK
A resort with RV Sites, Furnished Villas, & 3-Hole Golf Course. Within 3 miles of Atlantic-enjoy fishing, swimmiing, & boating. Easy drive to Cape Canaveral, Disney World, & Lion Country Safari. www.roadrunnertravelresort.com.

♦♦♦♦FACILITIES: 452 sites, typical site width 30 ft, 452 full hkups, (20, 30 & 50 amps), many extended stay sites (in winter), 10 pull-thrus, phone Internet access central location, tenting, cabins, RV storage, dump station, non-guest dumping $, laundry, full svc store, RV supplies, LP gas by weight/by meter, ice, tables, patios, controlled access gate.

♦♦♦♦♦RECREATION: rec hall, rec room/area, equipped pavilion, swim pool, pond fishing, golf nearby, bsktball, 4 shuffleboard courts, planned activities, tennis, horseshoes, v-ball.

Pets welcome, breed restrict. Partial handicap access. Open all yr. Big rigs welcome. Internet friendly. Clubs welcome. Rate in 2007 $38-42 for 2 persons. MC/VISA/DISC/Debit. ATM. Member ARVC, FLARVC. Phone: (800)833-7108. FMCA discount.

e-mail: rvroadrun@aol.com

SEE AD NEXT PAGE

FORT PIERCE—Continued on next page

Woodall's Tip #28... Woodall's ratings depend on the quality and quantity of our criteria elements. The more W's a park has generally reflects the presence of more development at the park, and usually more facilities.

FORT PIERCE—Continued

(SW) TREASURE COAST RV PARK—(St. Lucie) *From jct I-95 (exit 129) & Hwy 70: Go 1 block W on Hwy 70, then 1/4 mi N on Peters Rd./Crossroads Pkwy. Enter on R.*

WELCOME

◇◇◇◇◇FACILITIES: 165 sites, typical site width 28 ft, 165 full hkups, (20, 30 & 50 amps), some extended stay sites (in winter), 4 pull-thrus, cable TV, wireless Instant Internet access at site, dump station, non-guest dumping $, laundry, tables, patios, controlled access gate.

◇◇◇RECREATION: rec hall, swim pool, whirlpool, pond fishing, golf nearby, planned activities, horseshoes.

Pets welcome, quantity restrict. Partial handicap access. No tents. Open all yr. Big rigs welcome. Internet friendly. Escort to site. Clubs welcome. Rate in 2007 $35-49 per vehicle. MC/VISA/DISC/AMEX/Debit. Member ARVC, FLARVC. Phone: (772)468-2099. FCRV 10% discount. FMCA discount.

e-mail: treasurecoastrv@mail.com

SEE AD PAGE 123

FORT WALTON BEACH—F-2

See listings at Destin, Navarre & Santa Rosa Beach

✲ **(W) OPEN ROAD RV CENTER**—*From jct Hwy 189 & US 98: Go 3 mi W on US 98. Enter on L.* SALES: pre-owned unit sales. SERVICES: full-time mech, engine/chassis repair, RV appliance repair, body work/collision repair, sells parts/accessories, installs hitches. Open all yr. MC/VISA/DISC. Phone: (850)244-4020.

WELCOME

e-mail: ken@openroad.gccoxmail.com

SEE AD THIS PAGE

(NW) PLAYGROUND RV PARK—(Okaloosa) *From jct US-98 & Hwy-189: Go 4-1/2 mi N on Hwy-189. Enter on R.*

WELCOME

◇◇◇FACILITIES: 64 sites, typical site width 20 ft, 64 full hkups, (20, 30 & 50 amps), mostly extended stay sites, 9 pull-thrus, cable TV, wireless Instant Internet access at site, wireless Internet access central location, dump station, non-guest dumping $, laundry, RV supplies, tables, patios.

Pets welcome. Partial handicap access. No tents. Open all yr. Big rigs welcome. Internet friendly. Rate in 2007 $35-45 for 2 persons. MC/VISA. Member ARVC, FLARVC. Phone: (850)862-3513.

e-mail: camp@pgrv.gccoxmail.com

SEE AD THIS PAGE

FOUNTAIN—F-3

(N) PINE LAKE RV PARK—(Bay) *From I-10 (exit 130): Go 15 mi S on US 231. Enter on L.*

WELCOME

◇◇◇FACILITIES: 135 sites, typical site width 30 ft, 65 full hkups, 20 W&E, (30 & 50 amps), 50 amps ($), 50 no hkups, some extended stay sites, 75 pull-thrus, wireless Instant Internet access at site, phone Internet access central location, tenting, RV/park trailer rentals, cabins, RV storage, dump station, non-guest dumping $, laundry, RV supplies, LP gas by weight/by meter, tables.

◇◇◇RECREATION: rec hall, equipped pavilion, lake fishing, golf nearby, bsktball, planned activities (wkends only), horseshoes, hiking trails.

Pets welcome, breed restrict. Open all yr. Big rigs welcome. Internet friendly. Escort to site. Clubs welcome. Rate in 2007 $25-30 for 2 persons. MC/VISA/DISC/AMEX. Member ARVC, FLARVC. Phone: (850)722-1401.

e-mail: fun@pinelakerv.com

Reserve Online at Woodalls.com

SEE AD PANAMA CITY PAGE 157

FROSTPROOF—C-4

(NW) CAMP INN RESORT—(Polk) *From jct Hwy-630 & US-27: Go 3 mi N on US-27. Enter on L.*

WELCOME

◇◇◇◇FACILITIES: 796 sites, typical site width 26 ft, 763 full hkups, 33 W&E, (20, 30 & 50 amps), mostly extended stay sites (in winter), 193 pull-thrus, cable TV ($), phone/cable on-site Internet access (needs activ), wireless Internet access central location, tenting, RV/park trailer rentals, RV storage, dump station, non-guest dumping $, laundry, LP gas by weight/by meter, ice, tables, patios.

◇◇◇◇RECREATION: rec hall, rec room/area, 2 swim pools, whirlpool, pond fishing, golf nearby, bsktball, 8 shuffleboard courts, planned activities, horseshoes, v-ball, local tours.

Pets welcome, breed restrict, quantity restrict. Partial handicap access. Open all yr. Planned activities winter only. Big rigs welcome. Rate in 2007 $25 for 2 persons. MC/VISA/DISC. Phone: (800) 331-8030.

FROSTPROOF—Continued
CAMP INN RESORT—Continued

e-mail: campinn@newbury-management.com

SEE AD TRAVEL SECTION PAGE 73

(NW) Lakemont Ridge Home & RV Park—(Polk) *From jct US 27 US 98 & Hwy 630 (Fort Meade Rd): Go 1/2 mi E on Hwy 630, then continue 1/2 mi on Fort Meade Rd. Enter on R.* ◇◇◇FACILITIES: 100 sites, 100 full hkups, (30 & 50 amps), dump station, laundry, LP gas by weight/by meter, tables, patios. ◇◇◇◇RECREATION: rec hall, swim pool, 5 shuffleboard courts, planned activities, horseshoes. Pets welcome. Partial handicap access. No tents. Open all yr. Planned group activities winter only. Big rigs welcome. Rate in 2007 $40 for 2 persons. Phone: (863)635-4472. CCUSA discount.

(W) Rainbow Resort—(Polk) *From jct US 27 & Hwy 630A: Go 1/2 mi E on Hwy 630A. Enter on L.* ◇◇◇◇◇FACILITIES: 450 sites, typical site width 40 ft, 450 full hkups, (50 amps), 13 pull-thrus, laundry, patios. ◇◇◇◇RECREATION: rec hall, rec room/area, swim pool, pond fishing, 6 shuffleboard courts, planned activities, horseshoes. Pets welcome, size restrict, quantity restrict. Partial handicap access. No tents. Age restrictions may apply. Open all yr. Planned activities in season only. Big rigs welcome. Rate in 2007 $33 for 2 persons. Phone: (863)635-7541.

FRUITLAND PARK—B-3

(N) LAKE GRIFFIN STATE PARK—(Lake) *From jct US-27-441 & Hwy-446A: Go 2 mi S on US-27-441.* FACILITIES: 40 sites, 40 W&E, (50 amps), tenting, dump station, laundry, fire rings, grills, wood. RECREATION: pavilion, boating, canoeing, ramp, dock, 4 canoe rentals, lake fishing, playground, hiking trails. Pets welcome. Partial handicap access. Open all yr. Phone: (352)360-6760.

GAINESVILLE—B-3

✲ **(NW) J. D. SANDERS RV CENTER**—*From jct I-75 (exit 399) & Hwy 441: Go 6 mi E & SE on Hwy 441. Enter on R.* SALES: travel trailers, park trailers, 5th wheels, van campers, motor homes, fold-down camping trailers, pre-owned unit sales. SERVICES: full-time mech, RV appliance repair, body work/collision repair, LP gas by weight/by meter, RV storage, sells parts/accessories, installs hitches. Open all yr. MC/VISA/DISC/AMEX. Phone: (800)541-6439.

WELCOME

e-mail: jdsrv@worldnet.att.net

SEE AD THIS PAGE

GAINESVILLE—Continued on next page

GAINESVILLE—Continued

(S) PAYNES PRAIRIE PRESERVE STATE PARK—(Alachua) *From jct Hwy 121 & US 441: Go 10 mi S on US 441.* FACILITIES: 52 sites, 37 W&E, 15 E, tenting, dump station, portable dump, grills, wood. RECREATION: pavilion, boating, electric motors only, canoeing, ramp, canoe rentals, lake fishing, hiking trails. Rec open to public. No pets. Partial handicap access. Open all yr. Phone: (352)466-3397.

TRAVELERS CAMPGROUND—*From jct Hwy 26 & I-75: Go 12 mi N on I-75 to exit 399 (Old 78), then 200 feet E on US 441, then left at Waffle House, then 1 mi N on E Frontage Rd.*

SEE PRIMARY LISTING AT ALACHUA AND AD THIS PAGE

GEORGETOWN—B-4

(SE) Georgetown Marina, Lodge & RV Park—(Putnam) *From jct US 17 & CR 309: Go 21-3/4 mi S on CR 309. Enter on R.* ◇◇FACILITIES: 32 sites, typical site width 20 ft, 32 full hkups, (30 & 50 amps), many extended stay sites (in winter), 8 pull-thrus, heater not allowed, dump station, non-guest dumping $, laundry, ice, patios. ◇◇RECREATION: boating, ramp, dock, river fishing. Pets welcome. No tents. Open all yr. Big rigs welcome. Rate in 2007 $30 for 2 persons. Phone: (386)467-2002.

(W) Scruftys Riverwood RV Park—(Putnam) *From Hwy 17 & CR 308: Go 8 mi W on CR 308, then 2 -1/2 mi S on CR 309. Enter on R.* ◇◇◇FACILITIES: 36 sites, typical site width 30 ft, 36 full hkups, (30 & 50 amps), 2 pull-thrus, tenting, dump station, non-guest dumping $, laundry, ice, tables, patios. ◇◇RECREATION: equipped pavilion, boating, canoeing, dock, river fishing, horseshoes. Pets welcome. Partial handicap access. Open all yr. Big rigs welcome. Rate in 2007 $32-70 for 2 persons. Phone: (386)467-7147.

GRANT—C-5

(N) Orbit RV Park—(Brevard) *From jct I-95 (exit 173) & Hwy 514: Go 4 mi E on Hwy 514, then 3-1/2 mi S on US 1. Enter on R.* ◇◇◇◇FACILITIES: 62 sites, typical site width 30 ft, 42 full hkups, 20 W&E, (20, 30 & 50 amps), 11 pull-thrus, dump station, laundry, tables, patios. ◇◇◇RECREATION: rec hall, river swimming, boating, saltwater fishing, planned activities, horseshoes. Pets welcome, breed restrict, size restrict, quantity restrict. No tents. Age restrictions may apply. Open all yr. Big rigs welcome. Rate in 2007 $30-34 for 2 persons. Phone: (321)953-2555. CCUSA discount. FMCA discount.

GRAYTON BEACH—F-2

(E) GRAYTON BEACH STATE PARK—(Walton) *From jct US-98 & US-331: Go SW on Hwy-30A.* FACILITIES: 37 sites, 37 W&E, (30 amps), tenting, dump station, grills. RECREATION: pavilion, boating, canoeing, ramp, saltwater fishing, hiking trails. Pets welcome. Partial handicap access. Open all yr. Phone: (850)231-4210.

HAINES CITY—C-4

(W) Central Park—(Polk) *From jct I-4 (exit 55) & US 27: Go 8 mi S on US 27, then 1/4 mi W on Commerce Ave. Enter on L.* ◇◇◇◇FACILITIES: 351 sites, typical site width 30 ft, 351 full hkups, (30 & 50 amps), 50 amps ($), mostly extended stay sites (in winter), 26 pull-thrus, heater not allowed, tenting, dump station, laundry, LP gas by weight, tables, patios, fire rings. ◇◇◇RECREATION: rec hall, swim pool, pond fishing, 8 shuffleboard courts, planned activities, horseshoes. Pets welcome, breed restrict, size restrict. Open all yr. Most activities winter only. Big rigs welcome. Internet friendly. Rate in 2007 $26-29.50 for 2 persons. Phone: (863)422-5322.

Central Park II—(Polk) *From jct I-4 (exit 55) & US 27: Go 8 mi S on US 27, then 1/4 mi W on Commerce Ave. Enter on R.* ◇◇◇◇FACILITIES: 128 sites, typical site width 35 ft, 128 full hkups, (30 amps), many extended stay sites (in winter), heater not allowed, dump station, laundry, LP gas by weight, tables. ◇◇◇RECREATION: rec hall, swim pool, pond fishing, 4 shuffleboard courts, planned activities. Pets welcome, breed restrict, size restrict, quantity restrict. No tents. Age restrictions may apply. Open all yr. Seasonal sites available with minium stay of four months. Internet friendly. Phone: (863)421-2622.

(W) Oak Harbor RV Resort—(Polk) *From jct US-27 & US-17/92: Go 4-1/2 mi W on US-17/92, then 1 block N on Experiment Station Rd, then 1 mi E on Old Haines City/Lake Alford Rd, then 2-1/2 mi N & E on Lake Lowery Rd. Enter on R.* ◇◇◇FACILITIES: 191 sites, typical site width 28 ft, 186 full hkups, 5 W&E, (20, 30 & 50 amps), mostly extended stay sites (in winter), tenting, dump station, laundry, tables, patios. ◇◇◇◇RECREATION: rec hall, rec room/area, lake swimming, boating, ramp, dock, lake fishing, 4 shuffleboard courts, planned activities, horseshoes. Pets welcome, size restrict, quantity restrict. Open Oct 1 thru May 1. Planned group activities & church services winter only. Big rigs welcome. Rate in 2007 $25 per vehicle. Phone: (863)956-1341.

(S) Paradise Island RV Resort—(Polk) *From jct US 17 & 92 & US 27: Go 3 mi S on US 27. Enter on R.* ◇◇FACILITIES: 183 sites, 181 full hkups, 2 W&E, (30 & 50 amps), mostly extended stay sites (in winter), laundry, tables, patios. ◇◇◇RECREATION: rec room/area, swim pool, boating, ramp, dock, lake fishing, 2 shuffleboard courts, planned activities, horseshoes. Pets welcome, breed restrict, size restrict. No tents. Open all yr. Rate in 2007 $28 for 2 persons. Phone: (863)439-1350.

HALLANDALE—E-5

(W) HOLIDAY PARK—(Broward) *From jct I-95 (exit 18) & Hwy 858 (Hallandale Bch Blvd): Go 1/4 mi W on W Hallandale Beach Blvd. Enter on L.*

◇◇◇◇FACILITIES: 123 sites, typical site width 24 ft, 123 full hkups, (30 & 50 amps), many extended stay sites (in winter), 113 pull-thrus, dump station, non-guest dumping $, laundry, patios.

◇◇◇RECREATION: rec hall, swim pool, golf nearby, 2 shuffleboard courts, planned activities.

Pets welcome, breed restrict, size restrict. No tents. Open all yr. Planned group activities winter only. Children on limited basis only. Escort to site. Clubs welcome. Rate in 2007 $35-45 for 2 persons. MC/VISA/Debit. Member ARVC, FLARVC. Phone: (954)981-4414.

e-mail: holidayparks@aol.com

SEE AD THIS PAGE

HIGH SPRINGS—B-3

(W) Ginnie Springs Outdoors LLC—(Gilchrist) *From jct I-75 (exit 399) & US 441: Go 4 1/2 mi W on US 441, then 1/2 mi S on US 41, then 6 1/2 mi SW on CR 340, then 2 mi N on access road (NE 60th St). Enter at end.* ◇◇◇FACILITIES: 290 sites, typical site width 40 ft, 90 W&E, (20, 30 & 50 amps), 200 no hkups, 10 pull-thrus, tenting, dump station, laundry, ltd groceries, ice, tables, grills, wood. ◇◇◇RECREATION: equipped pavilion, river swimming, boating, canoeing, ramp, 40 canoe rentals, river fishing, playground, hiking trails, v-ball. Rec open to public. No pets. Open all yr. Rate in 2007 $18-25 for 1 persons. Member ARVC, FLARVC. Phone: (386)454-7188.

(N) O'LENO STATE PARK/RIVER RISE—(Columbia) *From jct I-10 & US-441-41: Go 20 mi S on US-441-41.* FACILITIES: 55 sites, 55 W&E, (30 & 50 amps), tenting, dump station. RECREATION: river swimming, boating, canoeing, dock, 4 canoe rentals, hiking trails. No pets. Partial handicap access. Open all yr. Phone: (386)454-1853.

HILLIARD—A-3

(N) CANOE COUNTRY OUTPOST—*From jct CR 108 & US 301/US 1: Go 6-1/2 mi N on US 301/US 1, then 3/4 mi E on Lake Hampton Rd, then 1/2 mi N on Scott Landing. Enter at end.* Canoe & kayak 165 miles of the St. Mary's River along the Fla/Ga stateline leading to the Okefenokee National Refuge. Sandbars for fishing, swimming and picnicking. Open all yr. MC/VISA/DISC. Phone: (866)845-4443.

e-mail: info@canoecountryoutpost.com

SEE AD THIS PAGE

(N) ST. MARY'S RIVER FISH CAMP & CAMPGROUND—(Nassau) *From jct CR 108 & US 301/US 1: Go 6-1/2 mi N on US 301/US 1; then 3/4 mi E on Lake Hampton Rd, then 1/2 mi N on Scotts Landing Rd. Enter at end.*

◇◇FACILITIES: 51 sites, typical site width 25 ft, 49 full hkups, 2 W&E, (20, 30 & 50 amps), some extended stay sites, 9 pull-thrus, tenting, RV/park trailer rentals, dump station, non-guest dumping $, laundry, ltd groceries, RV supplies, ice, tables, patios, fire rings, grills, wood.

◇◇◇RECREATION: river swimming, boating, canoeing, kayaking, ramp, 45 canoe/10 kayak/5 pedal boat/7 motorboat rentals, float trips, river

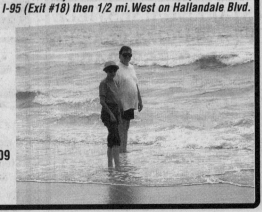

ST. MARY'S RIVER FISH CAMP & CAMPGROUND—Continued on next page

HILLIARD—Continued
ST. MARY'S RIVER FISH CAMP & CAMPGROUND—Continued

fishing, fishing supplies, bsktball, 5 bike rentals, planned activities (wkends only), horseshoes, hiking trails, v-ball.

Pets welcome, size restrict. Partial handicap access. Open all yr. Big rigs welcome. Escort to site. Clubs welcome. Rate in 2007 $25 for 2 persons. MC/VISA/DISC. Phone: (866)845-4443. FMCA discount.

e-mail: info@stmarysriverfishcamp.com

SEE AD PAGE 126

HOBE SOUND—D-5

(S) JONATHAN DICKINSON STATE PARK—(Martin) *From I-95 (Hobe Sound exit): Go E to US 1, then S on US 1.* FACILITIES: 135 sites, 35 ft max RV length, 135 W&E, tenting, dump station, ltd groceries, ice, fire rings, grills. RECREATION: river swimming, boating, canoeing, ramp, 75 canoe rentals, saltwater/lake/river fishing, playground, hiking trails. Rec open to public. Pets welcome. Open all yr. Phone: (772)546-2771.

HOLIDAY—C-3

(N) **HARBERSON RV**—*At jct Alt 19 & US 19: Go 1/2 mi N on US 19. Enter on R.*

WELCOME

SALES: travel trailers, 5th wheels, van campers, motor homes, mini-motor homes, micro-mini motor homes, pre-owned unit sales. SERVICES: full-time mech, engine/chassis repair, RV appliance repair, body work/collision repair, LP gas by weight/by meter, sells parts/accessories, installs hitches. Open all yr. Phone: (727)937-6176.

e-mail: harswan@aol.com

SEE AD THIS PAGE AND AD CLEARWATER PAGE 101

HOLLYWOOD—E-5

(W) **Lake Trinity Estates**—(Broward) *From jct I-95 (exit 19) & Hwy 824 (Pembroke Rd): Go 1/2 mi W on Pembroke Rd. Enter on L.* ◆◆◆◆FACILITIES: 255 sites, typical site width 20 ft, 255 full hkups, (30 & 50 amps), 50 amps ($), many extended stay sites (in winter), dump station, non-guest dumping $, laundry, patios. ◆◆◆RECREATION: 2 swim pools, lake fishing, 2 shuffleboard courts, planned activities. No pets. Partial handicap access. No tents. Open all yr. Internet friendly. Rate in 2007 $39-43 for 2 persons. Member ARVC, FLARVC. Phone: (954)962-7400.

HOLLYWOOD—Continued

(NW) TOPEEKEEGEE YUGNEE (T.Y.) Park (Broward County Park)—(Broward) *From jct I-95 & Sheridan St: Go 1/2 mi W on Sheridan St to N Park Rd. Enter on R.*

WELCOME

FACILITIES: 60 sites, 60 full hkups, (30 & 50 amps), 60 pull-thrus, cable TV, wireless Internet access central location, tenting, laundry, ice, tables, patios, grills.

RECREATION: 8 rowboat/24 pedal boat rentals, lake fishing, bsktball, playground, tennis, horseshoes, sports field, hiking trails, v-ball. Rec open to public.

Pets welcome. Partial handicap access. Open all yr. Internet friendly. Clubs welcome. MC/VISA/DISC. Phone: (954)985-1980.

e-mail: typark@broward.org

SEE AD TRAVEL SECTION PAGE 74

HOLT—E-1

(W) BLACKWATER RIVER STATE PARK—(Santa Rosa) *From US 90: Go 3 mi N.* FACILITIES: 30 sites, 30 W&E, tenting, dump station, grills. RECREATION: river swimming, boating, canoeing, river fishing, hiking trails. Pets welcome. Partial handicap access. Open all yr. Phone: (850)983-5363.

(S) **Eagle's Landing RV Park**—(Okaloosa) *From jct I-10 (exit 45) & Hwy 189: Go 1/4 mi N on Hwy 189. (Log Lake Rd). Enter on L.* ◆◆◆FACILITIES: 60 sites, 60 full hkups, (30 & 50 amps), 50 amps ($), mostly extended stay sites, 60 pull-thrus, dump station, non-guest dumping $, laundry, tables. ◆◆RECREATION: rec hall, pavilion, playground, horseshoes. Pets welcome. No tents. Open all yr. Big rigs welcome. Internet friendly. Rate in 2007 $19-21 for 2 persons. Phone: (850)537-9657.

(S) RIVER'S EDGE RV CAMPGROUND—(Okaloosa) *From jct I-10 (exit 45) & Hwy 189: Go 1-3/4 mi S on Hwy 189. Enter on L.*

WELCOME

◆◆◆FACILITIES: 104 sites, typical site width 45 ft, 83 full hkups, 11 W&E, (30 & 50 amps), 10 no hkups, some extended stay sites, 67 pull-thrus, phone Internet access central location, RV storage, dump station, non-guest dumping $, laundry, ltd groceries, RV supplies, LP gas by weight/by meter, ice, tables, wood.

HOLT—Continued
RIVER'S EDGE RV CAMPGROUND—Continued

◆◆◆◆RECREATION: rec hall, pavilion, river swimming, boating, canoeing, kayaking, ramp, river fishing, golf nearby, bsktball, playground, planned activities, horseshoes, sports field, hiking trails, local tours.

Pets welcome. Partial handicap access. No tents. Open all yr. Planned group activities in winter. Big rigs welcome. Internet friendly. Clubs welcome. Rate in 2007 $20-22 per family. Member ARVC, FLARVC. Phone: (850)537-2267. FMCA discount.

e-mail: riversedgerv@woolcom.net

SEE AD PENSACOLA PAGE 160

HOMESTEAD—E-5

(SW) EVERGLADES NATIONAL PARK (Long Pine Key) —(Miami-Dade) *From jct US 1 & Palm Dr/SW 344th St: Follow signs for Hwy 9336 (Everglades NP). Campground is 5 mi W from park entrance. Enter on L.* FACILITIES: 108 sites, 35 ft max RV length, 108 no hkups, tenting, dump station, portable dump, fire rings, grills. RECREATION: pond fishing, hiking trails. Rec open to public. Open all yr. 14 days max. stay Dec 1-Mar 31. No showers. Phone: (305)242-7700.

HOMESTEAD—Continued on next page

Woodall's Tip #3... The listings for public campgrounds are based upon information supplied by the appropriate government agency.

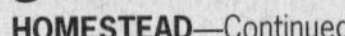

HOMESTEAD—Continued

(S) GOLDCOASTER MOBILE HOME & RV RESORT—(Dade) *From jct US 1 & Hwy 9336 (Palm Dr): Go 1 mi W on Palm Dr, then 1 block S on SW 187th Ave. Enter on R.*

◊◊◊◊◊FACILITIES: 150 sites, typical site width 40 ft, 150 full hkups, (30 & 50 amps), mostly extended stay sites (in winter), wireless Instant Internet access at site ($), phone Internet access central location, laundry, ice, tables, patios, controlled access gate.

◊◊◊◊◊RECREATION: rec hall, rec room/area, pavilion, swim pool, whirlpool, golf nearby, bsktball, playground, 6 shuffleboard courts, planned activities, horseshoes.

Pets welcome, breed restrict, quantity restrict. Partial handicap access. No tents. Open all yr. Big rigs welcome. Internet friendly. Clubs welcome. Rate in 2007 $30-44 for 2 persons. MC/VISA/DISC/Debit. Phone: (800)828-6992. CCUSA discount.

e-mail: sunresv@aol.com

SEE AD TRAVEL SECTION PAGE 73

(NE) K & K TRAILER SUPPLIES—*From jct Hwy 9336 (Palm Dr) & US 1: Go 8-1/4 mi N on US 1. Enter on R.* SERVICES: full-time mech, RV appliance repair, LP gas by weight/by meter, sells parts/accessories, installs hitches. Open all yr. MC/VISA/DISC/AMEX/Debit. Phone: (800)416-9041. FCRV 10% discount. FMCA discount.

SEE AD MIAMI PAGE 141

(NE) PINE ISLE MOBILE HOME PARK (RV SPACES)—(Dade) *From jct Hwy 9336 (Palm Dr) & US 1: Go 4 mi N on US 1, then 2 mi E on 288 St, then 500 ft N on 132 Ave. Enter on L.*

FACILITIES: 257 sites, typical site width 50 ft, 257 full hkups, (30 & 50 amps), mostly extended stay sites (in winter), 20 pull-thrus, wireless Internet access central location, laundry, patios.

RECREATION: rec hall, pavilion, swim pool, golf nearby, 3 shuffleboard courts, planned activities, horseshoes.

Pets welcome, quantity restrict. No tents. Age restrictions may apply. Open all yr. Planned activities in winter only. Big rigs welcome. Internet friendly. Clubs welcome. Rate in 2007 $20-25 for 2 persons. MC/VISA. Phone: (305)248-0783.

SEE AD PAGE 127

HOMESTEAD—Continued

(E) THE BOARDWALK—(Dade) *From jct Hwy 9336 (Palm Dr) & US 1: Go 2 mi N on US 1, then 1 block E on 328th St, then 200 feet N on 6th Ave. Enter on L.*

◊◊◊◊FACILITIES: 160 sites, typical site width 40 ft, 160 full hkups, (30 & 50 amps), 50 amps ($), mostly extended stay sites (in winter), cable Internet access central location, RV storage, laundry, tables, patios, controlled access gate.

◊◊◊◊RECREATION: rec hall, rec room/area, swim pool, golf nearby, playground, 5 shuffleboard courts, planned activities, horseshoes, v-ball.

Pets welcome. Partial handicap access. No tents. Open all yr. Big rigs welcome. Internet friendly. Clubs welcome. Rate in 2007 $40-70 for 2 persons. MC/VISA/Debit. Member ARVC, FLARVC. Phone: (305)248-2487.

e-mail: mirna.roger@newbymanagement.com

SEE AD MIAMI PAGE 141

HOMOSASSA—C-3

See listings at Chassahowitzka & Homosassa Springs

COMO TRUCK & RV SALES & SERVICE—*From jct Hwy 490A & US 19: Go 3/4 mi N on US 19. Enter on R.* SALES: travel trailers, park trailers, 5th wheels, van campers, motor homes, mini-motor homes, fold-down camping trailers, pre-owned unit sales. SERVICES: Open all yr. MC/VISA/DISC/AMEX. Phone: (866)344-1411.

e-mail: rcomo@tampabay.rr.com

SEE AD TRAVEL SECTION PAGE 73

(S) Covered Wagon Campground—(Citrus) *From jct Hwy-490 & US-19: Go 3 mi S on US-19. Enter on L.* ◊◊◊FACILITIES: 47 sites, typical site width 25 ft, 47 full hkups, (30 amps), many extended stay sites (in winter), 30 pull-thrus, dump station, tables, patios. ◊◊RECREATION: rec room/area, 2 shuffleboard courts, planned activities, horseshoes. Pets welcome. No tents. Open all yr. Planned activities winter only. Phone: (352)628-4669.

(NE) NATURE'S RESORT & MARINA—(Citrus) *From jct US 19 & Halls River Rd: Go 2 mi W on Halls River Rd. Enter on R.*

◊◊◊◊FACILITIES: 310 sites, 310 full hkups, (20, 30 & 50 amps), many extended stay sites (in winter), cable TV, phone on-site Internet access (needs activ), phone Internet access central location, tenting, cabins, RV storage, dump station, non-guest dumping $, laundry, groceries, RV supplies, LP gas by weight/by meter, gas, marine gas, ice, tables, patios, wood, controlled access gate.

◊◊◊◊RECREATION: rec hall, rec room/area, pavilion, swim pool, boating, canoeing, ramp, dock, 6 pontoon/6 canoe/4 kayak rentals, saltwater/river fishing, fishing supplies, golf nearby, bsktball, playground, 2 shuffleboard courts, planned activities, horseshoes, v-ball.

Pets welcome, quantity restrict. Partial handicap access. Open all yr. Big rigs welcome. Clubs welcome. Rate in 2007 $30-40 per family. MC/VISA. Phone: (800)301-7880.

SEE AD THIS PAGE

HOMOSASSA SPRINGS—C-3

(S) HOMOSASSA SPRINGS WILDLIFE STATE PARK—*From jct Hwy 490A & US 19 : Go 1/4 mi S on US 19. Enter on R.* Showcase for native Florida wildlife in their natural setting. Floating underwater observatory to view manatees and thousands of fish. Daily manatee, alligator programs and wildlife encounters. New whooping crane exhibit, bear cubs and reptile house. Open all yr. MC/VISA. Phone: (352)628-2311.

SEE AD NEXT PAGE

(S) TURTLE CREEK CAMPGROUND—(Citrus) *From jct US 19 & Hwy 490A: Go 1/2 mi W on 490A, then 1 mi SW on Fish Bowl Dr. Enter on L.*

◊◊◊FACILITIES: 225 sites, typical site width 30 ft, 225 full hkups, (30 & 50 amps), 50 amps ($), many extended stay sites (in winter), 32 pull-thrus, cable TV ($), wireless Instant Internet access at site, cable on-site Internet access (needs activ), wireless Internet access central location, tenting, cabins, dump station, laundry, RV supplies, LP gas by weight/by meter, ice, tables, patios.

◊◊◊RECREATION: rec hall, pavilion, swim pool, stream fishing, golf nearby, 2 shuffleboard courts, planned activities, horseshoes.

Pets welcome, breed restrict, quantity restrict. Partial handicap access. Open all yr. Planned acitivities during season only. Big rigs welcome. Internet friendly. Rate in 2007 $18-27 for 2 persons. MC/VISA/DISC. Phone: (800)471-3722.

e-mail: turtlecreek@gowebco.com

SEE AD HOMOSASSA THIS PAGE

HUDSON—C-3

(E) 7 Oaks RV Park & Sales—(Pasco) *From jct US 19 & Bolton Ave: Go 3/4 mi E on Bolton Ave. Enter on L.* ◊◊◊◊FACILITIES: 295 sites, 295 full hkups, (30 & 50 amps), 10 pull-thrus, dump station, laundry, tables, patios. ◊◊◊RECREATION: rec hall, swim pool, 3 shuffleboard courts, planned activities, horseshoes. Rec open to public. Pets welcome, size restrict, quantity restrict. No tents. Age restrictions may apply. Open all yr. Big rigs welcome. Rate in 2007 $20-26 for 2 persons. Phone: (727)862-3016.

HUDSON—Continued on next page

HUDSON—Continued

(NE) BARRINGTON HILLS RV RESORT—(Pasco) *From jct Hwy 52 & US 19: Go 3-1/2 mi N on US 19, then 1-1/2 mi E on New York Ave. Enter on R.*

◇◇◇◇FACILITIES: 100 sites, 100 full hkups, (30 & 50 amps), wireless Instant Internet access at site ($), phone/cable on-site Internet access (needs activ), wireless Internet access central location, RV/park trailer rentals, laundry, tables, patios.

◇◇◇RECREATION: rec hall, rec room/area, swim pool, golf nearby, 6 shuffleboard courts, planned activities, horseshoes.

Pets welcome, breed restrict, size restrict, quantity restrict. Partial handicap access. No tents. Age restrictions may apply. Open all yr. Planned activities winter only. Big rigs welcome. Internet friendly. Rate in 2007 $26-28 per vehicle. MC/VISA/DISC/AMEX. Phone: (877)287-2757.

e-mail: nhcflbh@gte.net

SEE AD TAMPA PAGE 176

(NE) THREE LAKES RV RESORT (Morgan RV Resorts)—(Pasco) *From jct Hwy 52 & US 19: Go 5 mi N on US 19, then 1 mi E on Denton Ave. Enter on R.*

◇◇◇◇FACILITIES: 310 sites, 310 full hkups, (20, 30 & 50 amps), wireless Instant Internet access at site, phone/cable on-site Internet access (needs activ), wireless Internet access central location, RV storage, laundry, patios, controlled access gate.

◇◇◇RECREATION: rec hall, rec room/area, swim pool, golf nearby, 4 shuffleboard courts, planned activities, horseshoes.

Pets welcome, breed restrict, quantity restrict. Partial handicap access. No tents. Age restrictions may apply. Open all yr. Planned activities in season

HUDSON—Continued
THREE LAKES RV RESORT (Morgan RV Resorts)—Continued

only. Big rigs welcome. Internet friendly. Clubs welcome. Rate in 2007 $35 for 2 persons. MC/VISA/DISC. Phone: (727)869-8511.

e-mail: rv@threelakesresort.com

SEE AD TAMPA PAGE 173 AND AD TRAVEL SECTION PAGE 73

(N) WINTER PARADISE TRAVEL RESORT—(Pasco) *From jct Hwy-52 & US-19: Go 5 mi N on US-19. Enter on R.*

◇◇◇FACILITIES: 302 sites, typical site width 30 ft, 35 ft max RV length, 302 full hkups, (20, 30 & 50 amps), many extended stay sites (in winter), phone/cable on-site Internet access (needs activ), phone Internet access central location, tenting, RV storage, dump station, non-guest dumping $, laundry, tables, patios.

◇◇◇RECREATION: rec hall, rec room/area, swim pool, golf nearby, 6 shuffleboard courts, planned activities, horseshoes.

Pets welcome. Open all yr. Planned activities & church services winter only. Clubs welcome. Rate in 2007 $25 for 2 persons. MC/VISA/DISC. Member ARVC, FLARVC. Phone: (800)328-0775.

e-mail: winterparadise@newbury-management.com

SEE AD TRAVEL SECTION PAGE 78

INVERNESS—C-3

✽ **COMO TRUCK & RV SALES & SERVICE**—*From north jct US 41 & Hwy 44: Go 1/2 mi W on Hwy 44. Enter on L.* SALES: travel trailers, park trailers, 5th wheels, van campers, motor homes, mini-motor homes, fold-down camping trailers, pre-owned unit sales. SERVICES: full-time mech, engine/chassis repair, RV appliance repair, body work/collision repair, mobile RV svc, sells parts/accessories. Open all yr. MC/VISA/DISC/AMEX. Phone: (866)344-1411.

e-mail: rcomo@tampabay.rr.com

SEE AD TRAVEL SECTION PAGE 73

RIVERSIDE LODGE—(Citrus) *From north jct Hwy 41 & Hwy 44: Go 7 mi E on Hwy 44. Enter on L.*

◇◇◇◇FACILITIES: 24 sites, typical site width 20 ft, 16 full hkups, 8 W&E, (30 & 50 amps), some extended stay sites, phone Internet access central location, tenting, cabins, laundry, tables, patios.

◇◇◇RECREATION: rec hall, boating, canoeing, kayaking, ramp, dock, rowboat/2 canoe/2 motorboat rentals, river fishing, golf nearby, planned activities.

Pets welcome ($), quantity restrict. Open all yr. Big rigs welcome. Internet friendly. Rate in 2007 $35-40 for 2 persons. MC/VISA. Member ARVC, FLARVC. Phone: (888)404-8382.

e-mail: info@riversidelodgerv.com

SEE AD CRYSTAL RIVER PAGE 103

Florida has belonged to five different nations: Spain, England, France, the Confederacy and the U.S.A.

JACKSONVILLE—A-3

COUNTRY OAKS CAMPGROUND & RV PARK—*From north jct I-295 & I-95: Go 19 mi N on I-95 (GA exit 1), then 1/4 mi W on St. Mary's Rd. Enter on L.*

SEE PRIMARY LISTING AT KINGSLAND, GA AND AD THIS PAGE

(N) FLAMINGO LAKE RV RESORT—(Duval) *From jct I-95 & J-295: Go 3 mi S on I-295 (exit 32), then 200 yds N on Hwy 115 (Lem Turner Blvd), then 200 yds SE on Newcomb Rd. Enter on L.*

HOSPITALITY BEGINS AND NEVER ENDS!!
Flamingo Lake RV Resort is Florida's Most Acclaimed Destination and More! Luxurious Amenities. Deluxe, Large Full Hookup Sites, Deluxe Bathhouse, New High-End Mall Nearby. WiFi Available. 800-782-4323. WWW.FLAMINGOLAKE.COM

◇◇◇◇◇FACILITIES: 288 sites, typical site width 40 ft, 288 full hkups, (20, 30 & 50 amps), many extended stay sites, 118 pull-thrus, cable TV, wireless Instant Internet access at site ($), phone Internet access central location, RV/park trailer rentals, cabins, dump station, non-guest dumping $, laundry, groceries, RV supplies, LP gas by weight/by meter, ice, tables, patios, controlled access gate.

◇◇◇◇◇RECREATION: rec hall, rec room/area, pavilion, equipped pavilion, swim pool, lake swimming, boating, electric motors only, canoeing, kayaking, dock, lake fishing, fishing supplies, golf nearby, bsktball, playground, planned activities (wkends only), horseshoes, v-ball.

Pets welcome, breed restrict. Partial handicap access. No tents. Open all yr. Big rigs welcome. Internet friendly. Escort to site. Clubs welcome. Rate in 2007 $40-65 for 2 persons. MC/VISA. Member ARVC, FLARVC. Phone: (800)782-4323.

e-mail: customer.service@flamingolake.com

SEE AD PAGE 131

GOLDEN ISLES RV PARK—*From north jct I-295 & I-95: Go 48 mi N on I-95 (exit 29 in GA), then 1/2 mi W on US 17, then 1/4 mi N on Hwy 303. Enter on L.*

SEE PRIMARY LISTING AT BRUNSWICK AND AD BRUNSWICK, GA PAGE 202

(E) HANNA PARK (City Park)—(Duval) *From jct Hwy 10 & Hwy A1A: Go 2-1/4 mi N on Hwy A1A, then 1 mi NE on Mayport Rd/Hwy 101, then 1 block E on Wonderwood Rd. Enter at end.* FACILITIES: 288 sites, typical site width 19 ft, 273 full hkups, 15 W&E, (20, 30 & 50 amps), 53 pull-thrus, tenting, dump station, non-guest dumping $, laundry, ltd groceries, ice, fire rings, grills, wood. RECREATION: rec room/area, pavilion, saltwater swimming, boating, no motors, canoeing, dock, 6 canoe/6 pedal boat rentals, saltwater/lake fishing, playground, shuffleboard court, planned activities (wkends only), sports field, hiking trails, v-ball. Rec open to public. Pets welcome, quantity restrict. Partial handicap access. Open all yr. Sprayground open seasonally, Height limit 54" & under. Big rigs welcome. Member ARVC, FLARVC. Phone: (904)249-4700.

(E) LITTLE TALBOT ISLAND STATE PARK—(Duval) *From jct I-95 & Hwy 105: Go 14 mi E on Hwy 105, then 3 mi N on Hwy A1A.* FACILITIES: 40 sites, 30 ft max RV length, 40 W&E, tenting, dump station. RECREATION: saltwater swimming, boating, canoeing, saltwater fishing, hiking trails. Pets welcome. Open all yr. Phone: (904)251-2320.

JACKSONVILLE—Continued on next page

Little Richard, singer, is from Florida.

See listing at Jacksonville, FL

JACKSONVILLE—Continued

(N) MILITARY PARK (Jacksonville NAS)—(Duval) Off base. *US 95S & US 295N: Go N on US 17.* FACILITIES: 43 sites, 28 full hkups, 9 W&E, 6 no hkups, tenting, grills. RECREATION: Open all yr. For Military Use Only-w/Military ID (Active duty has priority). Phone: (904)542-3227.

(N) **PECAN PARK FLEA & FARMERS MARKET**—*From I-95 (exit 366) & Pecan Park Rd: Go 1/8 mi W on Pecan Park Rd. Enter on L.* North Florida's largest Flea & Farmers Market adjacent to Jacksonville's newest & finest RV Resort, Pecan Park. Open all yr. Open Sat & Sun only.

e-mail: mrkt723@bellsouth.net

SEE AD PAGE 130

(N) **PECAN PARK RV RESORT**—(Duval) *From I-95 (exit 366) and Pecan Park Rd: Go 1/8 mi W on Pecan Park Rd. Enter on L.*

◆◆◆◆◆FACILITIES: 183 sites, typical site width 40 ft, 183 full hkups, (20, 30 & 50 amps), some extended stay sites, 183 pull-thrus, cable TV, wireless Instant Internet access at site ($), cable Internet access central location, RV storage, dump station, non-guest dumping, laundry, ltd groceries, RV supplies, ice, tables, patios.

◆◆◆RECREATION: rec hall, swim pool, lake fishing, bsktball, horseshoes.

Pets welcome. Partial handicap access. No tents. Open all yr. Big rigs welcome. Internet friendly. Clubs welcome. Rate in 2007 $40 for 2 persons. MC/VISA/DISC/AMEX. Member ARVC, FLARVC. Phone: (888)604-6770. FMCA discount.

e-mail: mrkt723@bellsouth.net

SEE AD PAGE 130

JENNINGS—A-2

(W) **JENNINGS OUTDOOR RESORT CAMPGROUND**—(Hamilton) *From jct I-75 (exit 467) & Hwy 143: Go 500 feet W on Hwy 143. Enter on R.*

◆◆◆◆◆FACILITIES: 102 sites, typical site width 25 ft, 102 full hkups, (30 & 50 amps), 102 pull-thrus, cable TV ($), wireless Internet access central location, tenting, RV storage, laundry, full svc store, RV supplies, LP gas by weight/by meter, ice, tables, patios.

◆◆◆◆RECREATION: rec hall, swim pool, boating, no motors, canoeing, kayaking, canoe/2 pedal boat rentals, lake fishing, fishing supplies, golf nearby, bsktball, playground, 2 shuffleboard courts, horseshoes, sports field.

Pets welcome. Partial handicap access. Open all yr. Big rigs welcome. Internet friendly. Clubs welcome. Rate in 2007 $24.95 for 2 persons. MC/VISA/DISC/AMEX. Member ARVC, FLARVC. Phone: (386)938-3321. FMCA discount.

e-mail: jor@alltel.net

SEE AD THIS PAGE

JENSEN BEACH—D-5

(N) **NETTLES ISLAND** (CAMP RESORT) —(St. Lucie) *From jct Hwy 716 & US 1: Go 2 mi S on US 1, then 3 mi E on Jensen Beach Blvd, then 1/2 mi N on Indian River, then 2 mi E on Hwy 732, then 1-1/2 mi N on A-1-A. Enter on L.*

FACILITIES: 100 sites, typical site width 35 ft, accepts full hkup units only, 100 full hkups, (20, 30 & 50 amps), cable TV, RV/park trailer rentals, laundry, full svc store, LP gas by weight/by meter, marine gas, ice, patios, controlled access gate.

RECREATION: rec hall, rec room/area, coin games, 2 swim pools, saltwater swimming, whirlpool, boating, ramp, dock, saltwater/river fishing, fishing supplies, mini-golf, golf nearby, bsktball, playground, 6 shuffleboard courts, planned activities, tennis, horseshoes, v-ball.

Pets welcome ($), breed restrict, size restrict, quantity restrict. Partial handicap access. No tents. Open all yr. Big rigs welcome. Rate in 2007 $37-64 for 4 persons. MC/VISA/Debit. Member ARVC, FLARVC. Phone: (772)229-1300.

e-mail: info@nettlescoastalrealty.com

SEE AD THIS PAGE

JUNO BEACH—D-5

(N) **JUNO OCEAN WALK RV RESORT** (CAMP RESORT)—(Palm Beach) *From jct Hwy 786 (PGA Blvd) & I-95: Go 3 mi N on I-95 (exit 83), then 4-1/2 mi E on Donald Ross Rd, then 3/4 mi N on US 1, then 1/4 mi W on Juno Ocean Walk. Enter at end.*

WALK TO THE OCEAN!
A vacation retreat in beautiful Palm Beach County. Miles of sandy beaches & St Louis Cardinal Spring Training nearby. Large heated pool with jacuzzi. First rate clubhouse. Free WiFi & Cable TV. Enjoy the carefree FL lifestyle!

FACILITIES: 246 sites, typical site width 30 ft, 246 full hkups, (30 & 50 amps), some extended stay sites, cable TV, wireless Instant Internet access at site, RV/park trailer rentals, RV storage, dump station, non-guest dumping $, laundry, tables, patios.

RECREATION: rec hall, rec room/area, swim pool, whirlpool, golf nearby, playground, 2 shuffleboard courts, planned activities, horseshoes, v-ball.

Pets welcome ($). Partial handicap access. No tents. Open all yr. Big rigs welcome. Internet friendly. Escort to site. Clubs welcome. Rate in 2007 $40-73 for 2 persons. MC/VISA/Debit. Phone: (561)622-7500.

SEE AD THIS PAGE

JUPITER—D-5

(W) **Land Yachts**—*From jct I-95 (exit 87) & Hwy 706 (Indian Town Rd): Go 1-1/4 mi E on Hwy 706, then 1/4 mi S on Maplewood Dr, then 1/4 mi E on Commerce Ln. Enter on R.* Warranty Work. SERVICES: full-time mech, engine/chassis repair, RV appliance repair, body work/collision repair, RV storage, sells parts/accessories, installs hitches. Open all yr. MC/VISA/DISC/AMEX/Debit. Phone: (561)745-0242.

JUPITER—Continued on next page

Home of the Kennedy Space Center

JUPITER—Continued

(W) WEST JUPITER CAMPING RESORT —(Palm Beach) *From jct I-95 (exit 87B) & Hwy 706 (Indiantown Rd): Go 5 mi W on Hwy 706, then 500 ft S on 130th Ave. Enter on R.*

WELCOME

◆◆◆FACILITIES: 84 sites, typical site width 30 ft, 84 full hkups, (15, 30 & 50 amps), 50 amps ($), some extended stay sites (in winter), cable TV ($), wireless Instant Internet access at site ($), RV/park trailer rentals, RV storage, dump station, non-guest dumping $, laundry, full svc store, RV supplies, LP bottle exch, ice, tables, patios, fire rings, wood, controlled access gate.

◆◆◆◆RECREATION: rec room/area, pavilion, swim pool, pond fishing, fishing supplies, golf nearby, bsktball, playground, 2 shuffleboard courts, planned activities, horseshoes, local tours.

Pets welcome, breed restrict. Partial handicap access. No tents. Open all yr. Big rigs welcome. Internet friendly. Clubs welcome. Rate in 2007 $27-45 for 2 persons. MC/VISA/DISC/Debit. Member ARVC, FLARVC. Phone: (888)746-6073. FMCA discount.

e-mail: wjcr@bellsouth.net

SEE AD WEST PALM BEACH PAGE 183

KENANSVILLE—C-4

(W) Lake Marion Paradise Marina & RV Resort (Not Visited)—(Osceola) *From jct US 441 & Hwy 523: Go 3-1/4 mi W on Hwy 523, then 1/2 mi S on Arnold Rd. Enter at end. FACILITIES: 59 sites, typical site width 35 ft, 59 full hkups, (30 & 50 amps), 4 pull-thrus, dump station, laundry, ltd groceries, LP bottle exch, ice, tables, patios, fire rings. RECREATION: rec hall, equipped pavilion, lake swimming, boating, canoeing, motorboat rentals, lake fishing, 2 shuffleboard courts, planned activities, horseshoes. Pets welcome. No tents. Open all yr. Big rigs welcome. Rate in 2007 $32-37 for 4 persons. Member ARVC. Phone: (407)436-1464.*

KEY LARGO—F-5

(N) JOHN PENNEKAMP CORAL REEF STATE PARK —(Monroe) *From jct Hwy 905 & US 1: Go 8 mi S on US 1 to milepost 102.5.* FACILITIES: 47 sites, 30 ft max RV length, 47 W&E, tenting, dump station, ice. RECREATION: saltwater swimming, boating, canoeing, ramp, dock, 10 canoe/10 motorboat rentals, saltwater fishing, hiking trails. Rec open to public. No pets. Partial handicap access. Open all yr. Phone: (800)326-3521.

(NE) KINGS KAMP, RV, TENT & MARINA —(Monroe) *On US 1 at milepost 103-1/2. Enter on R.*

WELCOME

◆◆◆FACILITIES: 60 sites, typical site width 25 ft, 35 ft max RV length, 52 full hkups, 8 W&E, (15, 30 & 50 amps), tenting, cabins, dump station, laundry, tables, patios, grills.

◆◆RECREATION: saltwater swimming, boating, canoeing, kayaking, ramp, dock, saltwater fishing.

Pets welcome, size restrict. Open all yr. Rate in 2007 $40-50 for 2 persons. MC/VISA. Member ARVC, FLARVC. Phone: (305)451-0010.

e-mail: keylargo@kingskamp.com

SEE AD THIS PAGE

KEY WEST—F-4

BIG PINE KEY & FLORIDA'S LOWER KEYS—*From jct US 1 & White St: Go 3 blocks E on White St. Enter on L.* Call for brochures & information on the Florida Keys. Open all yr. Phone: (800)352-5397.

WELCOME

SEE AD DISCOVER SECTION PAGE 42

The 10,000 islands of mangrove trees off the coast of Marco Island and the Everglades are formed from bits of shell, driftwood and seaweed that get trapped in the roots. As the trees mature and topple into the water, more trees take root. New islands are constantly being formed this way, so they are impossible to count. There may be as many as 20,000.

KEY WEST—Continued

(NE) BLUEWATER KEY RV RESORT (CAMP RESORT)—(Monroe) *On US 1 at mile marker 14-1/2. Enter on L.*

WELCOME

LUXURY OCEAN WATERFRONT RESORT
Enjoy paradise in the Florida Keys. Beautifully-landscaped exclusive ownership RV Resort only 10 mi from Key West. Lot rentals on large, private sites avail with Tiki Huts. Heated/cooled pool. Boating & fishing. www.bluewaterkey.com.

FACILITIES: 81 sites, typical site width 35 ft, accepts full hkup units only, 81 full hkups, (30 & 50 amps), some extended stay sites (in winter), cable TV, wireless Instant Internet access at site, laundry, ice, tables, patios, controlled access gate.

RECREATION: rec room/area, pavilion, swim pool, boating, canoeing, kayaking, ramp, dock, saltwater fishing, golf nearby, horseshoes.

Pets welcome, quantity restrict. Partial handicap access. No tents. Open all yr. RV minimum length

BLUEWATER KEY RV RESORT—Continued on next page

Little Richard, singer, is from Florida.

KEY WEST—Continued
BLUEWATER KEY RV RESORT—Continued

26'. Big rigs welcome. Internet friendly. Escort to site. Clubs welcome. MC/VISA/DISC/Debit. Phone: (305)745-2494.

e-mail: bluekeyrv@aol.com

SEE AD PAGE 133

(NE) BOYD'S KEY WEST CAMPGROUND —(Monroe) *From US 1 at milepost 5:Go 1 block S on 3rd St, then 1/4 mi E on Maloney (MacDonald) Ave. Enter on L.*

WELCOME

KEY WEST CAMPING
Our family owned and operated park is surrounded by the enchanting ocean on one side and exciting Key West on the other! Waterfront sites, marina with boat ramp and docks, heated pool, and wonderful tropical weather all year.

◊◊◊◊FACILITIES: 233 sites, typical site width 30 ft, 180 full hkups, 20 W&E, (20, 30 & 50 amps), 33 no hkups, some extended stay sites (in winter), cable TV, wireless Instant Internet access at site, tenting, RV storage, dump station, non-

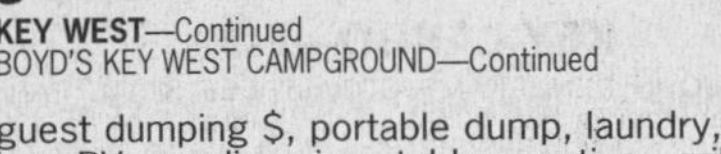

KEY WEST—Continued
BOYD'S KEY WEST CAMPGROUND—Continued

guest dumping $, portable dump, laundry, groceries, RV supplies, ice, tables, patios, grills, controlled access gate.

◊◊◊◊RECREATION: rec room/area, pavilion, equipped pavilion, coin games, swim pool, saltwater swimming, boating, canoeing, kayaking, ramp, dock, saltwater fishing, fishing supplies, golf nearby, planned activities.

Pets welcome, breed restrict. Partial handicap access. Open all yr. Storage available Apr 1 to Dec 1. Big rigs welcome. Internet friendly. Clubs welcome. MC/VISA/Debit. ATM. Member ARVC, FLARVC. Phone: (305)294-1465.

e-mail: info@boydscampground.com

SEE AD PAGE 133

MILITARY PARK (Key West NAS-Sigsbee Park)—(Monroe) *On US 1. On base.* FACILITIES: 70 sites, 70 full hkups, dump station, laundry, LP gas by weight, ice, grills. RECREATION: boating, ramp, canoe/16 motorboat rentals, saltwater fishing, playground, sports field, v-ball. Open all yr. For Military Use Only-w/Military ID Card. Phone: (888)539-7697.

KEYSTONE HEIGHTS—B-3

(NE) MIKE ROESS GOLD HEAD BRANCH STATE PARK —(Clay) *From jct Hwy-21 & Hwy-100: Go 6 mi NE on Hwy-21.* FACILITIES: 74 sites, 30 ft max RV length, 63 W&E, 11 no hkups, tenting, dump station, ice, grills. RECREATION: pavilion, lake swimming, boating, canoeing, ramp, dock, 10 canoe rentals, lake fishing, hiking trails. Pets welcome. Open all yr. Phone: (352)473-4701.

KISSIMMEE—C-4

(NE) EAST LAKE FISH CAMP—(Osceola) *From jct US 192 & Boggy Creek Rd: Go 6 mi NE on Boggy Creek Rd, then continue 1-1/2 SE on Boggy Creek Rd, the 1/2 mi S on Fish Camp Rd. Enter on L.*

◊◊FACILITIES: 220 sites, 220 full hkups, (30 & 50 amps), 25 pull-thrus, cable TV, phone/cable on-site Internet access (needs activ), wireless Internet access central location, tenting, cabins, dump station, laundry, ltd groceries, RV supplies, gas, marine gas, ice, tables, patios.

◊◊◊RECREATION: rec room/area, equipped pavilion, coin games, swim pool, boating, canoeing, kayaking, ramp, dock, 8 motorboat rentals, lake fishing, fishing supplies, golf nearby, bsktball, 2 shuffleboard courts, tennis, v-ball.

Pets welcome. Partial handicap access. Open all yr. Rate in 2007 $22 for 2 persons. MC/VISA/DISC/AMEX/Debit. Phone: (407)348-2040.

e-mail: info@eastlakefishcamp.net

SEE AD THIS PAGE AND AD TRAVEL SECTION PAGE 78

FORT SUMMIT KOA—*From jct US Hwy 192 amd I-4: Go 8 mi S on I-4 (exit 23/US 27), then 1/10 mi S on US 27, then 1000 feet W on S frontage Road. Enter on L.*

WELCOME

SEE PRIMARY LISTING AT LAKE BUENA VISTA AND AD ORLANDO PAGES 152-153

(N) Great Oak Campgrounds—(Osceola) *From jct US-17/441 & US-192: Go 3-1/2 mi W on US-192, then 3/4 mi S on Bass Rd, then 500 feet W on Yowell Rd. Enter on L.* ◊◊◊FACILITIES: 196 sites, typical site width 30 ft, 196 full hkups, (30 & 50 amps), some extended stay sites (in winter), 10 pull-thrus, tenting, dump station, laundry, tables, patios. ◊◊◊RECREATION: rec hall, swim pool, 2 shuffleboard courts, planned activities, horseshoes. Pets welcome, breed restrict. Partial handicap access. Open all yr. Church services & planned activities winter only. Rate in 2007 $30 for 2 persons. Phone: (407)396-9092.

KOA ORLANDO/KISSIMMEE—(Osceola) *From jct I-4 & US 192: Go 4-3/4 mi E on US 192, then left on Seven Dwarfs Lane (at Sam's Warehouse.) Enter on L.*

WELCOME

◊◊◊◊◊FACILITIES: 102 sites, typical site width 48 ft, 102 full hkups, (20, 30 & 50 amps), 46 pull-thrus, cable TV ($), wireless Instant Internet access at site, wireless Internet access central location, tenting, dump station, non-guest dumping $, laundry, ltd groceries, RV supplies, LP gas by weight/by meter, ice, tables, patios, fire rings, wood.

KOA ORLANDO/KISSIMMEE—Continued on next page

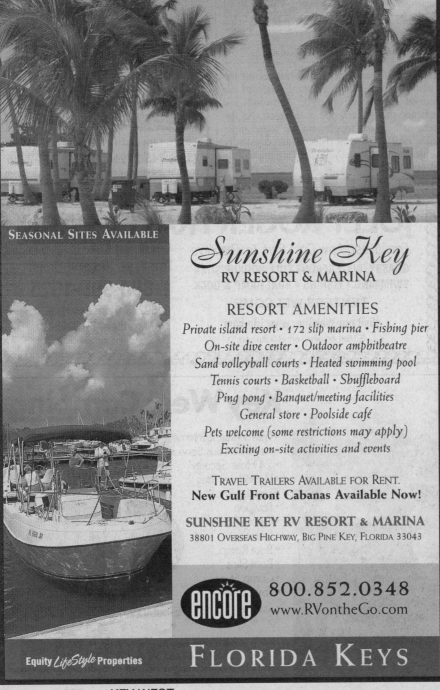

◊◊RECREATION: rec room/area, pavilion, swim pool, whirlpool, bsktball, 4 bike rentals, playground.

Pets welcome. Partial handicap access. Open all yr. Big rigs welcome. Internet friendly. Escort to site. Rate in 2007 $40-90 for 2 persons. MC/VISA/DISC/AMEX/DC. Phone: (407)396-2400. KOA 10% value card discount.

e-mail: kissimee@koa.net

SEE AD ORLANDO PAGE 151 AND AD DISCOVER SECTION PAGES 62 & 63

(S) Merry "D" RV Sanctuary—(Orange) *From jct US 17/92/441 (John Young Parkway) & US 192: Go 3-1/2 mi S on US 17/92, then 7 mi S on Hwy 531, (Pleasant Hill Rd). Enter on L.* ◊◊◊FACILITIES: 133 sites, typical site width 40 ft, 121 full hkups, 5 W&E, (20, 30 & 50 amps), 7 no hkups, 33 pull-thrus, tenting, dump station, non-guest dumping $, laundry, LP gas by weight/by meter, tables, patios. ◊◊◊RECREATION: rec hall, pavilion, pond fishing, playground, planned activities, horseshoes, hiking trails. Pets welcome. Partial handicap access. Open all yr. Planned group activities winter only. Big rigs welcome. Internet friendly. Rate in 2007 $28 for 2 persons. Phone: (407)870-0719.

(W) Mill Creek RV Resort—(Osceola) *From jct US 17/92 & US 192: Go 3/4 mi E on US 192, then 1-1/2 mi N on Hwy 531 (Michigan Ave). Enter on R.* ◊◊FACILITIES: 155 sites, typical site width 22 ft, 155 full hkups, (20, 30 & 50 amps), many extended stay sites (in winter), laundry, LP gas by weight/by meter, patios. ◊◊◊RECREATION: rec hall, swim pool, 4 shuffleboard courts, planned activities, horseshoes. Pets welcome, breed restrict. No tents. Open all yr. Planned group activities winter only. Office closed Sundays & holidays. Rate in 2007 $31 for 2 persons. Member ARVC, FLARVC. Phone: (407)847-6288.

(N) ORANGE GROVE CAMPGROUND—(Osceola) *From jct I-4 (exit 62) & US 192: Go 6-3/4 mi E on US 192, then 1-1/4 mi NW on Old Vineland Rd. Enter on R.*

WELCOME

◊◊◊FACILITIES: 200 sites, typical site width 25 ft, 176 full hkups, 24 W&E, (20, 30 & 50 amps), mostly extended stay sites (in winter), phone/wireless Instant Internet access at site, wireless Internet access central location ($), tenting, RV/park trailer rentals, dump station, non-guest dumping $, portable dump, laundry, full svc store, RV supplies, LP gas by meter, ice, tables, patios.

◊◊◊RECREATION: rec hall, swim pool, mini-golf, golf nearby, playground, 2 shuffleboard courts, planned activities, horseshoes, v-ball.

Pets welcome. Open all yr. Planned group activities winter only. Big rigs welcome. Internet friendly. Clubs welcome. Rate in 2007 $30-35 for 2 persons. MC/VISA/DISC. Phone: (407)396-6655.

SEE AD PAGE 134

Ponderosa RV Park—(Osceola) *From jct US 17/92/441 & US 192: Go 1-1/2 mi E on US 192 & 441, then 1 mi NE on Hwy C-530 (Boggy Creek Rd). Enter on L.* ◊◊◊◊FACILITIES: 190 sites, typical site width 30 ft, 180 full hkups, 10 W&E, (30 & 50 amps), many extended stay sites (in winter), tenting, dump station, portable dump, laundry, tables, patios. ◊◊◊◊RECREATION: rec hall, rec room/area, swim pool, playground, 3 shuffleboard courts, planned activities, horseshoes. Pets welcome. Open all yr. Planned activities winter only. Internet friendly. Rate in 2007 $29 for 2 persons. Phone: (407)847-6002. CCUSA discount.

SHERWOOD FOREST RV RESORT—(Osceola) *From jct I-4 & US-192: Go 3 mi E on US-192. Enter on R.*

WELCOME

◊◊◊◊FACILITIES: 512 sites, typical site width 30 ft, 512 full hkups, (30 & 50 amps), 50 amps ($), some extended stay sites (in winter), 450 pull-thrus, heater not allowed, wireless Instant Internet access at site, phone on-site Internet access (needs activ), wireless Internet access central location, tenting, laundry, groceries, RV supplies, ice, tables.

◊◊◊◊RECREATION: rec hall, equipped pavilion, swim pool, whirlpool, mini-golf, golf nearby, bsktball, playground, 14 shuffleboard courts, planned activities, horseshoes, v-ball, local tours.

Pets welcome, breed restrict, size restrict, quantity restrict. Partial handicap access. Open all yr. Planned activities winter only. Big rigs welcome. Internet friendly. Clubs welcome. MC/VISA/DISC/AMEX. Member ARVC, FLARVC. Phone: (407)396-7431.

e-mail: sherwood_forest_rv@mhchomes.com

SEE AD ORLANDO PAGE 155

TROPICAL PALMS FUN RESORT—(Osceola) *From jct I-4 & US 192: Go 1-1/2 mi E on US 192, then 1/2 mi S on Holiday Trail. Enter on R.*

WELCOME

◊◊◊◊◊FACILITIES: 540 sites, typical site width 40 ft, 400 full hkups, 120 W&E, (20, 30 & 50 amps), 20 no hkups, 400 pull-thrus, cable TV ($), wireless Instant Internet access at site, wireless Internet access central location, tenting, cabins, dump station, laundry, groceries, RV supplies, ice, tables, patios.

◊◊◊◊◊RECREATION: rec hall, rec room/area, equipped pavilion, swim pool, wading pool, pond fishing, fishing supplies, golf nearby, bsktball, playground, 6 shuffleboard courts, horseshoes, v-ball, local tours.

Pets welcome. Partial handicap access. Open all yr. Church services during season. Big rigs welcome. Escort to site. Clubs welcome. MC/VISA/DISC/AMEX. ATM. Phone: (800)64PALMS.

SEE AD ORLANDO PAGE 155

LA BELLE—D-4

(SW) GRANDMA'S GROVE RV PARK—(Hendry) *From jct Hwy 29 & Hwy 80: Go 3 mi W on Hwy 80. Enter on R.*

WELCOME

◊◊◊◊FACILITIES: 208 sites, typical site width 35 ft, 39 ft max RV length, 208 full hkups, (30 & 50 amps), some extended stay sites (in winter), dump station, non-guest dumping $, laundry, tables, patios.

◊◊◊RECREATION: rec hall, pavilion, swim pool, pond fishing, golf nearby, 2 shuffleboard courts, planned activities, horseshoes, hiking trails.

Pets welcome, size restrict, quantity restrict. Partial handicap access. No tents. Age restrictions may apply. Open all yr. Escort to site. Clubs welcome. Rate in 2007 $25 for 2 persons. Phone: (863)675-2567.

SEE AD THIS PAGE

(NE) Meadowlark Campground—(Glades) *From jct Hwy 80 & Hwy 29: Go 4 mi N on Hwy 29, then 6 mi E on Hwy 78, then 1-1/4 mi S on CR 78A, then 3/4 mi SE on Williams Rd. Enter on R.* ◊◊◊FACILITIES: 180 sites, typical site width 32 ft, 180 full hkups, (30 amps), many extended stay sites (in winter), 3 pull-thrus, tenting, shower$, dump station, non-guest dumping $, laundry, LP gas by weight/by meter, tables, patios. ◊◊◊◊RECREATION: rec hall, rec room/area, swim pool, boating, canoeing, ramp, dock, river fishing, 2 shuffleboard courts, planned activities, horseshoes. Pets welcome. Partial handicap access. Age restrictions may apply. Open all yr. Internet friendly. Rate in 2007 $22.50 for 2 persons. Member ARVC, FLARVC. Phone: (800)889-5636.

(E) THE GLADES RV, GOLF & MARINA RESORT—(Hendry) *From jct Hwy 29 & Hwy 80: Go 13 mi E on Hwy 80. Enter on L.*

WELCOME

480 ACRES OF FLORIDA'S PARADISE
Choose an RV site overlooking the Caloosahatchee Waterway and enjoy sunny days on our 9-hole Golf Course. Our deep-water Marina has access to a fisherman's dream-Lake Okeechobee. FREE WI-FI. New sites 2008 www.thegladesresort.com.

◊◊◊◊FACILITIES: 109 sites, typical site width 35 ft, 109 full hkups, (30 & 50 amps), many extended stay sites (in winter), 4 pull-thrus, wireless Instant Internet access at site, tenting, cabins, RV storage, dump station, non-guest dumping $, laundry, tables, patios.

◊◊◊◊RECREATION: rec hall, rec room/area, swim pool, boating, canoeing, kayaking, ramp, dock, river/pond fishing, golf nearby, 4 shuffleboard courts, planned activities, horseshoes, sports field, hiking trails.

Pets welcome, breed restrict. Partial handicap access. Open all yr. Big rigs welcome. Internet friendly. Escort to site. Clubs welcome. Rate in 2007 $30 for 2 persons. MC/VISA/DISC/AMEX/Debit. Member ARVC, FLARVC. Phone: (863)902-7034.

e-mail: info@thegladesresort.com

SEE AD TRAVEL SECTION PAGE 81 AND AD DISCOVER SECTION PAGE 46

Woodall's Tip #26... All privately-owned RV parks/campgrounds are personally inspected each year by one of our 28 Representative Teams, so you can feel confident that before you arrive, we've already been there.

(E) THE GLADES RV, GOLF & MARINA RESORT—*From jct Hwy 29 & Hwy 80: Go 13 mi E on Hwy 80. Enter on L.* Deep water marina with direct access to the Caloosahatchee River. Private boat launch for park guests, accommodates water craft up to 58 feet. Pump-out station available. Open all yr. MC/VISA/DISC/AMEX/Debit. Phone: (863)673-5653.

WELCOME

e-mail: info@thegladesresort.com

SEE AD TRAVEL SECTION PAGE 81

(E) THE GLADES RV, GOLF & MARINA RESORT—*From jct Hwy 29 & Hwy 80: Go 13 mi E on Hwy 80. Enter on L.* 3178 yard par-36 golf course with water features, natural landscaping, and a grill at the 9th hole. Open to public. Open all yr. MC/VISA/DISC/AMEX/Debit. Phone: (863)983-8464.

WELCOME

e-mail: info@thegladesresort.com

SEE AD TRAVEL SECTION PAGE 81

(N) Whisper Creek RV Resort—(Glades) *From jct Hwy 80 & Hwy 29: Go 1-3/4 mi N on Hwy 29. Enter on L.* ◊◊◊◊FACILITIES: 472 sites, typical site width 40 ft, 472 full hkups, (30 & 50 amps), mostly extended stay sites (in winter), dump station, laundry, patios. ◊◊◊◊RECREATION: rec hall, rec room/area, equipped pavilion, swim pool, 5 shuffleboard courts, planned activities, horseshoes. Pets welcome. Partial handicap access. No tents. Age restrictions may apply. Open all yr. Planned group activities winter only. Big rigs welcome. Internet friendly. Rate in 2007 $35 for 2 persons. Member ARVC, FLARVC. Phone: (863)675-6888.

LADY LAKE—B-3

The Recreation Plantation RV Resort—(Lake) *From jct US 27/441 & CR 466: Go 3/4 mi W on CR 466. Enter on R.* ◊◊◊◊◊FACILITIES: 850 sites, typical site width 35 ft, 850 full hkups, (30 & 50 amps), mostly extended stay sites (in winter), tenting, dump station, non-guest dumping $, laundry, LP gas by weight/by meter, ice, tables. ◊◊◊◊◊RECREATION: rec hall, rec room/area, swim pool, 8 shuffleboard courts, planned activities, tennis, horseshoes, v-ball. Pets welcome, breed restrict, quantity restrict. Partial handicap access. Age restrictions may apply. Open all yr. Big rigs welcome. Internet friendly. Rate in 2007 $37 for 2 persons. Member ARVC, FLARVC. Phone: (800)448-5646.

LAKE BUENA VISTA—C-4

LAKE BUENA VISTA AREA MAP

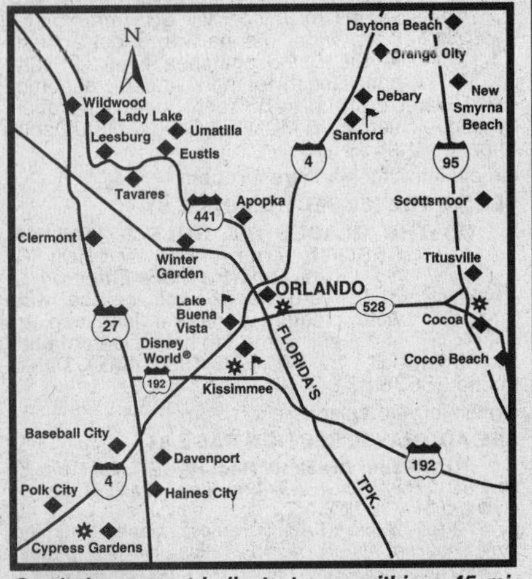

Symbols on map indicate towns within a 45 mi radius of Lake Buena Vista where campgrounds (diamonds), attractions (flags), & RV service centers & camping supply outlets (gears) are listed. Check listings for more information.

Tell Them Woodall's Sent You!

(W) DISNEY'S FORT WILDERNESS RESORT & CAMPGROUND—(Orange) *From jct I-4 & US 192: Go 1 mi W on US 192, then 1 mi N on World Dr. Enter on R.*

WELCOME

◆◆◆◆◆FACILITIES: 784 sites, typical site width 40 ft, 694 full hkups, 90 W&E, (20, 30 & 50 amps), cable TV, phone/cable Instant Internet access at site, wireless Internet access central location, tenting, cabins, laundry, full svc store, RV supplies, LP gas by weight/by meter, gas, ice, tables, patios, grills, controlled access gate.

◆◆◆◆◆RECREATION: rec room/area, coin games, 2 swim pools, boating, canoeing, dock, 20 canoe/10 pedal boat/60 motorboat rentals, lake fishing, fishing supplies, fishing guides, putting green, golf nearby, bsktball, 300 bike rentals, playground, 2 shuffleboard courts, planned activities, tennis, horseshoes, sports field, hiking trails, v-ball.

Pets welcome. Partial handicap access. Open all yr. $2.00 per person per night for third through tenth adults per campsite. Big rigs welcome. Internet friendly. Clubs welcome. Rate in 2007 $46-96 per family. MC/VISA/DISC/AMEX/DC/Debit. ATM. Member ARVC, FLARVC. Phone: (407)WDWCAMP.

SEE AD ORLANDO PAGE 150 AND AD TRAVEL SECTION PAGE 82 AND AD DISCOVER SECTION PAGE 41

Woodall's Tip #26... All privately-owned RV parks/campgrounds are personally inspected each year by one of our 28 Representative Teams, so you can feel confident that before you arrive, we've already been there.

LAKE BUENA VISTA—Continued

(SW) FORT SUMMIT KOA—(Polk) *From jct I-4 (exit 55) & US 27: Go 1 block S on US 27, then 1/4 mi W on S frontage road. Enter on L.*

WELCOME

THE BEST PARK IN THE "WORLD(S)"
Everything you'd expect from the best, and easy access to all Central Florida attractions. Free shuttle to Disney World, or just relax & enjoy great camping. Amenities galore and a super friendly staff to help you enjoy them.

◆◆◆◆◆FACILITIES: 289 sites, 251 full hkups, 38 W&E, (20, 30 & 50 amps), some extended stay sites (in winter), 100 pull-thrus, cable TV ($), wireless Instant Internet access at site, phone on-site Internet access (needs activ), wireless Internet access central location, tenting, cabins, RV storage, dump station, non-guest dumping $, laundry, full svc store, RV supplies, LP gas by weight/by meter, ice, tables, patios.

◆◆◆◆◆RECREATION: rec hall, rec room/area, coin games, swim pool, wading pool, mini-golf ($), golf nearby, bsktball, playground, planned activities, tennis, horseshoes, v-ball, local tours.

Pets welcome, quantity restrict. Partial handicap access. Open all yr. Planned activities winter only. Big rigs welcome. Internet friendly. Escort to site. Clubs welcome. Rate in 2007 $39-69 for 2 persons. MC/VISA/DISC/AMEX. Member ARVC, FLARVC. Phone: (800)424-1880. FCRV 10% discount. FMCA discount.

SEE AD ORLANDO PAGES 152-153 AND AD DISCOVER SECTION PAGES 62 & 63

(W) WALT DISNEY WORLD RESORT—*From jct I-4 & US-192: Go 1 mi W on US-192, then N to the park admission gate. Enter on R.* Walt Disney World Resort includes Magic Kingdom Park, Disney's Animal Kingdom Theme Park, Epcot, Disney MGM Studios, 2 water parks, 19 Disney owned hotels, 5 championship golf courses. Downtown Disney Marketplace and Pleasure Island Nightime entertainment. Open all yr. MC/VISA/DISC/AMEX/DC. ATM. Phone: (407)WDISNEY.

WELCOME

SEE AD ORLANDO PAGE 150 AND AD TRAVEL SECTION PAGE 82 AND AD DISCOVER SECTION PAGE 41

LAKE CITY—A-3

(SE) Casey Jones' RV Park—(Columbia) *From jct I-75 (exit 423) & Hwy 47: Go 1/10 mi W on Hwy 47, then 1/10 mi N on CR 242. Enter on R.* ◆◆◆FACILITIES: 80 sites, typical site width 32 ft, 80 full hkups, (30 & 50 amps), 50 amps ($), some extended stay sites (in winter), 50 pull-thrus, laundry, LP gas by weight/by meter, ice, tables. ◆◆RECREATION: rec hall, pavilion, horseshoes. Pets welcome, breed restrict, size restrict. Partial handicap access. No tents. Open all yr. Big rigs welcome. Internet friendly. Rate in 2007 $22 for 2 persons. Phone: (386)755-0471.

(S) E-Z Stop RV Park—(Columbia) *From jct I-75 (exit 414) & US-41/441: Go 1/8 mi W on US-41/441, then 1/10 mi N on Howell St. Enter on R.* ◆◆FACILITIES: 22 sites, typical site width 30 ft, 22 full hkups, (20, 30 & 50 amps), many extended stay sites, 11 pull-thrus, dump station, non-guest dumping $, tables. RECREATION: horseshoes. Pets welcome. Partial handicap access. No tents. Open all yr. Big rigs welcome. Rate in 2007 $19-22 for 2 persons. Member ARVC, FLARVC. Phone: (386)752-2279.

Woodall's Buyer's Guide—The best tool to arm yourself with as you shop for your next RV.

LAKE CITY—Continued

(W) INN & OUT RV PARK—(Columbia) *From jct I-75 & US 90 (exit 427): Go 1/4 mi E on US 90. Enter on R.*

WELCOME

◆◆◆FACILITIES: 80 sites, 80 full hkups, (30 & 50 amps), some extended stay sites (in winter), 78 pull-thrus, cable TV, wireless Internet access central location, tenting, cabins, RV storage, dump station, non-guest dumping $, laundry, groceries, LP gas by weight/by meter, gas, ice, tables.

RECREATION: lake fishing, golf nearby.

Pets welcome. Partial handicap access. Open all yr. Big rigs welcome. Internet friendly. Clubs welcome. Rate in 2007 $29.95 for 4 persons. MC/VISA/DISC/AMEX. ATM. Phone: (386)752-1648.

e-mail: Jrs929@hotmail.com

SEE AD THIS PAGE

(N) LAKE CITY CAMPGROUND—(Columbia) *From I-10 (exit 303) & Hwy 441: Go 1 mi N on Hwy 441. Enter on R.*

WELCOME

◆◆◆◆FACILITIES: 52 sites, typical site width 25 ft, 40 full hkups, 12 W&E, (30 & 50 amps), some extended stay sites, 40 pull-thrus, cable TV, wireless Instant Internet access at site ($), phone Internet access central location, tenting, cabins, RV storage, dump station, non-guest dumping $, laundry, groceries, RV supplies, LP gas by weight/by meter, ice, tables, fire rings, wood.

◆◆◆RECREATION: rec hall, coin games, swim pool, pond fishing, fishing supplies, golf nearby, playground, shuffleboard court, horseshoes, hiking trails, v-ball.

Pets welcome. Partial handicap access. Open all yr. Pool open during summer only. Big rigs welcome. Internet friendly. Clubs welcome. Rate in 2007 $30-32 for 2 persons. MC/VISA. Member ARVC, FLARVC. Phone: (386)752-9131. FMCA discount.

e-mail: lakecitycampground@yahoo.com

SEE AD THIS PAGE

(N) Oaks 'N Pines RV Campground—(Columbia) *From I-10 (exit 303) & Hwy 441: Go 2/10 mi N on Hwy 441. Enter on L.* ◆◆◆◆FACILITIES: 67 sites, typical site width 30 ft, 67 full hkups, (20, 30 & 50 amps), some extended stay sites, 67 pull-thrus, dump station, non-guest dumping $, laundry, LP gas by weight/by meter, ice, tables, patios. ◆◆RECREATION: rec hall, pavilion, pond fishing, planned activities, horseshoes. Pets welcome, breed restrict. Partial handicap access. No tents. Open all yr. Planned group activities in winter only. Big rigs welcome. Internet friendly. Rate in 2007 $33 for 2 persons. Member ARVC, FLARVC. Phone: (386)752-0830. FMCA discount.

(W) Wayne's RV Resort—(Columbia) *From jct I-75 (exit 427) & US 90: Go 1/4 mi W on US 90, then 1/4 mi W on CR 252-B. Enter on L.* ◆◆FACILITIES: 77 sites, typical site width 35 ft, 54 full hkups, 23 W&E, (20, 30 & 50 amps), 50 amps ($), mostly extended stay sites, 72 pull-thrus, tenting, laundry, ltd groceries, LP gas by weight/by meter, ice. ◆RECREATION: rec hall, swim pool, playground, shuffleboard court, v-ball. Pets welcome. Partial handicap access. Open all yr. Rate in 2007 $26-28 for 2 persons. Member ARVC, FLARVC. Phone: (386)752-5721.

LAKE PANASOFFKEE—C-3

(W) Countryside RV Park—(Sumter) *From jct I-75 (exit 321) & Hwy 470: Go 1/4 mi W on Hwy 470, then 1/2 mi W on Hwy 489. Enter on L.* ◆◆FACILITIES: 65 sites, 59 full hkups, 6 W&E, (20, 30 & 50 amps), many extended stay sites (in winter), 11 pull-thrus, tenting, dump station, non-guest dumping $, laundry, tables. ◆◆◆RECREATION: rec hall, 2 shuffleboard courts, planned activities, horseshoes, sports field. Pets welcome, breed restrict, size restrict. Open all yr. Big rigs welcome. Internet friendly. Rate in 2007 $27 for 2 persons. Phone: (352)793-8103.

LAKE PANASOFFKEE—Continued on next page

LAKE PANASOFFKEE—Continued

WELCOME

TURTLEBACK RV RESORT—*From jct I-75 (exit 321) & Hwy 470: Go 1/4 mi on Hwy 470. Enter on R.*

FACILITIES: 130 sites, 120 full hkups, 10 W&E, (20, 30 & 50 amps).

Open all yr. Rate in 2007 $28 per vehicle. Phone: (352)793-2051.

SEE AD THIS PAGE

LAKE PLACID—D-4

WELCOME

(S) CAMP FLORIDA RESORT—(Highlands) *From jct Hwy 70 & US 27: Go 4-1/2 mi N on US 27. Enter on R.*

◇◇◇◇FACILITIES: 397 sites, 397 full hkups, (30 & 50 amps), many extended stay sites (in winter), cable TV ($), phone/cable on-site Internet access (needs activ), phone Internet access central location, RV/park trailer rentals, dump station, non-guest dumping $, laundry, tables, patios, controlled access gate.

◇◇◇◇◇RECREATION: rec hall, rec room/area, swim pool, boating, ramp, dock, lake fishing, mini-golf, golf nearby, bsktball, 8 shuffleboard courts, planned activities, tennis, horseshoes, local tours.

Pets welcome, breed restrict, size restrict, quantity restrict. Partial handicap access. No tents. Open all yr. Big rigs welcome. Clubs welcome.

LAKE PLACID—Continued
CAMP FLORIDA RESORT—Continued

Rate in 2007 $35 per vehicle. MC/VISA/DISC/AMEX. Member ARVC, FLARVC. Phone: (863)699-1991. FMCA discount.

e-mail: campfla@strato.net

SEE AD THIS PAGE

(S) Sunshine RV Resort—(Highland) *From jct US 27S & Hwy 70: Go 1/4 mi E on Hwy 70. Enter on R.* ◇◇◇◇FACILITIES: 325 sites, typical site width 30 ft, 325 full hkups, (30 & 50 amps), mostly extended stay sites (in winter), 30 pull-thrus, laundry, patios. ◇◇◇◇RECREATION: rec hall, rec room/area, swim pool, lake fishing, 6 shuffleboard courts, planned activities, tennis, horseshoes. Pets welcome, breed restrict. Partial handicap access. No tents. Open all yr. Big rigs welcome. Internet friendly. Rate in 2007 $26-29 for 2 persons. Member ARVC, FLARVC. Phone: (877)317-2757.

LAKE WALES—C-4

(E) Camp Macks River Resort—(Polk) *From jct US 27 & Hwy 60: Go 10 mi E on Hwy 60, then 3-1/2 mi N on Boy Scout Rd, then 6 mi E on Camp Mack Rd. Enter on L.* ◇◇◇◇FACILITIES: 200 sites, 200 full hkups, (30 & 50 amps), some extended stay sites (in winter), tenting, dump station, non-guest dumping $, laundry, ltd groceries, LP gas by weight/by meter, ice, tables. ◇◇◇◇RECREATION: rec hall, swim pool, boating, ramp, dock, rowboat/motorboat rentals, lake/river fishing, planned activities, horseshoes. Pets welcome. Open all yr. Big rigs welcome. Rate in 2007 $32-36 for 4 persons. Phone: (863)696-1108.

LAKE WALES—Continued

(S) Camp'n Aire RV Resort—(Polk) *From jct Hwy 60 & US 27: Go 3-1/4 mi S on US 27. Enter on R.* ◇◇◇◇FACILITIES: 99 sites, typical site width 25 ft, 99 full hkups, (30 & 50 amps), many extended stay sites (in winter), 40 pull-thrus, heater not allowed, dump station, non-guest dumping $, laundry, LP gas by weight/by meter, tables, patios. ◇◇◇RECREATION: rec hall, swim pool, stream fishing, 2 shuffleboard courts, planned activities, horseshoes, sports field, hiking trails. Pets welcome, breed restrict, size restrict, quantity restrict. No tents. Age restrictions may apply. Open all yr. Planned activities in season only. Big rigs welcome. Internet friendly. Rate in 2007 $30 for 2 persons. Phone: (863)638-1015.

LAKE WALES—Continued on next page

LAKE WALES—Continued

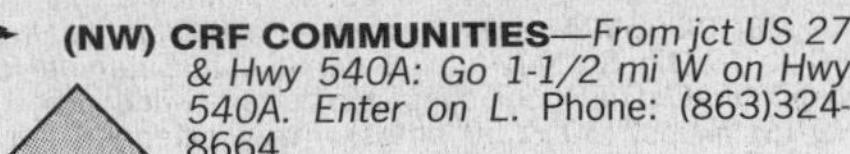

(NW) **CRF COMMUNITIES**—*From jct US 27 & Hwy 540A: Go 1-1/2 mi W on Hwy 540A. Enter on L.* Phone: (863)324-8664.

e-mail: jlawson@lakeashton.com

SEE AD TRAVEL SECTION PAGE 77 AND AD TRAVEL SECTION PAGE 83 AND AD DISCOVER SECTION PAGE 56

(E) LAKE KISSIMMEE STATE PARK—(Polk) *From town: Go 15 mi E on Hwy 60, then N on Camo Mack Rd.* FACILITIES: 60 sites, 60 W&E, tenting, dump station. RECREATION: pavilion, boating, canoeing, ramp, lake fishing, hiking trails. No pets. Open all yr. Phone: (863)696-1112.

(S) **Lake Wales Campground**—(Polk) *From jct Hwy 60 & US 27: Go 3 mi S on US 27. Enter on R.* ◊◊◊FACILITIES: 108 sites, typical site width 22 ft, 108 full hkups, (30 & 50 amps), 50 pull-thrus, heater not allowed, tenting, dump station, non-guest dumping $, laundry, ice, tables, fire rings, grills, wood. ◊◊◊◊RECREATION: rec hall, rec room/area, swim pool, pond fishing, 2 shuffleboard courts, planned activities, horseshoes. Pets welcome. Open all yr. Planned activities winter only. Big rigs welcome. Phone: (863)638-9011.

(E) **The Harbor RV Resort & Marina**—(Polk) *From jct US 27 & Hwy 60: Go 10 mi E on Hwy 60, then 3-1/2 mi N on Boy Scout Rd, then 1-3/4 mi E on Camp Mack Rd, then 1/4 mi SE on Kentucky, then 1/4 mi SE on N Marina Pkwy, then 1 block S on Monroe Ct. Enter at end.* ◊◊◊FACILITIES: 119 sites, 119 full hkups, (30 amps), many extended stay sites (in winter), tenting, dump station, non-guest dumping $, laundry, tables, patios. ◊◊◊◊RECREATION: rec hall, equipped pavilion, swim pool, boating, canoeing, ramp, dock, motorboat rentals, lake fishing, 2 shuffleboard courts, planned activities, horseshoes. Pets welcome. Open all yr. Planned group activities winter only. Internet friendly. Member ARVC, FLARVC. Phone: (863)696-1194. CCUSA discount. FMCA discount.

LAKE WORTH—D-5

(S) **JOHN PRINCE MEMORIAL PARK (Palm Beach County Park)**—(Palm Beach) *From jct Hwy 812 & I-95: Go 2 mi N on I-95 (exit 63), then 1-1/4 mi W on 6th Ave, then 1/2 mi S on Congress Ave. Enter on L.*

PEACEFUL, BEAUTIFUL & CLOSE TO NATURE

Enjoy a relaxing stay at one of our 277 rustic campsites, nestled throughout our 48-acre park, located on beautiful Lake Osborne in Lake Worth. Just minutes from the beach, shopping, restaurants, golfing, night life and more.

FACILITIES: 277 sites, typical site width 25 ft, 91 full hkups, 186 W&E, (30 & 50 amps), many extended stay sites (in winter), 18 pull-thrus, tenting, dump station, non-guest dumping $, portable dump, ice, tables, fire rings, grills, wood, controlled access gate.

RECREATION: pavilion, boating, canoeing, kayaking, ramp, dock, lake fishing, golf nearby, bsktball, playground, planned activities, tennis, horseshoes, sports field, hiking trails, v-ball. Rec open to public.

Pets welcome, quantity restrict. Partial handicap access. Open all yr. Planned activities in winter only. Clubs welcome. MC/VISA/Debit. Member ARVC, FLARVC. Phone: (877)992-9925.

e-mail: jppcamp@pbcgov.com

SEE AD THIS PAGE

LAKELAND—C-3

(N) **LAKELAND RV RESORT**—(Polk) *From I-4 (exit 33): Go 1/2 mi NE on Hwy 33, then 1/2 mi E on Old Combee Rd. Enter on R.*

WELCOME TO CAREFREE RV RESORTS!

Extra long, extra wide pull-thru's for big rigs! Recreation galore to keep you entertained. Drive just thirty minutes to Disney World. Book the Rec Hall for your private group function. We'll make your stay with us special!

◊◊◊◊FACILITIES: 230 sites, typical site width 35 ft, 230 full hkups, (20, 30 & 50 amps), 50 amps ($), some extended stay sites (in winter), 100 pull-thrus, wireless Instant Internet access at site, phone on-site Internet access (needs activ), wireless Internet access central location ($), tenting, cabins, RV storage, dump station, non-guest dumping $, laundry, RV supplies, LP gas by weight/by meter, tables, patios, controlled access gate.

◊◊◊◊RECREATION: rec hall, rec room/area, swim pool, wading pool, whirlpool, boating, 2 pedal boat rentals, pond fishing, mini-golf, golf nearby, bsktball, playground, 3 shuffleboard courts, planned activities, horseshoes, v-ball.

Pets welcome, breed restrict, quantity restrict. Open all yr. Church service & planned activities winter only. Big rigs welcome. Internet friendly.

LAKELAND RV RESORT—Continued on next page

Sidney Poitier, actor, is from Florida.

LAKELAND—Continued
LAKELAND RV RESORT—Continued

Clubs welcome. Rate in 2007 $36 for 2 persons. MC/VISA/DISC. Member ARVC, FLARVC. Phone: (888)622-4115. FMCA discount.

e-mail: lakelandrv@aol.com

SEE AD PAGE 138 AND AD DISCOVER SECTION PAGE 128

(N) Lazy Dazy Retreat—(Polk) *From jct I-4 & US-98: Go 3 mi N on US-98. Enter on R.* ◆◆FACILITIES: 86 sites, typical site width 30 ft, 86 full hkups, (15, 20 & 30 amps), many extended stay sites, 30 pull-thrus, tenting, dump station, non-guest dumping $, laundry, tables, patios. ◆◆RECREATION: rec room/area, 2 shuffleboard courts. Pets welcome. Open all yr. Rate in 2007 $22 for 2 persons. Phone: (863)858-2026.

✱ **(N) R.V. WORLD OF LAKELAND**—*From jct I-4 (exit 32) & US 98: Go 1 blk N on US 98, then 1/4 mi NE on Crevasse St. Enter on L.* SALES: travel trailers, truck campers, 5th wheels, van campers, motor homes, micro-mini motor homes, SERVICES: full-time mech, RV appliance repair, installs hitches. Open all yr. MC/VISA. Phone: (863)853-9177.

e-mail: info@rvworldinc.com

SEE AD PAGE 138

(S) Sanlan RV Park—(Polk) *From jct Polk Pkwy (570)(exit 10) & US 98: Go 1/2 mi S on US 98. Enter on R.* ◆◆◆◆FACILITIES: 531 sites, typical site width 40 ft, 531 full hkups, (20, 30 & 50 amps), some extended stay sites (in winter), 100 pull-thrus, tenting, dump station, non-guest dumping $, laundry, LP gas by weight/by meter, ice, tables, patios. ◆◆◆◆◆RECREATION: rec hall, rec room/area, 2 swim pools, boating, canoeing, lake fishing, playground, 18 shuffleboard courts, planned activities, horseshoes, hiking trails, v-ball. Rec open to public. Pets welcome ($), quantity restrict. Open all yr. Planned activities & church winter only. Children 2 weeks max. Big rigs welcome. Internet friendly. Rate in 2007 $18-42 for 2 persons. Member ARVC, FLARVC. Phone: (863)665-1726.

(N) Tiki Village Campground—(Polk) *From jct I-4 (exit 32) & US 98: Go 1 blk N on US 98, then 1/4 mi NE on Crevasse St. Enter on L.* ◆◆◆FACILITIES: 203 sites, typical site width 38 ft, 203 full hkups, (30 & 50 amps), 50 amps ($), many extended stay sites (in winter), 20 pull-thrus, laundry, ltd groceries, LP gas by weight/by meter, tables. ◆◆◆RECREATION: rec hall, swim pool, pond fishing, 2 shuffleboard courts, planned activities, horseshoes. Pets welcome. Partial handicap access. No tents. Open all yr. Planned activities winter only. Big rigs welcome. Member ARVC. Phone: (863) 858-5364.

(W) Woodall's Mobile Home Village (RV SPACES)—(Polk) *From jct I-4 & Memorial Blvd: Go 2 mi E on Memorial Blvd, then 1 mi S on Wabash Ave, then 1 block W on New Tampa Hwy.* FACILITIES: 101 sites, accepts self-contained units only, 101 full hkups, (30 & 50 amps), dump station, laundry, patios. RECREATION: rec hall, 6 shuffleboard courts, planned activities, horseshoes. No pets. Partial handicap access. No tents. Open all yr. Group activities winter season only. No restrooms. Rate in 2007 $30 for 2 persons. Phone: (863)686-7462.

LAKEPORT—D-4

(E) ARUBA RV PARK—(Glades) *From jct US-27 & Hwy-78: Go 9 mi N on Hwy-78, then 200 feet W on Lakeport Rd. Enter on L.*

◆◆◆FACILITIES: 137 sites, typical site width 40 ft, 137 full hkups, (30 & 50 amps), many extended stay sites (in winter), 6 pull-thrus, phone on-site Internet access (needs activ), RV storage, laundry, gas, ice, tables, patios.

◆◆◆◆RECREATION: rec hall, rec room/area, pavilion, swim pool, boating, ramp, dock, lake/river fishing, 2 shuffleboard courts, planned activities, horseshoes.

Pets welcome. Partial handicap access. No tents. Open all yr. Planned activities during winter only. Big rigs welcome. Clubs welcome. Rate in 2007 $30-35 for 2 persons. MC/VISA/DISC/Debit. Phone: (863)946-1324.

e-mail: arubarvpark@embargmail.com

SEE AD THIS PAGE

LAMONT—A-2

(S) A Camper's World—(Harrison) *From jct I-10 (exit 225) & US 19: Go 1 block N on US 19, then 400 yards W on Campground Rd. Enter on L.* ◆◆◆FACILITIES: 29 sites, typical site width 30 ft, 29 full hkups, (30 & 50 amps), 50 amps ($), some extended stay sites, 20 pull-thrus, laundry, LP gas by weight/by meter, tables. ◆RECREATION: swim pool, play equipment. Pets welcome. Partial handicap access. No tents. Open all yr. Big rigs welcome. Internet friendly. Rate in 2007 $25.25-28 for 2 persons. Member ARVC, FLARVC. Phone: (850)997-3300. FMCA discount.

LANTANA—D-5

(W) Palm Beach Traveler Park—(Palm Beach) *From jct Hwy 802 (Lake Worth Rd) & Hwy 809 (Military Trail): Go 2 mi S on Military Trail, then 1/2 mi E on Lantana, then 1 block S on Lawrence Rd. Enter on R.* ◆◆◆◆FACILITIES: 104 sites, typical site width 30 ft, 104 full hkups, (20, 30 & 50 amps), 50 amps ($), mostly extended stay sites (in winter), dump station, non-guest dumping $, laundry, patios. ◆◆RECREATION: rec hall, swim pool, 3 shuffleboard courts, planned activities, horseshoes. Pets welcome, breed restrict, size restrict. Partial handicap access. No tents. Open all yr. Internet friendly. Rate in 2007 $32-55 for 2 persons. Member ARVC, FLARVC. Phone: (561)967-3139.

LARGO—C-3

(S) Camper's Cove—(Pinellas) *From Jct Hwy 688 & Alt US 19 N: Go 1/4 mi S on Alt US 19 N. Enter on R.* ◆◆◆FACILITIES: 45 sites, 35 ft max RV length, 45 full hkups, (20 & 30 amps), some extended stay sites, laundry, tables, patios. ◆RECREATION: rec hall. Pets welcome. No tents. Open all yr. Rate in 2007 $20 for 2 persons. Phone: (727)584-2378.

(S) Lee's Travel Park—(Pinellas) *From jct US 19 & Hwy 688 (Ulmerton): Go 1 mi W on Hwy 688, then 1/2 mi N on Belcher Rd. Enter on L.* ◆◆◆FACILITIES: 158 sites, accepts full hkup units only, 158 full hkups, (30 amps), some extended stay sites (in winter), dump station, non-guest dumping $, laundry, patios. ◆◆◆RECREATION: rec hall, swim pool, 3 shuffleboard courts, planned activities. Pets welcome, size restrict, quantity restrict. No tents. Open all yr. Planned activities winter only. Limited hours on restrooms. Rate in 2007 $40 for 2 persons. Phone: (727)536-2050.

(S) RAINBOW VILLAGE RV RESORT—(Pinellas) *From jct I-275 & Hwy 688 (Ulmerton): Go 4 mi W on Hwy 688, then 3/4 mi S on 66th St N. Enter on L.*

◆◆◆◆◆FACILITIES: 307 sites, typical site width 35 ft, accepts full hkup units only, 307 full hkups, (20, 30 & 50 amps), mostly extended stay sites (in winter), shower$, laundry, LP gas by weight/by meter, patios.

◆◆◆◆RECREATION: rec hall, rec room/area, equipped pavilion, swim pool, golf nearby, 6 shuffleboard courts, planned activities, horseshoes.

Pets welcome. Partial handicap access. No tents. Age restrictions may apply. Open all yr. Big rigs welcome. Phone: (800)348-9607. CCUSA discount.

e-mail: rainbowvillagerv@aol.com

SEE AD ST. PETERSBURG PAGE 167 AND AD TAMPA PAGE 179 AND AD DISCOVER SECTION PAGE 128

(E) VACATION VILLAGE (CAMP RESORT)—(Pinellas) *From jct I-275 (exit 18) & Ulmerton Rd: Go 3 mi W on Ulmerton Rd. Enter on L.*

FACILITIES: 281 sites, typical site width 24 ft, 281 full hkups, (30 & 50 amps), mostly extended stay sites (in winter), wireless Instant Internet access at site ($), phone/cable on-site Internet access (needs activ), wireless Internet access central location ($), tenting, dump station, non-guest dumping $, laundry, patios.

RECREATION: rec hall, swim pool, golf nearby, 4 shuffleboard courts, planned activities, horseshoes, v-ball.

Pets welcome, breed restrict, quantity restrict. Partial handicap access. Age restrictions may apply. Open all yr. Planned activities winter only. Big rigs welcome. Internet friendly. Clubs welcome. Rate in 2007 $31-33 for 2 persons. MC/VISA/DISC/AMEX. Phone: (877)297-2757.

e-mail: nhcflvv@msn.com

SEE AD TAMPA PAGE 176

(S) YANKEE TRAVELER RV PARK—(Pinellas) *From jct I-275 (exit 31) (Southbound) & SR 688: Go 6 1/2 mi W on SR 688 (Ulmerton Rd.). From jct I-275 (exit 30) Northbound & SR 686: Go 1 8/10 mi NW on SR 686/Roosevelt, then 5 mi W on SR 688/Ulmerton Rd. Enter on L.*

◆◆◆◆FACILITIES: 210 sites, typical site width 30 ft, 210 full hkups, (20, 30 & 50 amps), mostly extended stay sites (in winter), wireless Instant Internet access at site, phone/cable on-site Internet access (needs activ), wireless Internet access central location, RV storage, dump station, non-guest dumping $, laundry, LP gas by weight/by meter, tables, patios.

◆◆◆◆RECREATION: rec hall, rec room/area, swim pool, golf nearby, bsktball, 7 shuffleboard courts, planned activities, horseshoes.

LARGO—Continued
YANKEE TRAVELER RV PARK—Continued

Pets welcome, size restrict, quantity restrict. No tents. Age restrictions may apply. Open all yr. Planned activities season only. Big rigs welcome. Rate in 2007 $31-35 for 2 persons. MC/VISA. Member ARVC, FLARVC. Phone: (866)202-9232.

e-mail: info@yankeetraveler.net

SEE AD CLEARWATER PAGE 101

LEESBURG—C-3

HOLIDAY TRAVEL RESORT—(Lake) *From jct FL Turnpike (exit 296) & CR 470: Go 3 mi E on CR 470, then 1 mi E on CR 33. Enter on L.*

◆◆◆◆FACILITIES: 935 sites, typical site width 50 ft, 935 full hkups, (30 & 50 amps), mostly extended stay sites (in winter), 935 pull-thrus, cable TV ($), wireless Internet access central location, tenting, dump station, non-guest dumping $, laundry, LP gas by weight/by meter, marine gas, ice, tables, controlled access gate.

◆◆◆◆◆RECREATION: rec hall, rec room/area, equipped pavilion, 2 swim pools, whirlpool, boating, canoeing, kayaking, ramp, dock, lake fishing, fishing supplies, mini-golf, golf nearby, bsktball, playground, 15 shuffleboard courts, planned activities, tennis, horseshoes, sports field, v-ball, local tours.

Pets welcome. Partial handicap access. Open all yr. Tenting in summer only. Non-guest dumping summer only. Big rigs welcome. Internet friendly. Clubs welcome. Rate in 2007 $33 for 2 persons. MC/VISA/DISC. Member ARVC, FLARVC. Phone: (800)428-5334.

SEE AD NEXT PAGE

LEESBURG—Continued on next page

LEESBURG—Continued

Ridgecrest RV & Mobile Home Resort—(Lake) *From jct CR 48 & US 27: Go 1-1/2 mi S on US 27. Enter on R.* ◆◆◆◆FACILITIES: 154 sites, typical site width 25 ft, 149 full hkups, 5 W&E, (30 & 50 amps), mostly extended stay sites (in winter), dump station, non-guest dumping $, laundry, LP gas by weight/by meter, tables, patios. ◆◆◆◆RECREATION: rec hall, rec room/area, equipped pavilion, swim pool, 2 shuffleboard courts, planned activities, horseshoes. Pets welcome, breed restrict, size restrict, quantity restrict. Partial handicap access. No tents. Age restrictions may apply. Open all yr. Big rigs welcome. Internet friendly. Rate in 2007 $26 for 2 persons. Member ARVC, FLARVC. Phone: (352)787-1504.

LIVE OAK—A-2

(N) Spirit of the Suwannee Music Park—(Suwannee) *From jct I-75 (exit 451) & US 129: Go 4 mi S on US 129. Enter on R.* ◆◆◆FACILITIES: 2300 sites, typical site width 25 ft, 250 full hkups, 1050 W&E, (30 amps), 1000 no hkups, 75 pull-thrus, tenting, dump station, non-guest dumping $, laundry, ltd groceries, ice, tables, wood. ◆◆◆◆RECREATION: rec hall, equipped pavilion, swim pool, boating, canoeing, ramp, 45 canoe rentals, lake/river fishing, mini-golf ($), playground, planned activities, horseshoes, sports field, hiking trails, v-ball. Pets welcome. Partial handicap access. Open all yr. Internet friendly. Rate in 2007 $20-40 for 4 persons. Member ARVC, FLARVC. Phone: (386) 364-1683.

(W) SUWANNEE RIVER STATE PARK—(Suwannee) *From town: Go 13 mi W on US 90.* FACILITIES: 31 sites, 32 ft max RV length, 22 W&E, (20 & 30 amps), 9 no hkups, tenting, dump station, grills. RECREATION: boating, canoeing, ramp, river fishing, playground, hiking trails. Pets welcome. Open all yr. Phone: (386)362-2746.

LONG KEY—F-4

(W) LONG KEY STATE PARK—(Monroe) *From town: Go 1 mi W on US 1. Milepost 67.5.* FACILITIES: 60 sites, 28 ft max RV length, 60 W&E, tenting, dump station, grills. RECREATION: saltwater swimming, boating, canoeing, 4 canoe rentals, saltwater fishing, hiking trails. No pets. Open all yr. Phone: (305)664-4815.

LUTZ—C-3

(N) WINTER QUARTERS-PASCO RV PARK—(Pasco) *From jct I-75 (exit 275) & Hwy 56: Go 5 mi W on Hwy 54/56. Enter on L.*

WELCOME

◆◆◆◆FACILITIES: 252 sites, 252 full hkups, (30 & 50 amps), many extended stay sites (in winter), wireless Instant Internet access at site, phone on-site Internet access (needs activ), phone Internet access central location, tenting, RV storage, dump station, non-guest dumping $, laundry, LP gas by weight/by meter, tables, patios.

◆◆◆◆RECREATION: rec hall, swim pool, whirlpool, lake fishing, golf nearby, 4 shuffleboard courts, planned activities, horseshoes, local tours.

Pets welcome, breed restrict, size restrict, quantity restrict. Partial handicap access. Open all yr. Planned activities winter only. Big rigs welcome.

Burt Reynolds, actor, is from Florida.

LUTZ—Continued
WINTER QUARTERS-PASCO RV PARK—Continued

Internet friendly. Clubs welcome. Rate in 2007 $25-35 for 2 persons. MC/VISA/DISC/AMEX. Member ARVC, FLARVC. Phone: (800)879-2131.

e-mail: info@rvonthego.com

SEE AD TAMPA PAGE 176

MADISON—A-2

(S) Deerwood Madison Campground & Motel—(Madison) *From I-10 (exit 258) & Hwy 53: Go 1/4 mi S on Hwy 53, then 1/10 mi W on SW Old St. Augustine Rd. Enter on L.* ◆FACILITIES: 75 sites, typical site width 35 ft, 38 full hkups, 37 W&E, (20, 30 & 50 amps), 50 amps ($), 75 pull-thrus, tenting, dump station, non-guest dumping $, laundry, ice, tables. ◆RECREATION: rec room/area, pavilion, swim pool, playground, 2 shuffleboard courts, tennis, horseshoes. Pets welcome. Partial handicap access. Open all yr. Pool open during summer only. Rate in 2007 $23-28 per family. Phone: (850)973-2504.

(S) Yogi Bear's Jellystone Park Camp Resort—(Madison) *From I-10 (exit 258) & Hwy 53: Go 1/4 mi S on Hwy 53, then 1/2 mi W on Ragans Lake Rd. Enter on L.* ◆◆◆◆FACILITIES: 135 sites, typical site width 25 ft, 64 full hkups, 62 W&E, (20, 30 & 50 amps), 50 amps ($), 9 no hkups, 83 pull-thrus, tenting, dump station, non-guest dumping $, portable dump, laundry, ltd groceries, LP gas by weight/by meter, ice, tables, fire rings, grills, wood. ◆◆◆◆◆RECREATION: rec hall, rec room/area, pavilion, equipped pavilion, swim pool, lake swimming, boating, electric motors only, canoeing, 8 pedal boat rentals, lake fishing, mini-golf ($), playground, planned activities, horseshoes, sports field, hiking trails, v-ball. Rec open to public. Pets welcome. Partial handicap access. Open all yr. Big rigs welcome. Internet friendly. Rate in 2007 $28-36 for 2 persons. Member ARVC, FLARVC. Phone: (800)347-0174.

MALABAR—C-5

(SW) CAMELOT RV PARK—(Brevard) *From jct I-95 (exit 173) & Hwy 514 (Malabar/Palm Bay exit): Go 4-1/2 mi E on Hwy 514, then 2 blocks S on US 1 (5 mi S of Melbourne on US 1). Enter on R.*

WELCOME

◆◆◆◆FACILITIES: 130 sites, typical site width 35 ft, 130 full hkups, (30 & 50 amps), 50 amps ($), some extended stay sites (in winter), 25 pull-thrus, heater not allowed, cable TV, wireless Instant Internet access at site, phone/cable on-site Internet access (needs activ), wireless Internet access central location, RV storage, dump station, laundry, LP gas by weight/by meter, ice, tables, patios, controlled access gate.

◆◆◆RECREATION: rec hall, saltwater/river fishing, golf nearby, bsktball, 2 shuffleboard courts, planned activities, horseshoes.

Pets welcome, breed restrict. Partial handicap access. No tents. Open all yr. Planned group activities winter only. Big rigs welcome. Internet friendly. Escort to site. Clubs welcome. Rate in 2007 $32-36 for 2 persons. MC/VISA/DISC/Debit. Phone: (321)724-5396.

SEE AD MELBOURNE NEXT PAGE

MARATHON—F-4

(NE) JOLLY ROGER TRAVEL PARK—(Monroe) *On US 1 at mile marker 59-1/2. Enter on R.*

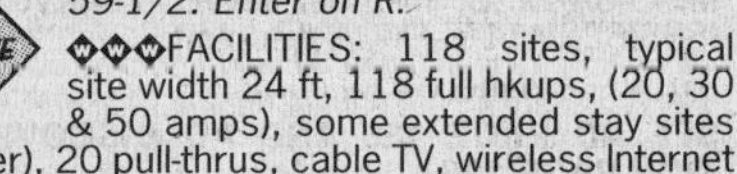

WELCOME

◆◆◆FACILITIES: 118 sites, typical site width 24 ft, 118 full hkups, (20, 30 & 50 amps), some extended stay sites (in winter), 20 pull-thrus, cable TV, wireless Internet access central location, tenting, laundry, ice, tables, patios.

◆◆RECREATION: pavilion, saltwater swimming, boating, canoeing, kayaking, ramp, dock, saltwater fishing, golf nearby, shuffleboard court.

Pets welcome, quantity restrict. Open all yr. Internet friendly. Escort to site. Clubs welcome. Rate in 2007 $60-70 for 2 persons. MC/VISA/DISC/Debit. Member ARVC, FLARVC. Phone: (800)995-1525. CCUSA discount.

e-mail: email@jrtp.com

SEE AD KEY WEST PAGE 133

MARIANNA—E-3

(E) ARROWHEAD CAMPSITES—(Jackson) *From jct I-10 (exit 142) & Hwy 71: Go 2 mi N on Hwy 71, then 1/2 mi W on US 90. Enter on R.*

WELCOME

◆◆◆FACILITIES: 245 sites, typical site width 30 ft, 200 full hkups, 45 W&E, (20 & 30 amps), some extended stay sites, 200 pull-thrus, cable TV, phone Internet access central location, tenting, cabins, dump station, non-guest dumping $, laundry, groceries, RV supplies, LP gas by weight/by meter, gas, ice, tables, fire rings, wood, controlled access gate.

◆◆◆◆RECREATION: rec hall, rec room/area, pavilion, swim pool, boating, canoeing, kayaking, ramp, dock, 13 canoe/6 pedal boat rentals, lake fishing, fishing supplies, golf nearby, bsktball, playground.

Pets welcome. Open all yr. Internet friendly. Rate in 2007 $26 for 2 persons. MC/VISA/DISC/AMEX. ATM. Member ARVC, FLARVC. Phone: (800)643-9166.

e-mail: arrowhead@phonl.com

SEE AD NEXT PAGE

✱ **(E) ARROWHEAD RV SALES**—*From jct I-10 (exit 142) & Hwy 71: Go 2 mi N on Hwy 71, then 1/2 mi W on US 90. Enter on R.* SALES: travel trailers, truck campers, 5th wheels, van campers, motor homes, mini-motor homes, fold-down camping trailers, pre-owned unit sales. SERVICES: full-time mech, RV appliance repair, body work/collision repair, LP gas by weight/by meter, dump station, sells parts/accessories, installs hitches. Open all yr. MC/VISA/DISC/AMEX. ATM. Phone: (866)277-6978.

WELCOME

SEE AD NEXT PAGE

(SE) Dove Rest RV Park & Campground—(Jackson) *From jct I-10 (exit 142) & Hwy-71: Go 1/2 mi S on Hwy-71. Enter on R.* ◆◆FACILITIES: 59 sites,

Dove Rest RV Park & Campground—Continued on next page

MARIANNA—Continued
Dove Rest RV Park & Campground—Continued

typical site width 35 ft, 45 full hkups, 14 W&E, (20, 30 & 50 amps), many extended stay sites, tenting, dump station, non-guest dumping $, laundry, tables. RECREATION: horseshoes. Pets welcome. Open all yr. Rate in 2007 $19.50-24.95 for 2 persons. Phone: (850)482-5313.

(N) FLORIDA CAVERNS STATE PARK—(Jackson) *From jct US 90 & Hwy 166: Go 3 mi N on Hwy 166.* FACILITIES: 35 sites, 30 ft max RV length, 35 W&E, tenting, dump station, grills. RECREATION: lake swimming, boating, canoeing, ramp, lake fishing, playground, hiking trails. Pets welcome. Open all yr. Phone: (850)482-9598.

MCINTOSH—B-3

(E) SPORTSMAN'S COVE RESORT—(Marion) *From jct Hwy 320 & US 441: Go 1 block N on US 441, then 1/2 mi E on Avenue F. Enter at end.*

WELCOME

◇◇◇FACILITIES: 36 sites, typical site width 30 ft, 36 full hkups, (30 & 50 amps), some extended stay sites, 5 pull-thrus, cable TV, wireless Instant Internet access at site, tenting, RV/park trailer rentals, dump station, non-guest dumping $, laundry, RV supplies, LP gas by weight/by meter, marine gas, ice, tables.

◇◇RECREATION: equipped pavilion, boating, canoeing, kayaking, ramp, dock, lake fishing, fishing supplies, golf nearby, horseshoes. Rec open to public.

Pets welcome. Open all yr. Big rigs welcome. Escort to site. Rate in 2007 $22 for 2 persons. Member ARVC, FLARVC. Phone: (352)591-1435.

SEE AD GAINESVILLE PAGE 125

MELBOURNE—C-5

(SE) Breezy Palms RV Park—(Brevard) *From I-95 (exit 173): Go 4 mi E on Hwy 514, then 1/2 mi N on US 1. Enter on L.* ◇◇◇FACILITIES: 65 sites, typical site width 25 ft, 65 full hkups, (30 & 50 amps), heater not allowed, laundry, tables, patios. ◇◇RECREATION: rec hall, saltwater fishing, horseshoes. Pets welcome. No tents. Open all yr. Big rigs welcome. Rate in 2007 $30-40 for 2 persons. Phone: (321)724-1639.

CAMELOT RV PARK—*From jct I-95 (exit 173) & Hwy 514: Go 4-1/2 mi E on Hwy 514, then 2 blocks S on US 1.*

WELCOME

SEE PRIMARY LISTING AT MALABAR AND AD THIS PAGE

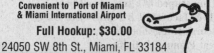

MELBOURNE—Continued

(N) Palm Shores RV Park—(Brevard) *From jct I-95 (exit 191) & Hwy 509 (Wickham Rd): Go 4-1/4 mi E & S on Hwy 509, then 1/2 mi E on Hwy 404, then 3/4 mi S on US 1. Enter on R.* ◇◇FACILITIES: 36 sites, typical site width 25 ft, 36 full hkups, (30 amps), heater not allowed, dump station, non-guest dumping $, laundry, tables, patios. ◇RECREATION: rec room/area, horseshoes. Pets welcome, breed restrict, size restrict, quantity restrict. No tents. Open all yr. Rate in 2007 $20 for 2 persons. Phone: (321)254-4388.

(NW) WICKHAM PARK (Brevard County Park)—(Brevard) *From US 192 & US-1: Go 7 mi N on US-1, then 1-1/2 mi W on Parkway Dr.* FACILITIES: 88 sites, 31 ft max RV length, 88 W&E, tenting, dump station, non-guest dumping $, laundry, ice, grills. RECREATION: rec room/area, equipped pavilion, lake swimming, pond fishing, playground, horseshoes, sports field, hiking trails, v-ball. Rec open to public. Pets welcome. Open all yr. Phone: (321)255-4307.

MELBOURNE BEACH—C-5

(S) Melbourne Beach Mobile Park (RV SPACES)—(Brevard) *From jct US-192 & Hwy-A1A: Go 3-1/2 mi S on Hwy-A1A. Enter on R.* FACILITIES: 75 sites, typical site width 25 ft, 36 ft max RV length, 75 full hkups, (20, 30 & 50 amps), some extended stay sites (in winter), 15 pull-thrus, dump station, non-guest dumping $, laundry, patios. RECREATION: rec room/area, saltwater swimming, saltwater/river fishing, 2 shuffleboard courts. No pets. No tents. Open all yr. Internet friendly. Phone: (321)723-4947.

MELBOURNE BEACH—Continued

(S) Outdoor Resorts/Melbourne Beach—(Brevard) *From jct US 192 & Hwy A1A: Go 4 mi S on Hwy A1A. Enter on R.* ◇◇◇◇FACILITIES: 75 sites, typical site width 34 ft, accepts full hkup units only, 75 full hkups, (20, 30 & 50 amps), laundry, patios. ◇◇◇RECREATION: 3 swim pools, saltwater swimming, boating, ramp, saltwater/river fishing, 8 shuffleboard courts, planned activities, tennis. Pets welcome. No tents. Open all yr. Planned activities winter only. Big rigs welcome. Internet friendly. Phone: (321)724-2600.

MIAMI—E-5

(W) GATOR PARK (RV SPACES)—(Dade) *From jct Hwy 997 & US 41: Go 6 mi W on US 41. Enter on L.*

WELCOME

FACILITIES: 60 sites, typical site width 20 ft, accepts self-contained units only, 15 full hkups, 15 W&E, (30 & 50 amps), 30 no hkups, some extended stay sites (in winter), dump station, non-guest dumping $.

RECREATION: local tours. Rec open to public.

Pets welcome, breed restrict, size restrict. No tents. Open all yr. No Showers. Escort to site. Rate in 2007 $30 per vehicle. MC/VISA/DISC/AMEX/DC/Debit. Phone: (800)559-2205.

SEE AD THIS PAGE

MIAMI—Continued on next page

MIAMI—Continued

(W) GATOR PARK AIRBOAT TOURS—*From jct of Hwy 997 & US 41: Go 6 mi W on US 41. Enter on L.* Fully narrated airboat tours of the Everglades National Park. Including Wildlife Shows & alligator exhibitions. Open all yr. MC/VISA/DISC/AMEX/DC/Debit. Phone: (800)559-2205.

SEE AD PAGE 141

(W) LARRY & PENNY THOMPSON PARK (Dade County Park)—(Dade) *From jct US 41 & Hwy 997: Go 11-1/2 mi S on Hwy 997, then 5 mi E on 184th St. Enter on R.*

FACILITIES: 240 sites, 240 full hkups, (20, 30 & 50 amps), some extended stay sites (in winter), 10 pull-thrus, phone Internet access central location, tenting, dump station, non-guest dumping $, laundry, ice, tables, fire rings.

RECREATION: equipped pavilion, lake swimming, lake fishing, playground, planned activities, sports field, hiking trails, v-ball, local tours.

Pets welcome. Partial handicap access. Open all yr. Big rigs welcome. Escort to site. Clubs welcome. MC/VISA/AMEX. Member ARVC, FLARVC. Phone: (305)232-1049.

e-mail: L&Pcampground@miamidade.gov

SEE AD PAGE 141

(SW) MIAMI EVERGLADES CAMPGROUND—(Dade) *From jct US 41 & Hwy 997: Go 12-1/2 mi S on Hwy 997, then 1-1/2 mi E on Quail Roost Dr, then 1/4 mi S on Farm Life School Rd. Enter on L.*

◆◆◆◆FACILITIES: 333 sites, typical site width 22 ft, 240 full hkups, 79 W&E, (30 & 50 amps), 50 amps ($), 14 no hkups, some extended stay sites (in winter), 229 pull-thrus, cable TV, wireless Instant Internet access at site ($), cable Internet access central location, tenting, cabins, RV storage, dump station, non-guest dumping $, laundry, full svc store, RV supplies, LP gas by weight/by meter, ice, tables, patios, grills.

◆◆◆◆RECREATION: rec hall, equipped pavilion, swim pool, whirlpool, golf nearby, bsktball, 7 bike rentals, playground, 8 shuffleboard courts, planned activities, horseshoes, sports field, hiking trails, v-ball, local tours.

Pets welcome, breed restrict. Partial handicap access. Open all yr. Planned group activities winter only. Big rigs welcome. Internet friendly. Escort to site. Clubs welcome. Rate in 2007 $35-65 for 2 persons. MC/VISA/Debit. ATM. Member ARVC, FLARVC. Phone: (800)917-4923.

e-mail: info@miamicamp.com

SEE AD DISCOVER SECTION PAGE 141

MILTON—F-1

(N) Adventures Unlimited Outdoor Center—(Santa Rosa) *From jct Hwy 90 & Hwy 87: Go 12 mi N on Hwy 87, then 1/2 mi E on Neal Kennington Rd, then 1/10 mi S on Lewis Rd, then 3 mi E on Springhill Rd.*

MILTON—Continued
Adventures Unlimited Outdoor Center—Continued

Enter on R. ◆◆FACILITIES: 24 sites, typical site width 25 ft, 32 ft max RV length, 22 W&E, (30 amps), 2 no hkups, tenting, dump station, ice, tables, fire rings, grills, wood. ◆◆◆RECREATION: river swimming, no motors, canoeing, 300 canoe rentals, river fishing, play equipment, sports field, hiking trails, v-ball. Rec open to public. No pets. Partial handicap access. Open all yr. Rate in 2007 $20 for 4 persons. Member ARVC. Phone: (800)239-6864.

(N) Cedar Pines Campground—(Santa Rosa) *From jct US 90 & Hwy 87: Go 4-1/2 mi N on Hwy 87. Enter on R.* ◆◆◆FACILITIES: 40 sites, typical site width 30 ft, 40 full hkups, (30 & 50 amps), 50 amps ($), many extended stay sites, 33 pull-thrus, tenting, dump station, laundry, tables, patios. ◆RECREATION: swim pool, horseshoes. Pets welcome. Open all yr. Internet friendly. Rate in 2007 $25.75-27.75 for 2 persons. Member ARVC, FLARVC. Phone: (850)623-8869.

(E) GULF PINES KOA—(Santa Rosa) *From jct I-10 (exit 31) & Hwy 87: Go 1 block N on Hwy 87, then 200 feet E on Gulf Pines Dr. Enter on R.*

◆◆◆◆FACILITIES: 122 sites, typical site width 30 ft, 100 full hkups, 11 W&E, (20, 30 & 50 amps), 11 no hkups, some extended stay sites, 100 pull-thrus, cable TV, wireless Instant Internet access at site, phone Internet access central location, tenting, cabins, RV storage, dump station, non-guest dumping $, laundry, groceries, RV supplies, LP gas by weight/by meter, ice, tables, patios.

◆◆◆◆◆RECREATION: rec hall, pavilion, coin games, swim pool, wading pool, mini-golf, bsktball, 14 bike rentals, playground, planned activities, horseshoes, sports field, hiking trails, v-ball.

Pets welcome, breed restrict. Partial handicap access. Open all yr. Big rigs welcome. Internet friendly. Escort to site. Clubs welcome. Rate in 2007 $31-46 for 2 persons. MC/VISA. Member ARVC, FLARVC. Phone: (877)684-2307. KOA 10% value card discount.

e-mail: info@gulfpinesrv.com

SEE AD DISCOVER SECTION PAGES 62 & 63 AND AD DISCOVER SECTION PAGE 141

(S) PELICAN PALMS RV PARK—(Santa Rosa) *From jct I-10 (exit 26) & Hwy 191: Go 1/10 mi S on Hwy 191. Enter on L.*

COUNTRY COMFORT - CITY CONVENIENCE! Location, Environment, Proximity - we've got it all! 1/10 mi off I-10 & close to Emerald Coast Gulf Beaches. Large, level, full-hookup sites. Swim or relax in our sunny pool after a day of driving or sightseeing. Visit us soon!

◆◆◆◆FACILITIES: 39 sites, typical site width 30 ft, 36 full hkups, 3 W&E, (20, 30 & 50 amps), 50 amps ($), some extended stay sites, 25 pull-thrus, wireless Instant Internet access at site ($), tenting, dump station, non-guest dumping $, laundry, RV supplies, LP gas by weight/by meter, ice.

MILTON—Continued
PELICAN PALMS RV PARK—Continued

◆◆RECREATION: rec room/area, equipped pavilion, swim pool.

Pets welcome. Open all yr. Big rigs welcome. Internet friendly. Clubs welcome. Rate in 2007 $25-27 for 2 persons. MC/VISA/DISC/AMEX. Member ARVC, FLARVC. Phone: (850)623-0576.

e-mail: pprvp@aol.com

SEE AD PENSACOLA PAGE 161

MONTICELLO—A-2

(S) KOA-Tallahassee East/Monticello—(Jefferson) *From jct I-10 (exit 225) & US 19: Go 1/4 mi S on US 19, then 2 mi W on CR 158B, then 1/2 mi N on CR 259, then 1/4 mi E on KOA Rd. Enter on R.* ◆◆◆FACILITIES: 72 sites, typical site width 35 ft, 64 full hkups, 8 W&E, (30 & 50 amps), 50 amps ($), many extended stay sites, 66 pull-thrus, tenting, dump station, non-guest dumping $, laundry, ltd groceries, LP gas by weight/by meter, ice, tables, fire rings, grills, wood. ◆◆RECREATION: rec hall, swim pool, lake fishing, playground. Pets welcome. Partial handicap access. Open all yr. Pool open Apr 1-Oct 1, weather permitting. Internet friendly. Rate in 2007 $34-38.50 for 2 persons. Phone: (800)562-3890. KOA 10% value card discount.

MOORE HAVEN—D-4

(E) Marina RV Resort—(Glades) *From east jct Hwy 78 & US 27: Go 1-1/2 mi S on US 27, then 1/2 mi N on 6th St, then 1/2 mi E on CR 720 NW (Tobias Ave) Enter at end.* ◆◆◆FACILITIES: 139 sites, typical site width 30 ft, 133 full hkups, 6 W&E, (20, 30 & 50 amps), many extended stay sites (in winter), tenting, laundry, tables, patios. ◆◆◆◆RECREATION: rec hall, swim pool, boating, canoeing, ramp, lake/river fishing, 2 shuffleboard courts, planned activities, horseshoes, hiking trails. Pets welcome. Partial handicap access. Open all yr. Internet friendly. Rate in 2007 $26.75 for 2 persons. Phone: (863)946-2255.

(NW) Robin's Nest RV Resort—(Glades) *From E jct Hwy 78 & US 27: Go 6-1/2 mi N on US 27. Enter on L.* ◆◆◆FACILITIES: 248 sites, typical site width 30 ft, 248 full hkups, (30 & 50 amps), some extended stay sites (in winter), dump station, laundry, ice, tables, patios. ◆◆◆RECREATION: rec hall, rec room/area, swim pool, pond fishing, 3 shuffleboard courts, planned activities, horseshoes, sports field. Pets welcome, size restrict. Partial handicap access. No tents. Age restrictions may apply. Open all yr. Big rigs welcome. Internet friendly. Rate in 2007 $25 for 2 persons. Phone: (863) 946-1298.

NAPLES—E-4

(E) CLUB NAPLES RV RESORT (Morgan RV Resorts)—(Collier) *From jct I-75 (exit 101) & Hwy 951: Go 1/4 mi S on Hwy 951, then 1 mi E on Old Hwy 84 (Alligator Alley). Enter on R.*

◆◆◆◆FACILITIES: 309 sites, typical site width 33 ft, 309 full hkups, (30 & 50 amps), mostly extended stay sites (in winter), 12 pull-thrus, heater not allowed, cable TV, wireless In-

CLUB NAPLES RV RESORT (Morgan RV Resorts)—Continued on next page

NAPLES—Continued
CLUB NAPLES RV RESORT (Morgan RV Resorts)—Continued

stant Internet access at site, tenting, dump station, non-guest dumping $, laundry, RV supplies, LP gas by weight/by meter, ice, tables, patios.

◆◆◆◆RECREATION: rec hall, swim pool, whirlpool, mini-golf, golf nearby, bsktball, 6 shuffleboard courts, planned activities, horseshoes.

Pets welcome, breed restrict. Partial handicap access. Open all yr. Group activities in season. Tents summer only. Internet friendly. Escort to site. Clubs welcome. Rate in 2007 $40-45 for 2 persons. MC/VISA/DISC/Debit. Member ARVC, FLARVC. Phone: (888)795-2780. CCUSA discount.

e-mail: clubnaples@yahoo.com

SEE AD THIS PAGE

(SE) COLLIER-SEMINOLE STATE PARK—(Collier) *From jct Hwy-84 & US-41: Go 15 mi S on US-41.* FACILITIES: 137 sites, 137 W&E, tenting, dump station, grills, wood. RECREATION: boating, canoeing, ramp, dock, 10 canoe rentals, saltwater fishing, playground, hiking trails. Partial handicap access. Open all yr. Phone: (239)394-3397.

Butterfly McQueen, actor, is from Florida.

NAPLES—Continued

(NE) CRYSTAL LAKE RV RESORT (CAMP RESORT)—(Collier) *From jct I-75 (exit 101) & Hwy 951: Go 7 mi N on Hwy 951. Enter on R.*

WELCOME

FACILITIES: 490 sites, typical site width 40 ft, accepts full hkup units only, 490 full hkups, (30 & 50 amps), mostly extended stay sites (in winter), cable TV, wireless Internet access central location, RV storage, dump station, laundry, tables, patios, controlled access gate.

CRYSTAL LAKE RV RESORT—Continued on next page

NAPLES—Continued
CRYSTAL LAKE RV RESORT—Continued

RECREATION: rec hall, rec room/area, equipped pavilion, 2 swim pools, whirlpool, boating, electric motors only, canoeing, kayaking, ramp, dock, lake fishing, putting green, golf nearby, 8 shuffleboard courts, planned activities, tennis, horseshoes, hiking trails, local tours.

Pets welcome, quantity restrict. Partial handicap access. No tents. Open all yr. Big rigs welcome. Internet friendly. Phone: (239)348-0017.

e-mail: crystalrealty@mindspring.com

SEE AD THIS PAGE

NAPLES—Continued on next page

NAPLES—Continued

(E) Endless Summer RV Park—(Collier) *From jct I-75 (exit 101) & Hwy 951: Go 1/4 mi S on Hwy 951 (Collier Blvd), then 1/2 mi W on Hwy 84 (Davis Blvd), then 2 mi W on CR 856 (Radio Rd). Enter on R.* ◊◊◊FACILITIES: 120 sites, typical site width 24 ft, 120 full hkups, (20, 30 & 50 amps), some extended stay sites (in winter), heater not allowed, tenting, dump station, non-guest dumping $, laundry, tables, patios. ◊◊RECREATION: rec hall, swim pool, 2 shuffleboard courts, planned activities, horseshoes. Pets welcome, size restrict. Open all yr. Planned group activities winter only. Internet friendly. Rate in 2007 $39-45 for 2 persons. Member ARVC, FLARVC. Phone: (239)643-1511.

(SE) KOA-Naples—(Collier) *From jct I-75 (exit 101) & Hwy 951: Go 7-3/4 mi S on Hwy 951, then 1/2 mi W on TV Tower Rd., then 500 feet S on Barefoot Williams Rd. Enter on L.* ◊◊◊◊FACILITIES: 182 sites, typical site width 20 ft, 143 full hkups, 29 W&E, (30 & 50 amps), 10 no hkups, some extended stay sites (in winter), 75 pull-thrus, tenting, dump station, laundry, groceries, LP gas by weight/by meter, ice, tables, patios. ◊◊◊◊◊RECREATION: rec hall, rec room/area, pavilion, swim pool, boating, canoeing, ramp, 4 canoe rentals, saltwater/river fishing, playground, 3 shuffleboard courts, planned activities, horseshoes. Pets welcome, breed restrict. Partial handicap access. Open all yr. Church services & planned group activities winter only. Internet friendly. Rate in 2007 $48-75 for 2 persons. Member ARVC, FLARVC. Phone: (800)562-7734. KOA 10% value card discount.

(SE) KOUNTREE KAMPINN RV RESORT—(Collier) *From jct I-75 (exit 101) & Hwy 951: Go 4-1/4 mi S on Hwy 951. Enter on L.*

◊◊◊◊FACILITIES: 161 sites, typical site width 32 ft, 161 full hkups, (30 & 50 amps), many extended stay sites (in winter), 15 pull-thrus, cable TV, wireless Instant Internet access at site, RV storage, dump station, non-guest dumping $, laundry, RV supplies, LP gas by weight/by meter, ice, tables, patios.

◊◊◊RECREATION: rec hall, swim pool, golf nearby, 3 shuffleboard courts, planned activities, horseshoes.

Pets welcome, breed restrict, size restrict, quantity restrict. Partial handicap access. No tents. Open all yr. Planned activities winter only. Internet friendly. Clubs welcome. MC/VISA/DISC/Debit. Member ARVC, FLARVC. Phone: (239)775-4340.

e-mail: Kountree-Kampinn@wfla.rr.com

SEE AD THIS PAGE

(N) LAKE SAN MARINO RV PARK—(Collier) *From jct Hwy 951 & I-75: Go 10 mi N on I-75 (exit 111), then 3-1/2 mi W on CR 846, then 1-1/2 mi N on US 41, then 1/4 mi E on Wiggins Pass Rd. Enter on R.*

◊◊◊FACILITIES: 411 sites, typical site width 35 ft, accepts full hkup units only, 411 full hkups, (30 & 50 amps), many extended stay sites (in winter), wireless Instant Internet access at site ($), dump station, non-guest dumping $, laundry, tables, patios.

◊◊◊◊RECREATION: rec hall, rec room/area, swim pool, boating, no motors, canoeing, kayaking, dock, lake fishing, golf nearby, 8 shuffleboard courts, planned activities, horseshoes.

Pets welcome, breed restrict, quantity restrict. Partial handicap access. No tents. Age restrictions may apply. Open all yr. Internet friendly. Clubs welcome. Rate in 2007 $35-46 for 2 persons. MC/VISA/DISC/Debit. Member ARVC, FLARVC. Phone: (239)597-4202.

e-mail: sunresv@aol.com

SEE AD TRAVEL SECTION PAGE 73

(SE) MARCO NAPLES HITCHING POST TRAVEL RESORT—(Collier) *From jct I-75 (exit 101) & Hwy 951: Go 7 mi S on 951 (Collier Blvd), then 1-1/4 mi N on US 41. Enter on L.*

◊◊◊FACILITIES: 305 sites, typical site width 30 ft, 295 full hkups, 10 W&E, (20 & 30 amps), mostly extended stay sites (in winter), 295 pull-thrus, heater not allowed, phone Internet access central location, dump station, non-guest dumping $, tables, patios.

◊◊◊◊RECREATION: rec hall, swim pool, golf nearby, 4 shuffleboard courts, planned activities, horseshoes.

Woodall's. The name that's trusted for over 70 years.

NAPLES—Continued
MARCO NAPLES HITCHING POST TRAVEL RESORT—Continued

Pets welcome. Partial handicap access. No tents. Age restrictions may apply. Open Oct 1 thru Apr 30. Planned group activities winter only. Internet friendly. Clubs welcome. Rate in 2007 $36 for 2 persons. Phone: (800)362-8968.

e-mail: lemorris@aol.com

SEE AD THIS PAGE

(SE) NAPLES REALTY SERVICES—Phone: (888)851-7677.

e-mail: SLRosol@aol.com

SEE AD THIS PAGE

Read interesting travel facts in the front of every state/province listing section.

NAPLES—Continued

(SE) NEAPOLITAN COVE RV RESORT—(Collier) *From jct I-75 (exit 101) & Hwy 951: Go 1/4 mi S on Hwy 951, then 5 mi W on Hwy 84, then 3/4 mi S on Airport Rd, then 1/2 mi SE on US 41. Enter on R.*

NEW LUXURIOUS RV RESORT

Beautiful landscaped RV Resort on Florida's West Coast. All the amenities of Naples nearby. Located near some of Florida's most beautiful beaches. Future clubhouse, laundry & pool. Enjoy fun & relaxation in a sunny paradise.

◊◊◊◊◊FACILITIES: 60 sites, typical site width 25 ft, accepts full hkup units only, 60 full hkups, (20 & 50 amps), some extended stay sites (in winter), 18 pull-thrus, cable TV, wireless Instant Internet access at site, laundry, tables, patios.

NEAPOLITAN COVE RV RESORT—Continued on next page

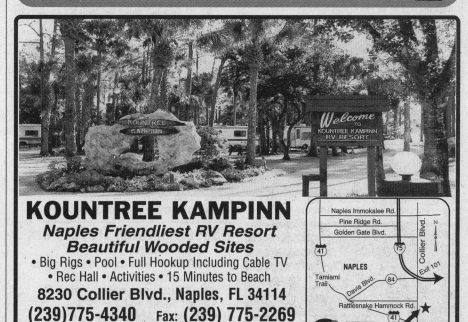

NAPLES—Continued
NEAPOLITAN COVE RV RESORT—Continued

◊◊RECREATION: pavilion, swim pool, golf nearby, planned activities.

Pets welcome, quantity restrict. Partial handicap access. No tents. Open all yr. Big rigs welcome. Internet friendly. Escort to site. Clubs welcome. MC/VISA. Member ARVC, FLARVC. Phone: (239) 793-0091.

e-mail: info@neapolitancoverv.com

SEE AD PAGE 144

OUTDOOR RESORTS/CHOKOLOSKEE ISLAND—*From Naples: Go 32 mi S on US 41, then 8 mi S on CR 29.*

WELCOME

SEE PRIMARY LISTING AT CHOKOLOSKEE AND AD CHOKOLOSKEE PAGE 101

(SE) **Paradise Pointe Luxury RV Resort**—(Collier) *From jct I-75 (exit 101) & Hwy 951: Go 7 mi S on Hwy 951 (Collier Blvd), then 2-1/2 mi E on US 41. Enter on R.* ◊◊◊◊FACILITIES: 383 sites, typical site width 40 ft, 383 full hkups, (30 & 50 amps), mostly extended stay sites (in winter), dump station, non-guest dumping $, laundry, tables, patios. ◊◊◊◊RECREATION: rec hall, swim pool, pond fishing, 6 shuffleboard courts, planned activities, tennis, horseshoes, v-ball. Pets welcome. Partial handicap access. No tents. Age restrictions may apply. Open all yr. Planned group activities winter season only. Big rigs welcome. Internet friendly. Rate in 2007 $40-45 for 2 persons. Phone: (877)462-7537.

(SE) **PELICAN LAKE MOTORCOACH RESORT**—(Collier) *From jct I-75 (exit 101) & Hwy 951: Go 9 mi S on Hwy 951. Enter on L.*

WELCOME

◊◊◊◊◊FACILITIES: 289 sites, typical site width 55 ft, accepts full hkup units only, 289 full hkups, (20, 30 & 50 amps), some extended stay sites (in winter), cable TV, wireless Instant Internet access at site, laundry, tables, patios, controlled access gate.

◊◊◊◊◊RECREATION: rec hall, equipped pavilion, swim pool, whirlpool, boating, electric motors only, canoeing, kayaking, dock, lake fishing, golf nearby, 4 shuffleboard courts, planned activities, tennis.

Pets welcome. Partial handicap access. No tents. Open all yr. Class A Motor Coaches only 26-ft minimum. Big rigs welcome. Internet friendly. Escort to site. Clubs welcome. Rate in 2007 $40-95 for 6 persons. MC/VISA. Phone: (800)835-4389.

e-mail: info@pelicanlake.com

SEE AD PAGE 143

(E) **ROCK CREEK RV RESORT & CAMPGROUND**—(Collier) *From jct I-75 (exit 101) & Hwy 951: Go 1/4 mi S on Hwy 951, then 1/2 mi W on Hwy 84, then 4-1/4 mi W on CR 856 (Radio Rd), then 1/2 mi S on CR 31 (Airport/Pulling Rd), then 500 feet W on North Rd. Enter on L.*

WELCOME

ROCK CREEK TROPICAL PARADISE

2 miles to Naples' exquisite beaches, downtown Historic District, & mall. A private family owned friendly business. Beautiful tropical setting of lush foilage, oaks, palms & a creek that flows to the Gulf. www.rockcreekrv.com

◊◊◊◊FACILITIES: 230 sites, typical site width 25 ft, 230 full hkups, (30 & 50 amps), 50 amps ($), some extended stay sites (in winter), 4 pull-thrus, cable TV, wireless Internet access central location, tenting, dump station, non-guest dumping $, laundry, RV supplies, ice, tables, patios.

◊◊◊◊RECREATION: rec hall, rec room/area, pavilion, swim pool, boating, canoeing, kayaking, ramp, dock, saltwater fishing, golf nearby, 2 shuffleboard courts, planned activities, horseshoes.

Pets welcome. Partial handicap access. Age restrictions may apply. Open all yr. Children limited stay only. Group activities winter only. Big rigs welcome. Internet friendly. Escort to site. Clubs wel-

NAPLES—Continued
ROCK CREEK RV RESORT & CAMPGROUND—Continued

come. Rate in 2007 $45-56 for 2 persons. MC/VISA. Member ARVC, FLARVC. Phone: (239)643-3100.

e-mail: rockcrkrv@aol.com

SEE AD PAGE 144

(SE) **SILVER LAKES RV RESORT AND GOLF CLUB**—(Collier) *From jct I-75 (exit 101) & Hwy 951: Go 9 mi S on Hwy 951. Enter on L.*

WELCOME

◊◊◊◊◊FACILITIES: 522 sites, typical site width 40 ft, accepts full hkup units only, 522 full hkups, (30 & 50 amps), many extended stay sites (in winter), 13 pull-thrus, cable TV, wireless Internet access central location, laundry, ice, tables, patios, controlled access gate.

◊◊◊◊◊RECREATION: rec hall, rec room/area, 2 swim pools, whirlpool, canoeing, kayaking, lake fishing, putting green, 8 shuffleboard courts, planned activities, tennis, horseshoes.

Pets welcome, breed restrict. Partial handicap access. No tents. Open all yr. 25 ft min RV. Big rigs welcome. Internet friendly. Escort to site. Clubs welcome. Rate in 2007 $45-85 for 6 persons. MC/VISA. Phone: (800)843-2836.

e-mail: silverlkes@aol.com

SEE AD PAGE 142

NAVARRE—F-1

(E) **EMERALD BEACH RV PARK**—(Santa Rosa) *From jct Hwy 87 & US 98: Go 1 mi E on US 98. (Big Rigs coming from east-turn on Navarre Sound Circle to make right turn into park.) Enter on R.*

WELCOME

◊◊◊◊◊FACILITIES: 72 sites, typical site width 25 ft, 72 full hkups, (20, 30 & 50 amps), many extended stay sites (in winter), 37 pull-thrus, cable TV, wireless Instant Internet access at site ($), cabins, dump station, non-guest dumping $, laundry, RV supplies, LP gas by weight/by meter, ice, tables, patios.

◊◊◊RECREATION: rec hall, equipped pavilion, swim pool, saltwater swimming, saltwater fishing, planned activities.

Pets welcome, breed restrict, quantity restrict. No tents. Open all yr. Planned group activities winter only. Big rigs welcome. Internet friendly. Clubs welcome. Rate in 2007 $37-52 for 2 persons. MC/VISA/DISC. Member ARVC, FLARVC. Phone: (866) 939-3431.

e-mail: emrldbch1@aol.com

SEE AD THIS PAGE

(E) **NAVARRE BEACH CAMPGROUND**—(Santa Rosa) *From jct Hwy 87 & US 98: Go 2 mi E on US 98. (Right at stoplight) Enter on R.*

WELCOME

◊◊◊◊◊FACILITIES: 146 sites, typical site width 32 ft, 146 full hkups, (30 & 50 amps), many extended stay sites (in winter), 42 pull-thrus, cable TV, wireless Instant Internet access at site ($), phone Internet access central location, tenting, cabins, dump station, non-guest dumping $, laundry, ltd groceries, RV supplies, LP gas by weight/by meter, ice, tables, patios, controlled access gate.

◊◊◊◊RECREATION: rec hall, equipped pavilion, coin games, swim pool, saltwater swimming, whirlpool, saltwater fishing, golf nearby, bsktball, 5 bike rentals, playground, 2 shuffleboard courts, planned activities, horseshoes.

Pets welcome. Partial handicap access. Open all yr. Planned group activites during winter & holidays only. Big rigs welcome. Internet friendly. Clubs welcome. Rate in 2007 $42-74 for 2 persons. MC/VISA. Member ARVC, FLARVC. Phone: (888)639-2188.

e-mail: info@navbeach.com

SEE AD DISCOVER SECTION PAGE 141

NEW PORT RICHEY—C-3

(E) **Orchid Lake RV Resort**—(Pasco) *From jct US 19 & Hwy 587A (Ridge Rd): Go 2-1/2 mi E on Hwy 587A, then 3/4 mi S on Little Rd, then 1/4 mi W on Arevee Dr. Enter at end.* ◊◊◊◊FACILITIES: 406 sites, accepts full hkup units only, 406 full hkups, (20, 30 & 50 amps), mostly extended stay sites (in winter), shower$, laundry, patios. ◊◊◊RECREATION: rec hall, swim pool, lake fishing, 10 shuffleboard courts, planned activities, horseshoes. Pets welcome. No tents. Age restrictions may apply. Open all yr. Church & planned activities winter only. Big rigs welcome. Internet friendly. Rate in 2007 $30 for 2 persons. Phone: (727)847-1925.

(SE) **SEVEN SPRINGS TRAVEL PARK**—(Pasco) *From jct US 19 & Hwy 54: Go 3-1/2 mi E on Hwy 54, then 1 block E on Old County Rd 54. Enter on L.*

WELCOME

◊◊◊◊FACILITIES: 120 sites, typical site width 32 ft, accepts full hkup units only, 120 full hkups, (30 amps), mostly extended stay sites (in winter), heater not allowed, wireless Instant Internet access at site, wireless Internet access central location ($), laundry, LP gas by weight/by meter, patios.

◊◊◊RECREATION: rec hall, swim pool, golf nearby, 3 shuffleboard courts, planned activities, horseshoes.

No pets. No tents. Age restrictions may apply. Open all yr. Planned activities winter only. Internet friendly. Rate in 2007 $25-30 for 2 persons. Phone: (727)376-0000.

SEE AD THIS PAGE

NEW SMYRNA BEACH—B-4

(SW) **NEW SMYRNA BEACH RV PARK**—(Volusia) *S'bnd from jct I-95 (exit 249A) & Hwy 44: Go 2-1/2 mi E on Hwy 44, then 2 mi S on Mission Dr. Entrance on right. N'bnd from jct I-95 (exit 244) & Hwy 442: Go 3/4 mi E on Hwy 442, then 3 mi N on Old Mission Dr. Entrance on left.*

WELCOME

◊◊◊◊◊FACILITIES: 250 sites, typical site width 30 ft, 193 full hkups, 9 W&E, (30 & 50 amps), 48 no hkups, some extended stay sites, 86 pull-thrus, cable TV, wireless Instant Internet access at site, cable Internet access central location, tenting, cabins, RV storage, dump station, non-guest dumping $, laundry, LP gas by weight/by meter, ice, tables.

◊◊◊◊◊RECREATION: rec hall, equipped pavilion, swim pool, mini-golf ($), golf nearby, bsktball, playground, shuffleboard court, planned activities, horseshoes, v-ball.

Pets welcome, quantity restrict. Partial handicap access. Open all yr. Rates adjusted during special events. Big rigs welcome. Internet friendly. Clubs welcome. Rate in 2007 $27 for 2 persons. MC/VISA/DISC. Member ARVC, FLARVC. Phone: (800) 928-9962. FCRV 10% discount. FMCA discount.

e-mail: beachcamp@beachcamp.net

SEE AD DAYTONA BEACH PAGE 106

(W) **Sugar Mill Ruins Travel Park**—(Volusia) *From jct I-95 (exit 249A) & Hwy-44: Go 3-1/2 mi E on Hwy-44, then 1-3/4 mi S on Mission Rd. Enter on R.* ◊◊◊FACILITIES: 180 sites, typical site width 25 ft, 176 full hkups, (30 & 50 amps), 4 no hkups, mostly extended stay sites (in winter), 100 pull-thrus, heater not allowed, tenting, dump station, non-guest dumping $, laundry, ltd groceries, LP gas by weight/by meter, ice, tables. ◊◊◊◊RECREATION: rec hall, swim pool, lake/pond fishing, playground, 3 shuffleboard courts, planned activities, horseshoes, sports field, hiking trails, v-ball. Pets welcome. Partial handicap access. Open all yr. Planned group activities winter only. Non-guest dumping allowed in summer only. Rate in 2007 $27.95-36.95 for 2 persons. Member ARVC, FLARVC. Phone: (386)427-2284.

NICEVILLE—F-2

(E) FRED GANNON ROCKY BAYOU STATE RECREATION AREA—(Okaloosa) *From jct Hwy-20 & Hwy-285: Go 3 mi E on Hwy-20.* FACILITIES: 42 sites, 30 ft max RV length, 42 W&E, tenting, dump station. RECREATION: boating, ramp, dock, saltwater fishing, playground, hiking trails. Pets welcome. Open all yr. Phone: (850)833-9144.

MILITARY PARK (Lake Pippin Rec Area-Maxwell/Gunter AFB AL)—(Okaloosa) *Off base. Off I-10 on Choctawhatchee Bay.* FACILITIES: 80 sites, 46 full hkups, 34 W&E, tenting, dump station. RECREATION: boating. Open all yr. Reservations required. For Military Use Only-w/Military ID Card. Phone: (334)953-3509.

Woodall's Tip #30... Rate information is based on the campground's published rate last year. These rates aren't guaranteed, and you should always call ahead for the most updated rate information.

NOKOMIS—D-3

(NW) ROYAL COACHMEN—(Sarasota) *From jct I-75 (exit 195) & Laurel Rd: Go 2-1/4 mi W on Laurel Rd. Enter on L.*

◊◊◊◊◊FACILITIES: 551 sites, typical site width 30 ft, 551 full hkups, (20, 30 & 50 amps), some extended stay sites (in winter), cable TV, phone/cable on-site Internet access (needs activ), phone Internet access central location, tenting, RV/park trailer rentals, RV storage, dump station, non-guest dumping $, laundry, RV supplies, ice, tables, controlled access gate.

◊◊◊◊◊RECREATION: rec hall, rec room/area, equipped pavilion, coin games, swim pool, boating, canoeing, saltwater fishing, mini-golf, putting green, golf nearby, bsktball, playground, 4 shuffleboard courts, planned activities, tennis, sports field, v-ball, local tours.

Pets welcome. Partial handicap access. Open all yr. Big rigs welcome. Internet friendly. Clubs welcome. Rate in 2007 $43-93 for 2 persons. MC/VISA/DISC/AMEX. Member ARVC, FLARVC. Phone: (800)548-8678.

e-mail: NHCFLRC@MSN.COM

SEE AD SARASOTA PAGE 169

OAKLAND PARK—E-5

(W) EASTERLIN PARK (Broward County Park)—(Broward) *From jct I-95 (exit 32) & Commerical Blvd: Go 1 block W on Commercial Blvd, then 3/4 mi S on Powerline Rd, then 1/2 mi W on NW 38th St. Enter on L.*

FACILITIES: 55 sites, 46 full hkups, 9 W&E, (20, 30 & 50 amps), 7 pull-thrus, tenting, dump station, non-guest dumping $, ice, tables, grills.

RECREATION: pavilion, playground, horseshoes, hiking trails, v-ball. Rec open to public.

Pets welcome. Partial handicap access. Open all yr. Clubs welcome. MC/VISA/DISC. Phone: (954) 938-0610.

e-mail: easterlinpark@broward.org

SEE AD TRAVEL SECTION PAGE 74

OCALA—B-3

(S) Camper Village—(Marion) *From jct I-75 & Hwy 200: Go 1/4 mi S on Hwy 200. Enter on R.* ◊◊◊FACILITIES: 250 sites, typical site width 25 ft, 250 full hkups, (30 & 50 amps), mostly extended stay sites, 150 pull-thrus, dump station, non-guest dumping $, laundry, LP gas by weight/by meter, ice. ◊◊RECREATION: rec hall, rec room/area, 4 shuffleboard courts, planned activities, horseshoes. Pets welcome. Partial handicap access. No tents. Age restrictions may apply. Open all yr. Entertainment winter months only. Big rigs welcome. Internet friendly. Rate in 2007 $21.95 for 2 persons. Phone: (352)237-3236.

ELITE RESORTS AT CRYSTAL RIVER—*From I-75 & SR 200: Go 26 mi S on SR 200, then 10 miles S on CR 491, then 2 miles W on SR 44, then 1.2 mi S on Rock Crusher Rd. Enter on L.*

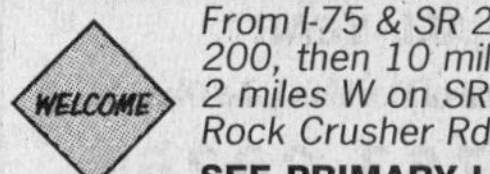

SEE PRIMARY LISTING AT CRYSTAL RIVER AND AD TRAVEL SECTION PAGE 79

(N) Grand Lake RV & Golf Resort—(Marion) *From jct I-75 (exit 368) & Hwy 318: Go 2-3/4 mi E on Hwy 318. Enter on L.* ◊◊◊◊◊FACILITIES: 409 sites, typical site width 40 ft, 409 full hkups, (30 & 50 amps), some extended stay sites, 270 pull-thrus, dump station, non-guest dumping $, laundry, groceries, LP gas by meter, ice, tables, patios. ◊◊◊◊◊RECREATION: rec hall, rec room/area, swim pool, boating, canoeing, dock, lake fishing, play equipment, 4 shuffleboard courts, planned activities, tennis, horseshoes, v-ball.

OCALA—Continued
Grand Lake RV & Golf Resort—Continued

Pets welcome. Partial handicap access. No tents. Open all yr. Church services winter season. Big rigs welcome. Internet friendly. Rate in 2007 $32.61 for 2 persons. Member ARVC, FLARVC. Phone: (800)435-2291. CCUSA discount. FMCA discount.

(SW) HOLIDAY TRAV-L-PARK RV RESORT—(Marion) *From jct I-75 (exit 352) & Hwy 40: Go 1000 feet W on Hwy 40. Enter on R.*

◊◊◊FACILITIES: 110 sites, typical site width 35 ft, 105 full hkups, 5 W&E, (30 & 50 amps), many extended stay sites (in winter), 103 pull-thrus, heater not allowed, cable TV, wireless Internet access central location, tenting, dump station, non-guest dumping $, laundry, ltd groceries, RV supplies, LP gas by weight/by meter, ice, tables.

◊◊◊RECREATION: rec room/area, pavilion, swim pool, play equipment, shuffleboard court, planned activities, local tours.

Pets welcome, breed restrict, quantity restrict. Partial handicap access. Open all yr. Big rigs welcome. Internet friendly. Clubs welcome. Rate in 2007 $26-34 for 2 persons. MC/VISA/DISC. Member ARVC, FLARVC. Phone: (800)833-2164.

SEE AD THIS PAGE

Oak Tree Village Campground—(Marion) *From jct I-75 (exit 354) & US 27: Go 1/8 mi W on US 27, then 1/4 mi N on Blitchton Rd. Enter on R.* ◊◊FACILITIES: 137 sites, typical site width 20 ft, 70 full hkups, 67 W&E, (20, 30 & 50 amps), some extended stay sites (in winter), 136 pull-thrus, dump station, non-guest dumping $, laundry, ice, tables. ◊◊◊RECREATION: rec hall, pavilion, swim pool, playground, 4 shuffleboard courts, planned activities (wkends only), tennis, horseshoes, sports field. Pets welcome. Partial handicap access. No tents. Open all yr. Planned group activities winter only. Rate in 2007 $22-25 for 2 persons. Phone: (352)629-1569.

(S) OCALA RV CAMP RESORT—(Marion) *From jct I-75, (exit 350) & HWY 200: Go 200 feet W on Hwy 200, then 1/2 mi N on SW 38th Ave. Enter on L.*

◊◊◊◊FACILITIES: 191 sites, typical site width 35 ft, 127 full hkups, 64 W&E, (20, 30 & 50 amps), 50 amps ($), some extended stay sites, 146 pull-thrus, cable TV ($), wireless Internet access central location, tenting, cabins, RV storage, dump station, non-guest dumping $, laundry, ltd groceries, RV supplies, LP gas by weight/by meter, ice, tables, wood.

◊◊◊◊◊RECREATION: rec hall, equipped pavilion, swim pool, wading pool, whirlpool, pond fishing, golf nearby, bsktball, playground, 2 shuffleboard courts, planned activities, horseshoes, sports field, v-ball.

Pets welcome, breed restrict. Partial handicap access. Open all yr. Planned group activities & heat-

OCALA—Continued
OCALA RV CAMP RESORT—Continued

ed pool winter only. Big rigs welcome. Internet friendly. Escort to site. Clubs welcome. Rate in 2007 $24.95-45.95 for 2 persons. MC/VISA/DISC/AMEX. Member ARVC, FLARVC. Phone: (866)858-3400.

e-mail: manager@ocalarvcampresort.com

SEE AD THIS PAGE

OCALA SUN RV RESORT—(Marion) *From jct I-75 (exit 341) & Hwy 484: Go 1/2 mi W on Hwy 484. Enter on R.*

◊◊◊FACILITIES: 165 sites, typical site width 35 ft, 165 full hkups, (30 & 50 amps), 50 amps ($), many extended stay sites, 47 pull-thrus, wireless Instant Internet access at site ($), phone Internet access central location, RV/park trailer rentals, RV storage, dump station, non-guest dumping $, laundry, RV supplies, LP gas by weight/by meter, ice, tables.

◊◊◊RECREATION: rec hall, swim pool, planned activities, horseshoes, hiking trails.

Pets welcome. Partial handicap access. No tents. Open all yr. Planned group activities winter only. Big rigs welcome. Escort to site. Clubs welcome. Rate in 2007 $33-36 for 2 persons. MC/VISA/DISC. Member ARVC, FLARVC. Phone: (877)809-1100. FMCA discount.

e-mail: info@ocalasunrvresort.com

SEE AD THIS PAGE AND AD DISCOVER SECTION PAGE 82

(E) SILVER SPRINGS CAMPERS GARDEN RV RESORT—(Marion) *From jct Hwy 35 & Hwy 40: Go 1 block E on Hwy 40. Enter on L.*

◊◊◊◊FACILITIES: 199 sites, typical site width 30 ft, 195 full hkups, 4 W&E, (20, 30 & 50 amps), many extended stay sites, 187 pull-thrus, cable TV ($), phone Internet access central location, tenting, dump station, non-guest dumping $, laundry, RV supplies, LP gas by weight/by meter, ice, tables.

◊◊◊◊RECREATION: rec hall, rec room/area, equipped pavilion, swim pool, golf nearby, play equipment, 2 shuffleboard courts, planned activities, horseshoes.

Pets welcome, breed restrict. Partial handicap access. Open all yr. Planned group activities winter only. Big rigs welcome. Internet friendly. Rate in 2007 $28.95 for 2 persons. Member ARVC, FLARVC. Phone: (800)640-3733.

SEE AD THIS PAGE AND AD SILVER SPRINGS PAGE 170

Wild Frontier Rally Park & Campground—(Marion) *From jct I-75 (exit 358) & SR 326: Go 1 mi E on SR 26, then 4 mi N on CR 25A. Enter on R.* ◊◊◊FACILITIES: 103 sites, typical site width 25 ft,

Wild Frontier Rally Park & Campground—Continued on next page

OCALA—Continued
Wild Frontier Rally Park & Campground—Continued

103 full hkups, (20, 30 & 50 amps), some extended stay sites (in winter), 1 pull-thrus, dump station, non-guest dumping $, laundry, ltd groceries, LP gas by weight/by meter, ice, tables, patios. ◆RECREATION: rec hall, horseshoes. Pets welcome, breed restrict, size restrict. Partial handicap access. No tents. Open all yr. Big rigs welcome. Rate in 2007 $25-32 per vehicle. Phone: (352)368-2451.

OCKLAWAHA—B-3

(NE) Lake Bryant MH & RV Park—(Marion) *From jct I-75 (exit 352) & SR 40: Go 22 mi E on SR 40, then 2-1/2 mi S on SE 183rd Ave.* ◆◆◆FACILITIES: 133 sites, typical site width 35 ft, 133 full hkups, (30 & 50 amps), some extended stay sites (in winter), 2 pull-thrus, tenting, dump station, non-guest dumping $, laundry, LP bottle exch, ice, tables, patios. ◆◆◆RECREATION: rec hall, lake swimming, boating, canoeing, ramp, dock, canoe/pedal boat/motorboat rentals, lake fishing, planned activities, horseshoes, v-ball. Pets welcome. Partial handicap access. Open all yr. Big rigs welcome. Internet friendly. Rate in 2007 $24 for 4 persons. Member ARVC, FLARVC. Phone: (352)625-2376.

ODESSA—C-3

(SW) Silver Dollar RV and Golf Resort—(Hillsborough) *From jct Hwy 587 & Hwy 582: Go 3-1/2 mi W on Hwy 582, then 1-3/4 mi S on Patterson Rd. Enter on R.* ◆◆◆FACILITIES: 113 sites, 35 full hkups, 78 W&E, (30 & 50 amps), mostly extended stay sites (in winter), dump station, non-guest dumping $, laundry, patios. ◆◆◆RECREATION: rec hall, rec room/area, swim pool, planned activities. Pets welcome. No tents. Open all yr. Big rigs welcome. Internet friendly. Rate in 2007 $21-50 for 2 persons. Member ARVC, FLARVC. Phone: (813)920-4185.

OKEECHOBEE—D-4

See listings at Belle Glade, Clewiston, Lakeport, Moore Haven, Palmdale & South Bay.

Norman Thargard, astronaut, is from Florida.

OKEECHOBEE—Continued

(SW) BUCKHEAD RIDGE MARINA RESORT—(Glades) *From jct Hwy 70 & US 441 & US 98: Go 3 mi S on US 441/US 98, then 8 mi W on Hwy 78, then 1 mi S on 14th St. Enter on L.*

WELCOME

◆◆◆FACILITIES: 102 sites, typical site width 25 ft, 102 full hkups, (30 & 50 amps), mostly extended stay sites (in winter), RV/park trailer rentals, dump station, laundry, ice, tables, patios.

◆◆◆◆RECREATION: rec hall, swim pool, boating, canoeing, ramp, dock, 2 motorboat rentals, lake/river fishing, fishing guides, golf nearby, shuffleboard court, planned activities, hiking trails.

Pets welcome, size restrict. Partial handicap access. No tents. Open all yr. Escort to site. Clubs welcome. Rate in 2007 $30-34 per vehicle. MC/VISA. Phone: (863)763-2826.

SEE AD THIS PAGE

(SE) Fijian RV Park—(Okeechobee) *From jct Hwy 78 & US 441/98: Go 5-3/4 mi SE on US 441/98. Enter on R.* ◆◆◆FACILITIES: 77 sites, typical site width 20 ft, 77 full hkups, (30 & 50 amps), many extended stay sites (in winter), laundry, ice, patios. ◆◆◆RECREATION: rec hall, boating, ramp, dock, lake/river fishing, planned activities. Pets welcome. No tents. Open all yr. Internet friendly. Rate in 2007 $22-38 for 2 persons. Member ARVC, FLARVC. Phone: (863)763-6200.

(N) OKEECHOBEE COUNTY TOURISM DEVELOPMENT COUNCIL—Offers over 5,000 camping sites. Centrally located on the North Shore of Lake Okeechobee, 2nd largest fresh water lake in USA. Local events include annual festivals, PRCA rodeos & an outdoor sportman's paradise. Open all yr. Phone: (800)871-4403.

WELCOME

e-mail: tourism@okeechobee.com

SEE AD THIS PAGE

(S) Okeechobee Resort KOA—(Okeechobee) *From jct Hwy-78 & US-441/98: Go 1/4 mi N on US 441/98. Enter on R.* ◆◆◆◆FACILITIES: 750 sites, typical site width 20 ft, 750 full hkups, (20, 30 & 50 amps), many extended stay sites (in winter), 14 pull-thrus, tenting, laundry, full svc store, LP gas by weight/by meter, ice, tables, patios. ◆◆◆◆◆RECREATION: rec hall, rec room/area, equipped pavilion, 2 swim pools, 2 motorboat rentals, mini-golf ($), playground, 9 shuffleboard courts, planned activities, tennis, horseshoes. Pets welcome, breed restrict. Partial handicap access. Open all yr. Big rigs welcome. Internet friendly. Rate in 2007 $40-78 for 2 persons. Member ARVC, FLARVC. Phone: (800)562-7748. KOA 10% value card discount.

(S) SILVER PALMS RV VILLAGE (UNDER CONSTRUCTION)—(Okeechobee) *From jct Hwy 70 & Hwy 441: Go 4 mi S on Hwy 441. Enter on R.*

WELCOME

FACILITIES: 509 sites, typical site width 40 ft, 509 full hkups, (30 & 50 amps), 16 pull-thrus, cable TV, wireless Instant Internet access at site, RV storage, dump station, laundry, LP gas by weight/by meter, controlled access gate.

RECREATION: rec hall, swim pool, whirlpool, golf nearby, bsktball, shuffleboard court, tennis, horseshoes, v-ball.

Pets welcome. Partial handicap access. No tents. Open all yr. Big rigs welcome. Internet friendly. MC/VISA.

e-mail: info@silverpalmsrv.com

SEE AD THIS PAGE

(SE) Zachary Taylor Resort—(Okeechobee) *From jct Hwy 78 & US 441/98: Go 2-1/4 mi SE on US 441/98, then 500 feet on 30th St. Enter on L.* ◆◆◆FACILITIES: 250 sites, typical site width 30 ft, 250 full hkups, (30 & 50 amps), many extended stay sites (in winter), 10 pull-thrus, heater not allowed, laundry, ice, tables. ◆◆◆RECREATION: rec hall, swim pool, boating, ramp, dock, lake/river fishing, 3 shuffleboard courts, planned activities, horseshoes. Pets welcome ($), breed restrict. Partial handicap access. No tents. Age restrictions may apply. Open all yr. Internet friendly. Rate in 2007 $43-50 for 2 persons. Member ARVC, FLARVC. Phone: (888)282-6523.

Woodall's Tip #32... If a campground does not have facilities for tenters, its listing will indicate "no tents" in the special info section or "accepts full hookup units only" in the facilities section.

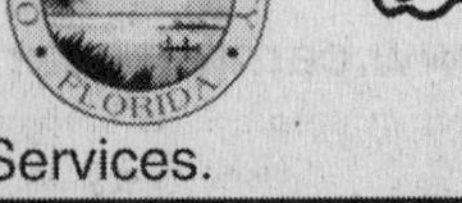

OKEECHOBEE LAKE—D-4

OKEECHOBEE LAKE AREA MAP

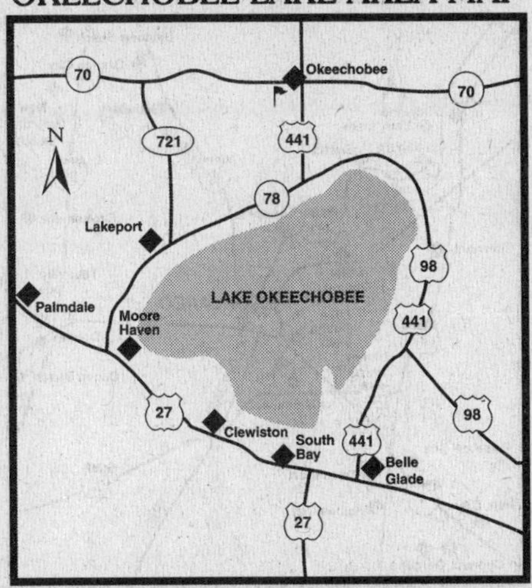

Symbols on map indicate towns within a 30 mi radius of Lake Okeechobee where campgrounds (diamonds), attractions (flags), & RV service centers & camping supply outlets (gears) are listed. Check listings for more information.

Tell Them Woodall's Sent You!

Woodall's Tip #38... Is a new Woodall's Directory needed every year? You bet! Each year the Woodall's North American Directory averages over 250,000 changes from the previous year.

OLD TOWN—B-2

OLD TOWN CAMPGROUND N' RETREAT —(Dixie) *From jct US 19N & Hwy 349S: Go 2 mi S on Hwy 349S. Enter on L.*

◆◆◆FACILITIES: 41 sites, typical site width 40 ft, 15 full hkups, 26 W&E, (30 & 50 amps), 50 amps ($), some extended stay sites, 6 pull-thrus, cable TV, phone Internet access central location, tenting, RV/park trailer rentals, RV storage, dump station, non-guest dumping $, laundry, ice, tables, fire rings, wood.

◆RECREATION: rec room/area, pavilion, horseshoes.

Pets welcome. Partial handicap access. Open all yr. Internet friendly. Clubs welcome. Rate in 2007 $18 for 2 persons. Member ARVC, FLARVC. Phone: (888)950-2267. CCUSA discount. FMCA discount.

e-mail: oldtowncampground@inetwZ.net

SEE AD THIS PAGE

Suwannee River Hideaway Campground, Inc. —(Dixie) *From jct US 19 & Hwy 349: Go 3 mi S on Hwy 349, then 1 mi E on Hwy 346A. Enter on R.* ◆◆◆FACILITIES: 73 sites, typical site width 35 ft, 34 full hkups, 25 W&E, (30 & 50 amps), 50 amps ($), 14 no hkups, some extended stay sites, 19 pull-thrus, dump station, laundry, ice, tables, fire rings, wood. ◆◆◆RECREATION: rec hall, river swimming, boating, canoeing, dock, river fishing, horseshoes, sports field. Pets welcome. Partial handicap access. Open Week before Labor Day thru Last week of July. Rate in 2007 $26-30 for 2 persons. Member ARVC, FLARVC. Phone: (352)542-7800. FMCA discount.

The Original Suwannee River Campground, Inc.—(Dixie) *From Suwannee River Bridge & US-19: Go 2 blocks N on US-19. Enter on L.* ◆◆FACILITIES: 70 sites, typical site width 35 ft, 60 full hkups, 10 W&E, (30 & 50 amps), some extended stay sites, 22 pull-thrus, dump station, laundry, ltd groceries, ice, tables, patios, fire rings. ◆◆RECREATION: rec hall, boating, dock, river fishing. Pets welcome, breed restrict. No tents. Open all yr. Rate in 2007 $25 for 2 persons. Member ARVC, FLARVC. Phone: (352)542-7680.

Woodall's. The name that's trusted for over 70 years.

OLD TOWN—Continued

(SW) YELLOW JACKET CAMPGROUND RESORT—(Dixie) *From jct US 19 & SR 349: Go 10 mi S on SR 349, then 1 mi E on SE 477 Rd. Enter at end.*

◆◆◆◆FACILITIES: 94 sites, typical site width 35 ft, 76 full hkups, 18 W&E, (30 & 50 amps), some extended stay sites (in winter), 10 pull-thrus, cable TV, wireless Instant Internet access at site, phone Internet access central location, tenting, cabins, RV storage, dump station, non-guest dumping $, laundry, ice, tables, fire rings, grills, wood.

◆◆◆◆RECREATION: rec hall, equipped pavilion, swim pool, whirlpool, boating, canoeing, kayaking, ramp, dock, 3 pontoon/6 canoe/3 motorboat rentals, river fishing, golf nearby, bsktball, playground, planned activities, hiking trails.

Pets welcome ($), quantity restrict. Partial handicap access. Open all yr. Internet friendly. Escort to site. Clubs welcome. Rate in 2007 $26.97-36.27 for 2 persons. MC/VISA. Member ARVC, FLARVC. Phone: (352)542-8365.

e-mail: star1@inetw.net

SEE AD THIS PAGE

OLUSTEE—A-3

(N) OSCEOLA NATIONAL FOREST (Ocean Pond Campground)—(Baker) *From jct Hwy 231 & US 90: Go 1 mi E on US 90, then 4 mi N on CR 250A, then 1 mi S on FR 268.*

OSCEOLA NATIONAL FOREST (Ocean Pond Campground)—Continued on next page

OLUSTEE—Continued
OSCEOLA NATIONAL FOREST (Ocean Pond Campground)—Continued

FACILITIES: 67 sites, typical site width 18 ft, 22 ft max RV length, 19 W&E, 48 no hkups, tenting, dump station, fire rings. RECREATION: lake swimming, boating, canoeing, ramp, lake fishing, hiking trails, v-ball. Rec open to public. Open all yr. No reservations. 30-day limit. Phone: (904)752-2577.

ORANGE CITY—B-4

(W) BLUE SPRING STATE PARK—(Volusia) *2 mi W of Orange City - off US-17-92.* FACILITIES: 57 sites, 57 W&E, tenting, dump station, groceries, ice, grills. RECREATION: boating, canoeing, ramp, dock, rowboat/4 canoe rentals, river fishing, hiking trails. Partial handicap access. Open all yr. Phone: (386) 775-3663.

(N) CLARK FAMILY CAMPGROUND—(Volusia) *From jct I-4 (exit 114) & Hwy 472: Go 1 1/2 mi NW on Hwy 472, then 1/3 mi W on Minnesota Ave. Enter on L.*

WELCOME

◊◊◊FACILITIES: 160 sites, typical site width 20 ft, 120 full hkups, 30 W&E, (20, 30 & 50 amps), 50 amps ($), 10 no hkups, many extended stay sites, 50 pull-thrus, wireless Instant Internet access at site ($), cable Internet access central location, tenting, cabins, dump station, non-guest dumping $, laundry, ltd groceries, RV supplies, LP gas by weight/by meter, ice, tables, patios, fire rings, grills, wood.

◊◊◊RECREATION: rec hall, rec room/area, coin games, swim pool, bsktball, playground, 2 shuffleboard courts, planned activities, horseshoes. Rec open to public.

ORANGE CITY—Continued
CLARK FAMILY CAMPGROUND—Continued

Pets welcome, breed restrict. Open all yr. Planned group activities winter season only. Escort to site. Rate in 2007 $27-41 for 2 persons. MC/VISA/DISC. Phone: (386)775-3996.

e-mail: delandkoa@yahoo.com

SEE AD DAYTONA PAGE 105

(NE) ORANGE CITY RV RESORT—(Volusia) *From I-4 (exit 114) & Hwy 472: Go 3/4 mi W on Hwy 472, then 3/4 mi S on CR 4101, then 1 block E on Graves. Enter on R.*

WELCOME

◊◊◊◊FACILITIES: 525 sites, typical site width 30 ft, 525 full hkups, (30 & 50 amps), some extended stay sites, 20 pull-thrus, cable TV, wireless Instant Internet access at site ($), tenting, dump station, non-guest dumping $, laundry, RV supplies, LP gas by weight/by meter, ice, tables, patios.

◊◊◊◊RECREATION: rec hall, equipped pavilion, swim pool, wading pool, whirlpool, mini-golf, 4 shuffleboard courts, planned activities, horseshoes.

Pets welcome, breed restrict, size restrict. Partial handicap access. Open all yr. Big rigs welcome. Internet friendly. Clubs welcome. Rate in 2007 $30-36 for 2 persons. MC/VISA/DISC. Member ARVC, FLARVC. Phone: (800)545-7354. CCUSA discount.

SEE AD ORLANDO THIS PAGE

ORLANDO—C-4

ORLANDO AREA MAP

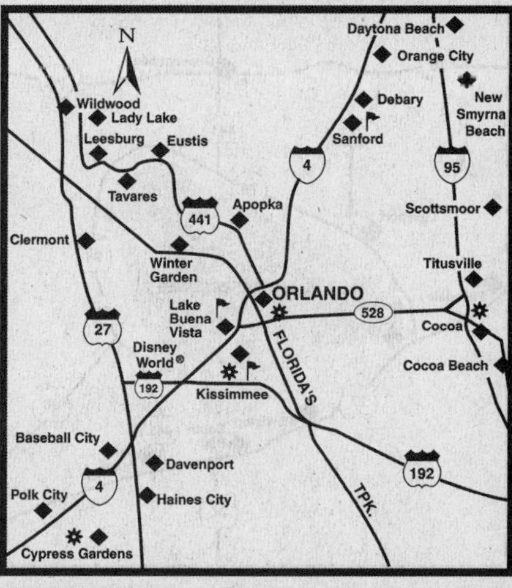

Symbols on map indicate towns within a 45 mi radius of Orlando where campgrounds (dia-monds), attractions (flags), & RV service centers & camping supply outlets (gears) are listed. Check listings for more information.

Tell Them Woodall's Sent You!

ORLANDO—Continued on next page

Woodall's Tip #36... Looking for a place to stay for an extended period of time? Check out our Extended Stay Guide (the yellow pages in the back of this Directory).

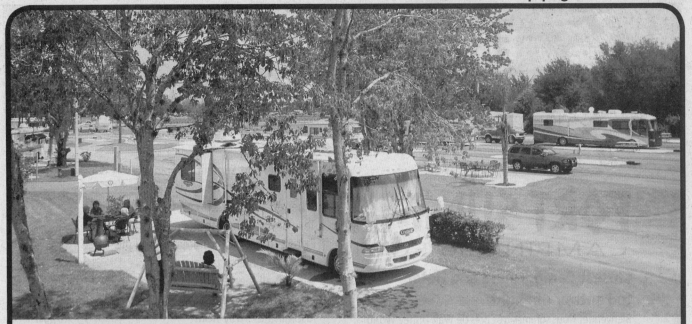

ORLANDO—Continued

(W) BILL FREDERICK PARK AT TURKEY LAKE (City Park)—(Orange) *From jct I-4 & Hwy 435: Go 1-1/2 mi N on Hwy 435 (Conroy Rd); Go 1-1/2 mi N on Hwy 435, then 1 mi N on Hiawassee Rd. Enter on R.*

FACILITIES: 136 sites, typical site width 85 ft, 15 full hkups, 21 W&E, (20 & 30 amps), 100 no hkups, tenting, cabins, dump station, laundry, tables, controlled access gate.

RECREATION: swim pool, boating, canoeing, 5 rowboat rentals, lake fishing, playground, sports field, hiking trails.

Pets welcome. Open all yr. Clubs welcome. MC/VISA. Phone: (407)299-5581.

SEE AD THIS PAGE

CAMP INN RESORT—*From jct US 192 & I-4: Go 9 mi W on I-4 (exit 23), then 33 mi S on US 27.*

SEE PRIMARY LISTING AT FROSTPROOF AND AD TRAVEL SECTION PAGE 73

(W) DISNEY'S FORT WILDERNESS RESORT & CAMPGROUND—(Orange) *From jct Hwy 91 (Florida's Turnpike) & I-4: Go 10 mi SW on I-4, then 2 mi W on W Ocala Pkwy, then 2-1/2 mi N on N World Dr. Enter on R.*

◊◊◊◊◊FACILITIES: 784 sites, typical site width 40 ft, 694 full hkups, 90 W&E, (20, 30 & 50 amps), cable TV ($), phone/cable Instant Internet access at site, wireless Internet access central location, tenting, cabins, laundry, full svc store, RV supplies, LP gas by weight/by meter, gas, ice, tables, patios, grills, controlled access gate.

◊◊◊◊◊RECREATION: rec room/area, coin games, 2 swim pools, boating, canoeing, dock, 20 canoe/10 pedal boat/60 motorboat rentals, lake fishing, fishing supplies, fishing guides, putting green, golf nearby, bsktball, 300 bike rentals, playground, 2 shuffleboard courts, planned activities, tennis, sports field, hiking trails, v-ball.

Pets welcome. Partial handicap access. Open all yr. $2.00 per person per night for third through tenth adult per campsite. Big rigs welcome. Internet friendly. Clubs welcome. Rate in 2007 $46-96 per family. MC/VISA/DISC/AMEX/DC/Debit. ATM. Member ARVC, FLARVC. Phone: (407)WDISNEY.

SEE PRIMARY LISTING AT LAKE BUENA VISTA AND AD TRAVEL SECTION PAGE 82

Book your reservation online at woodalls.com

FORT SUMMIT KOA—*From jct FL Tnkp & I-4: Go 15 mi W on I-4 (exit 23/US 27), then 1/10 mi S on US 27, then 1000 feet W on S frontage road.*

SEE PRIMARY LISTING AT LAKE BUENA VISTA AND AD PAGES 152-153

ORLANDO—Continued on next page

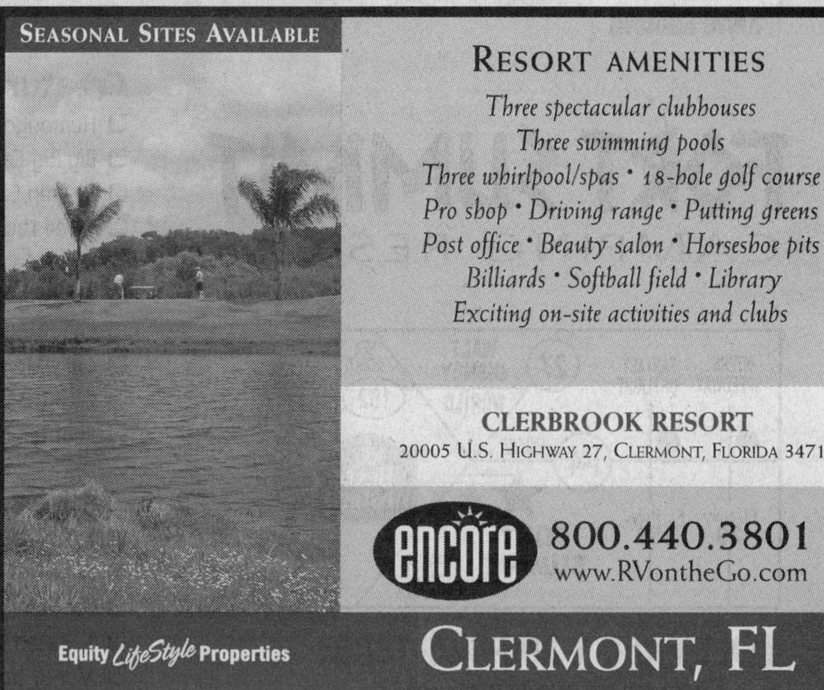

Three Worlds Resort

Florida at its Affordable Best!

RVs – Park Homes – Manufactured Homes

- Activities for everyone
- 5000 sq. ft. Rec Center
- Card Room
- Billiards
- Country Store
- Heated Pool
- 8 Shuffleboard Courts
- Horseshoes
- 3 Fishing Lakes
- Seasonal Activities
- 11 Miles from Disney World

Country Living! Close to all major attractions!

See listing at Davenport, FL

Toll Free (888) 293-3020 3700 U.S. Hwy. 17-92 North DAVENPORT, FL 33837

Relax and enjoy.

BILL FREDERICK PARK AT TURKEY LAKE

3401 S. Hiawassee Rd. • Orlando, FL 32835

407.299.5581 • Fax 407.290.2423

Open year-round with 36 sites on 175 acres, 14 full hookups and 30 amp service, Bill Frederick Park at Turkey Lake is the place to be for family fun! Located 2 miles from Universal Studios, we offer a wide variety of recreational activities, including picnicking, fishing, hiking, bicycling, roller blading/skating, and frisbee golf. There's a swimming pool available for all guests, restrooms with showers, laundry facilities, and picnic tables on every site. Rent a fishing boat for the day, a cabin for evening comfort, or a pavilion for your family gathering!

Swimming pool open summer months only. Credit cards accepted (MC/Visa). 29 nights maximum stay, unless other arrangements are made. RV limit 50'. Slideouts some sites.

CITY OF ORLANDO.net

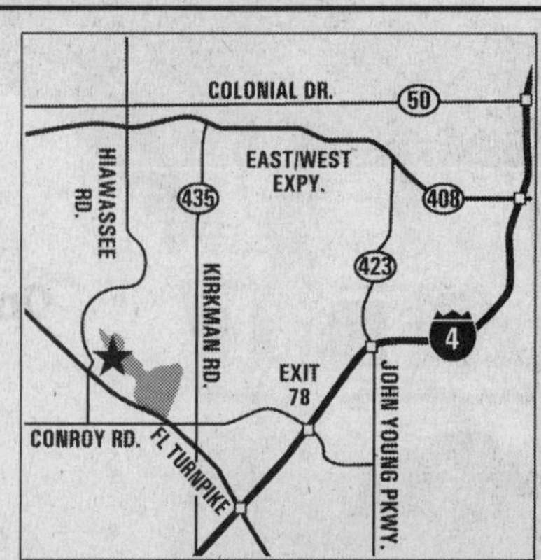

Take I-4 to Exit 78 (Conroy Rd.) Go west on Conroy for 3.2 miles. Go north on Hiawassee Rd. for 0.8 miles. The park will be on the right.

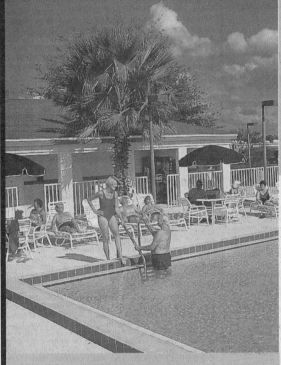

ORLANDO—Continued

HORSESHOE COVE RV RESORT—*From jct FL Tpk & I-4: Go 67 mi W on I-4, then 39 mi S on I-75 (exit 41), then 1-1/4 mi W on Hwy 70.*

WELCOME

SEE PRIMARY LISTING AT BRADENTON AND AD BRADENTON PAGE 97

ORANGE GROVE CAMPGROUND—*From jct I-4 (exit 62) & US 192: Go 6-3/4 mi E on US 192, then 1-1/4 mi NW on Old Vineland Rd. Enter on L.*

WELCOME

SEE PRIMARY LISTING AT KISSIMMEE AND AD KISSIMMEE PAGE 134

THE GREAT OUTDOORS RV-NATURE & GOLF RESORT—*From jct Hwy 417 (Central Florida Greeneway) & Hwy 50: Go 25 mi E on Hwy 50. Enter on R.*

WELCOME

SEE PRIMARY LISTING IN TITUSVILLE AND AD TITUSVILLE PAGE 181

THREE WORLDS RESORT—*From jct I-4 & US 17: Go 29 mi S on US 17. Enter on L.*

WELCOME

SEE PRIMARY LISTING AT DAVENPORT AND AD PAGE 154

ORMOND BEACH—B-4

HARRIS VILLAGE RV PARK—(Volusia) *From jct I-95 (exit 273) (old exit 89) & US 1: Go 2-1/2 mi S on US 1. Enter on R.*

WELCOME

◆◆◆◆FACILITIES: 25 sites, typical site width 25 ft, 25 full hkups, (20, 30 & 50 amps), some extended stay sites, 3 pull-thrus, cable TV, wireless Instant Internet access at site, RV/park trailer rentals, cabins, laundry, ice, tables, patios.

◆RECREATION: rec room/area.

Pets welcome, breed restrict, size restrict, quantity restrict. Partial handicap access. No tents. Age restrictions may apply. Open Oct 1 thru Apr 30. Big rigs welcome. Internet friendly. Escort to site. Rate in 2007 $42-47 for 2 persons. MC/VISA. Member ARVC, FLARVC. Phone: (386)673-0494. FMCA discount.

e-mail: harrisvillage@aol.com

SEE AD DAYTONA BEACH PAGE 107

(NE) SUNSHINE HOLIDAY RV PARK—(Volusia) *From jct I-95 (exit 273) & US-1: Go 1/2 mi NW on US-1. Enter on R.*

WELCOME

◆◆◆◆FACILITIES: 336 sites, typical site width 45 ft, 250 full hkups, 86 W&E, (20, 30 & 50 amps), many extended stay sites, 219 pull-thrus, cable TV ($), wireless Instant Internet access at site ($), phone Internet access central location, tenting, cabins, dump station, non-guest dumping $, portable dump, laundry, ltd groceries, RV supplies, LP gas by weight/by meter, ice, tables, patios.

◆◆◆◆◆RECREATION: rec hall, equipped pavilion, coin games, swim pool, pond fishing, fishing supplies, mini-golf, golf nearby, bsktball, playground, 2 shuffleboard courts, planned activities, tennis, horseshoes, v-ball.

Pets welcome. Partial handicap access. Open all yr. Big rigs welcome. Internet friendly. Escort to site. Clubs welcome. Rate in 2007 $38-53 per vehicle. MC/VISA/DISC/AMEX. Member ARVC, FLARVC. Phone: (386)672-3045.

e-mail: info@RVontheGO.com

SEE AD DAYTONA BEACH PAGE 108

ORMOND BEACH—Continued

(N) TOMOKA STATE PARK—(Volusia) *From jct US 1 & Hwy 40: Go 1/2 mi E on Hwy 40, then 3 mi N on North Beach St.* FACILITIES: 100 sites, 100 W&E, tenting, dump station, groceries, ice, grills. RECREATION: boating, canoeing, ramp, dock, 10 canoe rentals, saltwater fishing, playground, hiking trails. Pets welcome. Partial handicap access. Open all yr. Phone: (386)676-4050.

OSPREY—D-3

(S) OSCAR SCHERER STATE PARK—(Sarasota) *From US-41 & Hwy-72: Go S 4 mi on US-41.* FACILITIES: 104 sites, 104 W&E, tenting, dump station, wood. RECREATION: pavilion, lake swimming, boating, canoeing, ramp, dock, 10 canoe rentals, saltwater fishing, playground, hiking trails. Partial handicap access. Open all yr. Phone: (941)483-5956.

PACE—F-1

(N) Farmers' Opry House Campground—(Santa Rosa) *From jct US 90 & CR 197: Go 13 mi N on CR 197, then 1/2 mi W on Byrom Campbell Rd. Enter on R.* ◆◆FACILITIES: 158 sites, typical site width 30 ft, 30 full hkups, 128 W&E, (30 & 50 amps), 11 pull-thrus, dump station, ice. ◆◆RECREATION: rec hall, planned activities (wkends only), hiking trails. Pets welcome. No tents. Open all yr. Big rigs welcome. Rate in 2007 $18-22 for 2 persons. Phone: (850)994-6000.

PALATKA—B-4

(S) RODMAN (COE - Lake Ocklawaha)—(Putnam) *From jct Hwy 20 & Hwy 19: Go 12 mi S on Hwy 19, then 2 mi W on Rodman Dam Rd.* FACILITIES: 39 sites, 13 W&E, 26 no hkups, tenting, non-flush toilets only, dump station, fire rings, grills. RECREATION: boating, canoeing, ramp, lake/river fishing, hiking trails. Rec open to public. Open all yr. No showers. Max stay 30 days Nov 1-Apr 30; otherwise 14. Phone: (352)236-7413.

PALM COAST—B-4

FLAGLER COUNTY CHAMBER OF COMMERCE—The Tourist Dev Council & Chamber of Commerce provide information & brochures about campgrounds & RV Parks available in the Flagler County area. Open all yr. Phone: (800)670-2640.

WELCOME

e-mail: peggy@flaglerchamber.org

SEE AD TRAVEL SECTION PAGE 84

PALM HARBOR—C-3

(NW) Bay Aire Travel Trailer Park—(Pinellas) *From jct US 19 & Hwy 752: Go 2 mi W on Hwy 752, then 1-1/2 mi N on Alt US 19. Enter on R.* ◆◆◆FACILITIES: 152 sites, typical site width 20 ft, 152 full hkups, (20, 30 & 50 amps), 50 amps ($), mostly extended stay sites (in winter), tenting, laundry, LP gas by weight/by meter, ice, tables, patios. ◆◆◆RECREATION: rec hall, swim pool, 3 shuffleboard courts, planned activities, horseshoes. Pets welcome. Partial handicap access. Open all yr. Church & planned activities winter only. Tenters summer only. Big rigs welcome. Internet friendly. Rate in 2007 $25-45 for 2 persons. Member ARVC, FLARVC. Phone: (727)784-4082.

(NW) Caladesi RV Park—(Pinellas) *From jct US 19 & Hwy 752: Go 3 mi W on Hwy 752, then 1 block N on Dempsy Rd. Enter on L.* ◆◆◆FACILITIES: 86 sites, typical site width 30 ft, 86 full hkups, (20, 30 & 50 amps), mostly extended stay sites (in winter), dump station, laundry, LP gas by weight/by meter, tables. ◆RECREATION: swim pool. Pets welcome, quantity restrict. No tents. Open all yr. Big rigs welcome. Internet friendly. Rate in 2007 $28-40 for 2 persons. Phone: (727)784-3622.

(N) KOA-Clearwater/Tarpon Springs—(Pinellas) *From jct Hwy-584 & US-19: Go 2 mi N on US-19. Enter on R.* ◆◆◆FACILITIES: 116 sites, typical site width 28 ft, 75 full hkups, 41 W&E, (20, 30 & 50 amps), some extended stay sites (in winter), heater not allowed, tenting, dump station, non-guest dumping $, laundry, groceries, LP gas by weight/by meter, ice, tables, patios. ◆◆◆RECREATION: rec room/area, pavilion, equipped pavilion, swim pool, playground,

PALM HARBOR—Continued
KOA-Clearwater/Tarpon Springs—Continued

horseshoes. Pets welcome. Age restrictions may apply. Open all yr. Church winter only. Big rigs welcome. Rate in 2007 $28.95-44.95 for 2 persons. Member ARVC, FLARVC. Phone: (727)937-8412. KOA 10% value card discount.

(N) Sherwood Forest Travel RV Park—(Pinellas) *From jct US 19 & Hwy 752: Go 2 mi W on Hwy 752, then 1 block S on Alt US 19. Enter on R.* ◆◆◆FACILITIES: 111 sites, typical site width 40 ft, 104 full hkups, (20, 30 & 50 amps), 7 no hkups, many extended stay sites (in winter), tenting, laundry, tables. ◆◆◆RECREATION: rec hall, swim pool, pond fishing, planned activities, horseshoes. Pets welcome, breed restrict, size restrict, quantity restrict. Partial handicap access. Open all yr. Planned activities winter only. Big rigs welcome. Rate in 2007 $35-55 for 2 persons. Member ARVC, FLARVC. Phone: (727)784-4582.

PALMDALE—D-4

(S) Fisheating Creek Campground—(Glades) *From jct Hwy 29 & US 27: Go 1 mi N on US 27. Enter on L.* ◆◆◆FACILITIES: 124 sites, 52 full hkups, (20, 30 & 50 amps), 72 no hkups, tenting, dump station, non-guest dumping $, laundry, ltd groceries, ice, tables, fire rings, grills, wood. ◆◆◆RECREATION: rec room/area, pavilion, lake swimming, boating, electric motors only, canoeing, ramp, 29 canoe rentals, lake/stream fishing, 2 shuffleboard courts, horseshoes, v-ball. Pets welcome. Partial handicap access. Open all yr. Rate in 2007 $20 per vehicle. Phone: (863) 675-5999.

PALMETTO—D-3

(NE) FIESTA GROVE RV RESORT—(Manatee) *From jct I-75 (exit 228) & I-275: Go 1 mi W on I-275 (exit 1), then 3/4 mi N on US-41, then 1/4 mi SW on Bayshore Rd. Enter on R.*

WELCOME

◆◆◆◆FACILITIES: 220 sites, typical site width 40 ft, 205 full hkups, 15 W&E, (30 & 50 amps), many extended stay sites (in winter), cable TV ($), phone/cable on-site Internet access (needs activ), phone Internet access central location, RV storage, shower$, dump station, non-guest dumping $, laundry, RV supplies, tables, patios.

◆◆◆◆RECREATION: rec hall, swim pool, golf nearby, bsktball, 4 shuffleboard courts, planned activities, horseshoes, v-ball, local tours.

Pets welcome, breed restrict, quantity restrict. No tents. Age restrictions may apply. Open all yr. Planned activities winter only. Big rigs welcome. Internet friendly. Clubs welcome. Rate in 2007 $30-32 for 2 persons. Member ARVC, FLARVC. Phone: (941)722-7661.

SEE AD NEXT PAGE

(N) Fishermans Cove RV Resort—(Manatee) *From jct I-275 & US 41: Go 2-1/2 mi SE on US 41, then 1 mi N on US 19. Enter on R.* ◆◆◆◆FACILITIES: 75 sites, typical site width 24 ft, 75 full hkups, (30 & 50 amps), laundry, tables, patios. ◆◆◆◆RECREATION: rec hall, equipped pavilion, swim pool, boating, canoeing, ramp, dock, saltwater fishing, 2 shuffleboard courts, planned activities, tennis, horseshoes, v-ball. Pets welcome. No tents. Open all yr. Big rigs welcome. Rate in 2007 $30-50 for 2 persons. Phone: (941)729-3685.

(N) Frog Creek Campground—(Manatee) *From jct I-75 (exit 228) & I-275: Go 1 mi W on I-275 (exit 1), then 3/4 mi N on US 41, then 1/4 mi SW on Bayshore Rd. Enter on R.* ◆◆◆◆FACILITIES: 186 sites, typical site width 30 ft, 174 full hkups, 12 W&E, (30 & 50 amps), some extended stay sites (in winter), dump station, non-guest dumping $, laundry, tables, patios. ◆◆◆◆RECREATION: rec hall, pavilion, swim pool, boating, canoeing, stream fishing, 2 shuffleboard courts, planned activities, horseshoes. Pets welcome, breed restrict, size restrict, quantity restrict. Partial handicap access. No tents. Open all yr. Planned activities winter only. Big rigs welcome. Internet friendly. Rate in 2007 $28-41 for 2 persons. Member ARVC, FLARVC. Phone: (941)722-6154.

(NE) Manatee RV Park—(Sarasota) *From I-75 (exit 229): Go 2 mi W to US 41, then 4 mi N on US 41. Enter on R.* ◆◆◆FACILITIES: 325 sites, typical site width 35 ft, accepts full hkup units only, 325 full hkups, (30 & 50 amps), mostly extended stay sites (in winter), 18 pull-thrus, heater not allowed, dump station, non-guest dumping $, laundry, ltd groceries, LP gas by weight/by meter, ice, tables, patios. ◆◆◆◆RECREATION: rec hall, rec room/area, swim pool, pond fishing, mini-golf, 10 shuffleboard courts, planned activities, horseshoes. Pets welcome. No tents. Age restrictions may apply. Open all yr. Planned activities winter only. Church services (non-denominational) winter only. Big rigs welcome. Phone: (813)645-7652.

PALMETTO—Continued on next page

PALMETTO—Continued

(NE) TERRA CEIA VILLAGE (CAMP RESORT)—(Manatee) *From jct I-75 (exit 228) & I-275: Go 1 mi W on I-275 (exit 1), then 3/4 mi N on US 41. Enter on R.*

FACILITIES: 203 sites, typical site width 30 ft, accepts full hkup units only, 203 full hkups, (30 & 50 amps), many extended stay sites (in winter), wireless Instant Internet access at site ($), phone/cable on-site Internet access (needs activ), wireless Internet access central location, dump station, laundry, patios.

RECREATION: rec hall, swim pool, golf nearby, 4 shuffleboard courts, planned activities, horseshoes.

Pets welcome. No tents. Age restrictions may apply. Open all yr. Planned activities winter only. Big rigs welcome. Rate in 2007 $23-48 for 2 persons. MC/VISA. Phone: (941)729-4422.

e-mail: terra_ceia@MHChomes.com

SEE AD SARASOTA PAGE 169

(N) WINTERSET RV RESORT—(Manatee) *From jct I-275 (exit 2) & US 41: Go 1/4 mi E on US 41.*

◇◇◇◇FACILITIES: 221 sites, 221 full hkups, (30 & 50 amps), phone/cable on-site Internet access (needs activ), dump station, laundry, LP gas by weight, tables, patios.

◇◇◇◇RECREATION: rec hall, swim pool, boating, canoeing, kayaking, stream fishing, golf nearby, bsktball, 8 shuffleboard courts, planned activities, tennis, horseshoes.

Pets welcome, size restrict, quantity restrict. No tents. Open all yr. Big rigs welcome. Rate in 2007 $30 for 2 persons. Member ARVC. Phone: (941) 722-4884.

e-mail: john.vickiewinn@newbymanagement.com

SEE AD TAMPA PAGE 172

PANACEA—A-1

(W) Holiday Campground—(Wakulla) *From S jct US 98 & US 319: Go 7 mi S on US 98. Enter on R.*

◇◇◇FACILITIES: 77 sites, typical site width 20 ft, 75 full hkups, 2 W&E, (20, 30 & 50 amps), some extended stay sites, 4 pull-thrus, tenting, dump station, non-guest dumping $, laundry, LP gas by weight/by meter, ice, tables. ◇◇◇◇RECREATION: rec hall, pavilion, equipped pavilion, swim pool, boating, dock, saltwater fishing, playground, 2 shuffleboard courts, planned activities, horseshoes, sports field, v-ball. Pets welcome. Open all yr. Big rigs welcome. Internet friendly. Rate in 2007 $26.95-35.95 for 2 persons. Phone: (850)984-5757.

PANAMA CITY—F-2

MILITARY PARK (Tyndall AFB FAMCAMP)—(Bay) *On US 98. On base.* FACILITIES: 90 sites, 59 full hkups, 31 W&E, tenting, dump station, laundry, LP gas by weight/by meter, grills. RECREATION: boating, mini-golf, shuffleboard court, tennis, sports field. Open all yr. For Military Use Only-w/Military ID Card. Phone: (850)283-2798.

(W) RV CONNECTIONS—*From jct US-98 & US-231: Go 1-3/4 mi N on US-231. Enter on L.* SALES: travel trailers, 5th wheels, van campers, motor homes, pre-owned unit sales. SERVICES: full-time mech, RV appliance repair, installs hitches. Open all yr. MC/VISA/AMEX. Phone: (800) 958-6886.

e-mail: rvconnections@comcast.net

SEE AD THIS PAGE

RV CONNECTIONS—*From jct US 98 & Hwy 389: Go 1-1/2 mi E on US 98. Enter on R.* SALES: travel trailers, 5th wheels, van campers, motor homes, pre-owned unit sales. SERVICES: full-time mech, RV appliance repair, body work/collision repair, LP gas by weight/by meter, sells parts/accessories, installs hitches. Open all yr. MC/VISA/AMEX. Phone: (866)441-4678.

e-mail: rvcme@comcast.net

SEE AD THIS PAGE

PANAMA CITY BEACH—F-2

(SW) CAMPER'S INN—(Bay) *From east jct US 98 & Alt 98 (Scenic 98): Go 1-1/2 mi SW on Alt 98 (Scenic 98), then 9/10 mi S on Joan Ave, then 1/4 mi W on Thomas Dr (Hwy 392).*

◇◇◇FACILITIES: 114 sites, typical site width 40 ft, 104 full hkups, (30 & 50 amps), 10 no hkups, many extended stay sites (in winter), 10 pull-thrus, cable TV ($), wireless Internet access central location, tenting, cabins, RV storage,

PANAMA CITY BEACH—Continued
CAMPER'S INN—Continued

dump station, non-guest dumping $, laundry, full svc store, RV supplies, LP gas by weight/by meter, gas, ice, tables, patios, controlled access gate.

◇◇◇◇RECREATION: rec hall, equipped pavilion, coin games, swim pool, wading pool, pond fishing, fishing supplies, bsktball, playground, 4 shuffleboard courts, planned activities (wkends only), horseshoes, v-ball, local tours.

Pets welcome. Partial handicap access. Open all yr. Planned group activities winter season only. Big rigs welcome. Internet friendly. Clubs welcome. Rate in 2007 $32.95-54.95 for 2 persons. MC/VISA. ATM. Phone: (866)872-2267.

SEE AD THIS PAGE

(NW) EMERALD COAST RV BEACH RESORT—(Bay) *From Hathaway Bridge on Alt US 98: Go 2-3/10 mi W on Alt US 98, then 100 feet S on Allison Ave. Enter on L.*

AN EXCLUSIVE ELEGANT SECURE RESORT!
A Paradise RV Resort Nestled in the Heart Of Panama City Beach, "The Worlds Most Beautiful Beaches". Lush Landscaping, Concrete Pads, Paved Streets, Heated Pool, Spa, Clubhouse, ETC. 1-800-BEACHRV, 1-800-232-2478 WWW.RVRESORT.COM

◇◇◇◇◇FACILITIES: 138 sites, typical site width 35 ft, accepts full hkup units only, 138 full hkups, (20, 30 & 50 amps), some extended stay sites, 35 pull-thrus, cable TV ($), wireless Instant Internet access at site ($), wireless Internet access central location, RV storage, dump station, non-guest dumping $, laundry, RV supplies, LP gas by weight/by meter, ice, tables, patios, controlled access gate.

◇◇◇◇◇RECREATION: rec hall, swim pool, whirlpool, 2 pedal boat rentals, pond fishing, fishing supplies, putting green, golf nearby, bsktball, 15 bike rentals, playground, 2 shuffleboard courts, planned activities, horseshoes, sports field, v-ball.

Pets welcome, breed restrict. Partial handicap access. No tents. Open all yr. Big rigs welcome.

EMERALD COAST RV BEACH RESORT—Continued on page 160

Find a park or campground Woodall's doesn't list? Tell us!

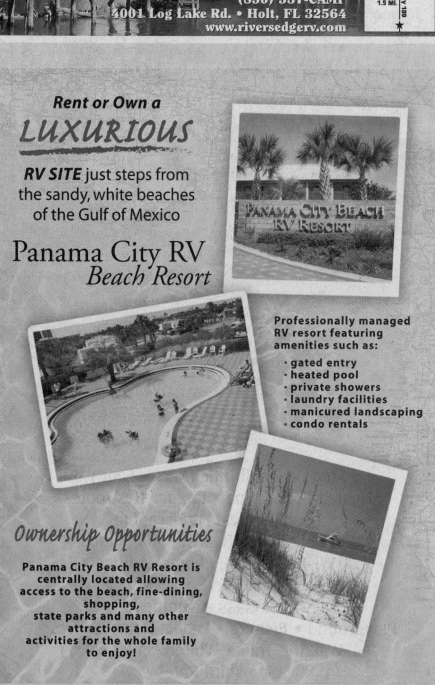

PANAMA CITY BEACH—Continued
EMERALD COAST RV BEACH RESORT—Continued

Internet friendly. Clubs welcome. Rate in 2007 $47.95-65.95 for 2 persons. MC/VISA. Member ARVC, FLARVC. Phone: (800)BEACHRV.

e-mail: rvinfo@rvresort.com

SEE AD PAGES 158-159 AND AD DESTIN PAGE 112

(E) PANAMA CITY BEACH RV RESORT—(Bay) *From jct US 98 & Thomas Rd: Go 3-1/2 mi S on Thomas Rd, then 2/10 mi SE on CR-392. Enter on L.*

WELCOME

◆◆◆◆◆FACILITIES: 69 sites, typical site width 30 ft, 69 full hkups, (30 & 50 amps), some extended stay sites (in winter), 14 pull-thrus, cable TV, wireless Instant Internet access at site, dump station, laundry, ice, patios, controlled access gate.

◆◆◆◆◆RECREATION: swim pool.

Pets welcome, quantity restrict. Partial handicap access. No tents. Open all yr. Big rigs welcome. Internet friendly. Rate in 2007 $49-69 for 2 persons. MC/VISA. Member ARVC, FLARVC. Phone: (866)631-3529.

e-mail: info@panamacityrvresort.com

SEE AD THIS PAGE AND AD DESTIN PAGE 113

(N) Pineglen Motorcoach & RV Park—(Bay) *From jct Hwy 79 & US 98: Go 4 mi E on US 98. Enter on L.* ◆◆◆◆FACILITIES: 60 sites, typical site width 25 ft, 60 full hkups, (30 & 50 amps), 50 amps ($), some extended stay sites, 23 pull-thrus, dump station, non-guest dumping $, laundry. ◆◆RECREATION: rec hall, swim pool, pond fishing, horseshoes. Pets welcome, breed restrict, size restrict, quantity restrict. Partial handicap access. No tents. Age restrictions may apply. Open all yr. Big rigs welcome. Internet friendly. Rate in 2007 $28.50-38.50 for 2 persons. Phone: (850)230-8535.

(N) Raccoon River Campground—(Bay) *From US 98A (Scenic Rt 98) & Hwy 392: Go 2-3/4 mi NW on Hwy 392 (Middle Beach Rd/Hutchinson Blvd). Enter on L.* ◆◆◆FACILITIES: 171 sites, typical site width 25 ft, 141 full hkups, (30 & 50 amps), 30 no hkups, some extended stay sites (in winter), 50 pull-thrus, tenting, dump station, non-guest dumping $, laundry, groceries, ice, tables, patios, fire rings. ◆◆◆◆RECREATION: rec room/area, 2 swim pools, lake fishing, playground, 2 shuffleboard courts, planned activities (wkends only), horseshoes, v-ball. Pets welcome ($), size restrict. Partial handicap access. Open all yr. Big rigs welcome. Internet friendly. Rate in 2007 $45-50 for 4 persons. Member ARVC, FLARVC. Phone: (877)234-0181.

(E) ST. ANDREWS STATE RECREATION AREA—(Bay) *From jct US 98 & SR 392 (Thomas Drive): Go 3-1/2 mi S on SR 392 (Thomas Drive), then 1/4 mi SE on SR 392 (Thomas Drive).* FACILITIES: 176 sites, 176 W&E, tenting, dump station, groceries, ice, fire rings, grills. RECREATION: pavilion, saltwater swimming, boating, canoeing, ramp, dock, saltwater fishing, playground, hiking trails. Pets welcome. Open all yr. Grocery open Apr to Sep only. Phone: (850)233-5140.

PEMBROKE PINES—E-5

(W) C.B. SMITH PARK (Broward County Park)—(Broward) *From jct I-95 (exit 20) & Hwy 820 (Hollywood Blvd): Go 9 mi W on Hollywood Blvd, then 1/2 mi N on Flamingo Rd. Enter on L.*

WELCOME

FACILITIES: 60 sites, 60 full hkups, (20, 30 & 50 amps), 30 pull-thrus, tenting, dump station, non-guest dumping $, laundry, ice, tables, patios, fire rings, grills, controlled access gate.

RECREATION: pavilion, swim pool, 30 canoe/25 pedal boat rentals, lake fishing, bsktball, playground, tennis, horseshoes, sports field, hiking trails, v-ball. Rec open to public.

Pets welcome. Partial handicap access. Open all yr. Big rigs welcome. Clubs welcome. MC/VISA/DISC. Phone: (954)437-2650.

e-mail: cbsmithpark@broward.org

SEE AD TRAVEL SECTION PAGE 74

PENSACOLA—F-1

See listings at Lillian, AL & Holt, Milton, Navarre and Perdido Key, FL

(E) BIG LAGOON STATE PARK—(Escambia) *From jct Hwy 292 & Hwy 292A: Go 2 mi E on Hwy 292A.* FACILITIES: 75 sites, 49 W&E, 26 no hkups, tenting, dump station, portable dump, grills. RECREATION: pavilion, saltwater swimming, boating, canoeing, ramp, dock, saltwater/pond fishing, playground, planned activities, hiking trails. Rec open to public. Open all yr. Phone: (850)492-1595.

PENSACOLA—Continued on next page

We are on the web! Come visit us at www.woodalls.com

PENSACOLA—Continued

GULF ISLANDS NATIONAL SEASHORE (Fort Pickens) —(Escambia) *From jct US-98 & Hwy-399: Go 15 mi SW on Hwy-399 & Ft. Pickens Rd.* FACILITIES: 200 sites, 136 E, 64 no hkups, tenting, dump station, laundry, ltd groceries, ice, grills. RECREATION: saltwater swimming, boating, saltwater fishing, planned activities, hiking trails. Rec open to public. Open all yr. Phone: (850)934-2621.

(W) MILITARY PARK (Oak Grove Fam-Camp-Pensacola NAS)—(Escambia) *From I-10 (exit 2): Go 2 mi S on Pine Forest Rd (Hwy 297), then 15 mi W & S on Hwy 297, which becomes Hwy 173 (Blue Angel Pkwy). On base.* FACILITIES: 59 sites, 51 full hkups, 8 no hkups, 10 pull-thrus, tenting, dump station, ice, fire rings, grills. RECREATION: pavilion, saltwater swimming, saltwater fishing, play equipment, hiking trails. Open all yr. For Military Use Only-w/Military ID Card. Phone: (904)452-2535.

(E) PENSACOLA CONVENTION & VISITOR INFORMATION CENTER— WELCOME *From jct US 98 & Bayfront Pkwy: Go N on E Gregory St. Enter on R.* Location for information on Pensacola, Pensacola Beach & Perdido Key. Open all yr. Phone: (800)874-1234.

SEE AD DISCOVER SECTION PAGE 54

PERDIDO KEY—F-1

(W) Playa del Rio RV Resort—(Escambia) *From jct I-10 (exit 7) & Hwy 297: Go 2-1/2 mi S on Hwy 297, then 10 mi SW on Hwy 173 (Blue Angel Pkwy), then 10-1/4 mi W on Hwy 292. Enter on R.* ◊◊◊◊FACILITIES: 30 sites, typical site width 30 ft, 30 full hkups, (30 & 50 amps), some extended stay sites (in winter), dump station, non-guest dumping $, laundry, ice, tables, patios. ◊◊◊◊RECREATION: rec hall, equipped pavilion, saltwater swimming, boating, canoeing, dock, saltwater fishing, planned activities. Pets welcome. Partial handicap access. No tents. Open all yr. Ongoing planned group activities Winter only; Some in Summer. Big rigs welcome. Internet friendly. Rate in 2007 $31-71 per family. Member ARVC, FLARVC. Phone: (888) 200-0904.

PERRY—A-2

(S) Perry KOA—(Taylor) *From jct US 98/19/27 & US 98/19/27A: Go 3 mi S on US 98/19/27A. Enter on R.* ◊◊◊FACILITIES: 75 sites, typical site width 25 ft, 71 full hkups, 4 W&E, (30 & 50 amps), 50 amps ($), some extended stay sites, 48 pull-thrus, tenting, laundry, ltd groceries, LP gas by weight/by meter, ice, tables. ◊◊◊RECREATION: rec hall, swim pool, playground, horseshoes. Pets welcome. Partial handicap access. Open all yr. Planned group activities in Fall & Winter only. Big rigs welcome. Internet friendly. Rate in 2007 $27-32 for 2 persons. Member ARVC, FLARVC. Phone: (850)584-3221. KOA 10% value card discount.

POLK CITY—C-3

(S) LELYNN RV RESORT—(Polk) WELCOME *From jct I-4 (exit 44) & Hwy 559: Go 1 block N on Hwy 559. Enter on L.*

◊◊◊◊FACILITIES: 360 sites, typical site width 35 ft, 360 full hkups, (30 & 50 amps), 10 pull-thrus, wireless Instant Internet access at site, phone on-site Internet access (needs activ), wireless Internet access central location, RV storage, dump station, non-guest dumping $, laundry, LP gas by weight/by meter, tables, patios.

◊◊◊◊RECREATION: rec hall, rec room/area, swim pool, boating, canoeing, ramp, dock, lake fishing, golf nearby, 4 shuffleboard courts, planned activities, horseshoes, local tours. Pets welcome, breed restrict, quantity restrict. Partial handicap access. No tents. Open all yr. Big rigs welcome. Internet friendly. Clubs welcome. Member ARVC, FLARVC. Phone: (800)736-0409.

SEE AD LAKELAND PAGE 138

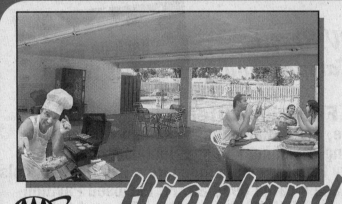

POMPANO BEACH—E-5

(W) CAMP USA—WELCOME *From jct I-95 (exit 39) & Hwy 834 (Sample Rd): Go 1-3/4 mi W on Sample Rd, then 2 mi S on Powerline Rd, then 1/2 mi W on Hammondville Rd. Enter on R.*

IT'S A GREAT DAY AT CAMP USA!
We are Florida's finest RV Rental Company, with locations in Ft. Lauderdale & Orlando. We have over 60 units to choose from. All sizes! New Units! Convenient locations! We set up and deliver too! www.campusarv.com.

SALES: travel trailers, motor homes, mini-motor homes, pre-owned unit sales. SERVICES: full-time

CAMP USA—Continued on next page

POMPANO BEACH—Continued
CAMP USA—Continued

mech, engine/chassis repair, RV appliance repair, body work/collision repair, 24-hr emerg rd svc, mobile RV svc, dump station, RV rentals, RV storage, sells parts/accessories, installs hitches. Open all yr. MC/VISA/DISC/Debit. Phone: (800) 971-8840.

e-mail: info@onfreewheels.com

SEE AD TRAVEL SECTION PAGE 85

(N) HIGHLAND PINES RV RESORT—(Broward) *From jct I-95 (exit 39) & Hwy 834 (Sample Rd): Go 3/4 mi E on Hwy 834, then 1 mi N on Hwy 811 (Dixie Hwy), then 1 block W on 48th St. Enter on R.*

◆◆◆◆FACILITIES: 416 sites, typical site width 20 ft, accepts full hkup units only, 416 full hkups, (20, 30 & 50 amps), many extended stay sites (in winter), wireless Internet access central location, RV storage, dump station, non-guest dumping $, laundry, patios.

◆◆◆◆RECREATION: rec hall, rec room/area, pavilion, swim pool, golf nearby, 3 shuffleboard courts, planned activities, horseshoes, local tours.

POMPANO BEACH—Continued
HIGHLAND PINES RV RESORT—Continued

Pets welcome, breed restrict, size restrict. Partial handicap access. No tents. Open all yr. Internet friendly. Escort to site. Clubs welcome. Rate in 2007 $35-42 for 2 persons. Phone: (954)421-5372.

e-mail: highlandpines@bellsouth.net

SEE AD PAGE 161

PONCE DE LEON—E-2

(N) Vortex Spring Camping and Diving Resort—(Holmes) *From jct I-10 (exit 96) & Hwy 81: Go 5 mi N on Hwy 81. Enter on R.* ◆◆FACILITIES: 23 sites, typical site width 50 ft, 4 full hkups, 19 W&E, (30 & 50 amps), 50 amps ($), 7 pull-thrus, tenting, dump station, non-guest dumping $, ltd groceries, ice, tables, fire rings, grills, wood. ◆◆◆RECREATION: equipped pavilion, lake swimming, canoeing, 6 canoe/8 pedal boat rentals, playground, sports field, hiking trails, v-ball. Rec open to public. No pets. Partial handicap access. Open all yr. Internet friendly. Rate in 2007 $17.50-25 for 2 persons. Phone: (800)342-0640.

PORT CHARLOTTE—D-3

✲ **(SE) CHARLOTTE RV SERVICE**—*From jct I-75 (exit 170) & Hwy 769 (Kings Hwy): Go 4 mi SW on Hwy 769 (Kings Hwy), then 1/4 mi E on Hwy 776 (Harborview Rd), then 1/4 mi S on Pinnacle St, then 1 blk W on Harper Ave.* SALES: pre-owned unit sales. SERVICES: full-time mech, engine/chassis repair, RV appliance repair, body work/collision repair, bus. hrs emerg rd svc, mobile RV svc, RV storage, sells parts/accessories, installs hitches. Open all yr. MC/VISA/DISC/AMEX/Debit. Phone: (941)883-5555.

e-mail: anita@charlottervservice.com

SEE AD THIS PAGE

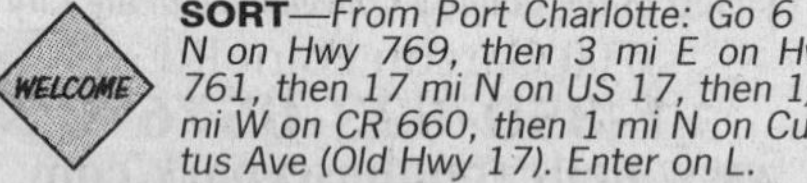

CROSS CREEK COUNTRY CLUB & RV RESORT—*From Port Charlotte: Go 6 mi N on Hwy 769, then 3 mi E on Hwy 761, then 17 mi N on US 17, then 1/4 mi W on CR 660, then 1 mi N on Cubitus Ave (Old Hwy 17). Enter on L.*

SEE PRIMARY LISTING AT ARCADIA AND AD ARCADIA PAGE 93

PORT CHARLOTTE—Continued

(W) HARBOR LAKES—(Charlotte) *From jct I-75 (exit 170) & Hwy 769 (Kings Hwy): Go 500 ft S on Hwy 769, then 10-1/2 mi W on Hwy 776. Enter on R.*

◆◆◆◆◆FACILITIES: 528 sites, typical site width 45 ft, 528 full hkups, (20, 30 & 50 amps), mostly extended stay sites (in winter), phone Internet access central location, RV/park trailer rentals, RV storage, dump station, non-guest dumping $, laundry, ice, tables, patios.

◆◆◆◆◆RECREATION: rec hall, rec room/area, equipped pavilion, swim pool, whirlpool, golf nearby, bsktball, 8 shuffleboard courts, planned activities, tennis, horseshoes, v-ball.

Pets welcome. Partial handicap access. Open all yr. Planned group activities, winter season only. Big rigs welcome. Internet friendly. Clubs welcome. Rate in 2007 $33-59 for 2 persons. MC/VISA/DISC/AMEX. Member ARVC, FLARVC. Phone: (800)468-5022.

e-mail: harbor_lakes@mhchomes.com

SEE AD FORT MYERS BEACH PAGE 123

(NE) Lettuce Lake Travel Resort—(DeSoto) *From jct I-75 (exit 170) & Hwy 769: Go 6 mi N on Hwy 769, then 2 mi E on Hwy 761, then 1/2 mi S on Lettuce Lake Rd. Enter on R.* ◆◆◆◆FACILITIES: 247 sites, typical site width 25 ft, 247 full hkups, (30 & 50 amps), some extended stay sites (in winter), 22 pull-thrus, heater not allowed, laundry, LP gas by weight, ice, tables, patios. ◆◆◆◆RECREATION: rec hall, pavilion, swim pool, boating, canoeing, saltwater/lake/river fishing, 6 shuffleboard courts, planned activities, horseshoes. Pets welcome, size restrict. Partial handicap access. No tents. Age restrictions may apply. Open all yr. Internet friendly. Rate in 2007 $34 for 2 persons. Member ARVC, FLARVC. Phone: (863)494-6057.

(NE) Oak Haven MH & RV Park—(DeSoto) *From jct I-75 (exit 170) & Hwy 769 (Kings Hwy): Go 6 mi N on Hwy 769 (Kings Hwy), then 2 mi E on Hwy 761, then 1/4 S mi on Lettuce Lake Ave. Enter on L.* ◆◆◆FACILITIES: 85 sites, typical site width 30 ft, 85 full hkups, (30 & 50 amps), mostly extended stay sites (in winter), 22 pull-thrus, laundry, patios. ◆◆◆RECREATION: rec hall,

Oak Haven MH & RV Park—Continued on next page

PORT CHARLOTTE—Continued
Oak Haven MH & RV Park—Continued

swim pool, 4 shuffleboard courts, planned activities, horseshoes. Pets welcome, breed restrict. No tents. Age restrictions may apply. Open all yr. Internet friendly. Rate in 2007 $30 for 2 persons. Phone: (888)611-4678.

(NE) RIVERSIDE RV RESORT & CAMPGROUND—(DeSoto) *From jct I-75 (exit 170) & Hwy 769 (Kings Hwy): Go 4-1/2 mi NE on Hwy 769. Enter on R.*

WELCOME

◊◊◊◊◊FACILITIES: 350 sites, typical site width 35 ft, 350 full hkups, (30 & 50 amps), 50 amps ($), many extended stay sites (in winter), 4 pull-thrus, wireless Instant Internet access at site ($), phone Internet access central location, tenting, RV/park trailer rentals, RV storage, dump station, non-guest dumping $, laundry, groceries, RV supplies, LP gas by weight/by meter, ice, tables, patios, fire rings, wood, controlled access gate.

◊◊◊◊◊RECREATION: rec hall, rec room/area, equipped pavilion, coin games, 2 swim pools, whirlpool, boating, canoeing, kayaking, ramp, dock, 6 canoe rentals, river fishing, fishing supplies, golf nearby, bsktball, playground, 4 shuffleboard courts, planned activities, horseshoes, v-ball, local tours.

Pets welcome. Partial handicap access. Open all yr. Big rigs welcome. Internet friendly. Escort to site. Clubs welcome. MC/VISA/DISC/Debit. Member ARVC, FLARVC. Phone: (800)795-9733.

e-mail: riverside@desoto.net

SEE AD PAGE 162

PORT ORANGE—B-4

(N) Daytona Beach KOA—(Volusia) *From jct I-95 (exit 261) & US 92: Go 3-1/4 mi E on US 92, then 4-1/2 mi S on Hwy 5A (Nova Rd). Enter on R.* ◊◊◊FACILITIES: 350 sites, typical site width 30 ft, 160 full hkups, 119 W&E, (20, 30 & 50 amps), 71 no hkups, some extended stay sites, tenting, dump station, non-guest dumping $, laundry, LP gas by weight/by meter, ice, tables, patios. ◊◊RECREATION: rec hall, swim pool, horseshoes. Pets welcome, size restrict. Partial handicap access. Open all yr. Big rigs welcome. Internet friendly. Rate in 2007 $28-33.60 for 2 persons. Member ARVC, FLARVC. Phone: (386)767-9170. KOA 10% value card discount.

PORT ORANGE—Continued

(S) Rose Bay Travel Park—(Volusia) *From I-95 (exit 256) & Hwy 421: Go 2-1/4 mi E on Hwy 421, then 1-1/2 mi S on Hwy 5-A. Enter on R.* ◊◊◊FACILITIES: 311 sites, typical site width 24 ft, 306 full hkups, 5 W&E, (30 & 50 amps), mostly extended stay sites, heater not allowed, tenting, portable dump, laundry, LP gas by weight/by meter, tables, patios. ◊◊◊◊RECREATION: rec hall, swim pool, boating, ramp, dock, saltwater fishing, 3 shuffleboard courts, planned activities, horseshoes. Pets welcome. Partial handicap access. Open all yr. Phone: (386)767-4308.

PORT RICHEY—C-3

(N) Ja-Mar Travel Park—(Pasco) *From jct Hwy 52 & US 19: Go 1-1/4 mi S on US 19. Enter on R.* ◊◊◊◊FACILITIES: 396 sites, 396 full hkups, (30 & 50 amps), 50 amps ($), laundry, patios. ◊◊◊◊RECREATION: rec hall, rec room/area, equipped pavilion, swim pool, pond fishing, shuffleboard court, planned activities, horseshoes. Pets welcome, breed restrict. No tents. Age restrictions may apply. Open all yr. Big rigs welcome. Internet friendly. Rate in 2007 $28 for 2 persons. FMCA discount.

(N) Suncoast RV Resort—(Pasco) *From jct Hwy 52 & US 19: Go 3 mi S on US 19. Enter on R.* ◊◊◊◊FACILITIES: 154 sites, typical site width 25 ft, 154 full hkups, (20, 30 & 50 amps), 64 pull-thrus, dump station, non-guest dumping $, laundry, tables, patios. ◊◊◊◊RECREATION: rec hall, rec room/area, equipped pavilion, swim pool, shuffleboard court, planned activities, horseshoes. Pets welcome, breed restrict, size restrict, quantity restrict. No tents. Open all yr. Planned activities in winter season. Big rigs welcome. Internet friendly. Rate in 2007 $25-28 for 2 persons. Member ARVC, FLARVC. Phone: (888)922-5603.

(N) Sundance Lakes RV Resort—(Pasco) *From Jct Hwy 52 & US 19: Go 1/2 mi S on US 19, then 1 block W on Hachem Dr. Enter on R.* ◊◊◊FACILITIES: 523 sites, typical site width 40 ft, 523 full hkups, (30 & 50 amps), mostly extended stay sites, laundry, LP gas by weight/by meter, tables, patios. ◊◊◊◊RECREATION: rec hall, rec room/area, swim pool, 8 shuffleboard courts, planned activities, tennis, horseshoes. Pets welcome, breed restrict, size restrict, quantity restrict. No tents. Age restrictions may apply. Open all yr. Big rigs welcome. Internet friendly. Rate in 2007 $27 for 2 persons. Phone: (727)862-3565.

(N) Tropic Breeze (RV SPACES)—(Pasco) *From jct Hwy 52 & US 19: Go 1 mi S on US 19. Enter on L.* FACILITIES: 44 sites, typical site width 35 ft, 44 full

PORT RICHEY—Continued
Tropic Breeze—Continued

hkups, (30 & 50 amps), mostly extended stay sites (in winter), tables, patios. RECREATION: rec hall, 2 shuffleboard courts, planned activities. Pets welcome. No tents. Age restrictions may apply. Open all yr. Phone: (727)868-1629.

PORT ST. JOE—F-3

(S) Presnell's Bayside Marina & RV Resort—(Gulf) *From jct Hwy 71 & US 98: Go 2 mi E on US 98, then 2 mi S on Hwy C-30A. Enter on R.* ◊◊FACILITIES: 22 sites, typical site width 30 ft, 22 W&E, (30 & 50 amps), some extended stay sites, 1 pull-thrus, tenting, dump station, non-guest dumping $, portable dump, ice, tables, fire rings. ◊◊◊RECREATION: boating, canoeing, ramp, dock, motorboat rentals, saltwater fishing, play equipment, sports field. Rec open to public. Pets welcome. Open all yr. No tenting May-Sep. Rate in 2007 $20-28 for 4 persons. Phone: (850)229-2710.

(S) ST. JOSEPH PENINSULA STATE PARK—(Gulf) *From jct Hwy 71 & US 98: Go 9 mi S on US 98 & paved road, then 4 mi W on Hwy 30, then 9 mi N on Hwy C-30 (Cape San Blas Rd).* FACILITIES: 119 sites, 28 ft max RV length, 119 W&E, tenting, dump station, groceries, ice, grills. RECREATION: pavilion, saltwater swimming, boating, canoeing, ramp, dock, saltwater fishing, playground, hiking trails. No pets. Open all yr. Phone: (850) 227-1327.

PORT ST. LUCIE—D-5

(SE) PORT ST LUCIE RV RESORT—(St. Lucie) *From jct Hwy 716 (W. Port St. Lucie Blvd) & I-95: Go 3 mi S on I-95 (exit 118), then 2-1/2 mi E on Gatlin Blvd, then 5-1/2 mi E on Port St. Lucie Blvd, then 1/2 mi N on US 1, then 1 block E on Jennings Rd. Enter on R.*

WELCOME

WE'RE NEAR EVERYTHING!
We offer a heated pool & sites with phone & cable access. 3 Month Specials. Valentine's Party — a favorite among campers. Great summer ocean breezes — a perfect get-away! www.portstluciervresort.com

◊◊◊◊FACILITIES: 117 sites, typical site width 35 ft, 117 full hkups, (20, 30 & 50 amps), some

PORT ST LUCIE RV RESORT—Continued on next page

PORT ST. LUCIE—Continued
PORT ST LUCIE RV RESORT—Continued

extended stay sites (in winter), 4 pull-thrus, cable TV ($), wireless Instant Internet access at site, RV storage, laundry, ice, tables, patios.

◇◇RECREATION: rec hall, pavilion, swim pool, golf nearby, planned activities, horseshoes.

Pets welcome ($), quantity restrict. Partial handicap access. No tents. Open all yr. Big rigs welcome. Internet friendly. Clubs welcome. Rate in 2007 $36.50-46.50 for 2 persons. MC/VISA/DISC/Debit. Member ARVC, FLARVC. Phone: (877) 405-2333. CCUSA discount. FMCA discount.

e-mail: portstluciervresort@juno.com

SEE AD PAGE 163

PUNTA GORDA—D-3

(S) GULF VIEW RV RESORT—(Charlotte) *From jct US 17 & I-75: Go 3 mi S on I-75 (exit 161), then 1-1/2 mi W on Hwy 768 (Jones Loop Rd), then 1/2 mi S on Burnt Store Rd. Enter on R.*

◇◇◇◇FACILITIES: 203 sites, typical site width 35 ft, 203 full hkups, (20, 30 & 50 amps), many extended stay sites (in winter), 138 pull-thrus, wireless Instant Internet access at site ($), cable Internet access central location, cabins, dump station, non-guest dumping $, laundry, tables, patios.

◇◇◇RECREATION: rec hall, swim pool, whirlpool, boating, ramp, dock, saltwater/river fishing, golf nearby, 4 shuffleboard courts, planned activities, horseshoes, local tours.

Pets welcome, breed restrict, quantity restrict. Partial handicap access. No tents. Open all yr. Group activities winter only. Big rigs welcome. Internet friendly. Rate in 2007 $30-45 for 2 persons. MC/VISA/DISC/AMEX/Debit. Phone: (877)237-2757.

e-mail: info@rvonthego.com

SEE AD FORT MYERS BEACH PAGE 123

(S) PUNTA GORDA RV RESORT—(Charlotte) *S'bnd: From I-75 (exit 164) & US 17: Go 2 mi W on US 17, then 2 mi S on US 41, then 500 ft W on Rio Villa Dr. Enter on L.*

◇◇◇◇FACILITIES: 223 sites, typical site width 25 ft, 223 full hkups, (30 & 50 amps), mostly extended stay sites (in winter), cable TV, wireless Instant Internet access at site ($), phone Internet access central location, RV/park trailer rentals, RV storage, laundry, RV supplies, tables.

◇◇◇◇RECREATION: rec hall, rec room/area, swim pool, whirlpool, boating, canoeing, kayaking, ramp, dock, saltwater fishing, golf nearby, 2 shuffleboard courts, planned activities, horseshoes.

Pets welcome. Partial handicap access. No tents. Age restrictions may apply. Open all yr. Internet friendly. Clubs welcome. Rate in 2007 $30-45 for 2 persons. MC/VISA/Debit. Member ARVC, FLARVC. Phone: (941)639-2010.

e-mail: puntagordarv@earthlink.net

SEE AD THIS PAGE

(SE) Sun 'N' Shade Campground—(Charlotte) *From jct US 17 & I-75: Go 6-1/2 mi S on I-75 (exit 158), then 1 mi W on Tucker Grade Rc, then 3-1/2 mi S on US 41. Enter on L.* ◇◇◇◇FACILITIES: 200 sites, typical site width 30 ft, 190 full hkups, 10 W&E, (20, 30 & 50 amps), many extended stay sites (in winter), heater not allowed, dump station, laundry, tables, patios. ◇◇◇RECREATION: rec hall, swim pool, 2 shuffleboard courts, planned activities, horseshoes, hiking trails. Pets welcome, breed restrict. Partial handicap access. No tents. Open all yr. Rate in 2007 $30-35 for 2 persons. Member ARVC, FLARVC. Phone: (941)639-5388.

(E) WATER'S EDGE RV RESORT OF PUNTA GORDA (CAMP RESORT)—(Charlotte) *From jct US 17 & I-75: Go 3 mi S on I-75 (exit 161), then 500 feet E on Jones Loop Rd, then 2-3/4 mi N on Piper Rd. Enter on R.*

FACILITIES: 187 sites, typical site width 30 ft, 171 full hkups, 16 W&E, (20, 30 & 50 amps), some extended stay sites (in winter), 37 pull-thrus, wireless Instant Internet access at site ($), phone Internet access central location, RV storage, dump station, non-guest dumping $, laundry, RV supplies, LP gas by weight/by meter, ice, tables, patios.

RECREATION: rec hall, rec room/area, pavilion, swim pool, whirlpool, boating, electric motors only, dock, lake fishing, golf nearby, planned activities, horseshoes.

Pets welcome. Partial handicap access. No tents. Age restrictions may apply. Open all yr. Planned activities winter only. Big rigs welcome. Internet friendly. Escort to site. Rate in 2007 $38 for 2 persons. MC/VISA/Debit. Member ARVC, FLARVC. Phone: (800)637-9224.

e-mail: watersedgerv@earthlink.net

SEE AD THIS PAGE

QUINCY—A-1

(S) BEAVER LAKE CAMPGROUND—(Gadsden) *From jct I-10 (exit 174) & Hwy 12: Go 1/4 mi N on Hwy 12. Enter on R.*

◇◇◇FACILITIES: 30 sites, typical site width 32 ft, 30 full hkups, (30 & 50 amps), some extended stay sites, 30 pull-thrus, tenting, RV storage, dump station, non-guest dumping $, laundry, groceries, gas, ice, tables.

RECREATION: golf nearby.

Pets welcome. Open all yr. Big rigs welcome. Rate in 2007 $27.95 for 2 persons. MC/VISA/DISC/AMEX. Phone: (850)856-9095.

SEE AD TALLAHASSEE PAGE 171

REDDICK—B-3

(W) Ocala North RV Park—(Athens) *From jct I-75 (exit 368). Go 1 block W on Hwy 318, then 1/2 mi S on Hwy 225. Enter on L.* ◇◇◇FACILITIES: 126 sites, typical site width 30 ft, 126 full hkups, (30 & 50 amps), some extended stay sites, 47 pull-thrus, tenting, dump station, non-guest dumping $, laundry, LP gas by weight/by meter, tables, patios. ◇◇◇◇RECREATION: rec hall, rec room/area, equipped pavilion, swim pool, 2 shuffleboard courts, planned activities, horseshoes, hiking trails, v-ball. Pets welcome, breed restrict. Partial handicap access. Open all yr. Big rigs welcome. Internet friendly. Rate in 2007 $28-32 for 2 persons. Member ARVC, FLARVC. Phone: (877)267-8737.

RIVERVIEW—C-3

(S) Hidden River Travel Resort—(Hillsborough) *From I-75 (exit 250) & Gibsonton Rd: Go 1-1/2 mi E on Gibsonton Rd, then 1-1/2 mi E on Boyette, then 3/4 mi NE McMullen Rd, then 1/2 mi E on McMullen Loop. Enter at end.* ◇◇◇FACILITIES: 340 sites, typical site width 25 ft, 320 full hkups, 20 W&E, (20, 30 & 50 amps), many extended stay sites (in winter), dump station, non-guest dumping $, laundry, LP gas by weight/by meter, tables, patios. ◇◇◇◇◇RECREATION: rec hall, rec room/area, equipped pavilion, swim pool, boating, canoeing, ramp, river/pond fishing, playground, 4 shuffleboard courts, planned activities, horseshoes, v-ball. Pets welcome. Partial handicap access. No tents. Age restrictions may apply. Open all yr. Planned activities winter only. Big rigs welcome. Internet friendly. Rate in 2007 $34 for 2 persons. Phone: (813)677-1515.

ROCKLEDGE—C-4

(S) SPACE COAST RV RESORT—(Brevard) *S'bound from I-95 (exit 195): Go 200 yards N on Fiske Blvd, then 200 yards E on Barnes Blvd. N'bound from I-95 (exit 195): Go 300 yards straight ahead from light. Enter on L.*

ENJOY THE EAST COAST'S FINEST RESORT!
Enjoy activities galore in the beautiful setting of the Cocoa Beach area! Visit Kennedy Space Center. Enjoy the Atlantic Ocean Beaches or just relax at one of our beautiful sites. Our RV Resort is near all area attractions

◇◇◇◇◇FACILITIES: 267 sites, typical site width 35 ft, 267 full hkups, (20, 30 & 50 amps), 50 amps ($), some extended stay sites (in winter), 85 pull-thrus, phone/cable on-site Internet access (needs activ), phone Internet access central location, tenting, RV storage, dump station, non-guest dumping $, laundry, RV supplies, LP gas by weight/by meter, tables, patios, grills.

◇◇◇◇RECREATION: rec hall, rec room/area, equipped pavilion, swim pool, wading pool, pond fishing, golf nearby, play equipment, 4 shuffleboard courts, planned activities, horseshoes.

Pets welcome, breed restrict, size restrict, quantity restrict. Age restrictions may apply. Open all yr. Planned group activities winter only. Big rigs welcome. Internet friendly. Escort to site. Clubs welcome. Rate in 2007 $35-55 for 2 persons. MC/VISA/DISC/AMEX. Phone: (800)982-4233.

e-mail: scrv@spacecoastrv.com

SEE AD COCOA PAGE 103 AND AD TRAVEL SECTION PAGE 71

RUSKIN—D-3

(S) HIDE-A-WAY RV RESORT—(Hillsborough) *From jct I-75 (exit 240) & Hwy 674: Go 3 mi W on Hwy 674, then 2-1/2 mi S on US 41, then 3/4 mi E on Chaney Dr. Enter on L.*

◇◇◇◇FACILITIES: 356 sites, typical site width 35 ft, 356 full hkups, (30 & 50 amps), many extended stay sites (in winter), 7 pull-thrus, wireless Instant Internet access at site, cable on-

HIDE-A-WAY RV RESORT—Continued on next page

Tell them Woodall's sent you!

RUSKIN—Continued
HIDE-A-WAY RV RESORT—Continued

site Internet access (needs activ), wireless Internet access central location ($), RV storage, dump station, non-guest dumping $, laundry, LP gas by weight/by meter, tables.

◊◊◊◊RECREATION: rec hall, rec room/area, swim pool, boating, ramp, dock, saltwater/river fishing, golf nearby, 8 shuffleboard courts, planned activities, horseshoes.

Pets welcome, size restrict, quantity restrict. Partial handicap access. No tents. Open all yr. Planned group activities winter only. Big rigs welcome. Internet friendly. Clubs welcome. Rate in 2007 $30 for 2 persons. MC/VISA/DISC/AMEX/ Debit. Member ARVC, FLARVC. Phone: (800)607-2532.

e-mail: hideawayrv@hotmail.com

SEE AD TAMPA PAGE 172

(SW) River Oaks RV Resort—(Hillsborough) *From jct I-75 (exit 240) & Hwy 674: Go 3 mi W on Hwy 674,then 3-1/4 mi S on US 41, then 1/4 mi E on Universal, then 2-1/2 mi Enter on L.* ◊◊FACILITIES: 97 sites, typical site width 22 ft, 97 full hkups, (20, 30 & 50 amps), many extended stay sites (in winter), laundry, tables, patios. ◊◊◊RECREATION: rec hall, boating, ramp, dock, river/pond fishing, 2 shuffleboard courts, planned activities, horseshoes. Pets welcome, breed restrict. No tents. Age restrictions may apply. Open all yr. Big rigs welcome. Rate in 2007 $30. Phone: (813) 645-2439.

WELCOME

(S) SUN LAKE RV RESORT—(Hillsborough) *From jct I-75 (exit 240B) & Hwy 674: Go 1/4 mi W on Hwy 674, then 3/4 mi S on 33rd St SE. N'bnd: Use exit 240. Enter on R.*

◊◊◊◊FACILITIES: 47 sites, typical site width 40 ft, 47 full hkups, (30 & 50 amps), 18 pull-thrus, cable TV ($), phone/cable on-site Internet access (needs activ), phone Internet access central location, tenting, RV storage, dump station, non-guest dumping $, laundry, tables, patios.

◊◊◊RECREATION: rec hall, swim pool, boating, dock, lake fishing, putting green, golf nearby, shuffleboard court, planned activities.

Pets welcome. Open all yr. Planned activities winter only. Big rigs welcome. Clubs welcome. Rate in 2007 $26 for 2 persons. MC/VISA. Phone: (800) 856-2105.

e-mail: sunlakerv@aol.com

SEE AD PAGE 164

WELCOME

(S) TAMPA SOUTH RV RESORT—(Hillsborough) *From jct I-75 (exit 240) & Hwy 674: Go 3 mi W on Hwy 674,then 2 mi S on US 41. Enter on L.*

◊◊◊FACILITIES: 121 sites, typical site width 30 ft, 121 full hkups, (20, 30 & 50 amps), mostly extended stay sites (in winter), 70 pull-thrus, wireless Instant Internet access at

RUSKIN—Continued
TAMPA SOUTH RV RESORT—Continued

site, wireless Internet access central location, RV storage, dump station, non-guest dumping $, laundry, tables, patios.

◊◊◊RECREATION: rec room/area, swim pool, boating, dock, saltwater fishing, golf nearby, 4 shuffleboard courts, planned activities, horseshoes.

Pets welcome, breed restrict. No tents. Age restrictions may apply. Open all yr. Planned activities during season only. Big rigs welcome. Internet friendly. Clubs welcome. Rate in 2007 $20-25 for 2 persons. MC/VISA. Phone: (813)645-1202.

e-mail: reservations@tampasouthrvresort.com

SEE AD PAGE 164

ST. AUGUSTINE—B-4

(S) ANASTASIA STATE PARK—(St. Johns) *From jct US 1 & Hwy A1A: Go 3 mi S on Hwy A1A at Hwy 3 (St. Augustine Beach). Enter on R.* FACILITIES: 139 sites, 30 ft max RV length, 139 W&E, tenting, dump station, laundry, ltd groceries, fire rings, grills. RECREATION: saltwater swimming, boating, canoeing, 10 canoe rentals, saltwater fishing, playground, hiking trails. Open all yr. Phone: (904)461-2033.

(S) Bryn Mawr Ocean Resort—(St. Johns) *From jct I-95 (exit 305) & Hwy 206: Go 7 mi E on Hwy 206, then 2-1/2 mi N on Hwy A1A. Enter on R.* ◊◊◊◊FACILITIES: 128 sites, typical site width 28 ft, accepts full hkup units only, 128 full hkups, (20, 30 & 50 amps), mostly extended stay sites, 70 pull-thrus, dump station, non-guest dumping $, laundry, LP gas by weight/by meter, ice, tables, patios. ◊◊◊◊RECREATION: rec hall, pavilion, swim pool, saltwater swimming, saltwater fishing, playground, 6 shuffleboard courts, tennis, horseshoes. Pets welcome ($). Partial handicap access. No tents. Open all yr. Big rigs welcome. Internet friendly. Rate in 2007 $53-71 for 2 persons. Member FLARVC. Phone: (888)768-9638.

(S) FAVER-DYKES STATE PARK—(St. Johns) *From town: Go 15 mi S on US-1.* FACILITIES: 30 sites, 30 ft max RV length, 30 W&E, tenting, dump station. RECREATION: pavilion, boating, canoeing, ramp, dock, 4 canoe rentals, saltwater fishing, playground, hiking trails. No pets. Open all yr. Phone: (904)794-0997.

(W) Indian Forest Campground—(St. Johns) *From jct I-95 (exit 311) & Hwy 207: Go 2 mi E on Hwy 207. Enter on L.* ◊◊◊FACILITIES: 105 sites, typical site width 30 ft, 86 full hkups, 19 W&E, (30 & 50 amps), some extended stay sites, 40 pull-thrus, dump station, non-guest dumping $, laundry, LP gas by weight/by meter, ice, tables. ◊◊RECREATION: rec hall, pond fishing, horseshoes, hiking trails. Pets welcome, breed restrict. Partial handicap access. No tents. Open all yr. Big rigs welcome. Rate in 2007 $28-38 for 2 persons. Member ARVC, FLARVC. Phone: (904)824-3574. FMCA discount.

ST. AUGUSTINE—Continued on next page

Stay with a Woodall's Advertised Campground!

ST. AUGUSTINE—Continued

(NE) NORTH BEACH CAMP RESORT—(St. Johns) *From jct Business US 1 & Hwy A1A: Go 4-1/4 mi N on Hwy A1A. Enter on L.*

OCEAN OUT FRONT & RIVER OUT BACK!
Sunrise on the Ocean, Sunset on the River, a bit of Olde Florida In Between! From Spectacular Ocean Sunrises to River Sunset Vistas and Endless Stars at Night, here's your ticket to the best camping vacation ever!

◆◆◆◆FACILITIES: 150 sites, typical site width 40 ft, 143 full hkups, 7 W&E, (30 & 50 amps), 50 amps ($), some extended stay sites, 35 pull-thrus, cable TV, wireless Instant Internet access at site, wireless Internet access central location, tenting, cabins, RV storage, dump station, non-guest dumping $, laundry, groceries, RV supplies, LP gas by weight/by meter, ice, tables, controlled access gate.

◆◆◆◆◆RECREATION: rec hall, rec room/area, coin games, swim pool, saltwater swimming, whirlpool, boating, ramp, dock, 5 motorboat rentals, saltwater/river fishing, fishing supplies, bsktball, playground, 4 shuffleboard courts, planned activities, horseshoes, v-ball.

Pets welcome, breed restrict, size restrict, quantity restrict. Partial handicap access. Open all yr. Group activities winter only. Big rigs welcome. Internet friendly. Clubs welcome. Rate in 2007 $47-55 for 2 persons. MC/VISA/DISC. Member ARVC, FLARVC. Phone: (800)542-8316.

e-mail: camping@aug.com

SEE AD PAGE 165

Visit Woodall's Advertised Attractions

ST. AUGUSTINE—Continued

(S) OCEAN GROVE CAMP RESORT—(St. Johns) *From jct I-95 (exit 305) & Hwy 206: Go 7 mi E on Hwy 206, then 3-1/2 mi N on Hwy A1A. Enter on L.*

◆◆◆FACILITIES: 198 sites, typical site width 35 ft, 198 full hkups, (20, 30 & 50 amps), some extended stay sites, 50 pull-thrus, cable TV ($), wireless Internet access central location, RV storage, laundry, ltd groceries, LP gas by weight/by meter, ice, tables, patios, controlled access gate.

◆◆◆◆◆RECREATION: rec hall, pavilion, equipped pavilion, swim pool, wading pool, whirlpool, boating, canoeing, kayaking, ramp, dock, saltwater/river fishing, bsktball, 20 bike rentals, playground, shuffleboard court, planned activities, horseshoes, v-ball, local tours.

Pets welcome, breed restrict. Partial handicap access. No tents. Open all yr. Big rigs welcome. Internet friendly. Clubs welcome. Rate in 2007 $50-75 for 4 persons. MC/VISA/DISC/AMEX. Member ARVC, FLARVC. Phone: (800)342-4007.

e-mail: debbie@oceangroveresort.com

SEE AD PAGE 165

(S) ST. AUGUSTINE BEACH KOA KAMPGROUND RESORT—(St. Johns) *From jct I-95 (exit 311-Old 94) & Hwy 207: Go 4 mi E on Hwy 207, then 4 mi E on Hwy 312, then 1/4 mi S on Hwy A1A, then 50 feet W on Pope Rd. Enter on L.*

◆◆◆◆FACILITIES: 119 sites, typical site width 40 ft, 84 full hkups, 35 W&E, (20, 30 & 50 amps), 61 pull-thrus, cable TV, wireless Instant Internet access at site, wireless Internet access central location, tenting, cabins, RV storage, dump station, non-guest dumping $, laundry, groceries, RV supplies, LP gas by weight/by meter, ice, tables, fire rings, grills, wood.

ST. AUGUSTINE—Continued
ST. AUGUSTINE BEACH KOA KAMPGROUND RESORT—Continued

◆◆◆◆RECREATION: rec hall, rec room/area, coin games, swim pool, dock, 5 pedal boat rentals, lake fishing, fishing supplies, golf nearby, 12 bike rentals, playground, planned activities, horseshoes, local tours.

Pets welcome. Partial handicap access. Open all yr. Planned group activities winter and holidays only. Big rigs welcome. Internet friendly. Escort to site. Clubs welcome. Rate in 2007 $48-91 for 2 persons. MC/VISA/DISC/AMEX. ATM. Member ARVC, FLARVC. Phone: (800)562-4022. KOA 10% value card discount.

e-mail: staugkoa@aol.com

SEE AD THIS PAGE AND AD DISCOVER SECTION PAGES 62 & 63

(SW) St. John's RV Park—(St. Johns) *From I-95 (exit 311) & Hwy 207: Go 1/4 mi E on Hwy 207. Enter on L.* ◆◆◆FACILITIES: 80 sites, 58 full hkups, 7 W&E, (20, 30 & 50 amps), 50 amps ($), 15 no hkups, many extended stay sites, 16 pull-thrus, dump station, laundry, tables. RECREATION: lake fishing, horseshoes. Pets welcome. Partial handicap access. No tents. Open all yr. Big rigs welcome. Rate in 2007 $25-30 for 2 persons. Phone: (904)824-9840.

(W) STAGECOACH RV PARK—(St. Johns) *From jct I-95 (exit 318) & Hwy 16: Go 3/10 mi W on Hwy 16, then 1 block S on Toms Rd, then 3/10 mi W on CR 208. Enter on L.*

◆◆◆FACILITIES: 80 sites, typical site width 45 ft, 80 full hkups, (30 & 50 amps), many extended stay sites (in winter), 60 pull-thrus, wireless Instant Internet access at site ($), RV storage, dump station, non-guest dumping $, laundry, RV supplies, LP gas by weight/by meter, ice, tables.

STAGECOACH RV PARK—Continued on next page

ST. AUGUSTINE—Continued
STAGECOACH RV PARK—Continued

◆◆RECREATION: rec hall, rec room/area, bsktball, play equipment, horseshoes.

Pets welcome, breed restrict. Partial handicap access. No tents. Open all yr. Big rigs welcome. Internet friendly. Clubs welcome. Rate in 2007 $33-35 for 2 persons. MC/VISA. Member ARVC, FLARVC. Phone: (904)824-2319. CCUSA discount. FMCA discount.

e-mail: stagecoachrvpark@bellsouth.net

SEE AD PAGE 166

ST. CLOUD—C-4

The Floridian RV Resort—(Osceola) *From jct Florida Tnpk (exit 254) & Hwy 528A/528: Go 12 mi E on Hwy 528A/528 (Bee Line Expwy), then 7 mi S on Hwy 15 to jct Hwy 530. Enter on L.* ◆◆◆FACILITIES: 308 sites, typical site width 30 ft, 233 full hkups, 75 W&E, (30 & 50 amps), some extended stay sites (in winter), 75 pull-thrus, tenting, dump station, non-guest dumping $, laundry, tables, patios. ◆◆◆◆RECREATION: rec hall, rec room/area, 2 swim pools, boating, ramp, lake fishing, playground, 4 shuffleboard courts, planned activities, tennis, horseshoes. Pets welcome, breed restrict, size restrict, quantity restrict. Open all yr. Planned activities & church services, winter only. Big rigs welcome. Rate in 2007 $30 for 2 persons. Phone: (407)892-5171.

(N) THE MARK MANUFACTURED HOME PARK—(Oceola) *From jct Florida's tnpk & US 192: Go 1-1/2 mi SE on US 192. Enter on L.*

WELCOME

◆◆◆FACILITIES: 55 sites, typical site width 33 ft, 55 full hkups, (30 & 50 amps), wireless Instant Internet access at site, wireless Internet access central location, laundry, patios.

◆◆◆RECREATION: rec hall, swim pool, whirlpool, golf nearby, 6 shuffleboard courts, planned activities, horseshoes.

Pets welcome, breed restrict, size restrict, quantity restrict. Partial handicap access. No tents. Open all yr. Big rigs welcome. Internet friendly. Rate in 2007 $40 for 2 persons. Phone: (407)892-3979.

e-mail: themark@arcinvestments.com

SEE AD ORLANDO PAGE 156

ST. GEORGE ISLAND—B-1

(E) ST. GEORGE ISLAND STATE PARK—(Franklin) *Cross the bridge to St George Island & go East.* FACILITIES: 60 sites, 33 ft max RV length, 60 W&E, tenting, dump station, grills. RECREATION: saltwater swimming, boating, canoeing, ramp, saltwater fishing, playground, hiking trails. Pets welcome. Open all yr. Phone: (850)927-2111.

ST. JAMES CITY—E-3

(N) PINE ISLAND RESORT—(Lee) *From jct Hwy 78 & Hwy 767: Go 5-1/2 mi S on Hwy 767. Enter on L.*

WELCOME

◆◆◆◆FACILITIES: 364 sites, typical site width 35 ft, 364 full hkups, (20, 30 & 50 amps), some extended stay sites (in winter), cable TV, wireless Instant Internet access at site, tenting, RV/park trailer rentals, cabins, dump station, non-guest dumping $, laundry, full svc store, RV supplies, LP gas by weight/by meter, ice, tables, patios.

◆◆◆◆RECREATION: rec hall, rec room/area, swim pool, saltwater swimming, whirlpool, lake fishing, fishing supplies, golf nearby, bsktball, 15

ST. JAMES CITY—Continued
PINE ISLAND RESORT—Continued

bike rentals, playground, 2 shuffleboard courts, planned activities, tennis, horseshoes, sports field, local tours.

Pets welcome, breed restrict. Partial handicap access. Open all yr. Local tours & group activities winter only. Internet friendly. Clubs welcome. Rate in 2007 $22.95-65.95 for 2 persons. MC/VISA/DISC/Debit. Member ARVC, FLARVC. Phone: (800) 562-8505.

e-mail: pineisland@mhcomes.com

SEE AD FORT MYERS PAGE 120

ST. PETERSBURG—C-3

(W) KOA-St. Petersburg—(Pinellas) *From jct I-275 (exit 25) & 38th Ave N: Go 5-1/2 mi N on 38th Ave, then 1-1/2 mi N on Tyrone (Bay Pines), then 1/2 mi N on 95th St. Enter at end.* ◆◆◆◆FACILITIES: 398 sites, typical site width 30 ft, 341 full hkups, 40 W&E, (20, 30 & 50 amps), 50 amps ($), 17 no hkups, mostly extended stay sites (in winter), 75 pull-thrus, tenting, dump station, non-guest dumping $, laundry, full svc store, LP gas by weight/by meter, ice, tables, patios. ◆◆◆◆◆RECREATION: rec hall, rec room/area, swim pool, boating, canoeing, ramp, dock, 6 canoe/motorboat rentals, saltwater fishing, mini-golf ($), playground, 8 shuffleboard courts, planned activities, horseshoes, v-ball. Pets welcome, quantity restrict. Partial handicap access. Open all yr. Planned activites winter & holiday weekends. Big rigs welcome. Internet friendly. Rate in 2007 $50-90 for 2 persons. Member ARVC, FLARVC. Phone: (800)562-7714. KOA 10% value card discount.

Visit our website www.woodalls.com

ST. PETERSBURG—Continued

(N) ROBERT'S MOBILE HOME & RV RESORT—(Pinellas) *From jct I-275 & Hwy 694: Go 1 mi W on Hwy 694. Enter on L.*

WELCOME

◆◆◆◆FACILITIES: 430 sites, typical site width 30 ft, 430 full hkups, (30 & 50 amps), some extended stay sites (in winter), cable TV ($), phone/cable on-site Internet access (needs activ), phone Internet access central location, RV storage, dump station, non-guest dumping $, laundry, ice, tables, patios.

◆◆◆◆◆RECREATION: rec hall, rec room/area, equipped pavilion, swim pool, whirlpool, mini-golf, golf nearby, bsktball, 12 shuffleboard courts, planned activities, tennis, horseshoes, v-ball.

Pets welcome, breed restrict, size restrict. No tents. Open all yr. Planned group activities winter only. Big rigs welcome. Internet friendly. Clubs welcome. Rate in 2007 $25 for 2 persons. MC/VISA. Phone: (727)577-6820.

e-mail: robertsresort@aol.com

SEE AD THIS PAGE

(N) Treasure Village MH/RV Park (RV SPACES) —(Pinellas) *From jct I-275 & 54th St: Go 1-1/2 mi E on 54th St, then 1 block S on Hwy 92. Enter on L.* FACILITIES: laundry. RECREATION: rec hall. Open all yr. Phone: (727)527-1701.

Woodall's Tip #44... If you're ever lost in the forest, you can tell your direction from the trees. The bark will be thicker on the north side of trees.

SALT SPRINGS—B-3

ELITE RESORTS AT SALT SPRINGS—(Marion) *From CR 314 & Hwy 19: Go 1 mi N on Hwy 19, then 1/10 mi W on CR 316. Enter on L.*

RV RESORT IN THE OCALA NATIONAL FOREST

Nestled on 70 acres along 1,300 linear feet of 2,800 acre Lake Kerr, Elite Resorts at Salt Springs offers RV and cottage rental sites with 2 large pools and amenities ranging from large lodge, boat ramp and other activities.

◊◊◊◊FACILITIES: 472 sites, typical site width 50 ft, 472 full hkups, (20, 30 & 50 amps), mostly extended stay sites, 31 pull-thrus, cable TV, phone/cable on-site Internet access (needs activ), wireless Internet access central location, cabins, laundry, ltd groceries, RV supplies, ice, tables, patios, controlled access gate.

◊◊◊◊◊RECREATION: rec hall, rec room/area, pavilion, 2 swim pools, wading pool, lake swimming, whirlpool, boating, canoeing, kayaking, ramp, dock, lake fishing, mini-golf, golf nearby, bsktball, playground, 3 shuffleboard courts, planned activities, tennis, horseshoes, v-ball.

Pets welcome, quantity restrict. Partial handicap access. No tents. Open all yr. Big rigs welcome. Internet friendly. Clubs welcome. Rate in 2007 $32 for 2 persons. MC/VISA. Member ARVC, FLARVC. Phone: (800)356-2460.

e-mail: info@eliteresorts.com

SEE AD TRAVEL SECTION PAGE 79

Read interesting travel facts in the front of every state/province listing section.

SALT SPRINGS—Continued

(N) OCALA NATIONAL FOREST (Salt Springs Rec. Area)—(Marion) *From jct Hwy-314 & Hwy-19: Go 1 mi N on Hwy-19.* FACILITIES: 106 sites, typical site width 14 ft, 32 ft max RV length, 106 full hkups, tenting, dump station, fire rings, wood. RECREATION: rec room/area, pavilion, lake swimming, boating, canoeing, ramp, lake fishing, tennis. Rec open to public. Partial handicap access. Open all yr. Phone: (352)685-2048.

SANFORD—C-4

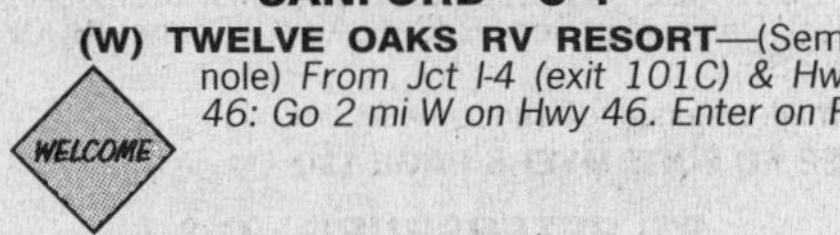

(W) TWELVE OAKS RV RESORT—(Seminole) *From Jct I-4 (exit 101C) & Hwy 46: Go 2 mi W on Hwy 46. Enter on R.*

FUNZONE BETWEEN DAYTONA AND DISNEY

Twelve Oaks is a pristine park in a shady country setting but close to all the goodies. Full facilities and activities. Near mall shopping, restaurants, golfing, gambling, fishing, canoeing, beaches and Disney minutes away.

◊◊◊◊FACILITIES: 247 sites, typical site width 30 ft, 247 full hkups, (20, 30 & 50 amps), many extended stay sites, 34 pull-thrus, phone Internet access central location, RV storage, dump station, laundry, RV supplies, LP gas by weight/by meter, tables, patios.

◊◊◊◊RECREATION: rec hall, rec room/area, swim pool, golf nearby, 2 shuffleboard courts, planned activities, horseshoes, v-ball, local tours.

Pets welcome. Partial handicap access. No tents. Open all yr. Big rigs welcome. Internet friendly. Escort to site. Clubs welcome. Rate in 2007 $30 for 2 persons. MC/VISA. Member ARVC, FLARVC. Phone: (800)633-9529.

SEE AD THIS PAGE

Save time! Plan ahead with WOODALL'S!

SANTA ROSA BEACH—F-2

(W) TOPSAIL HILL PRESERVE STATE PARK—(Walton) *Eastbound from Destin City limits: Go 8 mi E on US 98, then 1/4 mi S on Hwy 30A. Westbound from jct US 331 & US 98: Go 5 mi W on US 98, then 1/4 mi S on Hwy 30A. Enter on R.* FACILITIES: 156 sites, typical site width 45 ft, accepts full hkup units only, 156 full hkups, (20, 30 & 50 amps), 20 pull thrus, laundry, ltd groceries, ice, patios. RECREATION: rec hall, pavilion, swim pool, saltwater swimming, saltwater/lake fishing, 4 shuffleboard courts, planned activities, tennis, horseshoes, hiking trails. Pets welcome. Partial handicap access. No tents. Open all yr. Big rigs welcome. Internet friendly. Phone: (800)326-3521.

SARASOTA—D-3

WELCOME

✲ **(E) CAMPBELL RV INC**—*From jct I-75 (exit 210) and Hwy 780 (Fruitville Rd): Go 1 block W on Hwy 780, then 1 mi S on Cattlemen Rd.* SALES: travel trailers, 5th wheels, motor homes, mini-motor homes, pre-owned unit sales. SERVICES: full-time mech, engine/chassis repair, RV appliance repair, body work/collision repair, bus. hrs emerg rd svc, mobile RV svc, RV towing, sells parts/accessories, installs hitches. Open all yr. MC/VISA/AMEX. Phone: (941)342-4313.

e-mail: campbellrv1@aol.com

SEE AD NEXT PAGE

WELCOME

HORSESHOE COVE RV RESORT—*From jct Hwy 780 (Fruitville Rd) & I-75: Go 7 mi N on I-75 (exit 41), then 1-1/4 mi W on Hwy 70.*

SEE PRIMARY LISTING AT BRADENTON AND AD BRADENTON PAGE 97

(SE) MYAKKA RIVER STATE PARK—(Sarasota) *From jct US 41 & Hwy 72: Go 12 mi E on Hwy 72.* FACILITIES: 76 sites, 35 ft max RV length, 76 W&E, tenting, dump station, groceries, grills. RECREATION: boating, canoeing, ramp, dock, rowboat/4 canoe rentals, lake/river fishing, playground, hiking trails. No pets. Open all yr. Phone: (941)361-6511.

SARASOTA—Continued on next page

SARASOTA—Continued

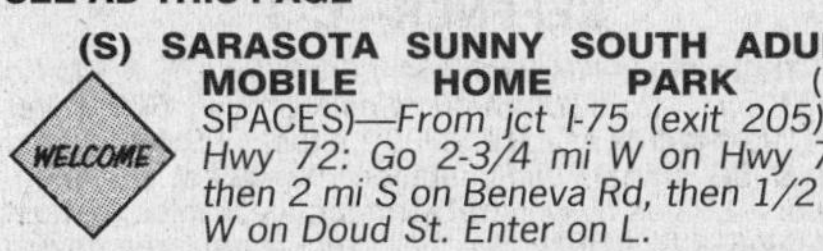

(NW) SARASOTA LAKES CAMPING RESORT—(Sarasota) *From jct I-75 (exit 213) & University Prkwy: Go 5 1/2 mi W on University Prkwy. Enter on L.*

◊◊◊◊FACILITIES: 420 sites, 420 full hkups, (20, 30 & 50 amps), cable TV, phone/cable on-site Internet access (needs activ), dump station, non-guest dumping $, laundry, tables, patios, controlled access gate.

◊◊◊◊RECREATION: rec hall, rec room/area, swim pool, wading pool, golf nearby, bsktball, playground, 8 shuffleboard courts, planned activities, tennis, horseshoes, local tours.

Pets welcome, quantity restrict. No tents. Open all yr. Big rigs welcome. MC/VISA. Phone: (941)355-8585.

SEE AD THIS PAGE

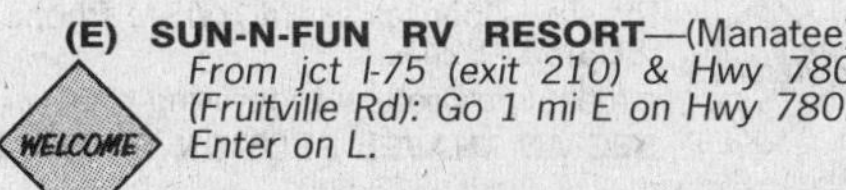

(S) SARASOTA SUNNY SOUTH ADULT MOBILE HOME PARK (RV SPACES)—*From jct I-75 (exit 205) & Hwy 72: Go 2-3/4 mi W on Hwy 72, then 2 mi S on Beneva Rd, then 1/2 mi W on Doud St. Enter on L.*

FACILITIES: 17 sites, typical site width 30 ft, 17 full hkups, (30 & 50 amps), phone/cable on-site Internet access (needs activ), dump station.

Pets welcome. No tents. Age restrictions may apply. Open all yr. Big rigs welcome. Phone: (941) 921-4444.

SEE AD THIS PAGE AND AD TRAVEL SECTION PAGE 76

(E) SUN-N-FUN RV RESORT—(Manatee) *From jct I-75 (exit 210) & Hwy 780 (Fruitville Rd): Go 1 mi E on Hwy 780. Enter on L.*

WHEN ONLY THE BEST IS GOOD ENOUGH
Great camping with all amenities & endless fun. Huge swimming pool, 18 shuffleboard courts, mini golf, pro horsehoe courts, hot tubs, billiard room, lawn boules, lighted tennis courts, 10 acre fishing lake & much more.

◊◊◊◊◊FACILITIES: 1483 sites, typical site width 35 ft, 1483 full hkups, (30 & 50 amps), many extended stay sites (in winter), 50 pull-thrus, cable TV, wireless Instant Internet access at site, cable on-site Internet access (needs activ), wireless Internet access central location, RV/park trailer rentals, RV storage, dump station, non-guest dumping $, laundry, LP gas by weight/by meter, patios, controlled access gate.

◊◊◊◊◊RECREATION: rec hall, rec room/area, equipped pavilion, swim pool, wading pool, whirlpool, boating, no motors, canoeing, lake fishing, mini-golf, golf nearby, bsktball, playground, 18 shuffleboard courts, planned activities, tennis, horseshoes, sports field, v-ball, local tours.

Pets welcome, quantity restrict. No tents. Open all yr. Group activities winter season only. Big rigs welcome. Internet friendly. Clubs welcome. Rate in 2007 $30-73 per vehicle. MC/VISA/DISC/AMEX. Member ARVC, FLARVC. Phone: (800)843-2421. FMCA discount.

SEE AD PAGE 168 AND AD DISCOVER SECTION PAGE 44

Visit a Woodall's Advertised Dealer/Service Location.

Shop at Woodall's Advertised Dealers

Check out our web site www.woodalls.com

SCOTTSMOOR—C-4

(W) Crystal Lake RV Park—(Brevard) *From jct I-95 (exit 231) & Stuckway Rd (formerly CR 5A): Go 1/10 mi on Stuckway Rd. Enter on L.* ◊◊◊FACILITIES: 62 sites, typical site width 25 ft, 60 full hkups, (20, 30 & 50 amps), 2 no hkups, many extended stay sites, 44 pull-thrus, heater not allowed, tenting, laundry, tables. ◊◊RECREATION: rec hall, swim pool, lake fishing, 2 shuffleboard courts. Pets welcome, quantity restrict. Open all yr. Rate in 2007 $26-32 for 2 persons. Member ARVC, FLARVC. Phone: (321)268-8555. CCUSA discount.

SEBASTIAN—C-5

(N) LONG POINT PARK (Brevard County Park)—(Brevard) *From town: Go 7 mi N on Hwy-A1A.* FACILITIES: 194 sites, 15 full hkups, 139 W&E, (20 & 30 amps), 40 no hkups, tenting, dump station, laundry, ltd groceries, ice. RECREATION: pavilion, pond swimming, ramp, dock, saltwater fishing, playground, horseshoes, hiking trails, v-ball. Open all yr. Phone: (321)952-4532.

(E) PELICAN'S LANDING—*From jct I-95 (exit 156) & Hwy 512: Go 6-1/4 mi E on Hwy 512, then 1 mi S on Indian River Dr. Enter on L.*

WELCOME

◊◊◊◊FACILITIES: 16 sites, typical site width 35 ft, accepts self-contained units only, 16 full hkups, (20, 30 & 50 amps), phone/wireless/cable Instant Internet access at site ($), cabins, laundry, patios.

◊◊◊RECREATION: boating, canoeing, kayaking, ramp, dock, saltwater fishing, golf nearby.

Pets welcome. No tents. Open all yr. No restrooms. No showers. Big rigs welcome. Rate in 2007 $40-50 for 2 persons. Phone: (772)589-5188.

e-mail: info@pelicanslandingresort.com

SEE AD THIS PAGE

(S) SEBASTIAN INLET STATE PARK—(Brevard) *From jct Hwy-510 & Hwy-A1A: Go 7 mi N on Hwy-A1A.* FACILITIES: 51 sites, 32 ft max RV length, 51 W&E, tenting, dump station, laundry, fire rings, grills. RECREATION: pavilion, saltwater swimming, boating, ramp, saltwater fishing, playground. Partial handicap access. Open all yr. Phone: (321)984-4852.

(SE) Vero Beach Kamp Inc—(Indian River) *From jct I-95 (exit 156) & Hwy 512: Go 6 mi E on Hwy 512, then 4-1/4 mi S on US 1. Enter on L.* ◊◊◊FACILITIES: 120 sites, typical site width 30 ft, 120 full hkups, (20, 30 & 50 amps), tenting, dump station, laundry, LP gas by weight/by meter, tables, patios. ◊◊◊RECREATION: rec hall, rec room/area, swim pool, playground, planned activities, horseshoes. Pets welcome. Open all yr. Group activities winter only. Big rigs welcome. Rate in 2007 $29.95 for 2 persons. Member ARVC, FLARVC. Phone: (877)589-5643.

(S) Whispering Palms RV Resort—(Indian River) *From jct I-95 (exit 156) & Hwy 512: Go 6 mi E on Hwy 512, then 2-1/4 mi S on US 1. Enter on R.* ◊◊◊◊FACILITIES: 250 sites, 250 full hkups, (30 & 50 amps), dump station, non-guest dumping $, laundry, LP gas by weight/by meter, tables, patios. ◊◊◊◊RECREATION: rec hall, rec room/area, 2 swim pools, 8 shuffleboard courts, planned activities, tennis, horseshoes, v-ball. Pets welcome. No tents. Open all yr. Big rigs welcome. Internet friendly. Member ARVC, FLARVC. Phone: (800)414-0814. CCUSA discount.

SEBRING—D-4

(SW) BUTTONWOOD BAY—(Highlands) *From jct Hwy 17 & US 27 & 98: Go 5 mi S on US 27. Enter on R.*

WELCOME

◊◊◊◊◊FACILITIES: 534 sites, typical site width 40 ft, 534 full hkups, (30 & 50 amps), cable TV ($), wireless Instant Internet access at site, phone/cable on-site Internet access (needs activ), phone Internet access central location, dump station, laundry, ice, tables, patios.

◊◊◊◊◊RECREATION: rec hall, rec room/area, 2 swim pools, boating, ramp, dock, lake fishing, mini-golf, golf nearby, bsktball, 14 shuffleboard courts, planned activities, tennis, horseshoes, sports field, hiking trails, v-ball, local tours.

Pets welcome, breed restrict, quantity restrict. Partial handicap access. No tents. Age restrictions may apply. Open all yr. Big rigs welcome. Internet friendly. Escort to site. Clubs welcome. Rate in 2007 $16-36 for 2 persons. MC/VISA/DISC. Phone: (866)655-5565. CCUSA discount.

e-mail: sunresv@aol.com

SEE AD TRAVEL SECTION PAGE 73

(SE) Highland Oaks RV Resort—(Highlands) *From jct US 27 & US 98: Go 1/2 mi E on US 98, then 1/2 mi N on CR 17, then 1/4 mi W on 6th St. Enter on R.* ◊◊◊◊FACILITIES: 106 sites, 106 full hkups, (30 amps), many extended stay sites (in winter), 3 pull-thrus, laundry, tables, patios. ◊◊◊RECREATION: rec hall, 2 shuffleboard courts, planned activities, tennis, horseshoes. Pets welcome, breed restrict. No tents. Open all yr. Planned activities in season only. Rate in 2007 $20 for 2 persons. Phone: (863)655-1685.

(NW) Highland Wheel Estates—(Highlands) *From jct US 27 & Hwy 634 (Hammock Rd): Go 1 block W on Hwy 634. Enter on R.* ◊◊◊FACILITIES: 120 sites, typical site width 30 ft, 120 full hkups, (30 & 50 amps), many extended stay sites (in winter), 25 pull-thrus, tenting, dump station, non-guest dumping $, laundry, tables, patios. ◊◊◊RECREATION: rec hall, swim pool, 4 shuffleboard courts, planned activities, horseshoes. Pets welcome, breed restrict, quantity restrict. Age restrictions may apply. Open all yr. Planned group activities winter only. Big rigs welcome. Rate in 2007 $30 for 2 persons. Phone: (800)493-0020.

(W) HIGHLANDS HAMMOCK STATE PARK—(Highlands) *From jct US-98 & US-27: Go 6 mi NW on US-27, exit Hwy-634.* FACILITIES: 112 sites, 30 ft max RV length, 112 W&E, tenting, dump station, laundry. RECREATION: rec hall, playground, hiking trails. Partial handicap access. Open all yr. Phone: (863)386-6094.

(S) LAKE JOSEPHINE RV RESORT—(Highlands) *From jct US 98 & US 27: Go 3 mi S on US 27. Enter on R.*

WELCOME

◊◊◊◊FACILITIES: 176 sites, typical site width 25 ft, 173 full hkups, 3 W&E, (30 & 50 amps), many extended stay sites (in winter), 24 pull-thrus, wireless Instant Internet access at site, phone/cable on-site Internet access (needs activ), wireless Internet access central location, dump station, non-guest dumping $, laundry, ltd groceries, RV supplies, LP gas by weight/by meter, ice, tables, patios.

◊◊◊◊RECREATION: rec hall, swim pool, boating, ramp, dock, lake fishing, golf nearby, 3 shuffleboard courts, planned activities, tennis, horseshoes.

Pets welcome, breed restrict. Partial handicap access. No tents. Open all yr. Planned activities winter only. Big rigs welcome. Internet friendly. Clubs welcome. Rate in 2007 $30-50 for 2 persons. MC/VISA. Phone: (863)655-0925.

SEE AD THIS PAGE

(S) Sebring Grove RV Resort—(Highlands) *From jct Hwy-17 & US-27/98: Go 1 mi S on US-27. Enter on R.* ◊◊◊FACILITIES: 114 sites, typical site width 27 ft, 114 full hkups, (30 & 50 amps), 8 pull-thrus, laundry, patios. ◊◊◊RECREATION: rec hall, swim pool, 2 shuffleboard courts, planned activities. Pets welcome, breed restrict. No tents. Age restrictions may apply. Open all yr. Planned activities winter only. Big rigs welcome. Rate in 2007 $28 for 2 persons. Phone: (863) 382-1660.

(NW) Sunny Pines—(Highlands) *From jct Hwy 634A & US 27: Go 1-1/2 mi S on US 27. Enter on L.* ◊◊FACILITIES: 134 sites, 134 full hkups, (30 & 50 amps), many extended stay sites (in winter), laundry, tables, patios. ◊◊◊RECREATION: rec hall, swim pool, shuffleboard court, planned activities, horseshoes.

Pets welcome, breed restrict, size restrict, quantity restrict. No tents. Open all yr. Planned group activities winter only. Big rigs welcome. Rate in 2007 $26 for 2 persons. Phone: (863)385-4144. FCRV 10% discount. FMCA discount.

(NW) The Outback RV Resort at Tanglewood—(Highlands) *From jct Hwy 634A & US 27: Go 3/4 mi N on US 27. Enter on L.* ◊◊◊◊◊FACILITIES: 272 sites, typical site width 50 ft, 272 full hkups, (20, 30 & 50 amps), 50 amps ($), dump station, laundry, tables, patios. ◊◊◊◊◊RECREATION: rec hall, rec room/area, swim pool, pond fishing, 8 shuffleboard courts, planned activities, tennis, horseshoes, hiking trails, v-ball. Pets welcome, breed restrict, quantity restrict. Partial handicap access. No tents. Open all yr. Big rigs welcome. Internet friendly. Phone: (888)402-1501.

SEFFNER—C-3

Rally Park—(Hillsborough) *From jct I-75 & I-4: Go 1 mi E on I-4 (exit 10), then1/4 mi N on Hwy 579. Enter on L.* ◊◊◊◊◊FACILITIES: 299 sites, 299 full hkups, (30 & 50 amps), dump station, non-guest dumping, laundry, LP gas by weight/by meter, ice, tables, patios. ◊◊◊◊RECREATION: rec hall, rec room/area, swim pool, 4 shuffleboard courts, planned activities, tennis, horseshoes. Pets welcome, breed restrict, size restrict. Partial handicap access. No tents. Open all yr. Maximum stay two weeks. Big rigs welcome. Internet friendly. Rate in 2007 $19.99-34.99 per vehicle. Member ARVC, FLARVC. Phone: (800)905-6627.

ROB'S AUTO DETAILING INC—Auto & RV cleaning & detailing. SERVICES: mobile RV svc. Open all yr. MC/VISA. Phone: (888)833-8245.

WELCOME

e-mail: info@robsautodetailing.com

SEE AD TRAVEL SECTION PAGE 71

SILVER SPRINGS—B-3

(E) Ben's Hitching Post Campground—(Marion) *From jct Hwy 314 & Hwy 40: Go 7/10 mi E on Hwy 40, then 50 yards S on NE 115th Ave. Enter on R.* ◊◊FACILITIES: 58 sites, typical site width 30 ft, 47 full hkups, 1 W&E, (30 amps), 10 no hkups, many extended stay sites, 5 pull-thrus, tenting, dump station, non-guest dumping $, laundry, tables. ◊◊◊RECREATION: rec hall, swim pool, 2 shuffleboard courts, planned activities, horseshoes. Pets welcome, breed restrict, quantity restrict. Partial handicap access. Age restrictions may apply. Open all yr. Planned group activities during winter only. Tenting Apr-Sep only. Rate in 2007 $20 for 2 persons. Phone: (352)625-4213.

(E) Lake Waldena Resort—(Marion) *From jct Hwy-35 & Hwy-40: Go 8 mi E on Hwy-40. Enter on R.* ◊◊FACILITIES: 105 sites, typical site width 30 ft, 103 full hkups, 2 W&E, (20, 30 & 50 amps), 50 amps ($), mostly extended stay sites (in winter), tenting, dump station, laundry, ltd groceries, ice, tables, patios, wood. ◊◊◊◊RECREATION: rec hall, pavilion, lake swimming, boating, electric motors only, canoeing, dock, 5 rowboat rentals, lake fishing, playground, 4 shuffleboard courts, planned activities, horseshoes. Pets welcome, quantity restrict. Open all yr. Closed Christmas, New Year's & Thanksgiving day. Big rigs welcome. Internet friendly. Rate in 2007 $22-25 for 4 persons. Member ARVC, FLARVC. Phone: (800)748-7898. CCUSA discount.

(E) OCALA NATIONAL FOREST (Fore Lake Campground)—(Marion) *From town: Go 11.8 mi E on Hwy 40, then 6 mi NE on Hwy 314. Enter on L.* FACILITIES: 31 sites, typical site width 12 ft, 35 ft max RV length, 31 no hkups, tenting, fire rings, grills. RECREATION: pavilion, lake swimming, boating, no motors, ramp, dock, lake fishing. Rec open to public. Open all yr. No showers. No reservations. 14-day limit. Phone: (352)625-2520.

(E) Whispering Pines RV Park—(Marion) *From jct Hwy 314 & Hwy 40: Go 1 mi E on Hwy 40, then 1/2 mi S on NE 118th Ave, then 1/4 mi W on NE 19th St, then 1/10 mi S on NE 115th Ave. Enter on R.* ◊◊◊FACILITIES: 65 sites, typical site width 30 ft, 62 full hkups, 3 W&E, (30 & 50 amps), 50 amps ($), mostly extended stay sites (in winter), 19 pull-thrus, dump station, laundry, tables, patios, wood. ◊◊RECREATION: rec hall,

Whispering Pines RV Park—Continued on next page

SILVER SPRINGS—Continued
Whispering Pines RV Park—Continued

shuffleboard court, planned activities, horseshoes. Pets welcome, quantity restrict. No tents. Open all yr. Planned group activities winter only. Rate in 2007 $20 for 2 persons. Member ARVC, FLARVC. Phone: (352) 625-1295. CCUSA discount.

WILDERNESS RV PARK ESTATES—(Marion) *From jct I-75 (exit 358) & Hwy 326: Go 9 mi E on Hwy 326, then 3 mi E on Hwy 40 (Just over bridge). Enter on L.*

WILDERNESS RV RESORT SELLS RV LOTS! 412 deeded 55+ RV lots at the Ocklawaha River along the Greenway. One condo features DELUXE big rig RV lots, and other park models. Enjoy nearby shopping convenience and nature in a serene setting. john@rvpe.com 877-900-9399.

◊◊◊◊FACILITIES: 346 sites, typical site width 30 ft, 346 full hkups, (30 & 50 amps), many extended stay sites, 80 pull-thrus, cable TV ($), wireless Instant Internet access at site, RV/park trailer rentals, dump station, non-guest dumping $, laundry, LP gas by weight/by meter, ice, tables, controlled access gate.

◊◊◊◊RECREATION: rec hall, pavilion, 2 swim pools, whirlpool, boating, canoeing, kayaking, ramp, 10 canoe/3 kayak rentals, river fishing, golf nearby, 4 shuffleboard courts, planned activities, horseshoes, v-ball.

Pets welcome, quantity restrict. Partial handicap access. No tents. Age restrictions may apply. Open all yr. Planned group activities during season only. Big rigs welcome. Internet friendly. Clubs welcome. Rate in 2007 $30 for 2 persons. MC/VISA/DISC/AMEX. Member ARVC, FLARVC. Phone: (352)625-1122.

e-mail: reservations@wildernessrvparkestates.com

SEE AD TRAVEL SECTION PAGE 76

SNEADS—E-3

(N) THREE RIVERS STATE PARK—(Jackson) *From jct US-90 & Hwy-271: Go 1 mi N on Hwy-271.* FACILITIES: 30 sites, 20 ft max RV length, 30 W&E, tenting, dump station, grills. RECREATION: pavilion, boating, canoeing, ramp, canoe rentals, lake fishing, playground, hiking trails. Open all yr. Phone: (850)482-9006.

SOPCHOPPY—A-1

(S) OCHLOCKONEE RIVER STATE PARK—(Wakulla) *From jct Hwy-375 & US-319: Go 4 mi S on US-319.* FACILITIES: 30 sites, 30 W&E, tenting, dump station, grills. RECREATION: river swimming, boating, canoeing, ramp, 4 canoe rentals, river fishing, hiking trails. Pets welcome. Open all yr. Phone: (850)962-2771.

SOUTH BAY—D-4

(N) SOUTH BAY RV CAMPGROUND (Palm Beach County Park)—(Palm Beach) *From jct Hwy 80 & US 27: Go 2 mi N on US 27. Enter on R.* FACILITIES: 72 sites, 72 W&E, (30 & 50 amps), 3 pull-thrus, tenting, dump station, portable dump, laundry, patios, grills. RECREATION: rec hall, equipped pavilion, boating, ramp, lake fishing, playground, v-ball. Partial handicap access. Open all yr. Phone: (561)992-9045.

SPRING HILL—C-3

(E) TOPICS RV COMMUNITY—(Hernando) *From jct US 19 & Hwy 578 (County Line Rd): Go 7 mi E on Hwy 578. Enter on L.*

◊◊◊FACILITIES: 231 sites, typical site width 40 ft, 231 full hkups, (30 & 50 amps), RV storage, laundry, tables, patios.

◊◊◊RECREATION: rec hall, swim pool, golf nearby, 4 shuffleboard courts, planned activities, horseshoes.

Pets welcome, breed restrict, size restrict, quantity restrict. No tents. Age restrictions may apply. Open all yr. Rate in 2007 $40 for 2 persons. MC/VISA. Phone: (352)796-0625.

SEE AD TAMPA PAGE 176

STARKE—B-3

✽ **(S) REVELS NATIONWIDE RV SALES**—*From jct Hwy 100 & US 301: Go 1/10 mi E on Hwy 100. Enter on R.* SERVICES: sells parts/accessories. Open all yr. MC/VISA/DC. Phone: (904)966-2020.

SEE AD GAINESVILLE PAGE 125

Woodall's Tip #2... Looking for a particular campground? Use our Alphabetical Quick Reference near the end of this Directory.

STARKE—Continued

(S) STARKE/GAINESVILLE NE KOA—(Bradford) *From jct Hwy-100 & US-301: Go 1 mi S on US-301. Enter on R.*

◊◊◊◊◊FACILITIES: 138 sites, typical site width 50 ft, 133 full hkups, 5 W&E, (30 & 50 amps), some extended stay sites (in winter), 80 pull-thrus, cable TV, wireless Instant Internet access at site, phone Internet access central location, tenting, RV/park trailer rentals, cabins, RV storage, dump station, non-guest dumping $, laundry, groceries, RV supplies, LP gas by weight/by meter, ice, tables, patios, wood.

◊◊◊◊◊RECREATION: rec hall, rec room/area, equipped pavilion, swim pool, pond fishing, golf nearby, bsktball, playground, 2 shuffleboard courts, planned activities, horseshoes, hiking trails, v-ball.

Pets welcome, breed restrict, size restrict, quantity restrict. Partial handicap access. Open all yr. Rates higher during special events. Big rigs welcome. Internet friendly. Escort to site. Clubs welcome. Rate in 2007 $30-39 for 2 persons. MC/VISA/DISC/AMEX. Member ARVC. Phone: (800)562-8498. KOA 10% value card discount.

e-mail: info@starkekoa.com

SEE AD GAINESVILLE PAGE 125 AND AD DISCOVER SECTION PAGES 62 & 63

STEINHATCHEE—B-2

(E) NATURE'S COAST RV RESORT—(Dixie) *From jct US 19 & CR-358: Go 4.7 mi W on CR-358. Enter on R.*

FACILITIES: 15 sites, 15 full hkups, (30 & 50 amps).

Open all yr. Rate in 2007 $25 for 2 persons. Phone: (352)498-7344.

e-mail: rv@naturescoastrvresort.com

SEE AD THIS PAGE

SUGARLOAF KEY—F-4

See listings at Key West

(S) KOA-Sugarloaf Key West—(Monroe) *On US-1 at mile marker 20. Enter on L.* ◊◊◊◊FACILITIES: 346 sites, typical site width 25 ft, 160 full hkups, 36 W&E, (30 & 50 amps), 150 no hkups, tenting, dump station, non-guest dumping $, portable dump, laundry, full svc store, LP gas by weight/by meter, ice, tables, wood. ◊◊◊◊◊RECREATION: rec room/area, pavilion, swim pool, saltwater swimming, boating, canoeing, ramp, dock, 4 canoe/6 motorboat rentals, saltwater fishing, playground, planned activities, v-ball. Pets welcome. Partial handicap access. Open all yr. Big rigs welcome. Internet friendly. Rate in 2007 $75-112 for 2 persons. Phone: (305)745-3549. KOA 10% value card discount.

SUMATRA—F-3

(S) APALACHICOLA NATIONAL FOREST (Wright Lake Campground)—(Liberty) *From jct CR 379 & Hwy 65: Go 2 mi S on Hwy 65, then 2 mi W on FR 101. Enter on R.* FACILITIES: 19 sites, typical site width 19 ft, 19 no hkups, tenting, dump station, fire rings, grills. RECREATION: lake swimming, boating, no motors, lake fishing, hiking trails. Rec open to public. Partial handicap access. Open all yr. No reservations. 14 day max stay. Phone: (850)643-2282.

SUMTERVILLE—C-3

(NW) Shady Brook Golf & RV Resort—(Sumter) *From jct I-75 (exit 321) & Hwy 470: Go 2-1/2 mi E on Hwy 470, then 3/4 mi N on US 301. Enter on L.* ◊◊◊FACILITIES: 170 sites, 170 full hkups, (30 & 50 amps), 3 pull-thrus, tenting, laundry, tables. ◊◊◊RECREATION: rec hall, rec room/area, lake fishing, planned activities, horseshoes, hiking trails, v-ball. Pets welcome. Partial handicap access. Age restrictions may apply. Open all yr. Tenting in off season only. Big rigs welcome. Rate in 2007 $20-30 for 2 persons. Phone: (352)568-2244. FMCA discount.

Save Money—Plan Ahead with WOODALL'S!

SUNRISE—E-5

(SW) MARKHAM PARK (Broward County Park)—(Broward) *From jct I-95 & I-595: Go W on I-595 (exit 1A), then continue W on Hwy 84 to second traffic light. Enter on R.*

FACILITIES: 88 sites, 88 full hkups, (20, 30 & 50 amps), 8 pull-thrus, dump station, non-guest dumping $, ice, tables, fire rings, grills, wood.

RECREATION: pavilion, swim pool, boating, canoeing, kayaking, ramp, 6 rowboat/18 canoe/8 kayak/8 pedal boat rentals, lake fishing, playground, tennis, horseshoes, sports field, hiking trails, v-ball. Rec open to public.

Pets welcome. Age restrictions may apply. Open all yr. Big rigs welcome. Clubs welcome. MC/VISA/DISC. Phone: (954)389-2000.

e-mail: markhampark@broward.org

SEE AD TRAVEL SECTION PAGE 74

SUNSHINE KEY—F-4

See listing at Marathon.

SUWANNEE RIVER—B-2

See listings at Old Town

TALLAHASSEE—A-1

(N) Big Oak RV Park—(Leon) *From jct I-10 (exit 199) & US 27: Go 2-1/2 mi N on US 27. Enter on L.* ◊◊◊◊FACILITIES: 100 sites, accepts full hkup units only, 100 full hkups, (30 & 50 amps), some extended stay sites, 37 pull-thrus, dump station, non-guest dumping $, laundry, ice, tables, patios. ◊◊RECREATION: rec hall, equipped pavilion, play equipment. Pets welcome. No tents. Open all yr. Big rigs welcome. Internet friendly. Rate in 2007 $33 for 2 persons. Member ARVC, FLARVC. Phone: (850)562-4660. FMCA discount.

(W) Lakeside Travel Park—(Leon) *From jct I-10 (exit 192) & US 90: Go 4 mi E on US 90. Enter on R.* ◊◊FACILITIES: 65 sites, typical site width 30 ft, 65 full hkups, (30 & 50 amps), 50 amps ($), many extended stay sites, 25 pull-thrus, tenting, dump station, non-guest dumping $, laundry, patios. RECREATION: lake fishing. Pets welcome, breed restrict, quantity restrict. Open all yr. 2 night max. on tenting!. Big rigs welcome. Internet friendly. Rate in 2007 $30-35 for 2 persons. Phone: (850)574-5998.

TALLAHASSEE—Continued on next page

TALLAHASSEE—Continued

(E) **TALLAHASSEE RV PARK**—(Leon) *From jct I-10 (exit 209A) & US 90: Go 1/2 mi W on US 90. Enter on R.*

WELCOME

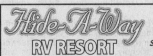

SOUTHERN HOSPITALITY AT ITS FINEST!
A Country Setting Convenient to all of Tallahassee's Dining and Entertainment. Big Rig 50 AMP, X-Long Pull-Thrus, Beautiful Flowers, Pool, FREE WI-FI & CABLE, Sparkling Restrooms, 1-850-878-7641 - WWW.TALLAHASSEERVPARK.COM

◆◆◆◆FACILITIES: 66 sites, typical site width 25 ft, 66 full hkups, (30 & 50 amps), many extended stay sites, 59 pull-thrus, cable TV, wireless Instant Internet access at site, phone Internet access central location, dump station, non-guest dumping $, laundry, tables.

◆◆RECREATION: rec hall, swim pool, golf nearby, horseshoes.

Pets welcome. Partial handicap access. No tents. Open all yr. Big rigs welcome. Internet friendly. Escort to site. Clubs welcome. Rate in 2007 $32-36 per vehicle. MC/VISA/DISC. Member ARVC, FLARVC. Phone: (850)878-7641.

e-mail: manager@tallahasseervpark.com

SEE AD THIS PAGE

TAMPA—C-3

(E) **Abbey's WigWam RV Park**—(Hillsborough) *From jct I-75 (exit 260A) & Martin Luther King Blvd (Hwy 574): Go 1/2 mi E on Martin Luther King Blvd, then 4 mi N on Williams Rd. Enter on R.* ◆◆◆FACILITIES: 110 sites, typical site width 21 ft, 110 full hkups, (30 & 50 amps), tenting, laundry, tables. ◆RECREATION: rec hall. Pets welcome, breed restrict. Open all yr. Big rigs welcome. Internet friendly. Rate in 2007 $30 per family. Phone: (813)935-1118.

AVALON RV RESORT—*From jct I-275 & Hwy 60: Go 12-3/4 mi W on Hwy 60, then 2 mi S on US 19, then 1/4 mi S on Whitney/Frontage Rd.*

WELCOME

SEE PRIMARY LISTING AT CLEARWATER. AND AD TRAVEL SECTION PAGE 75

TAMPA—Continued on next page

We all know that one of the best parts about camping is the food! Woodall's Campsite Cookbook is a classic cookbook containing such fun campsite and RV recipes as Roadside Spuds, The Fastest Sauce in the West, and Hairy Squares (which taste a lot better than they sound!) To order your copy go to www.woodalls.com/shop.

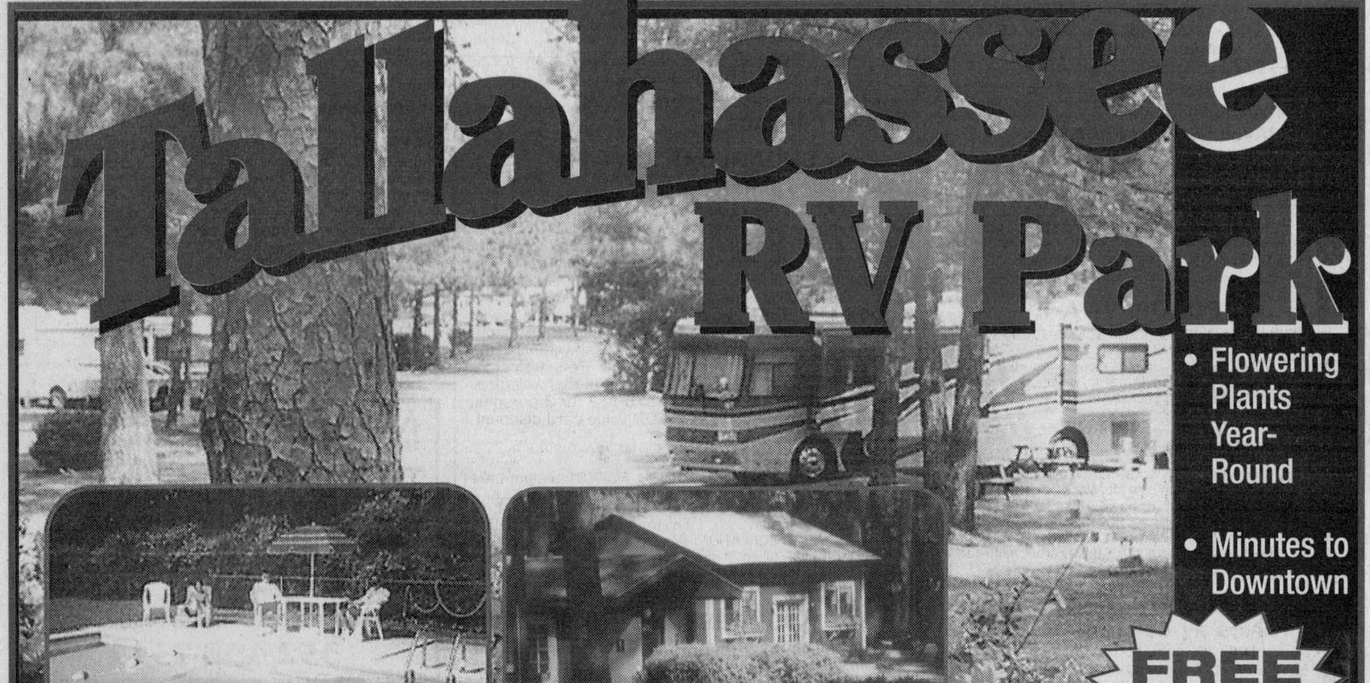

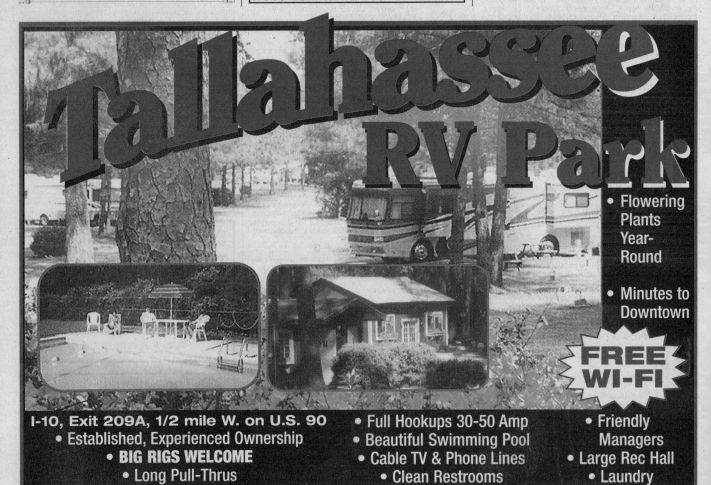

TAMPA BAY'S FINEST RV RESORT

A Setting of Beautiful, Ancient Oaks
241 Oversized Sites with Patio & Picnic Tables
30 & 50 Amp Electric Service
Full Sewer, Water, Telephone, etc. Hook-ups
3 new A/C Bathhouses and Laundry Facilities
Fenced Dog Run
Fishing & Viewing Docks, Plus Kayak Rentals
Large Heated Pool with Jacuzzi and Tiki Hut
Shuffleboard, Horseshoes, Bocce Ball & Billiards
New 6,000 sq.ft. Clubhouse with Full Kitchen;
Exercise Equipment, Convenience Store & Planned Activities
High-Speed Internet Access with FREE Wi-Fi Throughout the Park

Good Sam Park

12622 Memorial Highway
Tampa, FL 33635
888-MYBAYOU (888-692-2968)
info@baybayou.com • www.baybayou.com

See listing: Tampa, FL

TAMPA—Continued

(NW) BAY BAYOU RV RESORT (CAMP RESORT)—(Hillsborough) *From jct I-275 (exit 47) & Hillsborough Ave (SR 580): Go 10-1/2 mi W on Hillsborough Ave (SR 580), then 1/2 mi N on Country Way Blvd, then 3/4 mi W on Memorial Hwy. Enter on L.*

WELCOME

BEAUTIFUL WATERFRONT CAMPING

Spacious heavily wooded sites in a rural setting yet only minutes from the beach and all Tampa, St. Petersburg, Clearwater area attractions. A full amenity park with a friendly staff to help you enjoy your stay.

FACILITIES: 249 sites, typical site width 40 ft, 249 full hkups, (30 & 50 amps), some extended stay sites (in winter), wireless Instant Internet access at site, phone on-site Internet access (needs activ), wireless Internet access central location, RV storage, dump station, non-guest dumping $, laundry, RV supplies, LP gas by weight/by meter, tables, patios, controlled access gate.

RECREATION: rec hall, rec room/area, equipped pavilion, swim pool, whirlpool, boating, canoeing, kayaking, 2 kayak rentals, saltwater/pond fishing, golf nearby, 4 bike rentals, shuffleboard court, planned activities, horseshoes.

Pets welcome, size restrict, quantity restrict. Partial handicap access. No tents. Open all yr. Children accepted, 21 day limit. Big rigs welcome. Internet friendly. Clubs welcome. Rate in 2007 $45-48 for 2 persons. MC/VISA/DISC/Debit. Member ARVC, FLARVC. Phone: (813)855-1000. CCUSA discount.

e-mail: info@baybayou.com

SEE AD PAGE 174 AND AD TRAVEL SECTION PAGE 80

TAMPA—Continued on next page

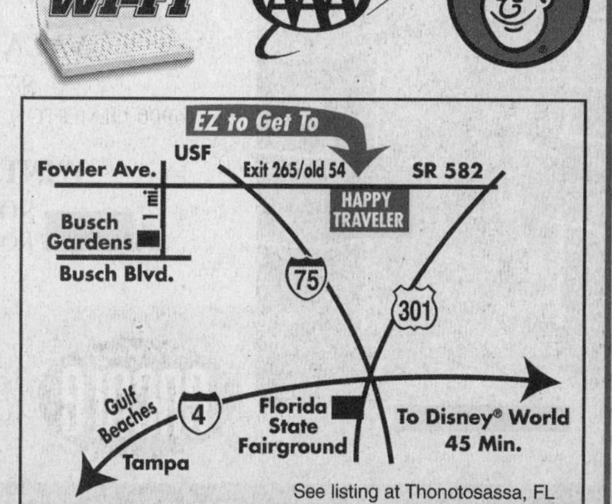

Woodall's Tip #5... Understand our ratings—Turn to the "How to Use" pages in the front of this Directory.

Woodall's Tip #6... For details on how to read the listings, turn to the "How to Use" pages in the front of the Directory.

TAMPA—Continued

BLUEBERRY HILL RV RESORT—*From jct I-275 & I-75: Go 41 mi N on I-75 (exit 314), then 1 block E on Hwy 48. Enter on R.*

SEE PRIMARY LISTING AT BUSHNELL AND AD BUSHNELL PAGE 99

(NE) CAMP NEBRASKA—(Hillsborough) *From jct I-4 & I-275: Go 5-1/2 mi N on I-275 (exit 51), then 1 block E on Fowler Ave, then 3/4 mi S on US 41, then 1 block W on Bouganvillea Ave. Enter on L.*

◇◇◇FACILITIES: 86 sites, typical site width 25 ft, 86 full hkups, (20, 30 & 50 amps), some extended stay sites (in winter), 40 pull-thrus, phone/cable on-site Internet access (needs activ), tenting, dump station, non-guest dumping $, laundry, tables.

RECREATION: golf nearby.

Pets welcome, breed restrict, size restrict, quantity restrict. Open all yr. Big rigs welcome. Clubs welcome. Rate in 2007 $25 for 2 persons. MC/VISA/Debit. Member ARVC, FLARVC. Phone: (877) 971-6990.

SEE AD PAGE 175

TAMPA—Continued on next page

Florida is the only state that has 2 rivers both with the same name. There is a Withlacoochee in north central Florida (Madison County) and a Withlacoochee in central Florida (Polk County).

DUNEDIN RV RESORT—*From jct I-275 & Hwy 60: Go 17 mi NW on Hwy 60, then 4-1/2 mi N on Alt US-19. Enter on R.*
WELCOME
SEE PRIMARY LISTING AT DUNEDIN AND AD TRAVEL SECTION PAGE 78

FLORIDA RV TRADE ASSOCIATION (FRVTA)—*From jct I-75 (exit 250) & Gibsonton Rd: Go 1 mi E on Gibsonton Rd.* Producer & Sponsor of World's largest RV Supershow held in Tampa, FL in January of each year, plus many other RV shows in various locations. Open Jan 15 thru Jan 19. Phone: (813)741-0488.
WELCOME
e-mail: davekelly@frvta.org
SEE AD PAGE 178

TAMPA—Continued on next page

Where Will You Camp Tonight? Stay With a Woodall's Advertised Campground.

Woodall's Tip #7... Get FREE Information—Use the Reader Service card.

TAMPA—Continued

HORSESHOE COVE RV RESORT—*From jct I-4 & I-75: Go 39 mi S on I-75 (exit 41), then 1-1/4 mi W on Hwy 70.*

SEE PRIMARY LISTING AT BRADENTON AND AD BRADENTON PAGE 97

THREE LAKES RV RESORT (Morgan RV Resorts)—*From jct Hwy 60 & US 19: Go 30 mi N on US 19, then 1 mi E on Denton Ave. Enter on R.*

WELCOME

SEE PRIMARY LISTING AT HUDSON. AND AD PAGE 173

Staying close to home next year? Pre-order the 2009 Directory in a smaller regional version. It contains all the great information Woodall's North American Directory contains, but in a handy to-go version, specific to the states or provinces you need.

TAVARES—C-3

(S) Fisherman's Cove Golf Marina & RV Resort—(Lake) *From jct US-441 & Hwy-19: Go 3-1/4 mi SW on Hwy-19. Enter on R.* ◊◊◊FACILITIES: 333 sites, typical site width 40 ft, 333 full hkups, (30 & 50 amps), mostly extended stay sites (in winter), dump station, non-guest dumping $, laundry, LP gas by weight/by meter, ice, tables. ◊◊◊◊RECREATION: rec hall, swim pool, boating, canoeing, ramp, dock, stream fishing, 4 shuffleboard courts, planned activities, horseshoes. Pets welcome, breed restrict. Partial handicap access. No tents. Age restrictions may apply. Open all yr. Internet friendly. Rate in 2007 $35 for 2 persons. Phone: (800)254-9993.

THONOTOSASSA—C-3

(NE) Camp Lemora RV Park—(Hillsborough) *From jct 75 (exit 265) & Fowler Ave: Go 1-1/4 mi E on Fowler Ave, then 8 mi NE on US 301, then 1 block N on Dead River Rd. Enter on L.* ◊◊◊◊FACILITIES: 302 sites, typical site width 40 ft, 302 full hkups, (20 & 30 amps), some extended stay sites (in winter), dump station, laundry, full svc store, LP gas by weight/by meter, ice, patios. ◊◊◊◊RECREATION: rec hall, equipped pavilion, swim pool, 8 shuffleboard courts, planned activities, horseshoes, hiking trails. Pets welcome, breed restrict. Partial handicap access. No tents. Open all yr. Planned activities winter only. Rate in 2007 $25 for 2 persons. Phone: (813)986-4456.

WELCOME

(W) HAPPY TRAVELER RV PARK—(Hillsborough) *From jct I-75 (exit 265) & Fowler Ave: Go 1/2 mi E on Fowler Ave. Enter on R.*

◊◊◊FACILITIES: 224 sites, typical site width 35 ft, 224 full hkups, (20, 30 & 50 amps), some extended stay sites (in winter), 4 pull-thrus, cable TV ($), wireless Instant Internet access at site, phone Internet access central location, RV/park trailer rentals, cabins, RV storage, dump station, non-guest dumping $, laundry, LP gas by meter, ice, tables, patios.

◊◊◊RECREATION: rec hall, swim pool, golf nearby, 2 shuffleboard courts, planned activities, horseshoes.

Pets welcome, quantity restrict. No tents. Age restrictions may apply. Open all yr. Children allowed for max 2 weeks stay. Planned activities winter season only. Big rigs welcome. Internet friendly. Clubs welcome. Rate in 2007 $27.64-35.20 for 2 persons. MC/VISA/DISC. Phone: (800)758-2795. FCRV 10% discount. FMCA discount.

e-mail: htrvpk@aol.com

SEE AD TAMPA PAGE 175

(S) HILLSBOROUGH RIVER STATE PARK—(Hillsborough) *From town: Go 8 mi S on US 301.* FACILITIES: 108 sites, 36 ft max RV length, 76 W&E, 32 no hkups, tenting, dump station, laundry, ltd groceries, ice, fire rings, grills. RECREATION: equipped pavilion, swim pool, boating, 5 hp limit, canoeing, 30 canoe/6 pedal boat rentals, river fishing, playground, sports field, hiking trails. Rec open to public. Partial handicap access. Open all yr. Phone: (813)987-6771.

WELCOME

(N) SPANISH MAIN RV RESORT—(Hillsborough) *From jct Hwy-582 E & I-75 (exit 265 Temple Terrace-Hwy-582 E): Go 1/2 mi E on Fowler, then 1-1/2 mi N on US-301. Enter on R.*

WELCOME TO CAREFREE RV RESORTS!
Large, grassy sites provide plenty of room to enjoy your stay. We offer recreation for all, including fishing ponds, heated pool, wading pool for the kids and much more! We welcome everyone, including our Canadian friends!

◊◊◊◊FACILITIES: 331 sites, typical site width 35 ft, 331 full hkups, (30 & 50 amps), many extended stay sites (in winter), 6 pull-thrus, wireless Internet access central location, tenting, RV storage, laundry, LP gas by weight/by meter, tables, patios.

◊◊◊◊RECREATION: rec hall, rec room/area, swim pool, pond fishing, golf nearby, bsktball, playground, 6 shuffleboard courts, planned activities.

Pets welcome, quantity restrict. Age restrictions may apply. Open all yr. Planned activities winter only. Big rigs welcome. Rate in 2007 $30 for 2 persons. Member ARVC, FLARVC. Phone: (813) 986-2415. CCUSA discount.

SEE AD TAMPA THIS PAGE

THONOTOSASSA—Continued on next page

Woodall's Tip #3... The listings for public campgrounds are based upon information supplied by the appropriate government agency.

Visit a Woodall's Advertised Dealer/Service Location.

We are on the web! Come visit us at www.woodalls.com

Woodall's Tip #19... Completely Revised and Updated Annually to Serve You Better

Woodall's Tip #20... Find free Tourism Information in the Travel Section

THONOTOSASSA—Continued

(S) Windward Knoll (RV SPACES)—(Hillsborough) *From jct I-4 (exit 14) & MacIntosh Rd: Go 3-1/2 mi N on MacIntosh Rd, then 1/2 mi W on Thonotosassa Rd. Enter on L.* FACILITIES: 11 sites, accepts full hkup units only, 11 full hkups, (15, 30 & 50 amps), laundry, patios. RECREATION: rec hall, swim pool, 4 shuffleboard courts, planned activities. Pets welcome, breed restrict, size restrict, quantity restrict. No tents. Age restrictions may apply. Open all yr. No restrooms. Rate in 2007 $28 for 2 persons. Phone: (813)986-2525.

TITUSVILLE—C-4

✲ **EAGLE'S PRIDE AT THE GREAT OUTDOORS**—*From jct I-95 (exit 215) & Hwy 50 (Cheney Hwy): Go 1/2 mi W on Hwy 50. Enter on L.* SALES: travel trailers, 5th wheels, motor homes, mini-motor homes, pre-owned unit sales. SERVICES: full-time mech, engine/chassis repair, RV appliance repair, body work/collision repair, mobile RV svc, LP gas by weight/by meter, dump station, sells parts/accessories, installs hitches. Open all yr. MC/VISA/DISC. Phone: (800)552-3555.

SEE AD THIS PAGE

(NW) KOA-Cape Kennedy—(Brevard) *From jct I-95 (exit 223) & Hwy 46: Go 1/4 mi W on Hwy 46. Enter on L.* ◇◇◇FACILITIES: 147 sites, typical site width 25 ft, 125 full hkups, 22 W&E, (15, 20, 30 & 50 amps), many extended stay sites (in winter), 15 pull-thrus, tenting, dump station, non-guest dumping $, laundry, groceries, LP gas by weight/by meter, ice, tables. ◇◇◇◇RECREATION: rec hall, rec room/area, equipped pavilion, swim pool, playground, 2 shuffleboard courts, planned activities, horseshoes. Pets welcome, breed restrict. Open all yr. Planned group activities winter only. Big rigs welcome. Internet friendly. Rate in 2007 $31-33 for 2 persons. Member ARVC, FLARVC. Phone: (321)269-7361. KOA 10% value card discount.

(S) MANATEE HAMMOCK PARK (Brevard County Park)—(Brevard) *From jct Hwy 50 & US 1: Go 3 mi S on US 1 to 7275 S US 1 (Bellwood).* FACILITIES: 182 sites, 147 full hkups, 35 W&E, (30 & 50 amps), tenting, dump station, laundry, fire rings, grills. RECREATION: rec hall, equipped pavilion, swim pool, saltwater/river swimming, saltwater/river fishing, shuffleboard court, horseshoes, v-ball. Open all yr. Phone: (321)264-5083.

(SW) THE GREAT OUTDOORS RV-NATURE & GOLF RESORT—(Brevard) *From jct I-95 (exit 215) & Hwy 50 (Cheney Hwy): Go 1/2 mi W on Hwy 50 (Cheney Hwy) to entrance. Enter on L.*

STAY A NIGHT OR A LIFETIME!

Conveniently located near Florida's premier attractions-Kennedy Space Center, Orlando, Daytona & miles of beaches-or enjoy our resort's own amenities: golf, fishing, tennis, swimming & more w/RV service facility on site.

◇◇◇◇FACILITIES: 626 sites, typical site width 40 ft, accepts full hkup units only, 626 full hkups, (30 & 50 amps), cable TV, phone/cable Instant Internet access at site, phone/cable on-site Internet access (needs activ), wireless Internet access central location, dump station, laundry, full svc store, RV supplies, LP gas by weight/by meter, ice, tables, patios, controlled access gate.

◇◇◇◇◇RECREATION: rec hall, equipped pavilion, 2 swim pools, whirlpool, lake fishing, fishing supplies, putting green, golf nearby, 8 shuffleboard courts, planned activities, tennis, horseshoes, hiking trails, local tours.

Pets welcome, quantity restrict. Partial handicap access. No tents. Open all yr. Water & electric sites for rallies. Big rigs welcome. Internet friendly. Clubs welcome. Rate in 2007 $35-65 for 2 persons. MC/VISA/DISC/AMEX. ATM. Phone: (800) 621-2267.

e-mail: info@tgoresort.com

SEE AD NEXT PAGE

Willow Lakes RV & Golf Resort—(Brevard) *From jct I-95 (exit 223) & Hwy 46: Go 1-1/2 mi E on Hwy 46, then 1/2 mi S on US 1. Enter on L.* ◇◇◇◇FACILITIES: 260 sites, 260 full hkups, (30 & 50 amps), laundry, patios. ◇◇◇◇RECREATION: rec hall, swim pool, lake fishing, 2 shuffleboard courts, planned activities, tennis, horseshoes, hiking trails. Pets welcome, size restrict, quantity restrict. Partial handicap access. No tents. Open all yr. Big rigs welcome. Internet friendly. Rate in 2007 $25-35 per vehicle. Phone: (321)269-7440.

TRENTON—B-2

(N) Otter Springs RV Resort—(Gilchrist) *From jct US 19/US 27 Alt & Hwy 26: Go 1-1/4 mi N on Hwy 26, then 1-3/4 mi N on CR 232, then 1 mi W on SW 70th St, then 1/2 mi N on SW 80th Ave. Enter on R.*

Otter Springs RV Resort—Continued on next page

TRENTON—Continued
Otter Springs RV Resort—Continued

◇◇◇FACILITIES: 110 sites, 100 full hkups, 10 W&E, (20, 30 & 50 amps), some extended stay sites (in winter), 99 pull-thrus, tenting, dump station, non-guest dumping $, laundry, ice. ◇◇◇RECREATION: rec room/area, swim pool, boating, canoeing, ramp, river fishing, 2 shuffleboard courts, planned activities, horseshoes, sports field, hiking trails, v-ball. Rec open to public. Pets welcome, breed restrict. Partial handicap access. Open all yr. Big rigs welcome. Internet friendly. Rate in 2007 $25 for 2 persons. Phone: (352)463-0800.

UMATILLA—B-4

(E) OCALA NATIONAL FOREST (Clearwater Lake Campground)—(Lake) *From jct Hwy 19 & 42: Go 6.6 mi E on Hwy 42. Enter on L.* FACILITIES: 41 sites, typical site width 8 ft, 22 ft max RV length, 41 no hkups, tenting, dump station, fire rings, grills, wood. RECREATION: lake swimming, boating, no motors, canoeing, lake fishing, hiking trails. Rec open to public. Open all yr. No reservations. 14-day limit Oct 15-Apr 15. Phone: (352)669-3153.

UMATILLA—Continued

(N) OCALA NATIONAL FOREST (Lake Dorr Campground)—(Lake) *From jct Hwy 42 & Hwy 19: Go 3 mi N on Hwy 19.* FACILITIES: 34 sites, typical site width 11 ft, 22 ft max RV length, 34 no hkups, tenting, fire rings, grills. RECREATION: lake swimming, boating, ramp, lake fishing. Rec open to public. Open all yr. No reservations. 14-day limit. Phone: (352)669-3153.

VALPARAISO—F-2

(S) MILITARY PARK (FAMCAMP-Eglin AFB)—(Okaloosa) *From jct I-10 & Hwy 85: Go S on Hwy 85 to Hwy 20 (John Sims Pkwy), then follow signs to Eglin AFB.* FACILITIES: 22 sites, 22 W&E, 22 pull-thrus, tenting, dump station, laundry, ltd groceries, LP gas by weight, ice, grills. RECREATION: pavilion, swim pool, saltwater swimming, boating, canoeing, ramp, dock, 15 rowboat/24 canoe/40 motorboat rentals, saltwater/lake/river fishing, playground, tennis, sports field, hiking trails, v-ball. Open all yr. For Military Use Only-w/Military ID Card. Phone: (850)882-6581.

Woodall's Tip #8... Turn to the Travel Section for "at-a-glance" RV Sales & Service Locations.

VENICE—D-3

(E) **FLORIDA PINES MOBILE HOME COURT**—(Sarasota) *From jct I-75 (exit 193) & Jacaranda Blvd: Go 5-1/2 mi S on Jacaranda Blvd, then 1/4 mi NW on Hwy 776. Enter on L.*

WELCOME

◇◇◇FACILITIES: 30 sites, typical site width 35 ft, accepts full hkup units only, 30 full hkups, (20, 30 & 50 amps), cable TV, phone/cable on-site Internet access (needs activ), RV storage, dump station, laundry, patios.

◇◇◇◇RECREATION: rec hall, lake fishing, golf nearby, 3 shuffleboard courts, planned activities, horseshoes.

No pets. No tents. Age restrictions may apply. Open all yr. Planned group activities winter only. Big rigs welcome. Clubs welcome. Rate in 2007 $25.50-38 for 2 persons. Phone: (941)493-0019.

SEE AD NEXT PAGE

VENICE—Continued on next page

VENICE—Continued

(SE) MYAKKA RV RESORT—(Sarasota) *From jct I-75 (exit 19) & River Rd: Go 5-1/2 mi SE on River Rd, then 3/4 mi NE on US 41. Enter on R.*

A RIVER RESORT WITH ITS OWN ISLAND

Lots to see and do nearby. Minutes from Gulf beaches and freeway close to Tampa Bay and Florida's west coast attractions. Or just relax in a full amenity park where our friendly staff will make your stay one to repeat.

◇◇◇FACILITIES: 77 sites, typical site width 35 ft, 77 full hkups, (30 & 50 amps), 1 pull-thrus, wireless Instant Internet access at site, phone/cable on-site Internet access (needs activ), wireless Internet access central location, dump station, non-guest dumping $, laundry, LP gas by weight/by meter, tables.

◇◇◇RECREATION: rec room/area, equipped pavilion, swim pool, boating, kayaking, ramp, dock, 3 kayak rentals, saltwater fishing, golf nearby, bsktball, 2 shuffleboard courts, horseshoes, sports field.

Pets welcome, breed restrict, size restrict, quantity restrict. No tents. Open all yr. Big rigs welcome. Internet friendly. Rate in 2007 $33-43 for 2 persons. MC/VISA/DISC/Debit. Member ARVC.

e-mail: myakkariver@hotmail.com

SEE AD PAGE 181 AND AD TRAVEL SECTION PAGE 85

(SE) RAMBLERS REST RESORT CAMPGROUND—(Sarasota) *From jct I-75 (exit 191) & River Rd: Go 3 mi S on River Rd. Enter on L.*

◇◇◇◇FACILITIES: 640 sites, typical site width 35 ft, 620 full hkups, 20 W&E, (20, 30 & 50 amps), mostly extended stay sites (in winter), heater not allowed, wireless Instant Internet access at site, phone on-site Internet access (needs activ), phone Internet access central location, tenting, RV storage, laundry, ltd groceries, RV supplies, LP gas by weight/by meter, ice, tables, controlled access gate.

◇◇◇◇◇RECREATION: rec hall, rec room/area, equipped pavilion, swim pool, whirlpool, boating, ramp, river fishing, golf nearby, bsktball, playground, 12 shuffleboard courts, planned activities, horseshoes, v-ball, local tours.

Pets welcome, size restrict, quantity restrict. Partial handicap access. Open all yr. Group activities winter only. Big rigs welcome. Clubs welcome. Rate in 2007 $40-55 for 2 persons. MC/VISA/DISC/AMEX/Debit. Member ARVC, FLARVC. Phone: (941)493-4354.

e-mail: ramblersrest@netzero.net

SEE AD SARASOTA PAGE 169

VENICE—Continued

(N) RV WORLD INC OF NOKOMIS—*From jct I-75 (exit 195) & Laurel Rd: Go 3 mi W on Laurel Rd, then 1 mi N on US 41. Enter on R.* SALES: travel trailers, 5th wheels, van campers, motor homes, mini-motor homes, micro-mini motor homes, pre-owned unit sales. SERVICES: full-time mech, engine/chassis repair, RV appliance repair, body work/collision repair, bus. hrs emerg rd svc, LP gas by weight/by meter, sells parts/accessories, installs hitches. Open all yr. MC/VISA/DISC/AMEX. Phone: (800)262-2182.

e-mail: sales@rvworldinc.com

SEE AD THIS PAGE

(E) Venice Campground & RV Park—(Sarasota) *From jct I-75 (exit 191) & River Rd: Go 3/4 mi S on River Rd. Enter on L.* ◇◇◇FACILITIES: 133 sites, typical site width 30 ft, 104 full hkups, 20 W&E, (20, 30 & 50 amps), 9 no hkups, some extended stay sites (in winter), 20 pull-thrus, tenting, dump station, laundry, LP gas by weight/by meter, ice, tables. ◇◇◇RECREATION: rec room/area, swim pool, boating, canoeing, ramp, 10 canoe rentals, saltwater/river fishing, play equipment, 2 shuffleboard courts, planned activities, horseshoes, hiking trails, v-ball. Pets welcome, breed restrict, quantity restrict. Open all yr. Planned activities during season. Big rigs welcome. Internet friendly. Rate in 2007 $40-50 for 4 persons. Member ARVC, FLARVC. Phone: (941)488-0850.

VERO BEACH—D-5

(NW) Sunshine Travel—(Indian River) *From jct I-95 (exit 156) & Hwy 512: Go 1 block E on Hwy 512. Enter on R.* ◇◇◇◇◇FACILITIES: 304 sites, typical site width 20 ft, 304 full hkups, (30 & 50 amps), some extended stay sites (in winter), 10 pull-thrus, tenting, dump station, non-guest dumping $, laundry, LP gas by meter, tables. ◇◇◇◇RECREATION: rec hall, rec room/area, swim pool, mini-golf, playground, 4 shuffleboard courts, planned activities, horseshoes. Pets welcome. Partial handicap access. Open all yr. Big rigs welcome. Internet friendly. Rate in 2007 $33-41 for 2 persons. Member ARVC. Phone: (800)628-7081.

WAUCHULA—D-3

(N) Crystal Lake Village—(Hardee) *From jct Hwy 62 & US 17: Go 1/4 mi S on US 17. Enter on L.* ◇◇◇◇FACILITIES: 361 sites, accepts full hkup units only, 361 full hkups, (30 & 50 amps), laundry, LP gas by weight, patios. ◇◇◇◇RECREATION: rec hall, rec room/area, swim pool, pond fishing, 6 shuffleboard courts, planned activities, horseshoes. Pets welcome, breed restrict. Partial handicap access. No tents. Open all yr. Big rigs welcome. Internet friendly. Rate in 2007 $20-25 for 2 persons. Phone: (800)661-3582.

(N) Little Charlie Creek RV Park—(Hardee) *From jct Hwy 62 & US 17: Go 1-1/4 mi S on US 17, then 1/2 mi E on Rea Rd, then 3/4 mi NE on Heard Bridge Rd. Enter on R.* ◇◇◇◇FACILITIES: 188 sites, typical site width 32 ft, 188 full hkups, (30 & 50 amps), laundry, LP gas by weight/by meter, patios. ◇◇◇RECREATION:

WAUCHULA—Continued
Little Charlie Creek RV Park—Continued

rec hall, river/pond fishing, 4 shuffleboard courts, planned activities, horseshoes. Pets welcome, breed restrict. No tents. Age restrictions may apply. Open all yr. Big rigs welcome. Rate in 2007 $30 for 2 persons. Phone: (863)773-0088.

WEBSTER—C-3

(W) Webster Travel Park—(Sumter) *From jct Hwy 78 & Hwy 471: Go 1/4 mi S on Hwy 471, then 1 mi W on E Central Ave (CR 740). Enter on L.* ◇◇◇◇FACILITIES: 249 sites, typical site width 35 ft, 240 full hkups, 9 W&E, (30 & 50 amps), mostly extended stay sites, dump station, laundry, tables, patios. ◇◇◇◇RECREATION: rec hall, rec room/area, equipped pavilion, swim pool, pond fishing, 3 shuffleboard courts, planned activities, horseshoes. Pets welcome, breed restrict, size restrict, quantity restrict. Partial handicap access. No tents. Open all yr. Big rigs welcome. Internet friendly. Rate in 2007 $27 for 2 persons. Member ARVC. Phone: (352)793-6765.

WEEKI WACHEE—C-3

(N) Hawks Nest RV Park & Campground—(Hernando) *From jct Hwy 50 & US 19: Go 5 mi N on US 19. Enter on L.* ◇◇FACILITIES: 42 sites, typical site width 28 ft, 34 full hkups, 4 W&E, (20 & 30 amps), 4 no hkups, many extended stay sites (in winter), tenting, dump station, laundry, tables, patios, fire rings. Pets welcome. Open all yr. Phone: (352)596-7959.

WESLEY CHAPEL—C-3

(W) QUAIL RUN RV PARK—(Pasco) *From jct I-75 (Zephrhills exit 279) & Hwy 54: Go 1/2 mi W on Hwy 54, then 2 mi N on Old Pasco Rd. Enter on R.*

◇◇◇◇FACILITIES: 145 sites, typical site width 35 ft, 145 full hkups, (20, 30 & 50 amps), some extended stay sites (in winter), 40 pull-thrus, cable TV, wireless Instant Internet access at site, wireless Internet access central location, RV storage, dump station, non-guest dumping $, laundry, full svc store, RV supplies, LP gas by weight/by meter, ice, tables, controlled access gate.

◇◇◇◇RECREATION: rec hall, rec room/area, swim pool, golf nearby, play equipment, 4 shuffleboard courts, planned activities, horseshoes.

Pets welcome, breed restrict. Partial handicap access. No tents. Open all yr. Planned activities winter only. Big rigs welcome. Internet friendly. Escort to site. Clubs welcome. Rate in 2007 $32 for 2 persons. MC/VISA. Member ARVC, FLARVC. Phone: (800)582-7084. FMCA discount.

e-mail: qrrv@usa.net

SEE AD NEXT PAGE AND AD TRAVEL SECTION PAGE 76

WEST PALM BEACH—D-5

JUNO OCEAN WALK RV RESORT—*From West Palm Beach: Go 12-1/4 mi N on I-95 (exit 83), then 4-1/2 mi E on Donald Ross Rd, then 3/4 mi N on US 1, then 1/4 mi W on Juno Ocean Walk. Enter at end.*

SEE PRIMARY LISTING AT JUNO BEACH AND AD JUNO BEACH PAGE 132

(NW) LION COUNTRY SAFARI KOA—(Palm Beach) *From jct I-95 (exit 68) & US 98/80 (Southern Blvd): Go 15 1/2 mi W on Southern Blvd. Enter on R.*

◇◇◇◇FACILITIES: 233 sites, typical site width 30 ft, 211 full hkups, 22 W&E, (20, 30 & 50 amps), 50 amps ($), mostly extended stay sites (in winter), 160 pull-thrus, heater not allowed, wireless Internet access central location, tenting, cabins, RV storage, dump station, non-guest dumping $, laundry, full svc store, RV supplies, LP gas by weight/by meter, ice, tables, patios, controlled access gate.

◇◇◇◇RECREATION: rec room/area, equipped pavilion, swim pool, golf nearby, bsktball, playground, 5 shuffleboard courts, planned activities, horseshoes, v-ball.

Pets welcome, breed restrict, quantity restrict. Partial handicap access. Open all yr. Planned activities in winter only. Limited activities in summer. Internet friendly. Escort to site. Clubs welcome. Rate in 2007 $49-50 for 2 persons. MC/VISA/DISC/AMEX/Debit. ATM. Member ARVC, FLARVC. Phone: (800)562-9115. KOA 10% value card discount. FMCA discount.

e-mail: koa@lioncountrysafari.com

SEE AD NEXT PAGE AND AD DISCOVER SECTION PAGES 62 & 63

WEST PALM BEACH—Continued on next page

WEST PALM BEACH—Continued

(N) Palm Beach Gardens RV Park—(Palm Beach) *From jct US 98/80 (Southern Blvd) & I-95: Go 11-1/2 mi N on I-95 (exit 79), then 1/2 mi W on Hwy 786 (PGA Blvd), then 1-3/4 mi N on Military Trail, then 1/4 mi E on Hood Rd. Enter on L.* ◇◇◇FACILITIES: 107 sites, 107 full hkups, (30 amps), many extended stay sites (in winter), 107 pull-thrus, heater not allowed, dump station, non-guest dumping $, laundry, LP gas by weight/by meter, ice, tables, patios. ◇RECREATION: rec room/area, swim pool. Pets welcome, quantity restrict. Partial handicap access. No tents. Open all yr. Planned activites weekends in winter only. Internet friendly. Rate in 2007 $35-37 for 2 persons. Phone: (561)622-8212.

✲ **(NW) PALM BEACH RV**—*From jct US 98/80 (Southern Blvd) & I-95: Go 8 mi N on I-95 (exit 76), then 1/2 mi W on Hwy 708 (Blue Heron Blvd), then 1-1/4 mi S on Hwy 809 (Military Tr). Enter on L.*

WELCOME

SALES: travel trailers, 5th wheels, pre-owned unit sales. SERVICES: full-time mech, RV appliance repair, body work/collision repair, LP gas by weight/by meter, sells parts/accessories, installs hitches. Open all yr. MC/VISA/DISC/AMEX/Debit. Phone: (561)689-5788.

e-mail: palmbeachrv@aol.com

SEE AD THIS PAGE

Woodall's Tip #42... Spray your garbage and trash with ammonia to keep the animals away.

WEWAHITCHKA—F-3

(N) DEAD LAKES STATE RECREATION AREA—(Gulf) *From jct Hwy-71 & Hwy-22: Go 4 mi N on Hwy-71.* FACILITIES: 20 sites, 35 ft max RV length, 10 E, 10 no hkups, tenting, dump station. RECREATION: boating, canoeing, ramp, lake fishing, hiking trails. Open all yr. Phone: (850)639-2702.

WHITE SPRINGS—A-3

(SE) Kelly's RV/MH Park—(Columbia) *From jct I-10 (exit 301) & US 41: Go 6 mi N on US 41. Enter on L.* ◇◇◇FACILITIES: 58 sites, typical site width 35 ft, 58 full hkups, (30 & 50 amps), mostly extended stay sites (in winter), 13 pull-thrus, dump station, laundry, LP gas by weight/by meter, ice, tables, patios. ◇◇◇RECREATION: rec hall, 2 shuffleboard courts, planned activities, horseshoes, hiking trails. Pets welcome, breed restrict. Partial handicap access. No tents. Open all yr. Planned group activities in Winter only. Big rigs welcome. Internet friendly. Rate in 2007 $27.52 for 2 persons. Member ARVC, FLARVC. Phone: (866)355-9600. CCUSA discount. FMCA discount.

WHITE SPRINGS—Continued on next page

WHITE SPRINGS—Continued

(SW) Lee's Country Campground—(Columbia) *From jct I-75 (exit 439) & Hwy 136: Go 7/10 mi E on Hwy 136. Enter on R.* ◊◊◊FACILITIES: 38 sites, typical site width 30 ft, 14 full hkups, 24 W&E, (20, 30 & 50 amps), 50 amps ($), 30 pull-thrus, tenting, dump station, non-guest dumping $, laundry, ice. RECREATION: horseshoes. Pets welcome, breed restrict. Partial handicap access. Open all yr. Big rigs welcome. Rate in 2007 $26 for 2 persons. Phone: (386)397-4132. CCUSA discount.

(NW) STEPHEN FOSTER FOLK CULTURE CENTER STATE PARK—(Hamilton) *From jct I-75 (exit 439) & Hwy 136: Go 3 mi E on Hwy 136, then 1/4 mi N on US 41 N. From I-10 (exit 301) & US 41 N: Go 9 mi on US 41 N Enter on L.*

FACILITIES: 45 sites, 45 W&E, (30 & 50 amps), 14 pull-thrus, tenting, cabins, dump station, non-guest dumping $, laundry, tables, fire rings, grills, wood, controlled access gate.

RECREATION: canoeing, river fishing, golf nearby, playground, hiking trails.

Pets welcome. Partial handicap access. Open all yr. Big rigs welcome. Clubs welcome. MC/VISA/DISC. Phone: (386)397-4331.

SEE AD THIS PAGE

WILDWOOD—B-3

KOA-Wildwood—(Sumter) *From jct I-75 (exit 329 - old 66) & Hwy 44: Go 100 feet E on Hwy 44. Enter on L.* ◊◊◊FACILITIES: 125 sites, typical site width 30 ft, 108 full hkups, 2 E, (30 & 50 amps), 15 no hkups, some extended stay sites (in winter), 88 pull-thrus, tenting, laundry, ltd groceries, LP gas by weight/by meter, ice, tables, wood. ◊◊◊RECREATION: rec hall, swim pool, mini-golf, playground, 2 shuffleboard courts, planned activities, horseshoes, sports field. Pets welcome, breed restrict, quantity restrict. Partial handicap access. Open all yr. Planned group activities winter only. Internet friendly. Rate in 2007 $36-51 for 2 persons. Phone: (352)748-2774. KOA 10% value card discount.

WILLISTON—B-3

(NW) Devil's Den Springs Resort—(Levy) *From jct US 41 & US 27A: Go 1 mi W on US 27A, then 1 mi N on NE 180th Ave. Enter on L.* ◊◊◊FACILITIES: 42 sites, typical site width 20 ft, 36 full hkups, (20, 30 & 50 amps), 6 no hkups, 20 pull-thrus, tenting, dump station, non-guest dumping $, tables, fire rings, grills. ◊◊◊RECREATION: pavilion, swim pool, play equipment, horseshoes, v-ball. Rec open to public. Pets welcome. Partial handicap access. Open all yr. Christmas Day closed. Big rigs welcome. Rate in 2007 $22 for 2 persons. Phone: (352)528-3344.

(NE) Williston Crossings RV Resort—(Iguy) *From W jct US 41 & Us 27A: Go 1 mi E on US 27A, then 300 ft N on NE 5th St. Enter on R.* ◊◊◊◊◊FACILITIES: 162 sites, typical site width 45 ft, 162 full hkups, (30 & 50 amps), many extended stay sites, dump station, non-guest dumping $, laundry, ice, patios. ◊◊◊◊RECREATION: rec hall, rec room/area, equipped pavilion, swim pool, lake swimming, dock, 3 pedal boat rentals, lake fishing, 2 shuffleboard courts,

Say you saw it in Woodall's!

WILLISTON—Continued

Williston Crossings RV Resort—Continued

planned activities, tennis, hiking trails. Pets welcome, breed restrict. Partial handicap access. No tents. Open all yr. Big rigs welcome. Internet friendly. Rate in 2007 $26.95-36.95 for 2 persons. Member ARVC, FLARVC. Phone: (800)615-5774.

WIMAUMA—D-3

(S) LITTLE MANATEE RIVER STATE RECREATION AREA—(Hillsborough) *From jct Hwy 674 & US 301: Go 5 mi S on US 301, then W on Lightfoot Rd.* FACILITIES: 34 sites, 34 W&E, tenting, dump station, fire rings, grills. RECREATION: pavilion, boating, 5 hp limit, canoeing, river fishing, playground, hiking trails. Rec open to public. Partial handicap access. Open all yr. Phone: (813)671-5005.

WINTER GARDEN—C-4

(W) ORLANDO WINTER GARDEN CAMPGROUND—(Orange) *From Florida Turnpike (exit 267): Go 2 mi W on Hwy 50. Enter on R.*

◊◊◊FACILITIES: 377 sites, typical site width 25 ft, 377 full hkups, (20, 30 & 50 amps), many extended stay sites (in winter), 50 pull-thrus, cable TV, phone/wireless/cable Instant Internet access at site ($), wireless Internet access central location, RV storage, dump station, laundry, LP gas by weight/by meter, tables, patios.

◊◊◊◊RECREATION: rec hall, equipped pavilion, 2 swim pools, golf nearby, bsktball, playground, 4 shuffleboard courts, planned activities, horseshoes.

Pets welcome, breed restrict. Partial handicap access. No tents. Open all yr. Church & planned activities winter only. Big rigs welcome. Internet friendly. Clubs welcome. Rate in 2007 $35 for 2 persons. MC/VISA. Member ARVC, FLARVC. Phone: (407)656-1415.

e-mail: wintergarden@intergate.com

SEE AD ORLANDO PAGE 155

(W) Stage Stop Campground—(Orange) *From jct Florida Tpk (exit 267) & Hwy 50: Go 2-1/2 mi W on Hwy 50. Enter on L.* ◊◊◊FACILITIES: 248 sites, typical site width 27 ft, 248 full hkups, (20, 30 & 50 amps), many extended stay sites (in winter), tenting, dump station, non-guest dumping $, laundry, groceries, ice, tables, patios. ◊◊◊RECREATION: rec room/area, pavilion, swim pool, pond fishing, playground, 2 shuffleboard courts, planned activities, horseshoes, v-ball. Pets welcome. Open all yr. Planned activities Nov thru mid Apr. A/C charge May 1-Sep 30. Big rigs welcome. Rate in 2007 $25 for 2 persons. Phone: (407)656-8000.

WINTER HAVEN—C-4

(E) East Haven RV Park—(DeSoto) *From jct US 27 & Hwy 542 W: Go 1-1/2 mi W on Hwy 542 W. Enter on L.* ◊◊◊◊FACILITIES: 73 sites, typical site width 20 ft, 73 full hkups, (30 & 50 amps), 12 pull-thrus, laundry, tables, patios. ◊◊◊RECREATION: rec hall, swim pool, 2 shuffleboard courts, planned activities, horseshoes. Pets welcome. No tents. Age restrictions may apply. Open all yr. Big rigs welcome. Rate in 2007 $35 for 2 persons. Phone: (863)324-2624.

(SE) HAMMONDELL CAMPGROUND—(Polk) *From jct US 27 & Hwy 540: Go 1-3/4 mi W on Hwy 540, then 1/2 mi N on Cypress Gardens Rd. Enter on L.*

◊◊◊FACILITIES: 80 sites, 80 full hkups, (30 & 50 amps), wireless Instant Internet access at site, phone/cable on-site Internet access (needs activ), wireless Internet access central location, cabins, dump station, non-guest dumping $, laundry, LP gas by weight/by meter, ice, tables, patios.

◊◊◊RECREATION: rec hall, swim pool, golf nearby, 4 shuffleboard courts, planned activities, horseshoes.

Pets welcome, quantity restrict. Partial handicap access. No tents. Open all yr. Planned activities in

WINTER HAVEN—Continued

HAMMONDELL CAMPGROUND—Continued

winter only. Big rigs welcome. Internet friendly. Clubs welcome. Rate in 2007 $28 for 2 persons. MC/VISA. Phone: (863)324-5775.

e-mail: hammondell@verizon.net

SEE AD THIS PAGE

(E) Holiday Travel Park—(Polk) *From jct Hwy-540 & US-27: Go 1-1/2 mi W on Hwy-540. Enter on L.* ◊◊FACILITIES: 227 sites, typical site width 32 ft, 200 full hkups, 27 W&E, (20, 30 & 50 amps), 50 amps ($), some extended stay sites (in winter), 140 pull-thrus, heater not allowed, tenting, dump station, laundry, LP gas by weight/by meter, ice, tables, patios. ◊◊RECREATION: rec hall, rec room/area, swim pool, mini-golf ($), 2 shuffleboard courts, planned activities, horseshoes. Pets welcome ($). Partial handicap access. Open all yr. Big rigs welcome. Rate in 2007 $23.95-26.95 for 2 persons. Phone: (800)858-7275.

YANKEETOWN—B-3

(W) CATTAIL CREEK RV PARK—(Levy) *From jct Hwy 19 & Hwy 40: Go 3 mi W on Hwy 40. Enter on L.*

◊◊FACILITIES: 82 sites, typical site width 40 ft, 72 full hkups, (30 & 50 amps), 10 no hkups, some extended stay sites, 5 pull-thrus, tenting, RV/park trailer rentals, RV storage, dump station, laundry, RV supplies, tables.

◊◊RECREATION: rec hall, swim pool, canoeing, 2 canoe rentals, golf nearby, horseshoes.

Pets welcome. Partial handicap access. Open all yr. Rate in 2007 $25 for 2 persons. MC/VISA/DISC. Phone: (352)447-3050.

SEE AD THIS PAGE

YULEE—A-3

(S) BOW & ARROW CAMPGROUND—(Nassau) *From jct I-95 (exit 373) and Hwy 200: Go 3 mi E on Hwy 200, then 2 mi S on US 17. Enter on L.*

◊◊◊FACILITIES: 56 sites, 56 full hkups, (30 & 50 amps), 50 amps ($), mostly extended stay sites, 25 pull-thrus, cable TV, wireless Internet access central location, dump station, non-guest dumping $, laundry, RV supplies, LP gas by weight/by meter, ice, tables.

◊◊RECREATION: equipped pavilion, swim pool, golf nearby.

Pets welcome. No tents. Open all yr. Pool open May 1 - Nov 30, weather permitting. Big rigs welcome. Internet friendly. Clubs welcome. Rate in 2007 $25 for 2 persons. MC/VISA. Phone: (904) 225-5577.

SEE AD JACKSONVILLE PAGE 129

(N) Osprey First In Florida RV Park—(Nassau) *From jct I-95 & US 17 (exit 380): Go 100 yards E on US 17, then 1 block N on Hance's Pkwy. Enter on L.* ◊◊◊FACILITIES: 73 sites, typical site width 30 ft, 73 full hkups, (30 & 50 amps), many extended stay sites, 72 pull-thrus, dump station, non-guest dumping $, laundry, groceries, LP gas by weight/by meter, ice, tables, patios. ◊◊◊RECREATION: rec room/area, swim pool, playground, horseshoes. Pets welcome. Partial handicap access. No tents. Open all yr. Big rigs welcome. Internet friendly. Rate in 2007 $30 for 2 persons. Phone: (904)225-2080. FMCA discount.

ZEPHYRHILLS—C-3

(NE) BAKER ACRES RV RESORT—(Pasco) *From N jct US 301 & Hwy 54: Go 1/4 mi E on Hwy 54, then 1-1/2 mi N on Wire Rd. Enter on R.*

◊◊◊◊FACILITIES: 355 sites, typical site width 30 ft, accepts full hkup units only, 355 full hkups, (20, 30 & 50 amps), mostly extended stay sites (in winter), wireless Instant Internet access at site, phone/cable on-site Internet

BAKER ACRES RV RESORT—Continued on next page

access (needs activ), phone Internet access central location, dump station, non-guest dumping $, laundry, tables, patios.

◆◆◆◆RECREATION: rec hall, rec room/area, swim pool, golf nearby, 12 shuffleboard courts, planned activities, horseshoes.

Pets welcome ($), breed restrict. No tents. Age restrictions may apply. Open all yr. Church services winter only. No showers. Big rigs welcome. Internet friendly. Member ARVC, FLARVC. Phone: (813)782-3950. CCUSA discount.

e-mail: bel-aire@3oaks.com

SEE AD TAMPA PAGE 178 AND AD TRAVEL SECTION PAGE 75 AND AD DISCOVER SECTION PAGE 128

(SW) GLEN HAVEN RV RESORT—(Pasco) *From S jct Hwy 54 & US 301: Go 2 mi S on US 301, then 1/2 mi W on Chancey Rd. Enter on R.*

WELCOME

◆◆◆◆FACILITIES: 218 sites, 218 full hkups, (30 & 50 amps), many extended stay sites (in winter), wireless Instant Internet access at site, phone/cable on-site Internet access (needs activ), phone Internet access central location, shower$, dump station, laundry, tables, patios.

◆◆◆◆RECREATION: rec hall, rec room/area, swim pool, whirlpool, golf nearby, 12 shuffleboard courts, planned activities, horseshoes.

Pets welcome, breed restrict, size restrict, quantity restrict. Partial handicap access. No tents. Age restrictions may apply. Open all yr. Big rigs welcome. Internet friendly. Rate in 2007 $28 for 2 persons. Phone: (813)782-1856. CCUSA discount.

e-mail: averm@photec.com

SEE AD TAMPA PAGE 180 AND AD TRAVEL SECTION PAGE 75 AND AD DISCOVER SECTION PAGE 128

(SW) HAPPY DAYS RV PARK—(Pasco) *From jct I-75 (exit 58) & SR 54: Go 8 mi E on SR 54, then 2 blocks S on Allen Rd. Enter on R.*

WELCOME

◆◆◆FACILITIES: 300 sites, typical site width 30 ft, 300 full hkups, (20 & 30 amps), many extended stay sites (in winter), cable TV ($), phone/cable on-site Internet access (needs activ), RV storage, dump station, non-guest dumping $, laundry.

◆◆◆RECREATION: rec hall, rec room/area, swim pool, golf nearby, 4 shuffleboard courts, planned activities, horseshoes.

Pets welcome, breed restrict, quantity restrict. No tents. Age restrictions may apply. Open all yr. Church services during winter only. Rate in 2007 $29 for 2 persons. MC/VISA. Member ARVC, FLARVC. Phone: (813)788-4858.

SEE AD THIS PAGE

(SW) HILLCREST RV RESORT—(Pasco) *From jct US 301 & Hwy 54: Go 1 mi W on Hwy 54, then 1/2 mi S on Lane Rd. Enter on R.*

WELCOME

◆◆◆FACILITIES: 497 sites, typical site width 35 ft, 497 full hkups, (30 & 50 amps), wireless Internet access central location, dump station, laundry, patios.

◆◆◆◆RECREATION: rec hall, rec room/area, swim pool, whirlpool, golf nearby, 6 shuffleboard courts, planned activities, horseshoes.

Pets welcome, breed restrict, size restrict, quantity restrict. No tents. Age restrictions may apply. Open all yr. Big rigs welcome. Rate in 2007 $29 for 2 persons. MC/VISA. Phone: (813)782-1947.

SEE AD THIS PAGE

(SW) Hunter's Run RV Resort—(Pasco) *From south jct SR 54 & US 301: Go 2 mi S on US 301, then 1-1/2 mi W on Chancey Rd. Enter on R.* ◆◆◆◆FACILITIES: 309 sites, 309 full hkups, (20, 30 & 50 amps), many extended stay sites (in winter), shower$, dump station, laundry, patios. ◆◆◆◆RECREATION: rec hall, rec room/area, swim pool, 8 shuffleboard courts, planned activities, horseshoes. Pets welcome. Partial handicap access. No tents. Age restrictions may apply. Open all yr. Big rigs welcome. Phone: (813)783-1133.

(W) Jim's RV Park—(Pasco) *From south jct US 301 & Hwy 54: Go 3 mi W on Hwy 54. Enter on L.* ◆◆◆FACILITIES: 155 sites, 147 full hkups, 8 W&E, (20 & 30 amps), many extended stay sites (in winter), 30 pull-thrus, dump station, laundry, LP gas by weight/by meter. ◆◆◆RECREATION: rec hall, rec room/area, swim pool, 2 shuffleboard courts, planned

activities, horseshoes. Pets welcome, breed restrict, size restrict, quantity restrict. No tents. Age restrictions may apply. Open all yr. Planned activities winter only. Rate in 2007 $25 for 2 persons. Phone: (813) 782-5610.

(W) LEISURE DAYS RV RESORT—*From jct I-75 (exit 279) & Hwy 54: Go 6-3/4 mi E on Hwy 54, then 1 block S on Hwy 579. Enter on R.*

WELCOME

◆◆◆FACILITIES: 44 sites, 44 full hkups, (30 & 50 amps), phone/cable on-site Internet access (needs activ), phone Internet access central location, dump station, laundry, LP gas by weight, patios.

◆◆◆RECREATION: rec hall, swim pool, golf nearby, 4 shuffleboard courts, planned activities, horseshoes.

Pets welcome, breed restrict, size restrict, quantity restrict. Partial handicap access. No tents. Open all yr. Big rigs welcome. Internet friendly. Rate in 2007 $23 for 2 persons. Phone: (813)788-2631.

SEE AD PAGE 184

(SE) MAJESTIC OAKS RV RESORT—(Pasco) *From jct SR 54 & US 301: Go 2 mi S on US 301, then 1-1/2 mi E on Chancey Rd. Enter on L.*

WELCOME

◆◆◆◆FACILITIES: 258 sites, 258 full hkups, (30 & 50 amps), wireless Instant Internet access at site, phone/cable on-site Internet access (needs activ), phone Internet access central location, laundry, ice, patios.

◆◆◆◆RECREATION: rec hall, swim pool, golf nearby, 8 shuffleboard courts, planned activities, tennis, horseshoes.

Pets welcome, breed restrict. Partial handicap access. No tents. Age restrictions may apply. Open all yr. Planned activities in winter only. Big rigs welcome. Internet friendly. Rate in 2007 $26 for 2 persons. MC/VISA. Member ARVC, FLARVC. Phone: (813)783-7518. CCUSA discount.

SEE AD TAMPA PAGE 177 AND AD DISCOVER SECTION PAGE 128

(SW) RAINBOW VILLAGE RV RESORT—(Pasco) *From jct US 301 & Hwy 54: Go 1 mi W on Hwy 54, then 1 mi S on Lane Rd. Enter on L.*

WELCOME

◆◆◆◆FACILITIES: 382 sites, typical site width 35 ft, accepts full hkup units only, 382 full hkups, (20, 30 & 50 amps), cable TV ($), wireless Instant Internet access at site, phone/cable on-site Internet access (needs activ), phone Internet access central location, laundry, patios.

◆◆◆◆RECREATION: rec hall, rec room/area, swim pool, golf nearby, bsktball, 6 shuffleboard courts, planned activities, horseshoes, v-ball.

Pets welcome, breed restrict, size restrict. Partial handicap access. No tents. Age restrictions may apply. Open all yr. Planned activities winter only. Big rigs welcome. Internet friendly. Rate in 2007 $25 for 2 persons. MC/VISA/DISC. Phone: (813) 782-5075. CCUSA discount.

e-mail: rainbowrv@webtv.net

SEE AD TRAVEL SECTION PAGE 75 AND AD DISCOVER SECTION PAGE 128

(W) Ralph's Travel Park—(Pasco) *From jct US 301 & Hwy 54: Go 2-1/2 mi W on Hwy 54. Enter on L.* ◆◆◆◆FACILITIES: 404 sites, typical site width 30 ft, 404 full hkups, (30 & 50 amps), dump station, non-guest dumping $, laundry, LP gas by meter, patios. ◆◆◆RECREATION: rec hall, rec room/area, swim pool, 8 shuffleboard courts, planned activities, horseshoes. Pets welcome, breed restrict, size restrict, quantity restrict. No tents. Age restrictions may apply. Open all yr. Big rigs welcome. Internet friendly. Rate in 2007 $22 for 2 persons. Phone: (813)782-8223.

(SW) Settlers Rest RV Park—(Pasco) *From S jct SR 54 & US 301: Go 2 mi S on US 301, then 1/2 mi W on Chancey Rd. Enter on R.* ◆◆FACILITIES: 379 sites, typical site width 30 ft, accepts full hkup units only, 379 full hkups, (20 & 30 amps), mostly extended stay sites (in winter), shower$, laundry. ◆◆RECREATION: rec hall, 8 shuffleboard courts, planned activities, horseshoes. Pets welcome, breed restrict. No tents. Age restrictions may apply. Open all yr. Church & planned activities winter only. Internet friendly. Phone: (813)782-2003.

ZEPHYRHILLS—Continued on next page

ZEPHYRHILLS—Continued

(SW) SOUTHERN CHARM RV RESORT—(Pasco) *From S jct Hwy 54 & US 301: Go 2 mi S on US 301, then 1/4 mi W on Chancey Rd. Enter on R.*

◆◆◆◆FACILITIES: 500 sites, typical site width 35 ft, accepts full hkup units only, 500 full hkups, (20, 30 & 50 amps), many extended stay sites (in winter), cable TV, wireless Instant Internet access at site, phone/cable on-site Internet access (needs activ), phone Internet access central location, RV/park trailer rentals, RV storage, dump station, laundry, tables, patios.

◆◆◆◆RECREATION: rec hall, swim pool, whirlpool, golf nearby, 8 shuffleboard courts, planned activities, horseshoes, v-ball.

Pets welcome, size restrict. Partial handicap access. No tents. Age restrictions may apply. Open all yr. Planned activities winter only. Big rigs welcome. Internet friendly. Phone: (813)783-3477. CCUSA discount.

e-mail: bel-aire@3oaks.com

SEE AD TAMPA PAGE 180 AND AD TRAVEL SECTION PAGE 75 AND AD DISCOVER SECTION PAGE 128

ZEPHYRHILLS—Continued

(SW) SWEETWATER RV PARK—(Pasco) *From south jct Hwy 54 & US 301: Go 2 mi S on US 301, then 1/4 mi W on Chancey Rd. Enter on R.*

◆◆◆FACILITIES: 289 sites, 289 full hkups, (30 & 50 amps), mostly extended stay sites (in winter), cable TV ($), wireless Instant Internet access at site, phone/cable on-site Internet access (needs activ), phone Internet access central location, dump station, laundry, tables.

◆◆◆RECREATION: rec hall, golf nearby, 6 shuffleboard courts, planned activities, horseshoes.

Pets welcome. Partial handicap access. No tents. Age restrictions may apply. Open all yr. Big rigs welcome. Internet friendly. Phone: (813)788-7513. CCUSA discount.

SEE AD TAMPA PAGE 176

ZEPHYRHILLS—Continued

(NE) WATER'S EDGE RV RESORT—(Pasco) *From north jct US 301 & Hwy 54: Go 1 block E on Hwy 54, then 2 mi N on Wire Rd, then 2 mi E on Otis Allen Rd. Enter on R.*

◆◆◆◆FACILITIES: 217 sites, typical site width 35 ft, accepts full hkup units only, 217 full hkups, (30 & 50 amps), many extended stay sites (in winter), cable TV ($), phone/cable on-site Internet access (needs activ), phone Internet access central location, laundry, tables.

◆◆◆RECREATION: rec hall, swim pool, golf nearby, 8 shuffleboard courts, horseshoes.

Pets welcome. Partial handicap access. No tents. Age restrictions may apply. Open all yr. Big rigs welcome. Internet friendly. Phone: (813)783-2708. CCUSA discount.

e-mail: bel-aire@3oaks.com

SEE AD TAMPA PAGE 175 AND AD TRAVEL SECTION PAGE 75 AND AD DISCOVER SECTION PAGE 128

Georgia

READER SERVICE INFO

The following businesses have placed an ad in the Georgia Travel Section. To receive free information, enter their Reader Service number on the Reader Service Card opposite page 48/Discover Section in the front of this directory:

Advertiser	RS#
Brunswick / Golden Isles Visitors Bureau	2424
Cedar Creek Park RV & Driving Range	3696
Country Boy's RV Park	3119
Flynn's Inn Camping Village	3221
Georgia Mountain Fairgrounds Campground	473
Georgia State Parks & Historic Sites	465
John Bleakley RV Ctr	3612
Lake Harmony RV Park & Campground	2883
Mountain Creek RV Resort	3697
Norman Campers	3053
Old Salem Park (Georgia Power)	849
Pine Mountain RVC	3734
Stone Mountain Family Campground	733

TIME ZONE

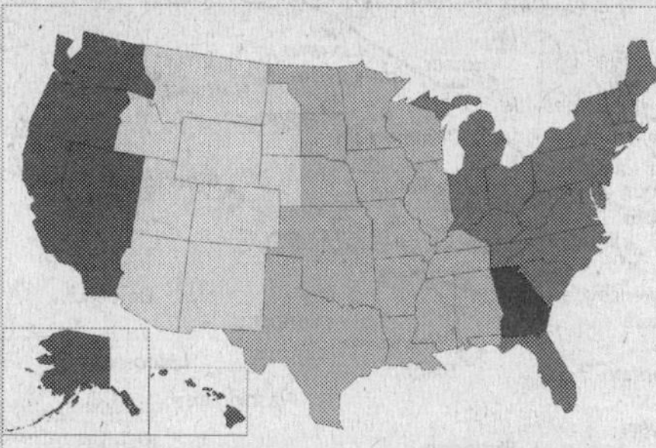

Georgia is in the Eastern Time Zone.

TOPOGRAPHY

Georgia's terrain ranges from mountains in the north to rolling hills in the central part; plains in the southwest and the coast in the southeast.

TEMPERATURE

Average yearly rainfall in Georgia ranges from 38 inches in the east-central area to 48 inches in the southwest. Average temperatures in January range from lows between 30° and 43° and highs between 34° and 46°. July temperatures vary from lows between 78° and 80° and highs from 80° to 83°.

TRAVEL & TOURISM INFO

State Agency:
Georgia Dept. of Economic Development
75 Fifth St., NW, Suite 1200
Atlanta, GA 30308
(404/962-4000)
www.georgiaonmymind.org

Local Agencies:
For local agencies not listed here, contact the Convention and Visitor's Bureau for the locality you are interested in.

Albany CVB
225 W. Broad Ave.
Albany, GA 31701
(800/475-8700 or 229/434-8700)
www.albanyga.com

Athens CVB
300 N. Thomas St.
Athens, GA 30601
(800/653-0603 or 706/357-4430)
www.visitathensga.com

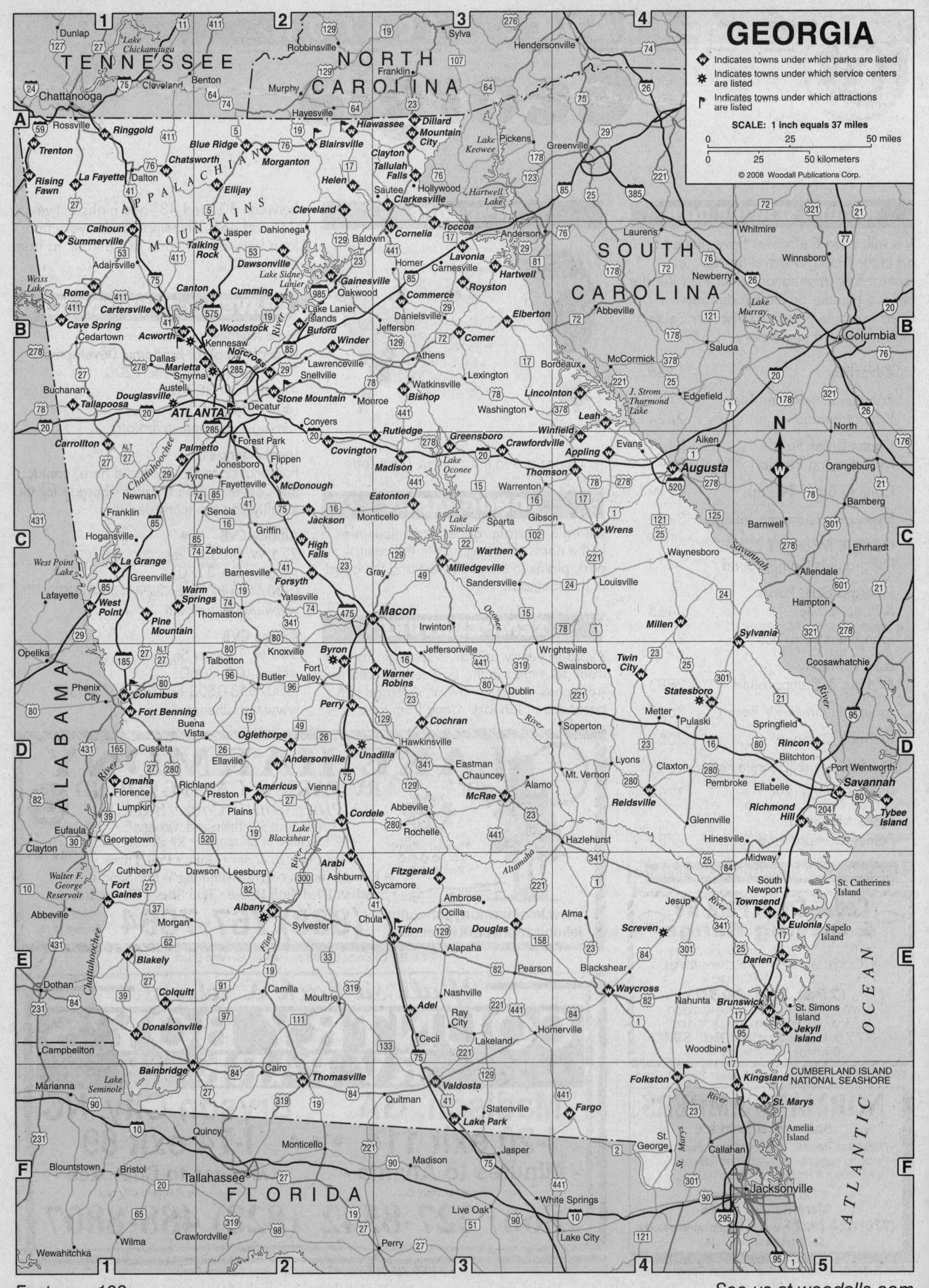
GEORGIA
Indicates towns under which parks are listed
Indicates towns under which service centers are listed
Indicates towns under which attractions are listed
SCALE: 1 inch equals 37 miles
0 25 50 miles
0 25 50 kilometers
© 2008 Woodall Publications Corp.
TENNESSEE
NORTH CAROLINA
SOUTH CAROLINA
ALABAMA
FLORIDA
ATLANTIC OCEAN
APPALACHIAN MOUNTAINS
N
Dunlap
Lake Chickamauga
Chattanooga
Cleveland
Benton
Robbinsville
Murphy
Franklin
Hayesville
Sylva
Hendersonville
Rossville
Ringgold
Trenton
Rising Fawn
La Fayette
Dalton
Chatsworth
Blue Ridge
Morganton
Blairsville
Hiawassee
Dillard
Mountain City
Clayton
Tallulah Falls
Lake Keowee
Pickens
Greenville
Ellijay
Helen
Sautee
Hollywood
Clarkesville
Hartwell Lake
Cleveland
Calhoun
Summerville
Jasper
Dahlonega
Talking Rock
Baldwin
Cornelia
Toccoa
Anderson
Laurens
Whitmire
Winnsboro
Adairsville
Dawsonville
Lake Sidney Lanier
Gainesville
Oakwood
Homer
Lavonia
Carnesville
Hartwell
Royston
Newberry
Weiss Lake
Rome
Canton
Cumming
Commerce
Lake Murray
Cartersville
Lake Lanier Islands
Danielsville
Elberton
Abbeville
Cave Spring
Cedartown
Acworth
Woodstock
Kennesaw
Buford
Jefferson
Comer
Columbia
Winder
Dallas
Marietta
Smyrna
Norcross
Lawrenceville
Athens
Bordeaux
McCormick
Saluda
Snellville
Lexington
Buchanan
Austell
Douglasville
Tallapoosa
ATLANTA
Decatur
Stone Mountain
Monroe
Watkinsville
Bishop
Lincolnton
J. Strom Thurmond Lake
Edgefield
Washington
Conyers
Leah
Carrollton
Forest Park
Rutledge
Greensboro
Crawfordville
Winfield
Palmetto
Covington
Lake Oconee
Appling
Evans
Aiken
North
Orangeburg
Jonesboro
Flippen
Madison
Thomson
Augusta
Chattahoochee
Tyrone
Fayetteville
McDonough
Warrenton
Newnan
Eatonton
Franklin
Senoia
Jackson
Monticello
Lake Sinclair
Sparta
Gibson
Bamberg
Griffin
Wrens
Barnwell
Hogansville
Zebulon
High Falls
Warthen
Milledgeville
Waynesboro
Ehrhardt
West Point Lake
La Grange
Greenville
Barnesville
Forsyth
Gray
Sandersville
Louisville
Allendale
Lafayette
West Point
Warm Springs
Yatesville
Savannah
Thomaston
Macon
Irwinton
Hampton
Pine Mountain
Oconee
Millen
Opelika
Talbotton
Knoxville
Byron
Jeffersonville
Wrightsville
Sylvania
Coosawhatchie
Fort Valley
Warner Robins
Swainsboro
Twin City
Phenix City
Columbus
Butler
Dublin
Statesboro
Fort Benning
Perry
Cochran
River
Metter
Pulaski
Springfield
Buena Vista
Soperton
Oglethorpe
Cusseta
Unadilla
Hawkinsville
Rincon
Blitchton
Ellaville
Andersonville
Eastman
Lyons
Claxton
Port Wentworth
Omaha
Chauncey
Pembroke
Ellabelle
Florence
Richland
Preston
Americus
Vienna
McRae
Alamo
Mt. Vernon
Reidsville
Lumpkin
Plains
Cordele
Abbeville
Glennville
Richmond Hill
Tybee Island
Eufaula
Georgetown
Lake Blackshear
Rochelle
Hazlehurst
Hinesville
Clayton
Altamaha
Midway
Cuthbert
Dawson
Leesburg
Arabi
Ashburn
Fitzgerald
Sycamore
South Newport
St. Catherines Island
Walter F. George Reservoir
Fort Gaines
Albany
Ambrose
Ocilla
Jesup
Townsend
Abbeville
Morgan
Sylvester
Chula
Tifton
Douglas
Alma
Screven
Eulonia
Sapelo Island
Blakely
Flint
Alapaha
Darien
Dothan
Camilla
Pearson
Blackshear
Waycross
Colquitt
Moultrie
Nashville
Nahunta
Brunswick
Adel
Ray City
St. Simons Island
Donalsonville
Cecil
Lakeland
Homerville
Jekyll Island
Campbellton
Woodbine
Bainbridge
Cairo
Lake Seminole
Thomasville
Valdosta
Folkston
Kingsland
CUMBERLAND ISLAND NATIONAL SEASHORE
Marianna
Quitman
St. Marys
Statenville
Lake Park
Fargo
Quincy
Amelia Island
Monticello
Jasper
St. George
St. Marys
Callahan
Blountstown
Bristol
Madison
Tallahassee
Jacksonville
White Springs
Live Oak
Wilma
Crawfordville
Perry
Lake City
Wewahitchka
A
B
C
D
E
F
1
2
3
4
5

Atlanta CVB
233 Peachtree St. NE
Atlanta, GA 30303
(800/285-2682 or 404/521-6688)
www.atlanta.net

Augusta Metropolitan CVB
1450 Greene St., Ste. 110
Augusta, GA 30901
(800/726-0243 or 706/823-6600)
www.augustaga.org

Brunswick-Golden Isles Chamber of Commerce
4 Glynn Ave.
Brunswick, GA 31520
(912/265-0620)
www.bgivb.com

Columbus CVB
900 Front Ave.
Columbus, GA 31902
(706/322-1613 or 800/999-1613)
www.columbusga.com

Jekyll Island CVB
PO Box 13186
Jekyll Island, GA 31527
(877/4-JEKYLL)
jekyllisland.com

RECREATIONAL INFO

Georgia Dept. of Natural Resources
2 Martin Luther King, Jr. Dr. S.E.
Suite 1252 East Tower,
Atlanta, GA 30334
(404/656-3500)
www.gadnr.org (links to information sites on fishing, boating, hunting, state parks and more)

Golf: Visit www.georgia.org/Travel/Rejuvenate/Golf.htm or www.golfgeorgia.org

History: Georgia State Parks & Historic Sites, 2 MLK Jr. Dr., Suite 1352, East Atlanta, GA 30334 (404/656-2770). www.gastateparks.org

DESTINATIONS

HISTORIC HIGH COUNTRY

Known as "the enchanted land" of the Cherokee Indians, this region has numerous driving, walking, pedaling or riding trails that lead you through the area's Native American roots, historic districts and homegrown attractions, from Civil War sites to national forests.

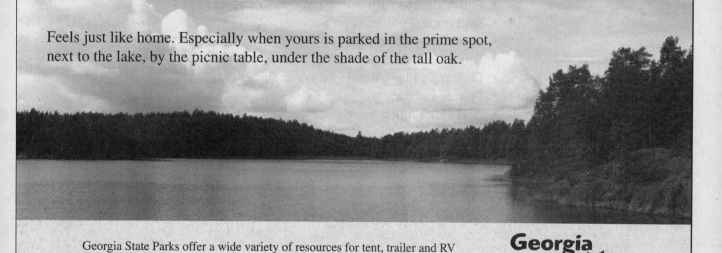

Pine Mountain RV Resort

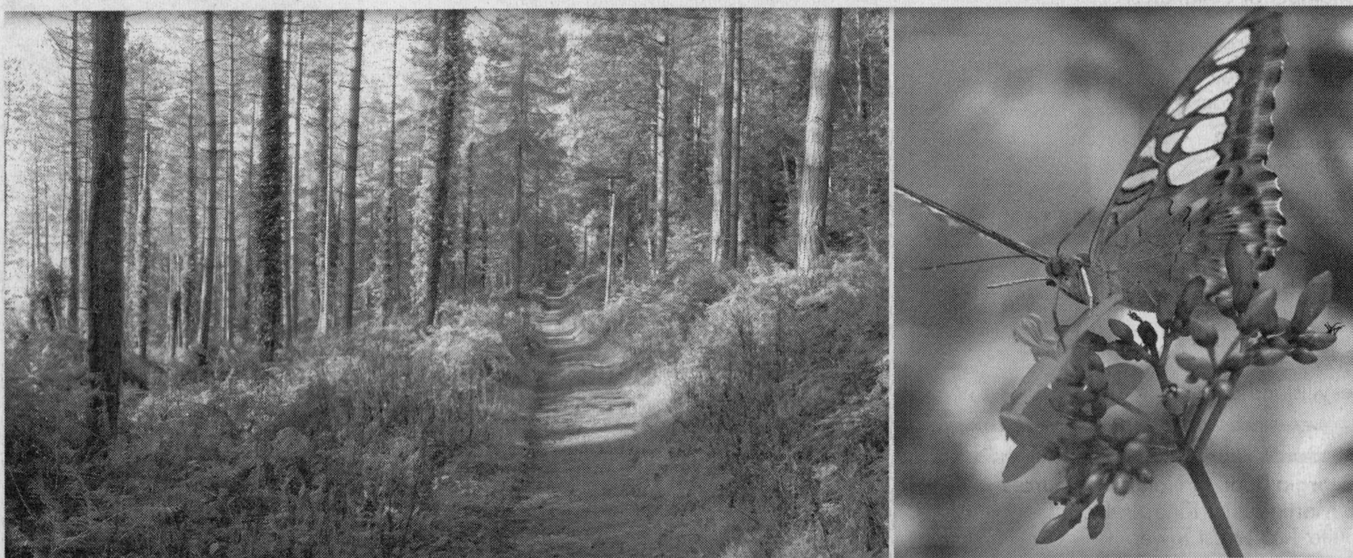

Your resort destination in the Georgia countryside.

Pine Mountain RV Resort is a beautiful RV and cabin community on Highway 27, located just over an hour from Atlanta and 3 miles from beautiful Callaway Gardens. Our lush facility features amenities and conveniences like no other, including:

- Pull-through, Level, and Paved Sites
- Full hook-ups with 30/50 amp service at all sites
- Swimming Pool and Spa Services
- Miniature Golf Course
- Gift & Convenience Store and Propane sales
- Children's Playground and Water Spray Park
- Private Cabins
- And much much more...

Please come visit our fully redeveloped 45-acre park in 2008!

8804 Hamilton Road • Highway 27 • Pine Mountain, Georgia 31822

(706) 663-4329 **www.PineMountainRVC.com**

FREE INFO! Enter #3734 on Reader Service Card

Cartersville. Featured attractions include: **The Bartow History Center**, portraying the workshops, farmsteads and mercantiles of north Georgian pioneers; **Allatoona Dam & Lake** with over 270 miles of shoreline and the **Red Top Mountain State Park & Lodge**, home to a variety of wildlife. **Barnsley Gardens** has over 30 acres of English-style gardens and dramatic ruins.

Chickamauga & Chattanooga National Military Park, located partially in Georgia at Fort Oglethorpe and partially in Tennessee. This is the site of the last major Confederate victory in the War Between the States. The oldest and largest military park in the country also offers 50 miles of hiking trails, a slide program, a bookstore and a 355-piece weapon collection of military shoulder arms.

Lookout Mountain. At the **Lookout Mountain Flight Park**, hang gliders launch from McCarty's Bluff in Dade County and soar 1,000 feet over the ridge. Lessons and training are available. Lush gardens, unique rock formations and a view of seven states from legendary Lover's Leap await visitors at **Rock City Gardens**. **Cloudland Canyon,** one of Georgia's most scenic areas, is located on the western edge of Lookout Mountain. Enjoy rugged canyons, waterfalls and beautiful views.

New Echota. Once the capital of the Cherokee Nation, it is now a State Historic Site in Calhoun. Before the treaty was signed in 1835, it was the seat of government for an independent Native American Nation that covered Georgia and four southeastern states. Buildings on-site include the Supreme Court House, Council House, Vann's Tavern, a missionary school and the print shop that published the bilingual Cherokee Phoenix, the only Native American language newspaper ever printed in North America.

NORTHEAST GEORGIA MOUNTAINS

The Mountain region is an area of breathtaking scenery and dramatic extremes. The villages and towns are filled with friendly, picturesque retreats, snow-capped in the winter and warm in the summer. Its foothills and mountains serve as the gateway to the Appalachian Mountains and the birthplace of the Chattahoochee River.

Anna Ruby Falls, located one and a half miles north of Unicoi State Park (near Helen), features fishing, hiking, picnicking, a visitor center and Braille trail.

Appalachian Trail. This famous hiking trail begins at Springer Mountain (Dawsonville) and runs 78 miles through Georgia and continues to Maine.

Dahlonega. Authentic 19th century buildings circle the courthouse museum, many of which are listed on the National Register of Historic Places. Try your luck at finding gold, or hike the Appalachian trail, fish, or take a scenic drive. Visit the **Appalachian Outfitters** downtown to arrange canoe, kayak and tube trips on the nearby Chestaee and Etowah Rivers. Stroll through the **Annual Wildflower Festival of the Arts** that takes place on the third weekend in May or Gold Rush Days, the third weekend in October.

De Soto Falls Scenic Area, 13 miles outside of Dahlonega. Visitors enjoy rugged mountainous country, exceptional views, beautiful waterfalls, hiking, fishing and wading in clear streams.

Russel-Brasstown Scenic Byway, just north of Helen. Take GA 348, one of two U.S. Forest Service-designated Scenic Byways in Georgia. This route will then take you close to Brasstown Bald, the highest mountain in Georgia at 4,784 ft. The interpretive center here offers a film, exhibits and an observation deck with a panoramic view of four states.

Hiawassee is home to the **Fred Hamilton Rhododendron Gardens**, displaying over 2,000 rhododendron and azalea plants plus native wildflowers and lakeside walking paths. In nearby **Young Harris** is "The Reach of Song," a summer epic musical celebration of the Appalachian Mountains. Attend the **Georgia Mountain Fair** in August.

Lake Lanier Islands, Buford/Gainesville, is home to a 1,200-acre family recreation resort with two hotels and a 300-site campground, located on the lake. The resort has facilities for golfing, swimming, sailing, houseboating and fishing. Also featured are an amphitheater and a 430-ft. waterslide.

ATLANTA METRO

This international city and surrounding area offers a unique blend of urban style and community charm. Around the city you'll find charming neighborhoods like Buckhead, Virginia-Highlands and College Park, each branching off from the city's center. Explore the magnificent architecture of downtown while walking through the tree-shaded streets that are so common throughout Atlanta. A short drive out of Atlanta provides you with charming communities and parks.

Atlanta. Visit the state capital in April for the week-long Dogwood Festival through Lenox Square and Phipps Plaza, located in Buckhead where you can visit the Governor's Mansion. While in Atlanta, don't miss the **Atlanta Botanical Gardens** or the **Atlanta History Center**. **Imagine It! Children's Museum of Atlanta** features hands-on colorful exhibits and activities. Visit the **Jimmy Carter Library & Museum** and see his Nobel Peace Prize on display. **Fernbank Science Center** is home to an exhibit hall, forest and planetarium. Check out **Underground Atlanta** and the **World of Coca-Cola,** then visit **CNN Center**, featuring studio tours of live news coverage. The

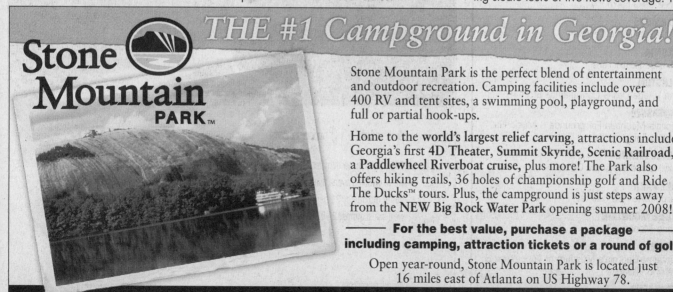

High Museum of Art, Folk Art and Photography is located at the **Woodruff Arts Center**, also the home of the Atlanta Symphony Orchestra. A must see is the **Zoo Atlanta**, known for its panda and gorilla habitats, where almost 1,000 animals reside in lush, naturalistic environments.

Atlanta Cyclorama. Visit one of the city's most beloved art treasures and learn the poignant tale of one of the pivotal events in Civil War history—the Battle of Atlanta (July 22, 1864). All the action of that terrible day is captured in a three-dimensional, 358-foot painting-in-the-round. Illustrations are made vivid by sound effects and narration of each facet of the battle. Setting the scene is an introductory film. See the museum of Civil War artifacts and the 1862 steam locomotive Texas.

The newly opened **Georgia Aquarium** has over eight million gallons of fresh and marine water and 100,000 animals representing 500 species from around the globe. With over 505,000 sq. ft of total space, it is the largest aquarium in the world. The different areas to explore include Cold Water Quest, Georgia Explorer, Ocean Voyager, River Scout and Tropical Diver. Also includes 4-D Theater, a cafe and gift shops.

Things to See & Do

ACWORTH
Lake Side Grill

AMERICUS
Brickyard Plantation Golf Club

ATLANTA
Georgia State Parks & Historic Sites

BLAIRSVILLE
Trackrock Stables

BRUNSWICK
Brunswick/Golden Isles Visitors Bureau
Fran's Place Restaurant
Three Oaks Farm

COLUMBUS
Lake Pines Event Center

EULONIA
Lakeside Restaurant

FOLKSTON
Pine Village Deli & Convenience Store

HIAWASSEE
Georgia Mountain Fairgrounds & Music Hall (County Fairgrounds)

JEKYLL ISLAND
Jekyll Island Welcome Center

LAKE PARK
Bargainville Flea Market

STONE MOUNTAIN
Stone Mountain Park

TIFTON
Agrirama-Georgia's Museum of Agriculture & Historic Village

TOWNSEND
Lake Harmony Bicycle Barn

The **Martin Luther King, Jr. National Historic Site** unveiled its **International Civil Rights Walk of Fame** in September 2004. The Walk of Fame was created to "pay homage to the brave warriors of justice who sacrificed and struggled to make equality a reality for all."

Georgia's Stone Mountain Park, Dekalb/Decatur. Experience the world's largest exposed granite monolith—a geological marvel featuring carvings of Confederate war heroes Jefferson Davis, Stonewall Jackson and Robert E. Lee on horseback on the side of the mountain. This 3,200-acre park offers a wide variety of attractions including the Stone Mountain Railroad, Paddlewheel Riverboat, Mountain Top Skylift, authentic Antebellum Plantation, Discovering Stone Mountain Museum, Antique Auto and Treasures Museum, Wildlife Preserve and Petting Zoo, a beach and waterslides, row boats, pedal boats, hydro-bikes, mini-golf, tennis, hiking trails, fishing, a 36-hole golf course, lodging, dining and shopping. The park also holds events and festivals throughout the year and features a laser show May—October.

Kennesaw Mountain National Battlefield Park, Kennesaw. This historic mountain top re-creates the fiercely contested battle where General Johnston's Confederate troops temporarily halted General Sherman's Union Army and their march to Atlanta. Visitors center open daily year-round.

Marietta Gone With the Wind Museum: Scarlett on the Square. Large collection of GWTW movie memorabilia including the bengaline gown worn by Scarlett in the honeymoon scene and a section dedicated to the African-American cast members.

Six Flags Over Georgia, Austell. Located on Riverside Pkwy, Six Flags is a 331-acre amusement park with more than 100 rides, several shows and various attractions. Ride BATMAN The Ride®, a suspended, outside looping themed roller coaster and visit Gotham City®.

Southeastern Railway Museum, Duluth. Georgia's largest railway museum displays over 90 pieces of railway equipment, including a WWII troop kitchen, steam locomotives and wooden freight cars.

Southern Museum of Civil War and Locomotive History, Kennesaw. Formerly the Civil War Museum, this newly renovated Smithsonian-affiliated museum features a reproduction of a turn-of-the-century locomotive factory and a glimpse into the daily lives of Americans during the Civil War.

MAGNOLIA MIDLANDS

Located in southeastern Georgia, this region provides a backdrop of beautiful scenery for any adventure you might seek, from outdoor sports to local festivals, from great food to a rich agricultural history.

Averitt Center for the Arts, Statesboro. Housed in two historic buildings, The Old Bank of Statesboro and The Springer Opera House, the center features the 362-seat Emma Kelly Theater and six small studios.

Douglas. Visit this Georgia Main Street City and find several interesting attractions such as the **Coffee County Bank**, which is listed on the National Historic Register. Also along the way are the **Coffee Art Walk** and **Heritage Art Walk**. Other stops to make include:

General Coffee State Park. Take advantage of the pool, nature trails, group shelters and group tours. Also on-site are a pioneer village and agricultural museum.

Lott's Grist Mill, Willacoochee. This working grist mill is more than a century old. See corn become grits and participate in hands-on activities.

Gordonia-Altamaha State Park & Golf Course, Reidsville. This 280-acre park has a swimming pool, boat dock, fishing, miniature golf, paddle boats and nine-hole golf course.

McRae is a hub of the Georgia pecan industry. Nature lovers will delight in the beautiful, old, spreading pecan trees, while pecan lovers can savor a variety of pecan products sold locally.

PRESIDENTIAL PATHWAYS

This west central Georgia region is deeply rooted in American history. Soak up reflections from the antebellum era, Civil War years, two U.S. presidents and the birth of the modern South.

Andersonville National Historic Site. National cemetery, Confederate prison site, museum, monuments, reconstructed portion of the stockade and special programs are available for viewing at the site where over 12,900 Union prisoners perished.

Georgia Veterans Memorial State Park & Golf Course, Cordele. An 18-hole golf course, camping, a swimming pool, a boat ramp and dock, a museum, water skiing and fishing are activities available at the park.

RV Sales & Service

	SALES	SERVICE
ACWORTH		
Georgia Boat Sales		
ALBANY		
Team RV Inc	•	•
BYRON		
Interstate RV Center		•
Mid-State RV Center	•	•
DOUGLASVILLE		
John Bleakley Motor Homes	•	•
John Bleakley RV Center	•	•
MARIETTA		
Norman Campers	•	•
SCREVEN		
Boyette Camper Sales	•	•
STATESBORO		
Ellis Travel Trailers	•	•
UNADILLA		
John Bleakley Motor Homes	•	•

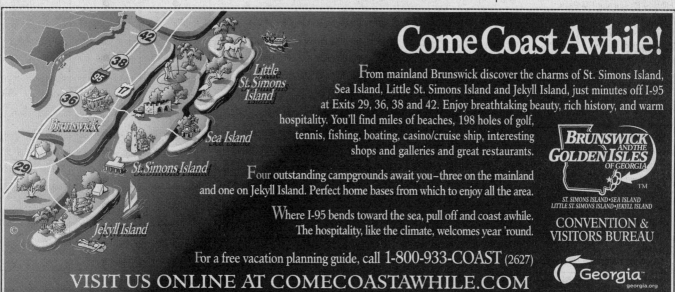

Woodall's Quick & Easy Reference for Georgia

	BIG RIGS WELCOME	INTERNET FRIENDLY	PETS WELCOME	WEB SAVER
ACWORTH				
Holiday Harbor Marina & Resort			■	
ADEL				
Reed Bingham State Park			■	
ALBANY				
Albany RV Resort	▲	●	■	
Creekside Plantation RV Campground	▲	●	■	
Team RV Inc				$
AMERICUS				
Brickyard Plantation RV Park	▲	●	■	
APPLING				
Mistletoe State Park			■	
AUGUSTA				
Flynn's Inn Camping Village	▲		■	
BAINBRIDGE				
The Place To Be RV Park	▲	●	■	
BLAIRSVILLE				
Lake Nottely RV Park	▲	●	■	
Mountain Creek RV Resort	▲	●	■	$
Trackrock Campground & Cabins	▲	●	■	
Vogel State Park	▲	●	■	
BLAKELY				
Kolomoki Mounds State Park	▲		■	
BRUNSWICK				
Blythe Island Regional Park Campground	▲	●	■	
Fran's Place Restaurant				$
Golden Isles RV Park	▲	●	■	
BYRON				
Interstate RV Campground	▲	●	■	
Interstate RV Center				$
Mid-State RV Center				$
CARROLLTON				
John Tanner State Park			■	
CARTERSVILLE				
Allatoona Landing Marine Resort & Campground	▲	●	■	
Red Top Mountain State Park	▲		■	
CAVE SPRING				
Cedar Creek Park RV & Driving Range	▲	●	■	
CHATSWORTH				
Fort Mountain State Park	▲		■	
CLARKESVILLE				
Moccasin Creek State Park			■	
COCHRAN				
Hillside Bluegrass RV Park	▲	●	■	
COLQUITT				
Emerald Lake RV Park	▲	●	■	$
COLUMBUS				
Blanton Creek Park (Georgia Power)	▲		■	
Lake Pines RV Park & Campground	▲	●	■	$
COMER				
Watson Mill Bridge State Park			■	
CORDELE				
Georgia Veterans Memorial State Park	▲		■	
COVINGTON				
Riverside Estates RV Park	▲		■	
CRAWFORDVILLE				
Alexander H. Stephens State Historic Park			■	
CUMMING				
Twin Lakes RV Park	▲	●	■	
DAWSONVILLE				
Amicalola Falls State Park & Lodge			■	
DILLARD				
River Vista Mountain Village	▲	●	■	

▲ = Big Rigs Welcome; ● = Internet Hookups; ● = (Wi-Fi available); ■ = Pets Welcome; $ = Web Saver Coupons

****Check out the "How to Use This Directory" section in the front of this book for a description of the criteria Woodall's uses in this chart.***

Woodall's Quick & Easy Reference for Georgia

	BIG RIGS WELCOME	INTERNET FRIENDLY	PETS WELCOME	WEB SAVER
DONALSONVILLE				
Seminole State Park	▲		■	
DOUGLAS				
General Coffee State Park			■	
DOUGLASVILLE				
John Bleakley RV Center				$
EATONTON				
Lawrence Shoals Park (Georgia Power)	▲		■	
ELBERTON				
Bobby Brown State Park	▲		■	
Richard B Russell State Park			■	
ELLIJAY				
Plum Nelly Campground	▲	●	■	
EULONIA				
Lakeside Restaurant				$
McIntosh Lake RV Park	▲	●	■	
FARGO				
Stephen C. Foster State Park	▲		■	
FOLKSTON				
Okefenokee RV Park	▲	●	■	
FORSYTH				
Forsyth KOA	▲	●	■	
GREENSBORO				
North Shore Resort at Lake Oconee	▲		■	
Old Salem Park (Georgia Power)	▲		■	
Parks Ferry Park (Georgia Power)	▲		■	
HARTWELL				
Hart State Park			■	
HELEN				
Cherokee Campground	▲	●	■	
Enota Mountain Retreat	▲	●	■	
Unicoi State Park	▲		■	
HIAWASSEE				
Bald Mountain Park Camping Resort	▲	●	■	
Georgia Mountain Fairgrounds Campground (County Park)	▲	●	■	
HIGH FALLS				
High Falls State Park	▲		■	
JACKSON				
Forest Glen Mobile Home & RV Park	▲		■	
Indian Springs State Park	▲		■	
JEKYLL ISLAND				
Jekyll Island Campground	▲	●	■	
KINGSLAND				
Country Oaks Campground & RV Park	▲	●	■	
LAKE PARK				
Eagles Roost RV Resort	▲	●	■	
LAVONIA				
Tugaloo State Park			■	
LINCOLNTON				
Elijah Clark State Park			■	
MACON				
Lake Juliette Dames Ferry Park (Georgia Power)	▲		■	
Lake Tobesofkee Recreation Area (Bibb Co.)	▲		■	
MADISON				
Country Boy's RV Park	▲	●	■	
MARIETTA				
Atlanta-Marietta RV Resort (formally Brookwood RV Park)	▲	●	■	
Norman Campers				$
MCDONOUGH				
Atlanta South RV Resort	▲	●	■	
MCRAE				
Little Ocmulgee State Park	▲		■	
MILLEDGEVILLE				
Scenic Mountain RV Park	▲	●	■	$

▲ = Big Rigs Welcome; ● = Internet Hookups; ● = (Wi-Fi available); ■ = Pets Welcome; $ = Web Saver Coupons

***Check out the "How to Use This Directory" section in the front of this book for a description of the criteria Woodall's uses in this chart.**

Woodall's Quick & Easy Reference for Georgia

	BIG RIGS WELCOME	INTERNET FRIENDLY	PETS WELCOME	WEB SAVER
MILLEN				
Magnolia Springs State Park			■	
MOUNTAIN CITY				
Black Rock Mountain State Park			■	
NORCROSS				
Jones RV Park	▲	●	■	
OMAHA				
Florence Marina State Park	▲		■	
PERRY				
Crossroads Holiday Trav-L-Park	▲	●	■	
Fair Harbor RV Park & Campground	▲	●	■	
Twin Oaks RV Park	▲	●	■	
PINE MOUNTAIN				
F. D. Roosevelt State Park	▲		■	
Pine Mountain RVC	▲	●	■	
REIDSVILLE				
Gordonia-Alatamaha State Park	▲		■	
RICHMOND HILL				
Fort McAllister State Historic Park	▲		■	
RISING FAWN				
Cloudland Canyon State Park			■	
ROYSTON				
Victoria Bryant State Park			■	
RUTLEDGE				
Hard Labor Creek State Park	▲		■	
SAVANNAH				
Savannah Oaks RV Resort	▲	●	■	
Skidaway Island State Park	▲		■	
SCREVEN				
Boyette Camper Sales				$
ST. MARYS				
Crooked River State Park			■	
STONE MOUNTAIN				
Stone Mountain Family Campground	▲	●	■	$
SUMMERVILLE				
James H. Floyd State Park	▲		■	
TALLULAH FALLS				
Tallulah Gorge State Park			■	
TIFTON				
Agrirama RV Park	▲		■	
Agrirama-Georgia's Museum of Agriculture & Historic Village				$
Amy's South Georgia RV Park	▲	●	■	
The Pines Campground	▲	●	■	
TOCCOA				
Toccoa RV Park			■	
TOWNSEND				
Lake Harmony RV Park & Campground	▲	●	■	$
TRENTON				
Lookout Mountain KOA-Chattanooga West	▲	●	■	
TWIN CITY				
George L. Smith State Park	▲		■	
TYBEE ISLAND				
River's End Campground & RV Park (City Park)	▲	●	■	
WARM SPRINGS				
Ramsey RV Park	▲		■	
WARTHEN				
Hamburg State Park			■	
WAYCROSS				
Laura S. Walker State Park	▲		■	
WINDER				
Fort Yargo State Park	▲		■	
WRENS				
Boss's RV Park	▲	●	■	

▲ = Big Rigs Welcome; ● = Internet Hookups; ● = (Wi-Fi available); ■ = Pets Welcome; $ = Web Saver Coupons

***Check out the "How to Use This Directory" section in the front of this book for a description of the criteria Woodall's uses in this chart.**

Habitat for Humanity Global Village & Discover Center, Americus. A multimedia museum and town dedicated to educating people about the worldwide need for adequate housing.

LaGrange. The historic 31-acre **Hills and Dales Estate** includes Ferrell Gardens which date to 1832 and consist of an elaborate blend of extensive boxwood plantings, fountains, descending terraces, a greenhouse and more. The centerpiece is the Italian-villa style house.

Warm Springs invites you to step back in time as you stroll down one sq. mile of shops and restaurants. Visit Roosevelt's **Little White House & Museum**, also in Warm Springs. It was built in 1932 by President Franklin Delano Roosevelt, so he could be close to Warm Springs for polio therapy. The house remains exactly the way it was the day he died there in 1945.

HISTORIC HEARTLAND

Enjoy true Southern hospitality in Georgia's Historic Heartland, just south of Atlanta. Step back in time in this region of quaint towns, antiques, scenic byways and local festivals.

Athens. Known as the "Classic City" in Georgia's Historic Heartland. **The Antebellum Trail** recaptures the romance and mystery of the Old South through glorious plantations and quaint town squares. Shop in picturesque downtown and lunch at a sidewalk cafe. Attractions within Athens include the **State Botanical Gardens of Georgia**, **Georgia Museum of Art** and **Founders Memorial Garden**. Stop by the **Athens Welcome Center** for information on easy-to-follow self-guided tours of local historic sites. The **Lyndon House Arts Center** contains galleries, a children's wing, artists' workshops, gift shop and more. The 1856 **Lyndon House** features authentic period furniture.

Macon. Home to six National Historic Districts with thousands of buildings dating to the 1830s. **The Hay House/Georgia Trust for Historic Preservation** features priceless furniture, a secret room and 18 hand-carved marble mantels. Also in Macon is **The Georgia Music Hall of Fame** dedicated to nurturing the cultural climate for music—its creators and those who enjoy it. Among the many artists featured are Toni Braxton, Otis Redding, Gladys Knight, Alan Jackson, Trisha Yearwood, Jimi Hendrix and many more, all with a connection to Georgia. **Museum of Arts & Sciences** has changing art and science exhibits, along with daily star shows. The **Georgia Sports Hall of Fame** includes Olympic champions, legendary coaches and professional superstars.

Museum of Aviation, Inc., Warner Robins. 90 historic aircraft plus 100,000 sq. ft. of indoor aviation exhibits, from WWII, Korea and Desert Storm.

PLANTATION TRACE

Located in rural southwestern Georgia, this region is full of plantations and historic farms that allow you to re-live Georgia's historic past.

Fort Valley features the **Blue Bird Body Company**, offering tours of their school bus and luxury RV building plant (by appointment). Also within Fort Valley is the **Historic Massee Lane Gardens**, complete with arboretum, lake, gazebo, rose garden, educational museum and extensive porcelain collection.

Georgia Agrirama, Tifton. This living history town depicts rural Georgia prior to 1900. More than 35 authentic restorations including a grist mill, a saw mill, a cotton gin and farm houses are displayed here.

Kolomoki Mounds State Park, Blakely. On-site are hiking trails, an interpretive museum, seven Native American mounds, fishing facilities, swimming, mini-golf and camping.

Lake Seminole, Bainbridge/ Donalsonville. Contained in these 37,500 acres are boating, swimming, water skiing, camping and great fishing. Anglers can expect to hook into largemouth, striper and hybrid bass.

Splash Island, Valdosta. This newly opened water park features the Rain Fortress, Paradise River, the Double Dip Zip and Cathawave Bay.

CLASSIC SOUTH

This region is considered Georgia's heart and soul. Offering a rich cultural heritage of music and literature along with its bountiful agriculture and entertaining festivals throughout the year, the Classic South has many restored antebellum homes and museums.

Augusta. A classic southern city, Augusta is known for its combination of beauty, elegance and tradition. The city is also home of six National Register districts and host to great sporting events such as the Masters Golf Tournament and the Southern National Dragboat Races. Also in Augusta is **The Morris Museum of Art**, featuring a unique collection of southern art as well as traveling exhibitions. **Riverwalk Augusta** is a beautiful outdoor walking path, set on the banks of the Savannah River. Tree-lined paths loaded with seasonal flowers provide the perfect backdrop for a charming array of restaurants, unique shops, museums and special events.

Madison. 19th century homes and buildings line the streets of this town recently voted "No. 1 Small Town in America." Museums dating back to the early 1800s include Heritage Hall, Madison-Morgan Cultural Center, Morgan County African American Museum and Rogers House/Rose Cottage.

Milledgeville. The Old Governor's Mansion in Milledgeville was recently reopened after a historic restoration. The Mansion, originally built in 1839, was home to eight of Georgia's governors until 1868 when the capital moved to Atlanta. It is considered one of the finest examples of High Greek Revival architecture in the country.

Reynolds Plantation, located midway between Atlanta and Augusta. Nestled against the banks of Lake Oconee, Reynolds Plantation has 32 miles of shoreline along this fabulous 19,000 acre lake.

COAST

Here you will find beauty and serenity in the coastal towns. Soak up the warm sea air as you walk among the moss-draped oaks of the coastal communities. Explore beyond the city streets and roam the lands of Georgia's pristine barrier islands, quiet swamps, unspoiled beaches and marshes – all thriving with wildlife. A variety of birds, fish, snakes, alligators, otters and sea turtles live within the lush vegetation of the area. Take an outdoor expedition through the trails of **Blackbeard Island** or **Okefenokee National Wildlife Refuge** and witness creatures in their natural habitat. This region also offers world-class golf courses, tennis, canoe trips along the waterways of the Atlantic and a variety of other recreational sports.

Brunswick. The Gateway to the Golden Isles also features many wildlife management areas, historic buildings, a 900-year-old oak tree and the **Mary Miller Doll Museum**, housing over 3,000 dolls.

Okefenokee Swamp. The swamp is a wilderness area accessible through Fargo, Folkston and Waycross. Guided boat tours take passengers through the swamp for views of wildlife and plant life. Also available are hiking trails, fishing, canoeing and camping.

Savannah. Savannah's Historic District is the largest registered urban landmark district in the nation. **Riverfront Plaza** provides a nine-block concourse dotted with fountains, benches, plantings, museums, pubs, restaurants, artists' galleries and boutiques. Tours of a former whaling vessel are also available. Railroad buffs will enjoy the **Central of Georgia Railroad Roundhouse Complex**. Guided tours are plentiful throughout Savannah. Aside from the usual walking/driving tours, visitors can also tour via horse-drawn carriage or riverboat. Before you begin, stop by the Savannah Visitor Center (301 Martin Luther King Blvd.).

St. Simons, **Sea Island**, **Jekyll Island** and **Little St. Simons Island**. Each of these beach resort areas are accessible only from Brunswick. Features of the islands include historical sites, crabbing, horseback riding, shelling, swimming, golf, tennis and fishing.

Georgia

ACWORTH—B-1

(W) CLARK CREEK SOUTH (Allatoona Lake COE)—(Bartow) *From I-75 (exit 121/278) & Glade Rd: Go 3 mi NE on Glade Rd.* FACILITIES: 40 sites, typical site width 20 ft, 24 W&E, (30 amps), 16 no hkups, tenting, dump station, laundry, fire rings, grills. RECREATION: lake swimming, boating, ramp, dock, lake fishing. Partial handicap access. Open Apr 14 thru Sep 5. Phone: (678)721-6700.

(N) GEORGIA BOAT SALES—*From jct I-75 (exit 278) & Glade Rd: Go 3/4 mi E on Glade Rd, then 1 mi N on Tanyard Creek Rd, then 3/4 mi E on Groovers Landing Rd. Enter at end.* SERVICES: Open all yr. MC/VISA/AMEX/Debit. Phone: (770)974-2575.

e-mail: eric@gaboatsales.com

SEE AD THIS PAGE

(N) HOLIDAY HARBOR MARINA & RESORT (REBUILDING)—(Bartow) *From jct I-75 (exit 278) & Glade Rd: Go 3/4 mi E on Glade Rd, then 1 mi N on Tanyard Creek Rd, then 3/4 mi E on Groovers Landing Rd. Enter at end.*

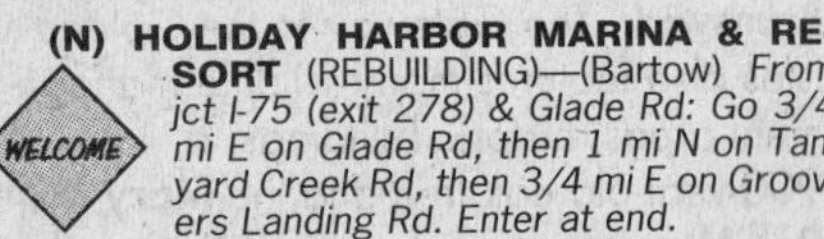

FACILITIES: 27 sites, 27 W&E, (20, 30 & 50 amps), 1 pull-thrus, cabins, RV storage, dump station, non-guest dumping $, portable dump, laundry, ltd groceries, RV supplies, marine gas, ice, tables, fire rings, wood, controlled access gate.

ACWORTH—Continued
HOLIDAY HARBOR MARINA & RESORT—Continued

RECREATION: boating, canoeing, kayaking, ramp, dock, 6 pontoon/2 motorboat rentals, lake fishing, fishing supplies, horseshoes, hiking trails.

Pets welcome. Partial handicap access. No tents. Open all yr. Big rigs welcome. Escort to site. Clubs welcome. Rate in 2007 $30 per family. MC/VISA/AMEX/Debit. Member ARVC, GARVC. Phone: (770) 974-2575.

e-mail: reservations@lakeallatoona.net

SEE AD THIS PAGE

(N) LAKE SIDE GRILL—*From jct I-75 (exit 78) & Glade Rd: Go 3/4 mi E on Glade Rd, then 1 mi N on Tanyard Creek Rd, then 3/4 mi E on Groovers Landing Rd. Enter at end.* Full service restaurant. Open Thur - Sun for lunch & dinner. Beer & wine available. Entertainment & Karaoke. Open all yr. MC/VISA/AMEX/Debit. Phone: (770) 974-2575.

e-mail: reservations@lakeallatoona.net

SEE AD THIS PAGE

(N) Lakemont RV Park—(Bartow) *From jct I-75 (exit 278) & Glade Rd: Go 1/2 mi W on Glade Rd, then 2-1/4 mi NW on Hwy 92, then 3/4 mi N on US 41. Enter on L.* ◇◇◇FACILITIES: 100 sites, typical site width 25 ft, accepts full hkup units only, 100 full hkups, (20, 30 & 50 amps), mostly extended stay sites, laundry, LP gas by weight/by meter, ice, tables. ◇◇RECREATION: boating, dock, lake fishing, play equipment, sports field. Pets welcome. No tents. Open all yr. Big rigs welcome. Internet friendly. Rate in 2007 $18 for 4 persons. Member ARVC. Phone: (770)966-0302.

(W) MCKINNEY CAMPGROUND (Allatoona Lake COE)—(Bartow) *From jct I-75 (exit 121/278) & Glade Rd: Go 4 mi NE on Glade Rd, then 3/4 mi W on King's Camp Rd & follow signs.* FACILITIES: 150 sites, typical site width 8 ft, 150 W&E, (30 amps), many extended stay sites, 25 pull-thrus, tenting, dump station, laundry, patios, fire rings, grills. RECREATION: lake swimming, boating, ramp, dock, lake fishing. Partial handicap access. Open all yr. Facilities fully operational Apr 1 thru Oct 31. No reservations. Phone: (678)721-6700.

(S) MILITARY PARK (World Famous Navy Lake Site-Atlanta NAS)—(Bartow) *From I-75 (exit 122/283-Emerson): Go 4 mi S on Sandtown Rd. Off base.* FACILITIES: 13 sites, typical site width 14 ft, 13 W&E, (30 amps), 1 pull-thrus, tenting, dump station, laundry, ltd groceries, fire rings, grills. RECREATION: pavilion, equipped pavilion, lake swimming, boating, canoeing, ramp, dock, 6 canoe/10 motorboat rentals, lake fishing, playground, sports field, v-ball. Rec open to public. No pets. Open all yr. No reservations. For Military Use Only-w/Military ID Card. Phone: (770)974-6309.

(N) OLD 41 NO. 3 CAMPGROUND (COE Allatoona Lake)—(Bartow) *From town: Go 2-1/2 mi N on Hwy-293.* FACILITIES: 44 sites, typical site width 20 ft, 44 W&E, 4 pull-thrus, tenting, dump station, laundry, fire rings, grills. RECREATION: lake swimming, boating, ramp, dock, lake fishing, playground. Open Apr 29 thru Sep 5. Phone: (678)721-6700.

(NW) PAYNE CAMPGROUND (COE-Allatoona Lake)—(Cherokee) *From jct I-75 (exit 120/277) & Hwy 92: Go 1 mi N on Hwy 92, then 2-3/4 mi W on Kellogg Creek Rd. Enter on R.* FACILITIES: 60 sites, typical site width 20 ft, 2 full hkups, 39 W&E, (30 amps), 19 no hkups, 3 pull-thrus, tenting, dump station, laundry, fire rings, grills. RECREATION: lake swimming, boating, ramp, dock, lake fishing, playground. Partial handicap access. Open Apr 1 thru Sep 5. No reservations. Phone: (678)721-6700.

Georgia State Name: Named in honor of King George II

ADEL—E-3

(W) REED BINGHAM STATE PARK—(Colquitt) *From jct I-75 (exit 39) & Hwy 37: Go 5-3/4 mi W on Hwy 37, then 3/4 mi N on Reed Bingham Rd. Enter at end.*

FACILITIES: 46 sites, 46 W&E, (20, 30 & 50 amps), 8 pull-thrus, cable TV, tenting, dump station, non-guest dumping $, laundry, ice, tables, fire rings, grills, wood.

RECREATION: pavilion, lake swimming, boating, canoeing, kayaking, ramp, dock, 2 motorboat rentals, lake/river fishing, mini-golf ($), golf nearby, playground, sports field, hiking trails, v-ball. Rec open to public.

Pets welcome. Partial handicap access. Open all yr. Clubs welcome. MC/VISA/DISC/AMEX. Phone: (800) 864-7275.

e-mail: reedbinghampark@dnr.state.ga.us

SEE AD TRAVEL SECTION PAGE 189

ALBANY—E-2

(S) ALBANY RV RESORT—(Dougherty) *From jct US 82 & US 19/Hwy 300: Go 4-1/2 mi S on US 19/Hwy 300. Enter on L.*

◇◇◇◇◇FACILITIES: 82 sites, typical site width 40 ft, 82 full hkups, (20, 30 & 50 amps), some extended stay sites, 42 pull-thrus, cable TV, wireless Instant Internet access at site, phone on-site Internet access (needs activ), tenting, RV storage, laundry, RV supplies, tables, patios.

◇◇RECREATION: rec hall, pavilion, pond fishing, horseshoes.

Pets welcome. Partial handicap access. Open all yr. Big rigs welcome. Internet friendly. Clubs welcome. Rate in 2007 $28 for 2 persons. MC/VISA/DISC/AMEX. Phone: (866)792-1481. FMCA discount.

e-mail: info@albanyrvresort.com

SEE AD THIS PAGE

ALBANY—Continued on next page

Georgia State Motto: "Wisdom, Justice & Moderation"

See us at woodalls.com

ALBANY—Continued

(S) CREEKSIDE PLANTATION RV CAMPGROUND—(Dougherty) *From jct US 82 & US 19/Hwy 300: Go 8 mi S on US 19/Hwy 300, then 1 block E on Hancock Rd. Enter on L.*

◆◆◆◆FACILITIES: 75 sites, typical site width 40 ft, 75 full hkups, (30 & 50 amps), 50 amps ($), some extended stay sites, 24 pull-thrus, cable TV, wireless Instant Internet access at site, phone/cable on-site Internet access (needs activ), wireless Internet access central location, tenting, RV/park trailer rentals, RV storage, laundry, LP gas by weight/by meter, ice, tables, patios, fire rings.

◆◆RECREATION: rec room/area, pavilion, river swimming, pond fishing, golf nearby, bsktball, playground, shuffleboard court, horseshoes, hiking trails.

Pets welcome. Partial handicap access. Open all yr. Big rigs welcome. Internet friendly. Clubs welcome. Rate in 2007 $20-22 per vehicle. Phone: (229)886-0504. CCUSA discount.

e-mail: levesque46@aol.com

SEE AD PAGE 198

(S) TEAM RV INC—*From jct US 82 & US 19/Hwy 300: Go 4-1/2 mi S on US 19/Hwy 300. Enter on L.* SALES: travel trailers, park trailers, 5th wheels, fold-down camping trailers, pre-owned unit sales. SERVICES: full-time mech, RV appliance repair, body work/collision repair, LP gas by weight/by meter, dump station, RV storage, sells parts/accessories, installs hitches. Open all yr. MC/VISA/AMEX/Debit. Phone: (800) 424-6301.

e-mail: sales@teamrvinc.com

SEE AD PAGE 198

(N) THE PARKS AT CHEHAW CAMPGROUND (City Park)—(Dougherty) *From jct US 19 & Hwy 91: Go 1-1/4 mi NE on Hwy 91. Enter on L.* FACILITIES: 50 sites, typical site width 25 ft, 50 W&E, (20, 30 & 50 amps), 14 pull-thrus, tenting, dump station, laundry, ice, fire rings, grills, wood. RECREATION: pavilion, equipped pavilion, boating, canoeing, ramp, dock, lake/pond fishing, playground, sports field, hiking trails. Pets welcome. Partial handicap access. Open all yr. Max stay 14 days. Big rigs welcome. Phone: (229)430-5277.

AMERICUS—D-2

(E) BRICKYARD PLANTATION GOLF CLUB—*From east jct Hwy 27 & US 280: Go 7 mi E on US 280. From jct I-75 (exit 101) & US 280: Go 24 mi W on US 280. Enter on L.* 27-hole championship golf course, 2 PGA pros, driving range, senior activities Wed & Fri. Snack Bar. Open to public all year. M-Sat 8-6, Sun 12:30-6 except Thanksgiving & Christmas, Golf clinics & lessons. Open all yr. MC/VISA/DISC/AMEX/Debit. Phone: (229)874-1234.

e-mail: bpgcdeb@sowega.net

SEE AD THIS PAGE

(E) BRICKYARD PLANTATION RV PARK—(Sumter) *From jct Hwy 27 & US 280: Go 7 mi E on US 280, then 1/2 mi S on Parkers Crossing. From jct I-75 (exit 101) & US 280: Go 24 mi W on US 280. Enter on R.*

◆◆◆FACILITIES: 48 sites, typical site width 25 ft, 48 full hkups, (30 & 50 amps), 32 pull-thrus, phone Internet access central location, dump station, laundry, ice, tables, patios, fire rings, grills, wood.

AMERICUS—Continued
BRICKYARD PLANTATION RV PARK—Continued

◆◆◆RECREATION: equipped pavilion, pond fishing, putting green, golf nearby, planned activities, hiking trails.

Pets welcome, breed restrict, quantity restrict. Partial handicap access. No tents. Open all yr. Big rigs welcome. Internet friendly. Clubs welcome. Rate in 2007 $25 per vehicle. MC/VISA/DISC/AMEX. Member ARVC, GARVC. Phone: (229)874-1234. CCUSA discount.

e-mail: bpgcdeb@sowega.net

SEE AD THIS PAGE

ANDERSONVILLE—D-2

(W) CITY CAMPGROUND—(Sumter) *From jct Hwy 49 & Hwy 228: Go 1/4 mi W on Hwy 228, then 1 block S to Monument, then 1 block W (follow signs).* FACILITIES: 40 sites, 12 full hkups, 18 W&E, 10 no hkups, 12 pull-thrus, tenting, ltd groceries, wood. RECREATION: Open all yr. Phone: (229)924-2558.

APPLING—C-4

(N) MISTLETOE STATE PARK—(Columbia) *From jct I-20 (exit 175) & Hwy 150: Go 7 3/4 mi NE on Hwy 150, then 3 mi NW on Mistletoe Rd. Enter at end.*

FACILITIES: 92 sites, 92 W&E, (20, 30 & 50 amps), 26 pull-thrus, tenting, cabins, dump station, non-guest dumping $, laundry, ice, tables, fire rings, grills, wood.

RECREATION: pavilion, lake swimming, boating, canoeing, kayaking, ramp, dock, 6 canoe/2 motorboat rentals, lake fishing, playground, planned activities (wkends only), sports field, hiking trails, v-ball. Rec open to public.

Pets welcome. Partial handicap access. Open all yr. Clubs welcome. MC/VISA/DISC/AMEX. Phone: (800)864-7275.

SEE AD TRAVEL SECTION PAGE 189

(E) WILDWOOD PARK (Columbia County Park)—(Columbia) *From jct I-20 & US-221: Go 8 mi N on US-221, then 2 mi NW on Hwy-104, then 1 mi E.* FACILITIES: 61 sites, typical site width 12 ft, 61 W&E, (20 & 50 amps), 2 pull-thrus, tenting, dump station, fire rings, grills, wood. RECREATION: pavilion, lake swimming, boating, ramp, dock, lake fishing, playground, horseshoes, sports field, hiking trails, v-ball. Rec open to public. Open Mar thru Nov. Phone: (706)541-0586.

ARABI—E-2

(E) Southern Gates RV Park & Campground (REBUILDING)—(Crisp) *From I-75 (Exit 92) & First St: Go 1/4 mi W on First St, then 1/4 mi N on Campsite Rd. Enter on R.* FACILITIES: 44 sites, typical site width 25 ft, 26 full hkups, 18 W&E, (20, 30 & 50 amps), 23 pull-thrus, tenting, dump station, non-guest dumping $, laundry, ltd groceries, LP gas by weight/by meter, ice, tables, fire rings, wood. RECREATION: rec room/area, pavilion, swim pool, pond fishing, playground, shuffleboard court, horseshoes, sports field, hiking trails. Pets welcome. Open all yr. Big rigs welcome. Rate in 2007 $25 per family. Phone: (229)273-6464. FMCA discount.

ATHENS—B-3

See listings at Bishop, Comer, Commerce, Elberton, Royston, Rutledge, & Winder.

ATLANTA—B-2

ATLANTA AREA MAP

Symbols on map indicate towns within a 40 mi radius of Atlanta where campgrounds (dia-monds), attractions (flags), & RV service centers & camping supply outlets (gears) are listed. Check listings for more information.

Tell Them Woodall's Sent You!

ATLANTA-MARIETTA RV RESORT (formerly Brookwood RV Park)—*From jct I-75 & I-285: Go 2-3/4 mi N on I-75 (Exit 261), then 3/4 mi W on Hwy 280 (Delk Rd), then 1/2 mi N on US 41 (Cobb Pkwy), then 1 block E on Wylie Rd. Enter on R.*

SEE LISTING AT MARIETTA AND AD THIS PAGE

ATLANTA—Continued on next page

ATLANTA—Continued

FOREST GLEN MOBILE HOME & RV PARK —*From south jct I-675 & I-75: Go 23 mi S on I-75 (exit 205), then 500 feet W on Hwy 16, then 1/2 mi S on Glade Rd. Enter on L.*

SEE PRIMARY LISTING AT JACKSON AND AD THIS PAGE

(C) GEORGIA STATE PARKS & HISTORIC SITES—Georgia state parks & historic sites (a division of the Georgia Dept of Natural Resources). Open all yr. Phone: (800)864-7275.

SEE AD TRAVEL SECTION PAGE 189

ATLANTA—Continued

JONES RV PARK—*From jct I-285 (exit 33B) & I-85: Go 5-1/2 mi NE on I-85 (exit 101), then 400 feet E on Indian Trail, then 1 block S on Willowtrail Pkwy. Enter at end.*

SEE PRIMARY LISTING AT NORCROSS AND AD PAGE 199

It is illegal to eat chicken with a fork in Gainesville, the "Chicken Capital of the World".

AUGUSTA—C-4

(S) FLYNN'S INN CAMPING VILLAGE—(Richmond) *From jct I-20 (exit 196 A) & I-520 (Bobby Jones Expressway): Go 7 mi S on I-520 (exit 7), then 3-1/2 mi S on US 25 (Peach Orchard Rd). Enter on L.*

◆◆FACILITIES: 71 sites, typical site width 30 ft, 62 full hkups, (30 & 50 amps), 50 amps ($), 9 no hkups, some extended stay sites, 30 pull-thrus, laundry.

FLYNN'S INN CAMPING VILLAGE—Continued on next page

AUGUSTA—Continued
FLYNN'S INN CAMPING VILLAGE—Continued

◇RECREATION: golf nearby, horseshoes, v-ball.

Pets welcome. No tents. Open all yr. Big rigs welcome. Clubs welcome. Rate in 2007 $20 for 2 persons. Phone: (706)798-6912.

SEE AD TRAVEL SECTION PAGE 189

BAINBRIDGE—F-1

(S) THE PLACE TO BE RV PARK—(Decatur) *From jct US 84/27 Bypass & Shotwell St: Go 1/4 mi S on Shotwell St. Enter on L.*

◇◇◇◇FACILITIES: 85 sites, typical site width 30 ft, 85 full hkups, (20, 30 & 50 amps), 34 pull-thrus, cable TV, wireless Instant Internet access at site ($), phone on-site Internet access (needs activ), tenting, RV storage, dump station, non-guest dumping $, laundry, RV supplies, LP gas by meter, ice, tables, fire rings, wood.

◇◇◇RECREATION: rec hall, pavilion, boating, river fishing, mini-golf ($), golf nearby, playground, horseshoes, hiking trails.

Pets welcome. Partial handicap access. Open all yr. Big rigs welcome. Internet friendly. Clubs welcome. Rate in 2007 $27 for 4 persons. MC/VISA/Debit. Member ARVC, GARVC. Phone: (229)246-5802.

e-mail: davidbrantly@hotmail.com

SEE AD THIS PAGE

BISHOP—B-3

(W) Pine Lake RV Campground—(Oconee) *From jct US 441 & Hwy 186: Go 1-1/4 mi W on Hwy 186. Enter on L.* ◇◇◇FACILITIES: 32 sites, typical site width 25 ft, 25 full hkups, 7 W&E, (20, 30 & 50 amps), some extended stay sites, 10 pull-thrus, tenting, laundry, ltd groceries, ice, tables, fire rings, grills, wood. ◇◇RECREATION: rec room/area, pavilion, pond fishing, playground, horseshoes, hiking trails. Pets welcome. Open all yr. Internet friendly. Rate in 2007 $24-28 for 2 persons. Phone: (706)769-5486.

BLAIRSVILLE—A-2

(S) CHATTAHOOCHEE NATIONAL FOREST (Lake Winfield Scott Campground)—(Union) *From town: Go 10-1/4 mi S on US-19, then 6-1/2 mi W on Hwy-180.* FACILITIES: 32 sites, typical site width 15 ft, 22 ft max RV length, 32 no hkups, 6 pull-thrus, tenting, grills. RECREATION: pavilion, lake swimming, boating, electric motors only, ramp, lake fishing, playground, hiking trails. Partial handicap access. Open Apr 28 thru Oct 28. No reservations. Max stay 14 days. Phone: (706)747-6928.

(W) LAKE NOTTELY RV PARK—(Union) *From jct US 76 & US 19/129: Go 2-1/2 mi W on US 76, then 1-1/4 mi N on Kiutuestia Creek Rd. Enter on R.*

◇◇◇◇FACILITIES: 80 sites, 80 full hkups, (30 & 50 amps), mostly extended stay sites (in summer), 1 pull-thrus, wireless Internet access central location, laundry, ice, tables, patios, fire rings, wood.

◇◇◇RECREATION: equipped pavilion, boating, canoeing, kayaking, ramp, dock, lake fishing, golf nearby, horseshoes.

Pets welcome. Partial handicap access. No tents. Open Apr 1 thru Dec 1. Big rigs welcome. Internet friendly. Clubs welcome. Rate in 2007 $22-24 for 2 persons. Member ARVC. Phone: (706)745-4523. FMCA discount.

e-mail: lnrv@windstream.net

SEE AD THIS PAGE

BLAIRSVILLE—Continued

(W) MOUNTAIN CREEK RV RESORT (TOO NEW TO RATE)—(Union) *From jct GA Hwy 515 & US 76: Go 2-1/4 mi W on US 76 (Blue Ridge Hwy). From jct Ga Hwy 515 & Kiutuestia Creek Rd: Go 1-1/4 mi S on Kiutuestia Creek Rd, then 1/2 mi E on Blue Ridge Hwy. Enter on L.*

FACILITIES: 128 sites, typical site width 40 ft, 128 full hkups, (20, 30 & 50 amps), 28 pull-thrus, cable TV, wireless Instant Internet access at site, phone/cable on-site Internet access (needs activ), wireless Internet access central location, cabins, RV storage, laundry, ltd groceries, RV supplies, ice, patios.

RECREATION: rec hall, rec room/area, equipped pavilion, swim pool, whirlpool, stream fishing, fishing supplies, putting green, golf nearby, bsktball, 2 shuffleboard courts, planned activities, tennis, horseshoes, sports field, v-ball.

Pets welcome. Partial handicap access. No tents. Open all yr. Big rigs welcome. Internet friendly. Escort to site. Clubs welcome. Rate in 2007 $45-55 for 2 persons. MC/VISA/Debit. Phone: (706) 745-5600.

SEE AD TRAVEL SECTION PAGE 189

(W) POTEETE CREEK (Union County Park)—(Union) *From jct US-19/129 & Hwy-325: Go 3-1/2 mi W on Hwy-325, then follow signs 1 mi E on county road.* FACILITIES: 59 sites, 59 E, tenting, dump station, laundry, ice, fire rings. RECREATION: pavilion, lake swimming, boating, ramp, lake fishing, horseshoes, hiking trails, v-ball. Open Apr 1 thru Oct 15. Phone: (706)439-6103.

(E) TRACKROCK CAMPGROUND & CABINS—(Union) *From jct US 19/129 & US-76: Go 6-1/2 mi E on US-76, then 2-3/4 mi S on Trackrock Gap Rd, then 1 mi on Trackrock Church Rd. Enter on L.*

◇◇◇◇FACILITIES: 97 sites, 74 full hkups, 23 W&E, (30 & 50 amps), some extended stay sites (in summer), 26 pull-thrus, wireless Instant Internet access at site, phone on-site Internet access (needs activ), wireless Internet access central location, tenting, cabins, RV storage, laundry, LP gas by weight, ice, tables, fire rings, wood.

◇◇◇◇RECREATION: rec hall, pavilion, coin games, lake swimming, lake fishing, golf nearby, bsktball, playground, horseshoes, sports field, hiking trails, v-ball.

Pets welcome. Partial handicap access. Open all yr. Facilities fully operational Apr 1 thru Nov 1. Minimum reservation 2 nights; Holiday weekends require 3 nights. Big rigs welcome. Internet friendly. Clubs welcome. Rate in 2007 $22-27 per family. MC/VISA/Debit. Member ARVC. Phone: (706)745-2420. CCUSA discount.

e-mail: trackroc@windstream.net

SEE AD THIS PAGE

Georgia's State Nicknames: Peach State; Empire State of the South

BLAIRSVILLE—Continued

(E) TRACKROCK STABLES—*From jct US 19/129 & Hwy 180: Go 2-1/2 mi E on Hwy 180, then 2 mi N on Town Creek School Rd, then 2 mi NE on Trackrock Creek Rd. Enter on R.* Guided horseback rides on bridle trails through hills & mountain meadows. Bring your own horse for overnight or longer stay. Riding lessons available. Children are welcome. Summer Horse camp available. Open all yr. MC/VISA/DISC/AMEX/Debit. Phone: (800)826-0073.

SEE AD THIS PAGE

(S) VOGEL STATE PARK—(Union) *From jct US 76 & US 129/19: Go 11 mi S on US 129/19. Enter on R.*

FACILITIES: 121 sites, 103 W&E, (30 & 50 amps), 18 no hkups, 20 pull-thrus, phone Internet access central location, tenting, cabins, dump station, non-guest dumping $, laundry, ltd groceries, ice, tables, fire rings, grills, wood.

RECREATION: pavilion, lake swimming, 26 pedal boat rentals, lake fishing, fishing supplies, mini-golf ($), playground, planned activities, sports field, hiking trails, v-ball. Rec open to public.

Pets welcome. Partial handicap access. Open all yr. Big rigs welcome. Internet friendly. Clubs welcome. MC/VISA/DISC/AMEX. Phone: (800)864-7275.

e-mail: vogel@alltel.net

SEE AD TRAVEL SECTION PAGE 189

BLAKELY—E-1

(N) KOLOMOKI MOUNDS STATE PARK—(Early) *From jct Hwy 62, Hwy 39 & US 27: Go 1-1/2 mi N on US 27, then 6-1/2 mi N on SR 1940. Enter on R.*

FACILITIES: 43 sites, typical site width 30 ft, 43 W&E, (30 & 50 amps), 12 pull-thrus, tenting, dump station, non-guest dumping $, laundry, ice, tables, fire rings, grills, wood.

RECREATION: pavilion, swim pool, boating, 10 hp limit, canoeing, kayaking, ramp, dock, 5 rowboat/4 canoe/3 pedal boat rentals, lake/stream fishing, mini-golf ($), playground, sports field, hiking trails, v-ball. Rec open to public.

KOLOMOKI MOUNDS STATE PARK—Continued on next page

The name of the famous south Georgia swamp, the Okeefenokee, is derived from an Indian word meaning "the trembling earth".

BLAKELY—Continued
KOLOMOKI MOUNDS STATE PARK—Continued

Pets welcome. Partial handicap access. Open all yr. Big rigs welcome. Clubs welcome. MC/VISA/DISC/AMEX. Phone: (800) 864-7275.

e-mail: kolomoki@alltel.net

SEE AD TRAVEL SECTION PAGE 189

BLUE RIDGE—A-2

(SW) CHATTAHOOCHE NATIONAL FOREST (Mulky) —(Union) *From town: Go E 4.5 mi on Hwy 76 to Hwy 60, then S 16 mi to FR.4, then NE 4.9 mi on FR-4. Enter at end.* FACILITIES: 11 sites, typical site width 15 ft, 20 ft max RV length, 11 no hkups, non-flush toilets only, grills. RECREATION: stream fishing. Open Mar 26 thru Oct 31. No reservations. No showers. Max stay 14 days. Phone: (706)632-3031.

(E) CHATTAHOOCHE NATIONAL FOREST (Lake Blue Ridge Campground)—(Union) *From town: Go 1-1/2 mi E on Old US 76, then 3 mi S on Dry Branch Rd.* FACILITIES: 58 sites, 28 ft max RV length, 58 no hkups, cold showers only, grills. RECREATION: boating, ramp, lake fishing, hiking trails. Open Mid April thru Oct 31. Phone: (706)632-3031.

(E) Whispering Pines Campground—(Fannin) *From jct Hwy 5 & US 76: Go 8-3/4 mi E on US 76/515 (Appalachian Hwy), then 1000 feet S on Whispering Pines Rd.(CAUTION! STEEP GRADE & SHARP TURN AT ENTRANCE) Enter on R.* ◊◊◊FACILITIES: 30 sites, typical site width 25 ft, 19 full hkups, 11 W&E, (20, 30 & 50 amps), some extended stay sites, 3 pull-thrus, tenting, laundry, ice, tables, wood. ◊◊◊RECREATION: pavilion, swim pool, stream fishing, play equipment, hiking trails, v-ball. Rec open to public. Pets welcome. Partial handicap access. Open all yr. Internet friendly. Rate in 2007 $19-25 for 2 persons. Member ARVC, GARVC. Phone: (706)374-6494.

The "Little White House" in Warm Springs, is where Franklin D. Roosevelt died.

BRUNSWICK—E-5

(W) BLYTHE ISLAND REGIONAL PARK CAMPGROUND—(Glynn) *From jct I-95 (exit 29) & US 17: Go 1/2 mi W on US 17, then 2-3/4 mi NE on Hwy 303. Enter on R.*

FACILITIES: 97 sites, typical site width 28 ft, 40 full hkups, 57 W&E, (20, 30 & 50 amps), some extended stay sites, 32 pull-thrus, cable TV, wireless Instant Internet access at site, wireless Internet access central location, RV storage, dump station, non-guest dumping $, laundry, LP gas by weight/by meter, ice, tables, fire rings, wood, controlled access gate.

RECREATION: pavilion, lake swimming, boating, electric motors only, canoeing, kayaking, ramp, dock, 3 rowboat/6 canoe/6 kayak rentals, saltwater/lake fishing, golf nearby, playground, hiking trails, v-ball. Rec open to public.

Pets welcome. Partial handicap access. No tents. Open all yr. Big rigs welcome. Internet friendly. Clubs welcome. MC/VISA/AMEX/Debit. Phone: (800)343-7855.

SEE AD THIS PAGE

(E) BRUNSWICK/GOLDEN ISLES VISITORS BUREAU—*From jct I-95 (exit 38) & Hwy 25 Spur: Go 4-1/2 mi E on Hwy 25 Spur, then 2 mi S on US 17. Enter on R.*

COME COAST AWHILE!
From Mainland Brunswick discover the charms of St. Simons Island, Sea Island, Little St. Simons Island & Jekyll Island. Miles of beaches, golf, tennis, fishing, boating, casino/cruise ship, shops & galleries. www.BGICVB.com

Information center for Brunswick & Golden Isles (St. Simons Island, Little St. Simons Island, Sea

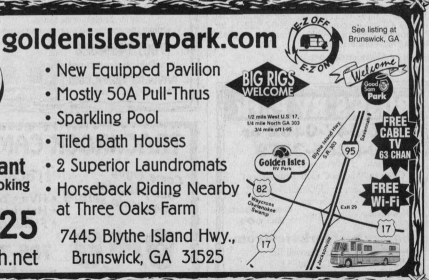

BRUNSWICK—Continued
BRUNSWICK/GOLDEN ISLES VISITORS BUREAU—Continued

Island & Jekyll Island). Welcome Center at US 17 & F.J. Torras Causeway. Open all yr. Phone: (800) 933-2627.

e-mail: visitorsbureau@bgicvb.com

SEE AD TRAVEL SECTION PAGE 193

(W) FRAN'S PLACE RESTAURANT—*From jct I-95 (exit 29) & US 17: Go 1/2 mi W on US 17, then 1/4 mi N on Hwy 303. Enter on L.* Full Service restaurant serving breakfast and lunch featuring country cooking & special menu items. Hrs 730am-2pm weekdays. Friday seafood buffet 5:30pm - 9pm. Open all yr. MC/VISA/DISC/AMEX/Debit. Phone: (912)262-9663.

e-mail: goldenislesrv@bellsouth.net

SEE AD THIS PAGE

(W) GOLDEN ISLES RV PARK—(Glynn) *From jct I-95 (exit 29) & US 17: Go 1/2 mi W on US 17, then 1/4 mi N on Hwy 303. Enter on L.*

ENJOY BRUNSWICK & THE GOLDEN ISLES!
Fresh local seafood prepared at Fran's Place. Beautiful beaches, golf, fishing, sightseeing, historic sites, free 63 channel cable TV, waterpark & cruise ship. Affordable family fun! Come relax by the pool or a campfire! Free WIFI!

◊◊◊FACILITIES: 137 sites, typical site width 21 ft, 126 full hkups, 11 W&E, (20, 30 & 50 amps), 50 amps ($), some extended stay sites, 88 pull-thrus, cable TV, wireless Instant Internet access at site, phone on-site Internet access (needs activ), cable Internet access central location, tenting, cabins, RV storage, dump station, non-guest dumping $, laundry, ltd groceries, RV supplies, LP gas by weight/by meter, ice, tables, fire rings, wood.

◊◊◊◊RECREATION: rec room/area, equipped pavilion, swim pool, golf nearby, bsktball, playground, shuffleboard court, horseshoes, sports field, v-ball.

Pets welcome. Partial handicap access. Open all yr. Big rigs welcome. Internet friendly. Clubs welcome. Rate in 2007 $30 for 2 persons. MC/VISA/DISC/AMEX/Debit. Phone: (912)261-1025. CCUSA discount.

e-mail: goldenislesrv@bellsouth.net

SEE AD THIS PAGE

(W) THREE OAKS FARM—*From jct I-95 (exit 29) & US 17/82: Go 2 mi W on US 82, then 1/4 mi N on Emanuel Church Rd, then 1 block E on Fish Hall Rd, then 1/2 mi N on Oyster Rd to entrance at Oyster Rd Extn. Enter on R.* 50 acre equine facility. Boarding, lessons, horseback riding, horse sales & leasing. Specializing in Hunter Jumpers,

THREE OAKS FARM—Continued on next page

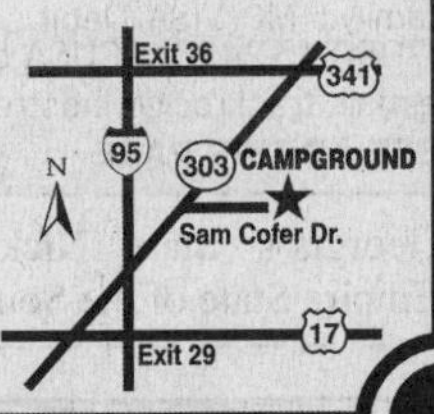

BRUNSWICK—Continued
THREE OAKS FARM—Continued

Dressage & Western Trail rides on beach & Forest. Horse transport available. Open all yr. Phone: (912)269-0623.

e-mail: tlcrum1@aol.com

SEE AD PAGE 202

BUFORD—B-2

(NW) CHESTNUT RIDGE PARK (COE-Lake Sidney Lanier)—(Forsyth) *From jct I-985 (exit 1/4) & Hwy 20: Go 2 mi W on Hwy 20, then 2-1/2 mi N on Peachtree Industrial Blvd, then 3/4 mi W on Gaines Ferry Rd, then N on Chestnut Ridge Rd. Enter at end.* FACILITIES: 84 sites, typical site width 12 ft, 51 W&E, (30 amps), 33 no hkups, 4 pull-thrus, tenting, dump station, laundry, fire rings, grills. RECREATION: lake swimming, boating, canoeing, ramp, dock, lake fishing, playground. Partial handicap access. Open Apr 26 thru Sep 10. Phone: (770)967-6710.

(N) Lake Lanier Islands Campground—(Forsyth) *From jct I-985 (exit 8) & Hwy 347: Go 4-1/2 mi NW on Hwy 347. Enter at end.* ◊◊◊◊FACILITIES: 147 sites, typical site width 25 ft, 58 full hkups, 79 W&E, (20 & 30 amps), 10 no hkups, 59 pull-thrus, tenting, dump station, laundry, ltd groceries, LP gas by meter, ice, tables, fire rings, grills, wood. ◊◊◊◊RECREATION: rec room/area, pavilion, lake swimming, boating, canoeing, ramp, dock, 90 motorboat rentals, lake fishing, mini-golf ($), play equipment, sports field, hiking trails, v-ball. Rec open to public. Pets welcome. Open all yr. Max stay 30 days in 60 day period. Rate in 2007 $33-42 for 2 persons. Phone: (770)932-7270.

(W) SHOAL CREEK CAMPING AREA (COE-Lake Sidney Lanier)—(Guinnett) *From jct I-985 (exit 1/4) & Hwy 20: Go 2 mi W on Hwy 20, then 2 mi N on Peachtree Industrial Blvd, then 1 mi NW on Shadburn Ferry Rd. Enter at end.* FACILITIES: 103 sites, typical site width 12 ft, 103 W&E, (30 amps), 14 pull-thrus, tenting, dump station, laundry, fire rings, grills, wood. RECREATION: lake swimming, boating, canoeing, ramp, dock, lake fishing, playground. Partial handicap access. Open Apr 1 thru Oct 9. No reservations. Phone: (770)945-9541.

BYRON—D-2

(E) INTERSTATE RV CAMPGROUND—(Peach) *From jct I-75 (exit 149) & Hwy 49: Go 500 ft W on Hwy 49, then 1/2 mi N on Chapman Rd. Enter on L.*

WELCOME

◊◊◊FACILITIES: 105 sites, typical site width 25 ft, 105 full hkups, (30 & 50 amps), many extended stay sites, 53 pull-thrus, heater not allowed, cable TV, phone on-site Internet access (needs activ), phone Internet access central location, RV storage, laundry, RV supplies, LP gas by weight/by meter, ice, tables.

◊◊RECREATION: pavilion, swim pool, golf nearby, play equipment, sports field.

Pets welcome. No tents. Open all yr. Big rigs welcome. Internet friendly. Clubs welcome. Rate in 2007 $22 for 2 persons. MC/VISA/DISC. Phone: (888)817-0906.

e-mail: irvcenter@alltel.net

SEE AD MACON PAGE 210

✽ **(E) INTERSTATE RV CENTER**—*From jct I-75 (exit 149) & Hwy 49: Go 500 fti W on US 49, then 1/2 mi N on Chapman Rd. Enter on L.* SERVICES: full-time mech, engine/chassis repair, RV appliance repair, body work/collision repair, LP gas by weight/by meter, RV storage, sells parts/accessories, installs hitches. Open all yr. MC/VISA/DISC/AMEX. Phone: (888)817-0906.

WELCOME

e-mail: irvcenter@alltel.net

SEE AD MACON PAGE 210

✽ **(E) MID-STATE RV CENTER**—*From jct I-75 (exit 149) & Hwy 49: Go 1/4 Mi E on Hwy 49,then 1/4 mi N on Peachtree Pkwy. Enter on L.* SALES: travel trailers, 5th wheels, motor homes, mini-motor homes, fold-down camping trailers, pre-owned unit sales. SERVICES: full-time mech, engine/chassis repair, RV appliance repair, body work/collision repair, bus. hrs emerg rd svc, RV towing, LP gas by weight/by meter, dump station, sells parts/accessories, installs hitches. Open all yr. MC/VISA/DISC/AMEX. Phone: (866) 293-9821.

WELCOME

e-mail: sales@midstaterv.com

SEE AD MACON PAGE 210

CALHOUN—B-1

(E) KOA-Calhoun—(Gordon) *From jct I-75 (exit 315) & Hwy 156: Go 1 1/2 mi E on Hwy 156. Enter on R.* ◊◊◊◊FACILITIES: 89 sites, typical site width 25 ft, 27 full hkups, 62 W&E, (15, 20, 30 & 50 amps), some extended stay sites, 50 pull-thrus, tenting, dump station, non-guest dumping $, laundry, ltd groceries, LP gas by weight/by meter, ice, tables, grills. ◊◊◊◊RECREATION: rec hall, pavilion, swim pool,

CALHOUN—Continued
KOA-Calhoun—Continued

pond fishing, mini-golf ($), playground, horseshoes, v-ball. Pets welcome. Partial handicap access. Open all yr. Big rigs welcome. Internet friendly. Rate in 2007 $30-45 for 2 persons. Member ARVC. Phone: (800) 562-7512. KOA 10% value card discount.

CANTON—B-2

(W) SWEETWATER CAMPGROUND (Allatoona Lake COE)—(Cherokee) *From town: Go 5-1/2 mi W on Hwy-20, then 2 mi S at Sweetwater Corner Store.* FACILITIES: 151 sites, typical site width 20 ft, 2 full hkups, 107 W&E, (30 amps), 42 no hkups, 10 pull-thrus, tenting, dump station, laundry, fire rings, grills. RECREATION: pavilion, lake swimming, boating, ramp, dock, lake fishing, playground. Partial handicap access. Open Apr 1 thru Sep 5. Phone: (678)721-6700.

CARROLLTON—C-1

(W) JOHN TANNER STATE PARK—(Carroll) *From jct US 27 & Hwy 16: Go 6 mi W on Hwy 16, then 1/2 mi S on Tanner Beach Rd. Enter at end.*

WELCOME

FACILITIES: 32 sites, typical site width 25 ft, 32 W&E, (20 & 30 amps), 6 pull-thrus, cable TV, tenting, dump station, non-guest dumping $, laundry, ice, tables, fire rings, grills, controlled access gate.

RECREATION: pavilion, lake swimming, boating, electric motors only, canoeing, kayaking, 4 rowboat/4 canoe/8 pedal boat rentals, lake fishing, mini-golf ($), golf nearby, playground, planned activities (wkends only), hiking trails, v-ball. Rec open to public.

Pets welcome. Partial handicap access. Open all yr. Clubs welcome. MC/VISA/DISC/AMEX/DC. Phone: (800) 864-7275.

e-mail: j_tanner@dnr.state.ga.us

SEE AD TRAVEL SECTION PAGE 189

CARTERSVILLE—B-1

(S) ALLATOONA LANDING MARINE RESORT & CAMPGROUND—(Bartow) *From jct I-75 (exit 283) & Emerson/Allatoona Rd: Go 2 mi E on Allatoona Landing Rd. Enter on L.*

WELCOME

◊◊◊◊FACILITIES: 120 sites, typical site width 25 ft, 17 full hkups, 103 W&E, (30 & 50 amps), some extended stay sites, 16 pull-thrus, cable TV, wireless Instant Internet access at site, phone Internet access central location, tenting, RV/park trailer rentals, RV storage, dump station, non-guest dumping $, portable dump, laundry, groceries, RV supplies, LP gas by weight/by meter, marine gas, ice, tables, fire rings, wood, controlled access gate.

◊◊◊◊RECREATION: rec hall, swim pool, lake swimming, boating, canoeing, kayaking, ramp, dock, lake fishing, fishing supplies, golf nearby, bsktball, playground, horseshoes, hiking trails, v-ball.

Pets welcome, breed restrict. Partial handicap access. Open all yr. Big rigs welcome. Internet friendly. Clubs welcome. Rate in 2007 $24-38 for 6 persons. MC/VISA/DISC/AMEX/Debit. Member ARVC. Phone: (800)346-7305.

e-mail: campground@allatoonalandingmarina.com

SEE AD ATLANTA PAGE 200

(N) Cartersville KOA—(Bartow) *From jct I-75 (exit 296) & Cass-White Rd: Go 1/4 mi W on Cass-White Rd. Enter on L.* ◊◊◊◊FACILITIES: 101 sites, typical site width 25 ft, 62 full hkups, 39 W&E, (30 & 50 amps), some extended stay sites, 91 pull-thrus, tenting, dump station, non-guest dumping $, laundry, ltd groceries, LP gas by weight/by meter, ice, tables. ◊◊RECREATION: rec hall, pavilion, swim pool, play equipment, sports field. Pets welcome, breed restrict. Open all yr. Big rigs welcome. Internet friendly. Rate in 2007 $25-35 for 2 persons. Member ARVC. Phone: (800)KOA-2841. KOA 10% value card discount.

(E) MCKASKEY CAMPGROUND (COE-Allatoona Lake) —(Bartow) *From jct I-75 (exit 125/290) & Hwy 20 Spur: Go 2 mi S on Hwy 20 Spur, then E on access road.* FACILITIES: 51 sites, typical site width 20 ft, 32 W&E, (30 amps), 19 no hkups, 2 pull-thrus, tenting, dump station, laundry, fire rings, grills. RECREATION: lake swimming, boating, ramp, dock, lake fishing, playground. Partial handicap access. Open Mar 31 thru Sep 5. No reservations. Phone: (678)721-6700.

(N) MILITARY PARK (Ft. McPherson-Lk Allatoona Army Rec Area)—(Bartow) *From I-75 (exit 122/283): Go 2-3/4 mi E off exit, then 1 block S on Old Sandtown Rd, then bear left and follow signs to office. Off Base: 45 mi N of Ft. McPherson.* FACILITIES: 20 sites, 12 full hkups, 8 W&E, tenting, dump station, laundry, ice, fire rings, grills. RECREATION: rec room/area, equipped pavilion, lake swimming, boating, ramp, dock, lake fishing, mini-golf ($), playground, hiking trails, v-ball. No pets. Open all yr. For Military Use Only-w/Military ID Card. Phone: (770)974-3413.

Georgia State Gem: Quartz

CARTERSVILLE—Continued

(E) RED TOP MOUNTAIN STATE PARK—(Bartow) *From I-75 (exit 285) & Red Top Mountain Rd: Go 3 mi E on Red Top Mountain Rd. Enter on L.*

WELCOME

FACILITIES: 92 sites, 68 W&E, (20, 30 & 50 amps), 24 no hkups, 12 pull-thrus, tenting, cabins, dump station, ice, tables, fire rings, grills, wood.

RECREATION: pavilion, lake swimming, boating, canoeing, kayaking, ramp, dock, lake fishing, mini-golf ($), playground, tennis, hiking trails. Rec open to public.

Pets welcome. Partial handicap access. Open all yr. Big rigs welcome. Clubs welcome. MC/VISA/DISC/AMEX/DC. Phone: (800) 864-7275.

SEE AD TRAVEL SECTION PAGE 189

CAVE SPRING—B-1

(N) CEDAR CREEK PARK RV & DRIVING RANGE—(Floyd) *From jct US 411 & US 27: Go 14 mi S on US 411. Enter on R.*

WELCOME

◊◊◊FACILITIES: 86 sites, typical site width 30 ft, 62 full hkups, 24 W&E, (20, 30 & 50 amps), some extended stay sites, 10 pull-thrus, wireless Instant Internet access at site, wireless Internet access central location, tenting, RV storage, dump station, non-guest dumping $, laundry, ltd groceries, RV supplies, LP gas by weight/by meter, LP bottle exch, ice, tables, fire rings, grills, wood.

◊◊◊RECREATION: equipped pavilion, river swimming, boating, canoeing, kayaking, ramp, dock, 5 canoe/5 kayak rentals, float trips, river fishing, fishing supplies, golf nearby, bsktball, planned activities (wkends only), horseshoes, sports field, v-ball.

Pets welcome. Partial handicap access. Open all yr. Big rigs welcome. Internet friendly. Escort to site. Clubs welcome. Rate in 2007 $18-20 for 5 persons. MC/VISA/DISC/AMEX/Debit. Member ARVC, GARVC. Phone: (706)777-3030.

e-mail: camp@bigcedarcreek.com

SEE AD TRAVEL SECTION PAGE 187

CHATSWORTH—A-1

(NE) CHATTAHOOCHEE NATIONAL FOREST (Lake Conasauga Campground)—(Murray) *From town: Go 4 mi N on US 411 to Eton, then 10 mi E on FR 18, then 10 mi NE on FR 68.* FACILITIES: 34 sites, 22 ft max RV length, 34 no hkups, 2 pull-thrus, tenting, grills. RECREATION: lake swimming, boating, electric motors only, ramp, lake fishing, hiking trails. Partial handicap access. Open Apr 14 thru Oct 29. No showers. No reservations. Max stay 14 days. Phone: (706)695-6736.

(S) FORT MOUNTAIN STATE PARK—(Murray) *From jct US 411 & Hwy 52/2 (in town): Go 7-1/4 mi E on Hwy 52/2.*

WELCOME

FACILITIES: 74 sites, 70 W&E, (30 & 50 amps), 4 no hkups, 35 pull-thrus, cable TV, tenting, cabins, dump station, non-guest dumping $, laundry, ice, tables, fire rings, grills, wood.

RECREATION: pavilion, lake swimming, canoeing, kayaking, 4 rowboat/20 pedal boat rentals, lake fishing, mini-golf ($), golf nearby, playground, hiking trails. Rec open to public.

Pets welcome. Partial handicap access. Open all yr. Big rigs welcome. Clubs welcome. MC/VISA/DISC/AMEX. Phone: (800) 864-7275.

e-mail: fortmnt@alltel.net

SEE AD TRAVEL SECTION PAGE 189

(SE) WOODRING BRANCH PUBLIC USE AREA (COE-Carters Lake)—(Gilmer) *From town: Go 20 mi S on US 411 & follow signs.* FACILITIES: 42 sites, typical site width 20 ft, 31 W&E, (20 & 30 amps), 11 no hkups, tenting, dump station, portable dump, laundry, fire rings, grills. RECREATION: boating, ramp, lake fishing, playground, planned activities, horseshoes, hiking trails. Rec open to public. Partial handicap access. Open Apr 7 thru Oct 28. Phone: (706)276-6050.

CLARKESVILLE—A-3

(N) MOCCASIN CREEK STATE PARK—(Rabun) *From jct Hwy 197 & US 441/23: Go 25 mi N on Hwy 197. Enter on R.*

WELCOME

FACILITIES: 55 sites, 55 W&E, (30 amps), 12 pull-thrus, tenting, dump station, non-guest dumping $, laundry, ice, tables, fire rings, grills, wood.

RECREATION: pavilion, boating, canoeing, kayaking, ramp, dock, 8 canoe rentals, lake/stream fishing, playground, hiking trails, v-ball. Rec open to public.

MOCCASIN CREEK STATE PARK—Continued on next page

Pets welcome. Partial handicap access. Open all yr. Clubs welcome. MC/VISA/DISC/AMEX. Phone: (800) 864-7275.

SEE AD TRAVEL SECTION PAGE 189

CLAYTON—A-3

(NW) CHATTAHOOCHE-OCONEE NATIONAL FOREST-TALLULAH RIVER—(Rabun) *From town: Go 8 mi W on US 76 to County Rd, then 4 mi N to FR-70, then 1 mi NW. Enter on L.* FACILITIES: 17 sites, typical site width 20 ft, 35 ft max RV length, 17 no hkups, 3 pull-thrus, non-flush toilets only, grills. RECREATION: river fishing, hiking trails. Partial handicap access. Open Mar 28 thru Nov 3. No reservations. No showers. Max stay 14 days. Phone: (706)782-3320.

(S) CHATTAHOOCHEE NATIONAL FOREST (Rabun Beach Campground)—(Rabun) *From town: Go 7 mi S on US 441/23, then 1/10 mi W on county road, then 2 mi S on Hwy 15, then 5 mi W on CR 10.* FACILITIES: 80 sites, typical site width 20 ft, 35 ft max RV length, 26 W&E, (20 amps), 54 no hkups, 3 pull-thrus, tenting, dump station, ltd groceries, grills, wood. RECREATION: lake swimming, boating, ramp, lake fishing, hiking trails. Partial handicap access. Open Apr 25 thru Nov 3. No reservations. Max stay 14 days. Phone: (706)782-3320.

(NW) CHATTAHOOCHEE-OCONEE NATIONAL FOREST-SANDY BOTTOM—(Rabun) *From town: Go 8 mi W on US-76 to County Rd, then 4 mi N to FM-70, then 5 mi Nw. Enter on L.* FACILITIES: 12 sites, typical site width 20 ft, 35 ft max RV length, 12 no hkups, non-flush toilets only, grills. RECREATION: river fishing. Open Mar 25 thru Nov 8. No reservations. No showers. Max stay 14 days. Phone: (706)782-3320.

(NW) CHATTAHOOCHEE-OCONEE NATIONAL FOREST-TATE BRANCH—(Raban) *From town: Go 8 mi W on US-76 to County Rd, then 4 mi W to FR-70, then 5 mi NW. Enter on R.* FACILITIES: 18 sites, typical site width 10 ft, 18 no hkups, tenting, non-flush toilets only, grills. RECREATION: river fishing. Open Mar 28 thru Nov 3. No Reservations. No showers. Max stay 14 days. Phone: (706)782-3320.

CLEVELAND—A-2

(N) Timber Ridge Resort in Mountain Lakes Resort—(White) *From Jct Hwy 129 & Alt Hwy 75: Go 2 1/2 mi N on Alt Hwy 75 to Mountain Lakes Resort. Enter on L.* ◇◇◇◇FACILITIES: 90 sites, 90 full hkups, (30 & 50 amps), 1 pull-thrus, tenting, laundry, tables, patios, fire rings, grills, wood. ◇◇◇◇◇RECREATION: rec hall, pavilion, 3 swim pools, boating, electric motors only, ramp, dock, 5 rowboat/7 pedal boat rentals, lake fishing, mini-golf, playground, planned activities, tennis, horseshoes, hiking trails, v-ball. Pets welcome. Open all yr. Rate in 2007 $15 for 2 persons. Phone: (706)865-0495.

(W) Turner Campsites—(Lumpkin) *From jct Hwy 75 & US 129: Go 10 mi NW on US 129, then 200 feet S on US 19. Enter on R.* ◇◇◇FACILITIES: 126 sites, typical site width 30 ft, 126 full hkups, (30 & 50 amps), some extended stay sites (in summer), 52 pull-thrus, laundry, LP gas by weight/by meter, ice, tables, fire rings, wood. ◇◇◇RECREATION: rec hall, pavilion, river swimming, river fishing, playground, sports field, v-ball. Pets welcome. No tents. Open all yr. Facilities fully operational Mar 15 thru Nov 15. Rate in 2007 $20-25 for 2 persons. Phone: (706)865-4757.

Georgia is the nation's number one producer of the three P's: peanuts, pecans, and peaches.

COCHRAN—D-3

(S) HILLSIDE BLUEGRASS RV PARK—(Bleckley) *From jct Alt US 129 & Bus US 23/Bus Ga Hwy 87: Go 2-1/2 mi S on GA Hwy 87. Enter on R.*

◇◇◇FACILITIES: 324 sites, typical site width 25 ft, 24 full hkups, 300 W&E, (30 & 50 amps), 50 pull-thrus, wireless Instant Internet access at site, phone on-site Internet access (needs activ), wireless Internet access central location, tenting, cabins, RV storage, dump station, non-guest dumping $, LP gas by weight/by meter, ice, tables, fire rings, wood.

◇◇◇RECREATION: rec hall, pavilion, pond fishing, golf nearby, bsktball, 3 bike rentals, playground, planned activities (wkends only), horseshoes, sports field, hiking trails.

Pets welcome. Partial handicap access. Open all yr. Big rigs welcome. Internet friendly. Escort to site. Clubs welcome. Rate in 2007 $20-22 per family. MC/VISA/DISC/AMEX/Debit. Member ARVC, GARVC. Phone: (478)934-6694. CCUSA discount. FMCA discount.

e-mail: hillsidervpark@bellsouth.net

SEE AD THIS PAGE

COLQUITT—E-1

(S) EMERALD LAKE RV PARK—(Miller) *From jct US 27 & Hwy 91: Go 5-1/2 mi S on Hwy 91. From jct US 84 & Hwy 91: Go 6 mi N on Hwy 91. (At intersection of Hwy 91 & Enterprise Rd).*

◇◇◇FACILITIES: 35 sites, typical site width 30 ft, 28 full hkups, 7 W&E, (20, 30 & 50 amps), some extended stay sites, 18 pull-thrus, wireless Instant Internet access at site, phone on-site Internet access (needs activ), wireless Internet access central location, tenting, RV/park trailer rentals, RV storage, dump station, non-guest dumping $, laundry, RV supplies, ice, tables, patios, grills, wood.

◇◇◇RECREATION: rec hall, rec room/area, pavilion, equipped pavilion, coin games, swim pool, boating, no motors, canoeing, kayaking, dock, pond fishing, fishing supplies, golf nearby, playground, horseshoes, sports field.

Pets welcome. Partial handicap access. Open all yr. Big rigs welcome. Internet friendly. Escort to site. Clubs welcome. Rate in 2007 $30 for 2 persons. MC/VISA. Phone: (888)758-9929. CCUSA discount.

e-mail: dcmathis@hughes.net

SEE AD THIS PAGE

COLUMBUS—D-1

(N) BLANTON CREEK PARK (Georgia Power)—(Harris) *From jct I-185 (exit 25) & Hwy 116: Go 1,000 feet W on Hwy 116, then 3-1/2 mi W on Hwy 103, then 1/4 mi S on Lickskillet Rd, then 3/4 mi W on Silva Dr. Enter on R.*

◇◇◇◇FACILITIES: 51 sites, typical site width 40 ft, 43 W&E, 8 E, (20, 30 & 50 amps), 2 pull-thrus, tenting, dump station, laundry, ice, tables, fire rings, grills, controlled access gate.

◇◇◇RECREATION: pavilion, lake swimming, boating, canoeing, kayaking, ramp, dock, lake fishing, golf nearby, playground, horseshoes, v-ball. Rec open to public.

Pets welcome. Partial handicap access. Open Mar thru Sep. Big rigs welcome. Clubs welcome. Rate in 2007 $18 per vehicle. Phone: (706)643-7737.

SEE AD TRAVEL SECTION PAGE 192

Georgia State Flower: Cherokee Rose

(E) LAKE PINES EVENT CENTER—*From jct I-185 & US 80: Go 9-1/2 mi E on US 80 (between milepost 12 & 13), then 1/4 mi S on Garrett Rd. Enter on L.* Specializing in weddings, family reunions, clubs & special meetings & gatherings. Open all yr. Phone: (706)561-9675.

SEE AD THIS PAGE

(E) LAKE PINES RV PARK & CAMPGROUND—(Muscogee) *From jct I-185 & US 80: Go 9-1/2 mi E on US 80, between milepost 12 & 13, then 1/4 mi S on Garrett Rd. Enter on L.*

◇◇◇◇FACILITIES: 75 sites, typical site width 25 ft, 65 full hkups, 10 W&E, (20, 30 & 50 amps), some extended stay sites (in winter), 37 pull-thrus, wireless Instant Internet access at site, phone on-site Internet access (needs activ), wireless Internet access central location, tenting, RV storage, dump station, non-guest dumping $, laundry, LP gas by weight/by meter, tables.

◇◇RECREATION: rec hall, swim pool, golf nearby, horseshoes, hiking trails.

Pets welcome. Open all yr. Big rigs welcome. Internet friendly. Escort to site. Clubs welcome. Rate in 2007 $28-30 for 2 persons. Member ARVC, GARVC. Phone: (706)561-9675.

SEE AD THIS PAGE

COMER—B-3

(S) WATSON MILL BRIDGE STATE PARK—(Oglethorpe) *From jct Hwy 72 & Hwy 22: Go 2-3/4 mi S on Hwy 22, then 3-1/2 mi E on Watson Mill Rd. Enter at end.*

FACILITIES: 21 sites, 21 W&E, (30 amps), 18 pull-thrus, tenting, dump station, non-guest dumping $, laundry, ice, tables, fire rings, grills, wood.

RECREATION: pavilion, river swimming, canoeing, kayaking, 9 canoe/3 pedal boat rentals, river fishing, golf nearby, playground, hiking trails, v-ball. Rec open to public.

Pets welcome. Partial handicap access. Open all yr. MC/VISA/DISC/AMEX. Phone: (800)864-7275.

e-mail: watson@negia.net

SEE AD TRAVEL SECTION PAGE 189

COMMERCE—B-3

(S) Country Boy's RV Park—(Jackson) *From jct I-85 (exit 149) & US 441: Go 1-1/2 mi S on US 441, then 1/4 mi W on Mt. Olive Rd. Enter on R.* ◇◇◇FACILITIES: 69 sites, typical site width 20 ft, 60 full hkups, 9 W&E, (20, 30 & 50 amps), 50 amps ($), some extended stay sites, 35 pull-thrus, laundry, ice, tables, fire rings, wood. ◇◇RECREATION: rec room/area, swim pool, playground, horseshoes, sports field. Pets welcome. No tents. Open all yr. Big rigs welcome. Internet friendly. Rate in 2007 $20 for 2 persons. Phone: (888)335-6130.

(N) The Pottery Campground—(Jackson) *From jct I-85 (exit 149) & US 441: Go 1000 feet S on US 441, then 1/4 mi W on Pottery Rd Enter on R.* ◇◇◇FACILITIES: 52 sites, typical site width 25 ft, 52 full hkups, (20 & 30 amps), 11 pull-thrus, tables, patios, grills. RECREATION: pavilion. Pets welcome. Partial handicap access. No tents. Open all yr. Rate in 2007 $22 for 2 persons. Phone: (800)223-0667. CCUSA discount.

With an elevation of 4,784 feet, Brasstown Bald Mountain is the highest point in Georgia.

CORDELE—D-2

(S) Cordele KOA—(Crisp) *From jct I-75 (exit 97) & Hwy 33 Conn: Go 1/4 mi W on Hwy 33 Conn. Enter on R.* ◆◆◆◆FACILITIES: 67 sites, typical site width 35 ft, 31 full hkups, 29 W&E, (20, 30 & 50 amps), 50 amps ($), 7 no hkups, 51 pull-thrus, tenting, dump station, non-guest dumping $, laundry, groceries, LP gas by weight/by meter, ice, tables, grills. ◆◆◆RECREATION: rec room/area, swim pool, playground, 2 shuffleboard courts, horseshoes, sports field, v-ball. Pets welcome. Partial handicap access. Open all yr. Rate in 2007 $26-30 for 2 persons. Phone: (229)273-5454. KOA 10% value card discount.

(S) Cordele RV Park—(Crisp) *From jct I-75 (exit 97) & Hwy 33 Conn: Go 500 feet E on Hwy 33 Conn, then 1/2 mi S on Floyd Rd. Enter on L.* ◆◆◆FACILITIES: 110 sites, typical site width 25 ft, 110 full hkups, (30 & 50 amps), 50 amps ($), some extended stay sites, 110 pull-thrus, tenting, dump station, laundry, ltd groceries, LP gas by weight/by meter, ice, tables, wood. ◆◆◆RECREATION: rec hall, pavilion, swim pool, lake fishing, horseshoes, sports field. Pets welcome. Open all yr. Internet friendly. Rate in 2007 $26 per vehicle. Phone: (229)273-4444. CCUSA discount. FMCA discount.

(W) GEORGIA VETERANS MEMORIAL STATE PARK—(Crisp) *From jct I-75 (exit 101) & US 280/Hwy 30: Go 9 mi W on US 280/Hwy 30. Enter on L.*

WELCOME

FACILITIES: 77 sites, 77 W&E, (30 & 50 amps), 43 pull-thrus, cable TV, tenting, cabins, dump station, laundry, ice, tables, fire rings, grills, wood.

RECREATION: pavilion, swim pool, lake swimming, boating, canoeing, kayaking, ramp, dock, lake fishing, golf nearby, playground, sports field, hiking trails, v-ball. Rec open to public.

Pets welcome. Partial handicap access. Open all yr. Big rigs welcome. Clubs welcome. MC/VISA/DISC/AMEX. Phone: (800) 864-7275.

e-mail: gavetstatepark@yahoo.com

SEE AD TRAVEL SECTION PAGE 189

CORNELIA—B-3

(E) CHATTAHOOCHEE NATIONAL FOREST (Lake Russell Campground)—(Habersham) *From town: Go 1-1/2 mi N on US 123, then 2 mi E on FR 59 (Lake Russell Rd).* FACILITIES: 42 sites, typical site width 12 ft, 35 ft max RV length, 42 no hkups, tenting, dump station, grills. RECREATION: pavilion, lake swimming, boating, electric motors only, canoeing, ramp, lake fishing, horseshoes, hiking trails. Partial handicap access. Open May 19 thru Sep 4. No reservations. Max stay 14 days. Phone: (706)754-6221.

COVINGTON—C-2

(W) RIVERSIDE ESTATES RV PARK—(Newton) *From jct I-20 (exit 88) & Almon Rd: Go 500 ft S on Almon Rd, then 1/2 mi E on south frontage road. Enter on R.*

WELCOME

◆◆FACILITIES: 172 sites, typical site width 25 ft, 172 full hkups, (30 & 50 amps), some extended stay sites, 23 pull-thrus, cable TV, phone on-site Internet access (needs activ), dump station, non-guest dumping $, laundry, LP gas by weight/by meter, ice.

◆◆RECREATION: pavilion, swim pool, river fishing, golf nearby, bsktball, playground, sports field.

Pets welcome. Partial handicap access. No tents. Open all yr. Big rigs welcome. Clubs welcome. Rate in 2007 $25 for 2 persons. MC/VISA. Phone: (770)787-3707.

SEE AD ATLANTA PAGE 200

CRAWFORDVILLE—C-3

(N) ALEXANDER H. STEPHENS STATE HISTORIC PARK—(Taliaferro) *From jct I-20 (exit 148) & Hwy 22: Go 2 mi N on Hwy 22, then 3/4 mi E on US 278. Enter on R.*

WELCOME

FACILITIES: 25 sites, typical site width 20 ft, 25 W&E, (20, 30 & 50 amps), 6 pull-thrus, tenting, cabins, dump station, non-guest dumping $, laundry, ice, tables, fire rings, grills, wood.

RECREATION: pavilion, swim pool, boating, electric motors only, ramp, 4 rowboat/2 canoe/6 pedal boat rentals, lake/pond fishing, playground, hiking trails, v-ball. Rec open to public.

Pets welcome. Partial handicap access. Open all yr. Clubs welcome. MC/VISA/DISC/AMEX. Phone: (800)864-7275.

e-mail: ah_stephens_park@mail.dnr.state.ga.us

SEE AD TRAVEL SECTION PAGE 189

CUMMING—B-2

(E) BALD RIDGE (COE-Lake Sidney Lanier)—(Forsyth) *From US 19/Hwy 400 (exit 16): Go 1 mi E and 1 mi S on Pilgrim Mill Rd, then 1/2 mi SW on Sinclair Shoals Rd, then E on Bald*

CUMMING—Continued
BALD RIDGE (COE-Lake Sidney Lanier)—Continued

Ridge Rd. Enter at end. FACILITIES: 82 sites, typical site width 25 ft, 82 W&E, (30 amps), 15 pull-thrus, tenting, dump station, laundry, fire rings, grills, wood. RECREATION: lake swimming, boating, canoeing, ramp, dock, lake fishing, playground. Partial handicap access. Open Mar 29 thru Oct 28. Phone: (770)889-1591.

(E) BOLDING MILL (COE-Lake Sidney Lanier)—(Hall) *From US 19/Hwy 400 (exit 17): Go 6 mi E on Hwy 306, then 4-1/2 mi NE on Hwy 53, then 1/2 mi N on Sardis Rd, then 3-1/2 mi W on Chestatee Rd. Enter at end.* FACILITIES: 97 sites, typical site width 12 ft, 88 W&E, (30 amps), 9 no hkups, 5 pull-thrus, tenting, dump station, laundry, fire rings, grills. RECREATION: lake swimming, boating, ramp, lake fishing, playground. Partial handicap access. Open Apr 26 thru Sep 10. Phone: (770)532-3650.

(SE) SAWNEE CAMPGROUND (COE-Lake Sidney Lanier)—(Forsyth) *From US 19/Hwy 400 (exit 14): Go 1/2 mi E on Hwy 20, then 1/2 mi N on Sanders Rd, then 2-1/2 mi E on Buford Dam Rd. Enter on L.* FACILITIES: 55 sites, typical site width 12 ft, 44 W&E, (30 amps), 11 no hkups, 6 pull-thrus, tenting, dump station, laundry, fire rings, grills, wood. RECREATION: lake swimming, boating, canoeing, ramp, dock, lake fishing, playground. Partial handicap access. Open Apr 1 thru Sep 10. No reservations. Phone: (770)887-0592.

(NE) SHADY GROVE PARK (COE-Lake Sidney Lanier)—(Forsyth) *From jct US 19/Hwy 400 & Hwy 369: Go 1 mi E on Hwy 369, then 2-1/2 mi SE on Shady Grove Rd. Enter at end.* FACILITIES: 126 sites, typical site width 12 ft, 76 W&E, (30 amps), 50 no hkups, tenting, dump station, laundry, fire rings, grills, wood. RECREATION: lake swimming, boating, canoeing, ramp, dock, lake fishing, playground. Partial handicap access. Open Apr 26 thru Sep 10. Phone: (770)887-2067.

(S) TWIN LAKES RV PARK—(Forsyth) *From jct US 19/Hwy 400 (exit 13) & Hwy 141: Go 500 ft N on Hwy 141, then 1 mi W on Hwy 9, then 1/4 mi N on Lake Rd. Enter at end.*

WELCOME

◆◆◆◆FACILITIES: 120 sites, typical site width 25 ft, accepts self-contained units only, 100 full hkups, 20 W&E, (30 & 50 amps), many extended stay sites, 6 pull-thrus, wireless Instant Internet access at site, phone on-site Internet access (needs activ), phone Internet access central location, dump station, non-guest dumping $, LP gas by weight/by meter, tables.

◆RECREATION: lake fishing, golf nearby, horseshoes.

Pets welcome. No tents. Open all yr. No restrooms. Big rigs welcome. Internet friendly. Rate in 2007 $20-25 for 2 persons. Phone: (770)887-4400.

SEE AD ATLANTA PAGE 200

DARIEN—E-5

(W) Inland Harbor RV Park—(McIntosh) *From SE jct I-95 (exit 49) & Hwy 251: Go 1/4 mi E on Hwy 251. Enter on R.* ◆◆◆◆FACILITIES: 50 sites, typical site width 30 ft, 50 full hkups, (20, 30 & 50 amps), some extended stay sites, 40 pull-thrus, laundry, tables. ◆RECREATION: equipped pavilion. Pets welcome. Partial handicap access. No tents. Open all yr. Big rigs welcome. Internet friendly. Rate in 2007 $25-28 for 2 persons. Phone: (912)437-6172.

DAWSONVILLE—B-2

(N) AMICALOLA FALLS STATE PARK & LODGE—(Dawson) *From jct Hwy 9 & Hwy 53: Go 3 mi W on Hwy 53, then 11 mi NW on Hwy 183, then 2 mi E on Hwy 52. (Steep mtn. grade - trailers over 16 ft not recommended). Enter on L.*

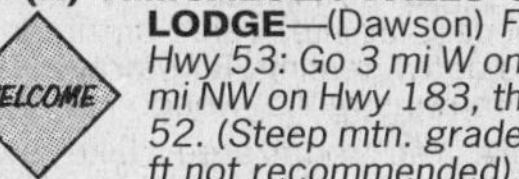

FACILITIES: 24 sites, 24 W&E, (20, 30 & 50 amps), 2 pull-thrus, tenting, cabins, dump station, laundry, ice, tables, patios, fire rings, grills, wood.

RECREATION: pavilion, pond/stream fishing, sports field, hiking trails, v-ball. Rec open to public.

Pets welcome. Partial handicap access. Open all yr. MC/VISA/DISC/AMEX. Phone: (800)864-7275.

SEE AD TRAVEL SECTION PAGE 189

DILLARD—A-3

(N) RIVER VISTA MOUNTAIN VILLAGE—(Rabun) *From jct US 441/23 & Hwy 246: Go 1 mi E on Hwy 246. Enter on R.*

WELCOME

◆◆◆◆◆FACILITIES: 143 sites, typical site width 35 ft, 143 full hkups, (20, 30 & 50 amps), some extended stay sites, 22 pull-thrus, cable TV, phone/wireless Instant Internet access at site ($), cabins, laundry, ltd groceries, LP gas by weight/by meter, ice, tables, grills.

◆◆◆◆RECREATION: rec hall, pavilion, 3 swim pools, whirlpool, golf nearby, bsktball, play equipment, horseshoes.

Pets welcome. Partial handicap access. No tents. Open all yr. Big rigs welcome. Internet friendly. Escort to site. Clubs welcome. Rate in 2007 $34.67-37.50 per vehicle. MC/VISA/DISC/AMEX/Debit. Member ARVC, GARVC. Phone: (888) 850-7275. FMCA discount.

e-mail: relax@rvmountainvillage.com

SEE AD THIS PAGE

DONALSONVILLE—E-1

(S) SEMINOLE STATE PARK—(Seminole) *From jct US 84 & Hwy 39: Go 16 mi S on Hwy 39, then 1/4 mi E on Hwy 253. Enter on R.*

WELCOME

FACILITIES: 50 sites, 50 W&E, (30 & 50 amps), 43 pull-thrus, tenting, cabins, dump station, non-guest dumping $, laundry, ice, tables, fire rings, grills, wood.

RECREATION: rec hall, pavilion, lake swimming, boating, canoeing, kayaking, ramp, dock, 8 canoe/3 kayak/6 pedal boat rentals, lake/pond fishing, mini-golf ($), planned activities, sports field, hiking trails, v-ball. Rec open to public.

Pets welcome. Open all yr. Big rigs welcome. MC/VISA/DISC/AMEX/DC. Phone: (800)864-7275.

e-mail: seminole-park@mail.dnr.state.ga.us

SEE AD TRAVEL SECTION PAGE 189

DOUGLAS—E-3

(N) GENERAL COFFEE STATE PARK—(Coffee) *From jct US 441 & Hwy 32: Go 6 mi E on Hwy 32. Enter on L.*

WELCOME

FACILITIES: 50 sites, 50 W&E, (20 & 30 amps), 51 pull-thrus, tenting, cabins, dump station, non-guest dumping $, laundry, ice, tables, fire rings, grills, wood.

RECREATION: rec hall, equipped pavilion, swim pool, wading pool, canoeing, kayaking, 7 canoe/3 pedal boat rentals, river/pond fishing, 7 bike rentals, playground, planned activities (wkends only), sports field, hiking trails, v-ball. Rec open to public.

Pets welcome. Partial handicap access. Open all yr. Clubs welcome. MC/VISA/DISC/AMEX. Phone: (800) 864-7275.

e-mail: gcpark@charterinternet.com

SEE AD TRAVEL SECTION PAGE 189

DOUGLASVILLE—B-1

✲ **(E) JOHN BLEAKLEY MOTOR HOMES**—*From Jct I-20 (exit 37) & Hwy 92 (Fairburn): Go 1-1/2 mi N on Hwy 92 (Fairburn Rd.), then 2 mi E on US 78(Bankhead Hwy). Enter on R.* SALES: motor homes, pre-owned unit sales. SERVICES: full-time mech, RV appliance repair, dump station. Open all yr. MC/VISA/DISC/AMEX/Debit. Phone: (877)247-3594.

WELCOME

e-mail: sales@bleakleyrv.com

SEE AD TRAVEL SECTION PAGE 189

DOUGLASVILLE—Continued on next page

DOUGLASVILLE—Continued

(E) JOHN BLEAKLEY RV CENTER—*From jct I-20 (exit 37) & Hwy 92 (Fairburn Rd): Go 1 mi N on Hwy 92 (Fairburn Rd). Enter on L.* SALES: van campers, motor homes, mini-motor homes, pre-owned unit sales. SERVICES: full-time mech, engine/chassis repair, RV appliance repair, body work/collision repair, LP gas by weight/by meter, sells parts/accessories, installs hitches. Open all yr. MC/VISA/DISC/AMEX/Debit. Phone: (888)527-8287.

e-mail: sales@bleakleyrv.com

SEE AD TRAVEL SECTION PAGE 189

EATONTON—C-3

(E) LAWRENCE SHOALS PARK (Georgia Power)—(Putnam) *From jct US 129/441 & Hwy 16: Go 14 1/2 mi E on Hwy 16. Enter on L.*

◆◆◆◆FACILITIES: 49 sites, typical site width 30 ft, 49 W&E, (20, 30 & 50 amps), some extended stay sites, tenting, RV storage, dump station, non-guest dumping $, laundry, ice, tables, fire rings, grills, controlled access gate.

◆◆◆RECREATION: pavilion, lake swimming, boating, canoeing, kayaking, ramp, dock, lake fishing, golf nearby, playground, hiking trails. Rec open to public.

Pets welcome. Partial handicap access. Open all yr. Big rigs welcome. Clubs welcome. Rate in 2007 $18 per vehicle. Phone: (706)485-5494.

SEE AD TRAVEL SECTION PAGE 192

(S) OCONEE NATIONAL FOREST (Lake Sinclair Campground)—(Putnam) *From town: Go 10 mi S on US 129, then 1 mi E on Hwy 212, then 2 mi N on FR 1062, follow signs.* FACILITIES: 44 sites, 22 ft max RV length, 5 W&E, 39 no hkups, tenting, dump station, grills. RECREATION: lake swimming, boating, ramp, lake fishing, playground, hiking trails. Open Mar 15 thru Dec 4. No reservations. Max stay 14 days. Phone: (706)485-7110.

(E) OCONEE SPRINGS PARK (Putnam County Park)—(Putnam) *From jct US 129/441 & Hwy 16: Go 10 mi E on Hwy 16, then 1-1/2 mi S on Oconee Springs Rd, then 1-3/4 mi SE on Rockville Rd, then continue 1-3/4 mi on S Spring Rd. Enter on L.* FACILITIES: 40 sites, 37 W&E, (30 amps), 3 no hkups, heater not allowed, tenting, dump station, laundry, ltd groceries, ice, patios, grills. RECREATION: pavilion, lake swimming, boating, canoeing, ramp, dock, lake fishing, playground, horseshoes. Open Feb thru Dec 14. Phone: (706)485-8423.

ELBERTON—B-3

(S) BOBBY BROWN STATE PARK—(Elbert) *From jct Hwy 17 & Hwy 72: Go 12-1/2 mi E on Hwy 72, then 6-1/2 mi S on Bobby Brown Park Rd. Enter at end.*

FACILITIES: 61 sites, 61 W&E, (30 & 50 amps), 7 pull-thrus, tenting, dump station, non-guest dumping $, laundry, ice, tables, fire rings, grills, wood.

RECREATION: pavilion, swim pool, boating, canoeing, kayaking, ramp, dock, 6 canoe/6 pedal boat/2 motorboat rentals, lake fishing, bsktball, playground, sports field, hiking trails. Rec open to public.

Pets welcome. Partial handicap access. Open all yr. Big rigs welcome. Clubs welcome. MC/VISA/DISC/AMEX. Phone: (800)864-7275.

e-mail: bobbyb@elbertonga.net

SEE AD TRAVEL SECTION PAGE 189

Ray Charles, singer, was from Georgia.

ELBERTON—Continued

(N) RICHARD B RUSSELL STATE PARK—(Elbert) *From jct Hwy 17/72 & Hwy 77: Go 2 mi N on Hwy 77, then 8 mi NE on Ruckersville Rd. Enter on R.*

FACILITIES: 28 sites, 28 W&E, (20 & 30 amps), 4 pull-thrus, cable TV, tenting, cabins, dump station, non-guest dumping $, laundry, ice, tables, fire rings, grills, wood.

RECREATION: pavilion, lake swimming, boating, canoeing, kayaking, ramp, dock, 2 pontoon/5 canoe/5 pedal boat rentals, lake fishing, golf nearby, play equipment, hiking trails, v-ball. Rec open to public.

Pets welcome. Partial handicap access. Open all yr. Clubs welcome. MC/VISA/DISC/AMEX. Phone: (800) 864-7275.

e-mail: rbrstpk@elbertonga.com

SEE AD TRAVEL SECTION PAGE 189

ELLIJAY—A-2

(W) DOLL MOUNTAIN CAMPGROUND (COE-Carters Lake)—(Gilmer) *From town: Go 5 mi S on Hwy-5, then 10 mi W on Hwy-382 to Doll Mountainsign, then 1 mi N.* FACILITIES: 66 sites, typical site width 20 ft, 39 W&E, (30 amps), 27 no hkups, 5 pull-thrus, tenting, dump station, portable dump, laundry, ltd groceries, fire rings, grills. RECREATION: lake swimming, ramp, lake fishing, playground, sports field. Rec open to public. Partial handicap access. Open Apr 6 thru Oct 27. Phone: (706)276-4413.

(S) PLUM NELLY CAMPGROUND—(Gilmer) *From jct US 76 & Hwy 515: Go 3-1/2 mi S on Hwy 515. Enter on R.*

◆◆FACILITIES: 32 sites, 32 full hkups, (20, 30 & 50 amps), 28 pull-thrus, wireless Instant Internet access at site, wireless Internet access central location, tenting, cabins, laundry, LP gas by weight/by meter, tables, wood.

◆◆RECREATION: pavilion, pond fishing, golf nearby, bsktball, play equipment.

Pets welcome. Open all yr. Big rigs welcome. Internet friendly. Clubs welcome. Rate in 2007 $21 per vehicle. MC/VISA. Phone: (706)698-7586.

e-mail: plumnellycampground@yahoo.com

SEE AD THIS PAGE

EULONIA—E-5

(W) LAKESIDE RESTAURANT—*From jct I-95 (exit 58) & Hwy 57: Go 1/2 mi W on Hwy 57. Enter on L.* Restaurant open for dinner only. Featuring seafood & local specialties. Food cooked to order. Open all yr. Phone: (912)242-2564.

e-mail: info@mcintoshlakervpark.com

SEE AD THIS PAGE

(W) MCINTOSH LAKE RV PARK—(McIntosh) *From jct I-95 (exit 58) & Hwy 57: Go 1/2 mi W on Hwy 57. Enter on L.*

◆◆◆FACILITIES: 39 sites, typical site width 24 ft, 35 full hkups, 4 W&E, (15, 30 & 50 amps), some extended stay sites (in winter), 22 pull-thrus, cable TV, wireless Instant Internet access at site, cable on-site Internet access (needs activ), tenting, RV storage, laundry, ice, tables, fire rings, grills, wood.

◆◆◆RECREATION: rec room/area, lake swimming, boating, electric motors only, canoeing, kayaking, dock, lake fishing, golf nearby, bsktball, horseshoes.

Pets welcome. Open all yr. Limited lake access. Big rigs welcome. Internet friendly. Clubs welcome. Rate in 2007 $20 per vehicle. Phone: (912) 832-6215.

e-mail: info@mcintoshlakervpark.com

SEE AD THIS PAGE

Oliver Hardy, comedian, was from Georgia.

FARGO—F-4

(E) STEPHEN C. FOSTER STATE PARK—(Charlton) *From jct Hwy-177 & Hwy-94: Go 18 mi NE on Hwy-177. Enter at end.*

FACILITIES: 66 sites, 66 W&E, (30 & 50 amps), 8 pull-thrus, cable TV, tenting, cabins, dump station, non-guest dumping $, laundry, ltd groceries, ice, tables, fire rings, grills, wood.

RECREATION: pavilion, boating, 10 hp limit, canoeing, kayaking, ramp, dock, 5 rowboat/52 canoe/36 motorboat rentals, lake fishing, fishing supplies, bsktball, playground, hiking trails, v-ball. Rec open to public.

Pets welcome. Partial handicap access. Open all yr. Big rigs welcome. MC/VISA/DISC/AMEX. Phone: (800)864-7275.

e-mail: stephen_c_foster@dnr.state.ga.us

SEE AD TRAVEL SECTION PAGE 189

FITZGERALD—E-3

(S) COLONY CITY CAMPGROUND (City Park)—(Turner) *From town: Go S on Perry House Rd, at Paulk Park.* FACILITIES: 36 sites, 6 full hkups, 30 W&E, dump station. RECREATION: boating, electric motors only, canoeing, dock, pond fishing, hiking trails. Open all yr. No showers. Phone: (229)426-5050.

FOLKSTON—F-4

(S) Okefenokee Pastimes Camping & Cabins—(Charlton) *From jct US 1/US 23/US 301 & Hwy 121/23 (Love St.): Go 7-3/4 mi S on Hwy 121/23 (Okefenokee Rd). Enter on L.* ◆◆◆FACILITIES: 22 sites, typical site width 30 ft, 5 full hkups, 7 W&E, (20 & 30 amps), 10 no hkups, 12 pull-thrus, tenting, dump station, non-guest dumping $, laundry, ltd groceries, ice, tables, wood. ◆◆RECREATION: canoeing, 6 canoe rentals, sports field, hiking trails. Pets welcome. Open all yr. Closed Wednesdays. Reservations recommended. Office hrs 2-6pm. Rate in 2007 $20-25 for 2 persons. Phone: (912)496-4472.

(N) OKEFENOKEE RV PARK—(Charlton) *From jct Hwy 40 & US 301: Go 1-1/2 mi N on US 301, then 1/2 mi W on Bowery Ln. Enter on L.*

◆◆◆◆FACILITIES: 52 sites, typical site width 35 ft, 52 full hkups, (20, 30 & 50 amps), 26 pull-thrus, wireless Instant Internet access at site, phone/cable on-site Internet access (needs activ), tenting, RV storage, laundry, groceries, RV supplies, LP gas by meter, ice, tables, patios, wood.

◆◆◆RECREATION: rec hall, rec room/area, equipped pavilion, bsktball, playground, 2 shuffleboard courts, horseshoes, local tours.

Pets welcome, breed restrict. Partial handicap access. Open all yr. Big rigs welcome. Internet friendly. Clubs welcome. Rate in 2007 $22-25 for 2 persons. MC/VISA/Debit. Member ARVC, GARVC. Phone: (912)496-3258. CCUSA discount.

e-mail: info@okefenokeerv.com

SEE AD THIS PAGE

(N) PINE VILLAGE DELI & CONVENIENCE STORE—*From jct Hwy 40 & US 301: Go 1-1/2 mi N on US 301, then 1/2 mi W on Bowery Ln. Enter on L.* Full breakfast, lunch & dinner featuring good home & country cooking. Daily specials & meals cooked to order. Open Mon - Sat 7am - 9pm. Open all yr. MC/VISA/Debit. Phone: (912) 496-3258.

e-mail: info@okefenokeerv.com

SEE AD THIS PAGE

(S) TRADERS HILL RECREATION AREA & CAMPGROUND (Charlton County)—(Charlton) *From jct US 1/23/301 & Hwys 23/40/121: Go 3 mi S on Hwys 23/121, then 1-1/4 mi E on paved road, then 1,000 feet N to park entrance.* FACILITIES: 38 sites, 12 full hkups, (20 & 30 amps), 26 no hkups, tenting, dump station. RECREATION: river swimming, boating, canoeing, ramp, dock, river fishing. Open all yr. Phone: (912)496-3412.

FORSYTH—C-2

(E) FORSYTH KOA—(Monroe) *From jct I-75 (exit 186) & Juliette Rd: Go 100 feet E on Juliette Rd, then 1/4 mi N on Frontage Rd. Enter on R.*

WELCOME

◆◆◆◆◆FACILITIES: 141 sites, typical site width 18 ft, 117 full hkups, 14 W&E, (20, 30 & 50 amps), 10 no hkups, many extended stay sites, 97 pull-thrus, cable TV ($), wireless Instant Internet access at site, phone on-site Internet access (needs activ), wireless Internet access central location, tenting, cabins, dump station, non-guest dumping $, laundry, groceries, RV supplies, LP gas by weight/by meter, ice, tables, wood.

◆◆◆◆RECREATION: rec hall, pavilion, swim pool, 2 pedal boat rentals, pond fishing, fishing supplies, golf nearby, bsktball, 6 bike rentals, playground, horseshoes, v-ball.

Pets welcome. Partial handicap access. Open all yr. Big rigs welcome. Internet friendly. Escort to site. Clubs welcome. Rate in 2007 $25-27 for 2 persons. MC/VISA/DISC/AMEX/Debit. ATM. Member ARVC. Phone: (800)562-8614. KOA 10% value card discount.

e-mail: ke123@msn.com

SEE AD THIS PAGE AND AD DISCOVER SECTION PAGES 62 & 63

(E) L & D RV Park—(Monroe) *From jct I-75 (exit 185) & Hwy 18: Go 2-1/2 mi E on Hwy 18. Enter on R.* ◆◆◆FACILITIES: 29 sites, typical site width 21 ft, 24 full hkups, 5 W&E, (30 & 50 amps), some extended stay sites, 20 pull-thrus, tenting, dump station, non-guest dumping $, laundry, tables, fire rings. ◆◆RECREATION: pavilion, swim pool, horseshoes, sports field, hiking trails. Pets welcome. Partial handicap access. Open all yr. Big rigs welcome. Rate in 2007 $20-23 for 2 persons. Phone: (478)994-5401.

FORT BENNING—D-1

MILITARY PARK (Uchee Creek Army Campground/Marina)—(Muscogee) *From I-185 (exit 1): Go 1-1/4 mi S on I-185 to Fort Benning entrance, then continue 2 mi S to jct of Dixie Rd & Firt Division Rd, then continue 3-3/4 mi SW on Dixie Rd., then follow signs. Enter at end.* FACILITIES: 100 sites, typical site width 40 ft, 72 full hkups, 28 W&E, (20, 30 & 50 amps), 11 pull-thrus, tenting, dump station, laundry, ltd groceries, LP gas by weight/by meter, ice, fire rings, grills, wood. RECREATION: rec

FORT BENNING—Continued
MILITARY PARK (Uchee Creek Army Campground/Marina)—Continued

hall, pavilion, swim pool, boating, canoeing, ramp, dock, 60 canoe/40 motorboat rentals, lake/river fishing, playground, 2 shuffleboard courts, sports field, hiking trails, v-ball. Partial handicap access. Open all yr. Closed Christmas & Thanksgiving. Phone: (706)545-7238.

FORT GAINES—E-1

(N) COTTON HILL PARK (COE-Walter F George Lake)—(Clay) *From jct Hwy 37 & Hwy 39: Go 7 mi N on Hwy 39, then 1-1/2 mi SW on access roads.* FACILITIES: 104 sites, typical site width 40 ft, 94 W&E, (20 & 30 amps), 10 no hkups, 10 pull-thrus, tenting, dump station, laundry, fire rings, grills, wood. RECREATION: pavilion, lake/river swimming, boating, ramp, dock, lake/river fishing, playground, hiking trails. Partial handicap access. Open all yr. Phone: (229)768-3061.

GAINESVILLE—B-2

(W) DUCKETT MILL (COE - Lake Sidney Lanier)—(Hall) *From US 19/Hwy 400 (exit 17): Go E on Hwy 53, then 1-1/2 mi S on Duckett Mill Rd. Follow signs.* FACILITIES: 111 sites, typical site width 12 ft, 97 W&E, (30 amps), 14 no hkups, 9 pull-thrus, tenting, dump station, laundry, fire rings, grills, wood. RECREATION: lake swimming, boating, canoeing, ramp, dock, lake fishing, playground. Partial handicap access. Open Apr 28 thru Sep 9. Phone: (770)532-9802.

(S) OLD FEDERAL ROAD PARK (COE-Lake Sidney Lanier)—(Hall) *From jct Hwy 369 & Hwy 53: Go 2 mi S on Hwy 53/McEver Rd, then 1/2 mi S on McEver Rd, then 2 mi S on Stephens Rd, then 1 mi W on Old Federal Rd.* FACILITIES: 83 sites, typical site width 12 ft, 59 W&E, (30 amps), 24 no hkups, 10 pull-thrus, tenting, dump station, laundry, fire rings, grills. RECREATION: pavilion, lake swimming, boating, canoeing, ramp, dock, lake fishing, playground. Open Mar 29 thru Oct 8. No reservations. Phone: (770)967-6757.

(W) RIVER FORKS PARK AND CAMPGROUND—(Hall) *From jct of Hwy 369 & Hwy 53: Go 1 mi W on Hwy 369, then 1/4 mi N on Keith Bridge Rd. Enter at end.* FACILITIES: 63 sites, typical site width 25 ft, 63 W&E, (30 & 50 amps), 8 pull-thrus, tenting, dump station, ice, fire rings, grills, wood. RECREATION: rec room/area, lake swimming, boating, ramp, dock, lake fishing, playground, horseshoes, v-ball. Pets welcome. Partial handicap access. Open Mar 1 thru Dec 31. Phone: (770)531-3952.

The pirate Edward "Blackbeard" Teach made a home on Blackbeard Island. The United States Congress designated the Blackbeard Island Wilderness Reserve in 1975 and it now has a total of 3,000 acres.

GREENSBORO—C-3

(W) NORTH SHORE RESORT AT LAKE OCONEE (CAMP RESORT)—(Greene) *From Jct I-20 (exit 130) & Hwy 44: Go W 5-1/2 S mi on Hwy 44, then 5 mi N on Carey Station Rd. Enter on L.*

WELCOME

FACILITIES: 102 sites, typical site width 30 ft, 96 full hkups, 6 W&E, (20, 30 & 50 amps), 6 pull-thrus, tenting, cabins, dump station, laundry, ltd groceries, LP gas by weight/by meter, tables, patios, grills, controlled access gate.

RECREATION: rec room/area, pavilion, equipped pavilion, 2 swim pools, boating, canoeing, kayaking, ramp, dock, lake fishing, fishing supplies, mini-golf, golf nearby, bsktball, playground, 2 shuffleboard courts, planned activities, tennis, horseshoes, sports field, hiking trails, v-ball.

Pets welcome. Age restrictions may apply. Open all yr. Big rigs welcome. VISA/DISC/DC/Debit. Phone: (706)453-4505.

e-mail: reservations@northshoreresort.net

SEE AD ATLANTA PAGE 199 AND AD PENSACOLA, FL PAGE 161

(S) OLD SALEM PARK (Georgia Power)—(Greene) *From jct I-20 (exit 130) & Hwy 44: Go 7 mi SW on Hwy 44, then 3/4 mi SE on Linger Longer Rd, then 1 mi SW on Old Salem Rd (following signs). Enter at end.*

WELCOME

◆◆◆◆FACILITIES: 92 sites, typical site width 30 ft, 92 W&E, (30 & 50 amps), some extended stay sites, 20 pull-thrus, tenting, RV storage, dump station, non-guest dumping $, laundry, ice, tables, fire rings, grills, wood, controlled access gate.

◆◆◆RECREATION: pavilion, lake swimming, boating, canoeing, kayaking, ramp, dock, lake fishing, golf nearby, playground, sports field, v-ball. Rec open to public.

Pets welcome. Partial handicap access. Open May 1 thru Nov 1. Big rigs welcome. Clubs welcome. Rate in 2007 $18 per vehicle. Phone: (706)467-2850.

SEE AD TRAVEL SECTION PAGE 192

GREENSBORO—Continued on next page

GREENSBORO—Continued

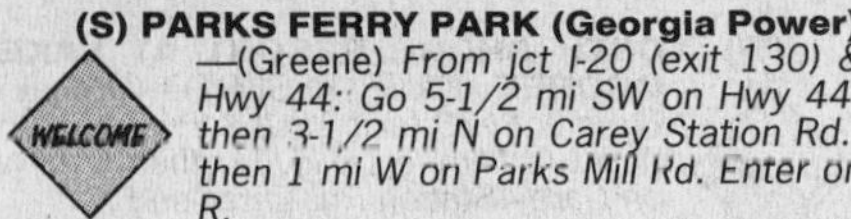

(S) PARKS FERRY PARK (Georgia Power) —(Greene) *From jct I-20 (exit 130) & Hwy 44: Go 5-1/2 mi SW on Hwy 44, then 3-1/2 mi N on Carey Station Rd., then 1 mi W on Parks Mill Rd. Enter on R.*

◆◆◆◆FACILITIES: 53 sites, typical site width 30 ft, 53 W&E, (20, 30 & 50 amps), some extended stay sites, 9 pull-thrus, tenting, RV storage, dump station, non-guest dumping $, laundry, ice, tables, grills, wood, controlled access gate.

◆◆◆RECREATION: pavilion, lake swimming, boating, canoeing, kayaking, ramp, dock, lake fishing, golf nearby, playground, horseshoes, sports field, v-ball. Rec open to public.

Pets welcome. Partial handicap access. Open Mar 1 thru Sep 30. Big rigs welcome. Clubs welcome. Rate in 2007 $18 per vehicle. Phone: (706)453-4308.

SEE AD TRAVEL SECTION PAGE 192

HARTWELL—B-3

(N) HART STATE PARK—(Hart) *From town: Go 1 mi E on US 29N, then 1-1/2 mi N on Ridge Rd, then follow signs. Enter at end.*

FACILITIES: 78 sites, 62 W&E, (20 & 30 amps), 16 no hkups, 33 pull-thrus, tenting, cabins, dump station, non-guest dumping $, laundry, ice, tables, fire rings, grills, wood.

RECREATION: pavilion, lake swimming, boating, canoeing, kayaking, ramp, dock, 5 canoe/2 pedal boat rentals, lake fishing, golf nearby, bsktball, playground, sports field, hiking trails, v-ball. Rec open to public.

Martin Luther King, Jr., civil rights activist, was from Georgia.

HARTWELL—Continued
HART STATE PARK—Continued

Pets welcome. Partial handicap access. Open all yr. Clubs welcome. MC/VISA/DISC/AMEX. Phone: (800) 864-7275.

e-mail: hartsp@dnr.state.ga.us

SEE AD TRAVEL SECTION PAGE 189

(N) MILLTOWN CAMPGROUND (COE - Hartwell Lake) —(Hart) *From town: Go 5 mi N on Hwy 51, then 6 mi E on CR 319 (New Prospect Rd), then 4 mi S on CR 310 to end.* FACILITIES: 25 sites, typical site width 20 ft, 25 no hkups, tenting, dump station, fire rings, grills. RECREATION: lake swimming, boating, ramp, lake fishing, playground. Open May 1 thru Sep 6. Phone: (888)893-0678.

(N) PAYNES CREEK CAMPGROUND (COE - Hartwell Lake)—(Hart) *From town: Go 12 mi N on Hwy-51, then 4 mi W on Cr-301, then 2 mi N onCR-279 to end.* FACILITIES: 44 sites, typical site width 20 ft, 44 W&E, (20, 30 & 50 amps), 31 pull-thrus, tenting, dump station, fire rings, grills. RECREATION: lake swimming, boating, ramp, lake fishing, playground. Open May 1 thru Sep 6. Phone: (888)893-0678.

(SE) WATSADLER CAMPGROUND (COE - Hartwell Lake)—(Hart) *From town: Go 5 mi E on US-29.* FACILITIES: 49 sites, typical site width 20 ft, 49 W&E, (50 amps), 18 pull-thrus, tenting, dump station, fire rings, grills. RECREATION: lake swimming, boating, ramp, dock, lake fishing, playground. Open all yr. Phone: (888)893-0678.

HELEN—A-2

See listings at Blairsville, Clayton, Clarkesville, Cleveland, Dillard, Dahlonega, Hiawassee, Mountain City, Toccoa, Tallulah Falls & Santee

(N) CHEROKEE CAMPGROUND—(White) *From jct Hwy 17/75 & Hwy 356: Go 5 mi NE on Hwy 356. Enter on R.*

◆◆◆◆FACILITIES: 47 sites, typical site width 35 ft, 41 full hkups, (20, 30 & 50 amps), 50 amps ($), 6 no hkups, some extended stay sites, 8 pull-thrus, cable TV ($), wireless Instant Internet access at site, cable Internet access central location, tenting, RV storage, laundry, ice, tables, fire rings, grills, wood.

HELEN—Continued
CHEROKEE CAMPGROUND—Continued

◆◆RECREATION: rec room/area, golf nearby, bsktball, playground, shuffleboard court, horseshoes, sports field.

Pets welcome. Partial handicap access. Open all yr. Big rigs welcome. Internet friendly. Clubs welcome. Rate in 2007 $22 for 2 persons. MC/VISA/Debit. Member ARVC, GARVC. Phone: (888)878-2268.

e-mail: cherokeecamp@alltel.net

SEE AD THIS PAGE

(N) Creekwood Resort Campground & Cabins —(White) *From jct Hwy 75/17 & Hwy 356: Go 5-3/4 mi NE on Hwy 356. Enter on R.* ◆◆◆FACILITIES: 18 sites, typical site width 30 ft, 18 full hkups, (20, 30 & 50 amps), some extended stay sites (in winter), laundry, tables, patios, fire rings, wood. ◆RECREATION: horseshoes, sports field, hiking trails. Pets welcome, breed restrict, quantity restrict. No tents. Open all yr. Big rigs welcome. Internet friendly. Rate in 2007 $25-35 for 4 persons. Member ARVC, GARVC. Phone: (706) 878-2164.

(S) ENOTA MOUNTAIN RETREAT—(Towns) *From east jct US 76 & Hwy 75/17: Go 6 mi S on Hwy 75/17, then 2-1/2 mi W on Hwy 180. Enter on L.*

◆◆◆◆◆FACILITIES: 35 sites, typical site width 32 ft, 35 full hkups, (30 & 50 amps), some extended stay sites, 3 pull-thrus, wireless Instant Internet access at site, phone Internet access central location, tenting, cabins, laundry, full svc store, RV supplies, ice, tables, patios, fire rings, grills, wood.

◆◆◆◆◆RECREATION: rec hall, rec room/area, pavilion, equipped pavilion, river swimming, whirlpool, pond fishing, fishing supplies, fishing guides, golf nearby, playground, planned activities, horseshoes, sports field, hiking trails, v-ball. Rec open to public.

Pets welcome. Partial handicap access. Open all yr. Big rigs welcome. Internet friendly. Escort to site. Clubs welcome. Rate in 2007 $33-35 for 2 persons. MC/VISA/Debit. Member ARVC, GARVC. Phone: (800)990-8869.

e-mail: enota@enota.com

SEE AD THIS PAGE

(N) UNICOI STATE PARK—(White) *From jct Hwy 17/75 & Hwy 356: Go 1 mi E on Hwy 356. Enter on R.*

FACILITIES: 115 sites, 82 W&E, (20, 30 & 50 amps), 33 no hkups, tenting, cabins, dump station, non-guest dumping $, laundry, ltd groceries, ice, tables, fire rings, grills, wood.

RECREATION: rec room/area, coin games, lake swimming, 12 canoe/12 pedal boat rentals, lake/stream fishing, fishing supplies, golf nearby, playground, planned activities, tennis, sports field, hiking trails, v-ball. Rec open to public.

Pets welcome. Partial handicap access. Open all yr. Big rigs welcome. MC/VISA/DISC/AMEX/DC. Phone: (800)864-7275.

SEE AD TRAVEL SECTION PAGE 189

HIAWASSEE—A-2

(S) BALD MOUNTAIN PARK CAMPING RESORT—(Towns) *From east jct US 76 & Hwys 75/17: Go 1/4 mi NW on US 76/Hwys 75/17, then 1/4 mi W on Hwy 288, then 3-1/2 mi S on Fodder Creek Rd, then on Gander Gap Rd. Enter on L.*

◆◆◆◆◆FACILITIES: 282 sites, typical site width 30 ft, 265 full hkups, 15 W&E, (20, 30 & 50 amps), 2 no hkups, some extended stay sites, 47 pull-thrus, cable TV, wireless Instant Internet access at site, tenting, cabins, RV storage, dump

BALD MOUNTAIN PARK CAMPING RESORT—Continued on next page

station, non-guest dumping $, portable dump, laundry, ltd groceries, RV supplies, LP gas by weight/by meter, ice, tables, patios, fire rings, grills, wood.

◇◇◇◇◇RECREATION: rec room/area, pavilion, equipped pavilion, coin games, swim pool, boating, kayaking, 4 kayak/3 pedal boat rentals, lake fishing, fishing supplies, mini-golf, golf nearby, bsktball, playground, 2 shuffleboard courts, planned activities, horseshoes, sports field, hiking trails, v-ball.

Pets welcome, breed restrict. Partial handicap access. Open Apr 1 thru Nov 1. Big rigs welcome. Internet friendly. Escort to site. Clubs welcome. Rate in 2007 $25-30 per vehicle. MC/VISA/DISC/Debit. Member ARVC, GARVC. Phone: (706)896-8896.

SEE AD PAGE 208

WELCOME

(W) GEORGIA MOUNTAIN FAIRGROUNDS CAMPGROUND (County Park)—(Towns) *From west jct Hwy 75 & US 76/Hwy 17: Go 1 mi W on US 76/Hwy 17. Enter on R.*

FACILITIES: 189 sites, typical site width 30 ft, 97 full hkups, 92 W&E, (30 & 50 amps), some extended stay sites (in summer), cable TV, wireless Instant Internet access at site, wireless Internet access central location, tenting, dump station, non-guest dumping $, ice, tables, controlled access gate.

RECREATION: pavilion, lake swimming, boating, canoeing, kayaking, ramp, lake fishing, golf nearby, bsktball, playground, tennis, sports field, hiking trails, v-ball. Rec open to public.

Pets welcome. Open all yr. Big rigs welcome. Internet friendly. Clubs welcome. MC/VISA/DISC/AMEX/Debit. Phone: (706)896-4191.

e-mail: gamtfair@alltel.net

SEE AD TRAVEL SECTION PAGE 189

WELCOME

(W) GEORGIA MOUNTAIN FAIRGROUNDS & MUSIC HALL (County Fairgrounds)—*From west jct Hwy 75 & US 76/Hwy 17: Go 1 mi W on US 76/Hwy 17. Enter on R.* Fair held each Aug in 2,900-seat music hall; music festivals-May thru Oct; mountain fiddlers convention in Oct; Rhododendron Festival in May and more. Open May 1 thru Oct 31. MC/VISA/DISC/AMEX. Phone: (706)896-4191.

e-mail: gamtfair@alltel.net

SEE AD TRAVEL SECTION PAGE 189

(E) Mountain View Campground—(Towns) *From east jct Hwy 75 & US 76: Go 2 mi E on US 76, then 1 mi S on Swallow Creek Rd. Enter on L.* ◇◇FACILITIES: 40 sites, typical site width 25 ft, 40 full hkups, (30 & 50 amps), 4 pull-thrus, laundry, ice, tables. RECREATION: pavilion. Pets welcome. No tents. Open all yr. Internet friendly. Rate in 2007 $30-35 per vehicle. Phone: (706) 896-4589.

(S) River Bend Campground—(Towns) *From E jct Hwy 17/75: Go 3/4 mi S on Hwy 75, then 1 mi E on Streak Hill Rd Enter on R.* ◇◇◇FACILITIES: 85 sites, typical site width 30 ft, 70 full hkups, 15 W&E, (30 & 50 amps), some extended stay sites, 3 pull-thrus, tenting, dump station, ice, tables, fire rings, wood. ◇◇◇RECREATION: rec hall, rec room/area, pavilion, swim pool, canoeing, river fishing, playground, horseshoes, v-ball. Pets welcome, breed restrict. Partial handicap access. Open all yr. Big rigs welcome. Internet friendly. Rate in 2007 $25 per vehicle. Phone: (706)896-1415. FMCA discount.

HIGH FALLS—C-2

WELCOME

(S) HIGH FALLS STATE PARK—(Monroe) *From I-75 (exit 198) & Moreland Rd: Go 1-3/4 mi E on Moreland Rd. Enter on L.*

FACILITIES: 87 sites, 87 W&E, (30 & 50 amps), 6 pull-thrus, tenting, dump station, non-guest dumping $, laundry, tables, fire rings, grills, wood.

RECREATION: pavilion, swim pool, boating, 10 hp limit, canoeing, kayaking, ramp, dock, 8 rowboat/8 canoe/10 pedal boat rentals, lake/river fishing, mini-golf ($), golf nearby, playground, hiking trails. Rec open to public.

Pets welcome. Partial handicap access. Open all yr. Big rigs welcome. Clubs welcome. MC/VISA/DISC/AMEX. Phone: (800) 864-7275.

e-mail: highfallsstatepk@mindspring.com

SEE AD TRAVEL SECTION PAGE 189

Jackie Robinson, baseball player, was from Georgia.

JACKSON—C-2

WELCOME

(W) FOREST GLEN MOBILE HOME & RV PARK—(Butts) *From jct I-75 (exit 205) & Hwy 16: Go 500 feet W on Hwy 16, then 1/2 mi S on Glade Rd. Enter on L.*

◇◇◇◇FACILITIES: 58 sites, typical site width 30 ft, 58 full hkups, (30 & 50 amps), many extended stay sites, 41 pull-thrus, phone on-site Internet access (needs activ), RV storage, laundry, tables.

◇◇RECREATION: rec room/area, swim pool, golf nearby, horseshoes, sports field.

Pets welcome. Partial handicap access. No tents. Open all yr. Big rigs welcome. Clubs welcome. Rate in 2007 $20 for 2 persons. MC/VISA. Phone: (770)228-3399.

SEE AD ATLANTA PAGE 200

WELCOME

(S) INDIAN SPRINGS STATE PARK—(Butts) *From jct I-75 (exit 205) & Hwy 16: Go 7-3/4 mi NE on Hwy 16, then 7 mi SE on Hwy 42. Enter on R.*

FACILITIES: 88 sites, 88 W&E, (30 & 50 amps), cable TV, tenting, cabins, dump station, non-guest dumping $, laundry, ice, tables, fire rings, grills, wood, controlled access gate.

RECREATION: pavilion, lake swimming, boating, 10 hp limit, canoeing, kayaking, ramp, dock, 10 rowboat/6 pedal boat rentals, lake fishing, mini-golf ($), golf nearby, playground, hiking trails.

Pets welcome. Partial handicap access. Open all yr. Big rigs welcome. Clubs welcome. MC/VISA/DISC/AMEX. Phone: (800) 864-7275.

e-mail: indian-s@innerx.net

SEE AD TRAVEL SECTION PAGE 189

JEKYLL ISLAND—E-5

See listings at Brunswick

WELCOME

(N) JEKYLL ISLAND CAMPGROUND—(Glynn) *From jct I-95 (exit 29) & US 17N: Go 5 mi E on US 17N, then 6 mi SE on Hwy 520 (Jekyll Island Causeway), then 4-1/2 mi N on Beach View Dr/Riverview Dr. Enter on L.*

FACILITIES: 206 sites, typical site width 20 ft, 162 full hkups, 2 W&E, (30 & 50 amps), 42 no hkups, 40 pull-thrus, cable TV, wireless Instant Internet access at site, tenting, RV storage, dump station, non-guest dumping $, laundry, ltd groceries, RV supplies, LP gas by weight/by meter, ice, tables, fire rings, wood, controlled access gate.

RECREATION: sprayground, saltwater swimming, saltwater/lake fishing, fishing supplies, golf nearby, 27 bike rentals, tennis, horseshoes, hiking trails, local tours.

Pets welcome. Partial handicap access. Open all yr. Big rigs welcome. Internet friendly. Clubs welcome. MC/VISA/AMEX/Debit. Phone: (866)658-3021.

e-mail: campground@jekyllisland.com

SEE AD DISCOVER SECTION PAGE 40

WELCOME

(W) JEKYLL ISLAND WELCOME CENTER—*From jct I-95 (exit 6/29) & US 17N: Go 5 mi E on US 17N, then 4 mi SE on Hwy 520 (Jekyll Island Causeway). Enter on R.* Brochures, maps, schedules & lodging info. Daily tours of National Historic District- cottage retreats of turn-of-the-century millionaires. Deep sea fishing, sightseeing cruises, ocean beaches, guided nature walks, paved bike trails, fine dining and more. Open all yr. MC/VISA. Phone: (912)635-3636.

e-mail: cvb@jekyllisland.com

SEE AD DISCOVER SECTION PAGE 40

KINGSLAND—F-5

WELCOME

(E) COUNTRY OAKS CAMPGROUND & RV PARK—(Camden) *From I-95 (exit 1) & St. Mary's Rd.: Go 1/4 mi W on St. Mary's Rd. Enter on L.*

◇◇◇◇FACILITIES: 43 sites, typical site width 30 ft, 42 full hkups, 1 W&E, (30 & 50 amps), some extended stay sites, 18 pull-thrus, wireless Instant Internet access at site, RV storage, laundry, LP gas by weight/by meter, ice, tables, fire rings, wood.

◇◇RECREATION: rec room/area, pond fishing, golf nearby, horseshoes, v-ball.

Pets welcome. Partial handicap access. No tents. Open all yr. Big rigs welcome. Internet friendly. Clubs welcome. Rate in 2007 $24-26 for 2 persons. MC/VISA/DISC/Debit. Member ARVC, GARVC. Phone: (912)729-6212.

SEE AD JACKSONVILLE, FL PAGE 129

(E) Jacksonville North/Kingsland KOA—(Camden) *From I-95 (exit 1) & St Mary's Rd: Go 500 ft W on St Mary's Rd, then 1/4 mi S on Scrubby Bluff Rd. Enter on R.* ◇◇◇FACILITIES: 85 sites, typical site width 25 ft, 61 full hkups, 24 W&E, (30 & 50 amps), some extended stay sites, 85 pull-thrus, tenting, dump station, non-guest dumping $, laundry, ltd groceries, LP gas by weight/by meter, ice, tables, fire rings, wood. ◇◇◇◇RECREATION: pavilion, equipped pavilion, swim pool, mini-golf, playground, planned activities (wkends only), horseshoes, sports field, v-ball. Pets welcome. Partial handicap access. Open all yr. Big rigs welcome. Internet friendly. Rate in 2007 $24-36 for 2 persons. Phone: (800)562-5220. KOA 10% value card discount.

LA FAYETTE—A-1

(E) CHATTAHOOCHEE NATIONAL FOREST (The Pocket Campground)—(Walker) *From town: Go 13-1/2 mi E on Hwy 136, then (1/2 mi E of Villanow) go 8 mi S on Pocket Rd.* FACILITIES: 26 sites, typical site width 10 ft, 26 no hkups, cold showers only, grills. RECREATION: hiking trails. Partial handicap access. Open Mar 31 thru Nov 12. No showers. No reservations. Max stay 14 days. Phone: (706)638-1085.

LA GRANGE—C-1

(SW) HOLIDAY PARK (West Point Lake COE)—(Troup) *From town: Go 10 mi W on Hwy-109, then over Chattahoochee River & follow signs.* FACILITIES: 143 sites, 92 W&E, (30 amps), 51 no hkups, tenting, dump station, laundry, fire rings, grills. RECREATION: pavilion, boating, ramp, dock, lake fishing, playground, tennis, sports field, hiking trails. Open Feb 25 thru Sep 24. Phone: (706)884-6818.

(N) RINGER PARK (COE - West Point Lake)—(Troup) *From town: Go 10 mi N on US-27, follow signs.* FACILITIES: 37 sites, typical site width 15 ft, 37 no hkups, tenting, non-flush toilets only, grills. RECREATION: boating, ramp, dock, lake fishing, tennis. Open all yr. No showers. No reservations. Phone: (706)645-2937.

(SW) STATE LINE PARK (COE - West Point Lake)—(Troup) *From town: Go 14 mi W on Hwy-109 to Hwy-109 spur, then follow signs.* FACILITIES: 122 sites, typical site width 20 ft, 56 W&E, (20 & 30 amps), 66 no hkups, tenting, dump station, laundry, fire rings, grills. RECREATION: lake swimming, boating, ramp, dock, lake fishing, playground, tennis, sports field, hiking trails. Partial handicap access. Open Mar 25 thru Sep 4. Phone: (706)882-5439.

(SW) WHITETAIL RIDGE (COE - West Point Lake)—(Troup) *From town: Go 10 mi W on Hwy 109, then over Chattahoochee River and follow signs.* FACILITIES: 58 sites, typical site width 20 ft, 58 W&E, (20 & 30 amps), 8 pull-thrus, tenting, dump station, laundry, ltd groceries, fire rings, grills. RECREATION: pavilion, boating, ramp, lake fishing, playground, hiking trails. Partial handicap access. Open Mar 25 thru Nov 26. Phone: (706) 884-8972.

LAKE PARK—F-3

WELCOME

(W) BARGAINVILLE FLEA MARKET—*From jct I-75 (exit 5) & Hwy 376: Go 500 feet E, then 1/2 mi S on Mill Store Road. Enter on L.* New, old & used collectable merchandise. Over 150 dealers under cover adjoining Eagles Roost RV Resort. Open all yr. Open Sat & Sun only, 9 a.m.-5 p.m. Phone: (229)559-5192.

e-mail: camp@eaglesroostresort.com

SEE AD VALDOSTA PAGE 217

WELCOME

(W) EAGLES ROOST RV RESORT—(Lowndes) *From jct I-75 (exit 5) & Hwy 376: Go 500 feet E on Hwy 376, then 1/2 mi S on Mill Store Rd. Enter on L.*

◇◇◇◇FACILITIES: 140 sites, typical site width 25 ft, 116 full hkups, 24 W&E, (30 & 50 amps), 140 pull-thrus, cable TV ($), wireless Instant Internet access at site, phone on-site Internet access (needs activ), wireless Internet access central location, tenting, RV storage, dump station, non-guest dumping $, laundry, RV supplies, LP gas by weight/by meter, ice, tables.

◇◇◇RECREATION: rec hall, rec room/area, pavilion, swim pool, golf nearby, bsktball, playground, 4 shuffleboard courts, horseshoes.

Pets welcome. Open all yr. Big rigs welcome. Internet friendly. Clubs welcome. Rate in 2007 $29.95-39.95 for 4 persons. MC/VISA/DISC. Member ARVC, GARVC. Phone: (229)559-5192. FMCA discount.

e-mail: camp@EaglesRoostResort.com

SEE AD VALDOSTA PAGE 217

(S) MILITARY PARK (Grassy Pond Rec. Area)—(Lowndes) *Offbase, 25 mi S on Moody AFB. From jct I-75 (exit 2/5) & Hwy 376: Go W on Hwy 376, then S on Loch Laurel Rd. Follow signs.* FACILITIES: 42 sites, 42 full hkups, 2 pull-thrus, tenting, dump station, laundry, fire rings, grills. RECREATION: rec hall, equipped pavilion, boating, ramp, 3 rowboat/14 pedal boat/11 motorboat rentals, pond fishing, playground, hiking trails, v-ball. Open all yr. For Military Use Only-w/Military ID Card. Phone: (912)559-5840.

(W) Valdosta/Lake Park KOA—(Lowndes) *From jct I-75 (exit 5) & Hwy 376: Go 500 feet W on Hwy 376, then 1/2 mi S on Jewell Futch Rd. Enter at end.*

Valdosta/Lake Park KOA—Continued on next page

LAKE PARK—Continued
Valdosta/Lake Park KOA—Continued

◊◊◊◊FACILITIES: 127 sites, typical site width 35 ft, 127 full hkups, (30 & 50 amps), 67 pull-thrus, tenting, dump station, non-guest dumping, laundry, ltd groceries, LP gas by weight/by meter, ice, tables, fire rings, grills, wood. ◊◊◊◊RECREATION: rec hall, rec room/area, pavilion, swim pool, lake fishing, playground, shuffleboard court, planned activities, horseshoes. Pets welcome. Partial handicap access. Open all yr. Big rigs welcome. Internet friendly. Rate in 2007 $33-38.50 for 2 persons. Member ARVC, GARVC. Phone: (800)562-2124. KOA 10% value card discount.

LAVONIA—B-3

(N) Sunset Campground—(Franklin) *From jct I-85 (exit 173) & Hwy 17: Go 3 mi N on Hwy 17. Enter on L.* ◊◊◊FACILITIES: 39 sites, typical site width 28 ft, 39 full hkups, (20, 30 & 50 amps), 50 amps ($), some extended stay sites, 4 pull-thrus, tenting, laundry, ice, tables, fire rings. ◊◊RECREATION: rec hall, equipped pavilion, horseshoes, hiking trails. Pets welcome. Open all yr. Big rigs welcome. Rate in 2007 $20-24 for 2 persons. Phone: (706)356-8932.

Woodall's Tip #9... Turn to the Travel Section for a list of the RV Parks & Campgrounds that Welcome Big Rigs.

LAVONIA—Continued

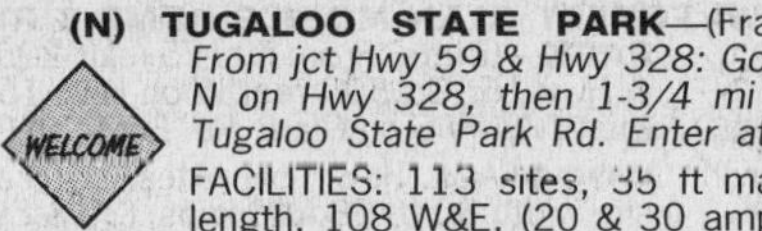

(N) TUGALOO STATE PARK—(Franklin) *From jct Hwy 59 & Hwy 328: Go 4 mi N on Hwy 328, then 1-3/4 mi E on Tugaloo State Park Rd. Enter at end.*

FACILITIES: 113 sites, 35 ft max RV length, 108 W&E, (20 & 30 amps), 5 no hkups, 30 pull-thrus, cable TV, tenting, cabins, dump station, non-guest dumping $, laundry, ice, tables, fire rings, grills, wood, controlled access gate.

RECREATION: pavilion, lake swimming, boating, canoeing, kayaking, ramp, dock, 6 canoe rentals, lake fishing, fishing supplies, mini-golf ($), golf nearby, tennis, sports field, hiking trails, v-ball. Rec open to public.

Pets welcome. Partial handicap access. Open all yr. Clubs welcome. MC/VISA/DISC/AMEX. Phone: (800)864-7275.

e-mail: tugaloosp@hartcom.net

SEE AD TRAVEL SECTION PAGE 189

LEAH—B-4

(N) MILITARY PARK (Fort Gordon Rec. Area)—*Off base, 23 mi N of Fort Gordon Military Reservation. From jct I-20 & Hwy 47/US 221: Go N on Hwy 47/Ray Owens Rd (Leah).* FACILITIES: 117 sites, 52 full hkups, 20 E, 45 no hkups, tenting, dump station, laundry, ltd groceries, ice, fire rings, grills, wood. RECRE-

LEAH—Continued
MILITARY PARK (Fort Gordon Rec. Area)—Continued

ATION: rec hall, equipped pavilion, lake swimming, boating, canoeing, ramp, dock, 5 canoe/10 pedal boat/38 motorboat rentals, lake fishing, playground, planned activities, hiking trails, v-ball. Pets welcome. Open all yr. No reservations. For Military Use Only-w/Military ID Card. Phone: (706)541-1057.

(SE) PETERSBURG CAMP AREA (COE - J. Strom Thurmond Lake)—(Columbia) *From town: Go 5 mi SE on Hwy-104, then 2 mi N on US-221.* FACILITIES: 93 sites, typical site width 20 ft, 85 W&E, (50 amps), 8 no hkups, 55 pull-thrus, tenting, dump station, laundry, grills. RECREATION: pavilion, lake swimming, boating, ramp, dock, lake fishing, playground, hiking trails. Open all yr. Phone: (706)541-9464.

(E) RIDGE ROAD CAMP AREA (COE-J. Strom Thurmond Lake)—(Columbia) *From town: Go 2 mi S on Hwy-104, then follow signs on paved county road.* FACILITIES: 69 sites, typical site width 20 ft, 27 ft max RV length, 63 W&E, (30 amps), 6 no hkups, 20 pull-thrus, tenting, dump station, laundry, grills. RECREATION: lake swimming, boating, ramp, dock, lake fishing, playground. Open Apr 1 thru Sep 29. Phone: (706)541-0282.

LINCOLNTON—B-4

WELCOME

(E) ELIJAH CLARK STATE PARK—(Lincoln) *From jct US 378 & Hwy 47: Go 6 mi NE on US 378. Enter on L.*

FACILITIES: 165 sites, 165 W&E, (20 & 30 amps), 68 pull-thrus, cable TV, tenting, cabins, dump station, non-guest dumping $, laundry, ice, tables, fire rings, grills, wood, controlled access gate.

RECREATION: pavilion, equipped pavilion, lake swimming, boating, canoeing, kayaking, ramp, dock, lake fishing, mini-golf ($), playground, shuffleboard court, sports field, hiking trails, v-ball. Rec open to public.

Pets welcome. Partial handicap access. Open all yr. Clubs welcome. MC/VISA/DISC/AMEX. Phone: (800) 864-7275.

e-mail: elijahclark@dnr.state.ga.us

SEE AD TRAVEL SECTION PAGE 189

(N) HESTERS FERRY CAMP AREA (COE - J. Strom Thurmond Lake)—(Lincoln) *From town: Go 12 mi N on Hwy 79, then 3 mi E on Hwy 44.* FACILITIES: 26 sites, typical site width 20 ft, 27 ft max RV length, 16 W&E, (30 amps), 10 no hkups, 6 pull-thrus, tenting, dump station, grills. RECREATION: lake swimming, boating, ramp, lake fishing, playground. Open Apr 1 thru Sep 29. Phone: (706)359-2746.

MACON—C-2

See listings at Byron, Forsyth, Perry & Warner Robins.

WELCOME

(N) LAKE JULIETTE DAMES FERRY PARK (Georgia Power)—(Monroe) *From jct I-75 (exit 171) & US 23/Hwy 87: Go 9-1/4 mi N on US 23/Hwy 87. Enter on L.*

◊◊◊FACILITIES: 50 sites, typical site width 35 ft, 45 W&E, (20, 30 & 50 amps), 5 no hkups, 6 pull-thrus, tenting, dump station, non-guest dumping $, ice, tables, fire rings, grills, wood, controlled access gate.

◊◊◊RECREATION: pavilion, lake swimming, boating, 25 hp limit, canoeing, kayaking, ramp, dock, lake fishing, golf nearby, hiking trails. Rec open to public.

Pets welcome. Partial handicap access. Open Mar 1 thru Oct 31. Big rigs welcome. Clubs welcome. Rate in 2007 $18 per vehicle. Phone: (478)994-7945.

SEE AD TRAVEL SECTION PAGE 192

WELCOME

(W) LAKE TOBESOFKEE RECREATION AREA (Bibb Co.)—(Bibb) *From jct I-475 (exit 5) & Hwy 74: Go 3/4 mi SW on Hwy 74, then 1-3/4 mi SW on Mosley Dixon Rd. Enter on L.*

FACILITIES: 116 sites, typical site width 22 ft, 106 W&E, 10 E, (30 & 50 amps), 10 pull-thrus, cable TV, tenting, dump station, non-guest dumping $, laundry, marine gas, ice, tables, fire rings, grills, controlled access gate.

RECREATION: pavilion, lake swimming, boating, canoeing, kayaking, ramp, dock, lake fishing, golf nearby, bsktball, playground, hiking trails, v-ball. Rec open to public.

Pets welcome. Partial handicap access. Open all yr. Big rigs welcome. Clubs welcome. Phone: (478)474-8770.

SEE AD THIS PAGE

Woodall's Tip #37... 100% Money Back Guarantee... If for any reason you're not satisfied with this Directory, please return it to us by December 31, 2008 along with your sales receipt, and we'll reimburse you for the amount you paid for the Directory.

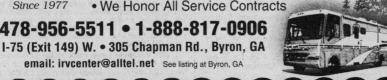

MADISON—C-3

(S) COUNTRY BOY'S RV PARK—(Morgan) *From jct I-20 (exit 114) & US 441/129: Go 1-1/2 mi S on US 441/129. Enter on L.*

◆◆◆FACILITIES: 150 sites, typical site width 25 ft, 150 full hkups, (30 & 50 amps), some extended stay sites, 100 pull-thrus, cable TV, phone on-site Internet access (needs activ), phone Internet access central location, RV storage, dump station, non-guest dumping $, laundry, RV supplies, ice, tables, fire rings, wood.

◆◆RECREATION: pavilion, swim pool, golf nearby, playground, horseshoes, sports field, hiking trails.

Pets welcome. No tents. Open all yr. Big rigs welcome. Internet friendly. Escort to site. Clubs welcome. Rate in 2007 $22 for 2 persons. Phone: (706)342-1799. FCRV 10% discount. FMCA discount.

e-mail: gacountrygirl60@yahoo.com

SEE AD TRAVEL SECTION PAGE 187

MARIETTA—B-2

(S) ATLANTA-MARIETTA RV RESORT (formerly Brookwood RV Park)—(Cobb) *From jct I-75 (exit 261) & Hwy 280: Go 3/4 mi W on Hwy 280, then 1/2 mi N on US 41 (Cobb Pkwy) then 1 block E on Wylie Rd. Enter on R.*

◆◆◆FACILITIES: 70 sites, typical site width 25 ft, 70 full hkups, (30 & 50 amps), many extended stay sites (in winter), cable TV, wireless Instant Internet access at site, wireless Internet access central location, laundry, ltd groceries, LP gas by weight/by meter, ice, tables, patios.

◆RECREATION: swim pool, golf nearby.

Pets welcome. Partial handicap access. No tents. Open all yr. Big rigs welcome. Internet friendly. Clubs welcome. Rate in 2007 $49.99 per vehicle. MC/VISA/DISC/AMEX. Member ARVC, GARVC. Phone: (877)727-5787. FMCA discount.

e-mail: information@amrvresort.com

SEE AD ATLANTA PAGE 199

(W) MILITARY PARK (Dobbins ARB Family Campground)—(Cobb) *From jct I-75 & Delk Rd/Hwy 280: Go 2 mi W on Delk Rd, then S on US 41 to 1st light. On base.* FACILITIES: 18 sites, 35 ft max RV length, 18 W&E, tenting, dump station, grills. RECREATION: pavilion, playground, tennis, sports field. Open all yr. For Military Use Only-w/Military ID Card. Phone: (678) 655-4870.

✽ **(S) NORMAN CAMPERS**—*From jct I-75 (exit 261) & Hwy 280: Go 6 mi S on Hwy 280, then 3/4 mi SW on Hwy 5 (Austell Rd). Enter on R.* SALES: travel trailers, truck campers, 5th wheels, fold-down camping trailers, pre-owned unit sales. SERVICES: full-time mech, RV appliance repair, body work/collision repair, bus. hrs emerg rd svc, RV towing, LP gas by weight/by meter, sells parts/accessories, installs hitches. Open all yr. MC/VISA. Phone: (770)424-7922.

e-mail: tim@normancampers.com

SEE AD TRAVEL SECTION PAGE 187

MCDONOUGH—C-2

(N) ATLANTA SOUTH RV RESORT—(Henry) *From jct I-75 (exit 222) & Jodeco Rd: Go 1000 feet W on Jodeco Rd, then 1/4 mi S on Mt. Olive Rd. Enter at end.*

ONE OF THE SOUTH'S FINEST RESORTS!
Easy on/off I-75 just 30 min from downtown Atlanta. Many of Georgia's most popular attractions are nearby. After sightseeing, relax by the pool, enjoy our resort amenities or sit by a fire. A fun and friendly place to stay!

◆◆◆◆◆FACILITIES: 170 sites, typical site width 25 ft, 170 full hkups, (30 & 50 amps), many extended stay sites, 80 pull-thrus, wireless Instant Internet access at site, phone on-site Internet access (needs activ), wireless Internet access central location, tenting, cabins, RV storage, dump station, laundry, RV supplies, LP gas by meter, ice, tables, fire rings, wood.

◆◆◆RECREATION: rec hall, rec room/area, pavilion, swim pool, pond fishing, golf nearby, bsktball, playground, planned activities (wkends only).

Find a park or campground Woodall's doesn't list? Tell us!

MCDONOUGH—Continued
ATLANTA SOUTH RV RESORT—Continued

Pets welcome. Partial handicap access. Open all yr. Big rigs welcome. Internet friendly. Escort to site. Clubs welcome. Rate in 2007 $35 for 2 persons. MC/VISA/DISC/AMEX. Phone: (678)583-1880.

SEE AD ATLANTA PAGE 200

MCRAE—D-3

(N) LITTLE OCMULGEE STATE PARK—(Telfair) *From jct US 441 & US 280: Go 1 mi N on US 441/319. Enter on L.*

FACILITIES: 55 sites, 55 W&E, (30 & 50 amps), 12 pull-thrus, cable TV, tenting, cabins, dump station, laundry, ice, tables, fire rings, grills, wood.

RECREATION: pavilion, lake swimming, boating, ramp, dock, lake fishing, mini-golf ($), golf nearby, playground, tennis, sports field, hiking trails, v-ball. Rec open to public.

Pets welcome. Partial handicap access. Open all yr. Big rigs welcome. Clubs welcome. MC/VISA/DISC/AMEX. Phone: (800) 864-7275.

SEE AD TRAVEL SECTION PAGE 189

MILLEDGEVILLE—C-3

(S) SCENIC MOUNTAIN RV PARK—(Baldwin) *From jct US 441 Bypass & Hwy 29: Go 1/4 mi N on US 441/Bus/SR 243 (Irwinton Rd). Enter on R.*

◆◆◆◆FACILITIES: 100 sites, typical site width 25 ft, 85 full hkups, 15 W&E, (30 & 50 amps), some extended stay sites, 10 pull-thrus, heater not allowed, cable TV, phone/cable on-site Internet access (needs activ), cable Internet access central location, RV/park trailer rentals, cabins, RV storage, laundry, ltd groceries, RV supplies, LP gas by weight/by meter, LP bottle exch, ice, tables, patios, fire rings, grills, wood.

◆◆◆◆RECREATION: rec hall, rec room/area, pavilion, equipped pavilion, coin games, swim pool, pond fishing, fishing supplies, golf nearby, bsktball, play equipment, planned activities, horseshoes, hiking trails, v-ball.

Pets welcome. No tents. Open all yr. Big rigs welcome. Internet friendly. Escort to site. Clubs welcome. Rate in 2007 $29 for 2 persons. MC/VISA/DISC/AMEX/Debit. Member ARVC. Phone: (800)716-3015. CCUSA discount.

e-mail: scenicmountainrv@windstream.net

SEE AD THIS PAGE

MILLEN—C-4

(N) MAGNOLIA SPRINGS STATE PARK—(Jenkins) *From jct US-25 & Hwy-23: Go 5 mi N on US-25. Enter on R.*

FACILITIES: 26 sites, 39 ft max RV length, 26 W&E, (20, 30 & 50 amps), 5 pull-thrus, tenting, cabins, dump station, non-guest dumping $, laundry, ice, tables, fire rings, grills, wood, controlled access gate.

RECREATION: pavilion, swim pool, boating, 10 hp limit, canoeing, kayaking, ramp, dock, 4 rowboat/7 canoe rentals, lake fishing, playground, sports field, hiking trails, v-ball. Rec open to public.

Pets welcome. Partial handicap access. Open all yr. Clubs welcome. MC/VISA/DISC/AMEX. Phone: (800) 864-7275.

e-mail: magsps@burke.net

SEE AD TRAVEL SECTION PAGE 189

MORGANTON—A-2

(W) CHATTAHOOCHEE NATIONAL FOREST (Morganton Point Campground)—(Fannin) *From jct Hwy 60 & CR 616: Go 1 mi SW on CR 616.* FACILITIES: 42 sites, typical site width 15 ft, 30 ft max RV length, 42 no hkups, 2 pull-thrus, tenting, ltd groceries, grills. RECREATION: pavilion, lake swimming, boating, ramp, lake fishing. Partial handicap access. Open Apr 15 thru Sep 20. No reservations. Max stay 14 days. Phone: (706)632-3031.

MOUNTAIN CITY—A-3

(W) BLACK ROCK MOUNTAIN STATE PARK—(Rabun) *From jct US 76 & US 441/23: Go 3 mi N on US 441/23 (Mountain City), then 3 mi W on Black Rock Mountain Pkwy. (Caution: steep grade). Enter at end.*

FACILITIES: 60 sites, 48 W&E, (20 & 30 amps), 12 no hkups, 1 pull-thru, cable TV, tenting, cabins, dump station, laundry, ltd groceries, ice, tables, fire rings, grills, wood.

RECREATION: lake fishing, playground, planned activities, hiking trails. Rec open to public.

MOUNTAIN CITY—Continued
BLACK ROCK MOUNTAIN STATE PARK—Continued

Pets welcome. Partial handicap access. Open all yr. Clubs welcome. MC/VISA/DISC/AMEX. Phone: (800)864-7275.

e-mail: brmp1@alltel.net

SEE AD TRAVEL SECTION PAGE 189

NORCROSS—B-2

(E) JONES RV PARK—(Gwinnett) *From jct I-85 (exit 101) & Indian Trl/Lilburn Rd: Go 400 ft E on Indian Trl/Lilburn Rd, then 1 block S on Willowtrail Pkwy. Enter at end.*

◆◆◆◆FACILITIES: 173 sites, typical site width 25 ft, 173 full hkups, (20, 30 & 50 amps), many extended stay sites, 55 pull-thrus, wireless Instant Internet access at site ($), RV storage, dump station, non-guest dumping $, laundry, LP gas by weight/by meter.

RECREATION: golf nearby.

Pets welcome. Partial handicap access. No tents. Open all yr. Reservations recommended. No cash accepted. Big rigs welcome. Internet friendly. Clubs welcome. Rate in 2007 $30 per vehicle. MC/VISA/AMEX/Debit. Phone: (770)923-0911.

e-mail: jonesrvpark@earthlink.net

SEE AD ATLANTA PAGE 199

OGLETHORPE—D-2

(N) WHITEWATER CREEK PARK (Macon County Park)—(Oglethorpe) *From jct Hwy 26 & Hwy 49/128: Go 6-1/4 mi N on Hwy 128 or Hwy 128 Bypass.* FACILITIES: 72 sites, 16 full hkups, 56 W&E, tenting, dump station, grills, wood. RECREATION: pavilion, lake swimming, boating, 10 hp limit, canoeing, ramp, dock, 2 rowboat rentals, lake fishing, playground, sports field, hiking trails, v-ball. Rec open to public. Partial handicap access. Open all yr. Phone: (478)472-8171.

OMAHA—D-1

(S) FLORENCE MARINA STATE PARK—(Stewart) *At jct Hwy 39C & Hwy 39.*

FACILITIES: 43 sites, 43 full hkups, (30 & 50 amps), 20 pull-thrus, cable TV, tenting, cabins, laundry, ltd groceries, ice, tables, fire rings, grills, wood.

RECREATION: pavilion, swim pool, boating, canoeing, kayaking, ramp, dock, 6 motorboat rentals, lake fishing, mini-golf ($), golf nearby, playground, tennis, hiking trails, v-ball. Rec open to public.

Pets welcome. Partial handicap access. Open all yr. Big rigs welcome. Clubs welcome. MC/VISA/DISC/AMEX. Phone: (800) 864-7275.

e-mail: flmarina@sowega.net

SEE AD TRAVEL SECTION PAGE 189

PALMETTO—C-1

(E) South Oaks Mobile Home Community RV Park (RV SPACES)—(Coweta) *From jct I-85 (exit 56) & Collingsworth Rd: Go 100 yds W on Collingsworth Rd, then 1/2 mi N on on Tingle Ln. Enter at end.* FACILITIES: 150 sites, accepts full hkup units only, 150 full hkups, (30 & 50 amps), some extended stay sites, 3 pull-thrus. RECREATION: playground. Pets welcome. No tents. Open all yr. No restrooms. Big rigs welcome. Internet friendly. Rate in 2007 $25 per vehicle. Phone: (770) 463-3070.

PERRY—D-2

(E) Boland's RV Park—(Houston) *From jct of I-75 (exit 136) & US 341: Go 1/4 mi E on US 341, then 1/4 mi N on Perimeter Rd. Enter on L.* ◆◆◆FACILITIES: 65 sites, typical site width 20 ft, 65 full hkups, (20, 30 & 50 amps), some extended stay sites (in winter), 64 pull-thrus, tenting, laundry, LP gas by weight/by meter, ice, tables, grills. ◆◆RECREATION: pavilion, swim pool, playground. Pets welcome. Open all yr. Internet friendly. Rate in 2007 $23 for 2 persons. Phone: (478) 987-3371. FCRV 10% discount.

PERRY—Continued on next page

PERRY—Continued

(N) CROSSROADS HOLIDAY TRAV-L-PARK—(Houston) *From I-75 (exit 136) & US 341: Go 500 ft W on US 341. Enter on L.*

WELCOME

◊◊◊◊FACILITIES: 64 sites, typical site width 28 ft, 58 full hkups, 6 W&E, (20, 30 & 50 amps), some extended stay sites (in winter), 34 pull-thrus, cable TV, phone on-site Internet access (needs activ), phone Internet access central location, tenting, RV storage, laundry, ltd groceries, RV supplies, LP gas by weight/by meter, ice, tables.

◊◊RECREATION: pavilion, swim pool, mini-golf, golf nearby, bsktball, play equipment.

Pets welcome. Open all yr. Big rigs welcome. Internet friendly. Clubs welcome. Rate in 2007 $21-23 for 2 persons. MC/VISA/DISC/AMEX/Debit. Phone: (478)987-3141. FCRV 10% discount. FMCA discount.

SEE AD THIS PAGE

(W) FAIR HARBOR RV PARK & CAMPGROUND—(Houston) *From jct I-75 (exit 135) & Hwy 127/224: Go 500 ft W on Hwy 127/224. Enter on R.*

WELCOME

◊◊◊◊FACILITIES: 153 sites, typical site width 30 ft, 153 full hkups, (20, 30 & 50 amps), some extended stay sites, 101 pull-thrus, cable TV, wireless Instant Internet access at site, phone on-site Internet access (needs activ), wireless Internet access central location, tenting, RV storage, laundry, RV supplies, LP gas by weight/by meter, ice, tables, fire rings, grills.

◊◊◊RECREATION: rec hall, rec room/area, pavilion, pond fishing, golf nearby, planned activities, horseshoes, hiking trails.

Pets welcome. Partial handicap access. Open all yr. Big rigs welcome. Internet friendly. Clubs welcome. Rate in 2007 $28 for 4 persons. MC/VISA/Debit. Member ARVC, GARVC. Phone: (877)988-8844. CCUSA discount. FMCA discount.

e-mail: fairharbor@yahoo.com

SEE AD THIS PAGE

(N) Perry Ponderosa Park—(Peach) *From jct I-75 (exit 142) & Hwy 96: Go 1/4 mi E on Hwy 96. Enter on L.* ◊◊◊◊FACILITIES: 65 sites, typical site width 25 ft, 65 full hkups, (30 & 50 amps), some extended stay sites, 65 pull-thrus, laundry, LP gas by weight/by meter, ice, tables, patios. ◊◊RECREATION: playground, 2 shuffleboard courts, sports field. Pets welcome. No tents. Open all yr. Big rigs welcome. Rate in 2007 $21-23 for 2 persons. Phone: (478)825-8030.

(S) TWIN OAKS RV PARK—(Houston) *From jct I-75 (exit 127) & Hwy 26: Go 1000 ft E on Hwy 26. Enter on L.*

WELCOME

RELAX IN A QUIET COUNTRY SETTING!
Spend a night & you'll want to stay a month! Conveniently located near Central Georgia attractions & historic sites. After a day of sightseeing, enjoy our Olympic sized pool or Gazebo covered hot tub. www.twinoaksrvpark.com

◊◊◊◊◊FACILITIES: 72 sites, typical site width 40 ft, 64 full hkups, 8 W&E, (30 & 50 amps), 40 pull-thrus, wireless Instant Internet access at site, phone on-site Internet access (needs activ), wireless Internet access central location, tenting, cabins, RV storage, dump station, non-guest dumping $, laundry, ltd groceries, RV supplies, LP gas by weight/by meter, ice, tables, patios, fire rings, wood.

◊◊◊◊RECREATION: rec hall, rec room/area, pavilion, equipped pavilion, swim pool, whirlpool, golf nearby, bsktball, horseshoes, sports field, v-ball.

Pets welcome. Partial handicap access. Open all yr. Big rigs welcome. Escort to site. Clubs welcome. Rate in 2007 $30 for 2 persons. MC/VISA/DISC/Debit. Member ARVC. Phone: (478)987-9361. CCUSA discount. FMCA discount.

e-mail: info@twinoaksrvpark.com

SEE AD THIS PAGE

PINE MOUNTAIN—C-1

(E) F. D. ROOSEVELT STATE PARK—(Harris) *From jct US 27 & Hwy 354: Go 3 mi E on Hwy 354 to Hwy 190. Enter on R.*

WELCOME

FACILITIES: 140 sites, 140 W&E, (20, 30 & 50 amps), 30 pull-thrus, tenting, cabins, dump station, non-guest dumping $, laundry, ltd groceries, ice, tables, fire rings, grills, wood, controlled access gate.

RECREATION: swim pool, boating, electric motors only, canoeing, dock, 4 rowboat rentals, lake fishing, golf nearby, playground, sports field, hiking trails. Rec open to public.

Pets welcome. Partial handicap access. Open all yr. Big rigs welcome. Clubs welcome. MC/VISA/DISC/AMEX/DC. Phone: (800) 864-7275.

e-mail: fdr.peachnet@peachnet.campuscwix.net

SEE AD TRAVEL SECTION PAGE 189

(N) PINE MOUNTAIN RVC—(Troup) *From jct US-27 & Hwy-18: Go 1 mi N on US-27. Enter on L.*

WELCOME

WE'RE IN THE HEART OF IT ALL Y'ALL!
Your resort destination in the Georgia countryside! Nearby Callaway Gardens, Roosevelt's little white house, Wild Animal Safari & National Pow Museum. Ideal for golfers, antique collectors, history buffs & gardening fans.

◊◊◊◊FACILITIES: 250 sites, typical site width 30 ft, 250 full hkups, (20, 30 & 50 amps), 48 pull-thrus, wireless Instant Internet access at site, phone on-site Internet access (needs activ), wireless Internet access central location, tenting, cabins, RV storage, dump station, non-guest dumping $, laundry, ltd groceries, RV supplies, LP gas by weight/by meter, ice, tables, fire rings, wood, controlled access gate.

◊◊◊◊RECREATION: rec hall, pavilion, swim pool, mini-golf ($), golf nearby, bsktball, 5 bike rentals, playground, horseshoes, sports field, v-ball.

Pets welcome. Partial handicap access. Open all yr. Big rigs welcome. Internet friendly. Escort to site. Clubs welcome. Rate in 2007 $25-45 for 2 persons. MC/VISA/Debit. Member ARVC, GARVC. Phone: (706)663-4329. FMCA discount.

e-mail: psanfilippo@rvcusa.com

SEE AD TRAVEL SECTION PAGE 190

REIDSVILLE—D-4

(C) GORDONIA-ALATAMAHA STATE PARK—(Tattnall) *In city limits at Jct US 280 & Park St.*

WELCOME

FACILITIES: 27 sites, 27 W&E, (30 & 50 amps), 3 pull-thrus, tenting, dump station, non-guest dumping $, laundry, ice, tables, fire rings, grills, wood.

RECREATION: swim pool, boating, electric motors only, dock, 5 rowboat/8 pedal boat rentals, lake fishing, mini-golf ($), golf nearby, tennis, v-ball. Rec open to public.

GORDONIA-ALATAMAHA STATE PARK—Continued on next page

REIDSVILLE—Continued
GORDONIA-ALATAMAHA STATE PARK—Continued

Pets welcome. Partial handicap access. Open all yr. Big rigs welcome. MC/VISA/DISC/AMEX. Phone: (800) 864-7275.

e-mail: gordoniast@alltel.net

SEE AD TRAVEL SECTION PAGE 189

(N) Wiregrass Trail RV Campground—(Tattnall) *From jct US 280 & Hwy 121/23: Go 3/4 mi E on US 280, then 1 mi N on Anderson St, then 1/4 mi W on Thomas K. Scott Rd, then 1/4 mi S on Catfish Ln. Enter on L.* ◆◆FACILITIES: 39 sites, typical site width 30 ft, 22 full hkups, 17 W&E, (30 & 50 amps), many extended stay sites, 8 pull-thrus, tenting, dump station, laundry, LP gas by weight, ice, tables, fire rings, wood. ◆◆RECREATION: rec hall, pavilion, boating, electric motors only, canoeing, pond fishing, play equipment, horseshoes. Pets welcome. Open all yr. Rate in 2007 $20-22 for 4 persons. Phone: (912)557-4185.

RICHMOND HILL—D-5

(SE) FORT MCALLISTER STATE HISTORIC PARK—*From jct I-95 (exit 15/90) & Hwy 144: Go 6-1/2 mi SE on Hwy 144, then E on Spur 144 to the end.*

FACILITIES: 65 sites, 65 W&E, (30 & 50 amps), 57 pull-thrus, tenting, cabins, dump station, laundry, ice, tables, fire rings, grills, wood, controlled access gate.

RECREATION: boating, canoeing, kayaking, ramp, dock, 3 canoe/2 kayak rentals, saltwater/river fishing, golf nearby, playground, hiking trails. Rec open to public.

Pets welcome. Partial handicap access. Open all yr. Big rigs welcome. MC/VISA/DISC/AMEX. Phone: (800) 864-7275.

e-mail: ftmcallr@coastalnow.net

SEE AD TRAVEL SECTION PAGE 189

(W) KOA-Savannah South—(Bryan) *From jct I-95 (exit 87) & US 17: Go 1/2 mi S on US 17. Enter on L.* ◆◆◆◆FACILITIES: 125 sites, typical site width 24 ft, 105 full hkups, 20 W&E, (30 & 50 amps), some extended stay sites, 100 pull-thrus, tenting, dump station, non-guest dumping $, laundry, groceries, LP gas by meter, ice, tables. ◆◆◆RECREATION: rec hall, swim pool, boating, electric motors only, canoeing, 2 rowboat rentals, lake fishing, playground. Pets welcome, quantity restrict. Open all yr. Big rigs welcome. Internet friendly. Rate in 2007 $36 for 2 persons. Phone: (912) 756-3396. KOA 10% value card discount.

RINCON—D-5

(S) Whispering Pines RV Park—(Effingham) *From jct I-95 (exit 109) & Hwy 21: Go 1/2 mi N on Hwy 21, then 3 mi W on Hwy 30, then 2 mi N on Hodgeville Rd. Enter on R.* ◆◆◆◆FACILITIES: 72 sites, typical site width 35 ft, 59 full hkups, 13 W&E, (50 amps), many extended stay sites (in winter), 15 pull-thrus, tenting, dump station, non-guest dumping $, laundry, LP gas by weight, ice, tables, patios. ◆◆◆RECREATION: pavilion, lake swimming, boating, canoeing, dock, rowboat rentals, lake fishing, playground, sports field, hiking trails. Pets welcome, size restrict. Partial handicap access. Open all yr. Big rigs welcome. Internet friendly. Rate in 2007 $34 for 2 persons. Phone: (912)728-7562.

RINGGOLD—A-1

(W) Chattanooga South-Lookout Mountain KOA—(Catoosa) *From jct I-75 (exit 350) & Hwy 2: Go 1/4 mi W on Hwy 2. Enter on R.* ◆◆◆◆FACILITIES: 145 sites, typical site width 35 ft, 60 full hkups, 82 W&E, (30 & 50 amps), 50 amps ($), 3 no hkups, 67 pull-thrus, tenting, laundry, groceries, LP gas by weight/by meter, ice, tables, fire rings, wood. ◆◆◆RECREATION: rec hall, rec room/area, pavilion, swim pool, playground, horseshoes, sports field, hiking trails. Pets welcome. Partial handicap access. Open all yr. Big rigs welcome. Internet friendly. Rate in 2007 $35-38 for 2 persons. Member ARVC, TNARVC. Phone: (800)562-4167. KOA 10% value card discount.

RISING FAWN—A-1

(N) CLOUDLAND CANYON STATE PARK—(Dade) *From I-59 (exit 11) & Hwy 136: Go 7 mi E on Hwy 136. Enter on L.*

FACILITIES: 103 sites, 73 W&E, (20 & 30 amps), 30 no hkups, 24 pull-thrus, tenting, cabins, dump station, non-guest dumping $, laundry, ltd groceries, ice, tables, fire rings, grills, wood.

RECREATION: pavilion, swim pool, golf nearby, playground, tennis, sports field, hiking trails, v-ball.

Pets welcome. Partial handicap access. Open all yr. Clubs welcome. MC/VISA/DISC/AMEX. Phone: (800)864-7275.

e-mail: cloudland-canyon-park@mail.dnr.state.ga.us

SEE AD TRAVEL SECTION PAGE 189

ROME—B-1

(S) COOSA RIVER CAMPGROUND (Rome-Floyd County Park) & Nature Center—(Floyd) *From Rome jct US 411 & US 27: Go 3 1/2 mi S on US 27/US 411 then 3 1/2 mi W on Walker Mountain Rd, then 1/2 mi N on Lock & Dam Rd. Enter at end.* FACILITIES: 33 sites, typical site width 30 ft, 33 full hkups, (30 & 50 amps), tenting, dump station, non-guest dumping $, laundry, ltd groceries, LP gas by weight, ice, fire rings, grills, wood. RECREATION: rec room/area, pavilion, boating, canoeing, ramp, dock, river fishing, playground, horseshoes, sports field, hiking trails, v-ball. Rec open to public. Partial handicap access. Open all yr. Phone: (706)234-5001.

ROYSTON—B-3

(W) VICTORIA BRYANT STATE PARK—(Franklin) *From jct Hwy 17 & US 29: Go 3 mi W on US 29S, then 1 mi N on Hwy 327. Enter on L.*

FACILITIES: 43 sites, 35 W&E, (30 & 50 amps), 8 no hkups, tenting, dump station, non-guest dumping $, laundry, ice, tables, fire rings, grills, wood, controlled access gate.

RECREATION: pavilion, swim pool, wading pool, river swimming, lake fishing, golf nearby, playground, planned activities, hiking trails, v-ball. Rec open to public.

Pets welcome. Partial handicap access. Open all yr. Clubs welcome. MC/VISA/DISC/AMEX. Phone: (800)864-7275.

e-mail: vbstparks@elbertonga.com

SEE AD TRAVEL SECTION PAGE 189

RUTLEDGE—C-3

(W) HARD LABOR CREEK STATE PARK—(Morgan) *From I-20 (exit 105) & Newborn Rd: Go 2-3/4 mi N on Newborn Rd, then 2 mi NE on Fairplay St. Enter on R.*

FACILITIES: 63 sites, typical site width 30 ft, 63 W&E, (30 & 50 amps), 8 pull-thrus, cable TV, tenting, cabins, dump station, non-guest dumping $, laundry, ltd groceries, ice, tables, fire rings, grills, wood.

RECREATION: pavilion, lake swimming, boating, 10 hp limit, canoeing, kayaking, ramp, dock, 5 rowboat/7 canoe/10 pedal boat rentals, lake fishing, golf nearby, playground, hiking trails. Rec open to public.

Pets welcome. Partial handicap access. Open all yr. Big rigs welcome. Clubs welcome. MC/VISA/DISC/AMEX. Phone: (800) 864-7275.

e-mail: hlcstpk@myexcel.com

SEE AD TRAVEL SECTION PAGE 189

ST. MARYS—F-5

(N) CROOKED RIVER STATE PARK—(Camden) *From jct I-95 (exit 3) & Hwy 40: Go 2-1/4 mi SE on Hwy 40, then 3 mi E on Kings Bay Rd, then 3-1/2 mi N on Spur 40. Enter on R.*

FACILITIES: 62 sites, 62 W&E, (30 & 50 amps), cable TV, tenting, cabins, dump station, non-guest dumping $, laundry, ice, tables, fire rings, grills, wood, controlled access gate.

RECREATION: pavilion, swim pool, boating, canoeing, kayaking, ramp, dock, saltwater fishing, mini-golf ($), golf nearby, playground, hiking trails.

Pets welcome. Partial handicap access. Open all yr. Clubs welcome. MC/VISA/DISC/AMEX. Phone: (800) 864-7275.

e-mail: crookstp@net-magic.net

SEE AD TRAVEL SECTION PAGE 189

SAVANNAH—D-5

See listings Richmond Hill, Rincon, Springfield, Statesboro & Tybee Island.

HARDEEVILLE RV-THOMAS' PARKS AND SITES—*From jct I-95 & I-16: Go 8-1/2 mi E on I-16 (exit 166), then 9 mi N on US 17, then 4 mi NE on 170-Alt Enter on R.*

SEE PRIMARY LISTING AT HARDEEVILLE, SC AND AD NEXT PAGE

KOA-POINT SOUTH—*From GA-SC border: Go 33 mi N on I-95 (exit 33), then 200 yds E on US 17, then S on Yemassee Rd, then 1/2 mi W on Campground Rd.*

SEE PRIMARY LISTING AT POINT SOUTH, SC AND AD NEXT PAGE

SAVANNAH—Continued on next page

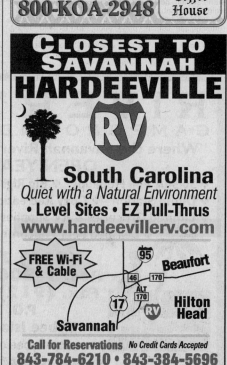

SAVANNAH—Continued

(E) MILITARY PARK (Hunter Army Airfield Trailer Camp) —(Chatham) *From jct I-95 & Hwy 204: Go 13 mi E on Hwy 204, then W on Stevenson Ave.* FACILITIES: 15 sites, 15 no hkups. RECREATION: Open all yr. For Military Use Only-w/Military ID Card. Phone: (912)315-9554.

RIVER'S END CAMPGROUND & RV PARK (City Park)—*From jct I-95 & I-16: Go 9 mi E on I-16 to(exit 167A), then 3/4 mi N on MLK Jr Blvd, then 1 mi E on Bay St, (stay in left hand lane), then 15 mi E on President St (becomes Island Expwy then US 80), then 2 blks N on Polk St. Enter on L.*

SEE PRIMARY LISTING AT TYBEE ISLAND AND AD PAGE 213

WELCOME

(W) SAVANNAH OAKS RV RESORT—(Chatham) *From jct I-95 (exit 94) & Hwy 204: Go 2 1/2 mi W on Hwy 204. Enter on L.*

◆◆◆◆FACILITIES: 139 sites, typical site width 30 ft, 111 full hkups, 28 W&E, (30 & 50 amps), some extended stay sites, 76 pull-thrus, cable TV, phone on-site Internet access (needs activ), wireless Internet access central location, dump station, non-guest dumping $, laundry, groceries, RV supplies, LP gas by weight/by meter, gas, marine gas, ice, tables, grills, controlled access gate.

◆◆◆RECREATION: rec room/area, pavilion, coin games, swim pool, boating, canoeing, kayaking, ramp, dock, lake fishing, golf nearby, playground.

Pets welcome. Partial handicap access. No tents. Open all yr. Big rigs welcome. Internet friendly. Escort to site. Clubs welcome. Rate in 2007

SAVANNAH OAKS RV RESORT—Continued on next page

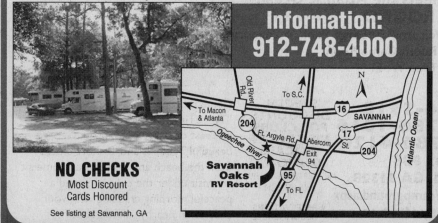

SAVANNAH—Continued
SAVANNAH OAKS RV RESORT—Continued

$38.50 for 2 persons. MC/VISA/DISC. Member ARVC, GARVC. Phone: (800)851-0717. FMCA discount.

e-mail: campinginsavannah@yahoo.com

SEE AD PAGE 214

(S) SKIDAWAY ISLAND STATE PARK—(Chatham) *From jct I-16 (exit 34A/164A) & Hwy 21: Go 5 mi SE on Hwy 21, then 2-1/2 mi S on Waters Ave, then 2-1/2 mi E on Diamond Causeway. Enter on L.*

FACILITIES: 88 sites, 88 W&E, (30 & 50 amps), 88 pull-thrus, cable TV, tenting, dump station, non-guest dumping $, laundry, ice, tables, fire rings, grills, wood.

RECREATION: swim pool, golf nearby, playground, hiking trails.

Pets welcome. Partial handicap access. Open all yr. Big rigs welcome. MC/VISA/DISC/AMEX. Phone: (800)864-7275.

e-mail: skidaway@g-net.net

SEE AD TRAVEL SECTION PAGE 189

SCREVEN—E-4

✽ **(N) BOYETTE CAMPER SALES**—*From jct US 341 & US 84/Hwy 38: Go 12 mi SW on US 84/Hwy 38. Enter on L.* SALES: travel trailers, 5th wheels, pre-owned unit sales. SERVICES: full-time mech, RV appliance repair, body work/collision repair, LP gas by weight/by meter, dump station, RV storage, sells parts/accessories, installs hitches. Open all yr. MC/VISA/Debit. Phone: (866)281-6787.

e-mail: heather@boyettecamper.com

SEE AD THIS PAGE

STATESBORO—D-4

✽ **(E) Ellis Travel Trailers**—*From jct US 301 Bypass & US 80: Go 1 mi E on US 80. Enter on L.* SALES: travel trailers, 5th wheels, pre-owned unit sales. SERVICES: RV appliance repair, RV towing, LP gas by weight/by meter, sells parts/accessories, installs hitches. Open all yr. MC/VISA/DISC/AMEX. Phone: (912)764-2043.

(S) Parkwood RV Park & Cottages—(Bulloch) *From jct I-16 (exit 116) & US 301: Go 8-1/2 mi N on US 301. Enter on R.* ◆◆◆◆FACILITIES: 48 sites, typical site width 30 ft, 48 full hkups, (20, 30 & 50 amps), some extended stay sites, 36 pull-thrus, laundry, ice, tables. ◆◆RECREATION: rec hall, swim pool, planned activities, horseshoes. Pets welcome. No tents. Open all yr. Big rigs welcome. Internet friendly. Rate in 2007 $23-27.50 Z. Phone: (912)681-3105. FMCA discount.

STONE MOUNTAIN—B-2

(N) STONE MOUNTAIN FAMILY CAMPGROUND—(DeKalb) *From east jct I-285 (exit 39B) & US 78: Go 7-1/2 mi E on US 78 (Stone Mountain Fwy), then 500 ft S to East Gate. Enter at end.*

◆◆◆◆FACILITIES: 441 sites, typical site width 20 ft, 144 full hkups, 253 W&E, (20, 30 & 50 amps), 44 no hkups, some extended stay sites (in winter), 17 pull-thrus, wireless Internet access central location ($), tenting, dump station, non-guest dumping $, laundry, groceries, RV supplies, LP gas by weight/by meter, ice, tables, fire rings, grills, wood, controlled access gate.

◆◆◆◆◆RECREATION: equipped pavilion, swim pool, boating, 10 hp limit, canoeing, kayaking, ramp, dock, 12 rowboat/50 pedal boat rentals, lake fishing, mini-golf ($), putting green, playground, planned activities, tennis, horseshoes, sports field, hiking trails, v-ball. Rec open to public.

Pets welcome. Partial handicap access. Open all yr. 14 day max stay Apr 1-Oct 31. 3 day min reservation Mem Day, 4th of July & Lab Day wknds. Big rigs welcome. Internet friendly. Clubs welcome. Rate in 2007 $28-50 per family. MC/VISA/DISC/AMEX/Debit. ATM. Phone: (800)385-9807.

e-mail: campground@stonemountainpark.com

SEE AD TRAVEL SECTION PAGE 191 AND AD DISCOVER SECTION PAGE 40

⚑ **(N) STONE MOUNTAIN PARK**—*From east jct I-285 (exit 39B) & US 78: Go 7-1/2 mi E on US 78 (Stone Mountain Fwy), then 500 ft S to East Gate. Enter at end.* Georgia's #1 attraction featuring 3200 acres of family fun including 1870s town of Crossroads, Scenic Railroad, Riverboat, Summit Skyride, world's largest Lasershow, 36-holes of golf, & Ride The Ducks. New water

STONE MOUNTAIN—Continued
STONE MOUNTAIN PARK—Continued

park opening May 2008. Open all yr. MC/VISA/DISC/AMEX/Debit. ATM. Phone: (800)317-2006.

e-mail: generalinfo@stonemountainpark.com

SEE AD TRAVEL SECTION PAGE 191 AND AD DISCOVER SECTION PAGE 40

SUMMERVILLE—B-1

(S) JAMES H. FLOYD STATE PARK—(Chattooga) *From jct US 27 & Sloppy Floyd Lake Rd: Go 3 mi SW on Sloppy Floyd Lake Rd. Enter at end.*

FACILITIES: 25 sites, 25 W&E, (20, 30 & 50 amps), 8 pull-thrus, tenting, cabins, dump station, non-guest dumping $, laundry, ice, tables, fire rings, grills, wood.

RECREATION: pavilion, boating, electric motors only, canoeing, kayaking, ramp, dock, 8 rowboat/8 pedal boat rentals, lake fishing, playground, hiking trails. Rec open to public.

Pets welcome. Partial handicap access. Open all yr. Big rigs welcome. MC/VISA/DISC/AMEX. Phone: (800) 864-7275.

e-mail: jhfloyd@roman.net

SEE AD TRAVEL SECTION PAGE 189

SYLVANIA—D-5

(S) Pinevale Campground—(Screven) *From jct Hwy-21 & US-301: Go 2-3/4 mi S on US-301. Enter on L.* ◆◆FACILITIES: 50 sites, typical site width 20 ft, 50 full hkups, (20, 30 & 50 amps), some extended stay sites, 50 pull-thrus, tenting, laundry. ◆◆RECREATION: boating, canoeing, pond fishing, sports field, hiking trails. Pets welcome. Open all yr. Rate in 2007 $15-17 for 2 persons. Phone: (912)863-4347.

TALKING ROCK—B-2

(N) Talona Creek Campground—(Gilmer) *From jct US 76 & Hwy 515: Go 11-1/2 mi S on 515, then 1/2 mi E on Carns Mill Rd. Enter on R.* ◆◆◆FACILITIES: 46 sites, typical site width 25 ft, 21 full hkups, 25 W&E, (30 & 50 amps), some extended stay sites, 4 pull-thrus, heater not allowed, laundry, ltd groceries, ice, tables, fire rings, grills, wood. ◆◆RECREATION: pavilion, river fishing, playground, sports field, v-ball. Pets welcome. Partial handicap access. Open all yr. Big rigs welcome. Internet friendly. Rate in 2007 $23 per family. Phone: (888)835-1266.

TALLAPOOSA—B-1

(S) Big Oak RV Park—(Haralson) *From jct I-20 (exit 5) & Hwy 100: Go 1/4 mi N on Hwy 100. Enter on R.* ◆◆◆FACILITIES: 50 sites, typical site width 25 ft, 50 full hkups, (20, 30 & 50 amps), some extended stay sites, 26 pull-thrus, tenting, dump station, laundry, LP gas by weight/by meter, tables, grills. RECREATION: pavilion. Pets welcome. Open all yr. Rate in 2007 $17-19 for 2 persons. Phone: (770)574-5522.

TALLULAH FALLS—A-3

(C) TALLULAH GORGE STATE PARK—(Rabun) *From Jct Tallulah Gorge Bridge & US 441: Go 1/2 mi N on US 441, then 1/2 mi SE on Jane Hurt Yarn Rd. Enter on R.*

FACILITIES: 50 sites, typical site width 30 ft, 50 W&E, (20 & 30 amps), 10 pull-thrus, tenting, dump station, non-guest dumping $, laundry, ice, tables, fire rings, grills, wood, controlled access gate.

RECREATION: pavilion, lake swimming, boating, electric motors only, canoeing, kayaking, lake/river fishing, playground, tennis, hiking trails. Rec open to public.

Pets welcome. Partial handicap access. Open all yr. Clubs welcome. MC/VISA/DISC/AMEX. Phone: (800)864-7275.

SEE AD TRAVEL SECTION PAGE 189

Visit Woodall's Advertised Attractions

THOMASVILLE—F-2

(N) Sugar Mill Plantation RV Park—(Thomas) *From N jct US 84 & US 19: Go 7 mi N on US 19, then 500 feet W on McMillan Rd. Enter on R.* ◆◆◆◆FACILITIES: 139 sites, typical site width 35 ft, 139 full hkups, (20, 30 & 50 amps), some extended stay sites, 25 pull-thrus, tenting, laundry, LP gas by meter, ice, tables. ◆◆◆RECREATION: rec hall, rec room/area, boating, no motors, canoeing, pond fishing, 2 shuffleboard courts, planned activities, horseshoes, sports field, hiking trails. Pets welcome. Partial handicap access. Open all yr. Big rigs welcome. Internet friendly. Rate in 2007 $25.68 per vehicle. Phone: (229)227-1451.

THOMSON—C-4

(W) BIG HART CAMP AREA (COE - J. Strom Thurmond Lake)—(McDuffie) *From town: Go 8 mi N on US 78, then 4 mi E on Russell Landing Rd.* FACILITIES: 31 sites, typical site width 20 ft, 30 ft max RV length, 24 W&E, (30 amps), 7 no hkups, 15 pull-thrus, tenting, dump station, fire rings, grills. RECREATION: pavilion, lake swimming, boating, ramp, dock, lake fishing, playground, hiking trails. Open Apr 1 thru Oct 31. Phone: (706)595-8613.

(W) RAYSVILLE BRIDGE CAMP AREA (COE - J. Strom Thurmond Lake)—(McDuffie) *From jct US-78 & Hwy-43: Go 7 mi N on Hwy-43.* FACILITIES: 55 sites, typical site width 20 ft, 30 ft max RV length, 55 W&E, (30 amps), 4 pull-thrus, tenting, dump station, grills. RECREATION: pavilion, lake swimming, boating, ramp, lake fishing, playground, sports field. Open Mar 1 thru Oct 30. Phone: (864)595-6759.

TIFTON—E-3

(W) AGRIRAMA RV PARK (RV SPACES)—(Tifton) *From jct I-75 (exit 63B) & Whiddon Mill Rd: Go 1/4 mi W on Whiddon Mill Rd. Enter on R.*

FACILITIES: 42 sites, typical site width 24 ft, accepts full hkup units only, 42 full hkups, (20, 30 & 50 amps).

RECREATION: pavilion, golf nearby.

Pets welcome. No tents. Open all yr. No restroom. Big rigs welcome. Rate in 2007 $20 per vehicle. DISC/AMEX. ATM. Phone: (800)767-1875.

e-mail: market@agrirama.com

SEE AD NEXT PAGE

⚑ **(W) AGRIRAMA-GEORGIA'S MUSEUM OF AGRICULTURE & HISTORIC VILLAGE**—*From jct I-75 (exit 63B) & Whiddon Mill Rd: Go 1/4 mi W on Whiddon Mill Rd. Enter on R.* Working farm and rural town with grist mill, cotton gin, sawmill, 19th century drug store and homes, turpentine still, country store, 35 restored buildings & machinery displays. Costumed interpreters. Large paved parking lot, picnic area. Open Tue - Sat. Open all yr. Clsd Thur & Fri for Thanksgiving, wk of Xmas & New Yrs Day. MC/VISA/AMEX. ATM. Phone: (800)767-1875.

e-mail: market@agrirama.com

SEE AD NEXT PAGE

(W) AMY'S SOUTH GEORGIA RV PARK—(Tift) *From jct I-75 (exit 60) & South Central Ave: Go 1 mi W on South Central Ave. Enter on R.*

◆◆◆FACILITIES: 86 sites, typical site width 30 ft, 61 full hkups, 25 W&E, (30 & 50 amps), some extended stay sites (in winter), 63 pull-thrus, wireless Instant Internet access at site, phone Internet access central location, tenting, cabins, RV storage, dump station, laundry, ltd groceries, RV supplies, LP gas by weight/by meter, ice, tables, fire rings, grills, wood, controlled access gate.

AMY'S SOUTH GEORGIA RV PARK—Continued on next page

TIFTON—Continued
AMY'S SOUTH GEORGIA RV PARK—Continued

◇◇◇RECREATION: rec hall, pavilion, swim pool, pond fishing, fishing supplies, golf nearby, playground, sports field.

Pets welcome. Open all yr. Big rigs welcome. Internet friendly. Clubs welcome. Rate in 2007 $25 for 2 persons. MC/VISA/AMEX/Debit. Member ARVC, GARVC. Phone: (229)386-8441. FMCA discount.

e-mail: amysrvpark@planttel.net

SEE AD THIS PAGE

Visit our website www.woodalls.com

TIFTON—Continued

(S) THE PINES CAMPGROUND—(Tift) *From jct I-75 (exit 61) & Omega Rd: Go 500 ft W on Omega Rd, then 300 feet S on Casseta Rd. Enter on R.*

WELCOME

◇◇◇FACILITIES: 34 sites, typical site width 25 ft, 34 full hkups, (20, 30 & 50 amps), 30 pull-thrus, cable TV, wireless Instant Internet access at site, tenting, laundry.

◇RECREATION: rec hall, golf nearby.

Pets welcome. Partial handicap access. Open all yr. Big rigs welcome. Internet friendly. Escort to site. Clubs welcome. Rate in 2007 $22 per vehicle. Phone: (229)382-3500.

SEE AD PAGE 215

TOCCOA—B-3

(S) TOCCOA RV PARK—(Stephens) *From jct I-85 (exit 173) & Hwy 17: Go 13 mi N on Hwy 17A, then 3-1/4 mi E on Oak Valley Rd. Enter on R.*

WELCOME

◇◇◇FACILITIES: 46 sites, typical site width 28 ft, 30 full hkups, 1 W&E, (30 & 50 amps), 50 amps ($), 15 no hkups, some extended stay sites, 20 pull-thrus, phone on-site Internet access (needs activ), tenting, dump station, non-guest dumping $, laundry, tables.

◇RECREATION: pavilion, golf nearby, horseshoes, sports field, hiking trails.

Pets welcome. Open all yr. Clubs welcome. Rate in 2007 $12 per vehicle. Phone: (706)886-2654.

SEE AD THIS PAGE

TOWNSEND—E-5

(E) LAKE HARMONY BICYCLE BARN—*From jct I-95 (exit 58) & Hwy 57: Go 1/4 mi W on Hwy 57. Enter on L.* Professional Bicycle Repair & Service. Located at Lake Harmony RV Park. Open all yr. Phone: (912)832-4338.

WELCOME

SEE AD TRAVEL SECTION PAGE 187

(E) LAKE HARMONY RV PARK & CAMPGROUND—(McIntosh) *From jct I-95 (exit 58) & Hwy 57: Go 1/4 mi W on Hwy 57. Enter on L.*

WELCOME

◇◇◇◇FACILITIES: 50 sites, typical site width 25 ft, 50 full hkups, (30 & 50 amps), some extended stay sites, 50 pull-thrus, cable TV, wireless Instant Internet access at site, tenting, RV storage, laundry, RV supplies, LP gas by weight/by meter, ice, tables, fire rings, wood.

◇◇◇◇RECREATION: rec hall, rec room/area, lake swimming, boating, electric motors only, canoeing, kayaking, 3 rowboat/6 kayak/pedal boat rentals, lake fishing, fishing supplies, golf nearby, bsktball, 2 shuffleboard courts, horseshoes, sports field.

Pets welcome. Partial handicap access. Open all yr. Big rigs welcome. Internet friendly. Escort to

LAKE HARMONY RV PARK & CAMPGROUND—Continued on next page

TOWNSEND—Continued
LAKE HARMONY RV PARK & CAMPGROUND—Continued

site. Clubs welcome. Rate in 2007 $27.50-29.50 for 2 persons. MC/VISA/Debit. Member ARVC, GARVC. Phone: (888)767-7864. FMCA discount.

e-mail: lakeharmonypark@aol.com

SEE AD TRAVEL SECTION PAGE 187

TRENTON—A-1

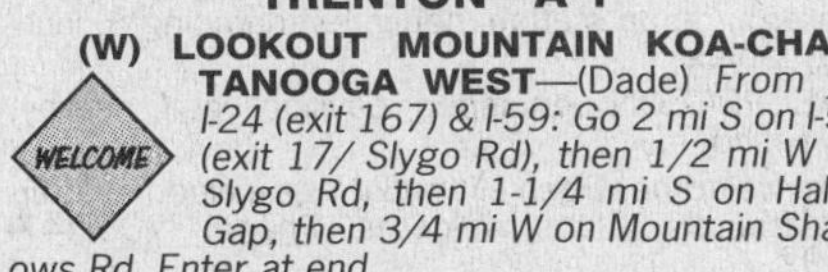

(W) LOOKOUT MOUNTAIN KOA-CHATTANOOGA WEST—(Dade) *From jct I-24 (exit 167) & I-59: Go 2 mi S on I-59 (exit 17/ Slygo Rd), then 1/2 mi W on Slygo Rd, then 1-1/4 mi S on Hales Gap, then 3/4 mi W on Mountain Shadows Rd. Enter at end.*

◆◆◆FACILITIES: 109 sites, typical site width 24 ft, 44 full hkups, 50 W&E, (20, 30 & 50 amps), 15 no hkups, 6 pull-thrus, wireless Instant Internet access at site, cable Internet access central location, tenting, cabins, RV storage, dump station, non-guest dumping $, laundry, ltd groceries, RV supplies, LP gas by weight/by meter, ice, tables, fire rings, grills, wood.

◆◆◆◆RECREATION: rec hall, pavilion, coin games, swim pool, golf nearby, playground, planned activities (wkends only), horseshoes, sports field, hiking trails, v-ball.

Pets welcome, breed restrict. Open all yr. Big rigs welcome. Internet friendly. Clubs welcome. Rate in 2007 $28-36 for 2 persons. MC/VISA/DISC/AMEX/Debit. Member ARVC, GARVC. Phone: (800) 562-1239. KOA 10% value card discount.

e-mail: lookoutmountainkoa@yahoo.com

SEE AD CHATTANOOGA, TN PAGE 790 AND AD DISCOVER SECTION PAGES 62 & 63

TWIN CITY—D-4

(E) GEORGE L. SMITH STATE PARK—(Emanuel) *From jct US 80 & Hwy 23: Go 3-1/2 mi SE on Hwy 23, then 1-3/4 mi E on George L Smith State Park Rd. Enter at end.*

FACILITIES: 25 sites, 25 W&E, (20, 30 & 50 amps), 5 pull-thrus, cable TV, tenting, cabins, dump station, non-guest dumping $, laundry, ice, tables, fire rings, grills, wood.

RECREATION: rec hall, pavilion, boating, 10 hp limit, canoeing, kayaking, ramp, dock, 10 rowboat/6 canoe/6 pedal boat rentals, lake/stream fishing, golf nearby, playground, sports field, hiking trails. Rec open to public.

Pets welcome. Partial handicap access. Open all yr. Big rigs welcome. Clubs welcome. MC/VISA/DISC/AMEX. Phone: (800) 864-7275.

e-mail: glsst@pineland.net

SEE AD TRAVEL SECTION PAGE 189

TYBEE ISLAND—D-5

(W) RIVER'S END CAMPGROUND & RV PARK (City Park)—(Chatham) *From jct I-95 & I-16: Go 9 mi E on I-16 to(exit 167A, then 3/4 mi N on MLK Jr Blvd, then 1 mi E on Bay St (stay in left hand lane), then 15 mi E on President St (Becomes Island Expwy then into US 80 to Tybee Island), then 2 blks N on Polk St. Enter on L.*

WHERE THE RIVER MEETS THE SEA!

A place for all seasons. Sandy beaches, great fishing & history at every turn. Only 3 blocks from beach & 15 miles to historic Savannah. Enjoy Tybee time under our live oak canopy. www.cityoftybee.ort/campground.aspx.

FACILITIES: 127 sites, typical site width 20 ft, 64 full hkups, 27 W&E, (30 & 50 amps), 36 no hkups, some extended stay sites (in winter), 34 pull-thrus, cable TV, wireless Instant Internet access at site, cable Internet access central location, tenting, dump station, non-guest dumping $, laundry, ltd groceries, RV supplies, LP gas by weight/by meter, ice, tables, wood.

RECREATION: rec hall, rec room/area, pavilion, swim pool, golf nearby, 7 bike rentals, planned activities, horseshoes, hiking trails.

Pets welcome, breed restrict, size restrict. Partial handicap access. Open all yr. Big rigs welcome. Internet friendly. Escort to site. Clubs welcome. MC/VISA/DISC/AMEX/Debit. Member ARVC, GARVC. Phone: (800)786-1016.

e-mail: campground@cityoftybee.org

SEE AD SAVANNAH PAGE 213

Save time! Plan ahead with WOODALL'S!

UNADILLA—D-2

(W) JOHN BLEAKLEY MOTOR HOMES—*From jct I-75 (exit 122) & Hwy 230: Go 1/4 mi W on Hwy 230, then 1/2 mi S on Bleakley Blvd. Enter on L.* SALES: motor homes, mini-motor homes, micro-mini motor homes, pre-owned unit sales. SERVICES: full-time mech, engine/chassis repair, RV appliance repair, body work/collision repair, mobile RV svc, sells parts/accessories, installs hitches. Open all yr. MC/VISA/DISC/AMEX. Phone: (877) 456-3700.

e-mail: sales@bleakleyrv.com

SEE AD TRAVEL SECTION PAGE 189

(S) Southern Trails RV Resort—(Dooly) *From jct I-75 (exit 121) & US 41: Go 1/4 mi E on US 41, then 500 ft E on Speeg Rd, then 1/2 mi S on E Railroad St/Arena Rd. Enter on L.* ◆◆◆FACILITIES: 208 sites, typical site width 30 ft, 148 full hkups, 60 W&E, (30 & 50 amps), 50 amps ($), 180 pull-thrus, tenting, dump station, laundry, LP gas by weight/by meter, ice, tables. ◆◆◆RECREATION: rec hall, swim pool, pond fishing, playground, planned activities, horseshoes, sports field. Pets welcome. Open all yr. Big rigs welcome. Internet friendly. Rate in 2007 $25 for 2 persons. Phone: (478)627-3255. CCUSA discount. FMCA discount.

VALDOSTA—F-3

EAGLES ROOST RV RESORT—*From jct I-75 (exit 16) & US 84: Go 11 mi S on I-75 (exit 5), then 500 ft E on Hwy 376, then 1/2 mi S on Mill Store Rd. Enter on L.*

SEE PRIMARY LISTING AT LAKE PARK AND AD THIS PAGE

(W) River Park RV Park—(Lowndes) *From jct I-75 (exit 18) & Hwy 133: Go 1 Block W on Hwy 133. Enter on R.* ◆◆◆FACILITIES: 57 sites, typical site width 20 ft, 57 full hkups, (30 & 50 amps), some extended stay sites, 57 pull-thrus, tenting, dump station, non-guest dumping $, laundry, tables, patios. ◆◆RECREATION: swim pool, pond fishing, hiking trails. Pets welcome. Open all yr. Big rigs welcome. Internet friendly. Phone: (229)244-8397.

WARM SPRINGS—C-1

(N) RAMSEY RV PARK—(Meriwether) *From jct Alt US 27/Hwy 41 & Alt Hwy 85: Go 1-1/4 mi N on Alt Hwy 85. (White House Pkwy) Enter on L.*

◆◆◆FACILITIES: 27 sites, typical site width 24 ft, 27 full hkups, (30 & 50 amps), 50 amps ($), some extended stay sites, 17 pull-thrus, tenting, laundry, tables.

◆RECREATION: swim pool, golf nearby.

Pets welcome. Partial handicap access. Open all yr. Big rigs welcome. Clubs welcome. Rate in 2007 $16.80-17.85 for 2 persons. Phone: (706) 655-2480.

SEE AD THIS PAGE

WARNER ROBINS—D-3

MILITARY PARK (Robins AFB FAMCAMP)—(Houston) *On I-75. On base.* FACILITIES: 30 sites, 18 W&E, 12 no hkups, tenting, laundry. RECREATION: canoeing. Open all yr. For Military Use Only-w/Military ID Card. Phone: (912)926-0918.

WARTHEN—C-3

(N) HAMBURG STATE PARK—(Washington) *From jct Hwy 15 & Hwy 102: Go 1 mi N on Hwy 102, then 5 mi N on Hamburg Rd.*

FACILITIES: 30 sites, 30 W&E, (30 amps), 7 pull-thrus, tenting, dump station, non-guest dumping $, laundry, ltd groceries, ice, tables, fire rings, grills, wood.

RECREATION: pavilion, boating, 10 hp limit, canoeing, kayaking, ramp, dock, 5 rowboat/6 canoe/8 pedal boat rentals, lake/river fishing, playground, sports field, hiking trails. Rec open to public.

WARTHEN—Continued
HAMBURG STATE PARK—Continued

Pets welcome. Partial handicap access. Open all yr. MC/VISA/DISC/AMEX. Phone: (800) 864-7275.

SEE AD TRAVEL SECTION PAGE 189

WAYCROSS—E-4

(S) LAURA S. WALKER STATE PARK—(Ware) *From jct US 1 & US 82: Go 10 mi SE on US 82, then 2 mi E on Hwy 177. Enter on L.*

FACILITIES: 44 sites, 44 W&E, (20, 30 & 50 amps), 4 pull-thrus, tenting, cabins, dump station, non-guest dumping $, laundry, ice, tables, fire rings, grills, wood.

RECREATION: swim pool, boating, canoeing, kayaking, ramp, dock, 12 canoe/4 motorboat rentals, lake fishing, golf nearby, playground, sports field, hiking trails, v-ball.

Pets welcome. Open all yr. Big rigs welcome. MC/VISA/DISC/AMEX. Phone: (800) 864-7275.

SEE AD TRAVEL SECTION PAGE 189

WEST POINT—C-1

(N) AMITY PARK (West Point Lake COE)—(Troup) *From town: Go 7 mi N on State Line Rd (crossing Georgia/Alabama border), then 1 mi E on CR 393. Park is in Alabama & Georgia.* FACILITIES: 96 sites, 93 W&E, 3 no hkups, tenting, dump station, laundry, grills. RECREATION: boating, ramp, dock, lake fishing, playground, tennis, sports field, hiking trails. Open Mar 18 thru Sep 10. Phone: (706)499-2404.

(N) R. SHAEFER HEARD (COE - West Point Lake)—(Troup) *From town: Go 3 mi N on US-29 & follow signs.* FACILITIES: 117 sites, typical site width 20 ft, 117 W&E, (20 & 30 amps), tenting, dump station, laundry, fire rings, grills. RECREATION: boating, ramp, dock, lake fishing, playground, tennis, sports field, hiking trails. Partial handicap access. Open all yr. Phone: (706)645-2404.

Staying close to home next year? Pre-order the 2009 Directory in a smaller regional version. It contains all the great information Woodall's North American Directory contains, but in a handy to-go version, specific to the states or provinces you need.

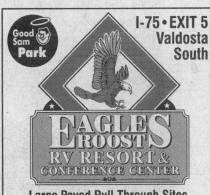

WINDER—B-2

(W) FORT YARGO STATE PARK—(Barrow) *From jct Hwy 8 & Hwy 81: Go 1 mi S on Hwy 81. Enter on L.*

WELCOME

FACILITIES: 47 sites, 40 W&E, (20, 30 & 50 amps), 7 no hkups, 4 pull-thrus, tenting, cabins, dump station, non-guest dumping $, laundry, ice, tables, fire rings, grills.

RECREATION: pavilion, lake swimming, boating, 10 hp limit, canoeing, ramp, dock, 10 rowboat/10 canoe/10 pedal boat rentals, lake fishing, mini-golf ($), golf nearby, tennis, hiking trails. Rec open to public.

Pets welcome. Partial handicap access. Open all yr. Big rigs welcome. Clubs welcome. MC/VISA/DISC/AMEX/DC. Phone: (800) 864-7275.

e-mail: fort_yargo_park@dnr.state.ga.us

SEE AD TRAVEL SECTION PAGE 189

WINFIELD—C-4

(N) WINFIELD CAMP AREA (COE - J. Strom Thurmond Lake)—(Mc Duffie) *From Hwy 150: Follow signs 4 mi N on Winfield Rd.* FACILITIES: 80 sites, typical site width 20 ft, 35 ft max RV length, 80 W&E, (30 amps), tenting, dump station, grills. RECREATION: lake swimming, boating, ramp, lake fishing, playground, hiking trails. Open Mar 1 thru Oct 30. Phone: (706)541-0147.

WOODSTOCK—B-2

(S) VICTORIA CAMPGROUND (Allatoona Lake COE) —(Cherokee) *From town: Go S on Hwy 5, then 6 mi W on Hwy 92, then 2 mi N on Bells Ferry Rd, then 2-1/2 mi W. Enter on L.* FACILITIES: 72 sites, typical site width 20 ft, 72 W&E, (30 amps), 8 pull-thrus, tenting, dump station, laundry, fire rings, grills. RECREATION: lake swimming, boating, ramp, dock, lake fishing, playground. Partial handicap access. Open Mar 1 thru Sep 13. No reservation. Phone: (678)721-6700.

We are on the web! Come visit us at www.woodalls.com

WRENS—C-4

(S) BOSS'S RV PARK—(Jefferson) *From N jct US 1/221 & Hwy 17: Go 1-1/2 mi S on US 1/221/Hwy 17 to Hoyte Braswell Rd. Enter on L.*

WELCOME

◆◆◆FACILITIES: 71 sites, typical site width 25 ft, 71 full hkups, (20, 30 & 50 amps), 50 amps ($), some extended stay sites, wireless Instant Internet access at site, tenting, RV storage, dump station, non-guest dumping $, laundry, tables.

◆RECREATION: equipped pavilion, golf nearby, horseshoes.

Pets welcome. Open all yr. Big rigs welcome. Internet friendly. Clubs welcome. Phone: (706)547-0402.

SEE AD AUGUSTA PAGE 201

A restaurant guide tells you where to eat when you
reach your destination.
Woodall's Cookbooks tell you how to eat delicious food
all the way there.
Save 30 to 50%!
Take these two cookbooks along on your next camping or RV trip. Cooking on the Road with Celebrity Chefs ($16.95) is the first-ever cookbook that suggests gourmet meals suitable for your RV kitchen. Campsite Cookbook ($4.95) gives suggestions for planning wholesome outdoor meals for the Tenter or RVer!
WOODALL'S
Cooking on the Road
Campsite Cookbook
To order, call 1-877-680-6155 and mention promo code 669 or order online at www.woodalls.com/shop.

Kentucky

READER SERVICE INFO

The following businesses have placed an ad in the Kentucky Travel Section. To receive free information, enter their Reader Service number on the Reader Service Card opposite page 48/Discover Section in the front of this directory:

Advertiser	RS#
Kentucky Lake KOA at Prizer Point	3429
Northside RV's	3371
Shepherdsville Bullitt County	3388
Wolf Creek Resort	3690

TIME ZONE

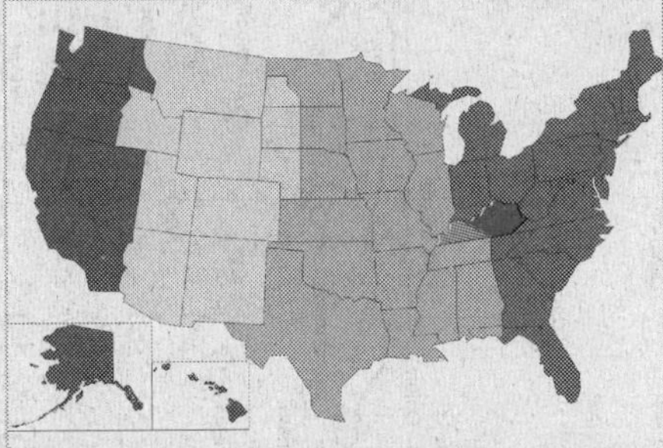

North central and eastern Kentucky are in the Eastern Time Zone and the south central and western part of the state are in the Central Time Zone.

TOPOGRAPHY

Kentucky's topography ranges from mountains in the east to uplands in the central portion to plains in the west. Elevation ranges from 260 feet along the Mississippi River to 4,145 feet at Black Mountain.

TRAVEL & TOURISM INFO

State Agency:
Kentucky Department of Tourism
Capital Plaza Tower, 22nd Floor
500 Mero Street
Frankfort, KY 40601
(800/225-8747 or 502/564-4930)
www.kentuckytourism.com

Regional Agencies:

Ashland Area CVB
1509 Winchester Ave.
Ashland, KY 41101
(800/377-6249 or 606/329-1007)
www.visitashlandky.com

Bell County Tourism Commission
2215 Cumberland Ave.
Middlesboro, KY 40965
(800/988-1075 or 606/248-2482)
www.MountainGateway.com

Bowling Green Area CVB
352 Three Springs Road
Bowling Green, KY 42104
(800/326-7465 or 270/782-0800)
www.visitbgky.com

Columbia/Adair County Tourism
201 Burkesville St., PO Box 116
Columbia, KY 42728
(270/284-6020)
www.columbia-adaircounty.com

Frankfort Area Chamber
100 Capital Avenue
Frankfort, KY 40601
(502/223-8261)
www.visitfrankfort.com

Henderson County Tourist Commission
101 N. Water Street, Suite B
Henderson, KY 42420
(800/648-3128 or 270/826-3128)
www.hendersonky.org

Louisville CVB
401 W. Main St., Suite 2300
Louisville, KY 40202
(888/LOUISVILLE or 800/626-5646)
www.gotolouisville.com

Northern Kentucky CVB
(800/STAY-NKY)
www.staynky.com

Paducah CVB
128 Broadway
Paducah, KY 42001
(800/PADUCAH or 270/443-8784)
www.paducah-tourism.org

Local Agencies:
Check with the Chamber of Commerce or Tourism Bureau for the locality you are interested in. Check with the state or regional agencies for phone numbers and addresses. Also visit the Kentucky Dept. of Tourism website for links to communities at www.kentuckytourism.com

SHOPPING

Factory Stores of America Outlet Center, Georgetown. Located off I-75 at exit 126, this outlet center includes Carolina Pottery and Levi's. (502/868-0682).

The Shops at Lexington Center, Lexington. Upscale shopping center in the newly renovated Lexington Convention Center features unique specialty stores and hand-crafted works of art. 430 W. Vine St. (859/233-4567)

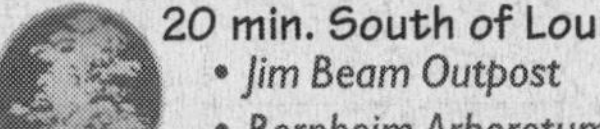

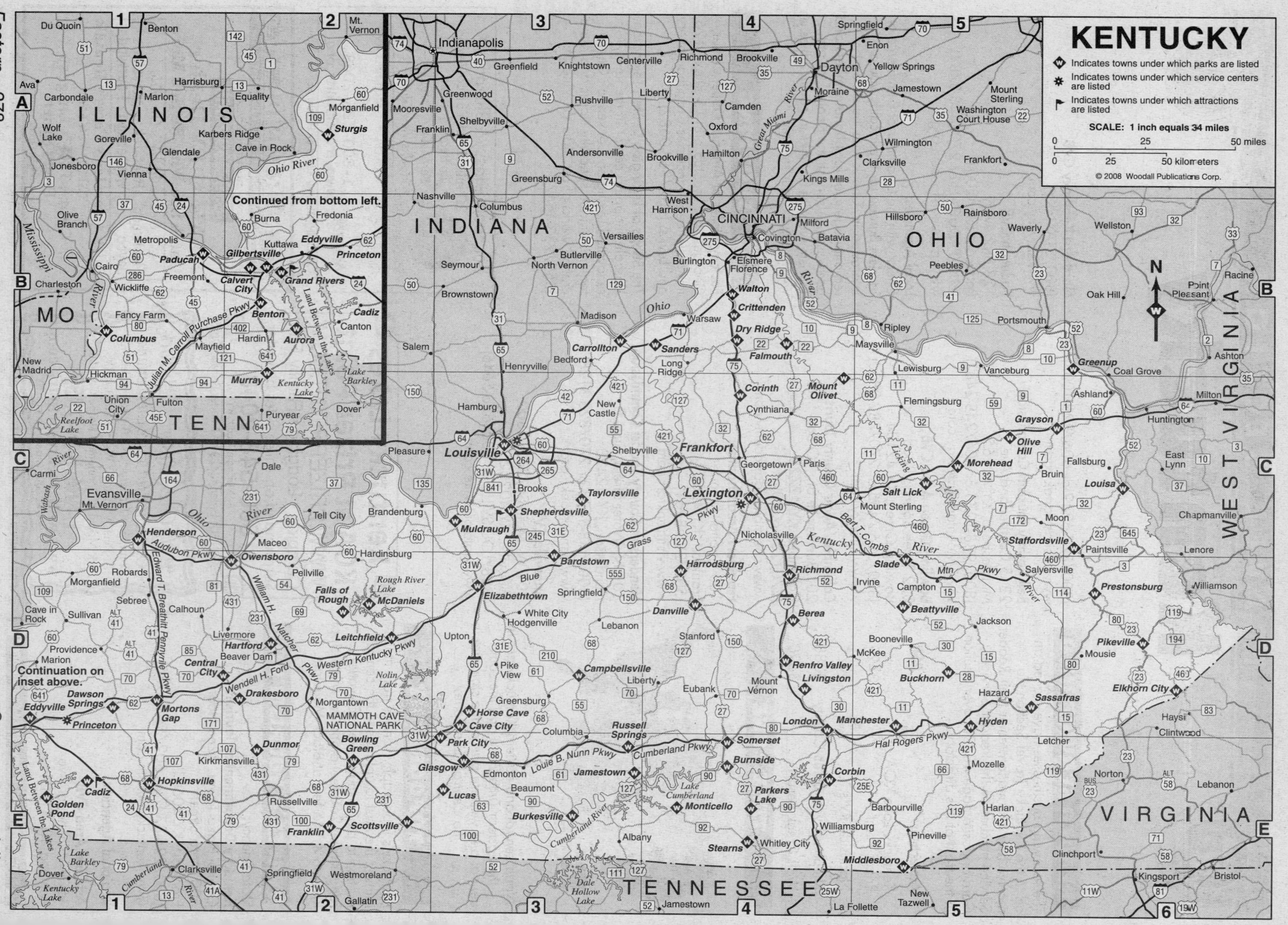
KENTUCKY
Indicates towns under which parks are listed
Indicates towns under which service centers are listed
Indicates towns under which attractions are listed
SCALE: 1 inch equals 34 miles
0 25 50 miles
0 25 50 kilometers
© 2008 Woodall Publications Corp.
INDIANA
OHIO
WEST VIRGINIA
VIRGINIA
TENNESSEE
ILLINOIS
MO
TENN
Continued from bottom left.
Continuation on inset above.

West Kentucky Factory Outlets, Eddyville. Shop at 42 outlet stores, located at US-62 at KY-730. (270/388-7379).

RECREATIONAL INFO

Hunting/Fishing Licenses: Kentucky Dept. of Fish and Wildlife Resources, #1 Sportsman's Lane, Frankfort, KY 40601 (800/858-1549) www.kdfwr.state.ky.us/

DESTINATIONS

BLUEGRASS REGION

Berea. See working studios of woodworkers, potters, quilters, jewelers, photographers, weavers and furniture makers in the "Folk Arts & Crafts Capital of Kentucky." **The Kentucky Artisan Center**, at Exit 77 on I-75, celebrates the accomplishments of Kentucky's artisans. Free admittance, shopping, demonstrations and restaurants.

Danville. History abounds in this picturesque community. Ten constitutional conventions took place at Danville's **Constitution Square State Historic Site** between 1784 and 1792.

Frankfort. It was here in the valley of the Kentucky River that Vice President Aaron Burr was first charged with treason. Today, Frankfort pays tribute to its past with museums such as the **Kentucky History Center** and the **Kentucky Military History Museum**. The **Frankfort Cemetery** contains the gravesites of Daniel and Rebecca Boone. Free tours of **Buffalo Trace Distillery** are offered. The **Old Governor's Mansion** is now open to public tours after renovation. Built in 1798, it was once referred to as the "Palace," hosting many presidents, officials of state and visiting dignitaries.

Harrodsburg. At **Old Fort Harrod State Park**, costumed interpreters guide visitors through the fort's daily activities. Also onsite are a pioneer cemetery, a cabin (believed to be where Abraham Lincoln's parents were married) and an 1830 Mansion Museum containing Native American and Civil War artifacts.

Kentucky Horse Park. Self-guided tours feature wide-screen films, covered wagon and pony rides and the Parade of Breeds. The American Saddle Horse Museum features a multi-image show and interactive exhibits.

Lawrenceburg. Wild Turkey Bourbon Distillery allows you to experience all the sights, sounds and smells of a real working distillery, located on the top of a scenic 300-foot Kentucky River gorge.

The Lexington Children's Museum has 7 galleries and 90 exhibits that can be touched and explored by children of all ages. There are experiment stations, traveling exhibits and workshops.

Mary Todd Lincoln House. Tour the first site in the U.S. dedicated to a woman.

Perryville. Kentucky's most important Civil War battle took place at **Perryville Battlefield State Historic Site** in October 1862. Perryville's downtown **Merchant's Row** buildings appear much as they did during the Civil War.

Shaker Village of Pleasant Hill contains 30 original buildings and over 20 miles of original stone fencing.

BLUEGRASS, BLUES AND BARBECUE REGION

Henderson. Founded and mapped with the guidance of Daniel Boone, Henderson has a wide array of 19th century homes. John James Audubon created many of his bird paintings while living here, many of which are on view at the **John James Audubon Museum** where visitors can also watch birds in a circular observation room and purchase limited edition prints.

Owensboro. The state's third largest city is home to the **International Bluebrass Music Museum** and headquarters of the **International Bluegrass Music Association.** Two floors of the state-of-the-art exhibits include a history of bluegrass, instruments used by well-known musicians and listening stations equipped with audio domes. The **Owensboro Area Museum** houses exhibits on astronomy, geology, paleontology, archaeology, biology and a hands-on physical science area.

CAVES, LAKES AND CORVETTES REGION

Bowling Green. Stop by the **Kentucky Museum** which preserves Kentucky's cultural heritage with a variety of photographs, manuscripts, artifacts and permanent and rotating exhibits. Also visit the **National Corvette Museum** to see the only place in the world where this classic American car is made.

Cave City. In the heart of Cave Country, the city boasts many famous area caves as well as activities for the whole family. Attractions include: Big Mike's Mystery House; Dinosaur World, an outdoor museum; Guntown Mountain with live entertainment, saloon shows, carnival rides and more; Kentucky Action Park with go-carts, bumper boats and shops; several museums and water activities on the Green River. The many area caves include:

Mammoth Cave National Park. A World Heritage Site and International Biosphere Reserve, Mammoth Cave's history stretches back 4,000 years. The longest cave system in the world holds over 350 miles of mapped corridors. Geologists estimate that there could be as many as 600 miles of undiscovered passageways. The 379 feet deep cave contains vast subterranean chambers. Several underground rivers, including Echo River and the River Styx, flow through the deepest chambers. Several guided tours are available ranging from one and a half to six hours long. Above ground, enjoy a myriad of outdoor activities including hiking, camping, boat rides, fishing and wildlife viewing as you explore the 53,000 acres of scenic beauty.

Horse Cave. Visit the **American Cave Museum** and learn of the adventures of early cavers. Exhibits include lifelike models of cave animals, modern cave exploration, history of Horse Cave and Mammoth Cave and groundwater science and conservation. Then visit **Hidden River Cave**, known as the greatest cave restoration in the U.S. Closed for 50 years due to pollution, the cave was revived due to conservation efforts and reopened a decade ago. At **Kentucky Down Under**, you can interact with Australian wildlife such as kangaroos, wallabies, Blue Tongued Skinks and Bearded Dragons; or learn to play a didgeridoo or throw a boomerang.

DANIEL BOONE COUNTRY

Cumberland Gap. One of America's most important historical sites is located in Kentucky's far southeast corner. Walk in the footsteps of Daniel Boone at the **Cumberland Gap National Historic Park,** the largest National Historic Park in the country.

RV Sales & Service

	SALES	SERVICE
LEXINGTON		
Northside RV'S	•	•
LOUISVILLE		
Louisville RV Center	•	•
Tinker's Toys Dixie RV	•	•
PRINCETON		
Murphy's RV's	•	•

Things to See & Do

CADIZ
The Landing Restaurant at Prizer Point Marina

GRAND RIVERS
Miss Scarlett's Restaurant

SHEPHERDSVILLE
Shepherdsville Bullitt County Tourism

Daniel Boone National Forest. Canoe and whitewater raft on the Cumberland, Rockcastle and Red rivers or hike on the **Sheltowee Trace National Recreation Trail.**

Natural Bridge, Slade. Located in the midst of the Daniel Boone National Forest, near the Red River Gorge Geological Area, the natural sandstone arch was formed over million of years. The arch spans 78 feet in length and 65 feet in height.

Renfro Valley. Travel the rhythm of the road in eastern Kentucky, where you'll find the Commonwealth's musical roots. Visit the **Renfro Valley Entertainment Center,**"Kentucky's Country Music Capital," for toe-tappin' tunes of the Bluegrass. Nearby, the **Kentucky Music Hall of Fame and Museum** showcases Kentucky's Musical Heritage.

KENTUCKY'S APPALACHIANS REGION

Carter Cave State Resort Park, located 38 miles west of Ashland. An underground waterfall 30 feet high is featured. Take a tour through **Saltpetre Cave, Cascade Cave** and **Bat Cave**.

Paintsville. The U.S. 23 Country Music Highway Museum opened in the spring of '05. It is dedicated to the country music entertainers that are listed on the brown state signs along U.S. 23. Entertainers featured in the museum are: Billy Ray Cyrus, The Judds, Ricky Skaggs, Hylo Brown, Loretta Lynn, Crystal Gayle, Dwight Yoakam, Patty Loveless, Tom T. Hall, Keith Whitley, Gary Stewart and Rebecca Lynn Howard.

Van Lear. The **Coal Miners' Museum** is located in the building that originally housed the headquarters of the Miller's Creek Division of the Consolidation Coal Company. Displays include: coal mining tools, a restored "company" doctor's office, a post office, a 1950's snack bar, a diorama of the town as it was in the 1930's, the old town jail, a Van Lear Schools collection and much more.

KENTUCKY'S DERBY REGION

Bardstown. A walking or driving tour includes attractions such as **Heaven Hill Distilleries**, offering guided tours; and **My Old Kentucky Home State Park,** which features "The Stephen Foster Story" outdoor musical during the summer months. **Federal Hill** is a Georgian-style mansion and formal gardens. **The Civil War Museum** contains rare artifacts, photos, uniforms, cannons, flags, battle wagons, medical equipment, weapons and person al items. The museum focuses on the western states involved in the war.

Elizabethtown. Walking tours are led by characters such as Carrie Nation, George Armstrong Custer, Sara Bush Lincoln, P.T. Barnum and Jenny Lind.

Louisville. Hop the **Toonerville II Trolley** or opt for a leisurely carriage ride on the **Louisville Horse Trams**. Cruise the Ohio River aboard the **Belle of Louisville**, or the **Star of Louisville. Louisville Zoo** offers seasonal camel and elephant rides. If it's a thrill you're looking for, check out **Six Flags Kentucky Kingdom.** Art enthusiasts won't want to miss the **Kentucky Center** with its 3 stages of entertainment, the **Speed Art Museum and GlassWorks**. For an all-star experience admire the world's largest baseball bat at the **Louisville Slugger Museum.** The **Kentucky Derby Festival** and the **Thunder Over Louisville** fireworks extravaganza is the prelude to the one and only **Kentucky Derby**. Visit the **Ken-**

Woodall's Quick & Easy Reference for Kentucky

	BIG RIGS WELCOME	INTERNET FRIENDLY	PETS WELCOME	WEB SAVER
BEREA				
Oh Kentucky Campground	▲	●	■	
Walnut Meadow RV Park	▲	●	■	
CADIZ				
Kentucky Lakes KOA at Prizer Point	▲	● (Wi-Fi)	■	
CAVE CITY				
Cave Country RV Campground	▲	● (Wi-Fi)	■	
CRITTENDEN				
Cincinnati South Rose Garden Resort		●	■	
EDDYVILLE				
Indian Point RV Park		●	■	
Lake Barkley RV Resort	▲	● (Wi-Fi)	■	
FRANKFORT				
Elkhorn Campground	▲	● (Wi-Fi)	■	
GRAND RIVERS				
Exit 31 RV Park	▲	● (Wi-Fi)	■	
HARRODSBURG				
Chimney Rock RV Park & Marina	▲	●	■	
MOREHEAD				
Poppy Mountain Campground			■	
PADUCAH				
Duck Creek RV Park	▲	● (Wi-Fi)	■	
RENFRO VALLEY				
KOA-Renfro Valley	▲	● (Wi-Fi)	■	$
RUSSELL SPRINGS				
Wolf Creek Resort Park		● (Wi-Fi)	■	
SHEPHERDSVILLE				
Louisville South KOA	▲	● (Wi-Fi)	■	
TAYLORSVILLE				
Rolling Hills Camping Resort	▲	● (Wi-Fi)	■	
WALTON				
Oak Creek Campground		● (Wi-Fi)	■	

▲ = Big Rigs Welcome; ● = Internet Hookups; ● = (Wi-Fi available); ■ = Pets Welcome; $ = Web Saver Coupons

***Check out the "How to Use This Directory" section in the front of this book for a description of the criteria Woodall's uses in this chart.**

tucky Derby Museum next to Churchill Downs. It features exhibits, computerized hands-on displays, memorabilia and a multimedia show that captures the thrill of the race.

NORTHERN KENTUCKY RIVER REGION

Covington Landing, Covington. This riverfront showcase offers outstanding views of the Cincinnati skyline and entertainment. **The Newport Aquarium** is located in the nearby Covington/Newport area.

SOUTHERN LAKES REGION

Big South Fork National River and Recreation Area offers a variety of natural and historical sights and activities. Visit the **K&T Special** railroad 16-mile round trip tour and ride next to spectacular gorges along the river. The train also includes visits to the **McCreary County Museum** and the **Blue Heron Coal Mining Camp**.

See some of the most pristine lakes in the country and be sure not to miss **Cumberland Falls** - the only place to see a moonbow during a full moon in the Northern Hemisphere.

WESTERN WATERLANDS REGION

Big South Fork National River & Recreation Area. Located at Kentucky's south-central border, this extensive recreation area is comprised of rugged, mountainous forestland. Whitewater rafting is excellent on the Big South Fork of the Cumberland River. Aboard the **Big South Fork Scenic Railway** you can view all that nature has to offer. One of the most scenic train rides in the country, the 11-mile, narrated, open-air excursion travels through the gorge with stops at the **Blue Heron Mining Community.**

Daniel Boone's Grave.
Photo courtesy Kentucky Tourism

Hopkinsville. The 19.7 acre Trail of Tears **Commemorative Park** is one of the few documented campsites along the 1,200 mile trail. The Heritage Center with history exhibits is located in a period log cabin.

Fort Campbell, 15 miles south of Hopkinsville, is the headquarters of the 101st Airborne "Screaming Eagles" Division. Exhibits can be seen at the **Don F. Pratt Memorial Museum**, which displays historic aircraft including WWII cargo gliders and those of the C-119 and C-47 series.

Great River Road. A 40-mile portion of this scenic car and bike route passes through western Kentucky's Reelfoot National Wildlife Refuge to Columbus-Belmont State Park. **Reelfoot Lake** was formed by earthquakes in the early 1800s. The national wildlife refuge has a vast cypress swamp that is home to many wetland plants and animals.

Land Between the Lakes. Located between Kentucky Lake and Lake Barkley, this 40-mile-long peninsula offers unlimited opportunities for camping, swimming, fishing, boating and hiking. Also on-site is the **Golden Pond Visitor Center** for maps and a list of attractions, nature center, planetarium and living history farm. In January, guides lead visitors to nesting sites of Bald and Golden eagles during the Gathering of Eagles weekend.

Paducah. Known as "Quilt City USA," visit the **Museum of the American Quilter's Society** located in this historic town. Various exhibits are on display in three galleries. The lobby features a quality museum shop and sunlit stained glass windows based on quilt patterns. Also see Paducah's colorful history depicted in over 30 spectacular murals painted on the city's floodwall. The 1905 brick Market House is home to the **Yeiser Art Center**, the **William Clark Market House Museum** and the **Market House Theatre.**

Venture River Water Park, Eddyville. This waterpark is home to such rides as Hurricane Bay, Dueling Demons and Old Man River.

The Woods and Wetlands Wildlife Center, west of Cadiz. See the huge 12,000-gallon aquarium, home to native fish, reptiles and amphibians. A walk through the park features birds of prey and wild mammals.

ANNUAL EVENTS

JANUARY

Winter Civil War Era Ball & Battle, Nancy; Annual Kentucky Opry Talent Show, Benton (through May).

FEBRUARY

Edison Birthday Celebration, Louisville.

MARCH

Bluegrass Series, Renfro Valley; Trigg County Civil War Days, West Cadiz Park; Celtic Fusion, Somerset; Chocolate Festival, Maysville; Battle of Paducah Celebration, Paducah.

APRIL

Thunder Over Louisville, Louisville; Kentucky Derby Festival, Louisville; Rolex Three Day Event, Lexington; Hillbilly Days, Pikeville; AQS National Quilt Show & Contest, Paducah.

MAY

International Barbecue Festival, Owensboro; Annual Kentucky Oaks, Louisville; Kentucky Derby, Louisville; Mountain Laurel Festival, Pineville; Kentucky Scottish Weekend, Carrollton; Corvette ZR-1 Gathering, Bowling Green.

JUNE

Horse Show, Shelbyville; Great American Brass Band Festival, Danville; Festival of the Bluegrass, Lexington; W.C. Handy Blues & Barbecue Festival, Henderson; Civil War Encampment, Harrodsburg.

JULY

Fourth of July Celebrations, Statewide; Freedom Fest, Murray; Newport Arts & Music Fest, Newport; Old Time Fiddlers Contest, Rough River Dam State Park.

AUGUST

Duncan Hines Festival, Bowling Green; Kentucky State Fair, Louisville; Kentucky Heartland Festival, Elizabethtown; Western Kentucky State Fair, Hopkinsville; US 127 Outdoor Sale, from Covington to Gadsden, AL; Battle of the Blue Licks, Mt. Olivet.

SEPTEMBER

Oktoberfest, Covington; Trail of Tears Indian Pow Wow, Hopkinsville; Marion Co. Ham Days, Lebanon; Festival of the Horse, Georgetown; Kentucky Bourbon Festival, Bardstown.

OCTOBER

Kentucky Apple Festival, Paintsville; Wooly Worm Fest, Beattyville; Bluegrass Fan Fest, Louisville; October Court Days, Mt. Sterling.

NOVEMBER

Christmas in the Valley, Renfro Valley; Southern Lights, Lexington; Festival of the Mountain Masters, Harlan.

DECEMBER

The Shaker Order of Christmas in the Village, Harrodsburg; Winter Wonderland of Lights, Ashland; Christmas Candlelight Tours, Bardstown.

Kentucky

AURORA—B-2

(W) Aurora Oaks Campground—(Marshall) *From jct US 68 & SR 80: Go 250 yds E on US 68/SR 80, then 500 yds N on KOA Ln. Enter at end.* ◊◊◊FACILITIES: 59 sites, typical site width 25 ft, accepts full hkup units only, 59 full hkups, (30 & 50 amps), mostly extended stay sites, 7 pull-thrus, laundry, ice, tables, fire rings, wood. ◊◊RECREATION: pavilion, swim pool, pond fishing, play equipment. Pets welcome. No tents. Open Mar 15 thru Nov 15. Big rigs welcome. Rate in 2007 $20-22 for 2 persons. Phone: (888)886-8704.

(E) KENLAKE STATE RESORT PARK—(Marshall) *From jct Hwy 80 & Hwy 94: Go 1/10 mi N on Hwy 94. Enter on R.* FACILITIES: 90 sites, 90 W&E, tenting, dump station, laundry, ice, fire rings, grills, wood. RECREATION: swim pool, boating, ramp, dock, lake fishing, playground, planned activities, tennis, horseshoes, hiking trails, v-ball. Pets welcome. Open Mar 31 thru Oct 31. Phone: (800)325-0143.

(W) Lakeside Campground & Marina—(Marshall) *From jct SR 80 & US 68: Go 3-3/4 mi N on US 68. Enter on R.* ◊◊◊FACILITIES: 135 sites, typical site width 20 ft, 50 full hkups, 85 W&E, (30 amps), many extended stay sites (in summer), 1 pull-thrus, tenting, dump station, non-guest dumping $, portable dump, laundry, ltd groceries, ice, tables, fire rings, grills, wood. ◊◊◊RECREATION: rec room/area, pavilion, swim pool, boating, ramp, dock, 4 motorboat rentals, lake fishing, playground. Pets welcome. Open 3rd wknd in Mar. thru Oct 31. Facilities fully operational Memorial Day thru Labor Day. Internet friendly. Rate in 2007 $24-26 for 2 persons. Phone: (270)354-8157.

(NW) Sportsman's Anchor Resort & Marina—(Marshall) *From jct SR 80 & US 68: Go 3-1/4 mi N on US 68. Enter on L.* ◊◊◊◊FACILITIES: 51 sites, typical site width 30 ft, 36 ft max RV length, 49 full hkups, 2 W&E, (30 amps), mostly extended stay sites (in summer), 3 pull-thrus, tenting, dump station, laundry, ltd

AURORA—Continued
Sportsman's Anchor Resort & Marina—Continued

groceries, ice, tables, fire rings, wood. ◊◊◊RECREATION: rec room/area, swim pool, lake swimming, boating, ramp, dock, 7 motorboat rentals, lake fishing, playground. Rec open to public. Pets welcome. Open Mid Mar thru Oct 31. Rate in 2007 $25-30 for 2 persons. Phone: (270)354-8493.

BARDSTOWN—D-3

(NW) Holt's Campground—(Nelson) *From jct Blue Grass Pky & US 31E: Go 2 mi N on US 31E, then 1/4 mi E on US 62, then 1-1/4 mi W on US 150, then 1-3/4 mi W on SR 245, then 100 yards S on SR 1430. Enter on R.* ◊◊◊FACILITIES: 60 sites, typical site width 30 ft, 8 full hkups, 32 W&E, (30 & 50 amps), 20 no hkups, some extended stay sites, 32 pull-thrus, tenting, dump station, non-guest dumping $, portable dump, ice, tables, patios, wood. ◊RECREATION: rec room/area, pavilion, lake fishing, sports field. Pets welcome. Open all yr. Big rigs welcome. Rate in 2007 $20 for 2 persons. Phone: (502)348-6717. FCRV 10% discount. FMCA discount.

(E) MY OLD KENTUCKY HOME SP—(Nelson) *From jct Blue-Grass Pky & US 31E: Go 2 mi N on US 31E, then 1/4 mi E on US 62, then 3/4 mi E on US 150, then 1/2 mi S on SR 49.* FACILITIES: 39 sites, 39 W&E, tenting, dump station, ice, fire rings, grills. RECREATION: playground, tennis. Pets welcome. Open Apr 1 thru Oct 31. Phone: (502)348-3502.

(W) White Acres Campground—(Nelson) *From jct Blue Grass Pky & US 31E: Go 2 mi N on US 31E, then 2-1/4 mi W on US 62. Enter on R.* ◊◊◊FACILITIES: 82 sites, typical site width 35 ft, 12 full hkups, 50 W&E, (30 & 50 amps), 20 no hkups, 40 pull-thrus, tenting, dump station, LP gas by weight/by meter, ice, tables, grills, wood. ◊◊RECREATION: pavilion, pond fishing, play equipment, sports field, hiking trails, v-ball. Rec open to public. Pets welcome. Open all yr. Big rigs welcome. Internet friendly. Rate in 2007 $24 for 2 persons. Member ARVC. Phone: (502)348-9677. FCRV 10% discount. FMCA discount.

BEATTYVILLE—D-5

(NW) Lago Linda Resort—(Lee) *From jct SH 402 & SH 11: Go 15 mi S on SH 11, then 3 mi W on SH 498, then 2-1/2 mi W on SH 52, then 1/2 mi S on SH 399. Enter on L.* ◊◊FACILITIES: 35 sites, typical site width 30 ft, 34 ft max RV length, 35 W&E, (20 & 30 amps), 14 pull-thrus, tenting, dump station, ice, tables, fire rings, wood. ◊◊RECREATION: boating, no motors, canoeing, dock, lake/pond fishing, horseshoes, sports field, hiking trails. Pets welcome. Open all yr. Call for reservations in winter months. Rate in 2007 $18-22 for 4 persons. Phone: (606)464-2876.

BENTON—B-2

(NE) Big Bear Resort—(Marshall) *From jct Purchase Pkwy & US 68: Go 4-3/4 mi S on US 68, then 3-1/2 mi E on Big Bear Pkwy/SR 58. Enter on L.* ◊◊FACILITIES: 73 sites, typical site width 24 ft, 32 ft max RV length, 15 full hkups, 55 W&E, (30 amps), 3 no hkups, many extended stay sites, 10 pull-thrus, tenting, dump station, portable dump, laundry, groceries, LP gas by weight, ice, tables, fire rings, wood. ◊◊◊RECREATION: swim pool, lake swimming, boating, ramp, dock, 6 rowboat/pedal boat/9 motorboat rentals, lake fishing, play equipment, shuffleboard court, planned activities (wkends only), sports field, v-ball. No pets. Open Apr 1 thru Oct 31. Facilities fully operational Memorial Day thru Labor Day. Rate in 2007 $20-30 for 2 persons. Phone: (800)922-BEAR.

Farmers in Kentucky grow large crops of tobacco, corn and hay.

BEREA—D-4

OH KENTUCKY CAMPGROUND—(Madison) *From jct I-75 (exit 76) & SR 21: Go 1/2 mi W on SR 21. Enter on R.*

WELCOME

◊◊◊FACILITIES: 80 sites, typical site width 20 ft, 42 full hkups, 29 W&E, (30 & 50 amps), 9 no hkups, many extended stay sites, 71 pull-thrus, phone Internet access central location, tenting, RV storage, dump station, non-guest dumping $, laundry, groceries, RV supplies, LP gas by weight/by meter, gas, ice, tables, fire rings, wood.

◊◊RECREATION: rec hall, 2 swim pools, playground, horseshoes, v-ball. Rec open to public.

Pets welcome. Partial handicap access. Open all yr. Pools open Memorial Day to Labor Day. Big rigs welcome. Internet friendly. Clubs welcome. Rate in 2007 $18-24 for 2 persons. MC/VISA/DISC/AMEX/Debit. Phone: (859)986-1150.

e-mail: dbowman765@adelphia.net

SEE AD THIS PAGE

WALNUT MEADOW RV PARK—(Madison) *From jct I-75 (exit 76) & SR 21: Go 3/4 mi W on SR 21. Enter on L.*

WELCOME

◊◊◊◊FACILITIES: 125 sites, typical site width 30 ft, 61 full hkups, 44 W&E, (50 amps), 20 no hkups, some extended stay sites, 59 pull-thrus, phone Internet access central location, tenting, RV storage, dump station, portable dump, laundry, LP gas by weight/by meter, ice, tables, fire rings, wood.

◊◊◊RECREATION: rec room/area, pavilion, bsktball, playground, planned activities (wkends only), horseshoes, hiking trails, v-ball.

Pets welcome. Partial handicap access. Open all yr. Big rigs welcome. Internet friendly. Escort to site. Clubs welcome. Rate in 2007 $22-24 for 2 persons. MC/VISA. Phone: (859)986-6180. CCUSA discount.

e-mail: contact@walnutmeadowrv.com

SEE AD THIS PAGE

BOWLING GREEN—E-2

(NW) Beech Bend Family Campground—(Warren) *From jct US 231 & I-65: Go 5-1/2 mi N on I-65, then 3/4 mi W on SR 446, then 3 mi W on US 68, then 2 mi N on Beech Bend Rd. Enter on R.* ◊◊◊FACILITIES: 498 sites, 298 full hkups, 200 W&E, (20, 30 & 50 amps), 150 pull-thrus, tenting, dump station, laundry, ice, tables, fire rings, wood. ◊◊◊◊RECREATION: rec hall, pavilion, swim pool, river fishing, horseshoes, sports field. Rec open to public. Pets welcome. Open all yr. Swimming - Memorial Day to Labor Day. Big rigs welcome. Internet friendly. Rate in 2007 $25 per vehicle. Phone: (270)781-7634.

(SE) KOA-Bowling Green—(Warren) *From jct I-65 & US 231: Go 1/2 mi N on US 231, then 1-1/2 mi S on Three Springs Rd. Enter on R.* ◊◊◊◊FACILITIES: 134 sites, typical site width 30 ft, 48 full hkups, 67 W&E, (30 & 50 amps), 19 no hkups, 81 pull-thrus, tenting, dump station, non-guest dumping $, laundry, groceries, LP gas by weight/by meter, ice, tables, fire rings, grills, wood. ◊◊◊◊RECREATION: rec room/area, equipped pavilion, swim pool, 2 pedal boat rentals, lake fishing, mini-golf ($), playground, planned activities (wkends only), horseshoes, sports field, hiking trails, v-ball. Rec open to public. Pets welcome. Partial handicap access. Open all yr. Facilities fully operational Swimming: Memorial Day thru Labor Day. Big rigs welcome. Internet friendly. Rate in 2007 $25-38 for 2 persons. Phone: (270)843-1919. KOA 10% value card discount.

BUCKHORN—D-5

(S) BUCKHORN DAM RECREATION AREA (COE-Buckhorn Lake)—(Perry) *From town: Go 1/2 mi S on Buckhorn Dam Rd.* FACILITIES: 33 sites, 29 W&E, 4 no hkups, tenting, non-flush toilets only, dump station, laundry, ice, fire rings, grills, wood. RECREATION: pavilion, lake swimming, boating, canoeing, ramp, dock, lake/river fishing, mini-golf ($), playground, tennis, horseshoes, hiking trails, v-ball. Rec open to public. Pets welcome. Open April thru Sep 30. Phone: (606)398-7251.

BUCKHORN—Continued on next page

Kentucky and neighboring Tennessee have enough coal to mine for thousands of years.

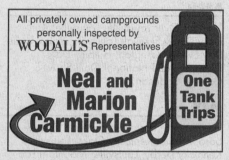

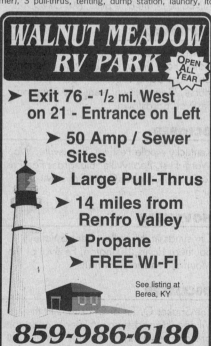

BUCKHORN—Continued

(S) TAILWATER CAMPGROUND (COE-Buckhorn Lake) —(Leslie) *From jct Hwy 28 & Old Hwy 28: Go 1/2 mi S on Old Hwy 28 (follow signs).* FACILITIES: 30 sites, 30 W&E, tenting, dump station, laundry, ice, fire rings, grills, wood. RECREATION: pavilion, ramp, lake/river fishing, playground, horseshoes, sports field. Pets welcome. Open Mid Apr thru Mid Oct. Phone: (606) 398-7220.

BURKESVILLE—E-3

(S) DALE HOLLOW LAKE STATE PARK—(Cumberland) *From town: Go 5 mi E on Hwy 90, then 5 mi SW on Hwy 449, then 3 mi S on Hwy 1206.* FACILITIES: 144 sites, 144 W&E, tenting, dump station, laundry, ice, grills, wood. RECREATION: swim pool, boating, ramp, dock, rowboat rentals, lake fishing, playground, planned activities, hiking trails. Pets welcome. Open all yr. Phone: (800)325-2282.

(S) Sulphur Creek Resort—(Cumberland) *From jct SR 90 & SR 61: Go 6-1/4 mi S on SR 61, then 1/2 mi E on Hwy 449, then 3-1/2 mi S on SR 485. Enter at end.* ◆◆◆FACILITIES: 22 sites, typical site width 22 ft, 9 full hkups, 13 W&E, (30 amps), 2 pull-thrus, tenting, dump station, laundry, groceries, LP gas by weight, ice, tables, fire rings. ◆◆RECREATION: rec room/area, lake swimming, boating, canoeing, ramp, dock, 4 rowboat/canoe/10 motorboat rentals, lake fishing, playground, hiking trails. Rec open to public. Pets welcome. Open Apr 1 thru Oct 31. Rate in 2007 $25 for 2 persons. Member COAK. Phone: (270)433-7200.

BURNSIDE—E-4

(S) GENERAL BURNSIDE STATE PARK—(Pulaski) *From jct US 27 & Hwy 90: Go 2 mi S on US 27.* FACILITIES: 94 sites, 94 W&E, tenting, dump station, laundry, ice, grills, wood. RECREATION: swim pool, lake swimming, boating, ramp, lake fishing, playground. Pets welcome. Open Apr 1 thru Oct 31. Phone: (606) 561-4104.

(SW) Lake Cumberland RV Park—(Pulaski) *From jct US 27 & SR 90: Go 1-1/2 mi W on Hwy 90, then 1/4 mi N on Gibson Ln. Enter on L.* ◆◆◆◆FACILITIES: 72 sites, typical site width 35 ft, 72 full hkups, (30 & 50 amps), many extended stay sites, 8 pull-thrus, tenting, laundry, tables. ◆◆RECREATION: rec room/area, swim pool, playground, horseshoes, v-ball. Pets welcome. Partial handicap access. Open all yr. Facilities fully operational May 1 thru Nov 1. Big rigs welcome. Internet friendly. Rate in 2007 $20-22 per family. Phone: (606)561-8222.

CADIZ—E-1

(W) Goose Hollow Campground—(Trigg) *From jct I-24 & SR 139 (exit 56): Go 1-1/4 mi S on SR 139, then 5-1/2 mi W on SR 276, then 1-1/4 m S on SR 274, then 1 mi S on Goose Hollow Rd. Enter on L.* ◆◆◆FACILITIES: 70 sites, typical site width 30 ft, 66 full hkups, 4 W&E, (30 & 50 amps), mostly extended stay sites, tenting, dump station, laundry, ice, tables, fire rings, wood. ◆◆RECREATION: rec room/area, pavilion, swim pool, play equipment, horseshoes, sports field, hiking trails, v-ball. Pets welcome. Open all yr. Facilities fully operational Mar 15 thru Nov 15. No water Nov to Mar. Rate in 2007 $18-20 per family. Phone: (270)522-2267.

(NW) HURRICANE CREEK RECREATIONAL AREA (COE-Lake Barkley)—(Trigg) *From jct US 68 & Hwy 139: Go 6-1/2 mi N on Hwy 139, then 7 mi W on Hwy 276, then 1/2 mi N on Hwy 274.* FACILITIES: 51 sites, 51 W&E, (20 & 30 amps), tenting, dump station, laundry, ltd groceries, fire rings, grills, wood. RECREATION: lake swimming, boating, ramp, lake fishing, playground. Pets welcome. Open Apr 29 thru Sep 5. Phone: (270) 522-8821.

(NW) KENTUCKY LAKES KOA AT PRIZER POINT—(Trigg) *From jct I-24 (exit 56) & Hwy 139: Go 1-1/2 mi S on Hwy 139, then 6 mi W on Hwy 276, then 1/4 mi S on Hwy 274, then 1 mi W on Prizer Point Rd. Enter on R.*

WELCOME

◆◆◆◆FACILITIES: 112 sites, typical site width 40 ft, 73 full hkups, 29 W&E, (30 & 50 amps), 50 amps ($), 10 no hkups, some extended stay sites, 52 pull-thrus, cable TV, wireless Instant Internet access at site, tenting, cabins, RV storage, dump station, laundry, full svc store, RV supplies, LP gas by weight/by meter, marine gas, ice, tables, patios, fire rings, grills, wood.

◆◆◆◆◆RECREATION: rec hall, rec room/area, equipped pavilion, coin games, 2 swim pools, wading pool, sprayground, lake swimming, boating, canoeing, kayaking, ramp, dock, 6 pontoon/4 kayak/10 pedal boat/9 motorboat rentals, lake fishing, fishing supplies, fishing guides, mini-golf ($), golf nearby, bsktball, 30 bike rentals, playground, planned activities, sports field, hiking trails, v-ball.

Pets welcome. Partial handicap access. Open Mar 18 thru Nov 6. Big rigs welcome. Internet friendly. Clubs welcome. Rate in 2007 $28-65 for 6 persons. MC/VISA/Debit. Member ARVC. Phone: (270)522-3762. KOA 10% value card discount.

e-mail: prizerpoint@prizerpoint.com

SEE AD TRAVEL SECTION PAGE 277 AND AD DISCOVER SECTION PAGES 62 & 63

CADIZ—Continued

(W) LAKE BARKLEY STATE RESORT PARK—(Trigg) *From jct Hwy 80 & US 68: Go 7 mi W on Hwy 80, then 2 mi N on Hwy 1489.* FACILITIES: 78 sites, 78 W&E, tenting, dump station, laundry, ice, grills, wood. RECREATION: pavilion, lake swimming, boating, ramp, dock, lake fishing, playground, planned activities, tennis, hiking trails, v-ball. Pets welcome. Open April thru October. Phone: (800)325-1708.

(NW) THE LANDING RESTAURANT AT PRIZER POINT MARINA—*From jct I-24 (exit 56) & Hwy 139: Go 1-1/2 mi S on Hwy 139, then 6 mi W on Hwy 276, the 1/4 mi S on Hwy 274, then 1 mi W on Prizer Point Rd. Enter on R.*

WELCOME

Floating restaurant featuring casual dining, serving breakfast, lunch & dinner all season. Overlooking Prizer Point & Lake Barkley. Open Apr 7 thru Nov 1. MC/VISA/Debit. Phone: (270)522-3762.

SEE AD TRAVEL SECTION PAGE 277

CALVERT CITY—B-2

(S) Cypress Lakes RV Park—(Marshall) *From jct I-24 (exit 27) & US 62: Go 1/2 mi W on US 62. Enter on R.* ◆◆◆FACILITIES: 130 sites, typical site width 30 ft, 122 full hkups, 8 W&E, (30 & 50 amps), some extended stay sites, 11 pull-thrus, tenting, dump station, non-guest dumping $, laundry, LP gas by weight/by meter, ice, tables, patios, fire rings, wood. ◆◆◆RECREATION: rec room/area, swim pool, lake fishing, playground, planned activities (wkends only), horseshoes, hiking trails, v-ball. Pets welcome. Open all yr. Big rigs welcome. Internet friendly. Rate in 2007 $19-21 for 2 persons. Phone: (270)395-4267.

(S) KOA-KY Lake Dam/Paducah—(Marshall) *From jct I-24 (exit 27) & US 62: Go 1-1/2 mi W on US 62. Enter on L.* ◆◆◆FACILITIES: 85 sites, typical site width 24 ft, 25 full hkups, 40 W&E, (20, 30 & 50 amps), 20 no hkups, 55 pull-thrus, tenting, dump station, non-guest dumping $, laundry, groceries, LP gas by weight/by meter, ice, tables, fire rings, grills, wood. ◆◆RECREATION: rec room/area, swim pool, pond fishing, playground, horseshoes, hiking trails, v-ball. Pets welcome. Open Mar 15 thru Nov 15. Facilities fully operational Memorial Day thru Labor Day. Big rigs welcome. Internet friendly. Rate in 2007 $28-36 for 2 persons. Phone: (270)395-5841. KOA 10% value card discount.

CAMPBELLSVILLE—D-3

(S) GREEN RIVER LAKE STATE PARK—(Taylor) *From jct Hwy 70 & Hwy 55: Go 8 mi S on Hwy 55.* FACILITIES: 157 sites, 157 W&E, tenting, dump station, laundry, groceries, ice, fire rings, grills, wood. RECREATION: lake swimming, boating, ramp, dock, rowboat rentals, river fishing, mini-golf, playground, horseshoes, hiking trails, v-ball. Pets welcome. Open Mar thru Nov. Phone: (270)465-8255.

(S) HOLMES BEND RECREATION AREA (COE-Green River Lake)—(Adair) *From jct Hwy 55 & Hwy 70: Go 12 mi S on Hwy 55, then 6 mi N on Holmes Bend Road, follow signs.* FACILITIES: 125 sites, 42 W&E, 60 E, 23 no hkups, tenting, dump station, groceries, ice, fire rings, wood. RECREATION: lake swimming, boating, ramp, dock, rowboat rentals, lake fishing, mini-golf, playground, hiking trails. Pets welcome. Open Apr 15 thru Oct 22. Phone: (270)384-4623.

(SW) PIKE RIDGE (COE-Green River Lake)—(Taylor) *From jct Hwy 55 & Hwy 70: Go 3 mi E on Hwy 70, then 3 mi SE on Hwy 76, then S at sign.* FACILITIES: 60 sites, 60 no hkups, tenting, non-flush toilets only, dump station, ltd groceries, fire rings, wood. RECREATION: lake swimming, boating, canoeing, ramp, lake/river/stream fishing, playground, hiking trails. Rec open to public. Pets welcome. Partial handicap access. Open Mid Apr thru Mid Sep. No showers. Phone: (270)465-6488.

(SE) SMITH RIDGE (COE - Green River Lake)—(Taylor) *From jct Hwy 55 & Hwy 70: Go 1 mi E on Hwy 70, then 4 mi S on Hwy 372.* FACILITIES: 80 sites, 31 W&E, 31 E, 18 no hkups, 1 pull-thrus, tenting, dump station, ltd groceries, ice, fire rings, wood. RECREATION: lake/river/pond swimming, boating, ramp, rowboat/motorboat rentals, lake/river/stream fishing, playground, planned activities (wkends only), horseshoes, hiking trails. Rec open to public. Pets welcome. Open mid Apr thru Mid Sep. Phone: (270)789-2743.

CARROLLTON—B-3

(S) GENERAL BUTLER STATE RESORT PARK—(Carroll) *From town: Go 1 mi S on US 227.* FACILITIES: 111 sites, 111 W&E, tenting, dump station, laundry, ice, grills, wood. RECREATION: boating, no motors, canoeing, ramp, dock, rowboat/pedal boat rentals, lake fishing, mini-golf, playground, shuffleboard court, planned activities, tennis, hiking trails. Pets welcome. Open all yr. Phone: (866)462-8853.

CAVE CITY—D-3

(E) CAVE COUNTRY RV CAMPGROUND—(Barren) *From jct I-65 & SR 70/90: Go 1/2 mi E on 70/90, then 350 yds N on Sanders St., then 350 yds E on Gaunce Dr. Enter at end.*

WELCOME

◆◆◆◆FACILITIES: 44 sites, typical site width 40 ft, 44 full hkups, (30 & 50 amps), some extended stay sites, 51 pull-thrus, cable TV ($), wireless Instant Internet access at site, laundry, RV supplies.

RECREATION: rec room/area, pavilion, golf nearby, horseshoes.

Pets welcome. Partial handicap access. No tents. Open all yr. Big rigs welcome. Internet friendly.

CAVE CITY—Continued
CAVE COUNTRY RV CAMPGROUND—Continued

Clubs welcome. Rate in 2007 $29-31 for 2 persons. MC/VISA/DISC/Debit. Member ARVC. Phone: (270)773-4678.

e-mail: office@cavecountryrv.com

SEE AD THIS PAGE

(W) Mammoth Cave Jellystone Park Camp Resort—(Barren) *From jct I-65 (Exit 53) & SR-70: Go 1 mi W on SR 70. Enter on R.* ◆◆◆◆FACILITIES: 191 sites, typical site width 30 ft, 98 full hkups, 43 W&E, (30 & 50 amps), 50 no hkups, 100 pull-thrus, tenting, dump station, non-guest dumping $, laundry, groceries, LP gas by weight/by meter, ice, tables, fire rings, grills, wood. ◆◆◆◆◆RECREATION: rec hall, rec room/area, pavilion, equipped pavilion, swim pool, pond fishing, mini-golf ($), playground, planned activities, horseshoes, sports field, hiking trails, v-ball. Rec open to public. Pets welcome. Partial handicap access. Open all yr. Big rigs welcome. Internet friendly. Rate in 2007 $18-49 per family. Member ARVC. Phone: (800)523-1854.

(W) Singin Hills Campground and RV Park—(Barren) *From jct I-65 (exit 53) & SR 70: Go 2-1/2 mi W on SR 70. Enter on R.* ◆◆◆FACILITIES: 31 sites, 17 full hkups, 14 W&E, (20, 30 & 50 amps), 22 pull-thrus, tenting, dump station, non-guest dumping $, LP gas by weight/by meter, ice, tables, fire rings, grills, wood. ◆RECREATION: swim pool, pond fishing, play equipment. Pets welcome. Partial handicap access. Open all yr. Big rigs welcome. Internet friendly. Rate in 2007 $28-32 for 2 persons. Phone: (270)773-3789. FMCA discount.

CENTRAL CITY—D-2

(S) Western Kentucky RV Park—(Muhlenberg) *From jct Western Ky Pkwy & US 431: Go 0.3 mi S on US 431 to Youngstown Rd. Turn left, park on L 0.3 mi. Enter on L.* ◆◆◆FACILITIES: 50 sites, typical site width 30 ft, accepts full hkup units only, 50 full hkups, (30 & 50 amps), 50 pull-thrus. RECREATION: pavilion, playground. Pets welcome. No tents. Open all yr. No restrooms. Big rigs welcome. Rate in 2007 $20 per vehicle. Phone: (270)757-0345. CCUSA discount.

COLUMBUS—B-1

(N) COLUMBUS - BELMONT STATE PARK—(Hickman) *From town: Take Hwy 80 & follow signs.* FACILITIES: 38 sites, 38 W&E, tenting, dump station, laundry, ice, fire rings, grills, wood. RECREATION: pavilion, river swimming, boating, ramp, mini-golf ($), playground, planned activities, hiking trails. Pets welcome. Open Apr 1 thru Oct 31. Phone: (270)677-2327.

CORBIN—E-4

(NE) Corbin-KOA—(Laurel) *From jct I-75 & US 25 E: Go 1/2 mi W on US 25E. Enter on L.* ◆◆◆◆FACILITIES: 65 sites, typical site width 18 ft, 25 full hkups, 25 W&E, (20, 30 & 50 amps), 15 no hkups, 36 pull-thrus, tenting, dump station, laundry, groceries, LP gas by weight/by meter, ice, tables, patios, fire rings, grills, wood. ◆◆RECREATION: rec room/area, swim pool, playground, horseshoes, hiking trails. Pets welcome. Open all yr. Pool open Memorial Day through Labor Day. Big rigs welcome. Internet friendly. Rate in 2007 $21-44 for 2 persons. Phone: (606)528-1534. KOA 10% value card discount.

(SW) CUMBERLAND FALLS STATE RESORT PARK—(Whitley) *From I-75 (Corbin exit): Go 8 mi S on US 25W, then 8 mi W on Hwy 90.* FACILITIES: 50 sites, 50 W&E, tenting, dump station, laundry, groceries, ice, fire rings, grills, wood. RECREATION: swim pool, river fishing, playground, shuffleboard court, planned activities, tennis, horseshoes, hiking trails. Pets welcome. Open Apr 1 thru Oct 31. Phone: (800)325-0063.

(W) DANIEL BOONE NATIONAL FOREST (Grove BoatIn Campground)—(Whitley) *From town: Go 5 mi SW on US 25, then 2 mi N on Hwy 1193, then 3-1/2 mi NE on FR 558 to boat ramp. Then 1 mi by private boat on the Laurel River Lake.* FACILI-

DANIEL BOONE NATIONAL FOREST (Grove BoatIn Campground)—Continued on next page

CORBIN—Continued
DANIEL BOONE NATIONAL FOREST (Grove Boatln Campground)—Continued

TIES: 31 sites, 31 no hkups, tenting, non-flush toilets only, dump station, fire rings, grills, wood. RECREATION: lake swimming, boating, canoeing, ramp, lake fishing, hiking trails. Pets welcome. Partial handicap access. Open all yr. Tents only, No RV's. No showers. Phone: (606)864-4163.

(W) DANIEL BOONE NATIONAL FOREST (Grove Campground)—(Whitley) *From town: Go 5 mi W on US 25, then 2 mi N on Hwy 1193, then 3 mi NE on FR 558.* FACILITIES: 52 sites, 32 ft max RV length, 52 W&E, (20 & 30 amps), tenting, dump station, ice, fire rings, grills, wood. RECREATION: lake swimming, boating, canoeing, ramp, dock, lake fishing, hiking trails. Pets welcome. Partial handicap access. Open Apr 13 thru Oct 28. Phone: (606)864-4163.

CORINTH—C-4

(SE) Three Springs Campground—(Harrison) *From jct I-75 & Hwy 330 (exit 144): Go 3/4 mi E to Saylor Point Rd, then 1/2 mi S on Saylor Point Rd, then 1/4 mi E on Campground Rd. Enter at end.* ◇◇◇FACILITIES: 48 sites, 24 W&E, (20 & 30 amps), 24 no hkups, some extended stay sites, 2 pull-thrus, tenting, dump station, non-guest dumping $, laundry, tables, fire rings. ◇◇RECREATION: rec hall, swim pool, pond fishing, playground, horseshoes, sports field, hiking trails. Rec open to public. Pets welcome. Open all yr. Facilities fully operational Memorial Day thru Labor Day. Rate in 2007 $22 for 2 persons. Phone: (859)806-3030. FCRV 10% discount. FMCA discount.

CRITTENDEN—B-4

(S) CINCINNATI SOUTH ROSE GARDEN RESORT—(Grant) *From jct I-75 & US 25 (exit 166): Go 1/4 mi E on Hwy 491, then 2-1/2 mi S on US 25. Enter on R.*

WELCOME

◇◇◇◇FACILITIES: 101 sites, typical site width 35 ft, 27 full hkups, 66 W&E, (30 & 50 amps), 50 amps ($), 8 no hkups, 59 pull-thrus, phone Internet access central location, tenting, cabins, RV storage, dump station, laundry, groceries, RV supplies, LP gas by weight/by meter, ice, tables, patios, fire rings, grills, wood.

◇◇◇◇RECREATION: rec room/area, pavilion, coin games, swim pool, boating, dock, 2 pedal boat rentals, lake fishing, fishing supplies, golf nearby, bsktball, playground, horseshoes, sports field, hiking trails.

Pets welcome. Partial handicap access. Open Mar 1 thru Dec 1. Pool open 5-25 to 9-15. Big rigs welcome. Internet friendly. Escort to site. Clubs welcome. Rate in 2007 $22-33 for 2 persons. MC/VISA/DISC/Debit. Member ARVC, OCOA. Phone: (866)477-0024.

SEE AD CINCINNATI, OH PAGE 683

DANVILLE—D-4

(NW) Pioneer Playhouse Trailer Park—(Boyle) *From jct US 127 & US 150: Go 1 mi E on US 150. Enter on L.* ◇◇FACILITIES: 70 sites, typical site width 25 ft, 50 W&E, (30 & 50 amps), 20 no hkups, 20 pull-thrus, tenting, dump station, non-guest dumping $, ice, tables, fire rings. ◇RECREATION: rec room/area, equipped pavilion. Rec open to public. Pets welcome. Open all yr. Facilities fully operational Apr 1 thru Oct 31. Rate in 2007 $15 for 4 persons. Member COAK. Phone: (859)236-2747.

DAWSON SPRINGS—D-1

(S) PENNYRILE FOREST STATE RESORT PARK—(Christian) *From jct US-62 & Hwy-109: Go 5 mi S on Hwy-109.* FACILITIES: 68 sites, 68 W&E, tenting, dump station, laundry, groceries, ice, grills. RECREATION: pavilion, lake swimming, boating, no motors, canoeing, dock, rowboat/canoe/2 pedal boat rentals, lake fishing, mini-golf, playground, tennis, hiking trails, v-ball. Pets welcome. Open Mar 15 thru Oct 31. Phone: (800)325-1711.

DRAKESBORO—D-2

(W) Gregory Lake RV Park—(Muhlenberg) *From US 431 & SR 176: Go 1-1/2 mi W on SR 176. Enter on L.* ◇◇◇◇FACILITIES: 117 sites, typical site width 50 ft, 84 full hkups, 33 W&E, (30 & 50 amps), mostly extended stay sites, 50 pull-thrus, heater not allowed, tenting, dump station, non-guest dumping $, portable dump, laundry, groceries, LP bottle exch, ice, tables, fire rings, wood. ◇◇◇RECREATION: rec hall, rec room/area, pavilion, boating, electric motors only, canoeing, ramp, lake fishing, planned activities (wkends only), horseshoes, hiking trails. Rec open to public. Pets welcome. Partial handicap access. Open all yr. Big rigs welcome. Internet friendly. Rate in 2007 $20-25 for 2 persons. Phone: (270)476-9223.

DRY RIDGE—B-4

(NW) I-75 Camper Village—(Grant) *From jct I-75 & Hwy 22: Go 50 yards W on Hwy 22, then 1 mi N on service road. Enter at end.* ◇◇◇FACILITIES: 70 sites, typical site width 30 ft, 50 full hkups, (20, 30 & 50 amps), 50 amps ($), 20 no hkups, some extended stay sites, 13 pull-thrus, tenting, dump station, non-guest dumping $, laundry, ice, tables, patios, fire rings, wood. ◇◇◇RECREATION: rec room/area, boating, 10 hp limit, ramp, dock, lake fishing, play equipment, sports field, hiking trails, v-ball. Pets welcome. Open all yr. Big rigs welcome. Internet friendly. Rate in 2007 $21.60-24 for 2 persons. Member ARVC. Phone: (859)824-5836.

DUNMOR—E-2

(E) Dogwood Lakes Camping & Resort—(Muhlenberg) *From jct US 431 & SR 973: Go 1 mi E on SR 973. Enter on R.* ◇◇◇FACILITIES: 160 sites, typical site width 25 ft, 110 full hkups, 50 W&E, (30 amps), 40 pull-thrus, tenting, dump station, non-guest dumping $, laundry, ltd groceries, ice, tables, fire rings, grills, wood. ◇◇◇◇RECREATION: rec room/area, lake swimming, 4 pedal boat rentals, pond fishing, mini-golf ($), playground, planned activities (wkends only), horseshoes, sports field, hiking trails, v-ball. Rec open to public. Pets welcome ($). Partial handicap access. Open all yr. Facilities fully operational Mar 15 thru Oct 15. Rate in 2007 $25-29. Phone: (270)657-8380.

(W) LAKE MALONE STATE PARK—(Muhlenberg) *From jct US 431 & 973: Go 3-1/4 mi W & N.* FACILITIES: 120 sites, 20 W&E, 100 no hkups, tenting, dump station, laundry, grills. RECREATION: pavilion, equipped pavilion, lake swimming, boating, ramp, dock, pedal boat rentals, lake fishing, playground, tennis, hiking trails. Pets welcome. Open Apr 1 thru Nov 15. Phone: (270)657-2111.

EDDYVILLE—D-1

(SE) Holiday Hills Resort—(Lyon) *From jct I-24 (exit 45) & SR 293: Go 100 yards W on SR 293, then 2 mi S on SR 93. Enter on L.* ◇◇◇◇FACILITIES: 135 sites, typical site width 22 ft, 32 ft max RV length, 90 full hkups, 45 W&E, (30 amps), some extended stay sites (in summer), 30 pull-thrus, tenting, dump station, portable dump, laundry, groceries, LP gas by weight/by meter, ice, tables, patios, fire rings, grills, wood. ◇◇◇◇RECREATION: rec room/area, pavilion, swim pool, lake swimming, boating, canoeing, ramp, dock, 2 canoe/4 motorboat rentals, lake fishing, playground, planned activities, horseshoes, hiking trails, v-ball. Pets welcome. Open Mid Mar thru Oct 31. Pool open Mid May to Oct. 1. Internet friendly. Rate in 2007 $30-32 for 4 persons. Phone: (800)337-8550.

(S) INDIAN POINT RV PARK—(Lyon) *From jct I-24 (exit 45) & Hwy 293: Go 2/10 mi W on Hwy 293, then 1/10 mi W on 1055, then 1 mi S on Indian Hills Trail. Enter on R.*

WELCOME

◇◇◇◇FACILITIES: 200 sites, typical site width 30 ft, 135 full hkups, 65 W&E, (30 amps), many extended stay sites, 5 pull-thrus, cable TV ($), phone Internet access central location, tenting, RV storage, dump station, laundry, ltd groceries, RV supplies, LP gas by weight/by meter, ice, tables, fire rings, wood.

◇◇◇◇RECREATION: rec hall, rec room/area, coin games, swim pool, wading pool, lake swimming, boating, canoeing, kayaking, ramp, dock, lake fishing, fishing supplies, fishing guides, golf nearby, bsktball, playground, horseshoes, sports field, v-ball.

Pets welcome. Open all yr. Facilities fully operational Apr 1 thru Nov 1. Internet friendly. Clubs welcome. Rate in 2007 $24-28 for 2 persons. MC/VISA/Debit. Phone: (270)388-2730.

e-mail: iprvpark@paducah.com

SEE AD THIS PAGE

(S) LAKE BARKLEY RV RESORT—(Lyon) *From jct I-24 (exit 45) & SR 293: Go 400 yards W on SR 293, then 1 mi S on SR 93. Enter on L.*

WELCOME

◇◇◇◇FACILITIES: 102 sites, typical site width 30 ft, 102 full hkups, (30 & 50 amps), many extended stay sites (in summer), 75 pull-thrus, wireless Instant Internet access at site, phone Internet access central location, RV storage, laundry, tables, fire rings.

◇◇◇RECREATION: rec room/area, equipped pavilion, coin games, swim pool, horseshoes, hiking trails.

Pets welcome. Partial handicap access. No tents. Open Apr 1 thru Nov 1. Facilities fully operational Memorial Day thru Labor Day. Big rigs welcome. Internet friendly. Escort to site. Clubs welcome. Rate in 2007 $30 for 2 persons. Phone: (800)910-7275.

SEE AD THIS PAGE

ELIZABETHTOWN—D-3

(NE) Elizabethtown Crossroads Campground—(Hardin) *From jct I-65 (Exit 94) & US-62: Go 1 mi E on US-62, then 1/4 mi N on Tunnel Hill Rd. Enter on L.* ◇◇◇FACILITIES: 50 sites, typical site width 30 ft, 23 full hkups, 27 W&E, (30 & 50 amps), 22 pull-thrus, tenting, dump station, non-guest dumping $, laundry, ltd groceries, LP gas by weight/by meter, ice, tables, fire rings, grills, wood. ◇◇◇RECREATION: pavilion, swim pool, playground, planned activities (wkends only), horseshoes, v-ball. Pets welcome. Open all yr. Big rigs welcome. Internet friendly. Rate in 2007 $25-29 for 2 persons. Member ARVC. Phone: (800)975-6521. KOA 10% value card discount.

(S) Glendale Campground—(Hardin) *From jct I-65 & SR 222: Go 1/2 mi E on SR 222 until T in road, then left 3/4 mi N on Sportsman Lake Rd. Enter on R.* ◇◇◇FACILITIES: 65 sites, typical site width 33 ft, 10 full hkups, 55 W&E, (20, 30 & 50 amps), 30 pull-thrus, tenting, dump station, laundry, ltd groceries, ice, tables, fire rings, wood. ◇◇◇◇RECREATION: rec hall, rec room/area, pavilion, swim pool, lake fishing, playground, planned activities (wkends only), horseshoes, sports field, hiking trails, v-ball. Pets welcome. Partial handicap access. Open all yr. Facilities fully operational Memorial Day thru Oct 31. Pool open from Memorial Day to Labor Day. Big rigs welcome. Internet friendly. Rate in 2007 $26-28 for 6 persons. Member ARVC. Phone: (270)369-7755. CCUSA discount.

ELKHORN CITY—D-6

(S) BREAKS INTERSTATE PARK—(Pike) *From town: Go 8 mi S on Hwy 80, then 2 mi NW on Park Rd. Enter on R.* FACILITIES: 122 sites, 34 ft max RV length, 37 full hkups, 58 W&E, 14 E, 13 no hkups, 20 pull-thrus, tenting, dump station, ice, grills, wood. RECREATION: swim pool, boating, electric motors only, canoeing, ramp, 18 pedal boat rentals, lake/river/pond fishing, playground, planned activities (wkends only), hiking trails. Pets welcome. Open Apr 1 thru Oct 31. Phone: (800)982-5122.

Christian County is wet while Bourbon County is dry and Barren County has the most fertile land in the state.

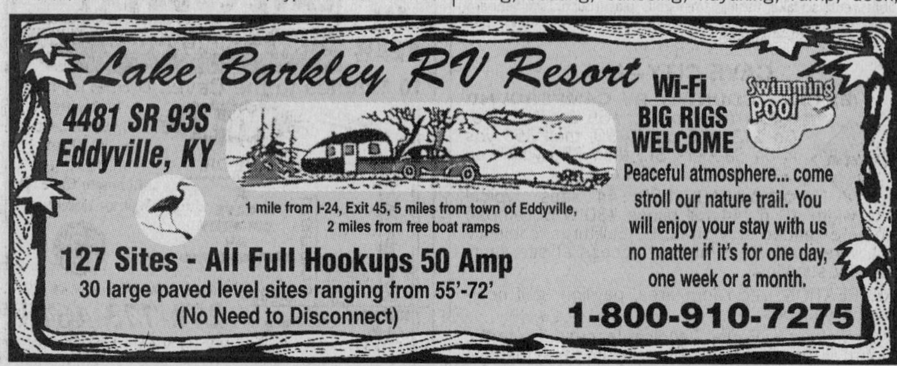

FALLS OF ROUGH—D-2

(S) CAVE CREEK (COE-Rough River Lake)—(Grayson) *From jct Hwy 79 & Hwy 736: Go 1 mi E on Hwy 736.* FACILITIES: 86 sites, 16 E, 70 no hkups, tenting, non-flush toilets only, dump station, fire rings, grills, wood. RECREATION: boating, canoeing, ramp, lake fishing, playground, hiking trails. Pets welcome. Open 3rd Fri in Apr thru 3rd Sun in Sep. No showers. 3 day min on holiday weekends. Phone: (270)879-4304.

(W) ROUGH RIVER DAM STATE RESORT PARK—(Grayson) *From jct Hwy 110 & Hwy 79: Go 3 mi NE on Hwy 79.* FACILITIES: 66 sites, 35 W&E, 31 E, tenting, dump station, laundry, ice, grills, wood. RECREATION: pavilion, lake swimming, boating, ramp, dock, rowboat/pedal boat rentals, lake fishing, mini-golf, playground, shuffleboard court, planned activities, tennis, hiking trails, v-ball. Pets welcome. Open Apr 1 thru Oct 31. Phone: (800)325-1713.

FALMOUTH—B-4

(E) KINCAID LAKE STATE PARK—(Pendleton) *From jct Hwy 22 & US 27: Go 4 mi N on Hwy 22 & Hwy 159.* FACILITIES: 84 sites, 84 W&E, (30 & 50 amps), tenting, dump station, laundry, groceries, ice, grills, wood. RECREATION: pavilion, swim pool, boating, 10 hp limit, ramp, dock, rowboat/pedal boat rentals, lake fishing, mini-golf ($), playground, shuffleboard court, planned activities, tennis, horseshoes, hiking trails, v-ball. Pets welcome. Open all yr. Phone: (859)654-3531.

FRANKFORT—C-4

(E) ELKHORN CAMPGROUND—(Franklin) *From I-64 & US 60: Go 2-1/2 mi N on US 60, then 2-1/4 mi E on US 460, then 1/4 mi S on Scruggs Ln. Enter on R.*

WELCOME

◊◊◊◊FACILITIES: 125 sites, typical site width 30 ft, 71 full hkups, 54 W&E, (30 & 50 amps), 50 amps ($), some extended stay sites, 30 pull-thrus, cable TV, phone/cable on-site Internet access (needs activ), wireless Internet access central location, tenting, RV storage, dump station, non-guest dumping $, laundry, ltd groceries, RV supplies, LP gas by weight/by meter, ice, tables, patios, fire rings, wood.

◊◊◊◊RECREATION: rec room/area, equipped pavilion, coin games, swim pool, river swimming, river fishing, fishing supplies, mini-golf ($), golf nearby, bsktball, playground, shuffleboard court, planned activities (wkends only), horseshoes, v-ball, local tours.

Pets welcome, breed restrict. Partial handicap access. Open all yr. Facilities fully operational Apr 1 thru Oct 31. Pool open Memorial Day to Labor Day. Big rigs welcome. Internet friendly. Clubs welcome. Rate in 2007 $21-26 for 2 persons. MC/VISA/DISC/Debit. Phone: (502)695-9154.

SEE AD THIS PAGE

(NE) Still Waters Campground—(Franklin) *From jct I-64 & US 60: Go 3 mi N on US 60, then 1-1/2 mi W on US 421 (Wilkenson Blvd), then 7-1/2 mi N on US 127, then 1/4 mi W on Strohmeier Rd. Enter at end.* ◊◊◊FACILITIES: 79 sites, typical site width 40 ft, 25 full hkups, 32 W&E, (20, 30 & 50 amps), 22 no hkups, some extended stay sites, tenting, dump station, non-guest dumping, ltd groceries, ice, tables, fire rings, wood. ◊◊RECREATION: river swimming, boating, canoeing, ramp, 12 canoe rentals, river/pond fishing, playground, horseshoes, sports field, hiking trails, v-ball. Pets welcome. Open all yr. Facilities fully operational Apr 1 thru Oct 31. Internet friendly. Rate in 2007 $16-22 per family. Member ARVC. Phone: (502)223-8896.

FRANKLIN—E-2

(E) Franklin RV Ranch—(Simpson) *From jct I-65 (exit 6) & Hwy 100: Go 1/4 mi W on Hwy 100. Enter on L.* ◊◊◊◊FACILITIES: 88 sites, typical site width 30 ft, 66 full hkups, (30 & 50 amps), 50 amps ($), 22 no hkups, some extended stay sites, 66 pull-thrus, tenting, dump station, non-guest dumping $, laundry, groceries, LP gas by weight/by meter, ice, tables, fire rings, grills, wood. ◊◊◊RECREATION: rec room/area, pavilion, swim pool, playground, planned activities (wkends only), horseshoes, sports field, v-ball. Rec open to public. Pets welcome. Open all yr. Pool open May 1 - Oct 1. Big rigs welcome. Internet friendly. Rate in 2007 $27.75-30 for 2 persons. Phone: (270)586-5622. CCUSA discount.

GILBERTSVILLE—B-2

(SW) KENTUCKY DAM VILLAGE STATE RESORT PARK—(Marshall) *At jct US 62 & US 641.* FACILITIES: 221 sites, 221 W&E, (50 amps), tenting, dump station, laundry, groceries, ice, grills, wood. RECREATION: rec hall, pavilion, lake swimming, boating, ramp, dock, rowboat/pedal boat rentals, lake fishing, mini-golf, playground, planned activities, tennis, horseshoes, hiking trails, v-ball. Pets welcome. Open all yr. Phone: (800)325-0146.

GLASGOW—E-3

(S) BARREN RIVER LAKE STATE RESORT PARK—(Barren) *From jct Hwy 90 & US 31E: Go 12 mi S on US 31E.* FACILITIES: 99 sites, 99 W&E, tenting, dump station, laundry, ice, grills, wood. RECREATION: lake swimming, boating, ramp, dock, playground, tennis, hiking trails, v-ball. Pets welcome. Open Apr 1 thru Oct 31. Phone: (800)325-0057.

GLASGOW—Continued

(SW) THE NARROWS (COE-Barren River Lake)—(Barren) *From jct Cumberland Pkwy & US 31E: Go 11 mi SW on US 31E, then W on CR (Lucas).* FACILITIES: 92 sites, 85 W&E, 7 no hkups, tenting, dump station, laundry, ice, fire rings, grills, wood. RECREATION: pavilion, lake swimming, boating, canoeing, ramp, lake fishing, playground, planned activities (wkends only), horseshoes, hiking trails, v-ball. Pets welcome. Open mid Apr thru mid Sep. Phone: (270)646-3094.

GOLDEN POND—E-1

(N) ENERGY LAKE (LBL) National Recreation Area—(Trigg) *From jct US 68 & Hwy 453 (The Trace): Go 6-1/2 mi N on The Trace, then 5 mi E on Mulberry Flat Rd, then 2 mi S on Energy Lake Rd.* FACILITIES: 48 sites, 35 E, (50 amps), 13 no hkups, 5 pull-thrus, tenting, laundry, ice, fire rings, grills, wood. RECREATION: lake swimming, boating, canoeing, 6 canoe rentals, lake fishing, playground, horseshoes, sports field, hiking trails, v-ball. Partial handicap access. Open Mar 1 thru Nov 30. Max stay 21 days. Phone: (270)924-2000.

(W) FENTON (LBL) National Recreation Area—(Trigg) *From jct The Trace (Hwy 453) & US 68: Go 3 mi W on US 68.* FACILITIES: 29 sites, 13 E, 16 no hkups, 9 pull-thrus, tenting, non-flush toilets only, grills. RECREATION: pavilion, boating, canoeing, ramp, lake fishing, hiking trails. Rec open to public. Open all yr. No showers. No reservations. Max stay 21 days. Phone: (270)924-2000.

(NE) HILLMAN FERRY CAMPGROUND (LBL)—(Lyon) *From jct Hwy 94/80/68: Go 5 mi E on Hwy 80/68, then 17 mi N on The Trace Rd, then 1/2 mi W on Rd 110. Enter at end.* FACILITIES: 379 sites, 88 full hkups, 143 W&E, 48 E, (30 & 50 amps), 100 no hkups, tenting, fire rings, wood. RECREATION: boating, ramp, dock, lake fishing, playground, sports field. Open all yr. Phone: (270)924-2000.

(S) RUSHING CREEK (LBL) National Recreation Area—(Stewart) *From jct US-68 & The Trace (Hwy-453): Go 8 mi S on The Trace, then 1-1/2 mi on Rushing Creek Rd.* FACILITIES: 56 sites, 1 E, 55 no hkups, tenting, ice, grills, wood. RECREATION: pavilion, boating, canoeing, ramp, dock, lake fishing, playground, hiking trails, v-ball. Rec open to public. Open all yr. Facilities fully operational mid Mar thru mid Oct. No reservations. Max stay 21 days. Phone: (270)924-2000.

WRANGLER (LBL) National Recreation Area—(Trigg) *From jct Hwy 94/80 & Hwy 453 (The Trace): Go 1/4 mi S on the Trace, then 6 mi E on CR 165. Enter on R.* FACILITIES: 168 sites, 18 full hkups, 2 W&E, 125 E, (50 amps), 23 no hkups, 7 pull-thrus, tenting, dump station, laundry, ltd groceries, ice, fire rings, grills, wood. RECREATION: pavilion, playground, planned activities, hiking trails, v-ball. Rec open to public. Partial handicap access. Open all yr. Horse stalls available. Max stay 21 days. Phone: (270)924-2000.

(SE) WRANGLERS CAMPGROUND (LBL)—(Trigg) *From jct Hwy 94/80/68: Go 5 mi E on Hwy 80/68, then 1 mi S on The Trace Rd, then 5 mi W on Rd 168. Enter on R.* FACILITIES: 184 sites, 18 full hkups, 2 W&E, 137 E, (30 amps), 27 no hkups, tenting, dump station, fire rings, wood. RECREATION: playground. Open all yr. Phone: (270)924-2000.

GRAND RIVERS—B-2

(S) BIRMINGHAM FERRY (LBL) National Recreation Area—(Livingston) *From jct I-24 & The Trace (Hwy 453): Go 9 mi S on The Trace, then 3 mi W on Rd 114 (Old Ferry Rd).* FACILITIES: 26 sites, 26 no hkups, 1 pull-thrus, tenting, non-flush toilets only, grills. RECREATION: boating, canoeing, ramp, lake fishing, hiking trails. Rec open to public. Partial handicap access. Open all yr. No showers. Phone: (502)924-2000.

(S) CANAL RECREATION AREA (COE-Lake Barkley)—(Livingston) *From town: Go 1 mi S on The Trace (Hwy-453).* FACILITIES: 110 sites, 110 W&E, tenting, dump station, grills. RECREATION: lake swimming, boating, canoeing, ramp, lake fishing, playground, hiking trails. Pets welcome. Open Apr 5 thru Oct 29. Phone: (270)362-4840.

(E) CRAVENS BAY (LBL) National Recreation Area—(Livingston) *From jct I-24 & The Trace (Hwy 453): Go 9 mi S on The Trace, then 5 mi E on Craven Bay Rd.* FACILITIES: 30 sites, 30 no hkups, tenting, grills. RECREATION: boating, canoeing, ramp, lake fishing, hiking trails. Rec open to public. Open all yr. No showers. No reservations. Phone: (270)924-2000.

The Bluegrass Country around Lexington is home to some of the world's finest racehorses.

GRAND RIVERS—Continued

(N) EXIT 31 RV PARK—(Livingston) *From jct I-24 and Hwy 453 (exit 31): Go 1/10 mi S on Hwy 453. Enter on R.*

WELCOME

◊◊◊◊FACILITIES: 31 sites, 31 full hkups, (15, 20, 30 & 50 amps), many extended stay sites, cable TV, wireless Instant Internet access at site, wireless Internet access central location, tables.

RECREATION: golf nearby, hiking trails.

Pets welcome, size restrict. No tents. Open all yr. Big rigs welcome. Internet friendly. Rate in 2007 $25-45 per vehicle. MC/VISA/DISC/AMEX/Debit. Phone: (800)971-1914.

e-mail: exit31_rv_park@yahoo.com

SEE AD THIS PAGE

(S) HILLMAN FERRY (LBL) National Recreation Area—(Livingston) *From jct I-24 & The Trace (Hwy-453): Go 5 mi S on The Trace, then 1 mi W on Hillman Ferry Rd. Enter at end.* FACILITIES: 366 sites, typical site width 28 ft, 65 full hkups, 157 W&E, 45 E, (20, 30 & 50 amps), 99 no hkups, 80 pull-thrus, tenting, dump station, laundry, ltd groceries, ice, patios, fire rings, grills, wood. RECREATION: equipped pavilion, lake swimming, boating, canoeing, ramp, dock, lake fishing, playground, planned activities, horseshoes, sports field, hiking trails, v-ball. Pets welcome. Partial handicap access. Open Mar 1 thru Nov 30. Max stay 21 days. Big rigs welcome. Phone: (270)924-2000.

(N) MISS SCARLETT'S RESTAURANT—*From jct I-24 & Hwy 453 (exit 31): Go 1/10 mi S on Hwy 453. Enter on R.* Restaurant at Exit 31 RV Park. Open all yr. MC/VISA/DISC/AMEX/Debit. Phone: (800)971-1914.

SEE AD THIS PAGE

GRAYSON—C-5

(SW) GRAYSON LAKE STATE PARK—(Carter) *From jct US 60 & Hwy 7: Go 10 mi S on Hwy 7.* FACILITIES: 71 sites, 71 W&E, tenting, dump station, laundry, ice, fire rings, grills, wood. RECREATION: lake swimming, boating, ramp, dock, lake fishing, playground, planned activities, horseshoes, hiking trails, v-ball. Pets welcome. Open Apr 1 thru Oct 31. Phone: (606)474-5107.

Valley Breeze RV Campground—(Carter) *From jct I-64 (exit 172) & SR 7: Go 150 feet N on SR 7, then 3/4 mi W on Hwy 1947. Enter on R.* ◊◊◊◊FACILITIES: 16 sites, typical site width 30 ft, accepts full hkup units only, 16 full hkups, (30 & 50 amps), 50 amps ($), 5 pull-thrus, tables. Pets welcome. No tents. Open all yr. No restrooms. Big rigs welcome. Rate in 2007 $23-26 for 2 persons. Phone: (606)474-6779.

GREENUP—B-6

(S) GREENBO LAKE STATE RESORT PARK—(Greenup) *From jct US 23 & Hwy 1: Go 8 mi SE on Hwy 1.* FACILITIES: 98 sites, 63 W&E, (20 & 30 amps), 35 no hkups, tenting, dump station, laundry, groceries, ice, grills, wood. RECREATION: pavilion, swim pool, boating, 10 hp limit, canoeing, ramp, dock, rowboat/canoe/pedal boat/motorboat rentals, lake fishing, mini-golf, playground, planned activities, tennis, horseshoes, hiking trails. Pets welcome. Open Apr 1 thru Oct 31. Phone: (800)325-0083.

HARRODSBURG—D-4

(E) CHIMNEY ROCK RV PARK & MARINA—(Mercer) *From jct US 127 & SR 152: Go 8-1/2 mi E on SR 152. Enter on L.*

◊◊◊FACILITIES: 70 sites, typical site width 24 ft, 55 full hkups, 15 W&E, (20, 30 & 50 amps), 50 amps ($), mostly extended stay sites (in summer), 2 pull-thrus, phone Internet access central location, tenting, RV storage, shower$, dump station, non-guest dumping $, laundry, ltd groceries, RV supplies, ice, tables, fire rings, wood.

CHIMNEY ROCK RV PARK & MARINA—Continued on next page

HARRODSBURG—Continued
CHIMNEY ROCK RV PARK & MARINA—Continued

◇◇◇RECREATION: pavilion, swim pool, lake swimming, boating, ramp, dock, 2 pontoon rentals, lake fishing, fishing supplies, golf nearby, bsktball, planned activities (wkends only), horseshoes, sports field, v-ball. Rec open to public.

Pets welcome. Open Apr 1 thru Nov 1. Big rigs welcome. Internet friendly. Clubs welcome. Rate in 2007 $20-30 for 2 persons. MC/VISA/DISC/DC. Phone: (859)748-5252.

e-mail: Chimneyrockkathy@yahoo.com

SEE AD THIS PAGE

HARTFORD—D-2

(E) OHIO COUNTY PARK—(Ohio) *From jct William Natcher Pkwy & Hwy 69: Go 1/2 mi N on Hwy 69. Enter on R.* FACILITIES: 50 sites, typical site width 24 ft, 50 W&E, (30 & 50 amps), mostly extended stay sites, 7 pull-thrus, tenting, dump station, non-guest dumping $, laundry, ice, patios, fire rings, grills, wood. RECREATION: pavilion, equipped pavilion, ramp, pond fishing, mini-golf, playground, planned activities (wkends only), tennis, horseshoes, sports field, hiking trails, v-ball. Rec open to public. Pets welcome. Open all yr. Phone: (270)298-4466.

HENDERSON—C-1

(N) JOHN JAMES AUDUBON STATE PARK—(Henderson) *From jct US 60 & US 41: Go 3 mi N on US 41.* FACILITIES: 69 sites, 69 W&E, (30 amps), tenting, dump station, laundry, ice, grills, wood. RECREATION: boating, no motors, canoeing, pedal boat rentals, lake fishing, mini-golf, playground, planned activities, tennis, hiking trails. Pets welcome. Partial handicap access. Open all yr. Closed week of xmas. Phone: (270)826-2247.

HOPKINSVILLE—E-1

MILITARY PARK (Eagle's Rest Army Travel Camp-Fort Campbell)—(Christian) *Off US 41A. On base.* FACILITIES: 41 sites, 16 full hkups, 25 W&E, tenting, dump station, laundry, ltd groceries, ice, fire rings, grills. RECREATION: boating, lake fishing, playground, hiking trails. Pets welcome. Open all yr. For Military Use Only-w/Military ID Card. Phone: (270)798-3126.

HORSE CAVE—D-3

(W) KOA-Horse Cave—(Hart) *From jct I-65 (exit 58) & SR 218: Go 100 yards W on SR 218. Enter on L.* ◇◇◇FACILITIES: 91 sites, typical site width 25 ft, 11 full hkups, 60 W&E, 20 E, (20 & 30 amps), 30 pull-thrus, tenting, dump station, non-guest dumping $, laundry, groceries, ice, tables, fire rings, wood. ◇◇◇RECREATION: rec room/area, pavilion, swim pool, pond fishing, mini-golf, playground, horseshoes, sports field, v-ball. Pets welcome. Open all yr. Facilities fully operational Memorial Day thru Labor Day. Rate in 2007 $20-28 for 2 persons. Phone: (270)786-2819. KOA 10% value card discount.

HYDEN—D-5

(N) TRACE BRANCH (COE-Buckhorn Lake)—(Leslie) *From town: Go 6 mi N on Hwy 257, after passing under Daniel Boone Pkwy, turn E and cross Dry Hill Bridge, then 6 mi N on Grassy Branch Rd.* FACILITIES: 15 sites, 25 ft max RV length, 15 W&E, tenting, dump station, laundry, ice, fire rings, grills, wood. RECREATION: lake swimming, boating, canoeing, ramp, dock, lake fishing, playground, horseshoes. Rec open to public. Pets welcome. Open May 1 thru Sep 30. Facilities fully operational Memorial Day thru Labor Day. Phone: (606)398-7251.

JAMESTOWN—E-3

(SW) KENDALL RECREATION AREA (COE-Lake Cumberland)—(Russell) *From jct US 127 & Hwy 92: Go 12 mi S on US 127.* FACILITIES: 102 sites, 102 W&E, tenting, dump station, laundry, ltd groceries, grills, wood. RECREATION: boating, canoeing, ramp, lake fishing, playground, horseshoes, hiking trails. Pets welcome. Open all yr. 3 day min on Holidays. Phone: (270) 343-4660.

(S) LAKE CUMBERLAND STATE RESORT PARK—(Russell) *From jct Hwy 92 & US 127: Go 14 mi S on US 127, then 5 mi E on Hwy 1370.* FACILITIES: 147 sites, 35 ft max RV length, 147 W&E, (30 & 50 amps), tenting, dump station, laundry, groceries, ice, fire rings, grills, wood. RECREATION: rec hall, pavilion, swim pool, boating, dock, lake fishing, mini-golf, playground, shuffleboard court, planned activities, tennis, hiking trails, v-ball. Pets welcome. Open Apr 1 thru Nov 26. Phone: (800)325-1709.

Kentucky State Tree: Tulip Poplar

LAND BETWEEN THE LAKES—B-2

See listings at Grand Rivers and Golden Pond.

LEITCHFIELD—D-2

(S) DOG CREEK (COE - Nolin River Lake)—(Grayson) *From jct Hwy-259 & US-62: Go 4 mi E on US-62, then 11 mi S on Hwy-88,then 1 mi W on Hwy-1015.* FACILITIES: 70 sites, 24 W&E, 46 no hkups, tenting, non-flush toilets only, dump station, fire rings, grills. RECREATION: lake swimming, boating, ramp, lake fishing, playground, hiking trails. Partial handicap access. Open Mid Apr thru Late Sep. No showers. Phone: (270)524-5454.

(S) MOUTARDIER (COE-Nolin River Lake)—(Edmonson) *From jct US-62 & Hwy-259: Go 10 mi S on Hwy-259, then E.* FACILITIES: 167 sites, 81 W&E, 86 no hkups, tenting, dump station, ltd groceries, ice, fire rings, grills. RECREATION: lake swimming, boating, canoeing, ramp, dock, motorboat rentals, lake fishing, playground, planned activities (wkends only), hiking trails. Partial handicap access. Open Mid Apr thru Late Oct. Phone: (270)286-4230.

(S) NOLIN LAKE STATE PARK—(Edmonson) *From jct US 62 & Hwy 259: Go 17 mi S on Hwy 259, then E and follow signs.* FACILITIES: 52 sites, 32 W&E, 20 no hkups, tenting, dump station, laundry, groceries, ice, fire rings, grills, wood. RECREATION: pavilion, lake swimming, boating, ramp, lake fishing, playground, hiking trails. Pets welcome. Partial handicap access. Open Mar thru Oct. Phone: (270)286-4240.

(W) WAX SITE (COE-Nolin River Lake)—(Edmonson) *From jct US 62 & Hwy 259: Go 4 mi E on US 62, then 14 mi S on Hwy 88.* FACILITIES: 110 sites, 56 W&E, 54 no hkups, tenting, dump station, groceries, ice, fire rings, grills. RECREATION: lake swimming, boating, ramp, dock, pedal boat/motorboat rentals, lake fishing, playground, planned activities (wkends only). Pets welcome. Partial handicap access. Open Mid Apr thru Late Sep. Phone: (270)242-7578.

LEXINGTON—C-4

KENTUCKY HORSE PARK (SP)—(Fayette) *From jct I-75 & US 27: Go 6-1/2 mi N on I-75, then 2 mi E on Ironworks Pike. Enter on L.* FACILITIES: 260 sites, typical site width 15 ft, 260 W&E, (50 amps), tenting, dump station, laundry, full svc store, ice, fire rings, wood. RECREATION: pavilion, swim pool, pond fishing, playground, planned activities, tennis, horseshoes, v-ball. Pets welcome. Partial handicap access. Open all yr. Big rigs welcome. Internet friendly. Phone: (859)233-4303.

✲ **(NE) NORTHSIDE RV'S**—*From jct I-75 & US 27: Go 1 mi S on US 27 (N Broadway). Enter on L.* SALES: travel trailers, 5th wheels, van campers, motor homes, mini-motor homes, fold-down camping trailers, pre-owned unit sales. SERVICES: full-time mech, RV appliance repair, body work/collision repair, LP gas by weight/by meter, RV rentals, sells parts/accessories, installs hitches. Open all yr. MC/VISA/DISC/AMEX/Debit. Phone: (859)299-8386.

WELCOME

e-mail: rvsales@northsidervs.com

SEE AD TRAVEL SECTION PAGE 277

LIVINGSTON—D-4

(NE) Red Hill Horse Camp—(Rockcastle) *From jct I-75 & US 25 S (exit 59): Go 7 mi E on US-25, then 4-1/2 mi N on SR-1955. Enter on R.* ◇FACILITIES: 48 sites, typical site width 30 ft, 48 W&E, (30 amps), tenting, dump station, tables. ◇◇RECREATION: equipped pavilion, horseshoes, hiking trails. Pets welcome. Open May thru Oct. Horse stalls available. Rate in 2007 $15 per vehicle. Phone: (606)758-4706.

LONDON—D-4

(W) DANIEL BOONE NATIONAL FOREST (Holly Bay Rec. Area)—(Laurel) *From town: Go 20 mi SW on Hwy-192, then 2 mi SW on Hwy-1193, then 1 mi S on Hwy-770, then 1-1/2 mi E on FR-611.* FACILITIES: 94 sites, 32 ft max RV length, 94 W&E, tenting, dump station, ice, fire rings, grills, wood. RECREATION: lake swimming, boating, canoeing, ramp, dock, lake fishing, hiking trails. Pets welcome. Open Apr 14 thru Oct 29. Phone: (606) 864-4163.

(SW) DANIEL BOONE NATIONAL FOREST (White Oak Boat-In Campground)—(Laurel) *From town: Go 10 mi SW on Hwy 192, then 2 mi S on FR 774, then 1 mi S by private boat on the Laurel River Lake.* FACILITIES: 51 sites, 51 no hkups, tenting, non-flush toilets only, fire rings, grills. RECREATION: lake swimming, boating, ramp, lake fishing, hiking trails. Open all yr. Tents only. No RV's. No showers. Phone: (606)864-4163.

LONDON—Continued

(S) LEVI JACKSON WILDERNESS ROAD STATE PARK—(Laurel) *From jct Hwy 80 & US 25: Go 3 mi S on US 25.* FACILITIES: 146 sites, 146 W&E, tenting, dump station, laundry, groceries, ice, grills, wood. RECREATION: pavilion, swim pool, mini-golf, playground, shuffleboard court, planned activities, tennis, horseshoes, hiking trails, v-ball. Pets welcome. Open all yr. Phone: (606)878-8000.

(NW) Westgate RV Camping—(Laurel) *From jct I-75 (exit 41) & Hwy 80: Go 100 yards W on Hwy 80. Enter on R.* ◇◇◇◇FACILITIES: 14 sites, typical site width 18 ft, 14 full hkups, (30 & 50 amps), some extended stay sites, 4 pull-thrus, tenting, ice, tables, grills. ◇◇RECREATION: rec room/area, pavilion, swim pool, playground. Pets welcome. Open all yr. Facilities fully operational Memorial Day thru Labor Day. Dump station at tourism office next door. Rate in 2007 $23-95 for 2 persons. Phone: (606)878-7330.

LOUISA—C-6

(NW) The Falls Campground—(Lawrence) *From jct US 23 & Hwy 3: Go 5-1/2 mi N on Hwy 3. Enter on R.* ◇◇FACILITIES: 93 sites, 7 full hkups, 86 W&E, (30 & 50 amps), 50 amps ($), 12 pull-thrus, tenting, dump station, portable dump, laundry, ice, tables, fire rings, wood. ◇◇◇RECREATION: rec room/area, pavilion, river swimming, canoeing, river fishing, playground, horseshoes, sports field, v-ball. Pets welcome. Partial handicap access. Facilities fully operational Apr 15 thru Nov 1. Big rigs welcome. Rate in 2007 $19-23 for 4 persons. Phone: (606)686-3398.

(W) YATESVILLE LAKE SP—(Lawrence) *From jct US 23 & Hwy 32W: Go 7 mi SW on Hwy 32 to Hwy 1325. Enter on R.* FACILITIES: 47 sites, 27 full hkups, 20 no hkups, tenting, dump station, laundry, groceries, fire rings, grills. RECREATION: lake swimming, boating, ramp, lake fishing, mini-golf, playground, planned activities, hiking trails, v-ball. Pets welcome. Open Apr 1 thru Oct 31. Phone: (606)673-1492.

LOUISVILLE—C-3

LOUISVILLE AREA MAP

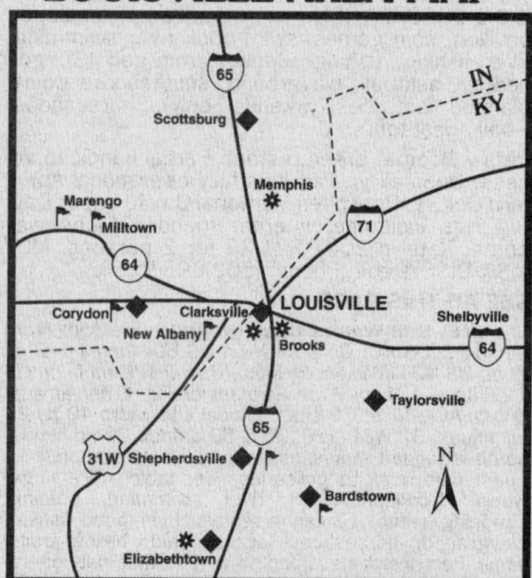

Symbols on map indicate towns within a 40 mi radius of Louisville where campgrounds (dia-monds), attractions (flags), & RV service centers & camping supply outlets (gears) are listed. Check listings for more information.

Tell Them Woodall's Sent You!

LOUISVILLE—Continued on next page

Diane Sawyer, broadcast journalist, is from Kentucky.

LOUISVILLE—Continued

✽ **(SW) LOUISVILLE RV CENTER**—*From jct I-65 & SR 841: Go N 2 mi on I-65, then W 1 mi. Enter on R.* SALES: travel trailers, 5th wheels, motor homes, preowned unit sales. SERVICES: full-time mech, engine/chassis repair, RV appliance repair, body work/collision repair, LP gas by weight/by meter, RV rentals, RV storage, sells parts/accessories, installs hitches. Open all yr. MC/VISA/DISC/AMEX/Debit. Phone: (502)966-0911.

SEE AD PAGE 286

LOUISVILLE SOUTH KOA—*From jct SR 841 & I-65: Go 8-1/2 mi S on I-65, then 1-1/2 mi E on SR 44. Enter on R.*

SEE PRIMARY LISTING AT SHEPHERDSVILLE AND AD THIS PAGE

(SW) OTTER CREEK PARK (City of Louisville)—(Meade) *From jct I-265 (Gene Snyder Fwy) & US 31W: Go 12-1/2 mi S on US 31W, then 2-1/2 mi W on Hwy 1638. Enter on R.* FACILITIES: 250 sites, typical site width 30 ft, 150 W&E, (30 & 50 amps), 100 no hkups, 12 pull-thrus, tenting, dump station, ltd groceries, ice, fire rings, grills, wood. RECREATION: pavilion, swim pool, boating, canoeing, ramp, river fishing, mini-golf ($), playground, horseshoes, hiking trails. Rec open to public. Pets welcome. Open all yr. Phone: (502)942-3211.

✽ **(SW) TINKER'S TOYS DIXIE RV**—*From jct I-65 & SR 841: Go 10 mi W on SR 841, then 2 mi N on 31 W. Enter on R.* SALES: travel trailers, 5th wheels, motor homes, mini-motor homes, preowned unit sales. SERVICES: full-time mech, engine/chassis repair, RV appliance repair, body work/collision repair, dump station, sells parts/accessories, installs hitches. Open all yr. MC/VISA. Phone: (502)933-3882.

SEE AD THIS PAGE

LUCAS—E-3

(SE) Spring Hill RV Park—(Barren) *From jct US 231 & US 31 E: Go 11-1/2 mi E on US 31 E, then 1/2 mi S on SR 87. Enter on R.* ◆◆◆FACILITIES: 40 sites, typical site width 30 ft, accepts full hkup units only, 40 full hkups, (30 & 50 amps), tables, fire rings, wood. RECREATION: pavilion. Pets welcome. No tents. Open all yr. Limited utilities in winter. No restrooms. Big rigs welcome. Rate in 2007 $16 for 2 persons. Phone: (270)646-3373.

MAMMOTH CAVE NATIONAL PARK—D-3

See listings at Bowling Green, Cave City, Horse Cave, Lucas & Park City

MANCHESTER—D-5

(E) Clay County Campground—(Clay) *From jct I-75 & SR 80: Go 1/2 E on SR 80, then 20-1/2 mi E on Daniel Boone Pkwy, then 1-1/2 mi S on SR 80. Enter on L.* ◆◆FACILITIES: 129 sites, 74 full hkups, 5 W&E, (30 & 50 amps), 50 no hkups, some extended stay sites, 10 pull-thrus, tenting, dump station, non-guest dumping $, laundry, ice, fire rings, wood. ◆◆RECREATION: equipped pavilion, stream fishing, sports field, hiking trails. Pets welcome. Open all yr. Facilities fully operational May 1 thru Oct 1. Big rigs welcome. Internet friendly. Rate in 2007 $15 per family. Phone: (606)598-3449.

MCDANIELS—D-2

(NW) AXTEL CAMPGROUND (COE - Rough River Lake)—(Grayson) *At jct Hwys-79 & 259.* FACILITIES: 158 sites, 43 W&E, 115 no hkups, tenting, dump station, ltd groceries, ice, fire rings, grills, wood. RECREATION: pavilion, lake swimming, boating, ramp, dock, 6 motorboat rentals, lake fishing, playground, shuffleboard court, horseshoes, v-ball. Pets welcome. Open 3rd Fri in Apr thru 3rd Sun in Sep. Facilities fully operational Apr 18 thru Sep 13. Phone: (270)257-2061.

(N) LAUREL BRANCH CAMPGROUND (COE- Rough River Lake)—(Breckinridge) *From jct Hwy 79 & Hwy 259: Go 1/2 mi SE on Hwy 259, then 1/2 mi S on Hwy 110.* FACILITIES: 77 sites, 25 W&E, 52 no hkups, tenting, non-flush toilets only, dump station, fire rings, grills. RECREATION: lake swimming, boating, ramp, lake fishing, playground, horseshoes, hiking trails. Pets welcome. Open all yr. Facilities fully operational May 1 thru Mid Sep. No showers. 3 days min on Holidays. Phone: (270)257-8839.

(N) NORTH FORK (Corps of Enigneers-Rough River Lake)—(Grayson) *From jct Hwy 79 & Hwy 259: Go W on Hwy 259 (follow signs).* FACILITIES: 107 sites, 81 W&E, (50 amps), 26 no hkups, tenting, dump station, ltd groceries, ice, fire rings, grills, wood. RECREATION: pavilion, lake swimming, boating, ramp, dock, lake fishing, playground, horseshoes, hiking trails. Rec open to public. Pets welcome. Open May 1 thru Mid Sep. Phone: (270)257-8139.

MIDDLESBORO—E-5

(SE) CUMBERLAND GAP NATIONAL HISTORICAL PARK (Wilderness Road Campground)—(Bell) *From jct US 25E & Hwy 74: Go 3 mi S on US 25E, then 1 mi E on US 58.* FACILITIES: 160 sites, 41 full hkups, 119 no hkups, tenting, dump station, grills, wood. RECREATION: hiking trails. Partial handicap access. Open all yr. Visitor center closed Christmas & New Years Day. No reservations. Phone: (606)248-2817.

MONTICELLO—E-4

(NW) Conley Bottom Resort—(Wayne) *From jct SR 90 & SR 1275: Go 6-1/2 mi W on SR 1275, then 1 mi N on SR 1765. Enter at end.* ◆◆◆◆FACILITIES: 200 sites, typical site width 24 ft, 20 full hkups, 180 W&E, (15, 20, 30 & 50 amps), some extended stay sites, 10 pull-thrus, tenting, dump station, non-guest dumping $, laundry, ltd groceries, LP gas by weight, ice, tables, fire rings, grills, wood. ◆◆◆RECREATION: lake swimming, boating, canoeing, ramp, dock, canoe/12 motorboat rentals, lake fishing, playground, horseshoes, hiking trails, v-ball. Rec open to public. Pets welcome. Partial handicap access. Open all yr. Facilities fully operational Apr thru Oct. Big rigs welcome. Rate in 2007 $14-33 for 4 persons. Phone: (606)348-6351.

(N) FALL CREEK CAMPGROUND (Corps of Engineers)—(Wayne) *From jct SR 90 & SR 1275: Go 5 mi N on SR 1275 (Follow signs) Enter on L.* FACILITIES: 10 sites, 10 E, tenting, dump station, fire rings, grills, wood. RECREATION: pavilion, lake swimming, boating, ramp, dock, playground. Open Apr 4 thru Oct 28. Phone: (606)348-6042.

MOREHEAD—C-5

(SW) DANIEL BOONE NATIONAL FOREST (Twin Knobs Rec. Area)—(Rowan) *From jct US-60 & Hwy-801: Go 5-1/2 mi SE on Hwy-801, then 1 mi W on FR-1017.* FACILITIES: 216 sites, 24 full hkups, 102 E, 90 no hkups, tenting, dump station, fire rings, grills, wood. RECREATION: lake swimming, boating, ramp, dock, lake fishing, horseshoes, sports field, hiking trails, v-ball. Partial handicap access. Open Mar 17 thru Oct 31. Phone: (606)784-8816.

MOREHEAD—Continued on next page

MOREHEAD—Continued

(NE) **POPPY MOUNTAIN BLUE GRASS FESTIVAL**—*From jct I-64 & SR 32: Go 3 mi S on SR 32, then 7 mi N on US 60. Enter on L.* Poppy Mountain is more than a Bluegrass Festival, we're a Bluegrass Event! Largest Bluegrass Festival in the US 3rd week in September. Open Apr 1 thru Oct 31. Summer Months. Phone: (606)780-4192.

e-mail: poppymtn@mis.net

SEE AD THIS PAGE

(NE) **POPPY MOUNTAIN CAMPGROUND**—(Rowan) *From jct I-64: Go 3 mi S on SR 32, then 7-1/2 mi N on US 60. Enter on L.*

◇◇◇FACILITIES: 6500 sites, typical site width 25 ft, 2500 W&E, (20, 30 & 50 amps), 50 amps ($), 4000 no hkups, tenting, dump station, portable dump, groceries.

◇◇RECREATION: rec hall, equipped pavilion, pond fishing, fishing supplies, golf nearby, playground, sports field, hiking trails.

Pets welcome. Open Apr 1 thru Oct 31. Reservations suggested 3rd week of Sep. Big rigs welcome. Clubs welcome. Rate in 2007 $14 per vehicle. Phone: (606)780-4192.

e-mail: poppymtn@mis.net

SEE AD THIS PAGE

MORTONS GAP—D-1

(SE) Pennyrile Campground/Best Western Motel (RV SPACES)—(Hopkins) *From jct Western Kentucky Pkwy & Pennyrile Pkwy: Go 2 mi N on Pennyrile Pkwy (exit 37), then 1/8 mi E on Hwy 813. Enter on R.* FACILITIES: 15 sites, typical site width 30 ft, 15 W&E, (20, 30 & 50 amps), mostly extended stay sites, 7 pull-thrus, dump station, non-guest dumping $, laundry, LP gas by weight/by meter, ice, tables. RECREATION: swim pool. Pets welcome. No tents. Open all yr. Rate in 2007 $18 for 2 persons. Phone: (270)258-5201.

MOUNT OLIVET—C-4

(SE) BLUE LICKS BATTLEFIELD STATE PARK—(Nicholas) *From jct US 62 & Hwy 65: Go 12 mi SE on Hwy 165* FACILITIES: 51 sites, 51 W&E, tenting, dump station, laundry, ice, fire rings, grills, wood. RECREATION: pavilion, swim pool, ramp, river fishing, mini-golf, playground, horseshoes, hiking trails, v-ball. Pets welcome. Open all yr. Facilities fully operational Apr thru Mid Nov. Phone: (800)443-7008.

MULDRAUGH—C-3

(W) MILITARY PARK (Camp Carlson Army Travel Camp)—(Meade) *From jct US 31W & US 60: Go 2-1/2 mi W on US 60. On base at Fort Knox Military Reservation.* FACILITIES: 83 sites, 40 full hkups, 18 W&E, 25 no hkups, 9 pull-thrus, tenting, dump station, laundry, ice, fire rings, grills. RECREATION: boating, electric motors only, lake/stream fishing, playground, horseshoes, sports field, v-ball. Pets welcome. Open all yr. For Military Use Only-w/Military ID Card. Phone: (502)624-4836.

MURRAY—B-2

(NE) Bullfrog Campground—(Calloway) *From SR 280 & SR 94: Go 10 mi N on SR 94, then 2 mi S on SR 497. Enter on L.* ◇◇FACILITIES: 25 sites, typical site width 28 ft, 35 ft max RV length, 12 full hkups, 13 W&E, (20 & 30 amps), many extended stay sites, tenting, dump station, portable dump, laundry, ltd groceries, ice, tables, fire rings, wood. ◇◇RECREATION: swim pool, lake fishing, playground, horseshoes, hiking trails. Pets welcome. Open all yr. Facilities fully operational Memorial Day thru Labor Day. Rate in 2007 $20 per family. Phone: (270)474-1144. CCUSA discount.

(NW) Holly Green RV Park—(Calloway) *From jct SR 280 & SR 94: Go 3-1/4 mi W on SR 94, then 1 mi N on US 641, then 3/4 mi W on SR 121, then 1/4 mi S on SR 774. Enter on L.* ◇◇◇FACILITIES: 50 sites, typical site width 24 ft, accepts full hkup units only, 50 full hkups, (20 & 30 amps), mostly extended stay sites, dump station, non-guest dumping $, tables. Pets welcome. No tents. Open all yr. Rate in 2007 $15 per vehicle. Phone: (270)753-5652.

(E) WILDCAT CREEK REC AREA—(Calloway) *From jct Hwy 94 & Hwy 280 E of town: Go 5-1/4 mi E on Hwy 280, then 2.1 mi NE on Hwy 614E. Follow signs. Enter on R.* FACILITIES: 54

MURRAY—Continued
WILDCAT CREEK REC AREA—Continued

sites, 54 W&E, (30 & 50 amps), 6 pull-thrus, tenting, dump station, laundry, ice, fire rings, grills, wood. RECREATION: lake swimming, boating, ramp, lake fishing. Rec open to public. Partial handicap access. Open all yr. Open Mar 1 thru Nov 30. Phone: (270)436-5628.

OLIVE HILL—C-5

(NE) CARTER CAVES STATE RESORT PARK—(Carter) *From jct Hwy 2 & US 60: Go 5 mi E on US 60, then 3 mi N on Hwy 182.* FACILITIES: 89 sites, 89 W&E, tenting, dump station, laundry, grills, wood. RECREATION: rec hall, boating, no motors, canoeing, ramp, rowboat/pedal boat rentals, lake fishing, mini-golf, playground, planned activities, tennis, hiking trails. Pets welcome. Open Apr thru Oct. Phone: (800)325-0059.

OWENSBORO—D-2

(SW) Diamond Lake Resort Campground—(Davies) *From jct SR 56 & US 60 bypass: Go 10 mi W on SR 56, then 100 yds S on SR 815, then 500 yds S on Hobbs Rd. Enter on L.* ◇◇◇FACILITIES: 270 sites, typical site width 40 ft, 225 full hkups, 45 W&E, (30 & 50 amps), many extended stay sites, 10 pull-thrus, dump station, non-guest dumping $, laundry, ltd groceries, ice, tables, patios, fire rings, wood. ◇◇◇◇RECREATION: rec hall, rec room/area, pavilion, swim pool, lake swimming, ramp, 2 pedal boat rentals, lake fishing, play equipment, planned activities (wkends only), horseshoes, sports field, hiking trails, v-ball. Rec open to public. Pets welcome. Partial handicap access. No tents. Open all yr. Big rigs welcome. Internet friendly. Rate in 2007 $21-25 for 2 persons. Phone: (270)229-4900.

(SW) Windy Hollow Campground & Recreation Area—(Daviess) *From jct SR 56/81 & US 60 bypass: Go 3/4 mi W on SR 56/81, then 6 mi S on SR 81, then 3/4 mi S on Old SR 81, then 2 mi W on Windy Hollow Rd. Enter on R.* ◇◇◇FACILITIES: 170 sites, typical site width 35 ft, 28 ft max RV length, 100 full hkups, 70 W&E, (30 & 50 amps), some extended stay sites, 14 pull-thrus, tenting, dump station, non-guest dumping $, laundry, ltd groceries, tables, fire rings, wood. ◇◇◇RECREATION: equipped pavilion, lake swimming, lake/pond fishing, mini-golf ($), playground, planned activities (wkends only), horseshoes, sports field, hiking trails, v-ball. Rec open to public. Pets welcome. Partial handicap access. Open all yr. Facilities fully operational Apr 1 thru Oct 31. Rate in 2007 $24-28 for 2 persons. Phone: (270)785-4150. CCUSA discount.

PADUCAH—B-1

(SE) **DUCK CREEK RV PARK**—(McCracken) *From jct US 45 & I-24: Go 4-1/4 mi E on US 24 (exit 11), then 1/2 mi N on John Puryear Dr. Enter on R.*

◇◇◇◇FACILITIES: 92 sites, typical site width 30 ft, 80 full hkups, 12 W&E, (30 & 50 amps), 50 amps ($), some extended stay sites, 51 pull-thrus, wireless Instant Internet access at site, phone Internet access central location, tenting, RV/park trailer rentals, cabins, RV storage, dump station, non-guest dumping $, laundry, ltd groceries, RV supplies, LP gas by weight/by meter, ice, tables, wood.

◇◇◇RECREATION: rec room/area, equipped pavilion, swim pool, pond/stream fishing, sports field.

Pets welcome. Partial handicap access. Open all yr. Facilities fully operational Memorial Day thru Labor Day. Big rigs welcome. Internet friendly. Clubs welcome. Rate in 2007 $23-25.50 for 2 persons. MC/VISA/DISC/AMEX/Debit. Member ARVC. Phone: (800)728-5109.

e-mail: mevessels@aol.com

SEE AD THIS PAGE

(SW) Fern Lake Campground—(McCracken) *From jct US 45 & I 24: Go 4 mi W on I-24, then 1/2 mi W on SR 305. Enter on R.* ◇◇◇◇FACILITIES: 90 sites, typical site width 30 ft, 50 full hkups, 30 W&E, (30 & 50 amps), 10 no hkups, some extended stay sites, 40 pull-thrus, tenting, dump station, non-guest dumping $, laundry, ice, tables, grills, wood. ◇◇RECREATION: pavilion, lake fishing, playground, shuffleboard court, sports field, v-ball. Pets welcome. Open all yr. Big rigs welcome. Internet friendly. Rate in 2007 $20-24.50 for 2 persons. Phone: (270)444-7939.

PARK CITY—E-3

(NW) Diamond Caverns Resort & Golf Club—(Barren) *From jct I 65 & SR 255: Go 1-1/4 mi N on SR 255.* ◇◇◇FACILITIES: 71 sites, typical site width 30 ft, 65 full hkups, 6 W&E, (30 & 50 amps), some extended stay sites, 32 pull-thrus, tenting, dump station, non-guest dumping, laundry, ltd groceries, LP gas by weight/by meter, ice, tables, patios, fire rings, wood. ◇◇◇◇RECREATION: rec hall, pavilion, equipped pavilion, 2 swim pools, mini-golf, playground, horseshoes, sports field, hiking trails, v-ball. Pets welcome. Open all yr. Facilities fully operational Mar 1 thru Nov 1. Swimming Memorial Day to Labor Day. Big rigs welcome. Rate in 2007 $27.50 for 2 persons. Phone: (270)749-2891.

(W) MAMMOTH CAVE NP (Headquarters Campground)—(Edmonson) *N'bound from jct I-65 (exit 48) & Hwy 255: Go 8 mi NW on Hwy 255. S'bound from jct I-65 (exit 53) & Hwy 70: Go 9 mi W on Hwy 70.* FACILITIES: 105 sites, 28 ft max RV length, 105 no hkups, tenting, shower$, dump station, laundry, ltd groceries, full svc store, ice, fire rings, grills, wood. RECREATION: boating, hiking trails. Open all yr. Facilities fully operational Mar 1 thru Nov 30. Phone: (270)758-2181.

PARKERS LAKE—E-4

(E) Eagle Falls Resort—(McCreary) *From jct I-75 & US 25W: Go 7 mi W on US 25W, then 9 mi W on SR 90. Enter on R.* ◇◇◇FACILITIES: 63 sites, typical site width 20 ft, 39 ft max RV length, 54 W&E, (20, 30 & 50 amps), 9 no hkups, tenting, dump station, laundry, groceries, ice, tables, fire rings, grills, wood. ◇◇◇◇RECREATION: rec room/area, pavilion, swim pool, lake fishing, playground, planned activities (wkends only), horseshoes. Rec open to public. Pets welcome. Partial handicap access. Open May 1 thru Nov 30. Pool open Memorial to Labor Day. Rate in 2007 $20-25 per vehicle. Phone: (888)318-2658. CCUSA discount.

PIKEVILLE—D-6

(S) GRAPEVINE CAMPGROUND (COE-Fishtrap Lake)—(Pike) *From jct Hwy 80 & US 119: Go 9-1/2 mi E on US 119 to Meta, then 16 mi S on Hwy 194.* FACILITIES: 28 sites, 10 W&E, 18 no hkups, tenting, dump station, laundry, groceries, ice, fire rings, grills. RECREATION: lake swimming, boating, canoeing, ramp, lake fishing, playground, hiking trails. Rec open to public. Pets welcome. Open Memorial Day thru Labor Day. Phone: (606) 835-4864.

PRESTONSBURG—D-6

(E) GERMAN BRIDGE CAMPING AREA (COE - Dewey Lake)—(Floyd) *From town: Go 6 mi S on Hwy-1428, then 7 mi on Hwy-194.* FACILITIES: 40 sites, 40 no hkups, tenting, dump station, laundry. RECREATION: boating, canoeing, ramp, lake fishing, playground. Open Memorial Day Wkend thru Labor Day Wkend. Phone: (606)789-4521.

(E) JENNY WILEY STATE RESORT PARK—(Floyd) *From jct US 23-460 & Hwy 80: Go 3 mi N on US 23-460, then 2 mi E on Hwy 3, then S on Hwy 302.* FACILITIES: 117 sites, 30 ft max RV length, 117 E, (30 & 50 amps), tenting, dump station, laundry, groceries, ice, fire rings, grills, wood. RECREATION: swim pool, boating, ramp, dock, pedal boat rentals, lake fishing, mini-golf, playground, planned activities, hiking trails. Pets welcome. Open Apr 1 thru Oct 31. Phone: (800)325-0142.

PRINCETON—D-1

✲ (E) **MURPHY'S RV'S**—*From jct US-62 & Hwy-91/Hwy-293: Go 2 mi E on US-62. Enter on L.* SALES: travel trailers, park trailers, 5th wheels, pre-owned unit sales. SERVICES: full-time mech, RV appliance repair, RV storage, sells parts/accessories, installs hitches. Open all yr. MC/VISA/Debit. Phone: (888)442-5000.

e-mail: murphysrv@bellsouth.net

SEE AD EDDYVILLE PAGE 284

RENFRO VALLEY—D-4

(NE) **KOA-RENFRO VALLEY**—(Rockcastle) *From jct I-75 (exit 62) & US 25: Go 1-1/2 mi N on US 25. Enter on R.*

◇◇◇◇FACILITIES: 133 sites, typical site width 30 ft, 68 full hkups, 35 W&E, (30 & 50 amps), 30 no hkups, 77 pull-thrus, cable TV ($), wireless Instant Internet access at site, wireless Internet access central location, tenting, RV/park trailer rentals, cabins, RV storage, dump station, non-guest dumping $, laundry, full svc store, RV supplies, LP gas by weight/by meter, ice, tables, fire rings, grills, wood.

◇◇◇◇RECREATION: rec hall, rec room/area, pavilion, equipped pavilion, coin games, swim pool, mini-golf ($), golf nearby, bsktball, bike rental, playground, shuffleboard court, planned activities, horseshoes, sports field, hiking trails, v-ball, local tours.

Pets welcome. Open all yr. Pool open May 1 - Oct 1. Big rigs welcome. Internet friendly. Escort to site. Clubs welcome. Rate in 2007 $27.90-39 per

KOA-RENFRO VALLEY—Continued on next page

RENFRO VALLEY—Continued
KOA-RENFRO VALLEY—Continued

family. MC/VISA/DISC/Debit. Member ARVC. Phone: (800)KOA-2475. KOA 10% value card discount.

e-mail: renfrovalleykoa@hotmail.com

SEE AD THIS PAGE AND AD DISCOVER SECTION PAGES 62 & 63

(SE) Renfro Valley RV Park—(Rockcastle) *From I-75 (exit 62) & US 25: Go 1/4 mi N on US 25. Enter on R.* ◊◊◊◊FACILITIES: 234 sites, typical site width 30 ft, 97 full hkups, 17 W&E, 120 E, (50 amps), 50 pull-thrus, tenting, dump station, non-guest dumping $, portable dump, laundry, LP gas by weight/by meter, ice, tables, fire rings, grills, wood. ◊◊◊RECREATION: pavilion, stream fishing, play equipment, shuffleboard court, planned activities, horseshoes, sports field, hiking trails, v-ball. Pets welcome. Partial handicap access. Open all yr. Facilities fully operational Mar thru Dec. Rate in 2007 $26.50-29 per vehicle. Member ARVC. Phone: (800)765-7464. FMCA discount.

RICHMOND—D-4

(N) FORT BOONESBOROUGH STATE PARK—(Madison) *From jct Hwy 338 & Hwy 627: Go 1/2 mi S on Hwy 338.* FACILITIES: 167 sites, 167 W&E, tenting, dump station, laundry, ltd groceries, ice, grills, wood. RECREATION: pavilion, swim pool, boating, ramp, river fishing, mini-golf, playground, shuffleboard court, planned activities, hiking trails. Pets welcome. Open all yr. Phone: (859)527-3131.

RUSSELL SPRINGS—E-3

(SE) KOA-Indian Hills—(Russell) *From jct US 127 & Hwy 80: Go 2-1/2 mi E on Hwy 80, then 2-1/2 mi S on Hwy 910, then 4-1/2 mi S on Hwy 76, then 1-1/2 mi S on Hwy 1383. Enter on L.* ◊◊◊FACILITIES: 156 sites, typical site width 24 ft, 32 full hkups, 118 W&E, (30 & 50 amps), 6 no hkups, some extended stay sites (in summer), 22 pull-thrus, tenting, dump station, non-guest dumping $, laundry, groceries, ice, tables, fire rings, wood. ◊◊◊◊RECREATION: rec hall, pavilion, swim pool, mini-golf ($), playground, planned activities (wkends only), tennis, horseshoes, sports field, hiking trails, v-ball. Rec open to public. Pets welcome. Open Apr 1 thru Nov 1. Facilities fully operational Memorial Day thru Labor Day. Rate in 2007 $25-34 for 2 persons. Phone: (270)866-5616. KOA 10% value card discount.

(SE) WOLF CREEK RESORT PARK (UNDER CONSTRUCTION)—(Russell) *From jct US 127 & Hwy 80: Go 2-1/2 mi E on Hwy 80, then 2-1/2 mi S on Hwy 910, then 4-1/2 mi S on Hwy 76, then 1/4 mi S on Hwy 1383. Enter on R.*

FACILITIES: 160 sites, typical site width 40 ft, 160 full hkups, (20, 30 & 50 amps), mostly extended stay sites, wireless Instant Internet access at site, controlled access gate.

RECREATION: rec room/area, swim pool, fishing guides, bsktball, playground, horseshoes, v-ball.

Pets welcome. No tents. Open all yr. Internet friendly. Rate in 2007 $35-40 per vehicle. Phone: (866)848-7855.

e-mail: chris@prosol.com

SEE AD TRAVEL SECTION PAGE 277

SALT LICK—C-5

(S) DANIEL BOONE NATIONAL FOREST (Zilpo Recreation Area)—(Bath) *From jct I-64 (exit 123) & US 60: Go 6-1/2 mi E on US 60, then 4 mi S on 211, then 3 mi E on FDR 129, then 9 mi N on FDR 918 (Nat'l Scenic Byway).* FACILITIES: 164 sites, 40 E, 124 no hkups, tenting, dump station, groceries, ice, fire rings, grills, wood. RECREATION: lake swimming, boating, ramp, dock, lake fishing, horseshoes, hiking trails. Rec open to public. Partial handicap access. Open Apr 14 thru Oct 17. Phone: (606) 768-2722.

SALT LICK—Continued

(SW) The Outpost RV Park—(Bath) *From jct SR 801 & US 60: Go 1-1/4 mi W on US 60, then 3/4 mi S on Cave Run Lake Rd. Enter on L.* ◊◊◊FACILITIES: 101 sites, typical site width 28 ft, 60 full hkups, 6 W&E, (30 & 50 amps), 35 no hkups, some extended stay sites, 30 pull-thrus, tenting, dump station, non-guest dumping $, laundry, groceries, ice, tables, fire rings, wood. ◊◊RECREATION: pavilion, swim pool, play equipment, horseshoes, sports field, v-ball. Rec open to public. Pets welcome. Open all yr. Facilities fully operational Memorial Day thru Labor Day. Big rigs welcome. Internet friendly. Rate in 2007 $16-18 for 4 persons. Phone: (606)683-2311.

SANDERS—B-4

(SW) Eagle Valley Camping Resort—(Owen) *From jct I-71 & Hwy 35 (exit 57): Go 2 mi S on Hwy 35, then 6-1/2 mi W on Hwy 467, then 1-1/2 mi S on Stephanus Rd. Enter on R.* ◊◊◊FACILITIES: 269 sites, typical site width 45 ft, 17 full hkups, 252 W&E, (30 & 50 amps), many extended stay sites, 1 pull-thrus, tenting, dump station, non-guest dumping $, laundry, groceries, ice, tables, fire rings, wood. ◊◊◊RECREATION: equipped pavilion, swim pool, boating, electric motors only, ramp, dock, 4 pedal boat rentals, lake fishing, playground, planned activities (wkends only), horseshoes, sports field, hiking trails, v-ball. Rec open to public. Pets welcome. Partial handicap access. Open all yr. Facilities fully operational Apr 1 thru Nov 1. Rate in 2007 $20-25 for 4 persons. Phone: (502)347-9361.

SASSAFRAS—D-5

(E) CARR CREEK STATE PARK—(Knott) *From town: Go E on Hwy 15.* FACILITIES: 39 sites, 39 W&E, tenting, dump station, laundry, ice, fire rings, grills, wood. RECREATION: pavilion, lake swimming, boating, ramp, dock, lake fishing, playground, horseshoes. Pets welcome. Partial handicap access. Open Apr 1 thru Oct 31. Phone: (606)642-4050.

SCOTTSVILLE—E-2

(N) BAILEY'S POINT CAMPGROUND (COE-Barren River Lake)—(Allen) *From jct US 231 & US 31E: Go 9 mi N on US 31E, then 1 mi W on Hwy 252, then 4 mi N on Hwy 517.* FACILITIES: 215 sites, 114 E, 101 no hkups, tenting, dump station, laundry, ltd groceries, ice, grills, wood. RECREATION: lake swimming, boating, canoeing, ramp, lake fishing, playground, planned activities (wkends only), horseshoes, hiking trails, v-ball. Pets welcome. Open Mid Apr thru 3rd Sat in Oct. Phone: (270)646-2055.

(N) THE TAILWATER BELOW DAM (COE-Barren River Lake)—(Allen) *From jct US 231 & US 31E: Go 9 mi N on US 31E, then 8 mi W on Hwy 252.* FACILITIES: 48 sites, 48 no hkups, tenting, fire rings, grills. RECREATION: lake swimming, boating, canoeing, ramp, lake/river fishing, playground, horseshoes, sports field, hiking trails, v-ball. Pets welcome. Open all yr. Facilities fully operational mid Apr thru mid Sep. No showers. Phone: (270)622-7732.

SHEPHERDSVILLE—C-3

(S) Grandma's RV Park—(Bullitt) *From jct SR 44 & I 65: Go 1 mi S on I 65, then 200 yds W on SR 40. Enter on R.* ◊◊◊◊FACILITIES: 65 sites, typical site width 25 ft, 65 full hkups, (30 & 50 amps), many extended stay sites, 30 pull-thrus, laundry, patios. RECREATION: pavilion. Pets welcome. Partial handicap access. No tents. Open all yr. Big rigs welcome. Internet friendly. Rate in 2007 $24 for 2 persons. Phone: (502) 543-7023.

(E) LOUISVILLE SOUTH KOA—(Bullitt) *From jct I-65 (exit 117) & Hwy-44: Go 1-1/2 mi E on Hwy-44. Enter on R.*

◊◊◊◊FACILITIES: 200 sites, typical site width 30 ft, 123 full hkups, 77 W&E, (30 & 50 amps), 50 amps ($), some extended stay sites, 68 pull-thrus, cable TV, wireless Instant Internet access at site, tenting, RV/park trailer rentals, cabins, RV storage, dump

SHEPHERDSVILLE—Continued
LOUISVILLE SOUTH KOA—Continued

station, laundry, groceries, RV supplies, LP gas by weight/by meter, ice, tables, fire rings, grills, wood.

◊◊◊◊RECREATION: rec room/area, equipped pavilion, coin games, swim pool, whirlpool, ramp, river/pond fishing, fishing supplies, fishing guides, mini-golf ($), golf nearby, bsktball, 8 bike rentals, playground, play equipment, planned activities (wkends only), horseshoes, sports field, hiking trails, v-ball. Rec open to public.

Pets welcome. Open all yr. Big rigs welcome. Internet friendly. Clubs welcome. Rate in 2007 $36-70 for 2 persons. MC/VISA/DISC/AMEX/Debit. Member ARVC. Phone: (800)KOA-1880. KOA 10% value card discount.

e-mail: louisvillesouth@koa.net

SEE AD LOUISVILLE PAGE 287 AND AD DISCOVER SECTION PAGES 62 & 63

(E) SHEPHERDSVILLE BULLITT COUNTY TOURISM—*From jct SR 44 & I-65: Go 100 yds W on SR 44, then 300 yds S on Paroquet Springs Dr. Enter on R.* Shepherdsville-Bullitt Cnty has weekend getaways to week long adventures. We have attractions for all ages which incl Jim Beam American Outpost, Bernheim Arboretum & Research Forest, Hawks Gallery & Cafe, & America's longest go cart track, Kart Kountry. Open all yr. Phone: (800)526-2068.

SEE AD TRAVEL SECTION PAGE 277

SLADE—D-5

(E) DANIEL BOONE NATIONAL FOREST (Koomer Ridge Campground)—(Wolfe) *From jct Mountain Parkway & Hwy-15: Go 3-1/2 mi SE on Hwy-15.* FACILITIES: 54 sites, 22 ft max RV length, 54 no hkups, tenting, fire rings, grills. RECREATION: hiking trails. Pets welcome. Partial handicap access. Open all yr. Facilities fully operational Mid Apr thru Late Oct. No showers. No reservations. Max stay 14 days. Phone: (606)668-7939.

(S) NATURAL BRIDGE STATE RESORT PARK—(Powell) *From jct Mountain Parkway & Hwy 11: Go 2-1/2 mi S on Hwy 11.* FACILITIES: 94 sites, 82 W&E, (20, 30 & 50 amps), 12 no hkups, tenting, dump station, laundry, ice, fire rings, grills, wood. RECREATION: pavilion, swim pool, boating, dock, rowboat/canoe/pedal boat rentals, lake fishing, mini-golf, playground, planned activities, tennis, hiking trails. Pets welcome. Open Apr 15 thru Oct 31. Phone: (800)325-1710.

SOMERSET—E-4

(W) CUMBERLAND POINT PUBLIC USE AREA (COE-Lake Cumberland)—(Wayne) *From jct Hwy 80 & US 27: Go 8 mi SW on Hwy 80, then 1 mi S on Hwy 235, then 10 mi E on Hwy 761.* FACILITIES: 30 sites, 30 W&E, tenting, dump station, laundry, grills. RECREATION: lake swimming, boating, ramp, lake fishing, playground, horseshoes. Pets welcome. Open Apr 19 thru Sep 24. Phone: (606)871-7886.

(W) FISHING CREEK PUBLIC USE AREA (COE-Lake Cumberland)—(Pulaski) *From jct Hwy 80 & US 27: Go 5 mi W on Hwy 80, then 3 mi N on Hwy 1248.* FACILITIES: 47 sites, 47 W&E, (30 & 50 amps), tenting, dump station, laundry, ltd groceries, grills. RECREATION: lake swimming, boating, ramp, lake fishing, playground. Pets welcome. Open Apr 18 thru Sep 24. Phone: (606)679-5174.

(S) WAITSBORO REC AREA (COE-Lake Cumberland)—(Pulaski) *From town: Go 5 mi S on US 27, then 1 mi W on Waitsboro Rd. Enter at end.* FACILITIES: 25 sites, 25 W&E, tenting, dump station, laundry, ice, fire rings, grills, wood. RECREATION: lake swimming, boating, canoeing, ramp, dock, lake fishing, playground. Pets welcome. Open Apr 4 thru Oct 13. Phone: (606)561-5513.

Jefferson Davis, President of the Confederacy, was from Kentucky.

STAFFORDSVILLE—C-6

(W) PAINTSVILLE LAKE STATE PARK—(Johnson) *From jct US 23 & SR 40: Go 1-1/4 mi W on SR 40, then 1 mi N on Rt 2275. Enter at end.* FACILITIES: 42 sites, typical site width 35 ft, 32 full hkups, (15, 30 & 50 amps), 10 no hkups, 12 pull-thrus, tenting, laundry, ice, fire rings, grills, wood. RECREATION: pavilion, boating, ramp, pedal boat rentals, lake fishing, playground, horseshoes, v-ball. Pets welcome. Partial handicap access. Open all yr. Big rigs welcome. Phone: (606)297-8486.

STEARNS—E-4

(S) BIG SOUTH FORK NAT'L RIVER & REC. AREA (Blue Heron Campground)—(McCreary) *From jct US 27 & Hwy 92: Go 1 mi W on Hwy 92, then 1 mi S on Hwy 1651, then 9 mi S on Hwy 741. Enter on R.* FACILITIES: 49 sites, 33 ft max RV length, 49 W&E, tenting, dump station, fire rings, grills. RECREATION: canoeing, river fishing, play equipment, hiking trails. Open Apr thru Nov. Phone: (606)376-5073.

STURGIS—A-2

(E) UNION COUNTY FAIR & EXPO CENTER—(Union) *From jct SR-109 & US-60: Go 1 mi E on US-60. Enter on L.* FACILITIES: 45 sites, typical site width 35 ft, accepts self-contained units only, 30 W&E, 15 E, (20, 30 & 50 amps), 20 pull-thrus. RECREATION: boating, electric motors only, ramp, lake fishing, sports field. Pets welcome. No tents. Open all yr. No restrooms, water available from March to Nov/Closed 3rd week in June & July. Big rigs welcome. Internet friendly. Phone: (270) 333-4107.

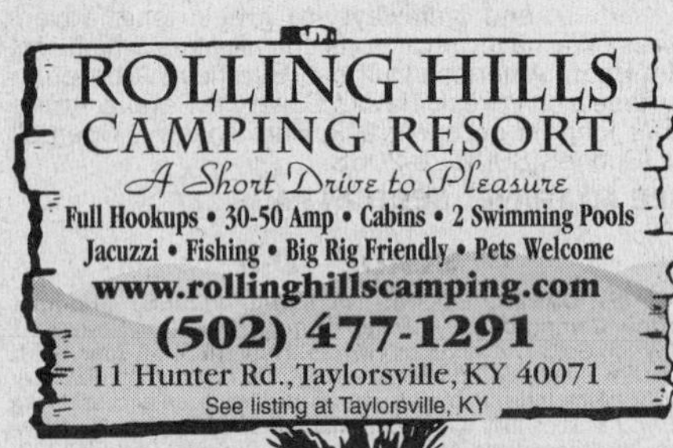

ROLLING HILLS
CAMPING RESORT
A Short Drive to Pleasure
Full Hookups • 30-50 Amp • Cabins • 2 Swimming Pools
Jacuzzi • Fishing • Big Rig Friendly • Pets Welcome
www.rollinghillscamping.com
(502) 477-1291
11 Hunter Rd., Taylorsville, KY 40071
See listing at Taylorsville, KY

TAYLORSVILLE—C-3

(E) ROLLING HILLS CAMPING RESORT —(Spencer) *From jct BlueGrass Pkwy & US 62: Go 12-3/4 mi N on US 62, then 2-1/4 mi E on SR 44. Enter on L.*

WELCOME

◆◆◆FACILITIES: 71 sites, 8 full hkups, 63 W&E, (30 & 50 amps), some extended stay sites, phone on-site Internet access (needs activ), wireless Internet access central location, tenting, cabins, dump station, non-guest dumping $, portable dump, laundry, ltd groceries, ice, tables, fire rings, grills, wood.

◆◆◆RECREATION: rec room/area, pavilion, 2 swim pools, lake swimming, whirlpool, lake fishing, mini-golf, golf nearby, bsktball, playground, planned activities (wkends only), horseshoes, sports field, v-ball.

Pets welcome. Partial handicap access. Open all yr. Facilities fully operational April thru Nov. Planned group activites holiday wknds only. Big rigs welcome. Internet friendly. Clubs welcome. Rate in 2007 $24-32 for 2 persons. MC/VISA/Debit. Member ARVC. Phone: (502)477-1291. CCUSA discount. FMCA discount.

e-mail: rollinghillscamping@hotmail.com

SEE AD THIS PAGE

(E) TAYLORSVILLE LAKE STATE PARK—(Spencer) *From jct Hwy 155 & Hwy 44: Go 3 mi E on Hwy 44. Enter on R.* FACILITIES: 45 sites, 45 W&E, tenting, dump station, laundry, ltd groceries, ice, fire rings, grills, wood. RECREATION: pavilion, boating, canoeing, ramp, dock, motorboat rentals, lake fishing, playground, planned activities, horseshoes, hiking trails. Pets welcome. Partial handicap access. Open Apr 1 thru Dec 15. Phone: (502)477-8713.

Farmers in Kentucky grow large crops of tobacco, corn and hay.

WALTON—B-4

(W) BIG BONE LICK STATE PARK—(Boone) *From jct I-75 & Hwy-1292: Go 4-1/2 mi W on Hwy-1292, then 3 mi on Hwy-338.* FACILITIES: 62 sites, 62 W&E, tenting, dump station, laundry, groceries, ice, grills. RECREATION: rec hall, pavilion, swim pool, stream fishing, mini-golf, playground, planned activities, tennis, horseshoes, hiking trails, v-ball. Pets welcome. Open all yr. Phone: (859)384-3522.

OAK CREEK CAMPGROUND—(Boone) *From jct I-75 & SR 16 (exit 171): Go S 1 mi on SR 16. Enter on R.*

WELCOME

◆◆◆FACILITIES: 105 sites, typical site width 30 ft, 100 W&E, (30 & 50 amps), 50 amps ($), 5 no hkups, some extended stay sites, 6 pull-thrus, cable TV, wireless Instant Internet access at site, wireless Internet access central location, tenting, RV storage, dump station, portable dump, laundry, groceries, RV supplies, ice, tables, fire rings, wood.

◆◆◆RECREATION: rec room/area, equipped pavilion, coin games, swim pool, stream fishing, golf nearby, bsktball, playground, planned activities (wkends only), horseshoes, hiking trails. Rec open to public.

Pets welcome. Open all yr. Facilities fully operational Mar 1 thru Nov 15. Pool open Memorial Day - Labor Day. Internet friendly. Clubs welcome. Rate in 2007 $20-28 for 2 persons. MC/VISA/DISC/AMEX. Phone: (859)485-9131. FCRV 10% discount. FMCA discount.

e-mail: oakcreek@fuse.com

SEE AD CINCINNATI, OH PAGE 682

Chevrolet Corvettes are manufactured in Bowling Green.

TRAVEL SECTION

Louisiana

READER SERVICE INFO

The following businesses have placed an ad in the Louisiana Travel Section. To receive free information, enter their Reader Service number on the Reader Service Card opposite page 48/Discover Section in the front of this directory:

Advertiser	RS#
Bayou Outdoor Supercenter	3791
Cajun Coast Visitors & Convention Bureau	2687
Houma Area Convention & Visitors Bureau	396
Lafayette Convention & Visitors Commission	2843
Louisiana Campground Owners Association	3255
Louisiana Travel Promotion Association	3767
Natalbany Creek Campground	3303
Paragon Casino	2589
Pavilion RV Park	3378
Prejean's Restaurant	2662
Randol's Restaurant & Cajun Dance Hall	3705
Shreveport/Bossier Convention & Tourist Bureau	837
Southwest Louisiana CVB	3013
St Tammany Parish Tourist Convention Commission	153
Tangipahoa Parish Tourist Community	773

TIME ZONE

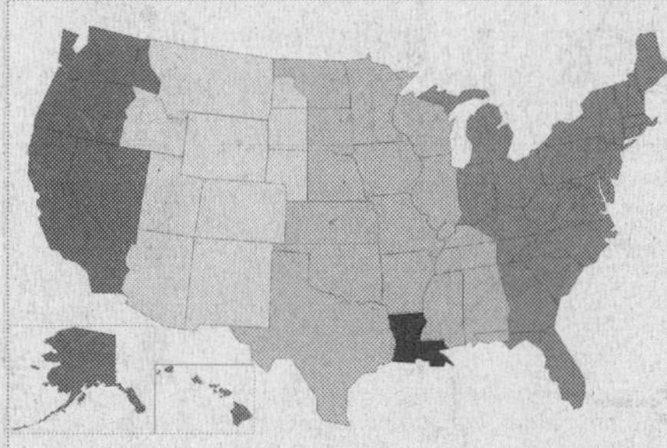

Louisiana is in the Central Time Zone.

Tell Them Woodall's Sent You!

TOPOGRAPHY

Louisiana's varied terrain encompasses rich alluvial plains, rolling hills, river bluffs, coastal marches, rivers and bayous.

TEMPERATURE

Snow rarely falls in the southern sections, with only light snowfall recorded in the northern regions. January's low/high temperatures are 25°/59° and July's low/high temperatures are 71°/92°.

TRAVEL & TOURISM INFO

Although the Louisiana coast was devastated by Hurricane Katrina, there is much that was untouched or has been reconstructed. Tourists are encouraged to visit and see the rebirth of the coastal region; however, you are encouraged to research your destination before leaving home. The following bureaus can give you up-to-date information on the area you are visiting:

State Agency:
Louisiana Office of Tourism
P.O. Box 94291
Baton Rouge, LA 70804
(225/342-8100)
www.louisanatravel.com

Local Agencies:
Acadia Parish Tourist Commission
P.O. Box 1342
Crowley, LA 70527
(337/783-2108)
www.acadiatourism.org

Alexandria-Pineville Area CVB
707 Main St.
Alexandria, LA 71301

FREE INFO! Enter #3705 on Reader Service Card

FREE INFO! Enter #3791 on Reader Service Card

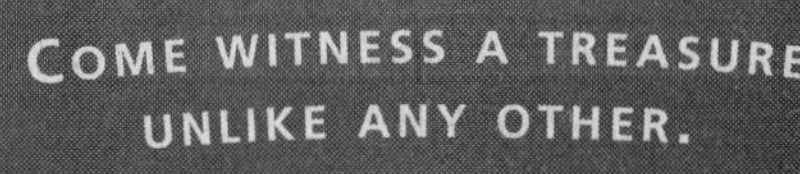

FREE INFO! Enter #2589 on Reader Service Card

FREE INFO! Enter #2662 on Reader Service Card

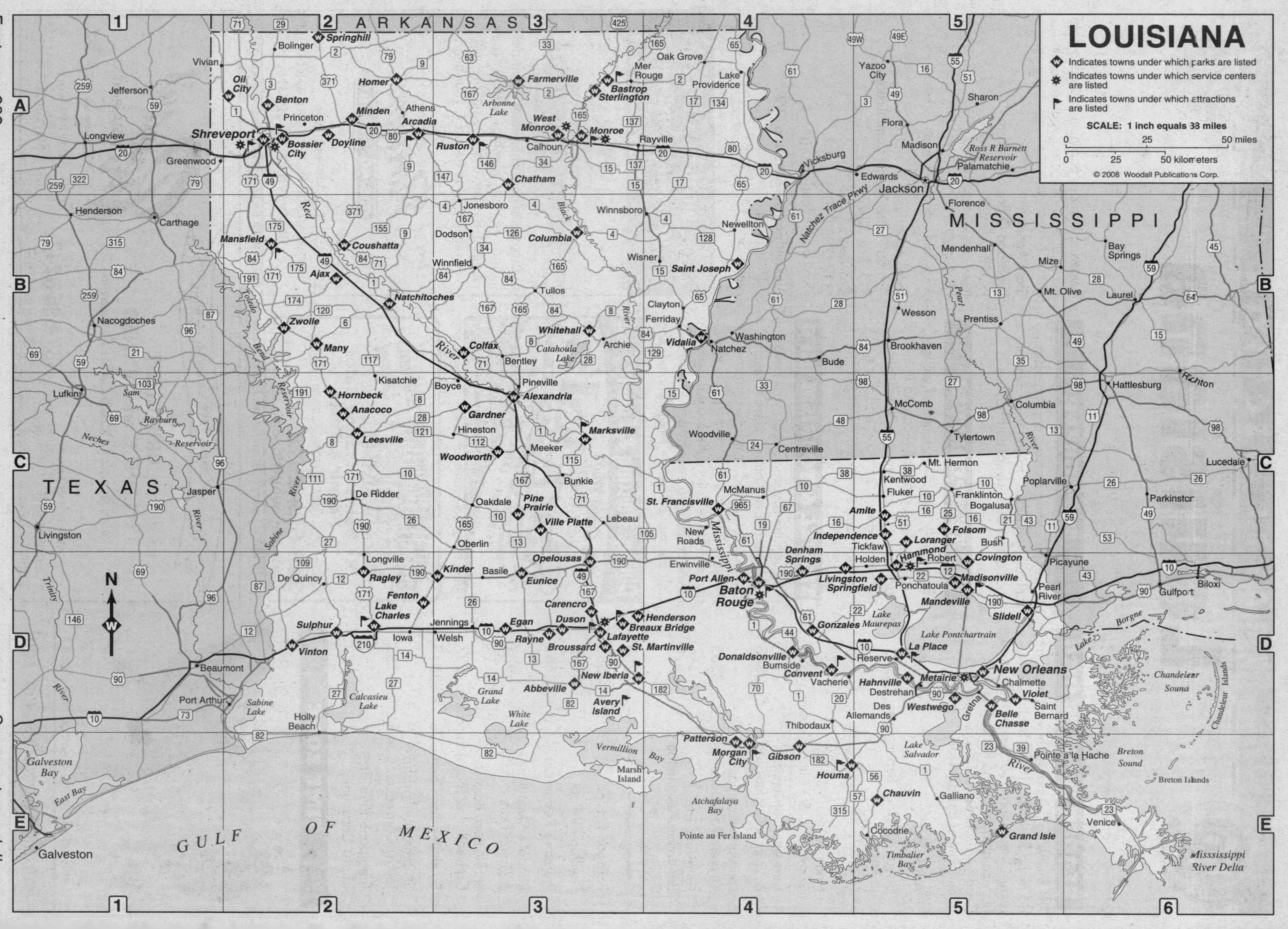

LOUISIANA
Indicates towns under which parks are listed
Indicates towns under which service centers are listed
Indicates towns under which attractions are listed
SCALE: 1 inch equals 33 miles
0 25 50 miles
0 25 50 kilometers
© 2008 Woodall Publications Corp.
ARKANSAS
MISSISSIPPI
TEXAS
GULF OF MEXICO
Shreveport
Bossier City
Monroe
Alexandria
Lafayette
Baton Rouge
New Orleans
Lake Charles
Jackson
Lake Pontchartrain
Mississippi River Delta

(800/551-9546 or 318/442-9546)
www.louisianafromhere.com

Allen Parish Tourist Commission
Box 1280
Oberlin, LA 70655
(888/639-4868 or 337/639-4868)
www.allenparish.com

Ascension Parish Tourist Commission
6967 Hwy. 22
Sorrento, LA 70778
(888/775-7990)
www.ascensiontourism.com

Avoyelles Parish Commission of Tourism Office
208 South Main St, P.O. Box 24
Marksville, LA 71351
(800/833-4195 or 318/253-0585)
www.travelavoyelles.com

Baton Rouge Area Convention & Visitors Bureau
730 North Blvd.
Baton Rouge, LA 70802
(800/527-6843)
www.visitbatonrouge.com

Bayou Teche Visitors Center (City of Breaux Bridge)
East Bridge Street
Breaux Bridge, LA 70517
(337/332-8500 or 888/565-5939)
www.BreauxBridgeLive.net

Cajun Coast Visitors & Convention Bureau
P.O. Box 2332
Morgan City, LA 70381
(800/256-2931)
www.cajuncoast.com

Caldwell Parish Chamber of Commerce
104 Main Street
Columbia, LA 71418
(318/649-0726)

Cameron Parish Police Jury
P.O. Box 366
Cameron, LA 70631
(337/775-5718)

Claiborne Chamber
519 S. Main Street
Homer, LA 71040
(318/927-3271)
www.claiborneone.org

East Carroll Parish (Byerley House Visitor & Community Center, Doorway to Louisiana, Inc.)
600 Lake St.
Lake Providence, LA 71254
(318/559-5125)
www.lapage.com/parishes/ecarr.htm

East Feliciana Tourist Commission
P.O. Box 667
Jackson, LA 70748
(225/634-7155)
www.felicianatourism.org

Evangeline Parish Tourism Commission
P.O. Box 412
306 West Main Street
Ville Platte, LA 70586
(337/363-1878 or 337/363-8687)
www.EvangelineTourism.com

Grant Parish Chamber
P.O. Box 32
Colfax, LA 71417
(318/627-2211)
www.grantcoc.org

Gretna (City of) Office of Tourism & Visitor Center
Jefferson Parish
P.O. Box 404
2nd Street @ Huey P. Long Ave.
Gretna, LA 70054
(504/363-1500)
www.gretnala.com

Houma Area CVB
P.O. Box 2792
Houma, LA 70361
(800/688-2732 or 985/868-2732)
www.houmatourism.com

Iberia Parish CVB
2513 Hwy. 14
New Iberia, LA 70560
(888/942-3742 or 337/365-1540)
www.iberiatravel.com

Jefferson Davis Parish Tourist Commission
100 Rue de l'Acadie
Jennings, LA 70546

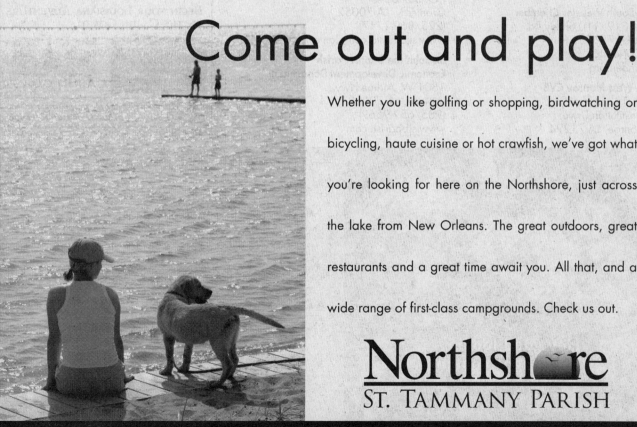

(800/264-5521 or 337/821-5521)
www.jeffdavis.org

Jefferson Convention & Visitors Bureau
Jefferson Parish Yenni Building
1221 Elmwood Park Blvd, Ste. 411
Jefferson, LA 70123
(877/572-7474 or 504/731-7083)
www.neworleansgateway.com

Kenner Convention and Visitors Bureau
2100 3rd St, Suite 11
Kenner, LA 70062
(504/464-9494 or 800/231-5282)
www.kennercvb.com

Lafayette Convention and Visitors Center
1400 N. W. Evangeline Throughway
Lafayette, LA 70501
(800/346-1958 U.S. or 800/543-5340 Canada)
www.lafayettetravel.com

Lafourche Parish Visitor Welcome Center
4484 LA Hwy. 1, P.O. Box 340
Raceland, LA 70394
(877/537-5800 or 985/537-5800)
www.visitlafourche.com

Livingston Parish CVB
30340 Catholic Hall Rd, P.O. Box 1057
Livingston, LA 70754
(888/317-7899 or 225/567-7899)
www.visitlivingstonparish.com

Madison Parish Tourist Commission
305 Dabney St.
Tallulah, LA 71282
(888/775-2987)

Minden-South Webster Chamber
P.O. Box 819, 110 Sibley Rd.
Minden, LA 71055
(318/377-4240)
www.minden.org

Monroe-West Monroe CVB
P.O. Box 1436
601 Constitution Drive
West Monroe, LA 71294
(800/843-1872 or 318/387-5691)
www.monroe-westmonroe.org

Natchitoches CVB
781 Front St.
Natchitoches, LA 71457
(800/259-1714 or 318/352-8072)
www.natchitoches.net

New Orleans Metropolitan Convention & Visitors Bureau
2020 St. Charles Ave.
New Orleans, LA 70130
(800/672-6124 or 504/566-5044)
www.neworleanscvb.com

Pointe Coupee Parish Office of Tourism
500 W. Main St, P.O. Box 733
New Roads, LA 70760
(800/259-2468 or 225/638-3998)
www.pctourism.org

Ruston-Lincoln Chamber
104 E. Mississippi St, P.O. Box 1383
Ruston, LA 71272
(800/392-9032 or 318/255-2031)
www.rustonlincoln.org

Sabine Parish Tourism Commission
1601 Texas Hwy.
Many, LA 71449
(318/256-3523)
www.SabineParish.com

St. Bernard Dept. of Tourism
(504/278-4242)
www.sbpg.net/tourism.htm

St. James Parish Tourist Commission
P.O. Box 629
Gramercy, LA 70052
(225/869-1717)
www.stjamesla.com/James/Tourist.htm

St. John the Baptist Parish Economic Development Department
1801 W. Airline Hwy.
Laplace, LA 70068
(985/652-9569)
www.sjbparish.com

St. Landry Parish Tourist Commission
P.O. Box 1415
Opelousas, LA 70571-1415
(877/948-8004)
www.cajuntravel.com

St. Martin Parish Tourist Commission
P.O. Box 9
St. Martinville, LA 70582
(337/298-3556)
www.CajunCountry.org

St. Tammany West Chamber
610 Hollycrest Blvd.
Covington, LA 70433
(985/892-3216)
www.sttammanychamber.org

Shreveport-Bossier Convention & Tourist Bureau
629 Spring St, P.O. Box 1761
Shreveport, LA 71166

(800/551-8682)
www.shreveport-bossier.org

Southwest Louisiana CVB

1205 N. Lakeshore Dr.

Lake Charles, LA 70601

(800/456-7952 or 337/436-9588)

www.visitlakecharles.org

Tangipahoa Parish CVB
42271 S. Morrison Blvd.
Hammond, LA 70403
(800/542-7520)
www.tangi-cvb.org

Vermilion Parish Tourist Commission
P.O. Box 1106
Abbeville, LA 70511
(337/898-6600)
www.vermilion.org

West Feliciana Parish Tourist Commission
P.O. Box 1548
St Francisville, LA 70775
(225/635-4224 or 800/789-4221)
www.stfrancisville.us

RECREATIONAL INFO

Louisiana Office of State Parks: P.O. Box 44426, Baton Rouge, LA 70804 (888/677-1400 or 225/342-8111). www.LaStateParks.com

Biking: For an official highway travel map or Parish road map, contact: Department of Transportation & Development, P.O. Box 94245, Baton Rouge, LA 70804-9245 (225/379-1100).

Hunting & Fishing Info: Louisiana Dept. of Wildlife and Fisheries, 2000 Quail Drive, Baton Rouge, LA 70808 (225/765-2800). www.wlf.state.la.us.

River Cruising: Delta Queen Steamboat Company, Inc. (800/543-1949) or visit www.deltaqueen.com. River Barge Excursion Lines (888/GO-BARGE) or visit www.riverbarge.com.

SHOPPING

America's Antique City, Ponchatoula. Historic District renovated in 1920-1930s featuring over 40 antique stores representing 200 dealers (800/617-4502).

The Shop at the Top, Ponchatoula. Located on the top floor of the Louisiana State Capitol, The Shop at the Top offers fantastic views and heritage souvenirs. Operated by Foundation for Historical Louisiana. LA State Capitol, 27th Floor, Baton Rouge, LA 70802 (225/342-5914).

Historic District and Antique Village, Denham Springs. Antique shops, apparel, fine gifts, ice cream parlor and more in a 3 block area. 133 Hummell St., Denham Springs, LA 70726 (225/667-8308).

Magazine Street, New Orleans. Six miles of antique shops, art galleries and specialty shops. Call for free map (866/679-4764 or 504/342-4435) www.magazinestreet.com

Maskarade, New Orleans. Handmade masks by local, national & international artists. Feather, ceramic, wood, tribal masks and more. 630 Ann St. (504/568-1018). www.themaskstore.com

Riverwalk Marketplace, New Orleans. Shop 140 stores plus food court with river views for a true taste of New Orleans. On the riverfront between Aquarium & Convention Center (504/522-1555). www.riverwalkmarketplace.com

UNIQUE FEATURES

CAJUN AND CREOLE CULTURES

Creole in its broadest sense can refer to a variety of combinations of French culture with Spanish, African and Caribbean cultures in colonial Louisiana. In early 19th century New Orleans, the term Creole was a way that these "born in the colony" cultural groups differentiated themselves from the many Americans who settled in the city after the Louisiana Purchase and from the waves of German and other immigrants arriving in the area. In rural Southwestern Louisiana, a blending of French, African and Caribbean cultures was considered Creole.

Cajun culture sprang from the Acadians who settled in South Louisiana following their explusion from Acadia, or Nova Scotia, in the 1700s. This French colonial culture melded with mainland French immigrant cultures and with Haitian, Spanish, English, German and Native American cultures as it evolved to form the distinctive and unique Cajun culture found today in South Louisiana.

MARDI GRAS

People all over the world may be starting their usual Tuesday routines, but in Louisiana it's Carnival Time! Every year locals outdo themselves in fun, fantasy and creativity. You can find Zulu warriors handing out gilded coconuts; a pregnant woman dressed like a Faberge egg; and a butterfly with wings as wide as the street. Be prepared for nonstop fun and frivolity on Mardi Gras day.

Mardi Gras is an ancient tradition, with origins in Greece and Rome, that celebrates food and fun just before the 40 days of Lent, the Catholic time of prayer and sacrifice. Brought to Louisiana by the French, it evolved from a simple celebration into the "Largest Free Show on Earth" with a healthy dose of irreverence for its own traditions of pomp and circumstance.

The season begins on Twelfth Night in the New Orleans area with more than 60 parades rolling during the two weeks before Fat Tuesday. But the parade route doesn't end in the Crescent City. Slidell and Madisonville celebrate with colorful boat parades. Monroe-West Monroe and Houma have lighted float parades, Shreveport-Bossier City boasts a citywide Mardi Gras tradition with a focus on family activities and the Alexandria Pineville area celebrates the season with family fun during the weekend before Fat Tuesday. Lake Charles celebrates with the Krewe of Barkus (a costumed dog parade). Lafayette has a unique tradition of naming the king and queen of festivities after their legendary Acadian lovers Gabriel and Evangeline. And in Church Point, Eunice, Mamou and other towns, men on horseback roam the countryside from farm to farm on a "Mardi Gras Ride," gathering the ingredients for their towns' communal gumbos.

From north to south, east to west, Mardi Gras is celebrated. A few parade organi-

LOUISIANA

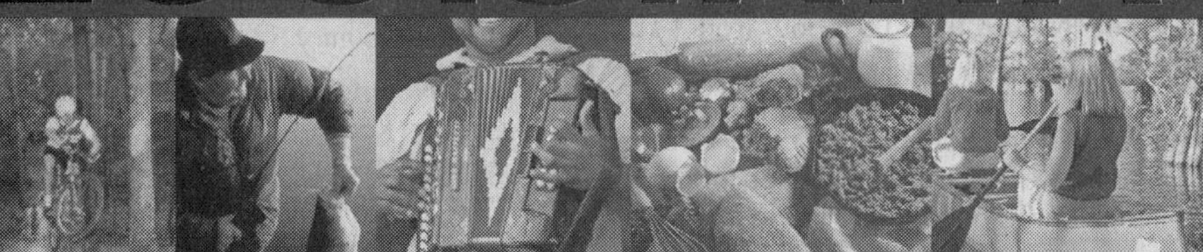

Sportsman's Paradise • Crossroads • Cajun Country • Plantation Country • Greater New Orleans

www.LouisianaTravel.com

1 DiamondJacks Casino & Resort

On-site casino, 4 restaurants, 32-spaces, water, full hookups, phone, cable hookups, showers, washers/dryers, vending.

866-5JAXMAX

www.diamondjacks.com

2 Ruston-Lincoln Convention & Visitors Bureau

30+ sites at Lincoln Parish Park with full hook-ups. Picnic Sites, beach area, fishing and boating.

800-392-9032

www.rustonlincoln.com

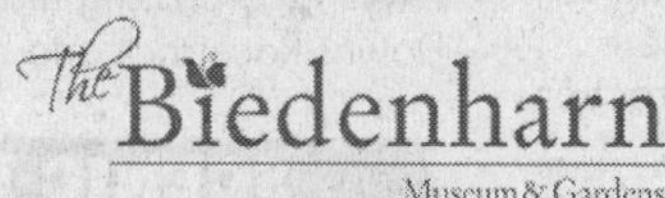

3 Biedenharn Museum & Gardens

We're always blooming. Surround yourself with the sheer majesty nature in our famous ELsong Garden & Conservatory. See us online.

318-387-5281

www.bmuseum.org

MOREHOUSE Parish

The Place to be Come on!

4 Morehouse Parish

Antiques, Theatre, Museums, Shopping, Chemin-A-Haut State Park, US Wildlife Refuges, Hunting, Fishing, Golf. Come On!

318-281-3794

www.bastroplacoc.org

5 Avoyelles Commission of Tourism

Campgrounds located in Central Louisiana offering festivals, history, gaming, golf, museums, nature trails, & recreation, on Red River. Day trip throughout Louisiana from Avoyelles Parish.

800-833-4195

www.travelavoyelles.com

6 Lafayette – the heart of Cajun Country

Lafayette – a cultural experience like no other. Dance to Cajun & Zydeco. Feast on Cajun food. We call it joie de vivre. You'll call it fun.

800-346-1958

www.LafayetteTravel.com

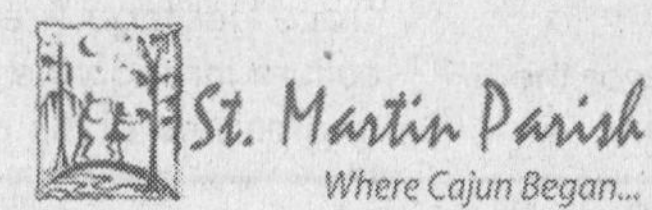

7 St. Martin Parish Tourist Commission

Campgrounds in the midst of Cajun Country and the Atchafalaya Basin. Breaux Bridge, Henderson, St. Martinville Area.

888-565-5939

www.cajuncountry.org

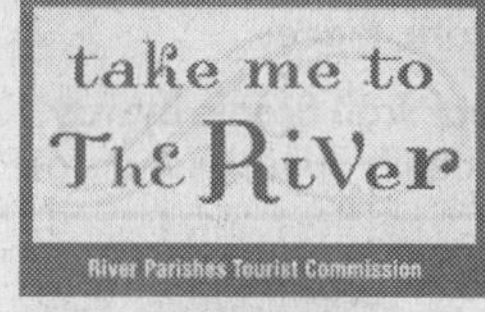

8 New Orleans Plantation Country

Explore beautiful and historic Plantations, experience a breathtaking Swamp Tour, and indulge in authentic Cajun & Creole Cuisine. Visit New Orleans Plantation Country.

866-204-7782

www.TakeMeToTheRiver.com

9 Iberia Parish Convention & Visitors Bureau

Get your HOTpak Getaway Package Guide New Iberia, Avery Island, Jefferson Island, Jeanerette, Loreauville, Delcambre.

888-942-3742

www.iberiatravel.com

10 KONRIKO® Rice Mill and Company Store

Guided tour of America's oldest rice mill. Company Store features Cajun crafts, food and folklore.

800-551-3245

www.conradricemill.com

JUNGLE GARDENS

11 Jungle Gardens

Avery Island's most spectacular feature. Camellias, azaleas & tropical plants, when in season, form a beautiful display. Admission Charge. Open daily 9-5.

337-369-6243

www.junglegardens.org

12 TABASCO® Brand Pepper Sauce

Take an inside look at TABASCO® Pepper Sauce and how it is produced. Open 7 days a week. Closed major holidays.

337-373-6129

www.TABASCO.com

FREE INFO! Enter #3767 on Reader Service Card

zations (krewes) even allow visitors to ride on floats. For more information, call the tourist bureau in the city you will be visiting. Or, if you can't attend Mardi Gras, check out the year-round Mardi Gras exhibit in the Louisiana State Museum's Presbytere in New Orleans.

SCENIC DRIVES

With so much to see and do in such an interesting state, the following are some of the more scenic drives through Louisiana:

Acadiana Trail, U.S. 190 from Baton Rouge to the Texas border. Paralleling I-10, this route leads past many of the scenic, recreational and historic attractions of Cajun Country.

Bayou Lafourche Tour. Shrimp fleets, quaint towns and fine plantations line Bayou Lafourche as it flows south to the Gulf. For a map, contact the Lafourche Parish Tourist Commission.

Bayou Teche Corridor. Follow Bayou Teche (a Native American word meaning snake), starting at Hwy. 31 & Hwy. 345 in St. Martinville, home of Longfellows Evangeline and continue on Hwy. 182 through New Iberia, home to Tabasco® & Konriko rice mill, to Franklin with over 400 historic properties listed on the National Register of Historic Places.

Longleaf Trail Scenic Byway. One of the most scenic drives in the state is in **Kisatchie National Forest** near Natchitoches. This 17-mile drive through rugged terrain with unique vistas includes mesas, buttes and sandstone outcrops among long leaf pine.

Creole Nature Trail. Loop tour from I-10 in Sulphur via Hwy. 27 to I-10 in Lake Charles, passing the Sabine and **Rockefeller Wildlife Refuges** and other bird and wildlife watching opportunities in the marshland along the Gulf Coast.

Old Spanish Trail. Drive this historic trail through Calcasieu Parish, via US 90 and Hwy. 109, passing historic landmarks, Delta Downs Racetrack and much natural beauty.

SCENIC BYWAYS

Louisiana's Scenic Byways are marked by distinctive signs throughout the state leading you through historic and cultural towns and past beautiful natural landscapes. For a map of all the scenic byways call (800/926-3758) or visit: www.louisianatravel.com/explorela/outdoors/scenicbyways/

The Atchafalaya Trace Heritage Area. America's largest freshwater swamp and the 14 parishes in and around the Atchafalaya Basin form the Atchafalaya Trace Heritage Area. Experience Louisiana culture through the stories, traditions, music and cuisine of the area.

Acadiana Trail. First used by Indians as a path that connected water routes, the Acadiana Trail now follows U.S. 190 from Baton Rouge to the Texas border. Paralleling I-10, this route leads past many of the scenic, recreational and historic attractions of Cajun Country.

Creole Nature Trail. One of only 20 All-American Roads—the highest ranking for a scenic byway in the United States—the trail travels through areas of breathtaking beauty. Loop tour from I-10 in Sulphur via Hwy. 27 to I-10 in Lake Charles, passing the Sabine and Rockefeller Wildlife Refuges and other bird and wildlife watching opportunities in the marshland along the Gulf Coast. Traversing Louisiana's outback, the 180-mile Creole Trail will lead you past where the notorious pirate Jean Lafitte hid treasure and where French traders did business with the Attakapas Indians. Prairie, marshland, thousands of acres of untouched wetlands and two national wildlife refuges are along the Byway. Wildlife abounds, especially alligators and waterfowl. Running along the Gulf of Mexico and up to Lake Charles, there are ample recreational opportunities including surf fishing, boating, hunting and swimming.

Mississippi River Road Corridor. A portion of the Great River Road runs through Louisiana between New Orleans and Baton Rouge. Passing through eight parishes, it is a historic stretch of road that affords views of romantic plantations, ancient cemeteries, quaint river towns and Civil War sites that take you back in time. There are numerous National Historic Districts, National Historic Landmarks, structures listed on the National Register of Historic Places and museums interpreting local history and river life. River outlooks along the way provide magnificent views of the Mississippi.

Longleaf Trail Scenic Byway. One of the most scenic drives in the state is in Kisatchie National Forest near Natchitoches. This 17-mile drive through rugged terrain with unique vistas includes mesas, buttes and sandstone outcrops among long leaf pine.

Louisiana Colonial Trails. This trail is comprised of the prehistoric and pioneer trail from Natchez to Natchitoches and into the Spanish Southwest. It begins at US 84 and Hwy. 6.

Louisiana's Western Corridor. This area transcends several regions along the western border of the state. Travel US 171 from I-10 to I-20, passing **Hodges Gardens, Kisatchie National Forest** and much more.

Old Spanish Trail. Drive this historic trail through Calcasieu Parish, via US 90 and Hwy. 109, passing historic landmarks, Delta Downs Racetrack and much natural beauty. For a map, contact the Southwest Convention & Visitors Bureau.

Promised Land Scenic Byway. So named because of a promise for land made to the exiled Acadians by the Spanish Governor of the Louisiana territory, the Byway borders the Henderson side of the Atchafalaya Basin.

DESTINATIONS

ANCIENT MOUNDS

Louisiana has more than 700 known earthen mound sites built hundreds to thousands of years ago. Prehistoric Native American cultures built them to serve as homes for tribal leaders, ceremonial sites and even burial sites. They can range in size from a few feet to over 70 feet tall. The Louisiana Ancient Mounds Trail is a current ongoing project to link the mounds in a trail with maps and interpretive guides. The first phase covering parts of northeast and central Louisiana links 40 mound sites and is interpreted in a 50 page map and interpretive guide.To order a copy visit

RV Sales & Service

	SALES	SERVICE
BATON ROUGE		
Blanchard Trailer Sales	•	•
Miller's RV Center	•	•
The RV Shop	•	•
BOSSIER CITY		
Bayou Outdoor Supercenter	•	•
HAMMOND		
Berryland Campers	•	•
Dixie RV SuperStores	•	•
LAFAYETTE		
G & J Mobile Home & RV Supplies		•
Gauthiers' RV Service Center	•	•
METAIRIE		
Bent's RV	•	•
MONROE		
Hope's Camper Corner	•	•
SHREVEPORT		
Campers RV Center	•	•
WEST MONROE		
Carter's Camping Center	•	•

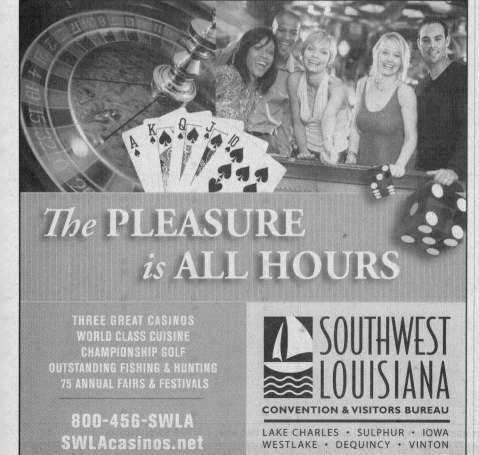

Things to See & Do

ARCADIA
Bonnie & Clyde Trade Days

AVERY ISLAND
Jungle Gardens
McIlHenny Co

BASTROP
Morehouse Parish Tourism Commission

BATON ROUGE
Louisiana Travel Promotion Association

BOSSIER CITY
Diamond Jacks Casino Resort

BREAUX BRIDGE
Breaux Bridge Tourist Commission
Poche's Market, Restaurant & Smokehouse

CONVENT
Felix Poche Plantation

HAMMOND
Tangipahoa Parish Tourist Commission

HOUMA
A Cajun Man's Swamp Cruise
Houma Area Convention & Visitors Bureau

LA PLACE
River Parishes Tourist Commission

LAFAYETTE
Lafayette Convention & Visitors Commission
Prejean's Restaurant
Randol's Restaurant & Cajun Dance Hall

LAKE CHARLES
Southwest Louisiana Convention & Visitors Bureau

MANDEVILLE
St. Tammany Parish Tourist & Convention Commission

MANSFIELD
New Rockdale Radio Shop

MARKSVILLE
Avoyelles Parish Tourism Commission
Paragon Casino

MONROE
Biedenharn Museum & Gardens

MORGAN CITY
Cajun Coast Visitors & Convention Bureau

NEW IBERIA
Iberia Parish Convention & Visitors Bureau
Konriko Rice Mill and Company Store

RUSTON
Ruston/Lincoln Convention & Visitors Bureau

SHREVEPORT
Shreveport/Bossier Convention & Tourist Bureau

Woodall's Quick & Easy Reference for Louisiana

	BIG RIGS WELCOME	INTERNET FRIENDLY	PETS WELCOME	WEB SAVER
ABBEVILLE				
Abbeville RV Park		●	■	
AMITE				
Natalbany Creek Campground	▲	●	■	
ARCADIA				
Bonnie & Clyde Trade Days & Campground	▲		■	
BENTON				
Cypress Black Bayou Recreation Area	▲		■	
BOSSIER CITY				
Cash Point Landing	▲		■	
BREAUX BRIDGE				
Poche's Fish-N-Camp	▲	●	■	
BROUSSARD				
Maxie's Campground	▲	●	■	
CONVENT				
Felix Poche Plantation RV Resort	▲	●	■	
DENHAM SPRINGS				
KOA-Baton Rouge East	▲	●	■	
DONALDSONVILLE				
B & B RV Park	▲		■	
DUSON				
Frog City RV Park	▲	●	■	$
EGAN				
Cajun Haven RV Park			■	
LAFAYETTE				
KOA-Lafayette	▲	●	■	
LAKE CHARLES				
Whispering Meadow RV Park	▲	●	■	
Yogi Bear's Jellystone Park Camp-Resort	▲	●	■	
LIVINGSTON				
Lakeside RV Park	▲	●	■	
MANSFIELD				
New Rockdale RV Park	▲		■	
MARKSVILLE				
Paragon Casino RV Resort	▲	●	■	
MINDEN				
Lakeside RV Park	▲	●	■	
MONROE				
Monroe's Shiloh Campground & RV Resort	▲	●	■	
NATCHITOCHES				
Nakatosh Campground	▲	●	■	
NEW IBERIA				
Chase's RV Park	▲		■	
KOC Kampground	▲	●	■	
NEW ORLEANS				
French Quarter RV Resort	▲	●		
KOA-New Orleans West	▲	●	■	
New Orleans RV Campground	▲	●	■	
PORT ALLEN				
Cajun Country Campground	▲		■	
SHREVEPORT				
Campers RV Center	▲		■	
KOA-Shreveport/Bossier City	▲	●	■	
SLIDELL				
New Orleans East Kampground	▲	●	■	
Pine Crest RV Park	▲	●	■	
ST. JOSEPH				
Shiloh's Lake Bruin Resort	▲	●	■	
SULPHUR				
Hidden Ponds RV Park	▲	●	■	
VINTON				
V RV Park-Lake Charles/Vinton	▲	●	■	
WEST MONROE				
Pavilion RV Park	▲	●	■	

▲ = Big Rigs Welcome; ● = Internet Hookups; ● = (Wi-Fi available); ■ = Pets Welcome; $ = Web Saver Coupons

**Check out the "How to Use This Directory" section in the front of this book for a description of the criteria Woodall's uses in this chart.*

www.louisianatravel.com/explorela/outdoors/ancientmounds/order.cfm.

SPORTSMAN'S PARADISE REGION

This area of northern Louisiana is filled with museums, parks, sporting and cultural events and is known for its fishing, hunting and outdoor recreation.

Arcadia. This peaceful town is located midway between Shreveport and Monroe and is surrounded by rolling hills and beautiful lakes. Visit Louisiana's largest flea market, Bonnie & Clyde Trade Days.

Mansfield State Historic Site. Located four miles south of Mansfield, this is the site of the most important Civil War battle fought west of the Mississippi. This 44-acre park includes a museum noted for its variety of military artifacts.

Monroe/West Monroe is located on the scenic **Ouachita River**. Visitors can enjoy diverse cultural experiences, along with riverboats, southern cuisine, festivals by the river and antique shopping. This area also offers a multitude of attractions including the **Emy-Lou Biedenharn Home**, built by Joseph Biedenharn, the first bottler of Coca-Cola. The **Louisiana Purchase Gardens & Zoo** houses 850 rare and exotic animals. Formal gardens, winding paths and waterways and huge live oaks provide a relaxing atmosphere. The **Masur Museum of Art** is the two-story English Tudor home of the Masur family.

Shreveport/Bossier City. Come experience roses, racing, riverboats and world class museums. Enjoy the Riverfront with year-round festivals and shopping.

CROSSROADS REGION

This area of central Louisiana has ancient Indian mounds, frontier towns, Civil War battlefields and the **Kisatchie National Forest**.

Alexandria/Pineville. This area is full of history with mementos of Native American villages, Spanish and French explorers, Civil War battles and American military heroes.

Alexandria Zoological Park is home to over 400 animals including endangered species from several continents.

Kent House is the oldest remaining "Crossroads" plantation, built circa 1800. The house, outbuildings and herb gardens reflect the early 1800s.

Loyd Hall Antebellum Home. Visit this restored working plantation (circa 1820-30), used by Confederate and Union troops.

Marksville is located in the southeastern section of the region. Marksville is home to the Marksville State Historic Site, an area of Indian culture and earthen mounds dating from 1,400 A.D. The **Tunica-Biloxi Regional Indian Center and Museum** houses the world's largest collection of Native American/European artifacts from Louisiana's colonial period. Located on the reservation is **Paragon Casino**, featuring live entertainment, more than 1,500 slot machines and 60 table games, a poker room, four restaurants and Kids Quest.

DeRidder. Parish attractions include a Gothic jail with hanging tower, the **Beauregard Museum**, a pioneer village and the first building built for the USO in World War II.

Many. While in the beautiful **Toledo Bend** country area, experience Louisiana's "Garden in the Forest," **Hodges Gardens**, featuring 4,700 acres of woodlands, waterfalls and multi-level botanical gardens, an old-fashioned rose garden, as well as hiking and nature trails.

Natchitoches. Points of interest in Natchitoches include the first French Settlement, **Fort St. Jean Baptists State Historic Site**, a National Historic Landmark District, the **American Cemetery**, the **Center for the History of Louisiana Education** and the **Louisiana Sports Hall of Fame**. Tours of the Landmark District are available aboard the trolley **"City Belle." Magnolia Plantation Home** is a National Bicentennial farm dating from 1753. View the extensive collection of Southern Empire and Louisiana furniture.

CAJUN COUNTRY

This southern area, full of lush, mysterious swamps and bayous has a time honored tradition of cultural and spiritual richness.

Houma. Established in 1834 is in the heart of America's wetland. Adventure awaits around every corner— swamp tours, plantations, museums, festivals, wildlife, shopping, Cajun foods. Let them entertain you in their well-known "Venice of America."

Kinder. Located on the **Coushatta Indian Reservation**, **Grand Casino Coushatta** offers more than 1,200 slot machines, 50 table games, a buffet, restaurant and lounge and Kids Quest— a supervised children's activity center.

Lafayette. The Capital of Cajun Country, Lafayette offers horse racing, boat tours of the **Atchafalaya Basin Swamp**, an authentically restored Acadian Village, nearby plantation homes, natural history, as well as contemporary and traditional art museums.

Acadian Village. This authentically restored folklife museum pays tribute to the uprooted Acadians who made southern Louisiana their own nearly two centuries ago.

Lafayette Planetarium. Experience a space odyssey created by projections on a domed ceiling.

Vermilionville is a 22-acre Cajun cultural attraction on the banks of Bayou Vermilion. A living history museum depicts various aspects of life in Acadiana from 1765 to 1890.

Lake Charles. Cajunland City, located in southwestern Louisiana, features freshwater, saltwater and deep sea fishing access. The city also offers duck hunting views of alligators in their natural habitat along the **Creole Nature Trail Scenic Byway** and the 1,000-acre **Sam Houston Jones State Park**. Enjoy the Historic "Charpentier" District, museums, palm beaches, quarter horse and thoroughbred racing, off-track betting, video poker and many casinos, including the Isle of Capri Casino.

New Iberia/Avery Island. Known as Cajun paradise, New Iberia offers everything from historic homes and gardens to fishing, golfing and is home of the world's most famous hot sauce—Tabasco®! In touring **McIlhenny Company's Tabasco® Factory**, you'll view an 8-minute film about the history of Tabasco® sauce, observe the bottling line and end the tour in the Tabasco® Country Store.

Avery Island's Jungle Gardens is southwest of New Iberia. In addition to the garden's lush plant life, the great number of egrets and herons are of special interest.

Jeanerette Museum. The museum features a pictorial history of Louisiana's 200-year old sugar cane industry.

Jefferson Island. The Victorian home of actor Joseph Jefferson features 25 acres of gardens in bloom year-round, **Café Jefferson**, a gift shop, a conference center and boat excursions.

Shadows-on-the-Teche. Built in 1834 for sugar planter David Weeks, the Shadows exhibits the lifestyle of the antebellum South through its 9 rooms.

St. Martinville. You'll find many buildings and homes with uniquely beautiful architecture and the Evangeline Oak made famous in Longfellow's poem about the love story of Evangeline and Gabriel.

St. Mary Parish. Follow the Cajun coast along the **Old Spanish Trail** to what National Geographic called this "hauntingly beautiful land." View museums, antebellum homes and plantations and take a swamp tour of the exotic **Atchafalaya River**. Nearby Berwick, the oldest settlement in St. Mary Parish, boasts of the **Great Wall**, a 22-foot sea wall with a moonwalk overlooking the Atchafalaya.

Thibodaux. Victorian homes, sugar plantations and numerous beautiful churches filled with history await you.

PLANTATION COUNTRY

Plantation Homes are to Louisiana what the "cottages" are to Newport, Rhode Island. Each one has a character all its own and there's a surprise at the top of every grand staircase.

Convent. Poche Plantation Bed and Breakfast and Guided Tours. Located less than an hour from New Orleans, on the majestic River Road, the Poche Plantation hosts a bed and breakfast and guided tours at this Louisiana plantation home that has been beautifully restored to its original splendor.

Baton Rouge. Attractions include old and new state capitals, the **LSU Rural Life Museum** and a zoo with more than 500 animals from 6 continents, plus plantation and river tours.

Magnolia Mound Plantation is a historic house and museum, open hearth kitchen.

U.S.S. Kidd. A national historic landmark, the Kidd is a restored World War II destroyer that was awarded 8 battle stars. A detailed tour takes you to over 50 inner spaces. The adjacent **Historic Center** contains a collection of ship models and a P-40 fighter plane.

West Baton Rouge Museum shows you how raw sugar cane becomes the stuff you twirl into your tea.

St. Francisville. Among the highlights in this part of "English Louisiana" are several beautiful plantation homes, as well as many historic landmarks. The **West Feliciana Historical Society Museum** features a glimpse into the area's past. Both the **Mount Carmel Roman Catholic Church**, (on a bluff overlooking the historic district) and the **Grace Episcopal Church** (where the graveyard is a history lesson in itself) are on the National Register.

Audubon State Historic Site is located on Hwy 965, 4 miles east of US 61. Visit this 3-story home, built in 1799 and occupied for a time by John James Audubon, famous painter of American birds. The home contains many of Audubon's prints and fine antiques.

Myrtles Plantation. Visit "America's Most Haunted House." Friday and Saturday night ghost tours begin at 9:30 p.m. Dinner by reservation.

Rosedown Plantation State Historic Site. This 140-year-old plantation home encompasses 30 acres of formal "Versailles" gardens. The house contains many paintings and primarily original furnishings.

San Francisco Plantation. Built in 1856, this beautiful plantation home is listed on the National Register of Historic Places and is a stunning example of mid 19th-century architecture.

West Feliciana Historical Society Museum. This former hardware store was restored to a house museum featuring flag-bedecked walls, wire sculptures of early residents and charming miniature rooms.

GREATER NEW ORLEANS REGION

In this southeast corner of the state you'll engage all your senses, from the sounds of jazz, to the scent of magnolias, rattles of the streetcars, or taste of hot sauce in your beans and rice.

Destrehan Plantation. Built in 1787, Destrehan is the oldest plantation left intact in the lower Mississippi Valley. It is located on the Great River Road. Daily tours are offered and a gift shop is located on the grounds.

Global Wildlife Center, Folsom. Hundreds of endangered, threatened and extinct wild animals roam free across 900 acres of hills, valleys, streams and lakes. Professionally guided tours allow visitors to interact with the animals, affording a unique wildlife experience.

New Orleans. The city boasts magnificent food, music, attractions and fun. Cruise on an authentic paddlewheeler through one of America's busiest ports to **Chalmette Battlefield**, the site of the Battle of New Orleans. Or, enjoy a dinner/jazz cruise, complete with a Creole buffet, a Dixieland jazz band and a sparkling city skyline. If you're interested in wildlife, take a swamp tour at **Jean Lafitte Swamp Tours**. See the gators jump, the owls hoot and moss-draped bayous. The **New Orleans Steamboat Company** offers an aquarium/zoo cruise on the riverboat John James Audubon that transports you to the **Audubon Zoo** and the **Aquarium of the Americas**. Ride on the only authentic steampowered stern wheeler, the Steamboat Natchez, on a 2-hour harbor cruise with live jazz music. Dine at **Mulate's—The World's Most Famous Cajun Restaurant** and have a memorable time dancing to a Cajun band and savoring Cajun cuisine. Enjoy the comfort of your own recreational vehicle on board the deck of the "Cruising Campground" with **RV River Charters** and experience the ever-changing scenery as you cruise America's inland waters. If you would rather stay on land, **Gray Line of New Orleans** offers a variety of daily tours to suit your interest: city, plantations and French Quarter walking tours. Get a glimpse of where Mardi Gras is made at **Blaine Kern's Mardi Gras World**. Try on costumes worn by Mardi Gras Royalty and marvel at figures of dinosaurs, monsters and more. **French Quarter (Vieux Carre).** The Quarter sets New Orleans apart from any other place in the world. Wander down any of the narrow streets and be drawn into the romance of the past and present. The French Market is 5 blocks of festive shopping in the French Quarter. Enjoy famous cafe au lait and beignets 24 hours a day, a flea market, Pirate's Alley with free music, entertainment, history and life-sized sculptures. **Jackson Square.** The hub of New Orleans is also the heart of the French Quarter. Surrounded on 3 sides by buildings and fronted by the Mississippi River, the square's landscaped tranquility belies the turbulent history it has witnessed. **LA Superdome.** The world's largest domed stadium is home to the New Orleans Saints and the Sugar Bowl. There are guided tours daily. **New Orleans Riverwalk.** Stroll along this half-mile festival marketplace filled with live entertainment.

St. Tammany Parish. In St. Tammany Parish, interstate highways give way to scenic country roads and the bustle of city life fades into a resort-like setting with beautifully landscaped motels and campgrounds.

Tangipahoa Parish. Some of the South's finest restaurants, as well as fairs, festivals and out-of-the-way bakeries are featured in Tangipahoa Parish.

ANNUAL EVENTS

MARCH

Courir de Mardi Gras, Church Point; Mardi Gras Celebration, Eunice/Mamou; Crawfish Festival, Chalmette.

APRIL

Catfish Festival, Winnsboro; Boggy Bayou Festival, Pine Prairie; Festival International de Louisiane, Lafayette; Food Festival, Belle Rose; French Quarter Festival, New Orleans; Jazz and Heritage Festival, New Orleans.

MAY

Crawfish Festival, Breaux Bridge.

JUNE

Buggy Festival, Church Point.

JULY

Fourth of July Celebrations, Statewide; Catfish Festival, Des Allemands.

AUGUST

Delcambre Shrimp Festival, Delcambre.

SEPTEMBER

Louisiana Folklife Festival, Monroe; Southern Pickin' & Ginnin' Festival, Rayville; Celebration Festival, Alexandria; Frog Festival, Rayne; Shrimp Festival, Meraux.

OCTOBER

Cotton Festival & Tournoi de la Ville Platte, Villa Platte; Roberts Cove Germanfest, Rayne; State Fair, Baton Rouge; Gumbo Festival, Bridge City; Swamp Festival, New Orleans.

NOVEMBER

Cajun Gumbo Festival, Ville Platte; Sunshine Festival, Donaldsonville.

DECEMBER

Festival of the Bonfires, Lutcher.

Louisiana

ABBEVILLE—D-3

(W) ABBEVILLE RV PARK—(Vermilion) *From jct US 167 & Bus. Hwy 14: Go 1/2 mi W on Bus. Hwy 14. Enter on L.*

WELCOME

FACILITIES: 53 sites, 47 full hkups, 6 W&E, (15, 30 & 50 amps), 50 amps ($), some extended stay sites, wireless Instant Internet access at site, cable Internet access central location, dump station, non-guest dumping $, tables, fire rings.

RECREATION: rec room/area, golf nearby, hiking trails.

Pets welcome, breed restrict, size restrict. Partial handicap access. No tents. Open all yr. Big rigs welcome. Internet friendly. Clubs welcome. Member ARVC, LCOA. Phone: (337)898-4042.

e-mail: info@abbevillervpark.com

SEE AD THIS PAGE

Betty's RV Park—(Vermilion) *From jct US 167 & Bus Hwy 14: Go 1/2 mi E on Bus Hwy 14, then 1-1/2 mi S on State St. Enter on R.* ◆◆◆FACILITIES: 15 sites, accepts full hkup units only, 15 full hkups, (20, 30 & 50 amps), 50 amps ($), some extended stay sites, tables. RECREATION: rec room/area. Pets welcome, breed restrict. No tents. Open all yr. Internet friendly. Rate in 2007 $15-18 for 2 persons. Phone: (337)893-7057.

AJAX—B-2

(C) Ajax Country Livin' at I-49 Rv Park, LLC—(Natchitoches) *From jct I-49 (exit 155) & Hwy 174: Go 3/10 mi W on Hwy 174. Enter on L.* ◆◆◆FACILITIES: 27 sites, typical site width 25 ft, 27 full hkups, (20, 30 & 50 amps), 50 amps ($), 22 pull-thrus, tenting, dump station, non-guest dumping $, laundry, LP gas by weight/by meter, ice, tables, wood. ◆RECREATION: rec room/area, pond fishing, horseshoes, sports field. Pets welcome. Open all yr. Big rigs welcome. Rate in 2007 $20 for 2 persons. Phone: (318)796-2543. CCUSA discount.

ALEXANDRIA—C-3

(W) RAPIDES COLISEUM (Parish Park)—(Rapides) *From jct US 71/US 165 & Hwy 28 W: Go 1 mi W on Hwy 28. Enter on R.* FACILITIES: 216 sites, accepts self-contained units only, 16 full hkups, 200 E, (30 amps). RECREATION: planned activities. Pets welcome. No tents. Open all yr. No restrooms. Phone: (318)442-1272.

AMITE—C-5

(W) NATALBANY CREEK CAMPGROUND—(St. Helena) *From jct I-55 (exit 46) & Hwy 16: Go 2-1/4 mi W on Hwy 16. Enter on R.*

WELCOME

◆◆◆◆◆FACILITIES: 135 sites, typical site width 40 ft, 135 full hkups, (20, 30 & 50 amps), 4 pull-thrus, phone Internet access central location, tenting, cabins, laundry, LP gas by weight/by meter, tables, patios, fire rings, grills, wood.

◆◆◆◆RECREATION: rec room/area, pavilion, equipped pavilion, coin games, swim pool, 3 pedal boat rentals, lake fishing, bsktball, playground, planned activities (wkends only), horseshoes, sports field, v-ball.

Pets welcome. Partial handicap access. Open all yr. Big rigs welcome. Internet friendly. Clubs welcome. Rate in 2007 $22-28 for 4 persons. MC/VISA/DISC/AMEX/Debit. ATM. Phone: (985)747-9909.

e-mail: minniehughes@bellsouth.net

SEE AD HAMMOND PAGE 307 AND AD TRAVEL SECTION PAGE 296

ARCADIA—A-2

(S) BONNIE & CLYDE TRADE DAYS—*From jct I-20 (exit 69) & Hwy 151: Go 1 mi S on Hwy 151, then continue S (straight ahead) 2-1/2 mi on Hwy 9. Enter on R.* Louisiana's largest trade fair and flea market with 650 dealer spaces and RV hookups. Your ultimate outdoor bargain shopping experience! Every month, the weekend before the 3rd Monday. Open all yr. MC/VISA/DISC. Phone: (318)263-2437.

WELCOME

e-mail: info@bonnieandclydetradedays.com

SEE AD THIS PAGE

(S) BONNIE & CLYDE TRADE DAYS & CAMPGROUND—(Bienville) *From jct I-20 (exit 69) & Hwy 151: Go 1 mi S on Hwy 151, then continue S (straight ahead) 2-1/2 mi on Hwy 9. Enter on R.*

WELCOME

◆◆◆FACILITIES: 72 sites, typical site width 24 ft, 32 full hkups, 40 W&E, (20, 30 & 50 amps), 50 amps ($), some extended stay sites, 25 pull-thrus, phone Internet access central location, tenting, cabins, dump station, non-guest dumping, laundry, ice.

RECREATION: equipped pavilion, pond fishing, planned activities (wkends only), sports field.

Pets welcome. Open all yr. Big rigs welcome. Clubs welcome. Rate in 2007 $18 per vehicle. MC/VISA/DISC/Debit. Phone: (318)263-2437. FMCA discount.

e-mail: info@bonnieandclydetradedays.com

SEE AD THIS PAGE

The town of Jean Lafitte was named after the famous pirate of the same name. The area in which it is located was once a hideaway for pirates.

AVERY ISLAND—D-3

(C) JUNGLE GARDENS—*From jct Hwy 90 & Hwy 329: Go 7 mi SW on Hwy 329. Enter at end.* A 250-acre garden with Chinese Garden & Budda Temple, bird sanctuary and a variety of flora & animal life native to southern Louisiana. View from your automobile or walk through the grounds. Open all yr. MC/VISA. Phone: (337)369-6243.

WELCOME

SEE AD TRAVEL SECTION PAGE 297

(C) MCILHENNY CO—*From jct US 90 & Hwy 329: Go 7 mi SW on Hwy 329 to Avery Island. Enter at end.* Tour Avery Island, home of World Famous Tabasco brand pepper sauce, and visit beautiful Jungle Gardens and Bird City. Open 7 days a week. Open all yr. MC/VISA/AMEX. Phone: (337) 365-8173.

WELCOME

SEE AD TRAVEL SECTION PAGE 297

BASTROP—A-3

(N) CHEMIN-A-HAUT STATE PARK—(Morehouse) *From jct US 165 & US 425: Go 10 mi N on US 425, then 1/2 mi E on Loop Park Rd/SR 2229.* FACILITIES: 26 sites, 26 W&E, (30 amps), tenting, dump station, laundry. RECREATION: swim pool, lake fishing, playground, hiking trails. Rec open to public. Pets welcome. Open all yr. Phone: (888)677-2436.

(C) MOREHOUSE PARISH TOURISM COMMISSION—*From jct Hwy 165 & Hwy 593 (Franklin St) in town. Enter on L.* Outdoor sports, antiques, museums, Rose Theatre, historic courthouse, cinema, Natural Wildlife Refuges, summer music on Main St & daily farmers market. Open all yr. Phone: (318)281-3794.

WELCOME

SEE AD TRAVEL SECTION PAGE 297

BATON ROUGE—D-4

(NE) BLANCHARD TRAILER SALES—*From jct I-12 (exit 2B) & US 61: Go 5-1/2 mi NW on US 61 (Airline Hwy). Enter on L.* SALES: travel trailers, 5th wheels, mini-motor homes, fold-down camping trailers, pre-owned unit sales. SERVICES: full-time mech, RV appliance repair, body work/collision repair, dump station, sells

WELCOME

BLANCHARD TRAILER SALES—Continued on next page

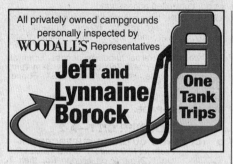

BATON ROUGE—Continued
BLANCHARD TRAILER SALES—Continued

parts/accessories, installs hitches. Open all yr. MC/VISA/DISC/AMEX/Debit. Phone: (225)355-4449.

e-mail: btsrv@hotmail.com

SEE AD THIS PAGE

(SW) FARR PARK CAMPGROUND & HORSE ACTIVITY CENTER—(East Baton Rouge) *From jct I-10 (exit 158) & College Dr: Go 5-1/2 mi S on College (which becomes Lee Dr, then becomes Brightside Lane), then 1/2 mi S on River Rd. Enter on L.* FACILITIES: 79 sites, typical site width 15 ft, 79 W&E, (20 & 30 amps), 79 pull-thrus, dump station, non-guest dumping $, laundry. RECREATION: pavilion, playground, planned activities, tennis, sports field, hiking trails. Rec open to public. Pets welcome. Partial handicap access. No tents. Open all yr. Phone: (225)769-7805.

FELIX POCHE PLANTATION RV RESORT *—From Baton Rouge jct I-12 & I-10: Go 20 mi S on I-10 (exit 179), then 15-3/4 mi S on Hwy 44. Enter on L.*

WELCOME

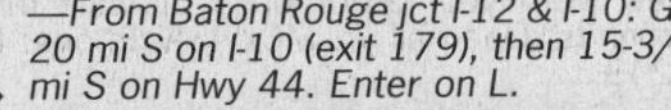

SEE PRIMARY LISTING AT CONVENT. AND AD CONVENT PAGE 306

LAKESIDE RV PARK—*From Baton Rouge (jct I-10 & I-12): Go 22 mi E on I-12, then 1-1/4 mi S on Hwy 63 (exit 22). Enter on R.*

WELCOME

SEE PRIMARY LISTING AT LIVINGSTON AND AD THIS PAGE

BATON ROUGE—Continued

(E) LOUISIANA TRAVEL PROMOTION ASSOCIATION—Explore the many regions of Louisiana and discover the diversity of its many cultures-from casinos to plantations to restaurants and museums. Open all yr. Phone: (225) 346-1857.

WELCOME

e-mail: info@ltpa.org

SEE AD TRAVEL SECTION PAGE 297

(E) MILLER'S RV CENTER—*From jct I-12 (exit 7) & O'Neal Lane: Go 1-1/2 mi N on O'Neal Lane. Enter on L.* SALES: motor homes, mini-motor homes, pre-owned unit sales. SERVICES: full-time mech, engine/chassis repair, RV appliance repair, body work/collision repair, RV rentals, sells parts/accessories. Open all yr. MC/VISA/DISC. Phone: (225)275-2940.

WELCOME

SEE AD PAGE 303

(E) The RV Shop—*From jct I-12 (exit 7) & O'Neal Lane: Go 3-1/2 mi N on O'Neal Lane (which becomes S Choctaw). Enter on L.* SALES: travel trailers, 5th wheels, motor homes, pre-owned unit sales. SERVICES: full-time mech, RV appliance repair, body work/collision repair, LP gas by weight/by meter, RV rentals, sells parts/accessories, installs hitches. Open all yr. MC/VISA/DISC. Phone: (225)272-8000.

BELLE CHASSE—D-5

(SE) MILITARY PARK (New Orleans NAS Travel Camp) —(PlaqueMines) *From I-10: Cross E over Miss. River to Business US 90/Westbank Expwy, then 9 mi SE on Hwy 23 (Lafayette St/Belle-Chase Hwy. On base. Enter on R.* FACILITIES: 30 sites, 30 full hkups, 2 pull-thrus, tenting, dump station, laundry, grills. RECREATION: swim pool. Open all yr. Resv. required. For Military Use Only- w/ Military ID Card. Phone: (504)678-3142.

BENTON—A-2

(N) CYPRESS BLACK BAYOU RECREATION AREA—(Bossier) *From jct I-220 & Airline Dr (Exit 12): Go 5-1/2 mi N on Airline Dr, then 4-1/4 mi E on Linton Rd. Enter on R.*

WELCOME

FACILITIES: 73 sites, typical site width 25 ft, 15 full hkups, 58 W&E, (30 & 50 amps), 21 pull-thrus, tenting, cabins, dump station, non-guest dumping $, gas, marine gas, ice, tables, fire rings, wood, controlled access gate.

RECREATION: lake swimming, boating, canoeing, ramp, dock, lake fishing, fishing supplies, golf nearby, playground, sports field, hiking trails, v-ball. Rec open to public.

Pets welcome. Partial handicap access. Open all yr. Nature Center and Zoo open daily 8am-4pm. Big rigs welcome. MC/VISA/DISC/AMEX. Phone: (318)965-0007.

e-mail: ed1202@cypressblackbayou.com

SEE AD THIS PAGE

BOSSIER CITY—A-2

(C) BAYOU OUTDOOR SUPERCENTER—*From jct I-20 (exit 21) & Old Minden Rd: Go 1/2 mi W on Minden Rd, then 1 block SE on Barksdale Blvd. Enter on R.* Boat service. SALES: travel trailers, 5th wheels, motor homes, mini-motor homes, fold-down camping trailers, pre-owned unit sales. SERVICES: full-time mech, RV appliance repair, body work/collision repair, LP gas by weight/by meter, RV rentals, sells parts/accessories, installs hitches. Open all yr. MC/VISA/DISC/AMEX. Phone: (318)629-2628.

WELCOME

e-mail: sales@bayououtdoor.com

SEE AD TRAVEL SECTION PAGE 291

BOSSIER CITY—Continued on next page

Woodall's Tip #28... Woodall's ratings depend on the quality and quantity of our criteria elements. The more W's a park has generally reflects the presence of more development at the park, and usually more facilities.

BOSSIER CITY—Continued

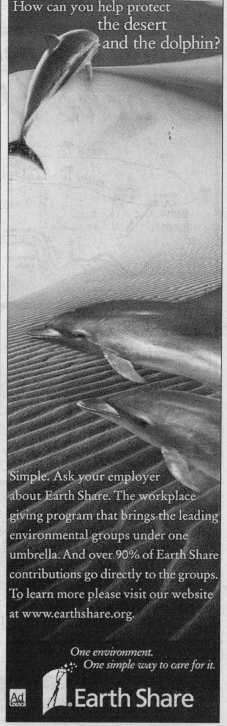

(N) CASH POINT LANDING—(Bossier) *From jct I-220 (exit 11) & LA 3: Go 3-3/4 mi N on LA 3. Enter on L.*

WELCOME

VERY CONVENIENT & PEACEFUL SETTING! Come to Cash Point Landing on the banks of the beautiful Red River. Launch your boat free and enjoy skiing or fishing. Or just relax watching the river glide by from the deck of Hot Rods & Hawgs Restaurant on site!

◇◇FACILITIES: 96 sites, typical site width 35 ft, 94 full hkups, 2 W&E, (20, 30 & 50 amps), 42 pull-thrus, tenting, cabins, RV storage, laundry, ltd groceries, ice.

◇◇RECREATION: boating, ramp, river fishing. Rec open to public.

Pets welcome. Open all yr. Big rigs welcome. Clubs welcome. Rate in 2007 $17.75 per vehicle. MC/VISA/DISC/AMEX. Phone: (318)742-4999.

e-mail: cashpointlanding@bellsouth.net

SEE AD SHREVEPORT PAGE 317

(C) DIAMOND JACKS CASINO RESORT—*From jct I-20 & Isle of Capri Blvd (exit 20): Go 1 block S on Isle of Capri Blvd. Enter at end.* 24 hour hot casino action, 4 restaurants, gift shop, live entertainment and special promotions! Convenient parking and meeting spaces. Open all yr. MC/VISA. Phone: (800)843-4753.

WELCOME

SEE AD TRAVEL SECTION PAGE 297

(C) Diamond Jacks RV Park—(Bossier) *From jct I-20 & Isle of Capri Blvd (exit 20A): Go 1 block S on Isle of Capri Blvd, then 1 block E on Access Rd. Enter at end.* ◇◇◇◇FACILITIES: 32 sites, 32 full hkups, (30 & 50 amps), 20 pull-thrus, laundry, ice, tables. ◇◇◇RECREATION: rec room/area, swim pool. Rec open to public. Pets welcome. Partial handicap access. No tents. Open all yr. Big rigs welcome. Rate in 2007 $25-40 for 2 persons. Phone: (318)678-7661.

(N) Maplewood RV Park—(Bossier) *From jct I-220 (exit 11) & Hwy 3: Go 3 mi N on Hwy 3. Enter on L.* ◇◇◇FACILITIES: 42 sites, 42 full hkups, (15, 30 & 50 amps), 50 amps ($), many extended stay sites, 12 pull-thrus, tenting, laundry, ice, tables, grills. Pets welcome. Open all yr. Big rigs welcome. Internet friendly. Rate in 2007 $22 per family. Phone: (800)569-2264.

MILITARY PARK (Barksdale AFB FAMCAMP)—(Caddo) *Off I-20 & US 71. On base.* FACILITIES: 22 sites, 22 W&E, tenting, dump station, laundry, ltd groceries. RECREATION: boating. Open all yr. For Military Use Only-w/Military ID Card. Phone: (318)456-3091.

BREAUX BRIDGE—D-3

(C) BREAUX BRIDGE TOURIST COMMISSION—*From jct I-10 (exit 109) & Hwy 328 (Rees St): Go 1-3/4 mi SE on Hwy 328 (Rees St), then 1 block SW on East Bridge St. Enter on R.* Along the banks of Bayou Teche. History, live music, dancing & shopping. Breaux Bridge-where the famous crawfish etouffee was created! Open all yr. Phone: (337)332-8500.

WELCOME

e-mail: bbcc@centurytel.net

SEE AD TRAVEL SECTION PAGE 297

(N) POCHE'S FISH-N-CAMP—(St. Martin) *From jct I-10 (exit 109) & Hwy 328: Go 1-3/4 mi NW on Hwy 328, then 1/4 mi N on Posche Bridge Rd, then 1/4 mi E on Hwy 31, then N 1-3/4 mi on Hwy 341, then 1/2 mi W on Hwy 354. Enter on R.*

WELCOME

◇◇◇◇FACILITIES: 89 sites, typical site width 32 ft, 89 full hkups, (20, 30 & 50 amps), 3 pull-thrus, wireless Instant Internet access at site ($), wireless Internet access central location ($), cabins, laundry, ltd groceries, ice, tables, fire rings, grills, wood.

◇◇◇RECREATION: rec hall, pavilion, swim pool, lake fishing, fishing supplies, play equipment, sports field.

Pets welcome. No tents. Open all yr. Big rigs welcome. Internet friendly. Clubs welcome. Rate in 2007 $25 for 2 persons. MC/VISA. Phone: (337) 332-0326. CCUSA discount.

e-mail: reservations@pochesmarket.com

SEE AD LAFAYETTE PAGE 308

The fantastic floats of New Orleans Mardi Gras are constructed and named by societies known as "Krewes".

BREAUX BRIDGE—Continued

(N) POCHE'S MARKET, RESTAURANT & SMOKEHOUSE—*From jct I-10 (exit 109) & Hwy 328: Go 1-3/4 mi NW on Hwy 328, then 1/4 mi N on Poche Bridge Rd, then 100 ft W on Hwy 31.* Specialty meats, market,restaurant and smokehouse. Many cajun specialties. Daily lunches served. Most items available for shipping. USDA inspected. Open all yr. MC/VISA/DISC. Phone: (337)332-2108.

WELCOME

e-mail: reservations@pochesmarket.com

SEE AD LAFAYETTE PAGE 308

BROUSSARD—D-3

(S) LaBoulaie RV Park & Campground—(St. Martin) *From Jct Hwy 182 & Hwy 90: Go 3 mi S on Hwy 90 (Evangeline Hwy). Enter on R.* ◇◇◇FACILITIES: 45 sites, typical site width 35 ft, 45 full hkups, (20, 30 & 50 amps), mostly extended stay sites, laundry. Pets welcome, breed restrict. Partial handicap access. No tents. Open all yr. Big rigs welcome. Internet friendly. Rate in 2007 $20 for 2 persons. Member LCOA. Phone: (337)856-0555. FMCA discount.

(N) MAXIE'S CAMPGROUND—(Lafayette) *From jct Hwy 182 & Hwy 90: Go 1 mi N on Hwy 90 (Evangeline Hwy). Enter on R.*

WELCOME

◇◇◇FACILITIES: 70 sites, typical site width 20 ft, 70 full hkups, (20, 30 & 50 amps), some extended stay sites, wireless Instant Internet access at site ($), phone Internet access central location, tenting, laundry, tables.

RECREATION: golf nearby.

Pets welcome. Open all yr. Big rigs welcome. Internet friendly. Rate in 2007 $24.64 for 2 persons. Member ARVC, LCOA. Phone: (337)837-6200. CCUSA discount.

e-mail: jason@maxiescampground.com

SEE AD LAFAYETTE PAGE 309

CARENCRO—D-3

(E) Bayou Wilderness RV Resort—(Lafayette) *From jct I-10 (exit 103B) & US 167/I-49N: Go 2-1/2 mi N on US 167/I-49, then 2-1/4 mi E on Gloria Switch (exit 2), then 3/4 mi N on North Wilderness Trail. Enter on R.* ◇◇◇◇FACILITIES: 120 sites, typical site width 25 ft, accepts full hkup units only, 120 full hkups, (20, 30 & 50 amps), 50 amps ($), some extended stay sites, 120 pull-thrus, laundry, ltd groceries, LP gas by meter, ice, tables. ◇◇◇RECREATION: rec room/area, swim pool, lake fishing, play equipment, shuffleboard court, planned activities (wkends only), tennis, sports field, v-ball. Pets welcome. Partial handicap access. No tents. Open all yr. Big rigs welcome. Rate in 2007 $35.25-38.64 for 2 persons. Member ARVC, LCOA. Phone: (337)896-0598. FMCA discount.

CHATHAM—A-3

(C) JIMMY DAVIS STATE PARK OF CANEY LAKE—(Jackson) *From jct US 167 & Hwy 4: Go 4 mi E on Hwy 4, exit on N Lakeshore Dr, then right on State Parks Rd.* FACILITIES: 73 sites, 73 W&E, (30 & 50 amps), tenting, dump station, laundry, fire rings, grills. RECREATION: pavilion, lake swimming, boating, ramp, lake fishing, playground. Rec open to public. Pets welcome. Open all yr. Phone: (888)677-2263.

CHAUVIN—E-5

Lapeyrouse Camping (RV SPACES)—(Terrebonne) *From jct Hwy 58 & Hwy 56: Go 11-1/2 mi S on Hwy 56. Enter on R.* FACILITIES: 53 sites, typical site width 28 ft, accepts self-contained units only, 53 full hkups, (30 & 50 amps), 50 amps ($), many extended stay sites, groceries, ice. RECREATION: equipped pavilion, boating, ramp, dock, lake fishing. Pets welcome. No tents. Open all yr. No restrooms. Rate in 2007 $28-35 per vehicle. Phone: (985)594-2600.

COLFAX—B-3

(NW) COLFAX RECREATION AREA RV PARK & CAMPGROUND—(Grant) *From jct I-49 (exit 99) & LA-8: Go 11-1/4 mi E on Hwy 8, then E on Main St 1/2 mi, then W on LA-158 1 mi to Lock & Dam sign, then 1/4 mi W to Area. Enter on R.* FACILITIES: 25 sites, 25 full hkups, (30 & 50 amps), tenting, dump station, non-guest dumping, laundry, patios, fire rings, grills. RECREATION: rec hall, pavilion, boating, ramp, river fishing, playground, sports field. Pets welcome. Partial handicap access. Open all yr. Big rigs welcome. Internet friendly. Phone: (318)627-2640.

COLUMBIA—B-3

(N) Riverton Lake Campground (RV SPACES)—(Caldwell) *From jct Hwy 4 & US 165: Go 6-3/4 mi N on US 165, then 3/4 mi W on asphalt road. Enter on L.* FACILITIES: 18 sites, typical site width 15 ft, 18 full hkups, (30 & 50 amps), some extended stay sites, 16 pull-thrus, tenting, laundry, tables, fire rings, grills. RECREATION: rec room/area, boating, ramp, lake/river fishing, hiking trails. Pets welcome. Open all yr. Rate in 2007 $15 per vehicle. Phone: (318)343-4658.

CONVENT—D-4

(C) FELIX POCHE PLANTATION—*From jct I-10 (exit 179) & Hwy 44: Go 15-3/4 mi S on Hwy 44. Enter on L.* Bed & Breakfast and guided tours, Poche Plantation listed on the National Register of historic places. Open all yr. MC/VISA/DISC/AMEX. Phone: (225)562-7728.

WELCOME

e-mail: innkeeper@pocheplantation.com

SEE AD NEXT PAGE

CONVENT—Continued on next page

Find a park or campground Woodall's does not list? Tell us about it! Use Reader Comment Forms located after the Alphabetical Quick Reference pages.

CONVENT—Continued

(C) FELIX POCHE PLANTATION RV RESORT—(St. James) *From jct I-10 (exit 179) & Hwy 44: Go 15-3/4 mi S on Hwy 44. Enter on L.*

WELCOME

◆◆◆◆◆FACILITIES: 80 sites, typical site width 30 ft, 80 full hkups, (20, 30 & 50 amps), some extended stay sites, 13 pull-thrus, cable TV, wireless Instant Internet access at site, phone on-site Internet access (needs activ), cable Internet access central location, cabins, dump station, non-guest dumping $, laundry, ice, tables, patios.

◆◆◆◆RECREATION: rec hall, rec room/area, pavilion, swim pool, whirlpool, golf nearby, bsktball, planned activities, sports field, hiking trails.

Pets welcome. No tents. Open all yr. Big rigs welcome. Internet friendly. Escort to site. Clubs welcome. Rate in 2007 $18-38 for 2 persons. MC/VISA/DISC/AMEX. Member ARVC, LCOA. Phone: (225)715-9510. FMCA discount.

e-mail: innkeeper@pocheplantation.com

SEE AD THIS PAGE

COUSHATTA—B-2

(SE) GRAND BAYOU RESORT—(Red River) *From jct I-49 (exit 162) & LA 177: Go 6 mi NE on LA 177, then 7-1/2 mi SE on US 84, then 1-1/4 mi E on Hwy 784. Enter on R.* FACILITIES: 59 sites, 49 W&E, (20, 30 & 50 amps), 50 amps ($), 10 no hkups, 11 pull-thrus, tenting, dump station, non-guest dumping $, laundry, fire rings, grills, wood. RECREATION: pavilion, lake swimming, boating, lake fishing. Pets welcome. Partial handicap access. Open all yr. Phone: (877)932-3821.

COVINGTON—D-5

(N) Land-O-Pines Family Campground—(St. Tammany) *From jct US 190 & Hwy 25: Go 4-1/2 mi NW on Hwy 25, then 2 mi E & N on Million Dollar Rd. Enter on L.* ◆◆FACILITIES: 270 sites, typical site width 35 ft, 150 full hkups, 120 W&E, (20, 30 & 50 amps), 50 amps ($), many extended stay sites (in summer), tenting, dump station, non-guest dumping $, laundry, groceries, LP gas by weight/by meter, ice, tables, wood. ◆◆◆RECREATION: rec room/area, pavilion, swim pool, river swimming, river/pond fishing, mini-golf ($), playground, planned activities (wkends only), horseshoes, sports field, v-ball. Rec open to public. Pets welcome. Open all yr. Facilities fully operational April thru Labor Day. Internet friendly. Rate in 2007 $28-40 for 4 persons. Member ARVC, LCOA. Phone: (985)892-6023.

DENHAM SPRINGS—D-4

(SW) KOA-BATON ROUGE EAST—(Livingston) *From jct US-61 & I-12: Go 6-1/2 mi E on I-12 (exit 10), then 1/2 mi S on Hwy-3002, then 1/2 mi W on Hwy 1034. Enter on L.*

WELCOME

◆◆◆◆FACILITIES: 112 sites, typical site width 35 ft, 96 full hkups, 10 W&E, (30 & 50 amps), 50 amps ($), 6 no hkups, some extended stay sites, 67 pull-thrus, cable TV, wireless Instant Internet access at site, phone Internet access central location, tenting, cabins, dump station, non-guest dumping $, laundry, groceries, RV supplies, LP gas by weight/by meter, ice, tables, patios, fire rings, grills.

◆◆◆◆RECREATION: rec hall, rec room/area, pavilion, coin games, swim pool, whirlpool, mini-golf ($), golf nearby, bsktball, playground, planned activities, sports field.

Pets welcome. Partial handicap access. Open all yr. Big rigs welcome. Internet friendly. Clubs welcome. Rate in 2007 $30-40 for 2 persons. MC/VISA/DISC/AMEX/Debit. Member ARVC, LCOA. Phone: (225)664-7281. KOA 10% value card discount.

e-mail: gbacot@ix.netcom.com

SEE AD BATON ROUGE PAGE 304 AND AD DISCOVER SECTION PAGES 62 & 63

DONALDSONVILLE—D-4

(C) B & B RV PARK (RV SPACES)—(Ascension) *From jct Hwy 18 & Hwy 1: Go 1 1/2 mi SW on Hwy 1, then 1 block N on Bellina Dr. Enter on R.*

WELCOME

FACILITIES: 48 sites, typical site width 25 ft, accepts full hkup units only, 48 full hkups, (30 & 50 amps), some extended stay sites, cable on-site Internet access (needs activ), laundry, patios.

Pets welcome. No tents. Open all yr. No restrooms. Big rigs welcome. Rate in 2007 $20 per vehicle. Phone: (225)473-4744.

e-mail: cjbellina@cox.net

SEE AD THIS PAGE

DOYLINE—A-2

(S) LAKE BISTINEAU STATE PARK—(Webster) *From jct I-20 (exit 47) & Hwy 7: Go 3-1/2 mi S on Hwy 7, then 6-1/2 mi W on Hwy 164, then 7 mi S on Hwy 163.* FACILITIES: 67 sites, 67 W&E, (30 & 50 amps), 6 pull-thrus, tenting, dump station, laundry, grills. RECREATION: pavilion, equipped pavilion, swim pool, boating, canoeing, ramp, 6 canoe rentals, lake fishing, playground, sports field, hiking trails. Rec open to public. Pets welcome. Open all yr. Phone: (888)677-2478.

DUSON—D-3

(NW) FROG CITY RV PARK—(Acadia) *From jct I-10 (exit 92): Go 1 block S, then 1 block N on SW Frontage Rd. Behind Super 8 Hotel. Enter at end.*

WELCOME

◆◆◆◆FACILITIES: 62 sites, typical site width 30 ft, 62 full hkups, (20, 30 & 50 amps), some extended stay sites, 45 pull-thrus, cable TV, wireless Instant Internet access at site, cable Internet access central location, laundry, tables.

◆RECREATION: rec room/area, play equipment, horseshoes.

Pets welcome, breed restrict, quantity restrict. Partial handicap access. No tents. Open all yr. Big rigs welcome. Internet friendly. Clubs welcome.

FROG CITY RV PARK—Continued on next page

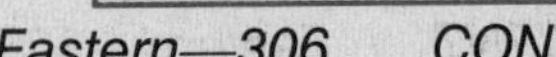

DUSON—Continued
FROG CITY RV PARK—Continued

Rate in 2007 $30 per vehicle. MC/VISA/DISC/AMEX/DC. Member LCOA. Phone: (337)873-9085.

e-mail: msthanki@cox.net

Reserve Online at Woodalls.com

SEE AD THIS PAGE AND AD LAFAYETTE PAGE 309

EGAN—D-3

(S) CAJUN HAVEN RV PARK—(Acadia) *From jct I-10 & Egan Hwy (exit 72): Go 1/4 mi N on Egan Hwy (Trumps Rd). Enter on R.*

WELCOME

◊◊FACILITIES: 20 sites, 10 full hkups, 10 W&E, (30 amps), some extended stay sites, 20 pull-thrus, tenting, RV/park trailer rentals, dump station, laundry, LP gas by weight/by meter, tables, grills.

◊◊RECREATION: equipped pavilion, pond fishing, play equipment, sports field.

Pets welcome. Open all yr. Rate in 2007 $15 for 2 persons. MC/VISA.

e-mail: jefdadawg@aol.com

SEE AD LAFAYETTE PAGE 309

EUNICE—D-3

(E) L'Acadie Inn RV Park (RV SPACES)—(St. Landry) *From jct Hwy 13 & US 190: Go 3-1/2 mi E, then 100 yds S on Hwy 95 (Tasso Loop). Enter on L.* FACILITIES: 17 sites, accepts full hkup units only, 17 full hkups, (20, 30 & 50 amps), some extended stay sites, ice. RECREATION: swim pool, pond fishing. Pets welcome, breed restrict. No tents. Open all yr. Big rigs welcome. Rate in 2007 $23 for 2 persons. Phone: (337)457-5211.

FARMERVILLE—A-3

(E) LAKE D'ARBONNE STATE PARK—(Union) *From town: Go 5 mi W on Hwy 2, then 1/4 mi S on Parish Rd 4410.* FACILITIES: 65 sites, 65 W&E, (20 & 30 amps), tenting, dump station, non-guest dumping, $, laundry, grills. RECREATION: rec room/area, pavilion, swim pool, boating, ramp, dock, 5 rowboat rentals, lake fishing, play equipment, tennis, hiking trails. Rec open to public. Pets welcome. Open all yr. Phone: (888)677-5200.

FENTON—D-2

(S) Quiet Oaks RV Park (REBUILDING)—(Jefferson) *From jct I-10 (exit 44) & US 165: Go 10 mi N on US 165, then 1/4 mi W on TV Tower Rd. Enter on L.* FACILITIES: 47 sites, typical site width 20 ft, 47 full hkups, (20, 30 & 50 amps), some extended stay sites, 23 pull-thrus, tenting, laundry, wood. RECREATION: rec room/area, pond fishing. Pets welcome. Open all yr. Rate in 2007 $17.60 for 2 persons. Phone: (888)755-2230. FCRV 10% discount. FMCA discount.

FOLSOM—C-5

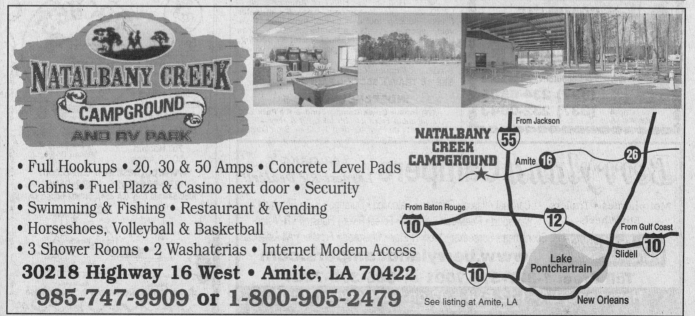

(W) Tchefuncte Family Campground—(Tangipahoa) *From jct Hwy 25 & Hwy 40: Go 4-1/2 mi W on Hwy 40, then 2-1/4 mi N on gravel road. Enter at end.* ◊◊FACILITIES: 109 sites, typical site width 25 ft, 43 full hkups, 66 W&E, (20, 30 & 50 amps), 50 amps ($), some extended stay sites, 8 pull-thrus, tenting, dump station, non-guest dumping $, laundry, ltd groceries,

FOLSOM—Continued
Tchefuncte Family Campground—Continued

ice, tables, wood. ◊◊◊RECREATION: rec hall, swim pool, river swimming, river/pond fishing, play equipment, horseshoes, sports field, hiking trails, v-ball. Pets welcome, breed restrict. Open all yr. Internet friendly. Rate in 2007 $30 for 5 persons. Phone: (985)796-3654.

GARDNER—C-3

(S) KISATCHIE NATIONAL FOREST (Kincaid Rec. Site)—(Rapides) *From jct Hwy 28 & Hwy 121: Go 1/4 mi SW on Hwy 121, then 5 mi S on FR 279, then 2 mi NE on FR 205.* FACILITIES: 40 sites, typical site width 10 ft, 40 E, tenting, cold showers only, dump station, fire rings, grills. RECREATION: lake swimming, boating, canoeing, ramp, lake fishing, hiking trails. Pets welcome. Partial handicap access. Open all yr. No reservations. Phone: (318)445-9396.

GIBSON—E-4

(N) Linda's Campground & RV Park—(Terrebonne) *From jct US 90 & Gibson exit: Go 1 mi W on Hwy 20, then 5 mi E on Hwy 182. Enter on R.* ◊◊FACILITIES: 28 sites, typical site width 30 ft, 34 ft max RV length, 24 full hkups, 4 W&E, (15, 20 & 30 amps), many extended stay sites, laundry, ice, tables. Pets welcome, size restrict. No tents. Open all yr. Rate in 2007 $18 for 2 persons. Phone: (985)575-3934.

GONZALES—D-4

(S) LAMAR DIXON EXPO CENTER RV PARK—(Ascension) *From jct I-10 & LA 30 (exit 177): Go 1/2 mi W on LA Hwy 30, then 1 mi S on St Landry Rd. Enter on R.* FACILITIES: 284 sites, 284 full hkups, (20, 30 & 50 amps), 50 amps ($), 100 pull-thrus. RECREATION: planned activities, sports field. Pets welcome. No tents. Open all yr. Phone: (225)621-1700.

GRAND ISLE—E-5

(SW) GRAND ISLE STATE PARK—(Jefferson) *From town: Go E on Hwy 1 to the end of the island. Enter at end.* FACILITIES: 49 sites, typical site width 30 ft, 49 W&E, (20, 30 & 50 amps), 49 pull-thrus, dump station. RECREATION: saltwater swimming, saltwater fishing, hiking trails. Rec open to public. Pets welcome. No tents. Open all yr. Phone: (888)787-2559.

HAMMOND—D-5

✱ **(S) BERRYLAND CAMPERS**—*From jct I-55 & I-12: Go 6 mi E on I-12 (exit 42), then 1 block S, then 3/4 mi W on Frontage Rd. Enter at end.* SALES: travel trailers, 5th wheels, motor homes, mini-motor homes, pre-owned unit sales. SERVICES: full-time mech, RV appliance repair, body work/collision repair, LP gas by weight/by meter, sells parts/accessories, installs hitches. Open all yr. MC/VISA/DISC/Debit. Phone: (877)370-7001.

WELCOME

e-mail: sales@berrylandcampers.com

SEE AD NEXT PAGE

HAMMOND—Continued

(S) Calloway RV & Campground—(Tangipahoa) *From jct I-12 & I-55: Go 1 mi S on I-55, then 1/2 mi N on US 51 (exit 28), then 3/4 mi W on Club Deluxe Rd. Enter on L.* ◇◇◇FACILITIES: 60 sites, typical site width 20 ft, 60 full hkups, (30 & 50 amps), 50 amps ($), many extended stay sites, 49 pull-thrus, tenting, dump station, non-guest dumping $, laundry, LP gas by weight/by meter, ice, tables. ◇◇RECREATION: rec hall, swim pool, 4 pedal boat rentals, lake fishing, mini-golf, playground, horseshoes, sports field, v-ball. Pets welcome. Open all yr. Big rigs welcome. Internet friendly. Rate in 2007 $24.42-33.30 for 2 persons. Member ARVC, LCOA. Phone: (985)542-8094.

(W) DIXIE RV SUPERSTORES—*From jct I-55 & I-12: Go 3 mi W on I-12 (exit 35), then 1 block N on CR 17. Enter on L.* SALES: travel trailers, 5th wheels, motor homes, mini-motor homes, pre-owned unit sales. SERVICES: full-time mech, engine/chassis repair, RV appliance repair, body work/collision repair, bus. hrs emerg rd svc, LP gas by weight/by meter, dump station, sells parts/accessories, installs hitches. Open all yr. MC/VISA/DISC/AMEX/Debit. Phone: (800)299-0321.

SEE AD PAGE 307

(E) Hidden Oaks Family Campground—(Tangipahoa) *From jct I-12 (exit 47) & Hwy-445: Go 2 mi N on Hwy-445, then 1-1/4 mi W on US-190. Enter on L.* ◇◇◇FACILITIES: 225 sites, typical site width 25 ft, 225 full hkups, (30 & 50 amps), some extended stay sites (in summer), 30 pull-thrus, tenting, dump station, laundry, ltd groceries, LP gas by weight/by meter, ice, tables, wood. ◇◇◇RECREATION: rec room/area, pavilion, swim pool, river swimming, boating, canoeing, 6 rowboat/20 canoe rentals, lake/river fishing, playground, planned activities (wkends only), horseshoes, sports field, hiking trails, v-ball. Pets welcome, breed restrict. Open all yr. Internet friendly. Rate in 2007 $27.50-30 for 5 persons. Phone: (800)359-0940.

(W) Punkin Park Campground—(Tangipahoa) *From jct I-55 & I-12: Go 3 mi W on I-12 (exit 35), then 1/2 mi N on CR 17, then 1/2 mi E on Hwy 1040, then 1/2 mi S on N Billville Rd. Enter on R.* ◇◇FACILITIES: 52 sites, typical site width 30 ft, 52 full hkups, (20, 30 & 50 amps), many extended stay sites, 10 pull-thrus, tenting, dump station, non-guest dumping $, laundry, tables, patios, fire rings. ◇◇RECREATION: pavilion, swim pool, lake fishing. Pets welcome. Open all yr. Internet friendly. Rate in 2007 $28.95 for 4 persons. Phone: (888)585-5519. FCRV 10% discount. FMCA discount.

(W) TANGIPAHOA PARISH TOURIST COMMISSION—*From jct I-12 & I-55: Go 2-3/4 mi N on I-55 to exit 32, then 1000 feet W on Wardline Rd. Enter on R.* Tangipahoa Parish offers a wide variety of restaurants, yearlong outdoor sporting and cultural events. Featuring wetlands, swamps & waterways in the south and rolling hills and pastures to the north. Seven campgrounds. Open all yr. Phone: (800)542-7520.

e-mail: betty@tangitourism.com

SEE AD TRAVEL SECTION PAGE 298

HENDERSON—D-3

(E) Frenchman's Wilderness—(St. Martin) *From jct I-10 (exit 121) & Hwy-3177: Go 3/4 mi S on Hwy-3177. Enter on R.* ◇◇◇FACILITIES: 140 sites, typical site width 50 ft, 140 full hkups, (30 & 50 amps), 50 amps ($), some extended stay sites, 2 pull-thrus, tenting, laundry, ltd groceries, LP gas by weight/by meter, ice, tables. ◇◇◇RECREATION: swim pool, boating, ramp, lake fishing, mini-golf ($), play equipment, v-ball. Pets welcome. Open all yr. Big rigs welcome. Internet friendly. Rate in 2007 $24.50 for 4 persons. Phone: (337)228-2616.

HOMER—A-2

(SE) LAKE CLAIBORNE STATE PARK—(Claiborne) *From jct I-20 (exit 61) & Hwy 154: Go 7 mi N on Hwy 154, then 8-1/2 mi NE on Hwy 518, then 1 mi S on Hwy 146.* FACILITIES: 87 sites, 87 W&E, (30 & 50 amps), 12 pull-thrus, tenting, dump station, laundry, fire rings. RECREATION: equipped pavilion, lake swimming, boating, ramp, rowboat rentals, lake fishing, playground, hiking trails. Rec open to public. Pets welcome. Open all yr. Phone: (888)677-2524.

HORNBECK—C-2

(SW) PLEASURE POINT/TOLEDO BEND LAKE (Sabine River Auth. Site 15)—(Sabine) *From jct US 171 & Hwy 473: Go 8 mi W on Hwy 473, then 10 mi S on Hwy 191, then W on access road. Enter on L.* FACILITIES: 124 sites, typical site width 25 ft, 50 full hkups, 74 W&E, (30 amps), tenting, dump station, non-guest dumping, ice, grills, wood. RECREATION: lake swimming, boating, ramp, dock, lake fishing, playground, hiking trails. Pets welcome. Partial handicap access. Open all yr. Member ARVC, LCOA. Phone: (318)565-4810.

HOUMA—E-4

(W) A Cajun Man's Swamp Cruise—*From jct of US 90 & Hwy 24: Go 7-3/4 mi S on Hwy 24, then 13 mi W on Hwy 182, then 1/4 mi SW on Marina Dr. Enter on L.* The Cajun Man provides Cajun music while you leisurely cruise a south Louisiana Swamp on a large canapi shaded boat. Tour times vary. Alligators, Birds, & Flora. Open all yr. Phone: (985)868-4625.

(E) Capri Court MHP—(Terrebonne) *From jct US 90 & Hwy 24: Go 2 mi S on Hwy 24, then 1-1/2 mi E on Hwy 660, then 1-1/2 mi NE on Country Estates Rd, then 1 mi S on Bayou Blue Rd. Enter on R.* ◇◇◇FACILITIES: 50 sites, typical site width 30 ft, 45 full hkups, 5 W&E, (15, 30 & 50 amps), 50 amps ($), some extended stay sites, 5 pull-thrus, tenting, dump station, non-guest dumping $, laundry, tables, patios, fire rings. ◇◇RECREATION: pavilion, swim pool, boating, ramp, dock, stream fishing, play equipment, sports field. Pets welcome, breed restrict, size restrict. Partial handicap access. Open all yr. Big rigs welcome. Rate in 2007 $27.45-30.75 for 2 persons. Member ARVC, LCOA. Phone: (800)428-8026. CCUSA discount. FMCA discount.

(E) Carriage Cove MH & RVP (RV SPACES)—(Terrebonne) *From jct US 90 & Hwy 24: Go 11-1/2 mi S on Hwy 24, then 1 block N on Prospect Rd, then 1/2 mi NW on West Park Rd. Enter on R.* FACILITIES: 40 sites, typical site width 18 ft, accepts full hkup units only, 40 full hkups, (20, 30 & 50 amps), many extended stay sites, laundry. Pets welcome. No tents. Open all yr. Rate in 2007 $20 for 2 persons. Phone: (985)872-2756.

(N) HOUMA AREA CONVENTION & VISITORS BUREAU—*From jct US 90 & Hwy 24: Go 1 block mi S on Hwy 24, then 1/4 mi W on W. Frontage Rd, then S on Tourist Dr. Enter on R.* Visit Houma, the Heart of America's WETLAND. Area info on camping, fresh & salt water fishing, swamp tours, gardens, museums, festivals, special events, attractions, Mardi Gras Parades, Cajun food & music. On site: RV parking, dump station & modem access. Open all yr. Phone: (800)688-2732.

e-mail: info@houmatourism.com

SEE AD TRAVEL SECTION PAGE 295

INDEPENDENCE—C-5

(W) Indian Creek Campground & RV Park LLC—(Tangipahoa) *From jct I-55 (exit 40) & Hwy 40: Go 1000 feet W on Hwy 40, then 1-1/2 mi S on Fontana Rd. Enter on R.* ◇◇◇FACILITIES: 185 sites, typical site width 25 ft, 45 full hkups, 140 W&E, (20, 30 & 50 amps), 50 amps ($), some extended stay sites (in summer), 20 pull-thrus, tenting, dump station, non-guest dumping $, portable dump, laundry, ltd groceries, LP gas by weight/by meter, ice, tables, wood. ◇◇◇◇RECREATION: rec room/area, pavilion, swim pool, canoeing, 5 canoe/4 pedal boat rentals, river/pond fishing, playground, planned activities (wkends only), horseshoes, hiking trails, v-ball. Rec open to public. Pets welcome. Open all yr. Big rigs welcome. Rate in 2007 $27-30 for 5 persons. Member ARVC, LCOA. Phone: (985)878-6567.

KINDER—D-3

(N) Coushatta Luxury RV Resort At Red Shoes Park—(Allen) *From jct US 190 & US 165: Go 3 mi N on US 165. Enter on L.* ◇◇◇◇FACILITIES: 107 sites, typical site width 30 ft, 107 full hkups, (20, 30 & 50 amps), 105 pull-thrus, dump station, non-guest dumping $, laundry, ltd groceries, ice, tables, patios. ◇◇◇◇RECREATION: rec room/area, swim pool, pond fishing, playground, shuffleboard court, tennis, v-ball. Pets welcome. Partial handicap access. No tents. Open all yr. Big rigs welcome. Internet friendly. Rate in 2007 $17-22 per vehicle. Member LCOA. Phone: (800)584-7263. FMCA discount.

LA PLACE—D-5

(E) La Place Trailer Park & Campground—(St. John the Baptist) *From jct I-10 (exit 209) & US 51: Go 3 mi SW on US 51, then 1-1/2 mi E on US 61. Enter on R.* ◇◇FACILITIES: 46 sites, typical site width 20 ft, accepts full hkup units only, 46 full hkups, (30 & 50 amps), 50 amps ($), many extended stay sites, laundry. RECREATION: pavilion. Pets welcome. No tents. Open all yr. Phone: (985)652-9712.

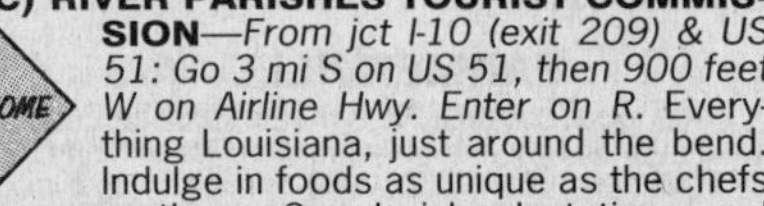

(C) RIVER PARISHES TOURIST COMMISSION—*From jct I-10 (exit 209) & US 51: Go 3 mi S on US 51, then 900 feet W on Airline Hwy. Enter on R.* Everything Louisiana, just around the bend. Indulge in foods as unique as the chefs that prepare them. See lavish plantations and dance to twin fiddles. Open all yr. Phone: (985) 359-2562.

SEE AD TRAVEL SECTION PAGE 297

LAFAYETTE—D-3

FROG CITY RV PARK—*From Lafayette: I-49 & I-10 (exit 103): Go 11 mi W on I-10 (exit 92) 1 block S. Behind Super 8 Motel. Enter at end.*

SEE PRIMARY LISTING AT DUSON AND AD DUSON PAGE 307

LAFAYETTE—Continued on next page

Louisiana State Bird: Brown Pelican

LAFAYETTE—Continued

✲ **(SE) G & J MOBILE HOME & RV SUPPLIES**—*From jct US 90 & Pinhook Rd: Go 2-1/2 mi S on W Pinhook Rd, then 1 mi W on Verot School Rd (Hwy 339), then 100 yards N on John Wayne Dr. Enter on R.* Complete Mobile Home Supplies too!. SERVICES: sells parts/accessories. Open all yr. MC/VISA/DISC/AMEX. Phone: (337) 234-6585.

WELCOME

e-mail: gjmobilehome@bellsouth.net

SEE AD PAGE 308

✲ **(NW) GAUTHIERS' RV SERVICE CENTER**—*From jct I-10 (exit 100): Go 200 ft N on Ambassador McCoffery Rd. Enter on R.* SALES: travel trailers, park trailers, 5th wheels, pre-owned unit sales. SERVICES: full-time mech, RV appliance repair, body work/collision repair, LP gas by weight/by meter, sells parts/accessories, installs hitches. Open all yr. MC/VISA/DISC/AMEX/Debit. Phone: (800)235-8547.

WELCOME

e-mail: sales@gauthiers.com

SEE AD THIS PAGE

Halfway Between Lk. Charles & Lafayette

Cajun Haven
RV Park
337-783-7330
I-10
Exit 72
EGAN, LA
See listing at Egan, LA
NEW BIG RIG SITES 2007!

Sales ❖ Service ❖ Parts
LAFAYETTE, LA
I-10 Exit 100 at Ambassador Caffery
EZ OFF / EZ ON
WWW.GAUTHIERSRV.COM
Mobile Scout • Brookside • Bristol Bay
Sunset Creek • Wildcat • Travel Supreme
Aspen • Explorer • Hyperlite
Durango & Montego Bay
See listing at Lafayette, LA
337-235-8547 ❖ 800-235-8547

LAFAYETTE—Continued

(W) KOA-LAFAYETTE—(Lafayette) *From jct US-167 & I-10: Go 5-1/4 mi W on I-10 (exit 97), then 100 feet S on Hwy 93, then 1/4 mi W on entry road. Enter at end.*

WELCOME

◊◊◊◊◊FACILITIES: 185 sites, typical site width 25 ft, 150 full hkups, 35 W&E, (15, 20, 30 & 50 amps), 50 amps ($), some extended stay sites, 100 pull-thrus, cable TV ($), wireless Instant Internet access at site, cable Internet access central location, tenting, cabins, RV storage, dump station, non-guest dumping $, laundry, full svc store, RV supplies, LP gas by weight/by meter, ice, tables, patios, fire rings, wood.

◊◊◊◊◊RECREATION: rec hall, rec room/area, pavilion, coin games, 2 swim pools, boating, 8 pedal boat rentals, lake fishing, fishing supplies, mini-golf ($), golf nearby, bsktball, playground, planned activities, v-ball, local tours. Rec open to public.

Pets welcome. Open all yr. Big rigs welcome. Internet friendly. Clubs welcome. Rate in 2007 $32.95-

---

Louisiana Nickname: Pelican State; Creole State; Sportsman's Paradise; Sugar State

---

LAFAYETTE—Continued
KOA-LAFAYETTE—Continued

45 for 2 persons. MC/VISA/DISC/Debit. Member ARVC, LCOA. Phone: (800)562-0809. KOA 10% value card discount.

SEE AD THIS PAGE AND AD DISCOVER SECTION PAGES 62 & 63

LAFAYETTE—Continued on next page

(337) 837-6200
Nestled under beautiful Live Oak Trees
Wi-Fi
CONVENIENT FOR SIGHTSEEING
"Vermillionville" A Cajun Living Museum
America's Oldest "Konriko Rice Mill"
Avery Island's "TABASCO" Sauce & "Jungle Gardens"
See listing at Broussard, LA
www.maxiescampground.com
4350 Hwy 90 E., Broussard, LA 70518

Award Winner

LAFAYETTE

Louisiana's only Double 5W Rated Kampground.

IN THE HEART OF CAJUN COUNTRY
537 Apollo Road, Scott, LA 70583

Kamping Kabins

Great people. Great camping.™

Recreation:
- Two Large Swimming Pools
- 18-Hole Mini-Golf
- Paddle Boats
- Playground • Arcade
- Fishing in our Stocked 10-Acre Lake
- Self Drive Tours of CAJUN COUNTRY

BIG RIGS WELCOME

Facilities: • Concrete Drive-Thru Sites • Lake Front Sites • Cable TV • Modem Access • Super Tent Sites • Monthly Rates • ON SITE RV REPAIRS • GIFT SHOP • Heat & Serve Cajun Dishes

"ASK ABOUT OUR EXTENDED STAY SPECIALS!"

WOODALL RATED
Facilities ◊◊◊◊◊
Recreation ◊◊◊◊◊

(337) 235-2739

(Reservations Only) (800) 562-0809

See listing at Lafayette, LA

www.KOAKampgrounds.com/where/LA/18101.htm

Plan your trip and make your reservations on koa.com

Bayou: French name for "slow-moving river"

Fats Domino, singer, was from Louisiana.

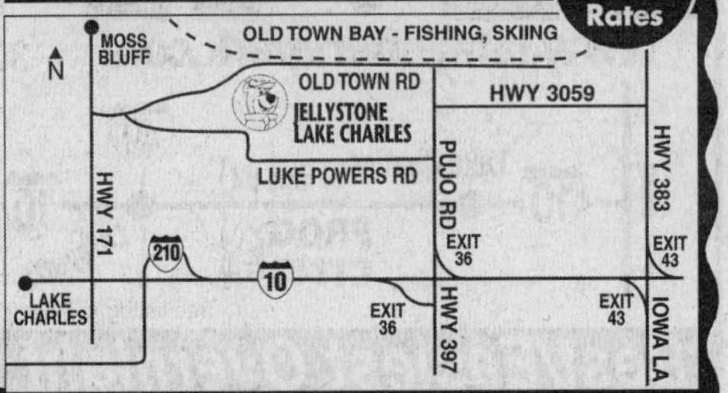

LAFAYETTE—Continued

(N) **LAFAYETTE CONVENTION & VISITORS COMMISSION**—*From jct I-49/I-10 (exit 103A) & US 167: Go 1 mi S on US 167. Enter on L.* The Lafayette Visitor Center is situated on an area surrounded by flora and fauna. Help is available with area maps, brochures and attractions in Cajun Country. Open all yr. Phone: (800) 346-1958.

e-mail: info@lafayettetravel.com

SEE AD TRAVEL SECTION PAGE 294 AND AD TRAVEL SECTION PAGE 297

(N) **PREJEAN'S RESTAURANT**—*From jct I-10 (exit 103B) & I-49: Go 2-1/2 mi N on I-49, then 1 block E on Gloria Switch Rd, then 1 mi N on E frontage road. Enter on R.* An authentic Cajun restaurant featuring seafood, steaks and wild game along with live Cajun music & dancing nightly. Open 7 days 7 am-9:30/10:30 p.m. Open all yr. Closed Christmas, Easter, Thanksgiving, New Year's Day. MC/VISA/DISC/AMEX/DC/Debit. Phone: (337)896-3247.

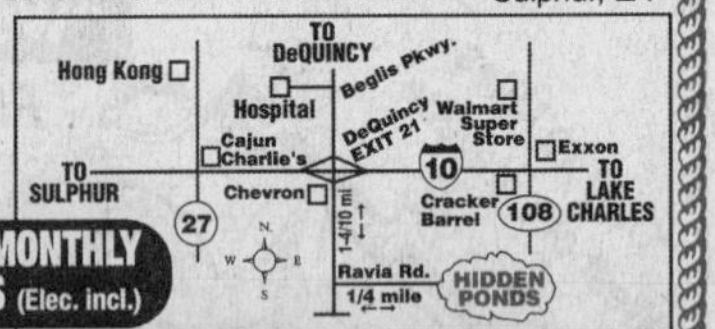

e-mail: prejeans@prejeans.com

SEE AD TRAVEL SECTION PAGE 291

(C) **RANDOL'S RESTAURANT & CAJUN DANCE HALL**—*From jct I-10 (exit 103) & I-49 N & Evangeline Thruway: Go 4-1/2 mi S on Evangeline Thruway, then 4 mi SW on Kaliste Saloom Rd. Enter on R.* An authentic Cajun restaurant featuring a full menu with seafood and steaks, and live Cajun music and dancing 7 days a week. Open at 5pm. Open all yr. MC/VISA. Phone: (337) 981-7080.

e-mail: randolsinfo@aol.com

SEE AD TRAVEL SECTION PAGE 291

LAKE CHARLES—D-2

See listings at Kinder, Sulphur & Vinton

(E) **I-10 Mobile Village & RV Campground**—(Calcasieu) *From east jct I-210 Bypass & I-10: Go 2-1/2 mi E on I-10 (exit 36), then 1 mi N on Pojol Rd., then 3 mi E on Mark Le Bleu Rd, then 3/4 mi S on Mobile Village Rd. Enter on L.* ◆FACILITIES: 58 sites, 57 full hkups, 1 W&E, (20 & 30 amps), many extended stay sites, 2 pull-thrus, tenting, dump station, non-guest dumping, laundry. RECREATION: pond fishing. Pets welcome. Open all yr. Rate in 2007 $20 for 2 persons. Phone: (337)433-2077.

(N) **Parkside Marina & RV Park** (RV SPACES)—(Calcasieu) *From jct I-10 & US 171: Go 4 mi N on US 171, then 3 mi W on Hwy 378, then 1/4 mi N on Spur 378. Enter on L.* FACILITIES: 10 sites, typical site width 20 ft, 38 ft max RV length, accepts self-contained units only, 10 W&E, (20 & 30 amps), groceries, LP gas by weight, ice, tables, grills. RECREATION: pavilion, boating, ramp, dock, river fishing. Pets welcome. No tents. Open all yr. Rate in 2007 $16 for 2 persons.

(N) SAM HOUSTON JONES STATE PARK—(Calcasieu) *From jct I-10 & US 171: Go 4 mi N on US 171, then 3 mi W on Hwy 378, then 1 mi NW on a blacktop road, then 1/2 mi W on*

SAM HOUSTON JONES STATE PARK—Continued on next page

LAKE CHARLES—Continued
SAM HOUSTON JONES STATE PARK—Continued

State Park Rd. FACILITIES: 62 sites, 16 full hkups, 46 W&E, (30 & 50 amps), 7 pull-thrus, tenting, dump station, grills. RECREATION: boating, canoeing, ramp, rowboat rentals, river/stream fishing, playground, hiking trails. Rec open to public. Pets welcome. Open all yr. Phone: (888)677-7264.

(SW) SOUTHWEST LOUISIANA CONVENTION & VISITORS BUREAU—*Eastbound: From jct I-10 (exit 29) & Lakeshore Dr: Go 50 feet E on Lakeshore Dr. Westbound: From jct I-10 (exit 30A) & Lakeshore Dr: Go 1 mi W on Lakeshore Dr (making U-turn under I-10), then 1/2 mi E on Lakeshore Dr. Enter on R.* Southwest Louisiana/Lake Charles is the Festival Capital of Louisiana w/Cajun food & culture around every corner! You can bet on the bayou at our casino complexes and then explore the Creole Nature Trail All-American Road. Open all yr. Phone: (800)456-7952.

SEE AD TRAVEL SECTION PAGE 299 AND AD DISCOVER SECTION PAGE 58

V RV PARK-LAKE CHARLES/VINTON—*From Lake Charles: Go 17 mi W on I-10 (exit 8), then 1/10 mi N on Hwy-108, then 1/10 mi W on Goodwin St. Enter on L.*

SEE PRIMARY LISTING AT VINTON AND AD PAGE 310

(W) WHISPERING MEADOW RV PARK—(Calcasieu) *From jct I-10 & Westlake (exit 27): Go 2 blks E on exit ramp, then 3 mi N on LA 378 (Sampson St). Enter on R.*

◇◇◇◇FACILITIES: 32 sites, typical site width 32 ft, 32 full hkups, (20, 30 & 50 amps), some extended stay sites, 32 pull-thrus, wireless Instant Internet access at site, wireless Internet access central location, laundry, tables.

◇RECREATION: rec hall, golf nearby.

Pets welcome. Partial handicap access. No tents. Open all yr. Big rigs welcome. Internet friendly. Escort to site. Clubs welcome. Rate in 2007 $25 per vehicle. MC/VISA. Member ARVC, LCOA. Phone: (337)433-8188. FCRV 10% discount. FMCA discount.

e-mail: whisperingmeadow@bellsouth.net

SEE AD PAGE 310

(NE) YOGI BEAR'S JELLYSTONE PARK CAMP-RESORT—(Calcasieu) *From east jct I-210 Bypass & I-10: Go 2-1/2 mi E on I-10 (exit 36), then 2 mi N on Pujol Rd, then 1 mi W & 1/4 mi N on Luke Powers Rd. Enter on R.*

◇◇◇◇FACILITIES: 63 sites, typical site width 25 ft, 63 full hkups, (20, 30 & 50 amps), some extended stay sites, 20 pull-thrus, wireless Internet access central location, tenting, cabins, RV storage, dump station, non-guest dumping $, laundry, ltd groceries, RV supplies, ice, tables, fire rings, wood.

◇◇◇◇RECREATION: rec room/area, equipped pavilion, coin games, swim pool, canoeing, 9 canoe/10 pedal boat rentals, lake fishing, fishing supplies, mini-golf ($), golf nearby, 13 bike rentals, playground, planned activities, horseshoes, sports field, v-ball. Rec open to public.

Pets welcome. Partial handicap access. Open all yr. Big rigs welcome. Internet friendly. Clubs welcome. Rate in 2007 $25-32 for 5 persons. MC/VISA/DISC/AMEX/Debit. Phone: (877)433-2400.

e-mail: jellystoneLCLA@aol.com

SEE AD PAGE 310

LEESVILLE—C-2

MILITARY PARK (Toledo Bend Rec Site-Fort Polk)—(Vernon) *Off base, on US 171 or Hwy 10.* FACILITIES: 27 sites, 12 full hkups, 15 W&E, tenting, dump station, groceries. RECREATION: lake swimming, boating, lake fishing. Open all yr. For Military Use Only-w/Military ID Card. Phone: (888)718-9088.

(S) Pecan Acres RV Park—(Vernon) *From S Jct Hwy 8 & US 171: Go 14-1/2 mi S on US 171, then W Feet on Hawks Rd. Enter on R.* ◇◇◇FACILITIES: 38 sites, typical site width 25 ft, accepts full hkup units only, 38 full hkups, (20, 30 & 50 amps), many extended stay sites, 16 pull-thrus, laundry, LP gas by weight/by meter. Pets welcome. No tents. Open all yr. Big rigs welcome. Internet friendly. Rate in 2007 $18-23 for 2 persons. Phone: (337)462-9999.

(N) Shady Lake RV Park—(Vernon) *From S Jct Hwy 8 & US 171: Go 2 mi N on US 171. Enter on R.* ◇◇◇FACILITIES: 30 sites, typical site width 30 ft, 30 full hkups, (20, 30 & 50 amps), 50 amps ($), many extended stay sites, 17 pull-thrus, dump station, laundry, tables. RECREATION: pond fishing. Pets welcome. No tents. Open all yr. Big rigs welcome. Rate in 2007 $18.36-20.52 for 2 persons. Phone: (866)742-3951.

LIVINGSTON—D-4

(N) LAKESIDE RV PARK—(Livingston) *From jct of I-12 & Hwy 63 (exit 22): Go 1 1/4 mi S on Hwy 63. Enter on L.*

◇◇◇◇FACILITIES: 139 sites, 139 full hkups, (20, 30 & 50 amps), some extended stay sites, 13 pull-thrus, wireless Instant Internet access at site, phone Internet access central location, cabins, RV storage, laundry, ltd groceries, RV supplies, LP gas by weight/by meter, ice, tables, patios, fire rings, grills, wood.

◇◇◇◇RECREATION: rec hall, rec room/area, swim pool, boating, electric motors only, lake fishing, golf nearby, bsktball, playground, planned activities, horseshoes, sports field, v-ball.

Pets welcome, breed restrict. Partial handicap access. No tents. Open all yr. Big rigs welcome. Internet friendly. Escort to site. Clubs welcome. Rate in 2007 $25-29 per family. MC/VISA/DISC/Debit. Member ARVC, LCOA. Phone: (225)686-7676.

e-mail: info@lakeside-rvpark.com

SEE AD BATON ROUGE PAGE 304

LORANGER—C-5

(N) Sweetwater Campground & RV Park—(Tangipahoa) *From jct I-55 (exit 40) & Hwy 40: Go 5 mi E on Hwy 40, then 1/10 mi N on Hwy 1054, then 4-1/2 mi E on Cooper Rd.* ◇◇FACILITIES: 225 sites, 185 full hkups, 40 W&E, (30 & 50 amps), many extended stay sites, tenting, dump station, laundry, groceries, ice, tables. ◇◇◇RECREATION: pavilion, swim pool, pond fishing, play equipment, planned activities, horseshoes, sports field, v-ball. Rec open to public. Pets welcome. Open all yr. Rate in 2007 $28-45 for 5 persons. Phone: (985)878-6868.

MADISONVILLE—D-5

(NE) FAIRVIEW-RIVERSIDE STATE PARK—(St. Tammany) *From jct Hwy 21 & Hwy 22: Go 1 mi E on Hwy 22.* FACILITIES: 81 sites, typical site width 30 ft, 81 W&E, (30 & 50 amps), tenting, dump station, non-guest dumping $, laundry, grills. RECREATION: boating, canoeing, ramp, river fishing, playground, hiking trails. Rec open to public. Pets welcome. Partial handicap access. Open all yr. Phone: (888)677-3247.

MANDEVILLE—D-5

(SE) FOUNTAINEBLEAU STATE PARK—(St. Tammany) *From jct Hwy 59 & US 190: Go 4 mi E on US 190.* FACILITIES: 303 sites, 66 W&E, (30 & 50 amps), 237 no hkups, 66 pull-thrus, tenting, dump station, laundry, grills. RECREATION: swim pool, lake swimming, boating, lake fishing, playground, hiking trails. Rec open to public. Pets welcome. Open all yr. Phone: (888)677-3668.

(N) ST. TAMMANY PARISH TOURIST & CONVENTION COMMISSION—*From jct I-12 (exit 65) & US 59: Go 1/4 mi N on US 59. Enter on L.* Tourism office for information on camping, attractions and special events. Brochures & quarterly newspaper detailing local festivals, shopping, restaurants & activities. Boardwalk nature trail on site. Open all yr. Phone: (800)634-9443.

e-mail: info@louisiananorthshore.com

SEE AD TRAVEL SECTION PAGE 293

MANSFIELD—B-2

(E) NEW ROCKDALE RADIO SHOP—*From jct I-49 (exit 172) & US 84: Go 4-1/4 mi W on US 84, then 1/4 mi S on Hwy 522. Enter on L.* Complete CB Radio Sales, installation & repair. Parts & accessories on site with RV Park. Open all yr. MC/VISA/DISC/AMEX. Phone: (318)871-6380.

e-mail: zeslott@cmaaccess.com

SEE AD THIS PAGE

(E) NEW ROCKDALE RV PARK—(De Soto) *From jct I-49 (exit 172) & US 84: Go 4-1/4 mi W on US 84, then 1/4 mi S on Hwy 522. Enter on L.*

◇◇◇FACILITIES: 86 sites, typical site width 26 ft, 86 full hkups, (20, 30 & 50 amps), 50 amps ($), 5 pull-thrus, cable on-site Internet access (needs activ), laundry, LP gas by weight/by meter.

◇RECREATION: pond fishing.

Pets welcome. Partial handicap access. No tents. Open all yr. Big rigs welcome. Rate in 2007 $20-26 for 2 persons. MC/VISA/DISC/AMEX. Phone: (318)871-6380.

e-mail: zeslott@cmaaccess.com

SEE AD THIS PAGE

Louisiana State Gem: Agate

MANY—B-2

(W) Bridge Bay Resort (RV SPACES)—(Sabine) *From NW jct US 171 & Hwy 6: Go 15 mi W on Hwy 6. Enter on L.* FACILITIES: 10 sites, typical site width 20 ft, 34 ft max RV length, 10 full hkups, (20, 30 & 50 amps), some extended stay sites, 7 pull-thrus, laundry, ice. RECREATION: pavilion, boating, ramp, dock, lake fishing. Pets welcome. No tents. Open all yr. Rate in 2007 $25 per vehicle. Phone: (318)256-6604.

(SW) CYPRESS BEND PARK/TOLEDO BEND LAKE (Sabine River Auth. Site 11)—(Sabine) *From jct US 171 & Hwy 6: Go 12 mi W on Hwy 6, then 3 mi S on Hwy 191. Enter on R.* FACILITIES: 67 sites, typical site width 20 ft, 26 full hkups, 41 W&E, (30 amps), some extended stay sites, tenting, dump station, non-guest dumping $, laundry, ice, grills. RECREATION: pavilion, lake swimming, boating, ramp, dock, lake fishing, playground, v-ball. Rec open to public. Pets welcome. Partial handicap access. Open all yr. 35 sites are monthly rentals. Member ARVC, LCOA. Phone: (318)256-4118.

MARKSVILLE—C-3

(W) AVOYELLES PARISH TOURISM COMMISSION—*From jct Hwy 107 & Hwy 115 (S Main St): Go 2 blocks N on S Main St. Enter on R.* Historic swamp and home tours, museums, French Acadian Culture, festivals, parades, casinos, agricultural attractions, hunting and fishing. Open all yr. Phone: (318)253-0585.

SEE AD TRAVEL SECTION PAGE 297

(S) PARAGON CASINO—*From jct LA 452 & Hwy 1: Go 3/4 mi S on Hwy 1. Enter on L.* Spacious, land based casino with supervised kids activity center, new 18 hole golf course, four restaurants & buffet. Over 2,000 slot machines. Table games and poker room. Great entertainment. Open 7 days a week, 24 hours. Open all yr. MC/VISA/DISC/DC. ATM. Phone: (800)946-1946.

SEE AD TRAVEL SECTION PAGE 291 AND AD DISCOVER SECTION PAGE 55

(S) PARAGON CASINO RV RESORT—(Avoyelles) *From jct LA 452 & Hwy 1: Go 1 mi S on Hwy 1, then 1/4 mi E on Slim Lemoine Rd. Enter on L.*

◇◇◇◇◇FACILITIES: 185 sites, typical site width 35 ft, 185 full hkups, (20, 30 & 50 amps), 166 pull-thrus, cable TV, wireless Instant Internet access at site ($), phone Internet access central location, cabins, dump station, non-guest dumping, laundry, ice, tables, patios.

◇◇◇◇◇RECREATION: rec room/area, equipped pavilion, 2 swim pools, whirlpool, golf nearby, playground, 4 shuffleboard courts, planned activities, horseshoes, sports field, v-ball. Rec open to public.

Pets welcome. Partial handicap access. No tents. Open all yr. Big rigs welcome. Internet friendly. Clubs welcome. Rate in 2007 $12.95-25.90 per vehicle. MC/VISA/DISC/AMEX/DC/Debit. ATM. Phone: (800)946-1946.

e-mail: avodlc@paragoncasinoresort.com

SEE AD TRAVEL SECTION PAGE 291 AND AD DISCOVER SECTION PAGE 55

METAIRIE—D-5

(SW) BENT'S RV—*From jct I-10 (exit 223B) & SR 49/Williams Blvd: Go 2 mi S on SR 49/Williams Blvd, then 1-1/4 mi E on US 61 (Airline Dr.) Enter on L.* Windshield repair. SALES: travel trailers, 5th wheels, motor homes, mini-motor homes, fold-down camping trailers, pre-owned unit sales. SERVICES: full-time mech, RV appliance repair, sells parts/accessories, installs hitches. Open all yr. MC/VISA/DISC/Debit. Phone: (866) 617-2368.

e-mail: rvsales@bentsrv.com

SEE AD NEW ORLEANS PAGE 315

MINDEN—A-2

(SW) Interstate RV Park (RV SPACES)—(Webster) *From jct I-20 (exit 38) & Goodwill Rd: Go 1 block S on Goodwill Rd. Enter on L.* FACILITIES: 27 sites, typical site width 22 ft, accepts full hkup units only, 27 full hkups, (20 & 50 amps), many extended stay sites, 27 pull-thrus, laundry. Pets welcome. No tents. Open all yr. Rate in 2007 $20 per vehicle. Phone: (318)377-1155.

(W) LAKESIDE RV PARK—(Webster) *From jct I-20 (exit 44) and Hwy 79/80: Go N 1/4 mi to Hwy 79/80, then E 1 mi on Hwy 79/80. Enter on R.*

WELCOME

◆◆◆◆FACILITIES: 39 sites, typical site width 28 ft, 39 full hkups, (20, 30 & 50 amps), some extended stay sites, 4 pull-thrus, wireless Instant Internet access at site, wireless Internet access central location, tenting, laundry.

◆RECREATION: lake swimming, lake fishing, hiking trails.

Pets welcome. Partial handicap access. Open all yr. Big rigs welcome. Internet friendly. Rate in 2007 $20 per vehicle.

SEE AD THIS PAGE

MONROE—A-3

See listings at Bastrop, Sterlington & West Monroe

(W) BIEDENHARN MUSEUM & GARDENS—*From jct I-20 (exit 115) & Mill St: Go 1/2 mi NE on Mill St, then continue NE on Hwy 80, then 1 mi NW on Riverside Dr. Enter on R.* Tours of Biedenharn home, built by Joseph Biedenharn, (first bottler of Coca-Cola) bible museum and formal gardens. Open Mon-Sat 10 a.m.-5 p.m. & Sun 2 p.m.-5 p.m. (last tour 1 hr before close). Open all yr. Phone: (800)362-0983.

WELCOME

e-mail: bmuseum@bayou.com

SEE AD TRAVEL SECTION PAGE 297

(E) HOPE'S CAMPER CORNER—*From jct I-20 & US 165: Go 2 mi E on I-20, then 1 block S on Garrett Rd (exit 120), then 3/4 mi E on Frontage Rd. Enter on R.* SALES: travel trailers, 5th wheels, motor homes, mini-motor homes, pre-owned unit sales. SERVICES: full-time mech, RV appliance repair, body work/collision repair, LP gas by weight/by meter, sells parts/accessories, installs hitches. Open all yr. MC/VISA/DISC/AMEX. Phone: (318)345-1691.

WELCOME

e-mail: hopes@hopescampers.com

SEE AD THIS PAGE

MONROE—Continued

(E) MONROE'S SHILOH CAMPGROUND & RV RESORT—(Ouachita) *From jct I-20 & US 165: Go 2 mi E on I-20 to exit 120, then 1 block S at Garrett Rd, then 1-1/2 mi E on Frontage Rd. Enter on R.*

WELCOME

◆◆◆FACILITIES: 91 sites, typical site width 30 ft, 80 full hkups, 11 W&E, (20, 30 & 50 amps), 50 amps ($), 50 pull-thrus, wireless Instant Internet access at site, wireless Internet access central location, tenting, cabins, RV storage, dump station, non-guest dumping $, laundry, ltd groceries, RV supplies, ice, tables, grills.

◆◆◆◆RECREATION: rec room/area, swim pool, whirlpool, lake fishing, bsktball, playground, 2 shuffleboard courts, horseshoes, v-ball.

Pets welcome. Open all yr. Big rigs welcome. Internet friendly. Rate in 2007 $26.95-32.95 for 2 persons. MC/VISA/DISC/AMEX. Phone: (318)343-6098.

e-mail: happycamping10@aol.com

SEE AD THIS PAGE

MORGAN CITY—E-4

(N) CAJUN COAST VISITORS & CONVENTION BUREAU—*From jct Hwy 70 & US 90: Go 5-3/4 mi W on US 90. Enter on R.* Located between New Orleans & Lafayette on the banks of Bayou Teche, a sampler of evertything Louisiana offers in a friendly, relaxed atmosphere. Swamp tours, plantation homes, festivals, Casino, a Van Hagge designed golf course, Eagle tours & more. Open all yr. Phone: (800)256-2931.

WELCOME

e-mail: info@cajuncoast.com

SEE AD TRAVEL SECTION PAGE 294

(W) KEMPER WILLIAMS PARK (St. Mary Parish Park)—(St Mary) *From jct Hwy 70 & US 90: Go 5-3/4 mi W on US 90, then 1/2 mi S on Parish Rd 133. Enter on R.* FACILITIES: 209 sites, typical site width 16 ft, 44 full hkups, 165 W&E, (30 & 50 amps), 50 amps ($), 4 pull-thrus, tenting, dump station, non-guest dumping $, fire rings. RECREATION: pavilion, pond fishing, playground, tennis, sports field, hiking trails, v-ball. Rec open to public. Pets welcome. Partial handicap access. Open all yr. Big rigs welcome. Member ARVC, LCOA. Phone: (985)395-2298.

(N) LAKE END RV CAMPGROUND (Municipal Park)—(St. Mary) *From jct US 90 & Hwy 70: Go 1-1/2 mi N on Hwy 70. Enter on R.* FACILITIES: 114 sites, typical site width 36 ft, 94 full hkups, (20, 30 & 50 amps), 20 no hkups, 9 pull-thrus, tenting, dump station, non-guest dumping, laundry, ice, fire rings. RECREATION: pavilion, equipped pavilion, boating, ramp, dock, lake fishing, playground, sports field, hiking trails, v-ball. Rec open to public. Pets welcome. Partial handicap access. Open all yr. Big rigs welcome. Member ARVC, LCOA. Phone: (985)380-4623.

The Eastern Brown Pelican is Louisiana's official state bird.

NATCHITOCHES—B-2

(S) NAKATOSH CAMPGROUND—(Natchitoches) *From jct I-49 (exit 138) & Hwy 6: Go 1/4 mi W on Hwy 6. Enter on R.*

WELCOME

◆◆◆FACILITIES: 41 sites, typical site width 30 ft, 41 full hkups, (15, 20, 30 & 50 amps), some extended stay sites, 22 pull-thrus, cable TV, wireless Instant Internet access at site, wireless Internet access central location, tenting, dump station, non-guest dumping, laundry, groceries, gas, ice.

◆RECREATION: rec hall, pond fishing, horseshoes.

Pets welcome. Partial handicap access. Open all yr. Big rigs welcome. Internet friendly. Clubs welcome. Rate in 2007 $19.34 for 2 persons. MC/VISA/DISC/AMEX. ATM. Phone: (318)352-0911.

SEE AD THIS PAGE

(NW) Sibley Lake Mini-Mart & Campground (RV SPACES)—(Natchitoches) *From jct I-49 (exit 138) & Hwy 6: Go 3 mi E on Hwy 6, then 3/4 mi N on Hwy 1 Bypass. Enter on L.* FACILITIES: 34 sites, typical site width 20 ft, 32 full hkups, 2 W&E, (20, 30 & 50 amps), 50 amps ($), many extended stay sites, tenting, dump station, non-guest dumping $, laundry, ltd groceries, LP gas by weight/by meter, ice. RECREATION: lake fishing. Pets welcome. Open all yr. Rate in 2007 $20 for 2 persons. Phone: (318)352-6708.

NEW IBERIA—D-3

CHASE'S RV PARK (REBUILDING)—(Iberia) *From jct US 90 & Hwy 83: Go 2/10 mi S on Hwy 83. Enter on R.*

WELCOME

FACILITIES: 91 sites, 91 full hkups, (15, 30 & 50 amps), 50 amps ($), many extended stay sites, 8 pull-thrus, laundry, tables.

RECREATION: swim pool.

Pets welcome. No tents. Open all yr. Big rigs welcome. Rate in 2007 $20-22 for 2 persons. Phone: (337)365-9865.

SEE AD NEXT PAGE

(C) IBERIA PARISH CONVENTION & VISITORS BUREAU—*From jct US 90 (New Iberia exit) & Hwy 14: Go 1/2 mi E on Hwy 14. Enter on R.* Tourist information office for Iberia Parish that assists with itinerary planning, touring maps, brochures, tips on dining coupons and accommodations. Travel the HOT side of Acadiana. Open all yr. Phone: (337)365-1540.

WELCOME

e-mail: info@iberiaparish.com

SEE AD TRAVEL SECTION PAGE 297

NEW IBERIA—Continued on next page

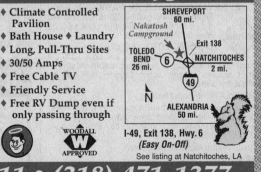

2008 RV Buyer's Guide is your best source. It contains all the information you need to make an intelligent buying decision. Over 450 vehicles are profiled with complete information about construction features, dimensions, popular options, and more, making comparing models easy. To order your copy go to www.woodalls.com/shop.

NEW ORLEANS—D-5

NEW ORLEANS AREA MAP

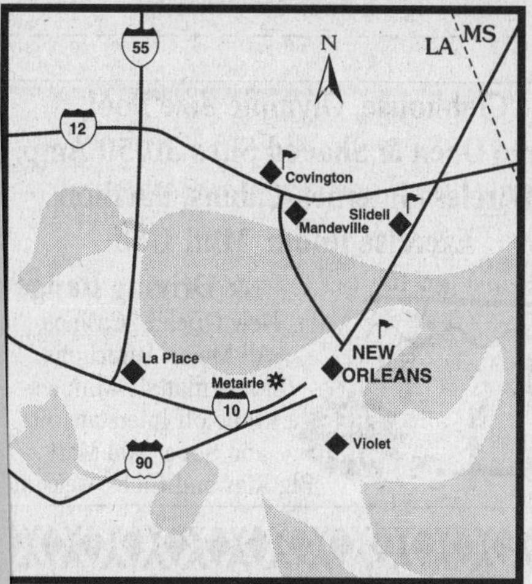

Symbols on map indicate towns within a 30 mi radius of New Orleans where campgrounds (dia-monds), attractions (flags), & RV service centers & camping supply outlets (gears) are listed. Check listings for more information.

Tell Them Woodall's Sent You!

FELIX POCHE PLANTATION RV RESORT —*From New Orleans jct Lake Pontchartrain Causeway & I-10: Go 34 mi W & N on I-10 (exit 199), then 5 mi S on 641 before Gramercy Bridge, then 12 mi N on Hwy 44. Enter on R.*

WELCOME

SEE PRIMARY LISTING AT CONVENT AND AD CONVENT PAGE 306

NEW ORLEANS—Continued

(C) FRENCH QUARTER RV RESORT—(Orleans) *From jct I-10 (exit 235A) (Orleans St/Vieux Carre) & Basin St: Go 1/4 mi S on Basin St, then 100 ft W on Crozat St (follow signs), then S through parking lot to entrance. Enter on L.*

WELCOME

◆◆◆◆FACILITIES: 52 sites, typical site width 30 ft, 52 full hkups, (50 amps), cable TV, wireless Instant Internet access at site, cable Internet access central location, laundry, ice, patios, controlled access gate.

◆◆◆◆RECREATION: rec hall, rec room/area, swim pool, whirlpool, golf nearby, planned activities, local tours.

Pets welcome. Partial handicap access. No tents. Open all yr. Big rigs welcome. Escort to site. Clubs welcome. MC/VISA/DISC/AMEX. ATM. Phone: (504)586-3000. FMCA discount.

e-mail: stay@fqrv.com

Reserve Online at Woodalls.com

SEE AD PAGE 315

NEW ORLEANS—Continued on next page

Louisiana was named in honor of King Louis XIV.

Famous Louisianan: Jazz musician Louis Armstrong—born in New Orleans

Louisiana is the only state in the union that does not have counties. Its political subdivisions are called parishes.

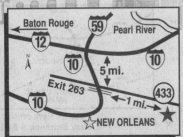

NEW ORLEANS—Continued

(NE) Jude Travel Park & Guest House (REBUILDING)—(Orleans) *From jct I-10 (exit 240B) & US 90 (Chef Menteur Hwy): Go 8 blocks E on Chef Menteur Hwy. Enter on R.* FACILITIES: 47 sites, typical site width 20 ft, 47 full hkups, (20, 30 & 50 amps), 50 amps ($), some extended stay sites, tenting, laundry, ice, tables. RECREATION: swim pool. Pets welcome. Open all yr. Internet friendly. Rate in 2007 $30-40 for 2 persons. Member ARVC, LCOA. Phone: (800)523-2196.

(W) KOA-NEW ORLEANS WEST—(Jefferson) *From jct I-10 (exit 223A) & Hwy 49 (Williams Blvd): Go 3 mi S on Hwy 49 (Williams Blvd), then 3/4 mi E on Hwy 48/3rd St (Jefferson Hwy). Enter on L.*

◆◆◆◆FACILITIES: 103 sites, typical site width 30 ft, 100 full hkups, 3 W&E, (20, 30 & 50 amps), 50 amps ($), some extended stay sites, cable TV, wireless Instant Internet access at site, wireless Internet access central location, tenting, dump station, non-guest dumping $, laundry, groceries, RV supplies, LP gas by weight/by meter, ice, tables, patios.

◆◆◆RECREATION: swim pool, bsktball, playground, horseshoes, v-ball, local tours.

Pets welcome. Partial handicap access. Open all yr. Big rigs welcome. Internet friendly. Escort to site. Clubs welcome. Rate in 2007 $30-55 for 2 persons. MC/VISA/DISC/AMEX/Debit. Member ARVC, LCOA. Phone: (504)467-1792. KOA 10% value card discount. FMCA discount.

e-mail: neworleanskoa@bellsouth.net

SEE AD PAGE 314 AND AD DISCOVER SECTION PAGES 62 & 63

(NE) Mardi Gras RV Park & Red Carpet Inn & Suites (REBUILDING)—(Orleans) *E'bound from jct I-10 (exit 240A) & Downman Rd: Go 1 block E on Chef Hwy (US 90). Entrance on right. W'bound from jct I-10 (exit 240B) & Chef Hwy (US 90): Go 2 blocks W on Chef Hwy (US 90). Enter on L.* FACILITIES: 83 sites, typical site width 30 ft, 83 full hkups, (20, 30 & 50 amps), mostly extended stay sites, 10 pull-thrus, tenting, dump station, non-guest dumping $, laundry, groceries, ice, tables, grills. RECREATION: swim pool. Pets welcome. Partial handicap access. Open all yr. Big rigs welcome. Internet friendly. Rate in 2007 $29.99 for 2 persons. Phone: (800)290-0085. FMCA discount.

NEW ORLEANS EAST KAMPGROUND—*From jct I-510 & I-10 in New Orleans: Go 21 mi NE on I-10 to exit 263, then 3/4 mi E on Hwy 433. Enter on R.*

SEE PRIMARY LISTING AT SLIDELL AND AD PAGE 314

(N) NEW ORLEANS RV CAMPGROUND (TOO NEW TO RATE)—(Orleans) *W'bnd: I-10 (exit 240B) & Chef Menteur Hwy/US 90: Go 1 mi W on Chef Menteur Hwy, then 1 mi N on France Rd. E'bnd: I-10 (exit 239B) & Louisa St: Go 250 yards N on Louisa St, then 1/4 mi E on Chef Menteur Hwy (stay right for France Rd), then 1-1/4 mi N. Enter on R.*

NEWEST CAMPGROUND IN NEW ORLEANS
Minutes off I-10 - Five miles east of the French Quarter. Full hook up sites 30/50 amp, bathhouse/laundry, free wifi & cable. Looking for an exciting vacation with authentic cajun food and great jazz - this is the place to be.

FACILITIES: 52 sites, typical site width 30 ft, 52 full hkups, (20, 30 & 50 amps), some extended stay sites, 17 pull-thrus, cable TV, wireless Instant Internet access at site, cable Internet access central location, laundry, LP gas by weight/by meter, tables, patios.

RECREATION: golf nearby.

Pets welcome, breed restrict, quantity restrict. Partial handicap access. No tents. Open all yr. Big rigs welcome. Internet friendly. Escort to site. Clubs welcome. Rate in 2007 $40-50 for 6 persons. MC/VISA. Member ARVC, LCOA. Phone: (504)274-0824. FMCA discount.

e-mail: info@neworleansrvcampground.com

SEE AD PAGE 314

PINE CREST RV PARK—*From jct I-510 & I-10: Go 16 mi E on I-10, then 1/4 mi SE on Hwy 433 (exit 263).*

SEE PRIMARY LISTING AT SLIDELL AND AD PAGE 313

(NE) Riverboat RV Park (REBUILDING)—(Orleans) *W-bnd from jct I-10 (exit 240B) & US 90 (Chef Menteur Hwy): Go 50 yards W on Chef Menteur Hwy. Entrance on left. E-bnd from I-10 (exit 240A) & Downman Rd: Go 1/4 mi N on Downman Rd, then 1/4 mi E*

Riverboat RV Park—Continued on next page

Because Covington is in a region referred to as the Ozone Belt, it has long been known for its clean air and water.

Louisiana was the 18th state admitted to the Union.

on US 90E (Chef Hwy). Enter on R. FACILITIES: 67 sites, typical site width 18 ft, 67 full hkups, (20, 30 & 50 amps), mostly extended stay sites, tenting, laundry. RECREATION: swim pool. Pets welcome. Open all yr. Big rigs welcome. Internet friendly. Rate in 2007 $25-28 for 2 persons. Phone: (504)246-2628. FMCA discount.

OIL CITY—A-2

(N) EARL WILLIAMSON PARK/CADDO LAKE PARK (Caddo Parish)—(Caddo) *From jct Hwy 220 & Hwy 1 (N Market): Go 18 mi N on Hwy 1.* FACILITIES: 25 sites, 10 W&E, 15 no hkups, tenting, dump station, fire rings, grills, wood. RECREATION: lake swimming, boating, canoeing, ramp, dock, lake fishing, playground, tennis, sports field, v-ball. Rec open to public. Pets welcome. Open all yr. Phone: (318)995-7139.

OPELOUSAS—D-3

(S) OPELOUSAS CITY PARK—(St. Landry) *From jct I-49 & US 190: Go 2 mi W on Hwy 190 (Landry), then 1/2 mi S on S Market St. Enter at end.* FACILITIES: 68 sites, typical site width 20 ft, 68 W&E, (20 & 30 amps), 30 pull-thrus, tenting, dump station, ice. RECREATION: pavilion, swim pool, playground, tennis, horseshoes, sports field, v-ball. Rec open to public. Pets welcome. Open all yr. Facilities fully operational mid May thru mid Aug. No showers. Phone: (337)948-2562.

PINE PRAIRIE—C-3

(NW) CROOKED CREEK REC. AREA—(Evangeline) *From jct Hwy 106 & Hwy 13 & Hwy 3187 (1 mi N of Pine Prairie): Go 4-1/2 mi W on Hwy 3187 to Entrance Rd, then 1/2 mi N on Entrance Rd. Enter at end.* FACILITIES: 150 sites, 10 full hkups, 140 W&E, (50 amps), tenting, dump station, laundry, ice, fire rings, grills, wood. RECREATION: pavilion, lake swimming, boating, canoeing, ramp, dock, motorboat rentals, lake fishing, playground, v-ball. Rec open to public. Pets welcome. Partial handicap access. Open Feb thru Nov. Internet friendly. Phone: (337)599-2661.

PORT ALLEN—D-4

(W) CAJUN COUNTRY CAMPGROUND—(West Baton Rouge) *From jct I-10 (exit 151) & Hwy 415: Go 3/4 mi N on Hwy 415, then 1/2 mi W on Hwy 76 (Rosedale Rd), then 1/2 mi W on Rebelle Lane. Enter on L.*

WELCOME

◆◆◆FACILITIES: 77 sites, typical site width 35 ft, 77 full hkups, (20, 30 & 50 amps), 50 amps ($), some extended stay sites, 54 pull-thrus, phone

Internet access central location, laundry, ltd groceries, RV supplies, LP gas by weight/by meter, ice, tables, wood.

◆◆◆RECREATION: rec room/area, equipped pavilion, coin games, swim pool, pond fishing, bsktball, play equipment, horseshoes, hiking trails, v-ball.

Pets welcome, breed restrict. No tents. Open all yr. Big rigs welcome. Clubs welcome. Rate in 2007 $22-27.72 per vehicle. MC/VISA. Member ARVC, LCOA. Phone: (800)264-8554. FCRV 10% discount. FMCA discount.

SEE AD BATON ROUGE PAGE 304

RAYNE—D-3

(C) CITY OF RAYNE RV PARK—(Acadia) *From jct I-10 (exit 87) & Hwy 98/35: Go 1/4 mi S on Hwy 98/35, then 200 yards W on Oak St, then NW on Gossen Memorial Dr to Frog Festival Blvd. Enter at end.* FACILITIES: 737 sites, typical site width 22 ft, 737 W&E, (20, 30 & 50 amps), dump station. RECREATION: rec hall, rec room/area, pavilion, swim pool, sports field. Pets welcome. Partial handicap access. No tents. Open all yr. Big rigs welcome. Phone: (337)334-6607.

RUSTON—A-3

(N) LINCOLN PARISH PARK—(Lincoln) *From jct I-20 (exit 86) & Hwy 33: Go 3-1/4 mi N on Hwy 33. Enter on L.* FACILITIES: 45 sites, 33 full hkups, (20, 30 & 50 amps), 12 no hkups, 4 pull-thrus, tenting, patios, fire rings, wood. RECREATION: rec hall, pavilion, equipped pavilion, lake swimming, boating, electric motors only, canoeing, ramp, dock, lake fishing, playground, sports field, hiking trails. Rec open to public. Pets welcome. Partial handicap access. Open all yr. Gate closes 5 pm Winter/7 pm Summer. Call ahead for gate code if arriving after close. Phone: (318)251-5156.

(C) RUSTON/LINCOLN CONVENTION & VISITORS BUREAU—*From jct I-20 (exit 85) & US 167S: Go 1 mi S to Mississippi, then 1 block E on Mississippi. Enter on R.* Area information on the MANY & VARIED attractions & activities including: 4 yearly festivals, museums, special events, Nat' mountain bike races, antique & specialty shops, over 100 craftsmen & artists, passion play, hunting & fishing. Mon-Fri 8:30-5. Open all yr. Phone: (800)392-9032.

WELCOME

e-mail: tbush@rustonlincoln.com

SEE AD TRAVEL SECTION PAGE 297

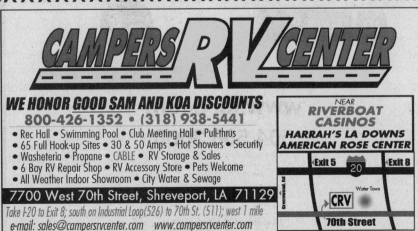

ST. FRANCISVILLE—C-4

(SE) Green Acres Campground & RV Park—(West Feliciana) *From jct US 61 & Hwy 965: Go 3 mi E on Hwy 965. Enter on L.* ◆◆◆FACILITIES: 48 sites, 46 full hkups, (30 & 50 amps), 50 amps ($), 2 no hkups, some extended stay sites, 4 pull-thrus, tenting, laundry, ice, tables. ◆◆RECREATION: equipped pavilion, swim pool, pond fishing. Pets welcome. Partial handicap access. Open all yr. Internet friendly. Rate in 2007 $20-23 for 2 persons. Phone: (225)635-4903.

ST. JOSEPH—B-4

(E) LAKE BRUIN STATE PARK—(Tensas) *From jct US 65 & Hwy 607: Go 1 mi E on Hwy 607, then 1/2 mi N on Hwy 605, then 7 mi E on Hwy 604, then 1/2 mi SW on Lake Bruin St.* FACILITIES: 25 sites, 35 ft max RV length, 25 W&E, (30 & 50 amps), 1 pull-thrus, dump station, laundry, grills. RECREATION: pavilion, lake swimming, boating, ramp, 5 rowboat rentals, lake fishing, playground. Rec open to public. Pets welcome. Partial handicap access. No tents. Open all yr. Phone: (888)677-2784.

(N) SHILOH'S LAKE BRUIN RESORT—(Tensas) *From Hwy 128 & US 65: Go 4-1/2 mi N on US 65, then 1 block E on Hwy 607, then 1/2 mi SW on Hwy 605. Enter on L.*

WELCOME

◆◆◆FACILITIES: 87 sites, typical site width 25 ft, 37 full hkups, 50 W&E, (20, 30 & 50 amps), 50 amps ($), 37 pull-thrus, wireless Instant Internet access at site, wireless Internet access central location, tenting, RV/park trailer rentals, RV storage, dump station, non-guest dumping $, portable dump, laundry, groceries, RV supplies, ice, tables, patios, grills, wood.

◆◆◆◆RECREATION: rec room/area, pavilion, coin games, swim pool, whirlpool, boating, ramp, dock, 4 pontoon/2 pedal boat/motorboat rentals, lake fishing, fishing supplies, mini-golf ($), playground, shuffleboard court, horseshoes, sports field, v-ball.

Pets welcome. Open all yr. Big rigs welcome. Internet friendly. Clubs welcome. Rate in 2007 $19-29.95 per vehicle. MC/VISA/DISC/AMEX/DC. Phone: (318)766-3334. FMCA discount.

e-mail: happycamping10@aol.com

Reserve Online at Woodalls.com

SEE AD MONROE PAGE 312

ST. MARTINVILLE—D-3

(E) LAKE FAUSSE POINTE STATE PARK—(Iberia) *From jct Hwy 96 & Hwy 679: Go 4 mi E on Hwy 679, then 4 mi E on Hwy 3083, then 7-1/2 mi S on W Atchafalaya protection levee road.* FACILITIES: 50 sites, 35 ft max RV length, 50 W&E, (20, 30 & 50 amps), tenting, dump station, laundry, grills. RECREATION: pavilion, boating, canoeing, ramp, dock, 8 rowboat/6 canoe rentals, lake/stream fishing, playground, hiking trails. Rec open to public. Pets welcome. Open all yr. Phone: (888)677-7200.

SHREVEPORT—A-2

(W) CAMPERS RV CENTER—*From jct I-20 (exit 8) & Hwy-526: Go 1/2 mi S on Hwy-526 (Industrial Loop), then 1-1/2 mi W on Hwy-511 (W 70th St). Enter on R.* SALES: travel trailers, 5th wheels, motor homes, mini-motor homes, preowned unit sales. SERVICES: full-time mech, RV appliance repair, body work/collision repair, bus. hrs emerg rd svc, LP gas by weight/by meter, dump station, RV storage, sells parts/accessories, installs hitches. Open all yr. MC/VISA/DISC/AMEX/Debit. Phone: (800)426-1352. FCRV 10% discount.

WELCOME

e-mail: sales@campersrvcenter.com

SEE AD THIS PAGE

(W) CAMPERS RV CENTER—(Caddo) *From jct I-20 (exit 8) & Hwy 526): Go 1/2 mi S on Hwy 526 (Industrial Loop), then 1-1/2 mi W on Hwy 511 W 70th St. Enter on R.*

WELCOME

◆◆◆FACILITIES: 58 sites, typical site width 30 ft, 58 full hkups, (20, 30 & 50 amps), mostly extended stay sites, 7 pull-thrus, cable TV, phone/cable on-site Internet access (needs activ), RV storage, dump station, non-guest dumping $, laundry, RV supplies, LP gas by meter, ice.

◆RECREATION: rec room/area, swim pool.

Pets welcome. No tents. Open all yr. Big rigs welcome. Clubs welcome. Rate in 2007 $27.47 for 2 persons. MC/VISA/DISC/AMEX/Debit. Phone: (800)426-1352.

e-mail: sales@campersrvcenter.com

SEE AD THIS PAGE

SHREVEPORT—Continued on next page

Van Cliburn, concern pianist, is from Louisiana.

SHREVEPORT—Continued

CASH POINT LANDING—*From Shreveport(jct Hwy 71 & I-220): Go 2 mi E on I-220, then 3-3/4 mi N on Hwy 3. Enter on L.*

SEE PRIMARY LISTING AT BOSSIER CITY AND AD THIS PAGE

(C) Kelly's RV Park—(Caddo) *E'bound from jct I-20 (exit 5) & Hwy 80: Go 50 yards N on Hwy 80, then 200 yards W on service road. W'bound: Continue straight across Hwy 80, then 200 yards W on service road. Enter on R.* ◊◊◊◊FACILITIES: 44 sites, typical site width 25 ft, 44 full hkups, (20, 30 & 50 amps), some extended stay sites, 10 pull-thrus, laundry, groceries, ice, tables, patios. ◊◊RECREATION: swim pool. Pets welcome. No tents. Open all yr. Big rigs welcome. Rate in 2007 $22 per vehicle. Phone: (318) 938-6360.

(W) KOA-SHREVEPORT/BOSSIER CITY—(Caddo) *From I-20 (exit 10): Go 3/4 mi S on Pines Rd, then 1 mi W on W 70th St. From jct I-49 (exit 201) & Hwy 3132 go: 6 1/4 mi W on Hwy 3132, then 2 mi W on W 70th. Enter on R.*

◊◊◊◊FACILITIES: 93 sites, typical site width 25 ft, 83 full hkups, 10 E, (15, 20, 30 & 50 amps), 50 amps ($), some extended stay sites, 51 pull-thrus, cable TV, wireless Instant Internet access at site, phone Internet access central location, tenting, cabins, dump station, non-guest dumping $, laundry, ltd groceries, RV supplies, LP gas by weight/by meter, ice, tables, patios, grills.

◊◊◊◊RECREATION: rec hall, rec room/area, coin games, swim pool, whirlpool, pond fishing, fishing supplies, golf nearby, bsktball, playground, horseshoes, sports field, v-ball.

Pets welcome, breed restrict. Partial handicap access. Open all yr. Pool open May 1. Big rigs welcome. Internet friendly. Clubs welcome. Rate in 2007 $24-69 for 2 persons. MC/VISA/DISC/AMEX/Debit. Phone: (318)687-1010. KOA 10% value card discount.

e-mail: shreveportkoa@bellsouth.net

SEE AD PAGE 316 AND AD DISCOVER SECTION PAGES 62 & 63

(C) SHREVEPORT/BOSSIER CONVENTION & TOURIST BUREAU—*From jct I-20 (exit 19A) & Spring St: Go 2 blocks N on Spring St. Enter on R.*

GAMING & PLAYING ON THE RED RIVER

Galloping Ponies, tumbling dice, spinning slots & the unique ark-la-tex heritage await you on the Red River in Shreveport-Bossier! www.shreveport-bossier.org 1-888-4SVISIT ext 805.

Contact for information on camping & attractions in the Shreveport-Bossier City area. Open all yr. Phone: (800)551-8682.

e-mail: info@sbctb.org

SEE AD TRAVEL SECTION PAGE 295

SLIDELL—D-5

(S) NEW ORLEANS EAST KAMPGROUND (REBUILDING)—(St. Tammany) *From jct I-59/I-12 & I-10: Go 4 mi SW on I-10 (exit 263), then 3/4 mi E on Hwy 433. Enter on R.*

FACILITIES: 107 sites, typical site width 20 ft, 84 full hkups, 23 W&E, (15, 20, 30 & 50 amps), some extended stay sites, 92 pull-thrus, wireless Instant Internet access at site, wireless Internet access central location, tenting, cabins, RV storage, dump station, non-guest dumping $, laundry, ltd groceries, RV supplies, LP gas by weight/by meter, ice, tables.

RECREATION: swim pool, stream fishing, mini-golf, v-ball, local tours.

SLIDELL—Continued
NEW ORLEANS EAST KAMPGROUND—Continued

Pets welcome. Open all yr. Big rigs welcome. Internet friendly. Clubs welcome. Rate in 2007 $29 for 2 persons. MC/VISA/DISC/Debit. Member ARVC, LCOA. Phone: (800)562-2128.

e-mail: noeast@sonic.net

SEE AD NEW ORLEANS PAGE 314

(S) PINE CREST RV PARK—(St. Tammany) *From jct I-59/I-12 & I-10: Go 4 mi SW on I-10 (exit 263), then 1/4 mi SE on 433. Enter on R.*

◊◊◊◊FACILITIES: 160 sites, typical site width 30 ft, accepts full hkup units only, 160 full hkups, (20, 30 & 50 amps), some extended stay sites, 130 pull-thrus, cable TV ($), phone Internet access central location, RV storage, dump station, laundry, RV supplies, LP gas by weight/by meter, ice, tables, patios.

◊◊RECREATION: rec hall, rec room/area, pavilion, lake fishing, golf nearby, play equipment, local tours.

Pets welcome, breed restrict. Partial handicap access. No tents. Open all yr. Big rigs welcome. Internet friendly. Clubs welcome. Rate in 2007 $30 for 2 persons. MC/VISA. Phone: (800)879-5936.

SEE AD NEW ORLEANS PAGE 313

SPRINGFIELD—D-5

(E) TICKFAW STATE PARK—(Livingston) *From jct I-12 & Hwy 43: Go 3 mi S on Hwy 43, then 1 mi E on Hwy 42, then 6 mi W on Hwy 1037, then 1-1/4 mi E on Patterson Rd. Enter at end.* FACILITIES: 50 sites, 30 W&E, (20, 30 & 50 amps), 20 no hkups, tenting, dump station, laundry, fire rings, grills. RECREATION: pavilion, canoeing, 35 canoe rentals, river fishing, playground, horseshoes, hiking trails, v-ball. Pets welcome. Partial handicap access. Open all yr. Phone: (888)981-2020.

SPRINGHILL—A-2

(E) SPRINGHILL RV PARK (City Park)—(Webster) *From jct Hwy 157 & US 371: Go 1 block S on US 371, then 2 blocks E on West Church St. Enter on R.* FACILITIES: 30 sites, accepts full hkup units only, 30 full hkups, (50 amps), dump station, grills. RECREATION: pavilion, hiking trails. Pets welcome. No tents. Open all yr. No restrooms. Phone: (318)539-5681.

STERLINGTON—A-3

(N) Bayou Boeuf RV Park—(Ouachita) *From Jct LA 2 & US 165: Go 3 mi N on US 165. Enter on L.* ◊◊FACILITIES: 53 sites, typical site width 25 ft, accepts full hkup units only, 53 full hkups, (20, 30 & 50 amps), 50 amps ($), mostly extended stay sites, 23 pull-thrus, dump station, non-guest dumping $, laundry, ice, tables. Pets welcome. No tents. Open all yr. No restrooms. Rate in 2007 $20-22 for 2 persons. Phone: (318)665-2405.

SULPHUR—D-2

(S) HIDDEN PONDS RV PARK—(Calcasieu) *From I-10 (DeQuincy, exit 21): Go 1-1/2 mi S to Ravia Rd, then 1/4 mi E on Ravia Rd. Enter on L.*

◊◊◊FACILITIES: 169 sites, typical site width 25 ft, 169 full hkups, (30 & 50 amps), some extended stay sites, 104 pull-thrus, wireless Instant Internet access at site, phone Internet access central location, cabins, laundry.

◊◊RECREATION: rec hall, rec room/area, pond fishing, sports field.

Pets welcome. Partial handicap access. No tents. Open all yr. Big rigs welcome. Internet friendly. Escort to site. Clubs welcome. Rate in 2007 $27 for 2 persons. MC/VISA. Member ARVC, LCOA. Phone: (800)440-4709. FCRV 10% discount. FMCA discount.

e-mail: hiddenponds@camtel.net

SEE AD LAKE CHARLES PAGE 310

TOLEDO BEND LAKE—B-2

See listings at Hornbeck, Many and Zwolle.

VIDALIA—B-4

(S) River View RV Park—(Concordia) *From jct US Hwy 65/84 & SR 131 (west end of Mississippi River Bridge): Go 1 mi S on SR 131, then one block E on Black Top Rd. Enter at end.* ◊◊◊FACILITIES: 197 sites, typical site width 35 ft, 192 full hkups, 5 W&E, (15, 20, 30 & 50 amps), 50 amps ($), 120 pull-thrus, tenting, laundry, ltd groceries, LP gas by weight/by meter, ice. ◊◊◊◊RECREATION: rec room/area, pavilion, swim pool, playground, hiking trails. Pets welcome. Partial handicap access. Open all yr. Big rigs welcome. Internet friendly. Rate in 2007 $27-32 for 2 persons. Member ARVC, LCOA. Phone: (318)336-1400. FCRV 10% discount. FMCA discount.

VILLE PLATTE—C-3

(N) CHICOT STATE PARK—(Evangeline) *From jct Hwy 29 & US 167: Go 3 mi W on US 167, then 7 mi N on Hwy 3042.* FACILITIES: 200 sites, 200 W&E, (20 & 30 amps), 7 pull-thrus, tenting, dump station, laundry, ice, grills, wood. RECREATION: pavilion, swim pool, boating, canoeing, ramp, dock, 13 rowboat/12 canoe rentals, lake fishing, playground, hiking trails. Rec open to public. Pets welcome. Open all yr. Phone: (888)677-2442.

VINTON—D-2

(SW) Texas Pelican Complex (RV SPACES)—(Calcasieu) *From jct I-10 (exit 4) & Hwy 109: Go 3/10 mi S on Hwy 109. Enter on R.* FACILITIES: 34 sites, typical site width 25 ft, 34 full hkups, (20, 30 & 50 amps), 50 amps ($), some extended stay sites, 8 pull-thrus, heater not allowed, tenting, dump station, non-guest dumping $, laundry, ltd groceries. Pets welcome. Partial handicap access. Open all yr. Rate in 2007 $10-16 for 2 persons. Phone: (337)589-5239.

(SE) V RV PARK-LAKE CHARLES/VINTON (REBUILDING)—(Calcasieu) *From jct I-10 (exit 8 Vinton) & Hwy-108: Go 1/10 mi N on Hwy-108, then 1/10 mi W on Goodwin St. Enter on L.*

FACILITIES: 141 sites, typical site width 30 ft, 141 full hkups, (20, 30 & 50 amps), 50 amps ($), 67 pull-thrus, wireless Instant Internet access at site, wireless Internet access central location, tenting, cabins, RV storage, dump station, non-guest dumping $, laundry, ltd groceries, RV supplies, LP gas by weight/by meter, ice, tables, patios, grills.

RECREATION: rec hall, rec room/area, pavilion, swim pool, golf nearby, playground, shuffleboard court, sports field, v-ball, local tours.

Pets welcome, breed restrict. Partial handicap access. Open all yr. Big rigs welcome. Internet friendly. Escort to site. Clubs welcome. Rate in 2007 $23-25.50 for 2 persons. MC/VISA/DISC/AMEX/Debit. Member ARVC. Phone: (337)589-2300. FMCA discount.

e-mail: vintonrv@bellsouth.net

SEE AD LAKE CHARLES PAGE 310

VIOLET—D-5

(E) SAINT BERNARD STATE PARK—(St. Bernard) *From jct I-510, I-10 & Hwy 47: Go 8 mi S on Hwy 47, then 10-1/2 mi E on Hwy 39. Enter on R.* FACILITIES: 51 sites, 51 W&E, tenting, dump station, laundry, grills. RECREATION: pavilion, swim pool, playground, hiking trails. Rec open to public. Pets welcome. Open all yr. Phone: (888)677-7823.

WEST MONROE—A-3

(NW) Bayou D'Arbonne Camping (RV SPACES)—(Ouachita) *From jct I-20 (Mill St exit 115) & Hwy 34: Go 1/4 mi NE on Hwy 34, then 4-1/2 mi N on Hwy 143, then 1/4 mi NE on G.B. Cooley Rd, then 1/4 mi E on Pinecrest Rd. Enter on L.* FACILITIES: 24 sites, typical

Bayou D'Arbonne Camping—Continued on next page

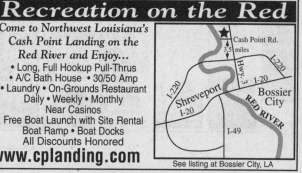

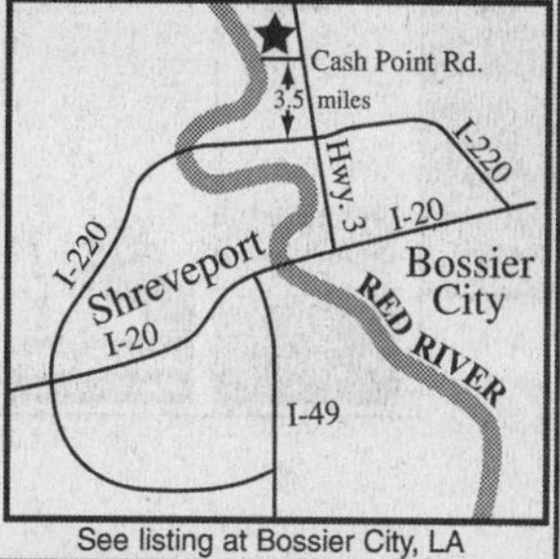

WEST MONROE—Continued
Bayou D'Arbonne Camping—Continued

site width 15 ft, 24 full hkups, (20, 30 & 50 amps), 50 amps ($), many extended stay sites, 1 pull-thrus, tenting, tables, wood. RECREATION: canoeing, river fishing, play equipment. Pets welcome. Open all yr. Rate in 2007 $14-15 for 2 persons. Phone: (318)396-1025.

(W) **CARTER'S CAMPING CENTER**—*From I-20 (Cheniere exit 108): Go 100 yards N on Cheniere. Enter on R.* SALES: travel trailers, park trailers, truck campers, 5th wheels, fold-down camping trailers, pre-owned unit sales. SERVICES: full-time mech, RV appliance repair, body work/collision repair, RV rentals, sells parts/accessories, installs hitches. Open all yr. MC/VISA/DISC/AMEX. Phone: (318)396-2225.

e-mail: hrjrec@bellsouth.net

SEE AD PAGE 317

(SW) **PAVILION RV PARK**—(Ouachita) *From jct I-20 (exit 112) & Well Rd: Go 1/4 mi S on Well Rd. Enter on L.*

◊◊◊◊FACILITIES: 104 sites, typical site width 32 ft, 104 full hkups, (15, 20, 30 & 50 amps), some extended stay sites, 29 pull-thrus, cable TV, wireless Instant Internet access at site ($), phone Internet access central location, cabins, laundry, ltd groceries, RV supplies, LP gas by weight/by meter.

WEST MONROE—Continued
PAVILION RV PARK—Continued

◊◊◊RECREATION: rec hall, rec room/area, pavilion, coin games, 2 swim pools, lake fishing, golf nearby, playground.

Pets welcome. Partial handicap access. No tents. Open all yr. Pool open May 1. Big rigs welcome. Internet friendly. Escort to site. Clubs welcome. Rate in 2007 $28 per vehicle. MC/VISA/DISC/Debit. Member ARVC, LCOA. Phone: (888)322-4216. FCRV 10% discount. FMCA discount.

e-mail: kmk@pavrv.com

SEE AD MONROE PAGE 312 AND AD TRAVEL SECTION PAGE 296

WHITEHALL—B-3

(NE) **Old River Campground**—(La Salle) *From jct Hwy 28 & US 84: Go 4 mi N on US 84, then 1/4 mi E on Old River Loop. Enter at end.* ◊◊◊FACILITIES: 18 sites, typical site width 22 ft, 14 full hkups, 4 W&E, (15, 20, 30 & 50 amps), 50 amps ($), some extended stay sites, 1 pull-thrus, tenting, tables. ◊RECREATION: river/pond fishing, sports field. Pets welcome. Open all yr. Rate in 2007 $15-18 for 4 persons. Phone: (318)992-6695.

WOODWORTH—C-3

(SE) INDIAN CREEK RECREATION AREA (Alexander SF)—(Rapides) *From town: Follow signs E off US-165.* FACILITIES: 109 sites, typical site width 20 ft, 109 W&E, (30 & 50 amps), 17 pull-thrus, tenting, dump station, fire rings, grills. RECREATION: pavilion, lake swimming, boating, canoeing, ramp, dock, lake fishing, playground, hiking trails. Rec open to public. Pets welcome. Partial handicap access. Open all yr. No reservations. Phone: (318)487-5058.

ZWOLLE—B-2

(W) NORTH TOLEDO BEND STATE PARK—(Sabine) *From jct Hwy 482 & Hwy 3229: Go 4 mi SW on Hwy 3229.* FACILITIES: 63 sites, 63 W&E, (20 & 30 amps), tenting, dump station, laundry, ice, fire rings, grills, wood. RECREATION: swim pool, boating, canoeing, ramp, 4 rowboat/4 canoe/4 pedal boat rentals, lake fishing, playground, hiking trails. Rec open to public. Pets welcome. Partial handicap access. Open all yr. Phone: (888) 677-6400.

(SW) SAN MIGUEL PARK/TOLEDO BEND LAKE (Sabine River Auth. Site 7-A)—(Sabine) *From jct Hwy 191 & Carter Ferry Rd: Go 2 mi W on Carter Ferry Rd. Enter on R.* FACILITIES: 40 sites, typical site width 25 ft, 20 full hkups, 20 W&E, (20 & 30 amps), tenting, dump station, ice, grills. RECREATION: pavilion, boating, ramp, dock, lake fishing, playground. Open all yr. Member ARVC, LCOA. Phone: (318)645-6748.

Find a park or campground Woodall's does not list? Tell us about it! Use Reader Comment Forms located after the Alphabetical Quick Reference pages.

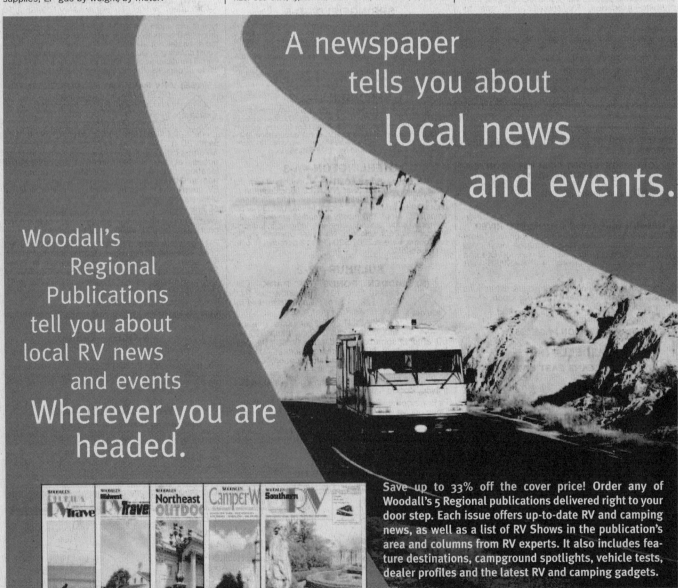

Mississippi

READER SERVICE INFO

The following businesses have placed an ad in the Mississippi Travel Section. To receive free information, enter their Reader Service number on the Reader Service Card opposite page 48/Discover Section in the front of this directory:

Advertiser	RS #
Hollywood Casino RV Resort	832
Mississippi State Parks	754
Natchez Trace Compact	3649
Plantation Pines RV Resort	3828

TIME ZONE

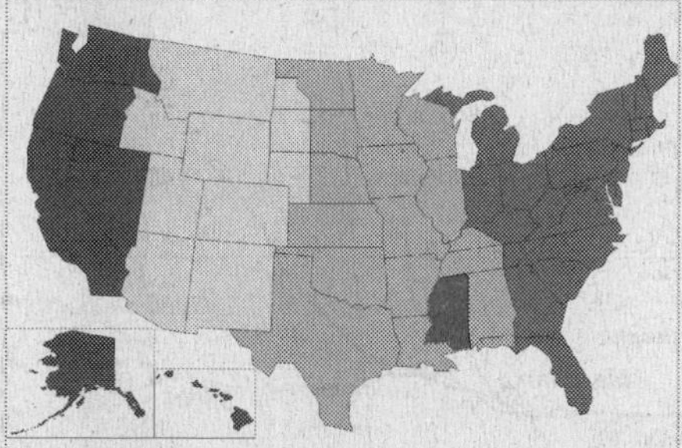

Mississippi is in the Central Time Zone.

TOPOGRAPHY

The greater part of the state is a rolling-to-hilly portion of the coastal plain, rising from the Gulf Coast to the north and west. From sea level on the Gulf Coast, elevation reaches 806 feet in northern Mississippi, though most of the state ranges from about 100 to 500 feet above sea level.

TEMPERATURE

While the state has a change of seasons, the moderate climate is mild all year. Average low in January is 50° and summer highs are in the 90s.

TRAVEL & TOURISM INFO

State Agency:
Mississippi Development Authority/ Tourism Division
PO Box 1705
Ocean Springs, MS 39566
(866/SEE-MISS)
www.visitmississippi.org

Regional Agencies:
Mississippi Gulf Coast CVB
PO Box 6128
Gulfport, MS 39506-6128
(888/467-4853 or 228/896-6699)
www.gulfcoast.org

Tenn-Tom Tourism Association
PO Drawer 671
Columbus, MS 39703
(888/Tenn-Tom or 662/328-3286)
www.tenntom.org

East Mississippi Tourism Council
PO Drawer 671
Columbus, MS 39703
(800/457-9739)
www.eastmississippi.org

Mississippi Delta Tourism Association
PO Box 68
Greenville, MS 38702
(877/DELTA-MS)
www.visitthedelta.com

Local Agencies:
For information on an area not listed here, contact the Chamber of Commerce or Tourism Bureau for the locality you are interested in visiting.

RECREATIONAL INFO

Biking: Mississippi Department of Transportation (for local cycling clubs, online maps, bike trails)
www.gomdot.com/bicycling

Birding: Audubon Mississippi (601/661-6189)
www.birdsource.org

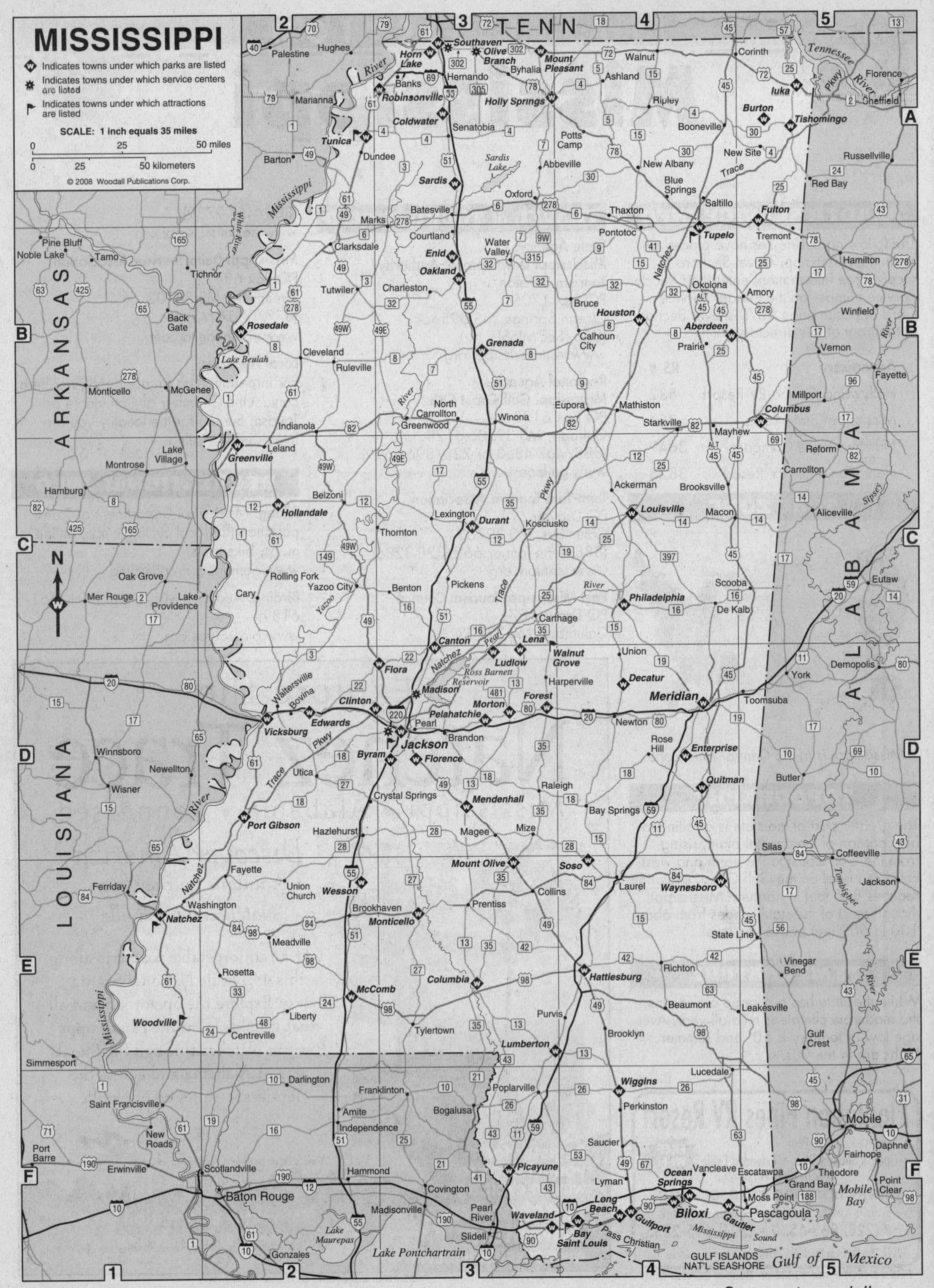
MISSISSIPPI
Indicates towns under which parks are listed
Indicates towns under which service centers are listed
Indicates towns under which attractions are listed
SCALE: 1 inch equals 35 miles
0 25 50 miles
0 25 50 kilometers
© 2008 Woodall Publications Corp.
TENN
ARKANSAS
LOUISIANA
ALABAMA
Southaven
Olive Branch
Horn Lake
Mount Pleasant
Hernando
Robinsonville
Holly Springs
Coldwater
Tunica
Senatobia
Sardis
Batesville
Oxford
Enid
Oakland
Corinth
Iuka
Burton
Tishomingo
Tupelo
Fulton
Houston
Aberdeen
Grenada
Rosedale
Greenville
Hollandale
Columbus
Louisville
Durant
Philadelphia
Canton
Lena
Ludlow
Walnut Grove
Flora
Madison
Clinton
Edwards
Vicksburg
Jackson
Byram
Florence
Pelahatchie
Morton
Forest
Decatur
Meridian
Enterprise
Quitman
Mendenhall
Port Gibson
Mount Olive
Soso
Waynesboro
Wesson
Monticello
Natchez
McComb
Columbia
Hattiesburg
Woodville
Lumberton
Wiggins
Picayune
Waveland
Bay Saint Louis
Long Beach
Gulfport
Ocean Springs
Biloxi
Gautier
Pascagoula
Mobile
Baton Rouge
Gulf of Mexico
GULF ISLANDS NAT'L SEASHORE
Lake Pontchartrain

Canoeing/Kayaking: Mississippi Canoe & Kayak Club
www.mscanoeclub.org

Fishing & Hunting: Mississippi Dept. of Wildlife, Fisheries & Parks, PO Box 451, Jackson, MS 39205-0451 (601/432-2400)
www.mdwfp.com

Golf: Mississippi Golf Information, PO Box 849, Jackson, MS 39205 (866/801-8551 or 601/359-3297)
www.visitmississippi.org/golf

Outfitters: Mississippi Outfitters and Guides Association (800/270-3358)
www.outfitters.org

SHOPPING

Factory Stores of MS, Batesville. This factory-direct outlet offers furnishings for the home, books, entertainment items, apparel and a food court. 325 Lakewood Dr., Batesville, MS (800/361-7406).
www.mississippioutletshopping.com

Gulfport Factory Stores, Gulfport. Famous-name merchandise is featured at over 70 exciting shops. A food court and playground is also on-site.10000 Factory Store Blvd., Gulfport, MS (228/867-6100).
www.gulf-coast.com/info/gpt_fact.html

Vicksburg Factory Outlet, Vicksburg. Shop at 24 nationally known stores, located across I-20 from the Vicksburg National Military Park. Off E. Clay St., overlooking I-20 at 4000 S. Frontage Rd., Vicksburg, MS (601/636-7434).
www.vicksburgfactoryoutlet.com/

DESTINATIONS

Antebellum mansions, historic homes and plantations are often open to the public through scheduled tours. Check with the local chamber of commerce in the city you are visiting for times and availability. The Mississippi Blues Trail is an unforgettable journey that allows visitors to follow the paths of blues musicians born in Mississippi. Walk where they walked, dance where they danced and experience the blues where they were born.

The Natchez Trace Parkway is renowned for its unspoiled, natural beauty. The Trace stretches diagonally across Mississippi from Natchez to Nashville, Tennessee and is lined with markers that point out important sites and fascinating history. First used by Native Americans thousands of years ago, it was later a major trade route during frontier days. Starting from Natchez, you travel through Port Gibson, Jackson, Ridgeland, Kosciusko and Tupelo. Sites along the way include magnificent antebellum homes, spectacular views of the Mississippi River, Cypress Swamp and Tishomingo State Park.

Tennessee-Tombigee Waterway. Located in the northeast corner of Mississippi, the Tenn-Tom boasts 234 miles of adventure. Thousands of acres of water and natural woodlands invite outdoor enthusiasts. Pleasure boaters and skiers delight in the easy current, while avid anglers partake in big money fishing tournaments. Nature trails, secluded campsites and abundant wildlife can be found along the Tenn-Tom's shores.

THE HILLS REGION

Corinth. Get a slugburger at Borroum's Drug Store, the oldest in the state; or stop by the Corinth Chamber of Commerce and pick up a brochure and tape describing the Corinth Driving Tour, providing hours of Civil War history.

Corinth National Cemetery/Memphis National Cemetery. This section of the Corinth Civil War Battlefield is the final resting place for 6,000 soldiers. Sadly, most of the tombstones read "Unknown Soldier."

Civil War Earthworks. Corinth has the largest number of intact Civil War earthworks in the nation. They were consructed by both the Confederate and Union armies stationed at Corinth and were used in the defense of the city.

Holly Springs. Known as the Antebellum Capital of the Mid-South, this town has over 100 antebellum structures still standing and more than 64 houses, churches and buildings that pre-date the Civil War.

Walter Place is the town's crown jewel antebellum home with a variety of architectural styles. The center section is Greek Revival, flanked by massive Medieval Gothic towers. Other attractions in Holly Springs include:

At the **Marshall County Historical Museum,** you can view artifacts that were used by the people of this county. On display are relics of wars from the War of 1812 to the Korean conflict, farm tools, quilts, as well as special Civil War rooms.

Montrose. Visit this Greek Revival brick mansion that was built in 1858 to serve as the Holly Springs Garden Club's headquarters. Today, the lushly landscaped grounds are designated as a state arboretum.

Oxford Rowan Oak. The antebellum home of Nobel prize-winner William Faulkner, the home features the outline of his novel, *A Fable*, written on the study wall.

University of Mississippi, Oxford. "Ole Miss" housed soldiers wounded from the Civil War battles of Shiloh and Corinth. Today the university provides visitors with a scenic and interesting walking tour. Don't miss the **Center for the Study of Southern Culture**—a unique research center which focuses on Southern music, history, lifestyles and folklore. University of Mississippi Blues Archives boasts an extensive blues collection including the personal collection of blues great B.B. King.

Tupelo. Popular attractions in Tupelo include **Tupelo National Battlefield Site**, the two-room home in which Elvis Presley was born and lived as a small child and the **Natchez Trace Parkway Visitors Center** with an audio-visual program on the history of the Trace. The Tupelo Buffalo Park is a thriving park and zoo. Visitors can ride through the park in open-air trolleys and see herds of buffalo or their family of giraffes. The park also features a rare white buffalo, camels, zebra, ostriches and more. It also includes a petting zoo and a re-created Chickasaw Indian village.

Things to See & Do

BAY ST. LOUIS
Hollywood Casino

JACKSON
Mississippi State Parks

NATCHEZ
Natchez Trace Compact

TUNICA
Hollywood Casino

TUPELO
Vanelli's Greek & Italian Restaurant

WALNUT GROVE
Golden Memorial State Park

WOODVILLE
Clark Creek Nature Park

THE PINES REGION

Aberdeen. Make an appointment to tour some of Mississippi's finest antebellum and Victorian homes. You'll enjoy the beautiful **Holiday Haven** (1850), **The Magnolias** (1850) and **Victoria** (1879), just to name a few.

Antebellum homes await your arrival in lovely **Columbus. Amzi Love, Lee Home Museum, Rosewood Manor, Temple Heights** and **Tennessee Williams Home** are all open to tourists year-round. **Waverly Plantation Mansion**, circa 1852, is a four story mansion with fluted columns and wrought-iron balcony railings topped with a magnificent octagonal cupola, completely renovated to its former glory over the last 45 years by the Snow family. Also in Columbus are riverboats, offering sightseeing and romantic dinner cruises on the **Tennessee-Tombigee Waterway**. **Friendship Cemetery** is the final resting place for 2,194 Confederate soldiers who fell at the Battle of Shiloh. Set among the towering oaks and magnolias are marble cherubs and angels, making it popular with photographers and film-makers.

Dunn's Falls, Enterprise. This 65-ft. waterfall was once a power source for the neighboring Carroll Richardson grist mill, which is open for tours. Also on-site are a natural wildlife refuge and gristmill pond.

Turkey Creek Water Park, located 15 miles southwest of Decatur, is part of the **Pat Harrison Waterway District**—a series of water parks offering a variety of recreation. Turkey Creek features excellent bass fishing, boating, water-skiing, camping, biking, an old-fashioned swimming hole and beach, boat rentals, a playground and a nature trail.

THE DELTA

Belzoni. Make an appointment to tour **Mama's Dream World**—the home of **Ethel Wright Mohamed** (the "Grandma Moses of Stitchery") featuring over 100 stitchery "memory pictures." Then view beauty of another sort at **Wister Gardens** with its 14 acres of scenic gardens and domestic and exotic birds.

Chatham. Take a step back in time on the **Lake Washington Scenic Tour**. Visit **Roy's Country Store** for a cold soda and a snack of hoop cheese and crackers.

Clarksdale. Learn about Mississippi and blues history in this town. Highlights include **Cat Head Delta Blues & Folk Art, Delta Blues Museum** and **Muddy Waters Cabin Site & Marker.**

Cleveland. Built in 1915, **Cleveland Depot Library** is one of the oldest surviving buildings in Cleveland. This historic depot contains local railroad history and literacy exhibits. The **Roy Lee Wiley Planetarium** location provides educational and entertaining programs related to astronomy.

Greenville. At **Winterville Mounds** view 17 earthen structures believed to be constructed by ancient ancestors of the known Mississippi tribes—Choctaw, Chickasaw and Natchez. Stroll through the museum to view artifacts discovered in the area. Other highlights include **Greenville Air Force Base Museum, Greenville History Museum** and **The Great Wall of Mississippi,** a levee system longer and taller than the Great Wall of China, constructed by the U.S. Army Corps of Engineers.

Greenwood. Cotton is certainly king in this Mississippi Delta town. The Delta's rich and varied history is presented at the **Cottonlandia Museum**. The museum has a large collection of Mississippi art work, an extensive archaeology collection and a room dedicated to the agricultural history of the region. A life-size, walk-through diorama of a Mississippi swamp (complete with sound effects), coupled with a hands-on natural science room are always favorites of younger visitors. The Leflore County Military History exhibit displays uniforms, veteran lists, victory posters and artifacts from the wars and the homefront.

Fort Pemberton. Located on a narrow strip of land between the Yazoo and Tallahatchie rivers, the fort was named for the Confederate commander-in-chief in Mississippi. The Union gunboat Star of the West was positioned here to prevent the advancement in the Yazoo Pass expedition.

Indianola. Scheduled to open this year, the **B.B. King Museum and Delta Interpretive Center** honors the blues icon and his delta heritage. Exhibits will explore the Delta, Beale Street, WDIA radio station and B.B.'s career. Plans also include an experi-

RV Sales & Service

	SALES	SERVICE
JACKSON S & S Apache Camping Center	•	•
MADISON Camper Corral	•	•
OLIVE BRANCH Southaven RV Centers	•	•
SOUTHAVEN Southaven RV Centers	•	•

Woodall's Quick & Easy Reference for Mississippi

	BIG RIGS WELCOME	INTERNET FRIENDLY	PETS WELCOME	WEB SAVER
BAY ST. LOUIS				
Bay Hide Away RV & Camping Resort	▲	●	■	
Bay Marina & RV Park		●	■	
Hollywood Casino RV Park	▲	●	■	
Shady Acres RV Community	▲	●		
BILOXI				
Cajun RV Park	▲	●	■	
Lakeview RV Resort	▲	●	■	
Majestic Oaks RV Resort	▲	●	■	
Mazalea Travel Park	▲		■	
Parker's Landing RV Park	▲	●	■	
Southern Comfort Camping Resort	▲	●	■	
COLDWATER				
Memphis South Campground & RV Park	▲		■	
COLUMBIA				
Mimosa Landing Campground	▲	●	■	
COLUMBUS				
Lake Lowndes SP			■	
DURANT				
Holmes County SP			■	
FLORENCE				
Wendy Oaks RV Resort	▲		■	
GAUTIER				
Indian Point RV Resort	▲	●	■	
Shepard SP			■	
GRENADA				
Hugh White SP			■	
GULFPORT				
Baywood RV Park and Campground, Inc.	▲		■	
Country Side RV Park & Tradin Post	▲		■	
HATTIESBURG				
Paul B Johnson SP			■	
HOLLANDALE				
Leroy Percy SP			■	
HOLLY SPRINGS				
Wall Doxey SP			■	
HORN LAKE				
Audubon Point RV Park	▲	●	■	
IUKA				
JP Coleman SP			■	
JACKSON				
LeFleur's Bluff SP & Golf Course			■	
LONG BEACH				
Plantation Pines RV Resort		●	■	
LOUISVILLE				
Legion SP			■	
MCCOMB				
Bogue Chitto Water Park Campground (Pearl River Basin Dev. Dist.)	▲		■	
Percy Quin SP & Quail Hollow Golf Course			■	
MERIDIAN				
Benchmark Coach and RV Park	▲	●	■	
KOA-Meridian East/Toomsuba	▲	●	■	
Nanabe Creek Campground	▲	●	■	
MORTON				
Roosevelt SP			■	
NATCHEZ				
Natchez SP			■	
OAKLAND				
George Payne Cossar SP			■	
OCEAN SPRINGS				
Camp Journey's End	▲	●	■	
PHILADELPHIA				
Frog Level RV Park	▲	●	■	
PICAYUNE				
Clearwater RV Park	▲	●	■	
Sun Roamers RV Resort	▲	●	■	

▲ = Big Rigs Welcome; ● = Internet Hookups; ● = (Wi-Fi available); ■ = Pets Welcome; $ = Web Saver Coupons

Check out the "How to Use This Directory" section in the front of this book for a description of the criteria Woodall's uses in this chart.

ential hands-on Blues Studio where visitors can create their own music.

Leland. Leland is the birthplace of the Frog. This town commemorates the Delta boyhood of Jim Hensen, creator of Sesame Street. The original Muppets are displayed in addition to Henson's Christmas card designs, videos of Hensen's early television appearances as well as other various memorabilia.

Tunica. While this town is known as the South's Casino Capital, Tunica also offers championship golf courses, antique shopping in a charming historic district and the **Tunica Museum** with exhibits on the town and Delta area. The **Tunica RiverPark** has a museum showcasing unique items and natural aquatic exhibits. The Tunica Queen offers paddlewheel cruises three times daily.

THE CAPITAL/RIVER REGION

Clinton. The **Clinton Community Nature Center** is comprised of thirty-three acres of woodlands near Olde Towne Clinton. It includes 2.5 miles of all weather walking trails, an array of native trees and flowers and a museum/education building.

Fayette. The **Springfield Plantation** (circa 1786-91) is the site of Andrew Jackson's wedding to Rachel Robars in 1791. This was one of the first houses in America to feature a full colonnade across the front facade and the first of its kind built in the Mississippi valley. Also noteworthy is its beautiful 18th century hand-carved interior woodwork.

Flora. Don't miss the **Mississippi Petrified Forest**. This natural landmark is the only petrified forest in the eastern U.S. It depicts 36 million years of geological history preserved in huge stone logs. It also features colorful Badlands, a nature trail, a campground, a museum and a lapidary shop.

Vicksburg. Visit the **Vicksburg National Military Park/U.S.S. Cairo Museum**. At the visitor center, view "In Memory of Men," an 18-minute film about the Confederate army. The 1,800-acre park features monuments built for both Confederate and Union forces. There is a large variety of antebellum homes as well. View scale models of several waterways, including Niagara Falls, at **Waterways Experiment Station**. This facility is the principal research, testing and development center for the Army Corps. of Engineers.

Woodville. The childhood home of Jefferson Davis, **Rosemont Plantation**, features original furnishings, a family cemetery and a windowsill carved with the names of the Davis children.

THE COASTAL REGION

Although the Mississippi coast was devasted by Hurricane Katrina, there is much that was untouched or has been reconstructed. Tourists are encouraged to visit and see the improved Gulf Coast; however, you are encouraged to research your coastal destination before leaving home. The following bureaus can give you up-to-date information on the area you are visiting: Mississippi Division of Tourism (866/733-6477); Hancock County Tourism Development Bureau (800/466-9048); Jackson County Chamber (228/762-3391); Mississippi Gulf Coast CVB (888/467-4853); Ocean Springs Chamber of Commerce (228/875-4424).

Bay St. Louis. For a sample of the infamous Mississippi Bayou, spend some time touring the marshes, the bayous, the Jordan River and the bay. Visit several historic sites near a charming bayside shopping district. The **Historic Downtown Walking Tour** begins at **Historical Society Home** on Cue Street. Take a guided tour of NASA's space shuttle main engine-testing complex at the **John C. Stennis Space Center**. Also on-site is a museum and a theater that features filmed and live presentations of space and related subjects. The Visitors Center exhibits include moon rocks, rockets and space suits. The Apollo 4 command module is also on display.

Biloxi/Gulfport Area is a popular vacation spot offering 26 miles of sandy beaches, golfing, deep sea fishing, boating, swimming, gambling cruises, nightclubs, historic sites and a scenic coast drive. The

Woodall's Quick & Easy Reference for Mississippi

	BIG RIGS WELCOME	INTERNET FRIENDLY	PETS WELCOME	WEB SAVER
QUITMAN				
Clarkco SP			■	
ROBINSONVILLE				
Buck Island MHC	▲		■	
ROSEDALE				
Great River Road SP			■	
SARDIS				
John Kyle SP & Mallard Point Golf Course			■	
SOUTHAVEN				
EZ Daze RV Park	▲	●	■	
Southaven RV Park	▲	●	■	
TISHOMINGO				
Tishomingo SP			■	
TUNICA				
Grand Casino RV Resort	▲	●	■	
Hollywood Casino RV Resort		●	■	
TUPELO				
Campgrounds at Barnes Crossing	▲	●	■	
Natchez Trace RV Park	▲	●	■	
Tombigbee SP			■	
Trace SP			■	
VICKSBURG				
Magnolia RV Park Resort	▲	●	■	
WAVELAND				
Buccaneer SP			■	
WESSON				
Lake Lincoln SP			■	

▲ = Big Rigs Welcome; ● = Internet Hookups; ● = (Wi-Fi available); ■ = Pets Welcome; $ = Web Saver Coupons

Check out the "How to Use This Directory" section in the front of this book for a description of the criteria Woodall's uses in this chart.

area is also known for its fine seafood restaurants.

Beauvoir Jefferson Davis Shrine, Biloxi. The historic last home of Jefferson Davis now contains a Confederate museum and a cemetery, where 700 Confederate soldiers are buried. The **Tomb of the Unknown Soldier of the Confederate States of America** was dedicated here. Although badly damaged by Katrina, the home survived and is currently undergoing an intensive historic restoration.

Biloxi Lighthouse has shined its beacon out across the Gulf for 157 years. Its light can be seen for 13 miles. Although its brick exterior suffered some hurricane damage, it survived and was photographed after the storm, standing on the ravaged beach with an American flag flying from its top.

Ship Island Excursions. This is the Biloxi point of departure for daily cruises to Ship Island, which is part of Gulf Islands National Seashore. **Fort Massachusetts**, used by Union General Benjamin "Beast" Butler during the Civil War as a POW camp, is also located here. In addition to being a beautiful beach and the place where the Mississippi Sound meets the Gulf of Mexico, this was also the launch site for Union forces in the battle for New Orleans.

Laurel. The **Lauren Rogers Museum of Art** in Laurel's historic district houses one of the most impressive collections of art in the South including works by Winslow Homer, John Singer Sargent, Mary Cassat, Grandma Moses and many more. Other Laurel attractions include **Landrum's Country Homestead and Village,** a re-creation of a late 1800's settlement with over 50 buildings and displays; **Veterans Memorial Museum** commemorating our military history and **Laurel's Historic District** which encompasses over 360 buildings.

ANNUAL EVENTS

JANUARY

Martin Luther King Celebration, Starkville; Martin Luther King, Jr. Day Parade & Celebration, Meridian; Eleventh Moon Storytelling Festival, Natchez; Tupelo Gigantic Flea Market and Crafts Show, Tupelo; Camp & Jam Bluegrass and Gospel Gathering, Meridian.

FEBRUARY

Dixie National Livestock Show and Rodeo, Jackson; Sportsmen Expo, Canton; Krewe of Kids Mardi Gras Parade, Bay St. Louis; Annual Camellia Show, Brookhaven; Magnolia Independent Film Festival, Starkville; Roosevelt State Park Music Festival, Morton.

MARCH

Delta Springfest, Greenville; Natchez Spring Pilgrimage, Natchez; Italian Festival Mississippi, Cleveland; Templeton Ragtime Festival, Starkville; Heritage Festival, Hattiesburg; Taste of Mississippi, Jackson; Biloxi Boat and RV Show, Biloxi; Pike County's Pathways of Beauty, McComb; Annual Bi-State Art Competition, Meridian;

APRIL

Natchez Bluff Blues Fest, Natchez; Blue Suede Cruise, Tupelo; Arts in the Park, Meridian; World Catfish Festival, Belzoni; International Fiesta, Starkville; Riverfest, Spring Arts and Crafts Show, Vicksburg; Confederate Memorial Day, Biloxi; Double Decker Arts Festival, Oxford; Tunica Rivergate Festival, Tunica; Juke Joint Festival, Clarksdale.

Springfield Plantation, Fayette. Photo courtesy Mississippi Tourism

MAY

The Jerry Clower Festival, Yazoo City; Arts and Crafts Festival, Calhoun City; Annual Gum Tree Festival, Tupelo; Market Street Festival, Columbus; Brick Streets Fine Arts Festival, Clinton; Deep Delta Festival, Rolling Fork; Dudies Burger Festival, Tupelo; Leland Crawfish Festival, Leland; Catfish Races 2007, Greenville.

JUNE

Old Tyme Festival, Olive Branch; Tomato Festival, Crystal Springs; Steamboat Race, Natchez; Balloon Glow, Ridgeland; Madison County Championship Hot Air Balloon Race, Canton; Juneteenth Heritage Celebration, Meridian.

JULY

Fourth of July celebrations, statewide; Slugburger Festival, Corinth; Choctaw Indian Fair, Choctaw; Annual Coast Coliseum Summer Fair, Biloxi; Hootenannies in Old Towne, Olive Branch; Slugburger Festival, Corinth; Mize Watermelon Festival, Mize; Lamar County Bluegrass Festival, Purvis.

AUGUST

Miss-Lou Wildlife Expo, Natchez; Watermelon Carnival, Water Valley; Sunflower River Blues and Gospel Festival, Clarksdale; Fiddlin' With the Frogs Bluegrass Festival, Grenada; Howlin' Wolf Memorial Blues Festival, West Point.

SEPTEMBER

Celtic Fest, Jackson; Delta Blues Week, Greenville; Seafood Festival, Biloxi; Pecan Festival, Richton; German Fest, Gluckstadt; Prairie Arts Festival, West Point; Mississippi Jazz & Heritage Festival, Greenville; Tennessee Williams Tribute Weekend, Columbus; Delta Blues Week, Greenville; Fall Fest Arts and Crafts, Clinton.

OCTOBER

Cruisin the Coast, Biloxi; Oktoberfest, Gulfport/Olive Branch/Carthage/ Cleveland; White Oak Fall Festival, Byhalia; Great MS River Balloon Race, Natchez.

NOVEMBER

Harvest Festival, Jackson; Victorian Christmas Festival, Canton.

DECEMBER

Victorian Christmas, Canton; Chimneyville Crafts Festival, Jackson; Christmas on the Tenn-Tom, Columbus; Trees of Christmas, Meridian; Holiday Home Tours, Columbus.

Mississippi

ABERDEEN—B-4

(N) BLUE BLUFF CAMPGROUND (COE-Tennessee/Tombigbee Waterway)—(Monroe) *from jct US 45 (Commerce St) & Meridian St (center of downtown): Go 1 mi N on Meridian St, then 1/2 mi E & N on paved roads.* FACILITIES: 92 sites, 92 W&E, (30 amps), tenting, shower$, dump station, laundry, ice, patios, fire rings, grills. RECREATION: pavilion, lake swimming, boating, canoeing, ramp, dock, lake/river fishing, playground, hiking trails, v-ball. Rec open to public. Pets welcome. Partial handicap access. Open all yr. Phone: (662)369-2832.

BAY ST. LOUIS—F-4

(W) BAY HIDE AWAY RV & CAMPING RESORT—(Hancock) *From jct I-10 W (exit 13) & Hwy 43/603: Go 6 mi S on Hwy 43/603, then 4.8 mi W on US 90, then 1/2 mi S on Lakeshore Rd. Enter on L.*

WELCOME

FRIENDLIEST CAMPING ON THE COAST!!!
Newly renovated/Better than ever! Best camping on the coast! Pool, Pavilion, AC/Heated Clubhouse, Spacious/Clean Bathhouse, Groups/Clubs welcome, Special Events/Cookouts, Close to everything! www.bayhideaway.com 228-466-0959

◆◆◆FACILITIES: 46 sites, typical site width 30 ft, 46 full hkups, (20, 30 & 50 amps), some extended stay sites, 41 pull-thrus, wireless Instant Internet access at site, phone Internet access central location, laundry, RV supplies, ice, tables, patios, fire rings, wood.

◆◆◆RECREATION: equipped pavilion, swim pool, playground, planned activities (wkends only), horseshoes, sports field, v-ball.

Pets welcome. Partial handicap access. No tents. Open all yr. Big rigs welcome. Internet friendly. Escort to site. Clubs welcome. Rate in 2007 $30 for 2 persons. MC/VISA. Member ARVC. Phone: (228)466-0959.

e-mail: bhacamping@aol.com

SEE AD THIS PAGE

Mississippi State Song: "Way Down South In Mississippi"

BAY ST. LOUIS—Continued

(N) BAY MARINA & RV PARK—(Hancock) *From jct I-10 (exit 13) & Hwy 603/43: Go 4-3/4 mi S on Hwy 603/43, then 1 block E on Longfellow, then 1/2 mi N on Chapman, then 2 blocks W on Washington. Enter on R.*

WELCOME

RELAX IN A SAFE QUIET RV PARK
A Marina atmosphere: Enjoy boating & fishing-close to the Gulf of Mexico. Emerald Coast white sand beaches. New Orleans and Biloxi Gulf Port Casinos and here in Bay Saint Louis the New Hollywood Casino.

◆◆◆FACILITIES: 28 sites, 28 full hkups, (20, 30 & 50 amps), 2 pull-thrus, cable TV, wireless Instant Internet access at site, dump station, laundry, ltd groceries, marine gas, ice, tables, patios, grills.

◆◆◆RECREATION: boating, canoeing, ramp, dock, 6 pontoon/6 motorboat rentals, saltwater/river fishing, fishing supplies, fishing guides, golf nearby.

Pets welcome. No tents. Open all yr. Internet friendly. Rate in 2007 $30 for 2 persons. MC/VISA/DISC/AMEX/Debit. Phone: (228)466-4970.

e-mail: bob@baymarina.com

SEE AD THIS PAGE

(N) HOLLYWOOD CASINO—*From jct I-10 (exit 13) & Hwy 43/603: Go 6 mi S on Hwy 43/603, then 2 mi E on US 90 to jct Main St & Blue Meadow Rd, then 1/2 mi N on Blue Meadow Rd, then 1 mi E on Hollywood Blvd. (follow signs). Enter on R.* Large, full-service casino on the Gulf Coast. Large, lighted free parking lot with plenty of room for RV's, plus full-hookup campground on premises. 24 hr Shuttle service. Open all yr. Open 24 hrs a day- 7 days a week. Phone: (228)463-4017.

WELCOME

e-mail: mary.hudson-bsl@pngaming.com

SEE AD TRAVEL SECTION PAGE 463

(N) HOLLYWOOD CASINO RV PARK—(Hancock) *From jct I-10 (exit 13) & Hwys 43/603: Go 6 mi S on Hwys 43/603, then 2 mi E on US 90 to jct Main St & Blue Meadow Rd, then 1/2 mi N on Blue Meadow Rd, then 1 mi E on Hollywood Blvd. (follow signs). Enter at end.*

WELCOME

◆◆◆◆◆FACILITIES: 100 sites, typical site width 45 ft, 100 full hkups, (30 & 50 amps), 6 pull-thrus, cable TV, wireless Instant Internet access at site, wireless Internet access central location, laundry, ice, tables, patios, grills.

◆◆◆◆RECREATION: pavilion, swim pool, whirlpool, boating, ramp, saltwater fishing, fishing guides, putting green, golf nearby.

Pets welcome. Partial handicap access. No tents. Open all yr. 7 day maximum stay. Big rigs welcome. Internet friendly. Clubs welcome. Rate in 2007 $28 per vehicle. MC/VISA/DISC/AMEX/DC/Debit. ATM. Phone: (800)WIN-BIG-2.

Mississippi State Rock: Petrified Wood

BAY ST. LOUIS—Continued
HOLLYWOOD CASINO RV PARK—Continued

e-mail: donna.peel@pngaming.com

SEE AD TRAVEL SECTION PAGE 463

MCLEOD WATER PARK—*From town: Go 10 mi N on Hwy 603, then turn W on Texas Flatt Rd.* FACILITIES: 70 sites, 70 W&E, tenting, dump station, laundry, ice, fire rings, grills, wood. RECREATION: pavilion, lake swimming, boating, canoeing, ramp, dock, pedal boat rentals, river fishing, playground, sports field, hiking trails. Rec open to public. Partial handicap access. Open all yr. Phone: (228)467-1894.

(W) SHADY ACRES RV COMMUNITY—(Hancock) *From jct I-10 & US Hwy 43/603: Go 6 mi S on Hwy 43/603, then 5 mi W on US Hwy 90. Enter on R.*

WELCOME

◆◆◆◆FACILITIES: 75 sites, 75 full hkups, (20, 30 & 50 amps), some extended stay sites (in winter), 5 pull-thrus, wireless Instant Internet access at site, wireless Internet access central location, laundry, LP gas by weight/by meter, ice, patios.

◆◆RECREATION: rec hall, swim pool, pond fishing, golf nearby, horseshoes.

Pets welcome, breed restrict. No tents. Open all yr. Big rigs welcome. Rate in 2007 $30 for 2 persons. Phone: (228)463-9670.

e-mail: julieberry8012@yahoo.com

SEE AD THIS PAGE

BILOXI—F-4

(C) CAJUN RV PARK—(Harrison) *From jct I-10 & I-110: Go 4 mi S on I-110, then 3 mi W on US 90. Enter on R.*

WELCOME

EXPLORE. PLAY. RELAX. IN BILOXI
Come enjoy our spacious sites, friendly staff and beautiful park. Across from the beach. Complimentary casino shuttles, Cable TV, Internet kiosk high-speed WIFI access. 1-877-225-8699 www.cajunrvpark.com

◆◆◆◆FACILITIES: 130 sites, typical site width 26 ft, 130 full hkups, (30 & 50 amps), 68 pull-

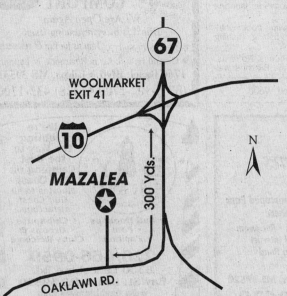

See listing at Biloxi, MS

BILOXI—Continued
CAJUN RV PARK—Continued

thrus, cable TV, wireless Instant Internet access at site, RV storage, dump station, non-guest dumping $, laundry, RV supplies, LP gas by weight/by meter, ice, tables.

◆◆RECREATION: rec room/area, pavilion, swim pool, play equipment, planned activities.

Pets welcome. No tents. Open all yr. Big rigs welcome. Internet friendly. Clubs welcome. Rate in 2007 $23.83-25.83 for 2 persons. MC/VISA. Member ARVC. Phone: (877)225-8699. FMCA discount.

e-mail: camp@cajunrvpark.com

SEE AD THIS PAGE

(N) LAKEVIEW RV RESORT—(Harrison) *From jct I-10 (exit 46B) & I-110/Hwy 15: Go 6-3/4 mi N on Hwy 15. Enter on R.*

WELCOME

YOUR HOME AWAY FROM HOME!
Nestled north of Biloxi - away from the city hustle - yet minutes from excitement, we are your home away from home. Special planned activities, recreation, clubhouse, swimming, store, WiFi: 30/50 amp full hookups concrete pads.

◆◆◆◆FACILITIES: 84 sites, 84 full hkups, (30 & 50 amps), some extended stay sites, 84 pull-thrus, wireless Instant Internet access at site, wireless Internet access central location, RV/park trailer rentals, cabins, RV storage, laundry, RV supplies, LP gas by weight/by meter.

◆◆◆◆RECREATION: rec hall, swim pool, boating, 2 pedal boat rentals, lake fishing, golf nearby, bsktball, horseshoes, sports field.

Pets welcome, breed restrict. Partial handicap access. No tents. Open all yr. Big rigs welcome. Internet friendly. Rate in 2007 $30-32 for 2 persons. Phone: (228)396-2211.

e-mail: lakeviewrvresort@aol.com

SEE AD PAGE 473

(C) MAJESTIC OAKS RV RESORT—(Harrison) *From jct I-110 & Hwy 90 (Beach Rd): Go 2-3/4 mi W on Hwy 90, then 1 mi N on Rodenberg Ave, then 1/8 mi W on Pass Rd. Enter on R.*

WELCOME

RAISING THE STANDARD OF RV TRAVEL!!
Biloxi is back! Come and stay with us at Biloxi's only new RV resort. We are here to raise the standards of RV travel. We have individually landscaped concrete sites, Lush green lawns and majestic oaks. www.majesticoaksrv.com

◆◆◆◆◆FACILITIES: 95 sites, 95 full hkups, (30 & 50 amps), some extended stay sites, 11 pull-thrus, cable TV, wireless Instant Internet access at site, wireless Internet access central location, laundry, RV supplies, LP gas by weight/by meter, ice, tables, patios.

◆◆RECREATION: rec room/area, swim pool, golf nearby, sports field.

Pets welcome, breed restrict, quantity restrict. Partial handicap access. No tents. Open all yr. Big rigs welcome. Internet friendly. Clubs welcome. Rate in 2007 $38.50-44 for 2 persons. MC/VISA/DISC/Debit. Phone: (228)436-4200. FMCA discount.

e-mail: majesticoaksrv@bellsouth.net

SEE AD PAGE 471

Mississippi State Fish: Largemouth or Black Bass

BILOXI—Continued

(N) MAZALEA TRAVEL PARK—(Harrison) *From jct I-110 & I-10 (exit 46): Go 4 mi W on I-10 (exit 41), then 300 yards S on Hwy 67. Enter on R.*

WELCOME

◆◆◆◆◆FACILITIES: 151 sites, typical site width 25 ft, 151 full hkups, (20, 30 & 50 amps), some extended stay sites, 45 pull-thrus, cable TV, phone on-site Internet access (needs activ), cabins, RV storage, dump station, non-guest dumping $, laundry, groceries, RV supplies, LP gas by weight/by meter, ice, tables, patios.

◆◆RECREATION: rec hall, rec room/area, equipped pavilion.

Pets welcome. No tents. Open all yr. Big rigs welcome. Escort to site. Clubs welcome. Rate in 2007 $25-28 for 2 persons. MC/VISA/Debit. Phone: (800)877-8575. FMCA discount.

SEE AD PAGE 470

(N) PARKER'S LANDING RV PARK—(Harrison) *From jct I-110 & I-10 (exit 46): Go 4 mi W on I-10 (exit 41), then 500 ft S on Hwy 67, then 1/4 mi E on Oaklawn Rd. Enter on R.*

WELCOME

◆◆◆◆◆FACILITIES: 130 sites, 130 full hkups, (20, 30 & 50 amps), some extended stay sites, 20 pull-thrus, cable TV, wireless Instant Internet access at site ($), phone on-site Internet access (needs activ), tenting, cabins, RV storage, laundry, ltd groceries, RV supplies, LP gas by weight/by meter, ice, tables, patios.

◆◆◆◆◆RECREATION: rec hall, rec room/area, swim pool, boating, canoeing, ramp, dock, 3 pedal boat rentals, river fishing, fishing guides, bsktball, playground, planned activities (wkends only), local tours.

Pets welcome. Partial handicap access. Open all yr. Big rigs welcome. Internet friendly. Escort to site. Clubs welcome. Rate in 2007 $28-30 for 2 persons. MC/VISA/AMEX/DC. ATM. Phone: (228) 392-7717. FMCA discount.

e-mail: parkerslan@aol.com

SEE AD PAGE 473

(C) SOUTHERN COMFORT CAMPING RESORT—(Harrison) *From jct I-10 (exit 46A) & I-110: Go 2 mi S on I-110, then 2-3/4 mi W on US 90. Enter on R.*

WELCOME

CLOSEST RV PARK TO CASINOS & BEACH
Mississippi's Gulf Coast is renewing itself. Join us to relax, have fun, play on the beach or casino's. Enjoy deep-sea fishing, restaurants & shopping. 1-1/2 hrs to New Orleans - 1 hr to Mobile. Nice large sites - Cable TV.

◆◆◆◆FACILITIES: 126 sites, typical site width 30 ft, 83 full hkups, 43 W&E, (20, 30 & 50 amps), some extended stay sites, 57 pull-thrus, cable TV, phone Internet access central location, tenting, RV storage, dump station, laundry, RV supplies, LP gas by weight/by meter, ice, tables, patios.

◆◆◆RECREATION: rec hall, rec room/area, coin games, swim pool, wading pool, local tours.

Pets welcome, breed restrict. Partial handicap access. Open all yr. Big rigs welcome. Internet friendly. Escort to site. Clubs welcome. Rate in 2007 $24-29 for 2 persons. MC/VISA. Phone: (877)302-1700.

SEE AD PAGE 469

BURTON—A-5

PINEY GROVE CAMPGROUND (COE-Tennessee/Tombigbee Waterway)—(Prentiss) *From jct Hwy 365 & Hwy 30: Go 2 mi W on Hwy 30, then 3 mi S on CR 3501, then*

BURTON—Continued
PINEY GROVE CAMPGROUND (COE-Tennessee/Tombigbee Waterway)—Continued

follow sign. FACILITIES: 141 sites, 141 W&E, tenting, dump station, laundry, grills. RECREATION: pavilion, lake swimming, boating, ramp, lake fishing, playground, sports field, hiking trails, v-ball. Partial handicap access. Open May 25 thru Nov 13. Phone: (662)728-1134.

BYRAM—D-3

(C) Swinging Bridge RV Park—(Hinds) *From I-55 (exit 85-Byram exit): Go 1 block E, then 1/4 mi N on Frontage Rd. Enter on R.* ◆◆◆◆FACILITIES: 118 sites, typical site width 30 ft, 118 full hkups, (20, 30 & 50 amps), many extended stay sites (in winter), laundry, LP gas by weight/by meter, ice, patios. ◆◆◆RECREATION: pavilion, swim pool, pond fishing, horseshoes, sports field. Pets welcome. Partial handicap access. No tents. Open all yr. Big rigs welcome. Internet friendly. Rate in 2007 $25 for 2 persons. Phone: (800)297-9127.

CANTON—D-3

(W) Movietown RV Resort—(Madison) *From jct I 55 (exit 119) & Hwy 22: Go 1/4 mi W on Hwy 22, then 1/4 mi N on Virlilia Rd. Enter on R.* ◆◆◆◆FACILITIES: 117 sites, 117 full hkups, (20, 30 & 50 amps), some extended stay sites, 75 pull-thrus, tenting, laundry, patios. ◆RECREATION: playground. Pets welcome. Partial handicap access. Open all yr. Big rigs welcome. Internet friendly. Rate in 2007 $20 per vehicle. Phone: (601)859-7990.

CLINTON—D-2

(SE) Springridge RV Park—(Hinds) *From I-20 (exit 36): Go 2 blocks S on Springridge Rd. Enter on L.* ◆◆◆◆FACILITIES: 42 sites, typical site width 25 ft, accepts full hkup units only, 42 full hkups, (30 & 50 amps), 50 amps ($), 30 pull-thrus, laundry, patios. ◆◆◆RECREATION: rec hall, swim pool, tennis. Pets welcome. No tents. Open all yr. Big rigs welcome. Phone: (601)924-0947.

COLDWATER—A-3

DUB PATTON CAMPGROUND (COE-Arkabutla Lake) —(Tate) *From town: Go 10 mi W on Arkabutla Rd. Follow signs N to the dam.* FACILITIES: 66 sites, 66 W&E, (20 & 30 amps), tenting, dump station, fire rings, grills. RECREATION: lake swimming, boating, ramp, lake fishing, hiking trails. Partial handicap access. Open all yr. Phone: (662)562-6261.

HERNANDO POINT (COE - Arkabutla Lake)—(Tate) *From town: Go 4 mi N on US-51, then 5 mi W on Wheeler Rd.* FACILITIES: 83 sites, 83 W&E, tenting, dump station, fire rings, grills. RECREATION: pavilion, lake swimming, boating, ramp, lake fishing, playground. Open all yr. Phone: (662)562-6261.

(C) MEMPHIS SOUTH CAMPGROUND & RV PARK—(Tate) *From I-55 (exit 271) & Hwy 306: Go 200 feet W on Hwy 306 (turn before gas station). Enter on L.*

WELCOME

SAFE, CLEAN, AND COUNTRY QUIET
Easy on/off I-55. 82 Full hkup pull-thru sites. Friendly folks. Close to Memphis for shopping, sight-seeing, or working. Nearby lakes for great fishing. Clean a/c nice bathrooms and showers. You can make friends for life here.

◆◆◆◆FACILITIES: 82 sites, typical site width 50 ft, 82 full hkups, (20, 30 & 50 amps), many extended stay sites, 82 pull-thrus, phone Internet access central location, tenting, RV storage, laundry, gas, tables.

◆RECREATION: swim pool, play equipment.

Pets welcome, breed restrict. Partial handicap access. Open all yr. Pool open May 15 thru Sep 1. Big rigs welcome. Clubs welcome. Rate in 2007 $22 for 2 persons. MC/VISA/DISC/AMEX. Phone: (662)622-0056.

e-mail: djpaulk@comcast.net

SEE AD MEMPHIS, TN PAGE 807

SOUTH ABUTMENT CAMPGROUND (COE-Arkabutla Lake)—(Tate) *From town: Go 10 mi W on Arkabutla Rd. Follow signs N to the dam.* FACILITIES: 80 sites, 80 W&E, tenting, dump station, fire rings, grills. RECREATION: lake swimming, boating, ramp, lake fishing, playground, hiking trails. Open all yr. Phone: (662)562-6261.

COLUMBIA—E-3

(N) MIMOSA LANDING CAMPGROUND —(Marion) *From Hwy 98 & Hwy 35: Go 3-3/4 mi NE on Hwy 35, then 1/4 mi N on Industrial Park Dr; then 100 ft W on Rustique Brick Dr. Enter at end.*

WELCOME

NEW OWNERS/COUNTRY SETTING
Come relax & enjoy camping on the Pearl River. Southern Hospitality at its best. Perfect for SNOWBIRDS. Spacious sites, full hookups & private baths. Activities include fishing-pool-rec hall and walking trails. www.mimosalanding.com

◆◆◆◆◆FACILITIES: 77 sites, typical site width 40 ft, 77 full hkups, (20, 30 & 50 amps), some extended stay sites, 13 pull-thrus, wireless Instant Internet access at site, wireless Internet access central location, cabins, dump station, laundry, ltd groceries, ice, tables, fire rings, grills, wood.

◆◆◆◆RECREATION: rec hall, equipped pavilion, swim pool, boating, dock, river/pond fishing, fishing supplies, golf nearby, bsktball, playground, planned activities (wkends only), horseshoes, sports field, hiking trails, v-ball.

Pets welcome, breed restrict. Partial handicap access. No tents. Open all yr. Big rigs welcome. Internet friendly. Clubs welcome. Rate in 2007 $26-28 for 2 persons. MC/VISA/DISC. Phone: (601)736-9700.

e-mail: info@mimosalanding.com

SEE AD THIS PAGE

COLUMBUS—B-5

DEWAYNE HAYES CAMPGROUND (COE-Tennessee/Tombigbee Waterway)—(Lowndes) *From jct US 45 & Hwy 50W/Hwy 373N: Go 1-1/2 mi NW on Hwy 373, then 1/2 mi left on Barton Ferry Rd.* FACILITIES: 110 sites, 100 W&E, (30 & 50 amps), 10 no hkups, tenting, dump station, laundry, ice, fire rings, grills. RECREATION: pavilion, lake swimming, boating, ramp, lake fishing, playground, sports field, hiking trails, v-ball. Pets welcome. Partial handicap access. Open all yr. Facilities fully operational in Summer. Phone: (662)434-6939.

(SE) LAKE LOWNDES SP—(Lowndes) *From town: Go 4 mi SE on Hwy-69, then 4 mi SE follow signs.*

WELCOME

FACILITIES: 50 sites, 32 ft max RV length, 10 full hkups, 40 W&E, tenting, cabins, dump station, laundry, tables, grills, wood.

RECREATION: rec hall, rec room/area, equipped pavilion, coin games, lake swimming, boating, ramp, dock, 6 rowboat/6 pedal boat rentals, lake fishing, bsktball, 8 bike rentals, playground, planned activities (wkends only), tennis, sports field, hiking trails, v-ball. Rec open to public.

Pets welcome. Open all yr. MC/VISA. Phone: (662) 328-2110.

e-mail: lowndesl@ayrix.net

SEE AD TRAVEL SECTION PAGE 464

(NW) TOWN CREEK CAMPGROUND (COE-Tennessee/Tombigbee Waterway)—(Clay) *From jct US 45 & Hwy 50: Go W on Hwy 50 to west side of Tenn-Tom Bridge, then follow signs N on county roads.* FACILITIES: 110 sites, 100 W&E, (30 amps), 10 no hkups, tenting, dump station, laundry, ice, fire rings, grills. RECREATION: pavilion, lake swimming, boating, ramp, dock, lake/river fishing, playground, sports field, hiking trails, v-ball. Pets welcome. Partial handicap access. Open all yr. Phone: (662)494-4885.

DECATUR—D-4

(W) TURKEY CREEK WATER PARK (Pat Harrison Waterway District)—(Newton) *From jct I-20 (exit 109) & Hwy 15: Go 7 mi N on Hwy 15 to Decatur, then 4-1/2 mi W on park road. Follow signs.* FACILITIES: 22 sites, typical site width 23 ft, 38 ft max RV

DECATUR—Continued
TURKEY CREEK WATER PARK (Pat Harrison Waterway District)—Continued

length, 22 W&E, some extended stay sites, tenting, dump station, laundry, patios, fire rings, grills, wood. RECREATION: pavilion, lake swimming, boating, canoeing, ramp, dock, 5 rowboat rentals, lake fishing, playground, sports field, hiking trails. Rec open to public. Open all yr. Phone: (601)635-3314.

DURANT—C-3

(S) HOLMES COUNTY SP—(Attala) *From jct I-55 (exit 156) & Hwy 12: Go 5 mi S on I-55 (exit 150), then 1 mi E on park access road.*

WELCOME

FACILITIES: 28 sites, 28 W&E, 2 pull-thrus, tenting, cabins, dump station, laundry, ice, tables.

RECREATION: rec hall, pavilion, coin games, lake swimming, boating, ramp, dock, 6 rowboat/6 pedal boat rentals, lake fishing, playground, sports field, hiking trails, v-ball. Rec open to public.

Pets welcome. Open all yr. MC/VISA. Phone: (662) 653-3351.

SEE AD TRAVEL SECTION PAGE 464

EDWARDS—D-2

Askew's Landing Campground—(Hinds) *From jct I-20 (exit 19, Edwards) & Askew Ferry Rd: Go 2-1/2 mi W on Askew Ferry Rd (north frontage road), then follow signs. Enter on R.* ◆◆◆FACILITIES: 99 sites, typical site width 60 ft, 51 full hkups, 48 W&E, (20, 30 & 50 amps), many extended stay sites, 50 pull-thrus, tenting, dump station, laundry, ltd groceries, LP gas by weight, ice, tables, fire rings, wood. ◆◆◆RECREATION: rec hall, equipped pavilion, swim pool, boating, electric motors only, canoeing, dock, lake fishing, play equipment, horseshoes, sports field, hiking trails, v-ball. Pets welcome, breed restrict. Open all yr. Big rigs welcome. Internet friendly. Rate in 2007 $16-20 per family. Phone: (601)852-2331.

ENID—B-3

CHICKASAW HILL CAMPGROUND (COE-Enid Lake)—(Yalobusha) *From jct I-55 (exit 233) & Enid Dam Rd (CR 36): Go 1 mi E on Enid Dam Rd, then 3 mi N on Chapel Hill Rd, then 7 mi E on Pope-Water Valley Rd, then 1-1/2 mi S on Chickasaw Rd.* FACILITIES: 51 sites, typical site width 12 ft, 51 W&E, (50 amps), tenting, dump station, fire rings, grills. RECREATION: pavilion, lake swimming, boating, ramp, lake fishing, playground, hiking trails. Open all yr. No reservations. Phone: (662)563-4571.

(NE) PERSIMMON HILL-SOUTH ABUTMENT (COE-Enid Lake)—(Yalobusha) *From jct I-55 (exit 233) & Enid Dam Rd (CR 36): Go 1 mi E on Enid Dam Rd (CR 36), then 2 mi S across top of the dam, then follow signs.* FACILITIES: 72 sites, typical

Mississippi State Motto: "By Valor and Arms"

ENID—Continued
PERSIMMON HILL-SOUTH ABUTMENT (COE-Enid Lake)—Continued

site width 12 ft, 72 W&E, (30 amps), tenting, dump station, fire rings, grills. RECREATION: lake swimming, boating, ramp, lake fishing, playground, hiking trails. Partial handicap access. Open all yr. Facilities fully operational Mar 1 thru Oct 31. Phone: (662) 563-4571.

WALLACE CREEK (COE-Enid Lake)—(Yalobusha) *From jct I-55 (exit 233) & CR 36: Go 2-1/2 mi E on CR 36 & follow signs.* FACILITIES: 99 sites, typical site width 12 ft, 99 W&E, (30 amps), 8 pull-thrus, tenting, dump station, fire rings, grills. RECREATION: pavilion, lake swimming, boating, ramp, lake fishing, playground, hiking trails. Pets welcome. Partial handicap access. Open all yr. Phone: (662)563-4571.

WATER VALLEY LANDING CAMPGROUND (COE-Enid Lake)—(Yalobusha) *From jct I-55 (exit 227) & Hwy 32: Go 1-1/4 mi E on Hwy 32, then 2 mi N on CR 553. Enter on R.* FACILITIES: 29 sites, 29 W&E, (30 amps), tenting, dump station, fire rings, grills. RECREATION: pavilion, lake swimming, boating, ramp, lake fishing, playground, hiking trails. Pets welcome. Partial handicap access. Open Mar 1 thru Oct 31. Phone: (662)563-4571.

ENTERPRISE—D-4

DUNN'S FALLS WATER PARK (Pat Harrison Waterway District)—(Clarke) *From jct I-20 & I-59: Go 6 mi S on I-59 (exit 142), then 4 mi W & S on paved road (cross back over I-59, follow signs).* FACILITIES: 15 sites, typical site width 20 ft, 15 no hkups, grills. RECREATION: lake swimming, canoeing, pedal boat rentals, lake/river fishing, hiking trails. Rec open to public. Open all yr. No showers. Phone: (601)655-8550.

FLORA—D-3

(SW) Mississippi Petrified Forest Campground (RV SPACES)—(Madison) *From jct US 49 & Hwy 22: Go 500 ft W on Hwy 22, then 1-3/4 mi S on asphalt road. Enter on R.* FACILITIES: 37 sites, typical site width 30 ft, 15 full hkups, 2 W&E, 20 no hkups, 5 pull-thrus, tenting, dump station, tables, fire rings, grills. RECREATION: hiking trails. No pets. Partial handicap access. Open all yr. Except Christmas Day. Rate in 2007 $15 for 2 persons. Phone: (601)879-8189.

FLORENCE—D-3

(S) WENDY OAKS RV RESORT—(Rankin) *From jct I-20 (exit 47) & Hwy 49: Go 13 mi S on Hwy 49 to Florence (traffic light), then 5 mi S on US Hwy 49, then go under railroad trestle, then cross over and go 1/2 mi N on Us Hwy 49. Enter on R.*

WELCOME

◆◆◆◆FACILITIES: 23 sites, 23 full hkups, (20, 30 & 50 amps), some extended stay sites, 10 pull-thrus, tenting, laundry, tables, fire rings, wood.

◆◆RECREATION: boating, electric motors only, canoeing, ramp, pedal boat rentals, lake fishing, fishing supplies, horseshoes.

WENDY OAKS RV RESORT—Continued on next page

FLORENCE—Continued
WENDY OAKS RV RESORT—Continued

Pets welcome, breed restrict. Partial handicap access. Open all yr. Big rigs welcome. Rate in 2007 $27 for 2 persons. Phone: (601)845-CAMP.

e-mail: grubep@bellsouth.net

SEE AD PAGE 475

FOREST—D-3

(SE) BIENVILLE NATIONAL FOREST (Marathon Campground)—(Smith) *From town: Go 11 mi SE on Hwy-501, then 3-1/2 mi SE on FR-506, then 1/3 mi S on FR 520.* FACILITIES: 32 sites, 22 ft max RV length, 32 W&E, (30 & 50 amps), tenting, dump station, grills. RECREATION: pavilion, lake swimming, boating, 10 hp limit, ramp, dock, lake fishing, hiking trails. Open all yr. No reservations. Maybe closed during winter, check with Ranger Dist. Office. Phone: (601)469-3811.

FULTON—A-5

WHITTEN PARK—(Itawamba) *From jct US 78 & Hwy 25: Go N on Hwy 25, then W on Main St to the waterway, then 2 mi N on access roads.* FACILITIES: 61 sites, 61 W&E, (30 amps), tenting, dump station, laundry, grills. RECREATION: pavilion, lake swimming, boating, ramp, dock, lake/river fishing, playground, sports field, hiking trails. Partial handicap access. Open all yr. Facilities fully operational in Summer. Phone: (662)862-5414.

GAUTIER—F-4

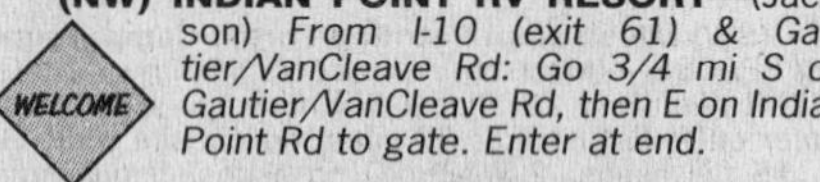

(NW) INDIAN POINT RV RESORT—(Jackson) *From I-10 (exit 61) & Gautier/VanCleave Rd: Go 3-1/4 mi S on Gautier/VanCleave Rd, then E on Indian Point Rd to gate. Enter at end.*

RELAX OR PLAY IN OUR 5W RESORT!
Located between Mobile & New Orleans - just minutes from Biloxi. Enjoy our 5W Resort on Sioux Bayou. Take a boat ride on the bayou. Swimming, Fishing, Acitivies & Restaurant on site. Near casinos, golf courses, shopping.

◇◇◇◇◇FACILITIES: 241 sites, typical site width 40 ft, 221 full hkups, 20 W&E, (20, 30 & 50 amps), some extended stay sites, 13 pull-thrus, cable TV, wireless Instant Internet access at site, wireless Internet access central location, tenting, RV/park trailer rentals, cabins, RV storage, dump station, non-guest dumping $, laundry, RV supplies, LP gas by weight/by meter, ice, tables, patios, wood.

◇◇◇◇◇RECREATION: rec hall, rec room/area, equipped pavilion, 2 swim pools, boating, canoeing, ramp, dock, river fishing, fishing guides, mini-golf, golf nearby, bsktball, playground, 2 shuffleboard courts, planned activities (wkends only), horseshoes, sports field, hiking trails.

Pets welcome. Partial handicap access. Open all yr. Big rigs welcome. Internet friendly. Clubs welcome. Rate in 2007 $25-30 for 2 persons. MC/VISA/DISC/AMEX/Debit. Member ARVC. Phone: (228)497-1011.

e-mail: ip@indianpt.com

SEE AD BILOXI PAGE 472

(S) SHEPARD SP—(Jackson) *From I-10 (exit 61): Go S on Van Cleave Rd, then E on US 90 to first stoplight, then 1-1/2 mi S to Graveline Rd.*

FACILITIES: 28 sites, 28 W&E, tenting, cabins, dump station, tables, grills, controlled access gate.

RECREATION: pavilion, boating, ramp, dock, 6 rowboat/6 canoe rentals, saltwater fishing, playground, sports field, hiking trails. Rec open to public.

GAUTIER—Continued
SHEPARD SP—Continued

Pets welcome. Open all yr. Phone: (228)497-2244.

SEE AD TRAVEL SECTION PAGE 464

GREENVILLE—C-2

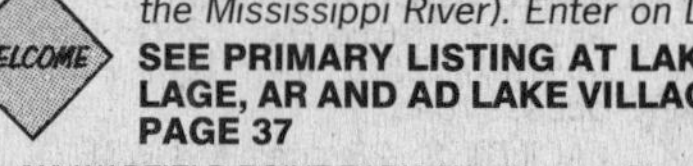

PECAN GROVE RV PARK—*From jct Hwy 1 & US 82: Go 19 mi W on US 82 (over the Mississippi River). Enter on L.*

SEE PRIMARY LISTING AT LAKE VILLAGE, AR AND AD LAKE VILLAGE, AR PAGE 37

(W) WARFIELD POINT PARK (Washington County Park)—(Washington) *From jct Hwy 1 & US 82: Go 5-1/2 mi W on US 82, then at Warfield Point Park sign go 3 mi N.* FACILITIES: 75 sites, typical site width 35 ft, 50 W&E, (20 & 30 amps), 25 no hkups, tenting, dump station, patios, fire rings, grills, wood. RECREATION: boating, canoeing, ramp, river fishing, playground, hiking trails. Rec open to public. Open all yr. Phone: (662)335-7275.

GRENADA—B-3

(N) Frog Hollow Campground/RV Park—(Grenada) *From north jct I-55 (exit 211) & Hwy 7: Go 500 feet E on Hwy 7. Enter on R.* ◇◇◇◇FACILITIES: 49 sites, typical site width 25 ft, 49 full hkups, (20, 30 & 50 amps), some extended stay sites, 24 pull-thrus, tenting, laundry, ltd groceries, LP gas by weight/by meter, ice, tables, patios. ◇◇RECREATION: rec hall, horseshoes, sports field. Pets welcome, breed restrict. Open all yr. Big rigs welcome. Internet friendly. Rate in 2007 $21-23 for 2 persons. Member ARVC. Phone: (662)226-9042.

(NE) HUGH WHITE SP—(Grenada) *From jct I-55 (exit 206) & Hwy 8: Go 5 mi E on Hwy 8, then 2-1/2 mi N on Hwy 333. Follow signs.*

FACILITIES: 173 sites, 34 ft max RV length, 173 W&E, tenting, cabins, dump station, laundry, ltd groceries, ice.

RECREATION: rec hall, pavilion, swim pool, lake swimming, boating, ramp, dock, 6 rowboat rentals, lake fishing, fishing supplies, bike rental, playground, tennis, hiking trails. Rec open to public.

Pets welcome. Open all yr. Phone: (662)226-4934.

SEE AD TRAVEL SECTION PAGE 464

GULFPORT—F-4

(W) Bay Berry RV Park—(Harrison) *From jct I-10 & Hwy 49 (exit 34): Go 2-1/2 mi W on I-10 (exit 31), then 200 yds N on Canal, then 200 yds E on Frontage Rd. Enter on L.* ◇◇◇◇FACILITIES: 36 sites, typical site width 25 ft, 36 full hkups, (30 & 50 amps), some extended stay sites, 6 pull-thrus, laundry, tables, patios. Pets welcome. Partial handicap access. No tents. Open all yr. Big rigs welcome. Rate in 2007 $30 for 3 persons. Phone: (877)777-0803.

(C) BAYWOOD RV PARK AND CAMPGROUND, INC.—(Harrison) *From jct I-10 (exit 38) & Lorraine/Cowen Rd: Go 3 mi S on Lorraine/Cowen Rd. Enter on L.*

◇◇◇◇FACILITIES: 118 sites, typical site width 25 ft, 118 full hkups, (15, 30 & 50 amps), some extended stay sites, 8 pull-thrus, cable TV, tenting, RV/park trailer rentals, RV storage, dump station, laundry, groceries, RV supplies, LP gas by weight/by meter, ice, tables, patios.

◇◇RECREATION: rec hall, swim pool, golf nearby, playground.

Pets welcome, breed restrict. Open all yr. Big rigs welcome. Escort to site. Clubs welcome. Rate in 2007 $25-28 for 2 persons. MC/VISA/Debit. Phone: (888)747-4840. FMCA discount.

e-mail: wmsentr@aol.com

SEE AD NEXT PAGE

Huge catches of seafood are taken from the gulf yearly.

GULFPORT—Continued

CAJUN RV PARK—*From Gulfport (I-10 & Hwy 49): Go 12 mi E on I-10 (exit 46) then 4 mi S on I-110, then 3 mi W on US 90. Enter on L.*

SEE PRIMARY LISTING AT BILOXI AND AD BILOXI PAGE 474

(N) COUNTRY SIDE RV PARK & TRADIN POST—(Harrison) *From jct I-10 (exit 34B) & US 49: Go 10 mi N on US 49. Enter on R.*

◇◇◇◇FACILITIES: 32 sites, typical site width 29 ft, 32 full hkups, (20, 30 & 50 amps), some extended stay sites (in winter), 2 pull-thrus, cable TV, tenting, RV/park trailer rentals, laundry, RV supplies, LP gas by weight/by meter, ice, tables.

◇◇◇RECREATION: rec room/area, pavilion, swim pool, pond fishing, golf nearby, planned activities, local tours.

Pets welcome. Partial handicap access. Open all yr. Big rigs welcome. Escort to site. Clubs welcome. Rate in 2007 $25 for 2 persons. Phone: (228)539-0807.

e-mail: csrv@bellsouth.net

SEE AD THIS PAGE

HARRISON COUNTY FAIRGROUNDS—(Harrison) *From jct I-10 (exit 28) & County Farm Rd: Go 7-1/2 mi N on County Farm Rd. Enter on L.* FACILITIES: 46 sites, 46 W&E. RECREATION: pavilion. Open all yr. Phone: (228)832-8620.

(N) SOUTHERN OAKS MH & RV COMMUNITY (RV SPACES)—(Harrison) *From jct I-10 (exit 34B) & US 49N: Go 1/4 mi N on US 49, then 3/4 mi E on Landon Rd, then 1/4 mi N on Three Rivers Rd. Enter on R.*

FACILITIES: 30 sites, accepts self-contained units only, 30 full hkups, (30 & 50 amps), cable TV, patios.

Pets welcome, breed restrict. No tents. Open all yr. Big rigs welcome. Escort to site. Rate in 2007 $30 for 2 persons. Phone: (228)832-5528.

e-mail: twosouth@bellsouth.net

SEE AD THIS PAGE

HATTIESBURG—E-4

MILITARY PARK (Lake Walker Family Campground-Camp Shelby)—(Forrest) *From jct I-59 & US 98: Go 3 mi E on US 98, then S on US 49 to South Gate. Check in at Bldg 1480. On base.* FACILITIES: 25 sites, 25 full hkups, (30 & 50 amps), laundry, grills. RECREATION: rec hall, equipped pavilion, swim pool, boating, electric motors only, ramp, 8 rowboat rentals, lake fishing, tennis, sports field, v-ball. Pets welcome. No tents. Open all yr. Facilities fully operational Apr thru Sep. No restrooms Oct 1-Mar 31. For Military Use Only-w/Military ID Card. Phone: (601) 558-2397.

(NW) Okatoma River Resort & RV Park—(Covington) *From jct I-59 (exit 67B) & US 49N: Go 8 mi N on Hwy 49, then 1 mi E on Lux Rd, then 1 mi N on Okatoma River Rd. Enter on L.* ◇◇◇FACILITIES: 60 sites, 60 full hkups, (30 & 50 amps), some extended stay sites, 16 pull-thrus, dump station, laundry, LP gas by weight/by meter, tables, wood. ◇◇◇RECREATION: rec hall, pavilion, equipped pavilion, swim pool, lake fishing, sports field. Pets welcome. No tents. Open all yr. Big rigs welcome. Rate in 2007 $30 for 2 persons. Phone: (601)268-6600.

(S) PAUL B JOHNSON SP—(Forrest) *From town: Go 14 mi S on Hwy 49.*

FACILITIES: 108 sites, 36 ft max RV length, 23 full hkups, 85 W&E, 22 pull-thrus, tenting, cabins, dump station, laundry, ice, tables, grills, wood, controlled access gate.

RECREATION: rec hall, pavilion, coin games, lake swimming, boating, canoeing, ramp, dock, 6 rowboat/6 canoe/6 pedal boat rentals, lake fishing, playground, sports field, hiking trails. Rec open to public.

Pets welcome. Open all yr. MC/VISA. Phone: (601) 582-7721.

SEE AD TRAVEL SECTION PAGE 464

(N) Shady Cove RV Park—(Forrest) *From jct I-59 (exit 67B) & US 49N: Go 5-1/2 mi N on US 49. Enter on R.* ◇◇◇◇FACILITIES: 49 sites, 39 full hkups, 10 W&E, (15, 20, 30 & 50 amps), 33 pull-thrus, tenting, laundry, LP gas by weight/by meter, ice, tables, fire rings, wood. ◇◇RECREATION: pavilion, pond fishing, play equipment, sports field. Pets welcome. Open all yr. Big rigs welcome. Internet friendly. Rate in 2007 $24 for 2 persons. Phone: (877)251-8169.

Greenwood is the home of Cotton Row, which is the second largest cotton exchange in the nation and is on the National Register of Historic Places.

Family Camping on the Gulf Coast

Good Sam Park

Newly Renovated

Baywood Campground, INC.

WOODALL W APPROVED

E-mail us at:
wmsentr@aol.com

- Grocery Store
- Pool • Playground • Rec Room • Laundry
- Fishing Pond • Cable TV
- Clean Restrooms
- Concrete Pads
- Full Hookups • Drive-thrus
- Weekly & Monthly Rates
- Open All Year
- AAA, AARP, FMCA and Good Sam Discounts
- LP Gas Available
- Car Rentals
- Serving You for 30 Years

Woodall's Rated:
Fac: WWWW Rec: WW

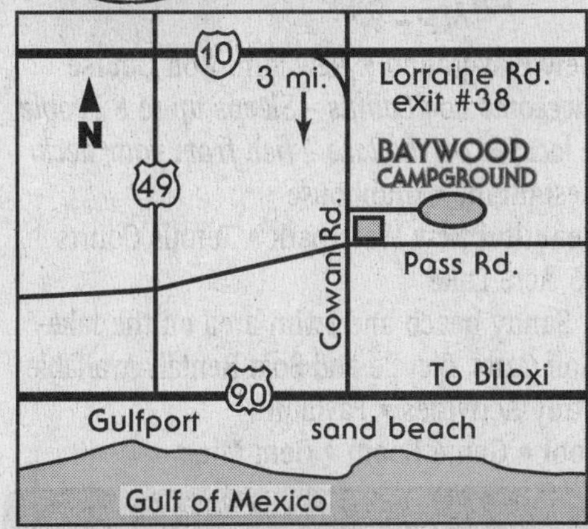

$1\frac{1}{4}$ mi North of U.S. 90 on Cowan Rd.
Take Exit #38 off I-10 then 3 miles South on left.

Toll-Free (888) 747-4840 • (228) 896-4840

www.southernrvparks/baywood/

1100 Cowan Road • Gulfport, MS 39507

See listing at Gulfport, MS

HOLLANDALE—C-2

(W) LEROY PERCY SP—(Washington) *From jct US 61 & Hwy 12: Go 6 mi W on Hwy 12.*

WELCOME

FACILITIES: 16 sites, typical site width 35 ft, 34 ft max RV length, 15 W&E, 1 no hkups, tenting, cabins, dump station, laundry, ltd groceries, ice, tables, patios, fire rings, grills, wood, controlled access gate.

RECREATION: pavilion, equipped pavilion, swim pool, boating, 10 hp limit, ramp, dock, 10 row-

HOLLANDALE—Continued
LEROY PERCY SP—Continued

boat/5 pedal boat rentals, lake fishing, playground, sports field, hiking trails, v-ball. Rec open to public.

Pets welcome. Open all yr. MC/VISA. Phone: (662) 827-5436.

SEE AD TRAVEL SECTION PAGE 464

HOLLY SPRINGS—A-3

HOLLY SPRINGS NATIONAL FOREST (Chewalla Lake Campground)—(Marshall) *From town: Go 5 mi NE on Hwy 4, then 1 mi S on CR 634, then 1 mi E on FR 611.* FACILITIES: 36 sites, 22 ft max RV length, 9 W&E, 27 no hkups, tenting, dump station, grills, wood. RECREATION: pavilion, lake swimming, boating, ramp, lake fishing, playground. Partial handicap access. Open all yr. Max stay 14 days. Phone: (662)236-6550.

(S) WALL DOXEY SP—(Benton) *From jct US 78 & Hwy 7: Go 6 mi S on Hwy 7.*

WELCOME

FACILITIES: 64 sites, 64 W&E, tenting, cabins, RV storage, dump station, laundry, ice, tables, patios, fire rings, grills, wood.

RECREATION: rec hall, pavilion, lake swimming, boating, electric motors only, canoeing, ramp, dock, 6 rowboat/6 canoe/6 pedal boat rentals, lake fishing, mini-golf, bsktball, playground, sports field, hiking trails, v-ball. Rec open to public.

Pets welcome. Open all yr. MC/VISA. Phone: (662) 252-4231.

SEE AD TRAVEL SECTION PAGE 464

HORN LAKE—A-3

(S) AUDUBON POINT RV PARK—(DeSoto) *Call for directions. Enter at end.*

MISSISSIPPI'S NEWEST RV PARK
Come join us At our new upscale RV Park. Conveniently located near Memphis, Graceland, Beal Street, Casinos and SE Veral Sports Complexes. Wi-Fi and cable to each site and a friendly staff to assist you.

◆◆◆◆◆FACILITIES: 114 sites, 114 full hkups, (20, 30 & 50 amps), some extended stay sites, 60 pull-thrus, cable TV, wireless Instant Internet ac-

HORN LAKE—Continued
AUDUBON POINT RV PARK—Continued

cess at site, wireless Internet access central location, RV storage, laundry, ltd groceries, RV supplies, LP gas by weight/by meter, ice, tables, patios.

◆◆◆RECREATION: rec hall, equipped pavilion, coin games, swim pool, golf nearby, playground, shuffleboard court.

Pets welcome, quantity restrict. Partial handicap access. No tents. Open all yr. Big rigs welcome. Internet friendly. Escort to site. Clubs welcome. Rate in 2007 $28-32 for 2 persons. MC/VISA/ Debit. Member ARVC. Phone: (662)280-8282.

e-mail: audubonpointrv1@bellsouth.net

SEE AD MEMPHIS, TN PAGE 805

HOUSTON—B-4

TOMBIGBEE NATIONAL FOREST (Davis Lake Campground)—(Chickasaw) *From town: Go 10 mi NE on Hwy-15, then 3 mi E on CR 903.* FACILITIES: 25 sites, 22 ft max RV length, 25 W&E, (20 amps), tenting, dump station, grills. RECREATION: pavilion, lake swimming, boating, ramp, dock, lake fishing. Pets welcome. Open all yr. Both facilities currently unavailable ; they are under construction. Phone: (662)285-3264.

IUKA—A-5

(NE) JP COLEMAN SP—(Tishomingo) *From jct US 17 & Hwy 25: Go 5 mi N on Hwy 25, then 8 mi NE on paved road. Follow signs.*

WELCOME

FACILITIES: 74 sites, 32 ft max RV length, 74 W&E, tenting, cabins, dump station, laundry, ice, tables, grills.

RECREATION: pavilion, swim pool, lake swimming, boating, ramp, dock, 6 rowboat rentals, lake fishing, mini-golf, playground, sports field. Rec open to public.

Pets welcome. Open all yr. MC/VISA. Phone: (662) 423-6515.

SEE AD TRAVEL SECTION PAGE 464

JACKSON—D-3

(NE) GOSHEN SPRINGS CAMPGROUND (Pearl River Valley Water Supply District)—(Rankin) *From Natchez Trace Pkwy & Hwy-43: Go 3 mi E on Hwy-43. Enter on L.* FACILITIES:

GOSHEN SPRINGS CAMPGROUND (Pearl River Valley Water Supply District)—Continued on next page

ACKSON—Continued
;OSHEN SPRINGS CAMPGROUND (Pearl River Valley Water Supply istrict)—Continued

74 sites, typical site width 25 ft, 174 full hkups, (20, 30 & 50 mps), mostly extended stay sites, dump station, laundry, patios, rills. RECREATION: pavilion, swim pool, lake/river swimming, oating, canoeing, ramp, dock, lake/river fishing, playground. ec open to public. Pets welcome. Partial handicap access. No ents. Open all yr. Big rigs welcome. Internet friendly. Phone: 601)829-2751.

(N) Homewood Manor MH & RV Park—GINDS) *From jct I-20 & I-55: Go 8 mi N on I-55 (exit 02B), then 1/2 mi W on Beasley, then 1 mi S on North State St. Enter on L.* ◊◊◊◊FACILITIES: 16 sites, typical site width 40 ft, accepts full hkup units only, 16 full hkups, (20, 30 & 50 amps), some extended stay sites. Pets welcome. No tents. Open all yr. Big rigs welcome. Rate in 2007 $22-25 per vehicle. Phone: (601)366-421.

(N) LEFLEUR'S BLUFF SP & GOLF COURSE—(Hinds) *From jct I-55 (exit 98B-Carthage/Lakeland) & Hwy 25N: Go 1 mi E on Hwy 25N to camping entrance.*

FACILITIES: 30 sites, 30 W&E, tenting, dump station, ltd groceries, tables, grills, wood, controlled access gate.

RECREATION: pavilion, swim pool, boating, electric motors only, canoeing, ramp, 8 rowboat/6 canoe/8 pedal boat rentals, lake fishing, putting green, playground, tennis, sports field, hiking trails. Rec open to public.

Pets welcome. Open all yr. Phone: (601)987-3923.

SEE AD TRAVEL SECTION PAGE 464

MISSISSIPPI STATE PARKS—*From I-55 (exit 98A) & Woodrow Wilson Ave: Go 3/4 mi W on Woodrow Wilson, then 1/2 mi N on State St.* Mississippi State Parks offer 22 campgrounds with developed campsites, tenting, group camping & cabins-rustic to deluxe. Food service available in most parks. E-mail tjack2013@mdwfp.state.ms.us. Phone: (601)364-2152.

e-mail: tjack2013@mowfp.state.ms.us

SEE AD TRAVEL SECTION PAGE 464

(S) S & S APACHE CAMPING CENTER—*From jct I-55 & I-20 (exit 45): Go 1 mi W on I-20 (exit 43B), then 1 blk N on Terry Rd North. Enter on R.* SALES: travel trailers, 5th wheels, van campers, motor homes, mini-motor homes, fold-down camping trailers, pre-owned unit sales. SERVICES: full-time mech, RV appliance repair, body work/collision repair, sells parts/accessories, installs hitches. Open all yr. MC/VISA/DISC. Phone: (601)372-6426.

e-mail: servicessapache@bellsouth.net

SEE AD PAGE 478

(NE) TIMBERLAKE CAMPGROUND (Pearl River Valley Water Supply District)—(Rankin) *From jct I-55 & Lakeland Dr: Go 7 mi E on Lakeland Dr, then 4 mi N on Old Fannin Rd. Enter on L.* FACILITIES: 272 sites, typical site width 25 ft, 272 full hkups, (15, 30 & 50 amps), many extended stay sites, tenting, dump station, laundry, ice, patios, grills. RECREATION: rec room/area, swim pool, lake swimming, boating, ramp, dock, lake fishing, playground, 2 shuffleboard courts, tennis, hiking trails. Rec open to public. Pets welcome. Partial handicap access. Open all yr. Big rigs welcome. Internet friendly. Phone: (601)992-9100.

LENA—D-3

(W) LEAKE COUNTY WATER PARK (Pearl River Valley Water Supply District)—(Leake) *From jct Natchez Trace Parkway & Hwy 43: Go 7 mi E on Hwy 43, then 10 mi N on Hwy 25, then 3 mi NW on Utah Rd, then 3 mi W on Park Rd (follow signs). Enter at end.* FACILITIES: 42 sites, typical site width 25 ft, 42 full hkups, (15, 30 & 50 amps), some extended stay sites, tenting, dump station, laundry, patios, grills. RECREATION: pavilion, swim pool, river swimming, boating, canoeing, ramp, dock, river fishing, playground, hiking trails, v-ball. Rec open to public. Pets welcome. Partial handicap access. Open all yr. Big rigs welcome. Phone: (601)654-9359.

(W) LOW HEAD DAM (Pearl River Valley Water Supply District)—(Leake) *From jct Natchez Trace Parkway & Hwy 43: Go 7 mi E on Hwy 43, then 10 mi N on Hwy 25, then 3 mi NW on Utah Rd, then 5 mi W on Lowhead Dam Rd. Enter at end.* FACILITIES: 13 sites, 13 W&E, (15, 30 & 50 amps), some extended stay sites, tenting, grills. RECREATION: swim pool, river swimming, boating, canoeing, ramp, river fishing. Pets welcome. Partial handicap access. Open all yr. Big rigs welcome. Phone: (601) 654-9359.

The Natchez Trace Parkway, named an All-American Road by the federal government, extends from Natchez to just south of Nashville, Tennessee. The Trace began as an Indian trail more than 8,000 years ago.

LONG BEACH—F4

(N) PLANTATION PINES RV RESORT—(Harrison) *From I-10 (exit 31) & Canal Rd: Go 2-3/4 mi S on Canal Rd, then 1-3/4 mi W on 28th St. Enter on L.*

◊◊◊FACILITIES: 69 sites, 55 full hkups, 4 W&E, (30 & 50 amps), 10 no hkups, some extended stay sites, 6 pull-thrus, cable TV, wireless Instant Internet access at site, wireless Internet access central location, RV storage, laundry.

◊◊RECREATION: rec room/area, swim pool, mini-golf ($), golf nearby, horseshoes.

Pets welcome, breed restrict. Partial handicap access. No tents. Open all yr. Internet friendly. Escort to site. Clubs welcome. Rate in 2007 $30-45 for 2 persons. MC/VISA. Phone: (228)863-6550.

e-mail: ian@plantationpinesrvresort.com

SEE AD TRAVEL SECTION PAGE 461

LOUISVILLE—C-4

(N) LEGION SP—(Winston) *From Hwy 14E (Main St) in town: Go 2 mi N on N Columbus Ave (Bypass Hwy 25). Enter on L.*

FACILITIES: 15 sites, 15 no hkups, tenting, cabins, tables, grills, wood, controlled access gate.

RECREATION: pavilion, boating, electric motors only, 6 rowboat/pedal boat rentals, lake fishing, bsktball, hiking trails. Rec open to public.

Pets welcome. Open all yr. For tent camping only. No RVs. Phone: (662)773-8323.

SEE AD TRAVEL SECTION PAGE 464

LUDLOW—D-3

(W) COAL BLUFF PARK (Pearl River Valley Water Supply District)—(Scott) *From jct Natchez Trace Parkway & Hwy 43: Go 7 mi E on Hwy 43, then 9 mi N on Hwy 25, then 3 mi W on Riverbend Rd, then 4 mi N on Coal Bluff Rd. Enter at end.* FACILITIES: 68 sites, typical site width 25 ft, 12 full hkups, 36 W&E, (15, 30 & 50 amps), 20 no hkups, some extended stay sites, 3 pull-thrus, tenting, dump station, laundry, patios, fire rings, grills. RECREATION: pavilion, equipped pavilion, swim pool, river swimming, boating, canoeing, ramp, river/pond fishing, playground, tennis, sports field, hiking trails, v-ball. Rec open to public. Pets welcome. Partial handicap access. Open all yr. Big rigs welcome. Phone: (601)654-7726.

LUMBERTON—E-3

LITTLE BLACK CREEK WATER PARK (Pat Harrison Waterway District)—(Lamar) *From jct I-59 (exit 41) & Hwy 13: Go 3 mi W on Hwy 13, then 1/3 mi N on US 11, then 7 mi NW on Mynich Rd. Follow signs.* FACILITIES: 106 sites, typical site width 23 ft, 82 full hkups, 24 W&E, (30 & 50 amps), some extended stay sites, tenting, dump station, laundry, ltd groceries, LP gas by weight, ice, patios, fire rings, grills, wood. RECREATION: equipped pavilion, lake swimming, boating, canoeing, ramp, dock, 8 rowboat/2 canoe/pedal boat rentals, lake fishing, playground, sports field, hiking trails, v-ball. Rec open to public. Open all yr. Phone: (601)794-2957.

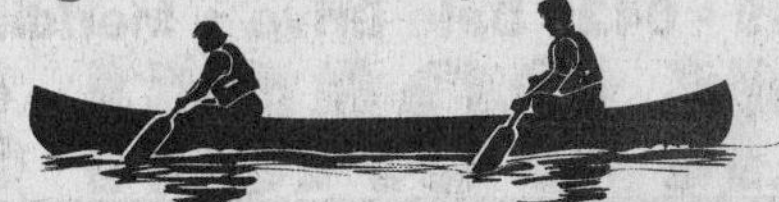

MADISON—D-3

(W) CAMPER CORRAL—*From jct I-55 (exit 112) & Gluckstadt Rd: Go 1/4 mi W on Gluckstadt Rd. then 1/2 mi S on Distribution Dr. Enter at end.* SALES: travel trailers, 5th wheels, mini-motor homes, micro-mini motor homes, pre-owned unit sales. SERVICES: full-time mech, RV appliance repair, body work/collision repair, dump station, sells parts/accessories, installs hitches. Open all yr. MC/VISA/DISC. Phone: (601)856-6070.

e-mail: camper@telapex.com

SEE AD THIS PAGE

MCCOMB—E-2

(E) BOGUE CHITTO WATER PARK CAMPGROUND (Pearl River Basin Dev. Dist.)—(Pike) *From jct I-55 & Hwy 98 east (exit 15A): Go 12 mi E on Hwy 98, then at Brown Bogue Chitto Water Park sign, go 1 mi S on Dogwood Trail. Enter at end.*

FACILITIES: 91 sites, typical site width 28 ft, 7 full hkups, 74 W&E, (30 & 50 amps), 10 no hkups, tenting, cabins, dump station, ice, tables, patios, fire rings, grills, wood, controlled access gate.

RECREATION: pavilion, equipped pavilion, boating, canoeing, ramp, float trips, river fishing, golf nearby, bsktball, playground, sports field, hiking trails, v-ball. Rec open to public.

Pets welcome. Partial handicap access. Open all yr. Big rigs welcome. Clubs welcome. Phone: (601)684-9568.

SEE AD THIS PAGE

(W) PERCY QUIN SP & QUAIL HOLLOW GOLF COURSE—(Pike) *From jct I-55 (exit 13) & Fernwood Rd: Go 3/4 mi W on Fernwood Rd, then 1/4 mi N on Hwy 48.*

FACILITIES: 100 sites, 32 ft max RV length, 100 W&E, tenting, cabins, dump station, laundry, ltd groceries, ice, tables, wood.

RECREATION: rec hall, pavilion, swim pool, lake swimming, boating, canoeing, ramp, dock, 6 rowboat/6 canoe/6 pedal boat rentals, lake fishing, mini-golf, bsktball, playground, tennis, sports field, hiking trails. Rec open to public.

Pets welcome. Open all yr. MC/VISA. Phone: (601) 684-3938.

SEE AD TRAVEL SECTION PAGE 464

In 1902, while on a hunting expedition in Sharkey County, President Theodore (Teddy) Roosevelt refused to shoot a captured baby bear. This act resulted in the creation of the world-famous "teddy bear".

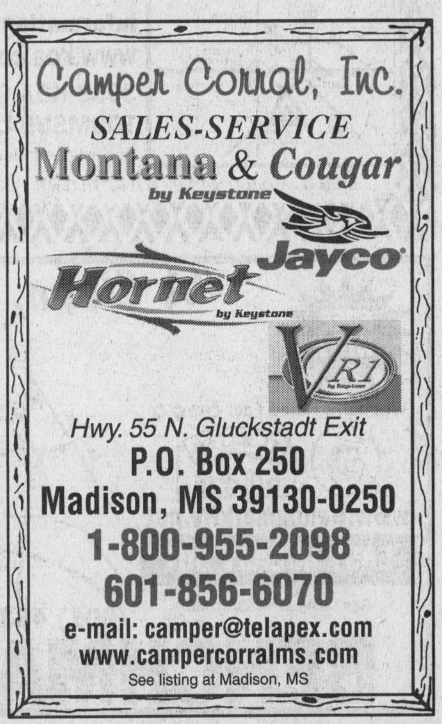

MENDENHALL—D-3

D'LO WATER PARK (Pearl River Basin Dev. Dist.)—(Simpson) *From town: Go 2 mi W on Old US 49 (D'Lo).* FACILITIES: 12 sites, 12 full hkups, (30 & 50 amps), dump station, non-guest dumping $, ice, fire rings, grills. RECREATION: pavilion, equipped pavilion, river swimming, boating, canoeing, ramp, dock, 43 canoe rentals, river fishing, playground, sports field. Rec open to public. Open all yr. Phone: (601)847-4310.

MERIDIAN—D-4

(E) BENCHMARK COACH AND RV PARK—(Lauderdale) *From jct I-20/59 (exit 157B) & Hwy 45: Go 2 mi N on US 45 N to Marion Russell exit, then 1 mi W on Marion Russell, then 1 mi N on Dale Dr.*

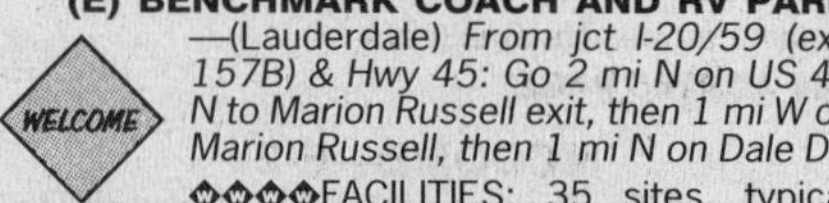

♦♦♦♦FACILITIES: 35 sites, typical site width 30 ft, 35 full hkups, (20, 30 & 50 amps), 27 pull-thrus, cable TV, wireless Instant Internet access at site, laundry, LP gas by weight/by meter, ice, tables.

Pets welcome, breed restrict. No tents. Open all yr. Big rigs welcome. Internet friendly. Clubs welcome. Rate in 2007 $25-30 for 2 persons. MC/VISA. Phone: (601)483-7999. CCUSA discount. FMCA discount.

e-mail: bigrigs@benchmarkrv.net

SEE AD THIS PAGE

(S) Bonita Lakes RV Park—(Lauderdale) *From jct I-20 (exit 157A) & Hwy 45 S: Go 1/4 mi S on Hwy 45, then 1/2 mi NW on Hwy 19. Enter on R.* ♦♦♦♦FACILITIES: 50 sites, 50 full hkups, (30 & 50 amps), many extended stay sites, 33 pull-thrus, laundry. ♦RECREATION: swim pool, pond fishing. Pets welcome. Partial handicap access. No tents. Open all yr. Big rigs welcome. Internet friendly. Rate in 2007 $25 per vehicle. Phone: (601)483-4330.

MERIDIAN—Continued

(E) KOA-MERIDIAN EAST/TOOMSUBA—(Lauderdale) *From jct US 45 & I-20/59: Go 8-1/4 mi E on I-20/59 (exit 165), then 1-1/4 mi S on Will Garrett Rd, then 1/2 mi W on KOA Campground Rd. Enter on R.*

♦♦♦♦FACILITIES: 49 sites, typical site width 23 ft, 26 full hkups, 23 W&E, (20, 30 & 50 amps), 26 pull-thrus, phone Internet access central location, tenting, cabins, dump station, laundry, groceries, RV supplies, LP gas by weight/by meter, ice, tables, fire rings, grills, wood.

♦♦♦♦RECREATION: rec hall, rec room/area, swim pool, bsktball, playground, horseshoes. Rec open to public.

Pets welcome. Partial handicap access. Open all yr. Big rigs welcome. Internet friendly. Escort to site. Clubs welcome. Rate in 2007 $25-32 for 2 persons. MC/VISA/DISC/AMEX. Phone: (800)KOA-4202. KOA 10% value card discount.

e-mail: koameridian@comcast.net

SEE AD THIS PAGE AND AD DISCOVER SECTION PAGES 62 & 63

(E) NANABE CREEK CAMPGROUND—(Lauderdale) *From jct US 45 & I-20/59 (exit 157): Go 3-1/2 mi E on I-20/59 (exit 160), then 1 mi N on Russell Rd. Enter on R.*

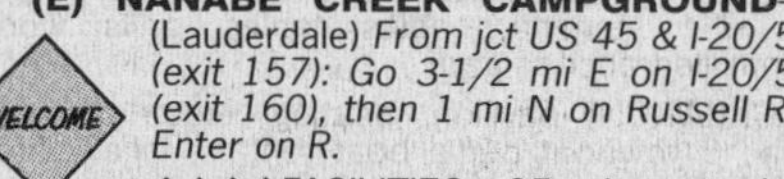

♦♦♦♦FACILITIES: 95 sites, typical site width 28 ft, 75 full hkups, 10 W&E, (20, 30 & 50 amps), 50 amps ($), 10 no hkups, some extended stay sites, 30 pull-thrus, phone Internet ac-

MERIDIAN—Continued
NANABE CREEK CAMPGROUND—Continued

cess central location, tenting, RV storage, laundry, ltd groceries, RV supplies, LP gas by weight/by meter, ice, tables, fire rings, wood.

♦♦♦RECREATION: rec room/area, pavilion, swim pool, pond fishing, bsktball, play equipment, sports field, v-ball. Rec open to public.

Pets welcome. Open all yr. Big rigs welcome. Internet friendly. Escort to site. Clubs welcome. Rate in 2007 $23-24.50 for 2 persons. Phone: (601)485-4711. FCRV 10% discount.

SEE AD THIS PAGE

OKATIBBEE WATER PARK (Pat Harrison Waterway District)—(Lauderdale) *From jct I-20/59 (exit 150) & Hwy 19: Go 5 mi N on Hwy 19, then 8 mi N on Pine Spring Rd. Follow signs.* FACILITIES: 105 sites, typical site width 25 ft, 75 full hkups, 30 W&E, (50 amps), some extended stay sites, 6 pull-thrus, tenting, dump station, laundry, patios, fire rings, grills, wood. RECREATION: equipped pavilion, swim pool, lake swimming, boating, canoeing, ramp, dock, lake fishing, playground, sports field, hiking trails, v-ball. Rec open to public. Open all yr. Phone: (601)737-2370.

TWILTLEY BRANCH CAMPING AREA (COE-Okatibbee Lake)—(Lauderdale) *From town: Go 10 mi NW on Hwy 19, then 2 mi E on CR 17.* FACILITIES: 61 sites, 50 W&E, (30 amps), 11 no hkups, 3 pull-thrus, tenting, dump station, laundry, fire rings, grills. RECREATION: pavilion, lake swimming, boating, canoeing, ramp, lake fishing, playground, hiking trails. Partial handicap access. Open all yr. Phone: (601)626-8068.

MONTICELLO—E-3

ATWOOD WATER PARK (Pearl River Basin Dev. Dist.)—(Lawrence) *From town: Go 1 mi E on Hwy-84.* FACILITIES: 44 sites, 44 W&E, tenting, dump station, non-guest dumping. RECREATION: pavilion, boating, ramp, river fishing, playground, tennis, sports field, hiking trails. Rec open to public. Partial handicap access. Open Mar thru Oct. Phone: (601)587-0045.

MORTON—D-3

(N) ROOSEVELT SP—(Scott) *From jct I-20 (exit 77) & Hwy 13: Go 1/2 mi N on Hwy 13.*

FACILITIES: 109 sites, 28 full hkups, 81 W&E, 1 pull-thrus, tenting, cabins, dump station, laundry, tables, patios.

RECREATION: rec hall, rec room/area, pavilion, swim pool, lake swimming, boating, canoeing, ramp, dock, 6 rowboat/6 canoe/6 pedal boat rent-

ROOSEVELT SP—Continued on next page

MORTON—Continued
ROOSEVELT SP—Continued

als, lake fishing, mini-golf, playground, tennis, sports field, hiking trails, v-ball. Rec open to public.

Pets welcome. Open all yr. MC/VISA. Phone: (601) 732-6316.

SEE AD TRAVEL SECTION PAGE 464

MOUNT OLIVE—E-3

DRY CREEK WATER PARK (Pat Harrison Waterway District)—(Covington) *From jct US 49 & park road: Go 4-1/2 mi W on park road. Follow signs.* FACILITIES: 28 sites, typical site width 23 ft, 38 ft max RV length, 28 W&E, some extended stay sites, tenting, dump station, patios, fire rings, grills, wood. RECREATION: pavilion, lake swimming, boating, canoeing, ramp, 4 rowboat rentals, lake fishing, playground, hiking trails. Rec open to public. Open all yr. Phone: (601)797-4619.

MT. PLEASANT—A-3

(NW) Pickard's RV Park (RV SPACES)—(Marshall) *From jct SH 302 & US Hwy 72: Go 3 mi W on US 72. Enter on L.* FACILITIES: 24 sites, accepts self-contained units only, 24 full hkups, (30 & 50 amps). Pets welcome. No tents. Open all yr. No restrooms. Rate in 2007 $15 per vehicle. Phone: (901)292-5000.

NATCHEZ—E-1

(NE) NATCHEZ SP—(Adams) *From north jct US 84/98 & US 61: Go 5-1/4 mi NE on US 61, then 3/4 mi E on park road.*

FACILITIES: 50 sites, 32 ft max RV length, 6 full hkups, 44 W&E, tenting, cabins, dump station, tables, grills.

RECREATION: pavilion, boating, ramp, dock, 6 rowboat/6 pedal boat rentals, lake fishing, playground, hiking trails. Rec open to public.

Pets welcome. Open all yr. Phone: (601)442-2658.

e-mail: natchez@tacinfo.com

SEE AD TRAVEL SECTION PAGE 464

NATCHEZ TRACE COMPACT—Take an unforgettable road trip along this 444 mi National Scenic Byway & All-American Road that stretches from the Mississippi River in Natchez through the Shoals area in Alabama and across the Tennessee Valley to Nashville. Open all yr. Phone: (800)305-7417.

e-mail: natr_superintendent@nps.gov

SEE AD TRAVEL SECTION PAGE 461 AND AD AL TRAVEL SECTION PAGE 1 AND AD TN TRAVEL SECTION PAGE 783

OAKLAND—B-3

(NE) GEORGE PAYNE COSSAR SP—(Tallahatchie) *From jct I-55 (exit 227) & Hwy 32: Go 2-1/2 mi E on Hwy 32, then 1-3/4 mi N on park access road.*

FACILITIES: 84 sites, 32 ft max RV length, 84 W&E, tenting, cabins, dump station, laundry, ice, tables, patios, fire rings, grills, wood, controlled access gate.

RECREATION: rec hall, pavilion, swim pool, boating, ramp, 6 rowboat rentals, lake fishing, mini-golf, 8 bike rentals, playground, sports field, hiking trails, v-ball. Rec open to public.

Pets welcome. Open all yr. Church services Memorial Day to Labor Day. MC/VISA. Phone: (662)623-7356.

SEE AD TRAVEL SECTION PAGE 464

OCEAN SPRINGS—F-4

(NE) CAMP JOURNEY'S END—(Jackson) *From jct I-10 (exit 57) & Hwy 57: Go 1/2 mi N on Hwy 57. Enter on L.*

CAMP JOURNEY'S END

A year round full service RV Park and campground. Great for a family summer getaway or a senior winter retreat. Conveniently located for exploring the Mississippi Gulf Coast, just north of interstate 10 at Exit 57.

◇◇◇◇◇FACILITIES: 117 sites, typical site width 28 ft, 105 full hkups, 12 W&E, (30 & 50 amps), many extended stay sites, 30 pull-thrus, cable TV, wireless Internet access central location, tenting, RV/park trailer rentals, cabins, dump station, laundry, ltd groceries, RV supplies, LP gas by weight/by meter, ice, tables, patios, controlled access gate.

◇◇◇◇◇RECREATION: rec hall, rec room/area, pavilion, swim pool, boating, ramp, dock, river/pond fishing, fishing supplies, golf nearby, bsktball, playground, planned activities (wkends only), horseshoes, v-ball.

Pets welcome, breed restrict. Open all yr. Big rigs welcome. Internet friendly. Escort to site. Clubs welcome. Rate in 2007 $32-38 for 2 persons. MC/VISA/DISC/AMEX/Debit. Member ARVC. Phone: (228)875-2100. FMCA discount.

e-mail: info@campjourneys-end.com

SEE AD BILOXI PAGE 472

GULF ISLANDS NATIONAL SEASHORE (Davis Bayou Area)—*From town: Go 2 mi E on US 90, then 1 mi S on Park Rd.* FACILITIES: 51 sites, 51 W&E, (30 amps), tenting, dump station, grills. RECREATION: pavilion, boating, ramp, dock, saltwater fishing, playground, planned activities, hiking trails. Rec open to public. Partial handicap access. Open all yr. Phone: (228)875-3962.

OLIVE BRANCH—A-3

(N) SOUTHAVEN RV CENTERS—*From jct I-240 (exit 21) & US 78/Lamar Ave (in Memphis): Go 9 mi SE on US 78, then 1 block E on Craft Rd, then 1/2 mi S on Craft-Goodman Rd (East Frontage Rd). Enter on L.* SALES: travel trailers, 5th wheels, motor homes, mini-motor homes, fold-down camping trailers, pre-owned unit sales. SERVICES: full-time mech, RV appliance repair, body work/collision repair, sells parts/accessories, installs hitches. Open all yr. MC/VISA/DISC. Phone: (888)307-6401.

SEE AD MEMPHIS, TN PAGE 807

PASCAGOULA—F-5

See listings at Escatawpa, Gautier, Ocean Springs

PELAHATCHIE—D-3

(N) YOGI ON THE LAKE (TOO NEW TO RATE)—(Rankin) *From I-20 (exit 68) & Hwy 43, then 2 mi N on Hwy 43, then 1/2 mi W on Lake Rd to Campgrounds Rd.*

FACILITIES: tenting.

Open all yr. Phone: (601)854-6859.

SEE AD JACKSON PAGE 478 AND AD DISCOVER SECTION PAGE 141

PHILADELPHIA—C-4

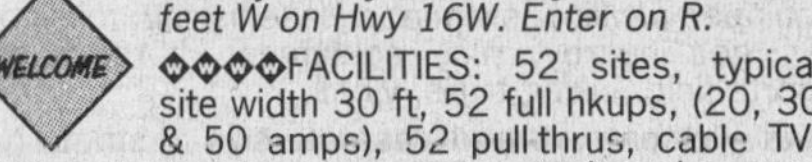

(W) FROG LEVEL RV PARK—(Neshoba) *From jct Hwy 15 & Hwy 16W: Go 500 feet W on Hwy 16W. Enter on R.*

◇◇◇◇FACILITIES: 52 sites, typical site width 30 ft, 52 full hkups, (20, 30 & 50 amps), 52 pull-thrus, cable TV, wireless Instant Internet access at site, phone on-site Internet access (needs activ), phone Internet access central location, laundry, full svc store, LP gas by weight, gas, ice, tables.

◇RECREATION: rec hall.

Pets welcome, breed restrict. Partial handicap access. No tents. Open all yr. Big rigs welcome. Internet friendly. Clubs welcome. Rate in 2007 $20 for 4 persons. MC/VISA/DISC/AMEX/DC. Phone: (601)650-0044.

e-mail: hop@froglevelrv.com

SEE AD THIS PAGE

PICAYUNE—F-3

(NE) CLEARWATER RV PARK—(Pearl River) *From jct I-59 & Hwy 43 (exit 4): Go 1 mi E on Hwy 43, then 7-1/2 mi N on Ceasar Rd. Enter on L.*

ENJOY SOUNDS OF THE OLD WATER WHEEL

As you swing by the waters edge. Take a walk back in time admiring rustic buildings, flowers all in a country setting. At dark stars appear within reach activities available or relax in peace and serenity. More info visit website.

◇◇◇◇FACILITIES: 65 sites, 65 full hkups, (20, 30 & 50 amps), some extended stay sites, 3 pull-thrus, wireless Instant Internet access at site, wireless Internet access central location, tenting, RV/park trailer rentals, cabins, RV storage, laundry, ltd groceries, RV supplies, LP gas by weight/by meter, ice, tables, fire rings, wood.

◇◇◇◇RECREATION: rec hall, pavilion, pond fishing, putting green, golf nearby, playground, planned activities (wkends only), horseshoes, sports field.

Pets welcome. Partial handicap access. Open all yr. Big rigs welcome. Internet friendly. Escort to site. Clubs welcome. Rate in 2007 $25 for 2 persons. MC/VISA/Debit. Phone: (601)749-8142.

e-mail: clearwater@datastar.net

SEE AD NEW ORLEANS, LA PAGE 313

(E) SUN ROAMERS RV RESORT—(Pearl River) *From jct I-59 & Hwy 43 (exit 4): Go 3/4 mi E on Hwy 43 then 1/2 mi S on Stafford Rd. Enter on R.*

RETREAT TO SUNNY MISSISSIPPI

Pleasantly placed between New Orleans, Casinos, Six Flags and all major attractions. Experience the wonderful, and beautiful, diversions that Southern Mississippi has to offer.

◇◇◇◇FACILITIES: 154 sites, typical site width 50 ft, 154 full hkups, (30 & 50 amps), some extended stay sites, wireless Instant Internet access at site, cabins, RV storage, dump station, non-guest dumping $, laundry, LP gas by weight/by meter, ice, tables.

SUN ROAMERS RV RESORT—Continued on next page

PICAYUNE—Continued
SUN ROAMERS RV RESORT—Continued

◆◆◆◆RECREATION: rec hall, rec room/area, equipped pavilion, swim pool, lake fishing, mini-golf ($), golf nearby, play equipment, horseshoes, sports field, hiking trails, v-ball.

Pets welcome, breed restrict, size restrict. No tents. Open all yr. Big rigs welcome. Internet friendly. Escort to site. Clubs welcome. Rate in 2007 $26-38 for 2 persons. MC/VISA/Debit. Phone: (601)798-5818. FMCA discount.

e-mail: info@sunroamers.com

Reserve Online at Woodalls.com

SEE AD NEW ORLEANS, LA PAGE 314

PORT GIBSON—D-2

(NW) GRAND GULF MILITARY PARK CAMPGROUND (State)—(Claiborne) *From jct US 61 & Hwy 462: Go 7 mi W on paved road (follow signs). Enter on R.* FACILITIES: 42 sites, typical site width 35 ft, 42 full hkups, (50 amps), 2 pull-thrus, tenting, dump station, laundry, patios, grills, wood. RECREATION: pavilion, sports field, hiking trails. Partial handicap access. Open all yr. Phone: (601)437-5911.

(NE) NATCHEZ TRACE PARKWAY (Rocky Springs Campground)—(Claiborne) *From jct Hwy 18 & Natchez Trace Pkwy: Go 13 mi N on Natchez Trace Pkwy. Enter on L.* FACILITIES: 22 sites, 35 ft max RV length, 22 no hkups, tenting, fire rings, grills. RECREATION: hiking trails. Pets welcome. Open all yr. No showers. No reservations. Phone: (662)680-4025.

QUITMAN—D-4

(NW) ARCHUSA CREEK WATER PARK (Pat Harrison Waterway District)—(Clarke) *From jct I-59 (exit 126) & Hwy 18: Go 9 mi E on Hwy 18, then 3 mi N on US 45/Hwy 18, then 1-1/4 mi E on Hwy 18, then 1 mi E on Hwy 511. Follow signs.* FACILITIES: 69 sites, typical site width 25 ft, 38 ft max RV length, 48 full hkups, 21 W&E, (30 & 50 amps), tenting, dump station, laundry, fire rings, grills, wood. RECREATION: rec hall, pavilion, equipped pavilion, lake swimming, boating, canoeing, ramp, dock, 6 rowboat rentals, lake fishing, playground, sports field, hiking trails. Rec open to public. Open all yr. Phone: (601)776-6956.

(N) CLARKCO SP—(Clarke) *From town: Go 5 mi N on US-45.*

FACILITIES: 43 sites, 32 ft max RV length, 43 W&E, 2 pull-thrus, cabins, dump station, laundry, groceries, tables, wood.

RECREATION: rec hall, pavilion, lake swimming, boating, canoeing, ramp, dock, 6 rowboat/6 canoe/6 pedal boat rentals, lake fishing, playground, tennis, sports field, hiking trails. Rec open to public.

Pets welcome. Open all yr. MC/VISA. Phone: (601) 776-6651.

SEE AD TRAVEL SECTION PAGE 464

ROBINSONVILLE—A-3

(E) BUCK ISLAND MHC (RV SPACES) —(TUNICA) *From jct Hwy 61 & CR-304: Go 1-1/2 mi E on CR 304, then 2 mi S on Kirby Rd.*

FACILITIES: 44 sites, accepts full hkup units only, 44 full hkups, (30 & 50 amps), some extended stay sites.

Pets welcome, breed restrict, size restrict. No tents. Open all yr. Big rigs welcome. Rate in 2007 $22 for 2 persons. Phone: (662)363-0121.

e-mail: buckisland@wildblue.net

SEE AD THIS PAGE AND AD MEMPHIS, TN PAGE 803 AND AD MILLINGTON, TN PAGE 808

The Mississippi River is the longest river in North America and is the nation's chief waterway. Its nicknames include "Old Man River" and "Ole Miss".

ROSEDALE—B-2

(W) GREAT RIVER ROAD SP—(Bolivar) *From jct Hwys 1/8: Go 1 mi W on park access road.*

FACILITIES: 61 sites, 61 W&E, tenting, dump station, laundry, ice, tables, patios, grills, wood, controlled access gate.

RECREATION: rec hall, rec room/area, pavilion, lake/river swimming, boating, no motors, canoeing, ramp, 6 rowboat/6 canoe/6 pedal boat rentals, lake/river fishing, bsktball, 8 bike rentals, playground, sports field, hiking trails. Rec open to public.

Pets welcome. Open all yr. MC/VISA. Phone: (662) 759-6762.

SEE AD TRAVEL SECTION PAGE 464

SARDIS—A-3

(E) JOHN KYLE SP & MALLARD POINT GOLF COURSE—(Panola) *From jct I-55 (exit 252) & Hwy 315: Go 7 mi SE on Hwy 315.*

FACILITIES: 200 sites, 200 W&E, tenting, cabins, dump station, laundry, ice, tables, grills, wood.

RECREATION: rec hall, pavilion, swim pool, lake swimming, boating, ramp, rowboat rentals, lake fishing, 8 bike rentals, playground, tennis, sports field, hiking trails. Rec open to public.

Pets welcome. Open all yr. MC/VISA. Phone: (662) 487-1345.

SEE AD TRAVEL SECTION PAGE 464

SOSO—E-4

(W) BIG CREEK WATER PARK (Pat Harrison Waterway District)—(Jones) *From jct I-59 & US 84: Go 12 mi W on US 84, then 1 mi S on park road. Follow signs.* FACILITIES: 46 sites, 38 ft max RV length, 20 full hkups, 26 W&E, tenting, dump station, laundry, fire rings, grills, wood. RECREATION: pavilion, lake swimming, boating, canoeing, ramp, dock, 4 rowboat rentals, lake fishing, playground, sports field, hiking trails. Rec open to public. Open all yr. Phone: (601)763-8555.

SOUTHAVEN—A-3

(S) EZ DAZE RV PARK (TOO NEW TO RATE) —(Desoto) *From jct I-55 (exit 287) & Church Rd: Go 1/8 mi W on Church Rd, then 3/4 mi N on Pepper Chase Dr, then 1 block W on WE Ross Parkway. Enter on R.*

BRAND NEW RV PARK DESIGNED JUST FOR YOU!

Location, Location - It's central to Memphis attractions and Tunica Casinos. Relax on our veranda, chill out in our gazebo - enclosed hot tub or let our massage therapist relax those tired muscles. It's a first-class RV Park.

FACILITIES: 87 sites, 87 full hkups, (20, 30 & 50 amps), 5 pull-thrus, cable TV, wireless Instant Internet access at site, phone Internet access central location, laundry, RV supplies, LP gas by weight/by meter, LP bottle exch, ice, tables, patios.

RECREATION: pavilion, swim pool, whirlpool.

Pets welcome. Partial handicap access. No tents. Open all yr. Big rigs welcome. Internet friendly. Clubs welcome. Rate in 2007 $30-32 for 2 persons. Phone: (662)342-7720. FMCA discount.

e-mail: ezdazervpark@yahoo.com

SEE AD MEMPHIS, TN PAGE 807

Natchez now has more than 500 buildings that are on the National Register of Historic Places.

SOUTHAVEN—Continued

(S) SOUTHAVEN RV CENTERS—*From I-55 (exit 287) & Church Rd: Go 1/8 mi W on Church Rd, then 1/2 mi N on Pepper Chase. Enter on L.* SALES: travel trailers, 5th wheels, motor homes, mini-motor homes, fold-down camping trailers, pre-owned unit sales. SERVICES: full-time mech, RV appliance repair, body work/collision repair, sells parts/accessories, installs hitches. Open all yr. MC/VISA/DISC. Phone: (662)393-9948.

e-mail: robinkingsrv@yahoo.com

SEE AD MEMPHIS, TN PAGE 807

(N) SOUTHAVEN RV PARK—(DeSoto) *From I-55 (exit 291/Stateline Rd): Go 2 blocks E. Enter on L.*

TOP RATED PARK-MINUTES TO GRACELAND

Stay in our 5W rated park while you visit Memphis attractions, Tunica Casinos or just relax. Conveniently located at the TN/MS State Line-2 blocks off I-55. Enjoy good shopping & excellent restaurants. Free WiFi & cable TV.

◆◆◆◆◆FACILITIES: 44 sites, typical site width 29 ft, 44 full hkups, (20, 30 & 50 amps), many extended stay sites, 14 pull-thrus, cable TV, wireless Instant Internet access at site, phone on-site Internet access (needs activ), laundry, LP gas by weight/by meter, patios.

Pets welcome, breed restrict. Partial handicap access. No tents. Open all yr. Big rigs welcome. Internet friendly. Rate in 2007 $30 for 2 persons. MC/VISA/DISC/AMEX. Phone: (662)393-8585.

e-mail: shrvpark@aol.com

SEE AD MEMPHIS, TN PAGE 807

TISHOMINGO—A-5

(SE) TISHOMINGO SP—(Tishomingo) *From town: Go 1 mi S on Hwy 25, then 2 mi E on park road.*

FACILITIES: 62 sites, 32 ft max RV length, 62 W&E, tenting, cabins, dump station, laundry, tables, wood.

RECREATION: pavilion, swim pool, boating, 10 hp limit, canoeing, ramp, dock, 6 rowboat/6 canoe/6 pedal boat rentals, float trips, lake/river fishing, mini-golf, bsktball, 8 bike rentals, playground, sports field, hiking trails, v-ball. Rec open to public.

Pets welcome. Open all yr. MC/VISA. Phone: (662) 438-6914.

SEE AD TRAVEL SECTION PAGE 464

TUNICA—A-2

(C) GRAND CASINO RV RESORT—(Tunica) *From jct US 61 & Grand Casino Pkwy: Go 2-1/2 mi W on Grand Casino Pkwy. Enter at end.*

◆◆◆◆◆FACILITIES: 200 sites, 200 full hkups, (20, 30 & 50 amps), 79 pull-thrus, cable TV, wireless Instant Internet access at site ($), wireless Internet access central location, laundry, ltd groceries, RV supplies, LP gas by weight/by meter, ice, tables, patios, controlled access gate.

◆◆◆◆RECREATION: rec room/area, pavilion, coin games, swim pool, putting green, bsktball, playground, shuffleboard court, tennis, sports field, v-ball.

Pets welcome. Partial handicap access. No tents. Open all yr. Big rigs welcome. Internet friendly. Clubs welcome. Rate in 2007 $22-32 per family. MC/VISA/DISC/AMEX/DC. Phone: (800)WIN 4-WIN.

SEE AD DISCOVER SECTION PAGE 37

(C) HOLLYWOOD CASINO—*From jct US 61 & Hwy 304: Go 5-1/2 mi W on Hwy 304. Enter on L.* Huge casino with dockside gambling, authentic Hollywood memorabilia and props, award-winning dining, RV park & hotel. Open all yr. MC/VISA/DISC/AMEX/DC. Phone: (800) 871-0711.

SEE AD TRAVEL SECTION PAGE 463 AND AD MEMPHIS, TN

TUNICA—Continued on next page

Jimmy Buffet, singer and songwriter, is from Mississippi.

TUNICA—Continued

(C) HOLLYWOOD CASINO RV RESORT—(Tunica) *From jct US 61 & Hwy 304: Go 5-1/2 mi W on Hwy 304. Enter at end.*

WELCOME

◆◆◆◆◆FACILITIES: 123 sites, typical site width 30 ft, accepts full hkup units only, 123 full hkups, (50 amps), 14 pull-thrus, cable TV, wireless Instant Internet access at site, dump station, laundry, RV supplies, LP gas by weight/by meter, ice, tables.

◆◆◆◆RECREATION: pavilion, coin games, swim pool, whirlpool, putting green.

Pets welcome. Partial handicap access. No tents. Open all yr. 7 day maximum stay. Holiday rates. Clubs welcome. Rate in 2007 $18 per vehicle. MC/VISA/DISC/AMEX/DC. ATM. Phone: (800)871-0711.

SEE AD MEMPHIS, TN PAGE 806 AND AD TRAVEL SECTION PAGE 463

(C) Sam's Town RV Park—*From jct 61 & Hwy 304 (Robinsonville exit): Go 5-1/2 mi W on Hwy 304 (Cross-over Mississippi River Levee) Follow Signs Enter on L.* ◆◆◆◆FACILITIES: 100 sites, typical site width 32 ft, 100 full hkups, (30 & 50 amps), 15 pull-thrus, laun-

TUNICA—Continued
Sam's Town RV Park—Continued

dry, ltd groceries, tables, patios, grills. ◆◆◆◆RECREATION: rec room/area, swim pool. Pets welcome. Partial handicap access. No tents. Open all yr. Big rigs welcome. Internet friendly. Rate in 2007 $12.99 per vehicle. Phone: (800)456-0711.

TUPELO—B-4

(N) CAMPGROUNDS AT BARNES CROSSING—(Lee) *From jct Natchez Trace Pkwy & US 78: Go 1-1/4 mi E on US 78, then 1-1/4 mi N on US 45, then 1/2 mi W on Barnes Crossing Rd, then 1/2 mi N on Old 45/145 to County Rd 1698. Enter on R.*

WELCOME

◆◆◆◆FACILITIES: 52 sites, 52 full hkups, (30 & 50 amps), some extended stay sites, 25 pull-thrus, cable TV, wireless Instant Internet access at site, phone Internet access central location, dump station, non-guest dumping $, laundry, RV supplies, ice, tables, patios.

RECREATION: golf nearby, hiking trails.

Pets welcome. No tents. Open all yr. Big rigs welcome. Internet friendly. Escort to site. Clubs welcome. Rate in 2007 $28 for 2 persons. Phone: (662)844-6063.

e-mail: cgbarnescrossing@bellsouth.net

SEE AD THIS PAGE

ELVIS PRESLEY LAKE & CAMPGROUND (County Park) —(Lee) *From jct US 45 & US 78: Go 1 mi E on US 78 (Veterans Blvd Exit), then 1 block N on Veterans Blvd, then 1 3/4 mi E on CR 1460, then 1/2 mi NE on CR 995. Enter on R.* FACILITIES: 66 sites, typical site width 30 ft, 16 W&E, 50 no hkups, 1 pull-thrus, tenting, dump station, fire rings, grills. RECREATION: pavilion, boating, ramp, dock, 3 rowboat/2 pedal boat rentals, lake fishing, hiking trails. Rec open to public. Open all yr. Phone: (662) 840-5172.

(SW) NATCHEZ TRACE RV PARK—(Lee) *From jct Hwy 78 & Natchez Trace Pkwy: Go 12 mi S on Natchez Trace Pkwy, exit between milepost 251 & 252, then 250 yards E on Pontocola Rd. Enter on R.*

WELCOME

◆◆◆◆FACILITIES: 30 sites, typical site width 30 ft, 14 full hkups, 11 W&E, (30 & 50 amps), 5 no hkups, some extended stay sites, 13 pull-thrus,

TUPELO—Continued
NATCHEZ TRACE RV PARK—Continued

phone Internet access central location, tenting, dump station, laundry, ltd groceries, RV supplies, LP gas by weight/by meter, ice, tables, wood.

◆◆◆RECREATION: rec room/area, pavilion, swim pool, pond fishing, fishing supplies, horseshoes.

Pets welcome. Open all yr. Big rigs welcome. Internet friendly. Clubs welcome. Rate in 2007 $20-22 per vehicle. Phone: (662)767-8609. CCUSA discount. FMCA discount.

e-mail: wez@dixieconnect.com

SEE AD THIS PAGE

(SE) TOMBIGBEE SP—(Lee) *From town: Go 3 mi SE on Hwy 6, then 3 mi E on state park road.*

WELCOME

FACILITIES: 20 sites, 20 W&E, tenting, cabins, dump station, laundry, ice, tables, fire rings, grills, wood.

RECREATION: rec hall, rec room/area, pavilion, lake swimming, boating, canoeing, ramp, dock, 8 rowboat/6 canoe/6 pedal boat rentals, lake fishing, playground, tennis, sports field, hiking trails, v-ball. Rec open to public.

Pets welcome. Open all yr. MC/VISA. Phone: (662) 842-7669.

e-mail: tombigb@bellsouth.net

SEE AD TRAVEL SECTION PAGE 464

(W) TRACE SP—(Lee) *From Natchez Trace Parkway: Go 6 mi W on Hwy 6, then 2-1/2 mi N on CR 65.*

WELCOME

FACILITIES: 52 sites, 32 ft max RV length, 52 W&E, 3 pull-thrus, tenting, cabins, RV storage, dump station, laundry, tables, grills, wood.

RECREATION: pavilion, lake swimming, boating, ramp, dock, 6 pedal boat rentals, lake fishing, 8 bike rentals, playground, sports field, hiking trails. Rec open to public.

TRACE SP—Continued on next page

TUPELO—Continued
TRACE SP—Continued

Pets welcome. Open all yr. Phone: (662)489-2958.

e-mail: tracesp@avrix.net

SEE AD TRAVEL SECTION PAGE 464

(N) VANELLI'S GREEK & ITALIAN RESTAURANT—*From jct US 78 & US 45: Go 1-3/4 mi S on US 45, then 1/2 mi W on McCullough Blvd, then 1/2 mi N on North Gloster. Enter on R.* Open all yr. MC/VISA/DISC/AMEX. Phone: (662)844-4410.

SEE AD PAGE 483

VICKSBURG—D-2

(C) Isle of Capri RV Park—(Warren) *From jct I-20 (exit 1A) & Washington St: Go 1/2 mi N on Washington St. Enter on R.* ◇◇◇◇FACILITIES: 67 sites, typical site width 30 ft, accepts full hkup units only, 67 full hkups, (30 & 50 amps), 67 pull-thrus, laundry, LP gas by weight/by meter, ice, tables, patios. ◇◇RECREATION: swim pool, play equipment. Pets welcome. No tents. Open all yr. Maximum stay one week. Big rigs welcome. Internet friendly. Rate in 2007 $17 per family. Phone: (800)WIN-ISLE.

(S) MAGNOLIA RV PARK RESORT—(Warren) *From jct I-20 (exit 1B) & US 61: Go 1 mi S on US 61, then 1/4 mi W on Miller St. Enter on R.*

◇◇◇◇FACILITIES: 66 sites, 66 full hkups, (20, 30 & 50 amps), 66 pull-thrus, cable TV ($), wireless Instant Internet access at site, wireless Internet access central location, RV storage, laundry, ltd groceries, RV supplies, LP gas by weight/by meter, ice, tables.

◇◇◇RECREATION: rec hall, rec room/area, swim pool, golf nearby, bsktball, playground, sports field, local tours.

Pets welcome, breed restrict, quantity restrict. Partial handicap access. No tents. Open all yr. Big rigs welcome. Internet friendly. Clubs welcome. Rate in 2007 $22-25 for 4 persons. MC/VISA/DISC/Debit. Phone: (601)631-0388. FMCA discount.

e-mail: guestservices@magnoliarvparkresort.com

SEE AD THIS PAGE

VICKSBURG—Continued

(S) River Town Campground—(Warren) *From I-20 (exit 1B) & US Hwy 61 S: Go 6 mi S on Hwy 61 S. Enter on L.* ◇◇◇◇FACILITIES: 148 sites, typical site width 45 ft, 108 full hkups, (20, 30 & 50 amps), 40 no hkups, some extended stay sites (in winter), 60 pull-thrus, tenting, dump station, laundry, ice, tables. ◇◇◇RECREATION: rec hall, swim pool, playground, horseshoes, sports field. Pets welcome. Partial handicap access. Open all yr. Big rigs welcome. Internet friendly. Rate in 2007 $18-22 per vehicle. Phone: (866) 442-2267.

WALNUT GROVE—D-3

(E) GOLDEN MEMORIAL STATE PARK—*From jct SH 35 & CR-492: Go 5 mi E on CR-492.* State Park - Day use only. For picnics, Nature Trails, playground & fishing. Open all yr. Day use only. Phone: (601)253-2237.

SEE AD TRAVEL SECTION PAGE 464

WAVELAND—F-3

(W) BUCCANEER SP—(Hancock) *From jct Hwys 43/603 & US 90: Go 1-3/4 mi S on Nicholson Ave, then 3-1/2 mi W on Beach Blvd.*

FACILITIES: 149 sites, 90 full hkups, 59 W&E, tenting, dump station, laundry, tables, patios, controlled access gate.

RECREATION: rec room/area, pavilion, swim pool, wading pool, saltwater swimming, boating, saltwater fishing, bsktball, playground, tennis, sports field, hiking trails. Rec open to public.

Pets welcome. Open all yr. MC/VISA. Phone: (228) 467-3822.

SEE AD TRAVEL SECTION PAGE 464

WAYNESBORO—E-4

(W) MAYNOR CREEK WATER PARK (Pat Harrison Waterway District)—(Wayne) *From town: Go 2 mi W on US 84, then 3 mi S on Reservoir Rd. Follow signs.* FACILITIES: 69 sites, typical site width 23 ft, 35 full hkups, 34 W&E, some extended stay sites, tenting, dump station, laundry, ice, patios, fire rings, grills, wood. RECREATION: rec hall, equipped pavilion, lake swimming, boating, canoeing, ramp, dock, 10 rowboat rentals, lake fishing, playground, sports field, hiking trails. Rec open to public. Open all yr. Phone: (601)735-4365.

WESSON—E-2

(E) LAKE LINCOLN SP—(Lincoln) *From town Go 6 mi E on Timberlane Rd.*

FACILITIES: 61 sites, 61 W&E, 61 pull-thrus, tenting, dump station, laundry, tables, fire rings, grills, controlled access gate.

RECREATION: pavilion, lake swimming, boating, canoeing, ramp, dock, 6 canoe/6 motorboat rentals, lake fishing, playground, sports field, hiking trails. Rec open to public.

Pets welcome. Open all yr. MC/VISA. Phone: (601) 643-9044.

SEE AD TRAVEL SECTION PAGE 464

WIGGINS—F-4

(NE) FLINT CREEK WATER PARK (Pat Harrison Waterway District)—(Stone) *From jct US 49 (Wiggins exit) & Hwy 29: Go 4 mi NE on Hwy 29. Follow signs.* FACILITIES: 156 sites, typical site width 22 ft, 77 full hkups, 79 W&E, (30 & 50 amps), 15 pull-thrus, tenting, dump station, laundry, ltd groceries, ice, patios, fire rings, grills, wood. RECREATION: rec hall, equipped pavilion, lake swimming, boating, canoeing, ramp, dock, 12 rowboat rentals, lake fishing, playground, sports field, hiking trails, v-ball. Rec open to public. Open all yr. Phone: (601)928-3051.

(S) Perk Beach RV Park and Campground—(Stone) *From jct Hwy 26 & US 49: Go 4 mi S on US 49. Enter on L.* ◇◇◇◇FACILITIES: 109 sites, 99 full hkups, (20, 30 & 50 amps), 10 no hkups, many extended stay sites, 24 pull-thrus, tenting, dump station, non-guest dumping $, laundry, LP gas by weight/by meter, ice, tables, patios, fire rings, grills. ◇◇RECREATION: rec hall, river swimming, river fishing, play equipment, hiking trails. Pets welcome. Open all yr. Big rigs welcome. Internet friendly. Rate in 2007 $20 for 4 persons. Phone: (800)547-7275.

WOODVILLE—E-1

(W) CLARK CREEK NATURE PARK—*From jct SH 61 & CR-24: Go 13 mi W on CR-34.* Daylight to dark park. Comprising more than 700 acres, it is highlighted by some 50 waterfalls, ranging in size 10 to more than 30 ft in height. Hiking, bird-watching, photography and botanizing are available on the established trails. Open all yr. Day use only. Phone: (601)888-6040.

SEE AD TRAVEL SECTION PAGE 464

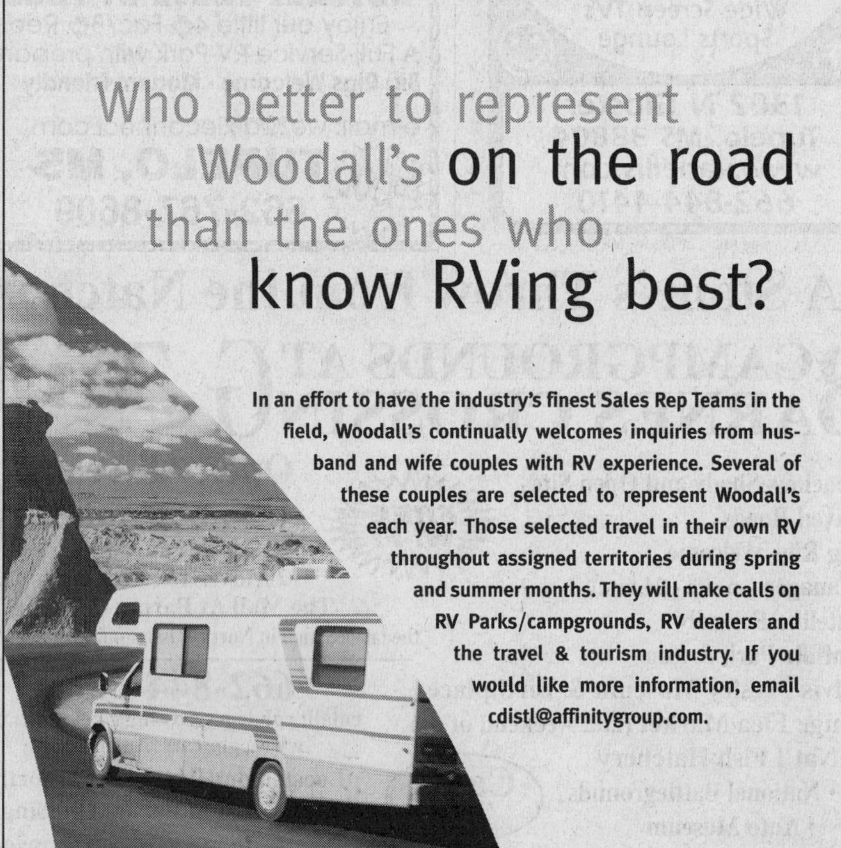

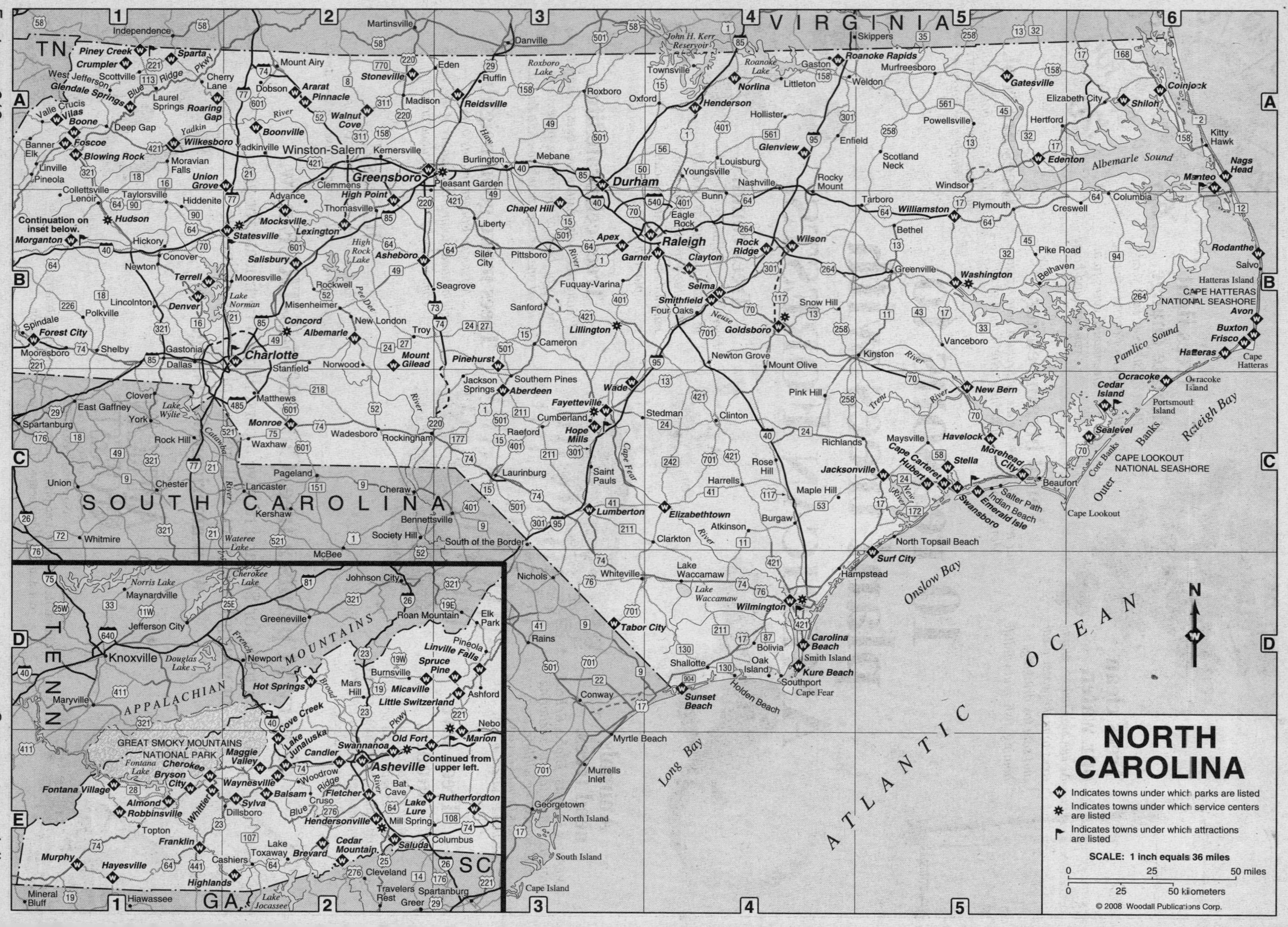
NORTH CAROLINA
Indicates towns under which parks are listed
Indicates towns under which service centers are listed
Indicates towns under which attractions are listed
SCALE: 1 inch equals 36 miles
0 25 50 miles
0 25 50 kilometers
© 2008 Woodall Publications Corp.
VIRGINIA
SOUTH CAROLINA
TENN
GA
SC
TN
ATLANTIC OCEAN
Continuation on inset below.
Continued from upper left.
GREAT SMOKY MOUNTAINS NATIONAL PARK
CAPE HATTERAS NATIONAL SEASHORE
CAPE LOOKOUT NATIONAL SEASHORE

North Carolina

READER SERVICE INFO

The following businesses have placed an ad in the North Carolina Travel Section. To receive free information, enter their Reader Service number on the Reader Service Card opposite page 48/Discover Section in the front of this directory:

Advertiser	RS#
Allsport RV Center	3531
Camp Hatteras	859
Cape Fear RV & Canoe Center	3695
Crisp RV Center	3386
Daly RV	3527
Franklin RV Park & CG	3617
Golden Pond Campground	3721
Happy Holiday RV Park & Campground	3548
Happy Holiday RV Park & Campground	3548
Howard RV Center	3452
Lake Norman MotorCoach Resort	3710
Mountain Camper Sales & Service	3723
Out of Doors Mart	3536
Rivers Edge Mountain RV Park	3437
The Family RV Center	3537
The Great Outdoors RV Resort	3558
The Refuge	3707
The RV Resort at Carolina Crossroads	3540
Tom Johnson Camping Ctr	3794
Valley River RV Resort	3764

Say You Saw It in Woodall's

TIME ZONE

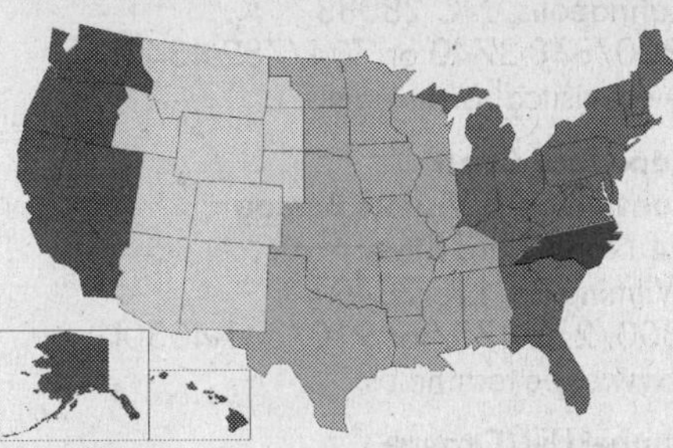

North Carolina is in the Eastern Time Zone.

TOPOGRAPHY

The state is divided into three distinct topographical regions: the Coastal Plain, the Heartland and the Mountains.

TEMPERATURE

North Carolina's average January temperatures range from 27° to 48.7°; July temperatures range from 59.2° to 80.2°.

TRAVEL & TOURISM INFO

State Agency:
North Carolina Department of Commerce Division of Tourism, Film and Sports Development
301 North Wilmington St.
Raleigh, NC 27699-4301
(800/VISIT-NC or 919/733-8372)
www.visitnc.com

Local Agencies:
Asheville Convention & Visitors Bureau
P.O. Box 1010
Asheville, NC 28802-1010
(828/258-6102 or 800/257-1300)
www.exploreasheville.com

TRAVEL & TOURISM (CONT.)

Blowing Rock Tourism Development Authority
P.O. Box 2445
Blowing Rock, NC 28605
(877/750-4636 or 828/295-4636)
www.visitblowingrock.com

Boone Convention & Visitors Bureau
208 Howard Street
Boone, NC 28607-4037
(828/262-3516 or 800/852-9506)
www.visitboonenc.com

NC Brunswick Islands
P.O. Box 1186
Shallotte, NC 28459
(800/795-7263 or 910/755-5517)
www.ncbrunswick.com

Burlington/Alamance County Convention & Visitors Bureau
610 S. Lexington Avenue
Burlington, NC 27215
(800/637-3804 or 336/570-1444)
www.burlington-area-nc.org

Cabarrus County Convention & Visitors Bureau
3003 Dale Earnhardt Blvd., Suite 200
Kannapolis, NC 28083
(800/848-3740 or 704/782-4340)
www.visitcabarrus.com

Cape Fear Coast Convention & Visitors Bureau
24 North Third Street
Wilmington, NC 28401
(800/222-4757 or 910/341-4030)
www.cape-fear.nc.us

Chapel Hill/Orange County Visitors Bureau
501 West Franklin Street
Chapel Hill, NC 27516
(888/968-2060 or 919/968-2060)
www.chocvb.org

Visit Charlotte The Convention and Visitors Bureau
500 South College Street, Suite 300
Charlotte, NC 28202
(800/231-4636 or 704/334-2282)
www.visitcharlotte.com

Cleveland County Economic Development/Travel & Tourism
P.O. Box 879
Shelby, NC 28151
(704/487-8521 or 800/480 8687
www.clevelandcounty.com

Columbus County Tourism Bureau
104 East Walter Street
P.O. Box 1352
Whiteville, NC 28472
(800/845-8419 or 910/640-2818)
www.discovercolumbus.org

Currituck County Department of Travel & Tourism
145 Courthouse Road
P.O. Box 39
Currituck, NC 27929
(252/232-0719 or 877/287-7488)
www.visitcurrituck.com

Durham Convention & Visitors Bureau
101 East Morgan Street
Durham, NC 27701
(800/446-8604 or 919/687-0288)
www.durham-nc.com

Elizabeth City Area Convention & Visitors Bureau
400 South Water Street, Suite 101
P.O. Box 573 (27907)
Elizabeth City, NC 27909
(252/335-4365)
www.elizabethcitychamber.org

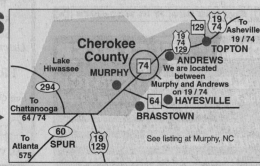

TRAVEL & TOURISM (CONT.)

Fayetteville Area Convention & Visitors Bureau
245 Person Street
Fayetteville, NC 28301
(800/255-8217 or 910/483-5311)
www.visitfayettevillenc.com

Gaston County Department of Tourism
620 North Main Street
Belmont, NC 28012
(800/849-9994 or 704/825-4044
www.gastontourism.com

Greensboro Area Convention & Visitors Bureau
317 South Greene Street
Greensboro, NC 27401-2615
(800/344-2282 or 336/274-2282)
www.visitgreensboro.com

Greenville-Pitt County Convention & Visitors Bureau
303 SW Greenville Blvd.
Greenville, NC 27835
(800/537-5564 or 252/329-4200)
www.visitgreenvillenc.com

Hickory Metro Convention and Visitors Bureau
1960-A Thirteenth Avenue Drive S.E.
Hickory, NC 28602
(800/509-2444 or 828/322-1335)
www.hickorymetro.com

Jackson County Travel & Tourism Authority
773 West Main Street
Sylva, NC 28779
(828/586-2155 or 800/962-1911)
www.mountainlovers.com

Johnston County Visitors Bureau
1115 Industrial Park Drive
Smithfield, NC 27577
(800/441-7829 or 919/989-8687)
www.johnstoncountync.org

Lake Norman Convention and Visitors Bureau
19900 West Catawaba Avenue
Cornelius, NC 28031
(704/987-3300)
www.lakenorman.org

Lexington Tourism Authority
16 East Center Street
P.O. Box 2103
Lexington, NC 27292
(336/236-4218 or 866/604-2389)
www.visitlexingtonnc.com

Martin County Travel & Tourism Authority
P.O. Box 382
Williamston, NC 27892
(800/776-8566 or 252/792-6605)
www.visitmartincounty.com

Monroe Tourism & Visitors Bureau
100 West Jefferson Street
Monroe, NC 28112
(704/225-1085)
www.visitmonroenc.org

New Bern/Craven County Convention & Visitors Bureau
203 South Front Street
New Bern, NC 28563
(800/437-5767 or 252/637-9400)
www.visitnewbern.com

Pinehurst, Southern Pines & Aberdeen Area CVB
10677 US Highway 15-501
Southern Pines, NC 28388
(800/346-5362 or 910/692-3330)
www.homeofgolf.com

Greater Raleigh Convention & Visitors Bureau
421 Fayetteville Street Mall, Suite 1505
P.O. Box 1879 (27602)
Raleigh, NC 27601-2946
(800/849-8499 or 919/834-5900)
www.visitraleigh.com

Randolph County Tourism Development Authority
222 Sunset Ave, Suite 107
Asheboro, NC 27203
(800/626-2672 or 336/626-0364)
www.visitrandolphcounty.com

TRAVEL & TOURISM (CONT.)

Rowan County Convention & Visitors Bureau
204 East Innes Street, Suite 120
Salisbury, NC 28144
(800/332-2343 or 704/638-3100)
www.visitsalisburync.com

Rutherford County Tourism Development Authority
1990 US Highway 221 South
Forest City, NC 28043
(800/849-5998 or 828/245-1492)
www.rutherfordtourism.com

Stanly County Convention & Visitors Bureau
116 East North Street
P.O. Box 1456
Albemarle, NC 28002
(704/986-2583 or 800/650-1476)
www.stanlycvb.org

Statesville Convention & Visitors Bureau
111 Depot Lane
P.O. Box 1109
Statesville, NC 28687
(704/878-3480 or 877/531-1819)
www.visitstatesville.org

Washington Tourism Development Authority
138 South Market Street
P.O. Box 1765
Washington, NC 27889
(800/999-3857 or 252/948-9415)
www.originalwashington.com

Wilson Visitors Bureau
124 East Nash Street
Wilson, NC 27894
(800/497-7398 or 252/243-8440)
www.wilson-nc.com

Winston-Salem Convention & Visitors Bureau
200 Brookstown Avenue
Winston-Salem, NC 27101
(866/728-4200 or 336/728-4200)
www.visitwinstonsalem.com

RECREATIONAL INFO

Fishing & Hunting: NC Wildlife Resources Commission, NCSU Centennial Campus, 1751 Varsity Dr., Raleigh, NC 27606 (919/707-0010) www.ncwildlife.org

Golf: For a free copy of the Official North Carolina Golf Guide, call 800/VISIT-NC or visit www.visitnc.com.

NC Beach Buggy Association, Box 940, Manteo, NC 27954. www.ncbba.org

SHOPPING

Appalachian Craft Center, Asheville. Authentic mountain handicrafts, pottery, face jugs, quilts, mountain-made toys, rugs and more. 10 N. Spruce St. www.appalachiancraftcenter.com

Carolina Premium Outlets, Smithfield. Shop at over 80 factory-direct designer and brand name outlets offering savings of 25%-65%. Off I-95, Exit 95, Smithfield, NC (919/989-8757). Web: www.premiumoutlets.com/carolina

Ninth Street Shopping District, Durham (919/286-3170). www.ninthst.com. Locally owned specialty shops in 25,000 square foot mall in the eclectic shopping district near Duke University East Campus at Main St. and Club Blvd.

North Carolina Remembered, Raleigh. The most complete NC products store in the state. A vast array of items, pottery, foods, suncatchers, flags, toys, pens, pencils, local sports items, etc. They will custom make gift baskets while you wait. 4325 Glenwood Ave. www.ncremembered.citysearch.com (919/782-5808).

In the Western North Carolina Mountains

RIVERS EDGE MOUNTAIN R.V. RESORT

NEW in 2008
Open All Year
Club House
Pool • Jacuzzi
Oversized Pavilion
Game Room
Camp Store
Laundry • LP Gas
24 hr. Security Monitor
Pets Welcome

HOME OF THE BIG RIG RV SUPER SITES

Two Hours or Less from:
Asheville, Franklin and Cherokee, NC; Chattanooga, Gatlinburg and Pigeon Forge, TN; and Atlanta, GA

Bikers Welcome

High-Speed Internet

Pull-Thrus and River Sites

Easy Access off 4-Lane
All Paved Roads • 30 & 50 Amp Service
Concrete Pads & Patios

Group Rates & Discounted Club Memberships up to 10%

Chattanooga, TN
Gatlinburg
Cherokee
on the banks of the Nottely River
64
64 74
Asheville
60
19 129
Blue Ridge, GA
Blairsville, GA

828-361-4517
828-644-5738
1750 Hilltop Rd., Murphy, NC
riversedgemountainrvresort.com

See listing at Murphy, NC

FREE INFO! Enter #3437 on Reader Service Card

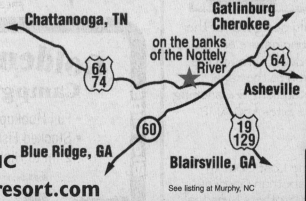

Wilcox Emporium Warehouse, Boone. Over 180 vendors in the historic downtown area selling unique antiques, art and collectibles. 161 Howard St., Boone, NC (828/262-1221).

DESTINATIONS

THE MOUNTAINS

Appalachian Trail. Over 2,150 miles of the wilderness route from Maine to Georgia follow high ridges in the **Pisgah National Park**, which is home to **Sliding Rock**, a natural water slide, Nantahala National Forest and the **Great Smoky Mountain National Park.**

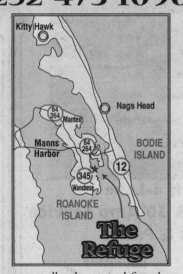

Belmont Abbey, Belmont. Once the only abbey cathedral in the nation, its beautiful painted-glass windows won a gold prize in 1893.

Blowing Rock. Enjoy a leisurely scenic walk overlooking John's River Gorge. The **Appalachian Heritage Museum** features costumed interpreters demonstrating skills of the period. **Mystery Hill** offers a fascinating way to explore science and optical illusion.

Blue Ridge Parkway. Over 250 miles of this scenic road skim the crest of the mountains between the North Carolina-Virginia line and the entrance to the **Great Smoky Mountains National Park** near Cherokee. The new Blue Ridge Parkway Destination Center houses exhibits featuring things to see and do in the region.

Boone. Step back into the 1800s in this historical town. At **Hickory Ridge Homestead**, a costumed interpreter will explain how early settlers lived and survived in the mountains of North Carolina. *Honor in the West* is an outdoor drama depicting the story of Daniel Boone and the Colonial Settlers in their struggle to free themselves from British tyranny.

Bottomless Pools is located in the hickory Nut Gorge of western North Carolina. The pools opened in 1916. Three pools each have their own waterfalll and unique, lovely natural setting.

Brevard/Cashiers Area. Known as the "Land of Waterfalls," the Brevard area contains many beautiful waterfalls, including **Connestee Falls, Looking Glass Falls, Toxaway Falls, High Falls, Rainbow Falls and Whitewater Falls. Brevard Station** is a museum portraying pictures, artifacts and documents from the past, including the discovery of the Bigleaf Magnolia in the area in 1795.

Cherokee/Qualla Boundary, located east of Bryson City at the Great Smoky Mountain National Park entrance, is now considered the **Cherokee Native American Reservation** by the descendants of the first mountain dwellers. See what life was like in an 18th-century Cherokee village. Visitors can follow the development of the Cherokee nation and learn about their language and important historical figures in tribal history at the **Museum of the Cherokee Indian**. Other attractions to visit include **Qualla Arts & Crafts Mutual; Unto These Hills,** an outdoor drama that illustrates the struggle of the Cherokee nation against the U.S.; **Aarrak's Cherokee Casino,** the size of 3 football fields; **Tribal Bingo**, with nightly games and **Santa's Land** amusement park.

Daniel Stow Botanical Garden is one of the finest perennial gardens in the Southeast with extensive landscaping, a glass-domed pavilion and more on 110 acres.

Grandfather Mountain (5,964 feet) is located in the Linville area and features a mile-high swinging bridge. The highest peaks can be reached only by trail in an undeveloped 5,000-acre area.

Great Smoky Mountains National Park. Located half in North Carolina and half in Tennessee, the park contains 514,093 acres and offers camping, fishing, hiking, picnicking, sightseeing, an observation tower and guided nature tours.

Green River Plantation, Rutherford. This 1804 mansion has 42 rooms on 366 acres of land bordered by lagoons. It is on the National Register of Historic Places.

Historic Hendersonville & Flat Rock Area, nestled in the beautiful Blue Ridge Mountains. Boasting antique stores, specialty shops and restaurants, this town has a history of tradition with a hometown charm. Visit the **Western North Carolina Air Museum,** the first of its kind in the "first in flight" state and **Jump Off Rock**, a scenic overlook which supplies a panoramic view of rolling pastures and Blue Ridge and Pisgah mountains. This rock also holds a Native American legend. The **Carl Sandburg Home** contains a collection of 10,000 books, notes and papers.

Labyrinth Center, Fairview dates back to prehistoric time and has been an integral part of many cultures including Celtic, Native American and Mayan.

Lake Lure has been named by National Geographic as one of the ten most spectacular man-made lakes in the world. Besides cruises and tours, boats of all kind are available for rent.

Linville Gorge Wilderness Area features one of eastern America's most scenic and rugged gorges. Stop by the district ranger's office (in Marion) for the permit required to enter the area. **Linville Caverns** is NC's only show cave– a natural limestone cavern with an underground stream.

Maggie Valley. Maggie Mountaineer Crafts has memorabilia and handcrafted items from local artisans. The newly reopened **Ghost Town in the Sky**, one of North Carolina's oldest family theme parks, features staged gunfights, special performances, historical and heritage exhibits.

Magic Mountain Gem Mine lets you mine for your own gems. Equipment is provided.

Oconaluflee Indian Village, Cherokee. An authentic replica of an 18th century Cherokee community. Artisans demonstrate their arts and crafts. Replica of a 7-sided Council House and Cherokee homes.

Schiele Museum of Natural History. Largest collection of land mammal species in the southeast; includes a planetarium with changing exhibits.

Sparta. Scheduled to open the summer of 2008 is the **Sparta Teapot Museum**, a multi-million dollar international collection of tea-themed treasures. The collection of more than 10,000 objects represents many cultures and includes priceless antique teapots from the 1700s, as well as contemporary ones.

Spruce Pine. Nearby is the **North Carolina Museum of Minerals**; the **Pemland School of Crafts**, the oldest and largest school for high quality mixed media arts and crafts; and the **Crossmore School**, home to the Weaving Room, where demonstrations of this traditional mountain craft are available.

THE HEARTLAND

Chapel Hill. This community is home to **Ackland Art Museum; Morehead Planetarium**, which offers daily public programs; and **North Carolina Botanical Garden**, a 307-acre woodland with a large collection of native plants and herbs.

Charlotte. Attractions in the Charlotte area include:

Paramount's Carowinds. Enjoy this theme park located on the border of North and South Carolina. Featured are over 30

RV Sales & Service

	SALES	SERVICE
CONCORD		
Tom Johnson Camping Center	•	•
FAYETTEVILLE		
Allsport Camping Center	•	•
Sunbird RV Repair Service		•
GOLDSBORO		
Daly RV	•	•
GREENSBORO		
Out-of-Doors Mart	•	•
HENDERSONVILLE		
Mountain Camper Sales & Service	•	•
HUDSON		
Bumgarner Camping Center	•	•
LILLINGTON		
Cape Fear RV & Canoe Center	•	•
MARION		
Tom Johnson Camping Center	•	•
STATESVILLE		
The Family RV Center	•	•
SWANNANOA		
Miles Motors RV Center	•	•
WASHINGTON		
Crisp RV Center	•	•
WILMINGTON		
Howard RV Center	•	•

rides, a wave pool, rock concerts and historic attractions.

Discovery Place & OMNI-MAX Theater is North Carolina's largest privately-owned museum of science and technology and offers a variety of exhibits and hands-on activities.

Things to See & Do

CEDAR ISLAND
The Pirates Chest

CHARLOTTE
Carowinds

EMERALD ISLE
Emerald Isle Wine Market

HOPE MILLS
The New Waldo's Beach Park

MANTEO
Outer Banks Visitors Bureau

MARION
Buck Creek Driving Range

MORGANTON
Jonas Ridge Snowtubing

PINEY CREEK
River Camp USA Canoe, Kayak & Tubing

STATESVILLE
Midway Trail of Horror

WILMINGTON
Battleship North Carolina

Woodall's Quick & Easy Reference for North Carolina

	BIG RIGS WELCOME	INTERNET FRIENDLY	PETS WELCOME	WEB SAVER
ABERDEEN				
Long Leaf Pine Oasis		●	■	
Pine Lake RV Resort		●	■	
ASHEBORO				
Deep River Campground & RV Park	▲	●	■	
Holly Bluff Family Campground	▲		■	
Trails End Family Camping	▲		■	
ASHEVILLE				
Asheville-Bear Creek RV Park	▲	●	■	
BALSAM				
Moonshine Creek Campground			■	
BOONE				
Flintlock Campground		●	■	
KOA-Boone	▲	●	■	
Waterwheel RV Park			■	
BRYSON CITY				
Country Boy's RV Park	▲		■	
Ela Campground		●	■	
BUXTON				
Cape Woods Campground		●	■	
CEDAR MOUNTAIN				
Black Forest Family Camping Resort	▲	●	■	
CHAPEL HILL				
Spring Hill Park	▲	●	■	
CHARLOTTE				
Cavowinds Camp Wilderness Resort	▲	●	■	
Fieldridge Acres	▲		■	
CHEROKEE				
Flaming Arrow Campground	▲	●	■	
Fort Wilderness Campground and RV Resort	▲	●	■	
Great Smokey Mountain RV Camping Resort			■	
Happy Holiday RV Park & Campground	▲	●	■	
KOA-Cherokee Great Smokies	▲	●	■	
Yogi in the Smokies		●	■	
CLAYTON				
Cooper's Mobile Home Park & RV's	▲		■	
EDENTON				
Rocky Hock Campground	▲		■	
EMERALD ISLE				
Holiday Trav-L-Park Resort For Campers	▲	●	■	$
FAYETTEVILLE				
Lazy Acres Campground		●	■	
FLETCHER				
Rutledge Lake RV Park	▲	●	■	$
FOSCOE				
Grandfather Campground	▲	●	■	
FRANKLIN				
Country Woods RV Park		●	■	
Franklin RV Park & Campground		●	■	
The Great Outdoors RV Resort	▲	●	■	
FRISCO				
Frisco Woods Campground		●	■	
GARNER				
70 East Mobile Acres & RV Park	▲		■	
GLENDALE SPRINGS				
Raccoon Holler Campground		●	■	
GREENSBORO				
Greensboro Campground	▲	●	■	
HATTERAS				
Hatteras Sands RV Resort	▲		■	
HENDERSONVILLE				
Apple Valley Travel Park		●	■	
Jaymar Travel Park	▲	●	■	
Lakewood RV Resort	▲	●	■	
Red Gates RV Park	▲		■	
Twin Ponds RV Park	▲	●	■	
HIGHLANDS				
Sky High Ridge Motorcoach Park	▲			
HOPE MILLS				
Lake Waldo's Beach Campground	▲		■	

▲ = Big Rigs Welcome; ● = Internet Hookups; ● = (Wi-Fi available); ■ = Pets Welcome; $ = Web Saver Coupons

*Check out the "How to Use This Directory" section in the front of this book for a description of the criteria Woodall's uses in this chart.

Woodall's Quick & Easy Reference for North Carolina

	BIG RIGS WELCOME	INTERNET FRIENDLY	PETS WELCOME	WEB SAVER
HUBERT				
Hawkins Creek Campground	▲		■	
JACKSONVILLE				
Cabin Creek Campground	▲	●	■	
LINVILLE FALLS				
Linville Falls Trailer Lodge & Campground			■	
LUMBERTON				
Sleepy Bear's RV Park	▲	●	■	
MANTEO				
The Refuge	▲	●	■	
MARION				
Buck Creek RV Park Campground & Driving Range	▲	●	■	
Mountain Stream RV Park	▲	●	■	
The Campground at Tom Johnson Camping Center	▲	●	■	
MOREHEAD CITY				
Whispering Pines Family Campground	▲	●	■	
MORGANTON				
Steele Creek Park		●	■	
MURPHY				
Rivers Edge Mountain RV Resort	▲	●	■	
NEW BERN				
Moonlight Lake RV Park & Campground	▲	●	■	
PINEHURST				
Village of Pinehurst RV Park	▲		■	
PINEY CREEK				
RiverCamp USA RV Park & Campground	▲	●	■	
ROANOKE RAPIDS				
The RV Resort at Carolina Crossroads	▲	●	■	
ROCK RIDGE				
Rock Ridge Campground			■	
RODANTHE				
Camp Hatteras	▲	●	■	$
SALISBURY				
Golden Pond Campground	▲	●	■	
Tamarac Marina & Campground	▲	●	■	
SALUDA				
Orchard Lake Campground & RV Park	▲	●	■	
SELMA				
RVacation Campground	▲	●	■	
SHILOH				
North River Campground & RV Park	▲		■	
STATESVILLE				
Midway Campground & RV Resort	▲	●	■	
STELLA				
White Oak Shores Camping & RV Resort	▲	●	■	
SURF CITY				
Lanier's Campground	▲	●	■	
SWANNANOA				
Asheville East-KOA		●	■	
Miles Motors RV Campground	▲	●	■	
SYLVA				
Ft Tatham RV Park		●	■	
TABOR CITY				
Yogi Bear's Jellystone Park at Daddy Joe's	▲	●	■	$
TERRELL				
Lake Norman Motor Coach Resort	▲	●	■	
VILAS				
Vanderpool Campground	▲		■	
WASHINGTON				
Tranter's Creek Resort & Campground	▲	●	■	
WAYNESVILLE				
Pride RV Resort	▲	●	■	
WILLIAMSTON				
Green Acres Family Campground		●	■	
WILSON				
Kamper's Lodge of America		●	■	

▲ = Big Rigs Welcome; ● = Internet Hookups; ● = (Wi-Fi available); ■ = Pets Welcome; $ = Web Saver Coupons

***Check out the "How to Use This Directory" section in the front of this book for a description of the criteria Woodall's uses in this chart.**

Mint Museum of Art. One of the leading museums in the Southeast, the Mint is not only the first branch of the U.S. Mint, but North Carolina's first art museum as well. Holdings include American and European paintings; African, Spanish and pre-Columbian art; furniture and decorative arts; regional crafts; historic costumes and an internationally acclaimed collection of pottery and porcelain.

Nature Museum. The museum features nature exhibits that encourage you to touch them, a nature trail, live animals, a planetarium and a puppet theater.

The U.S. National Whitewater Center (USNWC). This new outdoor recreation and environmental education center features the world's only multi-channel re-circulating whitewater river. With something for outdoor enthusiasts of all abilities, the facility offers mountain-biking and running trails, a climbing center, challenge course and the customized whitewater river for rafting and canoeing/kayaking.

Clemmons Educational State Forest, Clayton. Kids will enjoy the "talking" trees and rocks, telling tales about the forest.

Gold Hill is a preserved mining town once known as "the richest mining property east of the Mississippi."

Greensboro. Start your tour of this interesting town with a stroll through the Downtown Greensboro Historic District. On the North Carolina A&T University campus is the **African Heritage Museum,** which houses one of the finest collections of African artifacts in the nation. The **Natural Science Center** is a multi-dimensional experience. It contains a botanical garden, petting zoo, nature museum and trails, a marine gallery and a planetarium.

Lake Norman. North Carolina's "inland sea" offers 32,500 acres of water for swimming, boating and sailing.

National Railroad Museum, Hamlet. Located in the old depot, the museum's collection of railroad equipment includes rolling stock, maps and photographs.

North Carolina Museum of Life & Science, Durham. View extensive prehistoric exhibits, an outstanding aerospace exhibit, the zoo, a wildlife sanctuary and a mile-long, narrow gauge railroad for visitors to enjoy.

North Carolina Zoological Park, Asheboro. The park is the largest walk-through natural habitat zoo in the U.S., encompassing more than 550 acres, with both African and North American-style acreage.

Old Salem, Winston-Salem. Stroll through this restored town of Moravian ancestry and visit the **Museum of Early Southern Decorative Arts**, the **Herbst House**, where visitors may view candlemaking and saddlemaking, or the **Timothy Vogler Gun Shop**, a riflesmithing facility.

Piedmont Carolina Railroad Museum, Belmont. Located at the old Piedmont and Northern Railroad Depot, this museum houses a large collection of railroad equipment and rolling stock.

Pinehurst. Golfers thrill to this charming village with over 35 courses within a 15-mile radius of the Pinehurst-Southern Pines area. Stop by the **PGA World of Golf Hall of Fame** to view clubs, golf artifacts and portraits of golf legends inducted into the hall of fame.

Raleigh. Learn about the state's history and culture at North Carolina's capital and enjoy the arts and natural beauty of the city.

Exploris is the world's first global learning center and features hands-on exhibits for all ages.

North Carolina Museum of Art is home to the finest collection of Old Master paintings in the Southeast.

North Carolina State Museum of Natural Sciences offers hands-on programs every day. See the state's natural treasures, ranging from salamanders to a 2-toed sloth.

Reed Gold Mine State Historic Site, Georgeville. Visit the site of the first documented discovery of gold in the country. Found in 1799, mining of the gold took place from 1803 to 1912.

Sciworks, Winston Salem. Travel the Solar System, come face-to-face with river otters in our Environmental Park and enjoy interactive hands-on exhibits.

THE COAST

Bald Head Island. *Accessible only by ferry or boat, this picturesque island has many points of interest including* **Old Baldy Lighthouse** (1817), **Smith Island Museum of History** and the **Fort Holmes Site**.

Brunswick Islands. This colonial seaport, location of the Stamp Act Rebellion, was burned by British troops in 1776. Current attractions include the **Ingram Planetarium** featuring a domed theater and exhibits, the **Museum of Coastal Carolina**, a natural history museum with live reptile and turtle information programs and the **USS North Carolina Battleship Memorial.**

Calabash. Enjoy delicious Calabash cooking (lightly fried seafood) at this Intracoastal Waterway village.

Oak Island Beaches, Caswell, Long and Yaupon. These southern coastal vacation spots offer year-round fishing, boating, golfing and swimming, as well as a chance to see the **Oak Island Lighthouse.**

Cape Fear Coast is a world of history, sports, island beaches and incredible natural beauty—with four distinct yet mild seasons.

Highlights of the Cape Fear Coast include the newly renovated **Aquarium at Fort Fisher**, the historic **Wilmington** and the **Brunswick Islands**. Miles of beaches line the southeastern coast and offer excellent year-round recreational activities, including fishing, golf, boating and swimming.

The Battleship North Carolina. Take a tour to experience the inspiring "Through Their Eyes" exhibits. You'll see one of the few Kingfisher float planes still in existence.

Wilmington. The historic port of Wilmington affords visitors the unique opportunity to enjoy an exciting area rich in shopping, dining, culture and the arts, while being only minutes away from white sandy beaches. It has one of the largest districts listed in the National Register of Historic Places.

Cape Hatteras National Seashore was the first national seashore. It runs 75 miles along NC 12. The seashore is famous for windsailing, surf and deep sea fishing, as well as nature study and historic sites. **Pea Island National Wildlife Refuge** comprises 5,915 acres and has observation stands for wildlife viewing. The **Cape Hatteras Lighthouse** was built in 1870. At 208 ft. tall, it is the tallest lighthouse in the country. Visitors can climb the 268-step staircase for a spectacular view.

Cape Lookout National Seashore, Harkers Island. This 56-mile-long section of the Outer Banks consists of three undeveloped barrier islands that offer many natural and historical features.

Croatan National Forest. This coastal national forest covers over 155,000 acres and offers camping, picnicking, boating, canoeing, swimming, birdwatching and fishing.

Core Sound Waterfowl Museum, Harkers Island. Visit the exhibit gallery and artifacts and educational facilities.

Crystal Coast. Known as the "Southern Outer Banks," this area is recognized for its magnificent beaches and numerous water sports, such as swimming, fishing and surfing.

Duplin Wine Cellars, Rose Hill. North Carolina's largest and oldest operating winery offers tours and tastings.

Elizabeth City Historic District. Grab a brochure at the local Chamber of Commerce and take a self-guided tour of the downtown area, highlighting 32 National Register historic sites and structures.

Greenville Museum of Art, Greenville. The museum houses an impressive collection of 20th-century American art and the largest display of Jugtown Pottery in the eastern part of the state.

Historic Bath. Incorporated in 1705, Bath is the state's oldest town and was the first meeting place of the Colonial Assembly of the Province. Several important 18th- and 19th-century structures have been restored and contain period furnishings, all of which are open for public viewing. These include **Palmer Marse House, St. Thomas Church, William House, Van Der Veer House, Bonner House** and **Swindell's Store.**

History Place, Morehead City. View artifacts of Native Americans, costumes and furnishings of the 18th and 19th centuries, Civil War artifacts and visiting exhibits.

Museum of the Albemarle, Elizabeth City. Learn about the regional history of the 10-county area of northeastern North Carolina. Exhibits recount the area's government, education, religion and economy, as well as its geology and history.

North Carolina Maritime Museum, Beaufort. The exhibits explore maritime history and coastal natural history.

Outer Banks. Comprised of several barrier islands stretched along the coast, the Outer Banks offers historic sites, quaint villages, a variety of recreational activities and miles of scenery.

Cape Hatteras Lighthouse, Buxton. View the tallest brick lighthouse in North America.

Cape Hatteras National Seashore encompasses over 30,000 acres of land on Bodie, Hatteras and Ocracoke Islands. Enjoy camping, surf and sport fishing, swimming and the picturesque village of Ocracoke.

Cape Lookout National Seashore. Accessible only by boat, the seashore extends over 50 miles up to Ocracoke Inlet.

Roanoke Island is the site of the first English attempt to colonize the New World. **The Waterside Theatre,** home of America's oldest outdoor drama *The Lost Colony*, is found here. This drama tells the history of Sir Walter Raleigh's Roanoke Voyages.

Wright Brothers National Memorial, near Kitty Hawk and Kill Devil Hills. Site of the Wright Brothers' historic 1903 flight, the memorial is now home to a monument, markers, a museum, a reconstructed hangar and an airport.

ANNUAL EVENTS

JANUARY

Pooh Day, Greensboro; Boat Show, Raleigh; Ultimate Wine Glass Competition & Toast, Ocean Isle Beach.

FEBRUARY

Camper & RV Show, Concord; Art Exhibit, Marion; Carolina Chocolate Festival, Morehead City; Valentine Faire, Elizabeth City; Carolina Garden Expo, Charlotte; Annual Civil War Living History, Elizabeth City; Carolina Power & Sailboat Show, Raleigh; Folk Art Festival at Fearrington, Pittsboro; Native American Powwow, Durham; Native American Art Show, Raleigh.

MARCH

Fly a Kite Day, Tryon; Biltmore Estate's Festival of Flowers, Asheville; Annual Coastal Home and Garden Show, Morehead City; Rumba on the Lumber Festival, Lumberton; American Music Jubilee, Selma; Great Outdoor Expo, Morganton; Seafood Festival Fun Fest, Morehead City; Spring Craft Fair, Raleigh; Irish Festival, Ocean Isle Beach.

APRIL

Festival of Flowers, Asheville; NC Azalea Festival, Wilmington; NC Pickle Festival, Mount Olive; Annual National Juried Art Exhibition, Rocky Mount; Blue Ridge Wine Festival, Blowing Rock; Annual International Whistlers Convention, Louisburg; Annual Redbud Festival, Saxapahaw; Spring Wine Festival, Wagram; Antique Show and Sale, Greenville.

MAY

Ole Time Fiddlers' & Bluegrass Festival, Union Grove; Olde Tyme Music Festival, Hendersonville; Springfest, Saluda; NC Seafood Festival Golf Extravaganza, Morehead City; Spring Festival, Murphy; Annual North Carolina Forest Festival, Plymouth; Annual May Fest & Auto Show, Rutherfordton; Ramp Festival, Waynesville; Ribfest, Eden; Butterfly Festival, Hudson; Annual Celtic Festival and Highland Game, Winston-Salem.

JUNE

American Dance Festival, Durham; Big Rock Blue Marlin Fishing Tournament, Atlantic Beach; National Hollerin' Contest, Spivey's Corner; Eastern Music Festival, Greensboro; Annual Bluegrass Festival, Aberdeen; Festival of the Vino, Chapel Hill; Tar River Festival, Louisburg; Big Lick Bluegrass Festival, Oakboro; Annual Blue Ridge Barbecue Festival; Tryon; Annual Piedmont Pottery Festival, Eden; Bluff Mountain Festival, Marshall; Arts by the Sea Festival, Swansboro; Taste of Scotland, Franklin.

JULY

Hatteras Kite Festival, Hatteras; Jazz Festival, Morehead City; Doc Watson Music Fest, Sugar Grove; Art in the Park, Blowing Rock; Peach Festival, Candor; Cherokee Rodeo, Cherokee; Parade of Lawnmowers/Watermelon Festival, Cooleemee; Wright Kite Festival, Kill Devil Hills; Croaker Festival, Oriental; Blackberry Festival, Wilmington.

AUGUST

Art on Main, Hendersonville; Mountain Dance and Folk Festival, Asheville; Art & Craft Fair, Asheville; Sourwood Festival, Black Mountain; Mount Mitchell Craft Fair, Burnsville; Shrimp by the Bay, Edenton; Cape Lookout Lighthouse Open House, Harkers Island; Festival of Crafts, Hickory; Watermelon Festival, Murfreesboro; Blackberry Festival, Mars Hill; Annual Jack Tales Festival, Blowing Rock.

SEPTEMBER

NC Mountain State Fair, Asheville; Mule Days, Benson; Tomato Festival, Bryson City; Bull Durham Blues Festival, Durham; Apple Festival, Hendersonville; Bar-B-Q Blow Out, Maggie Valley; Grape Day/Gourd Festival, Raleigh; Purple Feet Festival, Ocean Isle Beach; Winston-Salem Crafts Guild Fall Craft Show, Winston Salem; Flatwoods Festival, Bennett; Historic Morganton Festival, Morganton; Greek Festival, Greensboro; Apple Festival, Winston-Salem; Mountain Heritage Festival, Sparta.

OCTOBER

North Carolina State Fair, Raleigh; International Sardine Festival, Aberdeen; Oktoberfest at Sugar Mountain, Banner Elk; Carolina Kite Fest, Atlantic Beach; Maple Leaf Festival, Bryson City; Great Grapes! Wine & Music Festival, Charlotte; Festifall, Chapel Hill; Dam Jam, Fontana Dam; North Carolina Seafood Festival, Morehead City; Oyster Festival, Ocean Isle Beach; Annual Cornshucking Frolic, Pinnacle; Hillbilly Heritage Festival, Spruce Pine.

NOVEMBER

Christmas at Biltmore Estate, Asheville; Weaverville Art Safari, Weaverville; Kites with Lights, Nags Head; Colossal Collard Day, Raleigh; Pecan Day, Raleigh; Wings Over Water, Kill Devil Hills; Pottery Festival, Seagrove; Storytelling Festival, Tryson; Holiday Season in Old Salem, Winston-Salem.

DECEMBER

Sugarfest, Banner Elk; Creekside Christmas, Archdale; A Carolina Mountain Christmas, Arden; Twilight Tour, Brevard; Winterfest, Burnsville; Island of Lights Tour of Homes, Carolina Beach; Window Wonderland, Franklin; Christmas Boat Parade, Lake Lure.

North Carolina

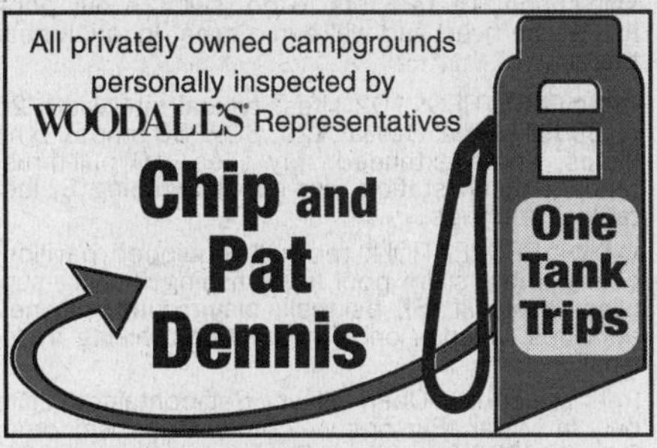

ABERDEEN—C-3

(S) LONG LEAF PINE OASIS (UNDER CONSTRUCTION)—(Scotland) *From jct of Hwy 211 & US 15/501: Go 14-1/2 mi S on US 15/501, then 2 mi W on Palmer Rd. Enter on L.*

WELCOME

FACILITIES: 1 sites, mostly extended stay sites, wireless Instant Internet access at site.

Pets welcome. Open all yr. Internet friendly. Rate in 2007 $30-45 per vehicle. Member ARVC, CARVC. Phone: (910)266-8372. CCUSA discount.

e-mail: longleafpineoasis@yahoo.com

Reserve Online at Woodalls.com

SEE AD PINEHURST PAGE 658

(SE) PINE LAKE RV RESORT—(Scotland) *From jct of Hwy 211 & US 15/US 501: Go 9.5 mi S on US 15/501, then 2 mi E on Hill Creek Rd. Enter on R.*

WELCOME

◊◊◊FACILITIES: 90 sites, typical site width 28 ft, 85 full hkups, 5 W&E, (30 & 50 amps), some extended stay sites, 80 pull-thrus, wireless Internet access central location, tenting, RV/park trailer rentals, cabins, RV storage, dump station, non-guest dumping $, laundry, RV supplies, LP gas by weight/by meter, ice, tables, fire rings, wood, controlled access gate.

◊◊◊RECREATION: rec hall, rec room/area, pavilion, coin games, swim pool, boating, no motors, canoeing, kayaking, pond fishing, fishing supplies, playground, horseshoes, hiking trails.

Pets welcome. Open all yr. Internet friendly. Clubs welcome. Rate in 2007 $26-29 per family. MC/VISA. Member ARVC, CARVC. Phone: (800)746-3505. CCUSA discount. FCRV 10% discount. FMCA discount.

e-mail: pinelakeresort@earthlink.net

SEE AD THIS PAGE

ALBEMARLE—B-2

(NE) MORROW MOUNTAIN STATE PARK—(Stanly) *From town: Go 5 mi E on Hwy 24/27/73/740.* FACILITIES: 106 sites, 26 ft max RV length, 106 no hkups, tenting, dump station, grills. RECREATION: swim pool, boating, canoeing, ramp, rowboat/canoe rentals, lake fishing, hiking trails. Rec open to public. Partial handicap access. Open Mar 15 thru Dec 15. Area C is open year round. Phone: (704)982-4402.

ALMOND—E-1

(W) NANTAHALA NATIONAL FOREST (Tsali Recreational Area)—(Swain) *From town: Go 2 mi W on Hwy 28, then 1-1/2 mi N on FR 361.* FACILITIES: 41 sites, 22 ft max RV length, 41 no hkups, tenting, fire rings, grills. RECREATION: boating, ramp, lake fishing, hiking trails. Partial handicap access. Open all yr. Facilities fully operational Apr 15 thru Nov 1. No reservations. $15 per day Apr thru Oct. $5 per day Nov thru Mar. Phone: (828)479-6431.

(NW) Tumbling Waters Campground—(Graham) *From west jct US 19/74 & Hwy 28: Go 5-1/4 mi NW on Hwy 28, then 1-3/4 mi W on Panther Creek Rd. Enter at end.* ◊◊◊FACILITIES: 30 sites, typical site width 18 ft, 30 full hkups, (15 & 30 amps), many extended stay sites, 5 pull-thrus, tenting, dump station, laundry, ice, tables, fire rings, wood. ◊RECREATION: river swimming, pond/stream fishing, horseshoes, v-ball. Rec open to public. Pets welcome. Open all yr. Rate in 2007 $20-23 for 2 persons. Phone: (828)479-3814.

(NW) Turkey Creek Campground—(Swain) *From west jct US 19/74 & Hwy 28: Go 2 mi NW on Hwy 28. Enter on R.* ◊◊FACILITIES: 60 sites, typical site width 30 ft, 32 ft max RV length, 60 W&E, (20 amps), tenting, dump station, laundry, ice, tables, fire rings, wood. ◊RECREATION: rec room/area, hiking trails, v-ball. Pets welcome, size restrict. Open Memorial Day Weekend thru Labor Day Weekend. Member ARVC, CARVC. Phone: (828)488-8966.

APEX—B-3

JORDAN LAKE STATE REC. AREA (Crosswinds Campground)—(Chatham) *From jct US 1 & US 64: Go 11 mi W on US 64.* FACILITIES: 129 sites, 129 W&E, tenting, dump station, fire rings, grills. RECREATION: boating, ramp, lake fishing, playground, hiking trails. Partial handicap access. Open all yr. Facilities fully operational May 20 thru Jul 18. Phone: (919)362-0586.

North Carolina State Nickname: "The Tarheel State"

APEX—Continued

JORDAN LAKE STATE REC. AREA (Parkers Creek)—(Chatham) *From jct Hwy 1 & US 64: Go W on US 64.* FACILITIES: 250 sites, 150 W&E, (20 amps), 100 no hkups, tenting, dump station, fire rings, grills. RECREATION: lake swimming, boating, canoeing, ramp, lake fishing, playground, hiking trails, v-ball. Rec open to public. No pets. Partial handicap access. Open all yr. No reservations. Phone: (919)362-0586.

JORDAN LAKE STATE REC. AREA (Poplar Point)—(Chatham) *From town: Go 10 mi W on US 64 to Wilsonville, then 2 mi S on Hwy 1008.* FACILITIES: 580 sites, 361 W&E, 219 no hkups, tenting, dump station, fire rings, grills. RECREATION: lake swimming, boating, canoeing, ramp, dock, lake fishing, playground, hiking trails. No pets. Open Mar 15 thru Nov 30. Phone: (919)362-0586.

JORDAN LAKE STATE REC. AREA (Vista Point)—(Chatham) *From town: Go 12 mi W on US 64 to Griffins Crossroads, then 3 mi S on Pea Ridge Rd.* FACILITIES: 50 sites, 50 W&E, dump station, grills. RECREATION: lake swimming, boating, canoeing, ramp, dock, lake fishing, hiking trails. No pets. No tents. Open Mar 15 thru Nov 30. Phone: (919)362-0586.

ASHEBORO—B-2

(NE) DEEP RIVER CAMPGROUND & RV PARK—(Randolph) *From jct I-73/I-74/US 220 & US 64/Hwy 40: Go 7 mi E on US 64/Hwy 49, then 1-1/2 mi N on Loflin Pond Rd, then 1/4 mi E on McDowell Country Trail. Enter on L.*

WELCOME

◊◊◊FACILITIES: 61 sites, typical site width 45 ft, 45 full hkups, 16 W&E, (20, 30 & 50 amps), some extended stay sites, 38 pull-thrus, wireless Instant Internet access at site, phone Internet access central location, tenting, cabins, dump station, non-guest dumping $, laundry, LP gas by weight/by meter, ice, tables, fire rings, wood.

DEEP RIVER CAMPGROUND & RV PARK—Continued on next page

ASHEBORO—Continued
DEEP RIVER CAMPGROUND & RV PARK—Continued

◆◆RECREATION: rec room/area, pavilion, coin games, 2 swim pools, canoeing, kayaking, canoe/2 kayak rentals, lake/river fishing, bsktball, play equipment, planned activities, horseshoes, v-ball. Rec open to public.

ASHEBORO—Continued
DEEP RIVER CAMPGROUND & RV PARK—Continued

Pets welcome, breed restrict. Open all yr. Big rigs welcome. Internet friendly. Clubs welcome. Rate in 2007 $20-28 for 4 persons. MC/VISA. Member ARVC, CARVC. Phone: (336)629-4069. CCUSA discount.

e-mail: drcampground@earthlink.net

SEE AD PAGE 633

ASHEBORO—Continued

(SW) HOLLY BLUFF FAMILY CAMPGROUND—(Randolph) *From jct I-73/I-74/US 220 & US 64/Hwy 49: Go 1/2 mi W on US 64/Hwy 49, then 7 mi S on Hwy 49. Enter on R.*

COME JOIN THE FUN!

We take pride in our family campground. Enjoy our mini-golf course. We keep everything up-to-date & ship-shape. There's lots to do (swim in our pool, fish at the river) and we're in a great location near the zoo.

◆◆◆FACILITIES: 102 sites, typical site width 25 ft, 89 full hkups, 8 W&E, (20, 30 & 50 amps), 5 no hkups, some extended stay sites, 10 pull-thrus, tenting, dump station, non-guest dumping $, ice, tables, fire rings.

◆◆◆◆RECREATION: rec hall, equipped pavilion, coin games, swim pool, river fishing, fishing supplies, mini-golf ($), bsktball, playground, planned activities (wkends only), horseshoes, hiking trails, v-ball.

Pets welcome. Open all yr. Self-contained units only in winter. Big rigs welcome. Clubs welcome. Rate in 2007 $25-27 for 3 persons. Phone: (336) 857-2761.

SEE AD PAGE 633

WELCOME

(SE) TRAILS END FAMILY CAMPING—(Randolph) *From SR 64 & Zoo Pkwy: Go 2 mi S on Zoo Pkwy, then SE 3 mi on Old Cox Rd. Enter on R.*

◆◆◆FACILITIES: 100 sites, typical site width 18 ft, 43 full hkups, 11 W&E, (30 & 50 amps), 46 no hkups, some extended stay sites (in summer), phone Internet access central location, tenting, dump station, laundry, ice, tables, fire rings, wood, controlled access gate.

◆◆RECREATION: equipped pavilion, coin games, swim pool, lake/stream fishing, planned activities (wkends only), horseshoes, hiking trails. Rec open to public.

Pets welcome. Open Apr 1 thru Nov 1. Big rigs welcome. Rate in 2007 $18-20 for 2 persons. Member ARVC, CARVC. Phone: (336)629-5353.

SEE AD THIS PAGE

ASHEVILLE—E-2

WELCOME

ASHEVILLE EAST-KOA—*From Asheville: Go E on I-40 to exit 59, then 1/2 mi N on Patton Cove Rd, then 1-1/2 mi E on US 70. Enter on L.*

SEE PRIMARY LISTING AT SWANNANOA AND AD THIS PAGE

ASHEVILLE—Continued on next page

In 1903 the Wright Brothers made the first successful powered flight by man at Kill Devil Hill near Kitty Hawk. The Wright Memorial at Kitty Hawk now commemorates their achievement.

RUTLEDGE LAKE
RV PARK
ARVC
Award
Winning
Park
2005/2006
PARK OF THE
YEAR
Small Park

Enjoy fishing, strolling wooded trails, canoeing, paddle boating, swimming in our new heated pool or just plain relaxing with all the beautiful mountains have to offer.

It's a quiet setting just minutes from the Blue Ridge Parkway, Biltmore Estate, Chimney Rock Park, and more!

I-26 - Exit 40, East one mile to Rutledge Road. One mile to RV Park.

GPS 35.440549, -82.523612

SPECIAL PACKAGE

Stay with us for SEVEN PAID CONSECUTIVE NIGHTS and get **TWO FREE TICKETS to BILTMORE ESTATE,** Asheville's premier attraction!

The Estate features the beautiful Vanderbilt home, the winery (complete with tastings!), wonderful eateries, and incredibly beautiful gardens.

Offer expires Oct. 31, 2008
Not valid during Biltmore Estate special events.
No other discounts apply.

Furnished cabins are available for you or your guests to enjoy the camping experience even without an RV!

Official Go RVing. Park

Simple, easy access to Biltmore Estate. Tickets available.

828-654-7873 • 800-368-3209 RESERVATIONS

Online Reservations

www.RutledgeLake.com

ASHEVILLE—Continued

(SW) ASHEVILLE-BEAR CREEK RV PARK —(Buncombe) *From jct I-40 (exit 47) & Hwy 191: Westbound: Go across Hwy 191, then 1/2 mi W on S Bear Creek Rd. Eastbound: Go 1/2 mi N on Hwy 191, then 1/2 mi W on S Bear Creek Rd. Enter on L.*

BILTMORE HOUSE VIEWS AND MORE

We're so close to the Biltmore House you can see it from our Park. Stay on our BIG, level concrete sites (Free WI-FI) and buy your tickets from us. You'll enjoy the sightseeing and the peace and quiet at the end of the day.

◆◆◆◆◆FACILITIES: 90 sites, typical site width 30 ft, 90 full hkups, (30 & 50 amps), 32 pull-thrus, cable TV, wireless Instant Internet access at site, wireless Internet access central location, cabins, dump station, laundry, RV supplies, LP gas by weight/by meter, ice, tables, patios.

◆◆◆RECREATION: rec hall, rec room/area, coin games, swim pool, golf nearby, bsktball, play equipment, v-ball.

Pets welcome. Partial handicap access. No tents. Open all yr. Big rigs welcome. Internet friendly. Clubs welcome. Rate in 2007 $36-45 for 2 persons. MC/VISA/Debit. Member ARVC, CARVC. Phone: (828)253-0798. FMCA discount.

e-mail: hbbercreek@bellsouth.net

SEE AD THIS PAGE

ASHEVILLE—Continued

BLUE RIDGE NATIONAL PARKWAY (Mt. Pisgah)—(Haywood) *From town: Go 24 mi W on Blue Ridge Pkwy at Milepost 409.* FACILITIES: 67 sites, 30 ft max RV length, 67 no hkups, tenting, dump station, ltd groceries, ice, grills, wood. RECREATION: hiking trails. Open May thru Oct 31. No showers. Phone: (828)298-0398.

(N) Campfire Lodgings—(Buncombe) *From jct I-40/ I-26 and I-240: Go 4 mi NE on I-240, then 5 3/4 mi N on US 19/23/70/I-26 Future (exit 21), then E to US 19, then 1/2 mi S on US 19 Bus., then 1/4 mi W on Old Marshall Hwy, then 1/4 mi SW on Appalachian Village Rd. Enter at end.* ◆◆◆◆FACILITIES: 30 sites, typical site width 40 ft, 19 full hkups, 5 W&E, (20, 30 & 50 amps), 6 no hkups, some extended stay sites, 0 pull-thrus, tenting, laundry, LP gas by weight/by meter, tables, patios, fire rings, grills, wood. ◆◆RECREATION: pond fishing, horseshoes, sports field, hiking trails. Pets welcome. Partial handicap access. Open all yr. Big rigs welcome. Internet friendly. Rate in 2007 $40-50 for 2 persons. Member ARVC, CARVC. Phone: (800)933-8012.

(S) PISGAH NATIONAL FOREST (Lake Powhatan Rec. Area)—(Haywood) *From town: Go 4 mi S on Hwy-191, then 3-1/2 mi W on FR-806.* FACILITIES: 97 sites, 35 ft max RV length, 97 no hkups, 7 pull-thrus, dump station, grills. RECREATION: lake swimming, lake fishing, hiking trails. Open May 13 thru Oct 28. Max stay 14 days. Phone: (828)670-5627.

(S) PISGAH NATIONAL FOREST (North Mills River Rec. Area)—(Haywood) *From town: Go 13-1/2 mi S on Hwy-19, then 5 mi W on FR-478.* FACILITIES: 32 sites, 22 ft max RV length, 32 no hkups, 1 pull-thrus, tenting, dump station, fire rings, grills. RECREATION: river fishing. Open all yr. No showers. Max stay 14 days. Phone: (828)890-3284.

ASHEVILLE—Continued

RUTLEDGE LAKE RV PARK—*From jct I-40 & I-26: Go 9 mi S on I-26 to exit 40, then 1 mi E on Hwy 280, then 3/4 mi S on Rutledge Rd. Enter on L.*

SEE PRIMARY LISTING AT FLETCHER AND AD PAGE 635

(E) Scenic Mobile Home/RV Park (RV SPACES) —(Buncombe) *From jct I-240-I-40/I-26: Go 9 mi N on I-40 to exit 55, then 1/2 mi W on US 70/Tunnel Rd, then up hill on Scenic Dr. Enter at end.* FACILITIES: 10 sites, typical site width 20 ft, 36 ft max RV length, 10 full hkups, (30 & 50 amps). No tents. Open Apr 15 thru Oct 31. Rate in 2007 $25 for 2 persons. Phone: (828)298-3822.

(E) Taps RV Park—(Buncombe) *From jct I-240 & I-40/I-26: Go 9 mi E on N I-40 (exit 55), then 1/4 mi W on US 70 (Tunnel Rd). Enter on L.* ◆◆◆FACILITIES: 46 sites, typical site width 35 ft, 32 full hkups, 14 W&E, (20, 30 & 50 amps), some extended stay sites, 23 pull-thrus, dump station, non-guest dumping $. ◆RECREATION: river fishing. Pets welcome. No tents. Open all yr. Big rigs welcome. Internet friendly. Rate in 2007 $26-30 for 2 persons. Phone: (800)831-4385.

AVON—B-6

(C) Sands of Time Campground—(Dare) *From jct of Hwy 12 & Harbor Rd: Go 1/4 mi W on Harbor Rd, then 300 feet N on N End Rd. Enter on R.* ◆◆◆FACILITIES: 62 sites, typical site width 30 ft, 57 full hkups, (30

Sands of Time Campground—Continued on next page

AVON—Continued
Sands of Time Campground—Continued

& 50 amps), 50 amps ($), 5 no hkups, some extended stay sites, tenting, dump station, laundry, tables. RECREATION: horseshoes, v-ball. Pets welcome ($), breed restrict. Open all yr. Call for reservations in Winter. Rate in 2007 $32-38 for 2 persons. Phone: (252)995 5596. CCUSA discount.

BALSAM—E-2

(SW) MOONSHINE CREEK CAMPGROUND—(Jackson) *From jct Blue Ridge Pkwy (exit MP 443.1) & US 23/US 74: Go 1/2 mi S & W on US 23/74, then 2 mi SW on Candlestick Lane/CR-1471. Enter on L.*

◆◆◆FACILITIES: 100 sites, typical site width 25 ft, 55 full hkups, 45 W&E, (20, 30 & 50 amps), some extended stay sites, cable TV ($), phone Internet access central location, tenting, RV/park trailer rentals, cabins, dump station, laundry, groceries, RV supplies, LP gas by weight/by meter, ice, tables, patios, fire rings, grills, wood.

◆◆RECREATION: rec hall, equipped pavilion, pond/stream fishing, fishing supplies, play equipment, horseshoes, hiking trails.

Pets welcome, breed restrict. Open Apr 1 thru Nov 1. Clubs welcome. Rate in 2007 $28-33 for 2 persons. MC/VISA. Member ARVC, CARVC. Phone: (828)586-6666.

e-mail: moonshinecreek@hotmail.com

SEE AD CHEROKEE PAGE 644

BLOWING ROCK—A-1

(S) BLUE RIDGE NATIONAL PARKWAY (Julian Price Memorial Campground)—*From town: Go 1 mi N on US-221 & 321, then 5 mi SW on Blue Ridge Pkwy to MP-297.* FACILITIES: 68 sites, 30 ft max RV length, 68 no hkups, tenting, dump station, grills, wood. RECREATION: boating, canoeing, ramp, dock, hiking trails. Partial handicap access. Open May 11 thru Oct 28. No showers. Phone: (828)963-5911.

BOONE—A-1

(SW) FLINTLOCK CAMPGROUND—(Watauga) *From jct US 321 & Hwy 105: Go 3 mi SW on Hwy 105. Enter on R.*

◆◆◆FACILITIES: 92 sites, typical site width 24 ft, 61 full hkups, 31 W&E, (15, 20, 30 & 50 amps), some extended stay sites, 6 pull-thrus, cable TV, wireless Instant Internet access at site, wireless Internet access central location, tenting, cabins, RV storage, dump station, laundry, RV supplies, ice, tables, patios, wood.

◆◆RECREATION: rec room/area, pavilion, coin games, bsktball, playground, horseshoes, v-ball.

North Carolina's mountains are the highest east of the Mississippi.

BOONE—Continued
FLINTLOCK CAMPGROUND—Continued

Pets welcome. Partial handicap access. Open Apr 1 thru Early Nov. Internet friendly. Clubs welcome. Rate in 2007 $24-29 for 2 persons. MC/VISA. Phone: (888)850-9997.

e-mail: FCG@charterinternet.com

SEE AD THIS PAGE

WELCOME

KOA-BOONE—(Watauga) *From jct US 421/Hwy 194 & US 321/221: Go 1 mi NE on US 221/194, then 3 mi NW on Hwy 194, then 1 mi W on Ray Brown Rd. Enter on R.*

◆◆◆FACILITIES: 135 sites, typical site width 45 ft, 115 full hkups, 20 W&E, (15, 20, 30 & 50 amps), some extended stay sites, 100 pull-thrus, wireless Instant Internet access at site, phone Internet access central location, tenting, cabins, dump station, laundry, ltd groceries, RV supplies, ice, tables, fire rings, grills, wood.

◆◆◆RECREATION: rec hall, rec room/area, coin games, swim pool, mini-golf ($), playground, planned activities (wkends only), horseshoes.

Pets welcome. Partial handicap access. Open May 1 thru Oct 31. Big rigs welcome. Internet friendly. Clubs welcome. Rate in 2007 $32-37 for 2 persons. MC/VISA. Member ARVC, CARVC. Phone: (828)264-7250. KOA 10% value card discount.

e-mail: boonekoa@bellsouth.net

SEE AD THIS PAGE AND AD DISCOVER SECTION PAGES 62 & 63

WELCOME

(NE) WATERWHEEL RV PARK—(Watauga) *From jct US 421/Hwy 194/105 & US 321/221: Go 1 mi NE on US 221/Hwy 194, then 1-1/2 mi NW on Hwy 194. Enter on L.*

◆◆◆FACILITIES: 27 sites, typical site width 20 ft, 27 full hkups, (15, 30 & 50 amps), 50 amps ($), some extended stay sites, 19 pull-thrus, cable TV, laundry, LP gas by weight/by meter, ice, tables.

Pets welcome. No tents. Open all yr. Rate in 2007 $24-26 for 2 persons. MC/VISA. Phone: (828)264-5165.

SEE AD THIS PAGE

BOONVILLE—A-2

(N) Holly Ridge Family Campground—(Yadkin) *From jct I-77 (exit 82) & Hwy 67: Go 6-1/2 mi E on Hwy 67, then 1-1/4 mi N on US 601, then 1/2 mi E on River Rd. Enter on L.* ◆◆◆FACILITIES: 62 sites, typical site width 30 ft, 42 full hkups, 20 W&E, (20, 30 & 50 amps), mostly extended stay sites, 17 pull-thrus, dump station, non-guest dumping $, laundry, ltd groceries, LP gas by weight/by meter, ice, tables, fire rings, wood. ◆◆◆RECREATION: rec room/area, pavilion, swim pool, mini-golf ($), playground, shuffleboard court, horseshoes, sports field, hiking trails, v-ball. Pets welcome. No tents. Open all yr. Big rigs welcome. Rate in 2007 $23-27 for 2 persons. Member ARVC, CARVC. Phone: (336)367-7756.

WELCOME

BREVARD—E-2

BLACK FOREST FAMILY CAMPING RESORT—*From jct US 64 & US 276: Go 12-1/2 mi S on US 276, then 1/4 mi E on Summer Rd.*

SEE PRIMARY LISTING AT CEDAR MOUNTAIN AND AD NEXT PAGE

BREVARD—Continued on next page

BREVARD—Continued

(N) PISGAH NATIONAL FOREST (Davidson River Campground)—(Transylvania) *From jct US-64 & US-276: Go 1-1/2 mi N on US-276.* FACILITIES: 160 sites, 12 full hkups, 3 E, (30 amps), 145 no hkups, 13 pull-thrus, tenting, dump station, fire rings. RECREATION: river fishing, play equipment, hiking trails. Partial handicap access. Open all yr. Max stay 14 days. Phone: (828)862-5960.

BRYSON CITY—E-1

(E) COUNTRY BOY'S RV PARK (REBUILDING)—(Swain) *From US 74 (exit 69): Go 1-1/4 mi N on Hyatt Creek Rd (SR 1190). Enter on L.*

WELCOME

FACILITIES: 85 sites, 85 full hkups, (30 & 50 amps), tenting, laundry, ice, wood.

Pets welcome, breed restrict. Open all yr. Big rigs welcome. Rate in 2007 $20 for 2 persons. Phone: (828)488-8807.

SEE AD CHEROKEE PAGE 645 AND AD GA TRAVEL SECTION PAGE 187

(NE) Deep Creek Tube Center & Campground—(Swain) *From US 74 (exit 67): Go 3/4 mi NW on Spring St, then 2 blocks E on US 19, then 1/4 mi N on Everett St, then 2 blocks E on Depot St, then 1-1/4 mi NE on Deep Creek Rd. Enter on R.* ◊◊◊FACILITIES: 46 sites, typical site width 25 ft, 30 full hkups, 3 W&E, (20, 30 & 50 amps), 50 amps ($), 13 no hkups, 3 pull-thrus, tenting, laundry, ltd groceries, ice, tables, grills, wood. ◊◊RECREATION: pavilion, river fishing, play equipment, v-ball. Rec open to public. Pets welcome. Partial handicap access. Open Apr 1 thru Oct 31. Big rigs welcome. Internet friendly. Rate in 2007 $24-32 for 4 persons. Member ARVC, CARVC. Phone: (828)488-6055.

(E) ELA CAMPGROUND (REBUILDING)—(Swain) *From US 74 (exit 69): Go 2 mi N on Hyatt Creek Rd (SR 1190), then 1/2 mi E on US 19. Enter on R.*

WELCOME

FACILITIES: 152 sites, typical site width 22 ft, 152 full hkups, (30 & 50 amps), mostly extended stay sites, 14 pull-thrus, cable TV, wireless Instant Internet access at site, wireless Internet access central location, tenting,

BRYSON CITY—Continued
ELA CAMPGROUND—Continued

RV/park trailer rentals, cabins, RV storage, dump station, full svc store, LP gas by weight/by meter, ice, tables, fire rings, wood.

RECREATION: rec hall, equipped pavilion, coin games, swim pool, river fishing, fishing supplies, bsktball, planned activities (wkends only), horseshoes, v-ball.

Pets welcome. Open all yr. Internet friendly. Escort to site. Rate in 2007 $25-40 for 4 persons. MC/VISA/DISC/AMEX. Member ARVC, CARVC.

e-mail: info@elacampground.com

SEE AD CHEROKEE PAGE 645

(N) GREAT SMOKY MOUNTAINS NATIONAL PARK (Deep Creek Campground)—(Swain) *From town: Follow brown & white signs 3 mi N.* FACILITIES: 92 sites, 26 ft max RV length, 92 no hkups, tenting, dump station, grills, wood. RECREATION: Open Apr 1 thru Oct 31. No showers. Phone: (865)436-1200.

BUXTON—B-6

(S) CAPE HATTERAS NATIONAL SEASHORE (Cape Point Campground)—(Dare) *From Hwy-12 in town: Go 3-1/2 mi SE on park road.* FACILITIES: 202 sites, 202 no hkups, tenting, cold showers only, dump station, groceries, grills. RECREATION: saltwater swimming, saltwater fishing, hiking trails. Open May 27 thru Sep 5. No Reservations. Phone: (252)473-2111.

(SW) CAPE WOODS CAMPGROUND—(Dare) *From north jct Hwy 12 & Hwy 1232 S (Buxton Back Rd): Go 1/2 mi S on Hwy 1232 (Buxton Back Rd). Enter on L.*

WELCOME

◊◊◊FACILITIES: 115 sites, typical site width 30 ft, 98 full hkups, 6 W&E, (30 & 50 amps), 11 no hkups, many extended stay sites, 10 pull-thrus, cable TV ($), wireless Internet access central location, tenting, cabins, dump station, laundry, ice, tables, patios, fire rings, grills, wood, controlled access gate.

◊◊◊RECREATION: rec room/area, pavilion, coin games, swim pool, pond fishing, playground.

Pets welcome. Partial handicap access. Open Mar 1 thru Late Dec. Rate in 2007 $27-52 per family. MC/VISA. Phone: (252)995-5850.

SEE AD THIS PAGE

CANDLER—E-2

(W) KOA-Asheville West—(Buncombe) *From jct I-40 (exit 37) & US Hwys 19/23/74: Go 200 yards S on connecting road, then 1/2 mi W on 19/23/74, then 200 yards N on Wiggins Rd. Enter on R.* ◊◊◊FACILITIES: 68 sites, typical site width 24 ft, 44 full hkups, 24 W&E, (20, 30 & 50 amps), 50 amps ($), some extended stay sites, 24 pull-thrus, tenting, dump station, laundry, ltd groceries, LP gas by weight/by meter, ice, tables, grills, wood. ◊◊RECREATION: rec room/area, swim pool, pond fishing, play equipment, hiking trails. Pets welcome, breed restrict. Partial handicap access. Open all yr. Internet friendly. Rate in 2007 $31-43 for 2 persons. Phone: (828)665-7015. KOA 10% value card discount.

CAPE CARTERET—C-5

(E) GOOSE CREEK RESORT FAMILY CAMPGROUND—(Carteret) *From jct Hwy 58 & Hwy 24: Go 4 mi NE on Hwy 24, then 3/4 mi S on Red Barn Rd. Enter on R.*

WELCOME

◊◊◊◊FACILITIES: 685 sites, typical site width 32 ft, 685 full hkups, (20, 30 & 50 amps), mostly extended stay sites, 12 pull-thrus, cable TV, wireless Internet access central location, tenting, RV storage, dump station, non-guest dumping $, laundry, groceries, RV supplies, LP gas by weight/by meter, ice, tables, controlled access gate.

◊◊◊◊◊RECREATION: rec hall, rec room/area, coin games, swim pool, saltwater swimming, boating, canoeing, kayaking, ramp, dock, saltwater fishing, fishing supplies, bsktball, playground, planned activities (wkends only), v-ball.

Pets welcome. Partial handicap access. Open all yr. Big rigs welcome. Clubs welcome. Rate in 2007 $32-52 per vehicle. MC/VISA/DISC. Member ARVC, CARVC. Phone: (252)393-2628.

e-mail: goose_creek_resort@mhchomes.com

SEE AD EMERALD ISLE PAGE 648

(W) WATERWAY RV RESORT—(Carteret) *From jct Hwy 58 & Hwy 24: Go 1-1/4 mi W on Hwy 24. Enter on L.*

◊◊◊◊FACILITIES: 337 sites, 337 full hkups, (30 & 50 amps), mostly extended stay sites, cable TV, laundry, ltd groceries, RV supplies, controlled access gate.

◊◊◊◊RECREATION: rec room/area, coin games, swim pool, boating, ramp, bsktball, planned activities, horseshoes, v-ball.

Pets welcome. Partial handicap access. No tents. Open all yr. Big rigs welcome. Rate in 2007 $36 MC/VISA. Member ARVC, CARVC. Phone: (252) 393-8915.

e-mail: info@rvonthego.com

SEE AD EMERALD ISLE PAGE 648

CAPE HATTERAS—B-6

See listings at Avon, Buxton, Frisco, Hatteras and Rodanthe

CAPE HATTERAS—Continued on next page

See listing at Hatteras, NC

50 ACRE OCEANFRONT & SOUNDFRONT RESORT

FREE WIRELESS INTERNET

- Pamlico Sound - 1000 ft. of Beach Frontage
- Atlantic Ocean - 1000 ft. of Beach Frontage
- Three Swimming Pools
  - Indoor Heated Pool • Large Outdoor Pool
  - Children's Pool • Jacuzzi Hot Tub
- 8000 Sq. Ft. of Recreation Rooms
  - Large Rec Room with Video Games
  - Great Room
  - Full Screen TV
- Many Activities - Recreation Staff
- Best Windsurfing Launch Areas on Hatteras
- Marina with Kayaking & Waverunners
- Lighted Tennis Courts & 9 Hole Mini Golf
- Playground • Oceanside Pavilion
- Volleyball • Horseshoes • Boat Ramp
- Three Stocked Fishing Ponds

- Open All Year • Full Hookups • 30/50 Amps • Patios
- Cable TV • Security • Clean Restrooms • Laundries
- Pull-Thrus • Paved Parking Pads • Paved Roads
- Camp Store - Tackle & RV Supplies
- Picnic Tables

WOODALL RATED
FAC: ◆◆◆◆
REC: ◆◆◆◆◆

A Complete Resort Facility on the Outer Banks

Clubs and Groups Welcome!

- Group Rates • 3200 Sq. Ft. Clubhouse Especially for Groups and Rallies - Full Kitchen Available
- Convenient to Outer Banks Activities & Restaurant

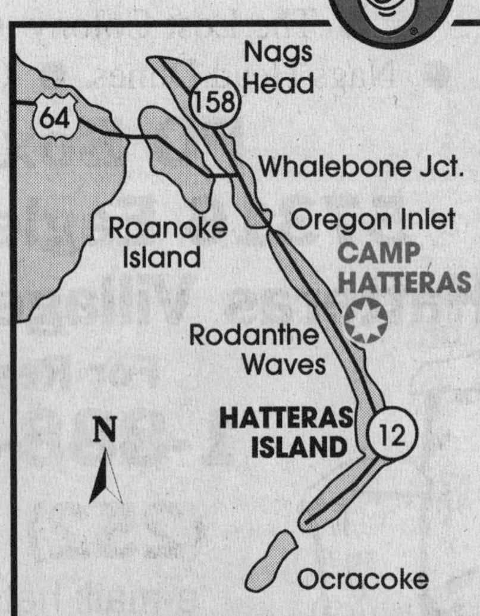

www.camphatteras.com **(252) 987-2777**

P. O. Box 10 - Waves, NC 27968 - See listing at Rodanthe, NC

CAPE HATTERAS—Continued

CAPE WOODS CAMPGROUND—*From Cape Hatteras Lighthouse: Go 1-1/2 mi S on Hwy 12, then 1/2 mi S on Buxton Back Rd. Enter on L.*

SEE PRIMARY LISTING AT BUXTON AND AD PAGE 638

FRISCO WOODS CAMPGROUND—*From Cape Hatteras Lighthouse: Go 5 mi S on Hwy 12. Enter on R.*

SEE PRIMARY LISTING AT FRISCO AND AD FRISCO PAGE 651

HATTERAS SANDS RV RESORT—*From the Ocracoke-Hatteras Ferry: Go 1/10 mi N on Hwy 12, then 1/4 mi E on Eagle Pass Rd. Enter on L.*

SEE PRIMARY LISTING AT HATTERAS AND AD PAGE 639

CAROLINA BEACH—D-4

(N) CAROLINA BEACH STATE PARK—(New hanover) *From town: Go 1 mi N on US-421, then 1/2 mi W on Dow Rd.* FACILITIES: 83 sites, 83 no hkups, tenting, dump station, non-guest dumping $, grills. RECREATION: boating, ramp, dock, river fishing, hiking trails. Partial handicap access. Open all yr. No showers. Max stay 14 days. Phone: (910)458-8206.

CEDAR ISLAND—C-6

(E) DRIFTWOOD CAMPGROUND—(Carteret) *On Hwy 12 at the terminal of the Cedar Island-Ocracoke Ferry Enter on R.*

◆◆FACILITIES: 65 sites, typical site width 25 ft, 20 full hkups, 38 W&E, (20 & 30 amps), 7 no hkups, 16 pull-thrus, tenting, dump station, ice, tables.

◆◆RECREATION: saltwater swimming, boating, canoeing, kayaking, ramp, dock, saltwater fishing, fishing supplies.

Pets welcome. Open all yr. Facilities fully operational Mar 1 thru Nov 30. Clubs welcome. Rate in 2007 $18 per vehicle. MC/VISA/DISC. Phone: (252)225-4861.

e-mail: driftwoodmotel@earthlink.net

SEE AD THIS PAGE

(E) THE PIRATES CHEST—*Located on Hwy 12 at the terminal of the Cedar Island-Ocracoke Ferry. Enter at end.* A local seafood specialty restaurant in a campground/motel/gift shop complex, located on a remote, historic island at the terminal of the Cedar Island-Ocracoke Ferry. Open all yr. MC/VISA/DISC. Phone: (252)225-4861.

e-mail: deg@clis.com

SEE AD THIS PAGE

CEDAR MOUNTAIN—E-2

(E) BLACK FOREST FAMILY CAMPING RESORT—(Transylvania) *From Cascade Ln & US 276: Go 1-1/2 mi S on 276, then 1/4 mi E on Summer Rd. Enter on R.*

◆◆◆◆FACILITIES: 110 sites, typical site width 35 ft, 52 full hkups, 46 W&E, 10 E, (20, 30 & 50 amps), 50 amps ($), 2 no hkups, phone Internet access central location, tenting, cabins, dump station, non-guest dumping $, laundry, groceries, RV supplies, ice, tables, fire rings, grills, wood, controlled access gate.

CEDAR MOUNTAIN—Continued
BLACK FOREST FAMILY CAMPING RESORT—Continued

◆◆◆◆RECREATION: rec hall, rec room/area, coin games, swim pool, golf nearby, playground, planned activities (wkends only), horseshoes, sports field, hiking trails, v-ball.

Pets welcome. Partial handicap access. Open all yr. Limited facilities in winter-call for availability. Big rigs welcome. Internet friendly. Rate in 2007 $30-36 for 2 persons. MC/VISA. Member ARVC, CARVC. Phone: (828)884-2267.

SEE AD BREVARD PAGE 638

CHAPEL HILL—B-3

(SW) SPRING HILL PARK—(Orange) *From jct I-40 & NC-54 (exit 273): Go 3 mi W on NC-54 (go under bridge and exit right) then continue 3-3/4 mi W on NC-54; then 1 mi SW on Jones Ferry Rd, then 4 mi W on Old Greensboro Rd, then 1/4 mi N on Spring Hill Rd.*

◆◆◆FACILITIES: 65 sites, typical site width 35 ft, accepts full hkup units only, 65 full hkups, (30 & 50 amps), many extended stay sites, 7 pull-thrus, cable TV, wireless Instant Internet access at site, RV storage, LP gas by meter.

RECREATION: golf nearby, play equipment, sports field.

Pets welcome. No tents. Open all yr. Reservations recommended. Big rigs welcome. Internet friendly. Rate in 2007 $25 per family. Phone: (800)824-8807.

SEE AD THIS PAGE

CHARLOTTE—B-2

(SW) CAROWINDS—*From jct I-85 & I-77: Go 13-1/2 mi S on I-77 (SC exit 90), then 3/4 mi W on Carowinds Blvd. Enter on R.* 100-acre family theme park. with the widest selection of rides, shows and attractions in the Carolinas. Open Late Mar thru Mid Oct. Open weekends only Spring & Fall. MC/VISA/DISC/AMEX. ATM. Phone: (800)888-4FUN.

SEE AD PAGE 643

(SW) CAVOWINDS CAMP WILDERNESS RESORT—(Mecklenburg) *From jct I-85 & I-77: Go 13-1/2 mi S on I-77 (SC exit 90), then 1 mi W on Carowinds Blvd, then 1/4 mi N on Catawba Trace. Enter on L.*

◆◆◆◆FACILITIES: 194 sites, typical site width 30 ft, 138 full hkups, 56 W&E, (20, 30 & 50 amps), 39 pull-thrus, wireless Instant Internet access at site, wireless Internet access central location, tenting, cabins, dump station, laundry, ltd groceries, RV supplies, ice, grills.

◆◆◆RECREATION: rec room/area, coin games, swim pool, mini-golf, playground, shuffleboard court, v-ball.

Pets welcome. Open all yr. Big rigs welcome. Internet friendly. Rate in 2007 $30-70 for 2 persons. MC/VISA/DISC/AMEX/Debit. Phone: (800)888-4386.

SEE AD PAGE 643

CHARLOTTE/FORT MILL KOA—*From jct I-85 & I-77: Go 15 mi S on I-77 to Gold Hill Rd (exit 88), then 1/2 mi W on Gold Hill Rd. Enter on R.*

SEE PRIMARY LISTING AT FORT MILL, SC AND AD NEXT PAGE

CHARLOTTE—Continued

(W) FIELDRIDGE ACRES—(Mecklenburg) *From jct I-77 & I-85: Go 9 mi S on I-85 to exit 30, then, 3/4 mi S on I-485 to exit 9, then 1/4 mi W on Wilkinson Blvd (US 74. Enter on R.*

◆◆◆FACILITIES: 94 sites, typical site width 25 ft, 94 full hkups, (20, 30 & 50 amps), 15 pull-thrus, tenting, dump station, non-guest dumping $.

RECREATION: pavilion, bsktball, horseshoes.

Pets welcome. Open all yr. Big rigs welcome. Rate in 2007 $20 per family. Phone: (704)399-3521.

e-mail: service@fieldridgeacres.com

SEE AD THIS PAGE

(NE) Fleetwood RV Racing Camping Resort at Charlotte—(Cabarrus) *From jct I-77 & I-85: Go 11 mi N on I-85 (exit 49), then 1-1/4 mi S on Fleetwood Blvd. Enter on L.* ◆◆◆◆FACILITIES: 460 sites, typical site width 20 ft, 460 full hkups, (20, 30 & 50 amps), 11 pull-thrus, dump station, non-guest dumping $, laundry, ice, tables. ◆RECREATION: equipped pavilion, pond fishing, play equipment, horseshoes. Pets welcome, size restrict. No tents. Open all yr. Big rigs welcome. Internet friendly. Rate in 2007 $25 per vehicle. Member ARVC, CARVC. Phone: (704)455-4445.

(SW) MCDOWELL NATURE PRESERVE—(Mecklenburg) *From jct I-85 & I-77: Go 13-1/2 mi S on I-77 (exit 90 in SC), then 2 mi NW on Carowinds Blvd, then 4-1/4 mi SW on York Rd (Hwy 49).* FACILITIES: 49 sites, 13 full hkups, 26 W&E, (30 & 50 amps), 10 no hkups, 13 pull-thrus, tenting, dump station, fire rings, grills. RECREATION: boating, canoeing, ramp, dock, 11 canoe/19 pedal boat rentals, lake fishing, playground, planned activities, horseshoes, hiking trails, v-ball. Rec open to public. Pets welcome. Partial handicap access. Open all yr. Limited facilities in winter. Max stay 7 days. Phone: (704)583-1284.

CHARLOTTE—Continued on next page

CHARLOTTE—Continued

(SW) MCDOWELL NATURE PRESERVE CAMPGROUND—(Mecklenburg) *From jct I-85 & I-77: Go 13-1/2 mi S on I-77 (exit 90), then 2 mi W on Carowinds Blvd, then 4 mi S on York Rd (Hwy 49). Enter on R.* FACILITIES: 56 sites, 46 W&E, (30 & 50 amps), 10 no hkups, 13 pull-thrus, tenting, dump station, ice, grills, wood. RECREATION: planned activities, horseshoes, v-ball. Pets welcome. Open all yr. Phone: (704)583-1284.

CHEROKEE—E-1

(S) Adventure Trail Campground—(Jackson) *From west jct US 19 & US 441: Go 2-1/4 mi S on US 441, then 1-3/4 mi SE on Camp Creek Rd. Enter on R.* ◆◆FACILITIES: 90 sites, typical site width 25 ft, 30 ft max RV length, 38 full hkups, 49 W&E, (15, 20 & 30 amps), 3 no hkups, some extended stay sites, 10 pull-thrus, tenting, dump station, laundry, ltd groceries, ice, tables, fire rings, wood. ◆◆◆◆RECREATION: rec room/area, pavilion, swim pool, playground, shuffleboard court, planned activities, horseshoes, sports field, hiking trails, v-ball. Rec open to public. Pets welcome. Open May 15 thru Oct 31. Rate in 2007 $30-35 for 4 persons. Phone: (828)497-3651.

ASHEVILLE - BEAR CREEK RV PARK—*From jct US 441 & US 19: Go E 26 mi, enter I-40 and continue E 20 mi to exit 47, then 1/2 mi N on Hwy 191, then 1/2 mi W on S. Bear Creek Rd. Enter on L.*

WELCOME

SEE PRIMARY LISTING AT ASHEVILLE AND AD ASHEVILLE PAGE 636

(N) Bradley's Campground—*From west jct US 441 & US 19/441: Go 1/2 mi W on US 19/441, then 2 mi N on US 441, then 3/4 mi W on Acquoni Rd. Enter*

CHEROKEE—Continued
Bradley's Campground—Continued

on L. ◆◆FACILITIES: 40 sites, typical site width 20 ft, 16 full hkups, 24 W&E, (20 & 30 amps), many extended stay sites, tenting, dump station, ice, tables. RECREATION: stream fishing. Pets welcome. Open all yr. Rate in 2007 $19 for 2 persons. Phone: (828)497-6051.

(E) Cherokee Campground—(Jackson) *From west jct US 441 and US 19: Go 1 mi NE on US 19 N. Enter on R.* ◆◆◆FACILITIES: 36 sites, typical site width 20 ft, 30 ft max RV length, 20 full hkups, (15, 20 & 30 amps), 16 no hkups, 1 pull-thrus, tenting, ice, tables, fire rings, grills, wood. ◆RECREATION: pavilion, stream fishing, play equipment. Pets welcome. Open mid Apr thru Oct 31. Rate in 2007 $32 for 2 persons. Phone: (828)497-9838.

(S) FLAMING ARROW CAMPGROUND—(Jackson) *From West jct US 19 and US 441: Go 2 1/2 mi S on US 441. Enter on L.*

WELCOME

HOSPITALITY - THE CHEROKEE WAY
Let Flaming Arrow spoil you with nice wide sites, great mountain views and friendly hosts. We're close to the museums & casino but outside the tourist hustle & bustle. You'll see all the sights and get a good night's sleep.

◆◆◆FACILITIES: 85 sites, typical site width 36 ft, 65 full hkups, 6 W&E, (20, 30 & 50 amps), 14 no hkups, 8 pull-thrus, cable TV, wireless Instant Inter-

CHEROKEE—Continued
FLAMING ARROW CAMPGROUND—Continued

net access at site, phone Internet access central location, tenting, laundry, ltd groceries, RV supplies, ice, tables, patios, fire rings, wood.

◆◆◆RECREATION: equipped pavilion, swim pool, bsktball, playground, shuffleboard court, horseshoes, v-ball.

Pets welcome. Open all yr. Facilities fully operational Apr 1 thru Oct 31. Big rigs welcome. Internet friendly. Escort to site. Clubs welcome. Rate in 2007 $37 for 2 persons. MC/VISA/DISC. Member ARVC, CARVC. Phone: (877)497-6161.

e-mail: info@flamingarrowcampground.com

SEE AD PAGE 645

(S) FORT WILDERNESS CAMPGROUND AND RV RESORT—(Jackson) *From west jct US 19 and US 441: Go 3 1/2 mi S on US 441, then 1/4 mi W on Shoal Creek Rd., then NE on County Road. Enter on R.*

WELCOME

◆◆◆FACILITIES: 130 sites, typical site width 25 ft, 110 full hkups, 10 W&E, (15, 30 & 50 amps), 10 no hkups, some extended stay sites, 15 pull-thrus, cable TV ($), wireless Instant Internet access at site, phone Internet access central location, tenting, RV/park trailer rentals, cabins, dump

FORT WILDERNESS CAMPGROUND AND RV RESORT—Continued on page 644

See listing at Terrell, NC

CHEROKEE—Continued
FORT WILDERNESS CAMPGROUND AND RV RESORT—Continued

station, non-guest dumping $, laundry, ltd groceries, RV supplies, ice, tables, patios, fire rings, wood.

◇◇◇RECREATION: rec room/area, pavilion, coin games, swim pool, bsktball, play equipment, planned activities (wkends only), v-ball.

Pets welcome. Open May 1 thru Oct 31. Big rigs welcome. Internet friendly. Rate in 2007 $30-35 per family. MC/VISA. Member ARVC. Phone: (828) 497-9331. CCUSA discount.

e-mail: fortwilderness@reservecampground.com

SEE AD THIS PAGE

(S) GREAT SMOKEY MOUNTAIN RV CAMPING RESORT—(Jackson) *From West jct US 19 & US 441: Go 1-1/2 mi S on US 441. Enter on L.*

WELCOME

CHEROKEE—Continued
GREAT SMOKEY MOUNTAIN RV CAMPING RESORT—Continued

CHEROKEE CASINO - BLUE RIDGE PRKWY
Quiet camping resort catering to adults - just 3/4 mi from Harrah's Casino. We've got everything you need here, and lots to do nearby. Enjoy great weather Spring, Summer & Fall.

◇◇◇FACILITIES: 251 sites, typical site width 20 ft, 251 full hkups, (20 & 30 amps), mostly extended stay sites, 100 pull-thrus, cable TV, laundry, ltd groceries, LP gas by weight/by meter, ice, tables, patios, fire rings, wood.

◇◇RECREATION: rec room/area, coin games, swim pool, river fishing, fishing supplies, bsktball, playground, 2 shuffleboard courts.

Pets welcome, size restrict. No tents. Open May 1 thru Oct 31. Clubs welcome. Rate in 2007 $30 for 2 persons. Member ARVC, CARVC. Phone: (828) 497-2470.

SEE AD THIS PAGE

CHEROKEE—Continued

GREAT SMOKY MOUNTAINS NATIONAL PARK (Balsam Mountain Campground)—(Swain) *From town: Go 4 mi N on US 441, 12 mi E on Blue Ridge Pkwy to MP 458, then 8 mi N on Balsam Mtn. Rd.* FACILITIES: 46 sites, 30 ft max RV length, 46 no hkups, tenting, wood. RECREATION: hiking trails. Open May 12 thru Oct 9. No showers. No reservations. Phone: (423)436-1200.

(N) GREAT SMOKY MOUNTAINS NATIONAL PARK (Smokemont Campground)—(Swain) *From town: Go 6 mi N on US-441.* FACILITIES: 142 sites, 27 ft max RV length, 142 no hkups, tenting, dump station, grills, wood. RECREATION: hiking trails. Open all yr. Facilities fully operational mid May thru Oct 31. No showers. Phone: (865)436-1200.

(E) HAPPY HOLIDAY RV PARK & CAMPGROUND—(Jackson) *From west jct US Business 441 & US 19: Go 3 mi NE on US 19 N. Enter on L.*

WELCOME

PRETTIEST PARK IN THE SMOKIES
Come for the Blue Grass Festivals, Cherokee cultural heritage, to trout fish, or just to relax. You'll enjoy the beauty of the mountains & our rushing streams. We're close to major attractions & offer free shuttle service.

◇◇◇◇FACILITIES: 389 sites, typical site width 45 ft, 300 full hkups, 66 W&E, (20, 30 & 50 amps), 23 no hkups, 159 pull-thrus, cable TV, wireless Instant Internet access at site ($), wireless Internet access central location, tenting, cabins, dump station, non-guest dumping $, laundry, groceries, RV supplies, LP gas by weight/by meter, ice, tables, wood, controlled access gate.

◇◇◇◇RECREATION: rec hall, rec room/area, pavilion, coin games, swim pool, pedal boat rentals, float trips, lake/stream fishing, fishing supplies, bsktball, playground, planned activities, horseshoes, v-ball, local tours.

Pets welcome. Partial handicap access. Open all yr. Facilities fully operational Apr 1 thru Nov 1. Big rigs welcome. Internet friendly. Clubs welcome. Rate in 2007 $31-44 for 3 persons. MC/VISA/DISC. Member ARVC, CARVC. Phone: (828)497-7250. FMCA discount.

SEE AD TRAVEL SECTION PAGE 622

CHEROKEE—Continued on next page

CHEROKEE—Continued
GREAT SMOKEY MOUNTAIN RV CAMPING RESORT—Continued

(NE) Indian Creek Campground—*From west jct US 441 & US 19/441: Go 1/2 mi W on US 19/441, then 2 mi N on US 441, then 100 yards W on Acquoni Rd, then 8 mi N on Big Cove Rd, then 1-1/4 mi E on Bunches Creek Rd. Enter on L.* ◇◇◇FACILITIES: 69 sites, typical site width 40 ft, 30 ft max RV length, 14 full hkups, 23 W&E, 12 E, (15, 20 & 30 amps), 20 no hkups, some extended stay sites, a/c not allowed, tenting, dump station, laundry, ltd groceries, ice, tables, fire rings, wood. ◇◇RECREATION: river swimming, stream fishing, playground, horseshoes, hiking trails. Pets welcome. Open Mar thru Oct 31. Internet friendly. Rate in 2007 $23-27 for 2 persons. Phone: (828)497-4361.

(NE) KOA-CHEROKEE GREAT SMOKIES—(Swain) *From jct US 441 & US 19/441: Go 2 mi N on US 441, then 4 1/4 mi N on Big Cove Rd. Enter on R.*

WELCOME

◇◇◇◇FACILITIES: 400 sites, typical site width 40 ft, 257 full hkups, 123 W&E, (30 & 50 amps), 20 no hkups, some extended stay sites, 133 pull-thrus, cable TV, wireless Instant Internet access at site, wireless Internet access central location, tenting, cabins, dump station, non-guest dumping $, laundry, full svc store, RV supplies, LP gas by weight/by meter, ice, tables, patios, fire rings, grills, wood, controlled access gate.

◇◇◇◇◇RECREATION: rec hall, rec room/area, pavilion, equipped pavilion, coin games, 2 swim pools, wading pool, river swimming, whirlpool, float trips, river/pond fishing, fishing supplies, mini-golf ($), bsktball, 36 bike rentals, playground, planned activities, horseshoes, hiking trails, v-ball, local tours.

Pets welcome. Partial handicap access. Open all yr. Big rigs welcome. Internet friendly. Clubs welcome. Rate in 2007 $30-99 for 2 persons. MC/VISA. ATM. Member ARVC, CARVC. Phone: (828) 497-9711. KOA 10% value card discount.

e-mail: cherokee@koa.net

SEE AD PAGE 644 AND AD DISCOVER SECTION PAGES 62 & 63

MOONSHINE CREEK CAMPGROUND—*From jct US 19 & US 441: Go 7-1/2 mi SE on US 441, then 8 mi NE on US 23/US 74, then 2 mi SW on Candlestick Rd/CR-1471. Enter on L.*

SEE PRIMARY LISTING AT BALSAM AND AD PAGE 644

(NE) River Valley Campground—(Swain) *From west jct US 441 & US 19/441: Go 1/2 mi W on US 19/441, then 2 mi N on US 441, then 100 yards W on Acquoni Rd, then 3-3/4 mi N on Big Cove Rd. Enter on R.* ◇◇◇FACILITIES: 200 sites, typical site width 25 ft, 151 full hkups, 49 W&E, (15, 30 & 50 amps), some extended stay sites, 56 pull-thrus, tenting, laundry, ice, tables, fire rings, grills, wood. ◇◇RECREATION: rec room/area, equipped pavilion, river fishing. Pets welcome, size restrict, quantity restrict. Partial handicap access. Open Late Mar thru Oct 31. Rate in 2007 $27-30 for 3 persons. Phone: (828)497-3540.

(NE) YOGI IN THE SMOKIES—(Swain) *From west jct US 441 & US 19/441: Go 1/2 mi W on US 19/441, then 2 mi N on US 441, then 100 yards E on Acquoni Rd, then 7 mi N on Big Cove Rd, then E on Galamore Bridge Rd. Continue 1/2 mi S on Sherrill Cove Rd. Enter at end.*

WELCOME

◇◇◇FACILITIES: 179 sites, typical site width 25 ft, 70 full hkups, 101 W&E, (15, 20, 30 & 50 amps), 8 no hkups, 20 pull-thrus, cable TV, wireless Instant Internet access at site, wireless Internet access central location, tenting, cabins, dump station, portable dump, laundry, groceries, RV supplies, LP gas by weight/by meter, ice, tables, fire rings, wood.

◇◇◇◇RECREATION: rec room/area, pavilion, coin games, swim pool, river swimming, river fishing, fishing supplies, bsktball, 4 bike rentals, play equipment, planned activities, horseshoes.

Pets welcome, breed restrict. Partial handicap access. Open Mar 15 thru Nov 12. Internet friendly. Clubs welcome. Rate in 2007 $29-38 for 2 persons. MC/VISA. Member ARVC, CARVC. Phone: (828)497-9151.

e-mail: yogibear@jellystone-cherokee.com

SEE AD DISCOVER SECTION PAGE 60

CLAYTON—B-4

(W) COOPER'S MOBILE HOME PARK & RV'S (RV SPACES)—(Johnston) *From jct I-40 (exit 306) & US 70: Go 4 mi E on US 70. Enter on L.*

WELCOME

FACILITIES: 40 sites, accepts full hkup units only, 40 full hkups, (20, 30 & 50 amps), mostly extended stay sites, cable TV.

CLAYTON—Continued
COOPER'S MOBILE HOME PARK RV'S—Continued

Pets welcome. No tents. Open all yr. No restrooms. Big rigs welcome. Rate in 2007 $35 per family. Phone: (919)868-4896.

SEE AD RALEIGH PAGE 659

COINJOCK—A-6

(NE) Hampton Lodge Camping Resort—(Currituck) *From US 158, Waterlilly Rd exit (South end of high bridge): Go 7-1/4 mi NE on Waterlilly Rd. Enter at end.* ◇◇FACILITIES: 268 sites, typical site width 25 ft, 140 full hkups, 128 W&E, (20 & 30 amps), many extended stay sites, 16 pull-thrus, tenting, dump station, non-guest dumping $, portable dump, laundry, groceries, LP gas by weight/by meter, ice, tables. ◇◇◇RECREATION: rec hall, rec room/area, lake swimming, boating, canoeing, ramp, dock, lake fishing, playground, 2 shuffleboard courts, sports field, v-ball. Pets welcome. Open all yr. Dec-Apr by reservation only. Rate in 2007 $25-30 for 2 persons. Phone: (252)453-2732.

CONCORD—B-2

✲ **(NE) TOM JOHNSON CAMPING CENTER**—*From jct I-77 & I-85: Go 11 mi N on I-85 (exit 49), then 1 1/4 mi E on US 29. Enter on L.* SALES: travel trailers, 5th wheels, motor homes, mini-motor homes, fold-down camping trailers, pre-owned unit sales. SERVICES: full-time mech, engine/chassis repair, RV appliance repair, body work/collision repair, LP gas by weight/by meter, dump station, RV rentals, installs hitches. Open all yr. MC/VISA. Phone: (888)450-1440.

WELCOME

e-mail: concordsales@tomjohnsoncamping.com

SEE AD TRAVEL SECTION PAGE 628

COVE CREEK—E-2

(SW) GREAT SMOKY MOUNTAINS NATIONAL PARK (Cataloochee Campground)—(Hawood) *From jct I-40 & US 276: Go 1/2 mi SW on US 276, then NW on Cove Creek Rd.* FACILITIES: 27 sites, 31 ft max RV length, 27 no hkups, tenting, grills. RECREATION: river fishing, hiking trails. Open Mar 10 thru Oct 31. No showers. Max stay 14 days. Phone: (423)436-1200.

CRUMPLER—A-1

(NE) Twin Rivers Family Campground—(Ashe) *From center of town: Go 1 mi S on US16, then 2 mi NE on Chestnut Hill Rd (SR-1567), then 2-1/2 mi NE on Geo McMillan Rd (SR-1565), then 1 mi NW on Garvey Bridge. Enter on R.* ◇◇FACILITIES: 60 sites, 8 full hkups, 14 W&E, (20 & 30 amps), 38 no hkups, some extended stay sites, tenting, dump station, ice, tables, wood. ◇RECREATION: boating, no motors, canoeing, river fishing. Pets welcome. Open Late Apr thru Late Oct. Rate in 2007 $18-20 for 2 persons. Phone: (336)982-3456.

DENVER—B-1

(N) Cross Country Campground—(Catawba) *From jct Hwy 16 & Hwy 150: Go 2-1/2 mi E on Hwy 150. Enter on L.* ◇◇◇◇FACILITIES: 407 sites, typical site width 25 ft, 347 full hkups, 60 W&E, (15, 20, 30 & 50 amps), some extended stay sites, 87 pull-thrus, tenting, dump station, non-guest dumping $, laundry, ltd groceries, LP gas by meter, ice, tables, fire rings. ◇◇◇◇RECREATION: rec room/area, swim pool, pond fishing, mini-golf ($), playground, 4 shuffleboard courts,

Cross Country Campground—Continued on next page

DENVER—Continued
Cross Country Campground—Continued

planned activities (wkends only), tennis, horseshoes, sports field, hiking trails, v-ball. Pets welcome, breed restrict, size restrict. Partial handicap access. Open all yr. Rate in 2007 $30 for 4 persons. Phone: (704)483 5897.

(N) Wildlife Woods Campground—(Catawba) *From jct I-77 & Hwy 150 (exit 36): Go 10-1/2 mi W on Hwy 150. Enter on L.* ◇◇◇FACILITIES: 305 sites, typical site width 30 ft, 260 full hkups, 45 W&E, (20, 30 & 50 amps), many extended stay sites, 80 pull-thrus, tenting, ice, tables, fire rings, wood. ◇◇◇◇RECREATION: rec hall, rec room/area, swim pool, lake swimming, boating, canoeing, ramp, dock, 4 canoe/5 pedal boat rentals, lake fishing, mini-golf, horseshoes, v-ball. Rec open to public. Pets welcome, breed restrict. Open all yr. Rate in 2007 $30-35 for 4 persons. Member ARVC, CARVC. Phone: (704)483-5611.

DURHAM—A-3

(SW) BIRCHWOOD RV PARK—(Orange) *From jct Hwy 40 & Hwy 86 (exit 266): Go 1-1/2 mi N on Hwy 86 then E 4-6/10 mi on Mt. Sinai Rd, then 3/10 mi S on Wilkins Dr. Enter on L.*

WELCOME

◇◇◇FACILITIES: 60 sites, typical site width 20 ft, accepts self-contained units only, 50 full hkups, 10 W&E, (30 & 50 amps), mostly extended stay sites, wireless Internet access central location, RV storage, dump station, laundry, LP gas by weight.

Pepsi was invented and first served in New Bern in 1898.

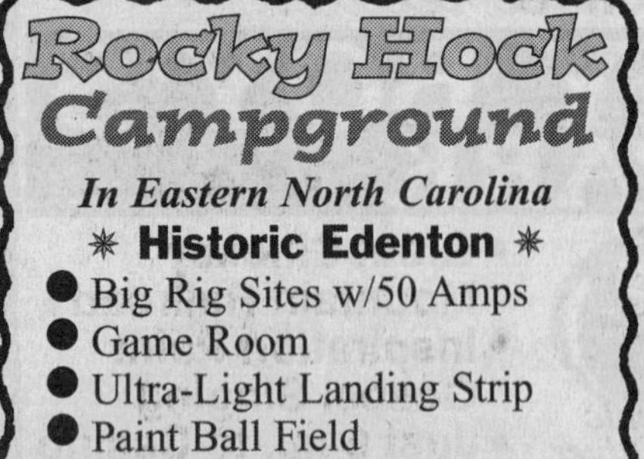

DURHAM—Continued
BIRCHWOOD RV PARK—Continued

RECREATION: golf nearby, play equipment.

Pets welcome. No tents. Open all yr. No restrooms. Rate in 2007 $29 for 2 persons. Phone: (919)493-1557.

e-mail: birchwoodrvpark@yahoo.com

SEE AD RALEIGH PAGE 659

EDENTON—A-5

(N) ROCKY HOCK CAMPGROUND—(Chowan) *From jct of US 17 and Hwy 32: Go 5 mi N on Hwy 32, then 1-1/4 mi W on Rocky Hock Rd, then 1/4 mi S on Rocky Hock Rd, then 1-3/4 mi W on Harris Landing Rd, then 3/4 mi N on Tynch Town Rd. Enter on L.*

◇◇◇FACILITIES: 32 sites, typical site width 35 ft, 32 full hkups, (30 & 50 amps), phone on-site Internet access (needs activ), tenting, RV storage, laundry, tables.

◇◇◇RECREATION: rec hall, boating, canoeing, pond fishing, planned activities (wkends only), v-ball.

Pets welcome. Open all yr. Big rigs welcome. Escort to site. Rate in 2007 $20-30 for 2 persons. MC/VISA/DISC/AMEX. Phone: (252)221-4695.

e-mail: rhcampground@net-change.com

SEE AD THIS PAGE

ELIZABETHTOWN—C-4

(N) JONES LAKE STATE PARK—(Bladen) *From town: Go 4 mi N on Hwy 242.* FACILITIES: 20 sites, 30 ft max RV length, 1 W&E, 19 no hkups, tenting, cold showers only, grills. RECREATION: lake swimming, canoeing, dock, rowboat/canoe rentals, lake fishing, hiking trails, v-ball. Open Mar 15 thru Dec 1. No showers. Phone: (910)588-4550.

EMERALD ISLE—C-5

EMERALD ISLE WINE MARKET—*From jct Hwy 24 & Hwy 58: Go 2 mi SE on Hwy 58, then W on Coast Guard Rd. Enter on L.* Extensive selection of wines from North Carolina and around the world, as well as gifts and accesories for wine lovers. Open all yr. MC/VISA. Phone: (252)354-2250.

SEE AD NEXT PAGE AND AD DISCOVER SECTION PAGE 60

EMERALD ISLE—Continued on next page

Read interesting travel facts in the front of every state/province listing section.

Woodall's Tip #29... The "Welcome" symbol before a listing identifies those parks that have purchased an advertisement because they want to tell you more about their business.

HOLIDAY TRAV-L-PARK RESORT FOR CAMPERS
Emerald Isle, N.C.

(252) 354-2250 - www.htpresort.com

9102 Coast Guard Road, Emerald Isle, North Carolina 28594

OCEAN FRONT CAMPING
Since 1976

Emerald Isle Wine Market

Snow Birds ❤ Us – Coming & Going

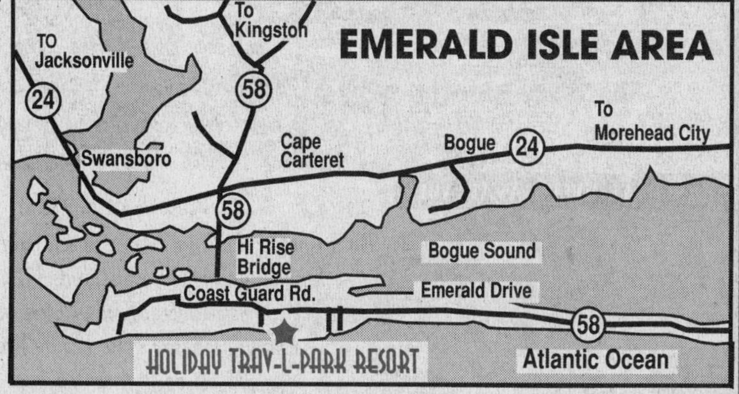

See listing at Emerald Isle, NC

Facilities: WWWWW

Recreation: WWWWW

- Golf Cart Parking Area at Beach
- Ocean Observation Deck & Concession Stand with Rafts, Boogie Boards, Umbrellas & Chair Rentals
- Handicap Access to Beach
- Swimming Pool ● Playground
- Game Room with Pool Tables & Video Games
- Home of Emerald Isle Speedway
- Ice Cream Shops ● Fudge Shop
- Line Dancing ● Live Music ● Movies
- Arts and Crafts ● Aquatic Games
- Bible School ● Worship Services

CLUBS WELCOMED

Covered Pavilion (can accommodate groups)

NEARBY GOLFING, SHOPPING & RESTAURANTS

- Grassy, Pull-Thru Sites with Picnic Tables & Full Hookups
- Wi-Fi & Cable TV
- Paved Roads ● Gated Entry
- A/C and Heated, Clean Restrooms w/ Ceramic-Tiled Showers
- Fully Handicap Accessible Restroom
- A/C and Heated Laundry Room
- LP Gas ● Gasoline ● Convenience Store
- Public Phones
- Special Tenting Area
- Dishwashing Area with Four Sinks

MasterCard VISA

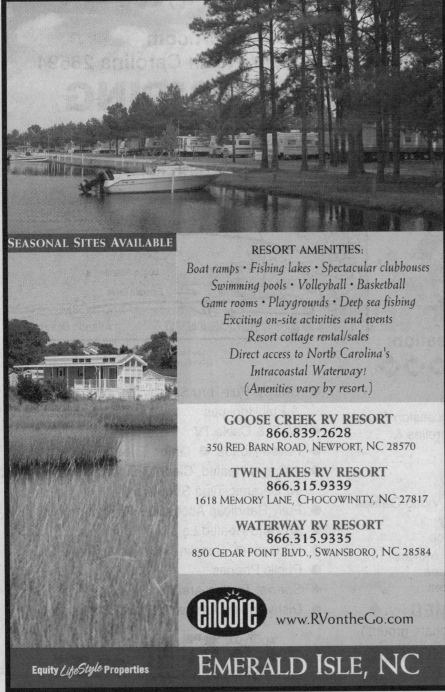

EMERALD ISLE—Continued

(C) HOLIDAY TRAV-L-PARK RESORT FOR CAMPERS—(Carteret) *From jct Hwy 24 & Hwy 58: Go 2 mi SE on Hwy 58, then W on Coast Guard Rd. Enter on L.*

WE'RE STILL HERE ON THE BEACH
Don't let the rumors fool you. We're still welcoming RV and tent campers to our beautiful 5W resort. All campsites are grassy and you can walk directly to the beach. Lots to do for all ages. Call now for reservations.

◇◇◇◇◇FACILITIES: 340 sites, typical site width 35 ft, 281 full hkups, 19 W&E, (20, 30 & 50 amps), 50 amps ($), 40 no hkups, some extended stay sites, 150 pull-thrus, cable TV, wireless Instant Internet access at site ($), tenting, RV storage, dump station, non-guest dumping $, laundry, groceries, RV supplies, LP gas by weight/by meter, gas, ice, tables, controlled access gate.

◇◇◇◇◇RECREATION: rec hall, pavilion, coin games, swim pool, wading pool, saltwater swimming, saltwater fishing, fishing supplies, mini-golf ($), 18 bike rentals, playground, planned activities, v-ball.

Pets welcome ($), breed restrict. Partial handicap access. Open March thru mid Dec. Big rigs welcome. Internet friendly. Clubs welcome. Rate in 2007 $45-75 for 2 persons. MC/VISA. ATM. Member ARVC, CARVC. Phone: (252)354-2250.

e-mail: htpresort@mynetrocks.com

SEE AD PAGE 647 AND AD DISCOVER SECTION PAGE 60

FAYETTEVILLE—C-3

✻ **(S) ALLSPORT CAMPING CENTER**—*N'bnd from jct I-95 (exit 40) & Bus I-95: Go 6 mi N on Bus I-95. S'bnd from jct I-95 (exit 56) & Bus I-95: Go 9 mi S on Bus I-95.* SALES: travel trailers, park trailers, 5th wheels, fold-down camping trailers, pre-owned unit sales. SERVICES: full-time mech, RV appliance repair, body work/collision repair, LP gas by weight/by meter, RV storage, sells parts/accessories, installs hitches. Open all yr. MC/VISA/DISC. Phone: (910)323-3888.

e-mail: allsportrv@aol.com

SEE AD TRAVEL SECTION PAGE 621

(SE) LAZY ACRES CAMPGROUND—(Cumberland) *From I-95 (exit 44): Go 1 mi N on Claude Lee Rd, then 1/4 mi E on Lazy Acres St. Enter at end.*

◇◇◇FACILITIES: 50 sites, typical site width 30 ft, 46 full hkups, 4 W&E, (30 & 50 amps), some extended stay sites, 45 pull-thrus, cable TV, wireless Instant Internet access at site, tenting, RV storage, dump station, non-guest dumping $, laundry, LP gas by weight/by meter, ice, tables, patios, fire rings, wood.

◇◇RECREATION: pavilion, swim pool, pond fishing, play equipment.

Pets welcome. Open all yr. Internet friendly. Escort to site. Rate in 2007 $23-28 for 2 persons. Member ARVC, CARVC. Phone: (910)425-9218.

e-mail: bob@lazyacrescampground.net

SEE AD NEXT PAGE

MILITARY PARK (Fort Bragg Travel Camp)—(Cumberland) *Off Hwy 24. On base. Adjacent to Smith Lake Rec. Area.* FACILITIES: 24 sites, 13 full hkups, 11 W&E, (30 & 50 amps), tenting, dump station, laundry, ice, fire rings, grills. RECREATION: lake swimming, boating, ramp, lake fishing, hiking trails. Open all yr. For Military Use Only-w/Military ID Card. Phone: (910)396-5979.

FAYETTEVILLE—Continued on next page

North Carolina was the 12th state admitted to the Union.

SUNBIRD RV REPAIR SERVICE—RVIA-RVDA Certified. SERVICES: full-time mech, RV appliance repair, mobile RV svc, sells parts/accessories, installs hitches. Open all yr. MC/VISA. Phone: (910)322-4065.

e-mail: sunbirdrv@yahoo.com

SEE AD PAGE 648

FLETCHER—E-2

(N) **RUTLEDGE LAKE RV PARK**—(Henderson) *From I-26 (exit 40) & Hwy 280: Go 1 mi E on Hwy 280, then 3/4 mi S on Rutledge Rd. Enter on L.*

IN THE HEART OF THE BLUE RIDGE

Close to Asheville's Biltmore Estate, Chimney Rock, Hendersonville, and the scenic Blue Ridge Parkway. Make us your base camp for exploring. Enjoy the fun right here with fishing, boat rentals and kid-friendly activities.

◇◇◇◇◇FACILITIES: 75 sites, typical site width 40 ft, 75 full hkups, (20, 30 & 50 amps), some extended stay sites, 8 pull-thrus, cable TV, wireless Instant Internet access at site, tenting, cabins, RV storage, laundry, ltd groceries, RV supplies, LP gas by weight/by meter, ice, tables, patios, fire rings, grills, wood, controlled access gate.

◇◇◇◇◇RECREATION: rec hall, pavilion, swim pool, boating, no motors, canoeing, kayaking, 2 canoe/2 kayak/7 pedal boat rentals, lake fishing, fishing supplies, golf nearby, bsktball, playground, planned activities (wkends only), horseshoes, sports field, hiking trails, v-ball.

Pets welcome, breed restrict. Partial handicap access. Open all yr. Big rigs welcome. Internet friendly. Clubs welcome. Rate in 2007 $40-43 for 2 persons. MC/VISA. Member ARVC, CARVC. Phone: (828)654-7873.

e-mail: info@campingnorthcarolina.com

SEE AD ASHEVILLE PAGE 635

FONTANA VILLAGE—E-1

(S) NANTAHALA NATIONAL FOREST (Cable Cove Campground)—(Graham) *From town: Go 4-1/2 mi NE on Hwy-28, then 1-1/2 mi NE on FR-3618.* FACILITIES: 26 sites, 26 no hkups, tenting, non-flush toilets only, grills. RECREATION: boating, ramp, lake fishing, hiking trails. Open all yr. Facilities fully operational Apr thru Oct. No showers. No reservations. Max stay 14 days. Phone: (828)479-6431.

FOREST CITY—B-1

(SW) Foothills Family Campground—(Rutherford) *From jct US 74 (exit 178) & Hwy 221: Go 7-1/4 mi S on Hwy 221, then 1 mi W on Hogan Rd. Enter on R.* ◇◇◇FACILITIES: 82 sites, 72 full hkups, 4 W&E, (20, 30 & 50 amps), 50 amps ($), 6 no hkups, some extended stay sites, 3 pull-thrus, tenting, laundry, ltd groceries, LP gas by meter, ice, tables, fire rings, wood. ◇◇RECREATION: rec room/area, equipped pavilion, swim pool, play equipment, hiking trails, v-ball. Pets welcome. Open all yr. Rate in 2007 $25 for 4 persons. Phone: (828)245-4064. CCUSA discount.

Reserve Online at Woodalls.com

FOSCOE—A-1

(S) **GRANDFATHER CAMPGROUND**—(Watauga) *From jct US 321 & Hwy 105: Go 8 mi S on Hwy 105. Enter on L.*

◇◇◇FACILITIES: 128 sites, typical site width 40 ft, 60 full hkups, 12 W&E, 7 E, (20, 30 & 50 amps), 49 no hkups, 19 pull-thrus, cable TV, wireless Instant Internet access at site, wireless Internet access central location, tenting, cabins, RV storage, dump station, non-guest dumping $, laundry, ltd groceries, RV supplies, ice, tables, fire rings, grills, wood.

◇◇RECREATION: rec room/area, pavilion, stream fishing, golf nearby, planned activities (wkends only), horseshoes, hiking trails.

Pets welcome. Partial handicap access. Open all yr. Big rigs welcome. Internet friendly. Clubs wel-

come. Rate in 2007 $24-33 for 2 persons. MC/VISA/DISC. Member ARVC, CARVC. Phone: (800) 788-2582.

e-mail: grandfatherrv@charter.net

SEE AD THIS PAGE

FRANKLIN—E-1

(W) Cartoogechaye Creek Campground—(Macon) *From west jct US 441 & US 64: Go 6-1/2 mi W on US 64. Enter on L.* ◇◇◇FACILITIES: 101 sites, typical site width 25 ft, 40 full hkups, 36 W&E, (30 & 50 amps), 25 no hkups, some extended stay sites, tenting, dump station, laundry, ice, tables, wood. RECREATION: stream fishing, v-ball. Pets welcome. Open Apr 1 thru Oct 31. Self-contained units only in winter. Phone: (828) 524-8553. FMCA discount.

FRANKLIN—Continued on next page

Howard Cosell, sports journalist, was from North Carolina.

FRANKLIN—Continued

(S) COUNTRY WOODS RV PARK—(Macon) *From west jct US 64 & US 441/23: Go 2-1/4 mi S on US 441/23. Entrance at time and temperature sign. Enter on R.*

◆◆◆FACILITIES: 72 sites, typical site width 35 ft, 72 full hkups, (30 amps), some extended stay sites, 3 pull-thrus, cable TV, wireless Instant Internet access at site, wireless Internet access central location, laundry, tables, patios, fire rings, wood.

◆◆RECREATION: rec room/area, equipped pavilion, hiking trails.

Pets welcome. No tents. Open Apr 1 thru Nov 30. Internet friendly. Escort to site. Clubs welcome. Rate in 2007 $27-30 for 2 persons. Phone: (828) 524-4339. CCUSA discount.

e-mail: cwoodrv@dnet.net

SEE AD PAGE 649

(S) FRANKLIN RV PARK & CAMPGROUND (TOO NEW TO RATE)—(Macon) *From jct US 64 & US 441 Bus: Go 3.1 mi S on US 441/23, then 300 feet SW on Addington Bridge Rd, then NW on Old Addington Bridge Rd. Enter on L.*

FACILITIES: 24 sites, typical site width 20 ft, 20 full hkups, 4 W&E, (20, 30 & 50 amps), cable TV, wireless Instant Internet access at site, tables, fire rings.

RECREATION: equipped pavilion.

Pets welcome, breed restrict, quantity restrict. No tents. Open May 1 thru Dec 31. Internet friendly. Rate in 2007 $25-28 for 2 persons. Phone: (828) 349-6200.

e-mail: info@franklinrvpark.com

SEE AD PAGE 649 AND AD TRAVEL SECTION PAGE 620

(NE) Mi Mountain Campground—(Macon) *From west jct US 64 & US 441/23: Go 5-1/2 mi N on US 441/23, then 1/4 mi E on Kirkland Rd. Enter on R.* ◆◆FACILITIES: 48 sites, typical site width 30 ft, 32 full hkups, 11 W&E, 5 E, (15, 30 & 50 amps), mostly extended stay sites, 7 pull-thrus, tenting, LP gas by meter, ice, tables, patios, fire rings, grills, wood. ◆RECREATION: pavilion, swim pool, pond fishing, play equipment, planned activities. Pets welcome. Partial handicap access. Open Apr 1 thru Oct 31. Rate in 2007 $20 per vehicle. Phone: (828)524-6155.

(S) NANTAHALA NATIONAL FOREST (Standing Indian Campground)—(Macoh) *From town: Go 10 mi SW on US 64, then 2 mi E on Wallace Gap Rd (Old US 64), then 2 mi S on FR 67.* FACILITIES: 81 sites, 22 ft max RV length, 81 no hkups, 4 pull-thrus, tenting, cold showers only. RECREATION: river swimming, river fishing, hiking trails. Facilities fully operational Apr 1 thru Dec 1. No showers. Phone: (828)524-6441.

(NW) Outside Inn Campground—*From jct US 64 & US 441: Go 1-1/4 mi N on US 441 Bus, then 3-1/2 mi N on Hwy 28, then 1/2 mi W on Iolta Church Rd, then 6-1/2 mi NW on Burningtown Rd. Enter on L.* ◆◆FACILITIES: 30 sites, typical site width 28 ft, 30 W&E, (20 & 30 amps), some extended stay sites, 15 pull-thrus, tenting, dump station, fire rings. ◆RECREATION: stream fishing. Open Mar 31 thru Oct 31. Phone: (828)349-1846.

(W) Pines RV Park—(Macon) *From west jct US 441 bypass & US 64: Go 4-3/4 mi W on US 64. Enter on L.* ◆◆◆FACILITIES: 69 sites, typical site width 24 ft, 57 full hkups, 12 W&E, (30 amps), some extended stay sites, tenting, dump station, laundry, ice, tables, patios, fire rings, wood. ◆◆RECREATION: rec room/area, playground, shuffleboard court, planned activities (wkends only). Pets welcome. Open all yr. Rate in 2007 $22-23 for 2 persons. Member ARVC, CARVC. Phone: (828)524-4490.

(N) THE GREAT OUTDOORS RV RESORT—(Macon) *From west jct US 64 & US 441/23: Go 6-1/2 mi N on US 441/23, then 100 yards W on Echo Valley Rd. Enter on R.*

JUST OPENED AND READY FOR YOU

We've opened the newest RV resort in the beautiful NC Mountains. Check out this first class facility. Terraced sites with unobstructed mountain views & paved roads are just part of what we offer. Easy Access & Big Rig Sites!

◆◆◆◆◆FACILITIES: 66 sites, typical site width 35 ft, accepts self-contained units only, 66 full hkups, (30 & 50 amps), cable TV, wireless Instant Internet access at site ($), laundry, ltd groceries, RV supplies, LP gas by weight/by meter, ice, tables.

◆◆RECREATION: rec hall, swim pool, golf nearby.

Pets welcome, breed restrict. Partial handicap access. No tents. Open all yr. Big rigs welcome. Internet friendly. Escort to site. Clubs welcome. Rate in 2007 $39 for 2 persons. MC/VISA/DISC/AMEX. Member ARVC, CARVC. Phone: (828)349-0412. CCUSA discount.

e-mail: gorvresort@aol.com

SEE AD TRAVEL SECTION PAGE 624

FRISCO—B-6

CAPE HATTERAS NATIONAL SEASHORE (Frisco Campground)—(Dare) *From center of town on Hwy 12: Go 2 mi E following signs.* FACILITIES: 127 sites, (20 & 30 amps), 127 no hkups, tenting, cold showers only, grills. RECREATION: saltwater swimming, saltwater fishing. Open Mar 25 thru Oct 10. No reservations. Phone: (252)473-2111.

(N) FRISCO WOODS CAMPGROUND—(Dare) *Located in center of town on Hwy 12. Enter on R.*

◆◆◆FACILITIES: 274 sites, typical site width 25 ft, 51 full hkups, 123 W&E, (15, 20, 30 & 50 amps), 100 no hkups, cable TV, wireless Instant Internet access at site, wireless Internet access central location, tenting, cabins, dump station, non-guest dumping $, laundry, full svc store, RV supplies, LP gas by weight/by meter, ice, tables.

◆◆◆RECREATION: swim pool, saltwater swimming, boating, canoeing, kayaking, 20 kayak rentals, saltwater fishing, play equipment, horseshoes, hiking trails, v-ball. Rec open to public.

Pets welcome. Open Mar 1 thru Dec 15. Internet friendly. Clubs welcome. Rate in 2007 $38-48 for 4 persons. MC/VISA/DISC/AMEX. Member ARVC, CARVC. Phone: (252)995-5208.

e-mail: friscowd@pinn.net

SEE AD NEXT PAGE

GARNER—B-4

(E) 70 EAST MOBILE ACRES & RV PARK (RV SPACES)—(Wake) *From jct I-40 (exit 306) & US 70: Go 2 mi E on US 70. Enter on L.*

FACILITIES: 60 sites, typical site width 40 ft, accepts full hkup units only, 60 full hkups, (20, 30 & 50 amps), some extended stay sites, 10 pull-thrus.

RECREATION: bsktball.

Pets welcome. No tents. Open all yr. No restrooms. Big rigs welcome. Rate in 2007 $30-35 per vehicle. Phone: (919)772-6568.

SEE AD RALEIGH PAGE 659

GATESVILLE—A-5

MERCHANTS MILLPOND STATE PARK—(Gates) *From town: Go 6 mi NE on Hwy 1403.* FACILITIES: 20 sites, 20 no hkups, tenting, grills. RECREATION: canoeing, canoe rentals, pond fishing, hiking trails. Partial handicap access. Open all yr. Facilities fully operational Mar 15 thru Nov 30. Family CG 3/15-11/30. No showers. No reservation. Phone: (252)357-1191.

GLENDALE SPRINGS—A-1

(N) RACCOON HOLLER CAMPGROUND—(Ashe) *From jct Blue Ridge Pkwy (milepost 257-3/4) & Raccoon Holler Rd: Go 1/4 mi W on Raccoon Holler Rd. Enter on R.*

◆◆◆◆FACILITIES: 250 sites, typical site width 25 ft, 165 full hkups, 35 W&E, (20, 30 & 50 amps), 50 no hkups, some extended stay sites, 12 pull-thrus, cable TV ($), wireless Instant Internet access at site ($), wireless Internet access central location, tenting, RV/park trailer rentals, RV storage, dump station, laundry, ltd groceries, RV supplies, LP gas by weight/by meter, ice, tables, fire rings, wood.

◆◆◆◆RECREATION: rec hall, rec room/area, coin games, lake fishing, fishing supplies, bsktball, playground, shuffleboard court, planned activities (wkends only), sports field, v-ball.

Pets welcome, breed restrict, quantity restrict. Partial handicap access. Open Apr 15 thru Oct 31. Clubs welcome. Rate in 2007 $18-24 for 2 persons. Member ARVC. Phone: (336)982-2706.

e-mail: janmill@skybest.com

SEE AD NEXT PAGE

GLENVIEW—A-4

(E) KOA-Enfield-Rocky Mt.—(Halifax) *From jct I-95 (exit 154) & Hwy 481: Go 3/4 mi W on Hwy 481. Enter on R.* ◆◆◆FACILITIES: 80 sites, typical site width 30 ft, 33 full hkups, 47 W&E, (15, 20, 30 & 50 amps), 50 amps ($), 67 pull-thrus, tenting, dump station, non-guest dumping $, laundry, ltd groceries, LP gas by weight/by meter, ice, tables, fire rings, wood. ◆◆RECREATION: rec hall, swim pool, mini-golf ($), playground, horseshoes, v-ball. Rec open to public. Pets welcome. Open all yr. Rate in 2007 $30-37 for 2 persons. Phone: (252)445-5925. KOA 10% value card discount.

GOLDSBORO—B-4

CLIFFS OF THE NEUSE STATE PARK—(Wayne) *From town: Go 14 mi SE on Hwy-111, then 1 mi E.* FACILITIES: 35 sites, 35 ft max RV length, 35 no hkups, tenting, dump station, grills. RECREATION: lake swimming, boating, rowboat rentals, river fishing, hiking trails. Open Mar 15 thru Nov 30. Phone: (919)778-6234.

GOLDSBORO—Continued on next page

The first English colony in America was located on Roanoke Island, founded by Walter Raleigh. The colonists mysteriously vanished with no trace except for the word "Croatoan" scrawled on a nearby tree.

GOLDSBORO—Continued

✽ **(W) DALY RV**—*From jct Hwy 581 & US 70: Go 1 mi W on US 70. Enter on L.* SALES: travel trailers, 5th wheels, pre-owned unit sales. SERVICES: full-time mech, engine/chassis repair, RV appliance repair, body work/collision repair, mobile RV svc, LP gas by weight/by meter, sells parts/accessories, installs hitches. Open all yr. MC/VISA/DISC. Phone: (919)734-4616.

e-mail: dalyrvoffice@bellsouth.net

SEE AD TRAVEL SECTION PAGE 624

Woodall's CampingLife magazine is the perfect camping companion to any of Woodall's Directories and Guides. With 8 monthly issues per year, containing camping stories, destination articles, buyers guides and more, CampingLife is a valuable resource for any Camper. Visit www.campinglife.com for more info.

In the Heart of the
Blue Ridge Mountains
RACCOON HOLLER
CAMPGROUND
336-982-2706
www.raccoonholler.com
493 Raccoon Holler Rd.
Glendale Springs, NC 28629
Between milepost 257 & 258
on the Blue Ridge Parkway
See listing at
Glendale Springs, NC
• 80 Acres
• 5 Acre Lake
• Wi-Fi
• Cable

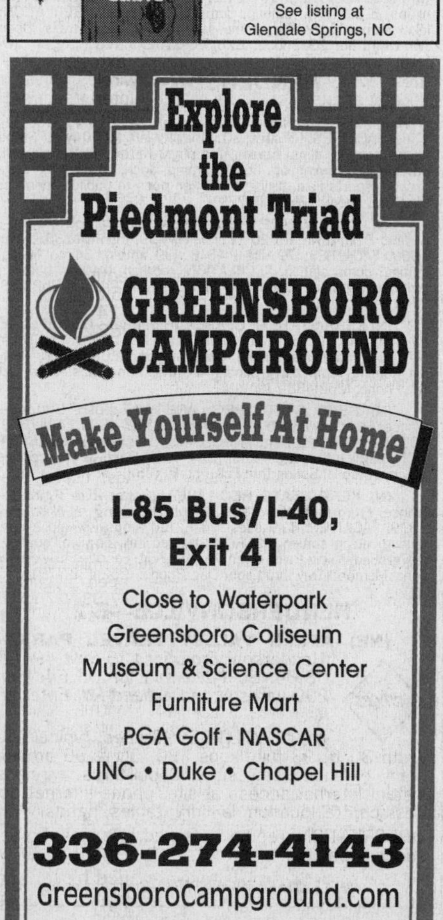

Explore the Piedmont Triad
GREENSBORO CAMPGROUND
Make Yourself At Home
I-85 Bus/I-40,
Exit 41
Close to Waterpark
Greensboro Coliseum
Museum & Science Center
Furniture Mart
PGA Golf - NASCAR
UNC • Duke • Chapel Hill
336-274-4143
GreensboroCampground.com
See listing at Greesboro, NC

GREENSBORO—A-2

(E) GREENSBORO CAMPGROUND—(Guilford) *From jct I-40 & Bus 85: Go 4-1/4 mi NE on Bus 85/I-40 to exit 41, then 1/4 mi SE on E Lee St, then 1 mi W on Sharpe Rd, then 1/4 mi N on Trox St. Enter on L.*

STAY A NIGHT OR FOREVER

EZ on/off I-40, but far enough that you'll want to stay awhile. The perfect home base while you enjoy everything the Piedmont is known for - shopping, museums, NASCAR, golf. Or just relax at our sparkling clean pool.

◆◆◆FACILITIES: 91 sites, 85 full hkups, 4 W&E, 2 E, (20, 30 & 50 amps), some extended stay sites, 70 pull-thrus, wireless Internet access central location, tenting, cabins, RV storage, dump station, laundry, ltd groceries, RV supplies, LP gas by weight/by meter, ice, tables, fire rings, wood, controlled access gate.

◆◆◆RECREATION: rec room/area, pavilion, swim pool, golf nearby, playground, planned activities, horseshoes, hiking trails, v-ball.

GREENSBORO—Continued
GREENSBORO CAMPGROUND—Continued

Pets welcome, breed restrict. Partial handicap access. Open all yr. Big rigs welcome. Internet friendly. Rate in 2007 $27-35 for 4 persons. MC/VISA. Member ARVC, CARVC. Phone: (336)274-4143. CCUSA discount.

e-mail: greensborocampgr@bellsouth.net

SEE AD THIS PAGE

✽ **(W) OUT-OF-DOORS MART**—*From jct I-85 & I-40: Go 11 mi W on I-40 (exit 208 Sandy Ridge Rd), then 1/10 mi S on Sandy Ridge Rd, then 1/4 mi W on Norcross Rd. Enter on R.* On-line Parts. SALES: travel trailers, truck campers, 5th wheels, van campers, fold-down camping trailers, pre-owned unit sales. SERVICES: full-time mech, RV appliance repair, body work/collision re-

OUT-OF-DOORS MART—Continued on next page

The first American born to English parents was born in North Carolina (Virginia Dare).

FRISCO WOODS CAMPGROUND

Cape Hatteras' Only Wooded Waterfront Campground

"We've put the camp back in camping"

- ◆ Full Hookups ◆ Laundry ◆ Wi-Fi
- ◆ LP Gas ◆ 30-50 Amps ◆ Cable TV
- ◆ Convenience Store ◆ Tent Sites
- ◆ 4 Bathhouses ◆ On Major Bike Trail
- ◆ 32 Camping Cabins ◆ Outdoor Pavilion
- ◆ One Mile to 4WD Accessible Beaches
- ◆ Large Pool Overlooking Pamlico Bay

Good Sam Park

Kite Surfing
Wind Surfing
Fishing
Crabbing
Oystering
Birdwatching
Boating
Kayaking
Horseshoes
Beach Equipment
Rentals

1-800-948-3942

See listing at Frisco, NC

Visit Our Web Site At:
www.outer-banks.com/friscowoods

Your Hosts: The Barnett Family
Box 159, Frisco, NC 27936

GREENSBORO—Continued
OUT-OF-DOORS MART—Continued

pair, LP gas by weight/by meter, RV storage, sells parts/accessories, installs hitches. Open all yr. MC/VISA/DISC/AMEX. Phone: (336)993-4518.

e-mail: joel@outofdoors.com

SEE AD TRAVEL SECTION PAGE 619

HATTERAS—B-6

(N) **HATTERAS SANDS RV RESORT**—(Dare) *From the Ocracoke-Hatteras Ferry: Go 1/4 mi N on Hwy 12, then 1/4 mi E on Eagle Pass Rd. Enter on L.*

WELCOME

◆◆◆◆FACILITIES: 111 sites, typical site width 30 ft, 48 full hkups, 51 W&E, (20, 30 & 50 amps), 12 no hkups, 20 pull-thrus, cable TV, phone on-site Internet access (needs activ), phone Internet access central location, tenting, RV/park trailer rentals, cabins, dump station, non-guest dumping $, portable dump, laundry, ltd groceries, RV supplies, ice, tables, controlled access gate.

◆◆◆◆RECREATION: rec room/area, pavilion, coin games, swim pool, wading pool, whirlpool, canoeing, kayaking, 2 pedal boat rentals, saltwater fishing, bsktball, 3 bike rentals, playground, planned activities, horseshoes, v-ball.

Pets welcome ($). Open Mar 1 thru Dec 1. Big rigs welcome. Escort to site. Clubs welcome. Rate in 2007 $44-60 for 2 persons. MC/VISA. Member ARVC, CARVC. Phone: (252)986-2422.

e-mail: hatsandscg@aol.com

SEE AD CAPE HATTERAS PAGE 639

HAVELOCK—C-5

MILITARY PARK (Cherry Point MCAS Travel Camp)—(Craven) *On Fontana Rd, on base.* FACILITIES: 15 sites, 15 full hkups, tenting, dump station, laundry, ltd groceries, grills. RECREATION: swim pool, boating, ramp. Open all yr. For Military Use Only-w/Military ID Card. Phone: (252)466-2197.

HAYESVILLE—E-1

(E) NANTAHALA NATIONAL FOREST (Jackrabbit Mountain Campground)—(Clay) *From town: Go 6 mi E on US-64, then 2-1/2 mi S on Hwy-175, then 1-1/2 mi W on CR-1155.* FACILITIES: 101 sites, 22 ft max RV length, 101 no hkups, 5 pull-thrus, tenting, dump station, grills. RECREATION: lake swimming, boating, ramp, lake fishing, hiking trails. Open Apr 1 thru Sep 29. Phone: (828)837-5152.

HENDERSON—A-4

(N) KERR STATE REC. AREA (Bullocksville)—(Vance) *From town: Go 6 mi N on US-1, then 5 mi NW on Hwy-1369, then 1366.* FACILITIES: 69 sites, 30 ft max RV length, 30 W&E, 39 no hkups, tenting, dump station, fire rings. RECREATION: rec hall, pavilion, lake swimming, boating, ramp, dock, lake fishing, playground, sports field, hiking trails. Rec open to public. Open Apr thru Sep. Phone: (252)438-7791.

(N) KERR STATE REC. AREA (Henderson Point)—(Vance) *From town: Go 20 mi N on Hwy-39, then CR-1356, then 1359.* FACILITIES: 79 sites, 45 E, (30 amps), 34 no hkups, tenting, dump station. RECREATION: rec hall, pavilion, boating, ramp, playground. Open Mar thru Sep 10. Phone: (252)438-7791.

(N) KERR STATE REC. AREA (Hibernia)—(Vance) *Go 15 mi N on Hwy 39, then right on to 1347.* FACILITIES: 150 sites, 50 E, 100 no hkups, tenting, dump station. RECREATION: pavilion, boating, ramp, playground, hiking trails. Open Easter thru Oct 31. Phone: (252)438-7791.

(N) KERR STATE REC. AREA (Nutbush Bridge)—(Vance) *From town: Go 6 mi N on Hwy-39, then 1308.* FACILITIES: 103 sites, 60 W&E, 43 no hkups, tenting, dump station. RECREATION: pavilion, boating, ramp, playground. Open all yr. Facilities fully operational Spring thru Fall. Phone: (252)438-7791.

(N) KERR STATE REC. AREA (Satterwhite Points)—(Vance) *From town: Take exit 217 off I-85, go 7 mi N on Hwy 1319.* FACILITIES: 119 sites, 60 E, (30 amps), 59 no hkups, tenting, dump station. RECREATION: rec hall, pavilion, boating, playground, hiking trails. Open May thru Aug. Facilities fully operational Memorial Day thru Labor Day. Phone: (252)438-7791.

HENDERSONVILLE—E-2

(NE) **APPLE VALLEY TRAVEL PARK**—(Henderson) *From jct I-26 (exit 49A) & US 64: Go 1-1/2 mi E on US 64, then 200 yards N on Fruitland Rd. Enter on R.*

WELCOME

◆◆◆FACILITIES: 93 sites, typical site width 30 ft, 93 full hkups, (20, 30 & 50 amps), many extended stay sites, 8 pull-thrus, wireless Instant Internet access at site, phone Internet access central location, laundry, tables, patios.

◆RECREATION: rec hall, planned activities, horseshoes, v-ball.

APPLE VALLEY TRAVEL PARK—Continued on next page

Richard Gatling, inventor, was from North Carolina.

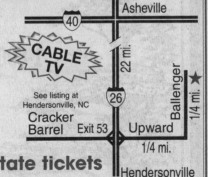

HENDERSONVILLE—Continued
APPLE VALLEY TRAVEL PARK—Continued

Pets welcome. No tents. Open Apr 1 thru Nov 1. Internet friendly. Escort to site. Clubs welcome. Rate in 2007 $24-25 for 2 persons. Phone: (828) 685-8000.

e-mail: applevalleytravelpark@yahoo.com

SEE AD THIS PAGE

WELCOME **(NE) JAYMAR TRAVEL PARK**—(Henderson) *From jct of I-26 (exit 49A) & US 64: Go 2 1/2 mi E on US 64. Enter on L.*

◆◆◆FACILITIES: 200 sites, typical site width 20 ft, accepts full hkup units only, 200 full hkups, (30 & 50 amps), mostly extended stay sites, 12 pull-thrus, cable TV, wireless Instant Internet access at site, wireless Internet access central location, laundry, tables.

◆◆RECREATION: rec hall, rec room/area, golf nearby, shuffleboard court, planned activities, horseshoes.

Pets welcome, quantity restrict. No tents. Open April 20 thru Nov 1. Big rigs welcome. Internet friendly. Escort to site. Rate in 2007 $23-28 per vehicle. Phone: (828)685-3771.

e-mail: jaymarnc@yahoo.com

SEE AD THIS PAGE

WELCOME **(SE) LAKEWOOD RV RESORT**—(Henderson) *From jct US 64 & I-26: Go 3-1/2 mi SE on I-26 to exit 53, then 1/4 mi E on Upward Rd, then 1/4 mi N on Ballenger Rd. Enter on R.*

◆◆◆◆FACILITIES: 100 sites, typical site width 24 ft, 100 full hkups, (30 & 50 amps), 24 pull-thrus, cable TV, wireless Instant Internet access at site, phone Internet access central location, RV storage, laundry, ice, tables, patios.

◆◆◆RECREATION: rec hall, swim pool, pond fishing, golf nearby, 2 shuffleboard courts, horseshoes.

Pets welcome, breed restrict. Partial handicap access. No tents. Open all yr. Big rigs welcome. Internet friendly. Rate in 2007 $39 for 4 persons. MC/VISA/DISC/AMEX. Member ARVC, CARVC. Phone: (888)819-4200. FMCA discount.

e-mail: info@lakewoodrvresort.com

SEE AD PAGE 652

(NE) Lazy Boy Travel Park—(Henderson) *From jct I-26 (exit 49A) & US 64: Go 1/2 mi E on US 64, then 1/4 mi SE on Howard Gap Rd, then 1/2 mi E on Old Sunset Hill Dr. Enter on R.* ◆◆FACILITIES: 83 sites, typical site width 30 ft, 73 full hkups, 10 W&E, (20 & 30 amps), some extended stay sites, 8 pull-thrus, tenting, dump station, non-guest dumping $, laundry, tables, patios. RECREATION: rec hall. Pets welcome. Open all yr. Phone: (828)697-7165.

✻ WELCOME **(NW) MOUNTAIN CAMPER SALES & SERVICE**—*From jct I-26 (exit 49A) and US 64: Go 200 yards E on US 64, then 4/10 mi S on Sugarloaf Rd. Enter on R.* SALES: pre-owned unit sales. SERVICES: full-time mech, engine/chassis repair, RV appliance repair, body work/collision repair, mobile RV svc, RV towing, LP gas by weight/by meter, dump station, RV rentals, RV storage, sells parts/accessories, installs hitches. Open all yr. MC/VISA/DISC/AMEX/DC/Debit. Phone: (828)697-6351.

e-mail: campersales@bellsouth.net

SEE AD TRAVEL SECTION PAGE 627

(SE) Park Place RV Park (RV SPACES)—(Henderson) *From jct US 64 & I-26: Go 3-1/2 mi SE on I-26E to exit 53, then 1/2 mi W on Upward Rd, then 50 feet*

HENDERSONVILLE—Continued
Park Place RV Park—Continued

N on South Allen Rd. Enter on L. FACILITIES: 48 sites, typical site width 25 ft, 48 full hkups, (30 & 50 amps), 50 amps ($), some extended stay sites, 47 pull-thrus, dump station, non-guest dumping $, laundry, tables, patios. RECREATION: Rec open to public. Pets welcome. No tents. Open all yr. Self check in. Phone: (828) 693-3831.

(SE) Phil & Ann's RV Service (RV SPACES)—(Henderson) *From jct US 64 & I-26: Go 3-1/2 mi SE on I-26 to exit 53, then 1/2 mi W on Upward Rd, then 1-1/2 mi N on Allen Rd, then 1/4 mi E on Tracy Grove Rd. Enter on R.* FACILITIES: 18 sites, accepts self-contained units only, 16 full hkups, 2 W&E, (30 & 50 amps), 50 amps ($), some extended stay sites, 10 pull-thrus, a/c not allowed, dump station, non-guest dumping $. Pets welcome. No tents. Open Apr 1 thru Nov 1. Phone: (800)753-8373.

WELCOME **(NE) RED GATES RV PARK**—(Henderson) *From jct I-26 (exit 49A) & US 64: Go 200 yards E on US 64, then 2-3/4 mi S on Sugarloaf Rd. Enter on R.*

◆◆◆FACILITIES: 20 sites, typical site width 35 ft, 18 full hkups, 2 W&E, (20, 30 & 50 amps), many extended stay sites, 4 pull-thrus, tenting, cabins, RV storage, laundry, tables.

◆◆RECREATION: pond swimming, boating, no motors, pedal boat rentals, pond fishing, golf nearby, shuffleboard court, horseshoes.

Pets welcome. Partial handicap access. Open Apr 1 thru Nov 1. Big rigs welcome. Clubs welcome. Rate in 2007 $23-25 for 2 persons. Phone: (828) 685-8787.

SEE AD THIS PAGE

WELCOME **RUTLEDGE LAKE RV PARK**—*From jct US 64 & I-26: Go 9 mi N on I-26 to exit 40, then 1 mi E on Hwy 280, then 3/4 mi S on Rutledge Rd. Enter on L.*

SEE PRIMARY LISTING AT FLETCHER AND AD ASHEVILLE PAGE 635

(SE) Town Mountain Travel Park—(Henderson) *From jct US 64 & I-26: Go 3-1/2 mi SE on I-26 to exit 53, then 3/4 mi W on Upward Rd, then 2/10 mi N & W on Upward Rd Ext., then 100 yards W on Old Spartanburg Rd. Enter on R.* ◆◆◆FACILITIES: 26 sites, typical site width 40 ft, 26 full hkups, (20, 30 & 50 amps), 50 amps ($), some extended stay sites, tables, patios. Pets welcome, breed restrict. No tents. Open all yr. No restrooms in winter. Rate in 2007 $26 for 2 persons. Phone: (828)697-6692.

WELCOME **(SE) TWIN PONDS RV PARK**—(Henderson) *From jct I-26 & Upward Rd (exit 53): Go 1/2 mi E on Upward Rd, then 4/10 mi N on S Orchard Rd. Enter on L.*

◆◆◆FACILITIES: 150 sites, typical site width 30 ft, 150 full hkups, (30 & 50 amps), some extended stay sites, 7 pull-thrus, cable TV ($), wireless Instant Internet access at site, phone Internet access central location, RV/park trailer rentals, RV storage, laundry, RV supplies, LP gas by weight/by meter, ice, tables, patios.

◆◆RECREATION: rec hall, rec room/area, swim pool, pond fishing.

Pets welcome, breed restrict. Partial handicap access. No tents. Open all yr. Big rigs welcome. Clubs welcome. Rate in 2007 $30-38 for 2 persons. MC/VISA. Member ARVC, CARVC. Phone: (828)693-4018.

e-mail: info@nctwinponds.com

SEE AD PAGE 652

HIGH POINT—B-2

OAK HOLLOW FAMILY CAMPGROUND (City Park)—(Davidson) *From I-85 (exit 111): Go 5-1/2 mi NW on US 311, then 1-3/4 mi E on Hwy 68, then 1-1/4 mi N on Centennial St, then 1/8 mi E on Oakview Rd. Enter on L.* FACILITIES: 127 sites, typical site width 25 ft, 116 full hkups, 11 W&E, (50 amps), tenting, dump station, laundry, grills. RECREATION: pavilion, swim pool, boating, ramp, dock, lake fishing, playground, tennis, v-ball. Open all yr. All sites first come, first served. Call for site availability during Apr & Oct. Phone: (336)883-3492.

HIGHLANDS—E-2

WELCOME **(W) SKY HIGH RIDGE MOTORCOACH PARK**—(Macon) *From jct US 64/NC 28 & NC 106: Go 10-2/10 mi SW on Hwy 106 (Dillard Rd), then 8/10 mi SE on Old Mudd Creek Rd to Sky Valley, then 1-1/10 mi N on Sky High Dr, then bear right on Moon Ridge Dr, then L on Ridge View Ln, then L on Thomas Knob Trail. Enter on L.*

FACILITIES: 9 sites, 9 full hkups, (30 & 50 amps).

Open all yr. Rate in 2007 $50-100 for 2 persons. Phone: (828)526-4189.

e-mail: info@skyhighridge.com

SEE AD NEXT PAGE

HOPE MILLS—C-3

(SE) **Fayetteville Spring Valley Park**—(Cumberland) *From jct I-95 (exit 41) & Hwy 59: Go 3/4 mi NW on Hwy 59, crossing I-95 Business Loop US 301, then 1 mi N on west service road. Enter on L.* ◆◆◆FACILITIES: 21 sites, typical site width 30 ft, 14 full hkups, 7 W&E, (30 & 50 amps), 50 amps ($), some extended stay sites, 22 pull-thrus, dump station, tables, fire rings, grills, wood. RECREATION: pavilion. Pets welcome. No tents. Open all yr. Big rigs welcome. Rate in 2007 $33-38 for 2 persons. Phone: (910)425-1505.

(W) LAKE WALDO'S BEACH CAMPGROUND—(Cumberland) *From jct I-95 (exit 41) & Hwy 59: Go 3 mi N on Hwy 59 (Main St), then 2 mi W on Rockfish Rd, then 1-1/4 mi W on Camden Rd, then 1-1/2 mi SW on Waldo's Beach Rd. Enter at end.*

◆◆◆FACILITIES: 23 sites, 23 full hkups, (30 & 50 amps), 3 pull-thrus, tenting, ice, tables, wood.

◆◆◆RECREATION: swim pool, wading pool, lake/pond fishing.

Pets welcome. Open all yr. Big rigs welcome. Clubs welcome. Rate in 2007 $25-36 for 2 persons. MC/VISA. Phone: (910)818-2618. CCUSA discount.

SEE AD FAYETTEVILLE PAGE 648

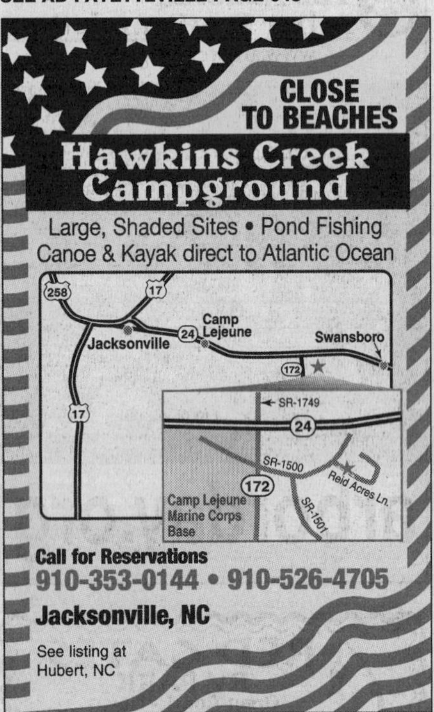

HOPE MILLS—Continued

(W) THE NEW WALDO'S BEACH PARK—*From jct I-95 (exit 41) & Hwy 59: Go 3 mi N on Hwy 59 (Main St), then 2 mi W on Rockfish Rd, then 1-1/4 W on Camden Rd, then 1-1/2 mi SW on Waldo's Beach Rd. Enter at end.* Small water park on large lake. Includes toddler's waterspray deck, water slide, lazy river and picnic facilities. Open Memorial Day thru Labor Day.

SEE AD FAYETTEVILLE PAGE 648

HOT SPRINGS—D-2

(C) **Hot Springs Campground & Suites**—(Madison) *From jct Hwy 209 & US 25/US 70: Go 1/4 mi E on US 25/US 70. Enter on R.* ◆◆FACILITIES: 104 sites, typical site width 40 ft, 34 full hkups, 9 W&E, (20, 30 & 50 amps), 61 no hkups, 2 pull-thrus, tenting, dump station, full svc store, LP gas by weight/by meter, ice, tables, fire rings, grills, wood. ◆◆RECREATION: canoeing, river fishing, play equipment, hiking trails, v-ball. Pets welcome. Partial handicap access. Open all yr. Rate in 2007 $35-40 for 4 persons. Phone: (828)622-7267.

(S) PISGAH NATIONAL FOREST (Rocky Bluff Campground)—(Madison) *From town: Go 3 mi S on Hwy-209.* FACILITIES: 30 sites, 30 ft max RV length, 30 no hkups, tenting, grills. RECREATION: hiking trails. Open May 1 thru Oct 31. No showers. No reservations. Max stay 14 days. Phone: (828)622-3202.

HUBERT—C-5

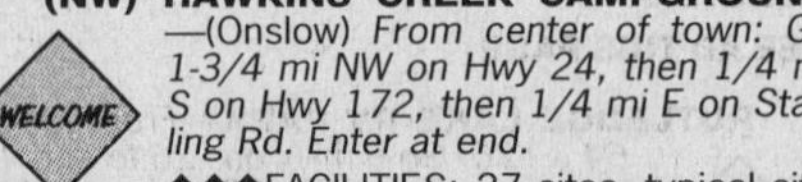

(NW) HAWKINS CREEK CAMPGROUND—(Onslow) *From center of town: Go 1-3/4 mi NW on Hwy 24, then 1/4 mi S on Hwy 172, then 1/4 mi E on Starling Rd. Enter at end.*

◆◆◆FACILITIES: 27 sites, typical site width 30 ft, accepts self-contained units only, 22 full hkups, 5 E, (30 & 50 amps), 4 pull-thrus, cable TV, non-flush toilets only, dump station.

HUBERT—Continued
HAWKINS CREEK CAMPGROUND—Continued

RECREATION: canoeing, kayaking, pond fishing.

Pets welcome. No tents. Open all yr. Big rigs welcome. Rate in 2007 $25 for 2 persons. Phone: (910)353-0144.

SEE AD THIS PAGE

HUDSON—B-1

(C) BUMGARNER CAMPING CENTER—*From jct US 321A & Cedar Valley Rd: Go 50 yards E on Cedar Valley Rd. Enter on R.* SALES: travel trailers, 5th wheels, fold-down camping trailers, pre-owned unit sales. SERVICES: full-time mech, RV appliance repair, LP gas by weight/by meter, sells parts/accessories, installs hitches. Open all yr. MC/VISA/DISC. Phone: (828) 728-5112.

e-mail: info@bumgarnercamping.com

SEE AD THIS PAGE

JACKSONVILLE—C-5

(SW) CABIN CREEK CAMPGROUND—(Onslow) *From west jct Hwy 24 & US 17: Go 4 3/4 mi S on US 17. Enter on R.*

NOTHING COULD BE FINER
Than to be at our Carolina campground. We take pride in all we do and provide friendly, personalized service to all our guests. Enjoy our great facilities with cable TV, WiFi and a golf driving range too!

◆◆◆FACILITIES: 174 sites, typical site width 30 ft, 62 full hkups, 12 W&E, (20, 30 & 50 amps), 100 no hkups, some extended stay sites, 30 pull-thrus, cable TV ($), wireless Instant Internet access at site, wireless Internet access central location, tenting, RV/park trailer rentals, cabins, RV storage, laundry, RV supplies, LP gas by weight/by meter, ice, tables, wood.

◆◆RECREATION: rec hall, rec room/area, pavilion, mini-golf ($), golf nearby, play equipment.

Pets welcome, quantity restrict. Open all yr. Big rigs welcome. Internet friendly. Escort to site. Rate in 2007 $29-35 per family. MC/VISA/AMEX/DC/Debit. Member ARVC, CARVC. Phone: (910)346-4808.

e-mail: cabincreekcampground@yahoo.com

SEE AD NEXT PAGE

MILITARY PARK (New River Rec. Area)—(Onslow) *From jct Hwy 24 & US 17: Go 5 mi S on US 17 to Main Gate. On base.* FACILITIES: 12 sites, 12 no hkups, tenting, ice, fire rings, grills, wood. RECREATION: pavilion, saltwater swimming, boating, canoeing, ramp, dock, canoe/motorboat rentals, saltwater fishing, playground, v-ball. Open all yr. For Military Use Only-w/Military ID Card. Phone: (910)449-6578.

JACKSONVILLE—Continued on next page

The Premier RV Park
Wi-Fi
IN HIGHLANDS, NC
Sky High Ridge Motorcoach Park

Explore the area that has attracted southern aristocratic families since 1875.
Experience nature at its best with premium views from every site.
Enjoy the cool climate, lush Nantahala National Forest & laid back atmosphere.

Specially designed for big motorcoaches with private decks and 100 amp service

(828) 526-4189
www.skyhighridge.com

2008 Grand Opening Special 50% Off Daily Rate

MILITARY PARK (Onslow Beach Recreation Area-Camp Lejeune MCB)—(Onslow) *Off jct US 17 & Hwy 24. On base.* FACILITIES: 71 sites, typical site width 15 ft, 52 full hkups, 19 W&E, (50 amps), tenting, dump station, laundry, ltd groceries, ice, patios. RECREATION: pavilion, saltwater swimming, saltwater fishing, play equipment. Open all yr. For Military Use Only-w/Military ID Card. Phone: (910)450-7502.

WHITE OAK SHORES CAMPING & RV RESORT—*From jct Hwy 24 & US 17: Go 15-1/2 mi NE towards Maysville on US 17, then 10 mi SE on Hwy 58, then 1 mi S on Morristown Rd, then W on Wetherington Rd, then 3/4 mi N Enter on L.*

SEE PRIMARY LISTING AT STELLA AND AD EMERALD ISLE PAGE 646

KURE BEACH—D-4

MILITARY PARK (Fort Fisher Air Force Rec. Area)—(New Hanover) *Off base, about 100 mi S of Seymour Johnson AFB (Goldsboro). Located 20 mi S of Wilmington on US 421 at Kure Beach.* FACILITIES: 36 sites, 16 full hkups, 20 no hkups, tenting, dump station, laundry, ltd groceries, ice. RECREATION: rec hall, swim pool, saltwater swimming, boating, canoeing, ramp, 6 canoe/5 pedal boat/motorboat rentals, saltwater/river fishing, playground, planned activities, tennis, v-ball. Open all yr. Reservations accepted. For Military use only-w/Military ID Card. Phone: (910)458-6549.

LAKE JUNALUSKA—E-2

(S) Camp Adventure Family Campground—(Haywood) *From jct I-40 (exit 127) & US 19/US 23: Go 3 mi SW on US 19. Enter on L.* ◊◊◊FACILITIES: 54 sites, typical site width 25 ft, 44 full hkups, 10 W&E, (30 & 50 amps), 12 pull-thrus, tenting, dump station, non-guest dumping $, tables, fire rings, grills, wood. ◊RECREATION: playground, hiking trails. Pets welcome. Partial handicap access. Open Apr 1 thru Oct 31. Big rigs welcome. Rate in 2007 $25-27 for 4 persons. Phone: (828)452-5887. CCUSA discount.

LAKE LURE—E-2

(E) River Creek Campground—(Rutherford) *From jct Hwy 9 & US 64/74A: Go 4-3/4 mi E on US 64/74A, then 100 feet S on Rock Springs Church Rd, then 1/4 mi E on River Creek Rd. Enter at end.* ◊◊◊FACILITIES: 57 sites, typical site width 25 ft, 27 full hkups, 30 W&E, (20, 30 & 50 amps), some extended stay sites, tenting, dump station, non-guest dumping $, laundry, ltd groceries, ice, tables, fire rings, wood. ◊◊RECREATION: rec room/area, river swimming, river fishing, play equipment. Pets welcome, breed restrict. Partial handicap access. Open all yr. Rate in 2007 $30 for 2 persons. Member ARVC, CARVC. Phone: (828)287-3915.

LEXINGTON—B-2

(S) High Rock Lake Marina & Campground—(Davidson) *From jct I-85 (exit 91) & Hwy 8: Go 7 mi S on Hwy 8, then 1-3/4 mi E on Wafford Rd. Enter on L.* ◊◊◊FACILITIES: 98 sites, typical site width 20 ft, 86 full hkups, 7 W&E, (20, 30 & 50 amps), 5 no hkups, many extended stay sites, 20 pull-thrus, tenting, dump station, non-guest dumping $, laundry, ltd groceries, LP gas by weight/by meter, ice, tables, fire rings, wood. ◊◊◊RECREATION: rec room/area, pavilion, swim pool, boating, canoeing, ramp, dock, lake fishing, playground, horseshoes. Pets welcome, breed restrict. Open all yr. Rate in 2007 $30-35 for 4 persons. Member ARVC. Phone: (800)382-3239. FMCA discount.

LILLINGTON—B-3

✽ **(C) CAPE FEAR RV & CANOE CENTER**—*From jct US 401 & 421: Go 4/10 mi N on US 401/421. Enter on L.* SALES: travel trailers, park trailers, 5th wheels, fold-down camping trailers, pre-owned unit sales. SERVICES: full-time mech, RV appliance repair, LP bottle exch, sells parts/accessories, installs hitches. Open all yr. MC/VISA. Phone: (910)814-1727.

e-mail: sales@capefearrv.com

SEE AD TRAVEL SECTION PAGE 626

Visit our website www.woodalls.com

LINVILLE FALLS—D-3

BLUE RIDGE NATIONAL PARKWAY (Linville Falls Campground)—(haywood) *At milepost 316 on Blue Ridge Pkwy.* FACILITIES: 70 sites, 30 ft max RV length, 70 no hkups, tenting, dump station, grills. RECREATION: lake/river fishing, hiking trails. Open Apr 1 thru Oct 23. No showers, limited facilities. Phone: (828)298-0398.

(NW) LINVILLE FALLS TRAILER LODGE & CAMPGROUND—(Avery) *From jct Blue Ridge Pkwy (between mileposts 317 & 318) & US 221: Go 500 feet S on US 221, then 3/4 mi W on Gurney Franklin Rd. Enter on L.*

◊◊◊FACILITIES: 48 sites, typical site width 20 ft, 35 full hkups, (15, 20 & 30 amps), 13 no hkups, some extended stay sites, phone Internet access central location, tenting, RV/park trailer rentals, cabins, laundry, ltd groceries, ice, tables, fire rings, wood.

◊RECREATION: pavilion, bsktball, play equipment, horseshoes, v-ball.

Pets welcome. Open May 1 thru Oct 31. Rate in 2007 $28-32 for 2 persons. Member ARVC, CARVC. Phone: (828)765-2681.

SEE AD THIS PAGE

LITTLE SWITZERLAND—D-3

BLUE RIDGE NATIONAL PARKWAY (Crabtree Meadows Campground)—(Haywood) *From town: Go 5 mi NE on Hwy-226A, then 3 mi S on Blue Ridge Pkwy to MP-339.* FACILITIES: 22 sites, 30 ft max RV length, 22 no hkups, tenting, dump station, grills. RECREATION: hiking trails. Open May 9 thru Oct 31. No water. Phone: (828)298-0398.

The Biltmore Estate in Asheville is America's largest home, and includes a 255-room chateau, an award-winning winery and extensive gardens.

LUMBERTON—C-3

(SW) SLEEPY BEAR'S RV PARK—(Robeson) *From jct I-95 (exit 17) & NC 72: Go 1/8 mi W on NC 72, then 2-1/2 mi S on Kenric Dr. Enter on R.*

OUR FAMILY WELCOMES YOUR FAMILY
We are proud to offer a restful retreat just off I-95. There's a lot to do here in the park and nearby - but feel free just to chill on your paved pull-thru site or beside our colorful pool. Just make yourself at home!

◊◊◊◊FACILITIES: 102 sites, typical site width 27 ft, 78 full hkups, 24 W&E, (20, 30 & 50 amps), 87 pull-thrus, wireless Instant Internet access at site, phone Internet access central location, tenting, RV/park trailer rentals, cabins, RV storage, dump station, non-guest dumping $, laundry, ltd groceries, RV supplies, LP gas by weight/by meter, ice, tables, fire rings, grills, wood.

◊◊◊◊RECREATION: rec hall, rec room/area, pavilion, coin games, swim pool, river fishing, mini-golf, golf nearby, bsktball, playground, shuffleboard court, planned activities, horseshoes, v-ball. Rec open to public.

Pets welcome. Partial handicap access. Open all yr. Big rigs welcome. Internet friendly. Clubs welcome. Rate in 2007 $28-30 for 2 persons. MC/VISA. Member ARVC, CARVC. Phone: (910)739-4372. FMCA discount.

e-mail: sleepybear@bellsouth.net

SEE AD THIS PAGE

MAGGIE VALLEY—E-2

(W) Rippling Waters Creekside RV Park—(Haywood) *From jct US 276 & US 19: Go 4 mi SW on US 19. Enter on R.* ◊◊◊◊FACILITIES: 36 sites, typical site width 28 ft, 36 full hkups, (30 & 50 amps), many

Rippling Waters Creekside RV Park—Continued on next page

MAGGIE VALLEY—Continued
Rippling Waters Creekside RV Park—Continued

extended stay sites, 12 pull-thrus, laundry, ice, tables. ◆◆RECREATION: rec hall, rec room/area, stream fishing. No tents. Open all yr. Facilities fully operational Apr 1 thru Oct 31. Call for reservations in Winter. Rate in 2007 $28-33 for 2 persons. Member ARVC, CARVC. Phone: (828)926-7787.

(E) Stone Bridge RV Park—(Haywood) *From west jct US 276 and US 19: Go 2 mi SW on US 19. Enter on R.* ◆◆◆FACILITIES: 380 sites, typical site width 25 ft, 380 full hkups, (20, 30 & 50 amps), some extended stay sites, 160 pull-thrus, tenting, laundry, ltd groceries, ice, tables, patios, fire rings, wood. ◆◆◆◆RECREATION: rec hall, pavilion, swim pool, river swimming, pond/stream fishing, play equipment, 2 shuffleboard courts, planned activities, v-ball. Pets welcome. Partial handicap access. Open Apr 1 thru Oct 31. Big rigs welcome. Rate in 2007 $25-40 for 4 persons. Phone: (828)926-1904.

Billy Graham, evangelist, is from North Carolina.

MANTEO—A-6

(W) OUTER BANKS VISITORS BUREAU —*From jct US 158 & US 64: Go 5 1-1/4 mi W on US 64/264.* Provides information about North Carolina's barrier islands: beaches, windsurfing, kite flying, surf & deep sea fishing, historical sites, outdoor dramas, NC Aquarium & Roanoak Island Festival Park. Open all yr. Phone: (877) 629-4386.

e-mail: detb-mccormick@outer-banks.com

SEE AD DISCOVER SECTION PAGE 60

(S) THE REFUGE (UNDER CONSTRUCTION) —(Dare) *From jct US 264/US 64 and Hwy 345: Go 2-3/4 mi S on Hwy 345. Enter on L.*

FACILITIES: 57 sites, typical site width 30 ft, 57 full hkups, (50 amps), some extended stay sites, wireless Instant Internet access at site.

RECREATION: pavilion, swim pool, canoeing, kayaking.

MANTEO—Continued
THE REFUGE—Continued

Pets welcome. Partial handicap access. No tents. Open all yr. Big rigs welcome. Internet friendly. Rate in 2007 $30-50 for 2 persons. Phone: (252) 473-1096.

SEE AD TRAVEL SECTION PAGE 626

MARION—E-3

(W) BUCK CREEK DRIVING RANGE— *From jct I-40W (exit 86) & Hwy 226: Go 6 mi N on Hwy 226/US 221 bypass, then 1-3/4 mi W on US 70, then 1-3/4 mi N on Hwy 80. From jct I-40E (exit 72) & US 70: Go 9 mi E on US 70, then 7 mi 1-3/4 W on US 70, then 1-3/4 mi N on Hwy 80. Enter on L.* Large, level driving range. Open Mar 1 thru Nov 30. Phone: (828)724-4888.

SEE AD THIS PAGE

(W) BUCK CREEK RV PARK CAMPGROUND & DRIVING RANGE— (McDowell) *From jct I-40W (exit 86) & Hwy 226: Go 6 mi N on Hwy 226/US 221 bypass, then 1-3/4 mi W on US 70, then 1-3/4 mi N on Hwy 80. From jct I-40E (exit 72) & US 70: Go 9 mi E on US 70, then 7 mi 1-3/4 W on US 70, then 1-3/4 mi N on Hwy 80. Enter on L.*

◆◆◆◆FACILITIES: 74 sites, typical site width 30 ft, 74 full hkups, (20, 30 & 50 amps), many extended stay sites (in summer), 5 pull-thrus, cable TV, wireless Instant Internet access at site, cable Internet access central location, RV storage, laundry, ice, tables, fire rings, grills, wood.

◆◆RECREATION: equipped pavilion, river swimming, river fishing, golf nearby, bsktball, horseshoes, sports field. Rec open to public.

Pets welcome. No tents. Open Apr 1 thru Nov 1. Off season by reservation only. Big rigs welcome. Internet friendly. Clubs welcome. Rate in 2007 $30-38 for 2 persons. Phone: (828)724-4888.

e-mail: buckcreekcampground@buckcreekcampground.com

SEE AD THIS PAGE

LAKE JAMES STATE PARK—(McDowell) *From town: Go 5 mi NE on Hwy 126.* FACILITIES: 20 sites, 20 no hkups, tenting, grills. RECREATION: lake swimming, boating, canoeing, ramp, lake fishing, hiking trails. Partial handicap access. Open Mar 15 thru Nov 30. Phone: (828)652-5047.

(W) MOUNTAIN STREAM RV PARK— (McDowell) *From jct I-40W (exit 86) & Hwy 226: Go 6 mi N on Hwy 226/US 221 bypass, then 1-3/4 mi W on US 70, then 7 mi N on Hwy 80. From jct I-40E (exit 72) & US 70: Go 9 mi E on US 70, then 7 mi N on Hwy 80. Enter on R.*

PRETTIEST PARK THIS SIDE OF HEAVEN
God gave us a beautiful creek side setting. We added the level, big rig sites with gravel pads and manicured lawns. Come enjoy nature at its best (and Sat. night Gospel music) just 5 mi off the scenic Blue Ridge Parkway.

◆◆◆◆FACILITIES: 37 sites, typical site width 30 ft, 37 full hkups, (20, 30 & 50 amps), 50 amps ($), wireless Instant Internet access at site, ltd groceries, RV supplies, ice, tables, fire rings, grills, wood.

◆◆RECREATION: rec room/area, pavilion, river swimming, stream fishing, fishing supplies, bsktball, horseshoes.

Pets welcome. Partial handicap access. No tents. Open Apr 1 thru Nov 30. Big rigs welcome. Internet friendly. Clubs welcome. Rate in 2007 $31-41 per family. MC/VISA/DISC. Member ARVC, CARVC. Phone: (828)724-9013. FMCA discount.

e-mail: camp@mountainstreamrvpark.com

SEE AD THIS PAGE

(W) THE CAMPGROUND AT TOM JOHNSON CAMPING CENTER—(Washington) *From jct I-40 (exit 86) & Hwy 226: Go 6 mi N on Hwy 226/US 221 Bypass, then 1-1/2 mi W on US 70. Enter on L. From jct I-40E (exit 72) & US 70: Go 9-1/2 mi E on US 70. Enter on R.*

FACILITIES: 60 sites, 60 full hkups, (50 amps).

Open all yr. Internet friendly. Rate in 2007 $30 per vehicle.

e-mail: camping@tomjohnsoncamping.com

SEE AD ASHEVILLE PAGE 634

MARION—Continued on next page

Ava Gardner, actress, was from North Carolina.

See listing at Waynesville, NC

MARION—Continued

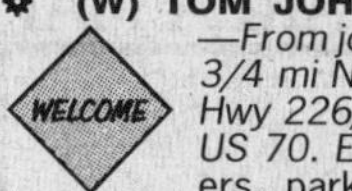

(W) TOM JOHNSON CAMPING CENTER —*From jct I-40 (exit 86) & Hwy 226: Go 3/4 mi N on Hwy 226, then 5 mi N on Hwy 226/US 221, then 1-1/2 mi W on US 70. Enter on L.* SALES: travel trailers, park trailers, 5th wheels, motor homes, mini-motor homes, fold-down camping trailers, pre-owned unit sales. SERVICES: full-time mech, engine/chassis repair, RV appliance repair, LP gas by weight/by meter, dump station, RV rentals, sells parts/accessories, installs hitches. Open all yr. MC/VISA/DISC. Phone: (800)225-7802.

e-mail: marionsales@tomjohnsoncamping.com

SEE AD TRAVEL SECTION PAGE 628

(SE) Yogi Bear's Jellystone Park Camp Resort —(McDowell) *From jct I-40 (exit 86) & Hwy 226: Go 300 yds on Hwy 226, then 1 mi E on Fairview Rd, then 1-1/4 mi SE on Deacon Dr. Enter on R.* ◇◇◇FACILITIES: 78 sites, typical site width 30 ft, 65 full hkups, 13 W&E, (30 amps), some extended stay sites, 10 pull-thrus, tenting, dump station, non-guest dumping $, laundry, ltd groceries, ice, tables, fire rings, wood. ◇◇◇◇RECREATION: rec hall, pavilion, swim pool, boating, electric motors only, lake fishing, mini-golf ($), playground, shuffleboard court, horseshoes, v-ball. Rec open to public. Pets welcome, breed restrict. Partial handicap access. Open Apr 1 thru Oct 31. Rate in 2007 $25-46 per family. Phone: (828)652-7208.

MICAVILLE—D-2

PISGAH NANTAHALA NATIONAL FOREST (Carolina Hemlock Park)—(Yancey) *From town: Go 8-3/4 mi S on Hwy-80.* FACILITIES: 33 sites, 22 ft max RV length, 33 no hkups, 4 pull-thrus, tenting, ltd groceries, grills. RECREATION: river swimming, river fishing, hiking trails. Facilities fully operational Apr 15 thru Oct 31. No showers. Max stay 14 days. No reservations. Phone: (828)837-5152.

PISGAH NATIONAL FOREST (Black Mountain Campground)—(Yancey) *From town: Go 12 mi S on Hwy-80, then 3 mi on FR-472.* FACILITIES: 48 sites, 22 ft max RV length, 48 no hkups, 2 pull-thrus, tenting, grills. RECREATION: river fishing, hiking trails. Open Apr 14 thru Nov 1. No showers. No reservations. Max stay is 14 days. Phone: (828)682-6146.

MOCKSVILLE—B-2

(NW) Lake Myers RV Resort—(Davie) *From jct I-40 (Mocksville exit 168) & US 64: Go 2-1/2 mi NW on US 64. Enter on R.* ◇◇◇FACILITIES: 425 sites, typical site width 25 ft, 400 full hkups, 25 W&E, (20, 30 & 50 amps), 50 amps ($), many extended stay sites, 17 pull-thrus, tenting, dump station, non-guest dumping $, laundry, ltd groceries, LP gas by weight/by meter, ice, tables, fire rings, wood. ◇◇◇◇◇RECREATION: rec hall, pavilion, 2 swim pools, electric motors only, canoeing, 20 canoe/6 pedal boat rentals, lake/pond fishing, mini-golf ($), playground, planned activities (wkends only), horseshoes, sports field. Rec open to public. Pets welcome. Partial handicap access. Open all yr. Facilities fully operational Memorial Day thru Labor Day. Rate in 2007 $35-53 per family. Member ARVC, NCARVC. Phone: (336)492-7736.

MONROE—C-2

CANE CREEK PARK (Union County Park)—(Union) *From town: Go 11 mi S on Hwy 200, then 3 mi SE on Potters Rd, then 2 mi SW on Cane Creek Rd. Enter on R.* FACILITIES: 108 sites, typical site width 25 ft, 49 full hkups, 59 W&E, (50 amps), tenting, dump station, non-guest dumping $, ltd groceries, ice, fire rings, grills, wood. RECREATION: equipped pavilion, lake swimming, boating, canoeing, ramp, 12 rowboat/6 canoe/18 pedal boat rentals, lake fishing, mini-golf, playground, sports field, hiking trails, v-ball. Rec open to public. Partial handicap access. Open all yr. Phone: (704)843-3919.

MOREHEAD CITY—C-5

(W) WHISPERING PINES FAMILY CAMPGROUND—(Carteret) *From jct US 70 & Hwy 24: Go 8 mi W on Hwy 24. Enter on L.*

◇◇◇◇FACILITIES: 184 sites, typical site width 30 ft, 184 full hkups, (30 & 50 amps), mostly extended stay sites, 12 pull-thrus, cable TV, wireless Instant Internet access at site, cable Internet access central location, tenting, RV storage, laundry, ltd groceries, RV supplies, ice, tables, wood.

◇◇RECREATION: swim pool, pond fishing, fishing supplies, bsktball, playground.

Pets welcome, quantity restrict. Partial handicap access. Open all yr. Big rigs welcome. Internet friendly. Rate in 2007 $35-40 for 4 persons. MC/VISA. Member ARVC, CARVC. Phone: (252)726-4902.

e-mail: whisperingpines@bizec.rr.com

SEE AD THIS PAGE

MORGANTON—B-1

(NW) JONAS RIDGE SNOWTUBING—*From jct I-40 (exit 105) & Hwy 18: Go 2-1/2 mi NW on Hwy 18, then 22 mi N on Hwy 181. Enter on R.* The sledding of the millennium, with no hill climbing. Fun for children over 7 and adults. Open Dec thru Feb. Phone: (828)733-4155.

SEE AD THIS PAGE

(NW) Optimistic Park RV Resort & Campground —(Burke) *From jct I-40 (exit 105) & Hwy 18: Go 2-1/2 mi NW on Hwy 18, then 13 mi N on Hwy 181. Enter on R.* ◇◇◇FACILITIES: 13 sites, typical site width 30 ft, 10 full hkups, 3 W&E, (20, 30 & 50 amps), 50 amps ($), dump station, non-guest dumping $, tables. RECREATION: river swimming, river fishing, sports field. Pets welcome. No tents. Age restrictions may apply. Open May thru Oct. Rate in 2007 $25-27 for 4 persons. Phone: (828)438-0550.

(NW) STEELE CREEK PARK—(Burke) *From jct I-40 (exit 105) & Hwy 18: Go 2-1/2 mi NW on Hwy 18, then 13-1/2 mi N on Hwy 181. Enter on L.*

◇◇◇FACILITIES: 334 sites, typical site width 30 ft, 249 full hkups, 60 W&E, (20, 30 & 50 amps), 25 no hkups, some extended stay sites, 9 pull-thrus, wireless Internet access central location, tenting, cabins, RV storage, dump station, non-guest dumping $, laundry, ltd groceries, RV supplies, LP gas by weight/by meter, ice, tables, fire rings, grills, wood, controlled access gate.

◇◇◇◇◇RECREATION: rec hall, pavilion, equipped pavilion, coin games, swim pool, river swimming, pond/stream fishing, fishing supplies, mini-golf ($), bsktball, playground, planned activities (wkends only), horseshoes, sports field, hiking trails, v-ball. Rec open to public.

Pets welcome, breed restrict, size restrict. Open all yr. Facilities fully operational Apr 1 thru Oct 31. Winter sites avail by reservation. Clubs welcome. Rate in 2007 $25-35 for 2 persons. Member ARVC, CARVC. Phone: (828)433-5660. FCRV 10% discount.

SEE AD THIS PAGE

MURPHY—E-1

(N) NANTAHALA NATIONAL FOREST (Hanging Dog Campground)—(Cherokee) *From town: Go 5 mi NW on Hwy-1326.* FACILITIES: 69 sites, 69 no hkups, 1 pull-thrus, tenting, grills. RECREATION: boating, ramp, lake fishing, hiking trails. Open Apr 1 thru Sep 29. No showers. Phone: (828)837-5152.

(NE) Peace Valley Campground & Cabins—(Cherokee) *From east jct US 64 and US 19/74/129: Go 4 mi NE on US 19/74/129. Enter on R.* ◇◇◇FACILITIES: 67 sites, typical site width 30 ft, 43 full hkups, 9 W&E, (30 & 50 amps), 15 no hkups, 20 pull-thrus,

Peace Valley Campground & Cabins—Continued on next page

MURPHY—Continued
Peace Valley Campground & Cabins—Continued

tenting, dump station, non-guest dumping $, laundry, ltd groceries, LP gas by meter, ice, tables, patios, fire rings, wood. ◆◆◆◆RECREATION: rec hall, equipped pavilion, swim pool, canoeing, 3 canoe rentals, river fishing, horseshoes, sports field, v-ball. Pets welcome. Open all yr. Big rigs welcome. Internet friendly. Rate in 2007 $25-30 for 2 persons. Member ARVC, CARVC. Phone: (828)837-6223.

(W) RIVERS EDGE MOUNTAIN RV RESORT (TOO NEW TO RATE)—(Cherokee) *From jct US/19/129/74 & US 64: Go 6-1/2 mi W on US 64/74. Enter on R.*

WELCOME

FACILITIES: 49 sites, typical site width 50 ft, 49 full hkups, (30 & 50 amps), 38 pull-thrus, cable TV, wireless Instant Internet access at site, LP gas by weight/by meter, tables, patios, fire rings, wood, controlled access gate.

RECREATION: pavilion, river fishing, golf nearby.

Pets welcome. No tents. Open all yr. Big rigs welcome. Internet friendly. Escort to site. Clubs welcome. Rate in 2007 $39-79 for 2 persons. MC/VISA/DISC/Debit. Phone: (828)361-4517.

SEE AD TRAVEL SECTION PAGE 625

(NE) VALLEY RIVER RV RESORT (PLANNED)—(Cherokee) *From east jct US 64 & US 19/74/129: Go 8 mi NE on US 19/74/129.*

WELCOME

Pets welcome. No tents. Open all yr. Big rigs welcome. Phone: (877)4RV-LOTS.

e-mail: info@valleyriverrvresort.com

SEE AD TRAVEL SECTION PAGE 620

NAGS HEAD—A-6

(S) CAPE HATTERAS NATIONAL SEASHORE (Oregon Inlet Campground)—(Dare) *From jct US-64/264 & Hwy-12: Go 8 mi S on Hwy-12.* FACILITIES: 120 sites, 120 no hkups, tenting, cold showers only, dump station, grills. RECREATION: saltwater swimming, saltwater fishing. Open Mar 25 thru Oct 10. No reservations. Phone: (252)473-2111.

NEW BERN—C-5

(E) MOONLIGHT LAKE RV PARK & CAMPGROUND—*From jct US 70 & US 17: Go 6 mi E on US 17/NC 55 toward Bayboro/Washington, then 6 mi E on Hwy 55. Enter on R.*

WELCOME

◆◆FACILITIES: 22 sites, accepts full hkup units only, 22 full hkups, (30 & 50 amps), some extended stay sites, wireless Instant Internet access at site, phone/cable on-site Internet access (needs activ), laundry, tables.

RECREATION: 2 pedal boat rentals.

Pets welcome. No tents. Open all yr. No restrooms. Big rigs welcome. Internet friendly. Rate in 2007 $20-25 per vehicle. Phone: (252)745-9800.

e-mail: 55emoonlightlake@gmail.com

SEE AD THIS PAGE

(NW) New Bern KOA—(Craven) *From jct US 70 & US 17: Go 8-1/2 mi E on US 17/NC 55 toward Bayboro/Washington. Enter on L.* ◆◆◆◆FACILITIES: 73 sites, typical site width 30 ft, 54 full hkups, 16 W&E, (30 & 50 amps), 3 no hkups, some extended stay sites, 31 pull-thrus, tenting, dump station, non-guest dumping $, laundry, groceries, LP gas by weight/by meter, ice, tables, patios, fire rings, grills, wood. ◆◆◆◆RECREATION: rec room/area, equipped pavilion, swim pool, boating, canoeing, ramp, dock, 3 pedal boat rentals,

NEW BERN—Continued
New Bern KOA—Continued

river/pond fishing, playground, horseshoes, sports field. Pets welcome, breed restrict. Open all yr. Big rigs welcome. Internet friendly. Rate in 2007 $35-70 for 2 persons. Member ARVC. Phone: (800)562-3341. KOA 10% value card discount.

NORLINA—A-4

KERR STATE REC. AREA (County Line Park)—(Vance) *From town: Take exit 223 off I-85: Go W on Manson Rd 2.5 mi to Drewry, turn right on Drewry-Valine Rd. Go 2.5 mi Turn left on Buchanan Store Rd. Go 1 mi, then right on County line rd 1.5 mi to the park.* FACILITIES: 85 sites, 41 W&E, 44 no hkups, tenting, dump station. RECREATION: lake swimming, boating, ramp, lake fishing, playground, hiking trails. Open Apr thru Mid Sept. Phone: (252)438-7791.

KERR STATE REC. AREA (Kimball Point Park)—(Vance) *From town: take exit 223 of I-85: Go W on Manson Rd 2.5 mi to Drewry. Go N on Drewry-Virgina Line Rd 5 mi. Turn let on Kimball Pt Rd. for 1.5 mi.* FACILITIES: 91 sites, 23 E, (30 amps), 68 no hkups, tenting, dump station. RECREATION: pavilion, lake swimming, boating, ramp, lake fishing, playground. Open Apr 1 thru Nov 1. Phone: (252)438-7791.

OCRACOKE—C-6

(C) Beachcomber Campground (RV SPACES)—(Hyde) *From Cedar Island-Ocracoke Ferry Landing: Go 1 mi N on Hwy 12. Enter on R.* FACILITIES: 29 sites, typical site width 15 ft, 29 W&E, (20, 30 & 50 amps), tenting, dump station, full svc store, ice, tables, grills. Pets welcome. Open all yr. Rate in 2007 $35-45 for 2 persons. Phone: (252)928-4031.

(E) CAPE HATTERAS NATIONAL SEASHORE (Ocracoke Campground)—(Hyde) *From town: Go 4 mi E on Hwy-12.* FACILITIES: 136 sites, 136 no hkups, tenting, cold showers only, dump station, groceries, grills. RECREATION: saltwater swimming, boating, ramp, dock, lake fishing. Partial handicap access. Open Mar 25 thru Oct 10. Reservations period Memorial Day through Labor Day. Phone: (800)365-CAMP.

OLD FORT—E-2

(SW) Catawaba Falls Campground—(McDowell) *From jct I-40 (exit 73) & Catawaba River Rd: Go 200 ft S, then 3 mi W on Catawaba River Rd. (south frontage road) Enter on L.* ◆FACILITIES: 40 sites, typical site width 24 ft, 30 ft max RV length, 18 full hkups, 7 W&E, (20, 30 & 50 amps), 15 no hkups, some extended stay sites, 1 pull-thrus, tenting, dump station, non-guest dumping $, ice, tables, fire rings, wood. ◆RECREATION: river/pond fishing, play equipment, horseshoes. Pets welcome. Open all yr. Phone: (828)668-4831.

(S) Cove Creek RV Park (TOO NEW TO RATE)—*Fromjct I-40 (exit 73) & Catabawa River Rd: Go 1/2 mi S on Catawba River Rd, then continue 4-1/2 mi S on Bat Cave Rd, then 1/4 mi E on Davis Town Church Rd. Enter on R.* FACILITIES: 10 sites, 10 full hkups, 10 pull-thrus, tenting, dump station. RECREATION: play equipment. Open all yr. Rate in 2007 $18-26 per vehicle. Phone: (828)668-7507.

OUTER BANKS—B-6

OUTER BANKS AREA MAP

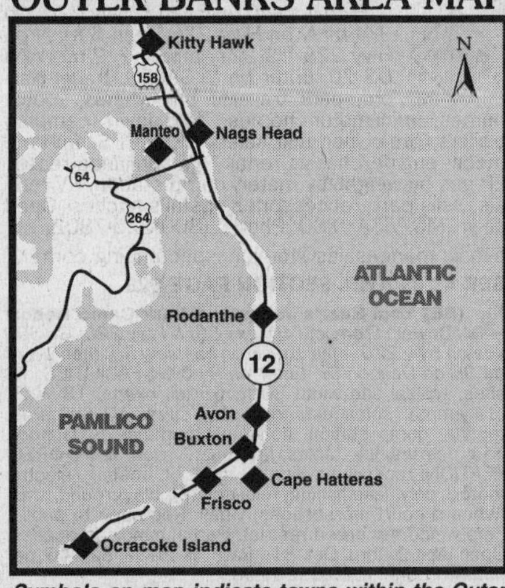

Symbols on map indicate towns within the Outer Banks where campgrounds (diamonds), attractions (flags), & RV service centers & camping supply outlets (gears) are listed. Check listings for more information.

HATTERAS SANDS RV RESORT—*From the jct US 64 & Hwy 12: Go 58 mi S on Hwy 12, then 1/4 mi E on Eagle Pass Rd.*

WELCOME

SEE PRIMARY LISTING AT HATTERAS AND AD CAPE HATTERAS PAGE 639

PINEHURST—B-3

(N) VILLAGE OF PINEHURST RV PARK—(Moore) *From jct Hwy 2 & US 15/US 501 (Pinehurst Traffic Cir); Go 1-1/2 mi N on US 15/US 501, then 1/4 mi NE on Campground Rd. Enter on R.*

WELCOME

◆◆◆◆FACILITIES: 55 sites, typical site width 20 ft, 55 full hkups, (20, 30 & 50 amps), some extended stay sites, 5 pull-thrus, phone Internet access central location, RV storage, dump station, non-guest dumping $, tables, fire rings, grills.

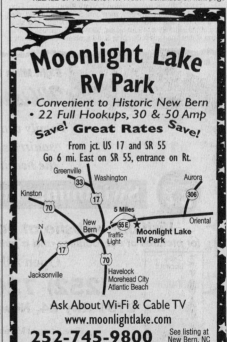

VILLAGE OF PINEHURST RV PARK—Continued on next page

PINEHURST—Continued
VILLAGE OF PINEHURST RV PARK—Continued

◆◆RECREATION: equipped pavilion, swim pool, lake fishing, bsktball, play equipment, horseshoes, v-ball.

Pets welcome, breed restrict, quantity restrict. Partial handicap access. No tents. Open all yr. Office open 10 am-8pm. No Haulers. Big rigs welcome. Escort to site. Clubs welcome. Rate in 2007 $24 per family. Member ARVC, CARVC. Phone: (910)295-5452.

e-mail: pinehurstrv@earthlink.net

SEE AD THIS PAGE

PINEY CREEK—A-1

(SW) RIVER CAMP USA CANOE, KAYAK & TUBING—*From jct US 221 & Hwy 113: Go 4-1/2 mi N on Hwy 113, then 1/2 mi W on South Fork Church Rd, then 2 mi W on Kings Creek Rd.* Leisurely float down the gentle New River - this 26.5 mile section designated a National Wild & Scenic River-on an affordable canoe, kayak or tube trip. Open Apr 15 thru Nov 1. Weather permitting. MC/VISA. Phone: (336)359-2267.

e-mail: info@rivercampusa.com

SEE AD THIS PAGE

(SW) RIVERCAMP USA RV PARK & CAMPGROUND—(Alleghany) *From jct US 221 & Hwy 113: Go 4-1/2 mi N on Hwy 113, then 1/2 mi W on South Fork Church Rd, then 2 mi W on Kings Creek Rd. Enter on L.*

◆◆◆FACILITIES: 61 sites, typical site width 35 ft, 38 full hkups, 13 W&E, (20, 30 & 50 amps), 50 amps ($), 10 no hkups, some extended stay sites, wireless Instant Internet access at site ($), phone

PINEY CREEK—Continued
RIVERCAMP USA RV PARK & CAMPGROUND—Continued

Internet access central location, tenting, cabins, RV storage, dump station, non-guest dumping $, laundry, ltd groceries, RV supplies, ice, tables, patios, fire rings, grills, wood, controlled access gate.

◆◆RECREATION: pavilion, boating, no motors, canoeing, kayaking, 80 canoe/26 kayak rentals, float trips, river fishing, fishing supplies, fishing guides, golf nearby, play equipment, horseshoes, v-ball. Rec open to public.

Pets welcome, breed restrict. Partial handicap access. Open Apr 15 thru Nov 1. Big rigs welcome. Internet friendly. Clubs welcome. Rate in 2007 $24 for 2 persons. MC/VISA. Member ARVC, CARVC. Phone: (336)359-2267. FMCA discount.

e-mail: info@rivercampusa.com

SEE AD THIS PAGE

PINNACLE—A-2

(N) PILOT MOUNTAIN STATE PARK—(Surry) *From town: Go 3 mi W on US 52.* FACILITIES: 49 sites, 49 no hkups, tenting, grills, wood. RECREATION: boating, canoeing, river fishing, hiking trails. Rec open to public. Open Mar 15 thru Nov 30. Phone: (336)325-2355.

RALEIGH—B-4

See listings at Chapel Hill, Clayton, Durham and Garner

FALLS LAKE STATE REC. AREA (Holly Point Campground)—(Wake) *From jct Hwy 50 & Hwy 98: Go 1/2 mi E on Hwy 98, then N on Ghoston Rd, then N on New Light Rd.* FACILITIES: 153 sites, 89 W&E, (20 & 30 amps), 64 no hkups, tenting, dump station, fire rings. RECREATION: lake swimming, boating, ramp, lake fishing, hiking trails. Partial handicap access. Open all yr. Phone: (919)676-1027.

(N) FALLS LAKE STATE REC. AREA (Rollingview Campground)—(Wake) *From jct Hwy 50 & Hwy 98: Go 8 mi W on Hwy 98, then N on Baptist Rd.* FACILITIES: 115 sites, 80 W&E, (20 & 30 amps), 35 no hkups, tenting, fire rings. RECREATION: lake swimming, boating, ramp, lake fishing, hiking trails. Open all yr. Phone: (919)676-1027.

Sugar Ray Leonard, boxer, is from North Carolina.

RALEIGH—Continued

RVACATION CAMPGROUND—*From Raleigh: Go E on US 70 to I-95, then 1-1/4 mi N on I-95 to exit 98, then 25 yds E on CR 1927 (Pine Level-Selma Rd), then 1/2 mi N on Campground Rd. Enter on R.*

SEE PRIMARY LISTING AT SELMA AND AD SMITHFIELD PAGE 661

(W) WILLIAM B UMSTEAD STATE PARK—(Wake) *From town: Go 6 mi NW on US 70.* FACILITIES: 28 sites, 20 ft max RV length, 28 no hkups, tenting, grills, wood. RECREATION: boating, rowboat rentals, lake fishing, hiking trails. Open Mar 15 thru Dec 15. No reservations. Phone: (919)571-4170.

REIDSVILLE—A-3

LAKE REIDSVILLE RECREATION PARK (City Park)—(Rockingham) *From town: Go 5 mi S on US 29, then 1 mi E on Waterworks Rd. Enter on L.* FACILITIES: 46 sites, typical site width 12 ft, 46 W&E, some extended stay sites, 10 pull-thrus, tenting, dump station, ltd groceries, ice, fire rings, wood. RECREATION: pavilion, boating, canoeing, ramp, dock, lake fishing, playground, planned activities (wkends only), sports field, hiking trails, v-ball. Rec open to public. Open Mar 1 thru Nov 1. Phone: (336) 349-4738.

Woodall's Tip #30... Rate information is based on the campground's published rate last year. These rates aren't guaranteed, and you should always call ahead for the most updated rate information.

ROANOKE RAPIDS—A-4

(S) THE RV RESORT AT CAROLINA CROSSROADS (UNDER CONSTRUCTION)—(Halifax) *From jct I-95 (exit 171) & Hwy 125: Go S on Hwy 125. Enter on L.*

SPECIAL SAVINGS FOR SNOWBIRDS
Easy On & Easy Off - I-95, exit 171. Overnite Express sites save you money. Extra long pull-thrus so no need to unhook! Dry camping $15. Premium sites $65.

FACILITIES: 89 sites, typical site width 35 ft, 89 full hkups, (50 amps), 68 pull-thrus, cable TV, wireless Instant Internet access at site, LP gas by weight/by meter, LP bottle exch.

RECREATION: golf nearby.

Pets welcome. Partial handicap access. No tents. Open all yr. Open Fall of 2007. Big rigs welcome. Internet friendly. Clubs welcome. Rate in 2007 $15-65 for 2 persons. MC/VISA/DISC/AMEX. Member ARVC, CARVC. Phone: (252)535-7000.

SEE AD TRAVEL SECTION PAGE 621

ROARING GAP—A-1

STONE MOUNTAIN STATE PARK—(Wilkes) *From jct US 21 & Hwy 1002: Go 7 mi SW on Hwy 1002 to John P. Frank Pkwy.* FACILITIES: 37 sites, 37 no hkups, tenting, laundry, grills. RECREATION: river fishing, hiking trails. Open all yr. Facilities fully operational Mar 15 thru Dec 15. No restrooms or showers. Phone: (336)957-8185.

ROBBINSVILLE—E-1

NANTAHALA NATIONAL FOREST (Cheoah Point Rec. Area)—(Graham) *From town: Go 8 mi NW on US-129.* FACILITIES: 26 sites, 22 ft max RV length, 26 no hkups, 1 pull-thrus, tenting, non-flush toilets only, fire rings, grills. RECREATION: boating, ramp, lake fishing. Facilities fully operational Apr thru Oct. No showers. Max stay 14 days. Phone: (828)479-6431.

ROCK RIDGE—B-4

(C) ROCK RIDGE CAMPGROUND—(Wilson) *From jct I-95 (exit 116) & Nc-42: Go 1 mi SW on NC-42, then 1 mi W on NC 1142. Enter on R.*

◊◊◊FACILITIES: 117 sites, 22 full hkups, 95 W&E, (30 & 50 amps), many extended stay sites, 40 pull-thrus, tenting, dump station, laundry, LP gas by weight, ice, tables.

◊◊RECREATION: pavilion, swim pool, pond fishing, golf nearby, bsktball, playground, sports field.

Pets welcome. Open all yr. Rate in 2007 $25-30 for 2 persons. MC/VISA. Member ARVC, CARVC. Phone: (252)291-4477.

SEE AD THIS PAGE

RODANTHE—B-6

(N) CAMP HATTERAS (CAMP RESORT) —(Dare) *From the business center: Go 1 mi S on Hwy 12. Enter on L.*

◊◊◊◊FACILITIES: 403 sites, typical site width 40 ft, 403 full hkups, (30 & 50 amps), 9 pull-thrus, cable TV ($), wireless Instant Internet access at site, tenting, laundry, ltd groceries, RV supplies, ice, tables, patios, controlled access gate.

◊◊◊◊◊RECREATION: rec hall, rec room/area, pavilion, coin games, 2 swim pools, wading pool, saltwater swimming, whirlpool, boating, canoeing, kayaking, ramp, 10 kayak rentals, saltwater/pond fishing, fishing supplies, mini-golf ($), bsktball, 6 bike rentals, playground, 4 shuffleboard courts, planned activities, tennis, v-ball.

Pets welcome. Partial handicap access. Open all yr. Big rigs welcome. Internet friendly. Clubs wel-

Save time! Plan ahead with WOODALL'S!

RODANTHE—Continued
CAMP HATTERAS—Continued

come. Rate in 2007 $32-81 for 2 persons. MC/VISA/DISC/AMEX. Member ARVC, CARVC. Phone: (252)987-2777. FMCA discount.

e-mail: camping@camphatteras.com

SEE AD CAPE HATTERAS PAGE 640 AND AD TRAVEL SECTION PAGE 619 AND AD DISCOVER SECTION PAGE 60

(S) Cape Hatteras KOA—(Dare) *From the business center: Go 1-1/4 mi S on Hwy 12. Enter on L.* ◊◊◊◊FACILITIES: 345 sites, typical site width 25 ft, 161 full hkups, 154 W&E, (20, 30 & 50 amps), 30 no hkups, 109 pull-thrus, tenting, dump station, laundry, groceries, ice, tables, grills, wood. ◊◊◊◊◊RECREATION: rec room/area, swim pool, saltwater swimming, canoeing, 3 pedal boat rentals, saltwater fishing, mini-golf ($), playground, planned activities, horseshoes, v-ball. Pets welcome. Partial handicap access. Open all yr. Big rigs welcome. Internet friendly. Rate in 2007 $37-85 for 2 persons. Phone: (252)987-2307. KOA 10% value card discount.

(S) Ocean Waves Campground—(Dare) *From business center: Go 1-1/2 mi S on Hwy 12. Enter on L.* ◊◊◊◊FACILITIES: 68 sites, typical site width 30 ft, 64 full hkups, (20, 30 & 50 amps), 4 no hkups, tenting, laundry, ltd groceries, ice, tables. ◊◊RECREATION: rec room/area, swim pool, saltwater swimming, saltwater fishing, play equipment. Pets welcome. Partial handicap access. Open Mar 15 thru Nov 15. Big rigs welcome. Internet friendly. Rate in 2007 $30-32 per family. Member ARVC, CARVC. Phone: (252)987-2556.

RUTHERFORDTON—E-3

(W) Four Paws Kingdom—(Rutherford) *From jct US 64/74A and Coopers Gap Rd: Go 3-1/4 mi W on Coopers Gap Rd to Lazy Creek Dr. Enter on R.* ◊◊◊FACILITIES: 47 sites, 41 full hkups, 6 W&E, (20, 30 & 50 amps), 50 amps ($), tenting, laundry, ltd groceries, ice, tables, fire rings, wood. ◊◊RECREATION: rec room/area, pavilion, pond swimming, pond fishing, play equipment, planned activities (wkends only), horseshoes, hiking trails. Pets welcome. Partial handicap access. Open Easter thru Oct 31. Big rigs welcome. Rate in 2007 $33-39 for 2 persons. Member ARVC, CARVC. Phone: (828)287-7324.

SALISBURY—B-2

(E) DAN NICHOLAS PARK (Rowan County Park)—(Rowan) *From jct US 52 & I-85: Go 1-3/4 mi N on I-85 (exit 79), then 1-1/4 mi SE on Choate Rd, then 1/2 mi SE on McCaules Rd, then 5 mi E on Bringle Ferry Rd. Enter on L.* FACILITIES: 75 sites, 50 W&E, (30 amps), 25 no hkups, 13 pull-thrus, tenting, dump station, non-guest dumping $, ltd groceries, ice, fire rings, grills, wood. RECREATION: rec room/area, pavilion, 50 pedal boat rentals, lake fishing, mini-golf ($), playground, tennis, horseshoes, sports field, hiking trails, v-ball. Rec open to public. Open all yr. Phone: (704)216-7803.

(E) GOLDEN POND CAMPGROUND (REBUILDING)—(Rowan) *From jct I-85 (exit 81) and Long Ferry Rd: Go 3 mi E on Long Ferry Rd, then 2/10 mi S on Harris Point Rd, then E on Keener Rd. Enter at end.*

FACILITIES: 10 sites, accepts full hkup units only, 10 full hkups, (50 amps), wireless Instant Internet access at site.

RECREATION: pavilion, pond fishing.

Pets welcome. No tents. Big rigs welcome. Internet friendly. Rate in 2007 $25 for 2 persons. Phone: (704)202-8812.

e-mail: reservations@goldenpondrvpark.com

SEE AD TRAVEL SECTION PAGE 626

Woodall's Tip #32... If a campground does not have facilities for tenters, its listing will indicate "no tents" in the special info section or "accepts full hookup units only" in the facilities section.

SALISBURY—Continued

(SE) TAMARAC MARINA & CAMPGROUND (TOO NEW TO RATE)—(Rowan) *From jct I-85 (exit 70) & US 52: Go 1/2 mi N on E Innes St (US 52), then 1/2 mi NE on N Long St, then 9-3/4 mi SE on Bringle Ferry Rd.*

FACILITIES: 23 sites, typical site width 30 ft, 23 full hkups, (30 & 50 amps), wireless Internet access central location, tenting, groceries, LP gas by weight/by meter, gas, marine gas, ice, tables.

RECREATION: boating, 2 pontoon rentals, lake fishing, fishing supplies, playground.

Pets welcome. Open all yr. Big rigs welcome. Rate in 2007 $30-35 for 2 persons. MC/VISA. Phone: (704)636-1918.

e-mail: tamaracmarina@bellsouth.net

SEE AD THIS PAGE

SALUDA—E-2

(SW) ORCHARD LAKE CAMPGROUND & RV PARK—(Polk) *From I-26 (exit 59, old 28-Saluda): Go 1-1/4 mi SW on Ozone Rd, then 1/2 mi SW on US 176, then 3 mi SE on Mountain Page Rd, then 1-1/2 mi E on left fork (Mine Mtn Rd), then 1/2 mi SE on Orchard Lake Rd. Enter on L.*

COME PLAY IN OUR COOL MOUNTAINS!
Affordable for your family - no extra charge for Wi-Fi, to swim, fish, play golf, use a canoe, paddleboat or kayak. If you hike, we're on the Palmetto Trail. There's also much to do and see in Saluda, Hendersonville, & Tryon.

◊◊◊FACILITIES: 125 sites, typical site width 25 ft, 104 full hkups, 21 W&E, (20, 30 & 50 amps), some extended stay sites, 10 pull-thrus, wireless Instant Internet access at site, phone Internet access central location, tenting, cabins, RV storage, dump station, laundry, ltd groceries, RV supplies, ice, tables, patios, fire rings, wood.

◊◊◊◊◊RECREATION: rec hall, pavilion, lake swimming, boating, electric motors only, canoeing, kayaking, dock, 4 rowboat/8 canoe/3 pedal boat rentals, lake/pond fishing, fishing supplies, bsktball, playground, shuffleboard court, planned activities (wkends only), horseshoes, sports field, hiking trails, v-ball. Rec open to public.

Pets welcome. Open Apr 1 thru Oct 31. Big rigs welcome. Internet friendly. Clubs welcome. Rate in 2007 $35 per family. MC/VISA/DISC. Phone: (828)749-3901.

e-mail: mgr@orchardlakecampground.com

SEE AD HENDERSONVILLE PAGE 653

SEALEVEL—C-6

(S) Cedar Creek Campground—(Carteret) *From jct Hwy 12 & US 70: Go 1-1/2 mi E on US 70, then 1/4 mi S on State Rd 1376 (Cedar Creek Rd). Enter on R.* ◊◊FACILITIES: 73 sites, typical site width 30 ft, 35 full hkups, 18 W&E, (20 & 30 amps), 20 no hkups, some extended stay sites, 3 pull-thrus, tenting, dump station, non-guest dumping $, ltd groceries, ice, tables. ◊◊RECREATION: swim pool, boating, canoeing, ramp, dock, saltwater fishing, play equipment. Rec open to public. Pets welcome. Open Apr 1 thru Nov 30. Member ARVC, NCARVC. Phone: (252)225-9571.

Woodall's Tip #15... Diamonds on maps indicate towns under which RV Park & Campground locations are listed.

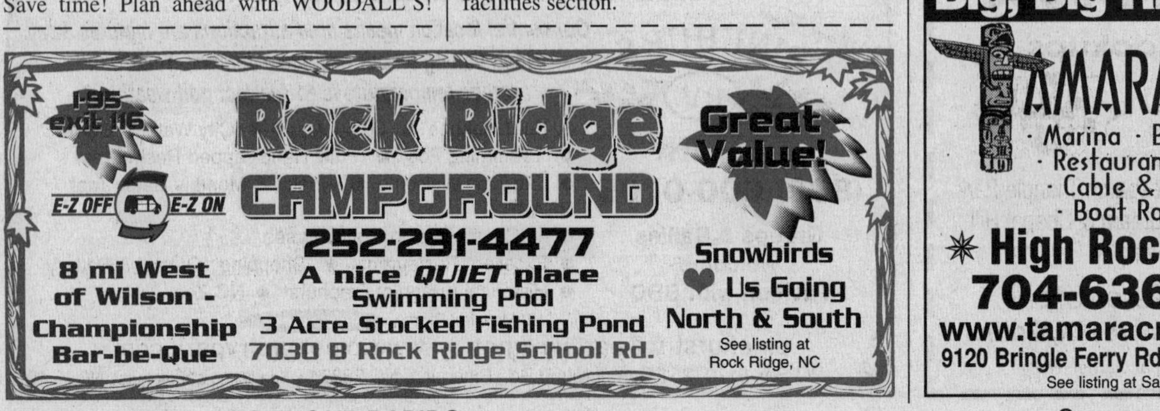

SELMA—B-4

(NE) RVACATION CAMPGROUND—(Johnston) *From jct US 70 & I-95: Go 1 mi N on I-95 to Exit 98, then E on CR 1927 (Pine Level-Selma Rd), then 1/2 mi N on Campground Rd Enter on R.*

LOWEST RATES IN SMITHFIELD/SELMA
Great stopover off I-95. Easy on/off to modern, spacious park with large, level sites up to 120'. Exceptionally clean bathhouse. Enjoy lake view and acres of open area to exercise pets. Restaurants and outlet malls nearby.

◆◆◆◆FACILITIES: 50 sites, typical site width 50 ft, 31 full hkups, 19 W&E, (30 & 50 amps), 45 pull-thrus, wireless Instant Internet access at site, phone Internet access central location, RV storage, dump station, non-guest dumping $, laundry, ltd groceries, RV supplies, LP gas by weight/by meter, ice, tables.

◆RECREATION: lake fishing, fishing supplies, golf nearby, playground.

Pets welcome. No tents. Open all yr. Big rigs welcome. Internet friendly. Escort to site. Clubs welcome. Rate in 2007 $25-35 for 2 persons. MC/VISA. Member ARVC, CARVC. Phone: (919)965-5923.

e-mail: camping@rvacation.us

SEE AD THIS PAGE

SHALLOTTE—D-4

See listing at Sunset Beach.

SHILOH—A-6

(E) NORTH RIVER CAMPGROUND & RV PARK—(Camden) *From town center: Go 3 mi SE on NC-343, then 2-1/2 mi N on Sassafras Ln, then 1-1/2 mi E on Garrington Island Rd. Enter at end.*

◆◆◆◆FACILITIES: 80 sites, typical site width 35 ft, 68 full hkups, 12 E, (20, 30 & 50 amps), some extended stay sites, 4 pull-thrus, phone Internet access central location, tenting, RV storage, dump station, non-guest dumping $, laundry, ltd groceries, LP gas by weight/by meter, ice, tables, grills, wood, controlled access gate.

◆◆◆RECREATION: rec hall, equipped pavilion, coin games, 5 pedal boat rentals, lake fishing, mini-golf ($), 6 bike rentals, horseshoes, sports field, v-ball.

SHILOH—Continued
NORTH RIVER CAMPGROUND & RV PARK—Continued

Pets welcome. Partial handicap access. Open all yr. Big rigs welcome. Escort to site. Clubs welcome. Rate in 2007 $35 for 2 persons. MC/VISA/DISC/AMEX. Phone: (252)336-4414. CCUSA discount.

SEE AD THIS PAGE

SMITHFIELD—B-4

(S) FOUR OAKS RV RESORT (NOT VISITED) —(Johnston) *From jct US 70 & I-95: Go 5 mi S on I-95 to exit 90, then 1/4 mi S on US 301. Enter on R.*

FACILITIES: 17 sites, typical site width 25 ft, accepts full hkup units only, 17 full hkups, (20, 30 & 50 amps), 3 pull-thrus, cable TV ($), wireless Instant Internet access at site, ice, tables.

Pets welcome. No tents. Open all yr. Escort to site. Rate in 2007 $18 for 2 persons. MC/VISA/DISC/AMEX. Member ARVC, CARVC. Phone: (919)963-3596.

e-mail: fouroakslodging@aol.com

SEE AD THIS PAGE

RVACATION CAMPGROUND—*From jct US 70 & I-95 (exit 95): Go 3 mi N on I-95 to exit 98, then 25 yds E on CR 1927 (Pine Level Selma Rd), then 1/2 mi N on Campground Rd. Enter on R.*

SEE PRIMARY LISTING AT SELMA AND AD THIS PAGE

(S) Smithfield KOA—(Johnston) *From jct US 70 & I-95: Go 5 mi S on I-95 to exit 90, then 1/4 mi S on US 701. Enter on L.* ◆◆◆FACILITIES: 60 sites, typical site width 25 ft, 56 full hkups, (30 & 50 amps), 4 no hkups, some extended stay sites, 56 pull-thrus, tenting, dump station, non-guest dumping $, laundry, groceries, LP gas by weight/by meter, ice, tables, fire rings, grills, wood. ◆◆RECREATION: rec hall, swim pool, playground, shuffleboard court, planned activities (wkends only), horseshoes, hiking trails, v-ball. Pets welcome. Partial handicap access. Open all yr. Big rigs welcome. Internet friendly. Rate in 2007 $37-44 for 2 persons. Member ARVC, CARVC. Phone: (800)562-5897. KOA 10% value card discount.

SPARTA—A-1

BLUE RIDGE NATIONAL PARKWAY (Doughton Park Campground)—(Alleghany) *From town: Go 7 mi S on US 21, then 13 mi S on Blue Ride Pkwy to milepost 239.* FACILITIES: 24 sites, 30 ft max RV length, 24 no hkups, tenting, dump station, grills. RECREATION: hiking trails. Open May thru Oct 31. No water. Phone: (336)372-8568.

SPRUCE PINE—D-3

(SE) Bear Den Campground—(McDowell) *From jct US 19 E & Hwy 226: Go 4-1/2 mi E on Hwy 226, then 6 mi N on Blue Ridge Pkwy to milepost 324.8. Enter on R.* ◆◆◆FACILITIES: 142 sites, typical site width 20 ft, 29 full hkups, 113 W&E, (20, 30 & 50 amps), some extended stay sites (in summer), 11 pull-thrus, tenting, dump station, portable dump, laundry, ltd groceries, LP gas by weight, ice, tables, fire rings, wood. ◆◆◆◆RECREATION: pavilion, equipped pavilion, lake swimming, canoe/pedal boat rentals, pond fishing, playground, 2 shuffleboard courts, planned activities (wkends only), horseshoes, hiking trails, v-ball. Pets welcome ($). Open Mar thru Nov. Self-contained RV sites available by reservation in Winter. Rate in 2007 $35-43 for 2 persons. Member ARVC, CARVC. Phone: (828)765-2888.

STATESVILLE—B-2

(S) KOA-Statesville—(Iredell) *From jct I-40 & I-77: Go 6 mi S on I-77 (exit 45), then 1/2 mi N on E frontage road. Enter on L.* ◆◆◆FACILITIES: 88 sites, typical site width 34 ft, 37 full hkups, 51 W&E, (20, 30 & 50 amps), 50 amps ($), some extended stay sites, 49 pull-thrus, tenting, dump station, non-guest dumping $, laundry, groceries, LP gas by weight/by meter, ice, tables, grills. ◆◆◆RECREATION: rec hall, pavilion, swim pool, playground, horseshoes. Pets welcome, breed restrict. Partial handicap access. Open all yr. Big rigs welcome. Internet friendly. Rate in 2007 $32-50 for 2 persons. Phone: (704)873-5560. KOA 10% value card discount.

LAKE NORMAN STATE PARK—(Iredell) *From town: Go 10 mi S on Hwy 1569.* FACILITIES: 33 sites, 33 no hkups, tenting, dump station, grills. RECREATION: lake swimming, boating, canoeing, ramp, rowboat/canoe/pedal boat rentals, lake fishing, hiking trails. Open Mar 15 thru Nov 30. Phone: (704)528-6350.

(NE) MIDWAY CAMPGROUND & RV RESORT—(Davie) *From jct I-77 & I-40: Go 9 mi E on I-40 to exit 162, then 1/4 mi S on US 64, then 1/4 mi E on Campground Road. Enter on L.*

◆◆◆◆FACILITIES: 83 sites, typical site width 25 ft, 47 full hkups, 25 W&E, (20, 30 & 50 amps), 11 no hkups, some extended stay sites, 39 pull-thrus, wireless Instant Internet access at site, phone Internet access central location, tenting, cabins, RV storage, dump station, non-guest

MIDWAY CAMPGROUND & RV RESORT—Continued on next page

Shop at Woodall's Advertised Dealers

dumping $, portable dump, laundry, groceries, RV supplies, LP gas by weight/by meter, ice, tables, fire rings, grills, wood.

◆◆◆◆RECREATION: rec room/area, pavilion, coin games, swim pool, wading pool, boating, electric motors only, canoeing, kayaking, lake fishing, fishing supplies, mini-golf ($), golf nearby, bsktball, playground, planned activities (wkends only), horseshoes, sports field, hiking trails, v-ball. Rec open to public.

Pets welcome, breed restrict. Open all yr. Big rigs welcome. Internet friendly. Escort to site. Clubs welcome. Rate in 2007 $32-44 for 2 persons. MC/VISA/DISC/AMEX. Member ARVC, CARVC. Phone: (888)754-4809.

e-mail: stay@midwaycampground.com

SEE AD PAGE 661

(NE) MIDWAY TRAIL OF HORROR—*From jct I-77 & I-40: Go 9 mi E on I-40 to exit 162, then 1/4 mi S on US 64, then 1/4 mi E on Campground Rd. Enter on L.* An outdoor Halloween adventure. Walk the trail on your own through scary buildings, the haunted graveyard and outside in the woods. Weekends in October. Phone: (704)546-7615.

SEE AD PAGE 661

(N) THE FAMILY RV CENTER—*From jct I-77 & I-40: Go 2 mi W on I-40 (exit 150), then 100 yards N on Hwy 115, then 1/4 mi W on Northside Dr. Enter on R.* SALES: travel trailers, park trailers, 5th wheels, motor homes, mini-motor homes, fold-down camping trailers, pre-owned unit sales. SERVICES: full-time mech, RV appliance repair, body work/collision repair, LP gas by weight/by meter, dump station, sells parts/accessories, installs hitches. Open all yr. MC/VISA. Phone: (800)872-3103. FMCA discount.

e-mail: sales@TheFamilyRVCenter.com

SEE AD TRAVEL SECTION PAGE 621

STELLA—C-5

(S) WHITE OAK SHORES CAMPING & RV RESORT—(Carteret) *From jct Hwy 24 & Hwy 58: Go 8-1/2 mi W on Hwy 58, then 1 mi S on Morristown Rd, then W on Wetherington Rd, then N 3/4 mi. Enter on L.*

◆◆◆◆FACILITIES: 100 sites, typical site width 30 ft, 100 full hkups, (20, 30 & 50 amps), 35 pull-thrus, cable TV, wireless Instant Internet access at site ($), tenting, RV storage, laundry, groceries, RV supplies, LP gas by weight/by meter, ice, tables, controlled access gate.

◆◆◆RECREATION: rec hall, swim pool, wading pool, canoeing, kayaking, river fishing, fishing supplies, bsktball, playground, planned activities (wkends only), horseshoes, sports field, hiking trails, v-ball.

Pets welcome, breed restrict. Open all yr. Big rigs welcome. Internet friendly. Clubs welcome. Rate in 2007 $35-50 for 4 persons. MC/VISA/DISC/AMEX. Phone: (252)393-3244.

e-mail: whiteoakshores@comerresorts.com

SEE AD EMERALD ISLE PAGE 646

STONEVILLE—A-2

(SW) Dan River Campground—(Rockingham) *From jct US 220 & Hwy 135: Go 1 blk W on Hwy 135, then 1/2 mi S on Dan Valley Rd, then 2 mi E on River Rd, then 1 mi SE on Webser Rd. Enter on R.* ◆◆FACILITIES: 42 sites, typical site width 35 ft, 20 full hkups, 18 W&E, (30 & 50 amps), 4 no hkups, many extended stay sites, tenting, dump station, ice, fire rings, wood. ◆◆RECREATION: pavilion, swim pool, canoeing, 8 canoe rentals, river fishing, play equipment, horseshoes, v-ball. Rec open to public. Open all yr. Rate in 2007 $22-25 for 2 persons. Member ARVC, CARVC. Phone: (336)427-8530.

SUNSET BEACH—D-4

(W) KOA Shallotte/Brunswick Beaches—(Brunswick) *From jct US 17 & Hwy 904: Go 1/4 mi SE on Hwy 904. Enter on R.* ◆◆◆◆FACILITIES: 93 sites, typical site width 30 ft, 70 full hkups, 23 W&E, (20, 30 & 50 amps), some extended stay sites, 80 pull-thrus, tenting, dump station, laundry, ltd groceries, LP gas by weight/by meter, ice, tables, patios, fire rings, grills, wood. ◆◆◆RECREATION: equipped pavilion, swim pool, pond fishing, playground, planned activities (wkends only), horseshoes, sports field, v-ball. Pets welcome. Partial handicap access. Open all yr. Big rigs welcome. Internet friendly. Rate in 2007 $30-50 for 2 persons. Phone: (888)562-4240. KOA 10% value card discount.

(W) Wishing Well Campground—(Brunswick) *From jct US 17 & Hwy 904: Go 1 mi SE on Hwy 904. Enter on R.* ◆◆FACILITIES: 31 sites, typical site width 30 ft, 15 full hkups, 16 W&E, (20 & 30 amps), some extended stay sites, tenting, tables. RECREATION: play equipment. Pets welcome. Open all yr. Full hookup units only Nov-March. Open 50 weeks (Please call for closed dates). Rate in 2007 $17 for 2 persons. Phone: (866) 433-7982.

SURF CITY—D-5

(C) LANIER'S CAMPGROUND—(Pender) *From jct US 17 & Hwy 210: Go 2-3/4 mi E on Hwy 210, continue 1 mi SE on Hwy 210, then 1/2 mi S on Little Kinston Rd., then 1/2 mi W on Spot Lane. Enter at end.*

COME LEARN ABOUT A NEW DEVELOPMENT

Our family has welcomed campers for over 30 years. Now we're building a dream RV park with 1st class sites & great amenities, including an executive golf course. Seasonal leases are available. (877)665-5347.

◆◆◆FACILITIES: 43 sites, typical site width 25 ft, 14 full hkups, 29 W&E, (30 & 50 amps), 3 pull-thrus, wireless Internet access central location, tenting, dump station, non-guest dumping $, laundry, ltd groceries, RV supplies, LP bottle exch, ice, tables, fire rings, wood, controlled access gate.

◆◆◆RECREATION: rec room/area, pavilion, coin games, swim pool, boating, canoeing, kayaking, ramp, dock, saltwater fishing, bsktball, playground, planned activities (wkends only), horseshoes.

Pets welcome, breed restrict. Partial handicap access. Open all yr. Big rigs welcome. Internet friendly. Clubs welcome. Rate in 2007 $28-38 for 5 persons. MC/VISA/AMEX. Member ARVC, CARVC. Phone: (910)328-9431. CCUSA discount.

e-mail: CampLanier@aol.com

SEE AD THIS PAGE

SURF CITY RESORTS (PLANNED)—(Pender)

SEE AD THIS PAGE

SWANNANOA—E-2

(E) ASHEVILLE EAST-KOA—(Buncombe) *From I-40 (exit 59) & Patton Cove Rd: Go 1/2 mi N on Patton Cove Rd, then 1-1/2 mi E on US 70. Enter on L.*

◆◆◆FACILITIES: 227 sites, typical site width 22 ft, 85 full hkups, 136 W&E, 4 E, (20, 30 & 50 amps), 2 no hkups, 15 pull-thrus, cable TV ($), wireless Instant Internet access at site, phone Internet access central location, tenting, RV/park trailer rentals, cabins, RV storage, dump station, non-guest dumping $, laundry, groceries, tables, RV supplies, LP gas by weight/by meter, ice, tables, fire rings, wood.

◆◆◆◆RECREATION: rec room/area, pavilion, coin games, swim pool, river swimming, boating, electric motors only, 3 rowboat/3 pedal boat rentals, lake/river fishing, fishing supplies, mini-golf ($), golf nearby, bsktball, 14 bike rentals, playground, planned activities (wkends only), horseshoes, hiking trails.

Pets welcome, breed restrict. Open all yr. Internet friendly. Escort to site. Clubs welcome. Rate in 2007 $30-37 for 2 persons. MC/VISA/DISC. Phone: (828)686-3121. KOA 10% value card discount.

e-mail: akoaeast@bellsouth.net

SEE AD ASHEVILLE PAGE 634 AND AD DISCOVER SECTION PAGES 62 & 63

(S) Mama Gertie's Hideaway Campground—(Buncombe) *From jct I-40 (exit 59) & Patton Cove Rd: Go 1/2 mi S on Patton Cove Rd. Enter on L.* ◆◆◆◆FACILITIES: 33 sites, typical site width 30 ft, 19 full hkups, 14 W&E, (20, 30 & 50 amps), 13 pull-thrus, tenting, dump station, laundry, ltd groceries, LP gas by weight/by meter, ice, tables, patios, fire rings, wood. ◆◆RECREATION: rec hall, rec room/area, equipped pavilion, horseshoes, hiking trails. Pets welcome. Partial handicap access. Open all yr. Big rigs welcome. Internet friendly. Rate in 2007 $27-42 for 2 persons. Member ARVC, CARVC. Phone: (828)686-4258. FMCA discount.

(W) MILES MOTORS RV CAMPGROUND—(Buncombe) *From jct I-40 (exit 59) & Patton Cove Rd: Go 1/4 mi N on Patton Cove Rd, then W on Reece Dr. Enter at end.*

◆◆◆FACILITIES: 60 sites, typical site width 24 ft, 60 full hkups, (30 & 50 amps), 8 pull-thrus, cable TV, wireless Instant Internet access at site, dump station, non-guest dumping $, RV supplies, LP gas by weight/by meter, tables, patios, fire rings.

◆RECREATION: equipped pavilion, bsktball, shuffleboard court, horseshoes.

MILES MOTORS RV CAMPGROUND—Continued on next page

SWANNANOA—Continued
MILES MOTORS RV CAMPGROUND—Continued

Pets welcome. No tents. Open all yr. Big rigs welcome. Internet friendly. Rate in 2007 $25 for 2 persons. MC/VISA. Phone: (800)982-5315.

e-mail: milesmotors@aol.com

SEE AD ASHEVILLE PAGE 634

✲ **(W) MILES MOTORS RV CENTER**—*From jct I-40 (exit 59) & Patton Cove Rd: Go 1/4 mi N on Patton Cove R, then W on Reece Dr. Enter at end.* SALES: travel trailers, 5th wheels, mini-motor homes, fold-down camping trailers, SERVICES: LP gas by weight/by meter, dump station, sells parts/accessories. Open all yr. MC/VISA. Phone: (828)686-3414.

SEE AD ASHEVILLE PAGE 634

SWANSBORO—C-5

(S) CROATAN NATIONAL FOREST (Cedar Point Campground)—(carterette) *From town: Go 3-1/4 mi SE on Hwy-24, then 3/4 mi NE on Hwy-58, then 1/2 mi NW on Hwy-1114, then 3/4 mi SW on FR-153A.* FACILITIES: 40 sites, 22 ft max RV length, 40 E, 1 pull-thrus, tenting, grills. RECREATION: boating, no motors, canoeing, ramp, river fishing, hiking trails. Partial handicap access. Open all yr. No showers. No reservations. Phone: (252)638-5628.

SYLVA—E-2

(SW) FT TATHAM RV PARK—(Jackson) *From jct US 23 & US 441: Go 6-1/2 mi S on US 441. Enter on L.*

◊◊◊FACILITIES: 90 sites, 86 full hkups, 4 W&E, (30 & 50 amps), mostly extended stay sites, wireless Instant Internet access at site, tenting, RV storage, dump station, laundry, ice, tables.

◊◊◊RECREATION: rec hall, equipped pavilion, swim pool, pond/stream fishing, bsktball, playground, 2 shuffleboard courts, planned activities, horseshoes, v-ball.

Pets welcome, breed restrict. Open Apr 1 thru Oct 31. Internet friendly. Escort to site. Clubs welcome. Rate in 2007 $22 for 2 persons. MC/VISA. Phone: (828)586-6662. CCUSA discount.

e-mail: fttathumrv@verizon.net

SEE AD FRANKLIN PAGE 650

TABOR CITY—D-3

(SE) YOGI BEAR'S JELLYSTONE PARK AT DADDY JOE'S—(Columbus) *From jct Hwy 410 & US 701: Go 1/2 mi S on US 701, then 1/2 mi E on Richard Wright Rd. Enter on R.*

WE MEAN IT! BIG RIG FRIENDLY!
Our sites are huge and accommodate the largest RVs and slideouts. Every site has a full concrete pad and Wi-Fi access. We've got a new grill/store and activities pool, plus a natural setting you won't want to leave.

◊◊◊◊FACILITIES: 78 sites, typical site width 45 ft, 78 full hkups, (20, 30 & 50 amps), some extended stay sites, 51 pull-thrus, wireless Instant Internet access at site, tenting, cabins, dump station, non-guest dumping $, laundry, groceries, RV supplies, LP gas by weight/by meter, ice, tables, patios, fire rings, grills, wood.

◊◊◊◊◊RECREATION: rec hall, pavilion, coin games, 2 swim pools, sprayground, boating, electric motors only, canoeing, kayaking, lake fishing, fishing supplies, bsktball, bike rental, playground, shuffleboard court, planned activities, horseshoes, sports field, hiking trails, v-ball.

Pets welcome. Partial handicap access. Open all yr. Big rigs welcome. Internet friendly. Clubs welcome. Rate in 2007 $32-45 for 4 persons. MC/VISA/AMEX. Member ARVC, CARVC. Phone: (910) 653-2155.

e-mail: yogi@taborcityjellystone.com

SEE AD MYRTLE BEACH, SC PAGE 775

TERRELL—B-1

(SW) LAKE NORMAN MOTOR COACH RESORT (UNDER CONSTRUCTION) —(Catawba) *From jct I-77 (exit 36) and Hwy 150: Go 10 mi W on Hwy 150. Enter on R.*

FACILITIES: 58 sites, typical site width 30 ft, 58 full hkups, (30 & 50 amps), wireless Instant Internet access at site, laundry, tables, patios, controlled access gate.

RECREATION: rec hall, boating, ramp, lake fishing, golf nearby, playground.

Pets welcome. Partial handicap access. No tents. Open all yr. Motorhomes only. Big rigs welcome.

TERRELL—Continued
LAKE NORMAN MOTOR COACH RESORT—Continued

Internet friendly. Escort to site. Rate in 2007 $35-65 for 2 persons. MC/VISA/DISC/AMEX. Phone: (704)489-6033.

SEE AD CHARLOTTE PAGE 643 AND AD TRAVEL SECTION PAGE 627

UNION GROVE—A-2

(E) Fiddlers Grove Campground—(Iredell) *From jct I-77 (exit 65) & US 901: Go 1-1/2 mi NW on US 901. Enter on L.* ◊◊FACILITIES: 47 sites, typical site width 20 ft, 9 full hkups, 38 W&E, (15, 30 & 50 amps), 27 pull-thrus, heater not allowed, tenting, dump station, tables, fire rings. ◊RECREATION: pavilion, lake fishing, sports field, v-ball. Pets welcome. Partial handicap access. Open all yr. Full hookup units only mid Nov thru mid Mar. Rate in 2007 $15-25 for 2 persons. Phone: (704)539-4417.

(E) Van Hoy Farms Family Campground—(Iredell) *From jct I-77 (exit 65) & Hwy-901: Go 200 yds E on Hwy 901, then 1/4 mi S on Jericho Rd. Enter on L.* ◊◊FACILITIES: 56 sites, typical site width 30 ft, 40 full hkups, 16 W&E, (15, 30 & 50 amps), some extended stay sites, 21 pull-thrus, tenting, laundry, LP gas by weight/by meter, ice, tables, wood. ◊◊RECREATION: pavilion, swim pool, horseshoes, sports field, hiking trails, v-ball. Rec open to public. Pets welcome. Open all yr. Big rigs welcome. Internet friendly. Rate in 2007 $30-35 for 2 persons. Member ARVC, CARVC. Phone: (704)539-5493.

VILAS—A-1

(E) VANDERPOOL CAMPGROUND—(Watauga) *From jct NC 321 & Hwy 421N: Go 7-1/4 mi NE on Hwy 421, then 100 yds S on Vanderpool Rd, then 50 ft S on Charlie Thompson Rd. Enter on R.*

WE'RE LIVING OUR DREAM
Come and be a part of Otha and Vicky's dream. Enjoy the beautiful mountain views and the quiet, peaceful sounds of the Appalachian Mountain nights. As new owners we are improving sites & adding activities for your pleasure.

◊◊◊FACILITIES: 42 sites, typical site width 27 ft, 34 full hkups, 8 W&E, (20, 30 & 50 amps), some extended stay sites, 8 pull-thrus, heater not allowed, cable TV, cable on-site Internet access (needs activ), phone Internet access central location, tenting, RV storage, dump station, non-guest dumping $, laundry, ltd groceries, RV supplies, ice, tables, patios, fire rings, wood.

Pets welcome. Open all yr. Big rigs welcome. Escort to site. Clubs welcome. Rate in 2007 $25 for 2 persons. Phone: (828)297-3486.

e-mail: omiller@vanderpoolcampground.com

SEE AD BOONE PAGE 637

WADE—C-3

(E) Fayetteville KOA—(Cumberland) *From jct I-95 (exit 61) & Wade Stedman Rd: Go 1/2 mi E on Wade Stedman Rd. Enter on L.* ◊◊◊FACILITIES: 85 sites, typical site width 45 ft, 50 full hkups, 25 W&E, (30 & 50 amps), 10 no hkups, 60 pull-thrus, tenting, dump station, non-guest dumping $, laundry, groceries, LP gas by weight/by meter, ice, tables, grills, wood. ◊◊◊RECREATION: rec hall, pavilion, swim pool, pond fishing, playground, horseshoes, hiking trails. Pets welcome. Partial handicap access. Open all yr. Big rigs welcome. Internet friendly. Rate in 2007 $30-52 for 2 persons. Member ARVC, CARVC. Phone: (910)484-5500. KOA 10% value card discount.

WALNUT COVE—A-2

HANGING ROCK STATE PARK—(Stokes) *From town: Go 11 mi NW on Hwy-89, then 12 mi SW on Hwy-1001.* FACILITIES: 73 sites, 73 no hkups, tenting, ice, grills, wood. RECREATION: lake swimming, rowboat/canoe rentals, lake fishing, hiking trails. Partial handicap access. Open all yr. Phone: (336)593-8480.

WASHINGTON—B-5

✲ **(S) CRISP RV CENTER**—*From jct US-264 & US-17: Go 2 mi S on US-17. Enter on R.*

WE'VE GOT IT ALL
RV Rentals, Service & Sales. For 31 years we've sold and serviced pop-ups, travel trailers, 5th wheels, motorhomes and park models. We have a large parts inventory and some of the best service techs in the business.

SALES: travel trailers, park trailers, 5th wheels, motor homes, mini-motor homes, fold-down camping trailers, pre-owned unit sales. SERVICES: full-time mech, RV appliance repair, body work/collision repair, LP gas by weight/by meter,

WASHINGTON—Continued
CRISP RV CENTER—Continued

dump station, RV rentals, sells parts/accessories, installs hitches. Open all yr. MC/VISA/DISC/AMEX. Phone: (252)946-0311.

e-mail: crisprv@earthlink.net

SEE AD TRAVEL SECTION PAGE 619

(NW) TRANTER'S CREEK RESORT & CAMPGROUND—(Pitt) *From jct US 17 & US 264: Go 1-1/2 mi W on US 264, then 1-1/2 mi S on Clarks Neck Rd. Enter on R.*

◊◊◊◊FACILITIES: 196 sites, typical site width 40 ft, 196 full hkups, (20, 30 & 50 amps), many extended stay sites, 12 pull-thrus, wireless Instant Internet access at site ($), phone Internet access central location, tenting, tent rentals, cabins, RV storage, laundry, ltd groceries, RV supplies, ice, tables, fire rings, wood, controlled access gate.

◊◊◊◊◊RECREATION: rec room/area, pavilion, equipped pavilion, coin games, swim pool, boating, canoeing, kayaking, ramp, dock, canoe/3 kayak/2 pedal boat rentals, river fishing, fishing supplies, mini-golf ($), bsktball, 2 bike rentals, playground, planned activities, horseshoes, sports field, v-ball.

Pets welcome. Partial handicap access. Open all yr. Big rigs welcome. Internet friendly. Clubs welcome. Rate in 2007 $30-36 for 2 persons. MC/VISA. Member ARVC, CARVC. Phone: (252)948-0850.

e-mail: camp@tranterscreekresort.com

SEE AD THIS PAGE

(S) TWIN LAKES CAMPING RESORT AND YACHT BASIN—(Beaufort) *From jct US 264 & US 17: Go 1-3/4 mi S on US 17, then 1-1/2 mi SE on Whichards Beach Rd. Enter on R.*

◊◊◊FACILITIES: 471 sites, typical site width 34 ft, 446 full hkups, (20, 30 & 50 amps), 25 no hkups, many extended stay sites, 55 pull-thrus, wireless Instant Internet access at site ($), tenting, cabins, RV storage, dump station, laundry, groceries, RV supplies, LP gas by weight/by meter, gas, marine gas, ice, tables, patios, wood.

◊◊◊◊RECREATION: rec hall, rec room/area, equipped pavilion, coin games, swim pool, boating, canoeing, kayaking, ramp, dock, lake/river/pond fishing, fishing supplies, bsktball, playground, planned activities (wkends only), v-ball.

Pets welcome. Open all yr. 2 day minimum stay. Big rigs welcome. Clubs welcome. Rate in 2007 $30-41 for 2 persons. MC/VISA. Member ARVC, CARVC. Phone: (252)946-5700.

e-mail: twin_lakes@MHChomes.com

SEE AD EMERALD ISLE PAGE 648

WAYNESVILLE—E-2

(NW) Creekwood Farm RV Park—(Haywood) *From jct I-40 (exit 20) & US 276: Go 1 mi S on US 276. Enter on L.* ◊◊◊◊FACILITIES: 125 sites, typical site width 25 ft, 125 full hkups, (30 & 50 amps), many extended stay sites, 15 pull-thrus, tenting, laundry, LP gas by weight/by meter, tables, wood. ◊◊RECREATION: rec hall, stream fishing, planned activities. Pets welcome. Open all yr. Big rigs welcome. Rate in 2007 $30-39 for 2 persons. Phone: (828)926-7977.

WAYNESVILLE—Continued on next page

WAYNESVILLE—Continued

(NW) **PRIDE CAFE**—*From jct I-40 (exit 20) & US 276: Go 1-1/4 mi S on US 276. Enter on L.* Comfortable casual dining. Open for breakfast buffet Monday thru Saturday and brunch on Sunday. Open Apr 15 thru Oct 31. Phone: (828)926-1645.

SEE AD MAGGIE VALLEY PAGE 656

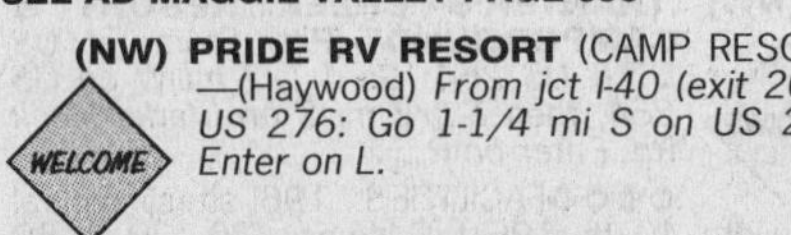

(NW) **PRIDE RV RESORT** (CAMP RESORT) —(Haywood) *From jct I-40 (exit 20) & US 276: Go 1-1/4 mi S on US 276. Enter on L.*

WE TAKE GREAT PRIDE...

From the time you check in you'll know that we've been working to make this a resort everyone takes pride in. Beautiful sites with WI-FI, a great breakfast buffet, sparkling pool & Jacuzzi are just some of what makes us proud.

◇◇◇◇FACILITIES: 148 sites, 140 full hkups, 8 W&E, (20, 30 & 50 amps), some extended stay sites, cable TV, wireless Instant Internet access at site, phone Internet access central location, tenting, cabins, RV storage, dump station, non-guest dumping $, laundry, LP gas by weight/by meter, ice, tables, wood.

◇◇◇◇RECREATION: rec hall, rec room/area, equipped pavilion, swim pool, pond/stream fishing, mini-golf, bsktball, playground, planned activities, horseshoes, v-ball.

Pets welcome, breed restrict, size restrict, quantity restrict. Partial handicap access. Open Mar 1 thru Nov 30. Big rigs welcome. Internet friendly. Clubs welcome. Rate in 2007 $30-40 for 2 persons. MC/VISA/DISC/AMEX. Phone: (800)926-8191.

SEE AD MAGGIE VALLEY PAGE 656

(NW) **Winngray Family Campground**—(Haywood) *From jct I-40 (exit 20) & US 276: Go 3 mi S on US 276. Enter on R.* ◇◇◇FACILITIES: 150 sites, typical site width 25 ft, 122 full hkups, 18 W&E, (20, 30 & 50 amps), 10 no hkups, many extended stay sites, 35 pull-thrus, tenting, dump station, non-guest dumping $, laundry, ltd groceries, LP gas by weight/by meter, ice, tables, patios. ◇RECREATION: rec room/area, equipped pavilion, river swimming, stream fishing, horseshoes. Pets welcome, size restrict. Open all yr. Self-contained units only in winter. Rate in 2007 $27-30 for 2 persons. Member ARVC, CARVC. Phone: (828) 926-3170.

WHITTIER—E-1

(SE) **Holly Cove & RV Resort & Cabins**—(Jackson) *From jct US 74 & US 441 : Go 4 mi SE on US 441/US 74 (mm 76.5), then 500 feet E on West Piney Mountain Rd, then 1/4 mi N on Holly Cove Rd. Enter at end.* ◇◇◇◇FACILITIES: 54 sites, typical site width 35 ft, 50 full hkups, 4 W&E, (20, 30 & 50 amps), some extended stay sites, 9 pull-thrus, tenting, dump station, laundry, ice, tables, fire rings, wood. ◇◇◇RECREATION: rec room/area, pavilion, swim pool, pond fishing, play equipment, horseshoes, hiking trails. Pets welcome. Partial handicap access. Open all yr. Facilities fully operational May 1 thru Nov 1. Big rigs welcome. Internet friendly. Rate in 2007 $28-31 for 2 persons. Member ARVC, CARVC. Phone: (828)631-0692.

The first English colony in America was located on Roanoke Island, founded by Walter Raleigh. The colonists mysteriously vanished with no trace except for the word "Croatoan" scrawled on a nearby tree.

WHITTIER—Continued
Holly Cove & RV Resort & Cabins—Continued

(S) **Timberlake Campground**—(Swain) *From jct US 441 & US 74: Go 1-1/2 mi W on US 74 (exit 72), then 1/4 mi N on Whittier Rd, then 1/4 mi W on Main St, then 1/2 mi S on Whittier Depot St, then 200 yards W on Old Bryson City Rd, then 3-1/4 mi S on Conleys Creek Rd. Enter on R.* ◇◇FACILITIES: 44 sites, typical site width 50 ft, 35 ft max RV length, 42 W&E, (20 & 30 amps), 2 no hkups, some extended stay sites, tenting, dump station, portable dump, laundry, ice, tables, fire rings, grills, wood. ◇◇RECREATION: pond swimming, pond fishing, sports field, hiking trails, v-ball. Pets welcome. Open May 1 thru Nov 1. Rate in 2007 $22-26 for 2 persons. Phone: (828)497-7320.

WILKESBORO—A-1

(W) BANDIT'S ROOST PARK (COE-W. Kerr Scott Reservoir)—(Wilkes) *From jct US-421 & Hwy-268: Go 5 mi W on Hwy-268, then 1/2 mi on RPR-1141.* FACILITIES: 100 sites, 30 ft max RV length, 80 W&E, (30 amps), 20 no hkups, 10 pull-thrus, tenting, dump station, laundry, fire rings, grills, wood. RECREATION: lake swimming, boating, ramp, dock, lake/river fishing, playground, hiking trails. Rec open to public. Open Apr 1 thru Oct 30. No shower. Phone: (336)921-3190.

(W) WARRIOR CREEK PARK (COE-W. Kerr Scott Reservoir)—(Wilkes) *From jct US-421 & Hwy-268: Go 7-1/2 mi W on Hwy-268.* FACILITIES: 71 sites, 30 ft max RV length, 36 W&E, (30 amps), 35 no hkups, 4 pull-thrus, tenting, dump station, fire rings, grills, wood. RECREATION: lake swimming, boating, lake fishing, playground, hiking trails. Rec open to public. Partial handicap access. Open Apr 15 thru Oct 14. Phone: (336)921-2177.

WILLIAMSTON—B-5

(S) **GREEN ACRES FAMILY CAMPGROUND**—(Martin) *From jct US 64/US 13 (exit 514) and US 17: Go 3 mi S on US 17, then 1 mi W on Rodgers School Rd. Enter on R.*

◇◇◇FACILITIES: 175 sites, typical site width 20 ft, 89 full hkups, 75 W&E, (20, 30 & 50 amps), 50 amps ($), 11 no hkups, some extended stay sites, 155 pull-thrus, wireless Instant Internet access at site, wireless Internet access central location, tenting, cabins, RV storage, dump station, non-guest dumping $, laundry, ltd groceries, RV supplies, LP gas by weight/by meter, ice, tables, fire rings, wood.

◇◇◇RECREATION: rec hall, rec room/area, equipped pavilion, coin games, 2 swim pools, no motors, canoeing, kayaking, 3 canoe/2 kayak/5 pedal boat rentals, pond fishing, fishing supplies, mini-golf ($), bsktball, playground, shuffleboard court, planned activities (wkends only), tennis, horseshoes, sports field, v-ball.

Pets welcome. Open all yr. Internet friendly. Clubs welcome. Rate in 2007 $23-28 for 2 persons. MC/VISA/DISC/AMEX. Member ARVC, CARVC. Phone: (252)792-3939.

e-mail: bgreene@embarqmail.com

SEE AD THIS PAGE

In 1903 the Wright Brothers made the first successful powered flight by man at Kill Devil Hill near Kitty Hawk. The Wright Memorial at Kitty Hawk now commemorates their achievement.

WILMINGTON—D-4

(W) **BATTLESHIP NORTH CAROLINA**—*On the west side of the Wilmington Bridge from jct US 17, US 74, US 76 & US 421: Go 1/2 mi N on US 421 North. Enter on R.* A WW II battleship museum and memorial. Visitors may take a self-guided tour. Located on the Cape Fear River across from historic downtown Wilmington. Parking for busses and RVs. No overnight camping. A National Historic Landmark. Open all yr. 7 days a wk; 8am-8pm Memorial Day weekend to Labor Day & 8am-5pm Labor Day to Memorial Day. MC/VISA. Phone: (910)251-5797.

e-mail: ncbb55@battleshipNC.com

SEE AD MYRTLE BEACH, SC PAGE 774 AND AD DISCOVER SECTION PAGE 60

(NE) **HOWARD RV CENTER**—*From jct I-40/Hwy 132 & Bus US 17N: Go 2-1/2 mi NE on Bus US 17N (Market St). Enter on L.* SALES: motor homes, preowned unit sales. SERVICES: full-time mech, RV appliance repair, sells parts/accessories. Open all yr. MC/VISA. Phone: (800)852-7148.

e-mail: sales@hrvc.com

SEE AD TRAVEL SECTION PAGE 621

Wilmington-KOA—(New Hanover) *From jct I-40 (exit 416) & Hwy 17: Go 4-3/4 mi N on Hwy 17, then 2-1/2 mi S on Bus 17 S. Enter on R.* ◇◇◇◇FACILITIES: 94 sites, typical site width 30 ft, 50 full hkups, 25 W&E, (15, 20, 30 & 50 amps), 19 no hkups, some extended stay sites, 45 pull-thrus, tenting, dump station, non-guest dumping $, laundry, ltd groceries, LP gas by weight/by meter, ice, tables, fire rings, wood. ◇◇◇◇RECREATION: rec room/area, pavilion, swim pool, playground, planned activities (wkends only), horseshoes, sports field, v-ball. Pets welcome, breed restrict. Open all yr. Big rigs welcome. Internet friendly. Rate in 2007 $39-52 per vehicle. Member ARVC, CARVC. Phone: (888)562-5699. KOA 10% value card discount.

WILSON—B-4

(N) **KAMPER'S LODGE OF AMERICA**—(Wilson) *From jct Alt US 264 & US 301: Go 2-1/4 mi NE on US 301. Enter on L.*

◇◇◇FACILITIES: 57 sites, typical site width 30 ft, 37 full hkups, 20 W&E, (30 & 50 amps), 45 pull-thrus, wireless Instant Internet access at site, phone Internet access central location, tenting, RV storage, laundry, LP gas by weight/by meter, ice, tables, patios, fire rings.

◇RECREATION: swim pool.

Pets welcome. Open all yr. Rate in 2007 $20-30 for 2 persons. Member ARVC, CARVC. Phone: (252)237-0905.

e-mail: kamperslodge@earthlink.net

SEE AD THIS PAGE

TRAVEL SECTION

South Carolina

READER SERVICE INFO

The following businesses have placed an ad in the South Carolina Travel Section. To receive free information, enter their Reader Service number on the Reader Service Card opposite page 48/Discover Section in the front of this directory:

Advertiser	RS#
Broxton Bridge Plantation	3659
Cane Creek Motor Coach Resort	3610
Cunningham RV Park	644
Don Mar RV Sales	3545
Florence KOA	3781
Hardeeville RV Thomas' Parks & Sites	3660
Magnolia RV Park & Campground	3667
New Green Acres RV Park	3518
Rocks Pond Campground & Marina	3664
South Carolina State Parks	522
Tony's RV Parts & Service	3663

TIME ZONE

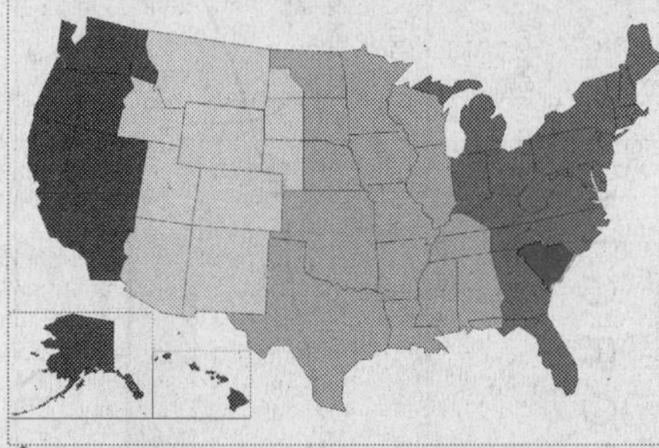

South Carolina is in the Eastern Time Zone.

TEMPERATURE

South Carolina's climate is generally mild and humid. The average temperature varies substantially across the state. During the winter months, the average temperature ranges from the mid-30s in the mountains to approximately 50° F near the southern coast. Summer average temperatures range from the low 70s to mid 80s. Rainfall varies across the state with the heaviest rain occurring in the northwest and the least rain falling in the central part of the state. Hurricane season annually runs from June through early November with peak activity occurring in August and September.

TRAVEL & TOURISM INFO

State Agency:
South Carolina Deptartment of Parks, Recreation & Tourism
1205 Pendleton St.
Columbia, SC 29201
(803/734-1700)
www.discoversouthcarolina.com

Regional Agencies:
Discover Upcountry Carolina Assn.
PO Box 3116
Greenville, SC 29601
(800/849-4766 or 864/233-2690)
www.TheUpcountry.com

Capital City/Lake Murray Country Tourism Region & Visitor Center
2184 N. Lake Dr.
Columbia, SC 29210
(866/725-3935 or 803/781-5940)
http://lakemurraycountry.com/

Lowcountry Visitors Center & Museum
PO Box 615
Yemassee, SC 29945
(800/528-6870 or 843/717-3090)
www.southcarolinalowcountry.com

Old 96 District Tourism Commission
204 E. Public Square
Laurens, SC 29360
(800/849-9633)
www.sctravelold96.com

Olde English District Tourism Commission
116 Gadsden Street
Chester, SC 29706

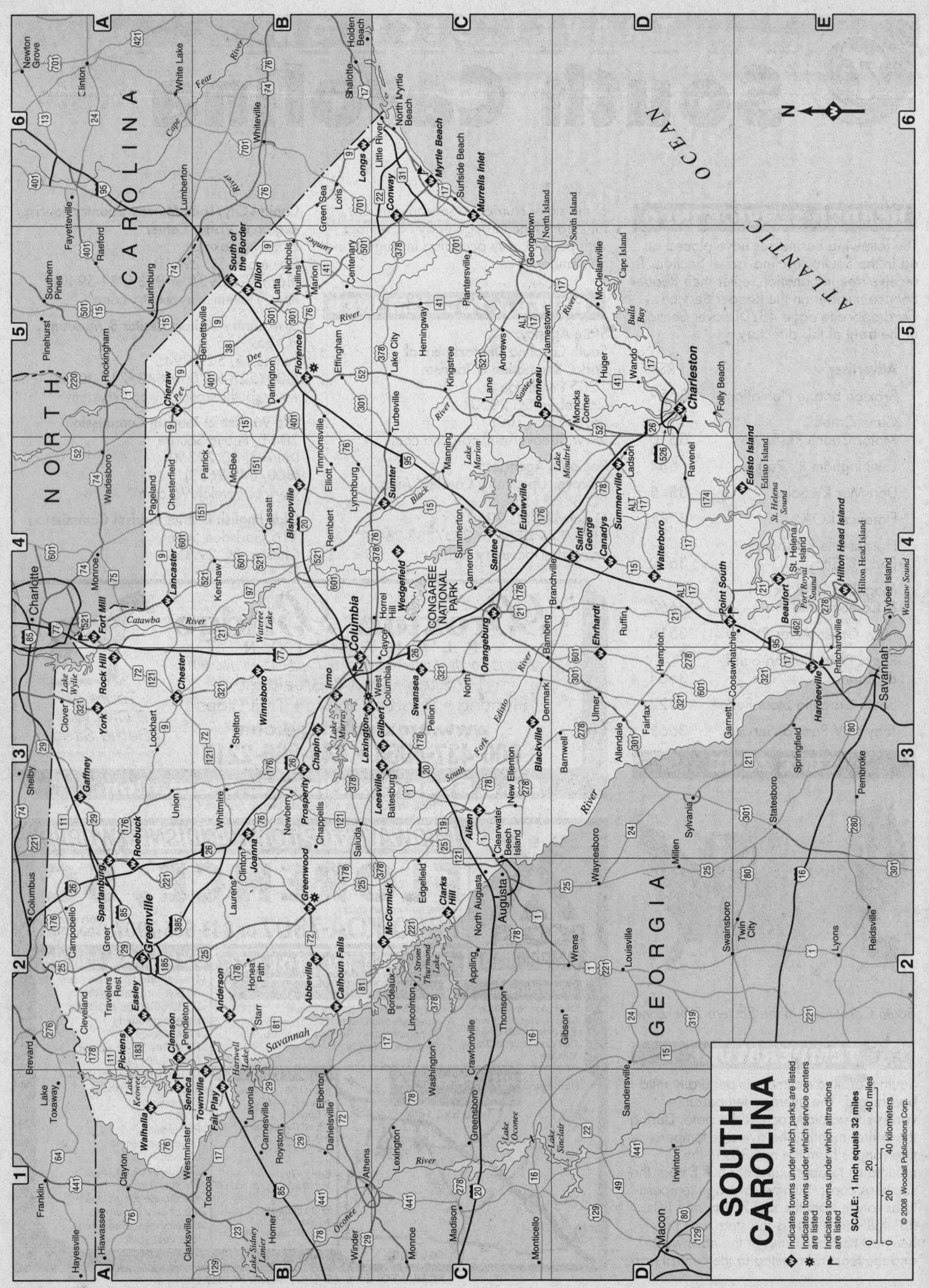
SOUTH CAROLINA
Indicates towns under which parks are listed
Indicates towns under which service centers are listed
Indicates towns under which attractions are listed
SCALE: 1 inch equals 32 miles
0 20 40 miles
0 20 40 kilometers
© 2008 Woodall Publications Corp.
NORTH CAROLINA
GEORGIA
ATLANTIC OCEAN

(800/968-5909 or 803/385-6800)
www.sctravel.net

Pee Dee Tourism Commission
3290 Radio Dr.
Florence, SC 29501
(800/325-9005 or 843/669-0950)
www.peedeetourism.com

Pendleton District Historical Recreational & Tourism Commission
125 East Queen St.
Pendleton, SC 29670
(800/862-1795 or 864/646-3782)
www.pendleton-district.org

Santee Cooper Counties Promotion Commission and Visitor Center
(800/227-8510 or 803/854-2131)
www.santeecoopercountry.org

Thoroughbred Country
PO Box 850
2748 Wagener Rd.
Aiken, SC 29802
(888/834-1654 or 803/649-7981)
www.tbredcountry.org

Local Agencies:
Charleston Area CVB
423 King St.
Charleston, SC 29403
(843/853-8000)
www.charlestoncvb.com

Clarendon Co. Chamber of Commerce
19 N. Brooks St.
Manning, SC 29102
(803/435-4405 or 800/731-5253)
www.clarendoncounty.com

Columbia Metropolitan CVB
1101 Lincoln St.
Columbia, SC 29201
(800/264-4884 or 803/545-0000)
www.columbiacvb.com

Edisto Chamber of Commerce
PO Box 206
Edisto Island, SC 29438
(843/869-3867 or 888/333-2781)
www.edistochamber.com

Hilton Head Island-Bluffton Chamber of Commerce & Visitor and Convention Center
1 Chamber Dr.
Hilton Head, SC 29938
(800/523-3373 or 843/785-3673)
www.hiltonheadisland.org

Kershaw County Chamber of Commerce Visitor Center
607 S. Broad St.
Camden, SC 29020
(800/968-4037 or 803/432-2525)
www.camden-sc.org

Lancaster County Chamber of Commerce
604 N. Main St.
Lancaster, SC 29721
(803/283-4105)
www.lancasterchambersc.org

Myrtle Beach Area
Chamber of Commerce & Visitor Center
1200 N. Oak St.
Myrtle Beach, SC 29577
(843/626-7444 or 800/356-3016)
www.myrtlebeachinfo.com

North Myrtle Beach Area
Chamber of Commerce & CVB
270 Hwy 17 N.
North Myrtle Beach, SC 29582
(877/332-2662 or 843/281-2662)
www.northmyrtlebeachchamber.com

Sumter Convention & Visitors Bureau
21 N. Main St.
Sumter, SC 29150
(803/436-2500)
www.sumter-sc.com

RECREATIONAL INFO

Arts & Culture: SC Arts Commission, 1800 Gervais St., Columbia, SC 29201 (803/734-8696). www.state.sc.us/arts

Fishing & Hunting: South Carolina Dept. of Natural Resources, Rembert C. Dennis Bldg., 100 Assembly St., Columbia, SC 29201 (803/734-3833).
www.dnr.state.sc.us

History: SC Dept. of Archives & History, 8301 Parklane Rd., Columbia, SC 29223 (803/896-6100).
Web: www.state.sc.us/scdah

SHOPPING

Barefoot Landing, North Myrtle Beach. Reminiscent of an old fishing village, over 100 shops and waterfront restaurants surround a 27-acre lake. On Hwy 17 S.

Broadway at the Beach, Myrtle Beach. A 350-acre shopping and dining complex features over 100 specialty shops. 1325 Celebrity Circle.

Catawba Cultural Center, Rock Hill. Features the distinctive Catawba pottery. 1536 Tom Stevens Rd.

The Old City Market, Charleston. Built in 1841, it features several small shops, restaurants and a flea market, offering everything from produce to antiques. Located on Market St., between Meeting and E Bay St.

Pee Dee State Farmers Market, Florence. This 55-acre site is home to a vast variety of plants and flowers, fresh fruits and vegetables, homemade goods and garden accessories.

South Carolina Artisans Center, Walterboro. Declared "The Official Folk Art and Craft Center for South Carolina" by the South Carolina Legislature. Representing the work of over 200 of the state's finest artists... blown and formed glass, sweetgrass baskets, furniture, carvings, pottery, jewelry, quilts, tatting, whimsical folk art, metalwork and much more. The center also offers a yearlong series of craft demonstrations on site. Located at 344 Wichman Street in Walterboro, SC. (843/549-0011)

State Farmers Market, Columbia. One of the largest produce markets in the Southeast receives truckloads of fresh fruits and vegetables daily in addition to perennial and annual flowers and plants. 1001 Bluff Rd.

DESTINATIONS

DISCOVER UPCOUNTRY REGION
This area in the far northwest section of the state is the most economically and geographically diverse area with foothills and the rugged mountains of the Blue Ridge.

Bob Jones University Museum & Gallery, Greenville, contains 30 galleries of art, tapestries, furniture, sculpture and architectural motifs from 5 centuries.

Chattooga National Wild & Scenic River. Forming 40 miles of the South Carolina/Georgia border, this famous whitewater paddling spot was featured in the movie *Deliverance*.

Greenville County Museum of Art, Greenville, contains works of art with a southern accent. See Andrew Wyeth pieces along with contemporary collections from artists such as Georgia O'Keefe and Andy Warhol.

Hollywild Animal Park in Inman is home to over 500 animals, many of which roam freely inside large natural enclosures or on man-made islands. The Outback Safari takes visitors through 80 acres of free-roaming animals.

The Peachoid is the best known, most photographed water tank in the U.S., painted to match the kind of peaches grown in Cherokee County. Along I-85 near Gaffney.

Pendleton Village Green is one of the largest historic districts in the nation featuring shops, restaurants and 19th century restored buildings.

Poinsett Bridge is the oldest intact bridge in South Carolina. Built in 1820, it is a 14-foot Gothic arch stone bridge and spans the Little Gap Creek.

SC Botanical Garden, Clemson features a unique collection of 12 nature-based sculptures. Also includes "niche gardens," a 70-acre arboretum, the **Bob Campbell Geology Museum** and the ca.1716 French Huguenot Hanover House.

Whitewater Falls is the highest series of falls in eastern North America with the Lower Falls having a 200-foot drop. Six different waterfalls along the NC/SC border comprise the chain. Off SC 130 at Duke Power's Bad Creek Hydroelectric Station.

OLDE ENGLISH DISTRICT

Andrew Jackson State Park, located north of Lancaster. On-site are a museum, one-room school, fishing, nature trail and year-round interpretive programs.

Carolina Sandhills National Wildlife Refuge, McBee. See a diverse species of flora and fauna from observation towers, biking trails or by car in this 45,000 acre national wildlife refuge.

Cheraw Historic District & Town Green. Laid out in 1768, more than 50 antebellum buildings and numerous Victorian and classical revival homes line the streets. The **Cheraw Museum and History Company** is part museum, part antique shop.

Museum of York County. Visit more than 200 animal exhibits from seven continents. This museum also houses Native American artifacts that mirror the heritage of the first Carolinians. A planetarium, three art galleries and a nature trail are also on-site.

Paramount's Carowinds, Fort Mill. Theme park with more than 50 rides; a water park and high-speed roller coaster highlight the park.

Rose Hill Plantation State Historic Site, Union. Home of SC's "Secession Governor," William H. Gist, the site offers a look at antebellum SC with a restored mansion, period furnishing and beautiful grounds.

PEE DEE COUNTRY

Florence. This bustling city began with the railroad in the 1880s. Located just west of the Pee Dee River, you'll find:

Pee Dee State Farmer's Market. Fresh fruits and veggies, flowers, hanging baskets and homemade goods are displayed Monday through Saturday.

Florence Museum of Art, Science & History. Changing art exhibits, regional history, Asian, African, ancient Mediterranean and southwest Pueblo cultures are featured.

Fryar's Topiary Garden, Bishopville. Three acres of meticulously sculpted plants include graceful arches, spirals, geometrics and fantasies.

SC Cotton Museum, Bishopville. Explore the state's cotton culture through interactive exhibits, stories, original tools and interpretive center.

OLD 96 DISTRICT

Old 96 is an area of living history, friendly towns, retirement communities, open country, deep woodlands and wide water. Area attractions include:

Burt-Stark Mansion, Abbeville. Built in the 1830s, this Greek Revival house was the site of the first reading of the secession papers, giving birth to the Confederacy. Contains family antiques.

Sumter National Forest. Explore over 118,000 acres of woodland wonderland filled with wildlife and recreation areas. Enjoy hiking, camping, picnicking and fishing.

CAPITAL CITY & LAKE MURRAY COUNTRY

Columbia. The capital city offers a multitude of activities and places of interest.

Columbia Museum of Art features collections of European and American fine and decorative art including masterpieces from the Italian Renaissance.

EdVenture, a children's museum, features a theater, library, two resource centers and eight galleries and contains 450 high-tech hands-on exhibits.

South Carolina State House. Bronze stars signify where General Sherman's army fired on the 145-year-old facility.

South Carolina State Museum. Visit four floors representing various fields of interest such as art, natural history, technology and science. There are hands-on exhibits about pioneering South Carolina inventors.

Lake Murray, just west of Columbia. A 50,000-acre impoundment, located just west of the metro-Columbia area, it has 520 miles of scenic shoreline, a host of marinas and campgrounds, excellent fishing and abundant water recreation.

Riverbanks Zoo and Botanical Garden, Riverbanks. This 170-acre park features 2,000 animals, a microcosmic rainforest, a desert, an undersea kingdom, a south-

ern farm, an aquarium/reptile complex and a botanical garden. The Ndoki Forest is Riverbank's new home for elephants, meerkats and gorillas. Also included are historic ruins, plant collections and 70 acres of woodland gardens.

THOROUGHBRED COUNTRY

Allendale County Art Gallery & Museum. Visit displays of Native American artifacts, war memorabilia and natural history exhibits. There are also ever-changing exhibits of arts and crafts.

Aiken. Aiken is unique in that the city is home to over 150 different species of trees that make up its Citywide Arboretum, which is spread over 176 parkways covering 15 miles in length. **Hitchcock Woods**, the largest urban forest in the U.S., offers peace and beauty in the midst of an urban area. To explore the city, take a 2-hour trolley tour that will take you past its many historic homes, churches, Civil War sites and more. **DuPont Planetarium,** located at the campus of USC-Aiken, the 45-seat theater has a 30-foot diameter tilted dome with a projector system that displays more than 9,000 stars. Other Aiken attractions include:

Hopelands Gardens is a 14 acre estate opened in 1969 as a public garden. Paths shaded by 100-year-old oaks, deodar cedars and magnolias curve through the gardens. Within the gardens is the **Thoroughbred Racing Hall of Fame & Museum**. Horses trained in Aiken who have gone on to become National Champions are enshrined in the Hall of Fame. Visitors may view trophies and photographs from the careers of some of America's best known equestrian riders, polo players and steeplechase riders. Adjacent to the property is **The Wetlands** featuring a floating boardwalk and a tranquil marshland setting.

SANTEE COOPER COUNTRY

Cypress Gardens, Moncks Corner. You can tour this 175-acre swamp garden on foot or in the famous beateaus (flat-bottomed boats). Features include a butterfly house, freshwater aquarium and reptile center.

Edisto Memorial Gardens & Horne Wetlands Park, Orangeburg. The north fork of the Edisto River winds through colorful and graceful gardens. Within the gardens, the Wetlands Park features an extensive boardwalk for viewing wetland wildlife. Adjacent to the gardens is the **Orangeburg Arts Center** with a gallery on the second floor.

Fort Watson, sight where a British outpost was located atop a 30-foot Indian ceremonial mound. Off US 301-15 at Santee Wildlife Refuge.

I.P. StaNBAck Museum & Planetarium, Orangeburg. The planetarium features Sky-Skan Automation and the NASA Educator Resource Center. An art museum offers African and African-American works.

Sumter. Swan Lake Iris Gardens surrounds the black waters of Swan Lake, where all eight known species of the world's swans swim.

MYRTLE BEACH AREA/ THE GRAND STRAND

The Grand Strand is a 60-mile stretch of white sandy beaches along the Atlantic Coast. Popular beaches include **Myrtle Beach, Huntington Beach State Park, Surfside Beach, Garden City, Litchfield Beach** and **Cherry Grove Beach**. Golfers thrill to over 100 championship courses, while anglers cast their lines into abundant fishing waters.

Georgetown. This first settlement in North America failed in 1526, but is now a thriving community with several marinas on the Intracoastal Waterway and the **Harborwalk**, an array of restaurants and shops. Sixteen blocks of the downtown area are listed on the National Historic Register.

Myrtle Beach. This is a camper's paradise for golf, beaches, shows, fishing and plantations. Attractions in Myrtle Beach include **NASCAR Speedpark**—a racing-theme park with seven race tracks, miniature golf and a 12,000-sq. ft. SpeedDome that features interactive arcade games and other racing memorabilia. See some of the most feared and fascinating members of the reptile world at **Alligator Adventure.** Visit **Ripley's Aquarium**, where you'll see an extensive aquatic collection in a unique way. Travel the aquarium's *Dangerous Reef* tunnel on a moving glide path surrounded on all sides by sharks up to 10 feet long. The Ripley complex also includes **Ripley's Believe It or Not! Museum** of the weird, incredible, rare and unbelievable in 12 galleries; **Ripley's Haunted Adventure** with high-tech animations and special effects; **Ripley's 4-D Moving Theater**, a movie that you actually ride featuring a digital 6-channel surround-sound system and giant 70mm films. The **Myrtle Beach Pavilion Amusement Park** is an 11-acre playground with a category 5 Hurricane roller coaster, an antique Herschel-Spillman Merry-Go-Round, 4-D Adventure Theater and a giant 1900 German Pipe Organ. See over 100 species of animals at the 500-acre **Waccatee Zoological Farm** which includes a wildlife sanctuary and breeding ground for several species of migratory birds and alligators.

LOWCOUNTRY & RESORT BEACHES REGION

Barrier Sea Islands is a string of barrier sea islands south of Charleston where modern resorts have been carved out of semi-tropical thickets. Golf, play tennis, beachcomb, boat, swim and camp in this peaceful environment. Major islands include **Seabrook, Kiawah, Edisto, Daufuskie, Hunting, Fripp** and **Hilton Head**.

Hilton Head Island. The **Coastal Discovery Museum** combines hands-on exhibits in coastal history and nature at its main location, with 15 different tours and cruises at various locations.

Lowcountry Visitors Center & Museum, Yemassee, features a re-created plantation parlor and displays from the region's 10 museums and the SC Artisans Center.

Parris Island Museum, Parris Island, focuses on the history of the island with exhibits that cover archaeology, Native Americans and 16th-century French and Spanish settlements.

Woodall's Quick & Easy Reference for South Carolina

	BIG RIGS WELCOME	INTERNET FRIENDLY	PETS WELCOME	WEB SAVER
AIKEN				
Pine Acres Campground	▲	●	■	
ANDERSON				
Lake Hartwell Camping & Cabins		●	■	
Tiger Cove Campground			■	
CHARLESTON				
Campground at James Island County Park	▲		■	$
KOA-Charleston	▲	●	■	
Lake Aire RV Park and Campground	▲	●	■	
Mt. Pleasant/Charleston KOA	▲	●	■	
Oak Plantation Campground	▲	●	■	
COLUMBIA				
Barnyard RV Park	▲	●	■	
CONWAY				
Big Cypress Lake RV Park & Fishing Retreat	▲	●	■	
EHRHARDT				
Broxton Bridge Plantation			■	
EUTAWVILLE				
Rocks Pond Campground & Marina	▲	●	■	$
FLORENCE				
Florence KOA	▲	●	■	
Swamp Fox Camping			■	
FORT MILL				
Charlotte/Fort Mill KOA	▲	●	■	
GREENVILLE				
Rainbow RV Park			■	
Springwood RV Park	▲	●	■	
HARDEEVILLE				
Hardeeville RV-Thomas' Parks and Sites	▲	●	■	
HILTON HEAD ISLAND				
Hilton Head Harbor RV Resort & Marina	▲	●	■	
Hilton Head Island Motor Coach Resort	▲	●	■	$
IRMO				
Woodsmoke Campground		●	■	
JOANNA				
Magnolia RV Park & Campground	▲	●	■	
LONGS				
WillowTree Resort	▲	●	■	
MYRTLE BEACH				
Apache Family Campground	▲	●	■	
KOA-Myrtle Beach	▲	●	■	
Lakewood Camping Resort	▲	●	■	$
Myrtle Beach Travel Park	▲	●	■	
Ocean Lakes Family Campground	▲	●	■	$
Pirateland Family Camping Resort	▲	●	■	$
POINT SOUTH				
KOA-Point South	▲	●	■	
ROEBUCK				
Pine Ridge Campground	▲	●	■	
SENECA				
Crooked Creek RV Park	▲	●	■	
SOUTH OF THE BORDER				
Camp Pedro			■	
SPARTANBURG				
Cunningham RV Park	▲	●	■	
SWANSEA				
River Bottom Farms Campground & R.V. Resort	▲	●	■	
WALTERBORO				
New Green Acres R.V. Park	▲	●	■	$

▲ = Big Rigs Welcome; ● = Internet Hookups; ● = (Wi-Fi available); ■ = Pets Welcome; $ = Web Saver Coupons

**Check out the "How to Use This Directory" section in the front of this book for a description of the criteria Woodall's uses in this chart.*

Photo courtesy South Carolina Department of Parks, Recreation and Tourism

HISTORIC CHARLESTON

Charleston. This aristocratic and historic port city offers privately guided or self-guided tours (using audio cassettes). Or, take a guided tour by horse-drawn carriage. Popular attractions in the area include Middleton Place House & Gardens, South Carolina Aquarium and The Old Exchange & Provost Dungeon. View the shoreline and estuaries from the vantage point of a shoreline cruise or charter boat which abound in the area. A newly constructed "historic home" at Charles Towne Landing is a living history exhibit that focuses on the struggles and contributions of indentured servants in early Charles Towne. The Charleston Museum, America's first (1773), contains everything from ancient fossils to a whale skeleton, costumes, crafts and exhibits, notably a major Civil War exhibit.

Johns Island. More than 1,400 years old, the **Angel Oak** is more than 65 feet high with a circumference of 25.5 feet. It is one of the largest living oak trees in the world.

Churches. There are a great many churches of historical interest and beauty in Charleston, including Emmanuel African Methodist Episcopal Church, First Baptist Church, French Huguenot Church, Old St. Andrew's Parish Church and First (Scots) Presbyterian Church.

Things to See & Do

CHARLESTON
Splash Zone Waterpark

COLUMBIA
Barnyard Flea Market
South Carolina State Parks

FORT MILL
Campground Massacre Haunted Attraction

HARDEEVILLE
The Pink Pig

MYRTLE BEACH
Myrtle Beach Campground Association

POINT SOUTH
KOA-Point South Carry Out Pizza
Swimming Mermaid Coffee House

SENECA
Crooked Creek Pizza Shoppe & Snack Bar

SOUTH OF THE BORDER
South of the Border

ANNUAL EVENTS

JANUARY

Winter Carnival, Hilton Head; Lowcountry Oyster Festival, Charleston.

FEBRUARY

Camellia Walks, Charleston.

MARCH

Springfest, St. Patrick's Day Parade, Hilton Head Island; Craftsmen's Classic Arts and Crafts Festival, Capital City; Triple Crown Street Fair, Aiken; Winefest, Hilton Head Island; Scottish Country Fair, Sumter; Georgetown Plantation Tours, Georgetown.

APRIL

Historic Spring Jubilee, Pendleton; Lowcountry Cajun Festival, Charleston; Southern Plant & Flower Festival, Columbia; Flowertown Festival, Summerville; Come-See-Me Festival, Rock Hill; International Festival, Clemson; Governor's Frog Jump Festival, Springfield; Tartan Fest, Columbia; Old Towne Artisan's Fair, North Augusta.

MAY

Art in the Park, Myrtle Beach; Hell Hole Swamp Festival, Jamestown; Fest-I-Fun, Fort Mill; Fox Trot Festival, Marion; Blue Crab Festival, Little River; Iris Festival, Sumter; Summer Concert Series (through Aug.), Aiken; Farmers Market (through Nov.), Aiken.

JUNE

Harbourfest, Hilton Head Island; Mighty Moo Festival, Cowpens; Art in the Park, Myrtle Beach.

JULY

Jammin' in July, Camden; Pageland Watermelon Festival, Pageland.

AUGUST

Gold Rush Festival, McCormick; Rice Walks, Charleston; Summerfest, York.

SEPTEMBER

Upcountry Folklife Festival, Pickens; Food Festival, Hilton Head Island; Fire Fest, Camden.

OCTOBER

SC State Fair, Columbia; Oktoberfest, Walhalla; Annual Antiques Show, Greenville; Halloween Hoopla, Aiken; Sweet Potato Festival, Langley; Beaufort Shrimp Festival, Beaufort; Apple Harvest Festival, York.

NOVEMBER

Revolutionary War Field Days, Camden; Plantation Days, Charleston; Society Hill Catfish Festival, Hartsville.

DECEMBER

Historic Christmas Open House, Irmo; Colonial Christmas, Camden; Holly Days in Aiken, Aiken.

RV Sales & Service

	SALES	SERVICE
FLORENCE		
Don Mar RV Sales	•	•
GREENWOOD		
Jody's RV	•	•
LEXINGTON		
Tony's RV Parts & Service	•	•

South Carolina

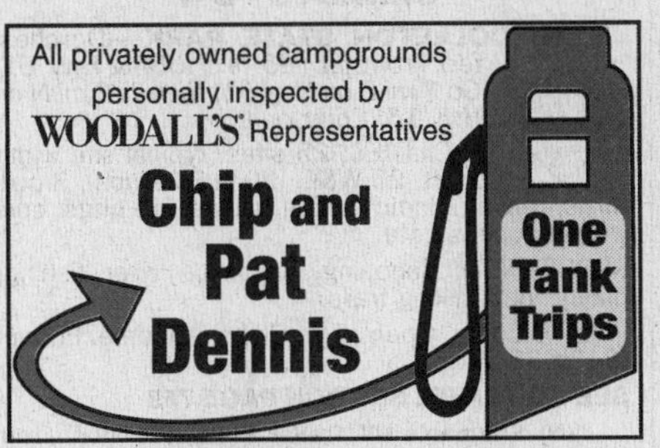

ABBEVILLE—B-2

(S) SUMTER NATIONAL FOREST (Parson's Mountain Lake Campground)—(Abbiville) *From town: Go 2 mi S on Hwy 28, then 1-1/2 mi E on FR SI-257.* FACILITIES: 23 sites, 22 ft max RV length, 23 no hkups, tenting, dump station, fire rings, grills, wood. RECREATION: lake swimming, boating, no motors, ramp, lake fishing, hiking trails. Partial handicap access. Open Apr 1 thru Dec 31. Phone: (803)637-5247.

AIKEN—C-3

(E) AIKEN STATE NATURAL AREA—(Aiken) *From jct Hwy 19 & US 78: Go 16 mi E on US 78, then 7 mi N on CR 53. Enter on R.*

WELCOME

FACILITIES: 25 sites, 35 ft max RV length, 25 W&E, 2 pull-thrus, tenting, dump station, tables, fire rings, controlled access gate.

RECREATION: boating, canoeing, kayaking, rowboat/canoe rentals, lake/river/pond fishing, hiking trails.

Pets welcome. Open all yr. Clubs welcome. Phone: (803)649-2857.

SEE AD TRAVEL SECTION PAGE 759

(S) Crossroads RV Park & Mobile Home Community (RV SPACES)—(Aiken) *From jct I-20 (exit 18) & Hwy 19: Go 11-3/10 mi S on Hwy 19, then 1-2/10 mi E on Talatha Church Rd. Enter on L.* FACILITIES: 22 sites, typical site width 37 ft, accepts full hkup units only, 22 full hkups, (20, 30 & 50 amps), 50 amps ($), many extended stay sites, laundry, patios. RECREATION: play equipment. Pets welcome. No tents. Open all yr. No restrooms. Reservations required. Big rigs welcome. Rate in 2007 $25-27 per vehicle. Phone: (803) 642-5702.

(NE) PINE ACRES CAMPGROUND (REBUILDING)—(Aiken) *From jct I-20 (exit 22) & US 1: Go 4-3/4 mi S on US 1. Enter on L.*

WELCOME

FACILITIES: 40 sites, typical site width 30 ft, 40 full hkups, (30 & 50 amps), some extended stay sites, 22 pull-thrus, cable TV, wireless Instant Internet access at site, phone on-site Internet access (needs activ), tenting, RV/park trailer rentals, dump station, non-guest dumping $, laundry, LP gas by weight/by meter, ice, tables, patios.

Pets welcome. Open all yr. Big rigs welcome. Internet friendly. Rate in 2007 $30 for 2 persons. MC/VISA/DISC/AMEX/Debit. Phone: (803)648-5715. CCUSA discount.

e-mail: pineacres@gforcecable.com

SEE AD THIS PAGE

ANDERSON—B-2

(NW) Anderson/Lake Hartwell KOA—(Anderson) *From jct I-85 (Exit 11) & Hwy 24: Go 3 mi E on I-85 (exit 14), then 1 mi SE on Hwy 187. Enter on L.* ◆◆◆FACILITIES: 86 sites, typical site width 35 ft, 49 full hkups, 33 W&E, (20, 30 & 50 amps), 50 amps ($), 4 no hkups, some extended stay sites, 65 pull-thrus, tenting, dump station, non-guest dumping $, laundry, ltd groceries, LP gas by weight/by meter, ice, tables, fire rings, grills, wood. ◆◆RECREATION: rec room/area, pavilion, swim pool, mini-golf ($), playground, horseshoes. Rec open to public. Pets welcome. Partial handicap access. Open all yr. Member ARVC, CARVC. Phone: (864)287-3161. KOA 10% value card discount.

ANDERSON—Continued on next page

ANDERSON—Continued

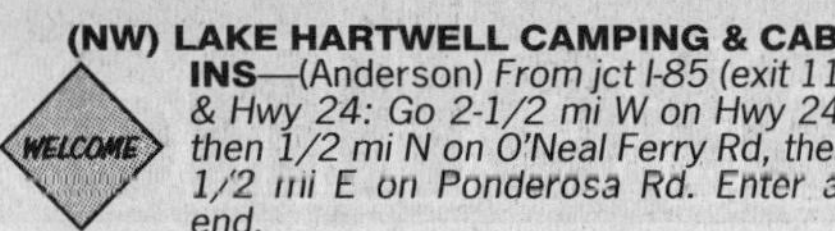

(NW) LAKE HARTWELL CAMPING & CABINS—(Anderson) *From jct I-85 (exit 11) & Hwy 24: Go 2-1/2 mi W on Hwy 24, then 1/2 mi N on O'Neal Ferry Rd, then 1/2 mi E on Ponderosa Rd. Enter at end.*

◆◆◆FACILITIES: 120 sites, typical site width 35 ft, 62 full hkups, 58 W&E, (20, 30 & 50 amps), some extended stay sites, 45 pull-thrus, wireless Instant Internet access at site, phone Internet access central location, tenting, RV/park trailer rentals, cabins, RV storage, dump station, non-guest dumping $, laundry, ltd groceries, RV supplies, LP gas by weight/by meter, ice, tables, fire rings, grills, wood.

◆◆◆◆RECREATION: rec hall, rec room/area, pavilion, coin games, swim pool, wading pool, boating, canoeing, kayaking, ramp, dock, 2 pontoon/6 canoe/2 motorboat rentals, lake fishing, fishing guides, mini-golf, bsktball, playground, tennis, horseshoes, hiking trails, v-ball. Rec open to public.

Pets welcome. Open all yr. Internet friendly. Clubs welcome. Rate in 2007 $22-30 for 4 persons. MC/VISA/DISC/AMEX. Phone: (888)427-8935. FMCA discount.

e-mail: info@camplakehartwell.com

SEE AD PAGE 765

(SW) SADLERS CREEK STATE RECREATION PARK—(Anderson) *From jct I-85 (exit 14) and Hwy 187: Go 14 mi S on Hwy 187, then 1 mi W on Sadlers Creek Rd.*

FACILITIES: 47 sites, typical site width 30 ft, 37 W&E, (20 & 30 amps), 10 no hkups, 8 pull-thrus, tenting, dump station, tables, controlled access gate.

RECREATION: pavilion, boating, ramp, lake fishing, playground, hiking trails.

Pets welcome. Open all yr. Clubs welcome. Phone: (864)226-8950.

SEE AD TRAVEL SECTION PAGE 759

(S) SPRINGFIELD CAMPGROUND (COE-Hartwell Lake) —(Anderson) *From jct I-85 (exit 14) & Hwy 187: Go 1-1/4 mi S on Hwy 187, then 2-3/4 mi E on Hwy 187/24, then 4-1/4 mi S on Hwy 187, then 2 mi W on Providence Ch Rd.* FACILITIES: 79 sites, 79 W&E, (50 amps), 31 pull-thrus, tenting, dump station, fire rings, grills. RECREATION: lake swimming, boating, ramp, lake fishing, playground. Open Apr 1 thru Sep 27. Phone: (888) 893-0678.

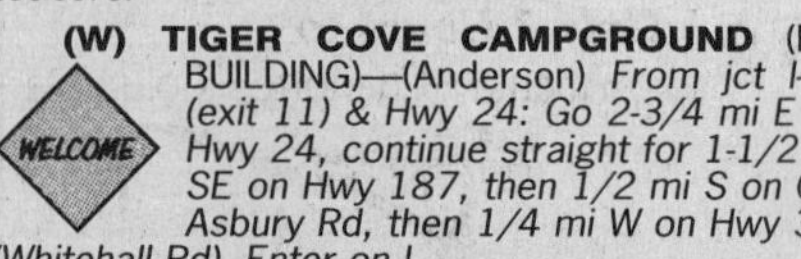

(W) TIGER COVE CAMPGROUND (REBUILDING)—(Anderson) *From jct I-85 (exit 11) & Hwy 24: Go 2-3/4 mi E on Hwy 24, continue straight for 1-1/2 mi SE on Hwy 187, then 1/2 mi S on Old Asbury Rd, then 1/4 mi W on Hwy 34, (Whitehall Rd). Enter on L.*

FACILITIES: 30 sites, 13 full hkups, 17 W&E, some extended stay sites, tenting, cabins, dump station, non-guest dumping $, tables, fire rings, wood.

RECREATION: lake swimming, canoeing, dock, 2 canoe rentals, lake fishing.

Pets welcome. Open all yr. Rate in 2007 $24-35 for 4 persons. MC/VISA. Member ARVC, CARVC. Phone: (864)225-5993.

e-mail: tigercovecampgrd@bellsouth.net

SEE AD PAGE 765

South Carolina State Bird: Carolina Wren

BEAUFORT—E-4

HUNTING ISLAND STATE PARK—(Beaufort) *From jct Hwy 170 & US 21: Go 16 mi SE on US 21.*

FACILITIES: 183 sites, typical site width 30 ft, 173 W&E, 10 no hkups, 43 pull-thrus, tenting, cabins, dump station, ltd groceries, ice, tables, controlled access gate.

RECREATION: saltwater swimming, boating, kayaking, ramp, dock, saltwater fishing, planned activities, hiking trails.

Pets welcome. Open all yr. MC/VISA. Phone: (843) 838-2011.

SEE AD TRAVEL SECTION PAGE 759

(E) Tuck In The Wood Campground—(Beaufort) *From jct Hwy 170 & US 21: Go 12 mi SE on US 21, then 2-1/4 mi W on Martin L King/Lands End Rd. Enter on L.* ◆◆◆FACILITIES: 74 sites, typical site width 30 ft, 65 full hkups, 9 W&E, (20, 30 & 50 amps), 50 amps ($), many extended stay sites, 11 pull-thrus, tenting, dump station, non-guest dumping $, laundry, ice, tables, wood. ◆◆RECREATION: equipped pavilion, pond fishing, playground, hiking trails, v-ball. Pets welcome. Partial handicap access. Open all yr. Rate in 2007 $22-25 for 6 persons. Phone: (843)838-2267.

BISHOPVILLE—B-4

(SE) LEE STATE NATURAL AREA—(Lee) *From jct I-20 & Hwy-341: Go 3 mi E on I-20, then 1-1/2 mi N on S-22.*

FACILITIES: 25 sites, typical site width 30 ft, 36 ft max RV length, 25 W&E, (20 & 30 amps), 11 pull-thrus, tenting, dump station, tables, controlled access gate.

RECREATION: river fishing, hiking trails.

Pets welcome. Partial handicap access. Open all yr. Clubs welcome. Phone: (803)428-5307.

SEE AD TRAVEL SECTION PAGE 759

BLACKVILLE—C-3

(SW) BARNWELL STATE PARK—(Barnwell) *From jct US 78 & Hwy 3: Go 2 mi S on Hwy 3.*

FACILITIES: 25 sites, 36 ft max RV length, 25 W&E, (20 & 30 amps), tenting, cabins, dump station, tables, controlled access gate.

RECREATION: rowboat rentals, lake fishing, playground, hiking trails.

Pets welcome. Open all yr. Clubs welcome. Phone: (803)284-2212.

SEE AD TRAVEL SECTION PAGE 759

BONNEAU—C-5

MILITARY PARK (Short Stay Rec Area-Charleston Naval Sta.)—(Berkeley) *Off base, 35 mi N of Charleston Naval Base. Located W of Bonneau, off US 52, on Lake Moultrie.* FACILITIES: 108 sites, 83 W&E, 25 no hkups, tenting, dump station, groceries, fire rings. RECREATION: rec room/area, pavilion, lake swimming, boating, pedal boat/motorboat rentals, lake fishing, mini-golf ($), playground. Open all yr. For Military Use Only- w/ Military ID Card. Phone: (800)447-2178.

CALHOUN FALLS—B-2

(N) CALHOUN FALLS STATE RECREATION AREA—(Abbeville) *From town: Go 1/2 mi N on Hwy 81. Enter on L.*

FACILITIES: 100 sites, 86 W&E, (20 & 30 amps), 14 no hkups, 31 pull-thrus, tenting, dump station, ltd groceries, marine gas, tables, fire rings, controlled access gate.

CALHOUN FALLS—Continued
CALHOUN FALLS STATE RECREATION AREA—Continued

RECREATION: rec hall, pavilion, lake swimming, boating, ramp, dock, rowboat rentals, lake fishing, bsktball, playground, tennis, hiking trails.

Pets welcome. Open all yr. MC/VISA. Phone: (864) 447-8267.

SEE AD TRAVEL SECTION PAGE 759

CANADYS—D-4

(N) COLLETON STATE PARK—(Dorchester) *From jct I-95 (exit 68) & Hwy 61: Go 3 mi E on Hwy 61, then 1/2 mi N on Hwy 15. Enter on L.*

FACILITIES: 25 sites, typical site width 20 ft, 25 W&E, (20 & 30 amps), 3 pull-thrus, tenting, dump station, tables, fire rings, controlled access gate.

RECREATION: canoeing, kayaking, river fishing, playground, hiking trails.

Pets welcome. Open all yr. Clubs welcome. Phone: (843)538-8206.

SEE AD TRAVEL SECTION PAGE 759

(N) Shuman's RV Trailer Park—(Colleton) *From I-95 (exit 68) & Hwy 61: Go 2-3/4 mi E on Hwy 61, then 1/4 mi N on Hwy 15. Enter on R.* ◆◆FACILITIES: 20 sites, typical site width 20 ft, accepts full hkup units only, 20 full hkups, (20, 30 & 50 amps), 50 amps ($), some extended stay sites, 11 pull-thrus, dump station, non-guest dumping $, LP gas by meter, tables, wood. Pets welcome. No tents. Open all yr. No restrooms. Rate in 2007 $14 per vehicle. Phone: (888)533-8731.

CHAPIN—B-3

(SW) DREHER ISLAND STATE RECREATION AREA—(Newberry) *From jct I-26 (exit 91) & Hwy 48: Go W on Hwy 48, then 1/8 mi S on US 76, then 4 mi S on CR 29, then 3 mi S on Hwy 231 (Dreher Isl Rd).*

FACILITIES: 112 sites, typical site width 30 ft, 97 W&E, (20 & 30 amps), 15 no hkups, 7 pull-thrus, tenting, cabins, dump station, ltd groceries, marine gas, tables, fire rings, controlled access gate.

RECREATION: rec hall, boating, ramp, lake fishing, playground, hiking trails.

Pets welcome. Open all yr. MC/VISA. Phone: (803) 364-4152.

SEE AD TRAVEL SECTION PAGE 759

CHARLESTON—D-5

(SW) CAMPGROUND AT JAMES ISLAND COUNTY PARK—(Charleston) *From jct I-26 (exit 221) & US 17: Go 2 mi S on US 17, then 1 mi S on Hwy 171, then 1-1/2 mi W on Hwy 700, then 1-3/4 mi S on Riverland Dr. Enter on R.*

EXPLORE CHARLESTON & THE LOWCOUNTRY
Discover the history, charm, fine dining, antiques, plantations, antebellum homes, parks and sandy beaches. All just minutes from your private retreat can be found within our 643-acre Park's beautiful campground.

FACILITIES: 124 sites, typical site width 25 ft, 118 full hkups, 6 W&E, (20, 30 & 50 amps), 50 amps ($), 11 pull-thrus, phone Internet access central location, tenting, cabins, dump station, non-guest dumping $, laundry, groceries, RV supplies, LP gas by weight/by meter, ice, tables, fire rings, grills, wood, controlled access gate.

RECREATION: rec room/area, pavilion, sprayground, boating, canoeing, kayaking, dock, canoe/8 kayak/16 pedal boat rentals, lake/stream fishing, 75 bike rentals, playground, sports field, hiking trails, v-ball, local tours. Rec open to public.

Pets welcome. Partial handicap access. Open all yr. Big rigs welcome. Clubs welcome. MC/VISA/DISC/AMEX. Phone: (843)795-7275.

e-mail: campground@ccprc.com

SEE AD NEXT PAGE AND AD DISCOVER SECTION PAGE 67

CHARLESTON—Continued on next page

South Carolina Firsts: Site of the First Museum in the U.S.A., Home of the First Real Theater, First Opera and First Symphony Orchestra heard in the U.S.A. were performed in South Carolina.

Woodall's Rated:
Good Sam Park
TL RATED 8.5/9.5★/9
Oak Plantation
CAMPGROUND, LP.

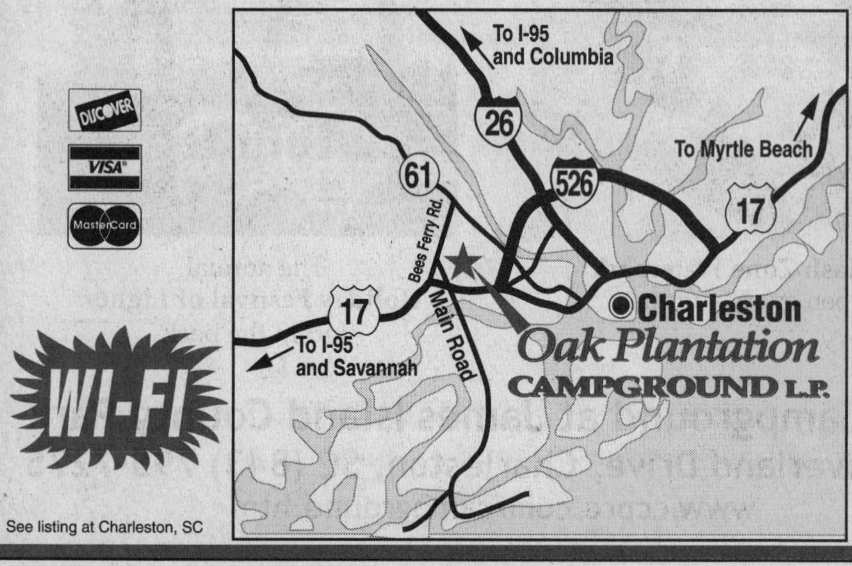

CHARLESTON—Continued

(NW) **KOA-CHARLESTON**—(Charleston) *From jct I-26 (exit 205) & US 78: Go 1 mi W on US 78. Enter on R.*

WELCOME

LOCATION-ENVIRONMENT-AMENITIES

We've got it all! Easy access to I-26 and Charleston's top tourist attractions, like Magnolia Plantation and Drayton Hall! Quiet, shaded camp sites and sunny swimming pool! And, our own resident alligator! Visit us soon!

◊◊◊◊FACILITIES: 150 sites, typical site width 35 ft, 105 full hkups, 45 W&E, (20, 30 & 50 amps), some extended stay sites, 65 pull-thrus, phone Internet access central location, tenting, cabins, RV storage, dump station, non-guest dumping $, laundry, groceries, RV supplies, LP gas by weight/by meter, ice, tables, wood.

◊◊◊RECREATION: rec hall, rec room/area, coin games, swim pool, bsktball, playground, horseshoes, sports field. Rec open to public.

Pets welcome. Partial handicap access. Open all yr. Big rigs welcome. Internet friendly. Clubs welcome. Rate in 2007 $24-27 for 2 persons. MC/VISA/AMEX. Member ARVC, CARVC. Phone: (800)KOA-5812. KOA 10% value card discount.

e-mail: charleston_koa@yahoo.com

SEE AD NEXT PAGE AND AD DISCOVER SECTION PAGES 62 & 63

(W) **LAKE AIRE RV PARK AND CAMPGROUND**—(Charleston) *From jct I-526 & US 17: Go 7-1/2 mi S on US 17, then 1000 feet S on Hwy 162. Enter on L.*

WELCOME

◊◊◊FACILITIES: 113 sites, 66 full hkups, 21 W&E, (20, 30 & 50 amps), 26 no hkups, some extended stay sites, 75 pull-thrus, heater not allowed, wireless Instant Internet access at site, phone Internet access central location, tenting, dump station, laundry, ltd groceries, RV supplies, LP gas by weight/by meter, ice, tables, fire rings, wood.

◊◊◊RECREATION: pavilion, swim pool, boating, electric motors only, canoeing, canoe/pedal boat rentals, lake fishing, bsktball, playground, horseshoes, sports field, hiking trails.

Pets welcome. Partial handicap access. Open all yr. Big rigs welcome. Internet friendly. Clubs welcome. Rate in 2007 $24-29 for 2 persons. MC/VISA/DISC. Phone: (843)571-1271. FMCA discount.

e-mail: lakeairerv@juno.com

SEE AD PAGE 766

MILITARY PARK (Shady Oaks Family Campground-Charleston AFB)—(Charleston) *From I-26 (exit 211-Aviation Ave): Go 1/2 mi W on Aviation Ave, then N on Arthur Rd around the runways, thru the gate to Outdoor Rec. Center. On base.* FACILITIES: 23 sites, 23 W&E, tenting, dump station, laundry, patios, grills. RECREATION: rec hall, pavilion, swim pool, lake/saltwater swimming, boating, canoeing, 14 rowboat/14 canoe rentals, saltwater/lake/river fishing, play equipment, tennis, sports field. Partial handicap access. Open all yr. For Military Use Only- w/ Military ID Card. No reservations. Phone: (803)566-5270.

(NE) **MT. PLEASANT/CHARLESTON KOA**—(Charleston) *From jct I-26 (exit 212C) & I-526: Go 12 mi E on I-526, then 5 mi N on US 17. Enter on R.*

WELCOME

STAY ON AN ANTEBELLUM PLANTATION

Enjoy a beautiful, quiet location on a 30-acre lake with lots of fun things to do. Fish, boat, bike or hike. Play mini-golf or join in other fun activities. And we're close to Charleston for dining, shopping and tours.

◊◊◊◊FACILITIES: 114 sites, typical site width 35 ft, 70 full hkups, 40 W&E, (20, 30 & 50 amps), 4 no hkups, some extended stay sites, 62 pull-thrus, cable TV, wireless Instant Internet access at site, phone Internet access central location, tenting, cabins, RV storage, dump station, non-guest dumping $, laundry, groceries, RV supplies, LP gas by weight/by meter, ice, tables, fire rings, grills, wood.

◊◊◊RECREATION: rec hall, swim pool, boating, no motors, canoeing, kayaking, 4 canoe/3 kayak/2 pedal boat rentals, lake fishing, fishing supplies, bsktball, 8 bike rentals, playground, sports field, hiking trails, v-ball.

Pets welcome. Partial handicap access. Open all yr. Big rigs welcome. Internet friendly. Clubs welcome. Rate in 2007 $37-51 for 2 persons. MC/

MT. PLEASANT/CHARLESTON KOA—Continued on next page

CHARLESTON—Continued
MT. PLEASANT/CHARLESTON KOA—Continued

VISA/DISC/AMEX/DC. Member ARVC, CARVC. Phone: (800)KOA-5796. KOA 10% value card discount.

e-mail: StayKOA@aol.com

SEE AD THIS PAGE AND AD DISCOVER SECTION PAGES 62 & 63

(W) OAK PLANTATION CAMPGROUND—(Charleston) *From west jct I-526 & US 17 South: Go 4 mi SW on US 17. Enter on R.*

15 MINUTES FROM HISTORIC CHARLESTON
Guests appreciate the friendly staff and picturesque facility as well as our convenient location to the many attractions in the Charleston area. For sightseeing or just relaxing, let us host your next camping experience.

◇◇◇◇◇FACILITIES: 298 sites, typical site width 28 ft, 144 full hkups, 80 W&E, (20, 30 & 50 amps), 74 no hkups, 87 pull-thrus, wireless Instant Internet access at site ($), wireless Internet access central location, RV storage, dump station, non-guest dumping $, laundry, ltd groceries, RV supplies, LP gas by meter, ice, tables, wood.

◇◇◇RECREATION: pavilion, swim pool, lake fishing, playground, horseshoes, sports field.

Pets welcome. No tents. Open all yr. Big rigs welcome. Internet friendly. Clubs welcome. Rate in 2007 $26-35 for 2 persons. MC/VISA/DISC. Phone: (866)658-2500.

e-mail: info@oakplantationcampground.com

SEE AD PAGE 768

(SW) SPLASH ZONE WATERPARK—*From jct I-26 (exit 221) & US 17: Go 2 mi S on US 17, then 1 mi S on Hwy 171, then 1 1/2 mi W on Hwy 700, then 1 3/4 mi S on Riverland Dr. Enter on R.* Fun for the entire family featuring tube and open slides, 500 foot lazy river, Caribbean play structure with slides, wheels and sprays plus a recreational pool. Open May thru Labor Day. Call for hours & days of operation. Phone: (843) 795-4386.

SEE AD PAGE 767

CHERAW—A-5

(S) CHERAW STATE RECREATION AREA—(Chesterfield) *From town: Go 4 mi S on US 52. Enter on R.*

FACILITIES: 17 sites, 17 W&E, (20 & 30 amps), 2 pull-thrus, tenting, cabins, dump station, tables, controlled access gate.

RECREATION: lake swimming, boating, 10 hp limit, canoeing, rowboat/kayak/pedal boat rentals, lake fishing, putting green, playground, hiking trails.

Pets welcome. Open all yr. MC/VISA. Phone: (843) 537-9656.

SEE AD TRAVEL SECTION PAGE 759

CHESTER—A-3

(SW) CHESTER STATE PARK—(Chester) *From jct Hwy 9 & Hwy 72: Go 3 mi SW on Hwy 72.*

FACILITIES: 25 sites, 33 ft max RV length, 25 W&E, (20 & 30 amps), 5 pull-thrus, tenting, dump station, tables, controlled access gate.

RECREATION: rowboat rentals, lake fishing, playground, hiking trails.

Pets welcome. Partial handicap access. Open all yr. Clubs welcome. Phone: (803)385-2680.

SEE AD TRAVEL SECTION PAGE 759

(W) SUMTER NF (Woods Ferry Campground)—(Chester) *From jct Hwy 72 & Hwy 25: Go 2 mi N on Hwy 25, then 3-1/2 mi N on Hwy 49, then 3-1/2 mi NW on Hwy 574.* FACILITIES: 28 sites, 22 ft max RV length, 28 no hkups, grills, wood. RECREATION: boating, ramp, hiking trails. Open all yr. No reservations. Phone: (864)427-9858.

CLARKS HILL—C-2

MODOC CAMPGROUND (COE-J. Strom Thurmond Lake)—(McCormick) *Northbound, from jct Hwy-28 & US-221: Go 3-1/2 mi N on US-221 (Modoc), then 1-1/2 mi SW on paved road.* FACILITIES: 49 sites, 35 W&E, (30 amps), 14 no hkups, 20 pull-thrus, tenting, dump station, laundry, grills. RECREATION: lake swimming, boating, ramp, lake fishing, playground, hiking trails. Open Apr 1 thru Nov 30. Phone: (864)333-2272.

CLEMSON—A-2

LAKE HARTWELL CAMPING & CABINS—*From jct US 123 & US 76: Go 5 mi S on US 76, then 6 mi E on Hwy 187 to I-85, then 3 mi S on I-85 to Exit 11, then 2-1/2 mi W on Hwy 24, then 1/2 mi N on O'Neal Ferry Rd, then 1/2 mi E on Ponderosa Rd. Enter at end.*

SEE PRIMARY LISTING AT ANDERSON AND AD ANDERSON PAGE 765

(SW) TWIN LAKES CAMPGROUND (COE-Hartwell Lake)—(Pickens) *From jct US 123 & US 76: Go 2 mi SE on US 76, then 5 mi SW on CR 56.* FACILITIES: 102 sites, 102 W&E, (50 amps), 25 pull-thrus, tenting, dump station, fire rings, grills. RECREATION: pavilion, lake swimming, boating, ramp, lake fishing, playground. Open Mar 1 thru Nov 27. Phone: (888)893-0678.

COLUMBIA—B-3

(W) BARNYARD FLEA MARKET—*From jct I-26 (exit 111A) & US 1: Go 3 mi SW on US 1. Or from jct I-20 (exit 58) & US 1: Go 2 mi NE on US 1. Enter on left. Enter on R.* One of the premier flea markets in South Carolina, with over 550 spaces stocked wtih a wide variety of items, new and old. Open Fri, Sat & Sun. Open all yr. Phone: (803)957-6570.

SEE AD THIS PAGE

We all know that one of the best parts about camping is the food! Woodall's Campsite Cookbook is a classic cookbook containing such fun campsite and RV recipes as Roadside Spuds, The Fastest Sauce in the West, and Hairy Squares (which taste a lot better than they sound!) To order your copy go to www.woodalls.com/shop.

COLUMBIA—Continued

(W) BARNYARD RV PARK—(Lexington) *From jct I-26 (exit 111A) & US 1: Go 3 mi SW on US 1. Or from jct I-20 (exit 58) & US 1: Go 2 mi NE on US 1.*

TALK ABOUT CONVENIENCE!
Located off Hwy 1, just minutes from I-20, I-26 and many area attractions. Come stay with us, kick back, relax and we will make you feel right at home. On weekends, experience Southern hospitality at our huge flea market.

◆◆◆◆FACILITIES: 129 sites, typical site width 40 ft, 129 full hkups, (30 & 50 amps), some extended stay sites, 82 pull-thrus, cable TV, wireless Instant Internet access at site ($), phone on-site Internet access (needs activ), phone Internet access central location, RV storage, dump station, non-guest dumping $, laundry, RV supplies, ice, tables, patios.

COLUMBIA—Continued
BARNYARD RV PARK—Continued

RECREATION: pavilion.

Pets welcome. Partial handicap access. No tents. Open all yr. Big rigs welcome. Internet friendly. Clubs welcome. Rate in 2007 $23.30 for 2 persons. MC/VISA/DISC. Phone: (803)957-1238.

e-mail: barnyardrvpark@sc.rr.com

SEE AD THIS PAGE

MILITARY PARK (Weston Lake Rec. Area-Ft. Jackson) —(Lexington) *From I-20 (exit 80): Go S on Clemson Rd to end, then E on Percival, then S on Wildcat, then 2-1/2 mi E on Hwy 262 (Leesburg Rd). On base.* FACILITIES: 28 sites, 13 full hkups, 5 W&E, 10 no hkups, tenting, dump station, ice, fire rings, grills. RECREATION: lake swimming, boating, canoeing, ramp, dock, 5 rowboat/30 canoe/20 pedal boat/15 motorboat rentals, lake fishing, sports field, hiking trails, v-ball. Open all yr. For Military Use Only- w/ Military ID Card. No reservations. Phone: (843)774-2690.

(NE) SESQUICENTENNIAL STATE PARK—(Richland) *From jct I-20 & US 1: Go 3 mi NE on US 1. Enter on R.*

FACILITIES: 87 sites, typical site width 30 ft, 35 ft max RV length, 87 W&E, (20 & 30 amps), 18 pull-thrus, tenting, dump station, tables, controlled access gate.

RECREATION: lake swimming, rowboat/pedal boat rentals, lake fishing, playground, planned activities, hiking trails.

Pets welcome. Partial handicap access. Open all yr. Clubs welcome. Phone: (803)788-2706.

SEE AD TRAVEL SECTION PAGE 759

(C) SOUTH CAROLINA STATE PARKS—Tourist information for South Carolina State Parks. Call for information. No RV Parking. Open all yr. Phone: (803)734-1779.

SEE AD TRAVEL SECTION PAGE 759

CONWAY—C-6

(NW) BIG CYPRESS LAKE RV PARK & FISHING RETREAT—(Horry) *From jct US 501 & Hwy 378: Go 1-1/2 mi SW on US 701, then 5-3/4 mi W on Janette St./Cates Bay Hwy. Then 1/2 mi S on Brown's Way Shortcut Rd. Enter on L.*

◆◆◆FACILITIES: 43 sites, typical site width 25 ft, 28 full hkups, (20, 30 & 50 amps), 50 amps ($), 15 no hkups, some extended stay sites, 10 pull-thrus, heater not allowed, phone Internet access central location, tenting, RV storage, tables, patios, fire rings, wood.

◆◆RECREATION: pavilion, boating, electric motors only, ramp, dock, lake fishing, hiking trails.

Pets welcome. Open all yr. Big rigs welcome. Internet friendly. Clubs welcome. Rate in 2007 $35-45 for 2 persons. MC/VISA. Member ARVC, CARVC. Phone: (843)397-1800. CCUSA discount.

e-mail: rvpark@sccoast.net

SEE AD MYRTLE BEACH PAGE 775

DILLON—B-5

(S) LITTLE PEE DEE STATE PARK—(Dillon) *From jct US 301 & Hwy 9: Go 9 mi SE on Hwy 9, then 2 mi SW on CR 22 (State Park Rd).*

FACILITIES: 50 sites, typical site width 22 ft, 32 W&E, (20 & 30 amps), 18 no hkups, 4 pull-thrus, tenting, dump station, tables, controlled access gate.

LITTLE PEE DEE STATE PARK—Continued on next page

DILLON—Continued
LITTLE PEE DEE STATE PARK—Continued

RECREATION: boating, rowboat/pedal boat rentals, lake fishing, playground, hiking trails.

Pets welcome. Partial handicap access. Open all yr. Clubs welcome. Phone: (843)774-8872.

SEE AD TRAVEL SECTION PAGE 759

EASLEY—A-2

(N) April Valley RV Park (TOO NEW TO RATE) —(Pickens) *From jct Hwy 123 & Hwy 135: Go 6-1/2 mi N on Hwy 135, then 2-1/4 mi W on Jameson Rd. Enter on R.* FACILITIES: 31 sites, accepts full hkup units only, 31 full hkups, (20, 30 & 50 amps). RECREATION: pavilion, lake/pond fishing, hiking trails. Pets welcome. No tents. Open all yr. Big rigs welcome. Rate in 2007 $20-25 per vehicle. Phone: (864)855-1200.

EDISTO ISLAND—E-4

(S) EDISTO BEACH STATE PARK—(Charleston) *From jct US 17 & Hwy 174: Go 28 mi S on Hwy 174.*

WELCOME

FACILITIES: 101 sites, typical site width 20 ft, 96 W&E, (30 & 50 amps), 5 no hkups, 3 pull-thrus, tenting, cabins, dump station, tables, controlled access gate.

RECREATION: saltwater swimming, boating, canoeing, ramp, saltwater fishing, playground, planned activities, hiking trails.

Pets welcome. Open all yr. MC/VISA. Phone: (843) 869-2156.

SEE AD TRAVEL SECTION PAGE 759

EHRHARDT—D-3

(S) BROXTON BRIDGE PLANTATION (TOO NEW TO RATE)—(Colleton) *From jct SC-64 & US-601: Go 7-1/4 mi S on US-601. Enter on R.*

WELCOME

FACILITIES: 130 sites, typical site width 60 ft, 30 full hkups, 100 W&E, (30 & 50 amps), 112 pull-thrus, tenting, dump station, laundry, ltd groceries, LP gas by weight/by meter, fire rings.

RECREATION: river swimming, river/pond fishing, hiking trails.

Pets welcome. Open all yr. Rate in 2007 $20 per vehicle. MC/VISA/DISC/AMEX. Phone: (800)437-4868.

e-mail: broxtonbridgeplantation@juno.com

SEE AD TRAVEL SECTION PAGE 757

EUTAWVILLE—C-4

(E) ROCKS POND CAMPGROUND & MARINA—(Orangeburg) *From jct Hwy 45 & Hwy 6: Go 5-3/4 mi E on Hwy 6 (Old Number Six Hwy), then 1-1/4 mi N on Rock Pond Road, then 1/2 mi E on Campground Rd. Enter at end.*

WELCOME

FAMILY RUN FOR FAMILY FUN
Come enjoy a week on the shores of Lake Marion! Fish, swim, play putt-putt & other games, or just relax on our sandy beach. Rent a boat, bike or golf cart. We have everything you'll need for great family fun on-site.

◊◊◊◊FACILITIES: 500 sites, typical site width 50 ft, 500 full hkups, (20, 30 & 50 amps), some extended stay sites, 290 pull-thrus, wireless Instant Internet access at site ($), phone Internet access central location, tenting, RV/park trailer rentals, RV storage, laundry, full svc store, RV supplies, LP gas by meter, gas, marine gas, ice, tables, fire rings, wood, controlled access gate.

EUTAWVILLE—Continued
ROCKS POND CAMPGROUND & MARINA—Continued

◊◊◊◊◊RECREATION: rec hall, rec room/area, equipped pavilion, coin games, lake swimming, boating, canoeing, kayaking, ramp, dock, 3 pontoon/7 rowboat/4 pedal boat/3 motorboat rentals, lake/pond fishing, fishing supplies, fishing guides, mini-golf ($), bsktball, 10 bike rentals, playground, planned activities, sports field, hiking trails. Rec open to public.

Pets welcome, breed restrict. Partial handicap access. Open all yr. Big rigs welcome. Internet friendly. Clubs welcome. Rate in 2007 $25-35 for 4 persons. MC/VISA. ATM. Member ARVC, CARVC. Phone: (803)492-7711.

e-mail: feedback@rockspondcampground.com

SEE AD TRAVEL SECTION PAGE 760

FAIR PLAY—B-1

LAKE HARTWELL RV PARK—(Oconee) *From jct I-85 (exit 1) & Hwy 11: Go 4 mi N on S. Hwy 11. Enter on R.*

WELCOME

FACILITIES: 14 sites, 14 full hkups, (30 & 50 amps).

Open all yr. Rate in 2007 $25 for 2 persons. Phone: (866)972-0378.

SEE AD ANDERSON PAGE 765

(W) LAKE HARTWELL STATE RECREATION AREA—(Oconee) *At jct I-85 & Hwy 11.*

WELCOME

FACILITIES: 148 sites, typical site width 25 ft, 117 W&E, (20 & 30 amps), 31 no hkups, 8 pull-thrus, tenting, dump station, laundry, ltd groceries, tables, controlled access gate.

RECREATION: boating, ramp, lake fishing, playground, hiking trails.

Pets welcome. Open all yr. Phone: (864)972-3352.

SEE AD TRAVEL SECTION PAGE 759

FLORENCE—B-5

✵ **(S) DON MAR RV SALES**—*From jct I-95 (exit 141) & Hwy 58/53: Go 1/4 mi E on Hwy 53, then 1/2 mi S on Hwy 58. Enter on L.* SALES: travel trailers, van campers, pre-owned unit sales. SERVICES: full-time mech, RV appliance repair, body work/collision repair, 24-hr emerg rd svc, RV towing, LP gas by weight/by meter, RV storage, sells parts/accessories, installs hitches. Open all yr. MC/VISA/AMEX. Phone: (803)453-5011.

WELCOME

e-mail: mary.don.marv@yahoo.com

SEE AD TRAVEL SECTION PAGE 762

South Carolina State Tree: Palmetto

FLORENCE—Continued

(NW) FLORENCE KOA—(Florence) *From jct I-95 (exit 169) & TV Rd: Go 1/10 mi S on TV Rd, then 1 mi N on E Frontage Rd. Enter on L.*

WELCOME

NEW OWNER, NEW LOOK
We've been working hard to improve our facilities and add new services. You'll notice the difference as soon as you pull in. Make us your base camp for exploring or just stopover on I-95. You'll come back!

◊◊◊◊FACILITIES: 135 sites, typical site width 24 ft, 85 full hkups, 50 W&E, (20, 30 & 50 amps), 135 pull-thrus, cable TV, wireless Instant Internet access at site, phone Internet access central location, tenting, cabins, RV storage, dump station, non-guest dumping $, laundry, full svc store, RV supplies, LP gas by weight/by meter, ice, tables, patios, fire rings, grills, wood.

◊◊◊RECREATION: rec hall, rec room/area, coin games, swim pool, pond fishing, bsktball, playground, sports field, v-ball.

Pets welcome. Open all yr. Big rigs welcome. Internet friendly. Escort to site. Clubs welcome. Rate in 2007 $30-34 for 2 persons. MC/VISA/DISC/AMEX. Member ARVC, CARVC. Phone: (843)665-7007. KOA 10% value card discount. FMCA discount.

e-mail: jeffhallkoa@bellsouth.net

SEE AD THIS PAGE AND AD TRAVEL SECTION PAGE 757 AND AD DISCOVER SECTION PAGES 62 & 63

(SW) SWAMP FOX CAMPING—(Florence) *From jct I-95 (exit 157) & US 76: Go 150 yds W on US 76, then 1/2 mi N on Meadors Rd, then 1/4 mi E on Gateway Rd. Enter at end.*

WELCOME

◊◊◊FACILITIES: 61 sites, typical site width 28 ft, 51 full hkups, 10 W&E, (30 & 50 amps), 50 amps ($), some extended stay sites, 55 pull-thrus, phone/cable on-site Internet access (needs activ), phone Internet access central location, tenting, dump station, non-guest dumping $, laundry, ice, tables.

◊◊RECREATION: rec room/area, swim pool, wading pool, whirlpool, golf nearby, bsktball, playground, tennis.

Pets welcome. Partial handicap access. Open all yr. Escort to site. Clubs welcome. Rate in 2007 $24-30 for 2 persons. MC/VISA/DISC/AMEX/DC. Phone: (877)251-2251.

e-mail: young-brothers@MSN.com

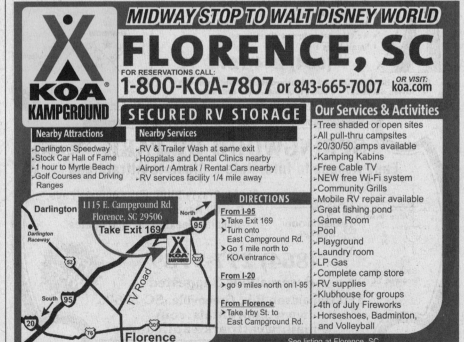

SEE AD THIS PAGE

FORT MILL—A-4

(N) CAMPGROUND MASSACRE HAUNTED ATTRACTION—*From jct I-77 (exit 88) & Gold Hill Rd: Go 1/2 mi W on Gold Hill Rd. Enter on R.* A haunted attraction on 2.5 acres with over 25 scare/scenes and 50 hi-tech automated props. Prepare to be scared! Open Oct 1 thru Oct 31. Open every Fri & Sat in October & nightly the last week of October. MC/VISA/DISC/AMEX. Phone: (866)SLASHER.

SEE AD CHARLOTTE, NC PAGE 642

(N) CHARLOTTE/FORT MILL KOA—(York) *From jct I-77 (exit 88) & Gold Hill Rd: Go 1/2 mi W on Gold Hill Rd. Enter on R.*

NOT YOUR TYPICAL CAMPGROUND
We brought the first JUMPING PILLOW to the U.S. It's 68' x 33' and great fun for the kids and exercise for adults. We've got everything here - fuel, groceries, handmade sandwiches, pizza, even a bar & lounge for adults.

♦♦♦♦FACILITIES: 236 sites, typical site width 35 ft, 164 full hkups, 47 W&E, 25 E, (20, 30 & 50 amps), some extended stay sites, 63 pull-thrus, cable TV, wireless Instant Internet access at site, phone on-site Internet access (needs activ), phone Internet access central location, tenting, cabins, dump station, non-guest dumping $, laundry, full svc store, RV supplies, LP gas by weight/by meter, gas, ice, tables, grills, wood.

♦♦♦RECREATION: rec room/area, pavilion, coin games, swim pool, mini-golf ($), playground.

Pets welcome. Partial handicap access. Open all yr. Big rigs welcome. Internet friendly. Escort to site. Clubs welcome. Rate in 2007 $30-60 for 2 persons. MC/VISA/DISC/AMEX/Debit. ATM. Member ARVC, CARVC. Phone: (888)562-4430. KOA 10% value card discount.

e-mail: charlottekoa@gmail.com

SEE AD CHARLOTTE, NC PAGE 642 AND AD DISCOVER SECTION PAGES 62 & 63

(NE) Lakeside Lodges & Campground—(York) *From jct I-77 & Carowinds Blvd (exit 90): Go 1 mi S on Hwy 21 to Regent Park Marble Entrance sign, then 1-3/4 mi E on Regents Pkwy, then 1/2 mi S on Heritage Blvd which becomes Regents. Enter on L.* ♦♦FACILITIES: 108 sites, 108 full hkups, (30 & 50 amps), 91 pull-thrus, tenting, dump station, non-guest dumping $, tables. Pets welcome. Open all yr. Rate in 2007 $25-35 per family. Phone: (803)547-3500.

GAFFNEY—A-3

(W) Pine Cone Campground—(Cherokee) *From jct I-85 (exit 87) & Road 39: Go 50 yds S on Rd-39, then 1 mi E on Overbrook Dr exit(east frontage rd), then 200 yds S on Sarratt School Rd. Enter on R.* ♦♦♦FACILITIES: 112 sites, typical site width 26 ft, 102 full hkups, 10 W&E, (20, 30 & 50 amps), some extended stay sites (in summer), 28 pull-thrus, tenting, dump station, non-guest dumping $, portable dump, laundry, LP gas by weight/by meter, ice, tables, fire rings, wood. ♦♦RECREATION: rec hall, swim pool, pond fishing, mini-golf ($), playground, hiking trails, v-ball. Rec open to public. Partial handicap access. Open all yr. Rate in 2007 $28 for 4 persons. Phone: (864)489-2022.

GREENVILLE—A-2

(N) PARIS MOUNTAIN STATE PARK—(Greenville) *From jct US 276 & Hwy 253: Go 6 mi NE on Hwy 253, then NW on park road.*

FACILITIES: 52 sites, typical site width 35 ft, 40 W&E, (20 & 30 amps), 12 no hkups, 3 pull-thrus, tenting, dump station, tables, controlled access gate.

RECREATION: lake swimming, pedal boat rentals, lake fishing, playground, hiking trails.

Pets welcome. Partial handicap access. Open all yr. Phone: (864)244-5565.

SEE AD TRAVEL SECTION PAGE 759

(NE) RAINBOW RV PARK (RV SPACES)—(Greenville) *N'bound from jct I-85 (exit 42) & US 29: Go 11-6/10 mi NE on US 29, then 200 feet NW on Rutherford Rd. S'bound from jct I-85 (exit 66) & US 29: Go 15 mi W on US 29, then 200 feet NW on Rutherford Rd. Enter on R.*

FACILITIES: 50 sites, typical site width 30 ft, accepts full hkup units only, 50 full hkups, (30 & 50 amps), mostly extended stay sites, 4 pull-thrus, patios.

Pets welcome, size restrict. No tents. Open all yr. No restrooms. Rate in 2007 $22-28 for 2 persons. Phone: (864)244-1271.

SEE AD THIS PAGE

(SE) Scuffletown USA Campground—(Greenville) *From jct I-85 (exit 51) & Hwy 146 (Woodruff Rd): Go 4-3/4 mi E on Hwy 146, then 1-1/2 mi S on Scuffletown Rd to campground. Enter on L.* ♦♦FACILITIES: 63 sites, typical site width 35 ft, 30 full hkups, 15 W&E, 8 E, (20, 30 & 50 amps), 50 amps ($), 10 no hkups, 4 pull-thrus, tenting, dump station, laundry, full svc

South Carolina State Rock: Blue Granite

GREENVILLE—Continued
Scuffletown USA Campground—Continued

store, LP gas by weight/by meter, ice, tables, wood. ♦RECREATION: lake fishing, play equipment, horseshoes. Pets welcome. Open all yr. Big rigs welcome. Internet friendly. Rate in 2007 $25-30 for 2 persons. Phone: (864)967-2276.

(S) SPRINGWOOD RV PARK—(Greenville) *From I-85 (exit 44) & US 25/White Horse Rd: go 2-3/4 mi S on White Horse Rd, then 1/2 mi S on Donaldson Rd. Enter on R.*

♦♦♦FACILITIES: 55 sites, typical site width 20 ft, accepts full hkup units only, 55 full hkups, (30 & 50 amps), mostly extended stay sites, 5 pull-thrus, wireless Internet access central location, patios.

Pets welcome. No tents. Open all yr. Big rigs welcome. Internet friendly. Rate in 2007 $23-29 for 2 persons. MC/VISA. Phone: (864)277-9789.

e-mail: wyattpark@aol.com

SEE AD THIS PAGE

GREENWOOD—B-2

(NE) CANE CREEK MOTOR COACH RESORT (UNDER CONSTRUCTION)—*From the jct of Hwy 72 & Hwy 39: Go 2 mi SE on Hwy 39, then 1-1/2 mi SW on Watts Bridge Rd, then 1-3/4 mi W on Whiteford Rd. Turn right at sign and go 1/4 mi. Enter on R.*

FACILITIES: 84 sites, 84 full hkups, (30 & 50 amps).

Open all yr. Phone: (864)992-3911.

SEE AD TRAVEL SECTION PAGE 761

(E) Jody's RV—*From jct US 178 Byp & US 221: Go 1 mi NE on US 221. Enter on L.* SALES: travel trailers, truck campers, 5th wheels, van campers, mini-motor homes, fold-down camping trailers, pre-owned unit sales. SERVICES: full-time mech, RV appliance repair, body work/collision repair, RV storage, sells parts/accessories, installs hitches. Open all yr. MC/VISA. Phone: (866)563-9778. FMCA discount.

(E) LAKE GREENWOOD STATE RECREATION AREA—(Greenwood) *From jct US 178-25 & Hwy 34: Go 14 mi E on Hwy 34, then 3 mi N on Hwy 702.*

FACILITIES: 130 sites, typical site width 25 ft, 125 W&E, (20 & 30 amps), 5 no hkups, 32 pull-thrus, tenting, dump station, ltd groceries, ice, tables, controlled access gate.

RECREATION: rec hall, boating, ramp, lake fishing, hiking trails.

Pets welcome. Open all yr. Phone: (864)543-3535.

SEE AD TRAVEL SECTION PAGE 759

HARDEEVILLE—E-3

(SE) HARDEEVILLE RV-THOMAS' PARKS AND SITES—(Jasper) *From I-95 (exit 5) & jct US 17: Go N 1 mi on US 17, then E 5 mi on Hwy 46, then 1/4 mi W on Hwy 170 and continue straight on Hwy 170-A for 3 mi. Enter on L.*

SMILING FACES. BEAUTIFUL PLACES.
We've got both! We're just minutes from Beaufort, Sun City, Hilton Head, and historic Savannah. Our sites are level with easy access and we provide FREE Wi-Fi & Cable TV. Come stay a few days and enjoy the Coastal Empire.

♦♦♦FACILITIES: 100 sites, typical site width 35 ft, accepts full hkup units only, 100 full hkups, (30 & 50 amps), 30 pull-thrus, cable TV, wireless Instant Internet access at site, laundry, ice, tables, fire rings, wood.

RECREATION: hiking trails.

Pets welcome. No tents. Open all yr. No restrooms. Big rigs welcome. Internet friendly. Rate in 2007 $30 for 2 persons. Member ARVC, CARVC. Phone: (843)784-6210.

SEE AD SAVANNAH, GA PAGE 214 AND AD TRAVEL SECTION PAGE 760

HARDEEVILLE—Continued on next page

Can you trust the Woodall's ratings? 28 evaluation teams have scoured North American campgrounds to provide you with accurate, up to date information & ratings. Find a rating you don't agree with? Send a letter or email our way, and we'll give it extra attention for 2009.

HARDEEVILLE—Continued

(SE) THE PINK PIG—*From jct I-95 (exit 5) & jct US 17: Go N 1 mi on US 17, then E 5 mi on Hwy 46, then 1/4 mi W on Hwy 170 and continue straight on Hwy 170-A for 2-1/2 mi. Enter on L.* The Pink Pig is a family owned and operated restaurant featuring a slow roasting bbq method. All sauces and other recipes were created by the founder. The restaurant has been featured on The Food Channel. Open all yr. Phone: (843)784-3635.

SEE AD TRAVEL SECTION PAGE 760

HILTON HEAD ISLAND—E-4

HILTON HEAD HARBOR RV RESORT & MARINA—(Beaufort) *From jct I-95 (exit 8) & US 278: Go 20 mi E on US 278, then 1/4 mi N on Jenkins Rd. Enter on L.*

◆◆◆◆FACILITIES: 200 sites, typical site width 40 ft, accepts full hkup units only, 200 full hkups, (20, 30 & 50 amps), cable TV, phone/wireless Instant Internet access at site, wireless Internet access central location, laundry, marine gas, ice, tables, patios, grills.

◆◆◆RECREATION: rec room/area, 2 swim pools, whirlpool, boating, canoeing, kayaking, ramp, dock, 2 kayak/motorboat rentals, saltwater/river fishing, fishing guides, golf nearby, playground, shuffleboard court, tennis.

Pets welcome. Partial handicap access. No tents. Open all yr. Big rigs welcome. Internet friendly. Clubs welcome. Rate in 2007 $45-59 for 4 persons. MC/VISA. Member ARVC, CARVC. Phone: (800)845-9560.

e-mail: info@hiltonheadharbor.com

SEE AD THIS PAGE

(C) **HILTON HEAD ISLAND MOTOR COACH RESORT**—(Beaufort) *From jct I-95 (exit 8) & US 278: Go 22 mi E on US 278, then 5-1/2 mi E on Cross Island Pkwy, then 1/4 mi N on Target Rd, then E on Arrow Rd. Enter on L.*

LUXURY ORA MOTORCOACH ONLY RESORT
401 beautiful sites on Hilton Head Island - just 45 minutes off I-95. Gated access with large swimming pool, 6 tennis courts, & fitness center. Beach, golf, dining, shopping with miles of bicycle trails surrounding resort.

◆◆◆◆◆FACILITIES: 401 sites, typical site width 40 ft, accepts full hkup units only, 401 full hkups, (30 & 50 amps), 6 pull-thrus, cable TV, wireless Instant Internet access at site, laundry, ice, tables, patios, controlled access gate.

◆◆◆◆RECREATION: rec hall, rec room/area, swim pool, whirlpool, pond fishing, golf nearby, bsktball, play equipment, 2 shuffleboard courts, planned activities, tennis.

Pets welcome. Partial handicap access. No tents. Open all yr. Motor Coaches Only. Big rigs welcome. Internet friendly. Escort to site. Clubs welcome. Rate in 2007 $47-53 for 4 persons. MC/VISA/AMEX. Member ARVC, CARVC. Phone: (800)722-2365. FMCA discount.

e-mail: outdooresort@hargray.com

SEE AD THIS PAGE

IRMO—B-3

(SE) **WOODSMOKE CAMPGROUND**—(Newberry) *From jct I-26 (exit 97) & US 176: Go 1 mi N on US 176.*

◆◆◆FACILITIES: 34 sites, 32 full hkups, 2 W&E, (30 & 50 amps), 50 amps ($), 10 pull-thrus, wireless Instant Internet access at site ($), tenting, dump station, non-guest dumping $, laundry, LP gas by weight, ice, tables, wood.

◆◆RECREATION: pond fishing, bsktball, playground, horseshoes, v-ball.

Pets welcome, breed restrict. Partial handicap access. Open all yr. Big rigs welcome. Internet friendly. Rate in 2007 $22-25 for 2 persons. Phone: (803)781-3451.

SEE AD COLUMBIA PAGE 770

JOANNA—B-3

MAGNOLIA RV PARK & CAMPGROUND—(Laurens) *From jct I-26 (exit 60) & Hwy 66: Go 1/10 mi W on Hwy 66, then 1/2 mi S on Fairview Church Rd. Enter on L.*

◆◆◆FACILITIES: 41 sites, typical site width 30 ft, 7 full hkups, 34 W&E, (20, 30 & 50 amps), some extended stay sites, 29 pull-thrus,

JOANNA—Continued
MAGNOLIA RV PARK & CAMPGROUND—Continued

wireless Instant Internet access at site, tenting, cabins, RV storage, dump station, non-guest dumping $, laundry, ltd groceries, RV supplies, LP gas by weight/by meter, ice, tables, fire rings, wood.

◆RECREATION: pavilion, swim pool, play equipment. Rec open to public.

Pets welcome, quantity restrict. Open all yr. Big rigs welcome. Internet friendly. Rate in 2007 $24-30 for 4 persons. MC/VISA/DISC. Phone: (864) 697-1214. CCUSA discount.

e-mail: info@magnoliarvparksc.com

SEE AD TRAVEL SECTION PAGE 761

LAKE HARTWELL—B-2

See lisings at Anderson, Clemson, Fair Play & Townville

LAKE KEOWEE—A-1

See listings at Clemson,Fairplay,Seneca,Townville

LANCASTER—A-4

(N) **ANDREW JACKSON STATE PARK**—(Lancaster) *Northbound, from jct Hwy 9 & US 521: Go 9 mi N on US 521. Enter on R.*

FACILITIES: 25 sites, typical site width 30 ft, 36 ft max RV length, 25 W&E, 5 pull-thrus, tenting, dump station, tables, controlled access gate.

RECREATION: rowboat rentals, lake fishing, playground, planned activities, hiking trails.

Pets welcome. Partial handicap access. Open all yr. Phone: (803)285-3344.

SEE AD TRAVEL SECTION PAGE 759

LEESVILLE—C-3

(SE) Cedar Pond Campground—(Lexington) *From jct I-20 (exit 39) & US 178: Go 1-1/2 mi E on US 178. Enter on R.* ◆◆FACILITIES: 32 sites, typical site width 30 ft, 26 full hkups, 6 W&E, (20, 30 & 50 amps), some extended stay sites, 6 pull-thrus, tenting, dump station, non-guest dumping $, laundry, LP gas by weight/by meter, tables. ◆RECREATION: pavilion, boating, electric motors only, dock, 3 rowboat/4 pedal boat rentals, pond fishing. Pets welcome. Open all yr. Rate in 2007 $18 for 4 persons. Phone: (803)657-5993.

LEXINGTON—B-3

(S) Edmund RV Park—(Lexington) *From jct I-20 & Hwy 6 (exit 55): Go 6 mi SE on Hwy 6, then 1/4 mi S on Hwy 302. Enter on R.* ◆◆◆FACILITIES: 225 sites, 150 full hkups, 75 W&E, (30 & 50 amps), 100 pull-thrus, dump station, laundry, tables, patios. Pets welcome. No tents. Open all yr. Big rigs welcome. Internet friendly. Rate in 2007 $25 for 2 persons. Phone: (800) 955-7957.

TONY'S RV PARTS & SERVICE—*From I-20 (exit 55) & Hwy 6: Go 3-3/4 mi S on Hwy 6, then 5 mi W on Platt Spring Rd (SC-34). Enter on R.* Renovations & Warranty Work. SALES: pre-owned unit sales. SERVICES: full-time mech, engine/chassis repair, RV appliance repair, body work/collision repair, LP gas by weight/by meter, dump station, RV storage, sells parts/accessories, installs hitches. Open all yr. MC/VISA/DISC/AMEX. Phone: (803)894-3071. FMCA discount.

e-mail: tonysrv@pbtcomm.net

SEE AD TRAVEL SECTION PAGE 760

South Carolina State Motto: "Dum Spiro Spero" (While I breathe, I hope)

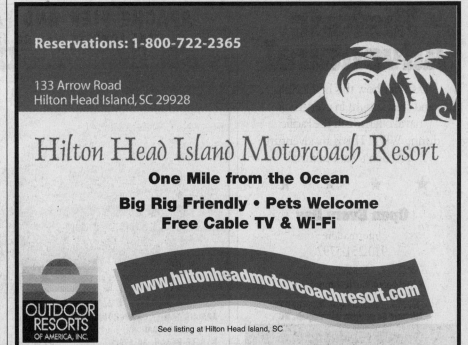

LONGS—B-6

(SE) WILLOWTREE RESORT—(Horry) *From jct SC-9 and SC 905: Go 1.8 mi NE on SC 905, then 1.5 mi N on Old Buck Creek Rd. Enter on R.*

NEWEST & BEST IN MYRTLE BEACH AREA
A true RV resort, planned and developed to meet the needs of today's discerning RVers. Large paved sites. Superior customer service. Picture-perfect setting. 21st century amenities.

◊◊◊◊◊FACILITIES: 107 sites, typical site width 45 ft, 107 full hkups, (20, 30 & 50 amps), 98 pull-thrus, wireless Instant Internet access at site, cabins, dump station, non-guest dumping $, laundry, ltd groceries, RV supplies, LP gas by meter, ice, tables, patios, fire rings, grills, wood, controlled access gate.

◊◊◊◊◊RECREATION: rec hall, rec room/area, coin games, swim pool, wading pool, whirlpool, boating, electric motors only, canoe/6 pedal boat/5 motorboat rentals, lake fishing, fishing supplies, golf nearby, bsktball, 12 bike rentals, playground, planned activities (wkends only), hiking trails, v-ball.

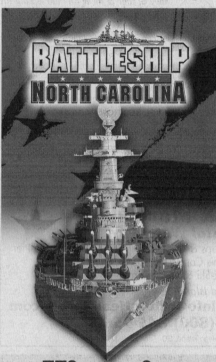

Pets welcome. Partial handicap access. No tents. Open all yr. Big rigs welcome. Internet friendly. Escort to site. Clubs welcome. Rate in 2007 $26-80 per family. MC/VISA/DISC. Member ARVC, CARVC. Phone: (866)207-2267.

e-mail: willowtreervr@aol.com

SEE AD MYRTLE BEACH PAGES 776-777 AND AD DISCOVER SECTION PAGE 65

MCCORMICK—C-2

(W) BAKER CREEK STATE PARK—(McCormick) *From jct Hwy 28 & US 378: Go 3-1/2 mi SW on US 378, then 1 mi N on park road. Enter on L.*

FACILITIES: 100 sites, 50 W&E, (20 & 30 amps), 50 no hkups, 8 pull-thrus, tenting, dump station, tables, controlled access gate.

RECREATION: boating, ramp, lake fishing, playground, hiking trails.

Pets welcome. Partial handicap access. Open all yr. Phone: (864)443-2457.

SEE AD TRAVEL SECTION PAGE 759

(SE) HAMILTON BRANCH STATE RECREATION AREA—(McCormick) *From town: Go 12 mi SE on US-221.*

FACILITIES: 180 sites, typical site width 32 ft, 140 W&E, 40 no hkups, 10 pull-thrus, tenting, dump station, tables, controlled access gate.

RECREATION: boating, ramp, lake fishing, playground.

Pets welcome. Open all yr. Clubs welcome. Phone: (864)333-2223.

SEE AD TRAVEL SECTION PAGE 759

(W) HAWE CREEK CAMPGROUND (COE-J. Strom Thurmond Lake)—(McCormick) *From jct US-221 & US-378: Go 2-1/2 mi SW on US-378, then 4 mi S on paved road.* FACILITIES: 28 sites, 10 W&E, (30 & 50 amps), 18 no hkups, 7 pull-thrus, tenting, dump station, grills. RECREATION: lake swimming, boating, ramp, lake fishing. Partial handicap access. Open Apr 1 thru Sep 30. Phone: (864)443-5441.

(W) HICKORY KNOB STATE RESORT PARK—(McCormick) *From town: Go 6 mi SW on US 378, then 2 mi N on Hwy 7, then 2 mi W on park road.*

FACILITIES: 44 sites, typical site width 20 ft, 30 ft max RV length, 44 W&E, 8 pull-thrus, tenting, cabins, dump station, marine gas, tables, grills, controlled access gate.

RECREATION: boating, ramp, dock, rowboat rentals, lake fishing, putting green, playground, tennis, hiking trails.

Pets welcome. Open all yr. MC/VISA. Phone: (800) 491-1764.

SEE AD TRAVEL SECTION PAGE 759

MT. CARMEL CAMPGROUND (COE-J. Strom Thurmond Lake)—(McCormick) *From jct Hwy-28 & US-378: Go 15 mi NW on Hwy-28 & Hwy-81.* FACILITIES: 43 sites, 21 W&E, (30 amps), 22 no hkups, 10 pull-thrus, tenting, dump station, grills. RECREATION: lake swimming, boating, ramp, lake fishing, playground. Open Apr 1 thru Sep 4. Phone: (864)391-2711.

MURRELLS INLET—C-6

(SW) HUNTINGTON BEACH STATE PARK—(Georgetown) *Westbound, from jct Hwy-544 & US-17: Go 4 mi S on US-17.*

FACILITIES: 137 sites, typical site width 40 ft, 24 full hkups, 113 W&E, (20 & 30 amps), 2 pull-thrus, tenting, dump station, ltd groceries, ice, tables, controlled access gate.

RECREATION: rec hall, saltwater swimming, saltwater fishing, bike rental, planned activities, hiking trails.

Pets welcome. Open all yr. MC/VISA. Phone: (843) 237-4440.

SEE AD TRAVEL SECTION PAGE 759

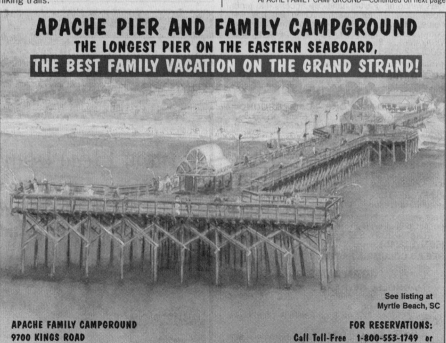

MYRTLE BEACH—C-6

(N) APACHE FAMILY CAMPGROUND—(Horry) *From jct US 501 & US 17: Go 9-3/4 mi N on US 17, then 1/2 mi E on Chestnut Rd, then 1/4 mi S on Kings Rd. Enter on L.*

LONGEST PIER ON EASTERN SEABOARD
Walk from your campsite or rental to great fishing, dining & fun on our 1220' pier. Enjoy cocktails from CROAKERS, ski-ball at the arcade, dancing in the moonlight. Close to all MB has to offer, we're a great family value.

◊◊◊◊FACILITIES: 937 sites, typical site width 32 ft, 931 full hkups, 6 W&E, (30 & 50 amps), some extended stay sites, 18 pull-thrus, cable TV, wireless Instant Internet access at site ($), phone Internet access central location, tenting, RV/park trailer rentals, RV storage, dump station, laundry, full svc store, RV supplies, LP gas by weight/by meter, ice, tables, controlled access gate.

◊◊◊◊RECREATION: rec room/area, equipped pavilion, coin games, swim pool, wading pool, saltwater swimming, saltwater fishing, fishing supplies, golf nearby, bsktball, playground, v-ball. Rec open to public.

Pets welcome, breed restrict, quantity restrict. Partial handicap access. Open all yr. Big rigs wel-

APACHE FAMILY CAMPGROUND—Continued on next page

MYRTLE BEACH—Continued
APACHE FAMILY CAMPGROUND—Continued

come. Internet friendly. Clubs welcome. Rate in 2007 $22-53 for 4 persons. MC/VISA. Member ARVC, CARVC. Phone: (800)553-1749.

e-mail: apache843@aol.com

SEE AD PAGE 774 AND AD DISCOVER SECTION PAGE 68

WELCOME **HOLIDAY TRAV-L-PARK RESORT FOR CAMPERS**—*From jct US 501 & US 17 in Myrtle Beach, SC: Go 103 mi N on US 17, then 22 mi SE on Hwy 24, then 2 mi SE on Hwy 58, then W on Coast Guard Rd. Enter on L.*

SEE PRIMARY LISTING AT EMERALD ISLE, NC AND AD EMERALD ISLE, NC PAGE 647

WELCOME **(C) KOA-MYRTLE BEACH**—(Horry) *From jct US 17 & US 501: Go 2-1/2 mi E on US 501, then 1 mi S on US 17 Bus, W on 5th Ave S. Enter on L.*

◊◊◊◊◊FACILITIES: 543 sites, typical site width 40 ft, 392 full hkups, 102 W&E, (20, 30 & 50 amps), 49 no hkups, some extended stay sites, 47 pull-thrus, cable TV, phone/wireless Instant Internet access at site, phone Internet access central location, tenting, RV/park trailer rentals, cabins, RV storage, dump station, non-guest dumping $, laundry, full svc store, RV supplies, LP gas by weight/by meter, gas, ice, tables, fire rings, grills, wood, controlled access gate.

◊◊◊◊RECREATION: rec room/area, coin games, swim pool, wading pool, pond fishing, bsktball, playground, planned activities, v-ball, local tours.

Pets welcome. Partial handicap access. Open all yr. Big rigs welcome. Internet friendly. Escort to site. Clubs welcome. Rate in 2007 $25-64 for 2 persons. MC/VISA/DISC. ATM. Member ARVC, CARVC. Phone: (800)255-7614. KOA 10% value card discount.

SEE AD PAGES 776-777 AND AD DISCOVER SECTION PAGES 62 & 63 AND AD DISCOVER SECTION PAGE 65

WELCOME **(S) LAKEWOOD CAMPING RESORT**—(Horry) *From jct US 501 & 544: Go E 14 mi on Hwy 544, then N 1/2 mi on US 17 Bus. Enter on R.*

FUN FOR THE WHOLE FAMILY
You choose - oceanfront or shaded camping, all with WI-FI! Then enjoy great new water attractions, fishing, miniature golf, pool parties, canoe and kayak rentals, planned activities for the kids & teens, bonfires and more.

◊◊◊◊◊FACILITIES: 1604 sites, typical site width 34 ft, 1578 full hkups, 26 W&E, (20, 30 & 50 amps), some extended stay sites, 37 pull-thrus, cable TV, phone/wireless Instant Internet access at site, tenting, RV/park trailer rentals, RV storage, dump station, laundry, full svc store, RV supplies, LP gas by weight/by meter, ice, tables, grills, wood, controlled access gate.

◊◊◊◊◊RECREATION: rec hall, rec room/area, equipped pavilion, coin games, 2 swim pools, wading pool, saltwater swimming, whirlpool, canoeing, kayaking, 9 canoe/10 kayak/20 pedal boat rentals, saltwater/lake/pond fishing, fishing supplies, mini-golf ($), bsktball, 50 bike rentals, playground, 3 shuffleboard courts, planned activities, v-ball, local tours.

Pets welcome. Partial handicap access. Open all yr. Big rigs welcome. Internet friendly. Clubs welcome. Rate in 2007 $25-60 for 5 persons. MC/VISA/DISC. ATM. Member ARVC, CARVC. Phone: (800)258-8309.

e-mail: marketing@lakewoodcampground.com

SEE AD PAGES 776-777 AND AD DISCOVER SECTION PAGE 65

MYRTLE BEACH—Continued

WELCOME **MYRTLE BEACH CAMPGROUND ASSOCIATION**—Association of Myrtle Beach Campgrounds which promotes tourism in the area. Phone: (800)356-3016x26001.

e-mail: ashepherd@brandonadvertising.com

SEE AD PAGES 776-777 AND AD DISCOVER SECTION PAGE 65

WELCOME **(SW) MYRTLE BEACH STATE PARK**—(Horry) *From jct US-501 & US-17: Go 3 mi S on US-17, then 1 mi on park road.*

FACILITIES: 347 sites, typical site width 30 ft, 302 W&E, (20 & 30 amps), 45 no hkups, 3 pull-thrus, tenting, cabins, dump station, laundry, ltd groceries, ice, tables, controlled access gate.

RECREATION: swim pool, saltwater swimming, dock, saltwater fishing, playground, planned activities, hiking trails.

Pets welcome. Open all yr. MC/VISA. Phone: (843) 238-5325.

SEE AD TRAVEL SECTION PAGE 759

WELCOME **(NE) MYRTLE BEACH TRAVEL PARK**—(Horry) *From jct US-501 & US-17: Go 9-3/4 mi N on US-17, then 1/2 mi E on Chestnut Rd, then 1/4 mi N on Kings Rd. Enter on R.*

125 ACRES OF OCEANFRONT CAMPING
Enjoy a wide variety of campsites, oceanfront lakeside, or wooded. We have beachcombing, swimming, fishing or just relaxing on the beach. Our restrooms are beautifully refurbished. www.myrtlebeachtravelpark.com

◊◊◊◊◊FACILITIES: 1100 sites, typical site width 35 ft, 1080 full hkups, 20 W&E, (20, 30 & 50 amps), some extended stay sites, 500 pull-thrus, cable TV, wireless Instant Internet access at site ($), phone Internet access central location, tenting, RV/park trailer rentals, RV storage, dump station, non-guest dumping, laundry, full svc store, RV supplies, LP gas by weight, ice, tables, controlled access gate.

◊◊◊◊◊RECREATION: rec room/area, pavilion, coin games, 3 swim pools, wading pool, saltwater swimming, whirlpool, dock, 8 pedal boat rentals, saltwater/pond fishing, golf nearby, bsktball, playground, 2 shuffleboard courts, planned activities, hiking trails, v-ball, local tours.

Pets welcome. Partial handicap access. Open all yr. Big rigs welcome. Internet friendly. Clubs welcome. Rate in 2007 $30-57 for 4 persons. MC/VISA/AMEX. Member ARVC, CARVC. Phone: (800) 255-3568.

e-mail: timbryant@scrr.com

SEE AD PAGES 776-777 AND AD DISCOVER SECTION PAGE 65

WELCOME **(S) OCEAN LAKES FAMILY CAMPGROUND**—(Horry) *From jct US-501 & SC Hwy 544: Go 14 mi E on SC Hwy 544. Enter at end.*

YOU MUST SEE IT TO BELIEVE IT!
Oceanfront & shaded sites. Big Rig friendly. Reserve by site number up to 18 mo in advance. All pull-thru sites. Large rally facility-no add'l fee. Concrete pads 45'x18' avail. All inclusive rates. www.oceanlakescamping.com

◊◊◊◊◊FACILITIES: 3412 sites, typical site width 40 ft, 3412 full hkups, (20, 30 & 50 amps), many extended stay sites, 893 pull-thrus, cable TV, phone/wireless Instant Internet access at site ($), wireless Internet access central location, tenting, cabins, RV storage, laundry, full svc store, RV supplies, LP gas by weight/by meter, ice, tables, controlled access gate.

◊◊◊◊◊RECREATION: rec hall, rec room/area, equipped pavilion, coin games, 3 swim pools, wading pool, saltwater swimming, saltwater/lake fishing, fishing supplies, mini-golf ($), golf nearby, bsktball, 15 bike rentals, playground, 3 shuffleboard courts, planned activities, horseshoes, v-ball, local tours.

Pets welcome, breed restrict. Partial handicap access. Open all yr. Big rigs welcome. Internet friendly. Clubs welcome. Rate in 2007 $27-62 per family. MC/VISA/DISC. ATM. Member ARVC, CARVC. Phone: (800)876-4306.

e-mail: camping@oceanlakes.com

SEE AD PAGES 776-777 AND AD DISCOVER SECTION PAGE 65

MYRTLE BEACH—Continued on next page

Find a park or campground Woodall's doesn't list? Tell us!

(S) PIRATELAND FAMILY CAMPING RESORT—(Horry) *From jct US 17 & US 544: Go 2 mi E on US 544, then 1 mi N on US 17 Bus. Enter on R.*

OCEANFRONT, PLUS 510' LAZY RIVER

Looking for the absolute best in oceanfront camping? Look no further. We have redefined the standards of family outdoor fun to bring you an unbeatable camping experience. Check out our specials at www.pirateland.com

◊◊◊◊◊FACILITIES: 1493 sites, typical site width 40 ft, 1493 full hkups, (30 & 50 amps), some extended stay sites, 37 pull-thrus, cable TV, wireless Instant Internet access at site ($), cable Internet access central location, tenting, RV/park trailer rentals, RV storage, laundry, full svc store, RV supplies, LP gas by weight/by meter, ice, tables, controlled access gate.

◊◊◊◊◊RECREATION: rec hall, rec room/area, equipped pavilion, coin games, 3 swim pools, wading pool, saltwater swimming, 4 canoe/15 pedal boat rentals, saltwater/lake/pond fishing, fishing supplies, mini-golf ($), golf nearby, bsktball, playground, planned activities, local tours.

Pets welcome, breed restrict. Partial handicap access. Open all yr. Facilities fully operational Easter Wknd, then memorial Day thru Labor Day. Big rigs welcome. Internet friendly. Clubs welcome. Rate in 2007 $24-65 for 4 persons. MC/VISA. ATM. Phone: (800)443-2267.

e-mail: pirateland@pirateland.com

SEE AD PAGES 776-777 AND AD DISCOVER SECTION PAGE 65

ORANGEBURG—C-4

(NE) Sweetwater Lake Campground (RV SPACES)—(Calhoun) *From jct I-26 (exit 139) & Rd-22: Go 2 mi W on Rd-22, then 1/2 mi N on Sweetwater Rd, then follow signs. Enter on R.* FACILITIES: 50 sites, typical site width 32 ft, 50 W&E, (20, 30 & 50 amps), tenting, dump station, non-guest dumping $, tables. RECREATION: pavilion, lake fishing. Pets welcome. Open all yr. Rate in 2007 $20 per vehicle. Phone: (803) 874-3547.

PICKENS—A-2

(NW) KEOWEE-TOXAWAY STATE NATURAL AREA—(Pickens) *From jct US 178 & Hwy 11: Go 9 mi W on Hwy 11.*

FACILITIES: 24 sites, typical site width 20 ft, 10 W&E, (20 & 30 amps), 14 no hkups, 2 pull-thrus, tenting, cabins, dump station, tables, fire rings, controlled access gate.

RECREATION: boating, lake fishing, hiking trails.

Pets welcome. Open all yr. Phone: (864)868-2605.

SEE AD TRAVEL SECTION PAGE 759

TABLE ROCK STATE PARK—(Pickens) *From jct Hwy 183 & US 178: Go 9 mi N on US 178, then 4 mi E on Hwy 11, then 1 mi N on park road.*

FACILITIES: 100 sites, typical site width 30 ft, 94 W&E, (20 & 30 amps), 6 no hkups, 27 pull-thrus, tenting, cabins, dump station, laundry, ltd groceries, tables, controlled access gate.

RECREATION: rec hall, lake swimming, boating, canoeing, kayaking, ramp, canoe/pedal boat rentals, lake fishing, mini-golf, planned activities, hiking trails.

Pets welcome. Open all yr. Clubs welcome. MC/VISA. Phone: (864)878-9813.

SEE AD TRAVEL SECTION PAGE 759

POINT SOUTH—D-4

(S) KOA-POINT SOUTH—(Jasper) *From jct I-95 (exit 33) & US 17: Go 200 yards E on US 17, then S on Yemassee Rd, then 1/2 mi W on Campground Rd. Enter at end.*

EXPLORE THE OLD SOUTH WITH KOA

We are surrounded! Visit the historic cities of Beaufort, Savannah and Charleston. Or explore the beaches of Hunting Island and the resort island of Hilton Head. Park once and travel the Low Country! Free Wi-Fi.

◊◊◊◊FACILITIES: 58 sites, typical site width 20 ft, 29 full hkups, 29 W&E, (20, 30 & 50 amps), 50 amps ($), 32 pull-thrus, cable TV ($), wireless Instant Internet access at site, phone Internet access central location, tenting, cabins, RV storage, dump station, non-guest dumping $, laundry, groceries, RV supplies, LP gas by weight/by meter, ice, tables, wood.

◊◊◊RECREATION: rec room/area, pavilion, swim pool, whirlpool, lake fishing, playground, horseshoes, hiking trails.

Pets welcome. Open all yr. Big rigs welcome. Internet friendly. Escort to site. Clubs welcome. Rate in 2007 $33-35 for 2 persons. MC/VISA/DISC/AMEX. Member ARVC, CARVC. Phone: (843)726-5733. KOA 10% value card discount.

e-mail: pskoa@hargray.com

SEE AD SAVANNAH, GA PAGE 214 AND AD DISCOVER SECTION PAGES 62 & 63

(S) KOA-POINT SOUTH CARRY OUT PIZZA—*From jct I-95 (exit 33) & US 17: Go 200 yards E on US 17, then S on Yemassee Rd, then 1/2 mi W on Campground Rd. Enter at end.* Carry out pizza. Fresh baked on premises and delivered to your site. Open all yr. Phone: (843)726-5733.

SEE AD SAVANNAH, GA PAGE 214

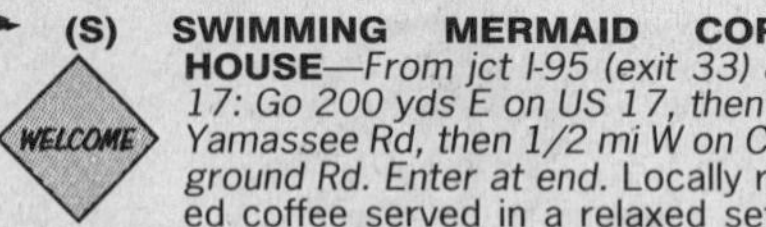

(S) SWIMMING MERMAID COFFEE HOUSE—*From jct I-95 (exit 33) & US 17: Go 200 yds E on US 17, then S on Yamassee Rd, then 1/2 mi W on Campground Rd. Enter at end.* Locally roasted coffee served in a relaxed setting. Open all yr.

SEE AD SAVANNAH, GA PAGE 214

(S) The Oaks at Point South RV Resort—(Jasper) *From jct I-95 (exit 33) & US 17: Go 1/4 mi E on US 17, then S on Yemassee Rd, then 1/2 mi E on Campground Rd. Enter on R.* ◊◊FACILITIES: 92 sites, typical site width 25 ft, 92 full hkups, (20, 30 & 50 amps), many extended stay sites, 88 pull-thrus, tenting, laundry, LP gas by weight/by meter, ice, tables. ◊◊◊RECREATION: rec room/area, pavilion, swim pool, lake fishing, mini-golf, playground, hiking trails. Pets welcome. Open all yr. Big rigs welcome. Rate in 2007 $26 for 2 persons. Phone: (843)726-5728.

ROCK HILL—A-3

(N) EBENEZER PARK—(York) *From jct I-77 & SR 161 (exit 82): Go 3/4 mi W on SR 161 to Mt. Gallant Rd., then 4 mi NE to Boatshore Rd., then 1/2 mi E to park. Enter on L.* FACILITIES: 69 sites, 69 full hkups, 3 pull-thrus, tenting, dump station, non-guest dumping $, fire rings, grills. RECREATION: lake swimming, boating, canoeing, ramp, dock, lake fishing, playground, hiking trails, v-ball. Partial handicap access. Open all yr. No reservations. Max stay 14 days. Phone: (803)366-6620.

Campbell's Covered Bridge built in 1909, is the only remaining covered bridge in South Carolina. It is located off Hwy 14 near Gowensville.

ROEBUCK—A-2

(SE) PINE RIDGE CAMPGROUND—(Spartanburg) *From jct I-26 (exit 28) & US 221: Go 500 yds NE on US 221, then 1 mi E on Stillhouse Rd, then 1 1/2 mi N on Otts Shoals Rd, then 1000 feet E on Pine Ridge Campground Rd. Enter at end.*

◊◊◊FACILITIES: 47 sites, typical site width 25 ft, 35 full hkups, 6 W&E, (30 & 50 amps), 6 no hkups, some extended stay sites, 11 pull-thrus, wireless Instant Internet access at site ($), tenting, RV/park trailer rentals, cabins, RV storage, dump station, non-guest dumping $, laundry, RV supplies, LP gas by weight/by meter, ice, tables, patios, fire rings, grills, wood.

◊◊RECREATION: rec hall, coin games, swim pool, pond fishing, play equipment, horseshoes.

Pets welcome. Open all yr. Big rigs welcome. Internet friendly. Escort to site. Clubs welcome. Rate in 2007 $23-25 for 3 persons. MC/VISA. Phone: (866)576-0302.

e-mail: camp@pineridgecampground.com

SEE AD THIS PAGE

ST. GEORGE—D-4

(W) Comfort Inn RV Park (RV SPACES)—(Dorchester) *From jct I-95 (exit 77) & Hwy 78: Go 1/4 mi E on Hwy 78, then 1/4 mi W on Frontage Rd. Enter at end.* FACILITIES: 20 sites, 20 full hkups, (20, 30 & 50 amps), 1 pull-thrus, laundry, ice. RECREATION: swim pool. Pets welcome. No tents. Open all yr. Rate in 2007 $20 per vehicle. Phone: (843)563-4180.

(E) Jolly Acres Camp & Storage—(Dorchester) *From jct I-95 (exit 77) & Hwy 78: Go 5-1/2 mi E on Hwy 78, then 1/2 mi N on Horne Taylor Rd. Enter on L.* ◊◊◊◊FACILITIES: 31 sites, typical site width 30 ft, 19 full hkups, 12 W&E, (20, 30 & 50 amps), 50 amps ($), some extended stay sites, 12 pull-thrus, dump station, laundry, ltd groceries, LP gas by weight/by meter, ice, tables, fire rings, grills, wood. ◊◊RECREATION: pond fishing, playground, planned activities (wkends only), hiking trails. Pets welcome. No tents. Open all yr. Big rigs welcome. Rate in 2007 $28 for 2 persons. Member CARVC. Phone: (843)563-8303. CCUSA discount.

SANTEE—C-4

ROCKS POND CAMPGROUND & MARINA—*From jct I-95 (exit 98) & Hwy 6: Go 16 mi E on Hwy 6, then 1-1/4 mi N on Rock Pond Rd, then 1/2 mi E on Campground Rd. Enter at end.*

SEE PRIMARY LISTING AT EUTAWVILLE, SC. AND AD TRAVEL SECTION PAGE 760

(NE) Santee Lakes Campground—(Clarendon) *From jct Hwy 6 & I-95 (exit 98): Go 4 mi N on I-95 to exit 102, then 200 yards E on Rd 400, then 1/4 mi S on Dingle Pond Rd. Enter on R.* ◊◊◊FACILITIES: 185 sites, typical site width 35 ft, 70 full hkups, 115 W&E, (30 amps), some extended stay sites, 185 pull-thrus, tenting, dump station, non-guest dumping $, laundry, groceries, ice, tables. ◊◊◊RECREATION: rec room/area, swim pool, lake swimming, boating, canoeing, ramp, dock, lake fishing, mini-golf, playground, vball. Pets welcome. Open all yr. Rate in 2007 $28-30 for 3 persons. Phone: (803)478-2262.

SANTEE STATE PARK—(Orangeburg) *From I-95 (exit 98) & Hwy 6: Go 3-1/2 mi NW on Hwy 6, then N on access road.*

FACILITIES: 158 sites, 158 W&E, 17 pull-thrus, tenting, cabins, dump station, laundry, ltd groceries, ice, tables, controlled access gate.

RECREATION: rec hall, lake swimming, boating, ramp, dock, rowboat/pedal boat rentals, lake fishing, playground, planned activities, tennis, hiking trails.

Pets welcome. Open all yr. MC/VISA. Phone: (803) 854-2408.

SEE AD TRAVEL SECTION PAGE 759

SENECA—A-1

(NW) CROOKED CREEK PIZZA SHOPPE & SNACK BAR—*From jct I-85 & US 76 W/SC 28 (exit 19B): Go 11 mi W on US 76 W/SC 28, then 9 mi W on US 76/US 123/SC 28, then 1-1/4 mi NW (Rt) on SC 28, then 3-3/10 mi NE (Rt) on SC 188 (Keowee Rd), then 1-7/10 mi N on Ebenezer Rd to Arvee Ln. Enter on R.* Pizza shoppe featuring fresh cooked pizza, hot dogs, chicken wings, sandwiche and hand dipped ice cream with a shad-

CROOKED CREEK PIZZA SHOPPE & SNACK BAR—Continued on next page

SENECA—Continued
CROOKED CREEK PIZZA SHOPPE & SNACK BAR—Continued

ed patio for lake side dining. Marina & marine gas available. Open all yr. MC/VISA/DISC/AMEX. ATM. Phone: (864)882-5040.

e-mail: CCRVP@trivergent.net

SEE AD THIS PAGE

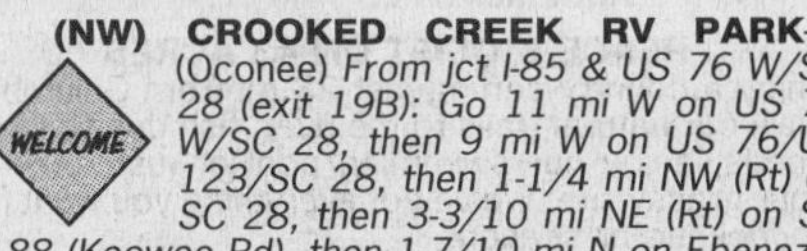

(NW) CROOKED CREEK RV PARK—(Oconee) *From jct I-85 & US 76 W/SC 28 (exit 19B): Go 11 mi W on US 76 W/SC 28, then 9 mi W on US 76/US 123/SC 28, then 1-1/4 mi NW (Rt) on SC 28, then 3-3/10 mi NE (Rt) on SC 188 (Keowee Rd), then 1-7/10 mi N on Ebenezer Rd to Arvee Ln. Enter on R.*

LAKE KEOWEE IS OUR HOME

Our family has owned this little piece of heaven for over 100 years. We just built a first-class RV park to share it with those who value beautiful mountains, pristine lakes and spectacular waterfalls. Come relax with us.

◊◊◊◊◊FACILITIES: 110 sites, typical site width 35 ft, 97 full hkups, 13 W&E, (20, 30 & 50 amps), 97 pull-thrus, cable TV, wireless Instant Internet access at site, phone on-site Internet access (needs activ), wireless Internet access central location, tenting, RV storage, laundry, groceries, RV supplies, LP gas by weight/by meter, marine gas, ice, tables, wood.

◊◊◊◊◊RECREATION: rec room/area, equipped pavilion, coin games, swim pool, wading pool, lake swimming, boating, canoeing, kayaking, ramp, dock, 2 pontoon/2 kayak/pedal boat rentals, lake fishing, fishing supplies, bsktball, playground, planned activities (wkends only), sports field, hiking trails, v-ball.

Pets welcome, breed restrict. Partial handicap access. Open all yr. Big rigs welcome. Internet friendly. Clubs welcome. Rate in 2007 $24-34 for 4 persons. MC/VISA/DISC/AMEX. ATM. Phone: (864)882-5040. FMCA discount.

e-mail: ccrvp@trivergent.net

SEE AD THIS PAGE AND AD DISCOVER SECTION PAGE 67

SOUTH OF THE BORDER—B-5

(C) CAMP PEDRO—(Dillon) *From jct I-95 & US-301: Go 1/10 mi S on US-301. Enter on L.*

◊◊◊◊FACILITIES: 100 sites, typical site width 35 ft, 100 full hkups, (20, 30 & 50 amps), 47 pull-thrus, RV storage, laundry, full svc store, RV supplies, LP gas by weight/by meter, gas, ice, tables, grills, controlled access gate.

◊◊◊RECREATION: rec room/area, coin games, 2 swim pools, whirlpool, mini-golf ($), bsktball, playground, tennis.

Pets welcome. Partial handicap access. No tents. Open all yr. Clubs welcome. Rate in 2007 $18-22 per vehicle. MC/VISA/DISC/AMEX/DC. ATM. Member ARVC, CARVC. Phone: (800)845-6011.

SEE AD NEXT PAGE

SOUTH OF THE BORDER—Continued

SOUTH OF THE BORDER—*From jct I-95 & US-301: Go 1/10 mi S on US-301. Enter on L.* Tourist complex with variety of six restaurants, shops, arcades and hotel/motel convention center. Also features children's amusement park, mini-golf, observation tower, post office and bingo (on weekends). Open all yr. MC/VISA/DISC/AMEX/DC. ATM. Phone: (843)774-2411.

SEE AD THIS PAGE

SPARTANBURG—A-2

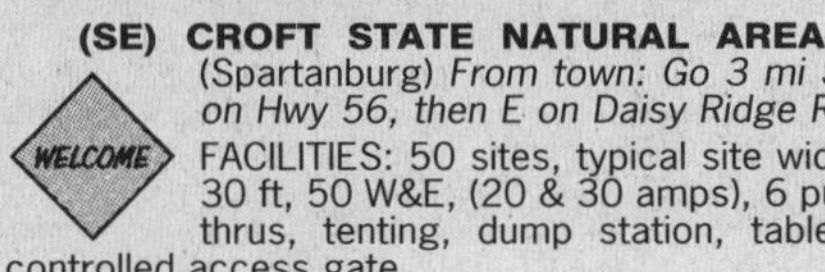

(SE) CROFT STATE NATURAL AREA—(Spartanburg) *From town: Go 3 mi SE on Hwy 56, then E on Daisy Ridge Rd.*

FACILITIES: 50 sites, typical site width 30 ft, 50 W&E, (20 & 30 amps), 6 pull-thrus, tenting, dump station, tables, controlled access gate.

RECREATION: swim pool, boating, electric motors only, rowboat rentals, lake fishing, playground, tennis, hiking trails.

Pets welcome. Open all yr. Phone: (864)585-1283.

SEE AD TRAVEL SECTION PAGE 759

(NW) CUNNINGHAM RV PARK—(Spartanburg) *From jct I-85 (exit 70) & I-26: Go 2-1/2 mi W on I-26 to exit 17, then 1/4 mi W on New Cut Rd, then 1 mi S on Campground Rd. Enter on R.*

◆◆◆FACILITIES: 95 sites, typical site width 40 ft, 57 full hkups, 38 W&E, (20, 30 & 50 amps), some extended stay sites, 69 pull-thrus, wireless Instant Internet access at site, wireless Internet access central location, tenting, RV storage, dump station, non-guest dumping $, laundry, ltd groceries, RV supplies, LP gas by weight/by meter, ice, tables, wood.

◆◆RECREATION: pavilion, swim pool, bsktball, playground, sports field, v-ball. Rec open to public.

Pets welcome. Partial handicap access. Open all yr. Big rigs welcome. Internet friendly. Clubs wel-

South Carolina State Gem: Amethyst

SPARTANBURG—Continued
CUNNINGHAM RV PARK—Continued

come. Rate in 2007 $26-30 for 2 persons. MC/VISA/DISC. Member ARVC, CARVC. Phone: (864)576-1973. CCUSA discount.

e-mail: cunninghamrvpark@bellsouth.net

SEE AD TRAVEL SECTION PAGE 761

PINE RIDGE CAMPGROUND—*From jct I-85 & I-26: Go E on I-26 to exit 28 (US 221 N), then 500 yds N on US 221,, then 1 mi E on Stillhouse Rd, then 1-1/2 mi N on Otts Shoal Rd, then 1000 feet E on Pine Ridge Campground Rd. Enter at end.*

SEE PRIMARY LISTING AT ROEBUCK AND AD ROEBUCK PAGE 778

SUMMERVILLE—D-4

(SW) GIVHANS FERRY STATE PARK—(Dorchester) *From jct US-78 & US-17A: Go 7 mi SW on US-17A, then 8 mi NW on Hwy-61.*

FACILITIES: 25 sites, typical site width 25 ft, 25 W&E, (20 & 30 amps), tenting, cabins, dump station, tables, controlled access gate.

RECREATION: boating, canoeing, kayaking, river fishing, hiking trails.

Pets welcome. Open all yr. Phone: (843)873-0692.

SEE AD TRAVEL SECTION PAGE 759

SUMTER—C-4

MILITARY PARK (Wateree Recreation Area and FAM-CAMP-Shaw AFB)—(Sumter) Off base. *From jct US 521 & Hwy 97: Go 10 mi NW on Hwy 97.* FACILITIES: 13 sites, 13 W&E, tenting, dump station, ltd groceries, ice, fire rings, grills. RECREATION: pavilion, lake swimming, boating, ramp, dock, rowboat rentals, lake fishing, playground, v-ball. Open all yr. For Military Use Only- w/ Military ID Card. Phone: (803)432-7976.

Stretching 60 miles from Little River to Georgetown, South Carolina's Grand Strand is one of the most popular tourist destinations in the United States.

SWANSEA—C-3

(SW) RIVER BOTTOM FARMS R.V. RESORT & CAMPGROUND—(Lexington) *From jct US 321 & S.C. 3: Go W 6-1/2 mi on S.C. 3, then NW 1/2 mi on US 178, then W 1/2 mi on Cedar Creek Rd. Enter on L.*

PEACE & QUIET ON 43 ACRES
Enjoy a country setting just 28 mi from Columbia! Walk our natural trails to the river, fish our stocked ponds, enjoy our swimming pool or just relax at your grassy site. We've got everything you want for a weekend or season!

◆◆◆◆FACILITIES: 78 sites, typical site width 40 ft, 61 full hkups, 14 W&E, 3 E, (20, 30 & 50 amps), some extended stay sites, 22 pull-thrus, wireless Instant Internet access at site, phone Internet access central location, tenting, cabins, RV storage, laundry, RV supplies, LP gas by weight/by meter, ice, tables, fire rings, grills, wood.

◆◆◆◆RECREATION: rec hall, equipped pavilion, swim pool, river/pond fishing, fishing supplies, play equipment, planned activities (wkends only), horseshoes, sports field, hiking trails, v-ball.

Pets welcome. Partial handicap access. Open all yr. Big rigs welcome. Internet friendly. Clubs welcome. Rate in 2007 $24-32 per family. MC/VISA. Member ARVC, CARVC. Phone: (803)568-4182. CCUSA discount.

e-mail: rbfrvresort@plotcomm.net

SEE AD COLUMBIA PAGE 770

TOWNVILLE—B-1

(N) CONEROSS CAMPGROUND (COE-Hartwell Lake)—(Oconee) *From town: Go 2 mi W on Hwy 24, then 1 mi N on CR 184, then 1 mi E on county road.* FACILITIES: 106 sites, 94 W&E, (30 & 50 amps), 12 no hkups, 36 pull-thrus, tenting, dump station, fire rings, grills. RECREATION: lake swimming, boating, ramp, dock, lake fishing, playground. Open May 1 thru Oct 28. Phone: (888)893-0678.

(N) OCONEE POINT CAMPGROUND (COE - Hartwell Lake)—(Oconee) *From town: Go 2 mi W on Hwy 24, then 4 mi N on CR 184, then 3 mi E on CR 21.* FACILITIES: 60 sites, 60 no hkups, tenting, dump station, fire rings, grills. RECREATION: lake swimming, boating, ramp, lake fishing, playground. Partial handicap access. Open May 1 thru Sep 6. Phone: (888)893-0678.

WALHALLA—A-1

(NE) DEVILS FORK STATE PARK—(Oconee) *From jct Hwy 183 & Hwy 11: Go 13 mi NE on Hwy 11, then 3 mi N on Hwy 25.*

FACILITIES: 84 sites, typical site width 22 ft, 36 ft max RV length, 59 W&E, (20 & 30 amps), 25 no hkups, 5 pull-thrus, tenting, cabins, dump station, laundry, ltd groceries, ice, tables, fire rings, grills, wood, controlled access gate.

RECREATION: boating, ramp, lake fishing, playground, hiking trails.

Pets welcome. Open all yr. MC/VISA. Phone: (864) 944-2639.

SEE AD TRAVEL SECTION PAGE 759

(N) OCONEE STATE PARK—(Oconee) *From jct Hwy-11 & Hwy-28: Go 10 mi NW on Hwy-28, then 2 mi N on Hwy-107.*

FACILITIES: 155 sites, typical site width 25 ft, 35 ft max RV length, 140 W&E, (20 & 30 amps), 15 no hkups, 46 pull-thrus, tenting, cabins, dump station, laundry, ltd groceries, ice, tables, controlled access gate.

RECREATION: rec hall, lake swimming, canoeing, rowboat/canoe/pedal boat rentals, lake fishing, mini-golf, playground, planned activities, hiking trails.

Pets welcome. Partial handicap access. Open all yr. MC/VISA. Phone: (864)638-5353.

SEE AD TRAVEL SECTION PAGE 759

(NW) SUMTER NF (Cherry Hill Campground)—(Oconee) *From jct Hwy-11 & Hwy-28: Go 9 mi NW on Hwy-28, then 7-1/3 mi N on Hwy-107. Enter on R.* FACILITIES: 28 sites, 22 ft max RV length, 28 no hkups, dump station, ltd groceries, grills. RECREATION: hiking trails. Open Apr 1 thru Oct 31. No reservations. Phone: (864)638-9568.

WALTERBORO—D-4

(SW) NEW GREEN ACRES R.V. PARK—(Colleton) *From jct I-95 (exit 53) & Hwy 63: Go W on Hwy 63, then take first right on Campground Rd. Enter on R.*

◆◆◆FACILITIES: 106 sites, typical site width 50 ft, 70 full hkups, 31 W&E, (30 & 50 amps), 50 amps ($), 5 no hkups, some extended stay sites, 101 pull-thrus, cable TV ($), wireless Instant Internet access at site, phone Internet access central location, tenting, RV storage, dump station, non-guest dumping $, laundry, RV supplies, LP gas by weight/by meter, ice, tables, patios, fire rings.

◆◆RECREATION: rec hall, swim pool, playground.

Pets welcome. Open all yr. Big rigs welcome. Internet friendly. Clubs welcome. Rate in 2007 $20-27 for 2 persons. MC/VISA. Member ARVC, CARVC. Phone: (800)474-3450.

e-mail: greenacres53@lowcountry.com

SEE AD TRAVEL SECTION PAGE 762

WEDGEFIELD—C-4

(S) POINSETT STATE PARK—(Sumter) *From jct Hwy 763 & Hwy 261: Go 6 mi S on Hwy 261, then 3 mi W on CR 34 & park road.*

FACILITIES: 50 sites, typical site width 20 ft, 24 W&E, (20 & 30 amps), 26 no hkups, tenting, cabins, dump station, tables, controlled access gate.

RECREATION: rowboat/pedal boat rentals, lake fishing, playground, hiking trails.

Pets welcome. Open all yr. Clubs welcome. Phone: (803)494-8177.

SEE AD TRAVEL SECTION PAGE 759

WINNSBORO—B-3

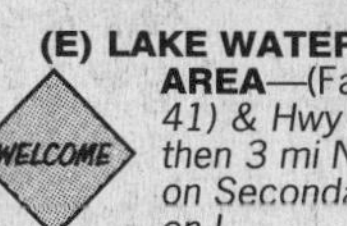

(E) LAKE WATEREE STATE RECREATION AREA—(Fairfield) *From jct I-77 (exit 41) & Hwy 41: Go 3 mi E on Hwy 41, then 3 mi N on US 21, then 5-1/2 mi E on Secondary Rd 101 (River Rd). Enter on L.*

FACILITIES: 72 sites, typical site width 20 ft, 72 W&E, (20 & 30 amps), 5 pull-thrus, tenting, dump station, ltd groceries, marine gas, tables, controlled access gate.

RECREATION: boating, ramp, dock, lake fishing, playground, hiking trails.

Pets welcome. Open all yr. MC/VISA. Phone: (803) 482-6401.

SEE AD TRAVEL SECTION PAGE 759

YORK—A-3

(E) KINGS MOUNTAIN STATE PARK—(York) *From jct Hwy 5 & US 321: Go 4 mi N on US 321, then 9 mi NW on Hwy 161, then 2 mi W on park road.*

FACILITIES: 125 sites, typical site width 30 ft, 115 W&E, (20 & 30 amps), 10 no hkups, 30 pull-thrus, tenting, dump station, laundry, ltd groceries, tables, controlled access gate.

RECREATION: lake swimming, canoeing, rowboat/canoe/pedal boat rentals, lake fishing, mini-golf, playground, planned activities, hiking trails.

Pets welcome. Open all yr. Phone: (803)222-3209.

SEE AD TRAVEL SECTION PAGE 759

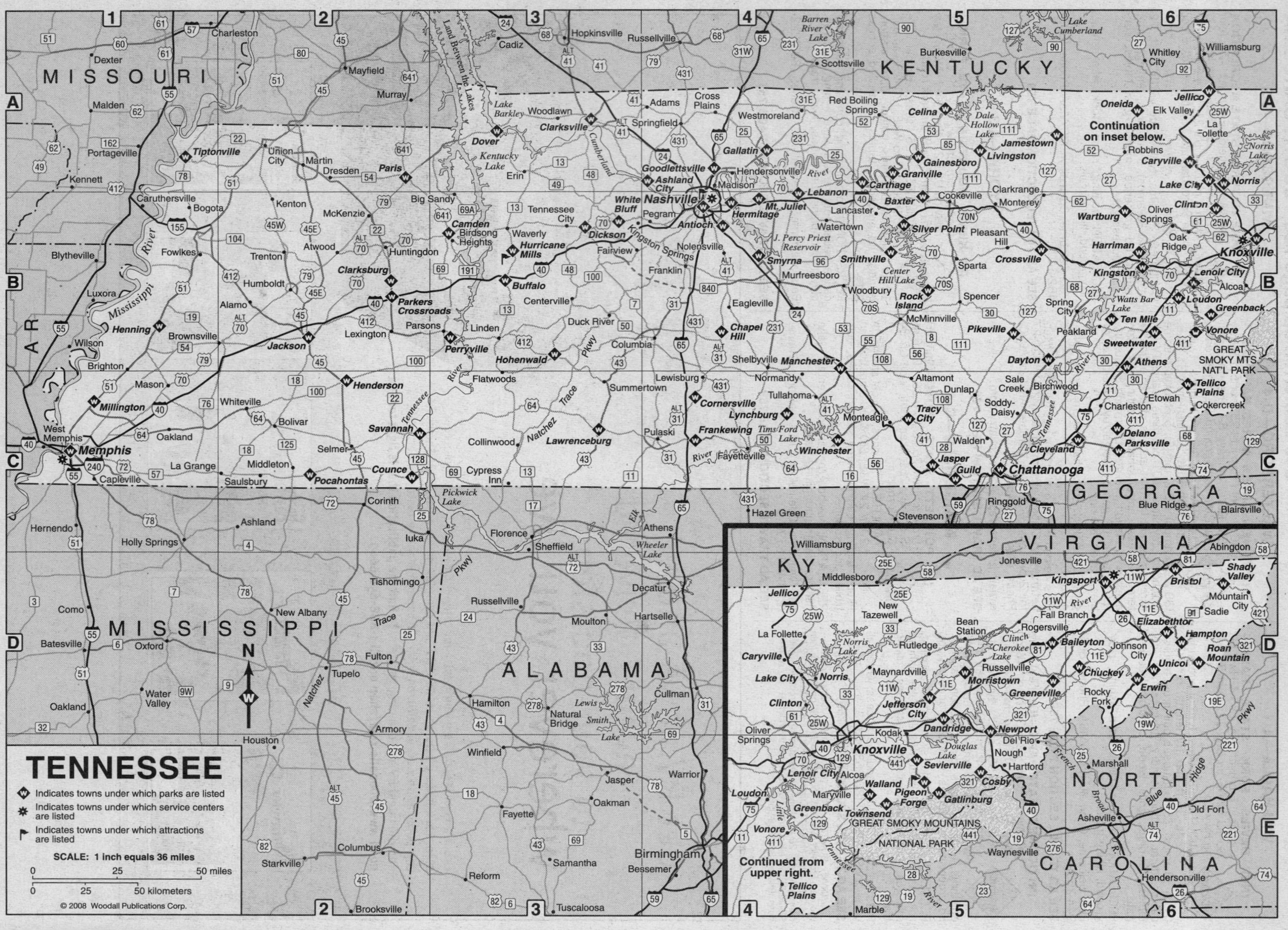
TENNESSEE
Indicates towns under which parks are listed
Indicates towns under which service centers are listed
Indicates towns under which attractions are listed
SCALE: 1 inch equals 36 miles
0 25 50 miles
0 25 50 kilometers
© 2008 Woodall Publications Corp.
Continuation on inset below.
Continued from upper right.

Tennessee

READER SERVICE INFO

The following businesses have placed an ad in the Tennessee Travel Section. To receive free information, enter their Reader Service number on the Reader Service Card opposite page 48/Discover Section in the front of this directory:

Advertiser	RS#
Casino Aztar RV Park	3455
Natchez Trace Compact	3650
Tennessee State Parks	3342

TIME ZONE

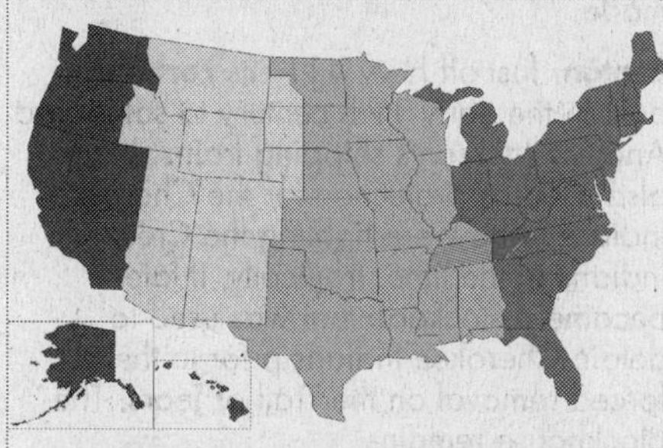

The eastern portion of Tennessee is on Eastern Standard Time. Middle and Western Tennessee are on Central Standard Time.

TOPOGRAPHY

Western Tennessee is marked by fertile bottomlands along the Mississippi River. From there, the land rises through the rolling hills and farmland of central Tennessee, to the deep valleys and forestlands of the Great Smoky Mountains in the east.

TEMPERATURE

Located in the Temperate Zone, Tennessee has a generally mild climate year-round, yet still has four distinct seasons. During the winter, the average high temperature is 49.4° and the average low is 30.4°. In the summer, the average high temperature is 89° and the average low is 67°. The average annual rainfall is 49.7".

TRAVEL & TOURISM INFO

State Agency:
Tennessee Department of Tourist Development
312 Eighth Ave. N., 25th Floor
William Snodgrass Building
Nashville, TN 37243
(615/741-9010)
www.tnvacation.com

Regional Agencies:

East Tennessee
www.easttnvacations.com

Memphis CVB
47 Union Ave.
Memphis, TN 38103
(901/543-5300)
www.memphistravel.com

Nashville CVB
One Nashville Place
150 Fourth Ave N., Ste. G-250
Nashville, TN 37219
(800/657-6910 or 615/259-4730)
www.musiccityusa.com

Middle East Tennessee Tourism Council
4420 Bucknell Dr.
Knoxville, TN 37938
(865/771-9250)
www.vacationeasttennessee.org

Middle Tennessee Tourism Council
501 Union St., 6th Flr.
Nashville, TN 37219
(615/862-8828)
www.middletennesseetourism.com

Northeast Tennessee Tourism Assn.
PO Box 415
Jonesborough, TN 37659
(800/468-6882 or 423/913-5550).
www.netta.com

Northwest Tennessee Tourism Council
PO Box 807
Paris, TN 38242
(866/698-6386 or 731/593-0171)
www.kentuckylaketourism.com

Southeast Tennessee Tourism Association
PO Box 4757
Chattanooga, TN 37405
(423/424-4263)
www.southeasttennessee.com

Tourism Association of Southwest Tennessee
PO Box 10543
Jackson, TN 38308
(800/462-8366 or 731/616-7474)
www.tast.tn.org

Upper Cumberland Tourism Assn.
PO Box 2411
Cookeville, TN 38502
(800/868-7237)
www.uppercumberland.org

RECREATIONAL INFO

Fishing/Hunting/Boating: Tennessee Wildlife Resources Agency (615/781-6500) www.state.tn.us/twra.

SHOPPING

Ada's, the Unusual Country Store, Bethel Springs. More than 75 Amish, Mennonite and Allergy-Free cookbooks. Also cheeses, teas and herbal remedies. On Hwy 45 N.

Belz Factory Outlet Center, Pigeon Forge. Buy direct from the manufacturer and save up to 75%. 2655 Teaster Ln., Pigeon Forge, TN.

Brooks Collection, Collierville. A unique gift and garden shop located in Collierville's Historic Town Square. 110 E. Mulberry St.

Market Street Antique Mall, Paris. Browse through one of the largest antique malls in the country. 414 N. Market St. (Hwy 641), Paris, TN.

Opry Mills, Nashville. Tennessee's newest retail, dining and entertainment destination with 200 interactive retailers offering value shopping, theme dining and entertainment. Adjacent to Grand Ole Opry at 433 Opry Mills Dr. www.oprymills.com.

Phillips General Store Antiques, Bell Buckle. Over 100-year-old dry goods store with original fixtures, vignettes of antique treasures, primitives, architectural fragments and textiles. 4 Railroad Square.

Rivergate Mall, Goodlettsville. More than 150 stores. Easy access off I-85 at exit 96.

DESTINATIONS

EAST REGION

An area of natural beauty, this region has the **Great Smoky Mountains National Park,** the largest wilderness area east of the Mississippi. Theme parks, shopping and sightseeing in resort towns make this an area of family fun.

American Museum of Science and Industry, Oak Ridge. Learn about and experiment with energy forms and discover their uses through demonstrations, audiovisuals, machines and other devices.

Athens. McMinn County Living Heritage Museum has 30 permanent exhibit areas over three floors that trace the history of McMinn County from the Cherokee through the 1940's. Special events and classes throughout the year, including an annual quilt show. At the **Mayfield Dairy Visitor Center,** you can tour the dairy plant to see how milk is bottled and ice cream is made.

Benton. Just off Hwy 411 sits **Fort Marr,** built in the early 19th century to safeguard Andrew Jackson's shipping trains. It was also used as protection for the Cherokee Indians, who were fighting the Creek Indians at the time. Ironically, it later became a stockade that was used to detain Cherokee Indians prior to their forced removal on the Trail of Tears. The blockhouse remains.

Bays Mountain Park & Planetarium, Kingsport. This 3,300-acre nature preserve has an excellent nature center, barge rides on a 44-acre lake, a museum, a planetarium, hiking trails, a saltwater tidal pool, marine aquariums, wildlife habitats and a variety of exhibits.

Bristol Caverns, Bristol. Caverns feature geologic formations and a paved walkway.

Butler Museum, Butler. View a replica of the train depot on "Old Butler" - the town that wouldn't drown. It houses artifacts and memorabilia of the only incorporated town "drowned" by the TVA.

Chattanooga. Many of Chattanooga's attractions reflect its early railroad history. **Chattanooga Choo Choo** is an immense complex of restaurants, shops, lounges and gardens. Enjoy trolley car rides, tennis courts and an ice skating rink. View one of the largest model railroad displays in the world. **Audubon Acres** has miles of hiking trails that enable naturalists to view a variety of birds and wildflowers. Other attractions include:

Creative Discovery Museum where you can pilot a riverboat, dig for dinosaur bones, make sculptures and build robots.

Lake Winnepesaukah Amusement Park. Over 30 rides and attractions including roller coasters, paddle boats, mini-golf and games.

Tennessee Aquarium. Learn the details of freshwater ecosystems; journey through two living forests and a 60-ft. canyon where over 7,000 animals fly, swim and crawl about their natural habitats. Enjoy the film at the IMAX® 3D Theater.

Houston Museum of Decorative Arts houses 18th-, 19th- and early 20th-century decorative art objects.

Cherokee National Forest consists of 600,000 acres of mountains, forests and meadows. Hiking, fishing, white water rafting, canoeing, skiing, hunting and camping keep visitors busy year-round.

Ducktown. Listed on the National Register of Historic Places, the **Ducktown Basin Museum** offers seasonal tours of the Burra Burra Mine Shops and Change House to complement permanent exhibits that depict the mining heritage of the Copper Basin. Near Ducktown and Copperhill is the **Ocoee Whitewater Center**. Built for the 1996 Olympic Whitewater Races, this visitor center includes the Olympic race channel, a native plant garden, paved walkways on both sides of the river, pools of water for wading or feeding fish and the historic Old Copper Road, open for hiking and biking.

Etowah. The 18-room **Louisville & Nashville Depot and Railroad Museum** resides in a restored Victorian Depot and features a museum "Growing Up With the L&N: Life and Times in a Railroad Town." In downtown Etowah, you'll find the historic **Gem Theater** with special events throughout the year.

Farragut Folklife Museum, Farragut. See a remarkable collection of East Tennessee artifacts including an extensive collection from Admiral David Farragut.

Gatlinburg. No longer a small mountain village, Gatlinburg has developed into a major resort area with over 400 shops and a large concentration of working craftspeople. At **Ober Gatlinburg Ski Resort & Amusement Park** you can enjoy indoor ice skating, alpine slide, a Black Bear Habitat, water raft rides, winter sports and a scenic aerial tramway.

Christus Gardens of Gatlinburg. Experience the Greatest Story Ever Told in a series of breathtaking dioramas, peopled with over 100 life-size wax figures in realistic settings. It's one of the Best Hours in the Smokies! Also featured at Christus Gardens is **The Promise**—a 900 square foot original mural featuring over 30 characters from the Old Testament, as well as **The Place of Parables**—a series of life-size paintings depicting the beloved stories told by Jesus. **Biblical Era Coins** features America's finest collection of Ancient coins from the Holy Land and Imperial Rome. **The Carraca Face of Christ** is a 6-ton marble sculpture of the head of Christ, so skillfully crafted not only the eyes but the entire face seems to follow your movements.

Guinness World of Records Museum, Gatlinburg. Hundreds of exhibits and 10 shows with memorabilia of famous record-holders.

Great Smoky Mountains Heritage Center. The Mission of the Great Smoky Mountain Heritage Center is to preserve, protect and promote the unique history and rich culture of the residents and Native Americans who inhabited the East Tennessee mountain communities. The Center will be a 15,000 square foot structure on three acres, including two classrooms, a museum, a store, an auditorium, a Native American gallery, an Early History gallery, a Temporary gallery, a Collection storage and a Fabrication shop. A 500 seat amphitheater will also be part of the new Heritage Center.

Great Smoky Mountains National Park, Gatlinburg. Located partly in North Carolina and partly in Tennessee, this 500,000-acre park has beautiful mountain scenery, over 800 miles of hiking trails, mile-high peaks and countless opportunities for fishing, biking, horseback riding and camping. Wildflowers abound in late April and early May and autumn's pageantry of color usually peaks during mid-October.

Hiwassee & Ocoee Scenic Rivers, Delano. Spend a leisurely afternoon canoeing, fishing, hiking and photographing nature along the Hiwassee River.

John Muir Trail. This 18.8 mile trail, which follows the Hiwassee River, begins at Childers Creek near Reliance and ends near Hwy 68 at Farner. The first three-mile section has been designed for senior citizens. Named for naturalist John Muir, the trail allows you to experience some of the most diverse and unique terrain in the Cherokee National Forest.

Knoxville. Enjoy the following areas, in and around Knoxville:

Ijams Nature Center offers 80 acres of trails, winding through wooded areas and wildflower meadows, past sink-holes, ponds and bluffs.

Knoxville Zoological Park features more than 1,000 animals, rides for adults and children, a playground, miniature golf and picnic facilities.

TVA Lakes. Located within 30 miles of Knoxville are six Tennessee Valley Authority lakes: **Norris, Douglas, Cherokee, Fort Loudon, Melton Hill and Watts Bar**. Most of the campgrounds around these lakes are open year-round; some have houseboats for rent and all offer year-round fishing.

Museum of Appalachia, Norris. Known as the most authentic and complete replica of pioneer Appalachian life in the world, this 65-acre museum has more than 250,000 pioneer relics, more than 30 log structures and the Appalachia Hall of Fame.

Paramount Center for the Arts, Bristol, is a historic 1931 landmark theater restored to its original art deco style.

Niota. Built in 1853, the **Niota Depot** is the oldest standing railroad depot in Tennessee. Now used as offices for the town, the depot is open for tours during business hours.

Ocoee Scenic Byway. US Highway 64. The first National Forest Scenic Byway in the United States is located in the Cherokee National Forest and consists of 26 miles of highway that winds alongside the Ocoee River in Polk County and up to the Chilhowee Campground on Forest Service Road 77. The highway passes through scenic areas dominated by rock bluffs,

Things to See & Do

HURRICANE MILLS
Loretta Lynn's Ranch

NASHVILLE
Tennessee State Parks Department of Environment and Conservation
US Army Corps of Engineers/Volunteer Clearing House

PIGEON FORGE
Pigeon Forge Department of Tourism

RV Sales & Service

	SALES	SERVICE
KINGSPORT		
Tri-City Travel Trailers	•	•
KNOXVILLE		
Bob Cox Camper Country	•	•
Tennessee RV	•	•
MEMPHIS		
Davis Motorhome/D & N Camper Sales	•	•
NASHVILLE		
Cullum & Maxey Camping Center	•	•
Nashville Easy Livin' Country	•	•

Woodall's Quick & Easy Reference for Tennessee

	BIG RIGS WELCOME	INTERNET FRIENDLY	PETS WELCOME	WEB SAVER
BAILEYTON				
Baileyton RV Park	▲	●	■	
BRISTOL				
Lakeview RV Park	▲	●	■	
CHATTANOOGA				
Best Holiday Trav-L-Park	▲	●	■	
CLARKSVILLE				
Clarksville RV Park & Campground	▲	●	■	
CLEVELAND				
Black Bear Cove	▲	●	■	
KOA-Chattanooga North/Cleveland	▲	●	■	
CLINTON				
Fox Inn Campground/Norris	▲	●	■	
CROSSVILLE				
Bean Pot Campground	▲	●	■	
DAYTON				
Blue Water Marina/Campground			■	
ELIZABETHTON				
Stoney Creek RV Park			■	
FRANKEWING				
Tennessee Valley R.V. Park		●	■	
GATLINBURG				
Great Smoky Jellystone Park Camp Resort	▲	●	■	
Smoky Bear Campground (formerly Huc A Bee)	▲	●	■	
Twin Creek RV Resort	▲	●	■	
GUILD				
Hale's Bar Marina & Resort	▲		■	
HARRIMAN				
Caney Creek RV Resort & Marina	▲	●	■	
HURRICANE MILLS				
Loretta Lynn's Ranch	▲		■	
JACKSON				
Jackson RV Park			■	
KINGSPORT				
KOA-Bristol/Kingsport	▲	●	■	
Rocky Top Campground	▲	●	■	
KNOXVILLE				
Southlake RV Park		●	■	
LAKE CITY				
Mountain Lake Marina & Campground	▲	●	■	
LEBANON				
Countryside RV Resort		●	■	
LENOIR CITY				
Soaring Eagle Campground & RV Park	▲	●	■	
LYNCHBURG				
Lynchburg Wilderness RV Park			■	$
MANCHESTER				
KOA-Manchester	▲	●	■	
MEMPHIS				
Memphis/Graceland RV Park & Campground	▲	●	■	
MILLINGTON				
Shady Oaks Community			■	
NASHVILLE				
Nashville Country RV Park	▲	●	■	
Nashville KOA		●	■	
Nashville's Jellystone Park	▲	●	■	
Two Rivers Campground	▲	●	■	
NEWPORT				
KOA-Newport I-40/Smoky Mtns	▲	●	■	
PARKERS CROSSROADS				
Parker's Crossroads Campground		●	■	

▲ = Big Rigs Welcome; ● = Internet Hookups; ● = (Wi-Fi available); ■ = Pets Welcome; $ = Web Saver Coupons

***Check out the "How to Use This Directory" section in the front of this book for a description of the criteria Woodall's uses in this chart.**

mountain peaks and historic sites such as the Ocoee Flume Line and Powerhouses, Confederate Camp and Old Copper Road. The panoramic views from the Chilhowee Overlooks and Boyd Gap are favorites of photographers.

Pigeon Forge. This family-fun town, located north of Gatlinburg, has numerous music shows, entertainment parks and more than 200 discount stores. Homespun fun can be found at **Dollywood**, a theme park which brings to life the fun and folklore of the Smoky Mountains. Flyaway, one of only three such facilities in the world, lets visitors experience the thrill of flying inside a wind tunnel.

Sweetwater. The **Tennessee Meji Gakuin Culture Enrichment Center** bridges the gap between Japanese and American cultures. Exhibits, classes and enrichment programs. Special events include the annual Japanese Quilt Show. Other highlights include: **Sweetwater Heritage Museum** featuring memorabilia and photographs that help visitors step back in time; **Lost Sea**, the world's largest underground lake. Designated a Registered National Landmark, the earliest known visitor to the cave was a saber-toothed tiger, whose fossilized remains are now in the Museum of Natural History. A guided walk to the bottom of the cavern is rewarded with a trip in a glass bottom boat.

Tellico Plains. Pause in this small mountain town and look for Babcock Street, where houses built by Babcock Lumber Company stand. At the end of the street, you'll see the old **Stokely Cannery**, where German prisoners of war worked in the cannery fields during WWII.

Vonore. Fort Loudon State Historic Area commemorates the first planned British fort in the land of the Overhill Cherokee. The reconstructed fort was originally built in 1756. Re-enactments and other celebrations add to museum exhibits on site. Picnicking and swimming. Other highlights include the **Sequoyah Birthplace Museum** located on the banks of Tellico Lake on tribal land. The museum examines the history of the Cherokee people and honors Sequoyah, creator of the Cherokee written language. Cherokee crafts and historical information are for sale in the gift shop.

MIDDLE REGION

Besides Nashville, the country music capital of the world, the middle region has picturesque communities, beautiful scenery, restored antebellum mansions and more.

101st Airborne Division's Don F. Pratt Memorial Museum at Clarksville tells the story of Fort Campbell and the 101st Airborne Division featuring a large collection of weapons, aircraft and vehicles.

Beachaven Vineyards & Winery, Clarksville, provides a look into historic wine making procedures. Free tours and tastings are available.

Cumberland River Walk, Clarksville. Meandering riverfront walk is the center of this 200-year-old city's River District.

Bell Witch Cave, Adams. This cave is associated with a famous spirit of the early 1800s and is considered to be one of the most haunted areas in America.

Big South Fork National River and Recreation Area, Jamestown. This area includes over 105,000 acres of the **Cumberland Plateau**. In addition to scenic beauty, the area offers camping, hiking, horseback riding, mountain biking, swimming, fishing, hunting, canoeing and whitewater paddling.

Fort Defiance, Clarksville. Well preserved Civil War fortification of earthen ramparts overlooks the Cumberland and Red rivers and the town of Clarksville.

Homeplace - 1850, A Living History Museum, Dover. Life in the mid 19th century is recreated with authentic houses and barns, interpreters in period clothing and demonstrations of daily chores.

Land Between the Lakes National Recreation Area, Dover, is made up of over 170,000 acres. Attractions include a living history farm, nature center, planetarium, wildlife viewing area and campgrounds.

Historic Mansker's Station Frontier Life Center, Goodlettsville. Fort reconstruction is considered to be one of the nation's most

Woodall's Quick & Easy Reference for Tennessee

	BIG RIGS WELCOME	INTERNET FRIENDLY	PETS WELCOME	WEB SAVER
PIGEON FORGE				
Clabough's Campground & RV Resort	▲	●	■	
Creekside RV Park	▲	●	■	
Eagle's Nest Campground	▲	●	■	
Foothills RV Park & Cabins			■	
King's Holly Haven RV Park	▲	●	■	
KOA-Pigeon Forge/Gatlinburg	▲	●	■	
River Plantation RV Park	▲	●	■	
Riverbend Campground	▲	●	■	
Riveredge RV Park	▲	●	■	
Shady Oaks Campground Pigeon Forge/Gatlinburg			■	
Smoker Holler RV Resort	▲	●	■	
Twin Mountain RV Park and Campground	▲	●	■	
Waldens Creek Campground	▲	●	■	
PIKEVILLE				
Mountain Glen RV Park	▲	●	■	
SEVIERVILLE				
Ripplin' Waters Campground	▲	●	■	
Riverside RV Park & Resort	▲	●	■	$
Two Rivers Landing Resort	▲	●	■	
SMYRNA				
Nashville I-24 Campground	▲	●	■	
SWEETWATER				
KOA-Sweetwater Valley	▲	●	■	
TOWNSEND				
Big Meadow Family Campground	▲	●	■	
Lazy Daze Campground		●	■	
Misty River Cabins & RV Resort, LLC	▲	●	■	

▲ = Big Rigs Welcome; ● = Internet Hookups; ● = (Wi-Fi available); ■ = Pets Welcome; $ = Web Saver Coupons

**Check out the "How to Use This Directory" section in the front of this book for a description of the criteria Woodall's uses in this chart.*

historically accurate. Tour with video and period dress interpreters.

Nashville. Welcome to "Music City USA," home of the famous **Grand Ole Opry,** dozens of recording studios, music shows and music-related attractions. The District in downtown Nashville has been renovated with imagination and flair; turn-of-the-century buildings house restaurants, trendy shops, contemporary art galleries and Nashville night spots. Visit the **Country Music Hall of Fame & Museum,** which offers displays of country music's greatest stars and live music daily. Interactive features will allow you to create a custom CD of songs. Other attractions include the **Adventure Science Center** where you can discover the wonders of science through interactive displays and exhibits; **Cheekwood Botanical Garden & Museum of Art, Belle Meade Plantation** and **Buchanan Log House**.

Stones River National Battlefield, Murfreesboro. These 509 acres commemorate the Civil War **Battle of Stones River**, where 23,000 casualties occurred in a 2-day period. On-site are a national cemetery, a visitors center and a museum.

Thomas Drugs, Cross Plains. Old-fashioned 1915 drugstore with operating soda fountain.

WEST REGION

Western Tennessee is a region of barbecues, blues and the mighty Mississippi.

Cotton Museum of the South, Bells, features a 1915 cotton gin located in a rural antique village with dining, shops, country church, arboretum, log buildings and one-room schoolhouse.

Dixie Gun Works Old Car Museum, Union City. View 36 antique autos, over 2,000 antique auto accessories, farm and steam engines and whistles.

Jackson. Visit the historic home of America's railroad legend at the **Casey Jones Home & Railroad Museum** with a 130-ton engine on display. Then head on over to the **International Rock-A-Billy Hall of Fame and Museum** featuring this country music sound with a blend of the blues.

Memphis. Hop aboard a **Main Street Trolley** for an entertaining tour of downtown. No trip to Memphis is complete without a walk through the **Beale Street Historic District,** known as the "birthplace of the blues." See Elvis Presley's home, **Graceland,** his auto collection and the Lisa Marie jet. The **National Civil Rights Museum** brings to life the sights, sounds and tensions of the Civil Rights Movement. See Ya Ya and Le Le, two giant pandas, at the **Memphis Zoo** along with more than 3,500 other animals. Then head to **Mud Island River Park** with its museum, riverwalk and recreation such as canoeing, kayaking and bicycling.

A. Schwab Dry Goods Store located on Beale St. was started in 1876 and is still owned and operated by three generations of the family. Incredible array of merchandise.

Art Museum of the University of Memphis contains changing exhibits of contemporary art throughout the year. Permanent collections include Egyptian Antiquities and the Neil Nokes West African Art Collection.

Peabody Hotel is home to the famous Peabody Ducks who have made their twice daily marches through the lobby since the 1930s.

Stax Museum of American Soul Music which presents the legacy of Stax Records whose recording artists included such legends as Otis Redding, Isaac Hayes, Booker T and more.

Shiloh was the site of one of the Civil War's bloodiest battles. Union and Confederate casualties reached a combined total of 23,746. **Shiloh National Military Park** commemorates this battle with 150 monuments, 217 cannons and 450 historic markers throughout its 4,000 acres. The Shiloh Civil War Relics & Museum features bullets, cannons, books, buckles and many more authentic Civil War artifacts.

Tennessee River Fresh Water Pearl Farm, Camden. Located on Kentucky Lake, this working farm produces America's most precious cultured pearls. The three-hour guided tour requires reservations.

CALENDAR OF EVENTS

JANUARY

Reelfoot Eagle Watch Tours, Tiptonville; Elvis Presley Birthday Celebration, Memphis; Wilderness Wildlife Week, Pigeon Forge.

FEBRUARY

Cherokee Indian Heritage & Sandhill Crane Viewing Days, Birchwood; Taste of Chattanooga, Chattanooga; Antiques & Garden Show of Nashville, Nashville; Smoky Mountains Storytelling Festival, Pigeon Forge; Boat, Sport, Travel & RV Show, Jackson; Annual American Sampler, Nashville.

MARCH

Lawn & Garden Show, Nashville; Heart of Country Antiques Show, Nashville; A Mountain Quiltfest, Pigeon Forge; Wearing of the Green, Erin; Cheez-It 250 & Food City 500, Bristol.

APRIL

Blount County Dogwood Arts Festival, Maryville; Mule Day, Columbia; Dolly Spring Parade, Pigeon Forge; Smoky Mountain Quilt Show and Competition, Knoxville; Dogwood Arts Festival, Knoxville.

MAY

Memphis in May, Memphis; Old Timers Day, Dickson; Smokin' in the Smokies Barbecue Cookoff, Townsend; Colonial Fair, Goodlettsville; West Tennessee Strawberry Festival, Humboldt/Dayton/Portland; Running the Iroquois Memorial Steeplechase, Nashville; Festival of British and Appalachian Culture, Rugby; Scottish Festival & Highland Games, Mills Park.

JUNE

Sumner County Museum Fleece Festival, Gallatin; Native American Festival, Sycamore Shoals State Historic Area; Independent Film Festival, Nashville; Riverbend Festival, Chattanooga.

JULY

Fiddler's Jamboree and Crafts Festival, Smithville; Bluegrass Festival, Savannah; Cedarfest, Lebanon; Jazz Festival, Watertown; Uncle Dave Macon Days Festival, Murfreesboro; Folklife Festival, Kingsport; Gem & Mineral Show, Centerville.

AUGUST

Cotton Festival, Crockett Mills; Reelfoot Lake Catfish Festival, Tiptonville; Waterfowl Festival, Big Sandy; Elvis Week, Memphis; Cherokee Days of Recognition, Cleveland.

SEPTEMBER

Stone Soul Picnic, Memphis; Fall Funfest, Cookeville; Goat Days International Family Festival, Millington; Tennessee State Fair, Nashville; Riverfest, Clarksville; 18th Century Trade Faire, Vonore.

OCTOBER

Davy Crockett Days, Rutherford; Erwin/Unicoi County Apple Festival, Erwin; National Storytelling Festival, Jonesborough; Jack Daniel's World Championship Cookoff, Lynchburg; Pioneer Day on the Mountain, Crossville; Candlelight Cemetery Tour, Gallatin; Liberty Square Celebration, Sparta.

NOVEMBER

Winterfest Kick-off, Pigeon Forge; Christmas at Graceland, Memphis; Smoky Mountain Winterfest, Gatlinburg.

DECEMBER

Tennessee Plantation Christmas Tour, Columbia/Mt. Pleasant/Spring Hill; Dickens of a Christmas, Franklin; First Night, Kingsport.

Tennessee

All privately owned campgrounds
personally inspected by
WOODALL'S Representatives
Lee and Mary Franck
One Tank Trips

ANTIOCH—B-4

ANDERSON ROAD CAMPGROUND (Corps of Engineers)—(Davison) *From I-40, exit 219, and Stewarts Ferry Pike.: Go S on Stewarts Ferry Pike, becomes Bell Rd., then 5 mi E on Smith Springs Rd., then 1 mi N on Anderson Rd. Enter on L.* FACILITIES: 37 sites, 37 no hkups, tenting, dump station, laundry, fire rings, grills. RECREATION: lake swimming, boating, ramp, lake fishing, playground, hiking trails. Partial handicap access. Open Apr 1 thru Sep 2. Phone: (615)361-1980.

ASHLAND CITY—A-4

LOCK A CAMPGROUND (COE - Chatham Lake)—(Cheatham) *From jct Ashland City: Go W 8 mi on US 12 to Cheap Hill, then W 4 mi on Cheatham Dam Rd. Enter on R.* FACILITIES: 45 sites, 45 W&E, (30 amps), tenting, dump station, laundry. RECREATION: lake swimming, boating, canoeing, ramp, lake fishing, playground, tennis, horseshoes, hiking trails, v-ball. Pets welcome. Partial handicap access. Open Apr 1 thru Oct 10. Phone: (615)792-3715.

ATHENS—B-6

(W) Athens I-75 Campground—(McMinn) *From jct I-75 (Exit 49) & Hwy-30: Go 1000 feet E on Hwy-30. Enter on R.* ◇◇FACILITIES: 60 sites, typical site width 25 ft, 44 full hkups, 6 W&E, (20, 30 & 50 amps), 50 amps ($), 10 no hkups, 24 pull-thrus, tenting, dump station, non-guest dumping $, laundry, LP gas by weight/by meter, tables, fire rings. ◇◇RECREATION: equipped pavilion, swim pool, stream fishing, play equipment, horseshoes, v-ball. Pets welcome. Open all yr. Facilities fully operational Jun 1 thru Sep 1. Internet friendly. Rate in 2007 $17-18 for 2 persons. Phone: (423)745-9199.

(N) Over-Niter RV Park—(McMinn) *From jct I-75 (exit 52) & Hwy 305: Go 3/4 mi E on US 305. Enter on L.* ◇◇◇FACILITIES: 16 sites, typical site width 30 ft, 16 full hkups, (20, 30 & 50 amps), some extended stay sites, 11 pull-thrus, tenting. RECREATION: rec room/area. Pets welcome. Open all yr. Big rigs welcome. Rate in 2007 $20-23 for 2 persons. Phone: (423)507-0069.

The Great Smoky Mountains National Park is the most visited national park in the United States. The park was named for the smoke-like bluish haze that often envelops these fabled mountains.

BAILEYTON—D-5

(E) BAILEYTON RV PARK—(Greene) *From jct I-81 (exit 36): Go 7/10 mi N, then 1 mi E on Horton Hwy. Enter on L.*

WELCOME

PEACE & QUIET ON 40 ACRES
Enjoy a country setting just minutes from Bristol, Pigeon Forge and Sevierville. Practice your swing on our 300 yd golf driving range, then visit the golf club next door for a round of golf. We look forward to your visit!

◇◇◇◇FACILITIES: 60 sites, typical site width 30 ft, 55 full hkups, 5 W&E, (20, 30 & 50 amps), some extended stay sites, 30 pull-thrus, cable TV, wireless Instant Internet access at site, phone on-site Internet access (needs activ), phone Internet access central location, tenting, RV/park trailer rentals, RV storage, dump station, non-guest dumping $, laundry, RV supplies, LP gas by weight/by meter, ice, tables, grills, wood.

◇◇RECREATION: equipped pavilion, pond fishing, fishing supplies, golf nearby, horseshoes, hiking trails, v-ball.

Pets welcome. Open all yr. Big rigs welcome. Internet friendly. Escort to site. Clubs welcome. Rate in 2007 $28-30 for 2 persons. MC/VISA/DISC/Debit. Member ARVC, TNARVC. Phone: (423)234-4992. FMCA discount.

e-mail: patricialinn@mac.com

SEE AD GREENEVILLE PAGE 798

BAXTER—B-5

(W) Twin Lakes Catfish Farm & Campground—(Putnam) *From jct I-40 & Hwy 56 (exit 280): Go 2-3/4 mi N on Hwy 56 Enter on L.* ◇◇◇FACILITIES: 32 sites, typical site width 30 ft, 28 full hkups, (20, 30 & 50 amps), 4 no hkups, some extended stay sites, 9 pull-

BAXTER—Continued
Twin Lakes Catfish Farm & Campground—Continued

thrus, tenting, ice, tables. ◇◇RECREATION: pavilion, lake fishing, planned activities (wkends only), horseshoes, v-ball. Pets welcome. Partial handicap access. Open all yr. Big rigs welcome. Internet friendly. Rate in 2007 $25 for 2 persons. Phone: (931)858-2333.

BRISTOL—D-6

See listing at Bristol, VA & Blountville, Johnson City & Kingsport, TN

CHEROKEE NATIONAL FOREST (Little Oak Campground)—(Sullivan) *From town: Go 14 mi E on US-421, then 7 mi SW on FR-87.* FACILITIES: 72 sites, 72 no hkups, tenting, dump station, fire rings, grills. RECREATION: lake swimming, boating, canoeing, ramp, lake fishing, hiking trails. Open Mar 17 thru Dec 1. No reservations. Phone: (423)476-9700.

(S) LAKEVIEW RV PARK—(Sullivan) *From jct I-81 (exit 69) & SR 394: Go 5-1/4 mi E on SR-394, then 3 mi S on Hwy 11E. Enter on R.*

WELCOME

NEW CAMPGROUND-GREAT SCENIC SETTING
Just 3 miles from Bristol Motor Speedway overlooking Boone Lake. Relax & enjoy country setting in the Tri Cities (Bristol, Kingsport & Johnson City). Big Rigs Welcome - 30/50 amps, full hookups, easy access sites. Free WiFi!

◇◇◇FACILITIES: 160 sites, typical site width 30 ft, 160 full hkups, (20, 30 & 50 amps), cable TV, wireless Instant Internet access at site, wireless Internet access central location, RV storage, laundry, ltd groceries, RV supplies, LP gas by weight/by meter, ice, tables.

◇◇◇RECREATION: rec room/area, dock, lake fishing, fishing supplies, golf nearby, planned activities, horseshoes, sports field, v-ball.

LAKEVIEW RV PARK—Continued on next page

BRISTOL—Continued
LAKEVIEW RV PARK—Continued

Pets welcome. No tents. Open all yr. Big rigs welcome. Internet friendly. Escort to site. Clubs welcome. Rate in 2007 $28-37 for 2 persons. MC/VISA/DISC/Debit. Member ARVC, TNARVC. Phone: (866)800-0777.

e-mail: camping@lakeviewrvpark.com

SEE AD PAGE 789

BUFFALO—B-3

(E) KOA-Buffalo—(Humphreys) *From jct I-40 (exit 143) & Hwy 13: Go 200 yards N on Hwy 13, then 1/4 mi E. Follow signs. Enter on R.* ◇◇◇◇FACILITIES: 62 sites, typical site width 22 ft, 26 full hkups, 26 W&E, 10 E, (20, 30 & 50 amps), 50 amps ($), 28 pull-thrus, tenting, dump station, laundry, full svc store, LP gas by weight/by meter, ice, tables, wood. ◇◇◇RECREATION: rec room/area, equipped pavilion, swim pool, playground, horseshoes, v-ball. Pets welcome, breed restrict. Open all yr. Swimming pool open May 15 - Sep 15. Big rigs welcome. Internet friendly. Rate in 2007 $24-32 for 2 persons. Phone: (931)296-1306. KOA 10% value card discount.

CAMDEN—B-3

(S) Birdsong Resort, Marina & Lakeside Campground—(Benton) *From I-40 (exit mile 133/Birdsong Rd/Hwy 191N): Go 9 mi N on scenic country highway, follow Birdsong logos. Enter on R.* ◇◇◇FACILITIES: 95 sites, typical site width 24 ft, 75 full hkups, (20, 30 & 50 amps), 20 no hkups, 10 pull-thrus, tenting, dump station, non-guest dumping $, portable dump, ltd groceries, LP gas by weight/by meter, ice, tables. ◇◇◇RECREATION: equipped pavilion, swim pool, lake swimming, boating, canoeing, ramp, dock, 6 rowboat/20 motorboat rentals, lake fishing, playground, shuffleboard court, planned activities, horseshoes, hiking trails, v-ball. Rec open to public. Pets welcome. Partial handicap access. Open all yr. Big rigs welcome. Internet friendly. Rate in 2007 $28.50-32.50 for 2 persons. Phone: (731)584-7880.

(E) NATHAN BEDFORD FORREST STATE PARK—(Benton) *From town: Go 10 mi NE on Hwy 191 (Eva). Enter at end.*

WELCOME

FACILITIES: 53 sites, 38 W&E, (20, 30 & 50 amps), 15 no hkups, tenting, cabins, dump station, tables, grills, wood.

RECREATION: lake swimming, boating, ramp, lake fishing, playground, planned activities, sports field, hiking trails, v-ball. Rec open to public.

Partial handicap access. Open Apr 1 thru Nov 15. No reservations. Phone: (731)584-6356.

SEE AD TRAVEL SECTION PAGE 784

CARTHAGE—A-5

(N) DEFEATED CREEK PARK (Corps of Engineers)—(Smith) *From Carthage: Go 4 mi W on SR 25, then N on US 80, then E on SR 85, 7 mi from Carthage.* FACILITIES: 155 sites, 63 full hkups, 92 W&E, (20 & 30 amps), 32 pull-thrus, tenting, dump station, laundry, fire rings. RECREATION: pavilion, swim pool, lake swimming, boating, ramp, dock, lake fishing, playground, tennis, v-ball. Partial handicap access. Open Apr 7 thru Oct 30. Phone: (615)774-3141.

CARYVILLE—A-6

(NE) COVE LAKE STATE PARK—(Campbell) *From jct I-75 & US 25W: Go 1/2 mi NE on US 25W. Enter on L.*

WELCOME

FACILITIES: 106 sites, 106 W&E, (30 amps), 2 pull-thrus, tenting, dump station, ice, tables, grills.

RECREATION: equipped pavilion, swim pool, boating, electric motors only, dock, 8 rowboat/10 pedal boat rentals, lake fishing, playground, shuffleboard court, planned activities, tennis, horseshoes, sports field, hiking trails, v-ball.

Pets welcome. Partial handicap access. Open all yr. Facilities fully operational Apr thru Labor Day. No reservations. Phone: (423)566-9701.

SEE AD TRAVEL SECTION PAGE 784

CELINA—A-5

(E) DALE HOLLOW DAM CAMPGROUND (COE-Dale Hollow Lake)—(Clay) *From town: Go 3 mi E on Hwy-53.* FACILITIES: 79 sites, 78 W&E, (50 amps), 1 no hkups, 13 pull-thrus, tenting, dump station, laundry, fire rings, grills. RECREATION: boating, canoeing, ramp, dock, river fishing, playground, hiking trails, v-ball. Rec open to public. Partial handicap access. Open Mar 31 thru Oct 28. Phone: (931)243-3554.

CHAPEL HILL—B-4

(S) HENRY HORTON STATE PARK—(Marshall) *From town: Go 3 mi S on US 31A. Enter on R.*

FACILITIES: 75 sites, 54 W&E, (30 amps), 21 no hkups, tenting, cabins, dump station, tables, grills.

RECREATION: pavilion, swim pool, boating, canoeing, ramp, river fishing, putting green, bsktball, playground, planned activities, tennis, sports field, hiking trails, v-ball.

Pets welcome. Open all yr. Facilities fully operational Apr 1 thru Dec 1. Phone: (931)364-2222.

SEE AD TRAVEL SECTION PAGE 784

The second largest earthquake in American history, the New Madrid Earthquake, occurred in the winter of 1811-12 in northwestern Tennessee. Reelfoot Lake located in Obion and Lake Counties was formed during this earthquake.

CHATTANOOGA—C-5

CHATTANOOGA AREA MAP

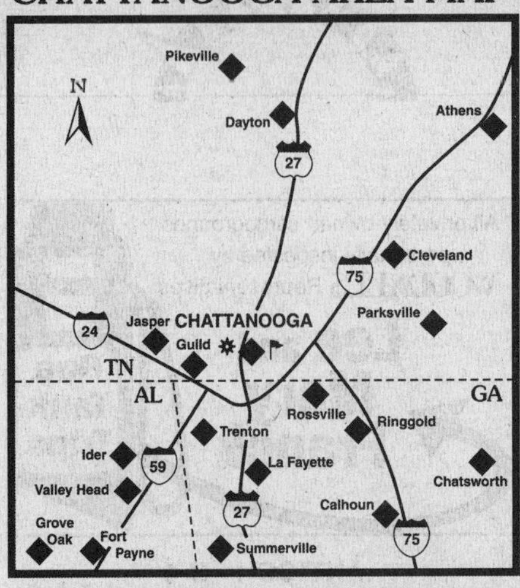

Symbols on map indicate towns within a 45 mi radius of Chattanooga where campgrounds (dia-monds), attractions (flags), & RV service centers & camping supply outlets (gears) are listed. Check listings for more information.

Tell Them Woodall's Sent You!

(S) BEST HOLIDAY TRAV-L-PARK—(Hamilton) *From jct I-24 & I-75: Go 1/2 mi S on I-75 (S bound exit 1, N bound exit 1B), then 1/4 mi W on US 41N, then 1/2 mi S on Mack Smith Rd. Enter on R.*

◇◇◇◇◇FACILITIES: 171 sites, typical site width 30 ft, 131 full hkups, 22 W&E, (20, 30 & 50 amps), 18 no hkups, some extended stay sites, 130 pull-thrus, cable TV, wireless Instant Internet access at site, phone on-site Internet access (needs activ), cable Internet access central location, tenting, cabins, RV storage, dump station, non-guest dumping $, laundry, groceries, RV supplies, LP gas by weight/by meter, ice, tables, patios, fire rings, wood.

BEST HOLIDAY TRAV-L-PARK—Continued on next page

CHATTANOOGA—Continued
BEST HOLIDAY TRAV-L-PARK—Continued

◇◇◇◇RECREATION: rec hall, rec room/area, pavilion, coin games, swim pool, golf nearby, bsktball, playground, 2 shuffleboard courts, horseshoes, sports field, v-ball.

Pets welcome, breed restrict. Partial handicap access. Open all yr. Big rigs welcome. Internet friendly. Clubs welcome. Rate in 2007 $31-33 for 2 persons. MC/VISA/Debit. Member ARVC, TNARVC. Phone: (800)693-2877. FCRV 10% discount. FMCA discount.

e-mail: campmail@chattacamp.com

SEE AD THIS PAGE

(W) Chattanooga's Raccoon Mtn. Caverns & Campground—(Hamilton) *From jct I-24 (exit 174) & US-41/64: Go 1-1/4 mi N on US-41/64, then 600 yards SW on West Hill Rd. Enter on L.* ◇◇◇◇FACILITIES: 130 sites, typical site width 22 ft, 55 full hkups, 44 W&E, (30 & 50 amps), 31 no hkups, 55 pull-thrus, tenting, dump station, non-guest dumping $, laundry, groceries, LP gas by weight/by meter, ice, tables, patios, fire rings, grills, wood. ◇◇◇◇RECREATION: rec hall, equipped pavilion, swim pool, playground, shuffleboard court, horseshoes, sports field, hiking trails. Pets welcome, breed restrict. Open all yr. Facilities fully operational Apr 1 thru Oct 31. Pool seasonal. Big rigs welcome. Internet friendly. Rate in 2007 $22-28 for 4 persons. Member ARVC, TNARVC. Phone: (423)821-9403. FMCA discount.

(N) CHESTER FROST PARK (Hamilton County Park) —(Hamilton) *From jct Hwy-153 & Hixson Pike: Go 10 mi N on Hixon Pike, then 1 mi N on Gold Point Circle.* FACILITIES: 254 sites, 191 W&E, (20 & 30 amps), 63 no hkups, 35 pull-thrus, tenting, dump station, grills. RECREATION: rec hall, pavilion, equipped pavilion, lake swimming, boating, ramp, dock, lake fishing, playground, tennis, horseshoes, hiking trails, v-ball. Open all yr. Facilities fully operational Apr thru Nov. No reservations. Phone: (423)842-3306.

HARRISON BAY STATE PARK—(Hamilton) *From town: Go 11 mi NE on Hwy 58. Enter on L.*

WELCOME

FACILITIES: 149 sites, 128 W&E, (30 amps), 21 no hkups, tenting, dump station, ltd groceries, marine gas, ice, tables, grills.

RECREATION: rec hall, pavilion, swim pool, boating, canoeing, ramp, dock, lake fishing, bsktball,

CHATTANOOGA—Continued
HARRISON BAY STATE PARK—Continued

playground, shuffleboard court, planned activities, tennis, horseshoes, sports field, hiking trails, v-ball.

Pets welcome. Partial handicap access. Open all yr. No reservations. MC/VISA/DISC/AMEX. Phone: (423)344-7966.

SEE AD TRAVEL SECTION PAGE 784

(S) Shipp's RV Center & Campground—(Hamilton) *From jct I-75 (exit 1) & US-41: Go 1/2 mi SE on US-41. Enter on R.* ◇◇◇FACILITIES: 80 sites, typical site width 20 ft, 50 full hkups, 30 W&E, (20, 30 & 50 amps), 50 amps ($), 50 pull-thrus, dump station, non-guest dumping $, ice, tables, patios, wood. ◇◇RECREATION: swim pool, boating, no motors, lake fishing, playground, hiking trails. Pets welcome. Partial handicap access. No tents. Open all yr. Internet friendly. Phone: (423)892-8275.

CHUCKEY—D-6

(S) Pebble Mountain Family Campground—(Greene) *From jct HE Bypass & Hwy 107: Go 7-1/2 mi E on Hwy 107, then 2 mi S on Horse Creek Park Rd, then 1/4 mi E on Durham Rd (follow signs). Enter on R.* ◇◇FACILITIES: 44 sites, typical site width 25 ft, 41 full hkups, (30 amps), 3 no hkups, 9 pull-thrus, tenting, dump station, non-guest dumping $, laundry, ice, tables, fire rings, wood. ◇◇RECREATION: equipped pavilion, swim pool, play equipment, horseshoes, hiking trails, v-ball. Pets welcome, breed restrict. Open all yr. Rate in 2007 $20 for 4 persons. Member ARVC, TNARVC. Phone: (423)257-2120. FCRV 10% discount.

CLARKSBURG—B-2

NATCHEZ TRACE STATE PARK—(Henderson) *From jct Hwy 114 & I-40 (exit 116): Follow signs.*

WELCOME

FACILITIES: 287 sites, 77 full hkups, 190 W&E, (30 & 50 amps), 20 no hkups, 9 pull-thrus, tenting, cabins, dump station, laundry, ltd groceries, tables, fire rings, grills.

RECREATION: lake swimming, boating, no motors, ramp, lake fishing, playground, hiking trails. Rec open to public.

Aretha Franklin, singer, is from Tennessee.

CLARKSBURG—Continued
NATCHEZ TRACE STATE PARK—Continued

Pets welcome. Partial handicap access. Open all yr. Facilities fully operational May thru Dec 15. No reservations. Phone: (731)968-8431.

SEE AD TRAVEL SECTION PAGE 784

CLARKSVILLE—A-3

(NE) CLARKSVILLE RV PARK & CAMPGROUND—(Montgomery) *From jct I-24 (exit 1) & Hwy-48: Go 700 feet N on Hwy-48, then follow signs 1/4 mi W. Enter on L.*

WELCOME

BIG RIG SITES!! 50 AMPS!! WIFI!!
We can handle your big rig with our long level pull thru 30/50 amp sites. We have high speed Internet access and we're close to restaurants & shopping. Stay with us once and you'll keep coming back. We also Welcome rallies.

◇◇◇◇FACILITIES: 75 sites, typical site width 25 ft, 55 full hkups, 12 W&E, (20, 30 & 50 amps), 8 no hkups, some extended stay sites, 51 pull-thrus, wireless Instant Internet access at site, phone Internet access central location, tenting, cabins, dump station, non-guest dumping $, laundry, ltd groceries, RV supplies, LP gas by weight/by meter, ice, tables, wood.

◇◇◇RECREATION: rec hall, swim pool, golf nearby, playground, horseshoes, sports field, v-ball.

Pets welcome. Open all yr. Swimming Pool open Memorial Day thru Labor Day. Big rigs welcome. Internet friendly. Clubs welcome. Rate in 2007 $28-31 for 2 persons. MC/VISA/DISC/Debit. Member ARVC, TNARVC. Phone: (888)287-8638.

e-mail: info@clarksvillervpark.com

SEE AD NEXT PAGE

The Ocoee River in southeastern Tennessee is rated among the top white water recreational rivers in the nation and was the site for the Olympic white water canoe/kayak competition in the 1996 Olympics.

CLEVELAND—C-6

(E) BLACK BEAR COVE—(Polk) *From jct I-75 (exit 20) & Bypass 64: Go 6-1/2 mi NE on Bypass 64, then 8 mi E on Hwy 64, then 12 mi N on Hwy 411, then 1/2 mi E on Hwy 30. Enter on L.*

WELCOME

◆◆◆◆FACILITIES: 41 sites, typical site width 30 ft, 41 full hkups, (20, 30 & 50 amps), 50 amps ($), 9 pull-thrus, cable TV, wireless Instant Internet access at site ($), phone Internet access central location, tenting, RV/park trailer rentals, laundry, ltd groceries, RV supplies, LP bottle exch, ice, tables, fire rings, wood.

◆◆◆RECREATION: pavilion, swim pool, river fishing, planned activities, horseshoes, sports field, v-ball.

Pets welcome. Open all yr. Big rigs welcome. Internet friendly. Clubs welcome. Rate in 2007 $29-40 for 2 persons. MC/VISA/Debit. Member ARVC, TNARVC. Phone: (866)438-4399.

e-mail: angie@blackbearcove.com

SEE AD THIS PAGE

(E) CHEROKEE NATIONAL FOREST (Chilhowee Campgrounds)—(Polk) *From town: Go 17-3/10 mi E on US-64, then 7-4/10 mi NW on FR-77.* FACILITIES: 83 sites, 83 no hkups, tenting, cold showers only, dump station, grills. RECREATION: lake swimming, boating, electric motors only, canoeing, lake fishing, hiking trails. Partial handicap access. Open May 1 thru Nov 1. Phone: (615)338-5201.

(SW) KOA-CHATTANOOGA NORTH/ CLEVELAND—(Bradley) *From jct I-75 (exit 20) & US 64 Bypass: Go 1/2 mi W on county road, then follow signs 1/2 mi SW. Enter on R.*

WELCOME

◆◆◆◆FACILITIES: 97 sites, typical site width 30 ft, 38 full hkups, 37 W&E, (20, 30 & 50 amps), 50 amps ($), 22 no hkups, 20 pull-thrus, cable TV, wireless Instant Internet access at site, phone Internet access central location, tenting, cabins, RV storage, dump station, laundry, groceries, RV supplies, LP gas by weight/by meter, ice, tables, patios, fire rings, grills, wood.

◆◆◆RECREATION: rec room/area, equipped pavilion, coin games, swim pool, golf nearby, bsktball, playground, planned activities (wkends only), horseshoes, v-ball.

Pets welcome, breed restrict. Partial handicap access. Open all yr. Planned activities weekends & holidays. Big rigs welcome. Internet friendly. Escort to site. Clubs welcome. Rate in 2007 $26-37 for 2 persons. MC/VISA/DISC/Debit. Phone: (423) 472-8928. KOA 10% value card discount.

e-mail: koacleveland@charter.net

SEE AD CHATTANOOGA PAGE 790 AND AD DISCOVER SECTION PAGES 62 & 63

Tennessee was the 16th state admitted to the Union

CLINTON—B-6

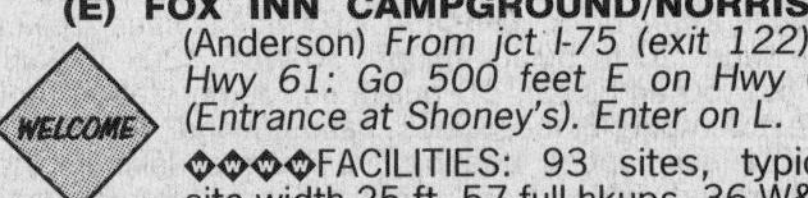

(E) FOX INN CAMPGROUND/NORRIS—(Anderson) *From jct I-75 (exit 122) & Hwy 61: Go 500 feet E on Hwy 61 (Entrance at Shoney's). Enter on L.*

◆◆◆◆FACILITIES: 93 sites, typical site width 25 ft, 57 full hkups, 36 W&E, (20, 30 & 50 amps), some extended stay sites, 70 pull-thrus, cable TV, wireless Instant Internet access at site, phone Internet access central location, tenting, cabins, dump station, non-guest dumping $, laundry, ltd groceries, RV supplies, LP gas by weight/by meter, LP bottle exch, ice, tables, fire rings, wood.

◆◆◆◆RECREATION: rec hall, equipped pavilion, coin games, swim pool, wading pool, golf nearby, bsktball, play equipment, horseshoes, sports field, v-ball.

Pets welcome. Open all yr. Full hookups year round. Big rigs welcome. Internet friendly. Escort to site. Clubs welcome. Rate in 2007 $26-30 for 2 persons. MC/VISA/Debit. Member ARVC, TNARVC. Phone: (865)494-9386. FMCA discount.

e-mail: foxinncamp@comcast.net

SEE AD KNOXVILLE PAGE 801

CORNERSVILLE—C-4

(W) Texas "T" Campground—(Marshall) *From jct I-65 (exit 27) & Hwy 129: Go 200 feet E on Hwy 129. Enter on R.* ◆◆◆FACILITIES: 40 sites, typical site width 30 ft, 36 full hkups, 4 W&E, (30 & 50 amps), some extended stay sites, 40 pull-thrus, heater not allowed, tenting, dump station, non-guest dumping $, laundry, LP gas by weight/by meter, ice, tables. ◆◆RECREATION: rec room/area, play equipment, sports field. Pets welcome, breed restrict. Open all yr. Big rigs welcome. Internet friendly. Rate in 2007 $20.93-28.49 per family. Phone: (931)293-2500.

COSBY—E-5

(S) Fox Den Campground—(Cocke) *From jct I-40 (exit 443) & Foothills Pkwy: Go 6 mi S on Foothills Pkwy, then 1 mi SE on Hwy 32. Enter on R.* ◆◆FACILITIES: 75 sites, typical site width 30 ft, 29 full hkups, 36 W&E, (30 & 50 amps), 10 no hkups, 7 pull-thrus, tenting, laundry, LP gas by weight, ice, tables, fire rings, wood. ◆◆RECREATION: rec room/area, pavilion, swim pool, pond fishing, playground, horseshoes. Pets welcome. Open all yr. Internet friendly. Rate in 2007 $20-25 for 4 persons. Member ARVC, TNARVC. Phone: (423)487-3178.

(S) GREAT SMOKY MOUNTAINS NATIONAL PARK (Cosby Campground)—(Sevier) *From town: Go 2 mi S on Hwy 32.* FACILITIES: 175 sites, 25 ft max RV length, 175 no hkups, tenting, dump station, grills, wood. RECREATION: stream fishing, hiking trails. Pets welcome. Open May thru Oct 31. No showers. No reservations. Phone: (865)436-1200.

(S) Triple Creek Campground—(Cocke) *From I-40 (exit 435): Go 5 mi S on Hwy 32/Hwy 321, then 1/2 mi right on old Hwy 32, then right on Lower Bogard Rd. Enter on L.* ◆◆FACILITIES: 79 sites, typical site width 25 ft, 34 full hkups, 30 W&E, (20, 30 & 50 amps), 15 no hkups, 3 pull-thrus, tenting, dump station, non-guest dumping $, laundry, tables, fire rings, wood. ◆RECREATION: pavilion, river swimming, stream fishing, play equipment, horseshoes, sports field, v-ball. Pets welcome. Open all yr. Self contained units only from Nov 15-Apr 15. Rate in 2007 $22-30 for 4 persons. Phone: (423)623-2020.

COUNCE—C-2

(N) PICKWICK DAM (TVA-Pickwick Lake)—(Hardin) *From jct Hwy-57 & Hwy-128: Go 1-1/2 mi N on Hwy-128 across dam, then W below dam.* FACILITIES: 95 sites, 66 W&E, (30 & 50 amps), 29 no hkups, 20 pull-thrus, tenting, dump station, grills. RECREATION: boating, ramp, river fishing. Pets welcome. Open all yr. Phone: (256)386-2560.

CROSSVILLE—B-5

(S) Ballyhoo Family Campground—(Cumberland) *From jct I-40 (exit 322) & Peavine Rd: Go 1/2 mi S on Peavine Rd, then 2-1/2 mi W on US 70/Hwy 101, then 2 mi W on Hwy 101, then 2-1/4 mi S on Hwy 419, following signs. Enter on R.* ◆◆◆FACILITIES: 74 sites, typical site width 40 ft, 24 full hkups, 46 W&E, (20, 30 & 50 amps), 50 amps ($), 4 no hkups, 16 pull-thrus, tenting, dump station, non-guest dumping $, laundry, ltd groceries, LP gas by weight/by meter, ice, tables, fire rings, wood. ◆◆◆◆RECREATION: rec hall, swim pool, boating, canoeing, 2 rowboat/2 canoe/pedal boat rentals, pond fishing, mini-golf, playground, planned activities (wkends only), horseshoes, v-ball. Pets welcome, breed restrict. Open all yr. Planned activities weekends during season. Rate in 2007 $25-27 for 2 persons. Member ARVC, TNARVC. Phone: (888) 336-3703.

(NE) BEAN POT CAMPGROUND—(Cumberland) *From jct I-40 (exit 322) & Peavine Rd: Go 1-1/2 mi N on Peavine Rd, then follow signs 1000 feet E. Enter on R.*

LONG 50 AMP/CABLE TV PULL THRUS
Only 5 minutes off I-40 - our resort features shady prepared sites, clean modern bathhouse, Free WiFi, rec hall, pool, propane, cabin rentals and our gift shop! Quiet & reasonable family rates.

◆◆◆◆FACILITIES: 64 sites, typical site width 28 ft, 36 full hkups, 28 W&E, (20, 30 & 50 amps), some extended stay sites, 50 pull-thrus, cable TV, wireless Instant Internet access at site, wireless Internet access central location, tenting, cabins, RV storage, dump station, non-guest dumping $, laundry, groceries, RV supplies, LP gas by weight/by meter, ice, tables, fire rings, grills, wood.

◆◆◆RECREATION: rec hall, swim pool, golf nearby, bsktball, playground, horseshoes, hiking trails, v-ball.

Pets welcome, breed restrict. Partial handicap access. Open all yr. Big rigs welcome. Internet friendly. Escort to site. Clubs welcome. Rate in 2007

BEAN POT CAMPGROUND—Continued on next page

Tennessee State Motto: "Agriculture and Commerce"

CROSSVILLE—Continued
BEAN POT CAMPGROUND—Continued

$18-26 for 2 persons. MC/VISA/Debit. Member ARVC, TNARVC. Phone: (877)848-7958. FCRV 10% discount. FMCA discount.

e-mail: beanpotcampground@yahoo.com

SEE AD PAGE 792

(E) Crossville KOA—(Cumberland) *(W-bound) From jct I-40 (exit 329) & Hwy 70: Go right to Hwy 70 & continue 4 mi W on Hwy 70. (E-bound) From jct I-40 (exit 332) & Hwy 101/Peavine Rd: Go 1 mi S on Hwy 101, then 4 mi E on Hwy 70 Enter at end.* ◇◇◇FACILITIES: 48 sites, typical site width 35 ft, 17 full hkups, 21 W&E, (20, 30 & 50 amps), 10 no hkups, 22 pull-thrus, tenting, laundry, groceries, LP bottle exch, ice, tables, fire rings, wood. ◇◇◇◇RECREATION: rec hall, rec room/area, pond fishing, playground, planned activities, horseshoes, sports field, hiking trails. Pets welcome. Partial handicap access. Open all yr. Big rigs welcome. Internet friendly. Rate in 2007 $29-36 for 2 persons. Phone: (931)484-2682. KOA 10% value card discount.

(S) CUMBERLAND MOUNTAIN STATE PARK—(Cumberland) *From I-40 (exit 317): Go 8-1/2 mi S on US 127. Enter on R.*

FACILITIES: 145 sites, 145 W&E, (30 amps), tenting, cabins, dump station, ltd groceries, ice, tables, grills.

RECREATION: rec hall, swim pool, wading pool, boating, no motors, canoeing, dock, 10 row-boat/8 canoe/24 pedal boat rentals, lake fishing, bsktball, playground, planned activities, tennis, sports field, hiking trails, v-ball. Rec open to public.

Pets welcome. Partial handicap access. Open all yr. Facilities fully operational May thru Oct. No reservations. No boat dock in winter. MC/VISA/DISC/AMEX/DC. Phone: (931)484-6138.

SEE AD TRAVEL SECTION PAGE 784

(NE) Deer Run RV Park—(Cumberland) *From jct I-40 (exit 322) & Peavine Rd: Go 2 mi N on Peavine Rd, then 3-1/2 mi W on Firetower Rd. Enter on L.* ◇◇◇◇FACILITIES: 100 sites, 100 full hkups, (20, 30 & 50 amps), tenting, laundry, groceries, LP gas by weight/by meter, ice, tables, fire rings, grills. ◇◇◇◇RECREATION: rec hall, equipped pavilion, swim pool, lake swimming, no motors, canoeing, lake fishing, playground, shuffleboard court, tennis, horseshoes, sports field. Pets welcome, quantity restrict. Partial handicap access. Open all yr. Rate in 2007 $25 per family. Member ARVC, TNARVC. Phone: (931)484-3333. CCUSA discount.

(NE) Spring Lake RV Resort (formerly known as Roam & Roost RV Campground)—(Cumberland) *From jct I-40 (exit 322) & Hwy 101 (Peavine Rd): Go 3-1/2 mi N on Peavine Rd, then turn 1/2 mi E on Fairview. Enter on L.* ◇◇◇◇FACILITIES: 24 sites, typical site width 50 ft, 21 full hkups, 3 W&E, (30 & 50 amps), 7 pull-thrus, laundry, tables, patios, fire rings. ◇◇RECREATION: equipped pavilion, 4 pedal boat rentals, lake fishing, horseshoes, sports field, v-ball. Pets welcome. No tents. Open all yr. Rate in 2007 $22.50-25 for 2 persons. Phone: (877)707-1414. FMCA discount.

DANDRIDGE—D-5

(E) Lake Cove Resort—(Jefferson) *From jct I-40 & Oak Grove Rd: Go 2 mi W on Oak Grove Rd (stay in middle lane). Enter on L.* ◇◇◇FACILITIES: 38 sites, 36 ft max RV length, 25 full hkups, 3 W&E, (30 amps), 10 no hkups, 6 pull-thrus, tenting, ice, patios, fire rings. ◇◇◇RECREATION: pavilion, playground, horseshoes, v-ball. Pets welcome. Open Apr 15 thru Nov 1. Rate in 2007 $25 for 2 persons. CCUSA discount.

(W) Mountain Lake Campground—(Sevier) *(Wbound) From jct I-40 (exit 412) & Deep Springs Rd: Go 3 mi S to Deep Springs Rd, then 2 mi W on Hwy 139. (Ebound) From jct I-40 (exit 407) & Hwy 66: Go 2 mi S on Hwy 66, then 3-1/4 mi E on Hwy 139. Enter on R.* ◇◇FACILITIES: 30 sites, 30 full hkups, (20, 30 & 50 amps), some extended stay sites, 3 pull-thrus, tenting, laundry, ice, tables, fire rings, grills, wood. ◇◇RECREATION: canoeing, pond fishing, playground, horseshoes, hiking trails, v-ball. Pets welcome. Open all yr. Rate in 2007 $20-25 for 2 persons. Phone: (865)397-1000.

DAYTON—B-5

(E) BLUE WATER MARINA/CAMPGROUND—(Rhea) *From jct US-27 Bypass & Hwy-30: Go 1/2 mi E on Hwy-30 to Double "S" Rd, then 1-3/4 mi S on blacktop road. Follow signs. Enter at end.*

◇◇◇FACILITIES: 37 sites, typical site width 25 ft, 10 full hkups, 7 W&E, (20, 30 & 50 amps), 20 no hkups, 2 pull-thrus, cable TV, tenting, dump station, ltd groceries, RV supplies, marine gas, ice, tables.

◇◇RECREATION: rec room/area, coin games, boating, ramp, dock, lake fishing, fishing supplies, golf nearby, play equipment, horseshoes.

Pets welcome. Open all yr. Rate in 2007 $17.71-19.99 for 2 persons. MC/VISA/Debit. Phone: (423)775-3265.

SEE AD THIS PAGE

DELANO—C-6

HIAWASSEE STATE SCENIC RIVER & OCOEE RIVER (Gee Creek Campground)—(Polk) *From north jct Hwy 30 & US 411: Go 6 mi S on US 411 to Hwy 163, then 1 mi SE on Spring Creek Rd. Enter on L.*

FACILITIES: 47 sites, 47 no hkups, 47 pull-thrus, tenting, tables, fire rings, grills, controlled access gate.

RECREATION: river swimming, boating, canoeing, ramp, river fishing, horseshoes, hiking trails, v-ball.

Pets welcome. Partial handicap access. Open all yr. Facilities fully operational Apr 1 thru Nov 30. No reservations. Phone: (423)263-0050.

SEE AD TRAVEL SECTION PAGE 784

DICKSON—B-3

(S) Dickson RV Park—(Dickson) *At jct I-40 (exit 172) & Hwy 46: Go N on Hwy 46, then turn W immediately on W Christie Rd. Enter on L.* ◇◇◇FACILITIES: 60 sites, typical site width 30 ft, 38 ft max RV length, 51 full hkups, 5 W&E, 4 E, (20, 30 & 50 amps), 50 amps ($), 60 pull-thrus, tenting, laundry, groceries, LP gas by weight/by meter, ice, tables, grills. ◇◇RECREATION: swim pool, playground, v-ball. Pets welcome. Open all yr. Facilities fully operational Memorial Day thru Labor Day. Rate in 2007 $27-28 for 2 persons. Phone: (615) 446-9925.

(S) Tanbark Campground—(Hickman) *From jct I-40 (exit 163) & Hwy 48: Go 1/4 mi S on Hwy 48, then 1/4 mi E on campground road. Enter on L.* ◇◇FACILITIES: 30 sites, typical site width 25 ft, 24 full hkups, 6 W&E, (20, 30 & 50 amps), 50 amps ($), 18 pull-thrus, tenting, laundry, ltd groceries, tables. Pets welcome. Open all yr. Rate in 2007 $12.50-16.50 for 2 persons. Phone: (866)441-1613.

DOVER—A-3

BUMPUS MILLS RECREATIONAL AREA (COE-Lk Barkley)—(Stewart) *From town: Go 13 mi NW on Hwy-120.* FACILITIES: 33 sites, 18 W&E, (20 & 30 amps), 15 no hkups, tenting, dump station, ltd groceries, grills. RECREATION: lake swimming, boating, ramp, dock, lake fishing, playground. Partial handicap access. Open Apr 27 thru Sep 3. Phone: (931)232-8831.

(N) GATLIN POINT (LBL) National Recreation Area (Lake Access Site Only)—(Stewart) *From jct US 79 & The Trace: Go 4 mi N on The Trace, then follow signs 3 mi E.* FACILITIES: 25 sites, 25 no hkups, tenting, non-flush toilets only, grills. RECREATION: boating, ramp, lake fishing. Rec open to public. Open all yr. No showers.

(S) PINEY CAMPGROUND (LBL)—(Stewart) *From jct Hwy 94/80/68: Go 5 mi E on Hwy 80/68, then 21 mi S on The Trace Rd, then 18 mi W on Fort Henry Rd. Enter on R.* FACILITIES: 389 sites, 39 full hkups, 293 E, (30 & 50 amps), 57 no hkups, tenting, dump station, fire rings. RECREATION: lake swimming, boating, ramp, dock, pond fishing, playground, sports field. Open all yr. Phone: (270)924-2000.

(W) PINEY (LBL) National Recreation Area—(Stewart) *From town: Go 9-1/2 mi W on US 79, then 3 mi on CR 230 (Fort Henry Rd). Follow signs. Enter at end.* FACILITIES: 383 sites, 40 full hkups, 274 E, (30 amps), 69 no hkups, some extended stay sites, 6 pull-thrus, tenting, dump station, non-guest dumping,

DOVER—Continued
PINEY (LBL) National Recreation Area—Continued

laundry, groceries, ice, fire rings, grills, wood. RECREATION: pavilion, lake swimming, boating, ramp, dock, lake/pond fishing, playground, 3 shuffleboard courts, planned activities, sports field, hiking trails, v-ball. Pets welcome. Open Mar 1 thru Nov 30. Phone: (931)232-5331.

ELIZABETHTON—D-6

STONEY CREEK RV PARK—(Sullivan) *From I-26 (exit 24) & Hwy 321/67: Go 8 mi E on Hwy 321/67 to jct US 19E/321 & Hwy 91, then 2-9/10 mi N on Hwy 91, then 1/10 mi E on Blue Springs Rd, then 1-3/10 mi N on Willow Springs Rd (Stay left at Y), then 100 ft W on Price Rd. Enter on L.*

◇◇◇FACILITIES: 13 sites, typical site width 25 ft, accepts full hkup units only, 13 full hkups, (30 & 50 amps), 50 amps ($), 4 pull-thrus, dump station, non-guest dumping $, tables, fire rings, grills, wood.

RECREATION: horseshoes.

Pets welcome. No tents. Open all yr. No restrooms. Rate in 2007 $17-20 for 2 persons. Phone: (423)474-3505.

SEE AD THIS PAGE

ERWIN—D-6

CHEROKEE NATIONAL FOREST (Rock Creek Campgrounds)—(Unicoi) *From town: Go 1 mi N on US-23, then 3 mi E on FR-30.* FACILITIES: 29 sites, 13 E, (20 & 30 amps), 16 no hkups, tenting, dump station. RECREATION: lake swimming, lake fishing, hiking trails. Partial handicap access. Open May 1 thru Nov 1. No reservations. Phone: (615)743-4452.

FRANKEWING—C-4

(W) TENNESSEE VALLEY R.V. PARK—(Giles) *From jct I-65 (exit 14) & US 64: Go 1/4 mi E on US 64. Enter on R.*

◇◇◇FACILITIES: 60 sites, typical site width 22 ft, 16 full hkups, 44 W&E, (20, 30 & 50 amps), 48 pull-thrus, wireless Instant Internet access at site, tenting, cabins, RV storage, dump station, non-guest dumping $, laundry, RV supplies, LP bottle exch, ice, tables, fire rings, wood.

◇◇RECREATION: swim pool, golf nearby, playground, horseshoes, sports field, v-ball. Rec open to public.

Pets welcome. Open all yr. Big rigs welcome. Internet friendly. Escort to site. Clubs welcome. Rate in 2007 $23-26 for 2 persons. MC/VISA. Phone: (931)363-4600.

e-mail: info@tnvalleyrvpark.com

SEE AD THIS PAGE

GAINESBORO—A-5

SALT LICK CREEK CAMPGROUND (Corps of Engineers)—(Jackson) *From Carthage, TN: Go 4 mi W on SR 25, then N on US 80, then E on SR 85 to Gladdice, follow signs, then right on Smith Bend Rd.* FACILITIES: 150 sites, 31 full hkups, 119 W&E, (30 amps), tenting, dump station, laundry, fire rings. RECREATION: pavilion, lake swimming, boating, ramp, lake fishing, playground, v-ball. Open May 12 thru Sep 5. Phone: (931)678-4718.

GALLATIN—A-4

(E) BLEDSOE CREEK STATE CAMPING PARK—(Sumner) *From town: Go 6 mi E on Hwy 25, then 1-1/2 mi S on Zeigler Fort Rd. Enter on L.*

FACILITIES: 35 sites, 35 W&E, 8 pull-thrus, tenting, dump station, laundry, tables, fire rings, controlled access gate.

RECREATION: boating, ramp, lake fishing, playground, hiking trails.

Pets welcome. Partial handicap access. Open all yr. Day use only. Limited water avail in winter months. Phone: (615)452-3706.

SEE AD TRAVEL SECTION PAGE 784

GALLATIN—Continued on next page

GALLATIN—Continued

(S) CAGES BEND CAMPGROUND (COE-Old Hickory Lake)—(Sumner) *From town: Go 8 mi SW on US 31E, then 2-1/4 miS on Cages Bend Rd, then 1/2 mi E on Bender Ferry Rd.* FACILITIES: 43 sites, 43 W&E, (20, 30 & 50 amps), tenting, dump station, laundry, ltd groceries, LP gas by weight. RECREATION: lake swimming, boating, ramp, dock, lake fishing, playground. Partial handicap access. Open Apr 1 thru Oct 31. Phone: (615) 824-4989.

GATLINBURG—E-5

(E) Adventure Bound Camping Resort Gatlinburg (formerly Crazy Horse Camping & RV Resort)—(Sevier) *From jct US-441 & US 321 N: Go 12 mi E on US 321 N Enter on L.* ◆◆◆FACILITIES: 207 sites, typical site width 30 ft, 75 full hkups, 132 W&E, (20, 30 & 50 amps), 29 pull-thrus, tenting, dump station, non-guest dumping $, laundry, ltd groceries, LP gas by weight/by meter, ice, tables, patios, fire rings, wood. ◆◆◆◆RECREATION: rec hall, rec room/area, pavilion, swim pool, pond fishing, playground, planned activities (wkends only), horseshoes, hiking trails, v-ball. Pets welcome. Partial handicap access. Open Apr 1 thru Oct 29. Internet friendly. Rate in 2007 $28-48 for 2 persons. Member ARVC, TNARVC. Phone: (800)528-9003.

(E) Arrow Creek Campground—(Sevier) *From jct I-40 (exit #440) & Hwy 32/321: Go 14-1/2 mi S on Hwy 321. Enter on L.* ◆◆◆FACILITIES: 52 sites, typical site width 30 ft, 35 ft max RV length, 37 full hkups, 12 W&E, (30 amps), 3 no hkups, 3 pull-thrus, tenting, dump station, non-guest dumping $, laundry, ltd groceries, ice, tables, fire rings, wood. ◆◆RECREATION: rec room/area, pavilion, swim pool, playground, horseshoes, v-ball. Pets welcome. Open Apr 1 thru Nov 1. Internet friendly. Rate in 2007 $27.50-29.50 for 2 persons. Member ARVC, TNARVC. Phone: (865)430-7433.

(E) Camping in the Smokies—(Sevier) *From jct US 441 & Hwy 321: Go 3 mi E on Hwy 321. Enter on R.* ◆◆◆FACILITIES: 64 sites, typical site width 35 ft, 47 full hkups, 17 W&E, (20, 30 & 50 amps), 2 pull-thrus, laundry, ice, tables, fire rings, grills, wood. ◆RECREATION: swim pool. Pets welcome, breed restrict. No tents. Open Mar 15 thru Nov 30. Internet friendly. Rate in 2007 $24.95-36.95 for 2 persons. Member ARVC, TNARVC. Phone: (865)430-3594.

WELCOME

(E) GREAT SMOKY JELLYSTONE PARK CAMP RESORT—(Cocke) *E'bnd from jct I-40 (exit 435) & Hwy 321: GO 15 mi S (right) on Hwy 321 and follow signs. W'bnd from jct I-40 (exit 440) & Hwy 73: Go 15 mi S (left) on Hwy 321 and follow signs. Enter on L.*

◆◆◆◆◆FACILITIES: 89 sites, typical site width 35 ft, 44 full hkups, 30 W&E, (20, 30 & 50 amps), 15 no hkups, 4 pull-thrus, cable TV, wireless Instant Internet access at site, phone Internet access central location, tenting, cabins, dump station, non-guest dumping $, laundry, full svc store, RV supplies, LP gas by weight/by meter, ice, tables, fire rings, wood.

◆◆◆◆◆RECREATION: rec hall, pavilion, coin games, swim pool, wading pool, stream fishing, fishing supplies, mini-golf ($), golf nearby, bsktball, playground, planned activities, horseshoes, hiking trails.

Pets welcome, breed restrict. Partial handicap access. Open Mar 15 thru Oct 30. Big rigs welcome. Internet friendly. Escort to site. Clubs welcome. Rate in 2007 $26-44 for 2 persons. MC/VISA/Debit. Member ARVC, TNARVC. Phone: (423)487-5534.

e-mail: gatlyogi@comcast.net

SEE AD PIGEON FORGE PAGE 817

Sequoyah, a Tsalagi leader, created an alphabet for the Tsalagi or Cherokee people.

GATLINBURG—Continued

GREAT SMOKY MOUNTAINS NATIONAL PARK (Elkmont Campground)—(Sevier) *From town: Go 2 mi S on US 441, then 5 mi W on Little River Rd.* FACILITIES: 220 sites, 32 ft max RV length, 220 no hkups, tenting, grills, wood. RECREATION: planned activities, hiking trails. Open Mar 10 thru Nov 30. No showers. Phone: (865)436-1220.

Greenbrier Island Campground—(Sevier) *From jct US-441 & Hwy-321: Go 6-1/4 mi E on Hwy-321, then 250 yards N on Pittman-Center Rd. Enter on L.* ◆◆◆FACILITIES: 116 sites, typical site width 40 ft, 48 full hkups, 34 W&E, (20 & 30 amps), 34 no hkups, 10 pull-thrus, tenting, shower$, dump station, laundry, LP gas by weight, ice, tables, wood. ◆◆◆RECREATION: rec room/area, pavilion, river swimming, river fishing, play equipment, sports field. Pets welcome, quantity restrict. Open Mar 17 thru Nov 10. Rate in 2007 $24-26 for 2 persons. Phone: (865)436-4243.

(E) Le Conte Vista Campground Resort—(Sevier) *From jct US-441 & Hwy-321: Go 4 mi E on Hwy-321. Enter on L.* ◆◆◆FACILITIES: 75 sites, typical site width 22 ft, 50 full hkups, 25 W&E, (15, 30 & 50 amps), 50 amps ($), 15 pull-thrus, tenting, dump station, laundry, ice, tables, fire rings, grills, wood. ◆◆◆RECREATION: rec room/area, pavilion, swim pool, playground, shuffleboard court, planned activities, horseshoes. Pets welcome. Open Mar 1 thru Dec 1. Planned activities in season only. Rate in 2007 $30-37 for 2 persons. Phone: (865)436-5437.

WELCOME

(E) SMOKY BEAR CAMPGROUND (formerly Huc A Bee)—(Sevier) *From jct I-40 (exit 435 or 440) & Hwy 321S: Go 12 or 17 mi S on US 321. Enter on R.*

◆◆◆◆FACILITIES: 49 sites, typical site width 30 ft, 49 full hkups, (20, 30 & 50 amps), 9 pull-thrus, cable TV, wireless Instant Internet access at site, phone Internet access central location, tenting, RV/park trailer rentals, cabins, laundry, RV supplies, ice, tables, fire rings, wood.

◆◆◆RECREATION: rec hall, swim pool, whirlpool, golf nearby, bsktball, playground, planned activities.

Pets welcome. Partial handicap access. Open Mar thru Dec. Big rigs welcome. Internet friendly. Escort to site. Clubs welcome. Rate in 2007 $28-38 for 4 persons. MC/VISA/DISC/Debit. Member ARVC, TNARVC. Phone: (800)850-8372.

e-mail: smokybearcamp@comcast.net

Reserve Online at Woodalls.com

SEE AD THIS PAGE

GATLINBURG—Continued on next page

The first telephone directory, issued on February 21, 1878, by the New Haven Telephone Company, had 50 listings

Smoky Mountains

Gatlinburg - Pigeon Forge - Sevierville

Tennessee's Camping Capital

PIGEON FORGE/GATLINBURG KOA ①

(865) 453-7903

www.pigeonforgekoa.com

Reservations Only: 1-800-KOA-7703

Trolley Stop

PO Box 310 • 3122 Veterans Blvd., Pigeon Forge, TN 37868-0310

See listing at Pigeon Forge

Riveredge RV Park ⑤

&Log Cabins Rentals

Trolley Stop

1-800-477-1205

(865) 453-5813

See listing at Pigeon Forge

4220 Huskey St., Pigeon Forge, TN 37863 www.stayriveredge.com

& Resort

1-800-341-7534 ②

(Reservation Only)

(865) 453-7299

4280 Boyds Creek Hwy.
Sevierville, TN 37876
www.riversidecamp.com

See listing at Sevierville

Located on the Parkway (South) at the City Limits ⑥

(865) 428-3818

www.foothillsrvparkandcabins.com

See listing at Pigeon Forge

Trolley Stop **4235 Huskey St., Pigeon Forge, TN 37863**

Campground & Cabins

1930 Winfield Dunn Pkwy.
Sevierville, TN 37876

See listing at Sevierville

Toll Free Reservations Only ③

1-888-Ripplin
(747-7546)

or call (865) 453-4169

www.ripplinwatersrv.com

See listing at Pigeon Forge

(865) 453-5352 ⑦

For Reservations Only

Toll FREE: 1-888-204-0247

www.hollyhavenrvpark.com

647 Wears Valley Rd.
Pigeon Forge, TN 37863

Trolley Stop

RV PARK

See listing at Pigeon Forge

For Reservations Only: ④

1-800-758-5267

1004 Parkway
Sevierville, TN 37862

www.riverplantationrv.com

email: riverrv@aol.com

Toll Free: 1-866-453-8777 ⑧

or call (865) 453-8777

SMOKER HOLLER RV RESORT

www.smokerholler.us

4119 Wears Valley Rd., Sevierville, TN 37862

See listing at Pigeon Forge, TN

Free Wi-Fi
All Full Hookups
30/50 Amps

Trolley Stop

See listing at Gatlinburg ⑨

Reservations Only:

1-800-252-8077

(865) 436-7081

1202 E. Parkway, Gatlinburg, TN 37738

www.twincreekrvresort.com

....COME AND ENJOY ONE OF THE MANY GREAT RV RESORTS!

PICK THE ONE OF YOUR CHOICE!

(E) TWIN CREEK RV RESORT—(Sevier) *From jct US 441 & US 321 (traffic light #3): Go 2 1/4 mi E on US 321 N Enter on R.*

WELCOME

◆◆◆◆◆FACILITIES: 83 sites, typical site width 30 ft, 83 full hkups, (20, 30 & 50 amps), 15 pull-thrus, cable TV, wireless Instant Internet access at site, phone Internet access central location, cabins, laundry, groceries, RV supplies, ice, tables, patios, fire rings, grills, wood.

◆◆◆◆RECREATION: rec room/area, coin games, swim pool, wading pool, whirlpool, stream fishing, fishing supplies, golf nearby, playground, hiking trails, local tours.

Pets welcome, breed restrict, quantity restrict. Partial handicap access. No tents. Open Mar 16 thru Dec 9. Big rigs welcome. Internet friendly. Escort to site. Clubs welcome. MC/VISA/Debit. Member ARVC, TNARVC. Phone: (865)436-7081. FMCA discount.

SEE AD PAGES 796-797 AND AD PIGEON FORGE PAGE 813

GOODLETTSVILLE—A-4

(N) Nashville North Campground—(Davidson) *From jct I-24 West & I-65 North: Go 10 mi N on I-65, (exit 98) US 31 W, then 1/2 mi S on US 31 W. Enter on R.* ◆◆FACILITIES: 200 sites, typical site width 35 ft, 100 full hkups, 72 W&E, (15, 20, 30 & 50 amps), 50 amps ($), 28 no hkups, 120 pull-thrus, tenting, dump station, non-guest dumping $, laundry, groceries, LP gas by weight/by meter, ice, tables. RECREATION: rec room/area. Pets welcome. Open all yr. Rate in 2007 $22-28 for 2 persons. Phone: (615)859-0075. FCRV 10% discount. FMCA discount.

GRANVILLE—A-5

(S) Maple Grove Campground—(Jackson) *From jct I-40 (exit 268) & Rte 96: Go 4 mi N on Rte 96, then 4 mi W on Hwy 70N, then 4 mi N on Rte 53. Enter on L.* ◆◆◆FACILITIES: 44 sites, typical site width 25 ft, 44 full hkups, (20, 30 & 50 amps), 50 amps ($), 22 pull-thrus, tenting, dump station, non-guest dumping $, ltd groceries, tables. ◆◆RECREATION: swim pool, lake fishing, play equipment, hiking trails, v-ball. Pets welcome. Open all yr. Rate in 2007 $16-18 for 4 persons. Phone: (931)653-4486. CCUSA discount. FCRV 10% discount.

GREAT SMOKY MOUNTAINS NATIONAL PARK—E-5

See listings at Cosby, Gatlinburg, Pigeon Forge, Sevierville, Townsend, Walland & Newport

GREENBACK—B-6

LOTTERDALE COVE—(Loudon) *From jct Hwy 95 & US 411: Go 3-1/4 mi SW on US 411, then follow signs 4-1/4 mi N. Enter on L.* FACILITIES: 90 sites, 86 E, (30 & 50 amps), 4 no hkups, 8 pull-thrus, tenting, dump station, LP gas by weight, ice, fire rings, grills, wood. RECREATION: lake swimming, boating, canoeing, ramp, lake fishing, playground, horseshoes, hiking trails, v-ball. Pets welcome. Partial handicap access. Open Apr thru Oct. Phone: (865)856-3832.

The Tulip Poplar was chosen as the state tree because it was used extensively by the Tennessee pioneers to construct their houses, barns and other buildings.

GREENEVILLE—D-5

DAVY CROCKETT BIRTHPLACE HISTORICAL SP—(Greene) *From jct US 11E & Limestone Rd.: Go 3 mi S & follow signs. Enter on R.*

WELCOME

FACILITIES: 74 sites, 25 full hkups, 49 W&E, tenting, dump station, ice, tables, grills, controlled access gate.

RECREATION: swim pool, wading pool, boating, ramp, river fishing, bsktball, playground, hiking trails.

Pets welcome. Partial handicap access. Open all yr. Phone: (423)257-2167.

SEE AD TRAVEL SECTION PAGE 784

KINSER PARK (City Park)—(Greene) *From jct US 321 & Hwy 70: Go 5 mi S on Hwy 70, then 5 mi E on Allens Bridge Rd.* FACILITIES: 157 sites, 157 full hkups, (30 amps), tenting, groceries, ice, fire rings, grills, wood. RECREATION: pavilion, swim pool, boating, ramp, lake fishing, mini-golf ($), playground, tennis, horseshoes, sports field, v-ball. Pets welcome. Open Apr 1 thru Oct 31. Phone: (423)639-5912.

GUILD—C-5

(W) Camp on the Lake Campground—(Marion) *From jct I-24 (exit 161): Go 500 ft S; 15 mi NW of Chattanooga. Enter on R.* ◆◆FACILITIES: 42 sites, typical site width 35 ft, 19 W&E, (20, 30 & 50 amps), 23 no hkups, 3 pull-thrus, heater not allowed, tenting, dump station, non-guest dumping $, ice, tables, patios, fire rings, grills, wood. ◆◆RECREATION: lake swimming, boating, ramp, lake fishing, play equipment, planned activities (wkends only), horseshoes, v-ball. Pets welcome, breed restrict. Open all yr. Rate in 2007 $20-25 per family. Phone: (423)942-4078.

(W) HALE'S BAR MARINA & RESORT—(Marion) *From jct I-24 (exit 161) & Hwy 156: Go 1 mi N on Hwy 156/134, then 900 ft (quick turn) NE to Hales Bar Rd, then 1-1/2 mi NE on Hales Bar Rd. Enter on L.*

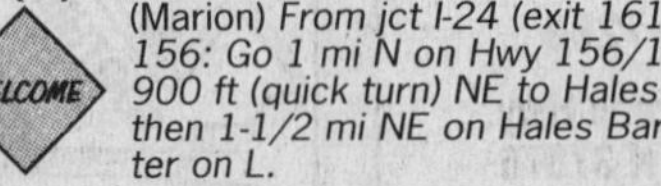

WELCOME

◆◆◆◆FACILITIES: 61 sites, typical site width 25 ft, 61 W&E, (20, 30 & 50 amps), 16 pull-thrus, cable TV, tenting, cabins, dump station, ltd groceries, gas, ice, tables, fire rings, controlled access gate.

◆◆◆◆RECREATION: rec hall, pavilion, swim pool, boating, ramp, dock, 4 pontoon/motorboat rentals, lake fishing, fishing supplies, fishing guides, golf nearby, horseshoes, hiking trails, v-ball.

Pets welcome. Partial handicap access. Open all yr. Big rigs welcome. Clubs welcome. Rate in 2007 $18-35 for 2 persons. MC/VISA/DISC/AMEX/Debit. Phone: (423)942-9000.

e-mail: info@halesbarmarina.com

SEE AD CHATTANOOGA PAGE 790

HAMPTON—D-6

CHEROKEE NATIONAL FOREST (Cardens Bluff Campground)—(Carter) *From town: Go 4 mi NE on US-321.* FACILITIES: 43 sites, 43 no hkups, tenting, cold showers only. RECREATION: boating, lake fishing, hiking trails. Partial handicap access. Open Apr 18 thru Oct 15. Phone: (615)542-2942.

Woodall's Tip #28... Woodall's ratings depend on the quality and quantity of our criteria elements. The more W's a park has generally reflects the presence of more development at the park, and usually more facilities.

HARRIMAN—B-6

(W) CANEY CREEK RV RESORT & MARINA—(Roane) *From jct I-40 (exit 350) & Hwy 29: Go 1/2 mi S on Hwy 29, then 3 mi W on Hwy 70. Enter on L.*

WELCOME

◆◆◆◆FACILITIES: 158 sites, 158 full hkups, (20, 30 & 50 amps), cable TV ($), wireless Instant Internet access at site, laundry, ltd groceries, RV supplies, LP gas by weight/by meter, LP bottle exch, ice, tables, patios, fire rings, grills, wood.

◆◆◆◆RECREATION: pavilion, swim pool, wading pool, boating, ramp, dock, 2 pontoon/2 canoe/2 pedal boat/2 motorboat rentals, lake fishing, fishing supplies, fishing guides, golf nearby, bsktball, 12 bike rentals, playground, shuffleboard court, planned activities (wkends only), horseshoes, sports field, hiking trails, v-ball.

Pets welcome, breed restrict, quantity restrict. No tents. Open all yr. Big rigs welcome. Internet friendly. Clubs welcome. Rate in 2007 $29-50 for 4 persons. MC/VISA/DISC/AMEX/Debit. Member ARVC, TNARVC. Phone: (865)882-4042.

e-mail: reservations@caneycreek.com

SEE AD NEXT PAGE

HENDERSON—C-2

(W) CHICKASAW STATE PARK—(Hardeman/Chester) *From jct Hwy 45 & Hwy 100 in Henderson: Go 8 mi W on Hwy 100. Enter on L.*

WELCOME

FACILITIES: 112 sites, 83 W&E, (30 amps), 29 no hkups, tenting, cabins, dump station, tables, grills.

RECREATION: pavilion, lake swimming, boating, no motors, ramp, 15 rowboat/30 pedal boat rentals, lake fishing, putting green, bsktball, playground, planned activities, tennis, sports field, hiking trails, v-ball. Rec open to public.

Pets welcome. Partial handicap access. Open all yr. MC/VISA/DISC/AMEX/DC/Debit. Phone: (731) 989-5141.

SEE AD TRAVEL SECTION PAGE 784

HENNING—B-1

FORT PILLOW STATE HISTORIC AREA—(Lauderdale) *From jct US 51 & Hwy 87: Go 17 mi W on 87, then 1 mi N on Hwy 207. Enter at end.*

WELCOME

FACILITIES: 35 sites, 35 no hkups, tenting, tables, grills.

RECREATION: lake/river fishing, playground, planned activities, hiking trails.

Pets welcome. Partial handicap access. Open all yr. For tent camping only. Phone: (731)738-5581.

SEE AD TRAVEL SECTION PAGE 784

HERMITAGE—B-4

(E) SEVEN POINTS CAMPGROUND (Corps of Engineers)—(Davison) *From jct I-40, exit 221B, and Old Hickory Blvd.: Go 1 mi S on Old Hickory Blvd., then 1 mi E on Bell Rd., then 1 mi S on New Hope Rd., then E on Stewart Ferry Rd. follow signs. Enter on R.* FACILITIES: 60 sites, 60 W&E, (30 & 50 amps), tenting, dump station, laundry, patios, fire rings, grills. RECREATION: pavilion, lake swimming, boating, canoeing, ramp, lake fishing. Partial handicap access. Open Apr 1 thru Oct 31. Phone: (615)889-5198.

HOHENWALD—B-3

(E) NATCHEZ TRACE PARKWAY (Meriwether Lewis Campground)—(Lewis) *From town: Go 7 mi E on Hwy-20.* FACILITIES: 32 sites, 32 no hkups, tenting, grills. RECREATION: hiking trails. Rec open to public. Pets welcome. Open all yr. No showers. No reservations. Phone: (800)305-7417.

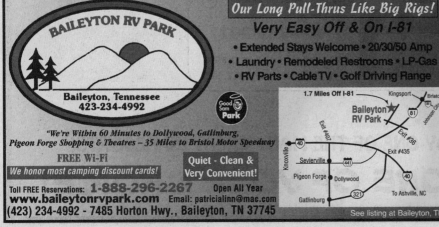

HURRICANE MILLS—B-3

LORETTA LYNN'S RANCH—(Humphreys) *From jct I-40 (exit 143) & Hwy-13: Go 8 mi N on Hwy-13. Enter on L.*

WELCOME

◆◆◆◆FACILITIES: 465 sites, typical site width 35 ft, 102 full hkups, 213 W&E, (20, 30 & 50 amps), 150 no hkups, 70 pull-thrus, tenting, cabins, dump station, laundry, groceries, RV supplies, ice, tables, fire rings, grills.

◆◆◆◆◆RECREATION: rec hall, equipped pavilion, coin games, swim pool, river swimming, boating, canoeing, 18 canoe/3 pedal boat rentals, pond/stream fishing, fishing supplies, 12 bike rentals, playground, 2 shuffleboard courts, planned activities, horseshoes, hiking trails, v-ball, local tours. Rec open to public.

LORETTA LYNN'S RANCH—Continued on next page

HURRICANE MILLS—Continued
LORETTA LYNN'S RANCH—Continued

Pets welcome. Open Apr 1 thru Oct 31. Facilities fully operational Memorial Day thru Labor Day. Big rigs welcome. Clubs welcome. MC/VISA/DISC/ Debit. Member ARVC. Phone: (931)296-7700.

e-mail: campground@lorettalynn.com

SEE AD NASHVILLE PAGE 808

LORETTA LYNN'S RANCH—*From jct I-40 (exit 143) & Hwy-13: Go 8 mi N on Hwy-13.* Tour this western town & museum and see the Old Grist Mill, coal mine, Loretta Lynn's plantation home and her childhood home in Butcher Holler. Complex also includes snack & gift shops. Open Apr 1 thru Oct 31. MC/VISA/DISC. Phone: (615)296-7700.

SEE AD NASHVILLE PAGE 808

JACKSON—B-2

(S) JACKSON RV PARK (RV SPACES) —(Madison) *From jct I-40 (exit 79) & Hwy-20: Go 1/4 mi S on Hwy-20. Enter on L.*

FACILITIES: 32 sites, typical site width 15 ft, accepts self-contained units only, 32 full hkups, (15, 30 & 50 amps), some extended stay sites, 15 pull-thrus, laundry.

RECREATION: bsktball.

Pets welcome. No tents. Open all yr. Rate in 2007 $18 per family. Phone: (731)668-1147.

SEE AD THIS PAGE

(N) Joy-O RV Park—(Madison) *From jct I-40 (exit 68) & Rte 138: Go 1/4 mi S on Rte 138. Enter on L.* ◇◇◇FACILITIES: 40 sites, 20 full hkups, 10 W&E, (30 & 50 amps), 50 amps ($), 10 no hkups, 20 pull-thrus, tenting, dump station, non-guest dumping $, laundry, tables. ◇RECREATION: rec room/area, swim pool. Pets welcome. Open all yr. Rate in 2007 $18.25-20.50 for 2 persons. Member ARVC, TNARVC. Phone: (731) 424-3725.

(W) Parkway Village (RV SPACES)—(Madison) *From I-40 (exit 87) & Hwy 70 SW: Go 3-1/2 mi SW on Hwy 70 W. Enter on R.* FACILITIES: 23 sites, typical site width 25 ft, accepts full hkup units only, 23 full hkups,

JACKSON—Continued
Parkway Village—Continued

(30 & 50 amps), laundry, tables, patios. RECREATION: rec hall, pavilion, swim pool, play equipment. Pets welcome, size restrict. No tents. Open all yr. Big rigs welcome. Rate in 2007 $18 per vehicle. Phone: (731)423-3331.

(W) Whispering Pines RV Park (RV SPACES) —(Madison) *From I-40 (exit 76): Go 3 mi S to US 70, then turn right & go 1/2 mi.* FACILITIES: 30 sites, accepts full hkup units only, 30 full hkups, (30 & 50 amps), 50 amps ($), heater not allowed, laundry, LP gas by weight/by meter. Pets welcome. No tents. Open all yr. No restrooms. Big rigs welcome. Internet friendly. Rate in 2007 $22 for 2 persons. Phone: (731)422-3682.

JAMESTOWN—A-5

(N) Maple Hill RV Park—(Fentress) *From jct I-40 (exit 317) & US 127: Go 36 mi N on US 127. Enter on R.* ◇◇◇FACILITIES: 22 sites, typical site width 25 ft, 19 full hkups, 3 W&E, (20, 30 & 50 amps), some extended stay sites, 9 pull-thrus, tenting, dump station, non-guest dumping $, laundry, tables, fire rings, wood. ◇◇RECREATION: pavilion, horseshoes, v-ball. Pets welcome. Partial handicap access. Open all yr. Big rigs welcome. Internet friendly. Rate in 2007 $15-20 for 2 persons. Phone: (931)879-3025. CCUSA discount.

Memphis, Tennessee is the site of Sun Studios... Elvis Presley's first recording studio.

JAMESTOWN—Continued

(NW) PICKETT STATE PARK—(Pickett) *From Jamestown: Go 15 mi NE on Hwy 154 Enter on L.*

FACILITIES: 32 sites, 25 ft max RV length, 32 W&E, (30 amps), tenting, cabins, dump station, laundry, ice, tables, grills, wood, controlled access gate.

RECREATION: rec hall, lake swimming, boating, no motors, canoeing, 5 rowboat/3 canoe rentals, lake fishing, bsktball, playground, tennis, hiking trails, v-ball. Rec open to public.

Pets welcome. Partial handicap access. Open all yr. Facilities fully operational Apr 1 thru Dec 1. No reservations. MC/VISA/DISC/AMEX. Phone: (931) 879-5821.

SEE AD TRAVEL SECTION PAGE 784

JASPER—C-5

SHELLMOUND-NICKAJACK DAM RESERVATION (TVA-Nickajack Lake)—(Marion) *From I-24 (exit 158): Go 2-1/4 mi S on paved TVA road to Nickajack Dam Reservation, then E at entrance to Shellmound Recreation Area.* FACILITIES: 50 sites, 50 W&E, (30 & 50 amps), tenting, dump station, ice, grills, wood. RECREATION: pavilion, lake swimming, boating, ramp, dock, lake/river fishing, playground, horseshoes, sports field, hiking trails. Pets welcome. Partial handicap access. Open mid Apr thru Oct 30. Phone: (423)942-9857.

The city of Murfreesboro lies in the exact geographical center of the state.

JEFFERSON CITY—D-5

(N) CHEROKEE DAM (TVA-Cherokee Lake)—(Grainger) *From town: Go 1-1/2 mi W on US-11-E, then follow signs 4-1/2 mi N to Cherokee Dam Reservation.* FACILITIES: 41 sites, 41 W&E, 10 pull-thrus, tenting, grills. RECREATION: lake swimming, boating, ramp, lake/river fishing, play equipment, hiking trails. Rec open to public. Open Mar 18 thru Nov 7. Phone: (423)587-5600.

(N) GREENLEE OF MAY SPRINGS—(Grainger) *From jct US 11-E & Hwy 92: Go 5 mi N on Hwy 92, then 4-1/2 mi NE on Hwy 375 (Lake Shore Dr), then follow signs 1/2 mi S.* FACILITIES: 170 sites, 100 full hkups, 35 W&E, 35 no hkups, tenting, dump station, laundry, ltd groceries, fire rings, grills. RECREATION: rec room/area, pavilion, lake swimming, boating, ramp, dock, lake fishing. Partial handicap access. Open all yr. Phone: (866)828-4802.

JELLICO—A-6

INDIAN MOUNTAIN STATE PARK—(Campbell) *From jct I-75 (exit #160 & US 25 NW: Follow signs 3 mi N to park. Enter on R.*

WELCOME

FACILITIES: 47 sites, 47 W&E, (20 & 30 amps), tenting, dump station, tables, grills.

RECREATION: swim pool, boating, no motors, 10 pedal boat rentals, lake fishing, playground, hiking trails.

Pets welcome. Open all yr. Facilities fully operational Apr 1 thru Nov. Phone: (423)784-7958.

SEE AD TRAVEL SECTION PAGE 784

JOHNSON CITY—D-6

See listings at Elizabethton, Kingsport & Unicoi

KINGSPORT—D-6

(E) KOA-BRISTOL/KINGSPORT—(Sullivan) *From I-81 (exit 63 Tri-City Airport): Follow signs yellow KOA signs 1-1/2 mi W. Enter on R.*

WELCOME

◆◆◆◆◆FACILITIES: 72 sites, typical site width 35 ft, 72 full hkups, (20, 30 & 50 amps), 50 amps ($), many extended stay sites, 12 pull-thrus, cable TV, wireless Instant Internet access at site, phone Internet access central location, tenting, cabins, RV storage, dump station, non-guest dumping $, laundry, groceries, RV supplies, LP gas by weight/by meter, ice, tables, patios, fire rings, grills, wood.

◆◆◆◆◆RECREATION: rec room/area, equipped pavilion, coin games, swim pool, golf nearby, bsktball, playground, planned activities, horseshoes, sports field, hiking trails, v-ball.

Pets welcome. Partial handicap access. Open all yr. Big rigs welcome. Internet friendly. Escort to site. Clubs welcome. Rate in 2007 $31-57 for 2

KINGSPORT—Continued
KOA-BRISTOL/KINGSPORT—Continued

persons. MC/VISA/DISC/AMEX/Debit. Member ARVC, TNARVC. Phone: (800)562-7640. KOA 10% value card discount.

e-mail: bristolkptkoa@charter.net

SEE AD BRISTOL PAGE 789 AND AD DISCOVER SECTION PAGES 62 & 63

(E) ROCKY TOP CAMPGROUND—(Sullivan) *From I-81 (exit 63 Tri-City Airport): Follow signs 1 mi W. Enter on R.*

WELCOME

◆◆◆◆FACILITIES: 35 sites, typical site width 25 ft, 35 full hkups, (20, 30 & 50 amps), 8 pull-thrus, cable TV, wireless Instant Internet access at site, phone Internet access central location, tenting, cabins, dump station, non-guest dumping $, laundry, groceries, RV supplies, LP gas by weight/by meter, ice, tables, patios, fire rings, grills, wood.

◆◆◆RECREATION: rec room/area, equipped pavilion, coin games, golf nearby, play equipment, horseshoes, hiking trails, v-ball.

Pets welcome. Open all yr. Big rigs welcome. Internet friendly. Escort to site. Clubs welcome. Rate in 2007 $31-34 for 2 persons. MC/VISA/DISC/AMEX/Debit. Member ARVC, TNARVC. Phone: (800)452-6456. FMCA discount.

e-mail: camping@rockytopcampground.com

SEE AD THIS PAGE

✲ **(E) Tri-City Travel Trailers**—*From jct I-81 (exit 74) & US 11W: Go 11 mi SW on US 11W. Enter on L.* SALES: travel trailers, 5th wheels, fold-down camping trailers, pre-owned unit sales. SERVICES: full-time mech, RV appliance repair, body work/collision repair, LP gas by weight/by meter, sells parts/accessories, installs hitches. Open all yr. MC/VISA/DISC/AMEX. Phone: (423)288-3131.

(E) WARRIOR'S PATH STATE PARK—(Sullivan) *From I-81 & Hwy 36: Go 1 mi NW on Hwy 36, then 1 mi N on access roads. Enter at end.*

WELCOME

FACILITIES: 135 sites, 94 W&E, (30 & 50 amps), 41 no hkups, tenting, dump station, marine gas, ice, tables, grills.

RECREATION: swim pool, boating, canoeing, ramp, dock, 2 canoe/2 kayak/10 pedal boat rentals, lake fishing, putting green, bsktball, playground, planned activities, tennis, horseshoes, hiking trails, v-ball.

Pets welcome. Partial handicap access. Open all yr. Phone: (423)239-8531.

SEE AD TRAVEL SECTION PAGE 784

Dolly Parton, singer, is from Tennessee.

KINGSTON—B-6

(E) Four Seasons Campground—(Roane) *From jct I-40 (exit 356A westbound) (356 eastbound): Go 1 block N. Enter on R.* ◆◆FACILITIES: 50 sites, typical site width 20 ft, 45 full hkups, 5 W&E, (20 & 30 amps), 25 pull-thrus, tenting, laundry, ltd groceries, LP gas by weight/by meter, ice, tables, fire rings, grills. ◆◆RECREATION: rec room/area, equipped pavilion, swim pool, play equipment, horseshoes, v-ball. Pets welcome. Open all yr. Internet friendly. Rate in 2007 $18-20 for 2 persons. Member ARVC, TNARVC. Phone: (800)990-CAMP. FCRV 10% discount. FMCA discount.

KNOXVILLE—B-6

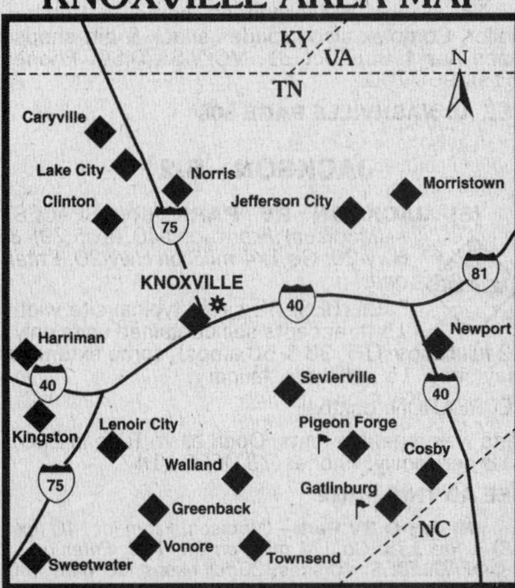

Symbols on map indicate towns within a 50 mi radius of Knoxville where campgrounds (dia-monds), attractions (flags), & RV service centers & camping supply outlets (gears) are listed. Check listings for more information.

Tell Them Woodall's Sent You!

KNOXVILLE—Continued on next page

Reputed "Turtle Capital of the World", Reelfoot Lake also features thousands of sliders, stinkpots, mud and map turtles.

KNOXVILLE—Continued

✽ **(N) BOB COX CAMPER COUNTRY**—*From jct I-75 (exit 108) & Merchant Rd: Go 3/4 mi W on Merchant Rd, then 1 mi N on US-25W (Clinton Hwy). Enter on R.* SALES: travel trailers, 5th wheels, motor homes, mini-motor homes, fold-down camping trailers, pre-owned unit sales. SERVICES: full-time mech, RV appliance repair, body work/collision repair, bus. hrs emerg rd svc, LP gas by weight/by meter, sells parts/accessories, installs hitches. Open all yr. MC/VISA/DISC/AMEX. Phone: (865)688-0823.

e-mail: david@bobcoxcampercountry.com

SEE AD PAGE 800

(N) Escapees Raccoon Valley RV Park—(Knox) *From jct I-640 & I-75: Go 9 mi N on I-75, take exit 117 (Racoon Valley Road), then 3/4 mi W on Raccoon Valley Road. Enter on L.* ◇◇◇FACILITIES: 77 sites, typical site width 27 ft, 77 full hkups, (20, 30 & 50 amps), 50 amps ($), 53 pull-thrus, tenting, dump station, non-guest dumping $, laundry, ice, tables. ◇◇◇RECREATION: rec room/area, swim pool, playground, planned activities, hiking trails. Pets welcome. Open all yr. Big rigs welcome. Internet friendly. Rate in 2007 $18.50-19.50 for 2 persons. Phone: (865)947-9776.

(S) SOUTHLAKE RV PARK—(Knox) *From jct I-40/75 (exit 376) and I-140: Go 14 mi SE on I-140/162, then 5 mi N on Hwy 33. Enter on L.*

◇◇◇FACILITIES: 123 sites, typical site width 35 ft, 98 full hkups, 25 W&E, (30 & 50 amps), 50 amps ($), some extended stay sites, 4 pull-thrus, cable TV, wireless Instant Internet access at site, phone Internet access central location, tenting, RV storage, dump station, non-guest dumping $, laundry, ltd groceries, RV supplies, ice, tables, grills, wood.

◇◇◇RECREATION: rec room/area, swim pool, boating, dock, lake fishing, fishing supplies, golf nearby, playground, horseshoes.

Pets welcome. Open all yr. Internet friendly. Clubs welcome. Rate in 2007 $22-30 for 2 persons. MC/VISA/DISC/AMEX/Debit. Phone: (865)573-1837.

e-mail: southlakervpark@yahoo.com

SEE AD THIS PAGE

✽ **(E) TENNESSEE RV**—*From jct I-40 (exit 398) & Strawberry Plains: Go 1/10 mi N on Strawberry Plains. Enter on L.* SALES: travel trailers, 5th wheels, motor homes, mini-motor homes, pre-owned unit sales. SERVICES: full-time mech, engine/chassis repair, RV appliance repair, body work/collision repair, bus. hrs emerg rd svc, LP gas by weight/by meter, sells parts/accessories, installs hitches. Open all yr. MC/VISA/DISC/AMEX. Phone: (800)678-2233.

e-mail: sales@tennesseerv.com

SEE AD PIGEON FORGE PAGE 813

(N) Volunteer Park—(Knox) *From jct I-640 & I-75: Go 9 mi N on I-75 (exit 117) then 1/4 mi W on Raccoon Valley Rd. Enter on L.* ◇◇◇◇FACILITIES: 144 sites, typical site width 35 ft, 100 full hkups, 44 W&E, (30 & 50 amps), some extended stay sites, 30 pull-thrus, tenting, dump station, non-guest dumping $, laundry, groceries, LP gas by weight/by meter, ice, tables, fire rings, wood. ◇◇◇◇RECREATION: rec hall, swim pool, playground, planned activities, horseshoes, hiking trails, v-ball. Pets welcome. Open all yr. fully operational Apr thru Oct 31. Big rigs welcome. Internet friendly. Rate in 2007 $30 for 4 persons. Phone: (865)938-6600. CCUSA discount. FMCA discount.

LAKE CITY—A-6

(N) MOUNTAIN LAKE MARINA & CAMPGROUND—(Anderson) *From jct I-75 (exit 128) & US 441: Go 1-1/4 mi SE on US 441, then 2 mi NE on Oak Grove Rd, then 3/4 mi E on Lindsey Mill Circle/Campground Rd. Follow signs. Enter at end.*

◇◇◇◇◇FACILITIES: 160 sites, 140 full hkups, 20 W&E, (20, 30 & 50 amps), 50 amps ($), some extended stay sites, 20 pull-thrus, cable TV ($), wireless Instant Internet access at site, phone Internet access central location, tenting, cabins, RV storage, dump station, laundry, ltd groceries, RV supplies, LP gas by weight/by meter, ice, tables, patios, fire rings, wood.

◇◇◇◇◇RECREATION: rec hall, rec room/area, coin games, swim pool, wading pool, lake swimming, boating, ramp, dock, 5 pontoon/3 motorboat rentals, lake fishing, fishing supplies, fishing guides, mini-golf ($), golf nearby, bsktball, 2 shuffleboard courts, planned activities, horseshoes, v-ball.

LAKE CITY—Continued
MOUNTAIN LAKE MARINA & CAMPGROUND—Continued

Pets welcome. Partial handicap access. Open all yr. Big rigs welcome. Internet friendly. Clubs welcome. Rate in 2007 $19-42 for 2 persons. MC/VISA/DISC/Debit. Member ARVC, TNARVC. Phone: (877)686-2267.

e-mail: mountainlakemarina@comcast.net

SEE AD KNOXVILLE PAGE 800

LAWRENCEBURG—C-3

(W) DAVID CROCKETT STATE PARK—(Lawrence) *From town: Go 1/2 mi W on US 64. Enter on R.*

FACILITIES: 107 sites, 107 W&E, (30 amps), tenting, dump station, ice, tables, grills, controlled access gate.

RECREATION: pavilion, swim pool, boating, no motors, dock, 7 pedal boat rentals, lake fishing, bsktball, playground, tennis, v-ball. Rec open to public.

Pets welcome. Partial handicap access. Open all yr. Swimming pool and boat rentals from Memorial Day to middle August. MC/VISA/DISC/AMEX/DC. Phone: (931)762-9408.

SEE AD TRAVEL SECTION PAGE 784

The Sequoyah Birthplace Museum in Vonore tells his story and is dedicated to the history and culture of Native Americans.

LEBANON—B-4

(S) CEDARS OF LEBANON STATE PARK—(Wilson) *From I-40 (exit 238) & US 231: Go 6 mi S on US 231. Enter on L.*

FACILITIES: 117 sites, 38 ft max RV length, 117 W&E, (20, 30 & 50 amps), 45 pull-thrus, tenting, cabins, dump station, laundry, ltd groceries, ice, tables, fire rings, grills.

RECREATION: rec hall, coin games, swim pool, playground, planned activities, tennis, horseshoes, sports field, hiking trails, v-ball. Rec open to public.

Pets welcome. Partial handicap access. Open all yr. Facilities fully operational Mar thru Nov. Camp store closed in winter. MC/VISA/DISC/AMEX. Phone: (615)443-2769.

SEE AD TRAVEL SECTION PAGE 784

(W) COUNTRYSIDE RV RESORT—(Wilson) *From jct I-40 (exit 232) & Hwy 109: Go 2/10 mi S to Safari Campground Rd, then 2 mi E on frontage road (Safari Campground Rd). Enter on R.*

◇◇◇◇FACILITIES: 120 sites, typical site width 35 ft, 68 full hkups, 52 W&E, (20, 30 & 50 amps), 50 amps ($), some extended stay sites (in summer), 40 pull-thrus, wireless Instant Internet access at site, phone Internet access central location, tenting, dump station, laundry, full svc store, RV supplies, LP gas by weight/by meter, ice, tables, fire rings, wood.

COUNTRYSIDE RV RESORT—Continued on next page

LEBANON—Continued
COUNTRYSIDE RV RESORT—Continued

◆◆◆RECREATION: equipped pavilion, swim pool, golf nearby, bsktball, playground, tennis, horseshoes, sports field, v-ball.

Pets welcome. Open all yr. Big rigs welcome. Internet friendly. Clubs welcome. Rate in 2007 $23-29 for 2 persons. MC/VISA/Debit. Member ARVC, TNARVC. Phone: (615)449-5527.

e-mail: countryside@countrysideresort.com

SEE AD NASHVILLE PAGE 810

(SE) Shady Acres Campground—(Wilson) *From jct I-40 (Exit 238) & US-231: Go 2 mi S on US-231. Enter on L.* ◆◆◆FACILITIES: 140 sites, typical site width 30 ft, 135 full hkups, 5 E, (30 & 50 amps), 50 amps ($), some extended stay sites (in summer), 115 pull-thrus, tenting, dump station, non-guest dumping $, laundry, ltd groceries, LP gas by weight/by meter, ice, tables. ◆◆◆RECREATION: equipped pavilion, swim pool, playground, shuffleboard court, horseshoes, sports field. Pets welcome. Open all yr. Big rigs welcome. Rate in 2007 $18-20 for 2 persons. Phone: (615)449-5400.

(SE) Timberline Campground—(Wilson) *From jct I-40 (exit 238) and US 231: Go 3/4 mi S on US 231. Enter on R.* ◆◆◆FACILITIES: 110 sites, 50 full hkups, 50 W&E, (30 & 50 amps), 50 amps ($), 10 no hkups, 29 pull-thrus, tenting, dump station, non-guest dumping $, laundry, LP gas by weight/by meter, ice, tables, patios, wood. ◆◆◆◆RECREATION: rec hall, swim pool, playground, shuffleboard court, planned activities, horseshoes, v-ball. Pets welcome. Open all yr. Big rigs welcome. Internet friendly. Rate in 2007 $23-27 for 2 persons. Phone: (615)449-2831. CCUSA discount.

LENOIR CITY—B-6

(W) Crosseyed Cricket—(Roane) *From jct I-40 (Exit 364) & Hwy-95: Go 1/4 mi N on Hwy-95, then 1/4 mi W on Buttermilk Road, then follow signs 1-3/4 mi S. Enter on R.* ◆◆◆FACILITIES: 50 sites, typical site width 30 ft, 32 full hkups, 18 W&E, (30 & 50 amps), many extended stay sites, 5 pull-thrus, tenting, dump station, non-guest dumping, laundry, ice, tables, fire rings, wood. ◆◆◆RECREATION: rec room/area, pavilion, swim pool, 2 canoe/2 pedal boat rentals, playground, horseshoes, v-ball. Pets welcome. Open all yr. Rate in 2007 $23-25 for 4 persons. Phone: (865)986-5435.

(N) MELTON HILL DAM (TVA-Melton Hill Reservoir)—(Anderson) *From jct I-40 (exit 364) & Hwy 95: Go 1/2 mi N on Hwy 95, then follow signs E to Melton Hill Dam Reservation.* FACILITIES: 56 sites, 56 no hkups, tenting, dump station, grills. RECREATION: pavilion, lake swimming, boating, ramp, lake/river fishing, planned activities, hiking trails. Partial handicap access. Open all yr. Facilities fully operational May 8 thru Sep 8. Phone: (865)632-1320.

Wilma Rudolph, athlete, was from Tennessee.

LENOIR CITY—Continued

(W) SOARING EAGLE CAMPGROUND & RV PARK—(Roane) *From jct I-40 (exit 360) & Buttermilk Rd: Go 100 feet N on Buttermilk Rd. Enter on R.*

◆◆◆FACILITIES: 125 sites, typical site width 28 ft, 76 full hkups, 39 W&E, (20, 30 & 50 amps), 50 amps ($), 10 no hkups, some extended stay sites, 44 pull-thrus, wireless Instant Internet access at site, wireless Internet access central location, tenting, RV storage, dump station, non-guest dumping $, laundry, ltd groceries, RV supplies, LP gas by weight/by meter, ice, tables, patios, grills, wood.

◆◆◆RECREATION: equipped pavilion, swim pool, boating, ramp, dock, lake fishing, golf nearby, bsktball, play equipment, horseshoes, v-ball.

Pets welcome, breed restrict. Partial handicap access. Open all yr. Facilities fully operational May 1 thru Oct 1. Big rigs welcome. Internet friendly. Clubs welcome. Rate in 2007 $21-24 for 2 persons. Member ARVC, TNARVC. Phone: (865)376-9017. FCRV 10% discount. FMCA discount.

SEE AD KNOXVILLE PAGE 800

LIVINGSTON—A-5

LILLYDALE CAMPGROUND (COE-Dale Hollow Lake)—(Clay) *From town: Go 5 mi NE on Hwy 111/294, then 14 mi N on Hwy 294, then 1 mi N on access road.* FACILITIES: 114 sites, 99 W&E, (20, 30 & 50 amps), 15 no hkups, 3 pull-thrus, tenting, dump station, laundry, grills. RECREATION: lake swimming, boating, ramp, lake fishing, playground, hiking trails, v-ball. Rec open to public. Open Apr 27 thru Sep3. Phone: (931)823-4155.

OBEY RIVER CAMPGROUND (COE-Dale Hollow Lake)—(Clay) *From town: Go 16 mi NE on Hwy-42 to the Obey River Bridge.* FACILITIES: 132 sites, 80 W&E, (30 & 50 amps), 52 no hkups, 13 pull-thrus, tenting, dump station, laundry, fire rings, grills. RECREATION: lake swimming, boating, ramp, lake fishing, playground, hiking trails, v-ball. Rec open to public. Partial handicap access. Open Apr 13 thru Oct 14. Phone: (931)864-6388.

(NW) STANDING STONE STATE PARK—(Overton) *From town: Go 12 mi NW on Hwy 52, then 2 mi S on Hwy 136. Enter on L.*

FACILITIES: 36 sites, 36 W&E, (30 amps), tenting, cabins, dump station, laundry, ice, tables, grills.

RECREATION: rec hall, equipped pavilion, swim pool, wading pool, boating, electric motors only, 10 rowboat rentals, lake/stream fishing, bsktball, playground, planned activities, tennis, sports field, hiking trails, v-ball. Rec open to public.

Pets welcome. Partial handicap access. Open all yr. MC/VISA/DISC/AMEX. Phone: (931)823-6347.

SEE AD TRAVEL SECTION PAGE 784

Tina Turner, singer, is from Tennessee.

LIVINGSTON—Continued

WILLOW GROVE (COE-Dale Hollow Lake)—(Clay) *From town: Go 5 mi NE on Hwy 111/294, then 16 mi N on Hwy 294. Enter at end.* FACILITIES: 83 sites, 62 W&E, (30 & 50 amps), 21 no hkups, tenting, dump station, laundry, fire rings, grills. RECREATION: lake swimming, boating, ramp, lake fishing, playground, hiking trails, v-ball. Rec open to public. Open May 18 thru Sep 3. Phone: (931)823-4285.

LOUDON—B-6

(E) EXPRESS RV PARK (RV SPACES)—(Loudon) *I-75 South exit 72: Turn right 1 block. I-75 North exit 72: Turn left 3 blocks. Enter on R.*

FACILITIES: 16 sites, 16 W&E, (30 & 50 amps), 16 pull-thrus, wireless Instant Internet access at site, tenting, dump station, non-guest dumping $, laundry.

RECREATION: swim pool.

Pets welcome, size restrict. Open all yr. Rate in 2007 $20-25 for 2 persons. MC/VISA/DISC/AMEX/DC/Debit. Phone: (865)458-5855.

SEE AD THIS PAGE

LYNCHBURG—C-4

(S) LYNCHBURG WILDERNESS RV PARK—(Moore) *From Lynchburg's only traffic light on Hwy 55 (Majors Blvd): Go 2 blocks west on Majors Blvd, then 1/2 mi S on Elm St which turns into Main St. Enter on L.*

◆◆◆FACILITIES: 48 sites, 48 full hkups, (20, 30 & 50 amps), 10 pull-thrus, tenting, RV storage, laundry, RV supplies, ice, tables, fire rings, wood.

◆◆RECREATION: rec room/area, equipped pavilion, stream fishing, bsktball, horseshoes, hiking trails.

Pets welcome. Partial handicap access. Open all yr. Clubs welcome. Rate in 2007 $20-35 per vehicle. MC/VISA/DISC. Member ARVC, TNARVC. Phone: (931)550-2680.

e-mail: gdspencer@cafes.net

SEE AD THIS PAGE

MANCHESTER—B-4

(S) KOA-MANCHESTER—(Coffee) *From jct I-24 (exit 114) & US 41: Go 100 yards on US 41, then 1/2 mi N on Kampground Rd (Frontage Rd). Enter on R.*

BIG RIG SITES!! FREE CABLE/WIFI!!
Easy on/off hwy, good signs between Nashville & Chattanooga. Close to shopping & dining. Big, long, wide pull-thrus, 50amps, onsite phone, cable, pool, Jacuzzi. Free fishing in stocked pond. Nice, new looking, shady country atmosphere.

◆◆◆◆◆FACILITIES: 59 sites, typical site width 33 ft, 24 full hkups, 15 W&E, (20, 30 & 50 amps), 20 no hkups, 42 pull-thrus, cable TV, wireless Instant Internet access at site, phone on-site Internet access (needs activ), phone Internet access central location, tenting, cabins, dump station, non-guest dumping $, laundry, full svc store, RV supplies, LP gas by weight/by meter, ice, tables, fire rings, grills, wood.

◆◆◆◆◆RECREATION: rec room/area, pavilion, coin games, swim pool, whirlpool, pond fishing,

KOA-MANCHESTER—Continued on next page

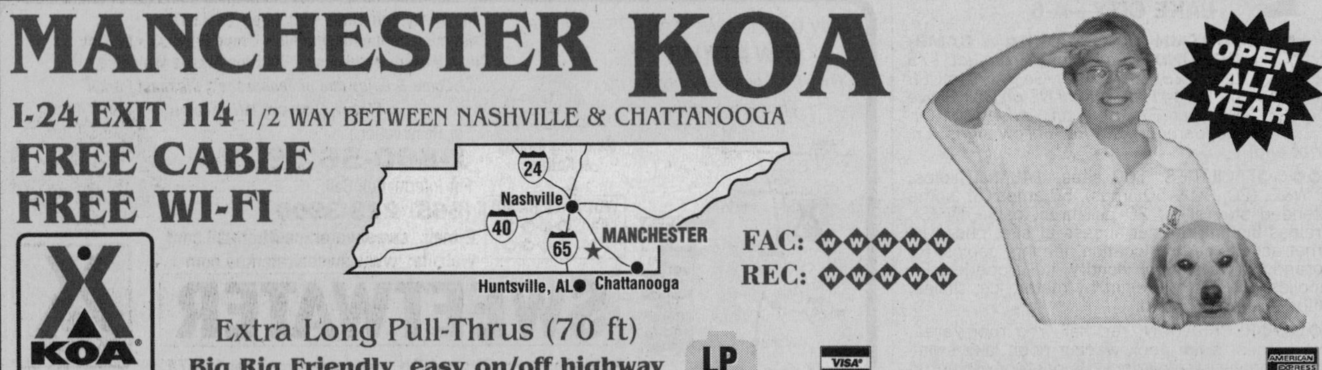

MANCHESTER—Continued
KOA-MANCHESTER—Continued

fishing supplies, golf nearby, bsktball, playground, planned activities (wkends only), horseshoes, sports field, hiking trails, v-ball, local tours.

Pets welcome. Open all yr. Big rigs welcome. Internet friendly. Escort to site. Clubs welcome. Rate in 2007 $25-40 for 2 persons. MC/VISA/DISC/AMEX/Debit. Member ARVC, TNARVC. Phone: (800)562-7785. KOA 10% value card discount.

e-mail: manchesterkoa@earthlink.net

SEE AD PAGE 802 AND AD DISCOVER SECTION PAGES 62 & 63

MILITARY PARK (FAMCAMP-Arnold AFB)—(Franklin) *From I-24 (exit 117): Go W on Wattendorf Hwy past Gate 2, then S on Pump Station Rd, then 1-1/2 mi W on Northshore Dr. On base. Enter on R.* FACILITIES: 83 sites, typical site width 14 ft, 25 ft max RV length, 26 W&E, 57 no hkups, 2 pull-thrus, tenting, dump station, laundry, ice, fire rings, grills. RECREATION: rec room/area, pavilion, lake swimming, boating, canoeing, ramp, dock, 2 canoe/5 motorboat rentals, lake fishing, playground, tennis, v-ball. Open Apr 1 thru Oct 1. For Military Use Only-w/Military ID Card. Reservations required. Phone: (615)454-4520.

Woodall's Tip #43... If you are camping in bear country, be sure to cook at least 300 feet downwind of your sleeping area. Use baking soda to rid your clothes and hands of cooking odors.

MANCHESTER—Continued

(W) OLD STONE FORT STATE ARCHAEOLOGICAL AREA—(Coffee) *From jct Hwy 53 & US 41: Go 1/2 mi W on US 41. Enter on L.*

WELCOME

FACILITIES: 51 sites, 51 W&E, tenting, dump station, tables, grills, controlled access gate.

RECREATION: boating, electric motors only, canoeing, lake/river fishing, playground, planned activities, hiking trails.

MANCHESTER—Continued
OLD STONE FORT STATE ARCHAEOLOGICAL AREA—Continued

Pets welcome. Partial handicap access. Open all yr. No reservations. MC/VISA/DISC/AMEX. Phone: (931)723-5073.

SEE AD TRAVEL SECTION PAGE 784

MEMPHIS—C-1

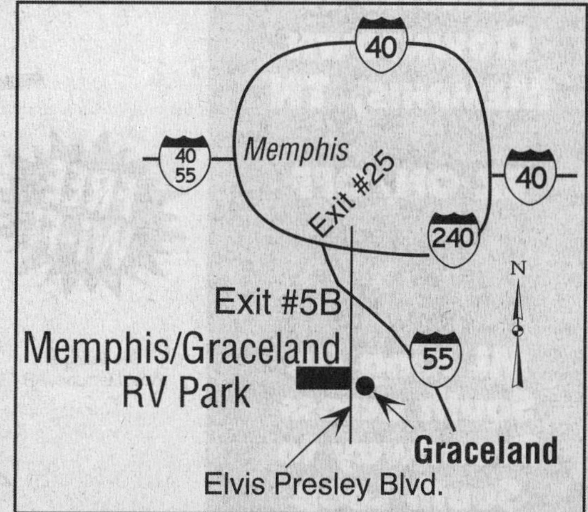

See listings at Millington, TN; West Memphis, AR; Southhaven, Tunica & Coldwater & Robinsonville, MS

MEMPHIS—Continued on next page

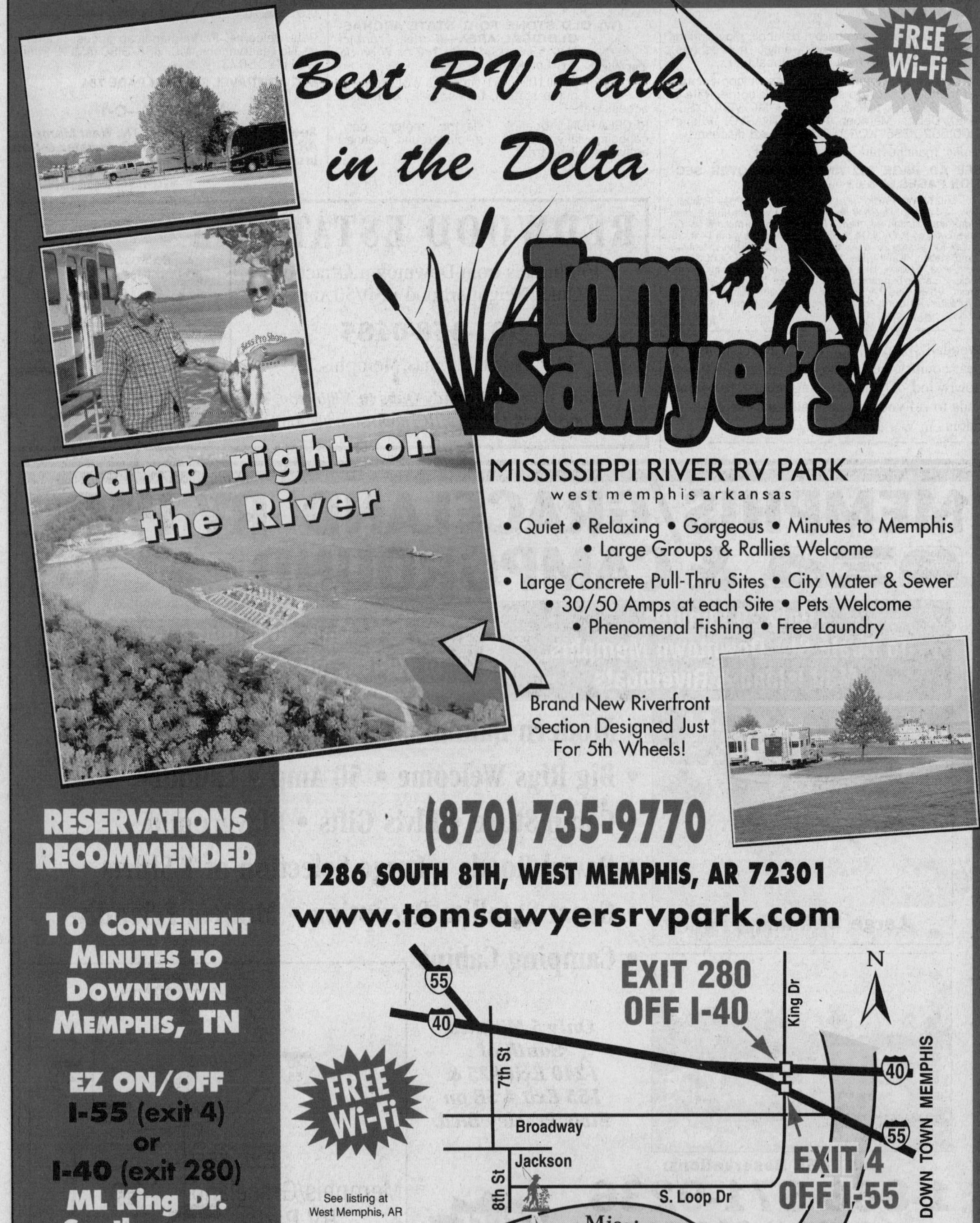
FREE Wi-Fi
Best RV Park in the Delta
Tom Sawyer's
MISSISSIPPI RIVER RV PARK
west memphis arkansas
• Quiet • Relaxing • Gorgeous • Minutes to Memphis
• Large Groups & Rallies Welcome
• Large Concrete Pull-Thru Sites • City Water & Sewer
• 30/50 Amps at each Site • Pets Welcome
• Phenomenal Fishing • Free Laundry
Camp right on the River
Brand New Riverfront Section Designed Just For 5th Wheels!
RESERVATIONS RECOMMENDED
10 Convenient Minutes to Downtown Memphis, TN
EZ ON/OFF I-55 (exit 4) or I-40 (exit 280) ML King Dr. South across Broadway to South Loop 2 1/2 Miles
(870) 735-9770
1286 SOUTH 8TH, WEST MEMPHIS, AR 72301
www.tomsawyersrvpark.com
55
40
EXIT 280 OFF I-40
King Dr
N
7th St
Broadway
Jackson
8th St
S. Loop Dr
EXIT 4 OFF I-55
DOWN TOWN MEMPHIS
Mississippi River
FREE Wi-Fi
See listing at West Memphis, AR
Tom Sawyer's R.V. Park

MEMPHIS—Continued

(S) AGRICENTER RV PARK—(Shelby) *From jct I-40 & Germantown Rd (W'bound exit 16A/E'bound exit 16): Go 4 mi S on Germantown Pkwy, then 2/10 mi W on Timber Creek Rd. Enter on R.* FACILITIES: 400 sites, 96 full hkups, 304 W&E, (30 amps), 96 pull-thrus, dump station, portable dump, laundry, ltd groceries, ice. RECREATION: pond fishing, hiking trails. Pets welcome. No tents. Open all yr. Phone: (901)355-1977.

✲ **Davis Motorhome/D & N Camper Sales**—*From I-55 (N'bnd exit 5). From I-55 (S'bnd 5B): Go 1 blk E on Brooks Rd.* SALES: travel trailers, 5th wheels, van campers, motor homes, mini-motor homes, pre-owned unit sales. SERVICES: full-time mech, RV appliance repair, body work/collision repair, sells parts/accessories. Open all yr. MC/VISA/DISC/AMEX. Phone: (800)772-3414.

(S) Elvis Presley Blvd RV Park—(Shelby) *From I-55 (S'Bnd exit 5B): Go 1-1/2 mi S on US 51 (Elvis Presley Blvd). Enter on R.* ◇◇FACILITIES: 60 sites, typical site width 20 ft, 60 full hkups, (20, 30 & 50 amps), 50 amps ($), some extended stay sites, 2 pull-thrus, tenting, dump station, non-guest dumping $, laundry, tables. Pets welcome. Open all yr. Rate in 2007 $32 for 2 persons. Phone: (901)332-3633.

(E) Memphis East Campground—(Shelby) *From jct I-40 (exit 20) & Canada Rd: Go 3/4 mi S on Canada Rd, then 1/4 mi E on Monroe St. Enter on L.* ◇◇◇FACILITIES: 82 sites, typical site width 22 ft, 64 full hkups, 10 W&E, 8 E, (20, 30 & 50 amps), 50 amps ($), many extended stay sites, 38 pull-thrus, tenting, dump station, non-guest dumping $, laundry, groceries,

Tell them Woodall's sent you!

MEMPHIS—Continued
Memphis East Campground—Continued

LP gas by weight/by meter, ice, tables. ◇◇RECREATION: rec room/area, pavilion, swim pool, pond fishing, playground. Pets welcome. Partial handicap access. Open all yr. Rate in 2007 $24.50-27 for 2 persons. Phone: (901)388-3053.

WELCOME **MEMPHIS KOA**—*From jct Mississippi River Bridge & I-40: Follow I-40/I-55 to I-55 N Cut off, then 7 mi N on I-55 to exit 14, then follow camping logo signs to entrance on west service road.*

SEE PRIMARY LISTING AT MARION, AR AND AD NEXT PAGE

WELCOME **MEMPHIS SOUTH CAMPGROUND & RV PARK**—*From Memphis (I-240 & I-55): Go 24 mi S on I-55 (exit 271) & Hwy 306 (MS), then 200 ft W on Hwy 306. Enter on L.*

SEE PRIMARY LISTING AT COLDWATER, MS AND AD PAGE 807

WELCOME **(S) MEMPHIS/GRACELAND RV PARK & CAMPGROUND**—(Shelby) *From I-55 (N'Bnd exit 5) follow Graceland signs. From I-55 (S'Bnd exit 5B): Go 1 mi S on US 51 (Elvis Presley Blvd), turn right at Heartbreak Hotel on Lonely St. Enter on R.*

◇◇◇◇FACILITIES: 107 sites, typical site width 22 ft, 72 full hkups, 16 W&E, (20, 30 & 50 amps), 19 no hkups, 30 pull-thrus, wireless Instant Internet access at site, phone Internet access central

MEMPHIS—Continued
MEMPHIS/GRACELAND RV PARK & CAMPGROUND—Continued

location, tenting, cabins, dump station, laundry, ltd groceries, RV supplies, LP gas by weight/by meter, ice, tables.

◇◇◇RECREATION: equipped pavilion, swim pool, golf nearby, bsktball, playground, horseshoes, sports field, v-ball, local tours.

Pets welcome. Partial handicap access. Open all yr. Big rigs welcome. Internet friendly. Clubs welcome. Rate in 2007 $39-42 for 2 persons. MC/VISA/DISC/Debit. Phone: (901)396-7125.

SEE AD PAGE 803

WELCOME **(N) REDWOOD ESTATES** (RV SPACES) —(Shelby) *From jct I-40 (exit 2A) & I-240: Go 3 mi N on US 51/North Thomas St. Enter on R.*

FACILITIES: 22 sites, accepts full hkup units only, 22 full hkups, (30 & 50 amps), phone on-site Internet access (needs activ), laundry.

RECREATION: bsktball.

Pets welcome, breed restrict. No tents. Open all yr. Phone: (901)358-0485.

SEE AD PAGE 803 AND AD MILLINGTON PAGE 808 AND AD TUNICA, MS PAGE 482

MEMPHIS—Continued on next page

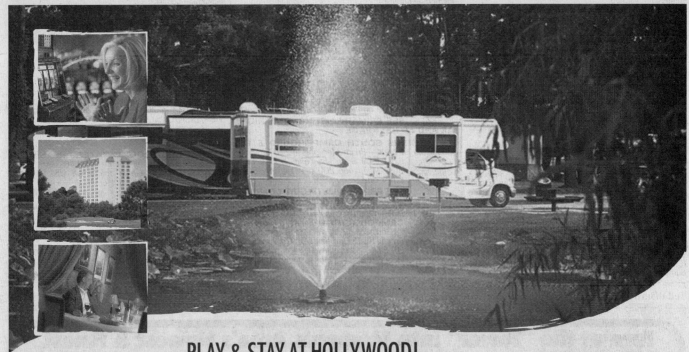

MEMPHIS—Continued

SOUTHAVEN RV PARK—*From jct I-240S & I-55: Go 5 mi S on I-55 (exit 291/Stateline Rd), then 2 blks E. Enter on L.*

SEE PRIMARY LISTING AT SOUTHAVEN, MS AND AD THIS PAGE

(SW) T.O. FULLER STATE PARK—(Shelby) *From I-55 & US 61: Go 2 mi S on US 61, then 6 mi W on Mitchell Rd, then S on Plant Rd, then 1/2 mi E on Boxtown Rd. Enter on L.*

FACILITIES: 45 sites, 45 W&E, (30 & 50 amps), 19 pull-thrus, tenting, dump station, laundry, tables, fire rings, grills.

RECREATION: equipped pavilion, swim pool, putting green, bsktball, playground, tennis, hiking trails.

Pets welcome. Partial handicap access. Open all yr. No reservations. MC/VISA/DISC/AMEX/DC. Phone: (901)543-7581.

SEE AD TRAVEL SECTION PAGE 784

MEMPHIS—Continued

TOM SAWYER'S MISSISSIPPI RIVER RV PARK—*From jct I-40 (exit 280) & ML King Dr: Go 3 mi S on ML King Dr (becomes South Loop). From jct I-55 (exit 4) & ML King Dr: Go 2-1/2 mi S on ML King Dr. Over levee to park. Enter on L.*

SEE PRIMARY LISTING AT WEST MEMPHIS, AR AND AD PAGE 804

MILLINGTON—C-1

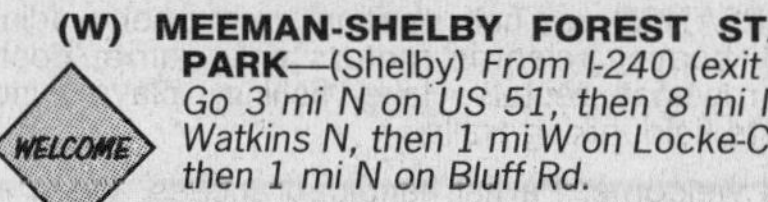

(W) MEEMAN-SHELBY FOREST STATE PARK—(Shelby) *From I-240 (exit 2A): Go 3 mi N on US 51, then 8 mi N on Watkins N, then 1 mi W on Locke-Cuba, then 1 mi N on Bluff Rd.*

FACILITIES: 49 sites, 49 W&E, (20, 30 & 50 amps), tenting, cabins, dump station, tables, fire rings, grills.

MEEMAN-SHELBY FOREST STATE PARK—Continued on next page

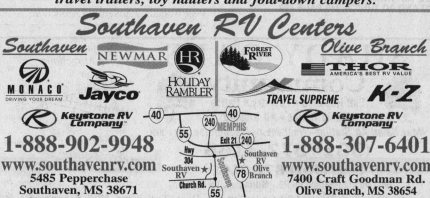

MILLINGTON—Continued
MEEMAN-SHELBY FOREST STATE PARK—Continued

RECREATION: rec hall, pavilion, swim pool, wading pool, boating, electric motors only, ramp, dock, 25 rowboat rentals, lake fishing, playground, sports field, hiking trails.

Pets welcome. Partial handicap access. Open all yr. MC/VISA/DISC/AMEX. Phone: (800)471-5293.

SEE AD TRAVEL SECTION PAGE 784

(E) SHADY OAKS COMMUNITY (RV SPACES)—(Shelby) *From jct US 51 & Navy Rd: Go 1 mi E on Navy Rd, then 1/2 block S on Raleigh Millington Rd. Enter on L.*

FACILITIES: 35 sites, typical site width 30 ft, accepts full hkup units only, 35 full hkups, (20 & 30 amps), heater not allowed, phone on-site Internet access (needs activ), laundry, patios.

RECREATION: golf nearby, play equipment.

Pets welcome, breed restrict. No tents. Open all yr. No restrooms. Phone: (901)872-3168.

e-mail: shadyoaks@bigriver.net

SEE AD THIS PAGE AND AD MEMPHIS PAGE 803 AND AD TUNICA, MS PAGE 482

MORRISTOWN—D-5

(W) PANTHER CREEK STATE PARK—(Hamblen) *From jct US 11E & Hwy 342: Go 2 mi W on Hwy 342. Enter on R.*

FACILITIES: 50 sites, 35 ft max RV length, 50 W&E, (30 amps), tenting, dump station, laundry, tables, patios, fire rings, grills, controlled access gate.

RECREATION: pavilion, swim pool, wading pool, boating, ramp, lake fishing, bsktball, playground, tennis, sports field, hiking trails, v-ball. Rec open to public.

Pets welcome. Partial handicap access. Open all yr. Phone: (423)587-7046.

SEE AD TRAVEL SECTION PAGE 784

MT. JULIET—B-4

CEDAR CREEK CAMPGROUND (COE-Old Hickory Lake)—(Wilson) *From jct Hwy 171 & US 70W: Go 1 mi W on US 70, then 2 mi N on Nonaville Rd, then 1 mi E on Saundersville Rd. Enter on L.* FACILITIES: 59 sites, typical site width 14 ft, 59 W&E, (30 & 50 amps), 4 pull-thrus, tenting, dump station, laundry, ltd groceries, LP gas by weight, ice, fire rings, grills, wood. RECREATION: pavilion, lake swimming, boating, ramp, dock, lake fishing, playground. Partial handicap access. Open Apr 1 thru Oct 31. Phone: (615)754-4947.

Visit Woodall's Advertised Attractions

NASHVILLE—B-4

NASHVILLE AREA MAP

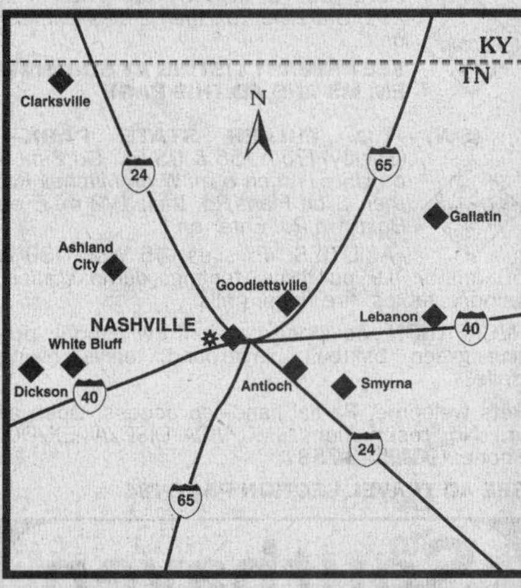

Symbols on map indicate towns within a 40 mi radius of Nashville where campgrounds (dia-monds), attractions (flags), & RV service centers & camping supply outlets (gears) are listed. Check listings for more information.

Tell Them Woodall's Sent You!

COUNTRYSIDE RV RESORT—*From jct I-265 & I-40: Go 17 mi E on I-40 (exit 232) & Hwy 109, then 2/10 mi S to Safari Campground Rd, then 2 mi E on front-age road (Safari Campground Rd).*

SEE PRIMARY LISTING AT LEBANON AND AD PAGE 810

NASHVILLE—Continued on next page

Only Two Miles From Grand Ole Opry®

NEXT DOOR TO CAMPING WORLD

Over 100 Spacious RV Sites • Full Hookups • 30/50 Amp Service • Concrete Patios, Tables & Benches • Laundry with New Machines • Clean Bath Houses • Playground • Game Room • Store & Gift Shop • Free Wi-Fi • Free Modem Hookup • Propane Available • Friendly Service

BEST RATES ON MUSIC VALLEY DRIVE
(GROUP RATES AVAILABLE)

Enjoy a "Muisc City Vacation." Let our friendly and experienced staff help you plan a "customized" vacation in Nashville. They will help you see Nashville like you've never seen it before. From tickets to the Grand Ole Opry to tours that suit your special interests our staff is here to make sure you enjoy yourself while visiting Music CIty U.S.A.

- EVENING ENTERTAINMENT (SEASONAL)
- TOURS OF ALL AREA ATTRACTIONS
- SHUTTLE BUS ($) TO GRAND OLE OPRY® AND OPRY MILLS MALL

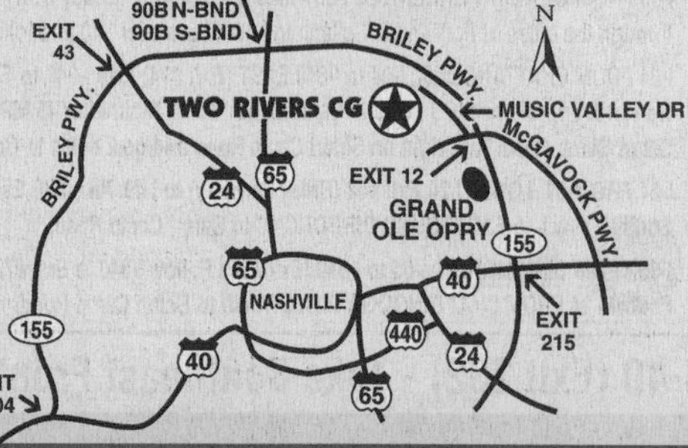

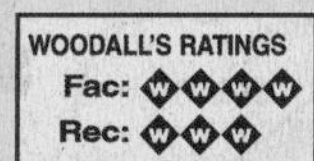

OPEN ALL YEAR

Campground Reservations & Information

(615) 883-8559 • (615) 883-8070

FAX (615) 889-5453 1 NIGHT DEPOSIT REQUIRED

2616 Music Valley Dr., Nashville, TN 37214

www.tworiverscampground.com

WEEKLY & MONTHLY RATES AVAILABLE

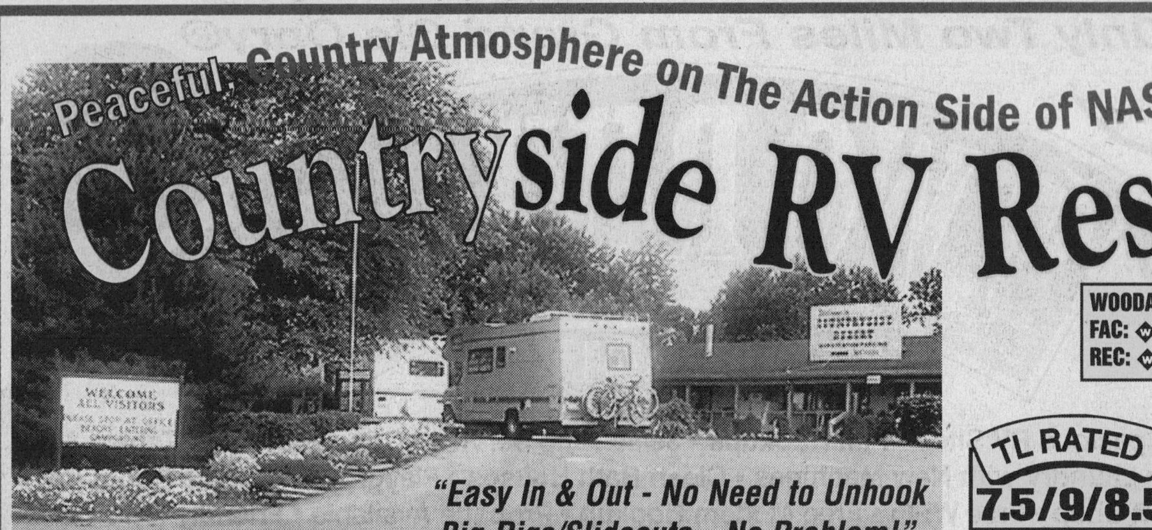

WOODALL RATED
FAC: ◈◈◈◈
REC: ◈◈◈

TL RATED 7.5/9/8.5

Good Sam Park

MasterCard VISA

See listings at Lebanon, TN & Nashville, TN

Visit us on the web: www.gocampingamerica.com/countrysidetn
E-Mail: countrysidetn@gocampingamerica.com

FREE HIGH SPEED WIRELESS INTERNET

BEST CAMPING VALUE IN NASHVILLE
COMPARE RATES-COMPARE RATINGS

...Only 25 Minutes to Nashville...
Grand Ole Opry® - The Hermitage.
Trinity Music City USA
Opry Mills Mall & Bass Pro Shop
10 Minutes to Lebanon TN, "Antique City of the South"
Outlet Village of Lebanon - Wal-Mart Super Center

"Big or Small" We Accommodate Them All

- **20/30/50 Amp Service • Long Pull Thrus**
- **Full Hookups • Swimming Pool • Tile Showers**
- **Full Store • RV Parts • Firewood-Ice • Playground**
- **Volleyball Courts • Laundry • LP-Gas**
- **9 Hole Target-Green Golf Course**
- **Covered Picnic Pavilion • TENTERS WELCOME**

WE WELCOME GROUPS-CLUBS-RALLIES

I-40 WESTBOUND FROM KNOXVILLE: I-40 Exit #232 (Highway 109). Turn left (SOUTH) onto Highway 109. As soon as you cross over I-40, the first left turn will be the I-40 East on-ramp. Go 1/10th mile farther to the next left turn, Safari Camp Road. LEFT on Safari Camp Road 2 miles to Countryside Resort.

I-40 EASTBOUND FROM NASHVILLE: I-40 Exit #2232A (Highway 109 South). As soon as you turn onto Highway 109, look for I-40 East on-ramp. Go 1/10th mile farther to the next left turn, Safari Camp Road. LEFT on Safari Camp Road 2 miles to Countryside Resort.

I-65 FROM BOWLING GREEN, KY: I-65 - Take KY Exit #2 (Highway 31W) to Hwy. 109. Left on Hwy. 109 through the cities of Portland & Gallatin to I-40. Cross over I-40 and follow I-40 WESTBOUND DIRECTIONS.

I-24 FROM CHATTANOOGA: I-24 to I-840 EAST (Exit #74) Take I-840 to Exit 72-B (Central Pike/Highway 265) Go North approximately 3 miles to Safari Camp Road. Right after 45 MPH speed limit sign, the next right is Safari Camp Road. Turn right on Safari Camp Road and go 2 miles to Countryside Resort.

I-24 FROM ST. LOUIS: I-24 Exit #43 (Briley Parkway) to I-40. Take I-40 East to Exit #232-A (Highway 109 South) Follw I-40 EASTBOUND DIRECTIONS to Safari Camp Road.

I-65 FROM BIRMINGHAM: I-65 to I-840 (Exit #59). Follow I-840 to Exit #72B (Highway 265/Central Pike). Follow I-24 FROM CHATTANOOGA DIRECTIONS to Safari Camp Road.

I-40 (Exit 232) - Take Southeast Frontage Rd. 2 Miles

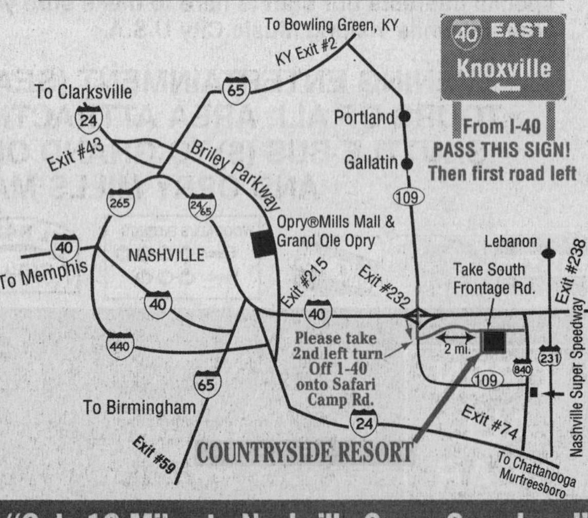

On Site Owners For Friendly Service
Please Call For Information and/or Reservations
(615) 449-5527
Your Hosts: Ron & Carol Fernandes
2100 Safari Camp Rd., Lebanon, TN 37090

"Only 12 Miles to Nashville Super Speedway"

Woodall's Directory is split, East/West. You can buy a Directory with all of North America, or you can buy only the Eastern or Western editions. Browse our bookstore at www.woodalls.com/shop for more details.

NASHVILLE—Continued

✽ **(NE) Cullum & Maxey Camping Center**—*From I-40 E (exit 215-Briley Pkwy): Go 5-1/2 mi N on Briley Pkwy, then 1/4 mi W on McGavock Pike, then 1 mi N on Music Valley Dr. Enter on L.* SALES: travel trailers, 5th wheels, motor homes, mini-motor homes, pre-owned unit sales. SERVICES: full-time mech, engine/chassis repair, RV appliance repair, body work/collision repair, LP gas by weight/by meter, dump station, sells parts/accessories, installs hitches. Open all yr. MC/VISA. Phone: (615)889-1600.

NASHVILLE—Continued

LORETTA LYNN'S RANCH—*From jct I-65 & I-40 (exit 208): Go 65 mi W on I-40 (exit 143), then 8 mi N on Hwy 13.*

WELCOME

SEE PRIMARY LISTING AT HURRICANE MILLS. AND AD PAGE 808

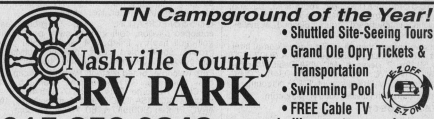

NASHVILLE—Continued on next page

NASHVILLE—Continued

NASHVILLE COUNTRY RV PARK—(Sumner) *From I-24 West & I-65 North: Go 10 mi N on I-65, (exit 98) US31 W, then 2 mi N on US 31 W. Enter on L.*

◇◇◇◇FACILITIES: 93 sites, typical site width 30 ft, 81 full hkups, 12 W&E, (20, 30 & 50 amps), 50 amps ($), some extended stay sites, 55 pull-thrus, cable TV, wireless Instant Internet access at site, phone Internet access central location, tenting, cabins, RV storage, dump station, non-guest dumping $, laundry, ltd groceries, RV supplies, LP gas by weight/by meter, ice, tables, patios.

◇◇◇◇◇RECREATION: rec room/area, pavilion, swim pool, stream fishing, golf nearby, playground, shuffleboard court, planned activities, horseshoes, hiking trails, local tours.

Pets welcome. Open all yr. Big rigs welcome. Internet friendly. Clubs welcome. Rate in 2007 $20-34.50 for 2 persons. MC/VISA/Debit. Member ARVC, TN ARVC. Phone: (615)859-0348. CCUSA discount. FCRV 10% discount. FMCA discount.

e-mail: camp@nashvillecountryrvpark.com

SEE AD PAGE 811

✱ **(SE) NASHVILLE EASY LIVIN' COUNTRY**—*From jct I-24 (exit 62): Go N 2 mi on Old Hickory Blvd, then 1/4 mi E on Murfreesboro Rd. Enter on R.* SALES: travel trailers, 5th wheels, motor homes, mini-motor homes, pre-owned unit sales. SERVICES: full-time mech, RV appliance repair, body work/collision repair, LP gas by weight/by meter, sells parts/accessories, installs hitches. Open all yr. MC/VISA/DISC/AMEX. Phone: (615)641-6302.

e-mail: info@nashvilleeasylivin.com

SEE AD PAGE 811

(NE) NASHVILLE KOA—(Davidson) *W'Bnd: From I-40E (exit 215-Briley Pkwy): Go 5-1/2 mi N on Briley Pkwy. S'Bnd: From I-65N (Opryland exit) & Briley Pkwy: Go 4-1/2 mi S on Briley Pkwy. Both From Briley Pkwy: Go 1/4 mi W on McGavock Pike, then 2 mi N on Music Valley Dr. Enter on L.*

◇◇◇◇FACILITIES: 389 sites, typical site width 30 ft, 271 full hkups, 62 W&E, (20, 30 & 50 amps), 50 amps ($), 56 no hkups, 112 pull-thrus, wireless Instant Internet access at site, phone Internet access central location, tenting, cabins, dump station, non-guest dumping $, laundry, full svc store, RV supplies, LP gas by weight/by meter, ice, tables, patios.

◇◇◇◇◇RECREATION: rec hall, rec room/area, coin games, swim pool, wading pool, mini-golf ($), golf nearby, bsktball, 12 bike rentals, playground, planned activities, horseshoes, local tours.

Pets welcome. Partial handicap access. Open all yr. Big rigs welcome. Internet friendly. Clubs welcome. MC/VISA/DISC/AMEX/Debit. Member ARVC, TN ARVC. Phone: (800)KOA-7789. KOA 10% value card discount.

e-mail: nashville@koa.net

SEE AD PAGE 811 AND AD DISCOVER SECTION PAGES 62 & 63

Tennessee ties with Missouri as the most neighborly state in the union. It is bordered by eight states.

NASHVILLE—Continued

(NE) NASHVILLE'S JELLYSTONE PARK—(Davidson) *Westbound: From I-40E (exit 215-Briley Pkwy): Go 5-1/2 mi N on Briley Pkwy. Southbound: From I-65 N & Briley Pkwy (Opryland exit): Go 4-1/2 mi S on Briley Pkwy. Both From Briley Pkwy: Go 1/4 mi W on McGavock Pike, then 1 mi N on Music Valley Dr. Enter on L.*

◇◇◇◇FACILITIES: 263 sites, typical site width 35 ft, 167 full hkups, 66 W&E, (20, 30 & 50 amps), 50 amps ($), 30 no hkups, 238 pull-thrus, wireless Instant Internet access at site, tenting, cabins, RV storage, dump station, non-guest dumping $, laundry, full svc store, RV supplies, LP gas by weight/by meter, ice, tables.

◇◇◇◇◇RECREATION: rec room/area, equipped pavilion, coin games, swim pool, mini-golf, golf nearby, bsktball, 4 bike rentals, playground, shuffleboard court, planned activities, horseshoes, sports field, v-ball, local tours.

Pets welcome, breed restrict. Partial handicap access. Open all yr. Big rigs welcome. Internet friendly. Clubs welcome. Rate in 2007 $35-48 for 2 persons. MC/VISA/DISC/Debit. Member ARVC, TN ARVC. Phone: (800)547-4480. FMCA discount.

e-mail: nashvillejellystone@yahoo.com

SEE AD PAGE 808

⚑ **TENNESSEE STATE PARKS DEPARTMENT OF ENVIRONMENT AND CONSERVATION**—Phone: (615)532-4580.

SEE AD TRAVEL SECTION PAGE 784

(NE) TWO RIVERS CAMPGROUND—(Davidson) *W'bnd: From I-40E (exit 215-Briley Pkwy): Go 5-1/2 mi N on Briley Pkwy (exit 12) S'bnd: From I-65N & Briley Pkwy (Opryland exit) 90 B: Go 4-1/2 mi S on Briley Pkwy. Both From Briley Pkwy: Go 1/4 mi W on McGavock Pike, then 1 mi N on Music Valley Dr. Enter on L.*

◇◇◇◇FACILITIES: 104 sites, typical site width 30 ft, 72 full hkups, 32 W&E, (30 & 50 amps), 50 amps ($), 11 pull-thrus, wireless Instant Internet access at site, phone Internet access central location, dump station, laundry, full svc store, RV supplies, LP gas by weight/by meter, ice, tables, patios.

◇◇◇RECREATION: rec room/area, coin games, swim pool, golf nearby, bsktball, playground, planned activities, local tours.

Pets welcome. Partial handicap access. No tents. Open all yr. Big rigs welcome. Internet friendly. Clubs welcome. Rate in 2007 $27-38 for 2 persons. MC/VISA/DISC/Debit. Member ARVC, TNARVC. Phone: (615)883-8559. FMCA discount.

e-mail: trcg@bellsouth.net

SEE AD PAGE 809

⚑ **US ARMY CORPS OF ENGINEERS/ VOLUNTEER CLEARING HOUSE**—Beautiful lakes, parks & visitor centers! the US Army offers nationwide volunteer opportunities to help in campgrounds & visitor centers, maintain park facilities, trails, wildlife habitat & more. Free campsite often provided. Phone: (800)865-8337.

e-mail: Volunteer.Clearinghouse@lrn02.usace.army.mil

SEE AD DISCOVER SECTION PAGE 71

NEWPORT—D-5

(W) KOA-NEWPORT I-40/SMOKY MTNS—(Cocke) *From jct I-40 (exit 432B) & US 25W/US 70: Go 1-1/2 mi E on US 25W/US 70, then follow signs 1/2 mi S. Enter on R.*

◇◇◇◇FACILITIES: 99 sites, typical site width 35 ft, 47 full hkups, 52 W&E, (20, 30 & 50 amps), 50 amps ($), 45 pull-thrus, cable TV ($),

NEWPORT—Continued
KOA-NEWPORT I-40/SMOKY MTNS—Continued

wireless Instant Internet access at site, phone Internet access central location, tenting, cabins, RV storage, dump station, non-guest dumping $, laundry, groceries, RV supplies, LP gas by weight/by meter, ice, tables, wood.

◇◇◇◇RECREATION: rec room/area, equipped pavilion, coin games, swim pool, pond fishing, golf nearby, bsktball, playground, horseshoes, v-ball. Rec open to public.

Pets welcome. Open all yr. Big rigs welcome. Internet friendly. Escort to site. Clubs welcome. Rate in 2007 $32-37 for 2 persons. MC/VISA/Debit. Phone: (800)562-9016. KOA 10% value card discount.

e-mail: k644@bellsouth.net

SEE AD THIS PAGE AND AD DISCOVER SECTION PAGES 62 & 63

NORRIS—A-6

BIG RIDGE STATE PARK—(Union) *From jct I-75 (exit 122) & Hwy 61: Go 12 mi E on Hwy 61. Enter on L.*

FACILITIES: 52 sites, 52 W&E, 3 pull-thrus, tenting, cabins, dump station, laundry, tables, fire rings, grills.

RECREATION: lake swimming, boating, canoeing, ramp, 6 rowboat/5 canoe/5 pedal boat rentals, lake fishing, bsktball, playground, planned activities, tennis, sports field, hiking trails, v-ball.

Pets welcome. Partial handicap access. Open all yr. No reservations. Bathhouses closed winter months. MC/VISA/DISC/AMEX. Phone: (865)992-5523.

SEE AD TRAVEL SECTION PAGE 784

(E) LOYSTON POINT (TVA - Norris Reservoir)—(Anderson) *From jct US-441 & Hwy-61: Go 2 mi E on Hwy-61, then 3-3/4 mi N on ParkRd, then 1/2 mi E on Boy Scout Rd, then follow signs 2-1/2 mi NE/S/E onLoyston Point Rd.* FACILITIES: 64 sites, 39 E, 25 no hkups, 8 pull-thrus, tenting, dump station. RECREATION: lake swimming, boating, ramp, lake fishing, hiking trails. Open Mar 21 thru Oct 31. Phone: (865)632-1320.

NORRIS DAM STATE PARK—(Campbell) *From jct I-75 (exit 128): Go 2-1/2 mi S on US 441. Enter on R.*

FACILITIES: 85 sites, 30 ft max RV length, 75 W&E, (20 & 30 amps), 10 no hkups, tenting, cabins, dump station, laundry, marine gas, tables, grills.

RECREATION: pavilion, boating, ramp, dock, motorboat rentals, lake fishing, playground, planned activities, tennis, hiking trails, v-ball. Rec open to public.

Pets welcome. Partial handicap access. Open all yr. Facilities fully operational Apr 15 thru Nov 16. some activities available in season only. Phone: (865)426-7461.

SEE AD TRAVEL SECTION PAGE 784

ONEIDA—A-6

BIG SOUTH FORK NAT'L. RIVER & REC. AREA (Bandy Creek Campground)—(Scott) *From jct US 27 & Hwy 297: Go 15 mi W on Hwy 297. Enter on R.* FACILITIES: 150 sites, 100 W&E, 50 no hkups, tenting, dump station, ice, fire rings, grills. RECREATION: swim pool, boating, no motors, canoeing, river fishing, play equipment, hiking trails. Partial handicap access. Open all yr. Phone: (423)569-8368.

PARIS—A-2

(E) Buchanan Resort—(Henry) *From jct US 641 & US 79: Go 12 mi NE on US 79, then 1-1/2 mi SE on Antioch Rd, then follow signs 3/4 mi NE. Enter on L.* ◇◇FACILITIES: 50 sites, typical site width 35 ft, 50 W&E, (20, 30 & 50 amps), many extended stay sites (in summer), 4 pull-thrus, tenting, dump station, non-guest dumping $, ice, tables, grills. ◇◇◇RECREATION: equipped pavilion, swim pool, lake swimming, boating, ramp, dock, 8 motorboat rentals, lake/river fishing, playground, 2 shuffleboard courts, tennis, horseshoes, v-ball. Pets welcome. Open Mar 15 thru Nov 1. Big rigs welcome. Internet friendly. Rate in 2007 $22 for 4 persons. Phone: (731)642-2828.

(E) KOA-Paris Landing—(Henry) *From jct US 641 & US 79: Go 12 mi NE on US 79, then 1000 feet SE on E Antioch Rd. Enter on L.* ◇◇◇◇FACILITIES: 75 sites, typical site width 25 ft, 19 full hkups, 21 W&E, 12 E, (20, 30 & 50 amps), 23 no hkups, 40 pull-thrus, tenting, dump station, laundry, groceries, ice, tables, wood. ◇◇◇RECREATION: rec room/area, equipped pavilion, swim pool, mini-golf ($), playground. Pets welcome. Open Apr 1 thru Sep 30. Big rigs welcome. Rate in 2007 $25-28 for 2 persons. Phone: (800)562-2815. KOA 10% value card discount.

(E) Little Eagle RV Park—(Henry) *From jct Hwy 641 & Hwy 79: Go 14 mi E on Hwy 79. Enter on R.* ◇◇◇◇FACILITIES: 38 sites, typical site width 35 ft,

Little Eagle RV Park—Continued on next page

PARIS—Continued
Little Eagle RV Park—Continued

38 full hkups, (20, 30 & 50 amps), some extended stay sites, tenting, laundry, tables. ◆◆RECREATION: pavilion, boating, ramp, dock, lake fishing, play equipment, sports field. Pets welcome. Partial handicap access. Open all yr. Big rigs welcome. Rate in 2007 $26 for 4 persons. Phone: (731)642-4669.

(NE) PARIS LANDING STATE PARK—(Henry) *From town: Go 16 mi NE on US 79. Enter on R.*

WELCOME

FACILITIES: 44 sites, 44 W&E, (30 amps), 4 pull-thrus, tenting, cabins, dump station, laundry, marine gas, ice, tables, grills, wood.

RECREATION: swim pool, lake/river swimming, boating, canoeing, ramp, dock, lake/river fishing, fishing supplies, bsktball, playground, tennis, horseshoes, hiking trails, v-ball. Rec open to public.

Pets welcome. Partial handicap access. Open all yr. Facilities fully operational late Mar thru Nov. No reservatons. Phone: (800)250-8614.

SEE AD TRAVEL SECTION PAGE 784

PARKERS CROSSROADS—B-2

(S) PARKER'S CROSSROADS CAMPGROUND—(Henderson) *From jct I-40 (exit 108) & Hwy 22: Go 1-1/4 mi N on Hwy 22. Enter on R.*

WELCOME

◆◆◆FACILITIES: 36 sites, 24 full hkups, 12 W&E, (30 & 50 amps), 30 pull-thrus, cable on-site Internet access (needs activ), phone Internet access central location, tenting, cabins, RV storage, dump station, non-guest dumping $, laundry, groceries, RV supplies, LP gas by weight/by meter, ice, tables, wood.

◆◆RECREATION: rec room/area, swim pool, pond fishing, golf nearby, play equipment, horseshoes, sports field.

Pets welcome. Partial handicap access. Open all yr. Internet friendly. Escort to site. Clubs welcome. Rate in 2007 $22.50-24.50 for 2 persons. MC/VISA/DISC/Debit. Phone: (731)968-9939.

e-mail: wessmith@charter.net

SEE AD JACKSON PAGE 799

PARKSVILLE—C-6

CHEROKEE NATIONAL FOREST (Parksville Lake Campground)—(Polk) *From jct US-64 & Hwy-30: Go 1/2 mi NE on Hwy-30.* FACILITIES: 41 sites, 41 E, (20 & 30 amps), 2 pull-thrus, tenting, dump station, grills. RECREATION: boating, ramp, lake fishing, hiking trails. Partial handicap access. Open all yr. No reservations. Phone: (423)338-5201.

PERRYVILLE—B-3

MOUSETAIL LANDING STATE PARK—(Perry) *From jct I-40 (exit 126) & Hwy 69: Go 14 mi S on Hwy 69, then 6 mi E on Hwy 412, then 2-1/2 mi S on Hwy 438. Enter on R.*

WELCOME

FACILITIES: 40 sites, 20 ft max RV length, 19 W&E, 21 no hkups, tenting, dump station, laundry, ice, tables, fire rings, grills.

RECREATION: equipped pavilion, river swimming, boating, canoeing, ramp, river/stream fishing, bsktball, playground, sports field, v-ball. Rec open to public.

Partial handicap access. Open all yr. Facilities fully operational Apr 1 thru Nov 1. Phone: (731)847-0841.

SEE AD TRAVEL SECTION PAGE 784

PIGEON FORGE—E-5

(W) BROOKSIDE RV RESORT—(Sevier) *From jct of Hwy 441 & Hwy 321: Go 2 mi W on Hwy 321 (Stoplight 3) Enter on L.*

WELCOME

◆◆◆◆FACILITIES: 65 sites, typical site width 25 ft, 65 full hkups, (30 & 50

PIGEON FORGE—Continued
BROOKSIDE RV RESORT—Continued

amps), 10 pull-thrus, cable TV, laundry, ice, tables, patios, fire rings.

◆◆RECREATION: swim pool, stream fishing, golf nearby, playground.

Pets welcome. Partial handicap access. No tents. Open all yr. Big rigs welcome. Rate in 2007 $29-34 per vehicle. MC/VISA/Debit. Phone: (865)428-7940.

e-mail: michelesxtn@yahoo.com

SEE AD PAGE 818

(W) CLABOUGH'S CAMPGROUND & RV RESORT—(Sevier) *From north city limits at jct US 441 & Wear's Valley Rd: Go 1/2 mi W on Wear's Valley Rd. Enter on L.*

WELCOME

◆◆◆◆FACILITIES: 320 sites, typical site width 30 ft, 320 full hkups, (30 & 50 amps), 50 amps ($), 90 pull-thrus, cable TV, wireless Instant Internet access at site, cable Internet access central location, tenting, cabins, laundry, full svc store, RV supplies, gas, ice, tables, grills, wood.

◆◆◆◆RECREATION: rec room/area, equipped pavilion, coin games, 2 swim pools, wading pool, stream fishing, golf nearby, bsktball, planned activities.

Pets welcome. Partial handicap access. Open all yr. Big rigs welcome. Internet friendly. Clubs welcome. Rate in 2007 $25-34 for 4 persons. MC/VISA/DISC/Debit. Member ARVC, TNARVC. Phone: (800)965-8524.

SEE AD PAGES 814-815

PIGEON FORGE—Continued on page 817

CAMPING IN PIGEON FORGE, TENNESSEE

To Knoxville
Exit# 407
Riverside RV Park & Resort
66
40
Boyd's Creek Hwy.
Sevierville
411
Pigeon Forge
441
321
Gatlinburg
See listing at Sevierville, TN

PIGEON FORGE—Continued
BROOKSIDE RV RESORT—Continued

(W) CREEKSIDE RV PARK—(Sevier) *From north city limits at US 441 & Wear's Valley Rd (US 321): Go 1/2 mi W on Wear's Valley Rd (US 321), then 1/4 mi NW on Henderson Springs Rd. Enter on R.*

WELCOME

◆◆◆◆FACILITIES: 110 sites, typical site width 30 ft, 110 full hkups, (30 & 50 amps), 50 amps ($), some extended stay sites, 5 pull-thrus, cable TV, wireless Instant Internet access at site, phone Internet access central location, laundry, RV supplies, ice, tables, patios, wood.

◆◆RECREATION: pavilion, swim pool, stream fishing, golf nearby, bsktball, play equipment, planned activities (wkends only).

Pets welcome. Partial handicap access. No tents. Open Mar 1 thru Jan 5. Big rigs welcome. Internet friendly. Clubs welcome. Rate in 2007 $24-32 for 2 persons. MC/VISA/DISC/Debit. Phone: (800) 498-4801.

e-mail: creeksidervpark@yahoo.com

SEE AD PAGES 814-815

(W) EAGLE'S NEST CAMPGROUND—(Sevier) *From north city limits at jct US 441 & Wear's Valley Rd: Go 1-1/2 mi W on Wear's Valley Rd/Hwy 321. Enter on L.*

WELCOME

◆◆◆FACILITIES: 244 sites, typical site width 35 ft, 135 full hkups, 50 W&E, (20, 30 & 50 amps), 50 amps ($), 59 no hkups, some extended stay sites, 24 pull-thrus, cable TV, wireless Instant Internet access at site, phone Internet access central location, tenting, cabins, dump station, laundry, RV supplies, ice, tables, fire rings, wood.

◆◆RECREATION: rec room/area, coin games, swim pool, stream fishing, golf nearby, play equipment, horseshoes, sports field.

Pets welcome. Partial handicap access. Open all yr. Big rigs welcome. Internet friendly. Escort to site. Clubs welcome. Rate in 2007 $23-27 for 2 persons. MC/VISA/DISC/Debit. Phone: (800)892-2714. CCUSA discount. FMCA discount.

e-mail: encamp@webtv.net

SEE AD PAGES 814-815

(S) FOOTHILLS RV PARK & CABINS—(Sevier) *At south city limits at jct US 441 & Huskey St & Parkway. Enter on L.*

WELCOME

◆◆◆◆FACILITIES: 39 sites, typical site width 22 ft, 37 full hkups, 2 W&E, (20, 30 & 50 amps), 50 amps ($), cable TV, cabins, laundry, RV supplies, ice, tables, patios, fire rings, wood.

◆RECREATION: swim pool, golf nearby.

Pets welcome. Partial handicap access. No tents. Open Apr 1 thru Oct 31. Rate in 2007 $29 for 2 persons. MC/VISA/Debit. Phone: (865)428-3818.

e-mail: foothillsrv@charterinternet.com

SEE AD PAGES 814-815 AND AD GATLINBURG PAGES 796-797

(W) KING'S HOLLY HAVEN RV PARK—(Sevier) *From north city limits at jct US 441 & Wear's Valley Rd (US 321) stop light #3: Go 1 mi W on Wear's Valley Rd (US 321). Enter on L.*

WELCOME

NEAR IT ALL-BUT AWAY FROM THE NOISE.
Our quiet family RV Park features creekside sites & long 50 amp pull thrus's, large pool, 2 laundries, pavilion & friendly folks await you. Near Outlet Malls & all attractions. Great Family Rates. Trolley stops at our entrance.

◆◆◆◆FACILITIES: 161 sites, typical site width 30 ft, 161 full hkups, (20, 30 & 50 amps), 50 amps ($), some extended stay sites, 12 pull-thrus, cable TV, phone Internet access central location, laundry, ltd groceries, RV supplies, ice, tables, patios, fire rings, grills, wood.

◆◆◆RECREATION: equipped pavilion, swim pool, stream fishing, golf nearby, playground, local tours.

Pets welcome. Partial handicap access. No tents. Open all yr. Big rigs welcome. Internet friendly. Clubs welcome. Rate in 2007 $20.50-30.50 for 2 persons. MC/VISA/Debit. Member ARVC, TNARVC. Phone: (865)453-5352.

e-mail: info@hollyhavenrvpark.com

SEE AD PAGES 814-815 AND AD GATLINBURG, PAGES 796-797

PIGEON FORGE—Continued

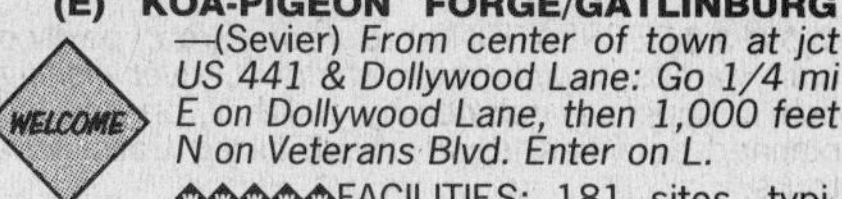

(E) KOA-PIGEON FORGE/GATLINBURG—(Sevier) *From center of town at jct US 441 & Dollywood Lane: Go 1/4 mi E on Dollywood Lane, then 1,000 feet N on Veterans Blvd. Enter on L.*

WELCOME

◆◆◆◆◆FACILITIES: 181 sites, typical site width 40 ft, 118 full hkups, 56 W&E, (30 & 50 amps), 50 amps ($), 7 no hkups, 80 pull-thrus, cable TV, wireless Instant Internet access at site, phone Internet access central location, tenting, cabins, dump station, non-guest dumping $, laundry, groceries, RV supplies, ice, tables, patios, fire rings, grills, wood.

KOA-PIGEON FORGE/GATLINBURG—Continued on next page

Memphis, Tennessee is the site of Sun Studios... Elvis Presley's first recording studio.

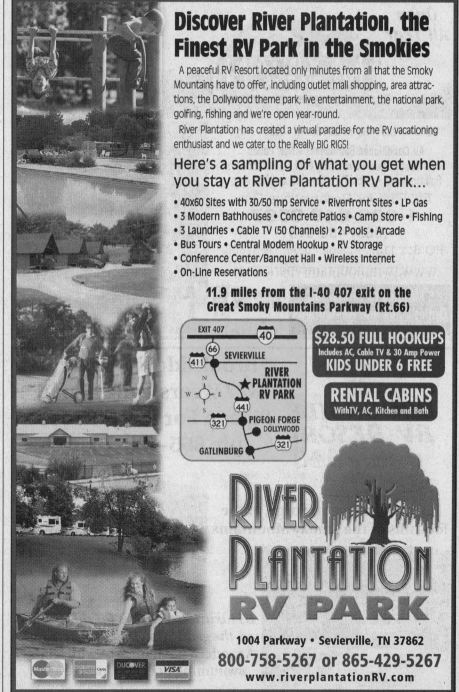

PIGEON FORGE—Continued
KOA-PIGEON FORGE/GATLINBURG—Continued

◆◆◆◆◆RECREATION: rec room/area, pavilion, coin games, swim pool, whirlpool, river fishing, fishing supplies, golf nearby, bsktball, playground, planned activities, sports field, hiking trails, local tours.

Pets welcome, quantity restrict. Partial handicap access. Open Apr 1 thru Nov 30. Big rigs welcome. Internet friendly. Clubs welcome. Rate in 2007 $32-80 for 2 persons. MC/VISA/Debit. ATM. Phone: (865)453-7903. KOA 10% value card discount.

e-mail: campingkoa@aol.com

SEE AD PAGES 814-815 AND AD GATLINBURG PAGES 796-797 AND AD DISCOVER SECTION PAGES 62 & 63

Tennessee has more than 3,800 documented caves.

PIGEON FORGE—Continued

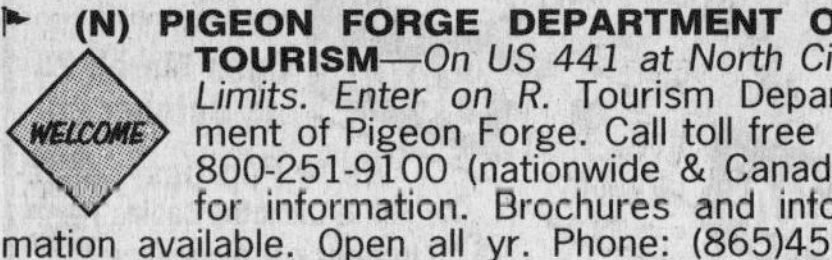

(N) PIGEON FORGE DEPARTMENT OF TOURISM—*On US 441 at North City Limits. Enter on R.* Tourism Department of Pigeon Forge. Call toll free 1-800-251-9100 (nationwide & Canada) for information. Brochures and information available. Open all yr. Phone: (865)453-8574.

e-mail: inquire@mypigeonforge.com

SEE AD PAGES 814-815

(N) RIVER PLANTATION RV PARK—(Sevier) *From jct Hwy 66 & US 441: Go 1 mi S on US 441. Enter on L.*

◆◆◆◆◆FACILITIES: 297 sites, typical site width 30 ft, 297 full hkups, (20, 30 & 50 amps), 50 amps ($), some extended stay sites (in summer), 58 pull-thrus, cable TV, wireless Instant Internet access at site, phone Internet access central location, cabins, RV storage, laundry, groceries, RV supplies, LP gas by weight/by meter, ice, tables, patios, fire rings, wood.

PIGEON FORGE—Continued
RIVER PLANTATION RV PARK—Continued

◆◆◆◆◆RECREATION: rec hall, rec room/area, equipped pavilion, coin games, 2 swim pools, wading pool, whirlpool, stream fishing, golf nearby, bsktball, playground, planned activities, horseshoes, v-ball, local tours.

Pets welcome. No tents. Open all yr. Big rigs welcome. Internet friendly. Clubs welcome. Rate in 2007 $22.50-49.50 for 2 persons. MC/VISA/DISC/Debit. Member ARVC, TNARVC. Phone: (865) 429-5267.

e-mail: riverrv@aol.com

SEE AD PAGE 817 AND AD GATLINBURG PAGES 796-797

(E) RIVERBEND CAMPGROUND—(Sevier) *From North city limits: Go 1/2 mi S on US 441, then turn right at the first traffic light, then 1/2 mi W on Henderson Chapel Rd. Enter on L.*

◆◆◆◆FACILITIES: 131 sites, typical site width 40 ft, 126 full hkups, 5 W&E, (30 & 50 amps), some extended stay sites, 35 pull-thrus, heater not allowed, cable TV, wireless Instant Internet access at site, phone Internet access central location, tenting, laundry, ice, tables, patios.

◆◆RECREATION: equipped pavilion, river swimming, river fishing, golf nearby.

Pets welcome. Open Apr 1 thru Dec 1. Church services during season only. Big rigs welcome. Internet friendly. Clubs welcome. Rate in 2007 $20-30 for 2 persons. Phone: (865)453-1224.

e-mail: riverbend@earthlink.net

SEE AD PAGES 814-815

(S) RIVEREDGE RV PARK—(Sevier) *South city limits at jct US 441 & Huskey St. Enter on L.*

◆◆◆◆◆FACILITIES: 169 sites, typical site width 30 ft, 169 full hkups, (20, 30 & 50 amps), 50 amps ($), cable TV, wireless Instant Internet access at site, phone Internet access central location, cabins, laundry, ltd groceries, RV supplies, ice, tables, patios, fire rings, wood.

◆◆◆◆RECREATION: rec room/area, coin games, swim pool, wading pool, whirlpool, stream fishing, golf nearby, playground, local tours.

Pets welcome. Partial handicap access. No tents. Open all yr. Big rigs welcome. Internet friendly. Clubs welcome. Rate in 2007 $35 for 2 persons. MC/VISA/Debit. Phone: (800)477-1205.

e-mail: info@stayriveredge.com

SEE AD PAGES 814-815 AND AD PAGE 813 AND AD GATLINBURG PAGES 796-797

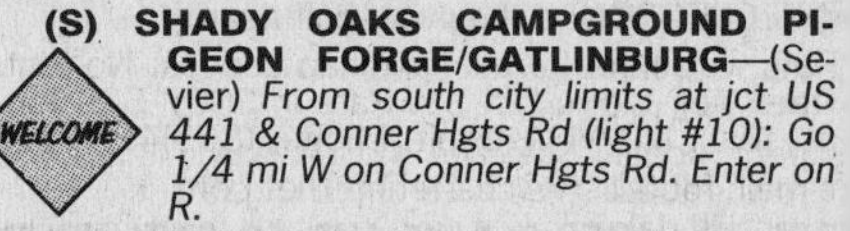

(S) SHADY OAKS CAMPGROUND PIGEON FORGE/GATLINBURG—(Sevier) *From south city limits at jct US 441 & Conner Hgts Rd (light #10): Go 1/4 mi W on Conner Hgts Rd. Enter on R.*

◆◆FACILITIES: 150 sites, typical site width 30 ft, 75 full hkups, 45 W&E, (15, 20, 30 & 50 amps), 30 no hkups, 4 pull-thrus, tenting, cabins, dump station, non-guest dumping $, laundry, RV supplies, ice, tables, grills, wood.

◆◆◆RECREATION: rec room/area, coin games, swim pool, wading pool, pond fishing, golf nearby, bsktball, playground, horseshoes.

Pets welcome. Open all yr. Phone: (865)453-3276.

SEE AD PAGES 814-815

(E) SMOKER HOLLER RV RESORT—(Sevier) *From jct US 441 & Hwy 321: Go 11 mi W on Hwy 321. Enter on L.*

◆◆◆FACILITIES: 33 sites, typical site width 38 ft, 33 full hkups, (20, 30 & 50 amps), some extended stay sites, 9 pull-thrus, cable TV, wireless Instant Internet access at site, phone Internet access central location, tenting, dump station, non-guest dumping $, RV supplies, ice, tables, fire rings, wood.

◆RECREATION: equipped pavilion, golf nearby, horseshoes, v-ball.

Pets welcome. Open all yr. Big rigs welcome. Internet friendly. Rate in 2007 $22-30 for 2 persons. MC/VISA/Debit. Member ARVC, TNARVC. Phone: (866)453-8777.

e-mail: smokerholler@aol.com

SEE AD GATLINBURG PAGES 796-797

PIGEON FORGE—Continued on next page

Brookside RV Resort
1327 Wears Valley Road
Pigeon Forge, TN 37863
ph: 865-428-7940

Located in Pigeon Forge, at the foothills of the Smoky Mountains

65 luxurious RV sites for sale or rent on the gently flowing Waldens Creek
A modern pavilion area with a large swimming pool and lounge area.

See listing at Pigeon Forge, TN

PIGEON FORGE—Continued

(S) TWIN MOUNTAIN RV PARK AND CAMPGROUND—(Sevier) *From jct US 321 & US 441: Go S on US 441 through traffic light #8, then 1/2 mi S, then E on Golf Dr at Duff's Rest, then 1/4 mi E on Golf Dr. Enter on R.*

EASY TO FIND HARD TO FORGET!
Enjoy our quiet riverfront campground on the foothills of the Smoky Mts, in the heart of Pigeon Forge that has been owned by our family for 35 years. Close to Dollywood, restaurants & attractions! Come visit us!

◊◊◊◊FACILITIES: 122 sites, typical site width 35 ft, 117 full hkups, (30 & 50 amps), 5 no hkups, cable TV, wireless Instant Internet access at site, phone Internet access central location, tenting, dump station, non-guest dumping $, laundry, RV supplies, ice, tables, fire rings, wood.

◊◊◊RECREATION: swim pool, float trips, river fishing, golf nearby, bsktball, tennis, local tours.

Pets welcome. Open all yr. Big rigs welcome. Clubs welcome. Rate in 2007 $23-36 for 2 persons. MC/VISA/Debit. Phone: (800)848-9097.

e-mail: creek@usit.net

SEE AD PAGES 814-815 AND AD PAGE 818

(E) WALDENS CREEK CAMPGROUND—(Sevier) *From north city limits at jct US 441 & Wear's Valley Rd (US 321): Go 1/2 mi W on Wear's Valley Rd (US 321), then 1/4 mi NW on Henderson Springs Rd. Enter on R.*

◊◊◊FACILITIES: 45 sites, typical site width 30 ft, 35 full hkups, 10 E, (20, 30 & 50 amps), 50 amps ($), some extended stay sites, cable TV, wireless Instant Internet access at site, wireless Internet access central location, tenting, laundry, ice, tables, patios, fire rings, wood.

◊◊RECREATION: pavilion, river swimming, stream fishing, golf nearby, bsktball, playground, planned activities (wkends only).

Pets welcome. Open all yr. Big rigs welcome. Internet friendly. Escort to site. Rate in 2007 $20-30 for 2 persons. MC/VISA/Debit. Phone: (865)908-2727.

e-mail: info@waldenscreekcampground.com

SEE AD PAGES 814-815

PIKEVILLE—B-5

(NW) FALL CREEK FALLS STATE PARK—(Van Buren) *From jct US 127 & Hwy 30: Go 14 mi W on Hwy 30, then 2 mi SW on Hwy 284, then at park entrance continue 7-1/2 mi to campground. Enter on L.*

FACILITIES: 228 sites, 228 W&E, (20 & 30 amps), tenting, cabins, dump station, laundry, ltd groceries, ice, tables, fire rings, grills.

RECREATION: rec hall, pavilion, swim pool, wading pool, boating, electric motors only, canoeing, 37 rowboat/11 canoe/18 pedal boat/37 motorboat rentals, lake fishing, putting green, bsktball, playground, planned activities, tennis, sports field, hiking trails, v-ball. Rec open to public.

Pets welcome. Partial handicap access. Open all yr. Facilities fully operational May thru Sep. MC/VISA/DISC. Phone: (800)250-8611.

SEE AD TRAVEL SECTION PAGE 784

(W) MOUNTAIN GLEN RV PARK (UNDER CONSTRUCTION)—(Bledsoe) *From jct State Hwy 111 & Hwy 284: Go 1 mi E on Hwy 284, then 1 mi S on Old Hwy 111, then 6-1/4 mi E on Brockdell Rd. Enter on R.*

FACILITIES: 42 sites, 42 full hkups, (50 amps), 42 pull-thrus, wireless Instant Internet access at site, laundry, ltd groceries, ice, tables, fire rings.

RECREATION: rec room/area, pond fishing, golf nearby.

Pets welcome. No tents. Open Apr 1 thru Nov 30. Big rigs welcome. Internet friendly. Rate in 2007 $28 for 2 persons. MC/VISA. Member ARVC, TNARVC. Phone: (877)716-4493.

e-mail: info@mountainglenonline.com

SEE AD THIS PAGE

Woodall's Tip #22... If you think Woodall's Ratings mean Good, Better, Best...think again. See the "How to Use" pages in the front of this Directory for an explanation of our Rating System.

POCAHONTAS—C-2

BIG HILL POND STATE PARK—(McNairy) *From town: Go 5 mi E on Hwy 57. Enter on R.*

FACILITIES: 30 sites, 30 no hkups, tenting, tables, grills, controlled access gate.

RECREATION: boating, electric motors only, canoeing, ramp, lake fishing, bsktball, playground, hiking trails.

Pets welcome. Partial handicap access. Open all yr. Phone: (731)645-7967.

SEE AD TRAVEL SECTION PAGE 784

ROAN MOUNTAIN—D-6

(S) ROAN MOUNTAIN STATE RESORT PARK—(Carter) *From jct US 9E & Hwy 143: Go 5 mi S on Hwy 143. Enter at end.*

FACILITIES: 107 sites, 87 W&E, (30 amps), 20 no hkups, tenting, cabins, dump station, laundry, ice, tables, fire rings, grills, wood, controlled access gate.

RECREATION: rec room/area, equipped pavilion, coin games, swim pool, river swimming, river/stream fishing, bsktball, playground, shuffleboard court, tennis, horseshoes, sports field, hiking trails, v-ball.

Pets welcome. Partial handicap access. Open all yr. Facilities fully operational Apr 1 thru Nov 15. No reservations. MC/VISA/DISC/AMEX. Phone: (423) 772-0190.

SEE AD TRAVEL SECTION PAGE 784

ROCK ISLAND—B-5

(W) ROCK ISLAND STATE PARK—(Warren) *From jct US 705 & Hwy 136: Go on Hwy 136 to Hwy 287, then W on Hwy 287 (follow signs). Enter on R.*

FACILITIES: 60 sites, 35 ft max RV length, 60 W&E, (30 amps), tenting, cabins, dump station, laundry, ltd groceries, ice, tables, grills, controlled access gate.

RECREATION: pavilion, lake swimming, boating, canoeing, ramp, lake/river fishing, bsktball, playground, tennis, sports field, hiking trails, v-ball. Rec open to public.

Pets welcome. Partial handicap access. Open all yr. Facilities fully operational Mar 15 thru Nov 15. MC/VISA/DISC/AMEX. Phone: (931)686-2471.

SEE AD TRAVEL SECTION PAGE 784

SAVANNAH—C-2

PICKWICK LANDING STATE RESORT PARK—(Hardin) *From town: Go 10 mi S on Hwy 128 to jct Hwy 28 & Hwy 57. Enter on L.*

FACILITIES: 48 sites, 48 W&E, (20, 30 & 50 amps), 2 pull-thrus, tenting, cabins, dump station, laundry, marine gas, tables, grills.

RECREATION: pavilion, lake swimming, boating, ramp, dock, 10 motorboat rentals, lake fishing, putting green, bsktball, playground, tennis, sports field, hiking trails, v-ball. Rec open to public.

Pets welcome. Partial handicap access. Open all yr. Facilities fully operational Apr 1 thru Dec 1. Phone: (800)250-8615.

SEE AD TRAVEL SECTION PAGE 784

SEVIERVILLE—E-5

(N) DOUGLAS DAM TAILWATER (TVA - Douglas Reservoir)—(Jefferson) *From jct US 411 & Hwy 66: Go 7 mi N on Hwy 66, then 3-1/2 mi E on Hwy 139, then 1/2 mi S on Hwy 338, follow signs.* FACILITIES: 64 sites, 30 W&E, (30 amps), 34 no hkups, 25 pull-thrus, tenting, ltd groceries, grills. RECREATION: boating, ramp, river fishing, play equipment. Partial handicap access. Open early Apr thru Oct. Phone: (423)587-5600.

(N) DOUGLAS HEADWATER (TVA - Douglas Reservoir)—(Jefferson) *From jct US 411 & Hwy 66: Go 7 mi N on Hwy 66, then 3-1/2 mi E on Hwy 139, then 2-1/2 mi S on Hwy 338, then follow signs 1 mi N.* FACILITIES: 65 sites, 61 W&E, 4 no hkups, tenting, dump station. RECREATION: lake swimming, boating, ramp, lake fishing, hiking trails. Partial handicap access. Open mid Apr thru late Oct. Phone: (423)587-5600.

Interested in receiving special discounts on camping and RVing books, directories and maps? Looking for the latest in RV travel destination spots? Log onto www.woodalls.com and register to receive FREE information and special offerings that will make your RV travel more enjoyable.

SEVIERVILLE—Continued

(N) RIPPLIN' WATERS CAMPGROUND—(Sevier) *From jct I-40 (exit 407) & Hwy 66: Go 5 mi S on Hwy 66. Enter on R.*

CHECK OUT OUR LOW LOW RATES!
Our quiet family campground features riverside sites & long 50 amp pull thrus! Our large pool, pavilion & country store await you. Near all the attractions with great facilities & great family rates.

◊◊◊◊FACILITIES: 155 sites, typical site width 25 ft, 155 full hkups, (20, 30 & 50 amps), 50 amps ($), 5 pull-thrus, cable TV, wireless Instant Internet access at site, cabins, laundry, groceries, RV supplies, LP gas by weight/by meter, LP bottle exch, ice, tables, patios, wood.

◊◊◊RECREATION: rec room/area, equipped pavilion, coin games, swim pool, river fishing, golf nearby, bsktball, playground.

Pets welcome. Partial handicap access. No tents. Open all yr. Big rigs welcome. Internet friendly. Escort to site. Clubs welcome. Rate in 2007 $26-31 for 2 persons. MC/VISA/DISC/Debit. ATM. Member ARVC, TNARVC. Phone: (888)-RIPPLIN.

e-mail: ripplinwaters@ripplinwatersrv.com

SEE AD NEXT PAGE AND AD GATLINBURG PAGES 796-797

(N) RIVERSIDE RV PARK & RESORT—(Sevier) *From jct I-40 (exit 407) & Hwy 66: Go 4 mi S on Hwy 66, then 1/4 mi W on Boyds Creek Rd (turn right at Marathon). Enter on R.*

LARGEST RV RESORT IN THE SMOKIES
At Riverside RV Park & Resort you have everything under the sun. Large full service sites with extra long pull thru's or deluxe riverfront sites with easy full hookups. A friendly staff. Celebrating 25 years!

◊◊◊◊◊FACILITIES: 316 sites, typical site width 30 ft, 296 full hkups, 20 W&E, (30 & 50 amps), 50 amps ($), some extended stay sites (in summer), 101 pull-thrus, cable TV, wireless Instant Internet access at site ($), RV/park trailer rentals, cabins, RV storage, laundry, groceries, RV supplies, LP gas by weight/by meter, ice, tables, patios, fire rings, grills, wood.

◊◊◊RECREATION: rec room/area, equipped pavilion, coin games, swim pool, boating, ramp, river fishing, fishing supplies, golf nearby, bsktball, playground, planned activities.

Pets welcome. No tents. Open all yr. Big rigs welcome. Internet friendly. Clubs welcome. Rate in 2007 $26-28 for 2 persons. MC/VISA/DISC/Debit. Phone: (800)341-7534.

e-mail: KVOLUNTEER@aol.com

SEE AD GATLINBURG PAGES 796-797 AND AD PIGEON FORGE PAGE 816

SEVIERVILLE—Continued on next page

Whether you're dreaming about buying a new RV or are actively shopping, WOODALL'S 2008 RV Buyer's Guide is your best source. It contains all the information you need to make an intelligent buying decision. Over 450 vehicles are profiled with complete information about construction features, dimensions, popular options, and more, making comparing models easy. To order your copy go to www.woodalls.com/shop.

SEVIERVILLE—Continued

(N) TWO RIVERS LANDING RESORT—(Sevier) *From jct I-40 (exit 407) & Hwy 66: Go 4 mi S on Hwy 66, then 1/4 mi W on Knife Works Ln, then 1/4 mi N on Business Center Circle. Enter on R.*

◆◆◆◆FACILITIES: 55 sites, typical site width 32 ft, 55 full hkups, (30 & 50 amps), cable TV, wireless Instant Internet access at site, laundry, ice, tables, patios.

◆◆◆RECREATION: rec hall, rec room/area, pavilion, swim pool, river fishing, golf nearby, playground.

Pets welcome. No tents. Open all yr. Big rigs welcome. Internet friendly. Clubs welcome. Rate in 2007 $45-65 for 6 persons. MC/VISA/AMEX. Phone: (866)727-5781.

e-mail: info@tworiversrvresort.com

SEE AD PAGE 820

SHADY VALLEY—D-6

CHEROKEE NATIONAL FOREST (Jacobs Creek Campgrounds)—(Sullivan) *From town: Go 9 mi NW on US-421, then 2 mi N on CR-32, then 7/10 mi W on FR-337.* FACILITIES: 29 sites, 29 no hkups, fire rings. RECREATION: lake swimming, boating, ramp, lake fishing, hiking trails. Partial handicap access. Open Apr 25 thru Oct 15. Phone: (615)476-9700.

SILVER POINT—B-5

FLOATING MILL (COE-Center Hill Reservoir)—(DeKalb) *From I-40 (exit 273): Go 5 mi S on Hwy-56 to Hurricane Dock Rd., then 1 mi W on Hurricane Dock Rd to campground.* FACILITIES: 118 sites, 30 ft max RV length, 30 W&E, (20 amps), 88 no hkups, tenting, dump station, laundry, ltd groceries, ice, grills. RECREATION: lake swimming, boating, canoeing, ramp, lake fishing, playground, hiking trails. Open Apr 9 thru Oct 21. Phone: (931)858-4845.

LONG BRANCH (COE - Center Hill Reservoir)—(DeKalb) *From I-40 (exit 268): Go 5 mi S on Bob Steber Rd, then 2 mi W on Hwy-141.* FACILITIES: 60 sites, 3 full hkups, 57 W&E, (20, 30 & 50 amps), tenting, dump station, portable dump, laundry, grills. RECREATION: lake swimming, boating, canoeing, ramp, lake fishing, playground, hiking trails. Rec open to public. Open Mar 31 thru Oct 30. Phone: (615)548-8002.

SMITHVILLE—B-5

EDGAR EVINS STATE RUSTIC PARK—(DeKalb) *From jct US 70 & Hwy 56: Go 16 mi N on Hwy 56, then 6 mi N on Hwy 141. Enter on L.*

FACILITIES: 70 sites, 36 ft max RV length, 60 W&E, (20, 30 & 50 amps), 10 no hkups, tenting, cabins, dump station, laundry, marine gas, ice, tables, fire rings, grills.

RECREATION: swim pool, lake swimming, boating, canoeing, ramp, dock, lake fishing, bsktball, playground, planned activities, hiking trails, v-ball. Rec open to public.

Pets welcome. Partial handicap access. Open all yr. No reservations. Phone: (931)858-2446.

SEE AD TRAVEL SECTION PAGE 784

(E) RAGLAND BOTTOM (COE - Center Hill Reservoir)—(DeKalb) *From jct Hwy-56 & Hwy-70: Go 8 mi E on Hwy-70, then 1 mi N on county road.* FACILITIES: 57 sites, 41 W&E, (30 & 50 amps), 16 no hkups, 15 pull-thrus, tenting, dump station, laundry, grills. RECREATION: lake swimming, boating, canoeing, ramp, lake fishing, playground, hiking trails. Open Apr 18 thru Oct 16. Phone: (931)761-3616.

SMYRNA—B-4

(SE) NASHVILLE I-24 CAMPGROUND—(Rutherford) *W'bound from I-24 (exit 66): Follow signs. E'bound from I-24 (exit 66B): Go 1 mi E on Sam Ridley Pkwy, then 2 mi S on Old Nashville Hwy, then 100 feet W on Rocky Fork Rd. Enter on R.*

◆◆◆FACILITIES: 155 sites, typical site width 25 ft, 90 full hkups, 65 W&E, (20, 30 & 50 amps), 50 amps ($), some extended stay sites (in summer), 75 pull-thrus, wireless Instant Internet access at site, phone Internet access central location, tenting, cabins, RV storage, dump station, non-guest dumping $, laundry, groceries, RV supplies, LP gas by weight/by meter, LP bottle exch, ice, tables.

◆◆RECREATION: rec room/area, coin games, swim pool, golf nearby, bsktball, playground, v-ball.

Pets welcome. Open all yr. Big rigs welcome. Internet friendly. Escort to site. Clubs welcome. Rate in 2007 $23-27 for 2 persons. MC/VISA/Debit. Member ARVC, TNARVC. Phone: (615)459-5818. FCRV 10% discount.

SEE AD NASHVILLE PAGE 812

Bristol is known as the "Birthplace of Country Music".

SWEETWATER—B-6

(W) KOA-SWEETWATER VALLEY—(Loudon) *From jct I-75 (exit 62) & Oakland Rd: Go 3/4 mi W on Oakland Road, then follow signs 1/4 mi S. Enter on L.*

◆◆◆◆FACILITIES: 58 sites, typical site width 30 ft, 46 full hkups, 12 W&E, (20, 30 & 50 amps), some extended stay sites, 58 pull-thrus, cable TV, wireless Instant Internet access at site, phone Internet access central location, tenting, cabins, RV storage, dump station, non-guest dumping $, laundry, groceries, RV supplies, LP gas by weight/by meter, LP bottle exch, ice, tables, fire rings, grills, wood.

◆◆◆◆RECREATION: rec hall, rec room/area, pavilion, equipped pavilion, coin games, swim pool, golf nearby, bsktball, playground, planned activities, horseshoes, sports field, v-ball.

Pets welcome. Open all yr. Planned group activities on holidays & special weekends. Big rigs welcome. Internet friendly. Escort to site. Clubs welcome. Rate in 2007 $25-43 for 2 persons. MC/VISA/DISC/AMEX/Debit. Phone: (800)562-9224. KOA 10% value card discount.

e-mail: sweetwaterkoa@hotmail.com

SEE AD KNOXVILLE PAGE 801 AND AD DISCOVER SECTION PAGES 62 & 63

(S) Tennessee Country Campground & RV Park—(McMinn) *From jct I-75 (exit 56) & CR 309: Go 500 feet E on CR 309. Enter on L.* ◆◆◆FACILITIES: 29 sites, typical site width 30 ft, 14 full hkups, 4 W&E, (20, 30 & 50 amps), 11 no hkups, some extended stay sites, 14 pull-thrus, tenting, laundry, LP bottle exch, ice, tables, wood. ◆◆RECREATION: rec hall, play equipment, v-ball. Pets welcome. Open all yr. Rate in 2007 $18-21 for 2 persons. Phone: (423)568-2939.

TELLICO PLAINS—C-6

(NE) CHEROKEE NATIONAL FOREST (Indian Boundary A & Overflow Areas)—(Monroe) *From jct Hwy 68 & Hwy 165: Go 15 mi NE on Hwy 165, then 1-1/2 mi NE on FR 35.* FACILITIES: 91 sites, 22 ft max RV length, 24 E, (20 amps), 67 no hkups, tenting, dump station. RECREATION: boating, no motors, canoeing, ramp, hiking trails. Partial handicap access. Open Apr 1 thru Oct 29. Phone: (423)253-2520.

(E) KOA Tellico Plains—(Monroe) *From jct I-75 (exit 60) & Hwy 68: Go 25 mi S on Hwy 68, then 1 mi E on Hwy 165, then N on Hwy 360 (in NW corner of Hwy 165 & Hwy 360). Enter on L.* ◆◆◆◆FACILITIES: 108 sites, 70 full hkups, 38 W&E, (30 & 50 amps), 56 pull-thrus, tenting, dump station, non-guest dumping $, laundry, groceries, LP bottle exch, ice, tables, grills, wood. ◆◆◆◆RECREATION: rec room/area, equipped pavilion, swim pool, river fishing, playground, horseshoes, hiking trails, v-ball. Pets welcome. Partial handicap access. Open Mar 14 thru Nov 16. Big rigs welcome. Internet friendly. Rate in 2007 $23-34 for 2 persons. Member ARVC, TNARVC. Phone: (423)253-2447. KOA 10% value card discount.

Shop at Woodall's Advertised Dealers

TEN MILE—B-6

(SW) FOOSHEE PASS—(Meigs) *From jct Hwy 68 & Hwy 304: Go 1-3/4 mi N on Hwy 304, then 1-3/4 mi W following signs. Enter on R.* FACILITIES: 55 sites, 52 W&E, (30 amps), 3 no hkups, tenting, dump station, non-guest dumping $, ice, fire rings, grills, wood. RECREATION: pavilion, lake swimming, ramp, lake fishing, playground, sports field. Partial handicap access. Open Apr 1 thru mid Sep. Phone: (423)334-4842.

(S) HORNSBY HOLLOW (Watts Bar Lake)—(Meigs) *From jct Hwy 68 & Hwy 58: Go 3-1/2 mi N on Hwy 58, then follow signs 2-1/2 mi W, then 1/2 mi N on Hwy 304. Enter on L.* FACILITIES: 99 sites, 99 W&E, (30 & 50 amps), tenting, dump station, non-guest dumping $, ice, patios, fire rings, grills, wood. RECREATION: pavilion, lake swimming, boating, canoeing, ramp, dock, lake fishing, playground, horseshoes, hiking trails. Pets welcome. Partial handicap access. Open Apr thru Oct. Phone: (423)334-1709.

TIPTONVILLE—A-1

(E) REELFOOT LAKE STATE PARK—(Lake) *From town: Go 5 mi E on Hwy 21. Enter on R.*

FACILITIES: 100 sites, 100 W&E, (30 amps), 4 pull-thrus, tenting, cabins, dump station, laundry, ice, tables, grills, controlled access gate.

RECREATION: pavilion, swim pool, boating, 10 hp limit, canoeing, ramp, dock, lake fishing, playground, tennis.

Pets welcome. Partial handicap access. Open May 1 thru Oct 31. No reservations. Phone: (731)253-7756.

SEE AD TRAVEL SECTION PAGE 784

TOWNSEND—E-5

(N) BIG MEADOW FAMILY CAMPGROUND—(Blount) *From jct Scenic Hwy 73 & US 321: Go 300 feet NE on US 321, then 1 block W on Cedar Creek Rd. Enter on L.*

TNARVC 2006 CAMPGROUND OF THE YEAR!

Come and enjoy a 360 degree mtn view on our extra long pull thru super sites. Minutes away from Smoky Mtns. Nat'l Park & Gatlinburg. Spend quality time with your family and ours in a gated, friendly, courteous and relaxing environment

◆◆◆◆FACILITIES: 77 sites, typical site width 35 ft, 77 full hkups, (30 & 50 amps), 58 pull-thrus, cable TV, wireless Instant Internet access at site, phone Internet access central location, RV storage, laundry, RV supplies, LP gas by weight/by meter, ice, tables, patios, fire rings, wood, controlled access gate.

◆◆◆◆RECREATION: rec room/area, equipped pavilion, coin games, river swimming, float trips, river fishing, golf nearby, bsktball, playground, planned activities, horseshoes, v-ball.

BIG MEADOW FAMILY CAMPGROUND—Continued on next page

Pets welcome. No tents. Open all yr. Planned activities & church services during season only. Big rigs welcome. Internet friendly. Escort to site. Clubs welcome. Rate in 2007 $35-45 for 4 persons. MC/VISA. Member ARVC, TNARVC. Phone: (888)497-0625.

e-mail: bigmeadow@msn.com

SEE AD PAGE 821

GREAT SMOKY MOUNTAINS NATIONAL PARK (Cades Cove Campground)—(Blount) *From jct US 321 & Scenic Hwy 73: Go 9 mi S on Scenic Hwy 73 to Laurel Creek Rd.* FACILITIES: 159 sites, 35 ft max RV length, 159 no hkups, tenting, dump station, groceries, grills, wood. RECREATION: hiking trails. Pets welcome. Open all yr. Facilities fully operational May 15 thru Oct 31. No showers. Phone: (865)436-1200.

LAZY DAZE CAMPGROUND—(Blount) *From jct Hwy 321 & Scenic Hwy 73: Go 1/2 mi E on Scenic Hwy 73. Enter on L.*

WELCOME

◊◊◊FACILITIES: 73 sites, typical site width 25 ft, 73 full hkups, (30 & 50 amps), 0 pull-thrus, cable TV, wireless Instant Internet access at site, phone Internet access central location, tenting, cabins, laundry, groceries, RV supplies, LP gas by weight/by meter, ice, tables, fire rings, wood.

◊◊◊◊RECREATION: rec room/area, equipped pavilion, coin games, swim pool, river swimming, float trips, river fishing, fishing supplies, golf nearby, bsktball, playground, planned activities, horseshoes.

Pets welcome. Open all yr. Clubs welcome. Rate in 2007 $30-41 for 2 persons. MC/VISA/Debit. Member ARVC, TNARVC. Phone: (865)448-6061.

SEE AD THIS PAGE

(S) Little River Village Campground—(Blount) *From jct Hwy-321 & Scenic Hwy-73: Go 1 mi E on Scenic Hwy-73. Enter on L.* ◊◊◊◊FACILITIES: 130 sites, typical site width 25 ft, 66 full hkups, 32 W&E, (20, 30 & 50 amps), 32 no hkups, 23 pull-thrus, tenting, dump station, laundry, full svc store, LP gas by weight/by meter, ice, tables, patios, fire rings, grills, wood. ◊◊◊◊◊RECREATION: rec room/area, pavilion, swim pool, river swimming, canoeing, stream fishing, playground, planned activities, horseshoes, hiking trails. Pets welcome, breed restrict. Partial handicap access. Open all yr. Special holiday activities. Big rigs welcome. Internet friendly. Rate in 2007 $25-53 for 2 persons. Member ARVC, TN ARVC. Phone: (865)448-2241.

(W) MISTY RIVER CABINS & RV RESORT, LLC—(Blount) *From jct US 321 & Hwy 73: Go 8 mi W on Hwy 321, then N on E Millers Cove, then 1/2 mi W on Old Walland Hwy (quick left off bridge). Enter on L.*

WELCOME

◊◊◊◊FACILITIES: 72 sites, typical site width 35 ft, 72 full hkups, (30 & 50 amps), some extended stay sites, 59 pull-thrus, cable TV, wireless Instant Internet access at site, phone Internet access central location, cabins, RV storage, laundry, ltd groceries, RV supplies, LP gas by weight/by meter, ice, tables, patios, fire rings, wood.

◊◊◊◊RECREATION: rec room/area, coin games, swim pool, whirlpool, canoeing, kayaking, river fishing, fishing supplies, golf nearby, playground, horseshoes, sports field, v-ball.

Pets welcome. Partial handicap access. No tents. Open all yr. Big rigs welcome. Internet friendly. Escort to site. Clubs welcome. Rate in 2007 $25-49 for 4 persons. MC/VISA. Member ARVC, TNARVC. Phone: (877)981-4306.

e-mail: info@mistyriverrv.com

SEE AD THIS PAGE

(E) Mountaineer Campground—(Blount) *From jct Hwy-321 & Scenic Hwy-73: Go 3/4 mi E on Scenic Hwy-73. Enter on L.* ◊◊◊FACILITIES: 50 sites, typical site width 25 ft, 39 full hkups, 11 W&E, (30 & 50 amps), 50 amps ($), tenting, dump station, non-guest dumping $, laundry, ltd groceries, ice, tables, patios, fire rings, grills, wood. ◊◊◊RECREATION: equipped pavilion, swim pool, river swimming, river fishing, playground. Pets welcome. Open Mar 1 thru Nov 15. Rate in 2007 $25-37 for 2 persons. Member ARVC, TNARVC. Phone: (865)448-6421.

(S) Tremont Outdoor Resort—(Blount) *From jct Hwy-321 & Scenic Hwy-73: Go 1-1/4 mi E on Scenic Hwy-73. Enter on L.* ◊◊◊◊FACILITIES: 121 sites, typical site width 35 ft, 90 full hkups, 23 W&E, (20, 30 & 50 amps), 8 no hkups, 3 pull-thrus, tenting, dump station, laundry, groceries, ice, tables, patios, fire rings, wood. ◊◊◊◊RECREATION: rec room/area, pavilion, equipped pavilion, swim pool, river swimming, river fishing, playground, planned activities, horseshoes, hiking trails. Pets welcome. Partial handicap access. Open all yr. Big rigs welcome. Internet friendly. Rate in 2007 $20-42 for 2 persons. Member ARVC, TNARVC. Phone: (800)448-6373.

(W) Tuckaleechee Campground—(Blount) *From jct Scenic Hwy 73 & US 321: Go 2-1/2 mi W on US 321. Enter on R.* ◊◊FACILITIES: 134 sites, typical site width 25 ft, 50 full hkups, 37 W&E, (20 & 30 amps), 47 no hkups, 25 pull-thrus, heater not allowed, tenting, dump station, non-guest dumping $, laundry, ice, tables, fire rings, wood. ◊◊◊RECREATION: pavilion, river swimming, river fishing, playground, horseshoes. Pets welcome. Open all yr. Rate in 2007 $20-30 for 2 persons. Phone: (865)448-9608.

TRACY CITY—C-5

FOSTER FALLS (TVA)—(Marion) *From town: Go 5 mi E on Hwy 150/US 41.* FACILITIES: 28 sites, 28 no hkups, tenting, grills. RECREATION: hiking trails. Partial handicap access. Open Apr 6 thru Nov 15. Phone: (423)942-5759.

UNICOI—D-6

(W) Woodsmoke Campground—(Unicoi) *From I-26 (exit 32, formerly US 19/23): Go 1/10 mi W. Follow sign. Enter on R.* ◊◊◊FACILITIES: 33 sites, 29 full hkups, (30 & 50 amps), 4 no hkups, some extended stay sites, tenting, tables, fire rings, wood. RECREATION: sports field. Pets welcome. Partial handicap access. Open Mar 15 thru Dec 1. Internet friendly. Rate in 2007 $24 for 2 persons. Phone: (423)743-2116.

VONORE—B-6

NOTCHY CREEK—(Monroe) *From jct US 411 & CR 400: Go 3 mi S on CR 400, then 1-3/4 mi E (follow signs). Enter on L.* FACILITIES: 51 sites, 51 E, (30 & 50 amps), tenting, dump station, ice, grills, wood. RECREATION: lake swimming, boating, ramp, lake fishing, v-ball. Open Apr thru Oct. Phone: (423)884-6280.

TOQUA BEACH CAMPGROUND—(Monroe) *From jct US 411 & Hwy 360: Go 3 mi E on Hwy 360. Enter on L.* FACILITIES: 24 sites, 20 E, (30 & 50 amps), 4 no hkups, tenting, dump station, ice, grills, wood. RECREATION: lake swimming, boating, ramp, dock, lake fishing, sports field, v-ball. Open Apr thru Oct. Phone: (423)884-2344.

WALLAND—E-5

GREAT SMOKY MOUNTAINS NATIONAL PARK (Look Rock Campground)—(Blount) *From town: Go 11 mi SW on Foothills Pkwy.* FACILITIES: 68 sites, 35 ft max RV length, 68 no hkups, tenting, grills, wood. RECREATION: hiking trails. Open May 12 thru Oct 31. No showers. No reservations. Phone: (865)436-1220.

WARTBURG—B-6

FROZEN HEAD STATE PARK—(Morgan) *From Hwy 27 in Harriman: Go N on Hwy 27, then 2 mi E on Hwy 62, then 4 mi N on Flat Fork Rd to park entrance.*

WELCOME

FACILITIES: 30 sites, 30 no hkups, tenting, tables, grills, wood.

RECREATION: bsktball, playground, horseshoes, sports field, hiking trails, v-ball.

Pets welcome. Open all yr. Phone: (423)346-3318.

SEE AD TRAVEL SECTION PAGE 784

WHITE BLUFF—B-3

MONTGOMERY BELL STATE PARK—(Dickson) *From town: Go 4 mi W on US 70. Enter on R.*

WELCOME

FACILITIES: 120 sites, 95 W&E, (20, 30 & 50 amps), 25 no hkups, 2 pull-thrus, tenting, cabins, dump station, tables, fire rings, grills.

RECREATION: pavilion, lake swimming, boating, electric motors only, ramp, canoe rentals, lake fishing, putting green, playground, shuffleboard court, sports field, hiking trails, v-ball, local tours. Rec open to public.

Pets welcome. Partial handicap access. Open all yr. Facilities fully operational Apr 1 thru Nov 1. MC/VISA/DISC/AMEX. Phone: (615)797-9052.

SEE AD TRAVEL SECTION PAGE 784

WINCHESTER—C-4

(NW) TIMS FORD STATE RUSTIC PARK—(Franklin) *From town: Go 5 mi W on Hwy 50, then 5 mi N on Mansford Rd. Enter on L.*

WELCOME

FACILITIES: 130 sites, 35 ft max RV length, 38 full hkups, 72 W&E, (30 amps), 20 no hkups, tenting, cabins, shower$, dump station, laundry, ice, tables, fire rings, grills.

RECREATION: rec hall, equipped pavilion, swim pool, wading pool, lake swimming, boating, canoeing, ramp, dock, lake/river fishing, putting green, playground, planned activities, hiking trails, v-ball. Rec open to public.

Pets welcome. Partial handicap access. Open all yr. Facilities fully operational Apr thru Oct. No reservations. MC/VISA/DISC/AMEX. Phone: (931) 962-1183.

SEE AD TRAVEL SECTION PAGE 784

WOODALL'S ALPHABETICAL QUICK REFERENCE

For Your Convenience Facilities are Listed Alphabetically by Name within each State/Province.

Types of Facilities Listed:

Campground/RV Parks ★ RV Sales/Service Centers ● Attractions & Tourism Locations

A Name in Bold Type indicates Advertisers who want your business

Campground/RV Parks Special Services Indicated:

□ Cabin Rentals, ® RV/Park Trailer Rentals, △ Tent Rentals

ALABAMA

AAA RV Park — ***FOLEY F-2***
● **Alabama Constitution Village — *HUNTSVILLE A-3***
● **Alabama Mountain Lakes Tourist Association — *MOORESVILLE A-3***
Alabama Port RV Park — *MOBILE F-1*
American Motor Coach Resorts — *GULF SHORES F-2*
Anchors Aweigh RV Resort — *FOLEY F-2*
Autauga Creek RV Campground — *PRATTVILLE D-3*
Azalea RV Park — *THEODORE F-1*
Bankhead NF (Clear Creek Rec Area) — ***JASPER B-2***
Bankhead NF (Corinth Rec Area) — ***DOUBLE SPRINGS B-2***
Bankhead NF (Houston Rec Area) — ***DOUBLE SPRINGS B-2***
® Bar W Campground — ***AUBURN D-4***
Barclay RV Parking — ***BOAZ B-4***
®□ Bay Breeze RV On the Bay — ***GULF SHORES F-2***
□ Bear Creek Dev Auth (Elliott Branch) — ***RUSSELLVILLE A-2***
Bear Creek Dev Auth (Horseshoe Bend) — ***HODGES A-2***
Bear Creek Dev Auth (Slickrock) — ***RUSSELLVILLE A-2***
Beech's Camping MHP — ***ORANGE BEACH F-2***
● **Bellingrath Gardens & Home — *MOBILE F-1***
□ **Birmingham South Campground — *PELHAM C-3***
Bladon Springs State Park — ***BLADON SPRINGS E-1***
□ Blakeley State Park — ***SPANISH FORT F-2***
Blue Springs SP — ***CLIO E-4***
Bluff Creek Park (COE-Walter F. George Lake) — ***COTTONTON D-5***
Buck's Pocket SP — ***GROVE OAK A-4***
● **Burritt on the Mountain — *HUNTSVILLE A-3***
★ **Burton's RV Service — *JASPER B-2***
Cane Creek RV Park & Campground — *HEFLIN B-4*
Capital City RV Park — *MONTGOMERY D-4*
Carson Village Mobile Home Community — ***BIRMINGHAM B-3***
Cathedral Caverns SP — ***WOODVILLE A-4***
□ Cheaha SP — ***DELTA C-4***
Cherokee Campground — *HELENA C-3*
□ Chewacla SP — ***AUBURN D-4***
Chickasabogue Park & CG (Mobile County Pk) — ***MOBILE F-1***
Chickasaw SP — ***GALLION D-2***
Chilatchee Creek Park (COE-Alabama River Lakes) — ***ALBERTA D-2***
Citronelle Lakeview RV Park (City Park) — ***CITRONELLE E-1***
□ Claude D. Kelley SP — ***ATMORE E-2***
Cochrane Campground (COE-Tennessee/Tombigbee Waterway) — ***COCHRANE C-1***
Conecuh NF (Open Pond Campground) — ***ANDALUSIA E-3***
Corinth Recreation Area — ***DOUBLE SPRINGS B-2***
Country Court RV Park — *ANNISTON B-4*
Country Sunshine RV Park — ***CASTLEBERRY E-3***
Country View RV Park — ***HANCEVILLE B-3***
Crawford RV Park — ***SCOTTSBORO A-4***
Cullman Campground — *CULLMAN B-3*
Dauphin Island Campground (City Park) — *DAUPHIN ISLAND F-1*
□ De Soto SP — ***FORT PAYNE A-4***
□ Dead Lake Marina & CG — ***CREOLA F-2***
Deer Run RV Park — *TROY E-4*
Deerlick Creek (COE-Holt Lake) — ***TUSCALOOSA C-2***
DeSoto Caverns Park Campground — ***CHILDERSBURG C-3***
□ DeSoto State Park Lodge — ***FORT PAYNE A-4***
Ditto Landing Marina Campground (City/County Park) — ***HUNTSVILLE A-3***
Doc's RV Park — ***GULF SHORES F-2***
® **Driftwood RV Park — *FAIRHOPE F-2***
● **Early Works Children's Museum — *HUNTSVILLE A-3***
East Bank Access Area (COE-Alabama River Lakes)/Millers Ferry Campground — ***CAMDEN D-2***
Escapees Rainbow Plantation — ***SUMMERDALE F-2***
□ Escatawpa Hollow Campground — ***WILMER F-1***
Florala SP — ***FLORALA E-4***
Forkland Park (COE-Demopolis Lake) — ***DEMOPOLIS D-2***
Fort Morgan RV Park — ***GULF SHORES F-2***
Fort Toulouse/Jackson Park (Ala. State Historical Commission) — ***WETUMPKA D-4***
Foscue Park (COE-Demopolis Lake) — ***DEMOPOLIS D-2***
Frank Jackson SP — ***OPP E-4***
Good Hope Campground — ***CULLMAN B-3***
□ Goose Pond Colony (City Park) — ***SCOTTSBORO A-4***
®□ **Gulf Breeze Resort — *GULF SHORES F-2***
Gulf Coast RV Park — ***GULF SHORES F-2***
□ Gulf SP — ***GULF SHORES F-2***
Gunter Hill Park (COE-Alabama River Lakes) — ***MONTGOMERY D-4***
Hardridge Creek Park (COE-Walter F. George Lake) — ***SHORTERVILLE E-5***
● **Harrison Brothers Hardware — *HUNTSVILLE A-3***
Heritage Acres RV Park — *TUSCUMBIA A-2*
★ **Heritage Coach & RV Center — *BIRMINGHAM B-3***
® Hidden Cove Outdoor Resort — ***ARLEY B-2***
Hilltop RV Park — *ROBERTSDALE F-2*
● **Historic Huntsville Depot — *HUNTSVILLE A-3***
Hoover RV Park — ***HOOVER C-3***
● **Huntsville Botanical Garden — *HUNTSVILLE A-3***
● **Huntsville Convention & Visitors Bureau — *HUNTSVILLE A-3***
● **Huntsville Museum of Art — *HUNTSVILLE A-3***
I-10 Kampground — *MOBILE F-1*
I-65 RV Campground — ***MOBILE F-1***
Isaac Creek Park (COE - Alabama River Lakes) — ***MONROEVILLE E-2***
Island Retreat RV Park — *GULF SHORES F-2*
□ Joe Wheeler SP — ***ROGERSVILLE A-2***
□ Joe Wheeler State Park Lodge — ***ROGERSVILLE A-2***
John's Campground & Grocery — ***CENTRE B-4***
Just Loafin' RV Park — ***SAMSON E-4***
K & K RV Park — ***PRATTVILLE D-3***
Knox Hill RV Resort — ***KNOXVILLE C-2***
®□ **KOA-Pensacola/Perdido Bay — *LILLIAN F-2***
□ **Kountry Air RV Park — *PRATTVILLE D-3***
Lake Eufaula Campground — ***EUFAULA D-5***
□ Lake Guntersville State Lodge — ***GUNTERSVILLE A-4***
□ Lake Lurleen SP — ***TUSCALOOSA C-2***
□ Lakepoint Resort Lodge — ***EUFAULA D-5***
□ Lakepoint SP — ***EUFAULA D-5***
Lakeside Landing RV Park & Marina — *PELL CITY B-4*
Lakeside RV Park — *OPELIKA C-5*
Lazy Acres — *ELBERTA F-2*
Lazy Lake RV Park — ***GULF SHORES F-2***

ALABAMA — Continued

Leisure Time Campgrounds — *AUBURN D-4*
®□ **Little Mountain Marina Camping Resort — *LANGSTON A-4***
® **Logan Landing RV Resort & Campground — *TALLADEGA C-4***
Luxury RV Resort — ***GULF SHORES F-2***
M & J RV Park — *BIRMINGHAM B-3*
Magnolia RV Park — *MAGNOLIA SPRINGS F-2*
Magnolia Springs RV Hideaway — ***FOLEY F-2***
Mallard Creek (TVA-Wheeler Lake) — ***DECATUR A-3***
Mc Farland Park (City Park) — ***FLORENCE A-2***
□ **McCalla Campground — *MCCALLA C-3***
Meaher SP — ***SPANISH FORT F-2***
□ MILITARY PARK (Coast Guard Rec Facility) — ***MOBILE F-1***
MILITARY PARK (Fort Rucker Campground) — ***OZARK E-4***
MILITARY PARK (Redstone Arsenal Travel Camp) — ***HUNTSVILLE A-3***
□ Monte Sano SP — ***HUNTSVILLE A-3***
□ **Montgomery Campground — *MONTGOMERY D-4***
Moundville Archaeological Park (Univ of Alabama) — ***MOUNDVILLE C-2***
Mountain Breeze RV Park — *HUNTSVILLE A-3*
□ Mr. D's — ***OZARK E-4***
● **Noccalula Falls — *GADSDEN B-4***
□ **Noccalula Falls Park & Campground (City Park) — *GADSDEN B-4***
Northshore Campground at the Big Rock — *LANGSTON A-4*
□ Oak Mountain SP — ***PELHAM C-3***
Owassa Lakeside RV — ***EVERGREEN E-3***
□ **Ozark Travel Park — *OZARK E-4***
Palm Lake Rv Park — *FOLEY F-2*
Parkway RV Camp — ***LOXLEY F-2***
□ Parnell Creek Campground — ***WOODVILLE A-4***
Paul M. Grist SP — ***SELMA D-3***
Payne's RV Park — *MOBILE F-1*
Peach Park RV Park — ***CLANTON C-3***
Peach Queen Campground — *JEMISON C-3*
Pecan Point RV Park — ***DOTHAN E-5***
Pickensville Campground (COE-Tennessee/Tombigbee Waterway) — ***PICKENSVILLE C-1***
Plantation Harbor RV Resort (Wolf Bay Plantations) — ***ELBERTA F-2***
Point Mallard Campground (City Park) — *DECATUR A-3*
Ponderosa RV Park — ***URIAH E-2***
Prairie Creek Park (COE-Alabama River Lakes) — ***LOWNDESBORO D-3***
★ **Prattville Auto & RV Repair Center — *MONTGOMERY D-4***
Rickwood Caverns SP — ***WARRIOR B-3***
River Country Campground — ***GADSDEN B-4***
□ Roland Cooper SP — ***CAMDEN D-2***
Rolling Hills RV Park — ***CALERA C-3***
Royal Palm Motor Coach Villages — *SUMMERDALE F-2*
Safe Harbor RV Park — *PELL CITY B-4*
● **Sci-Quest Hands-On Science Center — *HUNTSVILLE A-3***
Seibold Campground — *GUNTERSVILLE A-4*
Sequoyah Caverns & Ellis Homestead — ***VALLEY HEAD A-4***
Service Park (COE-Coffeeville Lake) — ***COFFEEVILLE E-1***
Shady Acres Campground — *MOBILE F-1*
□ **Shady Grove Campground — *MOBILE F-1***
Shallow Creek RV Park — *ASHFORD E-5*
Sharon Johnston Park — ***NEW MARKET A-3***
Sherling Lake Park & Campground (City Park) — *GREENVILLE D-3*
Six Mile Creek (COE-Alabama River Lakes) — ***SELMA D-3***
®□ **Sleepy Holler Campground — *JASPER B-2***
South Sauty Creek Resort — *LANGSTON A-4*
Southport Campgrounds — *GULF SHORES F-2*
□ **Southwind RV Park — *MAGNOLIA SPRINGS F-2***
® **Styx River Resort — *ROBERTSDALE F-2***
Sun-Runners RV Park — ***GULF SHORES F-2***
Sunset Travel Park — *TUSCALOOSA C-2*
Swan Creek Community — ***TANNER A-3***
□ **Talladega Creekside Resort — *TALLADEGA C-4***
Talladega NF (Coleman Lake) — ***HEFLIN B-4***
Talladega NF (Payne Lake West Side) — ***CENTREVILLE C-3***
Talladega NF (Pine Glen) — ***HEFLIN B-4***
□ Tannehill Ironworks Historical State Park — ***MCCALLA C-3***
The Woods RV Park and Campground — *MONTGOMERY D-4*
□ Thunder Canyon Campground — ***IDER A-4***
● **U.S. Army Aviation Museum — *FORT RUCKER E-4***
● **US Space & Rocket Center — *HUNTSVILLE A-3***
US Space & Rocket Center RV Campground — ***HUNTSVILLE A-3***
Veterans Memorial Park (City Park) — ***FLORENCE A-2***
● **Wales West Train & Garden Lovers — *FAIRHOPE F-2***
Wales West Train & Garden Lovers RV Resort — *FAIRHOPE F-2*
● **Weeden House Museum — *HUNTSVILLE A-3***
Wheeler Reservation Campground — ***ROGERSVILLE A-2***
White Oak Creek Park (COE-Walter F. George Lake) — ***EUFAULA D-5***
Wilderness RV Park — *ROBERTSDALE F-2*
Wilson Dam/Rockpile (TVA-Wilson Lake) — ***MUSCLE SHOALS A-2***
□ Wind Creek SP — ***ALEXANDER CITY C-4***
Wind Drift Campground — ***SHORTER D-4***

FLORIDA

® 21 Palms RV Resort — ***DAVENPORT C-4***
7 Oaks RV Park & Sales — ***HUDSON C-3***
A Camper's World — ***LAMONT A-2***
Abbey's WigWam RV Park — ***TAMPA C-3***
® Adelaide Shores RV Resort — ***AVON PARK D-4***
□ Adventures Unlimited Outdoor Center — ***MILTON F-1***
★ **Al's Motor Home & Trailer Sales — *FORT PIERCE D-5***
Anastasia State Park — ***ST. AUGUSTINE B-4***
Apalachicola National Forest (Wright Lake Campground) — ***SUMATRA F-3***
Arbor Terrace RV Resort — *BRADENTON D-3*
Arcadia Peace River Campground — *ARCADIA D-3*
★ Arrow RV Sales — ***CLEARWATER C-3***
□ **Arrowhead Campsites — *MARIANNA E-3***
★ **Arrowhead RV Sales — *MARIANNA E-3***
Aruba RV Park — *LAKEPORT D-4*
Avalon RV Resort — *CLEARWATER C-3*
□ Bahia Honda State Park — ***BAHIA HONDA KEY F-4***

FLORIDA — Continued

Baker Acres RV Resort — *ZEPHYRHILLS C-3*
® **Barrington Hills RV Resort — *HUDSON C-3***
Bay Aire Travel Trailer Park — ***PALM HARBOR C-3***
Bay Bayou RV Resort — *TAMPA C-3*
Beaver Lake Campground — *QUINCY A-1*
Belle Glade Campground (City Park) — ***BELLE GLADE D-5***
Ben's Hitching Post Campground — ***SILVER SPRINGS B-3***
Beverly Beach Camptown RV Resort — *FLAGLER BEACH B-4*
□ **Big Cypress RV Resort — *CLEWISTON D-4***
Big Lagoon State Park — ***PENSACOLA F-1***
Big Oak RV Park — ***TALLAHASSEE A-1***
● **Big Pine Key & Florida's Lower Keys — *KEY WEST F-4***
Big Tree RV Resort — *ARCADIA D-3*
□ **Bill Frederick Park at Turkey Lake (City Park) — *ORLANDO C-4***
Blackwater River State Park — ***HOLT E-1***
Blue Jay RV Park — *DADE CITY C-3*
□ Blue Spring State Park — ***ORANGE CITY B-4***
Blueberry Hill RV Resort — *BUSHNELL C-3*
Bluewater Key RV Resort — *KEY WEST F-4*
Bonita Lake RV Resort — *BONITA SPRINGS E-4*
Bow & Arrow Campground — *YULEE A-3*
Boyd's Key West Campground — *KEY WEST F-4*
Breezy Acres Campground — ***CHIEFLAND B-2***
Breezy Oaks RV Park — ***BUSHNELL C-3***
Breezy Palms RV Park — ***MELBOURNE C-5***
® Breezy Pines Campground — ***BIG PINE KEY F-4***
● **Broward County Parks & Recreation Division — *FORT LAUDERDALE E-5***
® Bryn Mawr Ocean Resort — ***ST. AUGUSTINE B-4***
® **Buckhead Ridge Marina Resort — *OKEECHOBEE D-4***
□ **Bulow Plantation RV Resort — *FLAGLER BEACH B-4***
Buttonwood Bay — *SEBRING D-4*
Caladesi RV Park — ***PALM HARBOR C-3***
Camelot RV Park — *MALABAR C-5*
® **Camp Florida Resort — *LAKE PLACID D-4***
® **Camp Inn Resort — *FROSTPROOF C-4***
Camp Lemora RV Park — ***THONOTOSASSA C-3***
□ Camp Macks River Resort — ***LAKE WALES C-4***
Camp Nebraska — *TAMPA C-3*
★ **Camp USA — *POMPANO BEACH E-5***
★ **Campbell RV Inc — *SARASOTA D-3***
Camper Village — ***OCALA B-3***
® Camper's Cove — ***LARGO C-3***
Campers Holiday — ***BROOKSVILLE C-3***
□ **Camper's Inn — *PANAMA CITY BEACH F-2***
□ **Camping on the Gulf — *DESTIN F-2***
Camp'n Aire RV Resort — ***LAKE WALES C-4***
● **Canoe Country Outpost — *HILLIARD A-3***
□ **Carrabelle Palms RV Park & Store — *CARRABELLE BEACH B-1***
Carver's Cove — *CAPE CANAVERAL C-5*
Casey Jones' RV Park — ***LAKE CITY A-3***
® **Cattail Creek RV Park — *YANKEETOWN B-3***
C.B. Smith Park (Broward County Park) — *PEMBROKE PINES E-5*
Cedar Key Sunset Isle RV Park — *CEDAR KEY B-2*
Cedar Pines Campground — ***MILTON F-1***
® Central Park — ***HAINES CITY C-4***
® Central Park II — ***HAINES CITY C-4***
★ **Charlotte RV Service — *PORT CHARLOTTE D-3***
Chassahowitzka River Campground (City Park) — ***CHASSAHOWITZKA C-3***
Chokoloskee Island Park & Campground — *CHOKOLOSKEE E-4*
Citrus Hill Park & Sales — *DADE CITY C-3*
Citrus Hills RV Park — ***DOVER C-3***
□ **Clark Family Campground — *ORANGE CITY B-4***
Clearwater Travel Resort — *CLEARWATER C-3*
Clerbrook Golf & RV Resort — *CLERMONT C-3*
®□ Clewiston/Lake Okeechobee KOA Campground — ***CLEWISTON D-4***
Cloverleaf Forest RV Resort — ***BROOKSVILLE C-3***
Club Naples RV Resort (Morgan RV Resorts) — *NAPLES E-4*
Collier-Seminole State Park — ***NAPLES E-4***
★ **Como Truck & RV Sales & Service — *HOMOSASSA C-3***
★ **Como Truck & RV Sales & Service — *INVERNESS C-3***
Countryside RV Park — ***LAKE PANASOFFKEE C-3***
Covered Wagon Campground — ***HOMOSASSA C-3***
Craig's RV Park — *ARCADIA D-3*
® Crescent City Campground — ***CRESCENT CITY B-4***
● **CRF Communities — *LAKE WALES C-4***
® Crooked Hook RV Resort — ***CLEWISTON D-4***
Cross Creek Country Club & RV Resort — *ARCADIA D-3*
□ **Crystal Isles — *CRYSTAL RIVER B-3***
Crystal Lake RV Park — ***SCOTTSMOOR C-4***
Crystal Lake RV Resort — *NAPLES E-4*
® Crystal Lake Village — ***WAUCHULA D-3***
Cypress Woods RV Resort — ***FORT MYERS D-3***
Daytona Beach Campground — *DAYTONA BEACH B-4*
Daytona Beach KOA — ***PORT ORANGE B-4***
Daytona Speedway KOA — ***DAYTONA BEACH B-4***
Dead Lakes State Recreation Area — ***WEWAHITCHKA F-3***
® **Deer Creek Golf & RV Resort — *DAVENPORT C-4***
Deerwood Madison Campground & Motel — ***MADISON A-2***
Del Raton RV Park — *DELRAY BEACH E-5*
□ Destin Recreation Area — ***DESTIN F-2***
Destin RV Beach Resort — *DESTIN F-2*
Destin Village RV Resort — *DESTIN F-2*
®□ Devil's Den Springs Resort — ***WILLISTON B-3***
□ **Disney's Fort Wilderness Resort & Campground — *LAKE BUENA VISTA C-4***
□ **Disney's Fort Wilderness Resort & Campground — *ORLANDO C-4***
★ **Dixie Trailer Supply — *FORT LAUDERDALE E-5***
Dove Rest RV Park & Campground — ***MARIANNA E-3***
Dunedin RV Resort — *DUNEDIN C-3*
E-Z Stop RV Park — ***LAKE CITY A-3***
Eagle's Landing RV Park — ***HOLT E-1***
★ **Eagle's Pride at the Great Outdoors — *TITUSVILLE C-4***
East Haven RV Park — ***WINTER HAVEN C-4***
□ **East Lake Fish Camp — *KISSIMMEE C-4***

ALPHABETICAL LISTINGS CONTINUED

FLORIDA — Continued

Easterlin Park (Broward County Park) — OAKLAND PARK E-5
Easy Livin' RV Park — FORT PIERCE D-5
® Elite Resorts at Citrus Valley (Not Visited) — CLERMONT C-3
Elite Resorts at Crystal River — CRYSTAL RIVER B-3
□ Elite Resorts At Salt Springs — SALT SPRINGS B-3
Ellenton Gardens Travel Resort — ELLENTON D-3
□ Emerald Beach RV Park — NAVARRE F-1
Emerald Coast RV Beach Resort — PANAMA CITY BEACH F-2
Endless Summer RV Park — NAPLES E-4
Everglades National Park (Long Pine Key) — HOMESTEAD E-5
Falling Waters State Park — CHIPLEY E-3
Farmers' Opry House Campground — PACE F-1
Faver-Dykes State Park — ST. AUGUSTINE B-4
Fiesta Grove RV Resort — PALMETTO D-3
Fijian RV Park — OKEECHOBEE D-4
□ Fisheating Creek Campground — PALMDALE D-4
® Fisherman's Cove Golf Marina & RV Resort — TAVARES C-3
Fishermans Cove RV Resort — PALMETTO D-3
Flagler by the Sea Campground — FLAGLER BEACH B-4
• Flagler County Chamber of Commerce — PALM COAST B-4
®□ Flamingo Lake RV Resort — JACKSONVILLE A-3
□ Florida Camp Inn — DAVENPORT C-4
Florida Caverns State Park — MARIANNA E-3
Florida City Campsite (City Park) — FLORIDA CITY E-5
Florida Pines Mobile Home Court — VENICE D-3
• Florida RV Trade Association (FRVTA) — TAMPA C-3
® Forest Village RV Resort — COCOA C-4
Fort Clinch State Park — FERNANDINA BEACH A-4
® Fort Myers Beach RV Resort — FORT MYERS BEACH E-3
□ Fort Summit KOA — CENTRAL FL'S WORLD OF THEME PARKS C-4
□ Fort Summit KOA — LAKE BUENA VISTA C-4
Fred Gannon Rocky Bayou State Recreation Area — NICEVILLE F-2
Frog Creek Campground — PALMETTO D-3
Gamble Rogers Memorial State Park at Flagler Beach — FLAGLER BEACH B-4
Gator Park — MIAMI E-5
• Gator Park Airboat Tours — MIAMI E-5
□ Georgetown Marina, Lodge & RV Park — GEORGETOWN B-4
Geronimo RV Resort — DESTIN F-2
□ Ginnie Springs Outdoors LLC — HIGH SPRINGS B-3
Glen Haven RV Resort — ZEPHYRHILLS C-3
Goldcoaster Mobile Home & RV Resort — HOMESTEAD E-5
Good Life RV Resort — BARTOW C-3
□ Grand Lake RV & Golf Resort — OCALA B-3
Grandma's Grove RV Park — LA BELLE D-4
□ Grayton Beach State Park — GRAYTON BEACH F-2
® Great Oak Campgrounds — KISSIMMEE C-4
Greenfield Village — DUNDEE C-4
® Grove Ridge RV Resort — DADE CITY C-3
® Gulf Air Travel Resort — FORT MYERS BEACH E-3
Gulf Islands National Seashore (Fort Pickens) — PENSACOLA F-1
□ Gulf Pines KOA — MILTON F-1
□ Gulf View RV Resort — PUNTA GORDA D-3
□ Hammondell Campground — WINTER HAVEN C-4
□ Hanna Park (City Park) — JACKSONVILLE A-3
Happy Days RV Park — ZEPHYRHILLS C-3
®□ Happy Traveler RV Park — THONOTOSASSA C-3
★ Harberson RV — HOLIDAY C-3
★ Harberson Swanston RV — CLEARWATER C-3
® Harbor Lakes — PORT CHARLOTTE D-3
®□ Harris Village RV Park — ORMOND BEACH B-4
Hawks Nest RV Park & Campground — WEEKI WACHEE C-3
Hidden River Travel Resort — RIVERVIEW C-3
Hidden Valley Campground — BROOKSVILLE C-3
Hide-A-Way RV Resort — RUSKIN D-3
□ Highbanks Marina & Campresort — DEBARY B-4
Highland Oaks RV Resort — SEBRING D-4
Highland Pines RV Resort — POMPANO BEACH E-5
® Highland Wheel Estates — SEBRING D-4
Highlands Hammock State Park — SEBRING D-4
Hillcrest RV Resort — ZEPHYRHILLS C-3
Hillsborough River State Park — THONOTOSASSA C-3
Ho-Hum RV Park — CARRABELLE B-1
Holiday Campground — PANACEA A-1
Holiday Cove RV Resort — BRADENTON D-3
Holiday Park — HALLANDALE E-5
Holiday Trav-L-Park RV Resort — OCALA B-3
® Holiday Travel Park — WINTER HAVEN C-4
Holiday Travel Resort — LEESBURG C-3
• Homosassa Springs Wildlife State Park — HOMOSASSA SPRINGS C-3
® Horseshoe Cove RV Resort — BRADENTON D-3
Hunter's Run RV Resort — ZEPHYRHILLS C-3
Imperial Bonita Estates RV Resort — BONITA SPRINGS E-4
Indian Creek Park — FORT MYERS BEACH E-3
Indian Forest Campground — ST. AUGUSTINE B-4
□ Inn & Out RV Park — LAKE CITY A-3
International RV Park & Campground — DAYTONA BEACH B-4
★ J. D. Sanders RV Center — GAINESVILLE B-3
Ja-Mar Travel Park — PORT RICHEY C-3
Jennings Outdoor Resort Campground — JENNINGS A-2
Jetty Park (Canaveral Port Auth) — CAPE CANAVERAL C-5
Jim's RV Park — ZEPHYRHILLS C-3
John Pennekamp Coral Reef State Park — KEY LARGO F-5
John Prince Memorial Park (Palm Beach County Park) — LAKE WORTH D-5
Jolly Roger Travel Park — MARATHON F-4
□ Jonathan Dickinson State Park — HOBE SOUND D-5
® Juno Ocean Walk RV Resort — JUNO BEACH D-5
★ K & K Trailer Supplies — HOMESTEAD E-5
Kelly's Countryside RV Park — CALLAHAN A-3
®□ Kelly's RV/MH Park — WHITE SPRINGS A-3
Key Way RV Park — CORTEZ D-3
□ Kings Kamp, RV, Tent & Marina — KEY LARGO F-5
KOA Orlando/Kissimmee — KISSIMMEE C-4
□ KOA-Cape Kennedy — TITUSVILLE C-4
□ KOA-Chattahoochee/Tallahassee West — CHATTAHOOCHEE A-1
KOA-Clearwater/Tarpon Springs — PALM HARBOR C-3
□ KOA-Naples — NAPLES E-4
□ KOA-St. Petersburg — ST. PETERSBURG C-3
® KOA-Sugarloaf Key West — SUGARLOAF KEY F-4
□ KOA-Tallahassee East/Monticello — MONTICELLO A-2
®□ KOA-Wildwood — WILDWOOD B-3
Koreshan State Park — ESTERO E-3
Kountree Kampinn RV Resort — NAPLES E-4
Kozy Kampers RV Park — FORT LAUDERDALE E-5
Labonte's Garden RV Park — FORT MYERS D-3
® Lake Bryant MH & RV Park — OCKLAWAHA B-3
□ Lake City Campground — LAKE CITY A-3
® Lake Glenada RV Park — AVON PARK D-4
Lake Griffin State Park — FRUITLAND PARK B-3
Lake Josephine RV Resort — SEBRING D-4
Lake Kissimmee State Park — LAKE WALES C-4
Lake Magic RV Park — CLERMONT C-3
Lake Manatee State Recreation Area — BRADENTON D-3
□ Lake Marion Marina & RV Resort (Not Visited) — KENANSVILLE C-4
Lake Monroe Park (Volusia County Park) — DEBARY B-4
® Lake Rousseau RV & Fishing Resort — CRYSTAL RIVER B-3
Lake San Marino RV Park — NAPLES E-4
Lake Trinity Estates — HOLLYWOOD E-5
Lake Waldena Resort — SILVER SPRINGS B-3
Lake Wales Campground — LAKE WALES C-4
□ Lakeland RV Resort — LAKELAND C-3
® Lakemont Ridge Home & RV Park — FROSTPROOF C-4
Lakeside Travel Park — TALLAHASSEE A-1
★ Land Yachts — JUPITER D-5
Larry & Penny Thompson Park (Dade County Park) — MIAMI E-5
Lazy Dazy Retreat — LAKELAND C-3
• Lee County Visitor & Convention — FORT MYERS D-3
Lee's Country Campground — WHITE SPRINGS A-3

FLORIDA — Continued

Lee's Travel Park — LARGO C-3
Leisure Days RV Resort — ZEPHYRHILLS C-3
LeLynn RV Resort — POLK CITY C-3
Lettuce Lake Travel Resort — PORT CHARLOTTE D-3
□ Lion Country Safari KOA — WEST PALM BEACH D-5
® Little Charlie Creek RV Park — WAUCHULA D-3
Little Manatee River State Recreation Area — WIMAUMA D-3
Little Talbot Island State Park — JACKSONVILLE A-3
Little Willies RV Resort — ARCADIA D-3
Long Key State Park — LONG KEY F-4
Long Point Park (Brevard County Park) — SEBASTIAN C-5
□ LongLeaf RV Park — DEFUNIAK SPRINGS E-2
Majestic Oaks RV Resort — ZEPHYRHILLS C-3
Manatee Hammock Park (Brevard County Park) — TITUSVILLE C-4
Manatee RV Park — PALMETTO D-3
Manatee Springs State Park — CHIEFLAND B-2
® Many Mansions RV Park — DADE CITY C-3
Marco Naples Hitching Post Travel Resort — NAPLES E-4
® Marina RV Resort — MOORE HAVEN D-4
Markham Park (Broward County Park) — SUNRISE E-5
Meadowlark Campground — LA BELLE D-4
Melbourne Beach Mobile Park — MELBOURNE BEACH C-5
Merry "D" RV Sanctuary — KISSIMMEE C-4
□ Miami Everglades Campground — MIAMI E-5
□ Mike Roess Gold Head Branch State Park — KEYSTONE HEIGHTS B-3
□ MILITARY PARK (Destin Recreation Area-Fort Benning GA) — DESTIN F-2
MILITARY PARK (FAMCAMP-Eglin AFB) — VALPARAISO F-2
MILITARY PARK (Jacksonville NAS) — JACKSONVILLE A-3
MILITARY PARK (Key West NAS-Sigsbee Park) — KEY WEST F-4
MILITARY PARK (Lake Pippin Rec Area-Maxwell/Gunter AFB AL) — NICEVILLE F-2
MILITARY PARK (Manatee Cove Campground-Patrick AFB) — COCOA BEACH C-5
®△□ MILITARY PARK (Oak Grove Fam-Camp-Pensacola NAS) — PENSACOLA F-1
MILITARY PARK (Tyndall AFB FAMCAMP) — PANAMA CITY F-2
Mill Creek RV Resort — KISSIMMEE C-4
Mouse Mountain RV Camping Resort — DAVENPORT C-4
□ Myakka River State Park — SARASOTA D-3
Myakka RV Resort — VENICE D-3
• Naples Realty Services — NAPLES E-4
Nature's Coast RV Resort — STEINHATCHEE B-2
□ Nature's Resort & Marina — HOMOSASSA C-3
□ Navarre Beach Campground — NAVARRE F-1
Neapolitan Cove RV Resort — NAPLES E-4
® Nettles Island — JENSEN BEACH D-5
□ New Smyrna Beach RV Park — NEW SMYRNA BEACH B-4
□ North Beach Camp Resort — ST. AUGUSTINE B-4
North Coast RV Park & Marina — FORT LAUDERDALE E-5
®□ Nova Family Campground — DAYTONA BEACH B-4
□ Oak Harbor RV Resort — HAINES CITY C-4
Oak Haven MH & RV Park — PORT CHARLOTTE D-3
Oak Tree Village Campground — OCALA B-3
®□ Oaks 'N Pines RV Campground — LAKE CITY A-3
Ocala National Forest (Alexander Springs Rec. Area) — ALTOONA B-4
Ocala National Forest (Big Bass Campground) — ALTOONA B-4
Ocala National Forest (Big Scrub Campground) — ALTOONA B-4
Ocala National Forest (Clearwater Lake Campground) — UMATILLA B-4
Ocala National Forest (Fore Lake Campground) — SILVER SPRINGS B-3
Ocala National Forest (Juniper Springs Rec. Area) — ASTOR B-4
Ocala National Forest (Lake Dorr Campground) — UMATILLA B-4
Ocala National Forest (Salt Springs Rec. Area) — SALT SPRINGS B-3
Ocala North RV Park — REDDICK B-3
□ Ocala RV Camp Resort — OCALA B-3
® Ocala Sun RV Resort — OCALA B-3
Ocean Grove Camp Resort — ST. AUGUSTINE B-4
Ochlockonee River State Park — SOPCHOPPY A-1
• Okeechobee County Tourism Development Council — OKEECHOBEE D-4
Okeechobee Landings — CLEWISTON D-4
®□ Okeechobee Resort KOA — OKEECHOBEE D-4
® Old Town Campground N' Retreat — OLD TOWN B-2
□ O'Leno State Park/River Rise — HIGH SPRINGS B-3
★ Open Road RV Center — FORT WALTON BEACH F-2
Orange Blossom Adult RV Park — BOWLING GREEN D-3
Orange Blossom RV Resort — APOPKA C-4
Orange City RV Resort — ORANGE CITY B-4
® Orange Grove Campground — KISSIMMEE C-4
Orange Grove Mobile Home & RV Park — FORT MYERS D-3
Orbit RV Park — GRANT C-5
® Orchid Lake RV Resort — NEW PORT RICHEY C-3
Orlando Winter Garden Campground — WINTER GARDEN C-4
Oscar Scherer State Park — OSPREY D-3
Osceola National Forest (Ocean Pond Campground) — OLUSTEE A-3
Osprey First In Florida RV Park — YULEE A-3
□ Otter Springs RV Resort — TRENTON B-2
® Outdoor Resorts At Orlando — CLERMONT C-3
□ Outdoor Resorts/Chokoloskee Island — CHOKOLOSKEE E-4
Outdoor Resorts/Melbourne Beach — MELBOURNE BEACH C-5
Palm Beach Gardens RV Park — WEST PALM BEACH D-5
★ Palm Beach RV — WEST PALM BEACH D-5
Palm Beach Traveler Park — LANTANA D-5
Palm Shores RV Park — MELBOURNE C-5
Panama City Beach RV Resort — PANAMA CITY BEACH F-2
Paradise Island — FORT LAUDERDALE E-5
® Paradise Island RV Resort — HAINES CITY C-4
Paradise Pointe Luxury RV Resort — NAPLES E-4
★ Park Model City & RV Sales — FORT MYERS D-3
□ Parramore's Campground — ASTOR B-4
Paynes Prairie Preserve State Park — GAINESVILLE B-3
• Pecan Park Flea & Farmers Market — JACKSONVILLE A-3
Pecan Park RV Resort — JACKSONVILLE A-3
Pelican Lake Motorcoach Resort — NAPLES E-4
Pelican Palms RV Park — MILTON F-1
□ Pelican's Landing — SEBASTIAN C-5
• Pensacola Convention & Visitor Information Center — PENSACOLA F-1
®□ Perry KOA — PERRY A-2
®□ Pine Island Resort — ST. JAMES CITY E-3
Pine Isle Mobile Home Park — HOMESTEAD E-5
®□ Pine Lake RV Park — FOUNTAIN F-3
Pineglen Motorcoach & RV Park — PANAMA CITY BEACH F-2
® Pioneer Village RV Resort (Encore) — FORT MYERS D-3
Playa del Rio RV Resort — PERDIDO KEY F-1
Playground RV Park — FORT WALTON BEACH F-2
Pleasant Lake RV Resort — BRADENTON D-3
® Ponderosa RV Park — KISSIMMEE C-4
Port St Lucie RV Resort — PORT ST. LUCIE D-5
Presnell's Bayside Marina & RV Resort — PORT ST. JOE F-3
® Punta Gorda RV Resort — PUNTA GORDA D-3
Quail Run RV Park — WESLEY CHAPEL C-3
△ Quiet Waters Park (Broward County Park) — DEERFIELD BEACH E-5
Raccoon River Campground — PANAMA CITY BEACH F-2
Rainbow Country RV Campground — CEDAR KEY B-2
Rainbow Resort — FROSTPROOF C-4
Rainbow Springs State Park — DUNNELLON B-3
Rainbow Village RV Resort — LARGO C-3
Rainbow Village RV Resort — ZEPHYRHILLS C-3
Raintree RV Resort — FORT MYERS D-3
Rally Park — SEFFNER C-3
Ralph's Travel Park — ZEPHYRHILLS C-3
Ramblers Rest Resort Campground — VENICE D-3
Red Barn Campground — BUSHNELL C-3
□ Red Coconut RV Resort on the Beach — FORT MYERS BEACH E-3
★ Revels Nationwide RV Sales — STARKE B-3
Ridgecrest RV & Mobile Home Resort — LEESBURG C-3

FLORIDA — Continued

River Oaks RV Resort — RUSKIN D-3
Riverbend Motorcoach Resort — FORT MYERS D-3
River's Edge RV Campground — HOLT E-1
□ Riverside Lodge — INVERNESS C-3
® Riverside RV Resort & Campground — PORT CHARLOTTE D-3
□ Road Runner Travel Resort — FORT PIERCE D-5
Robert's Mobile Home & RV Resort — ST. PETERSBURG C-3
® Robin's Nest RV Resort — MOORE HAVEN D-4
★ Rob's Auto Detailing Inc — SEFFNER C-3
Rock Creek RV Resort & Campground — NAPLES E-4
Rodman (COE - Lake Ocklawaha) — PALATKA B-4
Rolling Ridge RV Resort — CLERMONT C-3
Rose Bay Travel Park — PORT ORANGE B-4
® Royal Coachmen — NOKOMIS D-3
★ RV Connections — PANAMA CITY F-2
★ RV Connections — PANAMA CITY F-2
★ RV World Inc of Nokomis — VENICE D-3
★ R.V. World of Lakeland — LAKELAND C-3
St. Andrews State Recreation Area — PANAMA CITY BEACH F-2
□ St. Augustine Beach KOA Kampground Resort — ST. AUGUSTINE B-4
St. George Island State Park — ST. GEORGE ISLAND B-1
® St. John's RV Park — ST. AUGUSTINE B-4
□ St. Joseph Peninsula State Park — PORT ST. JOE F-3
® St. Mary's River Fish Camp & Campground — HILLIARD A-3
San Carlos RV Park & Islands — FORT MYERS BEACH E-3
Sanlan RV Park — LAKELAND C-3
Sarasota Bay RV Park — BRADENTON D-3
Sarasota Lakes Camping Resort — SARASOTA D-3
Sarasota Sunny South Adult Mobile Home Park — SARASOTA D-3
Scruftys Riverwood RV Park — GEORGETOWN B-4
Sebastian Inlet State Park — SEBASTIAN C-5
Sebring Grove RV Resort — SEBRING D-4
Settlers Rest RV Park — ZEPHYRHILLS C-3
Seven Springs Travel Park — NEW PORT RICHEY C-3
® Shady Acres RV Travel Park — FORT MYERS D-3
Shady Brook Golf & RV Resort — SUMTERVILLE C-3
Shady Oaks RV & Mobile Home Park, Inc — CROSS CITY B-2
Sherwood Forest RV Resort — KISSIMMEE C-4
Sherwood Forest Travel RV Park — PALM HARBOR C-3
Siesta Bay RV Resort — FORT MYERS BEACH E-3
Silver Dollar RV and Golf Resort — ODESSA C-3
Silver Lakes RV Resort and Golf Club — NAPLES E-4
Silver Palms RV Village — OKEECHOBEE D-4
Silver Springs Campers Garden RV Resort — OCALA B-3
® Sonrise Palms Christian RV Park — COCOA C-4
South Bay RV Campground (Palm Beach County Park) — SOUTH BAY D-4
® Southern Charm RV Resort — ZEPHYRHILLS C-3
® Southern Palms RV Resort — EUSTIS B-4
Space Coast RV Resort — ROCKLEDGE C-4
Spanish Main RV Resort — THONOTOSASSA C-3
®□ Spirit of the Suwannee Music Park — LIVE OAK A-2
® Sportsman's Cove Resort — MCINTOSH B-3
□ St Johns River Campground — ASTOR B-4
Stage Stop Campground — WINTER GARDEN C-4
Stagecoach RV Park — ST. AUGUSTINE B-4
®□ Starke/Gainesville NE KOA — STARKE B-3
□ Stephen Foster Folk Culture Center State Park — WHITE SPRINGS A-3
□ Sugar Mill Ruins Travel Park — NEW SMYRNA BEACH B-4
Sumter Oaks RV Park — BUSHNELL C-3
Sun Lake RV Resort — RUSKIN D-3
Sun 'N' Shade Campground — PUNTA GORDA D-3
® Sun-N-Fun RV Resort — SARASOTA D-3
Suncoast RV Resort — PORT RICHEY C-3
Sundance Lakes RV Resort — PORT RICHEY C-3
Sunny Pines — SEBRING D-4
® Sunseeker's RV Park — FORT MYERS D-3
®□ Sunset King Lake RV Resort — DEFUNIAK SPRINGS E-2
□ Sunshine Holiday RV Park — ORMOND BEACH B-4
® Sunshine Key Resort — BIG PINE KEY F-4
® Sunshine RV Resort — LAKE PLACID D-4
® Sunshine Travel — VERO BEACH D-5
Suwannee River Hideaway Campground, Inc. — OLD TOWN B-2
□ Suwannee River State Park — LIVE OAK A-2
• Swamp House Grill — DEBARY B-4
Swan Lake Village Manufactured Homes & RV Resort — FORT MYERS D-3
Sweetwater RV Park — ZEPHYRHILLS C-3
Tallahassee RV Park — TALLAHASSEE A-1
Tamiami RV Park — FORT MYERS D-3
□ Tampa East RV Resort — DOVER C-3
Tampa South RV Resort — RUSKIN D-3
Terra Ceia Village — PALMETTO D-3
The Boardwalk — HOMESTEAD E-5
The Floridian RV Resort — ST. CLOUD C-4
□ The Glades RV, Golf & Marina Resort — FORT MYERS D-3
• The Glades RV, Golf & Marina Resort — LA BELLE D-4
• The Glades RV, Golf & Marina Resort — LA BELLE D-4
□ The Glades RV, Golf & Marina Resort — LA BELLE D-4
The Great Outdoors RV-Nature & Golf Resort — TITUSVILLE C-4
The Groves RV Resort — FORT MYERS D-3
The Harbor RV Resort & Marina — LAKE WALES C-4
The Mark Manufactured Home Park — ST. CLOUD C-4
® The Oaks RV Resort — BUSHNELL C-3
□ The Original Suwannee River Campground, Inc. — OLD TOWN B-2
The Outback RV Resort at Tanglewood — SEBRING D-4
The Recreation Plantation RV Resort — LADY LAKE B-3
• The Shell Factory & Nature Park — FORT MYERS D-3
Themeworld RV Resort — DAVENPORT C-4
Three Lakes RV Resort (Morgan RV Resorts) — HUDSON C-3
□ Three Rivers State Park — SNEADS E-3
® Three Worlds Resort — DAVENPORT C-4
Tiki Village Campground — LAKELAND C-3
® Toby's RV Resort — ARCADIA D-3
Tomoka State Park — ORMOND BEACH B-4
Topeekeegee Yugnee (T.Y.) Park (Broward County Park) — HOLLYWOOD E-5
Topics RV Community — SPRING HILL C-3
□ Topsail Hill Preserve State Park — SANTA ROSA BEACH F-2
Torreya State Park — BRISTOL F-3
Town N' Country RV Resort — DADE CITY C-3
Travel World — CLEARWATER C-3
Travelers Campground — ALACHUA B-3
Travelers Rest Resort — DADE CITY C-3
Treasure Coast RV Park — FORT PIERCE D-5
Treasure Village MH/RV Park — ST. PETERSBURG C-3
Tropic Breeze — PORT RICHEY C-3
® Tropical Gardens RV Park — BRADENTON D-3
□ Tropical Palms Fun Resort — KISSIMMEE C-4
□ Turtle Creek Campground — HOMOSASSA SPRINGS C-3
Turtleback RV Resort — LAKE PANASOFFKEE C-3
Twelve Oaks RV Resort — SANFORD C-4
Upriver RV Resort — FORT MYERS D-3
Vacation Village — LARGO C-3
□ Venice Campground & RV Park — VENICE D-3
□ Vero Beach Kamp Inc — SEBASTIAN C-5
Vortex Spring Camping and Diving Resort — PONCE DE LEON E-2
® Wagon Wheel RV Park — BOWLING GREEN D-3
• Walt Disney World Resort — LAKE BUENA VISTA C-4
Water's Edge RV Resort — ZEPHYRHILLS C-3
Water's Edge RV Resort of Punta Gorda — PUNTA GORDA D-3
Wayne's RV Resort — LAKE CITY A-3
® Webster Travel Park — WEBSTER C-3
Wekiwa Springs State Park — APOPKA C-4
® West Jupiter Camping Resort — JUPITER D-5

FLORIDA — Continued

Whisper Creek RV Resort — ***LA BELLE D-4***
Whispering Palms RV Resort — ***SEBASTIAN C-5***
Whispering Pines RV Park — ***SILVER SPRINGS B-3***
Wickham Park (Brevard County Park) — ***MELBOURNE C-5***
® Wild Frontier Rally Park & Campground — ***OCALA B-3***
® **Wilderness RV Park Estates** — ***SILVER SPRINGS B-3***
Williston Crossings RV Resort — ***WILLISTON B-3***
® Willow Lakes RV & Golf Resort — ***TITUSVILLE C-4***
Windward Knoll — ***THONOTOSASSA C-3***
Winter Paradise Travel Resort — ***HUDSON C-3***
® **Winter Quarters Manatee RV Resort** — ***BRADENTON D-3***
Winter Quarters-Pasco RV Park — ***LUTZ C-3***
Winterset RV Resort — ***PALMETTO D-3***
□ Withlacoochee Backwaters RV Park — ***DUNNELLON B-3***
® Woodall's Mobile Home Village — ***LAKELAND C-3***
® **Woodsmoke Camping Resort** — ***FORT MYERS D-3***
Yacht Haven Park & Marina — ***FORT LAUDERDALE E-5***
Yankee Traveler RV Park — ***LARGO C-3***
□ **Yellow Jacket Campground Resort** — ***OLD TOWN B-2***
□ Yogi Bear's Jellystone Park Camp Resort — ***MADISON A-2***
□ Zachary Taylor Resort — ***OKEECHOBEE D-4***

GEORGIA

Agrirama RV Park — ***TIFTON E-3***
● **Agrirama-Georgia's Museum of Agriculture & Historic Village** — ***TIFTON E-3***
Albany RV Resort — ***ALBANY E-2***
□ **Alexander H. Stephens State Historic Park** — ***CRAWFORDVILLE C-3***
® **Alatoona Landing Marine Resort & Campground** — ***CARTERSVILLE B-1***
□ **Amicalola Falls State Park & Lodge** — ***DAWSONVILLE B-2***
Amity Park (West Point Lake COE) — ***WEST POINT C-1***
□ **Amy's South Georgia RV Park** — ***TIFTON E-3***
□ **Atlanta South RV Resort** — ***MCDONOUGH C-2***
Atlanta-Marietta RV Resort (formerly Brookwood RV Park) — ***MARIETTA B-2***
□ **Bald Mountain Park Camping Resort** — ***HIAWASSEE A-2***
Bald Ridge (COE-Lake Sidney Lanier) — ***CUMMING B-2***
● **Bargainville Flea Market** — ***LAKE PARK F-3***
Big Hart Camp Area (COE - J. Strom Thurmond Lake) — ***THOMSON C-4***
Big Oak RV Park — ***TALLAPOOSA B-1***
□ **Black Rock Mountain State Park** — ***MOUNTAIN CITY A-3***
Blanton Creek Park (Georgia Power) — ***COLUMBUS D-1***
Blythe Island Regional Park Campground — ***BRUNSWICK E-5***
Bobby Brown State Park — ***ELBERTON B-3***
Boland's RV Park — ***PERRY D-2***
Bolding Mill (COE-Lake Sidney Lanier) — ***CUMMING B-2***
Boss's RV Park — ***WRENS C-4***
★ **Boyette Camper Sales** — ***SCREVEN E-4***
● **Brickyard Plantation Golf Club** — ***AMERICUS D-2***
Brickyard Plantation RV Park — ***AMERICUS D-2***
● **Brunswick/Golden Isles Visitors Bureau** — ***BRUNSWICK E-5***
□ Cartersville KOA — ***CARTERSVILLE B-1***
Cedar Creek Park RV & Driving Range — ***CAVE SPRING B-1***
Chattahooche National Forest (Mulky) — ***BLUE RIDGE A-2***
Chattahooche-Oconee National Forest-Tallulah River — ***CLAYTON A-3***
Chattahoochee National Forest (Lake Blue Ridge Campground) — ***BLUE RIDGE A-2***
Chattahoochee National Forest (Lake Conasauga Campground) — ***CHATSWORTH A-1***
Chattahoochee National Forest (Lake Russell Campground) — ***CORNELIA B-3***
Chattahoochee National Forest (Lake Winfield Scott Campground) — ***BLAIRSVILLE A-2***
Chattahoochee National Forest (Morganton Point Campground) — ***MORGANTON A-2***
Chattahoochee National Forest (Rabun Beach Campground) — ***CLAYTON A-3***
Chattahoochee National Forest (The Pocket Campground) — ***LA FAYETTE A-1***
Chattahoochee-Oconee National Forest-Sandy Bottom — ***CLAYTON A-3***
Chattahoochee-Oconee National Forest-Tate Branch — ***CLAYTON A-3***
□ Chattanooga South-Lookout Mountain KOA — ***RINGGOLD A-1***
Cherokee Campground — ***HELEN A-2***
Chestnut Ridge Park (COE-Lake Sidney Lanier) — ***BUFORD B-2***
City Campground — ***ANDERSONVILLE D-2***
Clark Creek South (Allatoona Lake COE) — ***ACWORTH B-1***
□ **Cloudland Canyon State Park** — ***RISING FAWN A-1***
Colony City Campground (City Park) — ***FITZGERALD E-3***
Coosa River Campground (Rome-Floyd County Park) & Nature Center — ***ROME B-1***
□ Cordele KOA — ***CORDELE D-2***
Cordele RV Park — ***CORDELE D-2***
Cotton Hill Park (COE-Walter F George Lake) — ***FORT GAINES E-1***
□ Country Boy's RV Park — ***COMMERCE B-3***
Country Boy's RV Park — ***MADISON C-3***
Country Oaks Campground & RV Park — ***KINGSLAND F-5***
® **Creekside Plantation RV Campground** — ***ALBANY E-2***
□ Creekwood Resort Campground & Cabins — ***HELEN A-2***
□ **Crooked River State Park** — ***ST. MARYS F-5***
Crossroads Holiday Trav-L-Park — ***PERRY D-2***
Doll Mountain Campground (COE-Carters Lake) — ***ELLIJAY A-2***
Duckett Mill (COE - Lake Sidney Lanier) — ***GAINESVILLE B-2***
Eagles Roost RV Resort — ***LAKE PARK F-3***
□ **Elijah Clark State Park** — ***LINCOLNTON B-4***
★ Ellis Travel Trailers — ***STATESBORO D-4***
® **Emerald Lake RV Park** — ***COLQUITT E-1***
□ **Enota Mountain Retreat** — ***HELEN A-2***
□ **F. D. Roosevelt State Park** — ***PINE MOUNTAIN C-1***
Fair Harbor RV Park & Campground — ***PERRY D-2***
□ **Florence Marina State Park** — ***OMAHA D-1***
Flynn's Inn Camping Village — ***AUGUSTA C-4***
Forest Glen Mobile Home & RV Park — ***JACKSON C-2***
□ **Forsyth KOA** — ***FORSYTH C-2***
□ **Fort McAllister State Historic Park** — ***RICHMOND HILL D-5***
□ **Fort Mountain State Park** — ***CHATSWORTH A-1***
□ **Fort Yargo State Park** — ***WINDER B-2***
● **Fran's Place Restaurant** — ***BRUNSWICK E-5***
□ **General Coffee State Park** — ***DOUGLAS E-3***
□ **George L. Smith State Park** — ***TWIN CITY D-4***
★ **Georgia Boat Sales** — ***ACWORTH B-1***
Georgia Mountain Fairgrounds Campground (County Park) — ***HIAWASSEE A-2***
● **Georgia Mountain Fairgrounds & Music Hall (County Fairgrounds)** — ***HIAWASSEE A-2***
● **Georgia State Parks & Historic Sites** — ***ATLANTA B-2***
□ **Georgia Veterans Memorial State Park** — ***CORDELE D-2***
□ **Golden Isles RV Park** — ***BRUNSWICK E-5***
Gordonia-Alatamaha State Park — ***REIDSVILLE D-4***
Hamburg State Park — ***WARTHEN C-3***
□ **Hard Labor Creek State Park** — ***RUTLEDGE C-3***
□ **Hart State Park** — ***HARTWELL B-3***
Hesters Ferry Camp Area (COE - J. Strom Thurmond Lake) — ***LINCOLNTON B-4***
High Falls State Park — ***HIGH FALLS C-2***
□ **Hillside Bluegrass RV Park** — ***COCHRAN D-3***
□ **Holiday Harbor Marina & Resort** — ***ACWORTH B-1***
Holiday Park (West Point Lake COE) — ***LA GRANGE C-1***
□ **Indian Springs State Park** — ***JACKSON C-2***
Inland Harbor RV Park — ***DARIEN E-5***
Interstate RV Campground — ***BYRON D-2***
★ **Interstate RV Center** — ***BYRON D-2***
□ Jacksonville North/Kingsland KOA — ***KINGSLAND F-5***
□ **James H. Floyd State Park** — ***SUMMERVILLE B-1***
Jekyll Island Campground — ***JEKYLL ISLAND E-5***

GEORGIA — Continued

● **Jekyll Island Welcome Center** — ***JEKYLL ISLAND E-5***
★ **John Bleakley Motor Homes** — ***DOUGLASVILLE B-1***
★ **John Bleakley Motor Homes** — ***UNADILLA D-2***
★ **John Bleakley RV Center** — ***DOUGLASVILLE B-1***
John Tanner State Park — ***CARROLLTON C-1***
Jones RV Park — ***NORCROSS B-2***
□ KOA-Calhoun — ***CALHOUN B-1***
□ KOA-Savannah South — ***RICHMOND HILL D-5***
Kolomoki Mounds State Park — ***BLAKELY E-1***
L & D RV Park — ***FORSYTH C-2***
● **Lake Harmony Bicycle Barn** — ***TOWNSEND E-5***
Lake Harmony RV Park & Campground — ***TOWNSEND E-5***
Lake Juliette Dames Ferry Park (Georgia Power) — ***MACON C-2***
Lake Lanier Islands Campground — ***BUFORD B-2***
Lake Nottely RV Park — ***BLAIRSVILLE A-2***
● **Lake Pines Event Center** — ***COLUMBUS D-1***
Lake Pines RV Park & Campground — ***COLUMBUS D-1***
● **Lake Side Grill** — ***ACWORTH B-1***
Lake Tobesofkee Recreation Area (Bibb Co.) — ***MACON C-2***
Lakemont RV Park — ***ACWORTH B-1***
● **Lakeside Restaurant** — ***EULONIA E-5***
□ **Laura S. Walker State Park** — ***WAYCROSS E-4***
Lawrence Shoals Park (Georgia Power) — ***EATONTON C-3***
□ **Little Ocmulgee State Park** — ***MCRAE D-3***
□ **Lookout Mountain KOA-Chattanooga West** — ***TRENTON A-1***
□ **Magnolia Springs State Park** — ***MILLEN C-4***
McIntosh Lake RV Park — ***EULONIA E-5***
McKaskey Campground (COE-Allatoona Lake) — ***CARTERSVILLE B-1***
McKinney Campground (Allatoona Lake COE) — ***ACWORTH B-1***
★ **Mid-State RV Center** — ***BYRON D-2***
△ MILITARY PARK (Dobbins ARB Family Campground) — ***MARIETTA B-2***
MILITARY PARK (Fort Gordon Rec. Area) — ***LEAH B-4***
□ MILITARY PARK (Ft. McPherson-Lk Allatoona Army Rec Area) — ***CARTERSVILLE B-1***
MILITARY PARK (Grassy Pond Rec. Area) — ***LAKE PARK F-3***
MILITARY PARK (Hunter Army Airfield Trailer Camp) — ***SAVANNAH D-5***
MILITARY PARK (Robins AFB FAMCAMP) — ***WARNER ROBINS D-3***
®□ MILITARY PARK (Uchee Creek Army Campground/Marina) — ***FORT BENNING D-1***
□ MILITARY PARK (World Famous Navy Lake Site-Atlanta NAS) — ***ACWORTH B-1***
Milltown Campground (COE - Hartwell Lake) — ***HARTWELL B-3***
□ **Mistletoe State Park** — ***APPLING C-4***
Moccasin Creek State Park — ***CLARKESVILLE A-3***
□ **Moun[illegible] RV Resort** — ***BLAIRSVILLE A-2***
Mountain View Campground — ***HIAWASSEE A-2***
[illegible]han Campers — ***MARIETTA B-2***
□ **North Shore Resort at Lake Oconee** — ***GREENSBORO C-3***
Oconee National Forest (Lake Sinclair Campground) — ***EATONTON C-3***
□ Oconee Springs Park (Putnam County Park) — ***EATONTON C-3***
□ Okefenokee Pastimes Camping & Cabins — ***FOLKSTON F-4***
Okefenokee RV Park — ***FOLKSTON F-4***
Old 41 No. 3 Campground (COE Allatoona Lake) — ***ACWORTH B-1***
Old Federal Road Park (COE-Lake Sidney Lanier) — ***GAINESVILLE B-2***
Old Salem Park (Georgia Power) — ***GREENSBORO C-3***
Parks Ferry Park (Georgia Power) — ***GREENSBORO C-3***
□ Parkwood RV Park & Cottages — ***STATESBORO D-4***
Payne Campground (COE-Allatoona Lake) — ***ACWORTH B-1***
Paynes Creek Campground (COE - Hartwell Lake) — ***HARTWELL B-3***
Perry Ponderosa Park — ***PERRY D-2***
Petersburg Camp Area (COE - J. Strom Thurmond Lake) — ***LEAH B-4***
Pine Lake RV Campground — ***BISHOP B-3***
□ **Pine Mountain RVC** — ***PINE MOUNTAIN C-1***
● **Pine Village Deli & Convenience Store** — ***FOLKSTON F-4***
Pinevale Campground — ***SYLVANIA D-5***
□ **Plum Nelly Campground** — ***ELLIJAY A-2***
Poteete Creek (Union County Park) — ***BLAIRSVILLE A-2***
R. Shaefer Heard (COE - West Point Lake) — ***WEST POINT C-1***
Ramsey RV Park — ***WARM SPRINGS C-1***
Raysville Bridge Camp Area (COE - J. Strom Thurmond Lake) — ***THOMSON C-4***
□ **Red Top Mountain State Park** — ***CARTERSVILLE B-1***
Reed Bingham State Park — ***ADEL E-3***
□ **Richard B Russell State Park** — ***ELBERTON B-3***
Ridge Road Camp Area (COE-J. Strom Thurmond Lake) — ***LEAH B-4***
Ringer Park (COE - West Point Lake) — ***LA GRANGE C-1***
River Bend Campground — ***HIAWASSEE A-2***
River Forks Park and Campground — ***GAINESVILLE B-2***
River Park RV Park — ***VALDOSTA F-3***
□ **River Vista Mountain Village** — ***DILLARD A-3***
River's End Campground & RV Park (City Park) — ***TYBEE ISLAND D-5***
Riverside Estates RV Park — ***COVINGTON C-2***
Savannah Oaks RV Resort — ***SAVANNAH D-5***
Sawnee Campground (COE-Lake Sidney Lanier) — ***CUMMING B-2***
®□ **Scenic Mountain RV Park** — ***MILLEDGEVILLE C-3***
□ **Seminole State Park** — ***DONALSONVILLE E-1***
Shady Grove Park (COE Lake Sidney Lanier) — ***CUMMING B-2***
Shoal Creek Camping Area (COE-Lake Sidney Lanier) — ***BUFORD B-2***
Skidaway Island State Park — ***SAVANNAH D-5***
South Oaks Mobile Home Community RV Park — ***PALMETTO C-1***
□ Southern Gates RV Park & Campground — ***ARABI E-2***
Southern Trails RV Resort — ***UNADILLA D-2***
State Line Park (COE - West Point Lake) — ***LA GRANGE C-1***
□ **Stephen C. Foster State Park** — ***FARGO F-4***
Stone Mountain Family Campground — ***STONE MOUNTAIN B-2***
● **Stone Mountain Park** — ***STONE MOUNTAIN B-2***
Sugar Mill Plantation RV Park — ***THOMASVILLE F-2***
Sunset Campground — ***LAVONIA B-3***
Sweetwater Campground (Allatoona Lake COE) — ***CANTON B-2***
Tallulah Gorge State Park — ***TALLULAH FALLS A-3***
® Talona Creek Campground — ***TALKING ROCK B-2***
★ **Team RV Inc** — ***ALBANY E-2***
The Parks at Chehaw Campground (City Park) — ***ALBANY E-2***
The Pines Campground — ***TIFTON E-3***
The Place To Be RV Park — ***BAINBRIDGE F-1***
The Pottery Campground — ***COMMERCE B-3***
● **Three Oaks Farm** — ***BRUNSWICK E-5***
□ Timber Ridge Resort in Mountain Lakes Resort — ***CLEVELAND A-2***
Toccoa RV Park — ***TOCCOA B-3***
□ **Trackrock Campground & Cabins** — ***BLAIRSVILLE A-2***
● **Trackrock Stables** — ***BLAIRSVILLE A-2***
Traders Hill Recreation Area & Campground (Charlton County) — ***FOLKSTON F-4***
□ **Tugaloo State Park** — ***LAVONIA B-3***
Turner Campsites — ***CLEVELAND A-2***
Twin Lakes RV Park — ***CUMMING B-2***
□ **Twin Oaks RV Park** — ***PERRY D-2***
□ **Unicoi State Park** — ***HELEN A-2***
□ Valdosta/Lake Park KOA — ***LAKE PARK F-3***
Victoria Bryant State Park — ***ROYSTON B-3***
Victoria Campground (Allatoona Lake COE) — ***WOODSTOCK B-2***
□ **Vogel State Park** — ***BLAIRSVILLE A-2***
Watsadler Campground (COE - Hartwell Lake) — ***HARTWELL B-3***
Watson Mill Bridge State Park — ***COMER B-3***
□ Whispering Pines Campground — ***BLUE RIDGE A-2***
Whispering Pines RV Park — ***RINCON D-5***
Whitetail Ridge (COE - West Point Lake) — ***LA GRANGE C-1***
Whitewater Creek Park (Macon County Park) — ***OGLETHORPE D-2***
Wildwood Park (Columbia County Park) — ***APPLING C-4***
Winfield Camp Area (COE - J. Strom Thurmond Lake) — ***WINFIELD C-4***
□ Wiregrass Trail RV Campground — ***REIDSVILLE D-4***
Woodring Branch Public Use Area (COE-Carters Lake) — ***CHATSWORTH A-1***

KENTUCKY

□ Aurora Oaks Campground — ***AURORA B-2***
Axtel Campground (COE - Rough River Lake) — ***MCDANIELS D-2***
Bailey's Point Campground (COE-Barren River Lake) — ***SCOTTSVILLE E-2***
□ Barren River Lake State Resort Park — ***GLASGOW E-3***
Beech Bend Family Campground — ***BOWLING GREEN E-2***
□ Big Bear Resort — ***BENTON B-2***
Big Bone Lick State Park — ***WALTON B-4***
Big South Fork Nat'l River & Rec. Area (Blue Heron Campground) — ***STEARNS E-4***
Birmingham Ferry (LBL) National Recreation Area — ***GRAND RIVERS B-2***
Blue Licks Battlefield State Park — ***MOUNT OLIVET C-4***
□ Breaks Interstate Park — ***ELKHORN CITY D-6***
Buckhorn Dam Recreation Area (COE-Buckhorn Lake) — ***BUCKHORN D-5***
Bullfrog Campground — ***MURRAY B-2***
Canal Recreation Area (COE-Lake Barkley) — ***GRAND RIVERS B-2***
Carr Creek State Park — ***SASSAFRAS D-5***
□ Carter Caves State Resort Park — ***OLIVE HILL C-5***
Cave Country RV Campground — ***CAVE CITY D-3***
Cave Creek (COE-Rough River Lake) — ***FALLS OF ROUGH D-2***
Chimney Rock RV Park & Marina — ***HARRODSBURG D-4***
□ **Cincinnati South Rose Garden Resort** — ***CRITTENDEN B-4***
□ Clay County Campground — ***MANCHESTER D-5***
Columbus - Belmont State Park — ***COLUMBUS B-1***
□ Conley Bottom Resort — ***MONTICELLO E-4***
□ Corbin-KOA — ***CORBIN E-4***
Cravens Bay (LBL) National Recreation Area — ***GRAND RIVERS B-2***
□ Cumberland Falls State Resort Park — ***CORBIN E-4***
Cumberland Gap National Historical Park (Wilderness Road Campground) — ***MIDDLESBORO E-5***
Cumberland Point Public Use Area (COE-Lake Cumberland) — ***SOMERSET E-4***
Cypress Lakes RV Park — ***CALVERT CITY B-2***
Dale Hollow Lake State Park — ***BURKESVILLE E-3***
Daniel Boone National Forest (Grove Boat-In Campground) — ***CORBIN E-4***
Daniel Boone National Forest (Grove Campground) — ***CORBIN E-4***
Daniel Boone National Forest (Holly Bay Rec. Area) — ***LONDON D-4***
Daniel Boone National Forest (Koomer Ridge Campground) — ***SLADE D-5***
Daniel Boone National Forest (Twin Knobs Rec. Area) — ***MOREHEAD C-5***
Daniel Boone National Forest (White Oak Boat-In Campground) — ***LONDON D-4***
Daniel Boone National Forest (Zilpo Recreation Area) — ***SALT LICK C-5***
□ Diamond Caverns Resort & Golf Club — ***PARK CITY E-3***
® Diamond Lake Resort Campground — ***OWENSBORO D-2***
Dog Creek (COE - Nolin River Lake) — ***LEITCHFIELD D-2***
□ Dogwood Lakes Camping & Resort — ***DUNMOR E-2***
®□ **Duck Creek RV Park** — ***PADUCAH B-1***
Eagle Falls Resort — ***PARKERS LAKE E-4***
□ Eagle Valley Camping Resort — ***SANDERS B-4***
□ Elizabethtown Crossroads Campground — ***ELIZABETHTOWN D-3***
Elkhorn Campground — ***FRANKFORT C-4***
Energy Lake (LBL) National Recreation Area — ***GOLDEN POND E-1***
Exit 31 RV Park — ***GRAND RIVERS B-2***
Fall Creek Campground (Corps of Engineers) — ***MONTICELLO E-4***
Fenton (LBL) National Recreation Area — ***GOLDEN POND E-1***
Fern Lake Campground — ***PADUCAH B-1***
Fishing Creek Public Use Area (COE-Lake Cumberland) — ***SOMERSET E-4***
Fort Boonesborough State Park — ***RICHMOND D-4***
®□ Franklin RV Ranch — ***FRANKLIN E-2***
General Burnside State Park — ***BURNSIDE E-4***
□ General Butler State Resort Park — ***CARROLLTON B-3***
German Bridge Camping Area (COE - Dewey Lake) — ***PRESTONSBURG D-6***
Glendale Campground — ***ELIZABETHTOWN D-3***
Goose Hollow Campground — ***CADIZ E-1***
□ Grandma's RV Park — ***SHEPHERDSVILLE C-3***
Grapevine Campground (COE-Fishtrap Lake) — ***PIKEVILLE D-6***
Grayson Lake State Park — ***GRAYSON C-5***
Green River Lake State Park — ***CAMPBELLSVILLE D-3***
Greenbo Lake State Resort Park — ***GREENUP B-6***
Gregory Lake RV Park — ***DRAKESBORO D-2***
Hillman Ferry Campground (LBL) — ***GOLDEN POND E-1***
Hillman Ferry (LBL) National Recreation Area — ***GRAND RIVERS B-2***
□ Holiday Hills Resort — ***EDDYVILLE D-1***
Holly Green RV Park — ***MURRAY B-2***
Holmes Bend Recreation Area (COE-Green River Lake) — ***CAMPBELLSVILLE D-3***
Holt's Campground — ***BARDSTOWN D-3***
Hurricane Creek Recreational Area (COE-Lake Barkley) — ***CADIZ E-1***
®□ I-75 Camper Village — ***DRY RIDGE B-4***
Indian Point RV Park — ***EDDYVILLE D-1***
□ Jenny Wiley State Resort Park — ***PRESTONSBURG D-6***
□ John James Audubon State Park — ***HENDERSON C-1***
Kendall Recreation Area (COE-Lake Cumberland) — ***JAMESTOWN E-3***
□ Kenlake State Resort Park — ***AURORA B-2***
□ Kentucky Dam Village State Resort Park — ***GILBERTSVILLE B-2***
Kentucky Horse Park (SP) — ***LEXINGTON C-4***
□ **Kentucky Lakes KOA at Prizer Point** — ***CADIZ E-1***
Kincaid Lake State Park — ***FALMOUTH B-4***
□ KOA-Bowling Green — ***BOWLING GREEN E-2***
□ KOA-Horse Cave — ***HORSE CAVE D-3***
□ KOA-Indian Hills — ***RUSSELL SPRINGS E-3***
□ KOA-KY Lake Dam/Paducah — ***CALVERT CITY B-2***
®□ **KOA-Renfro Valley** — ***RENFRO VALLEY D-4***
□ Lago Linda Resort — ***BEATTYVILLE D-5***
Lake Barkley RV Resort — ***EDDYVILLE D-1***
□ Lake Barkley State Resort Park — ***CADIZ E-1***
Lake Cumberland RV Park — ***BURNSIDE E-4***
□ Lake Cumberland State Resort Park — ***JAMESTOWN E-3***
Lake Malone State Park — ***DUNMOR E-2***
Lakeside Campground & Marina — ***AURORA B-2***
Laurel Branch Campground (COE- Rough River Lake) — ***MCDANIELS D-2***
Levi Jackson Wilderness Road State Park — ***LONDON D-4***
★ **Louisville RV Center** — ***LOUISVILLE C-3***
®□ **Louisville South KOA** — ***SHEPHERDSVILLE C-3***
□ Mammoth Cave Jellystone Park Camp Resort — ***CAVE CITY D-3***
Mammoth Cave NP (Headquarters Campground) — ***PARK CITY E-3***
□ MILITARY PARK (Camp Carlson Army Travel Camp) — ***MULDRAUGH C-3***
□ MILITARY PARK (Eagle's Rest Army Travel Camp-Fort Campbell) — ***HOPKINSVILLE E-1***
● **Miss Scarlett's Restaurant** — ***GRAND RIVERS B-2***
Moutardier (COE-Nolin River Lake) — ***LEITCHFIELD D-2***
★ **Murphy's RV's** — ***PRINCETON D-1***
My Old Kentucky Home SP — ***BARDSTOWN D-3***
□ Natural Bridge State Resort Park — ***SLADE D-5***
Nolin Lake State Park — ***LEITCHFIELD D-2***
North Fork (Corps of Engineers-Rough River Lake) — ***MCDANIELS D-2***
★ **Northside RV'S** — ***LEXINGTON C-4***
Oak Creek Campground — ***WALTON B-4***
Oh Kentucky Campground — ***BEREA D-4***
Ohio County Park — ***HARTFORD D-2***
□ Otter Creek Park (City of Louisville) — ***LOUISVILLE C-3***
Paintsville Lake State Park — ***STAFFORDSVILLE C-6***
Pennyrile Campground/Best Western Motel — ***MORTONS GAP D-1***
□ Pennyrile Forest State Resort Park — ***DAWSON SPRINGS D-1***
Pike Ridge (COE-Green River Lake) — ***CAMPBELLSVILLE D-3***
Pioneer Playhouse Trailer Park — ***DANVILLE D-4***
● **Poppy Mountain Blue Grass Festival** — ***MOREHEAD C-5***

KENTUCKY — Continued

Poppy Mountain Campground — MOREHEAD C-5
Red Hill Horse Camp — LIVINGSTON D-4
□ Renfro Valley RV Park — RENFRO VALLEY D-4
□ Rolling Hills Camping Resort — TAYLORSVILLE C-3
□ Rough River Dam State Resort Park — FALLS OF ROUGH D-2
Rushing Creek (LBL) National Recreation Area — GOLDEN POND E-1
• Shepherdsville Bullitt County Tourism — SHEPHERDSVILLE C-3
Singin Hills Campground and RV Park — CAVE CITY D-3
□ Smith Ridge (COE - Green River Lake) — CAMPBELLSVILLE D-3
□ Sportsman's Anchor Resort & Marina — AURORA B-2
Spring Hill RV Park — LUCAS E-3
Still Waters Campground — FRANKFORT C-4
®□ Sulphur Creek Resort — BURKESVILLE E-3
Tailwater Campground (COE-Buckhorn Lake) — BUCKHORN D-5
Taylorsville Lake State Park — TAYLORSVILLE C-3
□ The Falls Campground — LOUISA C-6
• The Landing Restaurant at Prizer Point Marina — CADIZ E-1
The Narrows (COE-Barren River Lake) — GLASGOW E-3
The Outpost RV Park — SALT LICK C-5
The Tailwater Below Dam (COE-Barren River Lake) — SCOTTSVILLE E-2
□ Three Springs Campground — CORINTH C-4
★ Tinker's Toys Dixie RV — LOUISVILLE C-3
Trace Branch (COE-Buckhorn Lake) — HYDEN D-5
Union County Fair & Expo Center — STURGIS A-2
Valley Breeze RV Campground — GRAYSON C-5
Waitsboro Rec Area (COE-Lake Cumberland) — SOMERSET E-4
Walnut Meadow RV Park — BEREA D-4
Wax Site (COE-Nolin River Lake) — LEITCHFIELD D-2
Western Kentucky RV Park — CENTRAL CITY D-2
Westgate RV Camping — LONDON D-4
White Acres Campground — BARDSTOWN D-3
Wildcat Creek Rec Area — MURRAY B-2
®□ Windy Hollow Campground & Recreation Area — OWENSBORO D-2
Wolf Creek Resort Park — RUSSELL SPRINGS E-3
Wrangler (LBL) National Recreation Area — GOLDEN POND E-1
Wranglers Campground (LBL) — GOLDEN POND E-1
Yatesville Lake SP — LOUISA C-6

LOUISIANA

• A Cajun Man's Swamp Cruise — HOUMA E-4
Abbeville RV Park — ABBEVILLE D-3
Ajax Country Livin' at I-49 Rv Park, LLC — AJAX B-2
• Avoyelles Parish Tourism Commission — MARKSVILLE C-3
B & B RV Park — DONALDSONVILLE D-4
□ Bayou Boeuf RV Park — STERLINGTON A-3
Bayou D'Arbonne Camping — WEST MONROE A-3
★ Bayou Outdoor Supercenter — BOSSIER CITY A-2
Bayou Wilderness RV Resort — CARENCRO D-3
★ Bent's RV — METAIRIE D-5
★ Berryland Campers — HAMMOND D-5
Betty's RV Park — ABBEVILLE D-3
• Biedenharn Museum & Gardens — MONROE A-3
★ Blanchard Trailer Sales — BATON ROUGE D-4
• Bonnie & Clyde Trade Days — ARCADIA A-2
□ Bonnie & Clyde Trade Days & Campground — ARCADIA A-2
• Breaux Bridge Tourist Commission — BREAUX BRIDGE D-3
□ Bridge Bay Resort — MANY B-2
• Cajun Coast Visitors & Convention Bureau — MORGAN CITY E-4
Cajun Country Campground — PORT ALLEN D-4
® Cajun Haven RV Park — EGAN D-3
□ Calloway RV & Campground — HAMMOND D-5
★ Campers RV Center — SHREVEPORT A-2
Campers RV Center — SHREVEPORT A-2
Capri Court MHP — HOUMA E-4
Carriage Cove MH & RVP — HOUMA E-4
★ Carter's Camping Center — WEST MONROE A-3
□ Cash Point Landing — BOSSIER CITY A-2
Chase's RV Park — NEW IBERIA D-3
□ Chemin-A-Haut State Park — BASTROP A-3
□ Chicot State Park — VILLE PLATTE C-3
City of Rayne RV Park — RAYNE D-3
Colfax Recreation Area RV Park & Campground — COLFAX B-3
Coushatta Luxury RV Resort At Red Shoes Park — KINDER D-3
□ Crooked Creek Rec. Area — PINE PRAIRIE C-3
□ Cypress Bend Park/Toledo Bend Lake (Sabine River Auth. Site 11) — MANY B-2
□ Cypress Black Bayou Recreation Area — BENTON A-2
• Diamond Jacks Casino Resort — BOSSIER CITY A-2
Diamond Jacks RV Park — BOSSIER CITY A-2
• Dixie RV SuperStores — HAMMOND D-5
Earl Williamson Park/Caddo Lake Park (Caddo Parish) — OIL CITY A-2
Fairview-Riverside State Park — MADISONVILLE D-5
Farr Park Campground & Horse Activity Center — BATON ROUGE D-4
• Felix Poche Plantation — CONVENT D-4
□ Felix Poche Plantation RV Resort — CONVENT D-4
Fountainebleau State Park — MANDEVILLE D-5
French Quarter RV Resort — NEW ORLEANS D-5
□ Frenchman's Wilderness — HENDERSON D-3
Frog City RV Park — DUSON D-3
★ G & J Mobile Home & RV Supplies — LAFAYETTE D-3
★ Gauthiers' RV Service Center — LAFAYETTE D-3
□ Grand Bayou Resort — COUSHATTA B-2
Grand Isle State Park — GRAND ISLE E-5
Green Acres Campground & RV Park — ST. FRANCISVILLE C-4
□ Hidden Oaks Family Campground — HAMMOND D-5
□ Hidden Ponds RV Park — SULPHUR D-2
★ Hope's Camper Corner — MONROE A-3
• Houma Area Convention & Visitors Bureau — HOUMA E-4
I-10 Mobile Village & RV Campground — LAKE CHARLES D-2
• Iberia Parish Convention & Visitors Bureau — NEW IBERIA D-3
□ Indian Creek Campground & RV Park LLC — INDEPENDENCE C-5
Indian Creek Recreation Area (Alexander SF) — WOODWORTH C-3
Interstate RV Park — MINDEN A-2
□ Jimmy Davis State Park of Caney Lake — CHATHAM A-3
Jude Travel Park & Guest House — NEW ORLEANS D-5
• Jungle Gardens — AVERY ISLAND D-3
Kelly's RV Park — SHREVEPORT A-2
Kemper Williams Park (St. Mary Parish Park) — MORGAN CITY E-4
Kisatchie National Forest (Kincaid Rec. Site) — GARDNER C-3
□ KOA-Baton Rouge East — DENHAM SPRINGS D-4
□ KOA-Lafayette — LAFAYETTE D-3
KOA-New Orleans West — NEW ORLEANS D-5
□ KOA-Shreveport/Bossier City — SHREVEPORT A-2
KOC Kampground — NEW IBERIA D-3
• Konriko Rice Mill and Company Store — NEW IBERIA D-3
La Place Trailer Park & Campground — LA PLACE D-5
LaBoulaie RV Park & Campground — BROUSSARD D-3
□ L'Acadie Inn RV Park — EUNICE D-3
• Lafayette Convention & Visitors Commission — LAFAYETTE D-3
□ Lake Bistineau State Park — DOYLINE A-2
Lake Bruin State Park — ST. JOSEPH B-4
□ Lake Claiborne State Park — HOMER A-2
Lake D'Arbonne State Park — FARMERVILLE A-3
Lake End RV Campground (Municipal Park) — MORGAN CITY E-4
□ Lake Fausse Pointe State Park — ST. MARTINVILLE D-3
□ Lakeside RV Park — LIVINGSTON D-4
Lakeside RV Park — MINDEN A-2
Lamar Dixon Expo Center RV Park — GONZALES D-4
®□ Land-O-Pines Family Campground — COVINGTON D-5
Lapeyrouse Camping — CHAUVIN E-5
Lincoln Parish Park — RUSTON A-3
Linda's Campground & RV Park — GIBSON E-4
• Louisiana Travel Promotion Association — BATON ROUGE D-4
Maplewood RV Park — BOSSIER CITY A-2
Mardi Gras RV Park & Red Carpet Inn & Suites — NEW ORLEANS D-5

LOUISIANA — Continued

Maxie's Campground — BROUSSARD D-3
• McIlHenny Co — AVERY ISLAND D-3
MILITARY PARK (Barksdale AFB FAMCAMP) — BOSSIER CITY A-2
® MILITARY PARK (New Orleans NAS Travel Camp) — BELLE CHASSE D-5
MILITARY PARK (Toledo Bend Rec Site-Fort Polk) — LEESVILLE C-2
★ Miller's RV Center — BATON ROUGE D-4
□ Monroe's Shiloh Campground & RV Resort — MONROE A-3
• Morehouse Parish Tourism Commission — BASTROP A-3
Nakatosh Campground — NATCHITOCHES B-2
□ Natalbany Creek Campground — AMITE C-5
□ New Orleans East Kampground — SLIDELL D-5
New Orleans RV Campground — NEW ORLEANS D-5
• New Rockdale Radio Shop — MANSFIELD B-2
New Rockdale RV Park — MANSFIELD B-2
□ North Toledo Bend State Park — ZWOLLE B-2
Old River Campground — WHITEHALL B-3
Opelousas City Park — OPELOUSAS D-3
• Paragon Casino — MARKSVILLE C-3
□ Paragon Casino RV Resort — MARKSVILLE C-3
Parkside Marina & RV Park — LAKE CHARLES D-2
□ Pavilion RV Park — WEST MONROE A-3
Pecan Acres RV Park — LEESVILLE C-2
Pine Crest RV Park — SLIDELL D-5
□ Pleasure Point/Toledo Bend Lake (Sabine River Auth. Site 15) — HORNBECK C-2
□ Poche's Fish-N-Camp — BREAUX BRIDGE D-3
• Poche's Market, Restaurant & Smokehouse — BREAUX BRIDGE D-3
• Prejean's Restaurant — LAFAYETTE D-3
Punkin Park Campground — HAMMOND D-5
Quiet Oaks RV Park — FENTON D-2
• Randol's Restaurant & Cajun Dance Hall — LAFAYETTE D-3
Rapides Coliseum (Parish Park) — ALEXANDRIA C-3
• River Parishes Tourist Commission — LA PLACE D-5
River View RV Park — VIDALIA B-4
Riverboat RV Park — NEW ORLEANS D-5
Riverton Lake Campground — COLUMBIA B-3
• Ruston/Lincoln Convention & Visitors Bureau — RUSTON A-3
Saint Bernard State Park — VIOLET D-5
• St. Tammany Parish Tourist & Convention Commission — MANDEVILLE D-5
□ Sam Houston Jones State Park — LAKE CHARLES D-2
□ San Miguel Park/Toledo Bend Lake (Sabine River Auth. Site 7-A) — ZWOLLE B-2
Shady Lake RV Park — LEESVILLE C-2
® Shiloh's Lake Bruin Resort — ST. JOSEPH B-4
• Shreveport/Bossier Convention & Tourist Bureau — SHREVEPORT A-2
Sibley Lake Mini-Mart & Campground — NATCHITOCHES B-2
• Southwest Louisiana Convention & Visitors Bureau — LAKE CHARLES D-2
Springhill RV Park (City Park) — SPRINGHILL A-2
®□ Sweetwater Campground & RV Park — LORANGER C-5
• Tangipahoa Parish Tourist Commission — HAMMOND D-5
□ Tchefuncte Family Campground — FOLSOM C-5
Texas Pelican Complex — VINTON D-2
★ The RV Shop — BATON ROUGE D-4
□ Tickfaw State Park — SPRINGFIELD D-5
□ V RV Park-Lake Charles/Vinton — VINTON D-2
Whispering Meadow RV Park — LAKE CHARLES D-2
□ Yogi Bear's Jellystone Park Camp-Resort — LAKE CHARLES D-2

MISSISSIPPI

□ Archusa Creek Water Park (Pat Harrison Waterway District) — QUITMAN D-4
Askew's Landing Campground — EDWARDS D-2
Atwood Water Park (Pearl River Basin Dev. Dist.) — MONTICELLO E-3
Audubon Point RV Park — HORN LAKE A-3
Bay Berry RV Park — GULFPORT F-4
Bay Hide Away RV & Camping Resort — BAY ST. LOUIS F-4
Bay Marina & RV Park — BAY ST. LOUIS F-4
® Baywood RV Park and Campground, Inc. — GULFPORT F-4
Benchmark Coach and RV Park — MERIDIAN D-4
Bienville National Forest (Marathon Campground) — FOREST D-3
□ Big Creek Water Park (Pat Harrison Waterway District) — SOSO E-4
Blue Bluff Campground (COE-Tennessee/Tombigbee Waterway) — ABERDEEN B-4
□ Bogue Chitto Water Park Campground (Pearl River Basin Dev. Dist.) — MCCOMB E-2
Bonita Lakes RV Park — MERIDIAN D-4
Buccaneer SP — WAVELAND F-3
Buck Island MHC — ROBINSONVILLE A-3
Cajun RV Park — BILOXI F-4
®□ Camp Journey's End — OCEAN SPRINGS F-4
★ Camper Corral — MADISON D-3
Campgrounds at Barnes Crossing — TUPELO B-4
Chickasaw Hill Campground (COE-Enid Lake) — ENID B-3
• Clark Creek Nature Park — WOODVILLE E-1
□ Clarkco SP — QUITMAN D-4
®□ Clearwater RV Park — PICAYUNE F-3
Coal Bluff Park (Pearl River Valley Water Supply District) — LUDLOW D-3
® Country Side RV Park & Tradin Post — GULFPORT F-4
Dewayne Hayes Campground (COE-Tennessee/Tombigbee Waterway) — COLUMBUS B-5
□ D'Lo Water Park (Pearl River Basin Dev. Dist.) — MENDENHALL D-3
Dry Creek Water Park (Pat Harrison Waterway District) — MOUNT OLIVE E-3
Dub Patton Campground (COE-Arkabutla Lake) — COLDWATER A-3
□ Dunn's Falls Water Park (Pat Harrison Waterway District) — ENTERPRISE D-4
Elvis Presley Lake & Campground (County Park) — TUPELO B-4
EZ Daze RV Park — SOUTHAVEN A-3
□ Flint Creek Water Park (Pat Harrison Waterway District) — WIGGINS F-4
Frog Hollow Campground/RV Park — GRENADA B-3
Frog Level RV Park — PHILADELPHIA C-4
□ George Payne Cossar SP — OAKLAND B-3
• Golden Memorial State Park — WALNUT GROVE D-3
Goshen Springs Campground (Pearl River Valley Water Supply District) — JACKSON D-3
Grand Casino RV Resort — TUNICA A-2
Grand Gulf Military Park Campground (State) — PORT GIBSON D-2
Great River Road SP — ROSEDALE B-2
Gulf Islands National Seashore (Davis Bayou Area) — OCEAN SPRINGS F-4
Harrison County Fairgrounds — GULFPORT F-4
Hernando Point (COE - Arkabutla Lake) — COLDWATER A-3
Holly Springs National Forest (Chewalla Lake Campground) — HOLLY SPRINGS A-3
• Hollywood Casino — BAY ST. LOUIS F-4
• Hollywood Casino — TUNICA A-2
Hollywood Casino RV Park — BAY ST. LOUIS F-4
Hollywood Casino RV Resort — TUNICA A-2
□ Holmes County SP — DURANT C-3
Homewood Manor MH & RV Park — JACKSON D-3
□ Hugh White SP — GRENADA B-3
®□ Indian Point RV Resort — GAUTIER F-4
Isle of Capri RV Park — VICKSBURG D-2
□ John Kyle SP & Mallard Point Golf Course — SARDIS A-3
□ JP Coleman SP — IUKA A-5
□ KOA-Meridian East/Toomsuba — MERIDIAN D-4
Lake Lincoln SP — WESSON E-2
□ Lake Lowndes SP — COLUMBUS B-5
®□ Lakeview RV Resort — BILOXI F-4
Leake County Water Park (Pearl River Valley Water Supply District) — LENA D-3

MISSISSIPPI — Continued

LeFleur's Bluff SP & Golf Course — JACKSON D-3
□ Legion SP — LOUISVILLE C-4
□ Leroy Percy SP — HOLLANDALE C-2
□ Little Black Creek Water Park (Pat Harrison Waterway District) — LUMBERTON E-3
Low Head Dam (Pearl River Valley Water Supply District) — LENA D-3
Magnolia RV Park Resort — VICKSBURG D-2
Majestic Oaks RV Resort — BILOXI F-4
□ Maynor Creek Water Park (Pat Harrison Waterway District) — WAYNESBORO E-4
□ Mazalea Travel Park — BILOXI F-4
McLeod Water Park — BAY ST. LOUIS F-4
Memphis South Campground & RV Park — COLDWATER A-3
MILITARY PARK (Lake Walker Family Campground-Camp Shelby) — HATTIESBURG E-4
□ Mimosa Landing Campground — COLUMBIA E-3
Mississippi Petrified Forest Campground — FLORA D-3
• Mississippi State Parks — JACKSON D-3
®□ Movietown RV Resort — CANTON D-3
Nanabe Creek Campground — MERIDIAN D-4
□ Natchez SP — NATCHEZ E-1
• Natchez Trace Compact — NATCHEZ E-1
Natchez Trace Parkway (Rocky Springs Campground) — PORT GIBSON D-2
Natchez Trace RV Park — TUPELO B-4
□ Okatibbee Water Park (Pat Harrison Waterway District) — MERIDIAN D-4
®□ Okatoma River Resort & RV Park — HATTIESBURG E-4
□ Parker's Landing RV Park — BILOXI F-4
□ Paul B Johnson SP — HATTIESBURG E-4
□ Percy Quin SP & Quail Hollow Golf Course — MCCOMB E-2
Perk Beach RV Park and Campground — WIGGINS F-4
Persimmon Hill-South Abutment (COE-Enid Lake) — ENID B-3
® Pickard's RV Park — MT. PLEASANT A-3
Piney Grove Campground (COE-Tennessee/Tombigbee Waterway) — BURTON A-5
Plantation Pines RV Resort — LONG BEACH ??
River Town Campground — VICKSBURG D-2
□ Roosevelt SP — MORTON D-3
★ S & S Apache Camping Center — JACKSON D-3
Sam's Town RV Park — TUNICA A-2
Shady Acres RV Community — BAY ST. LOUIS F-4
Shady Cove RV Park — HATTIESBURG E-4
□ Shepard SP — GAUTIER F-4
South Abutment Campground (COE-Arkabutla Lake) — COLDWATER A-3
★ Southaven RV Centers — OLIVE BRANCH A-3
★ Southaven RV Centers — SOUTHAVEN A-3
Southaven RV Park — SOUTHAVEN A-3
Southern Comfort Camping Resort — BILOXI F-4
Southern Oaks MH & RV Community — GULFPORT F-4
Springridge RV Park — CLINTON D-2
Sun Roamers RV Resort — PICAYUNE F-3
Swinging Bridge RV Park — BYRAM D-3
Timberlake Campground (Pearl River Valley Water Supply District) — JACKSON D-3
□ Tishomingo SP — TISHOMINGO A-5
Tombigbee National Forest (Davis Lake Campground) — HOUSTON B-4
□ Tombigbee SP — TUPELO B-4
Town Creek Campground (COE-Tennessee/Tombigbee Waterway) — COLUMBUS B-5
□ Trace SP — TUPELO B-4
□ Turkey Creek Water Park (Pat Harrison Waterway District — DECATUR D-4
Twiltley Branch Camping Area (COE-Okatibbee Lake) — MERIDIAN D-4
• Vanelli's Greek & Italian Restaurant — TUPELO B-4
□ Wall Doxey SP — HOLLY SPRINGS A-3
Wallace Creek (COE-Enid Lake) — ENID B-3
Warfield Point Park (Washington County Park) — GREENVILLE C-2
Water Valley Landing Campground (COE-Enid Lake) — ENID B-3
Wendy Oaks RV Resort — FLORENCE D-3
Whitten Park — FULTON A-5
Yogi On The Lake — PELAHATCHIE D-3

NORTH CAROLINA

70 East Mobile Acres & RV Park — GARNER B-4
®□ Adventure Trail Campground — CHEROKEE E-1
★ Allsport Camping Center — FAYETTEVILLE C-3
Apple Valley Travel Park — HENDERSONVILLE E-2
®□ Asheville East-KOA — SWANNANOA E-2
□ Asheville-Bear Creek RV Park — ASHEVILLE E-2
Bandit's Roost Park (COE-W. Kerr Scott Reservoir) — WILKESBORO A-1
• Battleship North Carolina — WILMINGTON D-4
Beachcomber Campground — OCRACOKE C-6
□ Bear Den Campground — SPRUCE PINE D-3
□ Birchwood RV Park — DURHAM A-3
□ Black Forest Family Camping Resort — CEDAR MOUNTAIN E-2
Blue Ridge National Parkway (Crabtree Meadows Campground) — LITTLE SWITZERLAND D-3
Blue Ridge National Parkway (Doughton Park Campground) — SPARTA A-1
Blue Ridge National Parkway (Julian Price Memorial Campground) — BLOWING ROCK A-1
Blue Ridge National Parkway (Linville Falls Campground) — LINVILLE FALLS D-3
Blue Ridge National Parkway (Mt. Pisgah) — ASHEVILLE E-2
□ Bradley's Campground — CHEROKEE E-1
• Buck Creek Driving Range — MARION E-3
Buck Creek RV Park Campground & Driving Range — MARION E-3
★ Bumgarner Camping Center — HUDSON B-1
®□ Cabin Creek Campground — JACKSONVILLE C-5
□ Camp Adventure Family Campground — LAKE JUNALUSKA E-2
Camp Hatteras — RODANTHE B-6
□ Campfire Lodgings — ASHEVILLE E-2
□ Cane Creek Park (Union County Park) — MONROE C-2
★ Cape Fear RV & Canoe Center — LILLINGTON B-3
□ Cape Hatteras KOA — RODANTHE B-6
Cape Hatteras National Seashore (Cape Point Campground) — BUXTON B-6
Cape Hatteras National Seashore (Frisco Campground) — FRISCO B-6
Cape Hatteras National Seashore (Ocracoke Campground) — OCRACOKE C-6
Cape Hatteras National Seashore (Oregon Inlet Campground) — NAGS HEAD A-6
□ Cape Woods Campground — BUXTON B-6
Carolina Beach State Park — CAROLINA BEACH D-4
• Carowinds — CHARLOTTE B-2
®□ Cartoogechaye Creek Campground — FRANKLIN E-1
□ Catawaba Falls Campground — OLD FORT E-2
□ Cavowinds Camp Wilderness Resort — CHARLOTTE B-2
Cedar Creek Campground — SEALEVEL C-6
®□ Cherokee Campground — CHEROKEE E-1
Cliffs of the Neuse State Park — GOLDSBORO B-4
Cooper's Mobile Home Park & RV's — CLAYTON B-4
Country Boy's RV Park — BRYSON CITY E-1
Country Woods RV Park — FRANKLIN E-1
□ Cove Creek RV Park — OLD FORT E-2
□ Creekwood Farm RV Park — WAYNESVILLE E-2
★ Crisp RV Center — WASHINGTON B-5
Croatan National Forest (Cedar Point Campground) — SWANSBORO C-5

NORTH CAROLINA — Continued

Cross Country Campground — DENVER B-1
★ Daly RV — GOLDSBORO B-4
Dan Nicholas Park (Rowan County Park) — SALISBURY B-2
Dan River Campground — STONEVILLE A-2
□ Deep Creek Tube Center & Campground — BRYSON CITY E-1
□ Deep River Campground & RV Park — ASHEBORO B-2
Driftwood Campground — CEDAR ISLAND C-6
®□ Ela Campground — BRYSON CITY E-1
• Emerald Isle Wine Market — EMERALD ISLE C-5
Falls Lake State Rec. Area (Holly Point Campground) — RALEIGH B-4
Falls Lake State Rec. Area (Rollingview Campground) — RALEIGH B-4
□ Fayetteville KOA — WADE C-3
Fayetteville Spring Valley Park — HOPE MILLS C-3
Fiddlers Grove Campground — UNION GROVE A-2
Fieldridge Acres — CHARLOTTE B-2
Flaming Arrow Campground — CHEROKEE E-1
Fleetwood RV Racing Camping Resort at Charlotte — CHARLOTTE B-2
□ Flintlock Campground — BOONE A-1
□ Foothills Family Campground — FOREST CITY B-1
®□ Fort Wilderness Campground and RV Resort — CHEROKEE E-1
Four Oaks RV Resort — SMITHFIELD B-4
®□ Four Paws Kingdom — RUTHERFORDTON E-3
Franklin RV Park & Campground — FRANKLIN E-1
□ Frisco Woods Campground — FRISCO B-6
Ft Tatham RV Park — SYLVA E-2
Golden Pond Campground — SALISBURY B-2
Goose Creek Resort Family Campground — CAPE CARTERET C-5
□ Grandfather Campground — FOSCOE A-1
Great Smokey Mountain RV Camping Resort — CHEROKEE E-1
Great Smoky Mountains National Park (Balsam Mountain Campground) — CHEROKEE E-1
Great Smoky Mountains National Park (Cataloochee Campground) — COVE CREEK E-2
Great Smoky Mountains National Park (Deep Creek Campground) — BRYSON CITY E-1
Great Smoky Mountains National Park (Smokemont Campground) — CHEROKEE E-1
□ Green Acres Family Campground — WILLIAMSTON B-5
□ Greensboro Campground — GREENSBORO A-2
Hampton Lodge Camping Resort — COINJOCK A-6
□ Hanging Rock State Park — WALNUT COVE A-2
□ Happy Holiday RV Park & Campground — CHEROKEE E-1
®□ Hatteras Sands RV Resort — HATTERAS B-6
Hawkins Creek Campground — HUBERT C-5
□ High Rock Lake Marina & Campground — LEXINGTON B-2
Holiday Trav-L-Park Resort For Campers — EMERALD ISLE C-5
Holly Bluff Family Campground — ASHEBORO B-2
□ Holly Cove & RV Resort & Cabins — WHITTIER E-1
□ Holly Ridge Family Campground — BOONVILLE A-2
□ Hot Springs Campground & Suites — HOT SPRINGS D-2
★ Howard RV Center — WILMINGTON D-4
®□ Indian Creek Campground — CHEROKEE E-1
Jaymar Travel Park — HENDERSONVILLE E-2
• Jonas Ridge Snowtubing — MORGANTON B-1
Jones Lake State Park — ELIZABETHTOWN C-4
Jordan Lake State Rec. Area (Crosswinds Campground) — APEX B-3
Jordan Lake State Rec. Area (Parkers Creek) — APEX B-3
Jordan Lake State Rec. Area (Poplar Point) — APEX B-3
Jordan Lake State Rec. Area (Vista Point) — APEX B-3
Kamper's Lodge of America — WILSON B-4
Kerr State Rec. Area (Bullocksville) — HENDERSON A-4
Kerr State Rec. Area (County Line Park) — NORLINA A-4
Kerr State Rec. Area (Henderson Point) — HENDERSON A-4
Kerr State Rec. Area (Hibernia) — HENDERSON A-4
Kerr State Rec. Area (Kimball Point Park) — NORLINA A-4
Kerr State Rec. Area (Nutbush Bridge) — HENDERSON A-4
□ Kerr State Rec. Area (Satterwhite Points) — HENDERSON A-4
KOA Shallotte/Brunswick Beaches — SUNSET BEACH D-4
□ KOA-Asheville West — CANDLER E-2
□ KOA-Boone — BOONE A-1
□ KOA-Cherokee Great Smokies — CHEROKEE E-1
□ KOA-Enfield-Rocky Mt. — GLENVIEW A-4
□ KOA-Statesville — STATESVILLE B-2
Lake James State Park — MARION E-3
□ Lake Myers RV Resort — MOCKSVILLE B-2
Lake Norman Motor Coach Resort — TERRELL B-1
Lake Norman State Park — STATESVILLE B-2
Lake Reidsville Recreation Park (City Park) — REIDSVILLE A-3
Lake Waldo's Beach Campground — HOPE MILLS C-3
Lakewood RV Resort — HENDERSONVILLE E-2
Lanier's Campground — SURF CITY D-5
Lazy Acres Campground — FAYETTEVILLE C-3
® Lazy Boy Travel Park — HENDERSONVILLE E-2
®□ Linville Falls Trailer Lodge & Campground — LINVILLE FALLS D-3
Long Leaf Pine Oasis — ABERDEEN C-3
□ Mama Gertie's Hideaway Campground — SWANNANOA E-2
△ McDowell Nature Preserve — CHARLOTTE B-2
△□ McDowell Nature Preserve Campground — CHARLOTTE B-2
Merchants Millpond State Park — GATESVILLE A-5
□ Mi Mountain Campground — FRANKLIN E-1
□ Midway Campground & RV Resort — STATESVILLE B-2
• Midway Trail of Horror — STATESVILLE B-2
Miles Motors RV Campground — SWANNANOA E-2
★ Miles Motors RV Center — SWANNANOA E-2
MILITARY PARK (Cherry Point MCAS Travel Camp) — HAVELOCK C-5
MILITARY PARK (Fort Bragg Travel Camp) — FAYETTEVILLE C-3
□ MILITARY PARK (Fort Fisher Air Force Rec. Area) — KURE BEACH D-4
MILITARY PARK (New River Rec. Area) — JACKSONVILLE C-5
MILITARY PARK (Onslow Beach Recreation Area-Camp Lejeune MCB) — JACKSONVILLE C-5
Moonlight Lake RV Park & Campground — NEW BERN C-5
®□ Moonshine Creek Campground — BALSAM E-2
Morrow Mountain State Park — ALBEMARLE B-2
★ Mountain Camper Sales & Service — HENDERSONVILLE E-2
Mountain Stream RV Park — MARION E-3
Nantahala National Forest (Cable Cove Campground) — FONTANA VILLAGE E-1
Nantahala National Forest (Cheoah Point Rec. Area) — ROBBINSVILLE E-1
Nantahala National Forest (Hanging Dog Campground) — MURPHY E-1
Nantahala National Forest (Jackrabbit Mountain Campground) — HAYESVILLE E-1
Nantahala National Forest (Standing Indian Campground) — FRANKLIN E-1
Nantahala National Forest (Tsali Recreational Area) — ALMOND E-1
□ New Bern KOA — NEW BERN C-5
North River Campground & RV Park — SHILOH A-6
Oak Hollow Family Campground (City Park) — HIGH POINT B-2
Ocean Waves Campground — RODANTHE B-6
□ Optimistic Park RV Resort & Campground — MORGANTON B-1
□ Orchard Lake Campground & RV Park — SALUDA E-2
★ Out-of-Doors Mart — GREENSBORO A-2
• Outer Banks Visitors Bureau — MANTEO A-6
Outside Inn Campground — FRANKLIN E-1
Park Place RV Park — HENDERSONVILLE E-2
□ Peace Valley Campground & Cabins — MURPHY E-1
Phil & Ann's RV Service — HENDERSONVILLE E-2
Pilot Mountain State Park — PINNACLE A-2
®□ Pine Lake RV Resort — ABERDEEN C-3
□ Pines RV Park — FRANKLIN E-1
Pisgah Nantahala National Forest (Carolina Hemlock Park) — MICAVILLE D-2
Pisgah National Forest (Black Mountain Campground) — MICAVILLE D-2
Pisgah National Forest (Davidson River Campground) — BREVARD E-2
Pisgah National Forest (Lake Powhatan Rec. Area) — ASHEVILLE E-2
Pisgah National Forest (North Mills River Rec. Area) — ASHEVILLE E-2

NORTH CAROLINA — Continued

Pisgah National Forest (Rocky Bluff Campground) — HOT SPRINGS D-2
• Pride Cafe — WAYNESVILLE E-2
□ Pride RV Resort — WAYNESVILLE E-2
® Raccoon Holler Campground — GLENDALE SPRINGS A-1
□ Red Gates RV Park — HENDERSONVILLE E-2
□ Rippling Waters Creekside RV Park — MAGGIE VALLEY E-2
• River Camp USA Canoe, Kayak & Tubing — PINEY CREEK A-1
□ River Creek Campground — LAKE LURE E-2
River Valley Campground — CHEROKEE E-1
□ RiverCamp USA RV Park & Campground — PINEY CREEK A-1
Rivers Edge Mountain RV Resort — MURPHY E-1
Rock Ridge Campground — ROCK RIDGE B-4
Rocky Hock Campground — EDENTON A-5
□ Rutledge Lake RV Park — FLETCHER E-2
RVacation Campground — SELMA B-4
□ Sands of Time Campground — AVON B-6
Scenic Mobile Home/RV Park — ASHEVILLE E-2
Sky High Ridge Motorcoach Park — HIGHLANDS E-2
®□ Sleepy Bear's RV Park — LUMBERTON C-3
□ Smithfield KOA — SMITHFIELD B-4
Spring Hill Park — CHAPEL HILL B-3
□ Steele Creek Park — MORGANTON B-1
□ Stone Bridge RV Park — MAGGIE VALLEY E-2
Stone Mountain State Park — ROARING GAP A-1
★ Sunbird RV Repair Service — FAYETTEVILLE C-3
Surf City Resorts — SURF CITY D-5
Tamarac Marina & Campground — SALISBURY B-2
Taps RV Park — ASHEVILLE E-2
The Campground at Tom Johnson Camping Center — MARION E-3
★ The Family RV Center — STATESVILLE B-2
The Great Outdoors RV Resort — FRANKLIN E-1
• The New Waldo's Beach Park — HOPE MILLS C-3
• The Pirates Chest — CEDAR ISLAND C-6
The Refuge — MANTEO A-6
The RV Resort at Carolina Crossroads — ROANOKE RAPIDS A-4
Timberlake Campground — WHITTIER E-1
★ Tom Johnson Camping Center — CONCORD B-2
★ Tom Johnson Camping Center — MARION E-3
Town Mountain Travel Park — HENDERSONVILLE E-2
Trails End Family Camping — ASHEBORO B-2
△□ Tranter's Creek Resort & Campground — WASHINGTON B-5
®□ Tumbling Waters Campground — ALMOND E-1
Turkey Creek Campground — ALMOND E-1
□ Twin Lakes Camping Resort and Yacht Basin — WASHINGTON B-5
® Twin Ponds RV Park — HENDERSONVILLE E-2
Twin Rivers Family Campground — CRUMPLER A-1
Valley River RV Resort — MURPHY E-1
□ Van Hoy Farms Family Campground — UNION GROVE A-2
Vanderpool Campground — VILAS A-1
Village of Pinehurst RV Park — PINEHURST B-3
Warrior Creek Park (COE-W. Kerr Scott Reservoir) — WILKESBORO A-1
Waterway RV Resort — CAPE CARTERET C-5
Waterwheel RV Park — BOONE A-1
Whispering Pines Family Campground — MOREHEAD CITY C-5
White Oak Shores Camping & RV Resort — STELLA C-5
Wildlife Woods Campground — DENVER B-1
William B Umstead State Park — RALEIGH B-4
□ Wilmington-KOA — WILMINGTON D-4
□ Winngray Family Campground — WAYNESVILLE E-2
Wishing Well Campground — SUNSET BEACH D-4
□ Yogi Bear's Jellystone Park at Daddy Joe's — TABOR CITY D-3
Yogi Bear's Jellystone Park Camp Resort — MARION E-3
□ Yogi in the Smokies — CHEROKEE E-1

SOUTH CAROLINA

Aiken State Natural Area — AIKEN C-3
®□ Anderson/Lake Hartwell KOA — ANDERSON B-2
Andrew Jackson State Park — LANCASTER A-4
® Apache Family Campground — MYRTLE BEACH C-6
April Valley RV Park — EASLEY A-2
Baker Creek State Park — MCCORMICK C-2
□ Barnwell State Park — BLACKVILLE C-3
• Barnyard Flea Market — COLUMBIA B-3
Barnyard RV Park — COLUMBIA B-3
Big Cypress Lake RV Park & Fishing Retreat — CONWAY C-6
Broxton Bridge Plantation — EHRHARDT D-3
Calhoun Falls State Recreation Area — CALHOUN FALLS B-2
Camp Pedro — SOUTH OF THE BORDER B-5
□ Campground at James Island County Park — CHARLESTON D-5
• Campground Massacre Haunted Attraction — FORT MILL A-4
Cane Creek Motor Coach Resort — GREENWOOD B-2
Cedar Pond Campground — LEESVILLE C-3
□ Charlotte/Fort Mill KOA — FORT MILL A-4
□ Cheraw State Recreation Area — CHERAW A-5
Chester State Park — CHESTER A-3
Colleton State Park — CANADYS D-4
Comfort Inn RV Park — ST. GEORGE D-4
Coneross Campground (COE-Hartwell Lake) — TOWNVILLE B-1
Croft State Natural Area — SPARTANBURG A-2
• Crooked Creek Pizza Shoppe & Snack Bar — SENECA A-1
□ Crooked Creek RV Park — SENECA A-1
Crossroads RV Park & Mobile Home Community — AIKEN C-3
Cunningham RV Park — SPARTANBURG A-2
□ Devils Fork State Park — WALHALLA A-1
★ Don Mar RV Sales — FLORENCE B-5
□ Dreher Island State Recreation Area — CHAPIN B-3
Ebenezer Park — ROCK HILL A-3
□ Edisto Beach State Park — EDISTO ISLAND E-4
Edmund RV Park — LEXINGTON B-3
□ Florence KOA — FLORENCE B-5
□ Givhans Ferry State Park — SUMMERVILLE D-4
Hamilton Branch State Recreation Area — MCCORMICK C-2
Hardeeville RV-Thomas' Parks and Sites — HARDEEVILLE E-3
Hawe Creek Campground (COE-J. Strom Thurmond Lake) — MCCORMICK C-2
□ Hickory Knob State Resort Park — MCCORMICK C-2
Hilton Head Harbor RV Resort & Marina — HILTON HEAD ISLAND E-4
Hilton Head Island Motor Coach Resort — HILTON HEAD ISLAND E-4
□ Hunting Island State Park — BEAUFORT E-4
Huntington Beach State Park — MURRELLS INLET C-6
★ Jody's RV — GREENWOOD B-2
Jolly Acres Camp & Storage — ST. GEORGE D-4
□ Keowee-Toxaway State Natural Area — PICKENS A-2
Kings Mountain State Park — YORK A-3
□ KOA-Charleston — CHARLESTON D-5
®□ KOA-Myrtle Beach — MYRTLE BEACH C-6
□ KOA-Point South — POINT SOUTH D-4
• KOA-Point South Carry Out Pizza — POINT SOUTH D-4
Lake Aire RV Park and Campground — CHARLESTON D-5
Lake Greenwood State Recreation Area — GREENWOOD B-2
®□ Lake Hartwell Camping & Cabins — ANDERSON B-2
Lake Hartwell RV Park — FAIR PLAY B-1
Lake Hartwell State Recreation Area — FAIR PLAY B-1
Lake Wateree State Recreation Area — WINNSBORO B-3
□ Lakeside Lodges & Campground — FORT MILL A-4
® Lakewood Camping Resort — MYRTLE BEACH C-6
Lee State Natural Area — BISHOPVILLE B-4
Little Pee Dee State Park — DILLON B-5
□ Magnolia RV Park & Campground — JOANNA B-3
△ MILITARY PARK (Shady Oaks Family Campground-Charleston AFB) — CHARLESTON D-5

SOUTH CAROLINA — Continued

MILITARY PARK (Short Stay Rec Area-Charleston Naval Sta.) — BONNEAU C-5
®□ MILITARY PARK (Wateree Recreation Area and FAMCAMP-Shaw AFB) — SUMTER C-4
□ MILITARY PARK (Weston Lake Rec. Area-Ft. Jackson) — COLUMBIA B-3
Modoc Campground (COE-J. Strom Thurmond Lake) — CLARKS HILL C-2
Mt. Carmel Campground (COE-J. Strom Thurmond Lake) — MCCORMICK C-2
□ Mt. Pleasant/Charleston KOA — CHARLESTON D-5
• Myrtle Beach Campground Association — MYRTLE BEACH C-6
□ Myrtle Beach State Park — MYRTLE BEACH C-6
® Myrtle Beach Travel Park — MYRTLE BEACH C-6
New Green Acres R.V. Park — WALTERBORO D-4
Oak Plantation Campground — CHARLESTON D-5
□ Ocean Lakes Family Campground — MYRTLE BEACH C-6
Oconee Point Campground (COE - Hartwell Lake) — TOWNVILLE B-1
□ Oconee State Park — WALHALLA A-1
Paris Mountain State Park — GREENVILLE A-2
® Pine Acres Campground — AIKEN C-3
®□ Pine Cone Campground — GAFFNEY A-3
®□ Pine Ridge Campground — ROEBUCK A-2
® Pirateland Family Camping Resort — MYRTLE BEACH C-6
□ Poinsett State Park — WEDGEFIELD C-4
Rainbow RV Park — GREENVILLE A-2
□ River Bottom Farms Campground & R.V. Resort — SWANSEA C-3
® Rocks Pond Campground & Marina — EUTAWVILLE C-4
Sadlers Creek State Recreation Park — ANDERSON B-2
Santee Lakes Campground — SANTEE C-4
□ Santee State Park — SANTEE C-4
Scuffletown USA Campground — GREENVILLE A-2
Sesquicentennial State Park — COLUMBIA B-3
Shuman's RV Trailer Park — CANADYS D-4
• South Carolina State Parks — COLUMBIA B-3
• South of the Border — SOUTH OF THE BORDER B-5
• Splash Zone Waterpark — CHARLESTON D-5
Springfield Campground (COE-Hartwell Lake) — ANDERSON B-2
Springwood RV Park — GREENVILLE A-2
Sumter National Forest (Parson's Mountain Lake Campground) — ABBEVILLE B-2
Sumter NF (Cherry Hill Campground) — WALHALLA A-1
Sumter NF (Woods Ferry Campground) — CHESTER A-3
Swamp Fox Camping — FLORENCE B-5
Sweetwater Lake Campground — ORANGEBURG C-4
• Swimming Mermaid Coffee House — POINT SOUTH D-4
□ Table Rock State Park — PICKENS A-2
® The Oaks at Point South RV Resort — POINT SOUTH D-4
• The Pink Pig — HARDEEVILLE E-3
□ Tiger Cove Campground — ANDERSON B-2
★ Tony's RV Parts & Service — LEXINGTON B-3
Tuck In The Wood Campground — BEAUFORT E-4
Twin Lakes Campground (COE-Hartwell Lake) — CLEMSON A-2
□ WillowTree Resort — LONGS B-6
Woodsmoke Campground — IRMO B-3

TENNESSEE

□ Adventure Bound Camping Resort Gatlinburg (formerly Crazy Horse Camping & RV Resort) — GATLINBURG E-5
Agricenter RV Park — MEMPHIS C-1
Anderson Road Campground (Corps of Engineers) — ANTIOCH B-4
□ Arrow Creek Campground — GATLINBURG E-5
Athens I-75 Campground — ATHENS B-6
® Baileyton RV Park — BAILEYTON D-5
□ Ballyhoo Family Campground — CROSSVILLE B-5
□ Bean Pot Campground — CROSSVILLE B-5
Beech Bend (Decatur County Pk) — PERRYVILLE B-3
□ Best Holiday Trav-L-Park — CHATTANOOGA C-5
Big Hill Pond State Park — POCAHONTAS C-2
Big Meadow Family Campground — TOWNSEND E-5
□ Big Ridge State Park — NORRIS A-6
Big South Fork Nat'l. River & Rec. Area (Bandy Creek Campground) — ONEIDA A-6
□ Birdsong Resort, Marina & Lakeside Campground — CAMDEN B-3
® Black Bear Cove — CLEVELAND C-6
Bledsoe Creek State Camping Park — GALLATIN A-4
Blue Water Marina/Campground — DAYTON B-5
★ Bob Cox Camper Country — KNOXVILLE B-6
Brookside RV Resort — PIGEON FORGE E-5
□ Buchanan Resort — PARIS A-2
Bumpus Mills Recreational Area (COE-Lk Barkley) — DOVER A-3
Cages Bend Campground (COE-Old Hickory Lake) — GALLATIN A-4
® Camp on the Lake Campground — GUILD C-5
Camping in the Smokies — GATLINBURG E-5
Caney Creek RV Resort & Marina — HARRIMAN B-6
Cedar Creek Campground (COE-Old Hickory Lake) — MT. JULIET B-4
□ Cedars of Lebanon State Park — LEBANON B-4
□ Chattanooga's Raccoon Mtn. Caverns & Campground — CHATTANOOGA C-5
Cherokee Dam (TVA-Cherokee Lake) — JEFFERSON CITY D-5
Cherokee National Forest (Cardens Bluff Campground) — HAMPTON D-6
Cherokee National Forest (Chilhowee Campgrounds) — CLEVELAND C-6
Cherokee National Forest (Indian Boundary A & Overflow Areas) — TELLICO PLAINS C-6
Cherokee National Forest (Jacobs Creek Campgrounds) — SHADY VALLEY D-6
Cherokee National Forest (Little Oak Campground) — BRISTOL D-6
Cherokee National Forest (Parksville Lake Campground) — PARKSVILLE C-6
Cherokee National Forest (Rock Creek Campgrounds) — ERWIN D-6
Chester Frost Park (Hamilton County Park) — CHATTANOOGA C-5
□ Chickasaw State Park — HENDERSON C-2
□ Clabough's Campground & RV Resort — PIGEON FORGE E-5
□ Clarksville RV Park & Campground — CLARKSVILLE A-3
Countryside RV Resort — LEBANON B-4
Cove Lake State Park — CARYVILLE A-6
Creekside RV Park — PIGEON FORGE E-5
Crosseyed Cricket — LENOIR CITY B-6
□ Crossville KOA — CROSSVILLE B-5
★ Cullum & Maxey Camping Center — NASHVILLE B-4
□ Cumberland Mountain State Park — CROSSVILLE B-5
Dale Hollow Dam Campground (COE-Dale Hollow Lake) — CELINA A-5
David Crockett State Park — LAWRENCEBURG C-3
★ Davis Motorhome/D & N Camper Sales — MEMPHIS C-1
Davy Crockett Birthplace Historical SP — GREENEVILLE D-5
®□ Deer Run RV Park — CROSSVILLE B-5
Defeated Creek Park (Corps of Engineers) — CARTHAGE A-5
□ Dickson RV Park — DICKSON B-3
Douglas Dam Tailwater (TVA - Douglas Reservoir) — SEVIERVILLE E-5
Douglas Headwater (TVA - Douglas Reservoir) — SEVIERVILLE E-5
□ Eagle's Nest Campground — PIGEON FORGE E-5
□ Edgar Evins State Rustic Park — SMITHVILLE B-5
Elvis Presley Blvd RV Park — MEMPHIS C-1
Escapees Raccoon Valley RV Park — KNOXVILLE B-6
Express RV Park — LOUDON B-6
□ Fall Creek Falls State Park — PIKEVILLE B-5
Floating Mill (COE-Center Hill Reservoir) — SILVER POINT B-5
Fooshee Pass — TEN MILE B-6
□ Foothills RV Park & Cabins — PIGEON FORGE E-5
Fort Pillow State Historic Area — HENNING B-1
Foster Falls (TVA) — TRACY CITY C-5

ALPHABETICAL LISTINGS CONTINUED

TENNESSEE — Continued

Four Seasons Campground — ***KINGSTON B-6***
Fox Den Campground — ***COSBY E-5***
□ **Fox Inn Campground/Norris — *CLINTON B-6***
Frozen Head State Park — *WARTBURG B-6*
Gatlin Point (LBL) National Recreation Area (Lake Access Site Only) — ***DOVER A-3***
□ **Great Smoky Jellystone Park Camp Resort — *GATLINBURG E-5***
Great Smoky Mountains National Park (Cades Cove Campground) — ***TOWNSEND E-5***
Great Smoky Mountains National Park (Cosby Campground) — ***COSBY E-5***
Great Smoky Mountains National Park (Elkmont Campground) — ***GATLINBURG E-5***
Great Smoky Mountains National Park (Look Rock Campground) — ***WALLAND E-5***
Greenbrier Island Campground — ***GATLINBURG E-5***
□ Greenlee of May Springs — ***JEFFERSON CITY D-5***
□ **Hale's Bar Marina & Resort — *GUILD C-5***
Harrison Bay State Park — *CHATTANOOGA C-5*
□ **Henry Horton State Park — *CHAPEL HILL B-4***
Hiawassee State Scenic River & Ocoee River (Gee Creek Campground) — *DELANO C-6*
Hornsby Hollow (Watts Bar Lake) — ***TEN MILE B-6***
Indian Mountain State Park — *JELLICO A-6*
Jackson RV Park — *JACKSON B-2*
Joy-O RV Park — ***JACKSON B-2***
King's Holly Haven RV Park — *PIGEON FORGE E-5*
Kinser Park (City Park) — ***GREENEVILLE D-5***
□ KOA Tellico Plains — ***TELLICO PLAINS C-6***
□ **KOA-Bristol/Kingsport — *KINGSPORT D-6***
□ KOA-Buffalo — ***BUFFALO B-3***
□ **KOA-Chattanooga North/Cleveland — *CLEVELAND C-6***
□ **KOA-Manchester — *MANCHESTER B-4***
□ **KOA-Newport I-40/Smoky Mtns — *NEWPORT D-5***
□ KOA-Paris Landing — ***PARIS A-2***
□ **KOA-Pigeon Forge/Gatlinburg — *PIGEON FORGE E-5***
□ **KOA-Sweetwater Valley — *SWEETWATER B-6***
Lake Cove Resort — ***DANDRIDGE D-5***
Lakeview RV Park — *BRISTOL D-6*
□ **Lazy Daze Campground — *TOWNSEND E-5***
□ Le Conte Vista Campground Resort — ***GATLINBURG E-5***
Lillydale Campground (COE-Dale Hollow Lake) — ***LIVINGSTON A-5***
□ Little Eagle RV Park — ***PARIS A-2***
□ Little River Village Campground — ***TOWNSEND E-5***
Lock A Campground (COE - Chatham Lake) — ***ASHLAND CITY A-4***
Long Branch (COE - Center Hill Reservoir) — ***SILVER POINT B-5***
• **Loretta Lynn's Ranch — *HURRICANE MILLS B-3***
□ **Loretta Lynn's Ranch — *HURRICANE MILLS B-3***
Lotterdale Cove — ***GREENBACK B-6***
Loyston Point (TVA - Norris Reservoir) — ***NORRIS A-6***

TENNESSEE — Continued

Lynchburg Wilderness RV Park — *LYNCHBURG C-4*
Maple Grove Campground — ***GRANVILLE A-5***
® Maple Hill RV Park — ***JAMESTOWN A-5***
□ **Meeman-Shelby Forest State Park — *MILLINGTON C-1***
Melton Hill Dam (TVA-Melton Hill Reservoir) — ***LENOIR CITY B-6***
□ Memphis East Campground — ***MEMPHIS C-1***
□ **Memphis/Graceland RV Park & Campground — *MEMPHIS C-1***
®△ MILITARY PARK (FAMCAMP-Arnold AFB) — ***MANCHESTER B-4***
□ **Misty River Cabins & RV Resort, LLC — *TOWNSEND E-5***
□ **Montgomery Bell State Park — *WHITE BLUFF B-3***
Mountain Glen RV Park — *PIKEVILLE B-5*
□ Mountain Lake Campground — ***DANDRIDGE D-5***
□ **Mountain Lake Marina & Campground — *LAKE CITY A-6***
□ Mountaineer Campground — ***TOWNSEND E-5***
Mousetail Landing State Park — *PERRYVILLE B-3*
□ **Nashville Country RV Park — *NASHVILLE B-4***
★ **Nashville Easy Livin' Country — *NASHVILLE B-4***
□ **Nashville I-24 Campground — *SMYRNA B-4***
□ **Nashville KOA — *NASHVILLE B-4***
Nashville North Campground — ***GOODLETTSVILLE A-4***
□ **Nashville's Jellystone Park — *NASHVILLE B-4***
Natchez Trace Parkway (Meriwether Lewis Campground) — ***HOHENWALD B-3***
□ **Natchez Trace State Park — *CLARKSBURG B-2***
□ **Nathan Bedford Forrest State Park — *CAMDEN B-3***
□ **Norris Dam State Park — *NORRIS A-6***
Notchy Creek — ***VONORE B-6***
Obey River Campground (COE-Dale Hollow Lake) — ***LIVINGSTON A-5***
Old Stone Fort State Archaeological Area — *MANCHESTER B-4*
Over-Niter RV Park — ***ATHENS B-6***
Panther Creek State Park — *MORRISTOWN D-5*
□ **Paris Landing State Park — *PARIS A-2***
□ **Parker's Crossroads Campground — *PARKERS CROSSROADS B-2***
Parkway Village — ***JACKSON B-2***
Pebble Mountain Family Campground — ***CHUCKEY D-6***
□ **Pickett State Park — *JAMESTOWN A-5***
Pickwick Dam (TVA-Pickwick Lake) — ***COUNCE C-2***
□ **Pickwick Landing State Resort Park — *SAVANNAH C-2***
• **Pigeon Forge Department of Tourism — *PIGEON FORGE E-5***
Piney Campground (LBL) — ***DOVER A-3***
□ Piney (LBL) National Recreation Area — ***DOVER A-3***
Ragland Bottom (COE - Center Hill Reservoir) — ***SMITHVILLE B-5***
Redwood Estates — *MEMPHIS C-1*
□ **Reelfoot Lake State Park — *TIPTONVILLE A-1***
□ **Ripplin' Waters Campground — *SEVIERVILLE E-5***
□ **River Plantation RV Park — *PIGEON FORGE E-5***
Riverbend Campground — *PIGEON FORGE E-5*
□ **Riveredge RV Park — *PIGEON FORGE E-5***
®□ **Riverside RV Park & Resort — *SEVIERVILLE E-5***

TENNESSEE — Continued

□ **Roan Mountain State Resort Park — *ROAN MOUNTAIN D-6***
□ **Rock Island State Park — *ROCK ISLAND B-5***
□ **Rocky Top Campground — *KINGSPORT D-6***
Salt Lick Creek Campground (Corps of Engineers) — ***GAINESBORO A-5***
Seven Points Campground (Corps of Engineers) — ***HERMITAGE B-4***
Shady Acres Campground — ***LEBANON B-4***
□ **Shady Oaks Campground Pigeon Forge/Gatlinburg — *PIGEON FORGE E-5***
Shady Oaks Community — *MILLINGTON C-1*
Shellmound-Nickajack Dam Reservation (TVA-Nickajack Lake) — ***JASPER C-5***
Shipp's RV Center & Campground — ***CHATTANOOGA C-5***
Smoker Holler RV Resort — *PIGEON FORGE E-5*
®□ **Smoky Bear Campground (formerly Huc A Bee) — *GATLINBURG E-5***
Soaring Eagle Campground & RV Park — *LENOIR CITY B-6*
Southlake RV Park — *KNOXVILLE B-6*
Spring Lake RV Resort (formerly known as Roam & Roost RV Campground) — ***CROSSVILLE B-5***
□ **Standing Stone State Park — *LIVINGSTON A-5***
Stoney Creek RV Park — *ELIZABETHTON D-6*
® Tanbark Campground — ***DICKSON B-3***
Tennessee Country Campground & RV Park — ***SWEETWATER B-6***
★ **Tennessee RV — *KNOXVILLE B-6***
• **Tennessee State Parks Department of Environment and Conservation — *NASHVILLE B-4***
□ **Tennessee Valley R.V. Park — *FRANKEWING C-4***
Texas "T" Campground — ***CORNERSVILLE C-4***
Timberline Campground — ***LEBANON B-4***
□ **Tims Ford State Rustic Park — *WINCHESTER C-4***
T.O. Fuller State Park — *MEMPHIS C-1*
Toqua Beach Campground — ***VONORE B-6***
□ Tremont Outdoor Resort — ***TOWNSEND E-5***
★ Tri-City Travel Trailers — ***KINGSPORT D-6***
Triple Creek Campground — ***COSBY E-5***
Tuckaleechee Campground — ***TOWNSEND E-5***
□ **Twin Creek RV Resort — *GATLINBURG E-5***
Twin Lakes Catfish Farm & Campground — ***BAXTER B-5***
Twin Mountain RV Park and Campground — *PIGEON FORGE E-5*
Two Rivers Campground — *NASHVILLE B-4*
Two Rivers Landing Resort — *SEVIERVILLE E-5*
• **US Army Corps of Engineers/Volunteer Clearing House — *NASHVILLE B-4***
® Volunteer Park — ***KNOXVILLE B-6***
Waldens Creek Campground — *PIGEON FORGE E-5*
Warrior's Path State Park — *KINGSPORT D-6*
Whispering Pines RV Park — ***JACKSON B-2***
Willow Grove (COE-Dale Hollow Lake) — ***LIVINGSTON A-5***
Woodsmoke Campground — ***UNICOI D-6***

WOODALL'S® EXTENDED STAY

WEEKLY MONTHLY SEASONAL WEEKLY MONTHLY SEASONAL WEEKLY MONTHLY SEASONAL

SPRING SUMMER AUTUMN WINTER SPRING SUMMER AUTUMN WINTER SPRING

2008

GUIDE TO RV PARKS/CAMPGROUNDS

WOODALL'S 2008 EXTENDED STAY GUIDE TO RV PARKS/CAMPGROUNDS HELPS YOU MAKE YOUR PLANS!

If you'd like some great recommendations on where you can camp for a week, a month or an entire season, and which parks, RV dealerships and attractions cater to seasonal campers, then WOODALL'S 2008 EXTENDED STAY GUIDE TO RV PARKS/CAMPGROUNDS is for you! It has been specially designed for snowbirds, sunbirds and full-timers.

Throughout these pages, we have provided detailed listings and display advertising from RV parks and campgrounds that invite you to come stay with them.

The ADVERTISEMENTS show you what is unique about each listed facility. They may provide special seasonal rates, and tell you what attractions are nearby. They expand on the information in the listings. For example, the listing will tell you how many sites there are at an RV park. Their ad might say: Waterfront sites, or extra-wide pull-thrus. Additional information about hospital services, special entertainment programs, park trailer sales, distances to lakes and beaches is often provided, too. The LISTINGS tell you the "nuts and bolts" about the RV parks and campgrounds. They provide detailed driving directions, on-site facilities, and more. The reference line at the bottom of each advertiser listing tells you exactly where to find their ad.

The LISTINGS and ADVERTISEMENTS in this Guide are organized alphabetically, first by state in the United States, then by Canadian province. Within each state and province, the towns are listed in alphabetical order, and within each town, the facilities are also organized alphabetically.

WHAT DO THE NUMBERS MEAN AT THE BOTTOM OF EACH AD?

Reader Service Numbers are assigned to each advertiser in the EXTENDED STAY GUIDE. Look at the bottom of each ad for these numbers. Then, turn to the Reader Service Card following page 48 in the front of the book. In the spaces provided on the card, write the numbers of the facilities you are interested in. Drop the postage-paid card in the mail. It's that easy! You'll receive brochures and other information... sent directly to your home.

If you choose to inquire by phone, e-mail or web site, please let the RV Park/Campground know you found out about them by using WOODALL'S.

WHAT THE LISTINGS TELL YOU

(N) CARեFREE CAMPING RV PARK—(DuPage)

WELCOME

From jct I-94 (exit 24) & Golden Eagle Rd: Go 1/2 mi N on Golden Eagle Rd, then 4 mi W on Hwy 80, then 1 mi N on Carefree Rd. Enter on R.

FACILITIES: 320 sites, typical site width 40 feet, 175 full hkups, 100 W&E, 25 E, (20, 30 & 50 amp receptacles), 50 amps ($), 20 no hkups, 50 pull-thrus, heater not allowed, cable TV, phone on-site, Internet access (needs activ), cable Internet access central location ($), RV/park trailer rentals, cabins, dump station, non-guest dumping ($), laundry, groceries, LP gas by weight/meter, LP bottle exch, ice, tables, wood.

RECREATION: rec hall, equipped pavilion, coin games, 2 swim pools, wading pool, lake swimming, whirlpool, boating, 10 motor boat rentals, lake fishing, fishing supplies, mini-golf ($), 25 bike rentals, playground, planned activities, tennis, hiking trails, local tours.

Pet restrictions. Partial handicap access. Open all year. Big rigs welcome. Member of ARVC. ATM. Phone: (999) 555-6200.

e-mail: cmpn@carefree.com

SEE AD THIS PAGE

Reserve Online at Woodalls.com

COUNTY: Appears in parentheses after park name. May be useful in the event of severe weather, since most broadcast weather warnings are given by county.

FACILITIES: All of the facilities listed are available on site.

DRIVING DIRECTIONS: Detailed, easy-to-read driving information, including where the entrance to the campground is located.

INTERNET ACCESS: Phone and/or cable available upon activation by local phone company.

RECREATION: All of the recreation listed is available right at the campground.

PARTIAL HANDICAP ACCESS: Indicates the park has been adapted in one or more ways to accommodate RVers/campers with disabilities. If you or a family member has special needs, please call ahead to determine the type of services/facilities available.

SPECIAL INFORMATION: This area includes such information as no pets, age restrictions, and operating season. If the listing does not state "No Pets", pets are allowed. If you see "pet restrictions" in the listing, pets are allowed, but be sure to check with park management regarding stipulations they may have on pets.

ADVERTISER REFERENCE: This line will refer you to the specific page for this listing's advertisement.

E-MAIL ADDRESS: When available, advertiser listings contain e-mail addresses.

Free Camping Information Extended Stay Guide

SAVE HOURS OF RESEARCH!

The campgrounds/RV parks, RV service centers and attractions listed below want your business! Here is a quick and easy way to receive free information about seasonal camping, fun things to do, and where to service your RV or buy a new one. Simply enter their **Reader Service Number** (listed below) on the **Reader Service Card**, which is located opposite page 48 in the front of the **Discover Section**. Your request will be forwarded to the names you've indicated. Then, you'll receive brochures and/or pricing information, sent directly to your home. It's the no-hassle way to shop for the campground, attraction or RV dealership you are interested in!

Enter Number	
ARIZONA	
3444	Towerpoint Resort
3445	Good Life RV Resort
3681	Rincon Country East RV Park
3699	Arizona Maverik RV Park
3700	Mesa Spirit RV Resort
3715	Pueblo El Mirage RV Resort
3724	Desert's Edge RV Village
CALIFORNIA	
851	Rancho Los Coches RV Park
856	TwentyNine Palms Resort
2663	Pomona Fairplex KOA
2677	La Pacifica RV Resort
2965	Bernardo Shores RV Park
3532	Morena Mobile Village Office
3534	Woods Valley Kampground
3589	San Diego RV Resort
3590	Golden Village Palms RV Resort
3675	Flag City RV Resort
CONNECTICUT	
3770	Camper's World, Inc.
DELAWARE	
3409	Leisure Point Resort
FLORIDA	
884	Club Naples RV Resort (Morgan RV Resorts)
906	Road Runner Travel Resort
919	Upriver RV Resort
3544	John Prince Memorial Park
3554	Mill Creek RV Resort
3656	The Glades
GEORGIA	
3058	River's End Campground & RV Park
MICHIGAN	
926	Creek Valley
993	Wheel Inn Campground & Whitetail Acres Archery
1076	Greenwood Acres Family Campground
2124	Clearwater Campground
3441	Lake Chemung Outdoor Resort
MISSISSIPPI	
3732	Lakeview RV Resort
3792	Indian Point RV Resort
NEW JERSEY	
3081	Pleasant Valley Family Campground
NEW YORK	
925	Cliff & Ed's Trailer Park
ONTARIO	
3173	Rochester Place Resort Inc
3618	Spring Lake RV Resort
PENNSYLVANIA	
3765	Mountain Pines RV Resort
TEXAS	
3669	Parkview Riverside
3677	Llano Grande Lake Park
3678	Alamo Palms
3679	Victoria Palms Resort
VERMONT	
3630	Apple Island Resort
WISCONSIN	
3271	Lakeland Camping Resort

EXTENDED STAY GUIDE TO RV PARKS/CAMPGROUNDS

ALABAMA

HELENA

(S) Cherokee Campground—(Shelby) *From jct I-459 (exit 6) Hwy 52: Go 4 mi SW on Hwy 52/Morgan Rd, then 3/4 mi W on Hwy 93. Enter on L.* FACILITIES: 100 sites, typical site width 40 ft, 92 full hkups, 8 W&E, (30 & 50 amps), 50 amps ($), 22 pull-thrus, wireless Internet access central location, dump station, laundry, ltd groceries, LP bottle exch. RECREATION: rec room/area, pavilion, lake fishing, golf nearby, bsktball, hiking trails. Pets welcome. No tents. Open all yr. Big rigs welcome. Phone: (205)428-8339.

LANGSTON

(S) Little Mountain Marina Camping Resort—(Marshall) *From jct US 431 & Hwy 227: Go 12 mi S on Hwy 227 (Hwy 227 turns N), then 1/2 mi N on S Sauty Rd (Hwy 227 goes E at S Sauty Rd) to Murphy Hill Rd, then left on Murphy Hill Rd. Enter on L.* FACILITIES: 371 sites, typical site width 30 ft, 336 full hkups, 35 W&E, (20, 30 & 50 amps), 7 pull-thrus, phone Internet access central location, RV/park trailer rentals, cabins, RV storage, dump station, laundry, LP gas by weight, ice, tables, patios, grills, controlled access gate. RECREATION: rec hall, rec room/area, pavilion, equipped pavilion, coin games, 2 swim pools, wading pool, lake swimming, whirlpool, boating, canoeing, ramp, dock, lake fishing, mini-golf, bsktball, playground, 3 shuffleboard courts, planned activities, tennis, sports field, v-ball. Pets welcome. Partial handicap access. Open all yr. Big rigs welcome. Phone: (256)582-8211.

PELHAM

(W) Birmingham South Campground—(Shelby) *From jct I-65 (exit 242) & Hwy 52: Go 700 yards W on Hwy 52, then 300 yards N on Hwy 33. Enter on R.* FACILITIES: 108 sites, typical site width 50 ft, 102 full hkups, 6 W&E, (30 & 50 amps), 50 amps ($), 56 pull-thrus, cable TV, wireless Instant Internet access at site, phone Internet access central location, cabins, RV storage, dump station, non-guest dumping $, laundry, full svc store, RV supplies, LP gas by weight/by meter, ice, tables, patios, fire rings, grills, wood. RECREATION: rec hall, rec room/area, pavilion, equipped pavilion, coin games, swim pool, whirlpool, golf nearby, bsktball, playground, planned activities, horseshoes, v-ball. Rec open to public. Pets welcome. Partial handicap access. Open all yr. Big rigs welcome. Member ARVC, ALARVC. Phone: (205)664-8832.

PELL CITY

(S) Lakeside Landing RV Park & Marina—(St. Clair) *From jct I-20 (Eastbound exit 158, Westbound exit 158-B) & US 231: Go 6 mi S on US 231. Enter on L.* FACILITIES: 193 sites, typical site width 25 ft, 193 full hkups, (15, 30 & 50 amps), 164 pull-thrus, cable TV, wireless Internet access central location, RV storage, dump station, non-guest dumping $, laundry, full svc store, RV supplies, LP gas by weight, LP bottle exch, gas, marine gas, ice, tables, patios. RECREATION: rec hall, rec room/area, lake swimming, boating, canoeing, kayaking, ramp, dock, lake fishing, fishing supplies, golf nearby. Rec open to public. Pets welcome. Partial handicap access. Open all yr. Big rigs welcome. ATM. Phone: (205)525-5701.

ROBERTSDALE

(E) Wilderness RV Park (CAMP RESORT) —(Baldwin) *From I-10 (exit 53) & CR 64: Go S 1/4 mi on CR 64, then turn left on Patterson Rd for 1.3 mi.* FACILITIES: 74 sites, typical site width 46 ft, 74 full hkups, (20, 30 & 50 amps), 50 amps ($), 71 pull-thrus, wireless Internet access central location, dump station, laundry, LP gas by meter, tables, controlled access gate. RECREATION: rec hall, pavilion, swim pool, whirlpool, lake/pond fishing, golf nearby, planned activities, horseshoes, sports field. Pets welcome, quantity restrict. No tents. Open all yr. Big rigs welcome. Phone: (251)960-1195.

ALASKA

VALDEZ

(E) Eagle's Rest RV Park & Cabins—(Valdez-Cordova) *From Hwy 4 (Richardson Hwy) Mile Post 0: Go 3-1/2 mi S on Hwy 4, then 200 feet W on E Pioneer Dr. Enter on R.* FACILITIES: 230 sites, typical site width 20 ft, 180 full hkups, (20, 30 & 50 amps), 50 amps ($), 50 no hkups, 83 pull-thrus, cable TV, wireless Instant Internet access at site, phone Internet access central location, cabins, RV storage, dump station, non-guest dumping, laundry, ltd groceries, RV supplies, LP gas by meter, gas, ice, tables, fire rings, wood. RECREATION: float trips, fishing supplies, fishing guides, bike rental, horseshoes, local tours. Pets welcome. Partial handicap access. Open all yr. Facilities fully operational May thru Oct. Big rigs welcome. Member ARVC, ACOA. ATM. Phone: (800)553-7275.

Reserve Online at Woodalls.com

ARIZONA

APACHE JUNCTION

(E) SUNRISE RV RESORT—(Maricopa) *From jct Idaho Rd/Hwy 88 & US 60 (Superstition Fwy): Go 1 mi W on US 60 to (exit 195/Ironwood Dr), then 1-1/2 mi N on Ironwood, then 500 feet E on Broadway. Enter on R.*

FACILITIES: 498 sites, typical site width 36 ft, accepts full hkup units only, 498 full hkups, (30 & 50 amps), wireless Instant Internet access at site ($), wireless Internet access central location, laundry, patios, controlled access gate.

RECREATION: rec hall, rec room/area, equipped pavilion, swim pool, whirlpool, golf nearby, 6 shuffleboard courts, planned activities, tennis, horseshoes, local tours.

Pets welcome, breed restrict, quantity restrict. Partial handicap access. No tents. Age restrictions may apply. Open all yr. Big rigs welcome. Phone: (866)787-2754.

SEE AD EL MIRAGE THIS PAGE

BENSON

(C) Butterfield RV Resort—(Cochise) *From jct Hwy 90 & I-10: Go 2 mi E on I-10 (exit 304) Ocotillo Rd, then 3/4 mi S on Ocotillo Rd. Enter on L.* FACILITIES: 173 sites, typical site width 30 ft, accepts full hkup units only, 173 full hkups, (20, 30 & 50 amps), 24 pull-thrus, cable TV, wireless Instant Internet access at site ($), phone Internet access central location, dump station, non-guest dumping $, laundry, RV supplies, LP gas by meter, ice, tables. RECREATION: rec hall, rec room/area, equipped pavilion, swim pool, whirlpool, golf nearby, planned activities, local tours. Pets welcome, quantity restrict. Partial handicap access. No tents. Open all yr. Big rigs welcome. Member ARVC, ATPA. Phone: (800)863-8160.

Reserve Online at Woodalls.com

BRENDA

(E) Brenda RV Resort—(La Paz) *From jct I-10 (exit 31) & US 60: Go 3 mi E on US 60 (MP 34). Enter on L.* FACILITIES: 204 sites, typical site width 40 ft, 204 full hkups, (30 & 50 amps), 24 pull-thrus, cable TV, wireless Instant Internet access at site ($), RV storage, laundry, LP gas by meter, tables. RECREATION: rec hall, rec room/area, shuffleboard court, planned activities, horseshoes, hiking trails, local tours. Pets welcome, quantity restrict. No tents. Open all yr. Big rigs welcome. Phone: (877)927-5249.

(SE) Desert Gold RV Resort—(La Paz) *From jct I-10 (exit 31) & US 60: Go 4 mi NE on US 60 (MP 35). Enter on R.* FACILITIES: 550 sites, typical site width 35 ft, 550 full hkups, (20, 30 & 50 amps), 42 pull-thrus, cable TV, wireless Instant Internet access at site ($), RV storage, laundry, LP gas by meter, tables, patios. RECREATION: rec hall, rec room/area, swim pool, whirlpool, mini-golf, planned activities, horseshoes, hiking trails, local tours. Pets welcome. Partial handicap access. No tents. Open all yr. Big rigs welcome. Phone: (800)927-2101.

(E) Wagon West RV Park—(La Paz) *From jct I-10 (exit 31) & US 60: Go 7 mi E on US 60 (MP 39). Enter on R.* FACILITIES: 215 sites, typical site width 30 ft, 215 full hkups, (30 & 50 amps), 11 pull-thrus, cable TV, wireless Instant Internet access at site ($), phone Internet access central location, shower$, laundry, LP gas by meter, ice. RECREATION: rec hall, rec room/area, golf nearby, 3 shuffleboard courts, planned activities, horseshoes, hiking trails. Pets welcome, breed restrict, quantity restrict. No tents. Age restrictions may apply. Open Oct thru Apr. Big rigs welcome. Phone: (928)927-7077.

CASA GRANDE

(E) Palm Creek Golf & RV Resort—(Pinal) *From jct I-8 & I-10: Go 5 mi NW on I-10 (exit 194) Hwy 287, then 1/2 mi W on Hwy 287/Florence Blvd. Enter on R.* FACILITIES: 1888 sites, typical site width 40 ft, accepts full hkup units only, 1888 full hkups, (20, 30 & 50 amps), 25 pull-thrus, cable TV, wireless Instant Internet access at site ($), wireless Internet access central location, RV storage, laundry, ice, patios, controlled access gate. RECREATION: rec hall, rec room/area, equipped pavilion, 2 swim pools, whirlpool, putting green, golf nearby, 10 bike rentals, 16 shuffleboard courts, planned activities, tennis, horseshoes, sports field, hiking trails, v-ball, local tours. Pets welcome, quantity restrict. Partial handicap access. No tents. Age restrictions may apply. Open all yr. Big rigs welcome. Member ARVC, AZ ARVC. ATM. Phone: (800)421-7004.

(N) Val Vista Winter Village—(Pinal) *From jct I-8 & I-10: Go 14 mi W on I-10 to Hwy 387 (exit 185), then 2-1/4 mi S on Hwy 387 (N Pinal Rd), then 1/2 mi E on Val Vista. Enter on L.* FACILITIES: 344 sites, typical site width 30 ft, accepts full hkup units only, 344 full hkups, (30 & 50 amps), wireless Instant Internet access at site ($), phone Internet access central location, laundry, ice, patios. RECREATION: rec hall, rec room/area, equipped pavilion, swim pool, whirlpool, golf nearby, 4 shuffleboard courts, planned activities, horseshoes, hiking trails, local tours. Pets welcome. Partial handicap access. No tents. Age restrictions may apply. Open Sep 1 thru Jun 1. Big rigs welcome. Member ARVC, AZ ARVC. Phone: (877)836-7801.

EL MIRAGE

(E) PUEBLO EL MIRAGE RV RESORT & COUNTRY CLUB—(Maricopa) *From jct I-10 (exit 129) & Dysart Rd: Go 7-1/2 mi N on Dysart Rd, then 1 mi E on Olive, then 1 1/2 mi N on El Mirage Rd.*

FACILITIES: 1075 sites, typical site width 40 ft, accepts full hkup units only, 1075 full hkups, (30 & 50 amps), 10 pull-thrus, wireless Instant Internet access at site ($), phone on-site Internet access (needs activ), wireless Internet access central location, laundry, ice, patios, controlled access gate.

PUEBLO EL MIRAGE RV RESORT & COUNTRY CLUB—Continued on next page

EL MIRAGE—Continued
PUEBLO EL MIRAGE RV RESORT & COUNTRY CLUB—Continued

RECREATION: rec hall, rec room/area, 2 swim pools, whirlpool, putting green, golf nearby, 32 shuffleboard courts, planned activities, tennis, horseshoes, local tours. Rec open to public.

Pets welcome, breed restrict, quantity restrict. Partial handicap access. No tents. Age restrictions may apply. Open all yr. Big rigs welcome. Phone: (800)445-4115.

e-mail: puebloelmiragerv@aol.com

SEE AD PAGE 3

GOLD CANYON

(C) Canyon Vistas RV Resort—(Pinal) *From jct US 88 & US 60: Go 6-1/2 mi E on US 60. Enter on R.* FACILITIES: 634 sites, typical site width 40 ft, accepts full hkup units only, 634 full hkups, (30 & 50 amps), cable TV, wireless Instant Internet access at site, wireless Internet access central location, laundry, RV supplies, ice, patios, controlled access gate. RECREATION: rec hall, rec room/area, equipped pavilion, swim pool, whirlpool, mini-golf, golf nearby, 3 shuffleboard courts, planned activities, tennis, horseshoes, sports field, local tours. Pets welcome, breed restrict. Partial handicap access. No tents. Age restrictions may apply. Open all yr. Big rigs welcome. Phone: (888)940-8989.

(C) GOLD CANYON RV & GOLF RESORT—(Pinal) *From jct US 88 & US 60: Go 6-1/2 mi SE on US 60. Enter on R.*

WELCOME

FACILITIES: 756 sites, typical site width 34 ft, accepts self-contained units only, 756 full hkups, (30 & 50 amps), cable TV ($), phone/wireless Instant Internet access at site ($), wireless Internet access central location, RV storage, laundry, ltd groceries, ice, patios, controlled access gate.

RECREATION: rec hall, rec room/area, 2 swim pools, whirlpool, putting green, golf nearby, bsktball, 16 shuffleboard courts, planned activities, tennis, horseshoes, v-ball, local tours.

Pets welcome, breed restrict, quantity restrict. Partial handicap access. No tents. Age restrictions may apply. Open all yr. Planned group acitivites, winter months only. Big rigs welcome. Phone: (480)982-5800.

e-mail: gc@robertsresorts.com

SEE AD EL MIRAGE PAGE 3

GOODYEAR

(C) Destiny Phoenix RV Resort—(Maricopa) *From jct Loop 101 & I-10: Go 9 mi W on I-10 to (exit 124), Cotton lane then 3/4 mi S on Cotton Lane, then 1 mi W on Van Buren, then 100 yds N on Citrus Rd. Enter on L.* FACILITIES: 284 sites, typical site width 28 ft, 284 full hkups, (30 & 50 amps), 103 pull-thrus, wireless Instant Internet access at site ($), phone Internet access central location, RV storage, laundry, ltd groceries, RV supplies, LP gas by meter, ice, tables, patios,

GOODYEAR—Continued
Destiny Phoenix RV Resort—Continued

grills, controlled access gate. RECREATION: rec hall, rec room/area, equipped pavilion, swim pool, whirlpool, golf nearby, 2 shuffleboard courts, planned activities, horseshoes, v-ball, local tours. Pets welcome, breed restrict, quantity restrict. Partial handicap access. No tents. Open all yr. Daily $1.80 extra for electric. Big rigs welcome. Member ARVC, AZ ARVC. Phone: (888)667-2454.

MARANA

(SW) Valley of The Sun RV Mobile Home Resort—(Pima) *From jct I-10 (exit 236 Marana) & Sandario Rd: Go 1/2 mi S on Sandario Rd. Enter on R.* FACILITIES: 143 sites, typical site width 30 ft, 143 full hkups, (30 & 50 amps), 20 pull-thrus, wireless Instant Internet access at site, wireless Internet access central location, laundry, LP gas by meter, patios. RECREATION: rec hall, rec room/area, equipped pavilion, swim pool, whirlpool, golf nearby, shuffleboard court, planned activities, horseshoes. Pets welcome. Partial handicap access. Open all yr. Big rigs welcome. Phone: (520)682-3434.

Reserve Online at Woodalls.com

MESA

(NE) Apache Wells RV Resort—(Maricopa) *From jct Loop 101 & US 60 (Superstition Fwy): Go 10 mi E on US 60 to exit 186/Higley Rd, then 5-1/2 mi N on Higley Rd, then 1/2 mi E on McDowell Rd, then 200 feet S on 56th St. Enter on R.* FACILITIES: 318 sites, typical site width 32 ft, accepts full hkup units only, 318 full hkups, (30 & 50 amps), wireless Internet access central location, RV/park trailer rentals, laundry, patios. RECREATION: rec hall, rec room/area, swim pool, whirlpool, golf nearby, 8 shuffleboard courts, planned activities, tennis, local tours. Pets welcome, breed restrict. Partial handicap access. No tents. Age restrictions may apply. Open all yr. Big rigs welcome. Phone: (888)940-8989.

(E) ARIZONA MAVERIK RV PARK—(Maricopa) *From jct Loop 101 & US 60 (Superstition Fwy): Go 16-1/4 mi E on US 60 (exit 192/Crismon Rd), then 1-3/4 mi N on Crismon Rd. Enter on R.*

WELCOME

FACILITIES: 38 sites, typical site width 26 ft, accepts full hkup units only, 38 full hkups, (30 & 50 amps), wireless Instant Internet access at site ($), phone on-site Internet access (needs activ), phone Internet access central location, RV storage, laundry, patios, controlled access gate.

RECREATION: pavilion, golf nearby.

Pets welcome, breed restrict. Partial handicap access. No tents. Open all yr. Add'l chg for 50 amp during Summer months. Big rigs welcome. Member ARVC, AZ ARVC. Phone: (888)715-3700.

e-mail: azmaverikrv@aol.com

SEE AD THIS PAGE

MESA—Continued

(E) GOOD LIFE RV RESORT—(Maricopa) *From Loop 101 & US 60 (Superstition Fwy): Go 8 mi E on US 60 to (exit 184/Val Vista Dr), then 2 mi N on Val Vista Dr, then 1/4 mi W on Main. Enter on L.*

FACILITIES: 1156 sites, typical site width 32 ft, accepts full hkup units only, 1156 full hkups, (30 & 50 amps), wireless Instant Internet access at site ($), phone Internet access central location, RV/park trailer rentals, laundry, ice, patios, controlled access gate.

RECREATION: rec hall, rec room/area, pavilion, equipped pavilion, 2 swim pools, whirlpool, putting green, golf nearby, 24 shuffleboard courts, planned activities, tennis, horseshoes, local tours.

Pets welcome, breed restrict, size restrict, quantity restrict. Partial handicap access. No tents. Age restrictions may apply. Open all yr. Big rigs welcome. Member ARVC, AZ ARVC. Phone: (800)999-4990.

e-mail: info@goodliferv.com

SEE AD THIS PAGE

(E) Mesa Regal RV Resort—(Maricopa) *From jct Loop 101 & US 60 (Superstition Fwy): Go 9 mi E on US 60 to (exit 185/Greenfield Rd), then 2 mi N on Greenfield Rd, then 1/4 mi E on Main St. Enter on L.* FACILITIES: 2005 sites, typical site width 35 ft, accepts full hkup units only, 2005 full hkups, (30 & 50 amps), phone on-site Internet access (needs activ), wireless Internet access central location, RV/park trailer rentals, laundry, patios. RECREATION: rec hall, rec room/area, pavilion, equipped pavilion, 4 swim pools, whirlpool, putting green, golf nearby, 24 shuffleboard courts, planned activities, tennis, horseshoes, sports field, v-ball, local tours. Pets welcome, breed restrict. Partial handicap access. No tents. Age restrictions may apply. Open all yr. Big rigs welcome. Phone: (888)940-8989.

(E) MESA SPIRIT RV RESORT—(Maricopa) *From jct Loop 101 & US 60 (Superstition Fwy): Go 6 mi E on US 60 to (exit 182/Gilbert Rd), then 2 mi N on Gilbert Rd, then 1-1/4 mi E on Main St. Enter on L.*

FACILITIES: 1800 sites, typical site width 30 ft, accepts full hkup units only, 1800 full hkups, (30 & 50 amps), 28 pull-thrus, cable TV ($), wireless Instant Internet access at site ($), cable on-site

MESA SPIRIT RV RESORT—Continued on next page

Internet access (needs activ), cable Internet access central location, RV/park trailer rentals, RV storage, laundry, ice, patios, controlled access gate.

RECREATION: rec hall, rec room/area, pavilion, equipped pavilion, 3 swim pools, whirlpool, mini-golf, putting green, golf nearby, 32 shuffleboard courts, planned activities, tennis, horseshoes, local tours.

Pets welcome, breed restrict, quantity restrict. Partial handicap access. No tents. Age restrictions may apply. Open all yr. Big rigs welcome. Member ARVC, AZ ARVC. Phone: (877)924-6709.

e-mail: mesaspirit@azrvpark.com

SEE AD PAGE 4

(E) Silveridge RV Resort—(Maricopa) *From jct Loop 101 & US 60 (Superstition Fwy): Go 13-1/4 mi E on US 60 (exit 189)/Sossaman), then 1/2 mi N on Sossaman Rd, then 1 mi E on Southern. Enter on R.* FACILITIES: 687 sites, typical site width 40 ft, accepts full hkup units only, 687 full hkups, (30 & 50 amps), cable TV, phone Instant Internet access at site, wireless Internet access central location, RV/park trailer rentals, dump station, non-guest dumping $, laundry, ice, patios, controlled access gate. RECREATION: rec hall, rec room/area, swim pool, whirlpool, mini-golf, golf nearby, bsktball, 9 shuffleboard courts, planned activities, tennis, horseshoes, local tours. Pets welcome. Partial handicap access. No tents. Age restrictions may apply. Open all yr. Big rigs welcome. Member ARVC, AZ ARVC. Phone: (800)354-0054.

(E) Sun Life RV Resort—(Maricopa) *From jct Loop 101 & US 60 (Superstition Fwy): Go 10 mi E on US 60 to (exit 186/Higley Rd), then 2-1/2 mi N on Higley Rd, then 100 yards W on University Dr. Enter on L.* FACILITIES: 761 sites, typical site width 30 ft, accepts full hkup units only, 761 full hkups, (15, 30 & 50 amps), phone on-site Internet access (needs activ), wireless Internet access central location, RV/park trailer rentals, laundry, patios, controlled access gate. RECREATION: rec hall, rec room/area, pavilion, equipped pavilion, swim pool, whirlpool, golf nearby, bsktball, 12 shuffleboard courts, planned activities, tennis, horseshoes, local tours. Pets welcome, breed restrict, quantity restrict. Partial handicap access. No tents. Age restrictions may apply. Open all yr. Big rigs welcome. Phone: (888)940-8989.

(E) The Resort—(Maricopa) *From jct Loop 101& US 60 (Superstition Fwy): Go 15-1/4 mi E on US 60 (exit 191/Ellsworth Rd), then 1/2 mi N on Ellsworth Rd. Enter on R.* FACILITIES: 792 sites, typical site width 33 ft, accepts full hkup units only, 792 full hkups, (30 & 50 amps), cable TV, phone on-site Internet access (needs activ), wireless Internet access central location, laundry, ice, patios, controlled access gate. RECREATION: rec hall, rec room/area, pavilion, swim pool, whirlpool, putting green, golf nearby, 8 shuffleboard courts, planned activities, tennis, horseshoes, sports field, local tours. Pets welcome, breed restrict. Partial handicap access. No tents. Age restrictions may apply. Open all yr. Big rigs welcome. Member ARVC, AZ ARVC. Phone: (480)986-8404.

(E) TOWERPOINT RESORT—(Maricopa) *From jct Loop 101 & US 60 (Superstition Fwy): Go 9 mi E on US 60 to (exit 185/Greenfield Rd), then 2 mi N on Greenfield Rd, then 1/4 mi E on Main St. Enter on L.*

FACILITIES: 1112 sites, typical site width 33 ft, accepts full hkup units only, 1112 full hkups, (30 & 50 amps), wireless Instant Internet access at site ($), phone on-site Internet access (needs activ), phone Internet access central location, RV/park trailer rentals, RV storage, dump station, non-guest dumping $, laundry, ice, patios, controlled access gate.

RECREATION: rec hall, rec room/area, pavilion, equipped pavilion, 2 swim pools, whirlpool, golf nearby, 20 shuffleboard courts, planned activities, tennis, horseshoes, local tours.

Pets welcome, breed restrict, size restrict, quantity restrict. Partial handicap access. No tents. Age restrictions may apply. Open all yr. Big rigs welcome. Member ARVC, AZ ARVC. Phone: (800)444-4996.

e-mail: info@towerpointresort.com

SEE AD PAGE 4

(N) Val Vista Village RV Resort—(Maricopa) *From jct Loop 101 & US 60 (Superstition Fwy): Go 8 mi E on US 60 to (exit 184/Val Vista Dr), then 2-1/2 mi N on Val Vista Dr. Enter on R.* FACILITIES: 1533 sites, typical site width 30 ft, accepts full hkup units only, 1533 full hkups, (30 & 50 amps), 65 pull-thrus, cable TV ($), phone on-site Internet access (needs activ), wireless Internet access central location, RV/park trailer rentals, cabins, laundry, ice, patios, controlled access gate. RECREATION: rec hall, rec room/area, pavilion, equipped pavilion, 5 swim pools, whirlpool, mini-golf, putting green, golf nearby, bsktball, 32 shuffleboard courts, planned activities, tennis, horseshoes, v-ball, local tours. Pets welcome. Partial handicap access. No tents. Age restrictions may apply. Open all yr. Big rigs welcome. Phone: (888)940-8989.

(E) Valle Del Oro RV Resort—(Maricopa) *From jct Loop 101 & US 60 (Superstition Fwy): Go 15-1/4 mi E on US 60 to (exit 191/Ellsworth), then 200 yards N on Ellsworth Rd. Enter on L.* FACILITIES: 1760 sites, typical site width 35 ft, accepts full hkup units only, 1760 full hkups, (30 & 50 amps), phone on-site Internet access (needs activ), wireless Internet access central location, laundry, patios, controlled access gate. RECREATION: rec hall, rec room/area, pavilion, equipped pavilion, 2 swim pools, whirlpool, golf nearby, 16 shuffleboard courts, planned activities, tennis, horseshoes, sports field, local tours. Pets welcome, breed restrict. Partial handicap access. No tents. Age restrictions may apply. Open all yr. Big rigs welcome. Phone: (888)940-8989.

(E) Venture Out at Mesa—(Maricopa) *From jct Loop 101 & US 60 (Superstition Fwy): Go 9 mi E on US 60 (exit 185) Greenfield Rd, then 2 mi N on Greenfield, then 3/4 mi E on E Main St. Enter on R.* FACILITIES: 1782 sites, typical site width 15 ft, accepts full hkup units only, 1782 full hkups, (30 amps), 13 pull-thrus, cable TV, wireless Internet access central location, RV storage, dump station, laundry, ice, patios, controlled access gate. RECREATION: rec hall, rec room/area, 2 swim pools, whirlpool, putting green, golf nearby, bsktball, 20 shuffleboard courts, planned activities, tennis, horseshoes, sports field, local tours. No pets. Partial handicap access. No tents. Age restrictions may apply. Open all yr. Phone: (480)832-0200.

PHOENIX

(N) DESERT'S EDGE RV VILLAGE—(Maricopa) *From jct I-10 & I-17: Go 15 mi N on I-17 to (exit 217B/Deer Valley Rd), then 1/2 mi N on East Frontage Road, then 500 feet E on Williams Dr. Enter on L.*

FACILITIES: 202 sites, typical site width 28 ft, 202 full hkups, (20, 30 & 50 amps), 15 pull-thrus, cable TV, wireless Instant Internet access at site, phone on-site Internet access (needs activ), phone Internet access central location, RV storage, laundry, LP gas by meter, tables, patios.

RECREATION: rec hall, rec room/area, pavilion, coin games, swim pool, whirlpool, golf nearby, bsktball, playground, planned activities, horseshoes.

Pets welcome. Partial handicap access. No tents. Open all yr. Big rigs welcome. Member ARVC, AZ ARVC. Phone: (623)587-0940.

e-mail: dakarderv@aol.com

SEE AD THIS PAGE

(N) Phoenix Metro RV Park—(Maricopa) *From jct Loop 101 & I-17: Go 1 mi N on I-17 (Deer Valley exit 215B), then 3/4 mi N on east frontage road. Enter on R.* FACILITIES: 310 sites, typical site width 27 ft, accepts full hkup units only, 310 full hkups, (30 & 50 amps), wireless Instant Internet access at site, phone on-site Internet access (needs activ), wireless Internet access central location, RV storage, laundry, ice, grills. RECREATION: rec hall, rec room/area, equipped pavilion, swim pool, whirlpool, golf nearby, 2 shuffleboard courts, planned activities, horseshoes, local tours. Pets welcome, breed restrict, quantity restrict. Partial handicap access. No tents. Age restrictions may apply. Open all yr. Big rigs welcome. Member ARVC, AZ ARVC. Phone: (623)582-0390.

QUARTZSITE

(W) 88 Shades RV Resort—(La Paz) *From jct I-10 & Bus US 95 (exit 17): Go 1 mi E on Bus US 95. Enter on R.* FACILITIES: 238 sites, typical site width 26 ft, 238 full hkups, (30 & 50 amps), 26 pull-thrus, cable TV, wireless Instant Internet access at site ($), phone Internet access central location, RV/park trailer rentals, laundry, LP gas by meter, ice, tables, patios. RECREATION: rec hall, rec room/area, whirlpool, 2 shuffleboard courts, planned activities, horseshoes, local tours. Pets welcome. No tents. Open all yr. Big rigs welcome. Phone: (800)457-4392.

(W) Holiday Palms—(La Paz) *From jct I-10 & Bus US 95 (exit 17): Go 1-1/4 mi E on Bus US 95. Enter on L.* FACILITIES: 245 sites, typical site width 25 ft, accepts full hkup units only, 245 full hkups, (20, 30 & 50 amps), 14 pull-thrus, cable TV, wireless Instant Internet access at site ($), laundry, LP gas by meter, ice, patios. RECREATION: rec hall, rec room/area, whirlpool, 2 shuffleboard courts, planned activities, horseshoes, local tours. No pets. No tents. Open all yr. Planned group activities Nov 1 - April 1. Big rigs welcome. Phone: (800)635-5372.

SHOW LOW

(NE) Voyager At Juniper Ridge RV Resort—(Navajo) Altitude 6000 ft. *From jct Hwy 260 & US 60/Hwy 77: Go 5 mi NE on US 60/Hwy 77, then 7-1/4 mi N on Hwy 77, then 3-1/8 mi E on White Mountain Lake Rd. Enter on R.* FACILITIES: 100 sites, typical site width 45 ft, 100 full hkups, (30 & 50 amps), 16 pull-thrus, cable TV, wireless Instant Internet access at site ($), wireless Internet access central location, RV/park trailer rentals, cabins, RV storage, laundry, ltd groceries, RV supplies, ice, tables, patios, grills, controlled access gate. RECREATION: rec hall, rec room/area, pavilion, equipped pavilion, swim pool, whirlpool, dock, lake fishing, fishing supplies, putting green, golf nearby, 4 shuffleboard courts, planned activities, tennis, horseshoes, sports field, v-ball, local tours. Pets welcome. Partial handicap access. No tents. Age restrictions may apply. Open all yr. Facilities fully operational May 31 thru Sep 1. Big rigs welcome. Member ARVC, AZ ARVC. Phone: (866)534-3456.

SURPRISE

(N) Sunflower Resort—(Maricopa) *From jct I-17 (exit 215 W) & Loop 101: Go 8 mi W on Loop 101 (exit 14), then 5-1/2 mi W on Bell Rd, then 1/4 mi S on El Mirage Rd. Enter on L.* FACILITIES: 1155 sites, typical site width 35 ft, 1140 full hkups, 15 E, (30 & 50 amps), 39 pull-thrus, cable TV, phone on-site Internet access (needs activ), wireless Internet access central location, RV storage, dump station, laundry, ice, patios, controlled access gate. RECREATION: rec hall, rec room/area, equipped pavilion, 2 swim pools, whirlpool, mini-golf, putting green, golf nearby, 16 shuffleboard courts, planned activities, tennis, horseshoes, v-ball, local tours. Pets welcome, breed restrict. Partial handicap access. No tents. Age restrictions may apply. Open all yr. Big rigs welcome. Phone: (888)940-8989.

TUCSON

(E) Far Horizons Tucson Village RV Resort—(Pima) *From jct I-19 & I-10: Go 10 mi E on I-10 (exit 270) Kolb Rd, then 8 mi N on Kolb Rd, 1 mi E on Broadway, then 1/2 mi N on Pantano Rd, W 50 feet at 5th. Enter at end.* FACILITIES: 514 sites, typical site width 28 ft, accepts full hkup units only, 514 full hkups, (20, 30 & 50 amps), 2 pull-thrus, cable TV ($), wireless Instant Internet access at site ($), wireless Internet access central location, cabins, laundry, ice, patios, controlled access gate. RECREATION: rec hall, rec room/area, equipped pavilion, swim pool, whirlpool, mini-golf, golf nearby, 9 shuffleboard courts, planned activities, horseshoes, hiking trails, local tours. Pets welcome, quantity restrict. Partial handicap access. No tents. Age restrictions may apply. Open all yr. Big rigs welcome. Member ARVC, AZ ARVC. Phone: (800)480-3488.

TUCSON—Continued

(SE) RINCON COUNTRY EAST—(Pima) *From jct I-19 & I-10: Go 9-1/2 mi SE on I-10, exit 270, then 4-3/4 mi N on Kolb Rd, then 2 mi E on Escalante Rd. Enter on L.*

FACILITIES: 460 sites, typical site width 27 ft, accepts full hkup units only, 460 full hkups, (30 & 50 amps), wireless Instant Internet access at site ($), phone Internet access central location, RV storage, laundry, ice, patios, controlled access gate.

RECREATION: rec hall, rec room/area, pavilion, swim pool, whirlpool, putting green, golf nearby, 6 shuffleboard courts, planned activities, tennis, horseshoes, local tours.

Pets welcome, breed restrict, quantity restrict. Partial handicap access. No tents. Age restrictions may apply. Open all yr. Escort-winter season only. Big rigs welcome. Member ARVC, AZ ARVC. Phone: (888)401-8989.

e-mail: eastinfo@rinconcountry.com

Reserve Online at Woodalls.com

SEE AD PAGE 5

(SW) Rincon Country West—(Pima) *From jct of I-10 & I-19: Go 1-1/2 mi S on I-19 (exit 99) Ajo Way, then 1 mi W on Ajo Way, then 1/2 mi S on Mission Rd. Enter on L.* FACILITIES: 1083 sites, typical site width 35 ft, accepts full hkup units only, 1083 full hkups, (30 & 50 amps), 24 pull-thrus, cable TV, wireless Instant Internet access at site ($), phone Internet access central location, RV storage, laundry, patios, controlled access gate. RECREATION: rec hall, rec room/area, pavilion, equipped pavilion, swim pool, whirlpool, putting green, golf nearby, bsktball, 10 shuffleboard courts, planned activities, tennis, horseshoes, sports field, local tours. Pets welcome, breed restrict, quantity restrict. Partial handicap access. No tents. Age restrictions may apply. Open all yr. Escort winter season only. Big rigs welcome. Member ARVC, AZ ARVC. Phone: (800)782-7275.

Reserve Online at Woodalls.com

(SE) Voyager RV Resort—(Pima) *From jct I-19 & I-10: Go 10-1/4 mi E on I-10 (exit 270), then 1/2 mi S on Kolb Rd. Enter on L.* FACILITIES: 1576 sites, typical site width 34 ft, 1576 full hkups, (30 & 50 amps), 100 pull-thrus, cable TV, phone Instant Internet access at site, wireless Internet access central location, RV/park trailer rentals, RV storage, dump station, laundry, groceries, RV supplies, ice, tables, patios, controlled access gate. RECREATION: rec hall, rec room/area, equipped pavilion, 4 swim pools, whirlpool, mini-golf, putting green, golf nearby, bsktball, 18 shuffleboard courts, planned activities, tennis, horseshoes, sports field, v-ball, local tours. Pets welcome. Partial handicap access. No tents. Age restrictions may apply. Open all yr. Big rigs welcome. Member ARVC, AZ ARVC. ATM. Phone: (800)424-9191.

YUMA

(W) Cocopah RV & Golf Resort—(Yuma) *From jct I-8 (exit Winterhaven/4th Ave) & 4th Ave: Go 1/2 mi S on 4th Ave, then 2-1/2 mi W on 1st St, then 3 blocks S on Ave C, then 2 mi W on Riverside Drive, then 1 mi N on Strand Ave. Enter at end.* FACILITIES: 806 sites, typical site width 33 ft, accepts full hkup units only, 806 full hkups, (30 & 50 amps), cable TV, wireless Instant Internet access at site ($), phone on-site Internet access (needs activ), cable Internet access central location, RV storage, laundry, ltd groceries, RV supplies, ice, patios, controlled access gate. RECREATION: rec hall, rec room/area, pavilion, equipped pavilion, swim pool, whirlpool, river fishing, putting green, golf nearby, 8 shuffleboard courts, planned activities, tennis, horseshoes, hiking trails, local tours. Rec open to public. Pets welcome, quantity restrict. Partial handicap access. No tents. Age restrictions may apply. Open all yr. Big rigs welcome. ATM. Phone: (800)537-7901.

ARKANSAS

NORTH LITTLE ROCK

Hidden Grove RV Park (REBUILDING)—(Pulaski) *From jct I-40 & exit 142 (McArthur Dr): Go 4.5 mi N to Oak Grove East 1 block then N on Honysuckle 1 block. Enter on R.* FACILITIES: 12 sites, 12 full hkups, (30 & 50 amps), grills. Pets welcome. Open all yr. Big rigs welcome.

CALIFORNIA

ANAHEIM

POMONA/FAIRPLEX KOA—*From Anaheim: Go 18 mi N on Hwy 57, then 18 mi N on Hwy 57, then 2 1/2 mi E on I10, then 1-1/2 mi N on White Ave. Enter on R.*

FACILITIES: 185 sites, typical site width 20 ft, 158 full hkups, 27 W&E, (30 & 50 amps), 176 pull-thrus, wireless Instant Internet access at site, cabins, dump station, non-guest dumping $, laundry, groceries, RV supplies, ice, tables.

RECREATION: rec room/area, equipped pavilion, coin games, swim pool, whirlpool, golf nearby, planned activities, local tours.

Pets welcome, breed restrict, size restrict, quantity restrict. Partial handicap access. Open all yr. Big rigs welcome. Member ARVC, CTPA. ATM. Phone: (888)562-4230.

SEE PRIMARY LISTING AT POMONA AND AD POMONA NEXT PAGE

BAKERSFIELD

(E) Bakersfield River Run RV Park—(Kern) *From jct Hwy 99 & Hwy 58 (Rosedale Hwy): Go 1/2 mi W on Hwy 58 (Rosedale Hwy), then 1/2 mi S on Gibson Street, then 1/2 mi E on Burr St. Enter at end.* FACILITIES: 123 sites, typical site width 29 ft, 123 full hkups, (20, 30 & 50 amps), 31 pull-thrus, cable TV, phone/wireless Instant Internet access at site, dump station, non-guest dumping $, laundry, ltd groceries, RV supplies, LP gas by meter, ice, patios. RECREATION: rec hall, rec room/area, swim pool, whirlpool, golf nearby, hiking trails. Pets welcome ($), breed restrict, size restrict, quantity restrict. Partial handicap access. No tents. Open all yr. Pool open during summer months. Big rigs welcome. Member ARVC, CTPA. Phone: (888) 748-7786.

DESERT HOT SPRINGS

(SE) Sam's Family Spa Resort—(Riverside) *From jct Hwy 62 & I-10: Go 6 mi E on I-10, then 3 mi N on Palm Dr, then 4.8 mi E on Dillon Rd. Enter on R.* FACILITIES: 170 sites, typical site width 25 ft, 170 full hkups, (20, 30 & 50 amps), wireless Instant Internet access at site ($), laundry, ltd groceries, ice, patios. RECREATION: rec hall, pavilion, equipped pavilion, swim pool, whirlpool, golf nearby, bsktball, play equipment, planned activities, horseshoes, v-ball. Pets welcome. Open all yr. Planned group activities winter only. Big rigs welcome. Member ARVC, CTPA. Phone: (760)329-6457.

EL CAJON

(NE) CIRCLE RV RESORT—(San Diego) *From jct Hwy 67 & I-8: Go 2-1/2 mi E on I-8, then 1 block N on Greenfield Dr, then 1/4 mi E on E Main St. Enter on R.*

FACILITIES: 170 sites, typical site width 20 ft, 170 full hkups, (20, 30 & 50 amps), 8 pull-thrus, cable TV, wireless Instant Internet access at site ($), phone on-site Internet access (needs activ), phone Internet access central location, laundry, LP gas by meter, ice, tables, patios.

RECREATION: rec hall, rec room/area, equipped pavilion, swim pool, whirlpool, golf nearby, planned activities, horseshoes, local tours.

Pets welcome ($), breed restrict, quantity restrict. Partial handicap access. No tents. Open all yr. Advanced Reservations Suggested. Big rigs welcome. Member ARVC, CTPA. Phone: (800)422-1835.

e-mail: circlerv@sunlandrvresorts.com

SEE AD SAN DIEGO PAGE 8

(NE) OAK CREEK RV RESORT—(San Diego) *From jct I-15 & I-8: Go 16 mi E on I-8, then take Lake Jennings Park Rd exit, then 2-1/2 mi E (straight ahead) on Olde Hwy 80. Enter on L.*

FACILITIES: 121 sites, typical site width 20 ft, 121 full hkups, (30 & 50 amps), cable TV, wireless Instant Internet access at site ($), phone on-site Internet access (needs activ), phone Internet access central location, laundry, ice, tables, patios.

RECREATION: rec hall, equipped pavilion, swim pool, whirlpool, golf nearby, planned activities, horseshoes.

Pets welcome ($), breed restrict, quantity restrict. Partial handicap access. No tents. Open all yr.

Advanced Reservations Suggested. Big rigs welcome. Member ARVC, CTPA. Phone: (800)365-1274.

e-mail: oakcreekrv@sunlandrvresorts.com

SEE AD SAN DIEGO PAGE 8

(S) RANCHO LOS COCHES RV PARK—(San Diego) *From jct Hwy 67 & I-8: Go 4 mi E on I-8, then 1/2 mi N on Los Coches Rd, then 1/4 mi E on Hwy 8 Business. Enter on L.*

FACILITIES: 142 sites, typical site width 20 ft, 142 full hkups, (30 & 50 amps), cable TV, wireless Instant Internet access at site ($), dump station, non-guest dumping $, laundry, RV supplies, tables, patios.

RECREATION: rec hall, rec room/area, pavilion, equipped pavilion, swim pool, whirlpool, golf nearby, planned activities, horseshoes.

Pets welcome, breed restrict. Partial handicap access. Open all yr. Big rigs welcome. Member ARVC, CTPA. Phone: (800)630-0448.

e-mail: ranchorv@pacbell.net

Reserve Online at Woodalls.com

SEE AD SAN DIEGO PAGE 8

(E) THE VACATIONER RV RESORT—(San Diego) *From jct Hwy I-15 & I-8: Go 12-3/4 mi E on I-8 (Greenfield Dr exit), then 1 block N on Greenfield Dr, then 1/2 mi SW on E Main St. Enter on L.*

FACILITIES: 150 sites, typical site width 20 ft, 150 full hkups, (20, 30 & 50 amps), 12 pull-thrus, cable TV, wireless Instant Internet access at site ($), phone on-site Internet access (needs activ), phone Internet access central location, RV storage, laundry, LP gas by meter, ice, tables, patios.

RECREATION: rec room/area, equipped pavilion, swim pool, whirlpool, golf nearby, 2 shuffleboard courts, planned activities, horseshoes, local tours.

Pets welcome ($), breed restrict, quantity restrict. Partial handicap access. No tents. Open all yr. Advanced reservations suggested. Big rigs welcome. Member ARVC, CTPA. Phone: (866)490-5844.

e-mail: vacationerrv@sunlandrvresorts.com

SEE AD SAN DIEGO PAGE 8

ESCONDIDO

(N) ESCONDIDO RV RESORT—(San Diego) *From jct Hwy 78 & I-15: Go 1 mi N on I-15 (El Norte Pkwy exit), then 200 yds E on El Norte Pkwy, then 1 block N on Seven Oaks Rd. Enter on R.*

FACILITIES: 125 sites, typical site width 17 ft, 125 full hkups, (20, 30 & 50 amps), cable TV, wireless Instant Internet access at site ($), phone on-site Internet access (needs activ), phone Internet access central location, laundry, LP gas by meter, patios.

RECREATION: rec room/area, equipped pavilion, swim pool, whirlpool, golf nearby, playground, planned activities, horseshoes, sports field, hiking trails, local tours.

Pets welcome ($), breed restrict, quantity restrict. Partial handicap access. No tents. Open all yr. Advanced Reservations Suggested. Big rigs welcome. Member ARVC, CTPA. Phone: (800)331-3556.

e-mail: escondidorv@sunlandrvresorts.com

SEE AD SAN DIEGO PAGE 8

(NE) WOODS VALLEY KAMPGROUND—(San Diego) *From jct I-15 & CR-56 (Valley Parkway exit): Go 8-1/2 mi NE on CR-56, then 2 mi E on Woods Valley Rd. Enter on L.*

FACILITIES: 89 sites, typical site width 25 ft, 44 full hkups, 45 W&E, (20 & 30 amps), 1 pull-thrus, cable TV, dump station, laundry, ltd groceries, RV supplies, ice, tables, wood.

RECREATION: rec hall, rec room/area, coin games, swim pool, pond fishing, fishing supplies, golf nearby, playground, horseshoes, v-ball.

Pets welcome ($), breed restrict. Open all yr. Catch & release fishing only. Member ARVC, CTPA. Phone: (760)749-2905.

SEE AD SAN DIEGO PAGE 8

HEMET

(W) GOLDEN VILLAGE PALMS RV RESORT—(Riverside) *E'bnd from jct I-10 & Hwy 79S:Go 7-3/4 mi S on Hwy 79S, then 5-1/2 mi S across Ramona Expwy on Sanderson, then 1 blk W on Hwy 74/Florida Ave. W'bnd from jct I-15N & Winchester Rd exit: Go 14 mi N on Winchester Rd, then 6 mi E on Hwy 74E/Florida Ave. Enter on R.*

FACILITIES: 1041 sites, typical site width 35 ft, 1041 full hkups, (20, 30 & 50 amps), 103 pull-thrus, cable TV, wireless Instant Internet access at site ($), phone on-site Internet access (needs activ), phone Internet access central location, laundry, ice, patios, controlled access gate.

RECREATION: rec hall, rec room/area, equipped pavilion, 3 swim pools, whirlpool, putting green, golf nearby, 8 shuffleboard courts, planned activities, horseshoes, v-ball, local tours.

Pets welcome, breed restrict, quantity restrict. Partial handicap access. No tents. Age restrictions may apply. Open all yr. Advanced Reservation Suggested. Big rigs welcome. Member ARVC, CTPA. Phone: (800)323-9610.

e-mail: goldenrv@sunlandrvresorts.com

SEE AD PALM SPRINGS PAGE 9

IMPERIAL BEACH

(W) BERNARDO SHORES RV PARK—(San Diego) *From jct I-5 & Hwy 75 (Palm Ave): Go 2 mi W on Hwy 75 (Palm Ave). Enter on R.*

FACILITIES: 124 sites, typical site width 35 ft, accepts full hkup units only, 124 full hkups, (30 & 50 amps), wireless Instant Internet access at site, phone on-site Internet access (needs activ), phone Internet access central location, laundry, LP gas by meter, patios, controlled access gate.

RECREATION: rec room/area, putting green, golf nearby, shuffleboard court, planned activities, horseshoes.

Pets welcome ($), size restrict, quantity restrict. No tents. Age restrictions may apply. Open all yr. No restrooms. Big rigs welcome. Member ARVC, CTPA. Phone: (619)429-9000.

e-mail: Bernardo_ShoresRV@sbcglobal.net

Reserve Online at Woodalls.com

SEE AD SAN DIEGO PAGE 9

INDIO

(SE) Indian Wells RV Resort—(Riverside) *From jct Hwy 74 & I-10: Go 7-1/2 mi E on I-10, then 3 mi S on Jefferson St. Enter on L.* FACILITIES: 306 sites, typical site width 25 ft, 306 full hkups, (20, 30 & 50 amps), 168 pull-thrus, cable TV, wireless Instant Internet access at site ($), phone Internet access central location, RV storage, dump station, laundry, ice, patios. RECREATION: rec hall, rec room/area, equipped pavilion, 3 swim pools, whirlpool, putting green, golf nearby,

INDIO—Continued
Indian Wells RV Resort—Continued

bsktball, 4 shuffleboard courts, planned activities, horseshoes, v-ball. Pets welcome, quantity restrict. Partial handicap access. No tents. Open all yr. Big rigs welcome. Phone: (800)789-0895.

LA MESA

(W) SAN DIEGO RV RESORT—(San Diego) *From jct I-15 & I-8: Go 3 mi on I-8 to 70th St/Lake Murrray Blvd exit, then stay in the Lake Murray Blvd/Alvarado Rd left lane to south side of I-8, then 1/2 mi E on Alvarado Rd. Enter on R.*

FACILITIES: 171 sites, typical site width 25 ft, 171 full hkups, (15, 20, 30 & 50 amps), 2 pull-thrus, cable TV, wireless Instant Internet access at site ($), phone on-site Internet access (needs activ), phone Internet access central location, laundry, LP gas by meter, patios.

RECREATION: rec hall, rec room/area, equipped pavilion, swim pool, whirlpool, golf nearby, planned activities, local tours.

Pets welcome ($), breed restrict, quantity restrict. Partial handicap access. No tents. Open all yr. Advanced Reservations Suggested. Big rigs welcome. Member ARVC, CTPA. Phone: (877)787-6386.

e-mail: Sandiegorv@sunlandrvresorts.com

SEE AD SAN DIEGO NEXT PAGE

LODI

(W) FLAG CITY RV RESORT—(San Joaquin) *From jct I-5 & Hwy 12: Go 1/4 mi E on Hwy 12, then 1 block S on Star St, then 200 yds E on Banner St. Enter on R.*

FACILITIES: 180 sites, typical site width 26 ft, 180 full hkups, (20, 30 & 50 amps), 136 pull-thrus, cable TV, phone Instant Internet access at site, laundry, ltd groceries, RV supplies, LP gas by meter, ice, tables, patios.

RECREATION: rec hall, swim pool, whirlpool, golf nearby, planned activities, horseshoes, sports field, v-ball, local tours.

Pets welcome ($). Partial handicap access. No tents. Open all yr. Older rigs stay upon management discretion. Big rigs welcome. Member ARVC, CTPA. Phone: (866)371-4855.

e-mail: info@flagcityrvresort.com

SEE AD THIS PAGE

PALM SPRINGS

See listings at Cathedral City, Desert Hot Springs, Indio & Twentynine Palms

(SW) GOLDEN VILLAGE PALMS RV RESORT—(Riverside) *From Palm Springs: Go 28 mi W on I-10, 7-3/4 mi S on Hwy 795, then 5-1/2 mi S across Ramona Expressway on Sanderson Ave, then 1 block W on Hwy 74/Florida Ave. Enter on R.*

FACILITIES: 1041 sites, typical site width 35 ft, 1041 full hkups, (20, 30 & 50 amps), 103 pull-thrus, cable TV, wireless Instant Internet access at site ($), phone on-site Internet access (needs activ), phone Internet access central location, laundry, ice, patios, controlled access gate.

RECREATION: rec hall, rec room/area, equipped pavilion, 3 swim pools, whirlpool, putting green, golf nearby, 8 shuffleboard courts, planned activities, horseshoes, v-ball, local tours.

Pets welcome, breed restrict, quantity restrict. Partial handicap access. No tents. Age restrictions

Woodall's — Trusted for Over 70 Years.

PALM SPRINGS—Continued
GOLDEN VILLAGE PALMS RV RESORT—Continued

may apply. Open all yr. Advanced reservation suggested. Big rigs welcome. Member ARVC, CTPA. Phone: (800)323-9610.

e-mail: goldenrv@sunlandrvresorts.com

SEE PRIMARY LISTING AT HEMET AND AD PAGE 9

PARKER DAM

(W) Black Meadow Landing—(San Bernardino) *From jct Hwy 95 & Hwy 62: Go 16 mi E on Hwy 62, then 17 mi N on Parker Dam Rd, then 10 mi W on Black Meadow Rd (M.W.D. Rd). Enter at end.* FACILITIES: 398 sites, typical site width 25 ft, 350 full hkups, (30 & 50 amps), 50 amps ($), 48 no hkups, wireless Instant Internet access at site ($), cabins, RV storage, dump station, laundry, full svc store, RV supplies, LP gas by meter, gas, marine gas, ice, tables, fire rings, controlled access gate. RECREATION: rec hall, lake/river swimming, boating, canoeing, ramp, dock, river fishing, fishing supplies, golf nearby, bsktball, playground, planned activities, horseshoes, hiking trails. Pets welcome, breed restrict, quantity restrict. Open all yr. Member ARVC, CTPA. Phone: 800-742-8278.

PLYMOUTH

(S) Far Horizons 49er Village RV Resort—(Amador) *From jct Hwy-16 & Hwy-49: Go 2 mi N on Hwy-49. Enter on L.* FACILITIES: 329 sites, typical site width 33 ft, 329 full hkups, (30 & 50 amps), 50 amps ($), 16 pull-thrus, cable TV, wireless Instant Internet access at site ($), phone on-site Internet access (needs activ), phone Internet access central location, cabins, RV storage, dump station, non-guest dumping $, laundry, ltd groceries, RV supplies, LP gas by meter, ice, tables, patios. RECREATION: rec hall, rec room/area, equipped pavilion, 2 swim pools, whirlpool, pond fishing, golf nearby, bsktball, playground, 3 shuffleboard courts, planned activities (wkends only), horseshoes, v-ball, local tours. Pets welcome. Partial handicap access. No tents. Open all yr. Big rigs welcome. Member ARVC, CTPA. Phone: (800)339-6981.

POMONA

(N) POMONA/FAIRPLEX KOA—(Los Angeles) *E'bnd from jct Hwy 71 (Corona Expwy) & I-10: Go 2-1/2 mi NE on I-10, then 1-1/2 mi N on White Ave. W'bnd from jct Hwy 83 & I-10: Go 5-1/2 mi W on I-10, then 50 feet SW on Garey Ave, then 1/2 mi NW on McKinley Ave, then 1 mi N on White Ave. Enter on R.*

FACILITIES: 185 sites, typical site width 20 ft, 158 full hkups, 27 W&E, (30 & 50 amps), 176 pull-

POMONA/FAIRPLEX KOA—Continued on next page

POMONA—Continued
POMONA/FAIRPLEX KOA—Continued

thrus, wireless Instant Internet access at site, cabins, dump station, non-guest dumping $, laundry, groceries, RV supplies, ice, tables.

RECREATION: rec room/area, equipped pavilion, coin games, swim pool, whirlpool, golf nearby, local tours.

Pets welcome, breed restrict, size restrict, quantity restrict. Partial handicap access. Open all yr. Big rigs welcome. Member ARVC, CTPA. ATM. Phone: (888)562-4230.

SEE AD PAGE 7

SAN DIEGO

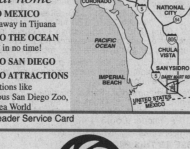

(N) Campland on the Bay—(San Diego) *Southbound: From jct I-5 & Hwy-274 (Balboa-Garnet exit): Go 1/2 mi S on Mission Bay Dr. then 1 mi W on Grand Ave, then 1/4 mi S on Olney St. Northbound: From jct I-5 & Garnet-Grand Ave: Go 1 mi W on Grand Ave, then 1/4 mi S on Olney St. Enter on R.* FACILITIES: 573 sites, typical site width 20 ft, 407 full hkups, 148 W&E, (20, 30 & 50 amps), 18 no hkups, 26 pull-thrus, cable TV, wireless Instant Internet access at site, phone Internet access central location, RV storage, dump station, laundry, full svc store, RV supplies, LP gas by meter, ice, tables, fire rings, wood, controlled access gate. RECREATION: rec hall, rec room/area, coin games, 2 swim pools, saltwater swimming, whirlpool, boating, canoeing, ramp, dock, 8 rowboat/8 canoe/16 pedal boat/2 motorboat rentals, saltwater fishing, fishing supplies, golf nearby, bsktball, 25 bike rentals, playground, planned activities, horseshoes, sports field, v-ball, local tours. Rec open to public. Pets welcome ($), breed restrict, quantity restrict. Open all yr. Big rigs welcome. Member ARVC, CTPA. ATM. Phone: (800)422-9386.

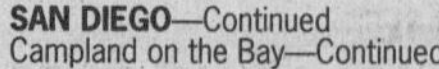

(N) CIRCLE RV RESORT—(San Diego) *From San Diego: Go 24 mi E on I-8, then 1 block on Greenfield Rd, then 1/4 mi E on E Main St.*

FACILITIES: 170 sites, typical site width 20 ft, 170 full hkups, (30 & 50 amps), 8 pull-thrus, cable TV, wireless Instant Internet access at site ($), phone on-site Internet access (needs activ), phone Internet access central location, laundry, LP gas by meter, ice, tables, patios.

RECREATION: rec hall, rec room/area, equipped pavilion, swim pool, whirlpool, golf nearby, planned activities, horseshoes, local tours.

CIRCLE RV RESORT—Continued on page 10

SAN DIEGO—Continued
CIRCLE RV RESORT—Continued

Pets welcome ($), breed restrict, quantity restrict. Partial handicap access. No tents. Open all yr. Advanced Reservations Suggested. Big rigs welcome. Member ARVC, CTPA. Phone: (800)422-1835.

e-mail: circlerv@sunlandrvresorts.com

SEE PRIMARY LISTING AT EL CAJON AND AD PAGE 8

(NE) ESCONDIDO RV RESORT—(San Diego) *From San Diego: Go 21 mi N on I-15 (El Norte Pkwy exit), then 1 block E on El Norte Pkwy, then 1 block N on Seven Oaks. Enter on R.*

FACILITIES: 125 sites, typical site width 17 ft, 125 full hkups, (20, 30 & 50 amps), cable TV, wireless Instant Internet access at site ($), phone on-site Internet access (needs activ), phone Internet access central location, laundry, LP gas by meter, patios.

RECREATION: rec room/area, equipped pavilion, swim pool, whirlpool, golf nearby, playground, planned activities, sports field, hiking trails, local tours.

Pets welcome ($), breed restrict, quantity restrict. Partial handicap access. No tents. Open all yr. Advanced Reservations Suggested. Big rigs welcome. Member ARVC, CTPA. Phone: (800)331-3556.

e-mail: escondidorv@sunlandrvresorts.com

SEE PRIMARY LISTING AT ESCONDIDO AND AD PAGE 8

(S) LA PACIFICA RV RESORT—(San Diego) *From jct Hwy 905 & I-5: Go 1 mi S on I-5, then 1 block E on Dairy Mart, then 1 block N on San Ysidro Blvd. Enter on L.*

FACILITIES: 179 sites, typical site width 22 ft, accepts full hkup units only, 179 full hkups, (20, 30 & 50 amps), 64 pull-thrus, wireless Internet access central location, dump station, non-guest dumping $, laundry, tables, patios.

RECREATION: rec room/area, swim pool, whirlpool, golf nearby, horseshoes.

Pets welcome, breed restrict, quantity restrict. Partial handicap access. No tents. Open all yr. Big rigs welcome. Member ARVC, CTPA. Phone: (619) 428-4411.

e-mail: lapacifica@rasnyder.com

SEE AD PAGE 8

(NE) MORENA MOBILE VILLAGE—(San Diego) *From jct I-8 & I-5: Go 1 m N on I-5, then 1 block E on Seaworld Dr/Tecolate Rd, then 1 block N on Morena Blvd. (entrance on Knoxville St). Enter on R.*

FACILITIES: 101 sites, accepts self-contained units only, 101 full hkups, (50 amps), phone on-site Internet access (needs activ), RV storage, laundry, patios.

RECREATION: rec room/area, swim pool.

Pets welcome ($). No tents. Open all yr. Min 2 months; Max 6-1/2 months. Phone: (619)276-5699.

SEE AD PAGE 8

(E) OAK CREEK RV RESORT—(San Diego) *From San Diego: Go 23 mi E on I-8 to Lake Jennings Rd exit, then 2-1/2 mi E on Olde Hwy 80. Enter on L.*

FACILITIES: 121 sites, typical site width 20 ft, 121 full hkups, (30 & 50 amps), wireless Instant Internet access at site ($), phone on-site Internet access (needs activ), phone Internet access central location, laundry, ice, tables, patios.

RECREATION: rec hall, equipped pavilion, swim pool, whirlpool, golf nearby, planned activities, horseshoes.

Pets welcome ($), breed restrict, quantity restrict. Partial handicap access. No tents. Advanced Reservations Suggested. Big rigs welcome. Member ARVC, CTPA. Phone: (800)365-1274.

SEE PRIMARY LISITNG AT EL CAJON AND AD PAGE 8

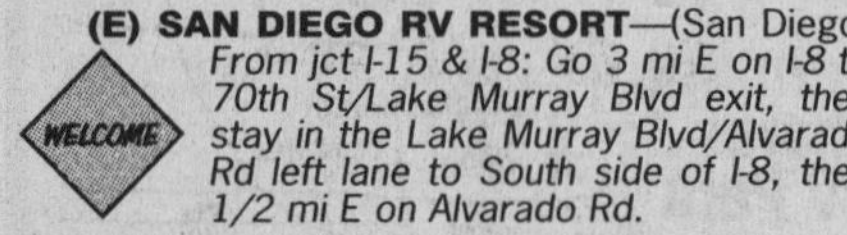

(E) SAN DIEGO RV RESORT—(San Diego) *From jct I-15 & I-8: Go 3 mi E on I-8 to 70th St/Lake Murray Blvd exit, then stay in the Lake Murray Blvd/Alvarado Rd left lane to South side of I-8, then 1/2 mi E on Alvarado Rd.*

FACILITIES: 171 sites, typical site width 25 ft, 171 full hkups, (15, 20, 30 & 50 amps), 2 pull-thrus, cable TV, wireless Instant Internet access at site ($), phone on-site Internet access (needs activ), phone Internet access central location, laundry, LP gas by meter, patios.

RECREATION: rec hall, rec room/area, equipped pavilion, swim pool, whirlpool, golf nearby, planned activities, local tours.

Pets welcome ($), breed restrict, quantity restrict. Partial handicap access. No tents. Open all yr. Advanced reservation suggested. Big rigs welcome. Member ARVC, CTPA. Phone: (877)787-6386.

e-mail: Sandiegorv@sunlandresorts.com

SEE PRIMARY LISTING AT LA MESA AND AD PAGE 8

(E) THE VACATIONER RV RESORT—(San Diego) *From San Diego: Go 20 mi E on I-8 (Greenfield Dr exit), then 1 block N under freeway, then 1/2 mi SW on Main St.*

FACILITIES: 150 sites, typical site width 20 ft, 150 full hkups, (20, 30 & 50 amps), 12 pull-thrus, cable TV, wireless Instant Internet access at site ($), phone on-site Internet access (needs activ), phone Internet access central location, RV storage, laundry, LP gas by meter, ice, tables, patios.

RECREATION: rec room/area, equipped pavilion, swim pool, whirlpool, golf nearby, 2 shuffleboard courts, planned activities, horseshoes, local tours.

Pets welcome ($), breed restrict, quantity restrict. Partial handicap access. No tents. Open all yr. Advanced Reservations Suggested. Big rigs welcome. Member ARVC, CTPA. Phone: (866)490-5844.

e-mail: vacationerrv@sunlandrvresorts.com

SEE PRIMARY LISTING AT EL CAJON AND AD PAGE 8

SHAFTER

(E) Bakersfield RV Park—(Kern) *From jct Hwy 99 (Shafter exit) & Lerdo Hwy: Go 1 mi W on Lerdo Hwy. Enter on L.* FACILITIES: 75 sites, typical site width 30 ft, 35 full hkups, 28 W&E, (20, 30 & 50 amps), 12 no hkups, 56 pull-thrus, phone Internet access central location, cabins, RV storage, dump station, non-guest dumping $, laundry, ltd groceries, RV supplies, LP gas by meter, ice, tables. RECREATION: rec room/area, swim pool, golf nearby, bsktball, play equipment, horseshoes, sports field. Pets welcome, breed restrict, size restrict. Partial handicap access. Open all yr. 11-1 thru 3-31 (pool open) 4-10. Member ARVC, CTPA. Phone: (661)399-3107.

SOUTH LAKE TAHOE

(S) Chris Haven RV Community—(El Dorado) Altitude 6300 ft. *From north jct Hwy 89 & US 50: Go 1/2 mi SW on Hwy 89/US 50, then 1 block E on E Street. Enter on L.* FACILITIES: 108 sites, typical site width 20 ft, 108 full hkups, (30 & 50 amps), 2 pull-thrus, cable TV ($), wireless Instant Internet access at site ($), dump station, non-guest dumping $, laundry, patios. RECREATION: golf nearby. Pets welcome, breed restrict, size restrict, quantity restrict. No tents. Open all yr. Phone: (530)541-1895.

TWENTYNINE PALMS

(NE) TWENTYNINE PALMS RESORT: RV PARK.COTTAGES.GOLF—(San Bernardino) *From jct I-10 & Hwy 62: Go 44 mi E on Hwy 62, then 2 mi N on Adobe Rd, then 1/2 mi E on Amboy Rd, then 100 yds N on Desert Knoll Ave. Enter on L.*

FACILITIES: 197 sites, typical site width 25 ft, 157 full hkups, 40 W&E, (30 & 50 amps), 31 pull-thrus, phone on-site Internet access (needs activ), wireless Internet access central location, cabins, RV storage, laundry, RV supplies, LP gas by meter, ice.

RECREATION: rec hall, rec room/area, swim pool, whirlpool, putting green, golf nearby, bsktball, 2 shuffleboard courts, planned activities, tennis, horseshoes.

Pets welcome, breed restrict, size restrict. Partial handicap access. Open all yr. Big rigs welcome. Member ARVC, CTPA. Phone: (800)874-4548.

e-mail: info@29palmsresort.com

SEE AD PALM SPRINGS PAGE 7

VAN NUYS

(W) Birmingham RV Park—(Los Angeles) *From jct I-405 & US 101 (Ventura Fwy): Go 2 mi W on US 101, then 2-3/4 mi N on Balboa Ave. Enter on R.* FACILITIES: 186 sites, 186 full hkups, (30 & 50 amps), cable TV, wireless Instant Internet access at site, phone Internet access central location, laundry, tables, patios, controlled access gate. RECREATION: rec hall. Pets welcome, breed restrict. Partial handicap access. No tents. Open all yr. Phone: (818)785-0949.

VENTURA

(N) Lake Casitas Recreation Area—(Ventura) *From jct Hwy 101 & Hwy 33: Go 11 mi N on Hwy 33, then 3 mi W on Hwy 150, then S on Santa Ana Rd. Enter on L.* FACILITIES: 410 sites, 50 full hkups, 100 W&E, (30 & 50 amps), 260 no hkups, 205 pull-thrus, cable TV, wireless Instant Internet access at site ($), phone Internet access central location, RV/park trailer rentals, RV storage, dump station, non-guest dumping $, groceries, RV supplies, LP gas by meter, marine gas, ice, tables, fire rings, grills, wood, controlled access gate. RECREATION: pavilion, wading pool, kayaking, ramp, dock, 10 pontoon/20 rowboat/20 canoe/20 kayak/5 pedal boat/40 motorboat rentals, lake fishing, fishing supplies, fishing guides, golf nearby, bsktball, 125 bike rentals, playground, horseshoes, sports field, hiking trails, v-ball. Rec open to public. Pets welcome ($). Partial handicap access. Open all yr. Long term stay 11-1 thru 3-31 only. Big rigs welcome. Member ARVC, CTPA. ATM. Phone: (805)649-2233.

WEST SACRAMENTO

(W) Capital West RV & MH Park—(Yolo) *From Jct I-80 & Bus I-80: Go 1 mi E on Bus I-80, then 1/4 mi N on Harbor Blvd, then 1/4 mi N on West Capital Ave, then 1 block E on Glide Ave. Enter on R.* FACILITIES: 70 sites, typical site width 24 ft, accepts self-contained units only, 70 full hkups, (30 & 50 amps), phone on-site Internet access (needs activ), laundry, patios. Pets welcome, quantity restrict. No tents. Open all yr. Big rigs welcome. Member CTPA. Phone: (916)371-6671.

CONNECTICUT

GRISWOLD

(N) CAMPER'S WORLD, INC.—(London) *From jct I-395 (exit 86) & SR201: Go 1/2 mi S on SR 201, then 1/4 mi SW on Edmond Rd, then 1/8 mi SE on Nowakowski Rd (gravel road). Enter at end.*

FACILITIES: 150 sites, 125 full hkups, 10 W&E, (30 & 50 amps), 15 no hkups, cable TV, wireless Internet access central location, tenting, dump station, RV supplies, tables, fire rings, controlled access gate.

RECREATION: pond, swimming, boating, dock, pond fishing, bsktball, playground, sports field.

Pets welcome. Open Apr 15 thru Oct 15. Rate in 2007 $32 per family. MC/VISA/AMEX. Member ARVC. Phone (860)376-2340.

e-mail: campersworld@aol.com

SEE AD THIS PAGE

Woodall's Tip #4... Rules of the Road information is located in the front of the Directory.

DELAWARE

FENWICK ISLAND

(W) Treasure Beach RV Park—(Sussex) *From jct US 1 & Hwy 54 (Lighthouse Rd): Go 1-1/2 mi W on Hwy 54. From jct US 113 & Hwy 54: Go 11 mi E on Hwy 54. Enter on R.* FACILITIES: 1000 sites, typical site width 25 ft, 1000 full hkups, (20, 30 & 50 amps), cable TV, phone/cable on-site Internet access (needs activ), cable Internet access central location, dump station, laundry, groceries, RV supplies, LP gas by weight/by meter, ice, tables, patios, grills, wood, controlled access gate. RECREATION: rec hall, rec room/area, equipped pavilion, coin games, 2 swim pools, wading pool, boating, canoeing, kayaking, ramp, saltwater/lake fishing, fishing supplies, golf nearby, bsktball, playground, planned activities, horseshoes, sports field, v-ball. Pets welcome. Partial handicap access. No tents. Open May 1 thru 2nd Sunday in Oct. Big rigs welcome. Phone: (302)436-8001.

LONG NECK

(W) LEISURE POINT RESORT (CAMP RESORT)—(Sussex) *From jct Hwy 24 & Hwy 23 (Longneck Rd): Go 1-1/2 mi SE on Hwy 23 then 1/4 mi NE on Radie Kay Lane, then 1 block SE on Dogwood Ln. Enter on L.*

FACILITIES: 43 sites, typical site width 34 ft, 43 full hkups, (20, 30 & 50 amps), cable TV, cable Internet access central location, RV/park trailer rentals, laundry, ltd groceries, RV supplies, LP gas by meter, marine gas, ice, tables, fire rings, grills, wood.

RECREATION: rec hall, rec room/area, equipped pavilion, coin games, swim pool, boating, canoeing, kayaking, ramp, dock, saltwater fishing, fishing supplies, golf nearby, bsktball, playground, planned activities, horseshoes, v-ball.

Pets welcome. Open Apr 15 thru Nov 15. Membership & Coast to Coast only. Big rigs welcome. Phone: (302)945-2000.

e-mail: information@leisurepoint.com

SEE AD THIS PAGE

FLORIDA

ARCADIA

(E) Big Tree RV Resort—(DeSoto) *From jct US-17 & Hwy-70: Go 2-1/2 mi E on Hwy-70. Enter on L.* FACILITIES: 390 sites, typical site width 40 ft, 390 full hkups, (20, 30 & 50 amps), wireless Instant Internet access at site ($), phone Internet access central location ($), dump station, non-guest dumping $, laundry, LP gas by weight, tables, patios. RECREATION: rec hall, rec room/area, swim pool, whirlpool, golf nearby, 6 shuffleboard courts, planned activities, horseshoes. Pets welcome, breed restrict, size restrict, quantity restrict. Partial handicap access. No tents. Age restrictions may apply. Open all yr. Big rigs welcome. Member ARVC, FLARVC. Phone: (863)494-7247.

ARCADIA—Continued

(N) Craig's RV Park—(DeSoto) *From jct Hwy 70 & US 17 N: Go 7 mi N on US 17 N, then 200 feet SW on Cubitis Ave. Enter on L.* FACILITIES: 349 sites, typical site width 35 ft, 349 full hkups, (20, 30 & 50 amps), 64 pull-thrus, wireless Instant Internet access at site ($), phone Internet access central location ($), RV storage, dump station, non-guest dumping $, laundry, RV supplies, LP gas by weight/by meter, patios. RECREATION: rec hall, rec room/area, pavilion, swim pool, putting green, golf nearby, bsktball, 8 shuffleboard courts, planned activities, horseshoes, hiking trails, local tours. No pets. Partial handicap access. No tents. Open all yr. Church services & planned activities during Nov-Apr. Member ARVC, FLARVC. Phone: (877)750-5129.

DUNNELLON

(W) Withlacoochee Backwaters RV Park—(Levy) *From jct US 41 & CR 40: Go 6 mi W on CR 40. Enter on L.* FACILITIES: 21 sites, typical site width 30 ft, 21 full hkups, (30 amps), 3 pull-thrus, phone on-site Internet access (needs activ), cabins, tables. RECREATION: rec hall, boating, ramp, dock, lake fishing, planned activities, horseshoes. Pets welcome. Partial handicap access. No tents. Age restrictions may apply. Open all yr. Phone: (352)489-6691.

FORT MYERS

(NE) UPRIVER RV RESORT—(Lee) *From jct Hwy 82 & I-75: Go 5-1/2 mi N on I-75 (exit 143), then 1-3/4 mi E on Hwy 78 (Bayshore Rd). Enter on R.*

FACILITIES: 350 sites, typical site width 35 ft, 350 full hkups, (20, 30 & 50 amps), 60 pull-thrus, cable TV, wireless Instant Internet access at site ($), phone Internet access central location, laundry, RV supplies, LP gas by weight/by meter, tables, patios.

RECREATION: rec hall, rec room/area, pavilion, swim pool, boating, canoeing, kayaking, ramp, dock, saltwater/river fishing, putting green, golf nearby, bsktball, 6 shuffleboard courts, planned activities, tennis, horseshoes, local tours.

Pets welcome, breed restrict, size restrict, quantity restrict. Partial handicap access. No tents. Age restrictions may apply. Open all yr. Group activities during winter season only. Big rigs welcome. Member ARVC, FLARVC. Phone: (800)848-1652.

e-mail: camping@upriver.com

SEE AD THIS PAGE

Woodall's Tip #20... Find free Tourism Information in the Travel Section

FORT PIERCE

(NW) ROAD RUNNER TRAVEL RESORT—(St. Lucie) *From jct I-95 (exit 129) & Hwy 70: Go 3/4 mi W on Hwy 70, then 5 mi N on Hwy 713, then 1-1/4 mi E on CR 608. Enter on L.*

FACILITIES: 452 sites, typical site width 30 ft, 452 full hkups, (20, 30 & 50 amps), 10 pull-thrus, phone Internet access central location, cabins, RV storage, dump station, non-guest dumping $, laundry, full svc store, RV supplies, LP gas by weight/by meter, ice, tables, patios, controlled access gate.

RECREATION: rec hall, rec room/area, equipped pavilion, swim pool, pond fishing, golf nearby, bsktball, 4 shuffleboard courts, planned activities, tennis, horseshoes, v-ball.

Pets welcome, breed restrict. Partial handicap access. Open all yr. Big rigs welcome. Member ARVC, FLARVC. ATM. Phone: (800)833-7108.

e-mail: rvroadrun@aol.com

SEE AD THIS PAGE

HOMESTEAD

(NE) Pine Isle Mobile Home Park—(Dade) *From jct Hwy 9336 (Palm Dr) & US 1: Go 4 mi N on US 1, then 2 mi E on 288 St, then 500 ft N on 132 Ave. Enter on L.* FACILITIES: 257 sites, typical site width 50 ft, 257 full hkups, (30 & 50 amps), 20 pull-thrus, wireless Internet access central location, laundry, patios. RECREATION: rec hall, pavilion, swim pool, golf nearby, 3 shuffleboard courts, planned activities, horseshoes. Pets welcome, quantity restrict. No tents. Age restrictions may apply. Open all yr. Planned activities in winter only. Big rigs welcome. Phone: (305)248-0783.

KISSIMMEE

(W) MILL CREEK RV RESORT—(Osceola) *From jct US 17/92 & US 192: Go 3/4 mi E on US 192, then 1-1/2 mi N on Hwy 531 (Michigan Ave). Enter on R.*

FACILITIES: 155 sites, typical site width 22 ft, 155 full hkups, (20, 30 & 50 amps), phone/cable on-site Internet access (needs activ), laundry, LP gas by weight/by meter, patios.

RECREATION: rec hall, swim pool, golf nearby, 4 shuffleboard courts, planned activities, horseshoes.

Pets welcome, breed restrict. No tents. Open all yr. Planned group activities winter only. Office closed Sundays & holidays. Member ARVC, FLARVC. Phone: (407)847-6288.

SEE AD NEXT PAGE

LA BELLE

(E) THE GLADES RV, GOLF & MARINA RESORT—(Hendry) *From jct Hwy 29 & Hwy 80: Go 13 mi E on Hwy 80. Enter on L.*

FACILITIES: 109 sites, typical site width 35 ft, 109 full hkups, (30 & 50 amps), 4 pull-thrus, wireless Instant Internet access at site, cabins, RV storage, dump station, non-guest dumping $, laundry, tables, patios.

RECREATION: rec hall, rec room/area, swim pool, boating, canoeing, kayaking, ramp, dock, river/pond fishing, golf nearby, 4 shuffleboard courts, planned activities, horseshoes, sports field, hiking trails.

Pets welcome, breed restrict. Partial handicap access. Open all yr. Big rigs welcome. Member ARVC, FLARVC. Phone: (863)902-7034.

e-mail: info@thegladesresort.com

SEE AD PAGE 11

LAKE WORTH

(S) JOHN PRINCE MEMORIAL PARK (Palm Beach County Park)—(Palm Beach) *From jct Hwy 812 & I-95: Go 2 mi N on I-95 (exit 63), then 1-1/4 mi W on 6th Ave, then 1/2 mi S on Congress Ave. Enter on L.*

FACILITIES: 277 sites, typical site width 25 ft, 91 full hkups, 186 W&E, (30 & 50 amps), 18 pull-thrus, dump station, non-guest dumping $, portable dump, ice, tables, fire rings, grills, wood, controlled access gate.

RECREATION: pavilion, boating, canoeing, kayaking, ramp, dock, lake fishing, golf nearby, bsktball, playground, planned activities, tennis, horseshoes, sports field, hiking trails, v-ball. Rec open to public.

Pets welcome, quantity restrict. Partial handicap access. Open all yr. Planned activities in winter only. Member ARVC, FLARVC. Phone: (877)992-9925.

e-mail: jppcamp@pbcgov.com

SEE AD THIS PAGE

LAKELAND

(N) Lakeland RV Resort—(Polk) *From I-4 (exit 33): Go 1/2 mi NE on Hwy 33, then 1/2 mi E on Old Combee Rd. Enter on R.* FACILITIES: 230 sites, typical site width 35 ft, 230 full hkups, (20, 30 & 50 amps), 50 amps ($), 100 pull-thrus, wireless Instant Internet access at site, phone on-site Internet access (needs activ), wireless

Internet access central location ($), cabins, RV storage, dump station, non-guest dumping $, laundry, RV supplies, LP gas by weight/by meter, tables, patios, controlled access gate. RECREATION: rec hall, rec room/area, swim pool, wading pool, whirlpool, boating, 2 pedal boat rentals, pond fishing, mini-golf, golf nearby, bsktball, playground, 3 shuffleboard courts, planned activities, horseshoes, v-ball. Pets welcome, breed restrict, quantity restrict. Open all yr. Church service & planned activities winter only. Big rigs welcome. Member ARVC, FLARVC. Phone: (888)622-4115.

NAPLES

(E) CLUB NAPLES RV RESORT (Morgan RV Resorts)—(Collier) *From jct I-75 (exit 101) & Hwy 951: Go 1/4 mi S on Hwy 951, then 1 mi E on Old Hwy 84 (Alligator Alley). Enter on R.*

FACILITIES: 309 sites, typical site width 33 ft, 309 full hkups, (30 & 50 amps), 12 pull-thrus, heater not allowed, cable TV, wireless Instant Internet access at site, dump station, non-guest dumping $, laundry, RV supplies, LP gas by weight/by meter, ice, tables, patios.

RECREATION: rec hall, swim pool, whirlpool, mini-golf, golf nearby, bsktball, 6 shuffleboard courts, planned activities, horseshoes.

Pets welcome, breed restrict. Partial handicap access. Open all yr. Group activities in season. Tents summer only. Member ARVC, FLARVC. Phone: (888)795-2780.

e-mail: clubnaples@yahoo.com

SEE AD THIS PAGE

PORT CHARLOTTE

(NE) Riverside RV Resort & Campground—(DeSoto) *From jct I-75 (exit 170) & Hwy 769 (Kings Hwy): Go 4-1/2 mi NE on Hwy 769. Enter on R.* FACILITIES: 350 sites, typical site width 35 ft, 350 full hkups, (30 & 50 amps), 50 amps ($), 4 pull-thrus, wireless Instant Internet access at site ($), phone Internet access central location, RV/park trailer rentals, RV storage, dump station, non-guest dumping $, laundry, groceries, RV supplies, LP gas by weight/by meter, ice, tables, patios, fire rings, wood, controlled access gate. RECREATION: rec hall, rec room/area, equipped pavilion, coin games, 2 swim pools, whirlpool, boating, canoeing, kayaking, ramp, dock, 6 canoe rentals, river fishing, fishing supplies, golf nearby, bsktball, playground, 4 shuffleboard courts, planned activities, horseshoes, v-ball, local tours. Pets welcome. Partial handicap access. Open all yr. Big rigs welcome. Member ARVC, FLARVC. Phone: (800)795-9733.

PORT ST. LUCIE

(SE) Port St Lucie RV Resort—(St. Lucie) *From jct Hwy 716 (W. Port St. Lucie Blvd) & I-95: Go 3 mi S on I-95 (exit 118), then 2-1/2 mi E on Gatlin Blvd, then 5-1/2 mi E on Port St. Lucie Blvd, then 1/2 mi N on US 1, then 1 block E on Jennings Rd. Enter on R.* FACILITIES: 117 sites, typical site width 35 ft, 117 full hkups, (20, 30 & 50 amps), 4 pull-thrus, cable TV ($), wireless Instant Internet access at site, RV storage, laundry, ice, tables, patios. RECREATION: rec hall, pavilion, swim pool, golf nearby, planned activities, horseshoes. Pets welcome ($), quantity restrict. Partial handicap access. No tents. Open all yr. Big rigs welcome. Member ARVC, FLARVC. Phone: (877)405-2333.

ZEPHYRHILLS

(NE) Baker Acres RV Resort—(Pasco) *From N jct US 301 & Hwy 54: Go 1/4 mi E on Hwy 54, then 1-1/2 mi N on Wire Rd. Enter on R.* FACILITIES: 355 sites, typical site width 30 ft, accepts full hkup units only, 355 full hkups, (20, 30 & 50 amps), wireless Instant Internet access at site, phone/cable on-site Internet access (needs activ), phone Internet access central location, dump station, non-guest dumping $, laundry, tables, patios. RECREATION: rec hall, rec room/area, swim pool, golf nearby, 12 shuffleboard courts, planned activities, horseshoes. Pets welcome ($), breed restrict. No tents. Age restrictions may apply. Open all yr. Church services winter only. No showers. Big rigs welcome. Member ARVC, FLARVC. Phone: (813)782-3950.

(SE) Majestic Oaks RV Resort—(Pasco) *From jct SR 54 & US 301: Go 2 mi S on US 301, then 1-1/2 mi E on Chancey Rd. Enter on L.* FACILITIES: 258 sites, 258 full hkups, (30 & 50 amps), wireless Instant Internet access at site, phone/cable on-site Internet access (needs activ), phone Internet access central location, laundry, ice, patios. RECREATION: rec hall, swim pool, golf nearby, 8 shuffleboard courts, planned activities, tennis, horseshoes. Pets welcome, breed restrict. Partial handicap access. No tents. Age restrictions may apply. Open all yr. Planned activities in winter only. Big rigs welcome. Member ARVC, FLARVC. Phone: (813) 783-7518.

(SW) Rainbow Village RV Resort—(Pasco) *From jct US 301 & Hwy 54: Go 1 mi W on Hwy 54, then 1 mi S on Lane Rd. Enter on L.* FACILITIES: 382 sites, typical site width 35 ft, accepts full hkup units only, 382 full hkups, (20, 30 & 50 amps), cable TV ($), wireless Instant Internet access at site, phone/cable on-site Internet access (needs activ), phone Internet access central location, laundry, patios. RECREATION: rec hall, rec room/area, swim pool, golf nearby, bsktball, 6 shuffleboard courts, planned activities, horseshoes, v-ball. Pets welcome, breed restrict, size restrict. Partial handicap access. No tents. Age restrictions may apply. Open all yr. Planned activities winter only. Big rigs welcome. Phone: (813)782-5075.

(SW) Southern Charm RV Resort—(Pasco) *From S jct Hwy 54 & US 301: Go 2 mi S on US 301, then 1/4 mi W on Chancey Rd. Enter on R.* FACILITIES: 500 sites, typical site width 35 ft, accepts full hkup units only, 500 full hkups, (20, 30 & 50 amps), cable TV, wireless Instant Internet access at site, phone/cable on-site Internet access (needs activ), phone Internet access central location, RV/park trailer rentals, RV storage, dump station, laundry, tables, patios. RECREATION: rec hall, swim pool, whirlpool, golf nearby, 8 shuffleboard courts, planned activities, horseshoes, v-ball. Pets welcome, size restrict. Partial handicap access. No tents. Age restrictions may apply. Open all yr. Planned activities winter only. Big rigs welcome. Phone: (813)783-3477.

Find a park or campground Woodall's doesn't list? Tell us!

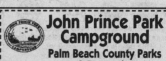

GEORGIA

ACWORTH

(N) Lakemont RV Park—(Bartow) *From jct I-75 (exit 278) & Glade Rd: Go 1/2 mi W on Glade Rd, then 2-1/4 mi NW on Hwy 92, then 3/4 mi N on US 41. Enter on L.* FACILITIES: 100 sites, typical site width 25 ft, accepts full hkup units only, 100 full hkups, (20, 30 & 50 amps), phone/cable on-site Internet access (needs activ), phone Internet access central location, laundry, LP gas by weight/by meter, ice, tables. RECREATION: boating, dock, lake fishing, golf nearby, play equipment, sports field. Pets welcome. No tents. Open all yr. Big rigs welcome. Member ARVC. Phone: (770)966-0302.

ALBANY

(S) Albany RV Resort—(Dougherty) *From jct US 82 & US 19/Hwy 300: Go 4-1/2 mi S on US 19/Hwy 300. Enter on L.* FACILITIES: 82 sites, typical site width 40 ft, 82 full hkups, (20, 30 & 50 amps), 42 pull-thrus, cable TV, wireless Instant Internet access at site, phone on-site Internet access (needs activ), RV storage, laundry, RV supplies, tables, patios. RECREATION: rec hall, pavilion, pond fishing, horseshoes. Pets welcome. Partial handicap access. Open all yr. Big rigs welcome. Phone: (866)792-1481.

(S) Creekside Plantation RV Campground—(Dougherty) *From jct US 82 & US 19/Hwy 300: Go 8 mi S on US 19/Hwy 300, then 1 block E on Hancock Rd. Enter on L.* FACILITIES: 75 sites, typical site width 40 ft, 75 full hkups, (30 & 50 amps), 50 amps ($), 24 pull-thrus, cable TV, wireless Instant Internet access at site, phone/cable on-site Internet access (needs activ), wireless Internet access central location, RV/park trailer rentals, RV storage, laundry, LP gas by weight/by meter, ice, tables, patios, fire rings. RECREATION: rec room/area, pavilion, river swimming, pond fishing, golf nearby, bsktball, playground, shuffleboard court, horseshoes, hiking trails. Pets welcome. Partial handicap access. Open all yr. Big rigs welcome. Phone: (229)886-0504.

AMERICUS

(E) Brickyard Plantation RV Park—(Sumter) *From jct Hwy 27 & US 280: Go 7 mi E on US 280, then 1/2 mi S on Parkers Crossing. From jct I-75 (exit 101) & US 280: Go 24 mi W on US 280. Enter on R.* FACILITIES: 48 sites, typical site width 25 ft, 48 full hkups, (30 & 50 amps), 32 pull-thrus, phone Internet access central location, dump station, laundry, ice, tables, patios, fire rings, grills, wood. RECREATION: equipped pavilion, pond fishing, putting green, golf nearby, planned activities, hiking trails. Pets welcome, breed restrict, quantity restrict. Partial handicap access. No tents. Open all yr. Big rigs welcome. Member ARVC, GARVC. Phone: (229) 874-1234.

BAINBRIDGE

(S) The Place To Be RV Park—(Decatur) *From jct US 84/27 Bypass & Shotwell St: Go 1/4 mi S on Shotwell St. Enter on L.* FACILITIES: 85 sites, typical site width 30 ft, 85 full hkups, (20, 30 & 50 amps), 34 pull-thrus, cable TV, wireless Instant Internet access at site ($), phone on-site Internet access (needs activ), RV storage, dump station, non-guest dumping $, laundry, RV supplies, LP gas by meter, ice, tables, fire rings, wood. RECREATION: rec hall, pavilion, boating, river fishing, mini-golf ($), golf nearby, playground, horseshoes, hiking trails. Pets welcome. Partial handicap access. Open all yr. Big rigs welcome. Member ARVC, GARVC. Phone: (229)246-5802.

BYRON

(E) Interstate RV Campground—(Peach) *From jct I-75 (exit 149) & Hwy 49: Go 500 ft W on Hwy 49, then 1/2 mi N on Chapman Rd. Enter on L.* FACILITIES: 105 sites, typical site width 25 ft, 105 full hkups, (30 & 50 amps), 53 pull-thrus, heater not allowed, cable TV, phone on-site Internet access (needs activ), phone Internet access central location, RV storage, laundry, RV supplies, LP gas by weight/by meter, ice, tables. RECREATION: pavilion, swim pool, golf nearby, play equipment, sports field. Pets welcome. No tents. Open all yr. Big rigs welcome. Phone: (888)817-0906.

COCHRAN

(S) Hillside Bluegrass RV Park—(Bleckley) *From jct Alt US 129 & Bus US 23/Bus Ga Hwy 87: Go 2-1/2 mi S on GA Hwy 87. Enter on R.* FACILITIES: 324 sites, typical site width 25 ft, 24 full hkups, 300 W&E, (30 & 50 amps), 50 pull-thrus, wireless Instant Internet access at site, phone on-site Internet access (needs activ), wireless Internet access central location, cabins, RV storage, dump station, non-guest dumping $, LP gas by weight/by meter, ice, tables, fire rings, wood. RECREATION: rec hall, pavilion, pond fishing, golf nearby, bsktball, 3 bike rentals, playground, planned activities (wkends only), horseshoes, sports field, hiking trails. Pets welcome. Partial handicap access. Open all yr. Big rigs welcome. Member ARVC, GARVC. Phone: (478) 934-6694.

COLQUITT

(S) Emerald Lake RV Park—(Miller) *From jct US 27 & Hwy 91: Go 5-1/2 mi S on Hwy 91. From jct US 84 & Hwy 91: Go 6 mi N on Hwy 91. (At intersection of Hwy 91 & Enterprise Rd).* FACILITIES: 35 sites, typical site width 30 ft, 28 full hkups, 7 W&E, (20, 30 & 50 amps), 18 pull-thrus, wireless Instant Internet access at site, phone on-site Internet access (needs activ), wireless Internet access central location, RV/park trailer rentals, RV storage, dump station, non-guest dumping $, laundry, RV supplies, ice, tables, patios, grills, wood. RECREATION: rec hall, rec room/area, pavilion, equipped pavilion, coin games, swim pool, boating, no motors, canoeing, kayaking, dock, pond fishing, fishing supplies, golf nearby, playground, horseshoes, sports field. Pets welcome. Partial handicap access. Open all yr. Big rigs welcome. Phone: (888)758-9929.

COLUMBUS

(E) Lake Pines RV Park & Campground—(Muscogee) *From jct I-185 & US 80: Go 9-1/2 mi E on US 80, between milepost 12 & 13, then 1/4 mi S on Garrett Rd. Enter on L.* FACILITIES: 75 sites, typical site width 25 ft, 65 full hkups, 10 W&E, (20, 30 & 50 amps), 37 pull-thrus, wireless Instant Internet access at site, phone on-site Internet access (needs activ), wireless Internet access central location, RV storage, dump station, non-guest dumping $, laundry, LP gas by weight/by meter, tables. RECREATION: rec hall, swim pool, golf nearby, horseshoes, hiking trails. Pets welcome. Open all yr. Big rigs welcome. Member ARVC, GARVC. Phone: (706)561-9675.

DILLARD

(N) River Vista Mountain Village—(Rabun) *From jct US 441/23 & Hwy 246: Go 1 mi E on Hwy 246. Enter on R.* FACILITIES: 143 sites, typical site width 35 ft, 143 full hkups, (20, 30 & 50 amps), 22 pull-thrus, cable TV, phone/wireless Instant Internet access at site ($), cabins, laundry, ltd groceries, LP gas by weight/by meter, ice, tables, grills. RECREATION: rec hall, pavilion, 3 swim pools, whirlpool, golf nearby, bsktball, play equipment, horseshoes. Pets welcome. Partial handicap access. No tents. Open all yr. Big rigs welcome. Member ARVC, GARVC. Phone: (888) 850-7275.

FOLKSTON

(N) Okefenokee RV Park—(Charlton) *From jct Hwy 40 & US 301: Go 1-1/2 mi N on US 301, then 1/2 mi W on Bowery Ln. Enter on L.* FACILITIES: 52 sites, typical site width 35 ft, 52 full hkups, (20, 30 & 50 amps), 26 pull-thrus, wireless Instant Internet access at site, phone/cable on-site Internet access (needs activ), RV storage, laundry, groceries, RV supplies, LP gas by meter, ice, tables, patios, wood. RECREATION: rec hall, rec room/area, equipped pavilion, bsktball, playground, 2 shuffleboard courts, horseshoes, local tours. Pets welcome, breed restrict. Partial handicap access. Open all yr. Big rigs welcome. Member ARVC, GARVC. Phone: (912)496-3258.

MADISON

(S) Country Boy's RV Park—(Morgan) *From jct I-20 (exit 114) & US 441/129: Go 1-1/2 mi S on US 441/129. Enter on L.* FACILITIES: 150 sites, typical site width 25 ft, 150 full hkups, (30 & 50 amps), 100 pull-thrus, cable TV, phone on-site Internet access (needs activ), phone Internet access central location, RV storage, dump station, non-guest dumping $, laundry, RV supplies, ice, tables, fire rings, wood. RECREATION: pavilion, swim pool, golf nearby, playground, horseshoes, sports field, hiking trails. Pets welcome. No tents. Open all yr. Big rigs welcome. Phone: (706)342-1799.

MARIETTA

(S) Atlanta-Marietta RV Resort (formerly Brookwood RV Park)—(Cobb) *From jct I-75 (exit 261) & Hwy 280: Go 3/4 mi W on Hwy 280, then 1/2 mi N on US 41 (Cobb Pkwy) then 1 block E on Wylie Rd. Enter on R.* FACILITIES: 70 sites, typical site width 25 ft, 70 full hkups, (30 & 50 amps), cable TV, wireless Instant Internet access at site, wireless Internet access central location, laundry, ltd groceries, LP gas by weight/by meter, ice, tables, patios. RECREATION: swim pool, golf nearby. Pets welcome. Partial handicap access. No tents. Open all yr. Big rigs welcome. Member ARVC, GARVC. Phone: (877)727-5787.

MCDONOUGH

(N) Atlanta South RV Resort—(Henry) *From jct I-75 (exit 222) & Jodeco Rd: Go 1000 feet W on Jodeco Rd, then 1/4 mi S on Mt. Olive Rd. Enter at end.* FACILITIES: 170 sites, typical site width 25 ft, 170 full hkups, (30 & 50 amps), 80 pull-thrus, wireless Instant Internet access at site, phone on-site Internet access (needs activ), wireless Internet access central location, cabins, RV storage, dump station, laundry, RV supplies, LP gas by meter, ice, tables, fire rings, wood. RECREATION: rec hall, rec room/area, pavilion, swim pool, pond fishing, golf nearby, bsktball, playground, planned activities (wkends only). Pets welcome. Partial handicap access. Open all yr. Big rigs welcome. Phone: (678)583-1880.

NORCROSS

(E) Jones RV Park—(Gwinnett) *From jct I-85 (exit 101) & Indian Trl/Lilburn Rd: Go 400 ft E on Indian Trl/Lilburn Rd, then 1 block S on Willowtrail Pkwy. Enter at end.* FACILITIES: 173 sites, typical site width 25 ft, 173 full hkups, (20, 30 & 50 amps), 55 pull-thrus, wireless Instant Internet access at site ($), RV storage, dump station, non-guest dumping $, laundry, LP gas by weight/by meter. RECREATION: golf nearby. Pets welcome. Partial handicap access. No tents. Open all yr. Reservations recommended. No cash accepted. Big rigs welcome. Phone: (770)923-0911.

PERRY

(N) Crossroads Holiday Trav-L-Park—(Houston) *From I-75 (exit 136) & US 341: Go 500 ft W on US 341. Enter on L.* FACILITIES: 64 sites, typical site width 28 ft, 58 full hkups, 6 W&E, (20, 30 & 50 amps), 34 pull-thrus, cable TV, phone on-site Internet access (needs activ), phone Internet access central location, RV storage, laundry, ltd groceries, RV supplies, LP gas by weight/by meter, ice, tables. RECREATION: pavilion, swim pool, mini-golf, golf nearby, bsktball, play equipment. Pets welcome. Open all yr. Big rigs welcome. Phone: (478)987-3141.

(W) Fair Harbor RV Park & Campground—(Houston) *From jct I-75 (exit 135) & Hwy 127/224: Go 500 ft W on Hwy 127/224. Enter on R.* FACILITIES: 153 sites, typical site width 30 ft, 153 full hkups, (20, 30 & 50 amps), 101 pull-thrus, cable TV, wireless Instant Internet access at site, phone on-site Internet access (needs activ), wireless Internet access central location, RV storage, laundry, RV supplies, LP gas by weight/by meter, ice, tables, fire rings, grills. RECREATION: rec hall, rec room/area, pavilion, pond fishing, golf nearby, planned activities, horseshoes, hiking trails. Pets welcome. Partial handicap access. Open all yr. Big rigs welcome. Member ARVC, GARVC. Phone: (877)988-8844.

(N) Perry Ponderosa Park—(Peach) *From jct I-75 (exit 142) & Hwy 96: Go 1/4 mi E on Hwy 96. Enter on L.* FACILITIES: 65 sites, typical site width 25 ft, 65 full hkups, (30 & 50 amps), 65 pull-thrus, phone on-site Internet access (needs activ), RV storage, laundry, LP gas by weight/by meter, ice, tables, patios. RECREATION: golf nearby, bsktball, playground, 2 shuffleboard courts, sports field. Pets welcome. No tents. Open all yr. Big rigs welcome. Phone: (478)825-8030.

(S) Twin Oaks RV Park—(Houston) *From jct I-75 (exit 127) & Hwy 26: Go 1000 ft E on Hwy 26. Enter on L.* FACILITIES: 72 sites, typical site width 40 ft, 64 full hkups, 8 W&E, (30 & 50 amps), 40 pull-thrus, wireless Instant Internet access at site, phone on-site Internet access (needs activ), wireless Internet access central location, cabins, RV storage, dump station, non-guest dumping $, laundry, ltd groceries, RV supplies, LP gas by weight/by meter, ice, tables, patios, fire rings, wood. RECREATION: rec hall, rec room/area, pavilion, equipped pavilion, swim pool, whirlpool, golf nearby, bsktball, horseshoes, sports field, v-ball. Pets welcome. Partial handicap access. Open all yr. Big rigs welcome. Member ARVC. Phone: (478)987-9361.

PINE MOUNTAIN

(N) Pine Mountain RVC—(Troup) *From jct US-27 & Hwy-18: Go 1 mi N on US-27. Enter on L.* FACILITIES: 250 sites, typical site width 30 ft, 250 full hkups, (20, 30 & 50 amps), 48 pull-thrus, wireless Instant Internet access at site, phone on-site Internet access (needs activ), wireless Internet access central location, cabins, RV storage, dump station, non-guest dumping $, laundry, ltd groceries, RV supplies, LP gas by weight/by meter, ice, tables, fire rings, wood, controlled access gate. RECREATION: rec hall, pavilion, swim pool, mini-golf ($), golf nearby, bsktball, 5 bike rentals, playground, horseshoes, sports field, v-ball. Pets welcome. Partial handicap access. Open all yr. Big rigs welcome. Member ARVC, GARVC. Phone: (706)663-4329.

SAVANNAH

(W) Savannah Oaks RV Resort—(Chatham) *From jct I-95 (exit 94) & Hwy 204: Go 2 1/2 mi W on Hwy 204. Enter on L.* FACILITIES: 139 sites, typical site width 30 ft, 111 full hkups, 28 W&E, (30 & 50 amps), 76 pull-thrus, cable TV, phone on-site Internet access (needs activ), wireless Internet access central location, dump station, non-guest dumping $, laundry, groceries, RV supplies, LP gas by weight/by meter, gas, marine gas, ice, tables, grills, controlled access gate. RECREATION: rec room/area, pavilion, coin games, swim pool, boating, canoeing, kayaking, ramp, dock, lake fishing, golf nearby, playground. Pets welcome. Partial handicap access. No tents. Open all yr. Big rigs welcome. Member ARVC, GARVC. Phone: (800)851-0717.

TYBEE ISLAND

(W) RIVER'S END CAMPGROUND & RV PARK (City Park)—(Chatham) *From jct I-95 & I-16: Go 9 mi E on I-16 to(exit 167A, then 3/4 mi N on MLK Jr Blvd, then 1 mi E on Bay St (stay in left hand lane), then 15 mi E on President St (Becomes Island Expwy then into US 80 to Tybee Island), then 2 blks N on Polk St. Enter on L.*

WELCOME

FACILITIES: 127 sites, typical site width 20 ft, 64 full hkups, 27 W&E, (30 & 50 amps), 36 no hkups, 34 pull-thrus, cable TV, cable Internet access central location, dump station, non-guest dumping $, laundry, ltd groceries, RV supplies, LP gas by weight/by meter, ice, tables, wood.

RECREATION: rec hall, rec room/area, pavilion, swim pool, golf nearby, 7 bike rentals, planned activities, horseshoes, hiking trails.

Pets welcome, breed restrict, size restrict. Partial handicap access. Open all yr. Big rigs welcome. Member ARVC, GARVC. Phone: (800)786-1016.

e-mail: campground@cityoftybee.org

SEE AD PAGE 13

WRENS

(S) Boss's RV Park—(Jefferson) *From N jct US 1/221 & Hwy 17: Go 1-1/2 mi S on US 1/221/Hwy 17 to Hoyte Braswell Rd. Enter on L.* FACILITIES: 71 sites, typical site width 25 ft, 71 full hkups, (20, 30 & 50 amps), 50 amps ($), wireless Instant Internet access at site, RV storage, dump station, non-guest dumping $, laundry, tables. RECREATION: equipped pavilion, golf nearby, horseshoes. Pets welcome. Open all yr. Big rigs welcome. Phone: (706)547-0402.

ILLINOIS

HERRIN

(N) Four Seasons Campground—(Williamson) *From jct Hwy 13 & Hwy 148: Go 5 mi N on Hwy 148, then 1-1/2 mi E on Herrin St, then 1 mi N on 3rd St (which becomes Carol Rd). Enter on R.* FACILITIES: 35 sites, typical site width 45 ft, 30 full hkups, 5 W&E, (30 & 50 amps), 50 amps ($), 12 pull-thrus, wireless Instant Internet access at site, cabins, dump station, non-guest dumping $, laundry, LP gas by weight/by meter, tables, fire rings. RECREATION: pond fishing, sports field. Pets welcome. Partial handicap access. No tents. Open all yr. Big rigs welcome. Phone: (618)942-2069.

POCAHONTAS

(S) Tomahawk Campground—(Bond) *From jct I-70 (exit 30) & Hwy 143: Go 6 mi E on Hwy 143, then 1 mi S on Jamestown Rd. Enter on L.* FACILITIES: 142 sites, typical site width 28 ft, 11 full hkups, 131 W&E, (20, 30 & 50 amps), 16 pull-thrus, wireless Instant Internet access at site, RV/park trailer rentals, RV storage, shower$, dump station, non-guest dumping $, portable dump, laundry, RV supplies, LP gas by weight, LP bottle exch, ice, tables, fire rings, wood. RECREATION: rec hall, pavilion, coin games, lake swimming, lake/pond fishing, bsktball, playground, horseshoes, sports field, v-ball. Rec open to public. Pets welcome. Open all yr. Facilities fully operational Apr 1 thru Nov 1. Big rigs welcome. Phone: (618)669-2781.

WILMINGTON

(W) Fossil Rock Recreation Area—(Will) *From jct I-80 & I-55: Go 10 mi S on I-55, then 1 mi S on Hwy 129, then 1/2 mi W on Strip Mine Rd. Enter on L.* FACILITIES: 290 sites, 215 full hkups, 10 E, (20, 30 & 50 amps), 65 no hkups, 10 pull-thrus, RV/park trailer rentals, cabins, dump station, ice, tables, patios, fire rings, controlled access gate. RECREATION: pavilion, lake swimming, boating, electric motors only, canoeing, lake fishing, golf nearby, bsktball, playground, planned activities (wkends only), horseshoes, sports field, hiking trails, v-ball. Pets welcome. Open all yr. Facilities fully operational Apr 1 thru Oct 31. Big rigs welcome. Member ARVC, ICA. Phone: (815)476-6784.

INDIANA

BLUFFTON

(E) Mendenhall's RV/Mobile Park—(Wells) *From jct SR 1 & SR 124: Go 1/2 mi E on SR 124. Enter on L.* FACILITIES: 14 sites, typical site width 30 ft, accepts self-contained units only, 12 full hkups, 2 W&E, (30 & 50 amps), 8 pull-thrus. Pets welcome. No tents. Open all yr. No restrooms. Big rigs welcome. Phone: (260) 824-5365.

GREENFIELD

Heartland Resort—(Hancock) *From I-70 (exit 96) & Mt Comfort Rd: Go 1/4 mi N on Mt Comfort Rd, then 4-1/2 mi E on CR W 300 N. Enter on R.* FACILITIES: 285 sites, typical site width 30 ft, 211 full hkups, 64 W&E, (30 & 50 amps), 50 amps ($), 10 no hkups, 55 pull-thrus, wireless Instant Internet access at site, wireless Internet access central location, RV storage, dump station, non-guest dumping $, laundry, ltd groceries, RV supplies, LP gas by weight/by meter, ice, tables, fire rings, wood. RECREATION: rec hall, rec room/area, pavilion, equipped pavilion, coin games, swim pool, lake swimming, lake fishing, mini-golf ($), golf nearby, bsktball, playground, planned activities (wkends only), tennis, horseshoes, sports field, v-ball. Rec open to public. Pets welcome. Partial handicap access. Open all yr. Facilities fully operational Memorial Day thru Labor Day. Indoor pool open Memorial to Labor Day. Big rigs welcome. Member ICOA. Phone: (317)326-3181.

IOWA

ALBIA

(S) Indian Hills RV Park—(Monroe) *From jct US 34 & SR 5: Go 100 yds E on US 34. Enter on R.* FACILITIES: 20 sites, typical site width 36 ft, 20 full hkups, (30 & 50 amps), 20 pull-thrus, cable TV, wireless Instant Internet access at site, wireless Internet access central location, dump station, non-guest dumping $, laundry, ltd groceries, LP gas by meter, ice. RECREATION: rec room/area, swim pool, whirlpool, golf nearby. Pets welcome. Partial handicap access. No tents. Open all yr. subject to snow conditions. Big rigs welcome. Phone: (800)728-4286.

ALTOONA

Griffs Valley View RV—(Polk) *From jct I-35 & Corporate Woods Dr (exit 89): Go 2-3/4 mi E on Corporate Woods Dr, then 1/4 mi N on NE 46th St. Enter on R.* FACILITIES: 120 sites, 120 full hkups, (30 & 50 amps), 20 pull-thrus, wireless Internet access central location,

ALTOONA—Continued
Griffs Valley View RV—Continued

laundry. RECREATION: rec room/area, pond swimming, pond fishing, golf nearby, play equipment. Pets welcome, quantity restrict. Partial handicap access. No tents. Open Mar 1 thru Dec 1. Big rigs welcome. Phone: (515)967-5474.

ARNOLDS PARK

(S) Fieldstone RV Park—(Dickinson) *From jct US 71 & 202nd St: Go 1/2 mi E on 202nd St. Enter on R.* FACILITIES: 107 sites, typical site width 36 ft, 107 full hkups, (30 & 50 amps), wireless Instant Internet access at site, wireless Internet access central location, RV storage, laundry, tables, fire rings. RECREATION: rec room/area. Pets welcome. Partial handicap access. No tents. Open May 15 thru Oct 15. Big rigs welcome. Phone: (712)332-7631.

SIGOURNEY

(N) Bridgeport Campground—(Keokula) *From jct SR 92 & SR 149 (Main Street): Go 1/2 mi N on Main St. Enter on R.* FACILITIES: 12 sites, 12 full hkups, (30 & 50 amps), phone on-site Internet access (needs activ), phone Internet access central location, shower$, dump station, non-guest dumping $, laundry, tables. Pets welcome. Open all yr. Big rigs welcome. Phone: (641)622-2306.

MAINE

BOOTHBAY HARBOR

(S) Gray Homestead Oceanfront Camping—*From jct Hwy 27 & Hwy 238: Go 2 mi S on Hwy 238. Enter on L.* FACILITIES: 40 sites, typical site width 22 ft, 19 full hkups, 9 W&E, (20, 30 & 50 amps), 12 no hkups, wireless Internet access central location, cabins, dump station, laundry, ice, tables, fire rings, wood. RECREATION: saltwater swimming, boating, canoeing, kayaking, 9 kayak rentals, saltwater fishing, golf nearby, bsktball, horseshoes, v-ball. Pets welcome, quantity restrict. Open May 1 thru Columbus Day. Member ARVC, MECOA. Phone: (207)633-4612.

WELLS

(S) BEACH ACRES CAMPGROUND—(York) *From jct I 95 (exit 19) & Hwy 109: Go 1-1/2 mi E on Hwy 109, then 2 mi S on US 1, then 1 block E on Eldridge Rd. Enter on L.*

WELCOME

FACILITIES: 400 sites, typical site width 40 ft, 320 full hkups, 20 W&E, 11 E, (20, 30 & 50 amps), 49 no hkups, cable on-site Internet access (needs activ), RV storage, shower$, dump station, non-guest dumping $, laundry, ice, tables, fire rings, wood, controlled access gate.

RECREATION: swim pool, golf nearby, bsktball, playground, shuffleboard court, planned activities (wkends only), horseshoes, sports field.

No pets. Open late May thru mid Sep. Big rigs welcome. Member ARVC, MECOA. Phone: (207) 646-5612.

e-mail: beachacres@beachacres.com

SEE AD THIS PAGE

MARYLAND

ABINGDON

(S) Bar Harbor RV Park & Marina—(Harford) *From jct I-95 (exit 80) & Hwy 543: Go 1-1/2 mi S on Hwy 543, then 1-1/2 mi W on US 40, then 3/4 mi S on Long Bar Rd, then 1/2 mi E on Baker Ave. Enter at end.* FACILITIES: 93 sites, typical site width 30 ft, 93 full hkups, (30 & 50 amps), 7 pull-thrus, cable TV, wireless Instant Internet access at site, phone/cable on-site Internet access (needs activ), wireless Internet access central location, dump station, laundry, ltd groceries, RV supplies, LP gas by weight/by meter, ice, tables, patios, fire rings, grills, wood, controlled access gate. RECREATION: rec hall, rec room/area, coin games, swim pool, boating, canoeing, kayaking, ramp, dock, 2 kayak/pedal boat rentals, saltwater/river fishing, fishing supplies, golf nearby, playground. Pets welcome. No tents. Open all yr. Facilities fully operational Mar 1 thru Dec 31. Dec 31 thru Mar 1, self-contained units only. Member ARVC, MAC. ATM. Phone: (800)351-2267.

OCEAN CITY

(E) Castaways RV Resort and Campground (REBUILDING)—(Worcestor) *From jct US 50 & CR 611: Go 5 mi S on CR-611, then 1-1/2 mi E on Eagles Nest Rd. Enter at end.* FACILITIES: 400 sites, typical site width 40 ft, 150 full hkups, 150 W&E, (20 & 30 amps), 100 no hkups, cable TV, RV storage, dump station, portable dump, laundry, ltd groceries, RV supplies, ice, tables, fire rings, wood. RECREATION: pavilion, coin games,

Castaways RV Resort and Campground—Continued on next page

OCEAN CITY—Continued
Castaways RV Resort and Campground—Continued

kayaking, ramp, dock, saltwater fishing, fishing supplies, golf nearby, bsktball, playground, horseshoes, sports field. Pets welcome, breed restrict, quantity restrict. Open May 15 thru Oct 15. Advance reservations peak season-minimum 3 nights. Phone: (410)213-0097.

PRINCESS ANNE

(N) Lake Somerset Campground—(Somerset) *From jct US 50 & US 13: Go 13 mi S on US 13. Enter on R.* FACILITIES: 151 sites, typical site width 30 ft, 140 full hkups, 11 W&E, (30 & 50 amps), 30 pull-thrus, phone Internet access central location, cabins, RV storage, dump station, non-guest dumping $, laundry, ltd groceries, RV supplies, LP gas by weight/by meter, ice, tables, fire rings, wood. RECREATION: rec room/area, pavilion, coin games, swim pool, boating, no motors, canoeing, kayaking, dock, 5 canoe/5 kayak/5 pedal boat rentals, lake/pond fishing, fishing supplies, mini-golf ($), golf nearby, bsktball, 12 bike rentals, playground, horseshoes, hiking trails, v-ball. Pets welcome. Partial handicap access. Open all yr. Big rigs welcome. Phone: (410)957-1866.

QUANTICO

(W) Sandy Hill Family Camp—(Wicomico) *From jct US 50 (Bus) & Hwy 349: Go 10 mi W on Hwy 349, then 3-1/2 mi N on Royal Oak Rd, then 3/4 mi E on Sandy Hill Rd. Enter at end.* FACILITIES: 110 sites, typical site width 25 ft, 110 W&E, (20 & 30 amps), 3 pull-thrus, dump station, portable dump, laundry, ltd groceries, RV supplies, LP gas by weight, ice, tables, fire rings, wood. RECREATION: rec hall, river swimming, boating, ramp, dock, river fishing, fishing supplies, golf nearby, playground, planned activities (wkends only), hiking trails. Pets welcome. Partial handicap access. Open Mar 1 thru Dec 15. Member ARVC, MAC. Phone: (410)873-2471.

THURMONT

(W) Ole Mink Farm Recreation Resort—(Frederick) *From jct US 15 & Hwy 77: Go 3 mi W on Hwy 77, then 3 mi S on Catoctin Hollow Rd, then 1-1/2 mi E on Mink Farm Rd. Enter on R.* FACILITIES: 110 sites, typical site width 50 ft, 35 ft max RV length, 110 full hkups, (20 & 30 amps), wireless Instant Internet access at site, cabins, dump station, portable dump, ltd groceries, RV supplies, LP gas by weight, ice, tables, fire rings, grills, wood, controlled access gate. RECREATION: rec hall, rec room/area, pavilion, equipped pavilion, coin games, swim pool, pond/stream fishing, fishing supplies, golf nearby, bsktball, playground, planned activities, horseshoes, hiking trails, v-ball. Pets welcome. Partial handicap access. No tents. Open all yr. Facilities fully operational Apr thru Oct. Phone: (877)OLE-MINK.

Woodall's Tip #33... Detailed, easy-to-read driving directions guide you right to the park entrance.

MASSACHUSETTS

WEBSTER

(E) Indian Ranch Campground—(Worcester) *From jct I-395 (exit 2) & Hwy 16: Go 1-1/4 mi E on Hwy 16. Enter on R.* FACILITIES: 210 sites, accepts full hkup units only, 210 full hkups, (20, 30 & 50 amps), cable TV, wireless Internet access central location, dump station, non-guest dumping $, portable dump, laundry, ice, tables. RECREATION: rec hall, rec room/area, equipped pavilion, coin games, lake swimming, boating, dock, lake fishing, golf nearby, horseshoes. Pets welcome, breed restrict, quantity restrict. No tents. Open May 1 thru Oct 15. Big rigs welcome. Member ARVC, MACO. Phone: (508)943-3871.

MICHIGAN

ALLENDALE

(NW) River Pines RV Park and Campground—(Ottawa) *From jct I-96 (exit 16) & CR B35/68th Ave: Go 4 mi S on 68th Ave, then 1-3/4 mi W on Warner St. Enter on R.* FACILITIES: 150 sites, typical site width 40 ft, 89 full hkups, 36 W&E, (20, 30 & 50 amps), 25 no hkups, cable TV ($), wireless Internet access central location, RV/park trailer rentals, RV storage, dump station, non-guest dumping $, portable dump, laundry, ltd groceries, RV supplies, ice, tables, patios, fire rings, wood. RECREATION: rec room/area, pavilion, swim pool, canoeing, kayaking, 6 canoe/2 kayak rentals, river/pond fishing, fishing supplies, golf nearby, bsktball, 10 bike rentals, playground, planned activities (wkends only), horseshoes, sports field, hiking trails, v-ball. Pets welcome, breed restrict. Partial handicap access. Open all yr. Facilities fully operational May 1 thru Oct 31. Big rigs welcome. Member ARVC, ARVC MI. Phone: (616) 895-6601.

BATTLE CREEK

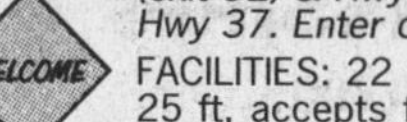

(N) CREEK VALLEY—(Calhoun) *From jct I-94 (exit 92) & Hwy 37: Go 8-1/2 mi N on Hwy 37. Enter on L.*

FACILITIES: 22 sites, typical site width 25 ft, accepts full hkup units only, 22 full hkups, (30 amps), 1 pull-thrus, RV storage, tables.

Pets welcome. No tents. Open all yr. No restrooms. Phone: (269)964-9577.

SEE AD THIS PAGE

DECATUR

(S) Leisure Valley RV Resort & Campground—(Van Buren) *From jct I-94 & Hwy 51: Go 6-1/4 mi S on Hwy 51, then 3 mi S on George St. then 1/4 mi W on Valley Rd (CR 669). Enter on L.* FACILITIES: 106 sites, typical site width 30 ft, 92 full hkups, 14 W&E, (20 & 30 amps), 1 pull-thrus, RV storage, dump station, non-guest dumping $, laundry, ltd groceries, RV supplies, LP gas by weight/by meter, ice, tables, fire rings,

DECATUR—Continued
Leisure Valley RV Resort & Campground—Continued

wood, controlled access gate. RECREATION: rec hall, rec room/area, pavilion, coin games, swim pool, lake swimming, boating, no motors, dock, rowboat/canoe/kayak/3 pedal boat rentals, lake fishing, fishing supplies, mini-golf ($), golf nearby, bsktball, playground, 2 shuffleboard courts, planned activities (wkends only), horseshoes, sports field, hiking trails, v-ball. Pets welcome. Partial handicap access. Open Apr 15 thru Oct 15. Member ARVC, ARVC MI. Phone: (269)423-7122.

HOWELL

(SE) LAKE CHEMUNG OUTDOOR RESORT—(Livingston) *From jct US 23 & I-96: Go 3 mi W on I-96 (exit 145), then 3 mi NW on Grand River Ave, then 2 mi N on Hughes Rd. Enter on L.*

FACILITIES: 340 sites, typical site width 30 ft, 340 full hkups, (30 & 50 amps), wireless Internet access central location, laundry, groceries, LP bottle exch, ice, tables, patios, fire rings, wood, controlled access gate.

RECREATION: rec room/area, equipped pavilion, swim pool, lake swimming, boating, canoeing, kayaking, lake/pond fishing, mini-golf, golf nearby, bsktball, playground, 2 shuffleboard courts, planned activities, tennis, horseshoes, sports field, v-ball.

Pets welcome, quantity restrict. Partial handicap access. No tents. Open all yr. Facilities fully operational Memorial Day thru Labor Day. Mid May thru mid Sep daily rates apply. Big rigs welcome. Phone: (517)546-6361.

e-mail: lcori@ismi.net

SEE AD THIS PAGE

JACKSON

(E) GREENWOOD ACRES FAMILY CAMPGROUND—(Jackson) *From jct US 127 S & I-94: Go 5 mi E on I-94 (exit 147), then 1 block S on Race Rd, then 3/4 mi W on Ann Arbor Rd, then 1-1/4 mi S on Portage Rd, then 1/2 mi E on Greenwood Rd, then N on Hilton to entrance. Enter on L.*

FACILITIES: 1080 sites, typical site width 40 ft, 500 full hkups, 580 W&E, (20, 30 & 50 amps), 35 pull-thrus, heater not allowed, phone Internet ac-

GREENWOOD ACRES FAMILY CAMPGROUND—Continued on next page

JACKSON—Continued
GREENWOOD ACRES FAMILY CAMPGROUND—Continued

cess central location, dump station, portable dump, laundry, ltd groceries, RV supplies, LP gas by weight/by meter, ice, tables, fire rings, wood, controlled access gate.

RECREATION: rec hall, rec room/area, pavilion, coin games, swim pool, lake swimming, boating, 5 hp limit, canoeing, kayaking, ramp, dock, lake fishing, fishing supplies, mini-golf, golf nearby, bsktball, playground, planned activities (wkends only), tennis, horseshoes, sports field, hiking trails, v-ball.

Pets welcome, quantity restrict. Partial handicap access. Open April 1 thru Oct 31. Facilities fully operational Memorial Day thru Labor Day. Member ARVC, ARVC MI. ATM. Phone: (517)522-8600.

SEE AD PAGE 15

(E) GREENWOOD ACRES GOLF—*From jct US 127 S & I-94: Go 5 mi E on I-94 (exit 147), then 1 block S on Race Rd, then 3/4 mi W on Ann Arbor Rd, then 1-1/4 mi S on Portage Rd, then 1/2 mi E on Greenwood Rd, then N on Hilton to entrance. Enter on L.* 9-hole golf course adjacent to an RV CAMPGROUND, golf included only when camping at Greenwood Acres, must have own equipment, artificial greens. Open Memorial Day thru Labor Day. MC/VISA/Debit. Phone: (517)522-8600.

SEE AD PAGE 15

LESLIE

(NE) WHEEL INN CAMPGROUND AND WHITE TAIL ACRES ARCHERY—(Ingham) *From jct Hwy 36 & US 127: Go 5 mi S on US 127, then 4-1/2 mi E on Barnes Rd, then 3-1/2 mi S on Meridian Rd, then 1/2 mi E on Fogg Rd. Enter on R.*

FACILITIES: 180 sites, typical site width 35 ft, 52 full hkups, 114 W&E, 14 E, (20 & 30 amps), 60 pull-thrus, phone Internet access central location, dump station, non-guest dumping $, portable dump, ice, tables, fire rings, wood.

RECREATION: rec hall, pond swimming, pond fishing, golf nearby, bsktball, playground, planned activities, horseshoes, sports field, hiking trails, v-ball. Rec open to public.

Pets welcome, breed restrict. Open all yr. Phone: (517)589-8097.

e-mail: ataylor3d@aol.com

SEE AD PAGE 15

(NE) WHITETAIL ACRES ARCHERY—*From jct Hwy 36 & US 127: Go 5 mi S on US 127, then 4-1/2 mi E on Barnes Rd, then 3-1/2 mi S on Meridian Rd, then 1/2 mi E on Fogg Rd. Enter on R.* Range with 30 3-D targets, two tree stands and competition archery shoots. Archery supplies, service & repair. Open Dec thru Sep. MC/VISA/DISC/Debit. Phone: (517)589-0133.

e-mail: ataylor3d@aol.com

SEE AD PAGE 15

MACKINAW CITY

(SE) Mackinaw Mill Creek Camping—(Cheboygan) *N'bound: From jct I-75 (exit 337) & Hwy 108 (Nicolet St): Go 1/2 mi N on Nicolet St, then 4 mi SE on US 23. S'bound: From jct I-75 (exit 338) & US 23: Go 4-1/4 mi SE on US 23. Enter on L.* FACILITIES: 600 sites, typical site width 35 ft, 300 full hkups, 100 W&E, 150 E, (20, 30 & 50 amps), 50 no hkups, 10 pull-thrus, wireless Instant Internet access at site ($), cabins, RV storage, dump station, non-guest dumping $, groceries, RV supplies, LP gas by weight/by meter, ice, tables, fire rings, grills, wood, controlled access gate. RECREATION: rec hall, pavilion, coin games, swim pool, lake swimming, boating, canoeing, kayaking, ramp, dock, lake fishing, fishing supplies, mini-golf ($), golf nearby, bsktball, 20 bike rentals, playground, planned activities, sports field, hiking trails, local tours. Pets welcome, breed restrict, quantity restrict. Partial handicap access. Open May 1 thru Oct 25. Store & pool operational late June to early Sept. Big rigs welcome. Member ARVC, ARVC MI. ATM. Phone: (231)436-5584.

ORTONVILLE

(SW) CLEARWATER CAMPGROUND—(Oakland) *From jct I-75 (exit 91) & Hwy 15: Go 6-1/4 mi N on Hwy 15. Enter on L.*

FACILITIES: 114 sites, typical site width 25 ft, 114 full hkups, (20, 30 & 50 amps), 10 pull-thrus, phone Internet access central location, RV/park trailer rentals, cabins, RV storage, laundry, ltd groceries, RV supplies, LP gas by weight, ice, tables, fire rings, wood, controlled access gate.

RECREATION: rec hall, pavilion, lake swimming, boating, electric motors only, canoeing, kayaking, lake fishing, fishing supplies, golf nearby, bsktball, playground, planned activities (wkends only), horseshoes, hiking trails, v-ball.

Pets welcome, breed restrict. Partial handicap access. Open Apr 15 thru Oct 15. Big rigs welcome. Phone: (248)627-3820.

e-mail: clearwatercampground@netzero.net

SEE AD THIS PAGE

MISSISSIPPI

BILOXI

(N) LAKEVIEW RV RESORT—(Harrison) *From jct I-10 (exit 46B) & I-110/Hwy 15: Go 6-3/4 mi N on Hwy 15. Enter on R.*

FACILITIES: 84 sites, 84 full hkups, (30 & 50 amps), 84 pull-thrus, wireless Instant Internet access at site, wireless Internet access central location, RV/park trailer rentals, cabins, RV storage, laundry, RV supplies, LP gas by weight/by meter.

RECREATION: rec hall, swim pool, boating, 2 pedal boat rentals, lake fishing, golf nearby, bsktball, horseshoes, sports field.

Pets welcome, breed restrict. Partial handicap access. No tents. Open all yr. Big rigs welcome. Phone: (228)396-2211.

e-mail: lakeviewrvresort@aol.com

SEE AD THIS PAGE

COLUMBIA

(N) Mimosa Landing Campground—(Marion) *From Hwy 98 & Hwy 35: Go 3-3/4 mi NE on Hwy 35, then 1/4 mi N on Industrial Park Dr; then 100 ft W on Rustique Brick Dr. Enter at end.* FACILITIES: 77 sites, typical site width 40 ft, 77 full hkups, (20, 30 & 50 amps), 13 pull-thrus, wireless Instant Internet access at site, wireless Internet access central location, cabins, dump station, laundry, ltd groceries, ice, tables, fire rings, grills, wood. RECREATION: rec hall, equipped pavilion, swim pool, boating, dock, river/pond fishing, fishing supplies, golf nearby, bsktball, playground, planned activities (wkends only), horseshoes, sports field, hiking trails, v-ball. Pets welcome, breed restrict. Partial handicap access. No tents. Open all yr. Big rigs welcome. Phone: (601)736-9700.

GAUTIER

(NW) INDIAN POINT RV RESORT—(Jackson) *From I-10 (exit 61) & Gautier/VanCleave Rd: Go 3/4 mi S on Gautier/VanCleave Rd, then E on Indian Point Rd to gate. Enter at end.*

FACILITIES: 241 sites, typical site width 40 ft, 221 full hkups, 20 W&E, (20, 30 & 50 amps), 13 pull-thrus, cable TV, wireless Instant Internet access at site, wireless Internet access central location, RV/park trailer rentals, cabins, RV storage, dump station, non-guest dumping $, laundry, RV supplies, LP gas by weight/by meter, ice, tables, patios, wood.

RECREATION: rec hall, rec room/area, equipped pavilion, 2 swim pools, boating, canoeing, ramp, dock, river fishing, fishing guides, mini-golf, golf nearby, bsktball, playground, 2 shuffleboard courts, planned activities (wkends only), horseshoes, sports field, hiking trails.

Pets welcome. Partial handicap access. Open all yr. Big rigs welcome. Member ARVC. Phone: (228) 497-1011.

e-mail: ip@indianpt.com

SEE AD BILOXI THIS PAGE

HORN LAKE

(S) Audubon Point RV Park—(DeSoto) *Call for directions. Enter at end.* FACILITIES: 114 sites, 114 full hkups, (20, 30 & 50 amps), 60 pull-thrus, cable TV, wireless Instant Internet access at site, wireless Internet access central location, RV storage, laundry, ltd groceries, RV supplies, LP gas by weight/by meter, ice, tables, patios. RECREATION: rec hall, equipped pavilion, coin games, swim pool, golf nearby, playground, shuffleboard court. Pets welcome, quantity restrict. Partial handicap access. No tents. Open all yr. Big rigs welcome. Member ARVC. Phone: (662)280-8282.

MISSOURI

BRANSON

(SW) Oak Grove RV Park—(Taney) *From jct US 65 & Hwy 248: Go 6 mi W on Hwy 248, (Hwy 248 turns into Gretna Rd) proceed straight ahead on Gretna Rd and cross US 76. Enter on L.* FACILITIES: 69 sites, 69 full hkups, (30 & 50 amps), 7 pull-thrus, cable TV, wireless Instant Internet access at site, laundry, LP gas by weight/by meter, ice, tables, grills. RECREATION: equipped pavilion. Pets welcome, size restrict, quantity restrict. Open all yr. Big rigs welcome. Member ARVC, MOARC. Phone: (888)334-4781.

MONTANA

ENNIS

(N) Ennis RV Village—(Madison) Altitude 4995 ft. *From jct Hwy 287 & US 287: Go 3/4 mi N on US 287. Enter on R.* FACILITIES: 90 sites, typical site width 30 ft, 76 full hkups, 14 W&E, (20, 30 & 50 amps), wireless Instant Internet access at site, phone on-site Internet access (needs activ), phone Internet access central location, RV storage, dump station, non-guest dumping $, laundry, ltd groceries, RV supplies, ice, tables, patios, grills. RECREATION: rec hall, fishing supplies, fishing

Ennis RV Village—Continued on next page

ENNIS—Continued
Ennis RV Village—Continued

guides, golf nearby, hiking trails. Pets welcome. Partial handicap access. Open Apr 1 thru Nov. 15. Big rigs welcome. Member ARVC, COAM. Phone: (866)682-5272.

NEBRASKA

OGALLALA

(NW) Eagle Canyon Hideaway—*From jct I-80 (exit 126): Go 3 mi N on US 26, then 7 mi W on US 26, then 3 mi N on Lakeview Rd, then 4-3/4 mi W on Lakeview West Rd (mostly gravel). Enter on L.* FACILITIES: 33 sites, typical site width 30 ft, 24 full hkups, (30 & 50 amps), 9 no hkups, 8 pull-thrus, phone/wireless Instant Internet access at site, wireless Internet access central location, cabins, RV storage, dump station, non-guest dumping $, laundry, ltd groceries, RV supplies, ice, tables, fire rings, wood. RECREATION: rec room/area, swim pool, wading pool, fishing supplies, bsktball, playground, horseshoes, sports field, hiking trails, v-ball. Pets welcome. Partial handicap access. Open all yr. Facilities fully operational Mar 1 thru Jan 1. Big rigs welcome. Phone: (866)866-LAKE.

NEVADA

CARSON CITY

(S) Camp-N-Town RV Park—(Carson) Altitude 4600 ft. *S'bound from jct of Hwy 395 & N Carson St exit: Go 1.7 mi S on N Carson St. Enter on R.* FACILITIES: 157 sites, typical site width 26 ft, 157 full hkups, (30 & 50 amps), 100 pull-thrus, cable TV ($), wireless Instant Internet access at site, dump station, non-guest dumping $, laundry, tables. RECREATION: rec room/area, coin games, golf nearby. Pets welcome ($). Partial handicap access. No tents. Open all yr. Phone: (775)883-1123.

NEW HAMPSHIRE

FREEDOM

(NW) Danforth Bay Camping Resort—(Carroll) *From jct Hwy 16 & Hwy 41: Go 1/2 mi N on Hwy 41, then 4-3/4 mi E on Ossippee Lake Rd, then 1 mi NE on Shawtown Rd. Enter on R.* FACILITIES: 295 sites, typical site width 30 ft, 249 full hkups, 46 W&E, (30 & 50 amps), 24 pull-thrus, cable TV, wireless Instant Internet access at site, wireless Internet access central location, cabins, RV storage, shower$, dump station, non-guest dumping $, laundry, groceries, RV supplies, LP gas by weight/by meter, LP bottle exch, ice, tables, fire rings, grills, wood, controlled access gate. RECREATION: rec hall, rec room/area, equipped pavilion, coin games, 2 swim pools, wading pool, lake swimming, boating, canoeing, kayaking, ramp, 2 rowboat/8 canoe/15 kayak/3 pedal boat/2 motorboat rentals, lake/river fishing, fishing supplies, golf nearby, bsktball, playground, planned activities, tennis, horseshoes, sports field, hiking trails, v-ball. Pets welcome, quantity restrict. Partial handicap access. Open all yr. Facilities fully operational Memorial Day thru Columbus Day. Big rigs welcome. Member NE-HA-CA. ATM. Phone: (603) 539-2069.

(NW) The Bluffs at Danforth Bay—(Carroll) *From jct Hwy 16 & Hwy 41: Go 1/2 mi N on Hwy 41, then 4-3/4 mi E on Ossippee Lake Rd, then 1-1/4 m NE on Shawtown Rd. Enter on R.* FACILITIES: 240 sites, typical site width 50 ft, 240 full hkups, (20, 30 & 50 amps), cable TV, wireless Instant Internet access at site, wireless Internet access central location, shower$, laundry, groceries, RV supplies, LP gas by weight/by meter, LP bottle exch, ice, tables, fire rings, grills, wood, controlled access gate. RECREATION: rec hall, rec room/area, coin games, 5 swim pools, lake swimming, boating, canoeing, kayaking, ramp, dock, 2 rowboat/8 canoe/15 kayak/3 pedal boat/2 motorboat rentals, lake/river fishing, fishing supplies, golf nearby, bsktball, planned activities, tennis, horseshoes, sports field, hiking trails, v-ball. Pets welcome, quantity restrict. Partial handicap access. No tents. Age restrictions may apply. Open Mid-April thru Mid-November. Facilities fully operational May 1 thru October 31. Big rigs welcome. Member ARVC, NE-HA-CA. ATM. Phone: (603)539-2069.

HAMPTON

(S) Tidewater Campground—(Rockingham) *From jct Hwy 101 & US 1: Go 160 yards S on US 1. Enter on R.* FACILITIES: 225 sites, typical site width 30 ft, 185 full hkups, (20, 30 & 50 amps), 50 amps ($), 40 no hkups, 4 pull-thrus, heater not allowed, shower$, portable dump, ltd groceries, RV supplies, ice, tables, fire rings, wood, controlled access gate. RECREATION: rec hall, coin games, swim pool, golf nearby, bsktball, playground, horseshoes, sports field. No pets. Partial handicap access. Open May 15 thru Oct 15. Big rigs welcome. Member ARVC, NE-HA-CA. Phone: (603)926-5474.

HENNIKER

(E) Keyser Pond Campground—(Merrimack) *From jct US 202, Hwy 127 & Old Concord Rd: Go 300 yards S on Old Concord Rd. Enter on R.* FACILITIES: 118 sites, typical site width 50 ft, 66 full hkups, 43 W&E, (20 & 30 amps), 9 no hkups, RV/park trailer rentals, shower$, dump station, non-guest dumping $, laundry, ltd groceries, RV supplies, LP gas by weight/by meter, ice, tables, fire rings, wood, controlled access gate. RECREATION: rec hall, coin games, pond swimming, boating, electric motors only, canoeing, kayaking, 2 rowboat/5 canoe/3 kayak/2 pedal boat rentals, pond fishing, fishing supplies, mini-golf ($), golf nearby, bsktball, playground, 3 shuffleboard courts, planned activities (wkends only), horseshoes, v-ball. Pets welcome. Open mid May thru mid Oct. Member ARVC, NE-HA-CA. Phone: (800)272-5221.

HINSDALE

(W) Hinsdale Campground—*From I-91 in VT, take exit 1 E on Rt 5: Go 1 mi, cross over Green Bridge. Follow Rte 119 4.8 mi E to Hinsdale Campground. Enter on L.* FACILITIES: 113 sites, typical site width 30 ft, 88 full hkups, 16 W&E, (20, 30 & 50 amps), 9 no hkups, cable TV ($), wireless Internet access central location, RV storage, dump station, non-guest dumping $, laundry, RV supplies, LP gas by weight/by meter, ice, tables, fire rings, grills, wood, controlled access gate. RECREATION: rec hall, rec room/area, equipped pavilion, coin games, swim pool, wading pool, play equipment, planned activities (wkends only), horseshoes, hiking trails, v-ball. Pets welcome, quantity restrict. Partial handicap access. Open Apr 1 thru Oct 31. Nov 1-Apr 1. Open Th-Fri-Sat-Sun-dry camping only. Big rigs welcome. Member NE-HA-CA. Phone: (603)336-8906.

MOULTONBOROUGH

(SW) Bear's Pine Woods Campground—(Carroll) *From jct Hwy 109 & Hwy 25: Go 4 mi SW on Hwy 25, then 4 mi S on Moultonborough Neck Rd. Enter on R.* FACILITIES: 100 sites, typical site width 25 ft, 97 full hkups, 3 W&E, (20, 30 & 50 amps), 8 pull-thrus, cable TV ($), wireless Instant Internet access at site, wireless Internet access central location, dump station, non-guest dumping $, laundry, ltd groceries, RV supplies, LP gas by weight/by meter, ice, tables, fire rings, wood, controlled access gate. RECREATION: rec room/area, pavilion, coin games, swim pool, golf nearby, bsktball, playground, planned activities (wkends only), horseshoes, v-ball. Pets welcome. Open Mid May thru Columbus Day. Member ARVC. Phone: (603)253-6251.

Long Island Bridge Campground—(Carroll) *From jct Hwy 109 & Hwy 25: Go 4 mi SW on Hwy 25, then 6-1/2 mi S on Moultonborough Neck Rd. Enter on L.* FACILITIES: 114 sites, typical site width 25 ft, 36 ft max RV length, 76 full hkups, 25 W&E, (20 & 30 amps), 13 no hkups, 4 pull-thrus, cable TV, phone Internet access central location, RV/park trailer rentals, cabins, shower$, dump station, laundry, RV supplies, ice, tables, fire rings, grills, wood, controlled access gate. RECREATION: lake swimming, boating, canoeing, kayaking, ramp, dock, 2 canoe rentals, lake fishing, golf nearby, bsktball, playground, sports field, v-ball. Pets welcome, breed restrict, quantity restrict. Partial handicap access. Open Mid May thru Mid Oct. Member ARVC, NE-HA-CA. Phone: (603)253-6053.

NEW BOSTON

(W) Friendly Beaver Campground—(Hillsborough) *From jct Hwy 77 & Hwy 136 & Hwy 13: Go 100 feet S on Hwy 13, then 2 mi W on Old Coach Rd. Enter on R.* FACILITIES: 278 sites, typical site width 40 ft, 213 full hkups, 62 W&E, (20, 30 & 50 amps), 3 no hkups, heater not allowed, phone Internet access central location, RV/park trailer rentals, dump station, portable dump, laundry, groceries, RV supplies, ice, tables, fire rings, grills, wood. RECREATION: rec hall, rec room/area, pavilion, coin games, 4 swim pools, wading pool, whirlpool, bsktball, playground, planned activities, horseshoes, sports field, hiking trails, v-ball. Pets welcome. Partial handicap access. Open all yr. Entire facility fully operational during Winter months. Big rigs welcome. Member ARVC, NE-HA-CA. ATM. Phone: (603)487-5570.

NORTH WOODSTOCK

(W) Lost River Valley Campground—(Grafton) *From jct I-93 (exit 32) & Hwy 112: Go 3-1/2 mi W on Hwy 112. Enter on L.* FACILITIES: 130 sites, typical site width 40 ft, 32 ft max RV length, 8 full hkups, 53 W&E, (20, 30 & 50 amps), 69 no hkups, 8 pull-thrus, phone Internet access central location, cabins, shower$, dump station, laundry, groceries, RV supplies, LP gas by weight/by meter, ice, tables, fire rings, grills, wood, controlled access gate. RECREATION: rec room/area, coin games, pond swimming, kayaking, 4 kayak/3 pedal boat rentals, stream fishing, fishing supplies, bsktball, playground, tennis, horseshoes, sports field, v-ball. Pets welcome, breed restrict, quantity restrict. Partial handicap access. Open May 15 thru Columbus Day. Member ARVC, NE-HA-CA. ATM. Phone: (800)370-5678.

RUMNEY

(E) Riverbrook RV Resort—(Grafton) *From jct I-93 (exit 26) & Hwy 25: Go 6 mi W on Hwy 25. Enter on R.* FACILITIES: 100 sites, 100 full hkups, (20, 30 & 50 amps), 8 pull-thrus, cable TV, wireless Instant Internet access at site, RV/park trailer rentals, RV storage, laundry, ltd groceries, RV supplies, LP gas by weight/by meter, ice, tables, fire rings, wood. RECREATION: rec hall, coin games, swim pool, river swimming, whirlpool, canoeing, kayaking, canoe rentals, river/stream fishing, golf nearby, playground, horseshoes, sports field, hiking trails. Pets welcome. Partial handicap access. Open Early May thru Late Oct. Winter camping late Nov. - early Mar w/some limitations. Big rigs welcome. Member NE-HA-CA. Phone: (888)786-2333.

NEW JERSEY

BARNEGAT

(W) Brookville Campground—(Ocean) *From Garden State Parkway South (exit 69) & Hwy 532: Go 4 mi W on Hwy 532, then 1-1/2 mi SW on Brookville Rd, then 1/2 mi E on Jones Rd. Enter on R.* FACILITIES: 100 sites, typical site width 35 ft, 72 full hkups, (20 & 30 amps), 28 no hkups, RV/park trailer rentals, RV storage, dump station, non-guest dumping $, ice, tables, wood. RECREATION: pavilion, swim pool, lake fishing, golf nearby, bsktball, playground, horseshoes, sports field, hiking trails, v-ball. Pets welcome. Open May 1 thru Oct 1. Member ARVC, NJCOA. Phone: (609)698-3134.

BUENA

(E) Buena Vista Camping Resort (Morgan RV Resorts)—(Atlantic) *From jct Hwy 54 & Hwy 40: Go 500 feet E on Hwy 40. Enter on L.* FACILITIES: 640 sites, typical site width 30 ft, 310 full hkups, 330 W&E, (20, 30 & 50 amps), cabins, RV storage, dump station, non-guest dumping $, laundry, groceries, RV supplies, LP gas by weight/by meter, ice, tables, fire rings, wood, controlled access gate. RECREATION: rec hall, rec room/area, pavilion, equipped pavilion, coin games, swim pool, wading pool, lake swimming, kayaking, 12 kayak rentals, pond fishing, fishing supplies, mini-golf ($), golf nearby, bsktball, playground, 4 shuffleboard courts, planned activities, tennis, horseshoes, sports field, v-ball. Rec open to public. Pets welcome, breed restrict. Partial handicap access. Open all yr. Most full hookup sites occupied by seasonal campers. Fun Zone & water activities $. Big rigs welcome. Member ARVC, NJCOA. Phone: (856)697-5555.

CAPE MAY

(N) Beachcomber Camping Resort—(Cape May) *From jct Hwy 47 & US 9: Go 1-1/4 mi S on US 9, then 1 block W on Sally Marshall Crossing, then 1 block N on Seashore Rd. Enter on L.* FACILITIES: 725 sites, typical site width 35 ft, 700 full hkups, 25 W&E, (30 & 50 amps), cable TV, wireless Instant Internet access at site ($), cabins, RV storage, shower$, dump station, laundry, groceries, RV supplies, LP gas by weight/by meter, ice, tables, patios, fire rings, wood, controlled access gate. RECREATION: rec hall, rec room/area, pavilion, coin games, 3 swim pools, wading pool, lake swimming, boating, no motors, canoeing, kayaking, 6 kayak/6 pedal boat rentals, lake fishing, fishing supplies, golf nearby, bsktball, playground, 6 shuffleboard courts, planned activities, horseshoes, v-ball, local tours. Pets welcome. Open Mid-April thru Oct 31. 7 day min. Jul & Aug. Big rigs welcome. Member ARVC, NJCOA. Phone: (609)886-6035.

(N) Seashore Campsites—(Cape May) *From jct Hwy 47 & US 9: Go 2-3/4 mi S on US 9, then 500 ft W over tracks on Bennetts Crossing, then 500 ft N on Hwy 626. (Seashore Rd). Enter on L.* FACILITIES: 700 sites, typical site width 40 ft, 514 full hkups, 130 W&E, (20, 30 & 50 amps), 56 no hkups, 13 pull-thrus, cable TV, wireless Instant Internet access at site ($), phone Internet access central location, shower$, dump station, non-guest dumping $, portable dump, laundry, groceries, RV supplies, LP gas by weight/by meter, ice, tables, patios, wood. RECREATION: rec hall, rec room/area, equipped pavilion, coin games, swim pool, wading pool, lake swimming, mini-golf ($), golf nearby, bsktball, bike rental, playground, 2 shuffleboard courts, planned activities, tennis, horseshoes, v-ball, local tours. Pets

Seashore Campsite—Continued on next page

CAPE MAY—Continued
Seashore Campsite—Continued

welcome. Open all yr. Facilities fully operational Apr 15 thru Oct 31. 3 day min. Jul & Aug with reservations. Self-contained units only Nov 1-Apr 15. Big rigs welcome. Member ARVC, NJCOA. ATM. Phone: (609)884-4010.

(N) The Depot Travel Park—(Cape May) *From jct Hwy 109 & US 9: Go 1/4 mi W on US 9, then 1-3/4 mi S on Seashore Rd (CR 626). Enter on R.* FACILITIES: 135 sites, typical site width 40 ft, 100 full hkups, 35 W&E, (20 & 30 amps), heater not allowed, RV/park trailer rentals, dump station, non-guest dumping $, LP gas by weight/by meter, ice, tables. RECREATION: pavilion, golf nearby, playground, horseshoes, sports field. Pets welcome. Open May 1 thru Oct 8. Member ARVC, NJCOA. Phone: (609)884-2533.

CLARKSBORO

(S) Timberlane Campground—(Gloucester) *N'bnd from jct I-295 & Timberlane Rd (exit 18): Go 3/4 mi SE on Timberlane Rd. Ent on rt. S'bnd from I-295 (exit 18AB):Go 1 mi S on Hwy 667 (Cohawkin Rd), then 1/4 mi SW on Friendship Rd, then 1/4 mi NW on Timberlane Rd.* FACILITIES: 96 sites, typical site width 30 ft, 82 full hkups, (20, 30 & 50 amps), 14 no hkups, 51 pull-thrus, cable TV, wireless Instant Internet access at site, wireless Internet access central location, cabins, RV storage, dump station, non-guest dumping $, laundry, RV supplies, LP gas by weight/by meter, ice, tables, fire rings, wood. RECREATION: rec room/area, pavilion, coin games, swim pool, wading pool, pond fishing, fishing supplies, golf nearby, bsktball, playground, shuffleboard court, horseshoes, sports field, v-ball. Pets welcome. Partial handicap access. Open all yr. Big rigs welcome. Member ARVC, NJCOA. Phone: (856)423-6677.

CLERMONT

(S) Avalon Campground—(Cape May) *From Garden State Parkway & Hwy 601 (exit 13): Go 1/2 mi W on Hwy 601, then 1-1/2 mi N on US 9. Enter on L.* FACILITIES: 360 sites, 200 full hkups, 120 W&E, (20, 30 & 50 amps), 40 no hkups, cable TV, wireless Internet access central location, RV/park trailer rentals, cabins, RV storage, dump station, non-guest dumping $, laundry, ltd groceries, RV supplies, LP gas by weight, ice, tables, fire rings, wood, controlled access gate. RECREATION: rec hall, rec room/area, equipped pavilion, coin games, 2 swim pools, mini-golf ($), golf nearby, bsktball, playground, 2 shuffleboard courts, planned activities, horseshoes, sports field, v-ball. Pets welcome. Open Apr 15 thru Sep 30. 3 Day Min Holiday Wknds by reservation. 4 Day Min Jul & Aug by reservation. Member ARVC, NJCOA. Phone: (609)624-0075.

EGG HARBOR CITY

(S) Best Holiday Trav-L-Park/Holly Acres—(Atlantic) *From jct Hwy 50 & US 30: Go 2 mi SE on US 30, then 1-1/2 mi NE on Frankfurt Ave. Enter on R.* FACILITIES: 175 sites, typical site width 35 ft, 125 full hkups, 50 W&E, (30 & 50 amps), 50 amps ($), 20 pull-thrus, cable TV, cabins, laundry, ltd groceries, ice, tables, fire rings, wood, controlled access gate. RECREATION: rec hall, rec room/area, equipped pavilion, coin games, swim pool, wading pool, pond fishing, fishing supplies, mini-golf ($), golf nearby, bsktball, playground, shuffleboard court, planned activities (wkends only), horseshoes, v-ball. Pets welcome. Partial handicap access. No tents. Open Apr 15 thru Oct 31. 3 Day Min. Holiday Weekends by Reservations. Big rigs welcome. Member ARVC, NJCOA. Phone: (609)965-2287.

ESTELL MANOR

(N) PLEASANT VALLEY FAMILY CAMPGROUND—(Weymouth) *From south jct Hwy 40 & Hwy 50: Go 1-1/4 mi S on Hwy 50. Enter on R.*

WELCOME

FACILITIES: 250 sites, 250 full hkups, (15, 20, 30 & 50 amps), cable TV, phone on-site Internet access (needs activ), cabins, RV storage, shower$, laundry, RV supplies, LP gas by weight/by meter, ice, tables, fire rings, wood, controlled access gate.

RECREATION: rec hall, rec room/area, pavilion, coin games, swim pool, wading pool, whirlpool, golf nearby, bsktball, playground, 2 shuffleboard

ESTELL MANOR—Continued
PLEASANT VALLEY FAMILY CAMPGROUND—Continued

courts, planned activities, horseshoes, sports field, v-ball.

Pets welcome, breed restrict. No tents. Open Apr 15 thru Oct 15. Big rigs welcome. Member NJCOA. Phone: (609)625-1238.

e-mail: pleasantvalley@gocampingamerica.com

SEE AD ATLANTIC CITY PAGE 17

FREEHOLD

(W) Pine Cone Resort—(Monmouth) *From jct Hwy 195 (exit 28) & Hwy 9: Go 1-1/2 mi N on Hwy 9, then 1-1/2 mi W on West Farms Rd. Enter on L.* FACILITIES: 125 sites, typical site width 40 ft, 35 full hkups, 90 W&E, (20, 30 & 50 amps), 15 pull-thrus, cable TV, wireless Internet access central location, cabins, RV storage, dump station, non-guest dumping $, portable dump, laundry, ltd groceries, RV supplies, ice, tables, fire rings, wood. RECREATION: rec room/area, coin games, swim pool, golf nearby, bsktball, playground, planned activities (wkends only), tennis, horseshoes, sports field, v-ball. Pets welcome. Partial handicap access. Open all yr. 3 day min holidays by reservation. Big rigs welcome. Member ARVC, NJCOA. Phone: (732)462-2230.

HAMMONTON

(S) Indian Branch Park—(Atlantic) *From jct Atlantic City Expressway (exit 28) & Hwy 54: Go 2 mi SW on Hwy 54, then 3-1/2 mi SE on US 322. (Skip Morgan Dr, under construction. Use Shoshoni Rd through 2008). Enter on L.* FACILITIES: 214 sites, typical site width 40 ft, 160 full hkups, 54 W&E, (20 & 30 amps), RV storage, shower$, dump station, laundry, groceries, RV supplies, LP gas by weight/by meter, ice, tables, fire rings, wood, controlled access gate. RECREATION: rec hall, rec room/area, coin games, lake/river swimming, boating, no motors, canoeing, kayaking, 7 canoe/6 kayak/3 pedal boat rentals, river fishing, golf nearby, bsktball, playground, 2 shuffleboard courts, horseshoes, sports field, hiking trails, v-ball. Pets welcome. Open May thru Sep. Member ARVC, NJCOA. Phone: (609)561-4719.

HOPE

(S) Triplebrook Camping Resort—(Warren) *From jct I-80 (exit 12) & CR 521: Go 1 mi S on CR 521, then 3 mi W on CR 609, then 1 mi N on Nightingale Rd, then 1/2 mi E on Honey Run Rd. Enter on L.* FACILITIES: 217 sites, typical site width 40 ft, 110 full hkups, 101 W&E, (20, 30 & 50 amps), 6 no hkups, 6 pull-thrus, cabins, RV storage, dump station, non-guest dumping $, portable dump, laundry, ltd groceries, RV supplies, LP gas by weight/by meter, ice, tables, wood. RECREATION: rec room/area, equipped pavilion, coin games, 2 swim pools, whirlpool, boating, canoeing, kayaking, 6 rowboat/3 kayak/4 pedal boat rentals, pond fishing, fishing supplies, mini-golf ($), golf nearby, bsktball, playground, shuffleboard court, planned activities, tennis, horseshoes, sports field, hiking trails, v-ball. No pets. Open all yr. 3 day min. stay holiday wkends with reservations. Dec 1-Mar 31 by reservation only. Big rigs welcome. Member ARVC, NJCOA. Phone: (908)459-4079.

JACKSON

(W) Indian Rock Resort—(Ocean) *From jct I-195 (exit 16B) & Hwy 537: Go 1 mi SE on Hwy 537, then 4-1/2 mi S on Hwy 571, then 1-1/2 mi W on Hwy 528. Enter on R.* FACILITIES: 210 sites, typical site width 40 ft, 90 full hkups, 120 W&E, (20 & 30 amps), wireless Internet access central location, RV/park trailer rentals, cabins, dump station, non-guest dumping $, laundry, groceries, RV supplies, LP gas by weight/by meter, ice, tables, fire rings, wood, controlled access gate. RECREATION: rec hall, pavilion, coin games, swim pool, pond fishing, mini-golf ($), golf nearby, bsktball, playground, planned activities (wkends only), horseshoes, sports field, v-ball. Pets welcome. Partial handicap access. Open all yr. Member ARVC, NJCOA. Phone: (732)928-0034.

MONROEVILLE

(S) Oldman's Creek Campground—(Gloucester) *From jct US 322 & Hwy 45: Go 3/4 mi S on Hwy 45, then 4 mi S on Hwy 77, then 1/2 mi E on Hwy 538, then 1/2 mi S on Hwy 641, then 3/4 mi S on Laux Rd. Enter on L.* FACILITIES: 143 sites, typical site width 32 ft, 140 full hkups, 3 W&E, (20, 30 & 50 amps), 2 pull-thrus, cable on-site Internet access (needs activ), RV/park trailer rentals, cabins, dump station, non-guest dumping $, laundry, RV supplies, LP gas by weight/by meter, ice, tables, fire rings, grills, wood, controlled access gate. RECREATION: rec hall, equipped pavilion, coin games, swim pool, lake swimming, boating, no motors, canoeing, kayaking, 4 pedal boat rentals, lake fishing, fishing supplies, golf nearby, playground, shuffleboard court, planned activities (wkends only), horseshoes, sports field, v-ball. Pets welcome, breed restrict. Open all yr. Member ARVC, NJCOA. Phone: (856)478-4502.

OCEAN VIEW

(S) Ocean View Resort Campground—(Cape May) *From jct Garden State Pkwy South (exit 17) & Hwy 625 (Sea Isle Blvd): Go 1/4 mi W on Hwy 625, then 1/4 mi N on US 9. Enter on L.* FACILITIES: 1175 sites, 1175 full hkups, (20, 30 & 50 amps), 40 pull-thrus, heater not allowed, cable TV, wireless Instant Internet access at site, wireless Internet access central location, RV/park trailer rentals, cabins, RV storage, shower$, laundry, full svc store, RV supplies, LP gas by weight/by meter, ice, tables, fire rings, wood, controlled access gate. RECREATION: rec hall, rec room/area, equipped pavilion, coin games, swim pool, wading pool, lake swimming, boating, 6 pedal boat rentals, pond fishing, fishing supplies, mini-golf ($), golf nearby, bsktball, playground, 2 shuffleboard courts, planned activities, tennis, sports field, v-ball, local tours. Pets welcome. Partial handicap access. Age restrictions may apply. Open Mid Apr thru Sep 30. Weekends only early season. Big rigs welcome. Member ARVC, NJCOA. Phone: (609)624-1675.

PORT REPUBLIC

(N) Atlantic City Blueberry Hill (Morgan RV Resorts)—(Atlantic) *From jct Garden State Parkway (South) exit 48 & US 9: Go 1/4 mi S on US 9, then 1-1/2 mi S on CR 575, then 1 mi S on CR 650, then 1/4 mi W on CR 624. Enter on L.* FACILITIES: 173 sites, typical site width 40 ft, 47 full hkups, 124 W&E, (20, 30 & 50 amps), 50 amps ($), 2 no hkups, 50 pull-thrus, heater not allowed, cable TV, wireless Internet access central location, RV/park trailer rentals, RV storage, dump station, portable dump, laundry, ltd groceries, RV supplies, LP gas by weight/by meter, ice, tables, fire rings, wood. RECREATION: rec hall, rec room/area, pavilion, coin games, swim pool, wading pool, whirlpool, golf nearby, bsktball, playground, planned activities (wkends only), horseshoes, v-ball. Pets welcome. Partial handicap access. Open Feb 1 thru Dec 15. 3 day minimum holiday with reservations. Member ARVC, NJCOA. Phone: (609)652-1644.

NEW YORK

CHERRY VALLEY

(S) Belvedere Lake Campground—(Otsego) *From jct Hwy 54 & Hwy 166: Go 4 mi S on Hwy 166, then 1/2 mi SE on Hwy 165, then 1/8 mi E on CR 57, then 3/4 mi N on Gage Rd. Enter on L.* FACILITIES: 160 sites, typical site width 35 ft, 120 full hkups, 40 W&E, (20 & 30 amps), phone on-site Internet access (needs activ), cabins, RV storage, shower$, dump station, portable dump, laundry, ltd groceries, RV supplies, LP bottle exch, ice, tables, fire rings, wood, controlled access gate. RECREATION: rec hall, pavilion, coin games, lake swimming, boating, electric motors only, dock, 6 rowboat rentals, lake fishing, mini-golf ($), bsktball, playground, planned activities (wkends only), tennis, horseshoes, sports field, hiking trails, v-ball. Pets welcome. Partial handicap access. Open May 1 thru Columbus Day. Member ARVC, CONY. Phone: (607)264-8182.

CUTCHOGUE

(C) CLIFF AND ED'S TRAILER PARK—(Suffolk) *From jct I-495 (exit 73) & Hwy 25: Go 15-1/4 mi E on Hwy 25, then 1 block N on Depot Lane, then 1 block W on Schoolhouse Rd. Enter on R.*

WELCOME

FACILITIES: 23 sites, typical site width 36 ft, accepts full hkup units only, 23 full hkups, (20, 30 & 50 amps), cable TV, phone/cable on-site Internet access (needs activ), RV/park trailer rentals, shower$, tables, patios.

RECREATION: golf nearby.

Pets welcome, breed restrict. Partial handicap access. No tents. Open Apr 1 thru Nov 1. Big rigs welcome. Member ARVC, CONY. Phone: (631)298-4091.

e-mail: cliffandeds@optonline.net

SEE AD THIS PAGE

DEWITTVILLE

(S) Chautauqua Heights Camping Resort—(Chautauqua) *From jct I-86 (exit 10) & Hwy 430: Go 6-1/2 mi W on Hyw 430, then 1/2 mi E on Thumb Rd. Enter on L.* FACILITIES: 182 sites, 153 full hkups, 28 W&E, (20, 30 & 50 amps), 1 no hkups, 40 pull-thrus, cable TV, wireless Instant Internet access at site, wireless Internet access central location, cabins, RV storage, dump station, laundry, ltd groceries, RV supplies, LP gas by weight, ice, tables, fire rings, wood, controlled access gate. RECREATION: rec hall, rec room/area, pavilion, coin games, swim pool, golf nearby, bsktball, playground, planned activities, horseshoes, sports field, hiking trails, v-ball. Pets welcome. Partial handicap access. Open May 1 thru Oct 15. Pets require rabies certification. Big rigs welcome. Member ARVC, CONY. Phone: (716)386-3804.

ELIZAVILLE

(N) Brook N Wood Family Campground—(Columbia) *From jct CR 199 & US 9: Go 9 mi N on US 9, then 2 mi E on CR 8. Enter on R.* FACILITIES: 174 sites, typical site width 40 ft, 124 full hkups, 30 W&E, (20, 30 & 50 amps), 20 no hkups, cable TV, wireless Instant Internet access at site, phone on-site Internet access (needs activ), phone Internet access central location, RV/park trailer rentals, cabins, dump station, non-guest dumping $, laundry, ltd groceries, RV supplies, LP gas by weight/by meter, ice, tables, fire rings, wood. RECREATION: rec hall, rec room/area, coin games, swim pool, stream fishing, fishing supplies, mini-golf ($), golf nearby, bsktball, play equipment, planned activities (wkends only), horseshoes, sports field, hiking trails, v-ball. Pets welcome, breed restrict. Open Apr 1 thru Mid Nov. Big rigs welcome. Member ARVC, CONY. Phone: (888)625-3186.

FLORIDA

(W) Black Bear Campground—(Orange) *From jct Hwy 17 (exit 124) & Hwy 17A: Go 5-1/2 mi SW on Hwy 17A, turn right at light (Bridge St), then 1-1/2 mi W on CR 41. Enter on L.* FACILITIES: 160 sites, typical site width 30 ft, 109 full hkups, 51 W&E, (20, 30 & 50 amps), 10 pull-thrus, cable TV, wireless Instant Internet access at site, RV/park trailer rentals, dump station, portable dump, laundry, ltd groceries, RV supplies, ice, tables, fire rings, grills, wood. RECREATION: equipped pavilion, coin games, swim pool, mini-golf, golf nearby, bsktball, play equipment, 2 shuffleboard courts, planned activities (wkends only), horseshoes, v-ball. Pets welcome, breed restrict. Partial handicap access. No tents. Open all yr. Big rigs welcome. Member ARVC, CONY. Phone: (845)651-7717.

HENDERSON HARBOR

(W) Association Island RV Resort & Marina—(Jefferson) *From I-81 (exit 41) & Hwy 178: Go 12 mi W on Hwy 178, then 2 mi N on Snowshoe Rd, cross bridge to 2nd Island. Enter at end.* FACILITIES: 305 sites, typical site width 40 ft, 305 full hkups, (20, 30 & 50 amps), 29 pull-thrus, cable TV, wireless Instant Internet access at site ($), wireless Internet access central location ($), cabins, dump station, laundry, ltd groceries, RV supplies, ice, tables, patios, fire rings, wood. RECREATION: rec hall, rec room/area, swim pool, lake swimming, boating, canoeing, kayaking, ramp, dock, 4 kayak rentals, lake fishing, fishing supplies, fishing guides, golf nearby, bsktball, playground, shuffleboard court, planned activities (wkends only), tennis, horseshoes, sports field, v-ball. Pets welcome, breed restrict, quantity restrict. Partial handicap access. No tents. Open May 15 thru Oct 15. Big rigs welcome. Member ARVC, CONY. Phone: (800)393-4189.

ITHACA

(N) Spruce Row Campground—(Tompkins) *From north jct Hwy 13 & Hwy 96: Go 7 mi NW on Hwy 96, then 1/2 mi N on Jacksonville Rd, then 1-1/4 mi E on Kraft Rd. Enter on R.* FACILITIES: 213 sites, typical site width 40 ft, 38 ft max RV length, 99 full hkups, 99 W&E, (20 & 30 amps), 15 no hkups, 30 pull-thrus, wireless Instant Internet access at site ($), wireless Internet access central location, RV/park trailer rentals, cabins, RV storage, dump station, non-guest dumping $, portable dump, ltd groceries, RV supplies, LP gas by weight/by meter, ice, tables, fire rings, wood. RECREATION: pavilion, coin games, swim pool, 2 pedal boat rentals, pond fishing, mini-golf ($), golf nearby, bsktball, 12 bike rentals, playground, planned activities (wkends only), horseshoes, sports field, hiking trails, v-ball. Pets welcome, quantity restrict. Partial handicap access. Open May 1 thru Columbus Day. Member ARVC, CONY. Phone: (607)387-9225.

LAKE GEORGE

(SE) Ledgeview RV Park—(Warren) *From jct I-87 (exit 20-Northway) & Hwy 149/US 9: Go 3/4 mi N on Hwy 149/US 9, then 1-1/2 mi E on Hwy 149. Enter on L.* FACILITIES: 130 sites, typical site width 50 ft, 130 full hkups, (30 & 50 amps), 50 amps ($), 17 pull-thrus, cable TV, wireless Internet access central location, RV storage, laundry, ltd groceries, RV supplies, ice, tables, fire rings, wood, controlled access gate. RECREATION: rec hall, pavilion, coin games, swim pool, golf nearby, bsktball, 10 bike rentals, playground, 2 shuffleboard courts, horseshoes, v-ball. No pets. Partial handicap access. No tents. Open May 1 thru Columbus Day. Big rigs welcome. Member ARVC, CONY. Phone: (518)798-6621.

PHELPS

(N) Cheerful Valley Campground—(Ontario) *From jct I-90 (exit 42) & Hwy-14: Go 1/2 mi N on Hwy-14. Enter on L.* FACILITIES: 130 sites, typical site width 45 ft, 37 full hkups, 88 W&E, (20 & 30 amps), 5 no hkups, 10 pull-thrus, phone Internet access central location, cabins, dump station, non-guest dumping $, portable dump, laundry, ltd groceries, RV supplies, LP gas by weight/by meter, ice, tables, fire rings, wood. RECREATION: rec room/area, pavilion, coin games,

PHELPS—Continued
Cheerful Valley Campground—Continued

swim pool, canoeing, kayaking, river fishing, golf nearby, bsktball, playground, 2 shuffleboard courts, planned activities (wkends only), horseshoes, sports field, v-ball. Pets welcome, quantity restrict. Open Apr 15 thru Oct 15. Pool open Memorial Day-Labor Day. Member ARVC, CONY. Phone: (315)781-1222.

VERONA

(SW) The Villages at Turning Stone RV Park—(Oneida) *From jct I-90 (NY Thruway) (exit 33) & Hwy 365: Go 1-1/2 mi W on Hwy 365. Enter on R.* FACILITIES: 176 sites, typical site width 40 ft, 176 full hkups, (20, 30 & 50 amps), 50 pull-thrus, cable TV, wireless Instant Internet access at site, cable Internet access central location, dump station, non-guest dumping $, laundry, ltd groceries, RV supplies, LP gas by weight/by meter, gas, ice, tables, patios, fire rings, grills, wood. RECREATION: rec hall, rec room/area, equipped pavilion, coin games, swim pool, wading pool, whirlpool, 5 pedal boat rentals, pond fishing, fishing supplies, putting green, golf nearby, bsktball, playground, planned activities (wkends only), tennis, horseshoes, hiking trails, v-ball, local tours. Pets welcome. Partial handicap access. No tents. Open Mid Apr thru Oct. Big rigs welcome. Member ARVC, CONY. Phone: (315)361-7275.

WARRENSBURG

(NE) Schroon River Campsites—(Warren) *From I-87 (exit 23-Warrensburg): Go 200 feet W on Diamond Point Rd, then 1/2 mi N on US-9, then 3 mi N on Horicon Ave/Schroon River Rd. Enter on R.* FACILITIES: 300 sites, typical site width 30 ft, 250 full hkups, 50 W&E, (15, 20, 30 & 50 amps), heater not allowed, cable TV, dump station, non-guest dumping $, laundry, groceries, RV supplies, LP gas by weight, ice, tables, fire rings, wood. RECREATION: rec room/area, coin games, swim pool, river swimming, boating, canoeing, kayaking, 2 rowboat/7 canoe/2 kayak rentals, float trips, river fishing, golf nearby, bsktball, playground, planned activities (wkends only), horseshoes, sports field, v-ball. Pets welcome. Open May 10 thru Oct 4. Member ARVC, CONY. Phone: (518)623-2171.

WOLCOTT

(E) Cherry Grove Campground—(Wayne) *From jct Hwy 414 & Hwy 104: Go 6 mi E on Hwy 104, then 300 feet NW on Ridge Rd. Enter on R.* FACILITIES: 110 sites, typical site width 40 ft, 105 full hkups, (20, 30 & 50 amps), 5 no hkups, 32 pull-thrus, wireless Instant Internet access at site, wireless Internet access central location, cabins, RV storage, dump station, non-guest dumping $, laundry, RV supplies, LP gas by weight/by meter, ice, tables, fire rings, wood. RECREATION: rec hall, coin games, swim pool, golf nearby, play equipment, 2 shuffleboard courts, horseshoes, sports field, v-ball. Pets welcome, breed restrict, quantity restrict. Open Apr 15 thru Oct 15. Big rigs welcome. Member ARVC, CONY. Phone: (315)594-8320.

NORTH CAROLINA

BRYSON CITY

(E) Country Boy's RV Park (REBUILDING) —(Swain) *From US 74 (exit 69): Go 1-1/4 mi N on Hyatt Creek Rd (SR 1190). Enter on L.* FACILITIES: 85 sites, 85 full hkups, (30 & 50 amps), laundry, ice, wood. Pets welcome, breed restrict. Open all yr. Big rigs welcome. Phone: (828)488-8807.

OHIO

BERLIN

(S) Scenic Hills RV Park—(Holmes) *From jct I-77 (exit 83) & SR-39: Go 18 mi W on SR-39, then 1/4 mi S on TR 367 (1 mi E of Berlin). Enter on R.* FACILITIES: 112 sites, typical site width 40 ft, accepts full hkup units only, 112 full hkups, (20, 30 & 50 amps), 40

BERLIN—Continued
Scenic Hills RV Park—Continued

pull-thrus, wireless Instant Internet access at site, RV storage, dump station, non-guest dumping $, RV supplies, LP bottle exch, tables, fire rings, wood. RECREATION: sports field. Pets welcome. No tents. Facilities fully operational Apr 1 thru Nov 1. No restrooms. Big rigs welcome. Member ARVC, OCOA. Phone: (330)893-3607.

LIMA

(SE) Sun Valley Family Campground—(Allen) *From jct US 33 & Hwy 196: Go 8 mi N on Hwy 196, then 3 mi E on Amherst Rd, then 2 mi N on May Rd, then 1 mi W on Faulkner Rd. Enter on R.* FACILITIES: 242 sites, typical site width 30 ft, 242 full hkups, (20, 30 & 50 amps), 5 pull-thrus, laundry, ltd groceries, RV supplies, LP gas by weight/by meter, ice, tables, fire rings, wood. RECREATION: rec room/area, pavilion, pond swimming, boating, electric motors only, dock, lake/pond fishing, fishing supplies, bsktball, playground, shuffleboard court, planned activities (wkends only), horseshoes, sports field, v-ball. Rec open to public. Pets welcome. Partial handicap access. Open Apr 15 thru Oct 31. Big rigs welcome. Member ARVC, OCOA. Phone: (419)648-2235.

NEW PARIS

(S) Natural Springs Resort—(Preble) *From jct I-70 (exit 156 B in Indiana) & US 40: Go 1 mi E on US 40, then 1 mi N on SR 320. Enter on L.* FACILITIES: 240 sites, typical site width 35 ft, 205 full hkups, 25 W&E, (20, 30 & 50 amps), 50 amps ($), 10 no hkups, 18 pull-thrus, cable TV ($), wireless Instant Internet access at site, cabins, RV storage, dump station, non-guest dumping $, laundry, groceries, RV supplies, LP gas by weight, ice, tables, patios, fire rings, grills, wood, controlled access gate. RECREATION: rec hall, rec room/area, pavilion, swim pool, lake/pond swimming, boating, electric motors only, canoeing, kayaking, ramp, dock, 4 pedal boat rentals, lake/pond fishing, fishing supplies, mini-golf ($), bsktball, playground, 3 shuffleboard courts, planned activities (wkends only), horseshoes, sports field, hiking trails, v-ball. Rec open to public. Pets welcome ($). Partial handicap access. Open all yr. Facilities fully operational Mid Apr thru Nov 1. Big rigs welcome. Member ARVC, OCOA. Phone: (937)437-5771.

NORTH BEND

(W) Indian Springs Campground—(Hamilton) *From jct I-74 & I-275: Go 8 mi SW on I-275 (exit 16), then 3 mi NE on US 50, then 1/2 N on State Line Rd. Enter on R.* FACILITIES: 73 sites, typical site width 31 ft, 73 W&E, (20, 30 & 50 amps), 13 pull-thrus, wireless Instant Internet access at site, dump station, RV supplies, LP gas by weight/by meter, ice, tables, fire rings, wood. RECREATION: rec room/area, coin games, boating, electric motors only, canoeing, kayaking, ramp, dock, 2 pontoon/5 rowboat/7 pedal boat rentals, lake fishing, playground, horseshoes. Pets welcome, breed restrict. No tents. Open all yr. Call for reservations Dec, Jan, Feb. Member ARVC, OCOA. Phone: (888)550-9244.

OKLAHOMA

AFTON

(SE) Grand Country Lakeside & RV Park—(Delaware) *From jct I-44 (exit 302) & US 59: Go 5 mi S & E on US 59, then 4 mi S on Hwy 125, then 1 mi W on Hwy 85A, then 1/4 mi S on CR 550. Enter on L.* FACILITIES: 32 sites, typical site width 30 ft, 32 full hkups, (20, 30 & 50 amps), 16 pull-thrus, tables. RECREATION: rec hall, lake swimming, boating, lake fishing, golf nearby, horseshoes, hiking trails. Pets welcome, breed restrict, size restrict. No tents. Open all yr. Big rigs welcome. Member ARVC. Phone: (918)257-5164.

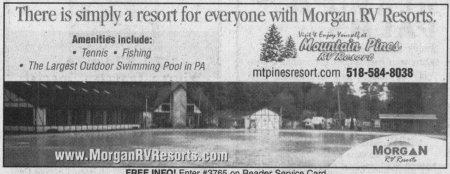

PENNSYLVANIA

CHAMPION

(S) MOUNTAIN PINES RV RESORT (Morgan Rv Resorts)—(Westmoreland) *From jct PA Turnpike & SR-31 (exit 91): Go 2 mi E on SR-31, then 2 mi S on SR-711. Enter on L.*

FACILITIES: 743 sites, typical site width 30 ft, 713 full hkups, 30 W&E, (20 & 30 amps), cable TV, cabins, dump station, non-guest dumping $, laundry, ltd groceries, RV supplies, LP gas by weight, ice, tables, fire rings, wood, controlled access gate.

RECREATION: rec hall, rec room/area, pavilion, coin games, 2 swim pools, wading pool, stream fishing, fishing supplies, mini-golf, golf nearby, bsktball, 15 bike rentals, playground, shuffleboard court, planned activities (wkends only), tennis, horseshoes, sports field, hiking trails, v-ball.

Pets welcome. Partial handicap access. Open Mid Apr thru Late Oct. Member ARVC, PCOA. Phone: (724)455-3300.

SEE AD PAGE 19

HATFIELD

(NW) Oak Grove Park & Sales—(Montgomery) *From jct SR 463 & Vine St: Go 1/4 mi N on SR 463 (Main St) then 3/4 mi N on N Main St/Cowpath Rd. Enter on R.* FACILITIES: 70 sites, 70 full hkups, (30 & 50 amps), 2 pull-thrus, phone/cable on-site Internet access (needs activ), wireless Internet access central location, RV storage, dump station, non-guest dumping $, laundry, LP gas by weight/by meter, tables. RECREATION: rec hall, playground. Pets welcome. No tents. Open all yr. Big rigs welcome. Phone: (215)723-2007.

JEFFERSON

(NE) Firehouse RV Campground—(Greene) *From jct I-79 (exit 19) & SR-19: Go 300 yds S on SR-19, then 4 mi E on SR-221, then 4 mi E on SR-188. Enter on L.* FACILITIES: 37 sites, typical site width 30 ft, accepts full hkup units only, 37 full hkups, (30 & 50 amps), 20 pull-thrus, cable TV ($), phone on-site Internet access (needs activ), ice, tables, patios. RECREATION: golf nearby, horseshoes. Pets welcome. No tents. Open all yr. Big rigs welcome. Phone: (724)883-3901.

SOUTH CAROLINA

SWANSEA

(SW) River Bottom Farms Campground & R.V. Resort—(Lexington) *From jct US 321 & S.C. 3: Go W 6-1/2 mi on S.C. 3, then NW 1/2 mi on US 178, then W 1/2 mi on Cedar Creek Rd. Enter on L.* FACILITIES: 78 sites, typical site width 40 ft, 61 full hkups, 14 W&E, 3 E, (20, 30 & 50 amps), 22 pull-thrus, wireless Instant Internet access at site, phone Internet access central location, cabins, RV storage, laundry, RV supplies, LP gas by weight/by meter, ice, tables, fire rings, grills, wood. RECREATION: rec hall, equipped pavilion, swim pool, river/pond fishing, fishing supplies, play equipment, planned activities (wkends only), horseshoes, sports field, hiking trails, v-ball. Pets welcome. Partial handicap access. Open all yr. Big rigs welcome. Member ARVC, CARVC. Phone: (803)568-4182.

Woodall's Tip #29... The "Welcome" symbol before a listing identifies those parks that have purchased an advertisement because they want to tell you more about their business.

TENNESSEE

BAILEYTON

(E) Baileyton RV Park—(Greene) *From jct I-81 (exit 36): Go 7/10 mi N, then 1 mi E on Horton Hwy. Enter on L.* FACILITIES: 60 sites, typical site width 30 ft, 55 full hkups, 5 W&E, (20, 30 & 50 amps), 30 pull-thrus, cable TV, wireless Instant Internet access at site, phone on-site Internet access (needs activ), phone Internet access central location, RV/park trailer rentals, RV storage, dump station, non-guest dumping $, laundry, RV supplies, LP gas by weight/by meter, ice, tables, grills, wood. RECREATION: equipped pavilion, pond fishing, fishing supplies, golf nearby, horseshoes, hiking trails, v-ball. Pets welcome. Open all yr. Big rigs welcome. Member ARVC, TNARVC. Phone: (423)234-4992.

BRISTOL

(S) Lakeview RV Park—(Sullivan) *From jct I-81 (exit 69) & SR 394: Go 5-1/4 mi E on SR-394, then 3 mi S on Hwy 11E. Enter on R.* FACILITIES: 160 sites, typical site width 30 ft, 160 full hkups, (20, 30 & 50 amps), cable TV, wireless Instant Internet access at site, wireless Internet access central location, RV storage, laundry, ltd groceries, RV supplies, LP gas by weight/by meter, ice, tables. RECREATION: rec room/area, dock, lake fishing, fishing supplies, golf nearby, planned activities, horseshoes, sports field, v-ball. Pets welcome. No tents. Open all yr. Big rigs welcome. Member ARVC, TNARVC. Phone: (866)800-0777.

MANCHESTER

(S) KOA-Manchester—(Coffee) *From jct I-24 (exit 114) & US 41: Go 100 yards on US 41, then 1/2 mi N on Kampground Rd (Frontage Rd). Enter on R.* FACILITIES: 59 sites, typical site width 33 ft, 24 full hkups, 15 W&E, (20, 30 & 50 amps), 20 no hkups, 42 pull-thrus, cable TV, wireless Instant Internet access at site, phone on-site Internet access (needs activ), phone Internet access central location, cabins, dump station, non-guest dumping $, laundry, full svc store, RV supplies, LP gas by weight/by meter, ice, tables, fire rings, grills, wood. RECREATION: rec room/area, pavilion, coin games, swim pool, whirlpool, pond fishing, fishing supplies, golf nearby, bsktball, playground, planned activities (wkends only), horseshoes, sports field, hiking trails, v-ball, local tours. Pets welcome. Open all yr. Big rigs welcome. Member ARVC, TNARVC. Phone: (800) 562-7785.

SEVIERVILLE

(N) Riverside RV Park & Resort—(Sevier) *From jct I-40 (exit 407) & Hwy 66: Go 4 mi S on Hwy 66, then 1/4 mi W on Boyds Creek Rd (turn right at Marathon). Enter on R.* FACILITIES: 316 sites, typical site width 30 ft, 296 full hkups, 20 W&E, (30 & 50 amps), 50 amps ($), 101 pull-thrus, cable TV, wireless Instant Internet access at site ($), RV/park trailer rentals, cabins, RV storage, laundry, groceries, RV supplies, LP gas by weight/by meter, ice, tables, patios, fire rings, grills, wood. RECREATION: rec room/area, equipped pavilion, coin games, swim pool, boating, ramp, river fishing, fishing supplies, golf nearby, bsktball, playground, planned activities. Pets welcome. No tents. Open all yr. Big rigs welcome. Phone: (800)341-7534.

Introducing gourmet meals for your RV kitchen! Woodall's Cooking on the Road with Celebrity Chefs includes dozens of tips and sidebars that makes recipes easier to use while traveling. Go to www.woodalls.com/shop and check it out.

TEXAS

ALAMO

(W) ALAMO PALMS—(Hidalgo) *From jct US-83 & FM-907: Go 1/2 mi S on FM-907, then 1/2 mi W on Bus US-83. Enter on L.*

FACILITIES: 642 sites, typical site width 20 ft, 642 full hkups, (30 & 50 amps), cable TV, wireless Instant Internet access at site, cable Internet access central location, RV storage, laundry, ice, patios, controlled access gate.

RECREATION: rec hall, rec room/area, swim pool, whirlpool, golf nearby, bsktball, 20 shuffleboard courts, planned activities, tennis, horseshoes, local tours.

Pets welcome. Partial handicap access. No tents. Age restrictions may apply. Open all yr. Member ARVC, TACO. Phone: (800)780-7571.

e-mail: info@alamopalms.com

SEE AD THIS PAGE

ARLINGTON

(S) Treetops RV Village—(Tarrant) *From jct I-20 (exit 449) & Hwy 157: Go 1/2 mi N on Hwy 157, then 1/4 mi W on Arbrook. Enter on R.* FACILITIES: 165 sites, typical site width 40 ft, 165 full hkups, (30 & 50 amps), 50 amps ($), 63 pull-thrus, cable TV, phone/wireless Instant Internet access at site ($), phone on-site Internet access (needs activ), phone Internet access central location, dump station, non-guest dumping $, laundry, RV supplies, LP gas by weight/by meter, tables, patios. RECREATION: pavilion, swim pool, golf nearby. Pets welcome, breed restrict. No tents. Open all yr. No pop-ups. Big rigs welcome. Member ARVC, TACO. Phone: (800)747-0787.

ATHENS

(W) Windsor Place RV Estates—(Henderson) *From jct Bus US 175, Hwy 19 & Bus Hwy 31: Go 3/4 mi W on Bus Hwy 31 (Corsicana St). Enter on R.* FACILITIES: 46 sites, typical site width 44 ft, accepts full hkup units only, 46 full hkups, (30 & 50 amps), phone/cable on-site Internet access (needs activ), RV storage, tables, patios, controlled access gate. RECREATION: rec hall, pavilion, golf nearby, planned activities. Pets welcome, breed restrict, size restrict. Partial handicap access. No tents. Open all yr. Big rigs welcome. Member ARVC, TACO. Phone: (903)477-4001.

CONCAN

(N) PARKVIEW RIVERSIDE RV PARK—(Uvalde) *From jct Hwy 127 & US 83: Go 8 mi N on US 83, then 1 mi E on FM 1050, then 1 1/2 mi S on CR 350. Enter on R.*

FACILITIES: 92 sites, typical site width 30 ft, 92 full hkups, (20, 30 & 50 amps), 17 pull-thrus, cable TV, wireless Instant Internet access at site ($), phone on-site Internet access (needs activ), RV/park trailer rentals, RV storage, dump station, non-guest dumping $, laundry, groceries, RV supplies, LP gas by weight/by meter, ice, tables, fire rings, grills, wood.

RECREATION: rec hall, pavilion, coin games, river swimming, canoeing, kayaking, float trips, river fishing, fishing supplies, golf nearby, shuffleboard court, planned activities, horseshoes, sports field, hiking trails, v-ball, local tours.

Pets welcome. Partial handicap access. No tents. Open all yr. Big rigs welcome. Member ARVC, TACO. Phone: (877)374-6748.

e-mail: parkviewrv@hctc.net

SEE AD THIS PAGE

CROCKETT

(NW) Crockett Family Resort & Marina—(Houston) *From jct Loop 304 & FM 229: Go 7 mi W on FM 229, then 2 mi N on Houston County Lake Rd (CR 2140). Enter at end.* FACILITIES: 116 sites, typical site width 25 ft, 86 full hkups, 30 W&E, (20, 30 & 50 amps), 50 amps ($), 76 pull-thrus, cable TV ($), wireless Instant Internet access at site, phone Internet access central location, cabins, RV storage, dump station, laundry, RV supplies, ice, tables, grills. RECREATION: rec hall, rec room/area, pavilion, swim pool, lake swimming, boating, canoeing, kayaking, ramp, dock, rowboat/canoe/kayak/4 pedal boat rentals, lake fishing, fishing supplies, fishing guides, mini-golf ($), bsktball, playground, 2 shuffleboard courts, planned activities, horseshoes, sports field, v-ball. Pets welcome. Open all yr. Member ARVC, TACO. Phone: (877)544-8466.

DONNA

(E) VICTORIA PALMS RESORT—(Hidalgo) *From jct FM-493 & US-83: Go 3/4 mi E on US-83, then 1/4 mi S on VictoriaRd. Enter on L.*

WELCOME

FACILITIES: 820 sites, typical site width 40 ft, 820 full hkups, (30 & 50 amps), 43 pull-thrus, cable TV, wireless Instant Internet access at site, cable Internet access central location, laundry, ice, patios, controlled access gate.

RECREATION: rec hall, rec room/area, 2 swim pools, whirlpool, golf nearby, bsktball, 16 shuffleboard courts, planned activities, tennis, horseshoes, local tours.

Pets welcome, breed restrict. Partial handicap access. No tents. Age restrictions may apply. Open all yr. Big rigs welcome. Member ARVC, TACO. Phone: (956)464-7801.

e-mail: vicpalms@sbcglobal.net

SEE AD PAGE 20

MCALLEN

(E) McAllen Mobile Park—(Hidalgo) *From jct Hwy 336 & US 83: Go 1-3/4 mi E on US 83, then 3-1/2 mi N on McColl Rd (2061). Enter on R.* FACILITIES: 318 sites, typical site width 25 ft, 318 full hkups, (30 & 50 amps), 50 amps ($), 70 pull-thrus, heater not allowed, wireless Instant Internet access at site, phone Internet access central location, RV storage, laundry, RV supplies, ice, patios. RECREATION: rec hall, rec room/area, swim pool, whirlpool, golf nearby, 6 shuffleboard courts, planned activities, horseshoes, local tours. No pets. Partial handicap access. No tents. Open all yr. Phone: (956)682-3304.

MERCEDES

(W) LLANO GRANDE LAKE PARK RESORT & COUNTRY CLUB—(Hidalgo) *From jct FM 491 & US 83: Go 1-1/2 mi W on US 83, then 1-3/4 mi S on Mile 2 W Rd. Enter at end.*

WELCOME

FACILITIES: 1012 sites, typical site width 40 ft, accepts full hkup units only, 1012 full hkups, (30 & 50 amps), 64 pull-thrus, cable TV, wireless Instant Internet access at site ($), cable Internet access central location, laundry, ice, patios, controlled access gate.

RECREATION: rec hall, rec room/area, 4 swim pools, whirlpool, boating, lake fishing, putting green, golf nearby, 18 shuffleboard courts, planned activities, tennis, horseshoes, local tours.

MERCEDES—Continued
LLANO GRANDE LAKE PARK RESORT & COUNTRY CLUB—Continued

Pets welcome. Partial handicap access. No tents. Age restrictions may apply. Open all yr. Big rigs welcome. Member ARVC, TACO. Phone: (956)565-2638.

e-mail: llanogrd@sbcglobal.net

SEE AD THIS PAGE

MISSION

(E) Mission Bell Tradewinds RV Resort—(Hidalgo) *From jct FM 1016 & US 83: Go 2-1/2 mi E on US 83, then 1 mi N on FM 494 (Shary Rd), then 3/4 mi W on Bus US 83. Enter on R.* FACILITIES: 716 sites, typical site width 25 ft, 716 full hkups, (30 & 50 amps), 13 pull-thrus, wireless Instant Internet access at site, laundry, ice, patios. RECREATION: rec hall, rec room/area, 2 swim pools, whirlpool, golf nearby, 12 shuffleboard courts, planned activities, horseshoes, local tours. Pets welcome. Partial handicap access. No tents. Open all yr. Big rigs welcome. Member ARVC, TACO. Phone: (956)585-4833.

Reserve Online at Woodalls.com

PORT ARANSAS

(SW) Gulf Waters Beach Front Resort—(Nueces) *From jct Hwy 358 (Park Rd 22) & Hwy 361: Go 9 mi N on Hwy 361. Enter on L.* FACILITIES: 158 sites, typical site width 46 ft, accepts full hkup units only, 158 full hkups, (20, 30 & 50 amps), cable TV, phone/wireless/cable Instant Internet access at site ($), wireless Internet access central location, patios. RECREATION: rec room/area, swim pool, saltwater swimming, whirlpool, saltwater fishing, golf nearby, planned activities, local tours. Pets welcome, breed restrict, quantity restrict. Partial handicap access. No tents. Open all yr. Big rigs welcome. Member ARVC, TACO. Phone: (361) 749-8888.

SCHULENBURG

(N) Schulenburg RV Park—(Fayette) *From jct I-10 (exit 674) & US 77: Go 1/4 mi S on US 77. Enter on R.* FACILITIES: 49 sites, typical site width 30 ft, 49 full hkups, (20, 30 & 50 amps), 50 amps ($), 45 pull-thrus, cable TV, wireless Instant Internet access at site, phone Internet access central location, dump station, non-guest dumping $, laundry, RV supplies, tables, grills. RECREATION: rec hall, rec room/area, equipped pavilion, pond fishing, fishing supplies, golf nearby, bsktball, planned activities, local tours. Pets welcome. Partial handicap access. Open all yr. Big rigs welcome. Member ARVC, TACO. Phone: (979)743-4388.

UTAH

GREEN RIVER

(S) A/OK RV PARK (REBUILDING)—(Emery) Altitude 4100 ft. *W'bnd from I-70 (exit 164): Go 2-3/4 mi W on Bus I-70, then 1/2 mi S on Green River Blvd. E'bnd from I-70 (exit 160): Go 1-3/4 mi E on Bus I-70, then 1/2 mi S on Green River Blvd. Enter on R.* FACILITIES: 77 sites, 26 full hkups, 51 W&E, (20 & 30 amps), 23 pull-thrus, cable TV, wireless Instant Internet access at site, wireless Internet access central location, dump station, non-guest dumping $, laundry, tables, grills. RECREATION: golf nearby. Pets welcome. No tents. Age restrictions may apply. Open Apr 1 thru Oct 1. Phone: (435)564-8372.

VERMONT

SOUTH HERO

(SE) APPLE ISLAND RESORT—(Grand Isle) *From I-89 (exit 17) & US-2: Go 6 mi NW on US-2. Enter on L.*

WELCOME

FACILITIES: 275 sites, typical site width 40 ft, 241 full hkups, 34 W&E, (30 & 50 amps), 20 pull-thrus, wireless Instant Internet access at site ($), cabins, RV storage, dump station, non-guest dumping $, laundry, groceries, RV supplies, marine gas, ice, tables, fire rings, wood.

SOUTH HERO—Continued
APPLE ISLAND RESORT—Continued

RECREATION: equipped pavilion, swim pool, whirlpool, boating, canoeing, kayaking, ramp, dock, pontoon/3 rowboat/2 canoe/4 kayak rentals, lake fishing, putting green, golf nearby, bsktball, playground, planned activities, horseshoes, sports field, hiking trails, v-ball.

Pets welcome, breed restrict, quantity restrict. Open May 1 thru Oct 20. Multiple night stay required on Holiday Wknds by reservation. Big rigs welcome. Member ARVC, VCA. Phone: (802)372-3800.

e-mail: info@appleislandresort.com

SEE AD THIS PAGE

VIRGINIA

VIRGINIA BEACH

(S) North Landing Beach Riverfront Campground and Resort—*From jct I-64 (exit 286) & Indian River Rd: Go 12 mi SE on Indian River Rd, then 10 mi S on Princess Anne Rd. Enter on R.* FACILITIES: 174 sites, typical site width 35 ft, 77 full hkups, 24 W&E, (20, 30 & 50 amps), 73 no hkups, 36 pull-thrus, cabins, RV storage, dump station, non-guest dumping $, laundry, ltd groceries, RV supplies, ice, tables, fire rings, wood. RECREATION: pavilion, swim pool, river swimming, boating, canoeing, kayaking, ramp, dock, 12 canoe/5 kayak/pedal boat rentals, river fishing, fishing supplies, golf nearby, bsktball, playground, planned activities (wkends only), horseshoes, sports field, hiking trails, v-ball. Pets welcome. Open all yr. Big rigs welcome. Member ARVC, VCA. Phone: (757)426-6241.

WASHINGTON

WALLA WALLA

(N) Fairway RV Resort—*E'bnd from jct US 12 & 2nd Ave exit: Go 2 blocks NW to second exit of on 2nd Ave, then turn N on 4th Ave for 1 block, then E on Rees Ave for 2 blocks, then N on Burns St. for 1 block, cross George St. Enter at end.* FACILITIES: 81 sites, typical site width 28 ft, 60 full hkups, 21 W&E, (20, 30 & 50 amps), 13 pull-thrus, cable TV, wireless Instant Internet access at site, laundry, ice, tables, patios. RECREATION: rec room/area, golf nearby, sports field, hiking trails. Pets welcome. Partial handicap access. Open all yr. Big rigs welcome. Phone: (509)525-8282.

WEST VIRGINIA

BECKLEY

(W) Lake Stephens Campground (Raleigh County Park) (Raleigh) *From jct I 77/64 (exit 44) & Hwy 3: Go 9 mi W on Hwy 3. Enter on R.* FACILITIES: 128 sites, 100 full hkups, (30 & 50 amps), 28 no hkups, 100 pull-thrus, laundry, ltd groceries, RV supplies, LP gas by weight/by meter, marine gas, ice, tables, patios, fire rings, wood. RECREATION: rec hall, rec room/area, pavilion, coin games, lake swimming, boating, canoeing, kayaking, ramp, dock, lake fishing, fishing supplies, golf nearby, bsktball, playground, tennis, horseshoes, sports field, hiking trails, v-ball. Rec
Lake Stephens Campground (Raleigh County Park)—Continued
open to public. Pets welcome. Partial handicap access. Open Apr 15 thru Oct 15. Big rigs welcome. Phone: (304)934-5323.

ROMNEY

(W) Wapocoma Campground—(Hampshire) *From jct US 220 & US 50: Go 6 mi E on US 50, then 4 mi S on South Branch River Rd. Enter on R.* FACILITIES: 186 sites, typical site width 36 ft, 95 W&E, (20, 30 & 50 amps), 91 no hkups, 50 pull-thrus, wireless Internet access central location, RV storage, dump station, ltd groceries, RV supplies, LP gas by weight, ice, tables, fire rings, wood. RECREATION: pavilion, river swimming, boating, canoeing, kayaking, ramp, river fishing, golf nearby, bsktball, playground, horseshoes, sports field, v-ball. Rec open to public. Pets welcome, quantity restrict. Facilities fully operational Apr 15 thru Oct 31. Phone: (304)822-5528.

WISCONSIN

MILTON

(W) LAKELAND CAMPING RESORT—(Rock) *From jct I-90 (exit 163) & Hwy 59: Go 2-1/4 mi E on Hwy 59. Enter on L.*

WELCOME

FACILITIES: 678 sites, typical site width 30 ft, 450 full hkups, 228 W&E, (30 & 50 amps), 8 pull-thrus, heater not allowed, phone on-site Internet access (needs activ), wireless Internet access central location, RV storage, dump station, portable dump, laundry, full svc store, RV supplies, LP gas by weight/by meter, ice, tables, wood, controlled access gate.

RECREATION: rec hall, rec room/area, equipped pavilion, coin games, swim pool, lake swimming, boating, canoeing, kayaking, ramp, dock, lake/pond fishing, fishing supplies, golf nearby, bsktball, playground, 2 shuffleboard courts, planned activities, tennis, horseshoes, sports field, hiking trails, v-ball.

Pets welcome. Partial handicap access. Open May 1 thru Oct 31. Big rigs welcome. Member ARVC, WACO. ATM. Phone: (608)868-4700.

e-mail: lakelandcampingresort@centurytel.net

SEE AD PAGE 21

✽ **(W) LAKELAND GOLF CART & CARE CENTER**—*From jct I-90 (exit 163) & Hwy 59: Go 2-1/4 mi E on Hwy 59. Enter on L.* New and pre-owned Golf Carts. SERVICES: Open all yr. MC/VISA/DISC/Debit. Phone: (608)868-4700.

WELCOME

SEE AD PAGE 21

✽ **(W) LAKELAND RV CENTER**—*From jct I-90 (exit 163) & Hwy 59: Go 2-1/4 mi E on Hwy 59. Enter on L.* Finance & Insurance available. SALES: travel trailers, park trailers, 5th wheels, fold-down camping trailers, pre-owned unit sales. SERVICES: full-time mech, engine/chassis repair, RV appliance repair, bus. hrs emerg rd svc, mobile RV svc, LP gas by weight/by meter, dump station, RV storage, sells parts/accessories, installs hitches. Open all yr. MC/VISA/DISC/Debit. Phone: (608)868-4700.

WELCOME

SEE AD PAGE 21

BRITISH COLUMBIA

SURREY

(S) Hazelmere RV Park & Campground—*From jct Hwy 1 & Hwy 15: Go 18.5 km / 11-1/2 mi S on Hwy 15, then 2.5 km / 1-1/2 mi E on 8 Ave. Enter on L.* FACILITIES: 200 sites, typical site width 22 ft, 164 full hkups, 28 W&E, (15 & 30 amps), 8 no hkups, cable TV, wireless Instant Internet access at site, wireless Internet access central location, cabins, RV storage, show-

SURREY—Continued
Hazelmere RV Park & Campground—Continued

er$, dump station, non-guest dumping $, laundry, groceries, RV supplies, LP gas by weight, ice, tables, fire rings, wood. RECREATION: rec room/area, equipped pavilion, coin games, swim pool, whirlpool, mini golf, golf nearby, bsktball, 3 bike rentals, playground, shuffleboard court, planned activities, horseshoes, sports field, hiking trails, v-ball, local tours. Pets welcome. Partial handicap access. Open all yr. Member BCLCA. Phone: (604)538-1167.

NEW BRUNSWICK

MIRAMICHI

(NE) Sunrise Campground—(Northumberland) *From jct Hwy 8 & Hwy 11 (at the Centennial Bridge): Go 11-1/4 km/7 mi N on Hwy 11. Enter on R.* FACILITIES: 95 sites, typical site width 30 ft, 70 full hkups, 25 W&E, (15 & 30 amps), 30 pull-thrus, dump station, non-guest dumping $, laundry, ltd groceries, ice, tables, fire rings, wood, controlled access gate. RECREATION: rec room/area, coin games, swim pool, canoeing, kayaking, ramp, river fishing, golf nearby, bsktball, playground, horseshoes, v-ball. Rec open to public. Pets welcome. Open May 15 thru Oct 9. Member COA of NB. Phone: (506)778-2282.

PENOBSQUIS

(w) Three Bears Family Camping & RV Park—(Kings) *From Hwy 1 (exit 211) & Hwy 114: Go 2 km/1-1/4 mi W on Hwy 114. Enter on L.* FACILITIES: 180 sites, 100 full hkups, 49 W&E, (15 & 30 amps), 31 no hkups, 15 pull-thrus, phone Internet access central location, cabins, dump station, non-guest dumping $, laundry, ltd groceries, LP gas by weight, ice, tables, fire rings, wood, controlled access gate. RECREATION: rec hall, coin games, swim pool, wading pool, canoeing, river fishing, mini-golf, golf nearby, bsktball, playground, 2 shuffleboard courts, planned activities (wkends only), horseshoes, sports field, v-ball. Pets welcome. Partial handicap access. Open May 1 thru Oct 1. Phone: (506)433-2870.

PETIT ROCHER NORD

(N) Camping Murraywood—(Gloucester) *From S town limits: Go 2.4 km/1-1/2 mi N on Hwy 134. Enter on R.* FACILITIES: 140 sites, typical site width 40 ft, 107 full hkups, 9 W&E, (15, 30 & 50 amps), 50 amps ($), 24 no hkups, 12 pull-thrus, wireless Instant Internet access at site, wireless Internet access central location, dump station, non-guest dumping $, laundry, ltd groceries, ice, tables, fire rings, wood, controlled access gate. RECREATION: rec hall, rec room/area, coin games, swim pool, saltwater swimming, golf nearby, bsktball, playground, 2 shuffleboard courts, planned activities (wkends only), horseshoes, sports field, hiking trails, v-ball. Pets welcome, breed restrict, size restrict, quantity restrict. Open May 15 thru Sep 23. Facilities fully operational Jun 15 thru Aug 20. Big rigs welcome. Member COA of NB. Phone: (506)783-2137.

SHEDIAC

(NW) Camping Oceanic—*From Hwy 15 (Exit 37) & Hwy 140: Go .08 km/3/4 mi N on Hwy 140. Enter on L.* FACILITIES: 240 sites, 220 full hkups, 20 W&E, (30 amps), cable TV, wireless Instant Internet access at site, ice, tables, fire rings, wood, controlled access gate. RECREATION: swim pool, golf nearby, play equipment. Pets welcome, breed restrict. Partial handicap access. No tents. Open May 15 thru Oct 15. Phone: (506)533-7006.

(NE) Etoile Filante Camping Wishing Star—(Westmorland) *From west town limits: Go 0.4 km/1/4 mi W on Hwy 133. Enter on R.* FACILITIES: 130 sites, typical site width 30 ft, 130 full hkups, (15 & 30 amps), cable TV, wireless Instant Internet access at site, wireless Internet access central location, dump station, non-guest dumping, laundry, ice, tables, fire rings, wood. RECREATION: rec hall, golf nearby, play equipment. Pets welcome. Open May 1 thru Oct 31. Member COA of NB. Phone: (506)532-6786.

WOODSTOCK

(S) Cosy Cabins Campground—*From Hwy 2 (exit 191) & Beardsley Rd: Go 1.5 km/1 mi E on Beardsley, then 30 m/100 ft N on Road 165. Enter on R.* FACILITIES: 25 sites, 21 full hkups, 4 W&E, (15, 30 & 50 amps), 12 pull-thrus, wireless Internet access central location, cabins, ice, tables. RECREATION: canoeing, kayaking, river fishing, golf nearby. Pets welcome. Open May 1 thru Nov 30. Big rigs welcome. Phone: (506)328-3344.

Woodall's Tip #22... If you think Woodall's Ratings mean Good, Better, Best...think again. See the "How to Use" pages in the front of this Directory for an explanation of our Rating System.

NEWFOUNDLAND AND LABRADOR

GAMBO

(NW) Square Pond Friends and Family RV Park—*From jct Hwy 320 & Hwy 1: Go 12 km/7-1/2 mi W on Hwy 1. Enter on L.* FACILITIES: 96 sites, 1 full hkups, 24 W&E, (15 & 30 amps), 71 no hkups, cable TV ($), wireless Internet access central location, RV storage, dump station, non-guest dumping $, laundry, ltd groceries, ice, tables, fire rings, wood, controlled access gate. RECREATION: rec room/area, coin games, pond swimming, boating, canoeing, kayaking, ramp, pond fishing, golf nearby, bsktball, playground, planned activities (wkends only), horseshoes, hiking trails, v-ball. Rec open to public. Pets welcome. Partial handicap access. Open May 15 thru Oct 15. Phone: (709)674-7566.

GREEN'S HARBOUR

(C) Golden Arm Trailer Park—*From jct Hwy 1 & Hwy 80 (exit 28): Go 24 km/15 mi N on Hwy 80. Enter on R.* FACILITIES: 140 sites, typical site width 30 ft, 90 full hkups, 50 W&E, (15 & 30 amps), 15 pull-thrus, cabins, dump station, non-guest dumping $, laundry, ltd groceries, ice, tables, fire rings, wood, controlled access gate. RECREATION: rec hall, swim pool, pond swimming, canoeing, kayaking, pond fishing, playground, horseshoes, hiking trails. Pets welcome. Partial handicap access. Open May 1 thru Oct 20. Phone: (709)582-3600.

PORT-AU-CHOIX

(SW) Oceanside RV Park—*From jct Hwy 430 & Hwy 430-28: Go 13 km/8 mi NW on Hwy 430-28. Enter on L.* FACILITIES: 46 sites, 26 W&E, (15 & 30 amps), 20 no hkups, dump station, non-guest dumping $, ice, tables, fire rings, wood. RECREATION: rec hall. Pets welcome. Open May 20 thru Sep 30. Phone: (709)861-2133.

QUIRPON

(W) Viking RV Park—*From jct Hwy 430 & 436: Go 24 km/15 mi E on Hwy 436, then 100 m/300 ft NE on Quirpon Intersection. Enter on L.* FACILITIES: 35 sites, 26 ft max RV length, 17 W&E, (15 & 30 amps), 18 no hkups, 2 pull-thrus, wireless Internet access central location ($), dump station, non-guest dumping $, laundry, ice, tables, fire rings, wood. RECREATION: rec room/area, play equipment. Pets welcome. Open mid May thru Sept 30. Phone: (709)623-2425.

NOVA SCOTIA

AMHERST

(NE) Gateway Parklands—(Cumberland) *From Hwy 104 (exit 1) & Fort Lawrence Rd: Go 100 meters/400 ft E on Fort Lawrence Rd. Enter on R.* FACILITIES: 123 sites, typical site width 30 ft, 98 full hkups, (15 & 30 amps), 25 no hkups, 80 pull-thrus, RV storage, dump station, non-guest dumping $, laundry, ice, tables, fire rings, wood. RECREATION: rec hall, golf nearby, bsktball, play equipment, horseshoes, v-ball. Pets welcome, breed restrict. Open May 15 thru Oct 15. Off season call (902)694-4492. Member COA of NS. Phone: (902)667-1106.

AYLESFORD

(E) Klahanie Kamping—(Kings) *From Hwy 101 (Exit 16): Go 1.6 km/1 mi S Enter on L.* FACILITIES: 150 sites, typical site width 40 ft, 85 full hkups, 23 W&E, (15 & 30 amps), 42 no hkups, cable TV ($), wireless Instant Internet access at site, phone Internet access central location, RV storage, dump station, non-guest dumping $, laundry, ltd groceries, LP gas by weight, ice, tables, fire rings, wood, controlled access gate. RECREATION: rec room/area, 2 swim pools, canoeing, rowboat/2 canoe/2 pedal boat rentals, pond fishing, mini-golf, golf nearby, bsktball, playground, 2 shuffleboard courts, planned activities (wkends only), horseshoes, sports field, hiking trails, v-ball. Pets welcome. Partial handicap access. Open Apr 15 thru Oct 30. Facilities fully operational May 15 thru Oct 15. Member COA of NS. Phone: (902)847-9316.

DELAPS COVE

(W) Fundy Trail Campground & Cottages—(Annapolis) *From E Delaps Cove City Limit: Go 2.1 km/1-1/3 mi W on Delaps Cove Rd. Enter at end.* FACILITIES: 73 sites, typical site width 35 ft, 30 full hkups, 20 W&E, (15 & 30 amps), 23 no hkups, phone Internet access central location, cabins, RV storage, shower$, dump station, non-guest dumping, laundry, ltd groceries, ice, tables, fire rings, wood. RECREATION: rec room/area, coin games, swim pool, canoeing, kayaking, ramp, saltwater fishing, mini-golf ($), golf nearby, playground, planned activities (wkends only), horseshoes, sports field. Pets welcome. Open May 15 thru Sep 30. Member COA of NS. Phone: (902)532-7711.

MARTIN'S RIVER

(N) Rayport Campground—(Lunenburg) *From jct Hwy 103 (exit 10) & Hwy 3: Go 3.5 km/2 mi E on Hwy 3, then .08 km/1/2 mi N. Enter at end.* FACILITIES: 70 sites, 60 W&E, (15, 30 & 50 amps), 50 amps ($), 10 no hkups, 6 pull-thrus, cable TV, wireless Instant Internet access at site ($), dump station, non-guest dumping $, portable dump, laundry, ltd groceries, ice, tables, fire rings, wood. RECREATION: rec room/area, coin games, swim pool, river fishing, golf nearby, play equipment, hiking trails. Pets welcome. Partial handicap access. Open May 15 thru Oct 15. Big rigs welcome. Member COA of NS. Phone: (902)627-2678.

PICTOU

(SW) Birchwood Campground—(Pictou) *From Hwy 104 (exit 22) & Hwy 106: Go 12.2 km/7-1/2 mi N on Hwy 106 to Pictou Rotary, then take Lyon's Brook exit off Rotary, then 3.2 km/2 mi W on Hwy 376. Enter on R.* FACILITIES: 55 sites, typical site width 30 ft, 33 full hkups, 17 W&E, (15 & 30 amps), 5 no hkups, 1 pull-thrus, wireless Instant Internet access at site, cabins, shower$, dump station, non-guest dumping $, ltd groceries, ice, tables, fire rings, wood. RECREATION: equipped pavilion, swim pool, golf nearby, bsktball, playground, planned activities (wkends only), horseshoes, sports field, v-ball. Pets welcome. Open May 15 thru Sep 30. Member COA of NS. Phone: (902)485-8565.

SOUTH RAWDON

(E) Boutiliers Glen—(Hants) *From jct Hwy 215 & Hwy 14: Go 4 km/2-1/2 mi E on Hwy 14, then 6.4 km/4 mi S on South Rawdon Rd (either Ashdale Rd). Enter on L.* FACILITIES: 80 sites, typical site width 35 ft, 61 full hkups, 11 W&E, (15, 30 & 50 amps), 8 no hkups, 10 pull-thrus, cabins, dump station, non-guest dumping $, laundry, ltd groceries, ice, tables, fire rings, wood, controlled access gate. RECREATION: rec hall, wading pool, river swimming, river fishing, golf nearby, bsktball, playground, planned activities (wkends only), horseshoes, sports field, hiking trails. Pets welcome. Partial handicap access. Open May 18 thru Oct 9. Phone: (902)757-2401.

YARMOUTH

(SE) Camper's Haven—(Yarmouth) *From jct Hwy 1 & Hwy 3: Go 7.3 km/4-1/2 mi SE on Hwy 3. Enter on L.* FACILITIES: 215 sites, typical site width 30 ft, 97 full hkups, 49 W&E, (15, 30 & 50 amps), 50 amps ($), 69 no hkups, 37 pull-thrus, wireless Internet access central location, RV/park trailer rentals, RV storage, dump station, non-guest dumping, laundry, ltd groceries, RV supplies, LP bottle exch, ice, tables, fire rings, wood. RECREATION: rec hall, coin games, swim pool, lake swimming, canoeing, kayaking, lake fishing, mini-golf ($), golf nearby, bsktball, playground, planned activities, sports field, hiking trails, v-ball. Pets welcome. Partial handicap access. Open Jun 1 thru Oct 1. Big rigs welcome. Member COA of NS. Phone: (902)742-4848.

ONTARIO

BELLE RIVER

ROCHESTER PLACE RV, GOLF & MARINE RESORT—(Essex) *From jct Hwy 401 (exit 40) & CR 31: Go 4.3km/2.7 mi N on CR 31, then go 0.1km/0.06 mi E on CR 42, then go 2.7km/1.7 mi N on CR 31, then go 0.3km/0.2 mi W on CR 2. Enter on R.*

FACILITIES: 274 sites, typical site width 30 ft, 274 full hkups, (20 & 30 amps), 2 pull-thrus, wireless Internet access central location, RV storage, dump station, non-guest dumping $, RV supplies, ice, tables, fire rings, wood.

RECREATION: rec hall, rec room/area, swim pool, boating, canoeing, kayaking, ramp, dock, lake/river/pond fishing, putting green, golf nearby, bsktball, playground, planned activities, horseshoes, sports field, hiking trails, v-ball.

Pets welcome. Partial handicap access. Open May 1 thru Oct 31. Pool open Mid Jun - Labor Day. Member OPCA. Phone: (800)563-5940.

e-mail: camping@rochesterplace.ca

SEE AD THIS PAGE

ROCHESTER PLACE RV, GOLF & MARINE RESORT—*From jct Hwy 401 (exit 40): Go 4.3 km/2.7 mi N on CR 31, then go .1 km/.06 mi E on CR 42, then go 2.7 km/1.7 mi N on CR 31, then go .3 km/.2 mi W on CR 2. Enter on R.* Marina with access to Lake St Claire, golf course & restaurant. Open Apr 7 thru Nov 15. MC/VISA/AMEX. Phone: (800)563-5940.

e-mail: golfing@rochesterplace.ca

SEE AD THIS PAGE

FERGUS

Highland Pines Campground—(Wellington) *From jct Hwy 6 & CR 19: Go 9 km/5-1/2 mi E on CR 19. Enter on R.* FACILITIES: 484 sites, typical site width 35 ft, 441 full hkups, 43 W&E, (30 amps), cabins, RV storage, dump station, non-guest dumping $, ltd groceries, RV supplies, ice, tables, patios, fire rings, wood, controlled access gate. RECREATION: rec hall, equipped pavilion, swim pool, wading pool, lake swimming, boating, canoeing, kayaking, ramp, dock, lake fishing, golf nearby, bsktball, 4 bike rentals, playground, 2 shuffleboard courts, planned activities (wkends only), horseshoes, sports field, hiking trails, v-ball. Pets welcome. Partial handicap access. Open First wk of May thru Mid Oct. Member ARVC, OPCA. ATM. Phone: (519)843-2537.

INGERSOLL

SPRING LAKE RV—*From jct Hwy 401 (exit 216) & Culloden Rd: Go 10.4 km/6-1/2 mi S on Culloden Rd, then .4 km/1/4 mi W on CR-27 (Prouse Rd).* SALES: travel trailers, park trailers, 5th wheels, pre-owned unit sales. SERVICES: full-time mech. Phone: (519)877-2315.

e-mail: slrvpark@execulink.com

SEE AD THIS PAGE

SPRING LAKE R.V. RESORT—(Oxford) *From jct Hwy 401 (exit 216) & Culloden Rd: Go 10.4 km/6-1/2 mi S on Culloden Rd, then .4 km/1/4 mi W on CR 27 (Prouse Rd). Enter on R.*

FACILITIES: 298 sites, typical site width 35 ft, accepts full hkup units only, 298 full hkups, (30 amps), 4 pull-thrus, phone Internet access central location ($), RV/park trailer rentals, RV storage, laundry, groceries, RV supplies, LP gas by weight, ice, tables, fire rings, wood, controlled access gate.

RECREATION: rec hall, rec room/area, coin games, sprayground, lake swimming, boating, electric motors only, canoeing, kayaking, 3 rowboat/6 canoe/kayak/5 pedal boat rentals, lake fishing, fishing supplies, mini-golf, golf nearby, bsktball, playground, 2 shuffleboard courts, planned activities, horseshoes, sports field, hiking trails, v-ball.

Pets welcome. No tents. Open May 1 thru Oct 31. Member ARVC, OPCA. Phone: (877)877-9265.

e-mail: slrvpark@execulink.com

SEE AD THIS PAGE

STOUFFVILLE

Cedar Beach Park—*Fron jct Hwy 48 & Aurora Rd. 15: Go 2 km/1-1/4 mi E on Aurora Rd. 15 then go 1/4 mile Enter on R.* FACILITIES: 570 sites, typical site width 40 ft, 519 full hkups, 41 W&E, (15, 30 & 50 amps), 50 amps ($), 10 no hkups, 16 pull-thrus, wireless Instant Internet access at site ($), wireless Internet access central location, RV storage, dump station, groceries, RV supplies, LP gas by weight, ice, tables, fire rings, wood, controlled access gate. RECREATION: rec hall, equipped pavilion, coin games, 2 swim pools, sprayground, lake swimming, whirlpool, boating, no motors, canoeing, kayaking, dock, 5 canoe/7 kayak/8 pedal boat rentals, lake fishing, fishing supplies, golf nearby, bsktball, playground, 4 shuffleboard courts, planned activities, tennis, horseshoes, sports field, hiking trails, v-ball. Rec open to public. Pets welcome. Open Apr 1 thru Oct 31. Big rigs welcome. Member OPCA. Phone: (877)588-8828.

SUNDERLAND

Trout Water Family Camping—*From jct Hwy 12 & Hwy 7: Go 2 km/1-1/2 mi E on Hwy 7. Enter on R.* FACILITIES: 150 sites, typical site width 40 ft, 75 full hkups, 35 W&E, (15 & 30 amps), 40 no hkups, 10 pull-thrus, wireless Instant Internet access at site ($), phone Internet access central location, RV storage, dump station, non-guest dumping $, laundry, ltd groceries, ice, tables, patios, fire rings, wood, controlled access gate. RECREATION: rec hall, 2 swim pools, boating, no motors, canoeing, kayaking, dock, 2 canoe/3 kayak/2 pedal boat rentals, river fishing, fishing supplies, putting green, golf nearby, bsktball, playground,

SUNDERLAND—Continued
Trout Water Family Camping—Continued

planned activities (wkends only), horseshoes, sports field, hiking trails, v-ball. Rec open to public. Pets welcome. Open May 1 thru mid Oct. Member OPCA. Phone: (705)357-1754.

PRINCE EDWARD ISLAND

BELLEVUE

(SE) Ben's Lake Campground & Trout Fishing—(Queens) *From jct Hwy 3 and Hwy 24: Go 15.7 km/9-1/2 mi S on Hwy 24; or from Wood Island Ferry: Go 12 km/7-1/2 mi N on Hwy 315, then 3 km/2 mi NW on Hwy 24. Enter on R.* FACILITIES: 30 sites, typical site width 24 ft, 35 ft max RV length, 14 full hkups, 6 W&E, (15 amps), 10 no hkups, RV/park trailer rentals, cabins, RV storage, dump station, non-guest dumping $, laundry, ice, tables, fire rings, wood. RECREATION: electric motors only, canoeing, ramp, dock, 8 rowboat/4 motorboat rentals, lake fishing, fishing supplies, golf nearby, horseshoes. Rec open to public. Pets welcome. Open May 5 thru Oct 15. Phone: (902)838-2706.

OYSTER BED BRIDGE

(N) Bayside RV Campground—(Queens) *From jct Hwy 7 & Hwy 6: Go 1.3 km/3/4 mi W on Hwy 6, then 0.8 km/1/2 mi N on a private road. Enter on R.* FACILITIES: 122 sites, typical site width 30 ft, 81 full hkups, 16 W&E, 3 E, (15 & 30 amps), 22 no hkups, 20 pull-thrus, phone Internet access central location, RV storage, dump station, non-guest dumping $, laundry, ltd groceries, ice, tables, fire rings, wood. RECREATION: rec room/area, equipped pavilion, coin games, swim pool, saltwater swimming, golf nearby, bsktball, playground, horseshoes, sports field, v-ball. Pets welcome, breed restrict, quantity restrict. Open May 23 thru Sep 27. Phone: (877)445-2489.

QUEBEC

BROMONT

(N) Camping Parc Bromont—*From Hwy 10 (exit 78) & Boul Bromont: Go .04 km/1/4 mi S on Boul Bromont, then 100 meters/ 325 ft E on Rue St-Denis, then 100 meters/325 ft S on Rue Lafontaine. Enter at end.* FACILITIES: 195 sites, 131 full hkups, 36 W&E, (15 & 30 amps), 28 no hkups, 35 pull-thrus, wireless Internet access central location, RV storage, dump station, non-guest dumping $, portable dump, laundry, groceries, ice, tables, fire rings, wood. RECREATION: pavilion, coin games, swim pool, mini-golf ($), golf nearby, bsktball, playground, horseshoes, v-ball. Pets welcome, quantity restrict. Open Apr 27 thru Oct 14. Member CQ. Phone: (450)534-2712.

CANTLEY

(SE) Camping Cantley—(Outaouais) *From jct Hwy 50 (exit 138) & Hwy 307: Go 14 km/8-3/4 mi N on Hwy 307, then 1.6 km/1 mi E on Chemin Ste-Elizabeth. Enter on R.* FACILITIES: 305 sites, 206 full hkups, 40 W&E, (15, 30 & 50 amps), 50 amps ($), 59 no hkups, heater not allowed, phone Internet access central location, RV/park trailer rentals, RV storage, shower$, dump station, non-guest dumping, laundry, ltd groceries, LP gas by weight, ice, tables, fire rings, wood, controlled access gate. RECREATION: rec hall, pavilion, equipped pavilion, 2 swim pools, wading pool, pond fishing, mini-golf, golf nearby, bsktball, playground, planned activities (wkends only), tennis, horseshoes, sports field, v-ball. Pets welcome. Partial handicap access. Open May 15 thru Sep 15. After closing date just on call. Big rigs welcome. Member CQ. Phone: (819) 827-1056.

CARLETON-SUR-MER

(W) Camping Motel L'Abri—*From East town city limit on Hwy 132: Go 2.7 km/1-3/4 mi E on Hwy 132. Enter on L.* FACILITIES: 18 sites, accepts full hkup units only, 18 full hkups, (30 & 50 amps), cable Internet access central location, ice, tables. RECREATION: golf nearby. Pets welcome. No tents. Open May 1 thru Oct 31. Member CQ. Phone: (800)827-7001.

GASPE

(NW) Camping Motel Fort Ramsay—(Gaspesie) *From west town limits at the bridge: Go 3.6 km/2-1/4 mi W on Hwy 132. Enter on R.* FACILITIES: 42 sites, 21 full hkups, (15 & 30 amps), 21 no hkups, wireless Instant Internet access at site, cabins, laundry, ice, tables, fire rings, wood. RECREATION: boating, canoeing, river fishing, fishing guides, bsktball, play equipment, horseshoes, v-ball. Pets welcome. Open May 22 thru Sep 30. Facilities fully operational Jun 1 thru Sep 30. Member CQ. Phone: (418)368-5094.

GRACEFIELD

(S) Camping Pionnier—(Outaouais) *From S city limit on Hwy 105: Go 3.7 km/2-1/4 mi S on Hwy 105. Enter on L.* FACILITIES: 125 sites, 125 full hkups, (15 & 30 amps), RV/park trailer rentals, RV storage, shower$, dump station, non-guest dumping $, laundry, ltd groceries, ice, tables, fire rings, wood. RECREATION: rec room/area, equipped pavilion, coin games, swim pool, boating, canoeing, kayaking, ramp, dock, motorboat rentals, river fishing, golf nearby, bsktball, playground, 2 shuffleboard courts, planned activities (wkends only), horseshoes, sports field, v-ball. Rec open to public. No pets. Open May 15 thru Oct 15. Facilities fully operational Jun 15 thru Sep 15. Member CQ. Phone: (819)463-4163.

HUDSON

(E) Camping D'Aoust—(Monteregie) *From Montreal: Take Hwy 40 (exit 26) & Hwy 342: Go 2.8 km/1-3/4 mi W on Hwy 342. Entrance on left. From Ottawa: Take Hwy 40 E (exit 22) & Hwy 342: Go 1.3 km/3/4 mi N on St Charles, then 2.6 km/1-1/2 mi E on Hwy 342. Entrance on right.* FACILITIES: 211 sites, 131 full hkups, 50 W&E, (15 & 30 amps), 30 no hkups, 5 pull-thrus, heater not allowed, phone Internet access central location, RV/park trailer rentals, RV storage, shower$, dump station, non-guest dumping $, laundry, ltd groceries, LP gas by weight, ice, tables, fire rings, wood. RECREATION: rec room/area, equipped pavilion, coin games, 2 swim pools, golf nearby, bsktball, 4 bike rentals, playground, planned activities (wkends only), horseshoes, sports field, hiking trails, v-ball. Rec open to public. Pets welcome ($). Open Apr 15 thru Oct 30. Facilities fully operational Jun 20 thru Sep 10. Member CQ. Phone: (450)458-7301.

MAGOG

(E) Domaine Parc Estrie—(Canton-de-l'est) *From Hwy 10-55 (exit 123): Go 0.8 km/1/2 mi W on Boul Bourque (Hwy 112), then 0.8 km/1/2 mi S on rue du Domaine. Enter on L.* FACILITIES: 450 sites, 273 full hkups, 101 W&E, (15 & 30 amps), 76 no hkups, 11 pull-thrus, wireless Instant Internet access at site ($), phone Internet access central location, RV storage, shower$, dump station, non-guest dumping $, laundry, ltd groceries, LP gas by weight, ice, tables, patios, fire rings, wood, controlled access gate. RECREATION: rec room/area, coin games, swim pool, wading pool, pond fishing, golf nearby, bsktball, playground, 4 shuffleboard courts, planned activities (wkends only), tennis, horseshoes, hiking trails, v-ball. Rec open to public. Pets welcome. Partial handicap access. Open Apr 25 thru Oct 25. Member CQ. Phone: (819)868-6944.

QUEBEC CITY

(N) Camping Aeroport—(Quebec) *From jct Hwy 138 & Route de l'Aeroport (either Hwy Duplessis): Go 4.8 km/3 mi N on Route de l'Aeroport. Enter on L.* FACILITIES: 200 sites, 120 full hkups, 49 W&E, (15, 30 & 50 amps), 50 amps ($), 31 no hkups, 24 pull-thrus, wireless Instant Internet access at site ($), phone Internet access central location, shower$, dump station, non-guest dumping, laundry, ltd groceries, RV supplies, ice, tables, fire rings, wood, controlled access gate. RECREATION: rec hall, swim pool, golf nearby, bsktball, playground, shuffleboard court, planned activities (wkends only), horseshoes, v-ball, local tours. Pets welcome. Partial handicap access. Open Apr 15 thru Oct 31. Facilities fully operational May 1 thru Sep 30. Big rigs welcome. Member CQ. Phone: (800)294-1574.

RIMOUSKI

(W) Camping Motel de l'Anse—*From jct Hwy 20 (exit 597) & Hwy 132E: Go 7.5 km/4-3/4 mi E on Hwy 132E. Enter on R.* FACILITIES: 87 sites, 48 full hkups, 4 E, (15, 30 & 50 amps), 50 amps ($), 35 no hkups, wireless Instant Internet access at site, dump station, non-guest dumping $, laundry, ice, tables. RECREATION: rec room/area, golf nearby, bsktball, play equipment, horseshoes. Pets welcome, breed restrict, quantity restrict. Open April 15 thru Nov 15. Facilities fully operational May 1 thru Oct 31. Big rigs welcome. Member CQ. Phone: (418)721-0322.

Woodall's Tip #12... Have a Question or Comment? Use Reader Comment Forms located after the Alphabetical Quick Reference pages.

SAINT-ALEXANDRE

(NE) Camping le Rayon de Soleil—*From Hwy 20 (exit 488): Go 230 meters/760 feet S, then 1.6 km/1 mi W on Rang St-Edouard Quest. Enter on L.* FACILITIES: 120 sites, 42 full hkups, 31 W&E, 4 E, (15 & 30 amps), 43 no hkups, 84 pull-thrus, wireless Internet access central location, cabins, dump station, non-guest dumping $, laundry, ltd groceries, ice, tables, fire rings, wood. RECREATION: rec room/area, swim pool, golf nearby, bsktball, playground, horseshoes, v-ball. Rec open to public. Pets welcome. Open May 12 thru Oct 4. Member CQ. Phone: (418)495-2677.

SAINT-ANDRE-AVELLIN

(C) Camping Saint-Andre-Avellin—*From jct Hwy 148 & Hwy 321: Go 13.2 km/8-1/4 mi N on Hwy 321, then .04 km/1/4 mi E on Du Moulin (Duquette). Enter on L.* FACILITIES: 169 sites, 148 full hkups, (15 & 30 amps), 21 no hkups, 1 pull-thrus, wireless Instant Internet access at site ($), shower$, dump station, non-guest dumping $, laundry, LP bottle exch, ice, tables, fire rings, wood. RECREATION: rec hall, pavilion, coin games, swim pool, sprayground, boating, 9 hp limit, canoeing, kayaking, dock, rowboat/4 canoe/3 kayak/pedal boat rentals, river fishing, mini-golf ($), golf nearby, bsktball, 7 bike rentals, playground, planned activities (wkends only), horseshoes, v-ball. Pets welcome. Open May 9 thru Oct 7. Facilities fully operational Jun 23 thru Sep 1. Member CQ. Phone: (819)983-3777.

SAINT-MATHIEU-DE-BELOEIL

(N) Camping Alouette Inc—(Monteregie) *From Hwy I-20 (exit 105): Go 1.6 km/1 mi NE on service road (ch.de l'Industrie). Enter on L.* FACILITIES: 400 sites, 344 full hkups, 33 W&E, (15, 30 & 50 amps), 50 amps ($), 23 no hkups, 150 pull-thrus, wireless Instant Internet access at site ($), phone Internet access central location, RV storage, shower$, dump station, non-guest dumping $, laundry, groceries, RV supplies, LP gas by weight/by meter, ice, tables, fire rings, wood, controlled access gate. RECREATION: rec hall, rec room/area, swim pool, wading pool, golf nearby, bsktball, playground, shuffleboard court, planned activities (wkends only), horseshoes, hiking trails, v-ball, local tours. Rec open to public. Pets welcome ($), quantity restrict. Partial handicap access. Open all yr. Facilities fully operational Apr 15 thru Oct 15. Big rigs welcome. Member CQ. Phone: (450)464-1661.

SAINT-MICHEL-DE-BELLECHASSE

(E) Camping Parc St-Michel—(Chaudiere-Appalaches) *From jct I 20 (exit 348) & Hwy 281: Go 1.6 km/1 mi N on Hwy 281, then 2.5 km/1-1/2 mi E on Hwy 132. Enter on L.* FACILITIES: 85 sites, 75 full hkups, 10 W&E, (15, 30 & 50 amps), 50 amps ($), 7 pull-thrus, dump station, non-guest dumping, laundry, ltd groceries, LP gas by weight, ice, tables, patios, fire rings, wood, controlled access gate. RECREATION: rec hall, swim pool, golf nearby, bsktball, playground, 2 shuffleboard courts, planned activities (wkends only), horseshoes, v-ball. Rec open to public. Pets welcome. Open May 15 thru Oct 15. Phone: (418)884-2621.

SAINT-NICOLAS

(sw) KOA-Quebec City—(Chaudiere-Appalaches) *1 mi W of I-73: Go W on I-20 (exit 311), then left at traffic light going E on I-20, (exit 311). Cross over I-20. Turn left at Oliver Rd (service road). Enter on R.* FACILITIES: 220 sites, 96 full hkups, 56 W&E, 12 E, (15, 30 & 50 amps), 50 amps ($), 56 no hkups, 134 pull-thrus, wireless Instant Internet access at site ($), phone Internet access central location, cabins, dump station, non-guest dumping $, laundry, groceries, RV supplies, LP gas by weight/by meter, ice, tables, fire rings, wood. RECREATION: rec hall, rec room/area, pavilion, coin games, swim pool, golf nearby, bsktball, playground, horseshoes, v-ball, local tours. Pets welcome ($), quantity restrict. Open May 1 thru Oct 12. Big rigs welcome. Member CQ. ATM. Phone: (418)831-1813.

SAINT-PHILIPPE-DE-LAPRAIRIE

(W) Camping Amerique Montreal—(Monteregie) *From Hwy 15 (exit 38): Go 1.6 km/1 mi E on Boul Monette, then 0.4 km/1/4 mi S on Rang St-Andre. Enter on R.* FACILITIES: 112 sites, 92 full hkups, 12 W&E, (15 & 30 amps), 8 no hkups, 2 pull-thrus, wireless Instant Internet access at site ($), wireless Internet access central location, RV/park trailer rentals, dump station, non-guest dumping $, laundry, ltd groceries, ice, tables, fire rings, wood. RECREATION: rec hall, coin games, swim pool, putting green, golf nearby, play equipment, 2 shuffleboard courts, planned activities (wkends only), horseshoes. Rec open to public. Pets welcome ($), breed restrict, size restrict, quantity restrict. Open Apr 1 thru Oct 31. Facilities fully operational Apr 20 thru Oct 15. Member CQ. Phone: (450)659-8282.

Tell them Woodall's sent you!

SAINT-PHILIPPE-DE-LAPRAIRIE—Continued
Camping la Cle des Champs—Continued

(E) Camping la Cle des Champs—(Monteregie) *From Hwy 30 (exit 104): Go 2.5 km/1-1/2 mi E on Hwy 104, then 3.5 km/2 mi S on Rang St-Raphael, then 1 km/3/4 mi W on Montee St-Claude. Enter on R.* FACILITIES: 120 sites, 108 full hkups, 12 W&E, (15 & 30 amps), phone Internet access central location, dump station, non-guest dumping $, laundry, ltd groceries, ice, tables, fire rings, wood, controlled access gate. RECREATION: rec room/area, swim pool, golf nearby, bsktball, play equipment, horseshoes, v-ball. Rec open to public. Pets welcome. No tents. Open Apr 22 thru Oct 22. Member CQ. Phone: (450)659-3389.

SAINT-ROCH-DE-RICHELIEU

(N) Camping Domaine des Erables—(Monteregie) *From the Ferry: Go 2.1 km/1-1/3 mi N on rue St. Pierre. Enter on L.* FACILITIES: 450 sites, 408 full hkups, 42 W&E, (15 & 30 amps), 51 pull-thrus, wireless Instant Internet access at site, shower$, dump station, non-guest dumping $, laundry, ltd groceries, LP gas by weight, ice, tables, fire rings, wood, controlled access gate. RECREATION: rec hall, rec room/area, equipped pavilion, coin games, swim pool, wading pool, sprayground, lake swimming, whirlpool, boating, canoeing, kayaking, dock, 4 kayak/5 pedal boat rentals, pond fishing, golf nearby, bsktball, playground, planned activities (wkends only), horseshoes, hiking trails, v-ball. Rec open to public. Pets welcome. Open Apr 28 thru Oct 29. Facilities fully operational Jun 5 thru Sep 5. Member CQ. Phone: (450)785-2805.

SAINTE-ANNE-DES-MONTS

(W) Camping du Rivage—(Gaspesie) *From west on Hwy 132: Go 5.7 km/3-1/2 mi E on Hwy 132E, then 30 meters/100 feet NW on 29c Avenue Quest, then 10 meters/30 feet on 1c Avenue Quest. Enter on R.* FACILITIES: 29 sites, 24 W&E, (15 & 30 amps), 5 no hkups, wireless Internet access central location ($), shower$, dump station, non-guest dumping $, laundry, ice, tables, wood. RECREATION: saltwater swimming, whirlpool, golf nearby, horseshoes. Pets welcome. Partial handicap access. No tents. Open May 15 thru Oct 30. Member CQ. Phone: (418)763-3529.

SAINTE-JULIENNE

(N) Camping Kelly—*From jct Hwy 346 & Hwy 125: Go 2 km/1-1/4 mi N on Hwy 125. Enter on L.* FACILITIES: 350 sites, 345 full hkups, 5 W&E, (15 & 30 amps), 25 pull-thrus, heater not allowed, RV storage, shower$, laundry, LP bottle exch, ice, tables, fire rings, wood, controlled access gate. RECREATION: rec hall, rec room/area, coin games, 2 swim pools, golf nearby, bsktball, playground, planned activities (wkends only), horseshoes, sports field, v-ball. Pets welcome, breed restrict, quantity restrict. Partial handicap access. No tents. Open May 15 thru Sep 15. Facilities fully operational Jun 20 thru Sep 2. Member CQ. Phone: (450)831-2422.

TROIS-RIVIERES

(N) Camping Lac St-Michel des Forges—(Mauricie Bois-Francs) *From Hwy I 55 (exit 191): Go 2.4 km/1 1/2 mi E on Boul St. Michel, then 3.6 km/2 1/4 mi N on Boul des Forges, then .04 km/1/4 mi E on rue des Pignons. Enter at end.* FACILITIES: 150 sites, 95 full hkups, 39 W&E, (15 & 30 amps), 16 no hkups, 12 pull-thrus, phone Internet access central location ($), cabins, dump station, non-guest dumping $, laundry, ltd groceries, LP bottle exch, ice, tables, fire rings, wood, controlled access gate. RECREATION: rec hall, equipped pavilion, 2 swim pools, golf nearby, bsktball, playground, planned activities (wkends only), horseshoes, sports field, v-ball. Rec open to public. Pets welcome. Open May 11 thru Sep 15. Facilities fully operational Jun 15 thru Sep 5. Member CQ. Phone: (877)374-8474.